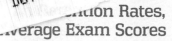
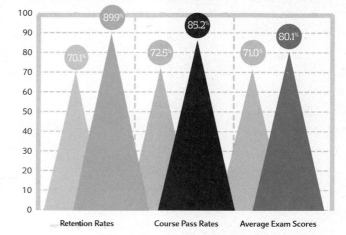

contents in brief

contents

2 Culture 17

3 Applying Anthropology 35

4 Doing Archaeology and Biological Anthropology *54*

5 Evolution and Genetics *70*

6 Human Variation and Adaptation

7 The Primates

8 Early Hominins *125*

9 The Genus *Homo* *144*

10 The Origin and Spread of Modern Humans *165*

11 The First Farmers *185*

12 The First Cities and States 206

13 Method and Theory in Cultural Anthropology 229

PART 3 APPRECIATING CULTURAL DIVERSITY

14 Language and Communication   *254*

17 Political Systems *320*

18 Gender *343*

19 Families, Kinship, and Descent *366*

20 Marriage *384*

21 Religion *403*

24 Anthropology's Role in a Globalizing World 468

list of boxes

appreciating ANTHROPOLOGY

appreciating DIVERSITY

focus on GLOBALIZATION

RECAP

about the author

Conrad Phillip Kottak

Conrad Phillip Kottak (A.B. Columbia College, Ph.D. Columbia University) is the Julian H. Steward Collegiate Professor Emeritus of Anthropology at the University of Michigan, where he served as anthropology department chair from 1996 to 2006. He has been honored for his undergraduate teaching by the university and the state of Michigan and by the American Anthropological Association. He is an elected member of the American Academy of Arts and Sciences and the National Academy of Sciences, where he chaired Section 51, Anthropology from 2010 to 2013.

Professor Kottak has done ethnographic fieldwork in Brazil, Madagascar, and the United States. His general interests are in the processes by which local cultures are incorporated—and resist incorporation—into larger systems. This interest links his earlier work on ecology and state formation in Africa and Madagascar to his more recent research on globalization, national and international culture, and the mass media, including new media and social media.

Kottak's popular case study *Assault on Paradise: The Globalization of a Little Community in Brazil* (2006) describes his long-term and continuing fieldwork in Arembepe, Bahia, Brazil. His book *Prime-Time Society: An Anthropological Analysis of Television and Culture* (2009) is a comparative study of the nature and impact of television in Brazil and the United States.

Kottak's other books include *The Past in the Present: History, Ecology and Cultural Variation in Highland Madagascar; Researching American Culture: A Guide for Student Anthropologists;* and *Madagascar: Society and History.* The most recent editions (17th) of his texts *Anthropology: Appreciating Human Diversity* (this book)

and *Cultural Anthropology: Appreciating Cultural Diversity* were published by McGraw-Hill in 2017. He also is the author of *Mirror for Humanity: A Concise Introduction to Cultural Anthropology* (10th ed., McGraw-Hill, 2016) and *Window on Humanity: A Concise Introduction to Anthropology* (7th ed., McGraw-Hill, 2016). With Kathryn A. Kozaitis, he wrote *On Being Different: Diversity and Multiculturalism in the North American Mainstream* (4th ed., McGraw-Hill, 2012).

Conrad Kottak's articles have appeared in academic journals, including *American Anthropologist, Journal of Anthropological Research, American Ethnologist, Ethnology, Human Organization,* and *Luso-Brazilian Review.* He also has written for popular journals, including *Transaction/SOCIETY, Natural History, Psychology Today,* and *General Anthropology.*

Kottak and his colleagues have researched television's impact in Brazil, environmental risk perception in Brazil, deforestation and biodiversity conservation in Madagascar, and economic development planning in northeastern Brazil. More recently, Kottak and his colleague Lara Descartes investigated how middle-class American families use various media in planning, managing, and evaluating the competing demands of work and family. That research is the basis of their book *Media and Middle Class Moms: Images and Realities of Work and Family* (Descartes and Kottak 2009). Professor Kottak currently is collaborating with Professor Richard Pace of Middle Tennessee State University and several graduate students on research investigating "The Evolution of Media Impact: A Longitudinal and Multi-Site Study of Television and New Electronic/Digital Media in Brazil."

Conrad Kottak appreciates comments about his books from professors and students. He can be reached by e-mail at the following address: **ckottak@bellsouth.net.**

a letter from the author

Welcome to the 17th Edition of *Anthropology: Appreciating Human Diversity!*

I wrote the first edition of this book during a time of rapid change in my favorite academic discipline—anthropology. My colleagues and I were excited about new discoveries and directions in all four of anthropology's subfields—biological anthropology, anthropological archaeology, sociocultural anthropology, and linguistic anthropology. My goal was to write a book that would capture that excitement, addressing key changes, while also providing a solid foundation of core concepts and the basics.

Just as anthropology is a dynamic discipline that encourages new discoveries and explores the profound changes now affecting people and societies, this edition of *Anthropology* makes a concerted effort to keep pace with changes in the way students read and learn core content today. Our digital program, **Connect Anthropology**, includes assignable and assessable quizzes, exercises, and interactive activities, organized around course-specific learning objectives. Furthermore, **Connect** includes an interactive eBook, **LearnSmart**, which is an adaptive testing program, and **SmartBook**, the first and only truly adaptive reading experience. The tools and resources provided in **Connect Anthropology** are designed to engage students and enable them to improve their performance in the course. This 17th edition has benefited from feedback from about 2,000 students who worked with these tools and programs while using the 16th edition of *Anthropology*. We were able to flag and respond to specific areas of difficulty that students encountered, chapter by chapter. I used this extensive feedback to revise, rethink, and clarify my writing in almost every chapter. In preparing this edition, I benefited tremendously from both students' and professors' reactions to my book.

As I work on each new edition, it becomes ever more apparent to me that while any competent and useful text must present anthropology's core, that text also must demonstrate anthropology's relevance to the 21st-century world we inhabit. Accordingly, each new edition contains substantial content changes as well as a series of features that examine our changing world. For example, several "Focus on Globalization" essays in this book examine topics as diverse as travel and tourism in the ancient and modern worlds, disease pandemics, world sports events (including the Olympics and the World Cup), and the expansion of international finance and branding. Several chapters contain discussions of new media, including social media. Many of the boxes titled "Appreciating Anthropology" and "Appreciating Diversity" (at least one per chapter) also present new discoveries and topics.

Each chapter begins with a discussion titled "Understanding Ourselves." These introductions, along with examples from popular culture throughout the book, show how anthropology relates to students' everyday lives. My overarching goal is to help students appreciate the field of anthropology and the various kinds of diversity it studies. How do anthropologists think and work? Where do we go, and how do we interpret what we see? How do we step back, compare, and analyze? How does anthropology contribute to our understanding of the world? The "Appreciating Anthropology" boxes focus on the value and usefulness of anthropological research and approaches while the "Appreciating Diversity" boxes focus on various forms and expressions of human biological and cultural diversity.

Most students who read this book will not go on to become anthropologists, or even anthropology majors. For those who do, this book should provide a solid foundation to build on. For those who don't—that is, for most of my readers—my goal is to instill a sense of appreciation: of human diversity, of anthropology as a field, and of how anthropology can build on, and help make sense of, the experience that students bring to the classroom. May this course and this text help students think differently about, and achieve greater understanding of, their own culture and its place within our globalizing world.

Conrad Phillip Kottak

Updates and Revisions—Informed by Student Data

Revisions to the 17th edition of *Anthropology* were extensively informed by student data, collected anonymously by McGraw-Hill's LearnSmart adaptive learning system. Using this data, we were able to graphically illustrate "hot spots," indicating content area students struggle with (see image below). This data provided feedback at the paragraph and even sentence level. Conrad Kottak relied on this data when making decisions about material to revise, update, and improve. Updates were also informed by the many excellent reviews provided by faculty at 2- and 4-year schools across the country.

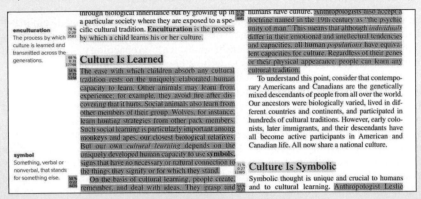

CHAPTER 1: WHAT IS ANTHROPOLOGY?
- Streamlined organization with clearer focus on core content
- Revised sections:
  - Biological Anthropology
  - Cultural Anthropology and Sociology
  - Theories, Associations, and Explanations, including a new Recap to emphasize key terms

CHAPTER 2: CULTURE
- Updated discussion on Makah whaling, including the latest available information on the dispute

CHAPTER 3: APPLYING ANTHROPOLOGY
- Coverage of "Early Applications" completely rewritten
- Key sections of "Development Anthropology" revised, including the discussions of equity impact and overinnovation
- "Medical Anthropology" section rewritten and reorganized, with the addition of three new subheads to group and organize content
- Updated coverage of all of the following:
  - Pros and cons of Western medicine
  - Health problems spawned by industrialization and globalization
  - The author's contention that Western systems would benefit from a more personal treatment of illness

CHAPTER 4: DOING ARCHAEOLOGY AND BIOLOGICAL ANTHROPOLOGY
- Revised section on "Molecular Anthropology"
- Updates throughout

CHAPTER 5: EVOLUTION AND GENETICS
- Revised and updated treatment of:
  - Evolution as both a scientific theory and a fact
  - Genetic drift
  - The four forces or mechanisms that cause change in gene frequencies (genetic evolution)
  - Mutation
- Revised section previously titled "The Modern Synthesis," now called "Microevolution, Macroevolution, and Extinction"
- New "Appreciating Anthropology" box, "Disease Evolution: A Case Study"

CHAPTER 6: HUMAN VARIATION AND ADAPTATION
- New discussion of racial perceptions in the ancient world
- New "Appreciating Anthropology" box, "What's Wrong with Race?" (previously in Chapter 15)
- Revised discussion of the following:
  - Problems of classifying people by skin color
  - How natural selection has affected skin color
  - Cultural alternatives to biological adaptation
  - The relationships between microbes and blood types
  - The increase in infectious diseases after food production (farming and herding)
  - The susceptibility of particular blood types to different diseases

CHAPTER 7: THE PRIMATES
- This chapter has received a thorough rewrite, including the following changes:
  - Replaced old prosimian/anthropoid taxonomic labels with phylogenetically correct strepsirrhine/haplorrhine categories
  - New discussion of angiosperm hypothesis for primate origins
  - New discussion of *Carpolestes simpsoni*
- Revised discussions of fitness theory, Eocene and Oligocene primates, and *Pierolapithecus*
- Two new figures, on the classification of primates and the distribution of the African great apes
- New "Appreciating Diversity" box, "Should Apes Have Human Rights?"

CHAPTER 8: EARLY HOMININS
- This chapter has been given a thorough rewrite, including the following changes:
  - The sections on South African australopiths and early tools have been completely rewritten
  - Changed terminology to reflect contemporary consensus—robust australopiths now called *Paranthropus* rather than *Australopithecus;* "australopithecine" now "australopith"
  - Revised discussion of anatomical features (e.g., pelvis, dentition, crests) of *Ardipithecus, Au. afarensis,* and South African australopiths
  - Rewritten "Understanding Ourselves" section, featuring Piltdown story
  - Updates including new dates for South African australopiths, earliest stone tools now 3.3 m.y.a., new body size estimates for fossil hominins
  - Two new figures, on the East African Rift Valley and early fossil hominins, and on Oldowan tools

CHAPTER 9: THE GENUS *HOMO*
- This chapter has been revised extensively, including the following changes:
  - Revised dating when available

- New section on "2015 Discoveries," covering recent finds of oldest *Homo* jaw from Kenya and *H. naledi* from South Africa
- New "Appreciating Anthropology" box, "The Rising Stars of a South African Cave"
- Middle Pleistocene hominins now discussed more precisely as *H. heidelbergensis;* no more use of the confusing term "archaic *Homo*"
- New maps and illustrations, including *H. heidelbergensis* map and illustrations, Neandertal site map, *H. naledi* illustrations

CHAPTER 10: THE ORIGIN AND SPREAD OF MODERN HUMANS

- Revised terminology as needed to reflect changes in prior chapters
- Five new illustrations of the Skhul skull, African anatomically modern humans (AMHs), and Clovis points
- Revised discussions of:
  - Mitochondrial eve
  - What Neandertal DNA tells us about last common ancestry of Neandertals and AMHs
  - The role of Polynesians and Melanesians in peopling the Pacific

CHAPTER 11: THE FIRST FARMERS

- Revised discussions of:
  - The spread of farming techniques in Europe
  - Changes in anthropological thought about the process of domestication in the Neolithic
  - The hardships, or costs, of food production
  - The decline of public health in societies based on food production
- New material on:
  - Dog domestication
  - Genetic changes due to migrations of farmers and herders into Europe
  - Millet as a transitional crop between foraging and food production across the Eurasian foothills

CHAPTER 12: THE FIRST CITIES AND STATES

- Treatment of the following topics has been revised for clarity:
  - The role of regional trade in state formation
  - The process of state formation itself
  - The attributes that distinguished states from earlier forms of society
  - Completely rewritten section on "Social Ranking and Chiefdoms"
  - Updated discussion of the Indus River Valley state
  - Revised discussion of warfare and the Zapotec state

CHAPTER 13: METHOD AND THEORY IN CULTURAL ANTHROPOLOGY

- Revised section on "Problem-Oriented Ethnography"
- Significant rewriting and reorganizing in the theory sections
- Updates throughout, referencing the latest sources

CHAPTER 14: LANGUAGE AND COMMUNICATION

- New "Appreciating Diversity" box, "Words of the Year"
- New discussion of "the language of food"
- Updates throughout

CHAPTER 15: ETHNICITY AND RACE

- This chapter has been almost completely rewritten. Changes include the following:
  - New section on the backlash to multiculturalism
  - New section on the Black Lives Matter movement
  - New discussion of the ongoing conflicts in Iraq and Syria
  - Updated statistics throughout, with the latest available figures on income, wealth, minority group poverty rates, and growth in ethnic diversity in the United States

CHAPTER 16: MAKING A LIVING

- Clarified discussion of the following topics:
  - The definition of foragers and the distribution of modern foragers
  - The relocation of the Basarwa San
  - Social distinctions in egalitarian foraging societies
  - The terms *horticulture, shifting cultivation,* and *slash-and-burn horticulture*
  - How agriculture affects society and the environment
  - The terms *redistribution* and *reciprocity*
  - The Potlatch

CHAPTER 17: POLITICAL SYSTEMS

- Revised treatment of the following topics:
  - The differences between contemporary and Stone Age hunter-gatherers
  - Changes in how anthropologists view foragers
  - The range of political systems associated with pastoralism and the status of pastoralism within modern nation-states.
  - How states enforce laws, how states intervene in disputes, and the significance of fiscal systems in states
  - Factors that curb and factors that enable public resistance

- The concepts of *public* and *hidden transcripts*
- How shame and gossip can function as effective processes of social control

CHAPTER 18: GENDER

- The chapter was heavily revised, including the following changes:
  - New information on deadly aspects of gender inequality in the contemporary world, including a discussion of the case of the Pakistani girl Malala, the teenage winner of the 2014 Nobel prize
  - New discussion of the increasing professionalization of the female labor force in the United States
  - New section titled "Work and Family: Reality and Stereotypes," which examines how contemporary families are balancing work and family responsibilities, how men have increased their contribution to housework and childcare, lingering stereotypes about male and female work, and the need for employers to offer more flexible work arrangements
  - Substantial updates to the section "Work and Happiness"
  - Updated discussion of transgender identity
  - Updated statistics throughout

CHAPTER 19: FAMILIES, KINSHIP, AND DESCENT

- Updated figures and statistics with data from 2014 and 2015
- Revised discussion of the following:
  - Descent groups
  - Expanded family households
  - How geographic mobility affects North American kinship
  - The zadruga family system
  - Stipulated descent
  - Ambilineal descent
  - Kinship calculation
  - Kin terms
  - Bifurcate merging kinship terminology and the kinds of societies that have it
  - Generational kinship terminology
  - Bifurcate collateral kinship terminology

CHAPTER 20: MARRIAGE

- New "Appreciating Anthropology" box, "What Anthropologists Could Teach the Supreme Court about the Definition of Marriage"
- Revised discussions of why marriage is difficult to define cross-culturally, and of the factors that promote or discourage polygyny.
- Updated section on "Same-Sex Marriage"
- New map showing countries now allowing same-sex marriage and the date of legalization

CHAPTER 21: RELIGION

- New "Appreciating Diversity" box, "This New-Time Religion," on changes in religious affiliation in the United States between 2007 and 2014
- Revised discussion of the following:
  - Durkheim's approach to religion
  - Anthony Wallace's definition of religion
  - The growth of Evangelical Protestantism
  - The relationship between antimodernism and religious fundamentalism in Christianity and Islam

CHAPTER 22: ARTS, MEDIA, AND SPORTS

- New "Appreciating Diversity" box, "Asian American Musicians: Internet Stars, Mainstream Wannabes," discussing successful Asian-American YouTube stars
- Revised discussions of:
  - The limitations of dictionary definitions of art
  - The varied forms of expressive culture included within the anthropological study of art
  - What the Kalabari case study reveals about art, aesthetics, and religion
- The interplay between the individual and the social in artistic production in non-Western and Western societies
- Updated and reworked section "Networking and Sociability On- and Offline"
- Clarified connections among the arts, media, and sports
- Amplified discussion of criticism of the arts in contemporary societies

CHAPTER 23: THE WORLD SYSTEM, COLONIALISM, AND INEQUALITY

- Updated throughout, especially in the section "The Persistence of Inequality," which has an entirely new subsection titled "Environmental Risks on the American Periphery"
- Clarified discussion of the following topics:
  - World-system theory
  - The Industrial Revolution
  - The domestic system of production
  - Reasons the Industrial Revolution began in England
  - Cultural and religious factors in England's industrialization
  - Ways in which the Industrial Revolution changed societies
- The colonies of Spain and Portugal
- The British Empire
- The impact of NAFTA on the Mexican economy
- New illustrations of changes in U.S. household income and the distribution of wealth in the United States

CHAPTER 24: ANTHROPOLOGY'S ROLE IN A GLOBALIZING WORLD

- New "Appreciating Diversity" box, "Diversity under Siege: Global Forces and Indigenous Peoples"
- Inclusion of 2015 American Anthropological Association (AAA) "Statement on Humanity and Climate Change"
- Revised discussions of:
  - The globalization of risk
  - The meaning of globalization
  - Emerging and zoonotic diseases
  - Why development projects and conservation efforts must pay attention to the needs and wishes of local people
  - Acculturation
  - Finance as a global force
  - Examples of a global culture of consumption

Learn Without Limits

Connect is proven effective

McGraw-Hill Connect® is a digital teaching and learning environment that improves performance over a variety of critical outcomes; it is easy to use; and it is proven effective. Connect® empowers students by continually adapting to deliver precisely what they need, when they need it, and how they need it, so your class time is more engaging and effective. Connect for *Anthropology* offers a wealth of interactive on-line content, including quizzes, exercises, and critical thinking questions, and "Applying Anthropology," "Anthropology on My Own," and "Anthropology on the Web" activities.

Connect also features these advanced capabilities

SMARTBOOK™ Available within Connect, **SmartBook®** makes study time as productive and efficient as possible by identifying and closing knowledge gaps. SmartBook is powered by the proven **LearnSmart®** engine, which identifies what an individual student knows and doesn't know based on the student's confidence level, responses to questions, and other factors. LearnSmart builds an optimal, personalized learning path for each student, so students spend less time on concepts they already understand and more time on those they don't. As a student engages with SmartBook, the reading experience continuously adapts by highlighting the most impactful content a student needs to learn at that moment in time. This ensures that every minute spent with SmartBook is returned to the student as the most value-added minute possible. The result? More confidence, better grades, and greater success.

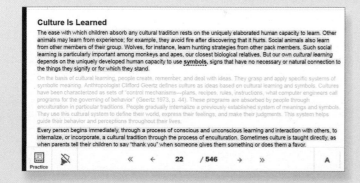

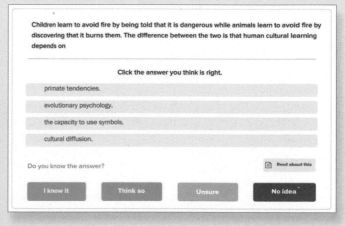

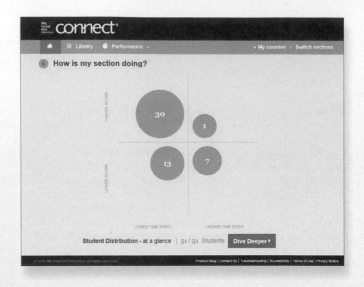

Connect Insight® is Connect's new one-of-a-kind visual analytics dashboard—now available for both instructors and students—that provides at-a-glance information regarding student performance, which is immediately actionable. By presenting assignment, assessment, and topical performance results together with a time metric that is easily visible for aggregate or individual results, Connect Insight gives the user the capability to take a just-in-time approach to teaching and learning, which was never before available. Connect Insight presents data that empowers students and helps instructors improve class performance in a way that is efficient and effective.

Your Course, Your Way

McGraw-Hill Create® is a self-service website that allows you to create customized course materials using McGraw-Hill Education's comprehensive, cross-disciplinary content and digital products. You can even access third-party content such as readings, articles, cases, videos, and more.

- Select and arrange content to fit your course scope and sequence.
- Upload your own course materials.
- Select the best format for your students—print or eBook.
- Select and personalize your cover.
- Edit and update your materials as often as you'd like.

Experience how McGraw-Hill Education's Create empowers you to teach your students your way: http://www.mcgrawhillcreate.com.

McGraw-Hill Campus® is a groundbreaking service that puts world-class digital learning resources just a click away for all faculty and students. All faculty—whether or not they use a McGraw-Hill title—can instantly browse, search, and access the entire library of McGraw-Hill instructional resources and services, including eBooks, test banks, PowerPoint slides, animations, and learning objects—from any Learning Management System (LMS), at no additional cost to an institution. Users also have single sign-on access to McGraw-Hill digital platforms, including Connect, Create, and Tegrity, a fully automated lecture caption solution.

Instructor Resources
Instructor resources available through Connect for *Anthropology* include an Instructor's Manual, Test Bank, Image Bank, and PowerPoint presentation for each chapter.

Acknowledgments

As always, I'm grateful to many colleagues at McGraw-Hill. Thanks to Gina Boedeker, McGraw-Hill's managing director for anthropology, and to Rhona Robbin, lead product developer, who was especially helpful and encouraging in launching this revision. I offer particular thanks to product developer Emily Pecora, with whom I've had the pleasure of working on multiple titles. I always appreciate Emily's keen editorial eye for style, language, and content, as she has helped guide me through several revisions. I thank marketing manager Kaitlyn Lombardo and McGraw-Hill's entire team of sales reps and regional managers for the work they do in helping professors and students gain access to my books.

I'm truly grateful as well for the superb work of the following: Rick Hecker, content project manager; George Theofanopoulous, digital project manager; Tara McDermott, designer; and Lori Slattery, content licensing specialist. I offer thanks as well to Charlotte Goldman, freelance photo researcher; Amy Marks, copyeditor; and Marlena Pechan, proofreader. I'm also very grateful to Christine Gimlin, who did an expert job of transferring my changes from Word files to pdfs. Thanks as well to Scott Lukas, Lake Tahoe Community College, who created the content for the Connect products for this book; and Helen Warner, who updated the materials for this latest edition. Special thanks, too, to Professor Richard Pace, who drafted the section on social media in Brazil in Chapter 17.

I'm especially indebted to the reviewers who evaluated the 16th edition of this book. I have followed many of their suggestions in this revision.

Dr. Jessica Thompson provided an especially detailed and useful critique of several chapters on primates and human evolution; those chapters benefited greatly, as I followed many of her suggestions.

Excellent suggestions were also provided by each of the following:

Bonny Christy, *Blinn College*
William Donner, *Kutztown University*
William Doonan, *Sacramento City College*
Max Kirsch, *Florida Atlantic University*
Amy Kowal, *Florida State University*
Merri Mattison, *Red Rocks Community College*
Reece Jon McGee, *Texas State University*
Kare McManama-Kearin, *Weber State University*
Andrew Nelson, *University of North Texas*
Leila Rodriguez, *University of Cincinnati*
Richard Sattler, *University of Montana*
Scott Sernau, *Indiana University South Bend*
Wayman Smith, *Georgia Perimeter College*

I'm also grateful to the reviewers of previous editions of this book and of my *Cultural Anthropology* text. Their names are as follows:

Julianna Acheson, Green Mountain College
Stephanie W. Alemán, Iowa State University
Mohammad Al-Madani, Seattle Central Community College
Maria Altemara, West Virginia University, Robert Morris University
Douglas J. Anderson, Front Range Community College
E. F. Aranyosi, University of Washington
Timi Lynne Barone, University of Nebraska, Omaha
Robert Bee, University of Connecticut
Joy A. Bilharz, SUNY at Fredonia
James R. Bindon, University of Alabama
Kira Blaisdell-Sloan, Louisiana State University
Kathleen T. Blue, Minnesota State University
Renée M. Bonzani, University of Kentucky
Daniel Boxberger, Western Washington University
Vicki Bradley, University of Houston
Lisa Kaye Brandt, North Dakota State University
Ethan M. Braunstein, Northern Arizona University
Ned Breschel, Morehead State University
Christopher A. Brooks, Virginia Commonwealth University
Peter J. Brown, Emory University
Margaret S. Bruchez, Blinn College

Vaughn M. Bryant, Texas A&M University
Andrew Buckser, Purdue University
Richard H. Buonforte, Brigham Young University
Karen Burns, University of Georgia
Richard Burns, Arkansas State University
Mary Cameron, Auburn University
Joseph L. Chartkoff, Michigan State University
Dianne Chidester, University of South Dakota
Stephen Childs, Valdosta State University
Inne Choi, California Polytechnic State University–San Luis Obispo
Wanda Clark, South Plains College
Jeffrey Cohen, Penn State University
Fred Conquest, Community College of Southern Nevada
Barbara Cook, California Polytechnic State University–San Luis Obispo
Maia Greenwell Cunningham, Citrus College
Sean M. Daley, Johnson County Community College
Karen Dalke, University of Wisconsin–Green Bay
Norbert Dannhaeuser, Texas A&M University
Michael Davis, Truman State University
Hillary Delprete, Wagner College
Paul Demers, University of Nebraska–Lincoln
Darryl de Ruiter, Texas A&M University
Robert Dirks, Illinois State University
William W. Donner, Kutztown University
Mary Durocher, Wayne State University
Paul Durrenberger, Pennsylvania State University
George Esber, Miami University of Ohio
Les W. Field, University of New Mexico
Grace Fraser, Plymouth State College
Todd Jeffrey French, University of New Hampshire, Durham
Richard H. Furlow, College of DuPage
Vance Geiger, University of Central Florida
Laurie Godfrey, University of Massachusetts–Amherst
Bob Goodby, Franklin Pierce College
Gloria Gozdzik, West Virginia University
Tom Greaves, Bucknell University

Mark Grey, University of Northern Iowa
Sharon Gursky, Texas A&M University
John Dwight Hines, University of California, Santa Barbara
Brian A. Hoey, Marshall University
Homes Hogue, Mississippi State University
Kara C. Hoover, Georgia State University
Charles W. Houck, University of North Carolina–Charlotte
Stevan R. Jackson, Virginia Tech
Alice James, Shippensburg University of Pennsylvania
Cara Roure Johnson, University of Connecticut
Kevin Keating, Broward College
Richard King, Drake University
Christine Kray, Rochester Institute of Technology
Eric Lassiter, Ball State University
Jill Leonard, University of Illinois–Urbana-Champaign
Kenneth Lewis, Michigan State University
David Lipset, University of Minnesota
Walter E. Little, University at Albany, SUNY
Jon K. Loessin, Wharton County Junior College
Brian Malley, University of Michigan
Jonathan Marks, University of North Carolina–Charlotte
H. Lyn Miles, University of Tennessee at Chattanooga
Barbara Miller, George Washington University
Richard G. Milo, Chicago State University
John Nass, Jr., California University of Pennsylvania
Frank Ng, California State University–Fresno
Constanza Ocampo-Raeder, University of Maine (Orono)
Divinity B. O'Connor DLR-Roberts, Des Moines Area
    Community College
Martin Ottenheimer, Kansas State University
De Ann Pendry, University of Tennessee–Knoxville
Holly Peters-Golden, University of Michigan
Leonard Plotnicov, University of Pittsburgh
Janet Pollak, William Paterson University
Christina Nicole Pomianek, University of Missouri–Columbia
Geoffrey G. Pope, William Paterson University
Howard Prince, CUNY–Borough of Manhattan Community
    College

Frances E. Purifoy, University of Louisville
Asa Randall, University of Florida
Mark A. Rees, University of Louisiana at Lafayette
Bruce D. Roberts, Minnesota State University Moorhead
Rita C. Rodabaugh, Central Piedmont Community College
Steven Rubenstein, Ohio University
Robert Rubinstein, Syracuse University
Richard A. Sattler, University of Montana
Richard Scaglion, University of Pittsburgh
Mary Scott, San Francisco State University
James Sewastynowicz, Jacksonville State University
Brian Siegel, Furman University
Michael Simonton, Northern Kentucky University
Megan Sinnott, University of Colorado–Boulder
Esther Skirboll, Slippery Rock University of Pennsylvania
Alexia Smith, University of Connecticut
Gregory Starrett, University of North Carolina–Charlotte
Karl Steinen, University of West Georgia
Noelle Stout, Foothill and Skyline Colleges
Merrily Stover, University of Maryland–University College
Elizabeth A. Throop, Eastern Kentucky University
Ruth Toulson, Brigham Young University
Susan Trencher, George Mason University
Mark Tromans, Broward Community College
Christina Turner, Virginia Commonwealth University
Donald Tyler, University of Idaho
Daniel Varisco, Hofstra University
Albert Wahrhaftig, Sonoma State University
Heather Walder, University of Wisconsin–La Crosse
Joe Watkins, University of New Mexico
David Webb, Kutztown University of Pennsylvania
George Westermark, Santa Clara University
Donald A. Whatley, Blinn College
Nancy White, University of South Florida
Katharine Wiegele, Northern Illinois University
Mary S. Willis, University of Nebraska–Lincoln
Brent Woodfill, University of Louisiana at Lafayette

Very, very, special thanks as well to the 2,000 or so students whose responses in LearnSmart helped me pinpoint content and writing that needed clarification. Never have so many voices contributed to a revision as to this one.

Other professors and students regularly share their insights about this and my other texts via e-mail and so have contributed to this book. I'm especially grateful to my Michigan colleagues who use my books and have suggested ways of making them better. Thanks especially to a 101 team that includes Tom Fricke, Stuart Kirsch, Holly Peters-Golden, and Andrew Shryock. By now, I've benefited from the knowledge, help, and advice of so many friends, colleagues, teaching assistants, graduate student instructors, and students that I can no longer fit their names into a short preface. I hope they know who they are and accept my thanks.

As usual, my family offers me understanding, support, and inspiration during the preparation of this book. Dr. Nicholas Kottak, who, like me, holds a doctorate in anthropology, regularly shares his insights with me, as does my daughter, Dr. Juliet Kottak Mavromatis, and my wife, Isabel Wagley Kottak. Isabel has been my companion in the field and in life during my entire career in anthropology, and I can't imagine being without her. I renew my dedication of this book to the memory of my mother, Mariana Kottak Roberts, who kindled my interest in the human condition and provided many insights about people and society.

Over my many years of teaching anthropology, feedback from students has kept me up to date on the interests and needs of my readers, as does my ongoing participation in workshops on the teaching of anthropology. I hope this product of my experience will be helpful to others.

Conrad Phillip Kottak
Seabrook Island, SC,
and Decatur, Georgia
ckottak@bellsouth.net

What Is Anthropology?

▶ **What distinguishes anthropology from other fields that study human beings?**

▶ **How do anthropologists study human diversity in time and space?**

▶ **Why is anthropology both scientific and humanistic?**

A produce market in Ubud, Bali, Indonesia.

understanding OURSELVES

When you grew up, which sport did you appreciate the most—soccer, swimming, football, baseball, tennis, golf, or some other sport (or perhaps none at all)? Is this because of "who you are" or because of the opportunities you had as a child to practice and participate in this particular activity? Think about the phrases and sentences you would use to describe yourself in a personal ad or on a networking site—your likes and dislikes, hobbies, and habits. How many of these descriptors would be the same if you had been born in a different place or time?

When you were young, your parents might have told you that drinking milk and eating vegetables would help you grow up "big and strong." They probably didn't recognize as readily the role that *culture* plays in shaping bodies, personalities, and personal health. If nutrition matters in growth, so, too, do cultural guidelines. What is proper behavior for boys and girls? What kinds of work should men and women do? Where should people live? What are proper uses of their leisure time? What role should religion play? How should people relate to their family, friends, and neighbors? Although our genetic attributes provide a foundation for our growth and development, human biology is fairly plastic—that is, it is malleable. Culture is an environmental force that affects our development as much as do nutrition, heat, cold, and altitude. Culture also guides our emotional and cognitive growth and helps determine the kinds of personalities we have as adults.

Among scholarly disciplines, anthropology stands out as the field that provides the cross-cultural test. How much would we know about human behavior, thought, and feeling if we studied only our own kind? What if our entire understanding of human behavior were based on analysis of questionnaires filled out by college students in Oregon? That is a radical question, but one that should make you think about the basis for statements about what humans are like, individually or as a group. A primary reason anthropology can uncover so much about what it means to be human is that the discipline is based on the cross-cultural perspective. A single culture simply cannot tell us everything we need to know about what it means to be human. We need to compare and contrast. Often culture is "invisible" (assumed to be normal, or just the way things are) until it is placed in comparison to another culture. For example, to appreciate how watching television affects us, as human beings, we need to study not just North America today but some other place—and perhaps some other time (such as Brazil in the 1980s; see Kottak 1990b, 2009). The cross-cultural test is fundamental to the anthropological approach, which orients this textbook.

HUMAN DIVERSITY

Anthropologists study human beings and their products wherever and whenever they find them—in rural Kenya, a Turkish café, a Mesopotamian tomb, or a North American shopping mall. Anthropology explores human diversity across time and space, seeking to understand as much as possible about the human condition. Of particular interest is the diversity that comes through human adaptability.

Humans are among the world's most adaptable animals. In the Andes of South America, people wake up in villages 16,000 feet above sea level and then trek 1,500 feet higher to work in tin mines. Tribes in the Australian desert worship animals and discuss philosophy. People survive malaria in the tropics. Men have walked on the moon. The model of the USS *Enterprise* in Washington's Smithsonian Institution symbolizes the desire to "seek out new life and civilizations, to boldly go where no one has gone before." Wishes to know the unknown, control the uncontrollable, and create order out of chaos find expression among all peoples. Creativity, adaptability, and flexibility are basic human attributes, and human diversity is the subject matter of anthropology.

Students often are surprised by the breadth of **anthropology,** which is the study of humans around the world and through time. Anthropology is a uniquely comparative and **holistic** science. *Holism* refers to the study of the whole of the human condition: past, present, and future; biology, society, language, and culture. Most people think that anthropologists study fossils and nonindustrial, non-Western cultures, and many of them do. But anthropology is much more than the study of nonindustrial peoples: It is a comparative field that examines all societies, ancient and modern, simple and complex, local and global. The other social sciences tend to focus on a single society, usually an industrial nation like the United States or Canada. Anthropology, however, offers a unique cross-cultural perspective by constantly comparing the customs of one society with those of others.

People share society—organized life in groups—with other animals, including baboons, wolves, mole rats, and even ants. Culture, however, is more distinctly human. **Cultures** are traditions and customs, transmitted through learning, that form and guide the beliefs and behavior of the people exposed to them. Children learn such a tradition by growing up in a particular society, through a process called enculturation. Cultural traditions include customs and opinions, developed over the generations, about proper and improper behavior. These traditions answer such questions as these: How should we do things? How do we make sense of the world? How

do we distinguish between what is right, and what is wrong? A culture produces a degree of consistency in behavior and thought among the people who live in a particular society.

The most critical element of cultural traditions is their transmission through learning rather than through biological inheritance. Culture is not itself biological, but it rests on certain features of human biology. For more than a million years, humans have possessed at least some of the biological capacities on which culture depends. These abilities are to learn, to think symbolically, to use language, and to make and use tools.

Anthropology confronts and ponders major questions about past and present human existence. By examining ancient bones and tools, we unravel the mysteries of human origins. When did our ancestors separate from those of the apes? Where and when did *Homo sapiens* originate? How has our species changed? What are we now, and where are we going? How have social and cultural changes influenced biological change? Our genus, *Homo,* has been changing for more than one million years. Humans continue to adapt and change both biologically and culturally.

Adaptation, Variation, and Change

Adaptation refers to the processes by which organisms cope with environmental forces and stresses. How do organisms change to fit their environments, such as dry climates or high mountain altitudes? Like other animals, humans have biological means of adaptation. But humans also habitually rely on cultural means of adaptation. Recap 1.1 summarizes the cultural and biological means that humans use to adapt to high altitudes.

Mountainous terrains pose particular challenges, those associated with altitude and oxygen deprivation. Consider four ways (one cultural and three biological) in which humans may cope with

anthropology
The study of humans around the world and through time.

holistic
Encompassing past, present, and future; biology, society, language, and culture.

culture
Traditions and customs transmitted through learning.

RECAP 1.1	Forms of Cultural and Biological Adaptation (to High Altitude)	
FORM OF ADAPTATION	**TYPE OF ADAPTATION**	**EXAMPLE**
Technology	Cultural	Pressurized airplane cabin with oxygen masks
Genetic adaptation (occurs over generations)	Biological	Larger "barrel chests" of native highlanders
Long-term physiological adaptation (occurs during growth and development of the individual organism)	Biological	More efficient respiratory system, to extract oxygen from "thin air"
Short-term physiological adaptation (occurs spontaneously when the individual organism enters a new environment)	Biological	Increased heart rate, hyperventilation

low oxygen pressure at high altitudes. Illustrating cultural (technological) adaptation would be a pressurized airplane cabin equipped with oxygen masks. There are three ways of adapting biologically to high altitudes: genetic adaptation, long-term physiological adaptation, and short-term physiological adaptation. First, native populations of high-altitude areas, such as the Andes of Peru and the Himalayas of Tibet and Nepal, seem to have acquired certain genetic advantages for life at very high altitudes. The Andean tendency to develop a voluminous chest and lungs probably has a genetic basis. Second, regardless of their genes, people who grow up at a high altitude become physiologically more efficient there than genetically similar people who have grown up at sea level would be. This illustrates long-term physiological adaptation during the body's growth and development. Third, humans also have the capacity for short-term or immediate physiological adaptation. Thus, when lowlanders arrive in the highlands, they immediately increase their breathing and heart rates. Hyperventilation increases the oxygen in their lungs and arteries. As the pulse also increases, blood reaches their tissues more rapidly. These varied adaptive responses—cultural and biological—all fulfill the need to supply an adequate amount of oxygen to the body.

As human history has unfolded, the social and cultural means of adaptation have become increasingly important. In this process, humans have devised diverse ways of coping with the range of environments they have occupied in time and space. The rate of cultural adaptation and change has accelerated, particularly during the last 10,000 years. For millions of years, hunting and gathering of nature's bounty—*foraging*—was the sole basis of human subsistence. However, it took only a few thousand years for **food production** (the cultivation of plants and domestication of animals), which originated some 12,000–10,000 years ago, to replace foraging in most areas. Between 6000 and 5000 B.P. (before the present), the first civilizations arose. These were large, powerful, and complex societies, such as ancient Egypt, that conquered and governed large geographic areas.

Much more recently, the spread of industrial production has profoundly affected human life. Throughout human history, major innovations have spread at the expense of earlier ones. Each economic revolution has had social and cultural repercussions. Today's global economy and communications link all contemporary people, directly or indirectly, in the modern world system. Nowadays, even remote villagers experience world forces and events. (See "Focus on Globalization" on p. 7.) The study of how local people adapt to global forces poses new challenges for anthropology: "The cultures of world peoples need to be constantly rediscovered as these people reinvent them in changing historical circumstances" (Marcus and Fischer 1986, p. 24).

Cultural Forces Shape Human Biology

Anthropology's comparative, biocultural perspective recognizes that cultural forces constantly mold human biology. (**Biocultural** refers to using and combining both biological and cultural perspectives and approaches to analyze and understand a particular issue or problem.) As we saw in "Understanding Ourselves," culture is a key environmental force in determining how human bodies grow and develop. Cultural traditions promote certain activities and abilities, discourage others, and set standards of physical well-being and attractiveness. Consider how this works in sports. North American girls are encouraged to pursue, and therefore do well in, competition involving figure skating, gymnastics, track and field, swimming, diving, and many other sports. Brazilian girls, although excelling in the team sports of basketball and volleyball, haven't fared nearly as well in individual sports as have their American and Canadian counterparts. Why are people encouraged to excel as athletes in some nations but not others? Why do people in some countries invest so much time and effort in competitive sports that their bodies change significantly as a result?

Cultural standards of attractiveness and propriety influence participation and achievement in sports. Americans run or swim not just to compete but also to keep trim and fit. Brazil's beauty standards traditionally have accepted more fat, especially in female buttocks and hips. Brazilian men have had significant international success in swimming and running, but Brazil rarely sends female swimmers or runners to the Olympics. One reason why Brazilian women avoid competitive swimming in particular may be that sport's effects on the body. Years of swimming sculpt a distinctive physique: an enlarged upper torso, a massive neck, and powerful shoulders and back. Successful female swimmers tend to be big, strong, and bulky. The countries that have produced them most consistently are the United States, Canada, Australia, Germany, the Scandinavian nations, the Netherlands, and the former Soviet Union, where this body type isn't as stigmatized as it is in Latin countries. For women, Brazilian culture prefers ample hips and buttocks to a muscled upper body. Many young female swimmers in Brazil choose to abandon the sport rather than their culture's "feminine" body ideal.

GENERAL ANTHROPOLOGY

The academic discipline of anthropology, also known as **general anthropology** or "four-field" anthropology, includes four main subdisciplines or subfields. They are sociocultural, archaeological, biological, and linguistic anthropology. (From here on, the shorter term *cultural anthropology*

biocultural
Combining biological and cultural approaches to a given problem.

food production
An economy based on plant cultivation and/or animal domestication.

general anthropology
Anthropology as a whole: cultural, archaeological, biological, and linguistic anthropology.

will be used as a synonym for "sociocultural anthropology.") Cultural anthropology focuses on societies of the present and recent past. Anthropological archaeology (the more common term for archaeological anthropology) reconstructs lifeways of ancient and more recent societies through analysis of material remains. Biological anthropology studies human biological variation through time and across geographic space. Linguistic anthropology examines language in its social and cultural contexts. Of the four subfields, cultural anthropology has the largest membership. Most departments of anthropology teach courses in all four subfields. (Note that general anthropology did not develop as a comparable field of study in most European countries, where the subdisciplines tend to exist separately.)

There are historical reasons for the inclusion of the four subfields in a single discipline in North America. The origin of anthropology as a scientific field, and of American anthropology in particular, can be traced back to the 19th century. Early American anthropologists were concerned especially with the history and cultures of the native

Early American anthropology was especially concerned with the history and cultures of Native North Americans. Ely S. Parker, or Ha-sa-noan-da, was a Seneca Indian who made important contributions to early anthropology. Parker also served as Commissioner of Indian Affairs for the United States.
SOURCE: National Archives and Records Administration

peoples of North America. Interest in the origins and diversity of Native Americans brought together studies of customs, social life, language, and physical traits. Anthropologists still are pondering such questions as these: Where did Native Americans come from? How many waves of migration brought them to the New World? What are the linguistic, cultural, and biological links among Native Americans and between them and Asians?

There also are logical reasons for including anthropology's four subfields in the same academic discipline. Answers to key questions in anthropology often require an understanding of both human biology and culture and of both the past and the present. Each subfield considers variation in time and space (that is, in different geographic areas). Cultural and archaeological anthropologists study (among many other topics) changes in social life and customs. Archaeologists have used studies of living societies and behavior patterns to imagine what life might have been like in the past. Biological anthropologists examine evolutionary changes in physical form, for example, anatomical

American swimmer Allison Schmitt starts the women's 100-meter freestyle championship final at the Arena Pro Swim Series on March 5, 2016 in Orlando, Florida. How might years of competitive swimming affect the human body?
© Alex Menendez/Getty Images

changes that might have been associated with the origin of tool use or language. Linguistic anthropologists may reconstruct the basics of ancient languages by studying modern ones.

The subdisciplines influence each other as members of the different subfields talk to each other, share books and journals, and associate in departments and at professional meetings. General anthropology explores the basics of human biology, society, and culture and considers their interrelations. Anthropologists share certain key assumptions. Perhaps the most fundamental is the idea that we cannot reach sound conclusions about "human nature" by studying a single nation, society, or cultural tradition. A comparative, cross-cultural approach is essential.

THE SUBDISCIPLINES OF ANTHROPOLOGY

Cultural Anthropology

Cultural anthropology, the study of human society and culture, is the subfield that describes, analyzes, interprets, and explains social and cultural similarities and differences. To study and interpret cultural diversity, cultural anthropologists engage in two kinds of activity: ethnography (based on fieldwork) and ethnology (based on cross-cultural comparison). **Ethnography** provides an account of a particular group, community, society, or culture. During ethnographic fieldwork, the ethnographer gathers data that he or she organizes, describes, analyzes, and interprets to build and present that account, which may be in the form of a book, an article, or a film. Traditionally, ethnographers lived in small communities, where they studied local behavior, beliefs, customs, social life, economic activities, politics, and religion. Today, any ethnographer will recognize that external forces and events have an increasing influence on such settings.

An anthropological perspective derived from ethnographic fieldwork often differs radically from that of economics or political science. Those fields focus on national and official organizations and policies and often on elites. However, the groups that anthropologists traditionally have studied usually have been relatively poor and powerless. Ethnographers often observe discriminatory practices directed toward such people, who experience food and water shortages, dietary deficiencies, and other aspects of poverty. Political scientists tend to study programs that national planners develop, while anthropologists discover how these programs work on the local level.

Communities and cultures are less isolated today than ever before. In fact, as the anthropologist Franz Boas noted many years ago (1940/1966), contact between neighboring tribes has always existed and has extended over enormous areas.

"Human populations construct their cultures in interaction with one another, and not in isolation" (Wolf 1982, p. ix). Villagers increasingly participate in regional, national, and world events. Exposure to external forces comes through the mass media, migration, and modern transportation. City, nation, and world increasingly invade local communities with the arrival of tourists, development agents, government and religious officials, and political candidates. Such linkages are prominent components of regional, national, and global systems of politics, economics, and information. These larger systems increasingly affect the people and places anthropology traditionally has studied. The study of such linkages and systems is part of the subject matter of modern anthropology. (See "Focus on Globalization" for a discussion of world events familiar to millions of people.)

Ethnology examines, interprets, and analyzes the results of ethnography—the data gathered in different societies. It uses such data to compare and contrast and to generalize about society and culture. Looking beyond the particular to the more general, ethnologists attempt to identify and explain cultural differences and similarities, to test hypotheses, and to build theory to enhance our understanding of how social and cultural systems work. (See the section "The Scientific Method" later in this chapter.) Ethnology gets its data for comparison not just from ethnography but also from the other subfields, particularly from archaeology, which reconstructs social systems of the past. (Recap 1.2 summarizes the main contrasts between ethnography and ethnology.)

Anthropological Archaeology

Anthropological archaeology (also known as archaeological anthropology or, most simply, "archaeology") reconstructs, describes, and interprets human behavior and cultural patterns through material remains. At sites where people live or have lived, archaeologists find artifacts, material items that humans have made, used, or modified, such as tools, weapons, campsites, buildings, and garbage. Plant and animal remains and garbage tell stories about consumption and activities. Wild and domesticated grains have different characteristics, which allow archaeologists to distinguish between the gathering and the cultivation of plants. Animal bones reveal the age and sex of slaughtered animals, providing other information useful in determining whether species were wild or domesticated.

Analyzing such data, archaeologists answer several questions about ancient economies. Did the group get its meat from hunting, or did it domesticate and breed animals, killing only those of a certain age and sex? Did plant food come from wild plants or from sowing, tending, and harvesting crops? Did the residents make, trade for, or buy particular items? Were raw materials available

ethnology
The study of sociocultural differences and similarities.

cultural anthropology
The comparative, cross-cultural study of human society and culture.

ethnography
Fieldwork in a particular cultural setting.

anthropological archaeology
The study of human behavior through material remains.

focus on GLOBALIZATION

World Events

People everywhere—even remote villagers—now participate in world events, especially through the mass media. The study of global–local linkages is a prominent part of modern anthropology. What kinds of events generate global interest? Disasters provide one example. Think of missing airplanes, nuclear plant meltdowns, and the earthquakes and tsunamis that have ravaged Thailand, Indonesia, and Japan. Think, too, of space—the final frontier: As many as 600 million people may have watched the first (Apollo 11) moon landing in 1969—a huge audience in the early days of global television. Also consider the British royal family, especially the photogenic ones. The wedding of Prince William and Catherine Middleton attracted 161 million viewers—twice the population of the United Kingdom. The birth, public presentation, and naming of their son George, an eventual heir to the British throne, in 2013 generated international interest. A generation earlier, millions of people had watched Lady Diana Spencer marry England's Prince Charles. Princess Diana's funeral also attracted a global audience.

And, of course, think of sports: Billions of people watched at least some of the 2016 Summer Olympics held in Rio de Janeiro, Brazil. Consider the FIFA World Cup (soccer), also held every four years. In 2006, an estimated 320 million people tuned in to the tournament's final game. This figure almost tripled to 909 million in 2010, and more than one billion viewers saw Germany defeat Argentina in the 2014 final. The World Cup generates huge global interest because it truly is a "world series," with 32 countries and five continents competing. Similarly, the Cricket World Cup, held every four years (most recently in 2015), is the world's third most watched event: Only the Summer Olympics and the FIFA World Cup exceed it. The 2015 Cricket World Cup was televised in over 200 countries, to over 2.2 billion potential viewers.

It's rather arrogant to call American baseball's ultimate championship "The World Series" when only one non-U.S. team, the Toronto Blue Jays, can play in it. (The title dates back to 1903, a time of less globalization and more American provincialism.) Baseball is popular in the United States (including Puerto Rico), Canada, Japan, Cuba, Mexico, Venezuela, and the Dominican Republic. South Korea, Taiwan, and China have professional leagues. Elsewhere the sport has little mass appeal.

On the other hand, when we focus on the players in American baseball we see a multiethnic world in miniature. With its prominent Latino and Japanese players, American baseball appears to be more ethnically diverse than American football or basketball. Particularly representative of this diversity is the list of finalists for the 2012 American League MVP (Most Valuable Player) award, won by Venezuelan Miguel Cabrera of the Detroit Tigers. In second place was New Jersey–born and non-Hispanic Mike Trout (Los Angeles Angels). Third and fourth were two more Latinos, Adrian Beltré and Robinson Cano. In fifth place came Josh Hamilton, a North Carolinian. The previous year's top five included Jacoby Ellsbury, a registered Native American, and Curtis Granderson, an African American. Can you think of a sport as ethnically diverse as baseball? What's the last world event that drew your attention?

locally? If not, where did they come from? From such information, archaeologists reconstruct patterns of production, trade, and consumption.

Archaeologists have spent much time studying potsherds, fragments of earthenware. Potsherds are more durable than many other artifacts, such as textiles and wood. The quantity of pottery fragments allows estimates of population size and density. The discovery that potters used materials unavailable locally suggests systems of trade. Similarities in manufacture and decoration at different sites may be proof of cultural connections. Groups with similar pots may share a common history. They might have common cultural ancestors. Perhaps they traded with each other or belonged to the same political system.

Many archaeologists examine paleoecology. *Ecology* is the study of interrelations among living things in an environment. The organisms and environment together constitute an ecosystem, a patterned arrangement of energy flows and exchanges. Human ecology studies ecosystems that include people, focusing on the ways in which human use "of nature influences and is influenced by social organization and cultural values" (Bennett 1969, pp. 10–11). *Paleoecology* looks at the ecosystems of the past.

In addition to reconstructing ecological patterns, archaeologists may infer cultural transformations, for example, by observing changes in the size and type of sites and the distance between them. A city develops in a region where only towns, villages, and hamlets existed a few centuries earlier. The number of settlement levels (city, town, village, hamlet) in a society is a measure of social complexity. Buildings offer clues about political and religious features. Temples and pyramids suggest that an ancient society had an authority structure capable of marshaling the labor needed to build such monuments. The presence or absence of certain structures, like the pyramids of ancient Egypt and Mexico, reveals differences in function between settlements. For example, some towns were places where people came to attend ceremonies. Others were burial sites; still others were farming communities.

Archaeologists also reconstruct behavior patterns and lifestyles of the past by excavating. This involves digging through a succession of levels at a particular site. In a given area, through time, settlements may change in form and purpose, as may the connections between settlements. Excavation can document changes in economic, social, and political activities.

Although archaeologists are best known for studying prehistory, that is, the period before the invention of writing, they also study the cultures of historical and even living peoples. Studying sunken ships off the Florida coast, underwater archaeologists have been able to verify the living conditions on the vessels that brought ancestral African Americans to the New World as enslaved

ETHNOGRAPHY	ETHNOLOGY
Requires fieldwork to collect data	Uses data collected by a series of researchers
Often descriptive	Usually synthetic
Group/community specific	Comparative/cross-cultural

people. In a research project begun in 1973 in Tucson, Arizona, archaeologist William Rathje has learned about contemporary life by studying modern garbage. The value of "garbology," as Rathje calls it, is that it provides "evidence of what people did, not what they think they did, what they think they should have done, or what the interviewer thinks they should have done" (Harrison, Rathje, and Hughes 1994, p. 108). What people report may contrast strongly with their real behavior as revealed by garbology. For example, the garbologists discovered that the three Tucson neighborhoods that reported the lowest beer consumption actually had the highest number of discarded beer cans per household (Podolefsky and Brown 1992, p. 100)! Findings from garbology also have challenged common misconceptions about the kinds and quantities of trash found in landfills: While most people thought that fast-food containers and disposable diapers were major waste problems, they were actually relatively insignificant compared with paper (Rathje and Murphy 2001; Zimring 2012).

Biological Anthropology

biological anthropology

The study of human biological variation through time and as it exists today.

Biological anthropology is the study of human biological diversity through time and as it exists in the world today. There are five specialties within biological anthropology:

1. Human biological evolution as revealed by the fossil record (paleoanthropology).

2. Human genetics.

3. Human growth and development.

4. Human biological plasticity (the living body's ability to change as it copes with environmental conditions, such as heat, cold, and altitude).

5. Primatology (the study of monkeys, apes, and other nonhuman primates).

A common thread that runs across all five specialties is an interest in biological variation among humans, including their ancestors and their closest animal relatives (monkeys and apes).

These varied interests link biological anthropology to other fields: biology, zoology, geology, anatomy, physiology, medicine, and public health. Knowledge of osteology—the study of bones—is essential for anthropologists who examine and interpret skulls, teeth, and bones, whether of living humans or of our fossilized ancestors. Paleontologists are scientists who study fossils. Paleoanthropologists study the fossil record of human evolution. Paleoanthropologists often collaborate with archaeologists, who study artifacts, in reconstructing biological and cultural aspects of human evolution. Fossils and tools often are found together. Different types of tools provide information about the habits, customs, and lifestyles of the ancestral humans who used them.

More than a century ago, Charles Darwin noticed that the variety that exists within any population permits some individuals (those with the favored characteristics) to do better than others at surviving and reproducing. Genetics, which developed after Darwin, enlightens us about the causes and transmission of the variety on which evolution depends. However, it isn't just genes that cause variety. During any individual's lifetime, the environment works along with heredity to determine biological features. For example, people with a genetic tendency to be tall will be shorter if they have poor nutrition during childhood. Thus, biological anthropology also investigates the influence of environment on the body as it grows and matures. Among the environmental factors that influence the body as it develops are nutrition, altitude, temperature, and disease, as well as cultural factors, such as the standards of attractiveness that were discussed previously.

Biological anthropology (along with zoology) also includes primatology. The primates include our closest relatives—apes and monkeys. Primatologists study their biology, evolution, behavior, and social life, often in their natural environments. Primatology assists paleoanthropology, because primate behavior and social organization may shed light on early human behavior and human nature.

Linguistic Anthropology

We don't know (and probably never will know) when our ancestors started speaking, although biological anthropologists have looked to the anatomy of the face and the skull to speculate about the origin of language. As well, primatologists have described the communication systems of monkeys and apes. We do know that well-developed, grammatically complex languages

Anthropological archaeologists from the University of Pennsylvania work to stabilize the original plaster at an Anasazi (Native American) site in Colorado's Mesa Verde National Park.
© George H.H. Huey/ Alamy Stock Photo

have existed for thousands of years. Linguistic anthropology offers further illustration of anthropology's interest in comparison, variation, and change. **Linguistic anthropology** studies language in its social and cultural context, throughout the world and over time. Some linguistic anthropologists also make inferences about universal features of language, linked perhaps to uniformities in the human brain. Others reconstruct ancient languages by comparing their contemporary descendants and in so doing make discoveries about history. Still others study linguistic differences to discover varied perceptions and patterns of thought in different cultures.

Historical linguistics considers variation over time, such as the changes in sounds, grammar, and vocabulary between Middle English (spoken from approximately 1050 to 1550 C.E.) and modern English. **Sociolinguistics** investigates relationships between social and linguistic variation. No language is a homogeneous system in which everyone speaks just like everyone else. How do different speakers use a given language? How do linguistic features correlate with social factors, including class and gender differences? One reason for variation is geography, as in regional dialects and accents. Linguistic variation also is expressed in the bilingualism of ethnic groups. Linguistic and cultural anthropologists collaborate in studying links between language and many other aspects of culture, such as how people reckon kinship and how they perceive and classify colors.

APPLIED ANTHROPOLOGY

What sort of man or woman do you envision when you hear the word *anthropologist*? Although anthropologists have been portrayed as quirky and eccentric, bearded and bespectacled, anthropology is not a science of the exotic carried on by quaint scholars in ivory towers. Rather, anthropology has a lot to tell the public. Anthropology's foremost professional organization, the American Anthropological Association (AAA), has formally acknowledged a public service role by recognizing that anthropology has two dimensions: (1) academic anthropology and (2) practicing, or **applied, anthropology.** The latter refers to the application of anthropological data, perspectives, theory, and methods to identify, assess, and solve contemporary social problems. As American anthropologist Erve Chambers (1987, p. 309) has stated, applied anthropology is "concerned with the relationships between anthropological knowledge and the uses of that knowledge in the world beyond anthropology." More and more anthropologists from the four subfields now work in "applied" areas such as public health, family planning, business, market research, economic development, and cultural resource management.

Because of anthropology's breadth, applied anthropology has many applications. For example, applied medical anthropologists consider both the sociocultural and the biological contexts and implications of disease and illness. Perceptions of good and bad health, along with actual health

linguistic anthropology
The study of language and linguistic diversity in time, space, and society.

sociolinguistics
The study of language in society.

applied anthropology
The use of anthropology to solve contemporary problems.

threats and problems, differ among societies. Various ethnic groups recognize different illnesses, symptoms, and causes and have developed different health care systems and treatment strategies.

Applied archaeology, usually called *public archaeology,* includes such activities as cultural resource management, public educational programs, and historic preservation. Legislation requiring evaluation of sites threatened by dams, highways, and other construction activities has created an important role for public archaeology. To decide what needs saving, and to preserve significant information about the past when sites cannot be saved, is the work of **cultural resource management** (CRM). CRM involves not only preserving sites but also allowing their destruction if they are not significant. The *management* part of the term refers to the evaluation and decision-making process. Cultural resource managers work for federal, state, and county agencies and other clients. Applied cultural anthropologists sometimes work with public archaeologists, assessing the human problems generated by the proposed change and determining how they can be reduced.

ANTHROPOLOGY AND OTHER ACADEMIC FIELDS

As mentioned previously, one of the main differences between anthropology and the other fields that study people is holism, anthropology's unique blend of biological, social, cultural, linguistic, historical, and contemporary perspectives. Paradoxically, while distinguishing anthropology, this breadth also is what links it to many other disciplines. Techniques used to date fossils and artifacts have come to anthropology from physics, chemistry, and geology. Because plant and animal remains often are found with human bones and artifacts, anthropologists collaborate with botanists, zoologists, and paleontologists.

Anthropology is a **science**—a "systematic field of study or body of knowledge that aims, through experiment, observation, and deduction, to produce reliable explanations of phenomena, with reference to the material and physical world" (*Webster's New World Encyclopedia* 1993, p. 937). This book presents anthropology as a *humanistic science* devoted to discovering, describing, understanding, appreciating, and explaining similarities and differences in time and space among humans and our ancestors. Clyde Kluckhohn (1944) described anthropology as "the science of human similarities and differences" (p. 9). His statement of the need for such a field still stands: "Anthropology provides a scientific basis for dealing with the crucial dilemma of the world today: how can peoples of different appearance, mutually unintelligible languages, and dissimilar ways of life get along peaceably together?" (p. 9).

Anthropology has compiled an impressive body of knowledge, which this textbook attempts to encapsulate.

Besides its links to the natural sciences (e.g., geology, zoology) and social sciences (e.g., sociology, psychology), anthropology also has strong links to the humanities. The humanities include English, comparative literature, classics, folklore, philosophy, and the arts. These fields study languages, texts, philosophies, arts, music, performances, and other forms of creative expression. Ethnomusicology, which studies forms of musical expression on a worldwide basis, has close links to anthropology. Also linked is folklore, the systematic study of tales, myths, and legends from a variety of cultures. One can make a strong case that anthropology is one of the most humanistic of all academic fields because of its fundamental respect for human diversity. Anthropologists listen to, record, and represent voices from a multitude of nations, cultures, times, and places. Anthropology values local knowledge, diverse worldviews, and alternative philosophies. Cultural anthropology and linguistic anthropology in particular bring a comparative and nonelitist perspective to forms of creative expression, including language, art, narratives, music, and dance, viewed in their social and cultural context.

Cultural Anthropology and Sociology

Sociology is probably the discipline that is closest to anthropology, specifically to sociocultural anthropology. Like anthropology (particularly cultural anthropology), sociologists study society—consisting of human social behavior, social relations, and social organization. Key differences between sociology and anthropology reflect the kinds of societies traditionally studied by each discipline. Sociologists typically have studied contemporary, Western, industrial societies. Anthropologists, by contrast, have focused on nonindustrial and non-Western societies. Sociologists and anthropologists developed different methods to study these different kinds of society. To study contemporary Western societies, which tend to be large-scale, complex nations, sociologists have relied on surveys and other means of gathering quantifiable data. Sociologists must use sampling and statistical techniques to collect and analyze such data, and statistical training has been fundamental in sociology. Working in much smaller societies, such as a village, anthropologists can get to know almost everyone and have less need for sampling and statistics. However, because anthropologists today are working increasingly in modern nations, use of sampling and statistics is becoming more common.

Traditionally, ethnographers studied small and nonliterate (without writing) populations and developed methods appropriate to that context. An ethnographer participates directly in the daily life of another culture and must be an attentive,

---

cultural resource management
Deciding what needs saving when entire archaeological sites cannot be saved.

science
A field of study that seeks reliable explanations, with reference to the material and physical world.

Applied anthropology in action. Professor Robin Nagle of New York University is also an anthropologist-in-residence at New York City's Department of Sanitation. Nagle studies curbside garbage as a mirror into the lives of New Yorkers. Here she accompanies sanitation worker Joe Damiano during his morning rounds, in August, 2015.

© Richard Drew/AP Images

detailed observer of what people do and say. The focus is on a real, living population, not just a sample of a population. During ethnographic fieldwork, the anthropologist takes part in the events she or he is observing, describing, and analyzing. Anthropology, we might say, is more personal and less formal than sociology.

In today's interconnected world, however, the interests and methods of anthropology and sociology are converging—coming together—because they are studying some of the same topics and areas. For example, many sociologists now work in non-Western countries, smaller communities, and other settings that used to be mainly within the anthropological orbit. As industrialization and urbanization have spread across the globe, anthropologists now work increasingly in industrial nations and cities, rather than villages. Among the many topics studied by contemporary sociocultural anthropologists are rural-urban and transnational (from one country to another) migration, urban adaptation, inner-city life, ethnic diversity and conflict, crime, and warfare. Anthropologists today may be as likely as sociologists are to study issues of globalization and inequality.

Anthropology and Psychology

Psychologists, like sociologists, typically do their research in only one—their own—society. Anthropologists know, however, that statements about "human" psychology cannot rely solely on observations made in a single society. Cross-cultural comparison suggests that certain psychological patterns may indeed be universal. Others occur in some but not all societies, while still others are confined to one or very few cultures. *Psychological anthropology* studies cross-cultural similarities and differences in psychological traits and conditions (see LeVine 2010). During the 1920s, 1930s, and 1940s several prominent anthropologists, including Bronislaw Malinowski (1927) and Margaret Mead (1935/1950; 1928/1961) described how particular cultures create distinctive adult personality types by inculcating in their children specific values, beliefs, and behavior patterns. Anthropologists have provided needed cross-cultural perspectives on aspects of developmental and cognitive psychology (Kronenfeld et al. 2011; Shore 1996), psychoanalytic interpretations (Gijswijt-Hofstra et al. 2005; Paul 1989), and psychiatric conditions (Gijswijt-Hofstra et al. 2005; Kleinman 1991).

Anthropologists are familiar, for example, with an array of *culturally specific syndromes*. These are patterns of unusual, aberrant, or abnormal behavior confined to a single culture or a group of related cultures (see Goleman 1995). One example is *koro*, the East Asian term for intense anxiety arising from the fear that one's sexual organs will recede into one's body and cause death. A distinctive Latin American syndrome is *susto*, or soul loss, whose symptoms are extreme sadness, lethargy, and listlessness. The victim typically falls prey to susto after experiencing a personal tragedy, such as the death of a loved one. A milder malady is *mal de ojo* ("evil eye"), most typically found in Mediterranean countries. Symptoms of evil eye, which mainly affects children, include fitful sleep, crying, sickness, and fever (Goleman 1995). Western cultures, too, have distinctive psychiatric syndromes, some of which appear now to be spreading internationally through globalization. This chapter's "Appreciating Anthropology" discusses how one such syndrome, anorexia nervosa, is spreading from the United States and Western Europe to other continents.

Like any other cultural anthropologist working in the 21st century, the student of psychological anthropology must recognize how local, indigenous patterns (psychological–psychiatric, in this case) interact with the forces of globalization, including the concepts and conditions it is spreading.

THE SCIENTIFIC METHOD

Anthropology, remember, is a science, although a very humanistic one. Any science aims for reliable explanations that *predict* future occurrences. Accurate predictions stand up to tests designed to disprove (falsify) them. Scientific explanations rely on data, which can come from experiments, observation, and other systematic procedures. Scientific causes are material, physical, or natural (e.g., viruses) rather than supernatural (e.g., ghosts).

Theories, Associations, and Explanations

In their 1997 article "Science in Anthropology," Melvin Ember and Carol R. Ember describe how scientists strive to improve our understanding of the world by hypothesis testing. A **hypothesis** is a *proposed* explanation for something. Until it is *tested*, it is merely hypothetical. If the test confirms the hypothesis, then that explanation is a good one. An *explanation* shows how and why one variable causes or is closely associated with another variable that we want to explain. An **association** refers to *covariation* of variables. Covariation means they vary together—when one variable changes, the other one also changes. *Theories provide explanations for associations* (Ember and Ember 1997). What exactly is a theory? A **theory** is a framework of logically connected ideas that helps us explain not just one, but many, associations. In other words, the most useful theories cover multiple cases.

We generalize when we say that a change in a particular variable usually follows or is usually associated with a change in another variable. A *law* is a *generalization* that applies to and explains all instances of an association. An example of a law is the statement "water freezes at 32 degrees

hypothesis
A suggested but as yet unverified explanation.

association
An observed relationship between two or more variables.

theory
A set of ideas formulated to explain something.

Fahrenheit." This law states a uniform association between two variables: the state of the water (whether liquid or ice) and the air temperature. We confirm the truth of the statement by repeated observations of freezing and by the fact that water does not solidify at higher temperatures. The existence of laws makes the world a more predictable place, helping us to understand the past and predict the future. Yesterday ice formed at 32 degrees F, and tomorrow it will still form at 32 degrees F.

The social sciences have few, if any, absolute laws of the water-freezing sort. "Laws" in social science tend to be imperfect generalizations, and explanations in social science tend to be probable rather than certain. They usually have exceptions; that is, sometimes the explanation does not hold. Does that mean such explanations are useless? Not at all. Imagine a law that said that water freezes at 32 degrees 83 percent of the time. Although we cannot make an exact prediction based on such a generalization, it still tells us something useful, even if there are exceptions. Most of the time, we would predict correctly that water was going to freeze. To take a real example from social science, we can generalize that "conflict tends to increase as a group's population size increases." Even if this statement applies only 83 percent of the time, it still is useful. In the social sciences, including anthropology, the variables of interest only *tend* to be associated in a predictable way; there are always exceptions. Recap 1.3 summarizes the key terms used in this section: association, hypothesis, explanation, theory, generalization, and law.

Case Study: Explaining the Postpartum Taboo

One classic cross-cultural study revealed a strong (but not 100 percent) association, or correlation, between a sexual restriction and a type of diet. A long postpartum sex taboo (a ban on sexual intercourse between husband and wife for a year or more after the birth of a child) tended to occur in societies where the diet was low in protein (Whiting 1964).

This association was confirmed by cross-cultural data (ethnographic information from a randomly chosen sample of several societies). How might one explain why the *dependent variable* (the thing to be explained, in this case the postpartum sex taboo) is related to the *predictor variable* (a low-protein diet). A likely explanation is that, when there is too little protein in their diets, babies can develop and die from a protein-deficiency disease called kwashiorkor. If the mother delays her next pregnancy, her current baby gets to breast-feed longer, thereby getting protein from the mother and enhancing its survival chances. Having another baby too soon—forcing early weaning—would jeopardize the

Key question: How do you explain associations?

ASSOCIATION	A systematic relationship between variables, so that when one variable changes (varies), the other does, too (covaries). **Example**: When temperatures fall, water solidifies.
HYPOTHESIS	A proposed explanation for an association; must be tested—may be confirmed or not. **Example**: Conflict will increase along with population size.
EXPLANATION	Reasons how and why a particular association exists. **Example**: Giraffes with longer necks have higher rates of survival and more surviving offspring than do shorter-necked giraffes, because they can feed themselves better when food is scarce.
THEORY	Explanatory framework of logically interconnected ideas used to explain multiple phenomena. **Example**: Darwinian evolutionary theory used to explain giraffes' long necks and other adaptive features in multiple species.
GENERALIZATION	A statement that change in one variable tends to follow or be associated with change in another variable. **Example**: When societies have low-protein diets, they tend to have longer postpartum taboos than when the diet is richer in protein.
LAW	Generalization that is universally valid. **Example**: When temperature reaches 32 degrees F, water turns from liquid to solid (ice).

survival of the previous one. The postpartum taboo thus enhances infant survival. When the taboo becomes institutionalized as a cultural expectation, people are more likely to comply, and less likely to succumb to momentary temptation.

Theories suggest patterns and relationships, and they generate additional hypotheses. Based, for example, on the theory that the postpartum taboo exists because it reduces infant mortality when the diet is low in protein, one could hypothesize that changes in the conditions that favor the taboo might cause it to disappear. By adopting birth control, for instance, families could space births without avoiding intercourse. The taboo might also disappear if babies started receiving protein supplements, which would reduce the threat of kwashiorkor.

Recap 1.4 summarizes the main steps in using the scientific method. In hypothesis testing, the relevant variables should be clearly defined (e.g., "height in centimeters" or "weight in kilograms" rather than "body size") and measured reliably. The strength and significance of the results should be evaluated using legitimate statistical methods (Bernard 2011). Scholars should be careful to avoid a common mistake in generalizing—citing only cases that confirm their hypothesis, while ignoring negative ones. The best procedure is random selection of cases from a wide sample of societies, not all of which are likely to fit the hypothesis.

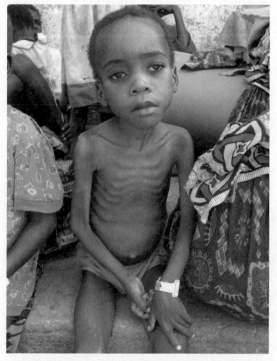

The name *kwashiorkor*, for a condition caused by severe protein deficiency, comes from a West African word meaning "one-two." Some cultures abruptly wean one infant when a second one is born. In today's world, refugees from civil wars, including the Angolan girl shown here, are among the most common victims of malnutrition.
© Ton Koene

appreciating ANTHROPOLOGY

Anorexia Goes Global

Both cultural and biological anthropologists contribute to *medical anthropology*, a growing field of study that examines how and why various health conditions affect particular populations, and how illness is socially constructed, diagnosed, managed, and treated in different societies. Particular cultures and ethnic groups recognize different illnesses, symptoms, and causes.

Well known to anthropology are *culturally specific syndromes*—health conditions, often with a mental-psychological component, that are confined to a single culture or a group of related cultures. Examples discussed in the text include *koro* (East Asia), *susto* (Latin America), and "evil eye" (Mediterranean countries). The influential *Diagnostic and Statistical Manual of Mental Disorders* published by the American Psychiatric Association (2013) now recognizes "culture-bound syndromes," another term for these culturally specific syndromes.

In our modern world system, as people migrate, they carry their cultural baggage, including their syndromes, with them across national boundaries. Today, diagnosticians in Western Europe and the United States may encounter cases of susto, evil eye, or even koro among recent immigrants. Furthermore, certain syndromes once confined to Western cultures are now spreading with globalization. One example is *anorexia nervosa* (food refusal or extreme dieting resulting in self-starvation), a syndrome once specific to Western industrialized societies that has been spreading internationally.

In the early 1990s (as reported by Watters 2010), Dr. Sing Lee, a Hong Kong-based psychiatrist and researcher, documented what was, at that time, a culturally specific, and very rare, form of anorexia nervosa in Hong Kong. Unlike American anorexics, Lee's patients did not worry about getting fat. Instead, they reduced their food intake in an attempt to fend off unwanted bodily symptoms—most frequently, bloated stomachs. Just as Dr. Lee started publishing his findings, however, the understanding of anorexia in Hong Kong suddenly shifted, after a teenage anorexic girl collapsed and died on a busy downtown street. Her death was featured prominently in local newspapers, with such headlines as "Anorexia Made Her All Skin and Bones."

Because anorexia was a rarity in Hong Kong at that time, local reporters did not know what to make of its symptoms. In reporting on the girl's death, many of them simply copied from American diagnostic manuals, thus spreading the idea that anorexia in Hong Kong was the same disorder that existed in the United States and Europe. As Hong Kongers became more familiar with the American diagnosis of anorexia, Lee's patients started mimicking the American symptoms, and the incidence of anorexia also increased. Lee's anorexic patient load rose rapidly, from two or three per year to that many per month. Eventually Lee concluded that up to 10 percent of young women in Hong Kong had fallen victim to eating disorders. Unlike his earlier patients, these women—eventually 90 percent of them—now cited a fear of getting fat as the key reason for not eating (Watters 2010).

Disorders and symptoms, both physical and mental, can easily cross national borders in today's globalized and socially networked world.

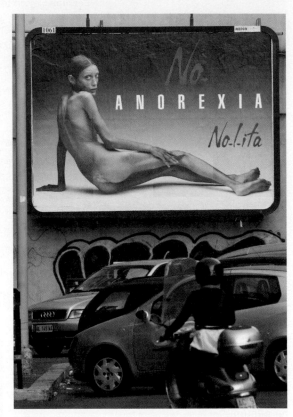

In Rome, a poster featuring an emaciated woman (in an advertisement for an Italian fashion house) bears the headline "No anorexia." How does anorexia illustrate a culturally specific syndrome?
© Riccardo De Luca/MAXPPP/Newscom

The *Diagnostic and Statistical Manual of Mental Disorders* serves as an increasingly transnational reference and standard. The Western form of anorexia surely would not have spread so quickly in Hong Kong without modern media. After all, it took more than half a century for Western mental health professionals to name, codify, and establish their definition of anorexia. By contrast, after a single widely reported death on a busy downtown street, it took just hours for the people of Hong Kong to learn about anorexia and its "Western" symptoms (Watters 2010), and just months for some of them to begin suffering from the ailment.

Have a research question.	Why do some societies have long postpartum taboos?
Construct a hypothesis.	Delaying marital sex reduces infant mortality when diets are low in protein.
Posit a mechanism.	Babies get more protein when they nurse longer; nursing is not a reliable method of contraception.
Get data to test your hypothesis.	Use a (random) sample of cross-cultural data (data from several societies; such data sets exist for cross-cultural research).
Devise a way of measuring.	Code societies 1 when they have a postpartum taboo of one year or longer, 0 when they do not; code 1 when diet is low in protein, 0 when it is not.
Analyze your data.	Notice patterns in the data: Long postpartum taboos generally are found in societies with low-protein diets, whereas societies with better diets tend to lack those taboos. Use appropriate statistical methods to evaluate the strength of these associations.
Draw a conclusion.	In most cases, the hypothesis is confirmed.
Derive implications.	Such taboos tend to disappear when diets get better or new reproductive technologies become available.
Contribute to larger theory.	Cultural practices can have adaptive value by enhancing the survival of offspring.

The Value, and Limitations, of Science

Science is one way—an excellent way—of understanding the world, but it certainly is not the only way. Indeed, the work of many prominent anthropologists has more in common with the humanities than with a strictly scientific approach. Many cultural anthropologists prefer to analyze and interpret aspects of culture, rather than trying to explain them scientifically. Accordingly, anthropological approaches that are interpretive, qualitative, and humanistic are considered in this book, along with those that are quantitative and scientific.

for REVIEW

summary

1. Anthropology is the holistic and comparative study of humanity. It is the systematic exploration of human biological and cultural diversity. Examining the origins of, and changes in, human biology and culture, anthropology provides explanations for similarities and differences. The four subfields of general anthropology are sociocultural, archaeological, biological, and linguistic. All consider variation in time and space. Each also examines adaptation—the process by which organisms cope with environmental stresses.

2. Cultural forces mold human biology, including our body types and images. Societies have particular standards of physical attractiveness. They also have specific ideas about what activities—for example, various sports—are appropriate for males and females.

3. Cultural anthropology explores the cultural diversity of the present and the recent past. Anthropological archaeology reconstructs cultural patterns, often of prehistoric populations. Biological anthropology documents variety, involving fossils, genetics, growth and development, bodily responses, and nonhuman primates. Linguistic anthropology considers diversity among languages. It also studies how speech changes in social situations and over time. Anthropology has two dimensions: academic and applied. Applied anthropology is the use of anthropological data, perspectives, theory, and methods to identify, assess, and solve contemporary social problems.

4. Concerns with biology, society, culture, and language link anthropology to many other fields—sciences and humanities. Anthropologists study

art, music, and literature across cultures. But their concern is more with the creative expressions of common people than with arts designed for elites. Anthropologists examine creators and products in their social context. Sociologists traditionally study Western industrial societies, whereas anthropologists have focused on rural, nonindustrial peoples. Psychological anthropology views human psychology in the context of social and cultural variation.

5. Ethnologists attempt to identify and explain cultural differences and similarities and to build theories about how social and cultural systems work. Scientists strive to improve understanding by testing hypotheses—suggested explanations. Explanations rely on associations and theories. An association is an observed relationship between variables. A theory is an explanatory framework capable of explaining many associations. The scientific method characterizes any anthropological endeavor that formulates research questions and gathers or uses systematic data to test hypotheses.

key terms

anthropological archaeology 6

anthropology 3

applied anthropology 9

association 12

biocultural 4

biological anthropology 8

cultural anthropology 6

cultural resource management 10

culture 3

ethnography 6

ethnology 6

food production 4

general anthropology 4

holistic 3

hypothesis 12

linguistic anthropology 9

science 10

sociolinguistics 9

theory 12

critical thinking

1. How might a *biocultural* approach help us understand the complex ways in which human populations adapt to their environments?

2. What themes and interests unify the subdisciplines of anthropology? In your answer, refer to historical reasons for the unity of anthropology. Are these historical reasons similar in all places where anthropology developed as a discipline?

3. If, as Franz Boas illustrated early on in American anthropology, cultures are not isolated, how can ethnography provide an account of a particular community, society, or culture? Note: There is no easy answer to this question! Anthropologists continue to deal with it as they define their research questions and projects.

4. The American Anthropological Association has formally acknowledged a public service role by recognizing that anthropology has two dimensions: (1) academic anthropology and (2) practicing, or applied, anthropology. What is applied anthropology? Based on your reading of this chapter, identify examples from current events where an anthropologist could help identify, assess, and solve contemporary social problems.

5. In this chapter, we learn that anthropology is a science, although a very humanistic one. What do you think this means? What role does hypothesis testing play in structuring anthropological research? What are the differences between theories, laws, and hypotheses?

CHAPTER 2

Culture

▶ What is culture and why do we study it?

▶ What is the relation between culture and the individual?

▶ How does culture change—especially with globalization?

© Chel Beeson/Photolibrary/Getty Images

Offerings at a temple in Bali, Indonesia. People learn and share beliefs and behavior as members of cultural groups.

understanding OURSELVES

How special are you? To what extent are you "your own person" and to what extent are you a product of your particular culture? How much does your cultural background influence your actions and decisions? Americans may not fully appreciate the power of culture because of the value their culture assigns to "the *individual*." Americans like to regard everyone as unique in some way. Yet individualism itself is a distinctive *shared* value, a feature of American culture, transmitted constantly in our daily lives. In the media, count how many stories focus on individuals versus groups. Agents of enculturation ranging from TV personalities to our parents, grandparents, and teachers, constantly insist that we all are "someone special." That we are individuals first and members of groups second is the opposite of this chapter's lesson about culture. To be sure, we have distinctive features because we are individuals, but we have other distinct attributes because we belong to cultural groups.

For example, a comparison of the United States with Brazil, Italy, or virtually any Latin nation reveals striking contrasts between a national culture (American) that discourages physical affection and national cultures in which the opposite is true. Brazilians touch, embrace, and kiss one another much more frequently than North Americans do. Such behavior reflects years of exposure to particular cultural traditions. Middle-class Brazilians teach their kids—both boys and girls—to kiss (on the cheek, two or three times, coming and going) every adult relative they see. Given the size of Brazilian extended families, this can mean hundreds of people. Women continue kissing all those people throughout their lives. Until they are adolescents, boys kiss all adult relatives. Men typically continue to kiss female relatives and friends, as well as their fathers and uncles, throughout their lives.

Do you kiss your father? Your uncle? Your grandfather? How about your mother, aunt, or grandmother? The answers to these questions may differ between men and women, and for male and female relatives. Culture can help us to make sense of these differences. In America, a cultural homophobia (fear of homosexuality) may prevent American men from engaging in displays of affection with other men; similarly, American girls typically are encouraged to show affection, while American boys typically are not. It's important to note that these cultural explanations rely upon example and expectation, and that no cultural trait exists because it is natural or right. *Ethnocentrism* is the error of viewing one's own culture as superior and applying one's own cultural values in judging people from other cultures. How easy is it for you to see beyond the ethnocentric blinders of your own experience? Do you have an ethnocentric position regarding displays of affection?

WHAT IS CULTURE?

The concept of culture is fundamental in anthropology. Well over a century ago, in his book *Primitive Culture,* the British anthropologist Sir Edward Tylor proposed that cultures—systems of human behavior and thought—obey natural laws and therefore can be studied scientifically. Tylor's definition of culture still offers an overview of the subject matter of anthropology, and it is widely quoted: "Culture . . . is that complex whole which includes knowledge, belief, arts, morals, law, custom, and any other capabilities and habits acquired by man as a member of society" (Tylor 1871/1958, p. 1). The crucial phrase here is "acquired . . . as a member of society." Tylor's definition focuses on attributes that people acquire not through biological inheritance but by growing up in a particular society where they are exposed to a specific cultural tradition. **Enculturation** is the process by which a child learns his or her culture.

Culture Is Learned

The ease with which children absorb any cultural tradition rests on the uniquely elaborated human capacity to learn. Other animals may learn from experience; for example, they avoid fire after discovering that it hurts. Social animals also learn from other members of their group. Wolves, for instance, learn hunting strategies from other pack members. Such social learning is particularly important among monkeys and apes, our closest biological relatives. But our own *cultural learning* depends on the uniquely developed human capacity to use **symbols,** signs that have no necessary or natural connection to the things they signify or for which they stand.

On the basis of cultural learning, people create, remember, and deal with ideas. They grasp and apply specific systems of symbolic meaning. Anthropologist Clifford Geertz defines culture as ideas based on cultural learning and symbols. Cultures have been characterized as sets of "control mechanisms—plans, recipes, rules, instructions, what computer engineers call programs for the governing of behavior" (Geertz 1973, p. 44). We absorb these programs through enculturation in a particular tradition. People gradually internalize a previously established system of meanings and symbols. This cultural system helps them define their world, express their feelings, and make their judgments. Our culture helps guide our behavior and perceptions throughout our lives.

Every person begins immediately, through a process of conscious and unconscious learning and interaction with others, to internalize, or incorporate, a cultural tradition through the process of enculturation. Sometimes culture is taught directly, as when parents tell their children to say "thank you" when someone gives them something or does them a favor.

We also acquire culture through observation. Children pay attention to the things that go on around them. They modify their behavior not only because other people tell them to do so, but also because of their own observations and growing awareness of what their culture considers right and wrong. Many aspects of culture are absorbed unconsciously. North Americans acquire their culture's notions about how far apart people should stand when they talk not by being told directly to maintain a certain distance but through a gradual process of observation, experience, and conscious and unconscious behavior modification. No one tells Latins to stand closer together than North Americans do, but they learn to do so anyway as part of their cultural tradition.

Anthropologists agree that cultural learning is uniquely elaborated among humans and that all humans have culture. Anthropologists also agree that although *individuals* differ in their emotional and intellectual tendencies and capacities, all human *populations* have equivalent capacities for culture. Regardless of their genes or their physical appearance, people can learn any cultural tradition.

To understand this point, consider that contemporary North Americans are the genetically mixed descendants of people from all over the world. Our ancestors lived in different countries and continent and participated in hundreds of cultural traditions. However, early colonists, later immigrants and their descendants have all become active participants in American or Canadian life. All now share a national culture.

Culture Is Symbolic

Symbolic thought is unique and crucial to humans and to cultural learning. Anthropologist Leslie White defined culture as

> dependent upon symbolling. . . . Culture consists of tools, implements, utensils, clothing, ornaments, customs, institutions, beliefs, rituals, games, works of art, language, etc. (White 1959, p. 3)

For White, culture originated when our ancestors acquired the ability to use symbols, that is, to originate and bestow meaning on a thing or an event, and, correspondingly, to grasp and appreciate such meanings (White 1959, p. 3).

A symbol is something verbal or nonverbal, within a particular language or culture, that comes to stand for something else. There is no obvious, natural, or necessary connection between the symbol and the thing that it symbolizes. A pet that barks is no more naturally a *dog* than a *chien, Hund,* or *mbwa,* to use the words for the animal we call "dog" in French, German, and Swahili. Language is one of the distinctive possessions of *Homo sapiens.* No other animal has developed anything approaching the complexity of language.

There also is a rich array of nonverbal symbols. Flags, for example, stand for countries, as arches do for a hamburger chain. Holy water is a potent symbol in Roman Catholicism. As is true of all symbols, the association between water and what it stands for (holiness) is arbitrary and conventional. Water is not intrinsically holier than milk, blood, or other natural liquids. Nor is holy water chemically different from ordinary water. Holy water is a symbol within Roman Catholicism, which is part of an international cultural system. A natural thing has been arbitrarily associated with a particular meaning for Catholics,

enculturation
The process by which culture is learned and transmitted across the generations.

symbol
Something, verbal or nonverbal, that stands for something else.

Some symbols are linguistic. Others are nonverbal, such as flags, which stand for countries. Here, colorful flags of several nations wave in front of the United Nations building in New York City.

© Ingram Publishing RF

who share common beliefs and experiences that are based on learning and that are transmitted across the generations. Our cultures immerse us in a world of symbols that are both linguistic and nonverbal. Particular items and brands of clothing, such as jeans, shirts, or shoes, can acquire symbolic meanings, as can our gestures, posture, and body decoration and ornamentation.

For hundreds of thousands of years, humans have possessed the abilities on which culture rests. These abilities are to learn, to think symbolically, to manipulate language, and to use tools and other cultural products in organizing their lives and coping with their environments. Every contemporary human population has the ability to use symbols and thus to create and maintain culture. Our nearest relatives—chimpanzees and gorillas—have rudimentary cultural abilities. No other animal, however, has elaborated cultural abilities—to learn, to communicate, and to store, process, and use information—to the extent that *Homo* has.

Culture Is Shared

Culture is an attribute not of individuals per se but of individuals as members of *groups*. Culture is transmitted in society. We learn our culture by observing, listening, talking, and interacting with many other people. Shared beliefs, values, memories, and expectations link people who grow up in the same culture. Enculturation unifies people by providing us with common experiences. Today's parents were yesterday's children. If they grew up

in North America, they absorbed certain values and beliefs transmitted over the generations. People become agents in the enculturation of their children, just as their parents were for them. Although a culture constantly changes, certain fundamental beliefs, values, worldviews, and child-rearing practices endure. One example of enduring shared enculturation is the American emphasis on self-reliance and independent achievement.

Despite characteristic American notions that people should "make up their own minds" and "have a right to their opinion," little of what we think is original or unique. We share our opinions and beliefs with many other people—nowadays not just in person but also via new media. Think about how often (and with whom) you share information or an opinion via texting, Facebook, Instagram, and Twitter. Illustrating the power of shared cultural background, we are most likely to agree with and feel comfortable with people who are socially, economically, and culturally similar to ourselves. This is one reason Americans abroad tend to socialize with each other, just as French and British colonials did in their overseas empires. Birds of a feather flock together, but for people, the familiar plumage is culture.

Culture and Nature

Culture takes the natural biological urges we share with other animals and teaches us how to express them in particular ways. People have to eat, but culture teaches us what, when, and how. In many cultures, people have their main meal at noon, but most North Americans prefer a large dinner. English people may eat fish for breakfast, while North Americans may prefer hot cakes and cold cereals. Brazilians put hot milk into strong coffee, whereas North Americans pour cold milk into a weaker brew. Midwesterners dine at 5 or 6 P.M., Spaniards at 10 P.M.

Culture molds "human nature" in many directions. People have to eliminate wastes from their bodies. But some cultures teach people to defecate squatting, while others tell them to do it sitting down. A generation ago, in Paris and other French cities, it was customary for men to urinate almost publicly, and seemingly without embarrassment, in barely shielded *pissoirs* located on city streets. Our "bathroom" habits, including waste elimination, bathing, and dental care, are parts of cultural traditions that have converted natural acts into cultural customs.

Our culture—and cultural changes—affect the ways in which we perceive nature, human nature, and "the natural." Through science, invention, and discovery, cultural advances have overcome many "natural" limitations. We prevent and cure diseases, such as polio and smallpox, that felled our ancestors. We can use pills to restore and enhance sexual potency. Through cloning, scientists have altered the way we think about biological identity and the meaning of life itself. Culture, of course, has not freed us from natural disasters. Hurricanes, earthquakes, tsunamis, and other natural forces regularly challenge our efforts to modify the environment through building, development, and expansion.

Culture Is All-Encompassing

For anthropologists, culture includes much more than refinement, taste, sophistication, education, and appreciation of the fine arts. Not only college graduates but all people are "cultured." The most interesting and significant cultural forces are those that affect people every day of their lives, particularly those that influence children during enculturation. *Culture,* as defined anthropologically, encompasses features that sometimes are considered trivial or unworthy of serious study, such as "popular" culture. To understand contemporary North American culture, however, we must consider social media, cell phones, the Internet, television, fast-food restaurants, sports, and games. As a cultural manifestation, a rock star may be as interesting as a symphony conductor, a comic book as significant as a book-award winner.

Culture Is Integrated

Cultures are not haphazard collections of customs and beliefs. Cultures are integrated, patterned systems. If one part of the system (e.g., the economy) changes, other parts also change. For example, during the 1950s, most American women planned

Cultures are integrated systems. When one behavior pattern changes, others also change. During the 1950s, most American women expected to have careers as wives, mothers, and domestic managers. As more and more women have entered the workforce, attitudes toward work and family have changed. In the earlier photo, a 1950s mom and kids do the dishes. In the recent photo, a doctor and two nurses examine a patient's record. What do you imagine these three women do when they get home?
Top: © William Gottlieb/Corbis; bottom: © Tom Tracy Photography/Alamy Stock Photo

domestic careers as homemakers and mothers. Since then, an increasing number of American women, including wives and mothers, have entered the workforce. Only 32 percent of married American women worked outside the home in 1960, compared to about 60 percent today.

Economic changes have social repercussions. Attitudes and behavior about marriage, family, and children have changed. Late marriage, "living together," and divorce have become commonplace. Work competes with marriage and family responsibilities and reduces the time available to invest in child care.

Cultures are integrated not simply by their dominant economic activities and related social

core values
Key, basic, or central values that integrate a culture.

hominid
Member of hominid family; any fossil or living human, chimp, or gorilla.

hominins
Hominids excluding the African apes; all the human species that ever have existed.

patterns but also by sets of values, ideas, symbols, and judgments. Cultures train their individual members to share certain personality traits. A set of **core values** (key, basic, or central values) integrates each culture and helps distinguish it from others. For instance, the work ethic and individualism are core values that have integrated American culture for generations. Different sets of dominant values exist in other cultures.

Culture Is Instrumental, Adaptive, and Maladaptive

Culture is the main reason for human adaptability and success. Other animals rely on biological means of adaptation (such as fur or blubber, which are adaptations to cold). Humans also adapt biologically—for example, by shivering when we get cold or sweating when we get hot. People, however, also have cultural ways of adapting. To cope with environmental stresses we habitually use technology, or tools. We hunt cold-adapted animals and use their fur coats as our own. We turn the thermostat up in the winter and down in the summer. Or we plan action to increase our comfort. We have a cold drink, jump in a pool, or travel to someplace cooler in the summer or warmer in the winter. People use culture instrumentally, that is, to fulfill their basic biological needs for food, drink, shelter, comfort, and reproduction.

People also use culture to fulfill psychological and emotional needs, such as friendship, companionship, approval, and sexual desirability. People seek informal support—help from people who care about them—as well as formal support from associations and institutions. To these ends, individuals cultivate ties with others based on common experiences, political interests, aesthetic sensibilities, or personal attraction. Increasingly, people use such Internet platforms as Facebook, Google+, and LinkedIn to create and maintain social or professional connections.

On one level, cultural traits (e.g., air conditioning) are adaptive because they help individuals cope with environmental stresses. On a different level, however, such traits can also be *maladaptive*. For example, emissions from our machines have environmental effects that can harm humans and other life forms. Many modern cultural patterns may be maladaptive in the long run. Examples of maladaptive aspects of culture include policies that encourage overpopulation, poor food-distribution systems, overconsumption, and environmental degradation.

CULTURE'S EVOLUTIONARY BASIS

The human capacity for culture has an evolutionary basis that extends back perhaps 3 million years, date of the earliest evidence of tool manufacture in the archaeological record. Tool making by our distant ancestors may extend even farther back, based on observations of tool manufacture by chimpanzees in their natural habitats (Mercader et al. 2002).

Similarities between humans and apes, our closest relatives, are evident in anatomy, brain structure, genetics, and biochemistry. Most closely related to us are the African great apes: chimpanzees and gorillas. *Hominidae* is the zoological family that includes fossil and living humans. Also included as **hominids** are chimps and gorillas. The term **hominins** is used for the group that leads to humans but not to chimps and gorillas and that encompasses all the human species that ever have existed.

Many human traits reflect the fact that our primate ancestors lived in the trees. These traits include grasping ability and manual dexterity (especially opposable thumbs), depth and color vision, learning ability based on a large brain, substantial parental investment in a limited number of offspring, and tendencies toward sociality and cooperation. Like other primates, humans have flexible, five-fingered hands and *opposable thumbs:* Each thumb can touch all the other fingers on the same hand. Like monkeys and apes, humans also have excellent depth and color vision. Our eyes are located forward in the skull and look directly ahead, so that their fields of vision overlap. Depth perception, impossible without overlapping visual fields, proved adaptive—for judging distance, for example—in the trees. Having color and depth vision also facilitates the identification of various food sources, as well as mutual grooming, picking out burrs, insects, and other small objects from hair. Such grooming is one way of forming and maintaining social bonds.

The combination of manual dexterity and depth perception allows monkeys, apes, and humans to pick up small objects, hold them in front of their eyes, and appraise them. Our ability to thread a needle reflects an intricate interplay of hands and eyes that took millions of years of primate evolution to achieve. Such dexterity, including the opposable thumb, confers a tremendous advantage in manipulating objects and is essential to a major human adaptive capacity: toolmaking. In primates, and especially in humans, the ratio of brain size to body size exceeds that of most mammals. Even more important, the brain's outer layer—concerned with memory, association, and integration—is relatively larger. Monkeys, apes, and humans store an array of images in their memories, which permits them to learn more. Such a capacity for learning is a tremendous adaptive advantage. Like most other primates, humans usually give birth to a single offspring rather than a litter. Receiving greater parental attention, that one infant has enhanced learning opportunities. The need for longer and more attentive care of offspring places a selective value on support by a social group. Humans have developed considerably the primate tendency to be social animals, living and interacting regularly with other members of their species.

What We Share with Other Primates

There is a substantial gap between primate *society* (organized life in groups) and fully developed human *culture,* which is based on symbolic thought. Nevertheless, studies of nonhuman primates reveal many similarities with humans, such as the ability to learn from experience and change behavior as a result. Apes and monkeys, like humans, learn throughout their lives. In one group of Japanese macaques (land-dwelling monkeys), for example, a 3-year-old female started washing sweet potatoes before she ate them. First her mother, then her age peers, and finally the entire troop began washing sweet potatoes as well. The ability to benefit from experience confers a tremendous adaptive advantage, permitting the avoidance of fatal mistakes. Faced with environmental change, humans and other primates don't have to wait for a genetic or physiological response. They can modify learned behavior and social patterns instead.

Although humans do employ tools much more than any other animal does, tool use also turns up among several nonhuman species, including birds, beavers, sea otters, and especially apes (see Campbell 2011). Nor are humans the only animals that make tools with a specific purpose in mind. Chimpanzees living in the Tai forest of Ivory Coast make and use stone tools to break open hard, golf-ball-sized nuts (Mercader, Panger, and Boesch 2002). At specific sites, the chimps gather nuts, place them on stumps or flat rocks, which are used as anvils, and pound the nuts with heavy stones. The chimps must select hammer stones suited to smashing the nuts and carry them to where the nut trees grow. Nut cracking is a learned skill, with mothers showing their young how to do it.

In 1960, Jane Goodall began observing wild chimps—including their tool use and hunting behavior—at Gombe Stream National Park in Tanzania, East Africa (see Goodall 2010). The most studied form of ape toolmaking involves "termiting," in which chimps make tools to probe termite hills. They choose twigs, which they modify by removing leaves and peeling off bark to expose the underlying sticky surface. They carry the twigs to termite hills, dig holes with their fingers, and insert the twigs. Finally, they pull out the twigs and dine on termites that have been attracted to the sticky surface. Given what we know about ape tool use and manufacture, it is almost certain that early hominins shared this ability, although the first evidence for hominin stone toolmaking dates back only about 3 million years. Upright bipedalism would have permitted the carrying and use of tools and weapons against predators and competitors.

The apes have other abilities essential to culture. Wild chimps and orangs aim and throw objects. Gorillas build nests, and they throw branches, grass, vines, and other objects. Hominins have elaborated the capacity to aim and throw, without which we never would have developed projectile technology and weaponry—or baseball.

As with toolmaking, anthropologists used to regard hunting as a distinctive human activity not shared with the apes. Again, however, primate research shows that other primates, especially chimpanzees, are habitual hunters. For example, in Uganda's Kibale National Park chimps form large hunting parties, including an average of 26 individuals (adult and adolescent males). Most hunts (78 percent) result in at least one prey item being caught—a much higher success rate than that among lions (26 percent), hyenas (34 percent), or cheetahs (30 percent). Chimps' favored prey there is the red colobus monkey (Mitani et al. 2012).

It is likely that human ancestors were doing some hunting by at least 3 million years ago, based on the existence of early stone tools designed to cut meat. Given our current understanding of chimp hunting and toolmaking, we can infer that hominids may have been hunting much earlier than the first archaeological evidence attests. Because chimps typically devour the monkeys they kill, leaving few remains, we may never find archaeological evidence for the first hominin hunt, especially if it proceeded without stone tools.

How We Differ from Other Primates

Although chimps often share meat from a hunt, apes and monkeys (except for nursing infants) tend to feed themselves individually. Cooperation and sharing are much more characteristic of humans. Until fairly recently (12,000 to 10,000 years ago), all humans were hunter-gatherers who lived in small groups called bands. In some world areas, the hunter-gatherer way of life persisted into recent times, permitting study by ethnographers. In such societies, men and women take resources back to the camp and share them. Everyone shares the meat from a large animal. Nourished and protected by younger band members, elders live past reproductive age and are respected for their knowledge and experience.

Primates have five-digited feet and hands, well suited for grasping. Flexible hands and feet that could encircle branches were important features in the early primates' arboreal life. In adapting to bipedal (two-footed) locomotion, hominins eliminated most of the foot's grasping ability—illustrated here by the chimpanzee.
© Kenneth Garrett/ National Geographic Creative

These two photos show different forms of tool use by chimps. Liberian chimps, like the one on the left, use hammer stones to crack palm nuts. On the right, chimps use prepared twigs to "fish" for termites from an ant hill.

Left: © Clive Bromhall/Oxford Scientific/Getty Images; right: © Stan Osolinski/Oxford Scientific/Getty Images

Humans are among the most cooperative of the primates—in the food quest and other social activities. In addition, the amount of information stored in a human band is far greater than that in any other primate group.

Another difference between humans and other primates involves mating. Among baboons and chimps, most mating occurs when females enter estrus, during which they ovulate. In estrus, the vaginal area swells and reddens, and receptive females form temporary bonds with, and mate with, males. Human females, by contrast, lack a visible estrus cycle, and their ovulation is concealed. Not knowing when ovulation is occurring, humans maximize their reproductive success by mating throughout the year. Human pair bonds for mating are more exclusive and more durable than are those of chimps. Related to our more constant sexuality, all human societies have some form of marriage. Marriage gives mating a reliable basis and grants to each spouse special, though not always exclusive, sexual rights to the other.

Marriage creates another major contrast between humans and nonhuman primates: exogamy and kinship systems. Most cultures have rules of exogamy requiring marriage outside one's kin or local group. Coupled with the recognition of kinship, exogamy confers adaptive advantages. It creates ties between the spouses' different groups of origin. Their children have relatives, and therefore allies, in two kin groups rather than just one. The key point here is that ties of affection and mutual support between members of different local groups tend to be absent among primates other than *Homo*. Other primates tend to disperse at adolescence. Among chimps and gorillas, females tend to migrate, seeking mates in other groups. Humans also choose mates from outside the natal group, and usually at least one spouse moves. However, *humans maintain lifelong ties with sons and daughters*. The systems of kinship and marriage that preserve these links provide a major contrast between humans and other primates.

UNIVERSALITY, GENERALITY, AND PARTICULARITY

In studying human diversity in time and space, anthropologists distinguish among the universal, the generalized, and the particular. Certain biological, psychological, social, and cultural features are **universal,** found in every culture. Others are merely **generalities,** common to several but not all human groups. Still other traits are **particularities,** unique to certain cultural traditions.

Universals and Generalities

Biologically based universals include a long period of infant dependency, year-round (rather than seasonal) sexuality, and a complex brain that enables us to use symbols, languages, and tools. Among the social universals is life in groups and in some kind of family. Generalities occur in certain times and places but not in all cultures. They may be widespread, but they are not universal. One cultural generality that is present in many but not all societies is the nuclear family, a kinship group consisting of parents and children. Many middle-class Americans still view the "traditional" nuclear family, consisting of a married man and woman and their children, as a proper and "natural" group. This view persists despite the fact that nuclear families now comprise only 20 percent of contemporary American households. Cross-culturally, too, this kind of "traditional" family is far from universal. Consider the Nayars, who live on the Malabar Coast of India. Traditionally, the Nayars lived in female-headed households, and husbands and wives did not live together. In many other societies, the nuclear family is submerged in larger kin groups, such as extended families, lineages, and clans.

Societies can share the same beliefs and customs because of borrowing or through (cultural) inheritance from a common cultural ancestor.

Speaking English is a generality shared by North Americans and Australians because both countries had English settlers. Another reason for generalities is domination, as in colonial rule, when a more powerful nation imposes its customs and procedures on another group. In many countries, use of the English language reflects colonial history. More recently, English has spread through diffusion (cultural borrowing) to many other countries, as it has become the world's foremost language for business, travel, and the Internet.

Particularity: Patterns of Culture

A cultural particularity is a trait or feature of culture that is not generalized or widespread; rather, it is confined to a single place, culture, or society. Yet because of cultural borrowing and exchanges, which have accelerated with globalization, traits that once were limited in their distribution have become more widespread. Traits that are useful, that have the capacity to please large audiences, and that don't clash with the cultural values of potential adopters are more likely to spread than others are. Nevertheless, certain cultural particularities persist. One example is a particular food dish (e.g., pork barbeque with a mustard-based sauce available in South Carolina, or the pastie—beef stew baked in pie dough—characteristic of Michigan's Upper Peninsula). Besides diffusion, which, for example, has spread McDonald's food outlets, once confined to San Bernardino, California, across the globe, there are other reasons cultural particularities are increasingly rare. Many cultural traits are shared as cultural universals because of independent invention. Facing similar problems, people in different places have come up with similar solutions.

At the level of the individual cultural trait or element (e.g., bow and arrow, hot dog, HBO), particularities may be getting rarer. At a higher level, however, particularity is more obvious. Different cultures emphasize different things. *Cultures are integrated and patterned differently and display tremendous variation and diversity.* When cultural traits are borrowed, they are modified to fit the culture that adopts them. They are reintegrated—patterned anew—to fit their new setting. The television show *Big Brother* in Germany or Brazil isn't at all the same thing as *Big Brother* in the United States. As was stated in the section "Culture Is Integrated," patterned beliefs, customs, and practices lend distinctiveness to particular cultural traditions.

Consider universal life-cycle events, such as birth, puberty, marriage, parenthood, and death, which many cultures observe and celebrate. The occasions (e.g., marriage, death) may be the same and universal, but the patterns of ceremonial observance may be dramatically different. Cultures vary in just which events merit special celebration. Americans, for example, regard expensive weddings as more socially appropriate than lavish funerals. However, the Betsileo of Madagascar take the opposite view.

Cultures use rituals to mark such universal life-cycle events as birth, puberty, marriage, parenthood, and death. But particular cultures differ as to which events merit special celebration and in the emotions expressed during their rituals. Compare the wedding party (top) in Bali, Indonesia, with the funeral (bottom) among the Tanala of eastern Madagascar. How would you describe the emotions suggested by the photos?
Top: © Hideo Haga/HAGA/The Image Works; bottom: © Carl D. Walsh/Aurora Photos

The marriage ceremony there is a minor event that brings together just the couple and a few close relatives. However, a funeral is a measure of the deceased person's social position and lifetime achievement, and it may attract a thousand people. Why use money on a house, the Betsileo say, when one can use it on the tomb where one will spend eternity in the company of dead relatives? How unlike contemporary Americans' dreams of home ownership and preference for quick and inexpensive funerals. Cremation, an increasingly common option in the United States (see Sack 2011), would horrify the Betsileo, for whom ancestral bones and relics are important ritual objects.

Cultures vary tremendously in their beliefs, practices, integration, and patterning. By focusing on and trying to explain alternative customs, anthropology forces us to reappraise our familiar ways of thinking. In a world full of cultural diversity, contemporary American culture is just one cultural variant, more powerful perhaps, but no more natural, than the others.

CULTURE AND THE INDIVIDUAL: AGENCY AND PRACTICE

Generations of anthropologists have theorized about the relationship between the "system," on the one hand, and the "person" or "individual," on the other. The "system" can refer to various concepts, including culture, society, social relations, and social structure. Individual human beings make up, or constitute, the system. Living within that system, humans also are constrained (to some extent, at least) by its rules and by the actions of other individuals. Cultural rules provide guidance about what to do and how to do it, but people don't always do what the rules say should be done. People use their culture actively and creatively, rather than blindly following its dictates. Humans are not passive beings who are doomed to follow their cultural traditions like programmed robots. Instead, people learn, interpret, and manipulate the same rules in different ways—or they emphasize different rules that better suit their interests. Culture is *contested:* Different groups in society struggle with one another over whose ideas, values, goals, and beliefs will prevail. Even common symbols may have radically different *meanings* to different individuals and groups in the same culture. Golden arches may cause one person to salivate, while another person plots a vegetarian protest. Different people may wave the same flag to support or to oppose a particular war.

Even when they agree about what should and should not be done, people don't always do as their culture directs or as other people expect. Many rules are violated, some very often (e.g., automobile speed limits). Some anthropologists find it useful to distinguish between ideal culture and real culture. The *ideal culture* consists of what people say they should do and what they say they do. *Real culture* refers to their actual behavior as observed by the anthropologist.

Culture is both public and individual, both in the world and in people's minds. Anthropologists are interested not only in public and collective behavior but also in how *individuals* think, feel, and act. As Roy D'Andrade (1984) has noted, the individual and culture are linked because human social life is a process in which individuals internalize the meanings of *public* (i.e., cultural) messages. Then, alone and in groups, people influence culture by converting their private (and often divergent) understandings into public expressions.

Conventionally, culture has been seen as social glue transmitted across the generations, binding people through their common past, rather than as something being continually created and reworked in the present. The tendency to view culture as an entity rather than a process is changing. Contemporary anthropologists now emphasize how day-to-day action, practice, or resistance can make and remake culture (Gupta and Ferguson 1997b). *Agency* refers to the actions that individuals take, both alone and in groups, in forming and transforming cultural identities.

The approach to culture known as *practice theory* (Ortner 1984) recognizes that individuals within a society or culture have diverse motives and intentions and different degrees of power and influence. Such contrasts may be associated with gender, age, ethnicity, class, and other social variables. Practice theory focuses on how such varied individuals—through their ordinary and extraordinary actions and practices—manage to influence, create, and transform the world they live in. Practice theory appropriately recognizes a reciprocal relation between culture (the system) and the individual. The system shapes the way individuals experience and respond to external events, but individuals also play an active role in the way society functions and changes. Practice theory recognizes both constraints on individuals and the flexibility and changeability of cultures and social systems.

Levels of Culture

We can distinguish levels of culture, which vary in their membership and geographic extent. **National culture** refers to those beliefs, learned behavior patterns, values, and institutions shared by citizens of the same nation. **International culture** is the term for cultural traditions that extend beyond and across national boundaries. Because culture is transmitted through learning rather than genetically, cultural traits can spread through borrowing, or *diffusion,* from one group to another.

Many cultural traits and patterns have become international in scope. For example, Roman Catholics in many different countries share beliefs, symbols, experiences, and values transmitted by their church. The contemporary United States, Canada, Great Britain, and Australia share cultural traits they have inherited from their common linguistic and cultural ancestors in Great Britain. The World Cup is an international cultural event, as people in many countries know the rules of, play, and follow soccer.

Cultures also can be smaller than nations. Although people who live in the same country partake in a national cultural tradition, all nations also contain diversity. Individuals, families, communities, regions, classes, and other groups within

national culture
Cultural features shared by citizens of the same nation.

international culture
Cultural traditions that extend beyond national boundaries.

a culture have different learning experiences as well as shared ones. **Subcultures** are different symbol-based patterns and traditions associated with particular groups in the same complex society. In a large nation like the United States or Canada, subcultures originate in region, ethnicity, language, class, and religion. The backgrounds of Christians, Jews, and Muslims—and the diverse branches of those religions, create subcultural differences among them. While sharing a common national culture, U.S. northerners and southerners also differ in aspects of their beliefs, values, and customary behavior. French-speaking Canadians contrast with English-speaking people in the same country. Italian Americans have ethnic traditions different from those of Irish, Polish, and African Americans. Using sports and foods, Table 2.1 gives some examples of international culture, national culture, and subculture. Soccer and basketball are played internationally. Monster-truck rallies occur throughout the United States. Bocci is a bowling-like sport from Italy still played in some Italian American neighborhoods.

Nowadays, many anthropologists are reluctant to use the term *subculture*. They feel that the prefix "sub-" is offensive because it means "below." "Subcultures" may thus be perceived as "less than" or somehow inferior to a dominant, elite, or national culture. In this discussion of levels of culture, I intend no such implication. My point is simply that nations may contain many different culturally defined groups. As mentioned earlier, culture is contested. Various groups may strive to promote the correctness and value of their own practices, values, and beliefs in comparison with those of other groups or of the nation as a whole. (See this chapter's "Appreciating Diversity" on how contemporary indigenous groups have to grapple with multiple levels of culture, contestation, and political regulation.)

TABLE 2.1 Levels of Culture, with Examples from Sports and Foods

LEVEL OF CULTURE	SPORTS EXAMPLES	FOOD EXAMPLES
International	Soccer, basketball	Pizza
National	Monster-truck rallies	Apple pie
Subculture	Bocci	Big Joe Pork Barbeque (South Carolina)

Illustrating the international level of culture, Roman Catholics in different nations share knowledge, symbols, beliefs, and behavior associated with their religion. Shown here, Chinese Catholics at an Easter mass in Beijing. In China, worship is allowed only in government-controlled churches, but an estimated 12 million Chinese Catholics belong to unofficial congregations loyal to Rome.
© Elizabeth Dalziel/AP Images

Ethnocentrism, Cultural Relativism, and Human Rights

Ethnocentrism is the tendency to view one's own culture as superior and to use one's own standards and values in judging outsiders. We witness ethnocentrism when people consider their own cultural beliefs to be truer, more proper, or more moral than those of other groups. However, fundamental to anthropology, as the study of human diversity, is the fact that what is alien (even disgusting) to us may be normal, proper, and prized elsewhere (see the previous discussion of cultural particularities, including burial customs). The fact of cultural diversity calls ethnocentrism into question, as anthropologists have shown all kinds of reasons for unfamiliar practices. During a course like this, anthropology students often reexamine their own ethnocentric beliefs. Sometimes as the strange becomes familiar, the familiar seems a bit stranger and less comfortable. One goal of anthropology is to show the value in the lives of others. But how far is too far? What happens when cultural practices, values, and rights come into conflict with human rights?

Several societies in Africa and the Middle East have customs requiring female genital modification. *Clitoridectomy* is the removal of a girl's clitoris. *Infibulation* involves sewing the lips (labia) of the vagina to constrict the vaginal opening. Both procedures reduce female sexual pleasure and, it is believed in some societies, the likelihood of adultery. Although traditional in the societies where they occur, such practices, characterized as

subcultures
Different cultural traditions associated with subgroups in the same complex society.

ethnocentrism
Judging other cultures using one's own cultural standards.

Who Owns Culture?

To what extent do and should indigenous peoples have the right to preserve traditional cultural practices? In today's world system, local people must contend not only with their own cultural rules and customs but also with agencies, laws, and lawsuits operating at the national and international levels. Consider the potential conflict between cultural rights, animal rights, economic rights, and legal rights. Consider as well the different levels of culture and administrative layers (local, regional, national, and international) that now determine how people live their lives.

Numbering about 1,500 people, the Makah are a Native American group who live on Washington's Olympic Peninsula. Traditionally, their economy relied on the Pacific Ocean for fishing and whaling. Ancestral Makah hunted the eastern North Pacific gray whale in seagoing canoes for more than a thousand years. External factors beyond their control have blocked Makah whaling for about a century, with the brief exception of a single whale hunt and kill in 1999.

Systematic Makah whaling ended in the 1920s, after commercial harvesting had depleted the population of the gray whales, which the United States eventually placed on the endangered species list. Over the years, national and international restrictions on whaling allowed the whales' numbers to recover and the U.S.

government removed the eastern North Pacific gray whale from the endangered list in 1994. Five years later, the Makah, who have never given up their desire to hunt whales, received permission to hunt again.

The brief resumption of Makah whaling took place in 1999. With the Makah whaling experience living only in the memory of oral tradition, no living Makah had ever witnessed a whale hunt, or even tasted the meat of the North Pacific gray whale. The 1999 hunt did result in a kill, by harpoons and a gunshot, of a 30-ton gray whale. Returning to shore, the whalers butchered, processed, and preserved its meat for future consumption. The event proceeded in the context of lawsuits and intense media coverage of the whalers and the protesters.

Animal rights groups, including the Humane Society of the United States, sued to stop Makah whaling. In response to that suit, an appeals court halted Makah whaling, declaring that the National Oceanic and Atmospheric Administration (NOAA) needed to conduct a thorough study of the impact of Makah hunting on the survival of the prey species.

The Makah, who consider whaling to be central to their culture, state that whaling is both a cultural right and a treaty right. They cite whaling's symbolic and spiritual meaning in addition to its material benefits and point out that an

1855 treaty between the United States and the Makah granted them the right to hunt whales, in exchange for large areas of Makah territory.

How unusual is the Makah situation? Several tribes of Native Alaskans, who are subsistence hunters of a different species, the bowhead whale, have received exemption from regulatory provisions of the 1972 Marine Mammal Protection Act. Despite their 1855 treaty rights, the Makah did not receive this exemption. They have petitioned the courts for a waiver that would grant them permanent rights to kill up to 20 gray whales in any five-year period.

The animal rights groups that have been so active against Makah whaling do *not* oppose the subsistence-oriented whaling of the Alaskan tribes. They claim that the Makah do not hunt for subsistence, but "merely" for cultural reasons, and that whale meat is not essential to their diet. The Makah and their supporters argue that their culture and subsistence are intertwined.

The future of Makah whaling currently rests with NOAA's Fisheries division. In the spring of 2015, NOAA issued a report outlining several possible alternatives for future Makah whaling, ranging from prohibiting an annual hunt to allowing the Makah to harvest up to five whales annually, but no more than 24 over a six-year period. NOAA plans eventually to issue a final document recommending whether the hunt can resume and, if so,

cultural relativism
The idea that behavior should be evaluated not by outside standards but in the context of the culture in which it occurs.

female genital mutilation (FGM), have been opposed by human rights advocates, especially women's rights groups. The idea is that the custom infringes on a basic human right: disposition over one's body and one's sexuality. Indeed, such practices are fading because of worldwide attention to the problem and changing sex/gender roles. Some African countries have banned or otherwise discouraged the procedures, as have Western nations that receive immigration from such cultures. Similar issues arise with circumcision and other male genital operations. Is it right to require

adolescent boys to undergo collective circumcision to fulfill cultural traditions, as has been done traditionally in parts of Africa and Australia? Is it right to circumcise a baby boy without his permission, as has been done routinely in the United States and as is customary among Jews and Muslims? (A 2011 initiative aimed at banning circumcision in San Francisco, California, failed to make it to the ballot.)

According to an idea known as **cultural relativism,** it is inappropriate to use outside standards to judge behavior in a given society;

A historic photo of a Makah whale hunt in 1910 (left). Protesting the resumption of Makah whaling (right). Do you think the Makah should be allowed to resume whaling?
Left: Miscellaneous Items in High Demand collection, Prints & Photographs Division, Library of Congress, LC-USZ62-107820; right: © Dan Levine/AFP/Getty Images

under what conditions. That recommendation must then go to an administrative judge, and thereafter to the head of NOAA Fisheries, who would need to approve the judicial ruling.

The Makah case illustrates how, in today's world full of lawyers, regulatory agencies, and activists, winning back a cultural right that also is a treaty right can be a long, arduous, and uncertain process.

For the latest on the Makah, see their own website at http://makah.com/makah-tribal-info/. See also http://indiancountrytodaymedia-network.com/2015/06/23/whale-wars-group-vs-makah-who-decides-if-traditions-are-authentic-160741

SOURCE: Hopper 2015, Kershaw 2005, and the Makah website.

we should evaluate such behavior with reference to the culture in which it occurs. Anthropologists employ cultural relativism not as a moral belief but as a methodological position: In order to understand another culture fully, we must try to understand how the people in that culture see things. What motivates them—what are they thinking when they do those things? Such an approach does not preclude making moral judgments. In the FGM example, one can understand the motivations for the practice only by looking at things from the point of view of the people who engage in it. Having done this, one then faces the moral question of what, if anything, to do about it.

We also should recognize that different people and groups within the same society—for example, women versus men or old versus young—can have very different opinions about what is proper, necessary, and moral. When there are power differentials in a society, a particular practice may be supported by some people more than others (e.g., old men versus young women). In trying to understand the meaning of a practice or belief within any cultural context, we should ask who benefits from that custom, and who does not.

The idea of **human rights** invokes a realm of justice and morality beyond and superior to particular countries, cultures, and religions. Human rights, usually seen as vested in individuals, include the right to speak freely, to hold religious beliefs without persecution, and not to be murdered, injured, enslaved, or imprisoned without charge. These rights are not ordinary laws that particular governments make and enforce. Human rights are seen as *inalienable* (nations cannot abridge or terminate them) and international (larger than and superior to individual nations and cultures). Four United Nations documents describe nearly all the human rights that have been internationally recognized. Those documents are the UN Charter; the Universal Declaration of Human Rights; the Covenant on Economic, Social and Cultural Rights; and the Covenant on Civil and Political Rights.

Alongside the human rights movement has arisen an awareness of the need to preserve cultural rights. Unlike human rights, **cultural rights** are vested not in individuals but in groups, including indigenous peoples and religious and ethnic minorities. Cultural rights include a group's ability to raise its children in the ways of its forebears, to continue its language, and not to be deprived of its economic base by the nation in which it is located. Many countries have signed pacts endorsing, for cultural minorities within nations, such rights as self-determination; some degree of home rule; and the right to practice the group's religion, culture, and language. The related notion of indigenous intellectual property rights (**IPR**) has arisen in an attempt to conserve each society's cultural base—its core beliefs and principles. IPR are claimed as a cultural right,

allowing indigenous groups to control who may know and use their collective knowledge and its applications. Much traditional cultural knowledge has commercial value. Examples include ethnomedicine (traditional medical knowledge and techniques), cosmetics, cultivated plants, foods, folklore, arts, crafts, songs, dances, costumes, and rituals. According to the IPR concept, a particular group may determine how its indigenous knowledge and the products of that knowledge are used and distributed, and the level of compensation required. (This chapter's "Appreciating Diversity" discusses how notions of legal, cultural, and animal rights may come into conflict.)

The notion of cultural rights recalls the previous discussion of cultural relativism, and the issue raised there arises again. What does one do about cultural rights that interfere with human rights? I believe that anthropology, as the scientific study of human diversity, should strive to present accurate accounts and explanations of cultural phenomena. Most ethnographers try to be objective, accurate, and sensitive in their accounts of other cultures. However, using objectivity, sensitivity, and a cross-cultural perspective doesn't mean that anthropologists have to ignore international standards of justice and morality. The anthropologist doesn't have to approve customs such as infanticide, cannibalism, and torture to recognize their existence and determine their causes and the motivations behind them. Each anthropologist has a choice about where he or she will do fieldwork. Some anthropologists choose not to study a particular culture because they discover in advance or early in fieldwork that behavior they consider morally repugnant is practiced there. When confronted with such behavior, each anthropologist must make a judgment about what, if anything, to do about it. What do you think?

The notion of indigenous property rights (IPR) has arisen in an attempt to conserve each society's cultural base, including its medicinal plants. The hoodia plant, shown on the left in Botswana, is a Kalahari Desert cactus traditionally used by the San people to stave off hunger. On the right we see HoodiaThin, a commercial appetite suppressant made from imported hoodia and distributed by Los Angeles–based Prime Life Nutritionals. Hoodia is grown today on a few commercial farms in southern Africa (including the San-owned farm on the left). For a film documentary on hoodia and the San see "Bushman's Secret" by Rehad Desai at https://www.youtube.com/watch?v=p1NamQj-E9I.

Left: © J.D. Dallet/age fotostock; right: © ZUMA Press, Inc./Alamy Stock Photo

MECHANISMS OF CULTURAL CHANGE

Why and how do cultures change? One way is through **diffusion,** or the borrowing of traits between cultures. Such exchange of information and products has gone on throughout human history because cultures never have been truly isolated. Contact between neighboring groups has always existed and has extended over vast areas (Boas 1940/1966). Diffusion is *direct* when two cultures trade, intermarry, or wage war on one another. Diffusion is *forced* when one culture subjugates another and imposes its customs on the dominated group. Diffusion is *indirect* when items move from group A to group C via group B without any firsthand contact between A and C. In this case, group B might consist of traders or merchants who take products from a variety of places to new markets. Or group B might be geographically situated between A and C, so that what it gets from A eventually winds up in C, and vice versa. In today's world, much transnational diffusion is due to the spread of the mass media and advanced information technology.

Acculturation, a second mechanism of cultural change, is the exchange of cultural features that results when groups have continuous firsthand contact. This contact may change the cultures of either group or both groups (Redfield, Linton, and Herskovits 1936). With acculturation, parts of the cultures change, but each group remains distinct. In situations of continuous contact, cultures may exchange and blend foods, recipes, music, dances, clothing, tools, technologies, and languages.

One example of acculturation is a *pidgin,* a mixed language that develops to ease communication between members of different societies in contact. This usually happens in situations of trade or colonialism. Pidgin English, for example, is a simplified form of English that blends English grammar with the grammar of a native language. Pidgin English first developed to facilitate commerce in Chinese ports. Similar pidgins developed later in Papua New Guinea and West Africa.

Independent invention—the process by which humans innovate, creatively finding solutions to problems—is a third mechanism of cultural change. Faced with similar problems and challenges, people in different societies have innovated and changed in similar ways, which is one reason cultural generalities exist. One example is the independent invention of agriculture in the Middle East and Mexico. Often a major invention, such as agriculture, triggers a series of subsequent interrelated changes. Thus, in both Mexico and the Middle East, agriculture led to many social, political, and legal changes, including notions of property and distinctions in wealth, class, and power.

GLOBALIZATION

The term **globalization** encompasses a series of processes that work transnationally to promote change in a world in which nations and people are increasingly interlinked and mutually dependent. (see Spooner 2015). The forces of globalization include international commerce and finance, travel and tourism, transnational migration, and the media—including the Internet and other high-tech information flows (see Friedman and Friedman 2008; Haugerud, Stone, and Little 2011; Kjaerulff 2010). New economic unions (which have met considerable resistance in their member nations) have been created through the World Trade Organization (WTO), the International Monetary Fund (IMF), and the European Union (EU).

The media, including the Internet and satellite and digital transmissions, play a key role in globalization. Long-distance communication is faster and easier than ever, and now it covers most of the globe. I can now e-mail, call, Skype, or Facebook friends in Arembepe, Brazil, which lacked phones and postal service when I first began to study the community. Information about Arembepe, including YouTube videos made by locals, is now available to anyone, including potential tourists, on hundreds of websites. Anything can be googled. The media help propel a transnational culture of consumption, as they spread information about products, services, rights, institutions, lifestyles, and the perceived costs and benefits of globalization. Emigrants transmit information and resources transnationally, as they maintain their ties with home (phoning, Skyping, Facetiming, tweeting, videoconferencing, texting, e-mailing, visiting, sending money). In a sense such people live multilocally—in different places and cultures at once. They learn to play various social roles and to change behavior and identity depending on the situation and context.

The effects of globalization are broad and not always welcome. Local people must deal increasingly with forces generated by larger systems—region, nation, and world. An army of outsiders and potential change agents now intrudes on people everywhere. Tourism has become the world's number one industry. Economic development agents and the media promote the idea that work should be for cash rather than mainly for subsistence. Indigenous peoples and traditional societies have devised various strategies to deal with threats to their autonomy, identity, and livelihood (Maybury-Lewis, Macdonald, and Maybury-Lewis, 2009). New forms of cultural expression and political mobilization, including the rights movements discussed previously, are emerging from the interplay of local, regional, national, and international cultural forces (see Ong and Collier 2005).

globalization
The accelerating interdependence of nations in the world system today.

diffusion
Borrowing of cultural traits between societies.

acculturation
An exchange of cultural features between groups in firsthand contact.

independent invention
The independent development of a cultural feature in different societies.

Globalization in its current form would not exist without the Internet. Shown here, Chinese youth in an Internet café in Beijing. Using cameras and ID card scanners, the Chinese government monitors activity in each of Beijing's more than 1,500 Internet cafés. Users must be 18 or older. Who monitors Internet use in your country?

© Wu changqing - Imaginechina/AP Images

Globalization: Its Meaning and Its Nature

Mark Smith and Michele Doyle (2002) distinguish between two meanings of globalization:

1. Globalization as fact: the spread and connectedness of production, communication, and technologies across the world. This is the principal meaning for this book.

2. Globalization as ideology and policy: efforts by the International Monetary Fund (IMF), the World Bank, and other international financial powers to create a global free market for goods and services. In this second sense, for its advocates, globalization is the way the world should go. For their opponents, it's the way the world should not go (Lewellen 2010).

The first meaning is more neutral. Globalization as systemic connectedness reflects the relentless and ongoing growth of the world system. In its current form, that system, which has existed for centuries, has some radical new aspects. Especially noteworthy are the speed of global communication, the scale (size and complexity) of global networks, and the volume of international transactions.

The fall of the Soviet empire (in 1989–1990) allowed a truly global economy to emerge (Lewellen 2010). Consider three key features of this new economy: (1) It is based on knowledge and information; (2) its networks are transnational; and (3) its core activities, no matter where they take place, can proceed as a unit in real time.

The Internet and cell phones have made possible the very rapid global transmission of money, resources, and information. Tasks that are spatially dispersed can now be coordinated in real time. Transactions that once involved face-to-face contact are now processed across vast distances. For example, when you order something using the Internet, the only human being you might speak to is the delivery driver, and a drone may soon replace that human! The computers that process your order from Amazon can be on different continents, and the products you order can come from a warehouse anywhere. The average food product now travels 1,300 miles and changes hands a dozen times before it reaches an American consumer (Lewellen 2010).

In such a world, Michael Burawoy suggests that anthropologists should shift "from studying 'sites' to studying 'fields,' that is, the relations between sites" (Burawoy 2000, p. xii). People increasingly live their lives across borders, maintaining social, financial, cultural, and political connections with more than one nation-state (see Lugo 1997). Examples of such "multiplaced" people include business and intellectual leaders, development workers, and members of multinational corporations, as well as migratory domestic, agricultural, and construction workers (see Lewellen 2010).

Multinational corporations move their operations to places where labor and materials are cheap. This globalization of labor creates unemployment "back home" as industries relocate and outsource abroad. Multinationals also seek out new markets. They strive to create new needs among specific target groups, especially young people, who increasingly construct their identities around consumption, especially of brand-name products. Successful multinationals, including Nike, Apple, and Coca-Cola invest huge sums in promoting their brands. The goal is to make a particular brand an integral part of the way people, especially young people, see themselves.

Multinational corporations ally themselves with, and influence, politicians and government officials, especially those who are most concerned with world trade. Financial globalization means that nations have less control over their own economies. Such institutions as the World Bank, the IMF, the European Union, and the European Central Bank routinely constrain and dictate the national economic policies of countries like Greece and Spain.

Illustrating political mobilization against globalization are regular protests at meetings of the principal agencies concerned with international trade. Protesters continue to show their disapproval of policies of the WTO, the IMF, and the World Bank. Anti-globalization activists fault those organizations for policies that, they say, promote corporate wealth at the expense of farmers, workers, and others at or near the bottom of the economy. Protesters also include environmentalists seeking tougher environmental regulations and trade unionists advocating global labor standards. Related to these protests was the 2011 Occupy movement, which spread quickly from Wall Street to other American (and Canadian) cities. That movement protested growing North American inequality—between the top 1 percent and everyone else. Similar sentiments motivated the 2016 Bernie Sanders Presidential campaign.

for REVIEW

summary

1. Culture, which is distinctive to humanity, refers to customary behavior and beliefs that are transmitted through enculturation. Culture rests on the human capacity for cultural learning. Culture encompasses rules for conduct internalized in human beings, which lead them to think and act in characteristic ways.

2. Although other animals learn, only humans have cultural learning, dependent on symbols. Humans think symbolically—arbitrarily bestowing meaning on things and events. By convention, a symbol stands for something with which it has no necessary or natural relation. Symbols have special meaning for people who share memories, values, and beliefs because of common enculturation. People absorb cultural lessons consciously and unconsciously.

3. Cultural traditions mold biologically based desires and needs in particular directions. Everyone is cultured, not just people with elite educations. Cultures may be integrated and patterned through economic and social forces, key symbols, and core values. Cultural rules don't rigidly dictate our behavior. There is room for creativity, flexibility, diversity, and disagreement within societies. Cultural means of adaptation have been crucial in human evolution. Aspects of culture also can be maladaptive.

4. The human capacity for culture has an evolutionary basis that extends back at least 3 million years—to early toolmakers whose products survive in the archaeological record (and most probably even farther back—based on observation of tool use and manufacture by apes). Humans share with monkeys and apes such traits as manual dexterity (especially opposable thumbs), depth and color vision, learning ability based on a large brain, substantial parental investment in a limited number of offspring, and tendencies toward sociality and cooperation.

5. Many hominin traits are foreshadowed in other primates, particularly in the African apes, which, like us, belong to the hominid family. The ability to learn, basic to culture, is an adaptive advantage available to monkeys and apes. Chimpanzees make tools for several purposes. They also hunt and share meat. Sharing and cooperation are more developed among humans than among the apes, and only humans have systems of kinship and marriage that permit us to maintain lifelong ties with relatives in different local groups.

6. Using a comparative perspective, anthropology examines biological, psychological, social, and cultural universals and generalities. There also are unique and distinctive aspects of the human condition (cultural particularities). North American cultural traditions are no more natural than any others. Levels of culture can be larger or smaller than a nation. Cultural traits may be shared across national boundaries. Nations also include cultural differences associated with ethnicity, region, and social class.

7. Ethnocentrism describes judging other cultures by using one's own cultural standards. Cultural relativism, which anthropologists may use as a methodological position rather than a moral stance, is the idea of avoiding the use of outside standards to judge behavior in a given society. Human rights are those based on justice and morality beyond and superior to particular countries, cultures, and religions. Cultural rights are vested in religious and ethnic minorities and indigenous societies, and IPR, or intellectual property rights, apply to an indigenous group's collective knowledge and its applications.

8. Diffusion, migration, and colonialism have carried cultural traits and patterns to different world areas. Mechanisms of cultural change include diffusion, acculturation, and independent invention.

9. Globalization describes a series of processes that promote change in a world in which nations and people are interlinked and mutually dependent. There is a distinction between globalization as fact (the primary meaning of globalization in this book) and globalization as contested ideology and policy (international efforts to create a global free market for goods and services).

key terms

acculturation 31

core values 22

cultural relativism 28

cultural rights 30

diffusion 31

enculturation 19

ethnocentrism 27

generality 24

globalization 31

hominid 22

hominins 22

human rights 30

independent invention 31

international culture 26

IPR 30

national culture 26

particularity 24

subcultures 27

symbol 19

universal 24

critical thinking

1. This chapter includes various authors' definitions of culture (e.g., those of Tylor, Geertz, and Kottak). How are these definitions similar? How are they different? How has reading this chapter altered your own understanding of what culture is?

2. Our culture—and cultural changes—affect how we perceive nature, human nature, and "the natural." This theme continues to fascinate science fiction writers. Recall a recent science fiction book, movie, or TV program that creatively explores the boundaries between nature and culture. How does the story develop the tension between nature and culture to craft a plot?

3. In American culture today, the term *diversity* is used in many contexts, usually referring to some positive attribute of our human experience, something to appreciate, to maintain, and even to increase. In what contexts have you heard the term used? To what precisely does the term refer?

4. What are some issues about which you find it hard to be culturally relativistic? If you were an anthropologist with the task of investigating these issues in real life, can you think of a series of steps that you would take to design a project that would, to the best of your ability, practice methodological cultural relativism? (You may want to review the use of the scientific method in an anthropological project presented in Chapter 1.)

5. What are the mechanisms of cultural change described in this chapter? Can you come up with additional examples of each mechanism? Also, recall the relationship between culture and the individual. Can individuals be agents of cultural change?

Applying Anthropology

▸ Can change be bad and, if so, how?

▸ How can anthropology be applied to medicine, education, and business?

▸ How does the study of anthropology fit into a career path?

© Michael Stuparyk/Toronto Star via Getty Images

Ph.D. Anthropologist Morgan Gerard works at Idea Couture, a global firm based in Toronto, Canada. A former "Resident Anthropologist" and "Chief Resident Anthropologist" there, his current title is "Chief Resident Storyteller." His job is to help develop compelling stories about people, brands, businesses, innovations, and corporate culture for varied organizations (see http://www.ideacouture.com/leadership-team/morgan-gerard).

understanding OURSELVES

Can change be bad? The idea that innovation is desirable is almost axiomatic and unquestioned in American culture—especially in advertising. "New and improved" is a slogan we hear all the time—a lot more often than "old reliable." Which do you think is best—change or the status quo?

That "new" isn't always "improved" is a painful lesson learned by the Coca-Cola Company (TCCC) in 1985 when it changed the formula of its premier soft drink and introduced "New Coke." After a national brouhaha, with hordes of customers protesting, TCCC brought back old, familiar, reliable Coke under the name "Coca-Cola Classic," which thrives today. New Coke, now history, offers a classic case of how not to treat consumers. TCCC tried a *top-down change* (a change initiated at the top of a hierarchy rather than inspired by the people most affected by the change). Customers didn't ask TCCC to change its product; executives made that decision.

Business executives, like public policy makers, run organizations that provide goods and services to people. The field of market research, which employs a good number of anthropologists, is based on the need to appreciate what actual and potential customers do, think, and want. Smart planners study and listen to people to try to determine *locally based demand*. In general, what's working well (assuming it's not discriminatory or illegal) should be maintained, encouraged, tweaked, and strengthened. If something's wrong, how can it best be fixed? What changes do the people—and which people—want? How can conflicting wishes and needs be accommodated? Applied anthropologists help answer these questions, which are crucial in understanding whether change is needed, and how it will work.

Innovation succeeds best when it is culturally appropriate. This axiom of applied anthropology could guide the international spread of programs aimed at social and economic change as well as of businesses. Each time an organization expands to a new nation, it must devise a culturally appropriate strategy for fitting into the new setting. In their international expansion, companies as diverse as McDonald's, Starbucks, and Ford have learned that more money can be made by fitting in with, rather than trying to Americanize, local habits.

Anthropology has two dimensions: academic and applied. **Applied anthropology** is the use of anthropological data, perspectives, theory, and methods to identify, assess, and solve contemporary problems (see Pelto 2013; Wasson, Butler, and Copeland-Carson 2012). Applied anthropologists help make anthropology relevant and useful to the world beyond anthropology (see Beck and Maida 2013). Medical anthropologists, for example, have worked as cultural interpreters in public health programs, helping such programs fit into local culture. Development anthropologists work for or with international development agencies, such as the World Bank and the U.S. Agency for International Development (USAID). The findings of garbology, the archaeological study of waste, are relevant to the Environmental Protection Agency, the paper industry, and packaging and trade associations. Archaeology also is applied in cultural resource management and historic preservation. Biological anthropologists apply their expertise in programs aimed at public health, nutrition, genetic counseling, aging, substance abuse, and mental health. Forensic anthropologists

ANTHROPOLOGY'S SUBFIELDS (ACADEMIC ANTHROPOLOGY)	EXAMPLES OF APPLICATION (APPLIED ANTHROPOLOGY)
Cultural anthropology	Development anthropology
Archaeological anthropology	Cultural resource management (CRM)
Biological anthropology	Forensic anthropology
Linguistic anthropology	Study of linguistic diversity in classrooms

Like other forensic anthropologists, Dr. Kathy Reichs (shown here) and her alter ego, Temperance Brennan (played on the TV show *Bones* by Emily Deschanel), work with the police, medical examiners, the courts, and international organizations to identify victims of crimes, accidents, wars, terrorism, and genocide.

© Will & Deni McIntyre/Corbis

statistics. However, the applied anthropologist's likely early request is some variant of "take me to the local people." Anthropologists know that people must play an active role in the changes that affect them and that "the people" have information that "the experts" lack.

Anthropological theory, the body of findings and generalizations of the four subfields, also guides applied anthropology. Just as theory aids practice, application fuels theory (see Rylko-Bauer, Singer, and Van Willigen 2006). As we compare social-change programs, our understanding of cause and effect increases. We add new generalizations about culture change to those discovered in traditional and ancient cultures.

applied anthropology
The use of anthropology to solve contemporary problems.

THE ROLE OF THE APPLIED ANTHROPOLOGIST

Early Applications

Anthropology is, and has long been, the main academic discipline that focuses on non-Western cultures. One example is the role that anthropologists played as agents of and advisors to colonial regimes during the first half of the 20th century. Under colonialism, some anthropologists worked as administrators in the colonies or held lower level positions as government agents, researchers, or advisors. Other anthropologists who supported colonialism were university professors who offered advice to colonial regimes. The main European colonial powers at that time—Britain, France, Portugal, and the Netherlands—all employed anthropologists. When those colonial empires began to collapse after World War II, as the former colonies gained independence, many anthropologists continued to offer advice to government agencies about the areas and cultures they knew the best.

In the United States, American anthropologists have worked extensively with the subjugated Native American populations within its borders. The 19th-century American anthropologist Lewis Henry Morgan studied the Seneca Iroquois tribe, Native Americans living in New York state, not far from his home in Rochester. Morgan was also

work with the police, medical examiners, the courts, and international organizations to identify victims of crimes, accidents, wars, and terrorism. Linguistic anthropologists have studied physician–patient speech interactions and have shown how dialect differences influence classroom learning. Most applied anthropologists seek humane and effective ways of helping local people. See Recap 3.1 for examples of applied anthropology in the four subdisciplines.

The ethnographic method is a particularly valuable tool in applying anthropology. Remember that ethnographers study societies firsthand, living with, observing, and learning from ordinary people. Nonanthropologists working in social-change programs often are content to converse with officials, read reports, and copy

a lawyer who represented the Iroquois in their disputes with a company that wanted to seize some of their land. Just as Morgan worked on behalf of the Seneca, there are anthropologists today who work on behalf of the non-Western groups they have studied. Other anthropologists, working as government employees and agents, have helped to establish and enforce policies developed by ruling classes and aimed at local populations.

Bronislaw Malinowski, a Polish-born scholar who spent most of his career teaching in England, was one of the most prominent cultural anthropologists of the early 20th century. Malinowski is well known for his ethnographic fieldwork with the Trobriand Islanders of the South Pacific and for his role in establishing ethnographic field methods. He also is recognized as one of the founders of applied anthropology, which he called "practical anthropology" (Malinowski 1929). Like many other anthropologists of his time, Malinowski worked *with* colonial regimes, rather than opposing the European subjugation of non-Western peoples.

Malinowski, who focused on Britain's African colonies, intended his "practical anthropology" to support and facilitate colonial rule. He believed that anthropologists could help European colonial officials to effectively administer non-Western societies. Anthropologists could help answer questions like the following: How much taxation and forced labor could "the natives" tolerate without resisting? How was contact with European settlers and colonial officials affecting tribal societies? Anthropologists could study local land ownership and use in order to determine how much of their own land "natives" could keep and how much Europeans could take from them. Malinowski did not question the right of Europeans to rule the societies they had conquered. For him, the anthropologist's job was not to question colonial rule, but to make it work as harmoniously as possible. Other colonial-era anthropologists offered similar advice to the French, Portuguese, and Dutch regimes (see also Duffield and Hewitt 2009; Lange 2009).

During World War II, American anthropologists applied anthropology by trying to gain insights about the motivations and behavior of the enemies of the United States—principally Germany and Japan. Margaret Mead (1977) estimated that during the 1940s, 95 percent of U.S. anthropologists were engaged in the war effort. For example, Ruth Benedict (1946) wrote an influential study of Japanese national culture not by doing fieldwork in Japan, but by studying Japanese literature, movies, and other cultural products and by interviewing Japanese in the United States. She called her approach "the study of culture at a distance." After World War II, American anthropologists worked to promote local-level cooperation with American policies on several Pacific islands that had been under Japanese control and were now administered by the United States.

Many of the early applications of anthropology described in this section were problematic because they aided and abetted the subjugation and control of non-Western cultures by militarily stronger societies. Most contemporary applied anthropologists see their work as radically removed from colonial-era applied anthropology. Applied anthropologists today usually see their work as a helping profession, designed to assist local people.

Academic and Applied Anthropology

The U.S. baby boom, which began in 1946 and peaked in 1957, fueled a tremendous expansion of the American educational system. New junior, community, and four-year colleges opened, and anthropology became a standard part of the college curriculum. During the 1950s and 1960s, most American anthropologists were college professors, although some still worked in agencies and museums.

Most anthropologists still worked in colleges and museums during the 1970s and 1980s. However, an increasing number of anthropologists were finding jobs in international organizations, governments, businesses, hospitals, and schools. Today, applied anthropologists work in extremely varied contexts, including large development organizations, communities and cultural groups, public institutions, government agencies, nongovernmental organizations (NGOs) and nonprofit organizations, international policy bodies, and private entities, such as unions, social movements, and increasingly businesses and corporations (Rylko-Bauer et al. 2006). The American Anthropological Association estimates that well over half of anthropology PhDs today seek nonacademic employment. This shift toward application has benefited the profession. It has forced anthropologists to consider the wider social value and implications of their research.

Applied Anthropology Today

According to Barbara Rylko-Bauer, Merrill Singer, and John van Willigen (2006), modern applied anthropology uses theories, concepts, and methods from anthropology to confront human problems, such as poverty, that often contribute to profound social suffering.

However, applied anthropologists also have clients who are neither poor nor powerless. An applied anthropologist working as a market researcher may be concerned with discovering how to increase sales of a particular product. Such commercial goals can pose ethical dilemmas, which also may arise in cultural resource management (CRM). The CRM anthropologist helps decide how to preserve significant remains when development threatens sites. The client that hires

Archaeologists Tim Griffith, left, and Ginny Hatfield of Fort Hood's (Texas) Cultural Resources Management Program, sift through sediment collected from an archaeological site. This CRM program manages resources representing more than 10,000 years of occupation of the land around Fort Hood. © Scott Gaulin/Temple Daily Telegram/AP Images

the CRM may be someone seeking to build a road or a factory. That client may have a strong interest in a CRM finding that no sites need protection, and the client may pressure the CRM firm in that direction. Among the ethical questions that arise in applied anthropology are these: To whom does the researcher owe loyalty? What problems are involved in holding firm to the truth? What happens when applied anthropologists don't make the policies they have to implement? How does one criticize programs in which one has participated? Anthropology's professional organizations have addressed such questions by establishing codes of ethics and ethics committees.

Anthropologists study, understand, and respect diverse cultural values. Because of this knowledge of human problems and social change, anthropologists are highly qualified to suggest, plan, and implement policies affecting people. Proper roles for applied anthropologists include (1) identifying needs for change that local people perceive, (2) collaborating with those people to design culturally appropriate and socially sensitive change, and (3) working to protect local people from harmful policies and projects that may threaten them.

For decades applied anthropologists have collaborated directly with communities to achieve community-directed change. Applied anthropologists not only work collaboratively with local people, but they may even be hired by such communities to advocate on their behalf. One example is Barbara Rose Johnston's (2005) research on behalf of Guatemalan communities that were adversely affected by the construction of the Chixoy Dam. Johnston's reports document the dam's long-term impact on these communities. She also offered recommendations and a plan for reparations.

DEVELOPMENT ANTHROPOLOGY

Development anthropology is the branch of applied anthropology that focuses on social issues in, and the cultural dimension of, economic development. Development anthropologists don't just carry out development policies planned by others; they also plan and guide policy. (For more detailed discussions of issues in development anthropology, see Crewe and Axelby 2013; Edelman and Haugerud 2005; Mosse 2011.)

Still, ethical dilemmas often confront development anthropologists (Escobar 2012; Venkatesan and Yarrow 2014). Foreign aid, including funds for economic development, usually does not go where need and suffering are greatest. Rather, such aid tends to support political, economic, and strategic priorities that are set by international donors, political leaders, and powerful interest groups. The goals and interests of the planners may ignore or conflict with the best interests of the local people. Although the stated aim of most development projects is to enhance the quality of life, living standards often decline in the affected area.

development anthropology
A field that examines the sociocultural dimensions of economic development.

Equity

An important stated goal of recent development projects has been to promote equity. **Increased equity** entails (1) reducing poverty and (2) evening out the distribution of wealth. Projects should not benefit only the "haves," but also the "have nots." If people who are already doing well get most of the benefits of a project, then it has not increased equity.

If projects are to increase equity, they must have the support of reform-minded governments. Wealthy and powerful people typically resist projects that offer more to the "have nots" than to the "haves." Often, they will actively oppose a project that threatens the status quo.

Negative Equity Impact

Some projects not only have not increased equity; they have actually widened the gap between the "haves" and "have nots." In this case, we say they have had a *negative equity impact*. I observed firsthand an example of negative equity impact in Arembepe, Bahia, Brazil, a fishing community on the Atlantic Ocean (see Kottak 2006). A development initiative there offered loans to buy motors for fishing boats, but only people who already owned boats ("haves") could get these loans. Nonowners ("have nots") did not qualify. After getting the loans, the boat owners, in order to repay them, increased the percentage of the catch they took from the men who fished in their boats. Their rising profits allowed them to eventually buy larger and more expensive boats. They cited their increased capital expense as a reason to pay their workers less. Over the years, the gap between "haves" and "have

nots" widened substantially. The eventual result was socioeconomic stratification—the creation of social classes in a community that had been egalitarian. In the past, Arembepe's fishing boats had been simple sailboats, relying only on wind power, and any enterprising young fisher could hope eventually to own one of his own. In the new economy, a fishing boat became so expensive that ambitious young men, who once would have sought careers in fishing, no longer could afford to buy a boat of their own. They sought wage labor on land instead. To avoid this kind of negative equity impact, credit-granting agencies must seek out and invest in enterprising young fishers, rather than giving loans only to owners and established businesspeople. A lesson here is that the stated goal of increased equity is easier said than done. Because the "haves" tend to have better connections than the "have nots," they are more likely to find out about and take advantage of new programs. They also tend to have more clout with government officials, who often decide who will benefit from a particular program.

STRATEGIES FOR INNOVATION

Development anthropologists should work collaboratively and proactively with local people, especially the "have nots," to assess, and help them realize, their own wishes and needs for change. Too many true local needs cry out for a solution to waste money funding projects in area A that are inappropriate there but needed in area B, or that are unnecessary anywhere. Development anthropology can help sort out the needs of the As and Bs and fit projects accordingly. Projects that put people first by consulting with them and responding to their expressed needs must be identified (Cernea 1991). To maximize social and economic benefits, projects must (1) be culturally compatible, (2) respond to locally perceived needs, (3) involve men and women in planning and carrying out the changes that affect them, (4) harness traditional organizations, and (5) be flexible (see Kottak 1990*b*, 1991).

Consider a recent example of a development initiative that failed because it ignored local culture. Working in Afghanistan after the fall of the Taliban, ethnographer Noah Coburn (2011) studied Istalif, a village of potters. During his fieldwork there Coburn discovered that an NGO had spent $20,000 on an electric kiln that could have greatly enhanced the productivity of local potters. The only problem was that the kiln was donated to a women's center that men could not enter. The misguided donors ignored the fact that Istalif's men did the work—pot-making and firing—that a kiln could facilitate. Women's role in pottery came later—in glazing and decorating.

A mix of boats harbored in Pucasana, a fishing village in Peru. A boat owner gets a loan to buy a motor. To repay it, he increases the share of the catch he takes from his crew. Later, he uses his rising profits to buy a more expensive boat and takes even more from his crew. Can a more equitable solution be found?

© Sean Sprague/The Image Works

Overinnovation

Development projects are most likely to succeed when they avoid the fallacy of **overinnovation** (too much change). People usually are willing to change just enough to maintain, or slightly improve on, what they already have. Motives for modifying behavior come from the traditional culture and the small concerns of ordinary life. Peasants' values are not such abstract ones as "learning a better way," "progressing," "increasing technical know-how," "improving efficiency," or "adopting modern techniques." Rather, their objectives are down-to-earth and specific. People want to grow and harvest their crops, amass resources for a ceremony, get a child through school, or have enough cash to pay bills. The goals and values of people who farm and fish for their own subsistence differ from those of people who work for cash, just as they differ from those of development planners.

Development projects that fail usually do so because they are either economically or culturally incompatible (or both). For example, one South Asian project tried to get farmers to start growing onions and peppers, expecting these cash crops to fit into the existing system of rice cultivation—the main local subsistence crop. However, it turned out that the labor peaks for these new cash crops coincided with those for rice, to which the farmers naturally gave priority. This project failed because it was overinnovative. It promoted too much change, introducing unfamiliar crops that conflicted with, rather than building on and complementing, an existing system. The planners should have realized that cultivation of the new crops would conflict with that of the main subsistence crop in the area. A good anthropologist could have told them as much.

Recent development efforts in Afghanistan also illustrate the problematic nature of overinnovation. Reporting on social change efforts in Afghanistan after the fall of the Taliban, anthropologists Noah Coburn (2011) and Thomas Barfield (2010) criticize various top-down initiatives that proved incompatible with local culture. Coburn suggests that the best strategy to maintain peace in the Afghan countryside is to work with existing resources, drawing on local beliefs and social organization. To be avoided are overinnovative plans from outside, whether from the national government or foreign donors. Destined for failure, according to Coburn, are attempts to create impersonal bureaucracies based on merit. Also doomed are attempts to impose liberal beliefs about gender at the village level. These are Western ideas that are particularly incompatible in rural areas. Barfield also cites the futility of direct attempts to change rural Afghans' beliefs about such entrenched matters as religion and gender equality. A better strategy, he suggests, is for change agents to work first in urban areas, where innovation is more welcome, and then let those changes spread gradually to the countryside.

Barfield also faults Western powers for trying to impose an autocratic system (the Karzai regime, which ended in 2014) on a country where autocracy is politically unsustainable. In 2014, Afghanistan elected an anthropologist as its president. Ashraf Ghani, who received his doctorate in anthropology from Columbia University in New York, had worked for the World Bank as a development anthropologist. Let us hope that Ghani's background in anthropology and development will encourage more culturally appropriate development strategies in the nation he now leads.

overinnovation
Trying to achieve too much change.

Underdifferentiation

The fallacy of **underdifferentiation** is planners' tendency to view "the less-developed countries" (LDCs) as more alike than they are. Often development agencies have ignored huge cultural contrasts (e.g., between Brazil and Botswana) and adopted a uniform approach to deal with very different societies. Planners often try to impose incompatible property concepts and social units. Most often, the faulty social design assumes either (1) units of production that are privately owned by an individual or a couple and worked by a nuclear family or (2) cooperatives based at least partially on models from the former Eastern bloc and Socialist countries.

One example of using an inappropriate First World model (the individual and the nuclear family) was a West African project designed for an area where the extended family was the basic social unit. The project succeeded despite its faulty

underdifferentiation
Seeing less-developed countries as all the same; ignoring cultural diversity.

Rural women attend a BRAC microfinance meeting in Tanzania's Kilimanjaro region. BRAC, the world's largest development NGO, provides affordable financial services, including credit, to the poor in many countries (see www.brac.net).
© Majority World/UIG via Getty Images

social design because the participants used their traditional extended family networks to attract additional settlers. Eventually, twice as many people as planned benefited as extended family members flocked to the project area. In this case, the settlers used their traditional social organization to modify the project design that planners had tried to impose on them.

The second dubious foreign social model that is common in development planning is the cooperative. In a comparative study of rural development projects, new cooperatives tended to succeed only when they harnessed preexisting local-level communal institutions. This is a corollary of a more general rule: Participants' groups are most effective when they are based on traditional social organization or on a socioeconomic similarity among members (Kottak 1990b, 1991).

An alternative to such foreign models is needed: greater use of indigenous social models in economic development. These are traditional social units, such as the clans, lineages, and other extended kin groups of Africa, Oceania, and many other nations, with their communally held estates and resources. The most humane and productive strategy for change is to base the social design for innovation on traditional social forms in each target area.

Indigenous Models

Many governments are not genuinely, or realistically, committed to improving the lives of their citizens. Interference by major powers also has kept governments from enacting needed reforms. Occasionally, however, a government does act as an agent of and for its people. One historic example is Madagascar, whose people, the Malagasy, were organized into descent groups prior to indigenous state formation in the 18th century. The Merina, creators of the major precolonial state of Madagascar, wove descent groups into its structure, making members of important groups advisers to the king and thus giving them authority in government. The Merina state made provisions for the people it ruled. It collected taxes and organized labor for public works projects. In return, it redistributed resources to peasants in need. It also granted them some protection against war and slave raids and allowed them to cultivate their rice fields in peace. The government maintained the water works for rice cultivation. It opened to ambitious peasant boys the chance of becoming, through hard work and study, state bureaucrats.

Throughout the history of the Merina state—and continuing to some extent in postcolonial Madagascar—there have been strong relationships between the individual, the descent group, and the state. Local Malagasy communities, where residence is based on descent, are more cohesive and homogeneous than are communities in Latin America or North America. Madagascar gained political independence from France in 1960. Its

new government had an economic development policy aimed at increasing the ability of the Malagasy to feed themselves. Government policy emphasized increased production of rice, a subsistence crop, rather than cash crops. Furthermore, local communities, with their traditional cooperative patterns and solidarity based on kinship and descent, were treated as partners in, not obstacles to, the development process.

In a sense, the descent group is preadapted to equitable national development. In Madagascar, descent groups pooled their resources to educate their most ambitious members. Once educated, these men and women gained economically secure positions in the nation. They then shared the advantages of their new positions with their kin. For example, they gave room and board to rural cousins attending school and helped them find jobs.

This Madagascar example suggests that when government officials are of "the people" (rather than the elites) and have strong personal ties to common folk, they are more likely to promote democratic economic development. In Latin America, by contrast, leaders and followers too often have been from different socioeconomic strata, with no connections based on kinship, descent, marriage, or common background. When elites rule, elites usually prosper. Recently, however, Latin America has elected some nonelite leaders. Brazil's lower class (indeed the entire nation) benefited socioeconomically when one of its own was elected president. Luiz Inácio da Silva, aka Lula, a former factory worker with only a fourth-grade education, served two terms (ending in 2011) as one of the Western Hemisphere's most popular leaders.

His better educated successor, Dilma Rousseff, from the same Workers' Party, has become one of Brazil's least popular presidents. As of this writing, she is embroiled in an impeachment process based on allegations that her administration violated fiscal laws.

Compatible and successful development projects promote change but not overinnovation. Many changes are possible if the aim is to preserve things while making them work better. Successful economic development projects respect, or at least don't attack, local cultural patterns. Effective development draws on indigenous cultural practices and social structures. As nations become more tied to the world capitalist economy, it is not inevitable that indigenous forms of social organization will break down into nuclear family organization, impersonality, and alienation. Descent groups, with their traditional communalism and solidarity, have important roles to play in economic development.

ANTHROPOLOGY AND EDUCATION

Attention to culture also is fundamental to **anthropology and education,** a field whose research extends from classrooms into homes, neighborhoods, and communities (see Anderson-Levitt 2012; Levinson and Pollock 2011; Spindler and Hammond 2006). In classrooms, anthropologists have observed interactions among teachers, students, parents, and visitors. Jules Henry's classic account of the American elementary school classroom (1972) shows how students learn to conform to and compete with their peers. Anthropologists view children as total cultural creatures whose enculturation and attitudes toward education belong to a context that includes family and peers. (see also Kontopodis et al. 2011; Reyhner et al. 2013)

Sociolinguists and cultural anthropologists have worked side by side in education research. In one classic study of Puerto Rican seventh graders in the urban Midwest (Hill-Burnett 1978), anthropologists uncovered some key misconceptions held by teachers. The teachers mistakenly had assumed that Puerto Rican parents valued education less than did non-Hispanics, but in-depth interviews revealed that the Puerto Rican parents valued it more. The anthropologists also identified certain practices that were preventing Hispanics from being adequately educated. For example, the teachers' union and the board of education had agreed to teach "English as a foreign language." However, they had provided no bilingual teachers to work with Spanish-speaking students. The school was assigning all students (including non-Hispanics) with low reading scores and behavior problems to the English-as-a-foreign-language classroom. This educational disaster brought together in the classroom a teacher who spoke no Spanish, children who barely spoke English, and a group of English-speaking students with reading and behavior problems. The Spanish speakers were falling behind not just in reading but in all subjects. They could at least have kept up in the other subjects if a Spanish speaker had been teaching them science, social studies, and math until they were ready for English-language instruction in those areas.

October, 2015: Lahore, Punjab, Pakistan: A young student peruses a book as her community prepares to celebrate World Teachers' Day. Observed annually on October 5, that globally-recognized day was established by UNESCO (the United Nations Educational, Scientific and Cultural Organization) in 1994 to focus attention on the contributions and achievements of teachers.
© Rana Sajid Hussain/Pacific Press/LightRocket via Getty Images

URBAN ANTHROPOLOGY

In today's world, media-transmitted images and information play an important role in attracting people to cities. Often, people move to cities for economic reasons, because jobs are scarce at home. Cities also attract people who want to be where the action is. Rural Brazilians routinely cite *movimento,* urban activity and excitement, as something to be valued. International migrants tend to settle in large cities, where a lot is going on and where they can feel at home in ethnic enclaves. Consider Canada, which, after Australia, is the country with the highest percentage of foreign-born population. Three-quarters of immigrants to Canada settle in Toronto, Vancouver, or Montreal. By 2031, it is estimated that nearly one-half (46 percent) of Canadians aged 15 and over will be foreign born or will have at least one foreign-born parent, up from 39 percent in 2006 (Statistics Canada 2010).

More than half of Earth's people live in cities—53 percent in 2014. That figure first surpassed 50 percent in 2008, and is projected to rise to 70 percent by 2050 (Handwerk 2008). Only about 3 percent of people were city dwellers in 1800, compared with 13 percent in 1900, 40 percent in 1980, and 53 percent today. The degree of urbanization (about 30 percent) in the less developed countries is well below the world average (50 percent). Even in the LDCs, however, the urban growth rate now exceeds the rural growth rate. By 2030, the percentage of city dwellers in the LDCs is projected to rise to 41 percent. In Africa and Asia alone, a million people a week migrate to cities. The world had only 16 cities with more than a million people in 1900, versus over 400 such cities today.

Over one billion people live in urban slums, mostly without reliable water, sanitation, public services, and legal security. If current trends continue, urban population increase and the concentration of people in slums will continue to be accompanied by rising rates of crime, along with water, air, and noise pollution (see Dürr and Jaffe 2010). These problems will be most severe in the LDCs.

As industrialization and urbanization spread globally, anthropologists increasingly study these processes and the social problems they create. **Urban anthropology,** which has theoretical (basic research) and applied dimensions, is the cross-cultural and ethnographic study of urbanization and life in cities (see Gmelch, Kemper, and Zenner 2010; Pardo and Prato 2012; Zukin et al. 2015). The United States and Canada have become popular arenas for urban anthropological research on topics such as immigration, ethnicity, poverty, class, and urban violence (Vigil 2010).

In any nation, urban and rural represent different social systems. However, cultural diffusion, or borrowing, occurs as people, products, images, and messages move from one to the other. Migrants bring rural practices and beliefs to cities and take urban patterns back home. The experiences and social forms of the rural area affect adaptation to city life. City folk also develop new institutions to meet specific urban needs.

An applied anthropology approach to urban planning starts by identifying key social groups in *specific* urban contexts—avoiding the fallacy of underdifferentiation. After identifying those groups, the anthropologist might elicit their wishes for change, convey those needs to funding agencies, and work with agencies and local people to realize those goals. In Africa relevant urban groups might include ethnic associations, occupational groups, social clubs, religious groups, and burial societies. Through membership in such groups, urban Africans maintain wide networks of personal contacts and support. The groups provide cash support and urban lodging for their rural relatives. Members may call one another "brother" and "sister." As in an extended family, richer members help their poorer relatives. A member's improper behavior, however, can lead to expulsion—an unhappy fate for a migrant in a large, ethnically heterogeneous city.

One role for the urban applied anthropologist is to help people deal with urban institutions, such as legal and social services, with which recent migrants may be unfamiliar. In certain North American cities, as in Africa, ethnic associations are relevant urban groups. One example comes from Los Angeles, which has the largest Samoan immigrant community in the United States (over 50,000 people). Samoans in Los Angeles draw on their traditional system of matai (respect for chiefs or elders) to deal with modern urban problems. When a white police officer shot and killed two unarmed Samoan brothers and a judge dismissed charges against the officer, local leaders used the matai system to calm angry youths (who have formed gangs, like other ethnic groups in the Los Angeles area). Clan leaders and elders organized a well-attended community meeting, in which they urged young members to be patient. The Samoans then brought a civil case against the officer in question and pressed the U.S. Justice Department to initiate a civil rights case in the matter (Mydans 1992b). Not all conflicts involving gangs and law enforcement end so peacefully.

James Vigil (2010) examines gang violence in the context of large-scale immigration to American cities. He notes that most gangs prior to the 1970s were located in white ethnic enclaves in eastern and midwestern cities. Back then, gang incidents typically were brawls involving fists, sticks, and knives. Today, gangs more often are composed of non-white ethnic groups, and handguns have replaced less lethal weapons. Gangs still consist mostly of male adolescents who have grown up together, usually in a low-income neighborhood, where it is estimated that about 10 percent of young men join gangs. Female gang members are much rarer. With gangs organized hierarchically by age, older members push younger ones (usually 14- to 18-year-olds) to carry out violent acts against rivals (Vigil 2010). How might an applied anthropologist approach the problem of urban violence? Which groups would have to be involved in the study?

MEDICAL ANTHROPOLOGY

Medical anthropology is the comparative, biocultural study of disease, health problems, and health care systems (see Wiley and Allen 2013). Both academic and applied, medical anthropology includes anthropologists from all four subfields (see Brown and Barrett 2010; Joralemon 2010; Singer and Baer 2012). Medical anthropology emerged out of applied work done in public health and international development (Foster and Anderson 1978). Current medical anthropology continues to have clear policy applications, partly because it so often deals with pressing human problems that cry out for solutions. Medical anthropologists examine such questions as which diseases and health conditions affect particular populations (and why) and how illness is socially constructed, diagnosed, managed, and treated in various societies (Lupton 2012; Singer and Erickson 2011).

Disease refers to a scientifically identified health threat caused genetically or by a bacterium, virus, fungus, parasite, or other pathogen. **Illness** is a condition of poor health perceived or felt by an individual within a particular culture. Particular cultures and ethnic groups recognize different illnesses, symptoms, and causes and have developed different health care systems and treatment strategies.

The incidence and severity of disease vary as well (see Baer, Singer, and Susser 2013). Group differences are evident in the United States. Consider, for example, health status indicators in relation to

U.S. census categories: white, black, Hispanic, American Indian or Alaska Native, and Asian or Pacific Islander. African Americans' rates for six indicators (total mortality, heart disease, lung cancer, breast cancer, stroke, and homicide) range from 2.5 to 10 times greater than those of the other groups. Other ethnic groups have higher rates for suicide (white Americans) and motor vehicle accidents (American Indians and Alaskan Natives). Overall, Asians have the longest lifespans (see Dressler, Oths, and Gravlee, 2005).

Reviewing the health conditions of the world's surviving indigenous populations (about 400 million people), anthropologists Claudia Vallegia and Josh Snodgrass (2015) found their health indicators to be uniformly low. Compared with nonindigenous people, indigenous groups tend to have shorter and riskier lives. Mothers are more likely to die in childbirth; infants and children have lower survival chances. Malnutrition stunts their growth, and they suffer more from infectious diseases. Reflecting their increasing exposure to global forces, they have rising rates of cardiovascular and other chronic diseases, as well as depression and substance abuse. They also have limited access to medical care. An increasing number of anthropologists are working in global health programs at academic and research institutions. This presence, no doubt, will increase understanding of the health concerns of indigenous peoples—but more is needed. Vallegia and Snodgrass (2015) urge medical anthropologists to involve themselves more in community outreach, which could help bring better health care to indigenous populations.

Anthropologists Magdalena Hurtado and her colleagues (2005) noted very high rates of early mortality among South America's indigenous populations, whose life expectancy at birth is at least 20 years shorter than that of other South Americans. Hurtado and colleagues (2005) suggest three ways in which applied anthropologists can help improve the health of indigenous peoples: (1) Identify their most pressing health problems; (2) gather information on possible solutions; and (3) implement solutions in partnership with the agencies that are in charge of public health programs for indigenous populations.

In many areas, the world system and colonialism worsened the health of indigenous peoples by spreading diseases, warfare, servitude, and other stressors. Traditionally and in ancient times, hunter-gatherers, because of their small numbers, mobility, and relative isolation from other groups, lacked most of the epidemic infectious diseases that affect agrarian and urban societies (Cohen and Armelagos 2013). Epidemic diseases such as cholera, typhoid, and bubonic plague thrive in dense populations, and thus among farmers and city dwellers. The spread of malaria has been linked to population growth and deforestation associated with food production.

Anthropologists have noted the significance of urban youth groups, including gangs, which now have transnational scope. This 29-year-old man, lodged in the Denver County jail, was one of several jailed gang members who discussed their lives on a 2010 History Channel special. Members look to gangs for social support and physical protection. How might this man's tattoos have social significance?
© Joe Amon/The Denver Post/AP Images

Disease Theory Systems

The kinds and incidence of disease vary among societies, and cultures perceive and treat illness differently (see Lupton 2012). Still, all societies have what George Foster and Barbara Anderson call "disease-theory systems" to identify, classify, and explain illness. Foster and Anderson (1978) identified three basic theories about the causes of illness: personalistic, naturalistic, and emotionalistic. Personalistic disease theories blame illness on agents, such as sorcerers, witches, ghosts, or ancestral spirits.

Naturalistic disease theories explain illness in impersonal terms. One example is Western medicine, or biomedicine, which aims to link illness to scientifically demonstrated agents that bear no personal malice toward their victims. Thus, Western medicine attributes illness to organisms (e.g., bacteria, viruses, fungi, or parasites), accidents, toxic materials, or genes. Other naturalistic systems blame poor health on unbalanced body fluids. Many Latin cultures classify food, drink, and environmental conditions as "hot" or "cold." People believe their health suffers when they eat or drink hot or cold substances together or under inappropriate conditions. For example, one shouldn't drink something cold after a hot bath or eat a pineapple (a "cold" fruit) when one is menstruating (a "hot" condition).

Emotionalistic disease theories assume that emotional experiences cause illness. For example, Latin Americans may develop *susto,* an illness brought on by anxiety, fright, or tragic news. Its symptoms (lethargy, vagueness, distraction) are similar to those of "soul loss," a diagnosis of similar symptoms made by people in Madagascar.

All societies have **health care systems** consisting of beliefs, customs, specialists, and techniques aimed at ensuring health and diagnosing and curing illness. A society's illness-causation theory is important for treatment. When illness has a personalistic cause, magicoreligious specialists may be effective curers. They draw on varied techniques (occult and practical), which constitute their special expertise. A shaman may cure soul loss by enticing the spirit back into the body. Shamans may ease difficult childbirths by asking spirits to travel up the birth canal to guide the baby out (Lévi-Strauss 1967). A shaman may cure a cough by counteracting a curse or removing a substance introduced by a sorcerer.

If there is a "world's oldest profession" besides hunter and gatherer, it is **curer,** often a shaman. The curer's role has some universal features (Foster and Anderson 1978). Thus, a curer emerges through a culturally defined process of selection (parental prodding, inheritance of the role, visions, dream instructions) and training (apprentice shamanship, medical school). Eventually, the curer is certified by older practitioners and acquires a professional image. Patients believe in the skills of the curer, whom they consult and compensate. Health interventions always have to fit into local cultures. When Western medicine is introduced, people usually preserve many of their old methods while also accepting new ones. Native curers may go on treating certain conditions (e.g., spirit possession), while physicians deal with others. The native curer may get as much credit as the physician for a cure.

Scientific Medicine versus Western Medicine

We should not lose sight, ethnocentrically, of the difference between scientific medicine and Western medicine per se. **Scientific medicine** relies on advances in technology, genomics, molecular biology, pathology, surgery, diagnostics, and applications. Scientific medicine surpasses tribal treatment in many ways. Although medicines such as quinine, coca, opium, ephedrine, and rauwolfia were discovered in nonindustrial societies, thousands of effective drugs are available today to treat myriad diseases. Today's surgical procedures are much safer and more effective than those of traditional societies. These are strong benefits of scientific medicine.

Western medicine refers to the practice of medicine in a particular modern Western nation, such as the United States. Of course, the practice of medicine and the quality and availability of heath care vary among Western nations. Some make free or low-cost health care available to all citizens, while other countries are not so generous. Millions of Americans, for example, remain uninsured.

Western medicine has both "pros" and "cons." The strongest "pro" of Western medicine is that it incorporates scientific medicine and its many benefits. "Cons" associated with Western medicine include overprescription of drugs, unnecessary surgeries, and the impersonality and inequality of the physician–patient relationship. In addition, overuse of antibiotics seems to be triggering an explosion of resistant microorganisms. Another "con" associated with Western medicine is that it tends to draw a rigid line between biomedical and psychological causation. Non-Western theories usually lack this sharp distinction, recognizing that poor health has intertwined physical, emotional, and social causes (see also Brown and Barrett 2010; Joralemon 2010; Strathern and Stewart 2010).

Treatment strategies that emulate the much more personal non-Western curer–patient–community relationship might benefit Western systems. Physician–patient encounters too often are rushed and truncated. Those who perform a surgical procedure or diagnose a condition often include specialists (e.g., radiologists and lab technicians) that the patient will never see. Surgeons are not renowned for their "bedside manner." Efforts are being made to improve physician–patient relationships. A recent trend in the United States is the rise of "concierge medicine," in which a physician charges an annual fee to each patient, limits the practice to a certain number of patients, and has ample time to spend with each patient because of the reduced caseload. To an extent, the Internet has empowered patients, who now have access to all kinds of medical information that used to be the sole property of physicians. This access, however, has its drawbacks. Information can make patients more informed as health care consumers, but it also prompts more questions than a physician usually can answer during a brief appointment.

Industrialization, Globalization, and Health

Despite the advances in scientific medicine, industrialization and globalization have spawned many significant health problems. Certain diseases, and physical conditions such as obesity, have spread with economic development and globalization (Inhorn and Wentzell 2012). Schistosomiasis, or bilharzia (liver flukes), is one of the fastest-spreading and most dangerous parasitic infections now known. People get schistosomiasis from snails living in ponds, lakes, and waterways, usually ones created by irrigation projects. The applied anthropology approach to reducing such diseases is to see if local people perceive a connection between the vector (e.g., snails in the water) and the disease. If not, local organizations, schools, and the media, including social media, can help spread the relevant information.

HIV/AIDS has been spread through international travel within the modern world system. The world's highest rates of HIV infection and AIDS-related deaths are in Africa, especially southern Africa (Mazzeo, Rödlach, and Brenton 2011). Sexually transmitted infections are spread through prostitution as young men from rural areas seek wage work in cities, labor camps, and mines, often across national borders. When the men return home, they infect their wives (see Baer et al. 2013). As it kills productive adults, AIDS leaves behind dependent children and seniors. Cultural factors affect the spread of HIV, which is less likely to spread when men are circumcised. (For more on the AIDS pandemic, see this chapter's "Focus on Globalization.")

Other problems associated with industrialization and globalization include the following: poor nutrition; dangerous machinery; impersonal work; isolation; poverty; homelessness; substance abuse; and noise, air, and water pollution (see McElroy and Townsend 2014). With industrialization and globalization, people turn from subsistence work, usually alongside family and neighbors, to cash employment in more impersonal settings such as factories. Rather than living in villages where everyone knows everyone else, people increasingly live in cities—and often in slums, where they tend to have poorer diets, more exposure to pathogens, poor sanitation, and polluted air. We all remember the scares caused by Ebola, H1N1, and other emergent viruses. Such pathogens, however, are not the only, or perhaps even the primary, cause of health problems associated with industrialization and globalization. Other stressors that endanger our health are economic (e.g., poverty), social (e.g., crowding, homelessness), political (e.g., terrorism), and cultural (e.g., ethnic conflict). Poverty contributes to many illnesses, including arthritis, heart conditions, back problems, and hearing and vision impairment.

In the United States and other developed countries, good health has become something of an ethical imperative (Foucault 1990). Individuals are expected to regulate their behavior so as to achieve bodies in keeping with new medical knowledge. Those who do so acquire the status of sanitary citizens—people with modern understanding of the body, health, and illness. Such citizens practice hygiene and look to health care professionals when they are sick. People who act differently (e.g., smokers, overeaters, those who avoid doctors) are stigmatized and blamed for their own health problems (Briggs 2005; Foucault 1990).

Nowadays, even getting an epidemic disease such as cholera may be viewed as a moral failure, because people did not take proper precautions. It's assumed that people who act rationally can avoid "preventable" diseases. Individuals are expected to follow scientifically based imperatives (e.g., "boil water," "don't smoke"). People (e.g., gay men, smokers, veterans) can become objects

Merina women plant paddy rice in the highlands south of Antsirabe, Madagascar. Schistosomiasis, of which all known varieties are found in Madagascar, is among the fastest-spreading and most dangerous parasitic infections now known. It is propagated by snails that live in ponds, lakes, and waterways (often ones created by irrigation systems, such as those associated with paddy rice cultivation).
© Carl D. Walsh/Aurora Photos

of avoidance and discrimination simply by belonging to a group seen as having a greater risk of poor health.

Medical anthropology also studies the impact of new scientific and medical techniques on ideas about life, death, and personhood (what it means to be a person). For decades, disagreements about personhood—such as about when life begins and ends—have been part of political and religious

At a market in Yangshuo, china, a woman undergoes a moxibustion treatment, in which mugwort, a small, spongy herb, is burned to facilitate healing.
© age fotostock/Alamy Stock Photo

The Deadliest Global Pandemic of Our Time

A pandemic is an infectious disease that spreads internationally and affects millions. In the case of HIV/AIDS, the pandemic has been global. HIV is the virus that causes the disease known as AIDS, which has killed about 39 million people since its discovery in 1981. Globally the number of people living with HIV has risen from about 8 million in 1990 to over 37 million today. In many countries, however, the number of new HIV infections and AIDS cases has declined because millions of people now take antiretroviral drugs. (HIV is classified as a retrovirus—a virus whose genes are encoded in RNA instead of DNA.) As Bono of U2 fame, a prominent campaigner against AIDS, notes, it's amazing what a difference "two little pills a day" can make (see Bono 2011). As of March 2015, around 15 million people living with HIV (41 percent of the total) had access to antiretroviral therapy.

Although HIV/AIDS is a global threat, some world areas are more infected than others are. More than two-thirds (70 percent) of all people living with HIV, 25.8 million, live in sub-Saharan Africa—including 88 percent of the world's HIV-positive children (see Foundation for AIDS Research 2015). The infection rate is highest in southern Africa. The following indicate the percentages of adults (ages 15–49) living with HIV in the nine contiguous southern Africa countries of Swaziland (26.1 percent), Botswana (23.9), Lesotho (23.2), South Africa (18.1), Namibia (15.3), Zimbabwe (15.3), Zambia (15.2), Mozambique (12.5), and Malawi (11.9). These are the highest rates in the world; in no other country does the figure rise above 10 percent. In these countries, HIV has spread through prostitution (mainly involving female sex workers and their clients). The infection rate is especially high among truckers, miners, and young rural men seeking wage work in cities and labor camps. Returning to their villages, these men infect their wives and the babies they bear.

Overall in Africa the adult infection rate is 5 percent. This is significantly higher than the rates of 1 percent in the Caribbean; 0.8 percent in Eastern Europe; 0.5 percent in North, Central, and South America; and 0.2 percent in Western and Central Europe, North Africa, and the Middle East. The rate in East Asia is minuscule—less than 0.1 percent. The HIV infection rates are below 1 percent in these populous countries: United States, 0.6 percent; Brazil, 0.4 percent; India, 0.3 percent; and China, 0.1 percent (Avert.org 2010).

American foreign aid has been instrumental in slowing the AIDS pandemic. Progress against HIV/AIDS is considered a signature accomplishment of the George W. Bush administration (2001–2009). In 2003, President Bush launched a five-year program aimed at fighting HIV/AIDS (and tuberculosis) in 15 high-risk countries. Congress extended the program in 2008, and it has continued under President Obama. American funding for HIV/AIDS increased from $2.3 billion in 2003 to $6 billion in 2008, and to $6.8 billion in 2011 (Ezekiel 2011). Although the United States was spending only 12 percent more on fighting HIV in 2011 than in 2008, twice as many people were benefiting because of reduced drug costs and streamlined program management (Ezekiel 2011).

Cultural practices play a clear role in HIV transmission. Sexual abstinence and condom use slow the spread of HIV. Infection rates are lower when men are circumcised (as is customary among Muslims) and there is little prostitution. It's estimated that male circumcision cuts HIV transmission by 60 percent. Since 2007, over a million men worldwide have been circumcised; three-fourths of those procedures were paid for by the U.S. government.

This tapestry by South African artist Jane Makhubele promotes condom use as a method of AIDS prevention.
Courtesy Melville J. Herskovits Library of African Studies, Northwestern University

discussions of contraception, abortion, and assisted suicide. Recent technological and scientific advances have raised new debates about personhood associated with stem cells, "harvested" embryos, assisted reproduction, genetic screening, cloning, and life-prolonging medical treatments.

Kaufman and Morgan (2005) emphasize the contrast between what they call low-tech and high-tech births and deaths. A desperately poor young mother dies of AIDS in Africa, while half a world away an American child of privilege is born as the result of a $50,000 in-vitro fertilization procedure.

Medical anthropologists increasingly are concerned with how the boundaries of life and death are being questioned and negotiated in our globalized world.

ANTHROPOLOGY AND BUSINESS

As David Price (2000) has noted, activities encompassed under the label "applied anthropology" are extremely diverse, ranging from research for activist NGOs to producing ethnographies and time-allocation studies of workplaces commissioned by and for management. For decades anthropologists have used ethnography to understand corporate settings and business (Arensberg 1987; Jordan 2013). Ethnographic research in a factory, for example, may view workers, managers, and executives as different social categories participating in a common system. Each group has characteristic attitudes and behavior patterns. These are transmitted through *microenculturation*, the process by which people learn particular roles within a limited social system. The free-ranging nature of ethnography can take the anthropologist back and forth across levels and microcultures—from worker to executive. Each employee is both an individual with a personal viewpoint and a cultural creature whose perspective is, to some extent, shared with other members of his or her group. Applied anthropologists have acted as "cultural brokers," translating managers' goals or workers' concerns to the other group (see Ferraro and Briody 2013).

Carol Taylor (1987) stressed the value of an "anthropologist-in-residence" in a large, complex organization, such as a hospital or corporation. A free-ranging ethnographer can be a perceptive oddball when information and decisions typically move through a rigid hierarchy. If allowed to observe and converse freely with all types and levels of personnel, the anthropologist may acquire a unique perspective on organizational conditions and problems (see Briody et al. 2010; Caulkins and Jordan 2013; Jordan 2013). Xerox, IBM, and Apple are among the companies that employ anthropologists. Closely observing how people actually use IT products, anthropologists have worked with engineers to design products that are more user friendly.

Key features of anthropology that are of value to business include (1) ethnography and observation as ways of gathering data, (2) a focus on diversity, and (3) cross-cultural expertise (see this chapter's "Appreciating Diversity"). Businesses have heard that anthropologists are specialists on cultural diversity and the observation of behavior. Hallmark Cards has hired anthropologists to observe parties, holidays, and celebrations of ethnic groups to improve its ability to design cards

Business anthropology in action: At the Intel Corporation in Hillsboro, Oregon, anthropologist Alexandra Zafiroglu displays a blanket with a huge photograph of the contents of one automobile. Zafiroglu works on a team directed by anthropologist Genevieve Bell (Intel's Director of User Experience Research) studying objects stored in cars. This research provides insights about how drivers use hand-held mobile devices in conjunction with technology built into their cars.
© Leah Nash/The New York Times/Redux

for targeted audiences. Applied anthropologists routinely go into people's homes to see how they actually use products (see Denny and Sunderland and 2014).

PUBLIC AND APPLIED ANTHROPOLOGY

Many academic anthropologists, myself included, occasionally work as applied anthropologists. Often, our role is to advise and consult about the direction of change in places where we originally did "academic" research. In my case, this has meant policy-relevant work on environmental preservation in Madagascar and poverty reduction in northeastern Brazil.

Other academics, while not doing applied anthropology per se, have urged the field of anthropology as a whole to engage more in what they call **public anthropology** (Borofsky 2000; Beck and Maida 2015) or *public interest anthropology* (Sanday 2003). Suggested ways of making anthropology more visible and relevant to the public include nonacademic publishing; testifying at government hearings; consulting; acting as an expert witness; and engaging in citizen activism, electoral campaigns, and political administrations (Sanjek 2004). The stated goals of public anthropology are to engage with public issues by opposing

public anthropology
Efforts to extend anthropology's visibility beyond academia and to demonstrate its public policy relevance.

Culturally Appropriate Marketing

Innovation succeeds best when it is culturally appropriate. This axiom of applied anthropology could guide the international spread not only of development projects but also of businesses, including fast food. Each time McDonald's or Burger King expands to a new nation, it must devise a culturally appropriate strategy for fitting into the new setting.

McDonald's has been very successful internationally. Almost 70 percent of its current annual revenue comes from sales outside the United States. As the world's most successful restaurant chain, McDonald's has more than 36,000 restaurants in some 120 countries. One place where McDonald's has expanded successfully is Brazil, where 100 million middle-class people, most living in densely packed cities, provide a concentrated market for a fast-food chain. Still, it took McDonald's some time to find the right marketing strategy for Brazil.

In 1980 when I visited Brazil after a seven-year absence, I first noticed, as a manifestation of Brazil's growing participation in the world economy, the appearance of two McDonald's restaurants in Rio de Janeiro. There wasn't much difference between Brazilian and North American McDonald's. The restaurants looked alike. The menus were more or less the same, as was the taste of the quarter-pounders. I picked up an artifact, a white paper bag with yellow lettering, exactly like the take-out bags then used in American McDonald's. An advertising device, it carried several messages about how Brazilians could bring McDonald's into their lives. However, it seemed to me that McDonald's Brazilian ad campaign was missing some important points about how fast food should be marketed in a culture that values large, leisurely lunches.

The bag proclaimed, "You're going to enjoy the [McDonald's] difference," and listed several "favorite places where you can enjoy McDonald's products." This list confirmed that the

marketing people were trying to adapt to Brazilian middle-class culture, but they were making some mistakes. "When you go out in the car with the kids" transferred the uniquely developed North American cultural combination of highways, affordable cars, and suburban living to the very different context of urban Brazil. A similar suggestion was "traveling to the country place." Even Brazilians who owned country places could not find McDonald's, still confined to the cities, on the road. The ad creator had apparently never attempted to drive up to a fast-food restaurant in a neighborhood with no parking spaces.

Several other suggestions pointed customers toward the beach, where *cariocas* (Rio natives) do spend much of their leisure time. One could eat McDonald's products "after a dip in the ocean," "at a picnic at the beach," or "watching the surfers." These suggestions ignored the Brazilian custom of consuming cold things, such as beer, soft drinks, ice cream, and ham and cheese sandwiches, at the beach. Brazilians don't consider a hot, greasy hamburger proper beach food. They view the sea as "cold" and hamburgers as "hot"; they avoid "hot" foods at the beach. Also culturally dubious was the suggestion to eat McDonald's hamburgers "lunching at the office." Brazilians prefer their main meal at midday, often eating at a leisurely pace with business associates. Many firms serve ample lunches to their employees. Other workers take advantage of a two-hour lunch break to go home to eat with the spouse and children. Nor did it make sense to suggest that children should eat hamburgers for lunch, since most kids attend school for half-day sessions and have lunch at home. Two other suggestions—"waiting for the bus" and "in the beauty parlor"—did describe common aspects of daily life in a Brazilian city. However, these settings have not proved especially inviting to hamburgers or fish filets.

The homes of Brazilians who can afford McDonald's products have cooks and maids to do many of the things that fast-food restaurants do in the United States. The suggestion that McDonald's products be eaten "while watching your favorite television program" is culturally appropriate, because Brazilians watch TV a lot. However, Brazil's consuming classes can ask the cook to make a snack when hunger strikes. Indeed, much televiewing occurs during the light dinner served when the husband gets home from the office.

Most appropriate to the Brazilian lifestyle was the suggestion to enjoy McDonald's "on the cook's day off." Throughout Brazil, Sunday is that day. The Sunday pattern for middle-class families who live on the coast is a trip to the beach, liters of beer, a full midday meal around 3 P.M., and a light evening snack. McDonald's found its niche in the Sunday evening meal, when families flock to the fast-food restaurant.

McDonald's has expanded rapidly in Brazil, where, as in North America, teenage appetites have fueled the fast-food explosion. As McDonald's outlets appeared in urban neighborhoods, Brazilian teenagers used them for after-school snacks, while families had evening meals there. As an anthropologist could have predicted, the fast-food industry has not revolutionized Brazilian food and meal customs. Rather, McDonald's is succeeding because it has adapted to preexisting Brazilian cultural patterns.

The main contrast with North America is that the Brazilian evening meal is lighter. McDonald's now caters to the evening meal rather than to lunch. Once McDonald's realized that more money could be made by fitting in with, rather than trying to Americanize, Brazilian meal habits, it started aiming its advertising at that goal. By 2015, McDonald's had more than 800 outlets in Brazil.

policies that promote injustice and by working to reframe discussions of key social issues in the media and by public officials. As Rylko-Bauer and her colleagues (2006) point out, there is, as well, a long tradition of work guided by such goals in applied anthropology.

New media are helping to disseminate anthropological knowledge to a wider public. The complete world of cyberspace, including the blogosphere, constantly grows richer in the resources and communication opportunities available to anthropologists. Some of the most widely read anthropological blogs include:

Savage Minds, a group blog
http://savageminds.org

Living Anthropologically, by Jason Antrosio
http://www.livinganthropologically.com

Neuroanthropology, by Greg Downey and Daniel Lende
http://blogs.plos.org/neuroanthropology/

Also see this detailed list of anthropology blogs, as updated for 2015:

http://anthropologyreport.com/anthropology-blogs-2015/

Anthropologists participate as well in various listservs and networking groups (e.g., on LinkedIn and Research Gate). A bit of googling on your part will take you to anthropologists' personal websites, as well as research project websites.

CAREERS AND ANTHROPOLOGY

Many college students find anthropology interesting and consider majoring in it. However, their parents or friends may discourage them by asking, "What kind of job are you going to get with an anthropology degree?" The first step in answering that question is to consider the more general question "What do you do with any college major?" The answer is "Not much, without a good bit of effort, thought, and planning." A survey of graduates of the University of Michigan's literary college showed that few had jobs that were clearly linked to their majors. Most professions, including medicine and law, require advanced degrees. Although many colleges offer bachelor's degrees in engineering, business, accounting, and social work, master's degrees often are needed to get the best jobs in those fields. Anthropologists, too, need an advanced degree, almost always a PhD, to find gainful employment.

A broad college education, and even a major in anthropology, can be an excellent foundation for success in many fields. One survey of women executives showed that most had majored not in business but in the social sciences or humanities. Only after graduating from college did they study business, leading to an MBA, a master's degree in business administration. These executives felt that the breadth of their college educations had contributed to their business careers. Anthropology majors go on to medical, law, and business schools and find success in many professions that often have little explicit connection to anthropology.

Anthropology's breadth provides knowledge and an outlook on the world that are useful in many kinds of work. For example, an anthropology major combined with a master's degree in business is excellent preparation for work in international business. Breadth is anthropology's hallmark. Anthropologists study people biologically, culturally, socially, and linguistically, across time and space, in various countries, in simple and complex settings. Most colleges offer anthropology courses that compare cultures, along with others that focus on particular world areas, such as Latin America, Asia, and Native North America. The knowledge of foreign areas acquired in such courses can be useful in many jobs. Anthropology's comparative outlook and its focus on diverse lifestyles combine to provide an excellent foundation for overseas employment (see Ellick and Watkins 2011; Omohundro 2001).

For work in modern North America, anthropology's focus on culture is increasingly relevant. Every day we hear about cultural differences and about problems whose solutions require a multicultural viewpoint—an ability to recognize and reconcile ethnic differences. Government, schools, hospitals, and businesses constantly deal with people from different social classes, ethnic groups, and cultural backgrounds. Physicians, attorneys, social workers, police officers, judges, teachers, and students can all do a better job if they understand cultural differences in a nation that is one of the most ethnically diverse in history.

Knowledge of the traditions and beliefs of the groups that make up a modern nation is important in planning and carrying out programs that affect those groups. Experience in planned social change—whether community organization in North America or economic development overseas—shows that a proper social study should be done before a project or policy is implemented. When local people want the change and it fits their lifestyle and traditions, it has a better chance of being successful, beneficial, and cost effective.

People with anthropology backgrounds do well in many fields. Even if one's job has little or nothing to do with anthropology in a formal or obvious sense, a background in anthropology provides a useful orientation when we work with our fellow human beings. For most of us, this means every day of our lives.

summary

1. Anthropology has two dimensions: academic and applied. Applied anthropology uses anthropological perspectives, theory, methods, and data to identify, assess, and solve problems. Applied anthropologists have a range of employers. Examples are government agencies; development organizations; NGOs; tribal, ethnic, and interest groups; businesses; social service and educational agencies. Applied anthropologists come from all four subfields. Ethnography is one of applied anthropology's most valuable research tools.

2. Development anthropology focuses on social issues in, and the cultural dimension of, economic development. Not all governments seek to increase equity and end poverty. Resistance by elites to reform is typical and hard to combat. At the same time, local people rarely cooperate with projects requiring major and risky changes in their daily lives. Many projects seek to impose inappropriate property notions and incompatible social units on their intended beneficiaries. The best strategy for change is to base the social design for innovation on traditional social forms in each target area.

3. Anthropology and education researchers work in classrooms, homes, and other settings relevant to education. Such studies may lead to policy recommendations. Both academic and applied anthropologists study migration from rural areas to cities and across national boundaries. North America has become a popular arena for urban anthropological research on migration, ethnicity, poverty, and related topics. Although rural and urban are different social systems, there is cultural diffusion from one to the other.

4. Medical anthropology is the cross-cultural, biocultural study of health problems and conditions, disease, illness, disease theories, and health care systems. Medical anthropology includes anthropologists from all four subfields and has theoretical (academic) and applied dimensions. In a given setting, the characteristic diseases reflect diet, population density, the economy, and social complexity. Native theories of illness may be personalistic, naturalistic, or emotionalistic. In applying anthropology to business, the key features are (1) ethnography and observation as ways of gathering data, (2) cross-cultural expertise, and (3) a focus on cultural diversity. Public anthropology describes efforts to extend anthropological knowledge of social problems and issues to a wider and more influential audience.

5. A broad college education, including anthropology and foreign-area courses, offers excellent background for many fields. Anthropology's comparative outlook and cultural relativism provide an excellent basis for overseas employment. Even for work in North America, a focus on culture and cultural diversity is valuable. Anthropology majors attend medical, law, and business schools and succeed in many fields, some of which have little explicit connection with anthropology.

key terms

anthropology and education 42

applied anthropology 36

curer 46

development anthropology 39

disease 44

health care systems 46

illness 44

increased equity 40

medical anthropology 44

overinnovation 41

public anthropology 49

scientific medicine 46

underdifferentiation 41

urban anthropology 44

critical thinking

1. This chapter uses the association between early anthropology and colonialism to illustrate some of the dangers of early applied anthropology. We also learn how American anthropologists studied Japanese "culture at a distance" in an attempt to predict the behavior of the enemies of the United States during World War II. Political and military conflicts with other nations and cultures continue today. What role, if any, could and/or should applied anthropologists play in these conflicts?

2. What roles could an applied anthropologist play in the design and implementation of a development project? Based on past experience and research on this topic, what could an applied anthropologist focus on avoiding and/or promoting?

3. This chapter describes some of the applications of anthropology in educational settings. Think back to your grade school or high school classroom. Were there any social issues that might have interested an anthropologist? Were there any problems that an applied anthropologist might have been able to help solve? How so?

4. Our culture—and cultural changes—affect how we perceive nature, human nature, and the "natural." Give examples of how medical anthropologists examine the shifting boundaries between culture and nature.

5. Indicate your career plans, if known, and describe how you might apply the knowledge learned through introductory anthropology in your future vocation. If you have not yet chosen a career, pick one of the following: economist, engineer, diplomat, architect, or elementary schoolteacher. Why is it important to understand the culture and social organization of the people who will be affected by your work?

CHAPTER 4

Doing Archaeology and Biological Anthropology

▸ How do biological anthropologists and archaeologists study the past?

▸ How do anthropologists determine the dates of sites, remains, and evolutionary events?

▸ What ethical concerns and issues affect biological anthropology and archaeology?

© Cesar Manso/AFP/Getty Images

Archaeologists excavating in June, 2015 at Gran Dolina, Atapuerca, Spain. The Atapuerca site has yielded fossils and stone tools of Europe's earliest known hominins, dating to around 780,000 years ago.

understanding OURSELVES

Consider Facebook, Twitter, Instagram, and other *social* networking websites. In how many such sites do you participate? For what do you use them? Do they extend or restrict your social network? Long before the Internet, all humans belonged to social networks. Anthropology studies people as members of groups—networks, societies, and cultures. Compared with our primate relatives, humans are unusually social. Even chimpanzees, our closest relatives, don't cooperate nearly as much as we do. There's reason to believe that our urge to cooperate emerged early in human evolution.

We'll never know all the causes of human sociality, and there is substantial cross-cultural variation in preferences for social contact versus solitude. In some societies sick people say, "I want to be alone," while in others it's "Please don't leave me." Which would it be for you?

Regardless of cultural variation, a human appreciation of the social appears to be based in features of human anatomy—from the brain to the pelvis. Consider the female pelvis, whose evolution has been guided by these facts: (1) Humans walk upright; (2) babies are born with big brains; and (3) babies have to negotiate a complicated birth canal during childbirth. There are striking contrasts between humans and other primates in anatomy and in the birthing process. Nonhuman primates aren't bipedal; they use four limbs rather than two to move about. Compared with humans, they have smaller brains, simpler birth canals, and more independent infants.

Human babies, in moving through the birth canal, must make several turns. Their heads and shoulders, the two body parts with the largest dimensions, must be aligned consistently with the widest parts of that canal. Monkeys and apes don't have this problem; their birth canals have a constant shape. Also, the primate infant emerges facing forward. The mother can grasp it, even pull it straight to her nipple. Human babies are born facing backward, away from the mother, so she has trouble assisting in the birth. The presence of someone else (e.g., a midwife or doctor) to help with delivery reduces the mortality risk for human infants and their mothers.

Birthing assistance is almost universal among human societies. The characteristic human wish to have supportive, familiar people around at childbirth probably goes way back in time. Based on pelvic openings and estimated infant skull sizes of fossilized human precursors, anthropologists Karen Rosenberg and Wenda Trevathan (2001) surmise that such assistance may date back millions of years. Nonhuman primate mothers seek seclusion when they give birth and act as their own midwives in the birthing process. Not so humans, who are as social as ever. Midwives, obstetricians, and baby showers are all manifestations of human sociality. The next time you encounter one, appreciate that such manifestations of human sociality have deep evolutionary roots.

"Been on any digs lately?" Ask your professor how many times she or he has heard this question. Then ask how often he or she actually has been on a dig. Remember that anthropology has four subfields, only two of which (archaeology and biological anthropology) require much digging—in the ground, at least. Even among biological anthropologists it is mainly paleoanthropologists (those concerned with the hominin fossil record) who must dig. Students of primate behavior in the wild, such as

Jane Goodall, don't do it. Nor, most of the time, is it done by forensic anthropologists, such as the title character in the TV series *Bones*.

Before this course, did you know the names of any anthropologists? If so, which ones—real or fictional? For the general public, biological anthropologists and archaeologists tend to be better known than cultural anthropologists because of what they study and discover—making them attractive subjects for the Discovery Channel. You're more likely to have watched *Bones* or seen a film of Jane Goodall with chimps or a paleoanthropologist holding a skull than to have seen a linguistic or cultural anthropologist at work. Archaeologists occasionally appear in the media to describe a new discovery or to debunk pseudo-archaeological arguments about how visitors from space have left traces on Earth.

This chapter is about what anthropologists do, focusing on archaeology and biological anthropology. Given space limitations, however, only some of the diverse methods and techniques employed by anthropological archaeologists and biological anthropologists can be covered here.

RESEARCH METHODS IN ARCHAEOLOGY AND BIOLOGICAL ANTHROPOLOGY

Archaeology and biological anthropology are two of anthropology's four subfields. Archaeologists tend to study material culture; biological anthropologists tend to study biological remains. Anthropological archaeology reconstructs human behavior, social patterns, and cultural features through the analysis of material remains (and other sources, including written records, if available). Biological anthropologists study living and recent humans (e.g., their genetics, growth, development, and physiological adaptation) and primates (e.g., their behavior and social organization) as well as deceased and ancient ones. Paleoanthropologists study human evolution through skeletal material and related material remains, such as biological traces (e.g., pollens, animal bones). Doing so, and as they attempt to date ancient human remains, biological anthropologists share many research interests and techniques with archaeologists. Members of both subfields must collaborate with many other kinds of scientists to do their work effectively.

Multidisciplinary Approaches

Scientists from diverse fields—for example, soil science and **paleontology** (the study of ancient life through the fossil record)—collaborate with archaeologists and biological anthropologists in the study of ancient sites. *Palynology,* the study of ancient plants through pollen samples, can help to determine a site's environment at the time of occupation. Physicists and chemists help anthropologists with dating techniques. *Bioarchaeologists* may form a picture of ancient life at a particular site by examining human skeletons to reconstruct their physical traits, health status, and diet (Buikstra and Beck 2006; Larsen 2015; Martin, Harrod, and Perez 2013; Stodder and Palkovich 2012). Evidence for social status can endure in hard materials—bones, jewels, buildings—through the ages. Diet influences bone growth and stature. Genetic differences aside, taller people often are that way because they eat better than shorter people do. Differences in the chemical composition of groups of bones at a site may help distinguish privileged nobles from less fortunate commoners.

To reconstruct ancient human biological and cultural features, anthropologists analyze material remains, including bones, teeth, and artifacts (manufactured items). Visible remains found at archaeological sites include animal and human bones, charcoal from ancient fires, remains in burials and storage pits, and worked stone and bone. Archaeologists today also draw on microscopic evidence, such as fossil pollen, phytoliths (plant crystals), and starch grains. After artifacts are collected from a site, they are sent to a lab, where, under sterile conditions, they are examined

paleontology
The study of ancient life through the fossil record.

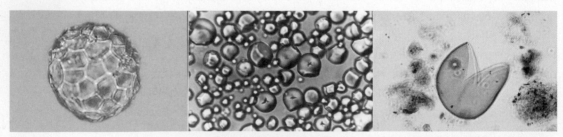

These photos illustrate three kinds of microscopic evidence of plant characteristics, including domestication. The photo on the left shows a phytolith (plant crystal) from domesticated squash, dated to 10,000 B.P., (years before the present) found in the soil at Ecuador's Vegas site. The middle photo shows reserve starch grains from the root of a modern manioc plant. The photo on the right shows a maize pollen grain dated to 5,000 B.P. from the Kob site in Belize.

Left: Courtesy of Dolores R. Piperno, National Museum of Natural History; center: Courtesy of Dolores R. Piperno, National Museum of Natural History; right: Courtesy of Dolores R. Piperno, National Museum of Natural History and John G. Jones, Washington State University

for microscopic traces of plant starch grains, phytoliths, and fossil pollen. These microscopic particles, which can be attached to almost any artifact, can offer valuable clues about ancient lifeways, especially diet and food preparation patterns (see Bryant 2013).

A phytolith ("plant stone") is a microscopic crystal found in many plants, including wheat, maize, rice, beans, squash, manioc (cassava), and other early domesticates. Because phytoliths are inorganic and do not decay, they can reveal which plants were present at a given site even when no other plant remains survive. Phytoliths trapped in the plaque of fossilized teeth have revealed, for example, that a recently discovered ancient hominin, *Australopithecus sediba,* had a diet that included fruit, leaves, and bark. Unlike other members of its genus, which fed in open grasslands, *Au. sediba* sought food in woodland areas, much like modern-day chimps and gorillas (Than 2012).

Starch grain analysis, another useful technique, recovers microfossils of food plants from the stone tools used to process them. Starch grains preserve well in areas—for example, the humid tropics—where other organic remains typically decay. These grains have been recovered from stone tools, pottery fragments, and basketry, and in human coprolites (ancient feces) (Bryant 2003, 2007*a,* 2007*b,* 2013). Vaughn Bryant (2007*b*) presents a strong case for the importance of such microscopic evidence in studying the past. As one example, he cites Bonnie Williamson's analysis of Middle to Late Stone Age tools from a cave site in South Africa. Examining hundreds of stone tools, Williamson found that many still had residues stuck to their cutting edges. Contradicting the prevailing assumption that such tools were used mainly to hunt and butcher game animals, Williamson found that over 50 percent of all the residues were from plants. Williamson's analysis suggested an important role for women (in gathering and processing plant foods) in early cultures.

Anthropologists also work with geologists, geographers, and other scientists in using satellite images to find ancient footpaths, roads, canals, and irrigation systems, which can then be investigated on the ground. Aerial photos (taken from airplanes) and satellite images are forms of **remote sensing** used in site location. For example, remote sensing enabled archaeologists to discover and study ancient footpaths in Costa Rica around a volcano called Arenal (Scott 2002). Volcanic ash, sediment, and vegetation had hidden the paths, which were up to 2,500 years old. A NASA aircraft discovered them using instruments that could "see" in a spectrum invisible to the naked human eye. The ancient trails showed up as thin red lines, reflecting the dense vegetation growing over them. The paths were dated based on the stratigraphy (layers of geological deposits) formed by multiple eruptions of the nearby Arenal volcano.

Many archaeological sites are visible from the air. Shown here, El Candelabro (the candelabra) is a giant ground drawing within the Paracas National Reserve, Peru. This drawing, located on the coast, can be seen from 12 miles out at sea. El Candelabro has been compared to Peru's Nazca lines, visible only from the air.
© Axel Fassio/Aurora/Getty Images

Village life arose in this area about 4,000 years ago and lasted through the Spanish Conquest around 500 years ago. Villagers periodically fled volcanic eruptions, returning when it was safe to resume farming in the rich volcanic soil. According to team leader Payson Sheets of the University of Colorado, "they inhabited a very large region and seemed to avoid conflict, conquest and serious disease. . . . They led comfortable lives, relying on an abundance of natural resources and a stable culture" (quoted in Scott 2002). When archaeologists excavated the footpaths, they found stone tools, pottery, and floors of ancient houses. The paths once connected a cemetery, a spring, and quarries where construction stone was mined. A goal of Sheets's field team was to understand ancient activities at the cemetery, where bodies were buried in stone coffins. Ceramics, vessels, and cooking stones confirmed that people had camped, cooked, and feasted at the cemetery (Scott 2002; Sheets 2006).

remote sensing
The use of aerial photos and satellite images to locate sites on the ground.

Anthropologists and other scientists also can use remote sensing to discover and understand events of the more recent past. Satellite images reveal, for example, patterns and sites of flooding and deforestation. By comparing a time series of satellite images of forest cover, scientists can identify regions where deforestation has been especially severe. Anthropologists can then travel to these areas to see what is happening on the ground—where people and biodiversity (including nonhuman primates) may be at risk. Working with anthropologist Lisa Gezon and geologist Glen Green, I did just this to understand the causes of deforestation in Madagascar (see Kottak 1999*b;* Kottak, Gezon, and Green 1994).

Studying the Past

Archaeologists and biological anthropologists share interests and techniques that enable them to reconstruct the human past. Paleoanthropologists continue to compile the fossil record of human evolution. **Fossils** are remains (e.g., bones), traces, or impressions (e.g., footprints) of ancient life forms. Typically, a team composed of scientists, students, and local workers participates in a paleoanthropological or archaeological study. Such teams may include biological anthropologists, archaeologists, paleontologists, geologists, palynologists, physicists, and chemists. Paleontologists help locate fossil beds containing remains of animals that can be dated and that are known to have coexisted with hominins at various times. Good preservation of faunal (animal) remains may suggest that hominin fossils have survived as well. Sometimes it's impossible to date the hominin fossils and artifacts found at a given site by using the most accurate and direct (radiometric) methods. In this case, comparison of the faunal remains at that site with similar, but more securely dated, fauna at another site may suggest a date for those animal fossils and the hominins and artifacts associated with them (see Gugliotta 2005).

Once potential sites have been identified, more intensive surveying begins (see Watzman 2006). If a site is shown to be a hominin site, much more concentrated work begins. Financial support may come from private donations and government agencies. Working under a lead anthropologist, the field crew will continue to survey and map the area and start searching carefully for bones and artifacts eroding out of the soil. In addition they will take pollen and soil samples for ecological analysis and rock samples for use in various dating techniques.

Consideration of the animal habitats suggested by the site (e.g., forest, woodland, or open country) will assist in the reconstruction of the environmental settings in which the hominins lived. Pollen samples help reveal diet. Sediments and other geological samples will suggest climatic conditions at the time of deposition. Sometimes fossils are encased in rock, from which they must be extracted

carefully. Once recovered and cleaned, fossils may be made into casts to permit wider study.

Survey and Excavation

Archaeologists typically work in teams and across time and space—adopting both local (e.g., excavation) and regional (e.g., survey) perspectives. The most common local approach is to excavate, or dig, through layers in a site. Regional approaches include remote sensing—for example, the discovery of ancient Costa Rican footpaths from space, as described earlier, and systematic survey on the ground. Archaeologists recognize that sites are not usually discrete and isolated but are parts of larger (regional) social systems. One example of such systems might be a series of villages that offered tribute to the same chief. Another example might be a few bands of hunter-gatherers that got together for annual ceremonies at a particular place. Let's examine some of the main techniques that archaeologists use to study patterns of behavior in ancient societies, based on their material remains.

Systematic Survey

Archaeologists have two key fieldwork strategies: systematic survey and excavation. **Systematic survey** provides a regional perspective by gathering information on settlement patterns over a large area. *Settlement pattern* refers to the distribution of sites within a region—how people grouped themselves and interacted spatially. Regional surveys reconstruct settlement patterns by addressing several questions: Where were sites located? How big were they? What kinds of buildings did they have? How old are the sites? Ideally, a systematic survey involves walking over the entire survey area and recording the location and size of all sites. From artifacts found on the surface, the surveyor estimates when each site was occupied. A full-coverage survey is not always possible. The ground cover may be impenetrable (e.g., thick jungle); certain parts of the survey area may be inaccessible. Landowners may deny permission to survey on their property. Archaeologists may have to rely on remote sensing to help locate and map sites.

With regional data, archaeologists can address many questions about the prehistoric communities that lived in a given area. Archaeologists use settlement pattern information to make population estimates and to assess levels of social complexity. Among hunter-gatherers and simple farmers, there are generally low numbers of people living in small campsites or hamlets with little variation in the architecture. Such sites tend to be scattered evenly across the landscape. With increasing social complexity, the settlement patterns become more elaborate. Population levels rise. Such social factors as trade and warfare have played a more important role in determining the location of sites (on hilltops, waterways, trade

fossils
Remains of ancient life.

systematic survey
The study of settlement patterns over a large area.

routes). In complex societies, a settlement hierarchy of sites emerges. Certain sites are larger than others, with greater architectural differentiation. Large sites with specialized architecture (elite residences, temples, administrative buildings, meeting places) were regional centers that exerted control over the smaller sites with less architectural differentiation.

Excavation

During an **excavation,** scientists dig through the layers of deposits that make up a site. These layers, or *strata,* are used to establish the time order of materials. This relative chronology is based on the principle of *superposition*: In an undisturbed sequence of strata, the oldest layer is on the bottom. Each successive layer above is younger than the one below. Thus, remains from lower strata are older than those recovered from higher strata in the same deposit. This relative time ordering of material remains lies at the heart of archaeological, paleoanthropological, and paleontological research.

The archaeological and fossil records are so rich, and excavation is so labor-intensive and expensive, that nobody digs a site without a good reason. Sites are excavated because they are endangered, or because they answer specific research questions (see Sabloff 2008). Cultural resource management (CRM) focuses on managing the preservation of archaeological sites that are threatened by modern development. Many countries require archaeological impact studies before construction can take place. If a site is at risk and the development cannot be stopped, CRM archaeologists are called in to salvage what information they can from the site (see King 2011).

Another reason for choosing a particular site to excavate is that it is well suited to answer specific research questions. An archaeologist studying the origins of agriculture would not want to excavate a large, fortified hilltop city with a series of buildings dating to a period well after the first appearance of farming communities. Rather, he or she would look for a small, hamlet-size site located near good farmland and a water source. Such a site would have evidence of an early occupation dating to the period when farming communities first appeared in that region.

Before a site is excavated, it is surface collected and mapped, so that the researchers can make an informed decision about where exactly to dig. The collecting of surface materials at a given site is similar to what is done over a much larger area in a regional survey. A grid is drawn to subdivide the site. Then collection units, which are equal-size sections of the grid, are marked off on the actual site (see the photo of the site at Teotihuacán, Mexico). This grid enables the researchers to record the exact location of any artifact, fossil, or feature found at the site. By examining all the materials on the surface of the site, archaeologists can direct their excavations toward those areas of the site most likely to yield information that will address their research interests. Once an area is selected, digging begins, and the location of every artifact or feature is recorded in three dimensions.

Digging may be done according to arbitrary levels. Thus, starting from the surface, consistent amounts of soil (usually 4 to 8 feet [1.2 to 2.4 meters]) are removed systematically from the excavation unit. This technique of excavation is a quick way of digging, because everything within a certain depth is removed at once. This kind of excavation usually is done in test pits, which are used to determine how deep the deposits of a site go and to establish a rough chronology for that site.

A more labor-intensive and refined way of excavating is to dig through the stratigraphy one layer at a time. The strata, which are separated by differences in color and texture, are studied one by one. This technique provides more information about the context of the artifacts, fossils, or features because the scientist works more slowly and in meaningful layers. A given 4-foot (1.2-meter) level may include within it a series of successive house floors, each with artifacts. If this deposit is excavated according to arbitrary levels, all the artifacts are mixed together. If it is excavated according to the natural stratigraphy, however, with each house floor excavated separately, the resulting picture is much more detailed. The procedure here is for the archaeologist to remove and bag all the artifacts from each house floor before proceeding to the level below that one.

excavation
Digging through layers at a site.

An archaeologist drives in another stake for a large grid at an excavation site in Teotihuacán, Mexico. Such a grid enables the researchers to record the exact location of any artifact or feature found at the site.
© Kenneth Garrett/National Geographic Creative

Any excavation recovers varied material remains, such as ceramics, stone artifacts (lithics), human and animal bones, and plant remains. Such remains may be small and fragmented. To increase the likelihood of recovering small remains the soil is passed through screens. To recover very small remains, such as fish bones and carbonized plant remains, archaeologists use a technique called *flotation*. Soil samples are sorted using water and a series of very fine meshes. When the water dissolves the soil, the carbonized plant remains float to the top. The fish bones and other heavier remains sink to the bottom. Flotation requires considerable time and labor. This makes it inappropriate to use on all the soil that is excavated from a site. Flotation samples are taken from a limited number of deposits, such as house floors, trash pits, and hearths.

KINDS OF ARCHAEOLOGY

taphonomy
The study of processes affecting remains of dead animals.

Archaeologists pursue diverse research topics, using a wide variety of methods (see Renfrew and Bahn 2012). Experimental archaeologists try to replicate ancient techniques and processes (e.g., toolmaking) under controlled conditions. Historical archaeologists use written records as guides and supplements to archaeological research. They work with remains more recent—often much more recent—than the advent of writing. Colonial archaeologists are historical archaeologists who use written records as guides to locate and excavate postcontact sites in North and South America, and to verify or question the written accounts. Classical archaeologists usually are affiliated with university departments of classics or the history of art, rather than with anthropology departments. These classical scholars tend to focus on the literate civilizations of the Old World, such as Greece, Rome, and Egypt. Classical archaeologists often are more interested in styles of architecture and sculpture than in the social, economic, and political features that typically interest anthropological archaeologists. Underwater archaeology is a growing field that investigates submerged sites, most often shipwrecks. Special techniques, including remotely operated vehicles, are used, but divers also do underwater survey and excavation.

An underwater archaeologist approaches a large amphora (tall jar) in the Aegean Sea, near Turkey's Datca Peninsula. Graduate degrees in underwater, or nautical, archaeology are available at East Carolina University, Florida State University, and Texas A&M University. This growing field of study investigates submerged sites, often shipwrecks.
© WaterFrame/Alamy Stock Photo

Cultural resource management is a type of applied anthropology that uses archaeological techniques to assess sites that are threatened by development, public works, and road building. Some CRM archaeologists are contract archaeologists, who typically negotiate specific contracts (rather than applying for research grants) for their studies. CRM often must be done rapidly, for example, when an immediate threat to archaeological materials becomes known. Based on a membership study done for the Society for American Archaeology, Melinda Zeder (1997) found that 40 percent of the respondents worked as contract archaeologists. Their employers included firms in the private sector, state and federal agencies, and educational institutions. An equivalent 40 percent held academic positions.

DATING THE PAST

The archaeological record has not revealed every ancient society that has existed on Earth; nor is the fossil record a representative sample of all the plants and animals that ever have lived. Some species and body parts are better represented than others are, for many reasons. Hard parts, such as bones and teeth, preserve better than do soft parts, such as flesh and skin. The chances of fossilization increase when remains are buried in silt, gravel, or sand. Good places for bone preservation include swamps, floodplains, river deltas, lakes, and caves. The species that live in such areas have a better chance to be preserved than do animals that live in other habitats. Fossilization also is favored in areas with volcanic ash. Once remains are buried, chemical conditions must be right for fossilization to occur. If the sediment is too acidic, even bones and teeth will dissolve. The study of the processes that affect the remains of dead animals is called **taphonomy,** from the Greek *taphos,* which means "tomb." Such processes include scattering by carnivores and scavengers, distortion by various forces, and the possible fossilization of the remains.

The conditions under which fossils are discovered also influence the fossil record. For example, fossils are more likely to be uncovered through erosion in arid areas than in wet areas. Sparse vegetation allows wind to scour the landscape and uncover fossils. The fossil record has been accumulating longer and is more extensive in Europe than in Africa because civil engineering projects and fossil hunting have been going on longer in Europe than in Africa. A world map showing where fossils have been found does not indicate the true range of ancient animals. Such a map tells us more about ancient geological activity, modern erosion, or recent human activity—such as paleontological research or road building. For the primate and hominin fossil records, for example, certain areas provide more abundant fossil evidence for particular time periods. This doesn't necessarily mean that primates or hominins were living only in that area at that time. Nor does failure to find a fossil species in a particular place always mean the species did not live there. In the words of paleoanthropologist Christopher Stringer, "absence of evidence does not necessarily prove evidence of absence" (quoted in Gugliotta 2005).

Paleontology is the study of ancient life through the fossil record and **paleoanthropology** is the study of ancient humans and their immediate ancestors. These fields have established a time frame, or chronology, for the evolution of life. Scientists use several techniques to date fossils. These methods offer different degrees of precision and are applicable to different periods of the past.

Relative Dating

Chronology is established by assigning dates to geological layers (strata) and to the material remains—the fossils and artifacts—within them. Dating may be relative or absolute. **Relative dating** establishes a time frame in relation to other strata or materials rather than absolute dates in numbers. Many dating methods are based on the geological study of **stratigraphy,** the science that examines the ways in which earth sediments accumulate in strata (singular, *stratum*). As was noted previously, in an undisturbed sequence of strata, age increases with depth. Soil that erodes from a hillside into a valley covers, and is younger than, the soil deposited there previously.

Stratigraphy permits relative dating. That is, the fossils in a given stratum are younger than those in the layers below and older than those in the layers above. We may not know the exact or absolute dates of the fossils, but we can place them in time relative to remains in other layers. Changing environmental forces, such as volcanic eruptions, or the alternation of land and sea, cause different materials to be deposited in a given sequence of strata; this allows scientists to distinguish between the strata.

Remains of animals and plants that lived at the same time are found in the same stratum. When scientists find fossils within a stratigraphic sequence, they know their dates relative to fossils in other strata; this is relative dating. For the fossils in a particular stratum, the associated geological features (such as frost patterning) and remains of particular plants and animals offer clues about the climate at the time of deposition.

Besides stratigraphic placement, another technique of relative dating is fluorine absorption analysis. Bones fossilizing in the same ground for the same length of time absorb the same proportion of fluorine from the local groundwater. Fluorine analysis uncovered a famous hoax involving the so-called Piltdown man, once considered an unusual and perplexing human ancestor (Stringer

Many dating methods rely on stratigraphy, the science that studies how sediments accumulate in layers, or strata. Labels make the strata evident as Professor Christopher Henshilwood excavates the south section of Blombos Cave, South Africa.

Image courtesy of Prof Christopher Henshilwood

2012*b*; Weiner 2003). The Piltdown "find," from England, turned out to be the jaw of a young orangutan attached to the skull of a modern human. Fluorine analysis showed the association to be false. The skull had much more fluorine than the jaw—impossible if they had come from the same individual and had been deposited in the same place at the same time. Someone had fabricated Piltdown man in an attempt to muddle the interpretation of the fossil record. (The attempt was partially successful—it did fool some scientists.)

Absolute Dating: Radiometric Techniques

Fossils can be dated more precisely, with dates in numbers (**absolute dating**), by using several methods. For example, the ^{14}C, or carbon-14, technique is used to date organic remains. This is a radiometric technique (so called because it measures radioactive decay). ^{14}C is an unstable radioactive isotope of normal carbon, ^{12}C. Cosmic radiation entering the Earth's atmosphere produces ^{14}C, and plants take in ^{14}C as they absorb carbon dioxide. ^{14}C moves up the food chain as animals eat plants and as predators eat other animals.

With death, the absorption of ^{14}C stops. This unstable isotope starts to break down into nitrogen (^{14}N). It takes 5,730 years for half the ^{14}C to change to nitrogen; this is the half-life of ^{14}C. After another 5,730 years, only one-quarter of the original ^{14}C will remain. After yet another 5,730 years, only one-eighth will be left. By measuring the proportion of ^{14}C in organic material, scientists can determine a fossil's date of death, or the date of an ancient campfire. However, because the half-life of ^{14}C is short, this dating technique is less dependable for specimens older than 40,000 years than it is for more recent remains.

paleoanthropology
The study of hominid, hominin, and human life through the fossil record.

relative dating
Establishing a time frame in relation to other strata or materials.

stratigraphy
The study of earth sediments deposited in demarcated layers (strata).

absolute dating
Establishing dates in numbers or ranges of numbers.

Early hominin fossils abound in Africa's Great Rift Valley, a vista of which is shown on the left. Past volcanic activity permits potassium–argon (K/A) dating in the valley, including at Olduvai Gorge, Tanzania, whose centerpiece is the rock formation on the right. Note the stratigraphy in the rock formation.

Left: © Nigel Pavitt/JWL/Aurora Photos; right: © Charles V. Angelo/Science Source

Fortunately, other radiometric dating techniques are available for earlier periods. One of the most widely used is the potassium–argon (K/A) technique. ^{40}K is a radioactive isotope of potassium that breaks down into argon-40, a gas. The half-life of ^{40}K is far longer than that of ^{14}C—1.3 billion years. With this method, the older the specimen, the more reliable the dating. Furthermore, whereas ^{14}C dating can be done only on organic remains, K/A dating can be used only for inorganic substances: rocks and minerals. ^{40}K in rocks gradually breaks down into argon-40. That gas is trapped in the rock until the rock is heated intensely (as with volcanic activity), at which point it may escape. When the rock cools, the breakdown of potassium into argon resumes. Dating is done by reheating the rock and measuring the escaping gas.

In Africa's Great Rift Valley, which runs down eastern Africa and in which early hominin fossils abound, past volcanic activity permits K/A dating. In studies of strata containing fossils, scientists find out how much argon has accumulated in rocks since they were last heated. They then determine, using the standard ^{40}K deterioration rate (half-life), the date of that heating. Considering volcanic rocks at the top of a stratum with fossil remains, scientists establish that the fossils are older than, say, 1.8 million years. By dating the volcanic rocks below the fossil remains, they determine that the fossils are younger than, say, two million years. Thus, the age of the fossils is set at between two million and 1.8 million years. Note that absolute dating is that in name only; it may give ranges of numbers rather than exact dates.

Many fossils were discovered before the advent of modern stratigraphy. Often we can no longer determine their original stratigraphic placement. Furthermore, fossils aren't always discovered in volcanic layers. Like ^{14}C dating, the K/A technique applies to a limited period of the fossil record. Because the half-life of ^{40}K is so long, the technique cannot be used with materials less than 500,000 years old.

Other radiometric dating techniques can be used to cross-check K/A dates, again by using minerals surrounding the fossils. One such method, uranium series dating, measures fission tracks produced during the decay of radioactive uranium (^{238}U) into lead. Two other radiometric techniques are especially useful for fossils that cannot be dated by ^{14}C (up to 40,000 years before the present, or B.P.) or ^{40}K (more than 500,000 B.P.). These methods are thermoluminescence (TL) and electron spin resonance (ESR). Both TL and ESR measure the electrons that are constantly being trapped in rocks and minerals. Once a date is obtained for a rock found associated with a fossil, that date also can be applied to that fossil. The time spans for which the various absolute dating techniques are applicable are summarized in Recap 4.1.

Absolute Dating: Dendrochronology

Dendrochronology, or tree-ring dating, is a method of absolute dating based on the study and comparison of patterns of tree-ring growth. Because trees grow by adding one ring every year, counting the rings reveals the age of a tree. Around 1920, A. E. Douglass of the University of Arizona noticed that wide rings grew during wet years, while narrow rings grew during dry years. Climatic

dendrochronology
Tree-ring dating; a form of absolute dating.

TECHNIQUE	ABBREVIATION	MATERIALS DATED	EFFECTIVE TIME RANGE
Carbon-14	^{14}C	Organic materials	Up to 40,000 years
Potassium–argon	K/A and ^{40}K	Volcanic rock	Older than 500,000 years
Uranium series	^{238}U	Minerals	Between 1,000 and 1,000,000 years
Thermoluminescence	TL	Rocks and minerals	Between 5,000 and 1,000,000 years
Electron spin resonance	ESR	Rocks and minerals	Between 1,000 and 1,000,000 years
Dendrochronology	Dendro	Wood and charcoal	Up to 11,000 years

variation, for example, moisture, cold, or drought, produces a distinctive year-by-year ring pattern—observable in all the trees that have grown over the same length of time in the same region. Ring patterns of trees can be compared and matched ring for ring. Charting such patterns back through time, scientists can compare wood from ancient buildings to known tree-ring chronologies, match the ring patterns, and determine precisely—to the year—the age of the wood used by the historic or prehistoric builder (see Schweingruber 2007; Speer 2010; Stoffel 2010).

Crossdating is the process of matching ring patterns among trees and assigning rings to specific calendar years. Both visual and statistical techniques are used to make the matches. Wood or charcoal samples from buildings and archaeological sites are crossdated with each other and with wood from living trees to extend the tree-ring chronology beyond the date of the oldest ring of the oldest living tree in the region.

Scientists first used tree-ring dating in the southwestern United States for Native American communities and historical settlements. The bristlecone pine chronology of the American Southwest now exceeds 8,500 years (see Miller 2004). A northern European chronology based on the study of oak and pine is over 11,000 years long. The objective of Cornell University's Aegean dendrochronology project (www.arts.cornell.edu/dendro/), directed by Peter Kuniholm, is to build a master chronology for the region of the Aegean Sea and the Middle East. So far this project has established over 6,000 years of tree-ring chronologies covering much of the period back to about 9,500 years ago. The project encompasses portions of the Aegean, the Balkans, and the Middle East, including Turkey, Cyprus, Greece, parts of Bulgaria and the former Yugoslavia, and some of Italy. (There is one major gap, for which matches have not yet been made, between about 1,500 and 2,500 years ago.) Scientists hope eventually to extend the chronology back to the period in which prehistoric peoples first started using significant amounts of wood in construction (Kuniholm 2004).

Dendrochronology is limited to certain tree species—those growing in a climate with marked seasons. The technique works with oak, pine, juniper, fir, boxwood, yew, spruce, and occasionally chestnut. The trees always have to come from the same region—thus having been exposed to the same environmental patterns—and long ring sequences are needed. Some charcoal fragments from the Neolithic site of Çatalhöyük in Turkey, where dendrochronology has established a 700-year sequence, have as many as 250 rings preserved (Özdoğan, Başgelen, and Kuniholm 2011). Not only do tree rings permit absolute dating; they also provide information about climatic patterns in specific regions.

Molecular Anthropology

Molecular anthropology studies genetic similarities and differences to assess evolutionary relationships among species. The more similar their basic genetic material—their DNA—the more

molecular anthropology
DNA comparisons used to determine evolutionary links and distances.

Research technician Lane Johnson applies dendrochronology in a newly-established (in January 2016) tree-ring laboratory at the Bureau of Land Management building in Santa Fe, New Mexico. What kinds of information can you get from studying tree rings? (see http://www.abqjournal.com/718878/news/tree-ring-analysis-helps-tells-ecological-history-of-area.html).
© ZUMA Press Inc/Alamy Stock Photo

All This from a Finger Bone?

Archaeologists and paleoanthropologists increasingly draw on genomics, including reconstructions of ancient DNA, to unravel the mysteries of hominin evolution, including its diverse branches. Their analysis of discovered fossils, no matter how miniscule, can often lead to significant findings. All that is known of an ancient hominin group called Denisovans comes from a tiny finger bone and two very large molar teeth found between 2008 and 2010 in Siberian caves. Neandertals and their cousins, the Denisovans, shared the world with anatomically modern humans. During their overlap in time, modern humans lived mainly in Africa, while Neandertals inhabited Europe and the Middle East; the Denisovans, Asia. Pay attention to the methodological advances described in this account. Such advances have transformed our understanding of hominin evolution.

In the Altay Mountains of southern Siberia . . . there is a cave called Denisova. . . . It was there that a young Russian archaeologist named Alexander Tsybankov was digging one day in July 2008, in deposits believed to be 30,000 to 50,000 years old, when he came upon a tiny piece of bone . . . about the size and shape of a pebble. . . .

Anatoly Derevianko, leader of the Altay excavations, . . . thought the bone might belong to . . . Homo sapiens. Sophisticated artifacts that could only be the work of modern humans, including a beautiful bracelet of polished green stone, had previously been found in the same deposits. But DNA from a fossil found earlier in a nearby cave had proved to be Neanderthal, so it was possible this bone was Neanderthal as well.

Derevianko . . . sent . . . [the bone] to Svante Pääbo, an evolutionary geneticist at the Max Planck Institute for Evolutionary Anthropology in Leipzig, Germany. . . .

When Pääbo received the package . . . , his team was hard at work producing the first sequence of the entire Neanderthal genome. . . . So it wasn't until late 2009 that the little Russian finger bone drew the attention of Johannes Krause, at the time a senior member of Pääbo's team. . . .

The tiny chip of a finger bone, it seemed, was not from a modern human at all. But it wasn't from a Neanderthal either. It belonged to a new kind of human being, never before seen [and thereafter called "Denisovan"]. . . .

DNA degrades over time, so usually very little remains in a bone tens of thousands of years old. Moreover, the DNA from the bone itself, called endogenous DNA, is typically just a tiny fraction of the total DNA in a specimen, most of which comes from soil bacteria and other contaminants. None of the Neanderthal fossils Pääbo and his colleagues had ever tested contained even 5 percent endogenous DNA. . . . To their amazement, the DNA in the finger bone was some 70 percent endogenous. Apparently, the cold cave had preserved it well.

Given so much DNA, the scientists easily ascertained that there was no sign of a male Y chromosome in the specimen. The fingertip had belonged to a little girl who had died in or near Denisova cave tens of thousands of years before. . . .

For a while they thought they might have her toe too. In the summer of 2010 a human toe bone had emerged. . . . The toe bone . . . turned out to be Neanderthal, deepening the mystery of the place.

The green stone bracelet found earlier . . . had almost surely been made by modern humans. The toe bone was Neanderthal. And the finger bone was something else entirely. One cave, three kinds of human being. . . .

When the researchers compared the Denisovan genome with those of various modern human populations, they found no trace of it in Russia or nearby China, or anywhere else, for that matter, except in the genomes of New Guineans, other people from islands in Melanesia, and Australian Aborigines. On average their genomes are about 5 percent Denisovan. . . .

In 2012 Pääbo's group published a new version of the finger bone's genome—astonishingly, one that in accuracy and completeness rivals any living human's genome that has been sequenced. The breakthrough came from a German postdoc in Pääbo's lab named Matthias Meyer. DNA consists of two interlocking strands, the familiar double helix. Previous methods for retrieving DNA from fossil bone could read out sequences only when both strands were preserved. Meyer had developed a technique for recovering short, single-stranded fragments of DNA as well, greatly increasing the amount of raw material to work with. The method produced a version of the Denisovan girl's genome so precise that the team could discriminate between genetic information inherited from her mother and that from her father. In effect, they now had two highly accurate Denisovan genomes, one from each parent. . . .

But what of the little girl herself? . . . She probably had dark hair, dark eyes, and dark skin. It isn't much, but at least it sketches in broad strokes what she looked like. . . .

SOURCE: Jamie Shreeve, "The Case of the Missing Ancestor: DNA from a Cave in Russia Adds a Mysterious New Member to the Human Family," *National Geographic,* July, 2013. http://nationalgeographic. com. Copyright © 2013 National Geographic Society. Reprinted with permission.

closely related they are. We know, for example, that chimps and humans are more similar to each other in their DNA than either species is to the gorilla. Humans and chimps share about 99 percent of their DNA, whereas the figure is only 98 percent for humans and gorillas (and, also for chimps and gorillas). This means that the common ancestors of humans and chimps lived more recently than did the common ancestors of humans and gorillas, or of chimps and gorillas.

Molecular studies have been used not only to assess the evolutionary relationships of humans and the apes (and other primate species), but also to estimate whether or not particular fossil hominin species were human ancestors. For example, when famed molecular anthropologist Svante Pääbo extracted ancient DNA from a Neandertal upper arm bone, he found 27 differences between that Neandertal DNA and the DNA of modern humans. By contrast, samples of DNA from modern populations worldwide showed only five to eight differences with the modern DNA sample he used. These differences supported other evidence (from paleoanthropology) that the Neandertals were too different to have been ancestors of modern humans. (This chapter's "Appreciating Anthropology" discusses the role of DNA analysis in the discovery and evaluation of an entirely new ancient hominin group—the Denisovans.)

Molecular anthropologists also use the analysis of genomes (a *genome* is the total genetic makeup of an organism, including all its DNA) to establish *when* ancient species lived, and *when* they diverged from other species. What is the basis for such a *genetic clock*? Differences in DNA arise from mutations—changes in genetic structure that are passed on through heredity. Through time, more and more mutations occur, so that the DNA of descendants differs increasingly from the DNA of their ancestors. Molecular anthropologists assume that mutations occur at a predictable rate. They can multiply that rate by the number of DNA differences to estimate the number of years that have passed between the ancestor and the descendant. Similarly, molecular anthropologists can multiply the mutation rate by the number of differences in DNA among species to estimate how many years they have been diverging from a common ancestor. Such DNA analysis and comparison enables molecular anthropologists to determine and date evolutionary relationships between ancient human ancestors and other primate ancestors. For example, molecular anthropology suggests that the common ancestors of humans and chimps probably lived around 6 million years ago (m.y.a.), while the common ancestor of humans, chimps, and gorillas lived about 7 m.y.a.

An additional use of molecular anthropology is to reconstruct waves and patterns of human migration and settlement. A *haplogroup* is a biological lineage (a large group of related people) defined by a specific cluster of genetic traits that occur together. Analysis of haplogroups of contemporary humans in various parts of the world has enabled molecular anthropologists to date a major wave of modern human migration out of Africa around 60,000 years ago. That wave eventually reached Europe, Asia, and Australia. The settlement of the Americas was more recent, occurring no more than 20,000 years ago. Native Americans have at least three major haplogroups, all of which are linked to East Asia.

KINDS OF BIOLOGICAL ANTHROPOLOGY

The past grades into the present when archaeologists do garbology—using garbage to interpret behavior among contemporary humans—or when biological anthropologists study patterns of movement or growth and development among living people. The interests of biological anthropologists are varied and encompass recent and living as well as ancient and deceased humans and other primates. Described in this chapter are many, but far from all, of the topics and methods within contemporary biological anthropology.

Bone Biology

Central to biological anthropology is **bone biology** (skeletal biology)—the study of bone as a biological tissue, including its genetics; cell structure; growth, development, and decay; and patterns of movement (biomechanics) (White, Black, and Folkens 2012). Bone biologists study skeletal characteristics of living and deceased humans and hominins. Any scientific interpretation of fossil remains relies on understanding the structure and function of the skeleton. **Paleopathology** is the

bone biology
The study of bone as a biological tissue.

paleopathology
The study of disease and injury in skeletons from archaeological sites.

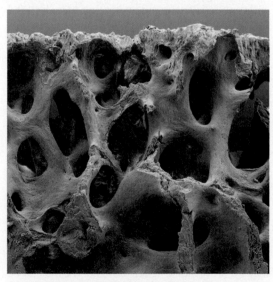

A color-enhanced image of bone affected by osteoporosis (brittle bone disease).
© Eye of Science/Science Source

study of disease and injury in skeletons from archaeological sites (see Buikstra and Roberts 2012; Cohen and Armelagos 2013). Some forms of cancer leave evidence in the bone. Breast cancer, for example, may spread (metastasize) skeletally, leaving holes or lesions in bones and skull. Certain infectious diseases (e.g., syphilis and tuberculosis) also mark bone, as do injuries and nutritional deficiencies (e.g., rickets, a vitamin D deficiency that deforms the bones).

In forensic anthropology, biological anthropologists work in a legal context, assisting coroners, medical examiners, and law enforcement agencies in recovering, analyzing, and identifying human remains and determining the cause of death (Byers 2011; Stefoff 2011; Tersigni-Tarrant and Shirley 2012). The television series *Bones* offers a view of such work. The creator of *Bones* (books and TV series) is biological/forensic anthropologist Kathy Reichs.

Anthropometry

Biological anthropologists use various techniques to study nutrition, growth, and development. **Anthropometry** is the measurement of human body parts and dimensions, including skeletal parts (osteometry). Anthropometry is done on living people as well as on skeletal remains from sites. Body mass and composition provide measures of nutritional status in living people. Body mass is calculated from height and weight. The body mass index (kg/m^2) is the ratio of weight in kilograms divided by height in meters squared. An adult body mass above 30 is considered at risk of overweight, while one below 18 is at risk of underweight or malnutrition.

Primatology

Primatology is considered a subfield of biological anthropology. Primate studies are useful to paleoanthropologists who are attempting to understand the behavior and social life of ancient hominins. Primatology also links with sociocultural anthropology (especially ethnography) through its focus on behavior and social life. Primate behavior has been observed in zoos (e.g., de Waal 1998) and through experimentation (e.g., Harlow 1971; Ottaviani and Meconis 2007), but the most significant studies have been done in natural settings, among free-ranging apes, monkeys, and lemurs. Since the 1950s, when primatologists began their shift from zoos to natural settings, numerous studies have been done of apes (chimps, gorillas, orangutans, and gibbons), monkeys (e.g., baboons, macaques), and lemurs (e.g., Madagascar's indri, sifaka, and ring-tailed lemurs). Arboreal primates (those that spend most of their time in the trees) are difficult to see and follow, but they typically make a lot of noise. Their howls and calls can be studied and teach us about how primates communicate. Studies of primate social systems and behavior, including their mating patterns, infant care, and patterns of contact and dispersal, suggest hypotheses about behavior that humans do or do not share with our nearest relatives—as well as with our hominin ancestors.

DOING ANTHROPOLOGY RIGHT AND WRONG: ETHICAL ISSUES

Science exists in society and in the context of law and ethics. Anthropologists can't study things simply because they might be scientifically interesting. We must consider ethical issues. Anthropologists typically have worked abroad, outside their own society. In the context of international contacts, different ethical codes and value systems will meet, and often compete.

Archaeologists and biological anthropologists, in particular, often work as members of multinational teams (see Dalton 2006). Some team members will be from the host country—the place (e.g., Ethiopia) where the research takes place. Anthropologists must inform officials and colleagues in the host country about the purpose, funding, and likely results, products, and impacts of their research. They need to negotiate the matter of where the materials produced by the research will be analyzed and stored—in the host country or in the anthropologists' country—and for how long. To whom do research materials such as bones, artifacts, and blood samples belong? What kinds of restrictions will apply to their use?

Contemporary anthropologists recognize that **informed consent** (agreement to take part in the research—after having been informed about its nature, procedures, and possible impacts) should be obtained from anyone who provides information or who might be affected by the research. Although nonhuman primates can't give informed consent, primatologists still must take steps to ensure that their research doesn't endanger the animals they study. Either government agencies or nongovernmental organizations (NGOs) may be entrusted with protecting primates. If this is the case, the anthropologist will need their permission and informed consent to conduct research.

With living humans, informed consent is a necessity, not only in gathering information but especially in obtaining biological samples such as blood or urine. The research subjects must be told how the samples will be collected, used, and identified, and about the potential costs and benefits to them. Informed consent is needed from anyone providing data or information, owning materials being studied, or otherwise having an interest that might be affected by the research.

It is appropriate for North American anthropologists working in another country to (1) include host country colleagues in their research planning and requests for funding, (2) establish truly collaborative relationships with those colleagues and their

anthropometry
The measurement of human body parts and dimensions.

informed consent
Agreement to take part in research, after being fully informed about it.

institutions before, during, and after fieldwork, (3) include host country colleagues in dissemination, including publication, of the research results, and (4) ensure that something is "given back" to host country colleagues. For example, research equipment and technology can remain in the host country. Additionally, funding can be provided for host country colleagues to do research, attend international meetings, or visit foreign institutions—especially those where their international collaborators work.

Ownership Issues

Even with broad efforts to respect diverse value systems and acknowledge the contributions of the host country and its colleagues, ethical issues continue to arise. Recently, several disputes have arisen over the ownership of human remains, artifacts, and heritage items. Lawsuits against museums by groups seeking the repatriation of remains and artifacts have become common (see Rothstein 2006). Peru, for instance, sued Yale University to recover objects removed during the exploration of Machu Picchu (an important Peruvian archaeological and tourist site) by Yale explorer Hiram Bingham in 1912. Native Australians have argued that images of native Australian fauna, such as the emu and kangaroo, belong exclusively to the Aboriginal people (Brown 2003). Michael F. Brown (2003) describes efforts by Hopi Indians to control and restrict historic photos of secret religious ceremonies.

Many anthropologists have worked to represent or assist indigenous groups, for example, when disasters strike or when disputes arise with external agents. Sometimes, however, issues involving access to, or ownership of, physical and archaeological remains place anthropologists and indigenous people in opposed camps. The Native American Graves Protection and Repatriation Act (NAGPRA) gives ownership of Native American remains to Native Americans. Hundreds of thousands of Native American remains are said to be in American museums. NAGPRA requires museums to return remains and artifacts to any tribe that requests them and can prove a "cultural affiliation" between itself and the remains or artifact.

The 1996 discovery in Washington state (on federal land) of a skeleton dubbed "Kennewick Man" led to a legal case between anthropologists and five Native American tribes (nations) with ancestral homelands in the area where Kennewick Man was discovered. The anthropologists wanted to conduct a thorough scientific study of the skeleton, which is one of the oldest (between 8,500 and 9,500 years old) and best preserved human remains ever discovered in North America. What might its anatomy and DNA reveal about the early settlement of the Americas? The Umatilla Indians and their allies in four other Native American nations believe they have always occupied the region where the skeleton was found. In their view, Kennewick Man was an ancestor, whom they wanted to rebury with dignity and without contamination from scientific testing.

Anthropometry in action: In Taranto, Italy, a biological anthropologist measures the 2,500-year-old skull of a Greek athlete.
© Gianni Tortoli/Science Source

In 2002, U.S. Magistrate Judge John Jelderks ruled that the Kennewick remains could be subjected to scientific study. The judge found little evidence linking the Kennewick find to any identifiable contemporary group or culture. He suggested that the culture to which Kennewick belonged may have ended thousands of years ago. The ruling, later backed by a federal appeals court, cleared the way for the scientists to begin their ongoing study (see Burke et al. 2008; Egan 2005; Walker and Owsley 2012).

The Code of Ethics

To guide its members in making decisions involving ethics and values, the American Anthropological Association (AAA) offers a Code of Ethics (http://aaanet.org/coe/Code_of_Ethics.pdf.) The

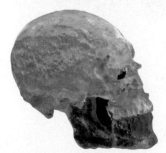
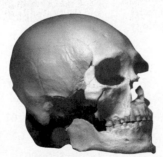

A four-stage reconstruction of "Kennewick Man," whose remains, discovered in 1996 and dating to between 8,500 and 9,500 B.P., represent one of the oldest and most complete skeletons ever found in North America.

photo 1: © Kevin P. Casey/AP Images; photo 2: © Elaine Thompson/AP Images; photo 3: © Emmanuel Laurent/Science Source; photo 4: © Emmanuel Laurent/Science Source

most recent code, approved in 2012, points out that anthropologists have obligations to their scholarly field, to the wider society and culture, and to the human species, other species, and the environment. Like physicians who take the Hippocratic oath, the anthropologist's first concern should be to *do no harm* to the people, animals, or artifacts being studied. The stated aim of the AAA code is to offer guidelines and to promote discussion and education, rather than to investigate possible misconduct. The code addresses several contexts in which anthropologists work. Some of its main points may be highlighted.

Anthropologists should be open and honest about their research projects with all parties affected by the research. These parties should be informed about the nature, procedures, purpose(s), potential impacts, and source(s) of support for the research. Researchers should pay attention to proper relations between themselves as guests and the host nations and communities where they work. The AAA does not advise anthropologists to avoid taking stands on issues. Indeed, seeking to shape actions and policies may be as ethically justifiable as inaction.

for REVIEW

summary

1. As they study the past, archaeologists and biological anthropologists may share research topics and methods, as well as work together in multidisciplinary teams. Remote sensing may be used to locate ancient footpaths, roads, canals, and irrigation systems, which can then be investigated on the ground. Archaeologists combine both local (excavation) and regional (systematic survey) perspectives. Sites are excavated because they are in danger of being destroyed or because they address specific research interests. There are many kinds of archaeology, such as historical, classical, and underwater archaeology.

2. The fossil record is not a representative sample of all the plants and animals that have ever lived. Hard parts, such as bones and teeth, preserve better than soft parts, such as flesh and skin. Stratigraphy and radiometric techniques are used to date fossils. Carbon-14 (^{14}C) dating is most effective with fossils less than 40,000 years old. Potassium–argon (K/A) dating can be used for fossils older than 500,000 years. Dendrochronology provides absolute dates by counting and matching tree rings. Molecular anthropology

uses genetic analysis (of DNA sequences) to assess and date evolutionary relationships.

3. Within biological anthropology, bone biology is the study of bone genetics; cell structure; growth, development, and decay; and patterns of movement. Paleopathology is the study of disease and injury in skeletons from archaeological sites. Anthropometry, the measurement of human body parts and dimensions, is done on living people and on skeletal remains from sites. Studies of primates suggest hypotheses about behavior that humans do or do not share with our nearest relatives—as well as with our hominid ancestors.

4. Because science exists in society, and in the context of law and ethics, anthropologists can't study things simply because they happen to be interesting or of scientific value. Anthropologists have obligations to their scholarly field, to the wider society and culture (including that of the host country), and to the human species, other species, and the environment. The AAA Code of Ethics offers ethical guidelines for anthropologists.

key terms

1. Imagine yourself to be an archaeologist researching early farming communities somewhere in the world. What guidelines might you use in choosing sites to investigate? What methods and techniques might you use in your study? What kinds of problems might you encounter during your research?

2. Imagine yourself to be a biological anthropologist working as part of an international team at an African site where early human fossils have been found. What other academic disciplines might be represented on your team? What kinds of jobs would there be for team members, and where would the members be recruited? What might happen to the fossils and other materials that were recovered? Who would be the authors of the scientific papers describing any discovery made by the team?

3. How can fossils be dated when radiometric dating is impossible?

4. This chapter is about how biological anthropologists and archaeologists conduct scientific studies of the past. Science, however, exists in society as well as in the context of law, values, and ethics. What are some examples of how this fact affects the work of biological anthropologists and archaeologists?

5. As this chapter illustrates, many of the ethical issues that affect the work of anthropologists have some legal dimension, whether in their own country, in another country, or even among several nations. Have you thought about law as a possible future career? (If not, think of a friend who has!) Write a convincing argument about why anthropology could be a valuable tool for a lawyer.

critical thinking

Evolution and Genetics

▶ What is evolution, and how does it occur?

▶ How does heredity work, and how is it studied?

▶ What forces contribute to genetic evolution?

© Ellen McKnight/Alamy Stock Photo

Witnessing a panorama of evolutionary diversity in the Hall of Biodiversity at the American Museum of Natural History in New York City.

understanding OURSELVES

"Hey, it's all in the genes." We routinely use assumptions about genetic determination to explain, say, why tall parents have tall kids or why obesity runs in families. But just how much do genes really influence our bodies? The genetics behind some physical traits (e.g., blood types) are clear, but the genetic roots of other traits are less so. For example, can you crease or fold your tongue by raising its sides? (See the photo below.) Some people easily can; some people never can; some people who never thought they could can do so after practicing. An apparent genetic limitation turns out to be more plastic (changeable).

Human biology is plastic, but only to a degree. If you're born with blood group O, you've got it for life. The same is true for hemophilia and sickle-cell anemia. Fortunately, cultural (medical) solutions now exist for many genetic disorders. Can you recognize in yourself or your family any genetic condition for which there has been a cultural (e.g., medical) intervention? Although we tend to view modern medical advances favorably, some people worry that culture may be intervening too much with human biology. Some people who are deaf, for example, spurn cochlear implants, because they view them as a threat to the Deaf culture, which they hold dear. Plastic surgery, genetic screening, and the possibility of genetic engineering of infants (e.g., "designer babies") concern those who imagine a future in which physical "perfection" might reduce human diversity and increase socioeconomic inequality.

Even as our culture struggles with issues of medically manipulated biological plasticity, many people still question the long-term plasticity of the human genome, a process known as evolution. Most basically, evolution is the idea that all living organisms come from ancestors that were different in some way. The oft-heard statement "evolution is only a theory" suggests

Tongue rolling—a genetic trait, at least partially, which this dad has transmitted to his son.
© Graham Dunn/Alamy Stock Photo

71

to the nonscientist that evolution has not been proven. Scientists, however, use the term *theory* differently—to refer to an interpretive framework that helps us understand the natural world. In science, evolution is both a theory and a fact. As a *scientific theory,* evolution is a central organizing principle of modern biology and anthropology. Evolution also is a fact. The following are examples of evolutionary facts: (1) All living forms come from older or previous living forms. (2) Birds arose from nonbirds; humans arose from nonhumans; and neither birds nor humans existed 250 million years ago. (3) Major ancient life forms (e.g., dinosaurs) are no longer around. (4) New life forms, such as viruses, are evolving right now. (5) Natural processes help us understand the origins and history of plants and animals, including humans and diseases.

What alternatives to evolution have you heard about? Are those scientific theories? Should they be taught in science classes? Do viruses mutate? Should people who reject evolution still get flu shots?

EVOLUTION

Compared with other animals, humans have uniquely varied ways—cultural and biological—of adapting to environmental stresses. Exemplifying cultural adaptation, we manipulate our artifacts and behavior in response to environmental conditions. Contemporary North Americans turn up thermostats or travel to Florida in the winter. We turn on fire hydrants, swim, or ride in air-conditioned cars from New York City to Maine to escape the summer's heat. Although such reliance on culture has increased in the course of human evolution, people haven't stopped adapting biologically. As in other species, human populations adapt genetically in response to environmental forces, and individuals react physiologically to stresses. Thus, when we work in the midday sun, sweating occurs spontaneously, cooling the skin and reducing the temperature of subsurface blood vessels.

Natural History before Darwin

We are ready now for a more detailed look at the principles that determine human biological adaptation, variation, and change.

During the 18th century, many scholars became interested in biological diversity, human origins, and our position within the classification of plants and animals. At that time, the commonly accepted explanation for the origin of species came from Genesis, the first book of the Bible: God had created all life during six days of Creation. According to *creationism,* biological similarities and differences originated at the Creation. Characteristics of life forms were immutable; they could not change. Through calculations based on genealogies in the Bible, the biblical scholars James Ussher and John Lightfoot even claimed to trace the Creation to a very specific time: October 23, 4004 B.C., at 9 A.M.

The Swedish naturalist Carolus Linnaeus (1707–1778) developed the first comprehensive and still influential classification, or taxonomy, of plants and animals. He grouped life forms based on similarities and differences in their physical characteristics. He used traits such as the presence of a backbone to distinguish vertebrates from invertebrates and the presence of mammary glands to distinguish mammals from birds. Linnaeus viewed the differences between life forms as part of the Creator's orderly plan. Biological similarities and differences, he thought, had been established at the time of Creation and had not changed.

Fossil discoveries during the 18th and 19th centuries raised doubts about creationism. Fossils showed that different kinds of life had once existed. If all life had originated at the same time, why weren't ancient species still around? Why weren't contemporary plants and animals found in the fossil record? A modified explanation combining creationism with *catastrophism* arose to

According to creationism, all life originated during the six days of Creation described in the Bible. Catastrophism proposed that fires and floods, including the biblical deluge involving Noah's ark (depicted in this painting by the American artist Edward Hicks), destroyed certain species. Note that creationism is not a scientific theory.

replace the original doctrine. In this view, fires, floods, and other catastrophes, including the biblical flood involving Noah's ark, had destroyed ancient species. After each destructive event, God had created again, leading to contemporary species. How did the catastrophists explain certain clear similarities between fossils and modern animals? They argued that some ancient species had managed to survive in isolated areas. For example, after the biblical flood, the progeny of the animals saved on Noah's ark spread throughout the world. (This chapter's "Appreciating Diversity" discusses a recent approach called "intelligent design," which has been judged to be a secular repackaging of old-time "creationism.")

The alternative to creationism and catastrophism was *transformism,* better known as **evolution.** Evolutionists believe that new species arise from old ones through a long and gradual process of transformation, or descent with modification over the generations. Charles Darwin became the best known of the evolutionists. However, he benefited from the work of earlier scholars, including his own grandfather. In a book called *Zoonomia* published in 1794, Erasmus Darwin had proclaimed the common ancestry of all animal species.

Another major influence on Charles Darwin was Sir Charles Lyell, the father of geology (see Eldredge and Pearson 2010). During Darwin's famous voyage to South America aboard the *Beagle,* he read Lyell's influential book *Principles of Geology* (1837/1969), which exposed him to Lyell's principle of **uniformitarianism.** Uniformitarianism states that the present is the key to the past. Thus, in the present we observe natural forces at work all around us. Given enough time, those same forces can produce major changes. Such natural forces as rainfall, soil deposition, earthquakes, and volcanic action have gradually built and modified geological features such as mountain ranges. The Earth's structure has been transformed gradually through natural forces operating for millions of years.

Uniformitarianism was a necessary building block for evolutionary theory. It cast serious doubt on the belief that the world was only 6,000 years old. It would take much longer than that for such ordinary forces as rain and wind to produce major geological changes. The longer time span also allowed enough time for the biological changes that fossil discoveries were revealing. Darwin applied the ideas of uniformitarianism and long-term transformation to living things. He argued that all life forms are related and that the number of species has increased over time.

Evolution: Theory and Fact

Charles Darwin provided a theoretical framework for understanding evolution. He offered natural selection as the principal mechanism that could explain changes in life forms. Darwin proposed a

theory of evolution in the strict sense. A *theory* is a set of logically connected ideas formulated to explain something. The main value of a theory is to promote new understanding. A theory suggests patterns, connections, and relationships that future research may confirm.

Evolution as a scientific theory is a central organizing principle of modern biology and anthropology. Evolution, however, is both a theory and a fact. Factually, there is absolutely no doubt that biological evolution has occurred and is still occurring. To be sure, scientists do debate *details* about evolutionary processes and events. Nevertheless, they accept certain facts, as the following examples illustrate. Fact: Our Earth with liquid water is more than 3.6 billion years old. Fact: Cellular life has been around for at least half that time. Fact: Multicellular life is at least 800 million years old. Fact: There were no birds or mammals 250 million years ago. Fact: The dinosaurs that once roamed the Earth are no longer with us. Facts: All life forms arose from ancestral forms that were different. Birds arose from nonbirds, and humans arose from nonhumans (see Moran 1993).

Fact: Viruses and other microorganisms mutate all the time, posing a problem for public health officials seeking to control disease transmission (see this chapter's "Appreciating Anthropology").

Although the *fact* that evolution has occurred was recognized before Charles Darwin, for example, by Erasmus Darwin, the *theory* of evolution, through natural selection (*how* evolution occurred), was Charles Darwin's major contribution. Actually, natural selection was not Darwin's unique discovery. Working independently, the British naturalist Alfred Russel Wallace had reached a similar conclusion (Shermer 2011; Smith and Beccaloni 2010). In a joint paper read to London's Linnaean Society in 1858, Darwin and Wallace made their discovery public. Darwin's book *On the Origin of Species* (1859/2009) offered much fuller documentation.

Natural selection is the process by which the life forms that are best suited to survive and reproduce in a particular environment do so in greater numbers than other members of the same population. Natural selection is most obvious when there is competition among members of a population for strategic resources. Such resources include those that are necessary for the survival of the individual, such as food and space, along with those that are necessary for the survival of the species— that is, mates. Members of a population compete not only for food, but also for mates—for the right to reproduce. More than survival of the fittest, natural selection is differential reproductive success. You can win the competition for food and space, but without a mate, you have no impact on the future of the species.

For natural selection to work on any population, there must be variety within that population, as

evolution
Transformation of species; descent with modification.

uniformitarianism
The belief that natural forces at work today also explain past events.

natural selection
Selection of favored forms through differential reproductive success.

Intelligent Design versus Evolutionary Theory

Evolutionary theory is basic to understanding and appreciating human diversity. Contemporary humans, members of the species *Homo sapiens,* represent one branch in the tree of life. Scientists, who seek natural rather than supernatural explanations, use evolutionary theory to explain how humans evolved from ancestors that were not human. Scientists also use Evolutionary theory to explain biological diversity among contemporary and recent human beings. One proposed alternative to evolution, known as "intelligent design (ID)," is not a scientific theory. In a 2005 ruling (the most recent definitive one on this issue), a federal district judge ruled that ID no longer could be taught in biology classes in Pennsylvania's Dover public school district. The judge found that Dover school board members had violated the U.S. Constitution by requiring their schools' biology curriculum to include the notion that life on Earth was produced by an unspecified intelligent designer. Before this ruling, administrators had been required to read a statement in biology classes asserting that evolution was a theory, not a fact; that the evidence for evolution had gaps; and that ID offered an alternative explanation laid out in a book (purchased by church funds) in the school library. According to the judge (a Republican appointed by President George W. Bush), that statement amounted to

an endorsement of religion. It could cause students to doubt a well-established scientific theory by presenting a religious alternative masquerading as a scientific theory (see *New York Times* 2005, p. A32).

The school board's attorneys claimed that board members were seeking to improve science education by exposing students to alternatives to Charles Darwin's theory that evolution occurs through natural selection. ID proponents argued that evolutionary theory cannot fully explain complex life forms. The ID movement asserts that life forms are too complex to have been formed by natural processes and must therefore have been created by a higher intelligence. The fundamental claim of ID proponents, such as William A. Dembski, is that "there are natural systems that cannot be adequately explained in terms of undirected natural forces and that exhibit features which in any other circumstance we would attribute to intelligence" (Dembski 2004). The source of this intelligence never is identified officially. But since the naturalness of the design is denied, its supernaturalness would seem to be assumed.

The Pennsylvania court case thoroughly examined the claim that ID was science. After a six-week trial featuring hours of expert testimony, that claim was rejected. Echoing the overwhelming majority of scientists, the judge

found that ID violated the ground rules of science. It relied on supernatural, rather than natural, causation and made assertions that could not be tested or proved wrong (falsified). By injecting ID into the science curriculum, the judge ruled, Dover's board was unconstitutionally endorsing a religious view that advances "a particular version of Christianity" (*New York Times* 2005, p. A32).

ID advocates were eventually voted off the Dover school board. Although the new board removed ID from science classes, interested students could still learn about ID in an elective course on comparative religion. ID did not belong in the *science* curriculum, the judge ruled, because it is "a religious view, a mere relabeling of creationism and not a scientific theory" (*New York Times* 2005, p. A32).

One key feature of science is to recognize the tentativeness and uncertainty of knowledge and understanding, which scientists try to improve. Scientists work to refine theories and to provide accurate explanations, and they strive for objectivity and impartiality. Science has many limitations and is not the only way we have of understanding things. Certainly, the study of religion is another path to understanding. But the goals of objectivity and impartiality do help distinguish science from ways of knowing that are more biased, more rigid, and more dogmatic.

there always is. The giraffe's neck can illustrate how natural selection works on variety within a population. In any group of giraffes, there always is variation in neck length. When food is adequate, the animals have no problem feeding themselves. But when there is pressure on strategic resources, so that dietary foliage is not as abundant as usual, giraffes with longer necks have an advantage. They can feed off the higher branches. If this ability permits longer-necked giraffes to survive and reproduce even slightly more effectively than shorter-necked ones, giraffes with longer necks will transmit more of

their genetic material to future generations than will giraffes with shorter necks.

An incorrect alternative to this (Darwinian) explanation would be the *inheritance of acquired characteristics.* That is the idea that in each generation, individual giraffes strain their necks to reach just a bit higher. This straining somehow modifies their genetic material. Over generations of strain, the average neck gradually gets longer through the accumulation of small increments of neck length acquired during the lifetime of each generation of giraffes. This is not how evolution

Contrast the speckled (peppered) moth on the left with the darker one on the right. Which environment would favor each of these variants?
© The Natural History Museum/The Image Works

works. If it did work in this way, weight lifters could expect to produce especially muscular babies. Instead, the process of natural selection takes advantage of the variety that is already present in a population.

Evolution through natural selection continues today. One classic recent example of natural selection is change in the coloring of the peppered moth that occurred in England following industrialization. The peppered moth naturally occurs in both light or dark variations (in either case with black speckles, thus the name "peppered"). Before the Industrial Revolution in Great Britain, the light colored variety, which camouflaged effectively against the light color of most tree bark, was prevalent. During the 1800s, as industrial pollution increased, soot coated buildings and trees, turning them a darker color. The lighter moths now stood out against these darker backgrounds and were easily visible to their predators, creating a major selective disadvantage. The dark moths, on the other hand, blended in with the soot. As a result, the darker moths survived and reproduced in greater numbers than lighter moths, and became the dominant moth for the industrial age. In the 20th century, the air quality in Great Britain improved, the soot disappeared from trees and buildings, and the lighter moths once again became the predominant species. We see here how natural selection favors darker moths in polluted environments and lighter-colored moths in nonindustrial or less polluted environments.

GENETICS

Charles Darwin recognized that for natural selection to operate, there must be variety in the population undergoing selection. Documenting and explaining such variety among humans—human biological diversity—is one of anthropology's major concerns (see Relethford 2012). Genetics, a science that emerged after Darwin, helps us understand the causes of biological variation. We now know that DNA (deoxyribonucleic acid) molecules make up genes and chromosomes, which are basic hereditary units. Biochemical changes (mutations) in DNA provide much of the variety on which natural selection operates. Through sexual reproduction, recombination of the genetic traits of mother and father in each generation leads to new arrangements of the hereditary units received from each parent. Such genetic recombination also adds variety on which natural selection may operate.

Mendel's Experiments

In 1856, in a monastery garden, the Austrian monk Gregor Mendel began a series of experiments that were to reveal the basic principles of genetics. Mendel studied the inheritance of seven traits in pea plants. For each trait there were only two forms. For example, plants were either tall (6 to 7 feet [1.8 to 2.1 meters]) or short (9 to 18 inches [23 to 46 centimeters]), with no intermediate forms. The ripe seeds could be either smooth and round, or wrinkled. The peas could be either yellow or green, again with no intermediate colors.

When Mendel began his experiments, one of the prevailing beliefs about heredity was what has been called the "paint-pot" theory. According to this theory, the traits of the two parents blended in their children much as two pigments are blended in a can of paint. Children were therefore a unique mixture of their parents, and when these children reproduced, their traits would inextricably blend with those of their mates. However, prevailing notions about heredity also recognized that occasionally the traits of one parent might swamp those of the other. If children looked far more like their mother than their father, people might say that her "blood" was stronger than his. Occasionally, too, there would be a "throwback," a child who was the image of his or her grandparent or

dominant
Term describing an allele that masks another allele in a heterozygote.

recessive
Term describing a genetic trait masked by a dominant trait.

chromosomes
Paired lengths of DNA, composed of multiple genes.

gene
The place (locus) on a chromosome that determines a particular trait.

allele
A variant of a particular gene.

Charles Darwin (1809–1882), the English naturalist made famous by his theory of evolution by means of natural selection.

© Photo Inc/Photo Researchers/Getty Images

Alfred Russel Wallace (1823–1913), the Welsh-born British naturalist who independently arrived at a theory of evolution similar to that of Charles Darwin.

© Print Collector/Hulton Archive/Getty Images

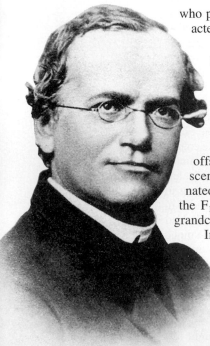

Gregor Mendel, the father of genetics.

© Time & Life Pictures/Getty Images

who possessed a distinctive chin or nose characteristic of a whole line of descent.

Through his experiments with pea plants, Mendel discovered that heredity is determined by discrete particles, or units. Although traits could disappear in one generation, they reemerged in their original form in later generations. For example, Mendel crossbred pure strains of tall and short plants. Their offspring were all tall. This was the first descending, or first filial, generation, designated F_1. Mendel then interbred the plants of the F_1 generation to produce a generation of grandchildren, the F_2 generation (Figure 5.1). In this generation, short plants reappeared. Among thousands of plants in the F_2 generation, there was approximately one short plant for every three tall ones.

From similar results with the other six traits, Mendel concluded that although a **dominant** form could mask the other form in *hybrid*, or mixed, individuals, the dominated trait—the **recessive**—was

not destroyed; it wasn't even changed. Recessive traits would appear in unaltered form in later generations because genetic traits were inherited as discrete units.

These basic genetic units that Mendel described were factors (now called genes or alleles) located on **chromosomes.** Chromosomes are arranged in matching (homologous) pairs. Humans have 46 chromosomes, arranged in 23 pairs, one in each pair from the father and the other from the mother.

For simplicity, a chromosome may be pictured as a surface (see Figure 5.2) with several positions, to each of which we assign a lowercase letter. Each position is a **gene.** Each gene determines, wholly or partially, a particular biological trait, such as whether one's blood is A, B, or O. **Alleles** (for example, b^1 and b^2 in Figure 5.2) are biochemically different forms of a given gene. In humans, A, B, AB, and O blood types reflect different combinations of alleles of a particular gene.

In Mendel's experiments, the seven contrasting traits were determined by genes on seven different pairs of chromosomes. The gene for height occurred in one of the seven pairs. When Mendel crossbred pure tall and pure short plants to produce his F_1 generation, each of the offspring

Trait Exhibited by F₁ Hybrids	F₂ Generation (produced by crossbreeding F₁ hybrids)	
	Exhibit Dominant Trait	Exhibit Recessive Trait
Smooth seed shape	Smooth 3	+	Wrinkled 1
Yellow seed interior	Yellow 3	+	Green 1
Gray seed coat	Gray 3	+	White 1
Inflated pod	Inflated 3	+	Pinched 1
Green pod	Green 3	+	Yellow 1
Axial pod	Axial 3	+	Terminal 1
Tall stem	Tall 3	+	Short 1
	Offspring exhibit dominant or recessive traits in ratio of 3:1.	

FIGURE 5.1 Mendel's Second Set of Experiments with Pea Plants. Dominant colors are shown unless otherwise indicated.

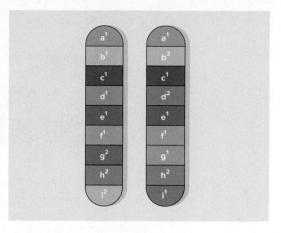

FIGURE 5.2 Simplified Representation of a Normal Chromosome Pair. Letters indicate genes; superscripts indicate alleles.

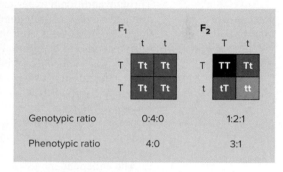

FIGURE 5.3 Punnett Squares of a Homozygous Cross and a Heterozygous Cross. These squares show how phenotypic ratios of the F₁ and F₂ generations are generated. Colors show genotypes.

received an allele for tallness (T) from one parent and one for shortness (t) from the other. These offspring were mixed, or **heterozygous,** with respect to height; each had two dissimilar alleles of that gene. Their parents, in contrast, had been **homozygous,** possessing two identical alleles of that gene (see Hartl 2014).

In the next generation (F₂), after the mixed plants were interbred, short plants reappeared in the ratio of one short to three talls. Because shorts only produced shorts, Mendel knew they were genetically pure. Another fourth of the F₂ plants produced only talls. The remaining half, like the F₁ generation, were heterozygous; when interbred, they produced three talls for each short. (See Figure 5.3.)

Dominance produces a distinction between **genotype,** or hereditary makeup, and **phenotype,** or expressed physical characteristics. Genotype is what you really are genetically; phenotype is what you appear as. Mendel's peas had three genotypes—TT, Tt, and tt—but only two phenotypes—tall and short. Because of dominance, the heterozygous plants were just as tall as the genetically pure tall ones. How do Mendel's discoveries apply to humans? Although some of our genetic traits follow Mendelian laws, with only two forms—dominant and recessive—other traits are determined differently. For instance, three alleles determine whether our blood type is A, B, AB, or O. People with two alleles for type O have that blood type. However, if they receive a gene for either A or B from one parent and one for O from the other, they will have blood type A or B. In other words, A and B are both dominant over O. A and B are said to be *codominant*. If people inherit a gene for A from one parent and one for B from the other, they will have type AB blood, which is chemically different from the other varieties, A, B, and O.

These three alleles produce four phenotypes—A, B, AB, and O—and six different genotypes—OO, AO, BO, AA, BB, and AB (Figure 5.4). There are fewer phenotypes than genotypes because O is recessive to both A and B.

heterozygous
Having dissimilar alleles of a given gene.

homozygous
Having identical alleles of a given gene.

genotype
An organism's hereditary makeup.

phenotype
An organism's evident biological traits.

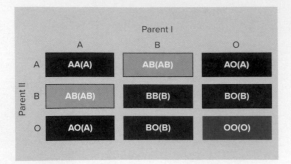

FIGURE 5.4 Determinants of Phenotypes (Blood Groups) in the ABO System.
The four phenotypes—A, B, AB, and O—are indicated in parentheses and by color.

Independent Assortment and Recombination

independent assortment
Chromosomes inherited independently of one another.

Through additional experiments, Mendel also formulated his law of **independent assortment.** He discovered that traits are inherited independently of one another. For example, he bred pure round yellow peas with pure wrinkled green ones. All the F$_1$ generation peas were round and yellow, the dominant forms. But when Mendel interbred the F$_1$ generation to produce the F$_2$, four phenotypes turned up. Round greens and wrinkled yellows had been added to the original round yellows and wrinkled greens.

The independent assortment and recombination of genetic traits provide one of the main ways by which variety is produced in any population. *Recombination* is important in biological evolution because it creates new types on which natural selection can operate.

The Role of DNA

If, as in Mendel's experiments, the same genetic traits always appeared in predictable ratios across the generations, there would be continuity rather than change. There would be no evolution. Various kinds of mutations produce the variety on which natural selection depends. Since Mendel's time, scientists have learned about **mutations**— changes in the DNA molecules of which genes and chromosomes are built. Mendel demonstrated that variety is produced by genetic recombination. Mutation, however, is even more important as a source of new biochemical forms on which natural selection may operate.

DNA does several things basic to life. DNA can copy itself, forming new cells, replacing old ones, and producing the sex cells, or *gametes,* that make new generations. DNA's chemical structure also guides the body's production of proteins— enzymes, antigens, antibodies, hormones, and hundreds of others.

The DNA molecule is a double helix (Crick 1962/1968; Watson 1970). Imagine it as a small

mutation
Change in DNA molecules.

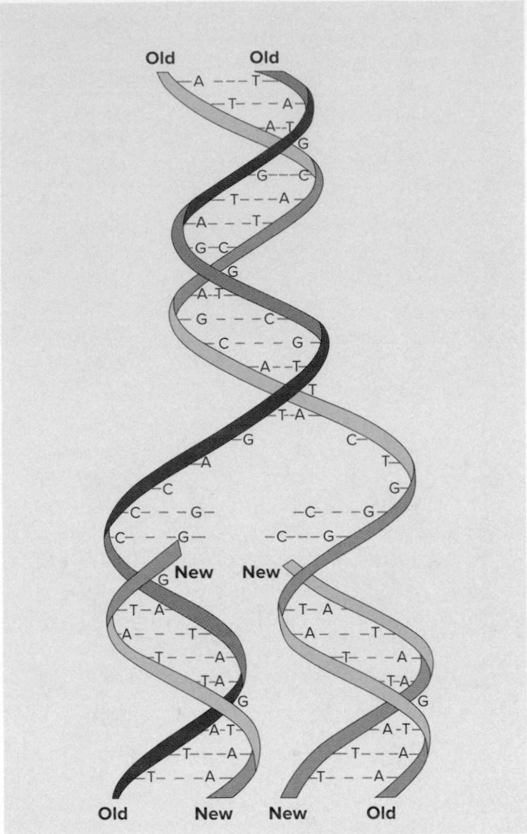

FIGURE 5.5 DNA Replication.
A double-stranded DNA molecule "unzips," and a new strand forms on each of the old ones, producing two molecules, and eventually two cells, each identical to the first.

rubber ladder that you can twist into a spiral. Its sides are held together by chemical bonds between four bases: thymine (T), adenine (A), cytosine (C), and guanine (G). DNA's duplication leads to ordinary cell division, as shown in Figure 5.5.

In protein building, another molecule, RNA, carries DNA's message from the cell's nucleus to its *cytoplasm* (outer area). The structure of RNA, with paired bases, matches that of DNA. This permits RNA to carry a message from DNA in the cell nucleus to guide the construction of proteins in the cytoplasm. A protein, which is a chain of amino acids, is constructed by "reading" a length of RNA. RNA's bases are read as three-letter "words," called *triplets*—for example, AAG. (Because DNA and RNA have four bases, which can occur anywhere in the "word," there are $4 \times 4 \times 4 = 64$ possible triplets.) Each triplet "calls" a particular amino acid, although there is some redundancy; for example, AAA and AAG both call for the amino acid lysine. A protein is made as amino acids are assembled in the proper sequence.

Thus, proteins are built following instructions sent by DNA, with RNA's assistance. In this way, DNA, the basic *hereditary* material, also initiates and guides the construction of hundreds of proteins necessary for bodily growth, maintenance, and repair (see Jobling 2013; Stoneking 2015; Strachan and Read 2011).

Cell Division

An organism develops from a fertilized egg, or *zygote,* created by the union of two sex cells (gametes), a sperm from the father and an egg (ovum) from the mother. The zygote grows rapidly through **mitosis,** or ordinary cell division, which continues as the organism grows. Mistakes in this process of cell division, including chromosomal breaks and rearrangements, can cause diseases such as cancer.

The special process by which sex cells are produced is called **meiosis.** Unlike ordinary cell division, in which two cells emerge from one, in meiosis four cells are produced from one. Each has half the genetic material of the original cell. In human meiosis, four cells, each with 23 individual chromosomes, are produced from an original cell with 23 pairs.

With fertilization of egg by sperm, the father's 23 chromosomes combine with the mother's 23 to re-create the pairs in every generation. However, the chromosomes sort independently, so that a child's genotype is a random combination of the DNA of its four grandparents. It is conceivable that one grandparent will contribute very little to his or her grandchild's heredity. Independent assortment of chromosomes is a major source of variety, because the parents' genotypes can be assorted in 2^{23}, or more than eight million, different ways.

Crossing Over

Another source of variety is **crossing over.** Before fertilization, early in meiosis, as a sperm or an egg is being formed, paired chromosomes temporarily

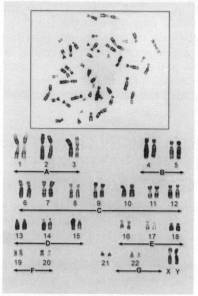

Shown here is a karyogram of a human genotype. A karyogram is a diagram or photograph of the chromosomes of a cell arranged in homologous pairs and in a numbered sequence. Each chromosome has a particular banding pattern representing its genetic composition.

CDC/Suzanne Trusler, MPH, DrPH

intertwine as they duplicate themselves. As they do this, they often exchange lengths of their DNA (Figure 5.6). Crossovers are the sites where homologous chromosomes have exchanged segments by breakage and reattachment.

Because of crossing over, each new chromosome is partially different from either member of the original pair. As a person produces sex cells, replacing, say, part of a chromosome one has received from one's mother with a corresponding

mitosis
Ordinary cell division.

meiosis
The process by which sex cells are produced.

crossing over
Homologous chromosomes intertwine and exchange DNA.

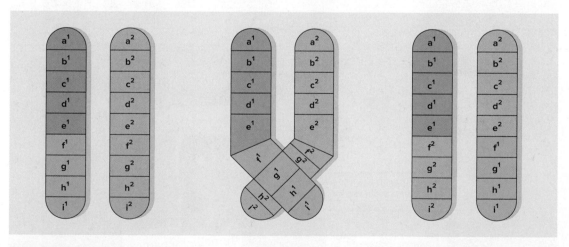

FIGURE 5.6 Crossing Over.
In the first phase of meiosis, homologous chromosomes intertwine as they duplicate themselves. As they do this, they often exchange lengths of their DNA, as shown here. This is known as crossing over. Note that the lower lengths of the original pair now differ. Each chromosome is therefore chemically different from either member of the original pair.

section of the homologous chromosome from one's father, crossing over partially contradicts Mendel's law of independent assortment and makes a new combination of genetic material available to the offspring. Because crossing over can occur with any chromosome pair, it is an important source of variety.

POPULATION GENETICS AND MECHANISMS OF GENETIC EVOLUTION

population genetics
The field that studies genetics of breeding populations.

gene pool
All the genetic material in a breeding population.

genetic evolution
Change in gene (allele) frequency in a breeding population.

Population genetics studies the genetic characteristics of populations in which most breeding normally takes place (see Hamilton 2009; Hartl 2014; Nielsen and Slatkin 2013). The term **gene pool** refers to all the alleles, genes, chromosomes, and genotypes within a breeding population—the "pool" of genetic material available. When population geneticists use the term *evolution,* they have a more specific definition in mind than the one given earlier ("descent with modification over the generations"). Geneticists define **genetic evolution** as change in gene frequencies (that is, in the frequency of alleles in a breeding population) over time, across the generations. The four principal forces or mechanisms that cause genetic evolution are natural selection, mutation, genetic drift, and gene flow (see Relethford 2012).

Natural Selection

Natural selection remains the first and best explanation for (genetic) evolution. Essential to understanding evolution through natural selection is the distinction between genotype and phenotype. *Genotype* refers just to hereditary factors—genes and chromosomes. Phenotype—an organism's evident or manifest biological characteristics—develops over the years as environmental forces influence that organism. (See the photo of the identical twins below. Identical twins have exactly the same genotype, but their actual biology, their phenotypes, will differ if they grow up in different environments.) Furthermore, because of dominance, individuals with different genotypes may have identical phenotypes (like Mendel's tall pea plants). Natural selection can operate only on phenotype—on what is exposed, not on what is hidden. For example, a harmful recessive gene cannot be eliminated from the gene pool if it is masked by a favored dominant.

Phenotype includes not only outward physical appearance but also internal organs, tissues and cells, and physiological processes and systems. Many biological reactions to foods, disease, heat, cold, sunlight, and other environmental factors are not automatic, genetically programmed responses but the product of years of exposure to particular environmental stresses. Human biology is not set at birth but has considerable *plasticity.*

Paula Bernstein and Elyse Schein, authors of *Identical Strangers: A Memoir of Twins Separated and Reunited.* These identical twins, adopted by different middle-class families in the 1960s, were the victims of a New York adoption agency's theory that identical twins would flourish if raised separately. Schein and Bernstein were reunited in 2004.
© Brian Zak/SIPA/ Newscom

That is, it is changeable, being affected by the environmental forces, such as diet and altitude, that we experience as we grow up (see Cameron and Bogin 2012).

The environment works on the genotype to build the phenotype, and certain phenotypes do better in some environments than other phenotypes do. However, remember that favored phenotypes can be produced by different genotypes. Because natural selection works only on genes that are expressed, maladaptive recessives can be eliminated only when they occur in homozygous form. When a heterozygote carries a maladaptive recessive, its effects are masked by the favored dominant. The process of perfecting the fit between organisms and their environment is gradual.

Directional Selection

After several generations of selection, gene frequencies will change. Adaptation through natural selection will have occurred. Once that happens, those traits that have proved to be the most **adaptive** (favored by natural selection) in that environment will be selected again and again from generation to generation. Given such *directional selection,* or long-term selection of the same trait(s), maladaptive recessive alleles will be eliminated from the gene pool.

Directional selection will continue as long as environmental forces stay the same. However, if the environment changes, new selective forces start working, favoring different phenotypes. This also happens when part of the population colonizes a new environment. Selection in the changed, or new, environment continues until a new equilibrium is reached. Then there is directional selection until another environmental change or migration takes place. Over millions of years, such a process of successive adaptation to a series of environments has led to biological modification and branching. The process of natural selection has led to the tremendous array of plant and animal forms found in the world today.

Selection operates *only* on traits that are present in a population. A favorable mutation *may* occur, but a population doesn't normally come up with a new genotype or phenotype just because one is needed or desirable. Many species have become extinct because they weren't sufficiently varied to adapt to environmental shifts.

Species that are adapted to a narrow range of environments may be especially endangered by environmental fluctuation. Others—*Homo sapiens* among them—tolerate much more environmental variation because their genetic potential permits many adaptive possibilities. Humans can adapt rapidly to changing conditions by modifying both biological responses and learned behavior. We don't have to delay adaptation until a favorable mutation appears.

Sexual Selection

Selection also operates through competition for mates in a breeding population. Males may openly compete for females, or females may choose to mate with particular males because they have desirable traits. Obviously, such traits vary from species to species. Familiar examples include color in birds; male birds, such as cardinals, tend to be more brightly colored than females are. Colorful males have a selective advantage because females are attracted to them. As, over the generations, females have opted for colorful mates, the alleles responsible for color have built up in the species. **Sexual selection,** based on differential success in mating, is the term for this process in which certain traits of one sex are selected because of advantages they confer in winning mates.

sexual selection
Selection of traits that enhance mating success.

Stabilizing Selection

We have seen that natural selection reduces variety in a population through directional selection—by favoring one trait or allele over another. Selective forces also can work to *maintain* variety through *stabilizing selection,* by favoring a **balanced polymorphism,** in which the frequencies of two or more alleles of a gene remain constant from generation to generation. This may be because the phenotypes they produce are neutral, or equally favored, or equally opposed by selective forces. Sometimes a particular force favors (or opposes) one allele while a different but equally effective force favors (or opposes) the other allele.

adaptive
Favored by natural selection.

balanced polymorphism
Alleles maintain a constant frequency in a population over time.

One well-studied example of a balanced polymorphism involves two alleles, Hb^A and Hb^S, that affect the production of the beta strain (Hb) of human hemoglobin. Hemoglobin, which is located in our red blood cells, carries oxygen from the lungs to the rest of the body via the circulatory system. The allele that produces normal hemoglobin is Hb^A. Another allele, Hb^S, produces a different hemoglobin. Individuals who are homozygous for Hb^S suffer from *sickle-cell anemia.* Such anemia, in which the red blood cells resemble crescents or sickles (see photo on the next page), is associated with a disease that usually is fatal. This condition interferes with the blood's ability to store oxygen. It increases the heart's burden by clogging the small blood vessels.

Given the fatal disease associated with Hb^S, geneticists were surprised to discover that certain populations in Africa, India, and the Mediterranean had very high frequencies of that allele. In some West African populations, the frequency of Hb^S is around 20 percent. Researchers eventually discovered that both Hb^A and Hb^S are maintained because selective forces in certain environments favor the heterozygote over either homozygote.

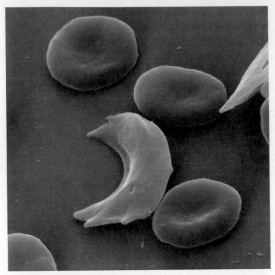

Sickle cells, magnified 7,400 times. Sickle-cell anemia is a painful disease that affects the red blood cells. The heterozygous phenotype resists both anemia and malaria.

© Eye of Science/Science Source

Initially, scientists wondered why, if most Hb^S homozygotes died before they reached reproductive age, the harmful allele had not been eliminated. Why was its frequency so high? The answer turned out to lie in the *heterozygote's* greater fitness. Only people who were homozygous for Hb^S died from sickle-cell anemia. Heterozygotes suffered very mild anemia, if any. On the other hand, although people homozygous for Hb^A did not suf-

fer from anemia, they were much more susceptible to *malaria*—a killer disease that continues to plague *Homo sapiens* in the tropics.

The heterozygote, with one sickle-cell allele and one normal one, was the fittest phenotype for a malarial environment. Heterozygotes have enough abnormal hemoglobin, in which malaria parasites cannot thrive, to protect against malaria. They also have enough normal hemoglobin to fend off sickle-cell anemia. The Hb^S allele has been maintained in these populations because the heterozygotes survived and reproduced in greater numbers than did people with any other phenotype.

The example of the sickle-cell allele demonstrates the relativity of evolution through natural selection: Adaptation and fitness are in relation to specific environments. Traits are not adaptive or maladaptive for all times and places. Even harmful alleles can be selected if heterozygotes have an advantage. Moreover, as the environment changes, favored phenotypes and gene frequencies can change. In malaria-free environments, normal-hemoglobin homozygotes reproduce more effectively than heterozygotes do. With no malaria, the frequency of Hb^S declines because Hb^S homozygotes can't compete in survival and reproduction with the other types. This has happened in areas of West Africa where malaria has been reduced through drainage programs and insecticides. Selection against Hb^S also has occurred in the United States among Americans descended from West Africans. (Compare Figures 5.7 and 5.8 to see the overlap between the geographic distributions of the sickle-call allele and of malaria.)

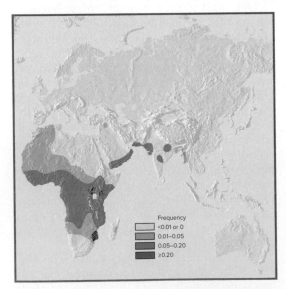

Frequency	
	<0.01 or 0
	0.01–0.05
	0.05–0.20
	≥0.20

FIGURE 5.7 Geographic Distribution of the Sickle-Cell Allele.

Compare with Figure 5.8.

SOURCE: From Agustín Fuentes, *Biological Anthropology: Concepts and Connections,* 2nd ed., p. 318. Copyright © 2012 by McGraw-Hill Education, LLC. Reprinted with permission.

FIGURE 5.8 Regions of the Old World Where Malaria Is Endemic.

Compare Figures 5.7 and 5.8.

SOURCE: From Agustín Fuentes, *Biological Anthropology: Concepts and Connections,* 2nd ed., p. 319. Copyright © 2012 by McGraw-Hill Education, LLC. Reprinted with permission.

Mutation

The second force or mechanism of genetic evolution is mutation. Mutations are the most important source of variety on which natural selection depends and operates. The simplest mutation results from substitution of just one base in a triplet by another. If such a mutation occurs in a sex cell that joins with another in a fertilized egg, the new organism will carry the mutation in every cell. As DNA directs protein building, a protein different from that produced by the nonmutant parent *may* be produced in the child. The child's protein building will differ from the parent's only if the new base codes for a different amino acid. Because the same amino acid can be coded by more than one triplet, a base substitution mutation doesn't always produce a different protein. However, the abnormal protein associated with sickle-cell anemia is caused by just such a difference in a single base between normal individuals and those afflicted with the disease.

Another form of mutation is *chromosomal rearrangement.* Pieces of a chromosome can break off, turn around and reattach, or migrate somewhere else on that chromosome. This can occur in the sex cell, or in the fertilized egg or the growing organism, during mitosis. A mismatch of chromosomes resulting from rearrangement can lead to speciation (the formation of new species). Scientists often find that separate but closely related species living in overlapping ranges cannot interbreed because their chromosomes, due to rearrangement, no longer match. Chromosomes also may fuse. When the ancestors of humans split off from those of chimpanzees around six million years ago, two ancestral chromosomes fused together in the human line. Humans have 23 chromosome pairs, versus 24 for chimps.

Mutation rates vary, but for base substitution mutations, the likely average is 10^{29} mutations per DNA base per generation. This means that approximately three mutations will occur in every sex cell (Strachan and Read 2011). Many geneticists believe that most mutations are neutral, conferring neither advantage nor disadvantage. Others argue that most mutations are harmful and will be eliminated because they deviate from types that have been selected over the generations. However, if the selective forces affecting a population change, mutations in its gene pool may acquire an adaptive advantage they lacked in the old environment.

Evolution depends on mutations as a major source of genetically transmitted variety, raw material on which natural selection can work. Alterations in genes and chromosomes may result in entirely new types of organisms, which may demonstrate some new selective advantage. Variants produced through mutation can be especially significant if there is a change in the environment. They may prove to have an advantage they lacked in the old environment, as is illustrated by the spread of the Hb^S allele in malarial environments (see this chapter's "Appreciating Anthropology" for an example of how a disease microorganism mutates and spreads).

Random Genetic Drift

A third mechanism of genetic evolution is **random genetic drift.** This term refers to random changes in gene frequencies, most typically seen in small populations. The changes are random; they happen by chance rather than because of natural selection. To illustrate how genetic drift works, let's compare the sorting of genes to a game involving a bag of only 12 marbles, 6 red and 6 blue. In step 1, you randomly draw 6 marbles from the bag. Statistically, your chances of drawing 3 reds and 3 blues are less than those of getting 4 of one color and 2 of the other. Step 2 is to fill a new bag with 12 marbles based on the ratio of marbles drawn in step 1. Let's say that in step 1 you drew 4 reds and 2 blues: The step 2 bag will have 8 red marbles and 4 blue ones. Step 3 is to randomly draw 6 marbles from the new bag. Your chances of drawing blues in step 3 are lower than they were in step 1, and the probability of drawing all reds increases. If you do draw all reds, the next bag (step 4) will have only red marbles.

This game is analogous to random genetic drift operating over a few generations. The blue marbles were lost purely by chance. Alleles of a gene also can be lost by chance rather than because of any disadvantage they confer.

Contrast this example with the discussion of how, because of natural selection, dark-colored moths replaced light-colored ones in industrial England. Dark replaced light because of a selective advantage. With this simulation of drift, however, red marbles replaced blue ones by chance, not because either color conferred any selective advantage or disadvantage. *Fixation* refers to the total replacement of blue by red. Imagine a human example in which everyone with brown eyes happens to die in an accident, and all the survivors have blue eyes. Blue has replaced brown merely by chance, not because of natural selection. The history of the human line features a series of small populations, migrations, and fixation due to genetic drift. One cannot understand human origins, human genetic variation, and a host of other important anthropological topics without recognizing the importance of genetic drift.

random genetic drift
Genetic change due to chance.

Disease Evolution: A Case Study

The same processes (e.g., mutation and environmental adaptation) that operate in the evolution of life in general also apply to the evolution of disease microorganisms. Consider syphilis, a sexually transmitted infection (STI) that appears to have originated as a childhood infection transmitted through skin contact. The syphilis bacterium *(T. pallidum)*, which most probably originated in the Americas, mutated and spread rapidly when it reached Europe via the return voyage of Christopher Columbus and his crew in 1493. In just a few years, the mutated bacterium—as the STI syphilis—spawned an epidemic and became a major killer during the European Renaissance. While the New World origin of syphilis is widely accepted, some believe that syphilis already existed in Europe before Columbus but did not become a major threat until the Renaissance, when it erupted in epidemic form, perhaps in response to environmental and social changes, including the growth of cities.

What kinds of evidence can help us solve the puzzle of the origin and evolution of syphilis? Anthropologists Kristin Harper, Molly Zuckerman, and George Armelagos (2014) consider bone biology, genetics, and nonhuman primates in their studies of syphilis and its close cousins, yaws and bejel (known together as treponemal diseases). Like syphilis, yaws and bejel are chronic, debilitating diseases, but neither spreads sexually. Yaws, found in tropical regions, spreads via skin-to-skin contact. Bejel, found in arid areas like the Middle East, spreads via contaminated utensils. All three diseases often leave skeletal evidence, including crater-like markings on the skull, and shinbones that are swollen and pitted.

From bone biology, there is indisputable evidence for *T. pallidum* infection throughout the Americas prior to Columbus. Many of the affected skeletons are of juvenile individuals, suggesting nonsexual transmission. By contrast, the skeletal evidence for pre-Columbian treponemal infection in the Old World is spotty and ambiguous. Based on an extensive review, Harper, Zuckerman, and Armelagos (2014) could find no European skeleton with both a confirmed diagnosis of *Treponema* and a reliable pre-Columbian date. For this reason, those researchers were unconvinced that the pathogen really did exist in Europe before Columbus. They do recognize, however, that *Treponema* may have existed in Africa, where monkeys and apes continue to experience treponemal infections.

Genetics is another important tool for studying the origin and evolution of syphilis. When researchers compared *T. pallidum* strains from around the world, the closest genetic match to syphilis was a yaws-causing strain of *T. pallidum* found in South America. This strain infects children in remote indigenous communities in Guyana; the children develop sores on their shins that resemble both yaws and syphilis. In terms of its genetics and clinical symptoms, this South American strain occupied a space midway between yaws and syphilis. The close genetic and clinical similarity of syphilis to this South American strain strongly suggests that syphilis descends from a non-sexually-transmitted yaws-like pathogen in the Americas. However, genetic comparison also suggests that some forms of treponemal disease were present in the pre-Columbian Old World as well, most probably in Africa.

Researchers working in national parks in Tanzania in the 1980s and 1990s reported a gruesome treponemal disease that attacked the genitals of baboons. One strain from these baboons was indistinguishable from a group of human yaws strains, suggesting the possibility

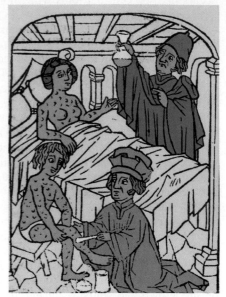

The scourge of syphilis: This historic (1497) woodcut depicts a bed-ridden woman and a young man seated on a stool—both covered with the lesions or skin pustules that are characteristic of the disease. The first European syphilis epidemics occurred in 1494. What is significant about that date?
© Jessica Wilson/Science Source

of cross-species transmission. Researchers are examining the risk of the bacterium jumping from animals to humans. The human diseases that are easiest to eradicate are those that cannot jump back and forth between animals and humans (e.g., polio and smallpox). We can seem to eradicate a disease such as yaws among humans, only to have it jump back later from its animal hosts.

We see in this account how biological anthropologists can combine the study of genetics, skeletons, clinical manifestations, and nonhuman primates to understand the origin, evolution, and spread of syphilis and its cousins. Anthropologists use a similar multipronged approach to study the evolution of other life forms, especially humans.

Gene Flow

A fourth mechanism of genetic evolution is **gene flow,** the exchange of genetic material between populations of the same species. Gene flow, like mutation, works in conjunction with natural selection by providing variety on which selection can work. Gene flow may consist of direct interbreeding between formerly separated populations of the same species (e.g., Europeans, Africans, and Native Americans in the United States), or it may be indirect.

Consider the following hypothetical case (Figure 5.9). In a certain part of the world live six local populations of a certain species. P_1 is the westernmost of these populations. P_2, which interbreeds with P_1, is located 50 miles to the east. P_2 also interbreeds with P_3, located 50 miles east of P_2. Assume that each population interbreeds with, and only with, the adjacent populations. P_6 is located 250 miles from P_1 and does not directly interbreed with P_1, but it is tied to P_1 through the chain of interbreeding that ultimately links all six populations.

Assume further that an allele exists in P_1 that isn't particularly advantageous in its environment. Because of gene flow, this allele may be passed on to P_2, by it to P_3, and so on, until it eventually reaches P_6. In P_6 or along the way, the allele may encounter an environment in which it does have a selective advantage. If this happens, it may serve, like a new mutation, as raw material on which natural selection can operate.

In the long run, natural selection works on the variety within a population, whatever its source—mutation or gene flow. Selection and gene flow have worked together to spread the Hb^S allele in Central Africa. Frequencies of Hb^S in Africa reflect not only the intensity of malaria but also the length of time gene flow has been going on (Livingstone 1969).

Gene flow is important in the study of the origin of species. A **species** is a group of related organisms whose members can interbreed to produce offspring that can live and reproduce. A species has to be able to reproduce itself through time. We know that horses and donkeys belong to different species because their offspring cannot meet the test of long-term survival. A horse and a donkey may breed to produce a mule, but mules are sterile. So are the offspring of lions with tigers. Gene flow tends to prevent **speciation**—the formation of new species—unless subgroups of the same species are separated for a sufficient length of time.

When gene flow is interrupted, and isolated subgroups are maintained, new species may arise. Imagine that an environmental barrier arises between P_3 and P_4, so that they no longer interbreed. If over time, because of isolation, P_1, P_2, and P_3 become incapable of interbreeding

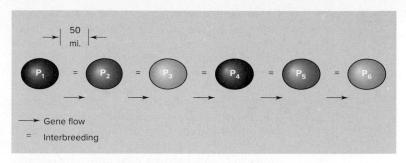

FIGURE 5.9 Gene Flow between Local Populations.

P_1–P_6 are six local populations of the same species. Each interbreeds (=) only with its neighbor(s). Although members of P_6 never interbreed with P_1, P_6 and P_1 are linked through gene flow. Genetic material that originates in P_1 eventually will reach P_6, and vice versa, as it is passed from one neighboring population to the next. Because they share genetic material in this way, P_1–P_6 remain members of the same species. In many species, local populations distributed throughout a larger territory than the 250 miles depicted here are linked through gene flow.

with the other three populations, speciation will have occurred.

gene flow
Exchange of genetic material through interbreeding.

MICROEVOLUTION, MACROEVOLUTION, AND EXTINCTION

Microevolution and macroevolution are two ends (short-term and long-term) of a continuum of evolutionary change in which gradually changing gene frequencies in a population eventually can lead to the formation of new species. *Microevolution* refers to genetic changes in a population or species over a few, several, or many generations, but without speciation. *Macroevolution* refers to larger-scale or more significant genetic changes in a population or species, usually over a longer time period, which result in speciation. Indeed, macroevolution is defined as speciation, the separation or divergence of one ancestral species into two (or more) descendant species. Most biologists assume that new species develop gradually as successive mutations accumulate in isolated populations, so that eventually the populations are too different to interbreed. In this case, the long-term operation of microevolution leads to macroevolution. However, the time and the number of generations required for microevolution to become macroevolution are highly variable.

Modern-day creationists sometimes use a misunderstanding of the contrast between microevolution and macroevolution to comment on evolution. They may say they accept microevolution, such as a change in a species' size or coloring, or as demonstrated in the laboratory or through studies of such traits as the sickle-cell allele. Macroevolution, they claim, by contrast, cannot be demonstrated, only inferred from the fossil record.

species
A population whose members can interbreed to produce offspring that can live and reproduce.

speciation
Formation of new species.

Note, however, that the term *macroevolution* implies no specific degree of obvious phenotypical difference between species. A simple chromosomal rearrangement can be sufficient to separate two closely related species whose ranges overlap. They now belong to different species not because they are spacially isolated from each other but because their chromosomes no longer match. They can no longer interbreed successfully. Although no phenotypic difference may be visible between these newly distinct species, this is a case of macroevolution rather than microevolution.

We should not exaggerate the contrast between microevolution and macroevolution. Microevolution and macroevolution happen in the same way and for the same reasons, reflecting the mechanisms of genetic evolution discussed in this chapter.

Punctuated Equilibrium

Charles Darwin saw species as arising from others over time, in a gradual and orderly fashion. Microevolutionary changes would accumulate over the generations and eventually produce macroevolution. In other words, minor alterations in the gene pool, accumulating generation after generation, would add up to major changes, including speciation, after thousands of years.

The **punctuated equilibrium** model of evolution (see Eldredge 2015; Gould 2007) points to the fact that long periods of stasis (stability), during which species change little, may be interrupted (punctuated) by evolutionary leaps. One reason for such apparent jumps (which are revealed by the fossil record) may be the extinction of one species followed by invasion by a closely related species. For example, a sea species may die out when a shallow body of water dries up, while a closely related species survives in deeper waters. Later, when the sea reinvades the first locale, the protected species extends its range to the first area. Another possibility is that when barriers are removed, a group may replace, rather than succeed, a related one because it has a trait that makes it adaptively fitter in the environment they now share.

When there is a sudden environmental change, rather than such extinction and replacement, another possibility is for the pace of evolution to speed up. Some highly significant mutation(s) or combination of genetic changes may permit the survival of a radically altered species in a new and very different environmental niche. Many scientists believe that the evolution of our hominin ancestors featured one or more such evolutionary leaps.

punctuated equilibrium
Long periods of stability, with occasional evolutionary leaps.

Extinction

Although species can survive radical environmental shifts, a more common fate is extinction (see Eldredge 2014). The Earth has witnessed several mass extinctions—worldwide catastrophes affecting multiple species. The biggest one divided the era of "ancient life" (the Paleozoic) from the era of "middle life" (the Mesozoic). This mass extinction occurred 245 million years ago, when 4.5 million of the Earth's estimated 5 million species (mostly invertebrates) were wiped out. The second-biggest extinction, around 65 million years ago, destroyed the dinosaurs. One explanation for the extinction of the dinosaurs is that a massive, long-lasting cloud of gas and dust arose from the impact of a giant meteorite at the end of the Mesozoic. The cloud blocked solar radiation and therefore photosynthesis, ultimately destroying most plants and the chain of animals that fed on them.

From the fossil record, including the hominin fossil record, we know there are periods of more intense evolutionary change. At the end of the Mesozoic, the extinction of the dinosaurs was accompanied by the rapid spread and speciation of mammals and birds. Speciation responds to many factors, including the rate of environmental change, the speed with which geographic barriers rise or fall, the degree of competition with other species, and the effectiveness of the group's adaptive response (see Michalak 2013).

Extinction! The skeleton of a T. Rex partially buried in what has become a desert—perhaps a common scene around 65 million years ago. Scientists think that the dinosaurs perished due to the global impact of a 10-kilometer comet that crashed into Earth.
© Mark Garlick/Science Photo Library/Getty Images

1. In the 18th century, Carolus Linnaeus developed biological taxonomy. He viewed differences and similarities among organisms as part of God's orderly plan rather than as evidence for evolution. Charles Darwin and Alfred Russel Wallace proposed that natural selection could explain the origin of species, biological diversity, and similarities among related life forms. Natural selection requires variety in the population undergoing selection.

2. Through breeding experiments with peas in 1856, Gregor Mendel discovered that genetic traits pass on as units. These are now known to be chromosomes, which occur in homologous pairs. Alleles, some dominant, some recessive, are the chemically different forms that occur at a given genetic locus. Mendel also formulated the law of independent assortment. Each of the seven traits he studied in peas was inherited independently of all the others. Independent assortment of chromosomes and their recombination provide some of the variety needed for natural selection. But the major source of such variety is mutation, an alteration in the DNA molecules of which genes are made.

3. Genetic changes that provide variety within a population include base substitution mutations, chromosomal rearrangements, and genetic recombination. Population genetics studies gene frequencies in stable and changing populations. Natural selection is the most important force or mechanism of evolutionary change. Others include mutation, genetic drift, and gene flow. Natural selection works with traits already present in the population. If variety is insufficient to permit adaptation to environmental change, extinction is likely. New types don't appear just because they are needed.

4. One well-documented case of natural selection in contemporary human populations is that of the sickle-cell allele. In homozygous form, the sickle-cell allele, Hb^S, produces an abnormal hemoglobin. This clogs the small blood vessels, impairing the blood's capacity to store oxygen. The result is sickle-cell anemia, which usually is fatal. The distribution of Hb^S has been linked to that of malaria. Homozygotes for normal hemoglobin are susceptible to malaria and die in great numbers. Homozygotes for the sickle-cell allele die from anemia. Heterozygotes get only mild anemia and are resistant to malaria. In a malarial environment, the heterozygote has the advantage. This explains why an apparently maladaptive allele is preserved. The preservation of Hb^A and Hb^S alleles within a breeding population is an example of a balanced polymorphism, in which the heterozygote has greater fitness than does either homozygote.

5. Other forces or mechanisms of genetic evolution complement natural selection. Mutation is the principal source of variety on which natural selection operates. Random genetic drift operates most obviously in small populations, where pure chance can easily change allele frequencies. Gene flow and interbreeding keep subgroups of the same species genetically connected and thus impede speciation.

6. Microevolution and macroevolution are two ends (short-term and long-term) of a continuum of evolutionary change in which gradually changing allele frequencies in a population eventually can lead to the formation of new species. Punctuated equilibrium theory states that long periods of stasis (stability), during which species change little, are interrupted (punctuated) by evolutionary leaps. Although species can survive radical environmental shifts, a more common fate is extinction.

adaptive 81

allele 76

balanced polymorphism 81

chromosomes 76

crossing over 79

dominant 76

evolution 73

gene 76

gene flow 85

gene pool 80

genetic evolution 80

genotype 77

heterozygous 77

homozygous 77

critical thinking

1. During the 18th century, many scholars became interested in biological diversity, human origins, and our position within the classification of plants and animals. Why do you think that this interest arose at this time, at least in Europe? Think of historical events that led to the realization that the world is much larger and much more diverse than previously thought.

2. In the context of understanding evolution, why is it important to distinguish between a theory and a fact?

3. Also in the context of understanding evolution, why is it important to distinguish between phenotype and genotype?

4. The strange consequences of mutations have been featured in science fiction books and movies. What is a mutation? What role do mutations play in evolution? Are they always bad?

Human Variation and Adaptation

▶ What is the race concept, and why have anthropologists rejected it?

▶ How does natural selection work on contemporary and recent human populations?

▶ Does biological adaptation occur during an individual's lifetime?

© Matt McClain for The Washington Post via Getty Images

Diversity at the mall. Black Friday shoppers wait in line at a Best Buy store in Fairfax, Virginia.

understanding OURSELVES

How do you imagine human "diversity"? Maybe you associate that word with "race" or "ethnicity." Perhaps you think of differences in skin or eye color, or something like height, which the naked eye can observe. In fact, human biological diversity encompasses much more than observable physical differences. It includes our abilities to digest various foods. It also includes our innate resistance or susceptibility to particular diseases. Consider smallpox, a virus that once plagued humankind. When I was a child, everyone was vaccinated against smallpox. Were you? Probably not, because smallpox has been eradicated in nature since 1979. The virus survives only in labs. The smallpox vaccine turned out to be highly effective but potentially lethal. At one time, when smallpox was nearing extinction, more people were dying from the vaccine than from the disease. Anthropologists know that people with certain blood types seem to be more at risk from smallpox and its vaccine than are people with other blood types. This type of knowledge about biological diversity can help us make important decisions about public policy and public safety in a society as diverse as our own.

Contemporary North America is strikingly rich in human biological diversity. The photos in this chapter and throughout this book illustrate just a fraction of the world's biological variation. Additional illustration comes from your own experience. Look around you in your classroom or at the mall or movie theater. Inevitably, you'll see people whose ancestors lived in many lands. The first (Native) Americans had to cross a land bridge that once linked Siberia to North America. For later immigrants, perhaps including your own parents or grandparents, the voyage may have been across the sea, or overland from nations to the south. They came for many reasons; some came voluntarily, while others came as enslaved human beings. The scale of migration in today's world is so vast that millions of people routinely cross national borders or live far from the homelands of their grandparents. Now meeting every day are diverse human beings whose biological features reflect adaptation to a wide range of environments other than the ones they now inhabit. Physical contrasts are evident to anyone. Anthropology's job is to explain them.

RACE: A DISCREDITED CONCEPT IN BIOLOGY

Historically, scientists have approached the study of human biological diversity in two main ways: (1) racial classification (now largely abandoned) versus (2) the current explanatory approach, which focuses on understanding specific differences. First, we'll consider problems with **racial classification** (the attempt to assign humans to discrete categories—races—based on common ancestry). Then we'll offer some explanations for specific aspects of human biological diversity.

What is race anyway? In theory, a biological race would be a geographically isolated subdivision of a species. Such a *subspecies* would be capable of interbreeding with other subspecies of the same species, but it would not actually do so because of its geographic isolation. Some biologists also use "race" to refer to "breeds," as of dogs or roses. Thus, a pit bull and a Chihuahua would be different races of dogs. Such domesticated "races" have been bred by humans for generations. Humanity (*Homo sapiens*) lacks such races because human populations have not been isolated enough from one another to develop into such discrete groups. Nor have humans experienced controlled breeding like that which has created the various kinds of dogs and roses.

Racial classification assumes that humans belong to distinct races and that each race has a biological basis (shared "blood" or genes). Discrimination against a group perceived to be biologically different is *racism*. However, race is actually a *cultural* category rather than a biological reality. That is, "races" are based on contrasts perceived and perpetuated in particular societies, rather than on scientific classifications based on common genes (see Fairbanks 2015). Racial distinctions and racial discrimination vary from one society to another. The chapter "Ethnicity and Race" has a fuller discussion of the social construction of race and racism (see also this chapter's "Appreciating Anthropology").

Racism has not always existed, nor is it intrinsic to humanity. Consider studies by the classics scholar Frank Snowden, Jr., of intergroup relations in the ancient world. Snowden (1970, 1995) draws on classical studies and ancient art to show that Europeans and Africans coexisted in the ancient world and that social relations and business transactions occurred free of discrimination based on skin color or other physical features. Most Roman slaves were foreigners, and slavery was not based on race. Slaves included prisoners of war and other people captured or bought outside Roman territory. Needy Roman citizens sometimes sold their own children into slavery. Slaves looked so similar to Roman citizens that the Senate once considered making them wear special clothing so that they could be easily identified. Although there were African slaves in the Roman Empire, other Africans were free and worked in varied professions, for example, as writers, philosophers, generals, and Roman officials.

According to Snowden, the ancient Greeks and Romans accepted the physical and cultural diversity in their midst. For example, they used the term "Ethiopian" for the dark-skinned peoples who lived south of Egypt. Portrayals of African blacks by Greeks and Romans spanned a range of physical types and a gradation of skin color. Terms for degrees of coloration (e.g., blackest, less sunburned, mildly dark) and contrasts by physical features (e.g., thick lips, tightly curled hair) denote recognition of a range of human diversity. Ancient art and literature also acknowledged variety in customs and social practices, for instance, facial scarification. The Greeks and Romans attributed variations in physical characteristics and cultural markers partly to environmental influences and partly to intermarriage between members of different groups (Snowden 1995).

Biological differences are real, important, and apparent to us all. Modern scientists find it most productive to seek explanations for this diversity, rather than trying to pigeonhole people into categories called races (see Tattersall and DeSalle 2011).

The photos in this chapter illustrate only a small part of the range of human biological diversity. Shown here is a Bai minority woman from Shapin, in China's Yunnan province.

© Paul Grebliunas/The Image Bank/Getty Images

Certainly, human groups do vary biologically—for example, in their genetic attributes. But often we observe gradual, rather than abrupt, shifts in gene frequencies between neighboring groups. Such gradual genetic shifts are called **clines,** and they are incompatible with discrete races (see Edgar and Hunley 2009; Mukhopadhyay, Henze, and Moses 2014).

A race is supposed to reflect shared genetic material (inherited from a common ancestor), but early scholars instead used phenotypical traits (such as skin color and facial features) for racial classification. *Phenotype* refers to an organism's evident traits, its "manifest biology"—anatomy and physiology. Humans display hundreds of evident (detectable) physical traits. They range from skin color, hair form, eye color, and facial features (which are visible) to blood groups, color blindness, and enzyme production (which become evident through testing).

Racial classifications based on phenotype raise the problem of deciding which trait(s) should be primary. Should races be defined by height, weight, body shape, facial features, teeth, skull form, or skin color? Like their fellow citizens, early European and American scientists gave priority to skin color. Many schoolbooks and

racial classification
Assigning humans to categories (purportedly) based on common ancestry.

cline
Gradual shift in gene (allele) frequencies between neighboring populations.

encyclopedias still proclaim the existence of three great races: the white, the black, and the yellow. This overly simplistic classification was compatible with the political use of race during the colonial period of the late 19th and early 20th centuries (see Gravlee 2009). Such a tripartite scheme kept white Europeans neatly separate from their African, Asian, and Native American subjects. Colonial empires began to break up, and scientists began to question established racial categories, after World War II (see Tattersall and DeSalle 2011).

Races Are Not Biologically Distinct

History and politics aside, one obvious problem with classifying people by skin color is that the terms "white," "black," and "yellow" do not accurately describe human skin colors. So-called "white" people are more pink, beige, or tan than white. "Black" people are various shades of brown, and "yellow" people are tan or beige. It does not make the tripartite division of human races any more accurate when we use the more scientific-*sounding* synonyms—Caucasoid, Negroid, and Mongoloid—rather than white, black, and yellow.

Another problem with classifying people by skin color is that many populations do not fit neatly into any one of the three "great races." For example, where would one put the Polynesians? *Polynesia* is a triangle of South Pacific islands formed by Hawaii to the north, Easter Island to the east, and New Zealand to the southwest. Does the "bronze" skin color of Polynesians connect them to the Caucasoids or to the Mongoloids? Some scientists, recognizing this problem, enlarged the original tripartite scheme to include the Polynesian "race." Native Americans presented a similar problem. Were they red or yellow? Some scientists added a fifth race—the "red," or Amerindian—to the major racial groups.

Many people in southern India have dark skins, but scientists have been reluctant to classify them with "black" Africans because of their Caucasoid facial features and hair form. Some, therefore, have created a separate race for these people. What about the Australian aborigines, hunters and gatherers native to what has been, throughout human history, the most isolated continent? By skin color, one might place some Native Australians in the same race as tropical Africans. However, similarities to Europeans in hair color (light or reddish) and facial features have led some scientists to classify them as Caucasoids. But there is no evidence that Australians are closer genetically to either of these groups than they are to Asians. Recognizing this problem, scientists often regard Native Australians as a separate race.

Finally, consider the *San* ("Bushmen") of the Kalahari Desert in southern Africa. Scientists have perceived their skin color as varying from brown to yellow. Some who regard San skin as "yellow" have placed them in the same category as Asians. In theory, people of the same race share more recent common ancestry with each other

A Quechua woman in Macha, Bolivia.

© Leonid Plotkin/Alamy Stock Photo

A boy at the Pushkar livestock fair, Rajasthan, India.

© Conrad P. Kottak

A Polynesian boy from Bora Bora, Society Islands, French Polynesia.
© Tom Cockrem/Lonely Planet Images/Getty Images

A Native Australian girl from East Arnhem Land, Northern Territory, Australia.
© Lynn Gail/Lonely Planet Images/Getty Images

than they do with anyone else. There is, however, no evidence for recent common ancestry between San and Asians. Somewhat more reasonably, some scholars assign the San to the Capoid race (from the Cape of Good Hope), which is seen as being different from other groups inhabiting tropical Africa.

Similar problems arise in using any single phenotypical trait for racial classification. An attempt to use facial features, height, hair type, or any other phenotypical trait is fraught with difficulties. For example, consider the *Nilotes,* natives of the upper Nile region of Uganda and South Sudan. Nilotes tend to be tall and to have long, narrow noses. Certain Scandinavians also are tall, with similar noses. Given the distance between their homelands, however, there is no reason to assume that Nilotes and Scandinavians are more closely related to each other than either is to shorter and nearer populations with different kinds of noses.

Would racial classifications be better if we based them on a combination of physical traits rather than a single trait such as skin color, height, or nose form? To do so would avoid some of the problems raised using a single trait, but other problems would arise. The main problem is that physical features do not go together in a coherent and consistent bundle. Some tall people have dark skin; others are lighter. Some short people have curly hair; others have straight hair. Imagine the various possible combinations of skin color, stature, and skull form. Add to that facial features such as nose form, eye shape, and lip thickness. People with dark skin may be tall or short and have hair ranging from straight to very curly. Dark-haired populations may have light or dark skin, along with various skull forms, facial features, and body sizes and shapes. The number of combinations is very large, and the amount that heredity (versus environment) contributes to such phenotypical traits is often unclear (see also Anemone 2011; Beall 2014). Using a combination of physical characteristics would not solve the problem of constructing an accurate racial classification scheme.

Genetic Markers Don't Correlate with Phenotype

The analysis of human DNA indicates that fully 94 percent of human genetic variation occurs *within* so-called races. Considering conventional geographic "racial" groupings such as Africans, Asians, and Europeans, there is only about 6 percent variation in genes from one group to the other. In other words, there is much greater variation within each of the traditional "races" than between them. Humans are much more alike genetically than are other hominoids (the living apes). This suggests a recently shared common ancestor (perhaps as recent as 70,000 to 50,000 years) for all members of modern *Homo sapiens*. Sampling the mitochondrial DNA (mtDNA) of various populations, Rebecca Cann, Mark Stoneking, and Allan C. Wilson (1987) concluded that humans are genetically uniform overall, suggesting recent common ancestry. The fact that African populations are the most diverse genetically provides evidence that Africa was the site where the human diaspora originated (see also Fairbanks 2015).

Contemporary work in genomics has allowed scientists to construct regional and global phylogenetic trees based on shared genetic markers. Such trees can be based on mtDNA (sampling females) and the Y chromosome (sampling males). As the human genome becomes better known, molecular anthropologists refine their models of genetic relationships among human groups (see Stoneking 2015). A **haplogroup** is a lineage or branch of such a genetic tree marked by one or more specific genetic mutations. For example, the global mtDNA tree includes branches known as M and N (among others). The Y chromosome tree includes branches known as C and F (among others). Those four branches (either M or N for

haplogroup
Lineage or branch of a genetic tree marked by one or more specific genetic mutations.

mtDNA and either C or F for the Y chromosome) are known to be associated with the spread of modern humans out of Africa between 70,000 and 50,000 B.P. Because Native Australians share those four branches, they are known to be part of that diaspora. The Americas were settled (from Asia) much later than Australia by multiple haplogroups, which reached North America at different times and came by different routes.

Although long-term genetic markers do exist, they do not correlate neatly with phenotypical similarities and differences. Because of changes in the environment that affect individuals during growth and development, the range of phenotypes characteristic of a population may change without any genetic change whatsoever. There are several examples. In the early 20th century, the anthropologist Franz Boas (1940/1966) described changes in skull form (e.g., toward rounder heads) among the children of Europeans who had migrated to North America. The reason for this was not a change in genes, for the European immigrants tended to marry among themselves. In addition, some of their children had been born in Europe and merely raised in the United States. Something in the environment, probably in the diet, was producing this change. From observations in the Americas, Europe, and Japan, we know now that changes in average height and weight produced by dietary differences in a few generations are common and may have nothing to do with "race" or genetics.

The AAA RACE Project

To broaden public understanding of human diversity, the American Anthropological Association (AAA) offers its RACE Project, which includes an award-winning public education program titled RACE Are We So Different? This program, whose intended audience is middle-school-aged children through adults, includes an interactive website and a traveling museum exhibit. You can visit the interactive website right now at www. understandingrace.org/home.html. The museum exhibit may be showing somewhere near you. For its touring schedule visit this website: www. understandingrace.org/about/tour.html.

RACE Are We So Different? examines the race concept through the eyes of history, science, and lived experience (see Goodman et al. 2013 for a collection of essays related to the project). It explains how human variation differs from race, when and why the idea of race was invented, and how race and racism affect our everyday lives. The program's three key messages are that (1) race is a recent human invention, (2) race is about culture, not biology, and (3) race and racism are embedded in institutions and everyday life (see also Gravlee 2009; Hartigan 2013).

In addition to its RACE project, the AAA has issued a statement on race, which is reprinted as

This young Syrian refugee arrived in Turkey in January 2014.

© David Gross/ZUMA Press/Newscom

this chapter's "Appreciating Anthropology." It discusses the social construction of race, for example, under colonialism. The AAA statement also stresses that inequalities among "racial" groups are not consequences of their biological inheritance but products of social, economic, educational, and political circumstances (see also Hartigan 2015).

HUMAN BIOLOGICAL ADAPTATION

Traditional racial classification assumed that biological characteristics such as skin color were determined by heredity and that they were stable (immutable) over many generations. We now know that a biological similarity does not necessarily indicate recent common ancestry. Tropical Africans and southern Indians, for example, can share dark skin color for reasons other than common ancestry. Scientists have made considerable progress in explaining variation in human skin color, along with many other features of human biological diversity (see Relethford 2009). We shift now from racial classification to explanation, in which natural selection plays a key role.

Explaining Skin Color

How has natural selection affected human skin color? Natural selection, remember, is the process by which the forms most fit to survive and reproduce in a given environment do so. Over the generations, the less fit organisms die out, and the favored types survive by producing more offspring. The role of natural selection in producing variation in skin color will illustrate the explanatory approach to human biological diversity. Explanations for many other aspects of human biological variation are provided later in this chapter.

Skin color is a complex biological trait—influenced by several genes (see Jablonski 2006, 2012). **Melanin,** the primary determinant of human skin color, is a chemical substance manufactured in the epidermis, or outer skin layer. The melanin cells of darker-skinned people produce more and larger granules of melanin than do those of lighter-skinned people. By screening out ultraviolet (UV) radiation from the sun, melanin offers protection against a variety of maladies, including sunburn and skin cancer. It is advantageous to have lots of melanin if one lives in the tropics, where UV radiation is intense.

Before the 16th century, most of the world's very dark-skinned peoples did live in the **tropics,** a belt extending about 23 degrees north and south of the equator, between the Tropic of Cancer and the Tropic of Capricorn. The association between dark skin color and a tropical habitat existed throughout the Old World, where humans and their ancestors have lived for millions of years.

Before the 16th century, almost all the very dark-skinned populations of the world lived in the tropics, as does this Samburu woman from Kenya.
© Jan Spieczny/Photolibrary/Getty Images

Princess Madeleine of Sweden at the wedding of Sweden's Crown Princess Victoria and Daniel Westling at the Stockholm Cathedral. Very light skin color, illustrated in this photo, maximizes absorption of ultraviolet radiation by those few parts of the body exposed to direct sunlight during northern winters.
© Antony Jones/Julian Parker/Mark Cuthbert/UK Press via Getty Images

melanin
"Natural sunscreen" produced by skin cells responsible for pigmentation.

tropics
Zone between 23 degrees north (Tropic of Cancer) and 23 degrees south (Tropic of Capricorn) of the equator.

appreciating **ANTHROPOLOGY**

What's Wrong with Race?

Anthropologists have a lot to say about the race concept. There is considerable public confusion about the meaning and relevance of "race," and false claims about biological differences among "races" continue to be advanced. Stemming from previous actions by the American Anthropological Association (AAA) designed to address public misconceptions about race and intelligence, the need was apparent for a clear AAA statement on the biology and politics of race that would be educational and informational (see also www.understandingrace.org).

The following statement was adopted by the AAA Executive Board, based on a draft prepared by a committee of representative anthropologists. This statement represents the thinking and scholarly positions of most anthropologists, including me—your textbook author.

In the United States both scholars and the general public have been conditioned to viewing human races as natural and separate divisions within the human species based on visible physical differences. With the vast expansion of scientific knowledge in this century, however, it has become clear that human populations are not unambiguous, clearly demarcated, biologically distinct groups. Evidence from the analysis of genetics (e.g., DNA) indicates that most physical variation, about 94%, lies within so-called racial groups. Conventional geographic "racial" groupings differ from one another only in about 6% of

their genes. This means that there is greater variation within "racial" groups than between them. In neighboring populations there is much overlapping of genes and their phenotypic (physical) expressions. Throughout history whenever different groups have come into contact, they have interbred. The continued sharing of genetic materials has maintained all of humankind as a single species.

Physical variations in any given trait tend to occur gradually rather than abruptly over geographic areas. And because physical traits are inherited independently of one another, knowing the range of one trait does not predict the presence of others. For example, skin color varies largely from light in the temperate areas in the north to dark in the tropical areas in the south; its intensity is not related to nose shape or hair texture. Dark skin may be associated with frizzy or kinky hair or curly or wavy or straight hair, all of which are found among different indigenous peoples in tropical regions. These facts render any attempt to establish lines of division among biological populations both arbitrary and subjective.

Historical research has shown that the idea of "race" has always carried more meanings than mere physical differences; indeed, physical variations in the human species have no meaning except the social ones that humans put on them. Today scholars in many fields argue that "race" as it is understood in the United States of America was a social mechanism invented during the

18th century to refer to those populations brought together in colonial America: the English and other European settlers, the conquered Indian (Native American) peoples, and those peoples of Africa brought in to provide slave labor.

From its inception, this modern concept of "race" was modeled after an ancient theorem of the Great Chain of Being, which posited natural categories on a hierarchy established by God or nature. Thus "race" was a mode of classification linked specifically to peoples in the colonial situation. It subsumed a growing ideology of inequality devised to rationalize European attitudes and treatment of the conquered and enslaved peoples. Proponents of slavery in particular during the 19th century used "race" to justify the retention of slavery. The ideology magnified the differences among Europeans, Africans, and Indians (Native Americans), established a rigid hierarchy of socially exclusive categories, underscored and bolstered unequal rank and status differences, and provided the rationalization that the inequality was natural or God-given. The different physical traits of African-Americans and Indians (Native Americans) became markers or symbols of their status differences.

As they were constructing US society, leaders among European-Americans fabricated the cultural/behavioral characteristics associated with each "race," linking superior traits with Europeans and negative and inferior ones to blacks and Indians (Native Americans). Numerous

The darkest populations of Africa evolved not in shady equatorial forests but in sunny open grassland, or savanna, country.

Outside the tropics, skin color tends to be lighter. Moving north in Africa, for example, there is a gradual transition from dark brown to medium brown. Average skin color continues to lighten as one moves through the Middle East,

into southern Europe, through central Europe, and to the north. South of the Old World tropic, skin color also is lighter. In the Americas, however, tropical populations do not have very dark skin. This is true because the settlement of the New World by light-skinned Asian ancestors of Native Americans was relatively recent, probably dating back no more than 20,000 years.

96   PART 2   Biological Anthropology and Archaeology

arbitrary and fictitious beliefs about the different peoples were institutionalized and deeply embedded in American thought. . . .

Ultimately "race" as an ideology about human differences was subsequently spread to other areas of the world. It became a strategy for dividing, ranking, and controlling colonized people used by colonial powers everywhere. But it was not limited to the colonial situation. In the latter part of the 19th century it was employed by Europeans to rank one another and to justify social, economic, and political inequalities among their peoples. During World War II, the Nazis under Adolf Hitler enjoined the expanded ideology of "race" and "racial" differences and took them to a logical end: the extermination of 11 million people of "inferior races" (e.g., Jews, Gypsies, Africans, homosexuals, and so forth) and other unspeakable brutalities of the Holocaust.

"Race" thus evolved as a world view, a body of prejudgments that distorts our ideas about human differences and group behavior. Racial beliefs constitute myths about the diversity in the human species and about the abilities and behavior of people homogenized into "racial" categories. The myths fused behavior and physical features together in the public mind, impeding our comprehension of both biological variations and cultural behavior, implying that both are genetically determined. Racial myths bear no relationship to the reality of human capabilities or behavior. . . .

We now understand that human cultural behavior is learned, conditioned into infants beginning at birth, and always subject to modification. No human is born with a built-in culture or language. Our temperaments, dispositions, and personalities, regardless of genetic propensities, are developed within sets of meanings and values that we call "culture." . . .

This photo, taken near Bucharest, Romania, shows a Rom (Gypsy) woman standing in front of another woman as she holds her baby daughter. Gypsies (Rom or Roma) have faced discrimination in many nations. During World War II, the Nazis led by Adolf Hitler murdered 11 million Jews, Gypsies, Africans, homosexuals, and others.
© Peter Turnley/Corbis

It is a basic tenet of anthropological knowledge that all normal human beings have the capacity to learn any cultural behavior. The American experience with immigrants from hundreds of different language and cultural backgrounds who have acquired some version of American culture traits and behavior is the clearest evidence of this fact. Moreover, people of all physical variations have learned different cultural behaviors and continue to do so as modern transportation moves millions of immigrants around the world.

How people have been accepted and treated within the context of a given society or culture has a direct impact on how they perform in that society. The "racial" world view was invented to assign some groups to perpetual low status, while others were permitted access to privilege, power, and wealth. The tragedy in the United States has been that the policies and practices stemming from this world view succeeded all too well in constructing unequal populations among Europeans, Native Americans, and peoples of African descent. Given what we know about the capacity of normal humans to achieve and function within any culture, we conclude that present-day inequalities between so-called "racial" groups are not consequences of their biological inheritance but products of historical and contemporary social, economic, educational, and political circumstances.

SOURCE: From the American Anthropological Association (AAA) Statement on "Race" (May 1998). American Anthropological Association, 1998.

How, aside from recent migrations, can we explain the geographic distribution of human skin color? Natural selection provides an answer. In the tropics, intense UV radiation poses a series of threats, including severe sunburn, which make light skin color an adaptive disadvantage (Recap 6.1 summarizes those threats). By damaging sweat glands, sunburn reduces the body's ability to perspire and thus to regulate its own temperature. Sunburn also can increase susceptibility to disease. Yet another disadvantage of having light skin color in the tropics is that exposure to UV radiation can cause skin cancer. Melanin, nature's own sunscreen, confers a selective advantage (i.e., a better chance to survive and reproduce) on darker-skinned people living in the tropics.

Also shown are cultural alternatives that can make up for biological disadvantages and examples of natural selection (NS) operating today in relation to skin color.

		CULTURAL ALTERNATIVES	NS IN ACTION TODAY
DARK SKIN COLOR	Melanin is natural sunscreen.		
Advantage	In tropics: screens out UV radiation		
	Reduces susceptibility to folate destruction and thus to neural tube defects (NTDs), including spina bifida		
	Prevents sunburn and thus enhances sweating and temperature regulation		
	Reduces disease susceptibility		
	Reduces risk of skin cancer		
Disadvantage	Outside tropics: reduces UV absorption		
	Increases susceptibility to rickets, osteoporosis	Foods, vitamin D supplements	East Asians in northern UK Inuit with modern diets
LIGHT SKIN COLOR	No natural sunscreen		
Advantage	Outside tropics: admits UV		
	Body manufactures vitamin D and thus prevents rickets and osteoporosis		
Disadvantage	Increases susceptibility to folate destruction and thus to NTDs, including spina bifida	Folic acid/folate supplements	Whites still have more NTDs
	Impaired spermatogenesis		
	Increases susceptibility to sunburn and thus to impaired sweating and poor temperature regulation	Shelter, sunscreens, lotions, etc.	
	Increases disease susceptibility		
	Increases susceptibility to skin cancer		

(Today, there are cultural alternatives that allow people with various skin colors to live wherever they choose. Thus, light-skinned people can survive in the tropics by staying indoors and by using cultural products, such as umbrellas and lotions, to screen sunlight.) Outside the tropics, however, melanin's role in blocking UV radiation can become a selective disadvantage.

Many years ago, W. F. Loomis (1967) focused on the role of UV radiation in stimulating the manufacture of vitamin D by the human body. The unclothed human body can produce its own vitamin D when exposed to sufficient sunlight. However, in a cloudy environment that also is so cold that people have to wear clothes much of the year (such as northern Europe, where very light skin color evolved), clothing interferes with the body's manufacture of vitamin D, as does having too much melanin in one's skin. The ensuing shortage of vitamin D diminishes the absorption of calcium in the intestines. A nutritional disease known as **rickets,** which softens and deforms the bones, may develop. In women, deformation of the pelvic bones from rickets can interfere with childbirth. In cold northern areas, light skin color maximizes the absorption of

UV radiation and the manufacture of vitamin D by the few parts of the body that are exposed to direct sunlight during northern winters. There has been selection against dark skin color in northern areas because melanin screens out UV radiation.

This natural selection continues today: East Asians who have migrated recently from India and Pakistan to northern areas of the United Kingdom have a higher incidence of rickets and osteoporosis (also related to vitamin D and calcium deficiency) than the general British population. A related example involves Eskimos (Inuit) and other indigenous inhabitants of northern Alaska and northern Canada. According to Nina Jablonski (quoted in Iqbal 2002), "Looking at Alaska, one would think that the native people should be pale as ghosts" (to maximize their UV absorption and vitamin D). One reason they are not pale is that they haven't inhabited this region very long in terms of geological time. Even more important, their traditional diet, rich in fish oils, supplied sufficient vitamin D to make a reduction in pigmentation unnecessary. (This is another example of how a cultural alternative can help overcome a disadvantageous biological trait.) However, and

rickets
Vitamin D deficiency marked by bone deformation.

again illustrating natural selection at work today, "when these people don't eat their aboriginal diets of fish and marine mammals, they suffer tremendously high rates of vitamin D–deficiency diseases such as rickets in children and osteoporosis in adults" (Jablonski quoted in Iqbal 2002). Far from being immutable, skin color can become an evolutionary liability very quickly.

According to Jablonski and George Chaplin (2000; see also Jablonski 2006, 2012), another way in which natural selection has affected human skin color involves the effects of UV radiation on folate, an essential nutrient that the human body manufactures from folic acid. Humans require folate for cell division and the production of new DNA. Pregnant women require large amounts of folate to support rapid cell division in the embryo, and there is a direct connection between folate and individual reproductive success. Folate deficiency causes neural tube defects (NTDs) in human embryos. NTDs are marked by the incomplete closure of the neural tube, so the spine and spinal cord fail to develop completely. One NTD, anencephaly (with the brain an exposed mass), results in stillbirth or death soon after delivery. With spina bifida, another NTD, survival rates are higher, but babies have severe disabilities, including paralysis. NTDs are the second most common human birth defect after cardiac abnormalities.

Spina bifida, a congenital (birth) disorder that leaves a portion of the spinal cord exposed, can be treated with surgery and physiotherapy. Shown here is an outing, including fishing, for children with spina bifida in Lee's Summit, Missouri. Why is light skin color correlated with a higher incidence of spina bifida?

© Brent Frazee/Kansas City Star/MCT via Getty Images

Dark skin color, as we have seen, is adaptive in the tropics because it protects against such UV hazards as sunburn and its consequences. UV radiation also destroys folate in the human body. By blocking UV and thus preventing this destruction, melanin helps conserve folate, thus protecting against NTDs, (Jablonski and Chaplin 2000). Africans and African Americans rarely experience severe folate deficiency, which primarily affects light-skinned people. Folate also plays a role in another process that is central to reproduction, spermatogenesis—the production of sperm. In mice and rats, folate deficiency can cause male sterility; it may well play a similar role in humans.

Today, of course, cultural alternatives to biological adaptation allow light-skinned people to survive in the tropics and darker-skinned people to live in the far north. Light-skinned people can clothe themselves seek shelter from the sun, and use artificial sunscreens. Dark-skinned people living in the north can, indeed must, get vitamin D from their diet or take supplements. Today, pregnant women are routinely advised to take folic acid or folate supplements as a hedge against NTDs. Even so, light skin color still is correlated with a higher incidence of spina bifida.

Jablonski and Chaplin (2000) explain variation in human skin color as resulting from a balancing act between the evolutionary needs to (1) protect against all UV hazards (thus favoring dark skin in the tropics) and (2) have an adequate supply of vitamin D (thus favoring lighter skin outside the tropics). This discussion of skin color shows that common ancestry, the presumed basis of race, is not the only reason for biological similarities. Natural selection, still at work today, makes a major contribution to variations in human skin color.

Facial Features

Natural selection also affects facial features. For instance, long noses seem to be adaptive in arid areas (Brace 2005), because membranes and blood vessels inside the nose moisten the air as it is breathed in. Long noses also are adaptive in cold environments, because blood vessels warm the air as it is breathed in. This form of nose distances the brain, which is sensitive to bitter cold, from raw outer air. These were adaptive biological features for humans who lived in cold climates before the invention of central heating.

The association between nose form and temperature is recognized as **Thomson's nose rule** (Thomson and Buxton 1923), which shows up statistically. In plotting the geographic distribution of nose length among human populations who have lived for many generations in the areas they now inhabit, the average nose tends to be longer in areas with lower mean annual temperatures.

Other facial features also illustrate adaptation to selective forces. Among contemporary humans, average tooth size is largest among Native

Thomson's nose rule
Average nose length increases in cold areas.

Australian hunters and gatherers, for whom large teeth had an adaptive advantage, given a diet based on foods with a considerable amount of sand and grit. People with small teeth—if false teeth and sand-free foods are unavailable—cannot feed themselves as effectively as people with more massive dentition can (see Brace 2005).

Size and Body Build

Certain body types have adaptive advantages for particular environments. In 1847, the German biologist Karl Christian Bergmann observed that

The Maasai (or Masai) are a Nilotic ethnic group of seminomadic people located in Kenya and northern Tanzania.

© Antonio Ciufo/Flickr Vision/Getty Images

In Nunavut, Canada, on the western shore of Hudson Bay, this Inuit couple wear traditional arctic attire in front of a caribou hide tent.

© Cindy Hopkins/Alamy Stock Photo

within the same species of warm-blooded animals, populations with smaller individuals are more often found in warm climates, while those with greater bulk, or mass, live in colder regions. **Bergmann's rule** states the following relation between body weight and temperature: The smaller of two bodies similar in shape has more surface area per unit of weight. Therefore, it sheds heat more efficiently. (Heat loss occurs on the body's surface—the skin perspires.) Average body size tends to increase in cold areas and to decrease in hot ones because big bodies hold heat better than small ones do. To be more precise, in a study of a large sample of native populations, average adult male weight increased by 0.66 pound (0.3 kilogram) for every 1 degree Fahrenheit fall in mean annual temperature (Roberts 1953; Steegman 1975). The "pygmies" and the San, who live in hot climates and weigh only 90 pounds on the average, illustrate this relation in reverse.

Body shape differences also reflect adaptation to temperature through natural selection. The zoologist J. A. Allen in 1877 recognized the relationship between temperature and body shape in animals and birds. **Allen's rule** states that the relative size of protruding body parts—ears, tails, bills, fingers, toes, limbs, and so on—increases with temperature. Among humans, slender bodies with long digits and limbs are advantageous in tropical climates. Such bodies increase body surface relative to mass and allow for more efficient heat dissipation. An opposite phenotype characterizes the cold-adapted Eskimos or Inuit. Their short limbs and stocky bodies conserve heat. Cold-area populations tend to have larger chests and shorter arms than do people from warm areas (Roberts 1953).

This discussion of adaptive relationships between climate and body size and shape illustrates that natural selection may achieve the same effect in different ways. East African Nilotes, who live in a hot area, have tall, linear bodies with elongated extremities that increase surface area relative to mass and thus maximize heat dissipation (illustrating Allen's rule). Among the "pygmies," the reduction of body size achieves the same result (illustrating Bergmann's rule). Similarly, the large bodies of northern Europeans and the compact stockiness of the Inuit serve the same function of heat conservation.

Genes and Disease

The remainder of this chapter examines additional examples of human biological diversity that reflect adaptation to environmental stresses, including disease, diet, and climate. There is abundant evidence for human genetic adaptation and thus for evolution (change in gene frequency) through selection working in specific environments. One example is the adaptive value of the Hb^S heterozygote in malarial environments. Adaptation and evolution go on in specific environments. There is no generally or ideally adaptive allele and no perfect phenotype. Nor can we assume that a given allele will be maladaptive for all times and all places. We have seen that even Hb^S, which produces a lethal anemia, has a selective advantage in the heterozygous form in malarial environments. Furthermore, alleles that once were maladaptive can lose their disadvantage if the environment shifts. Today's environment includes medical techniques that allow many people with many genetic disorders to live normal lives.

As food production (farming and herding) spread about 10,000 years ago, infectious diseases posed a mounting risk. Food production supports larger, denser populations and a more sedentary lifestyle than does hunting and gathering. People live closer to each other and to their own wastes, making it easier for microbes to survive and to find hosts. Domesticated animals also transmit diseases to people.

Until 1979, when the last case was reported, smallpox had been a major threat to humans and a determinant of blood group frequencies (Diamond 1990, 1997). The smallpox virus is a mutation from one of the pox viruses found in such domesticated animals as cows, sheep, goats, horses, and pigs. Smallpox appeared in human beings after people and animals started living together. Smallpox epidemics have played important roles in world history, often killing one-fourth to one-half of the affected populations. Smallpox contributed to Sparta's defeat of Athens in 430 B.C.E. and to the decline of the Roman Empire after C.E. 160.

Having a particular ABO blood type may confer resistance to certain microbes, including smallpox. In the ABO system, blood is typed according to the protein and sugar compounds on the surface of the red blood cells. Different substances (compounds) distinguish between type A and type B blood. The compounds on type A cells trigger the production of *antibodies* in type B blood, so that A cells clot in B blood (and vice versa). The different substances work like chemical passwords; they help us distinguish our own cells from invading cells, including microbes we ought to destroy. The surfaces of some microbes have compounds similar to ABO blood group compounds. We don't produce antibodies to compounds similar to those on our own blood cells.

It turns out that people with A or AB blood are more susceptible to smallpox than are people with type B or type O. Presumably this is because a compound on the smallpox virus mimics the type A compound, permitting the virus to slip by the defenses of a type A individual. By contrast, type B and type O individuals produce antibodies against smallpox because they recognize it as a foreign compound.

The relation between type A blood and susceptibility to smallpox was first suggested by the low

In New York City in 1947, the appearance of nine cases of smallpox, including two deaths, spurred a very successful mass vaccination program. Shown here, lines of people wait to be vaccinated at the New York Health Department on April 14, 1947. The threat made the cover of *Cosmopolitan* magazine.

Top: © Tony Camerano/ AP Images; bottom: SOURCE: NIH History of Medicine Divison, U.S. National Library of Medicine

frequencies of the A allele in areas of India and Africa where smallpox had been endemic. A comparative study done in rural India during a virulent smallpox epidemic did much to confirm this relationship. Drs. F. Vogel and M. R. Chakravartti analyzed blood samples from smallpox victims and their uninfected siblings (Diamond 1990). The researchers focused on 415 infected children, none ever vaccinated against smallpox. All but eight of these children had an uninfected (also unvaccinated) sibling.

A Devastating Encounter in the Columbian Exchange

The Columbian exchange (named for Christopher Columbus) was a key early form of globalization, because it forever linked our globe's Western and Eastern Hemispheres. The term refers to the exchange of products, populations, and pathogens between the Old World and the New World that occurred after Columbus reached the Americas in 1492.

One devastating aspect of the Columbian exchange was the global spread of diseases previously confined to the Old World. Having lived with these pathogens for generations, Old World populations had developed various forms of immunity to many of them. Native Americans had no such resistance to Old World diseases, which included smallpox, chicken pox, measles, malaria, yellow fever, cholera, typhoid, bubonic plague, influenza, and the common cold. Only syphilis moved the other way—from the New World to the Old.

By debilitating and decimating the Aztecs of Mexico and the Inca of Peru, severe smallpox epidemics helped the Spanish conquer those peoples and their territories. Up to 90 percent of the population of the New World may have perished from Old World pathogens between 1500 and 1650 (Nunn and Qian 2010).

The African slave trade emerged in the context of Native American depopulation and the demand for human labor to produce commodities on New World plantations. Plantation economies outside the southern United States (where cotton was a New World domesticate) grew mainly on Old World crops (especially sugar and tobacco) introduced to the Americas and the Caribbean as part of the Columbian exchange. About 12 million enslaved human beings were transported involuntarily from Africa to the New World during the centuries of the Atlantic slave trade—the 16th through the 19th centuries.

Europeans from Spain, Portugal, the Netherlands, England, and France extended their colonial empires from the Americas to Africa and Asia. Europeans had a degree of genetic resistance to many Old World pathogens, but not to malaria—the scourge of the tropics. Quinine was a New World product that—again through the Columbian exchange—eventually offered Europeans a degree of protection against malaria. Europeans might never have been able to maintain colonial empires in the tropics of Africa, Asia, and South America without quinine (Nunn and Qian 2010). Western expansion, and ultimately the formation of the modern world system, depended on the Columbian exchange.

Globalization remains an important factor in the spread of diseases today, as anyone knows who has seen the movie *World War Z* or *Contagion*. The spread of pathogens, such as H1N1, or swine flu, from animals (such as pigs, or swine) to humans became more common after people began living in proximity to domesticated pigs, poultry, sheep, and cattle. These animals, originally domesticated in the Old World, now have a global distribution. How have humans adapted to the diseases their animals transmit?

The results of the study were clear: Susceptibility to smallpox varied with ABO type. Of the 415 infected children, 261 had the A allele; 154 lacked it. Among their 407 uninfected siblings, the ratio was reversed. Only 80 had the A allele; 327 lacked it. The researchers calculated that a type A or type AB person had a seven times greater chance of getting smallpox than did an O or B person.

In most human populations, the O allele is more common than A and B combined. Type A is most common in Europe; type B frequencies are highest in Asia. Since smallpox was once widespread in the Old World, we might wonder why natural selection did not eliminate the A allele entirely. The answer appears to be this: Other diseases spared the type A people and penalized those with other blood groups.

For example, type O people seem to be especially susceptible to bubonic plague. Type O people also are more likely to get cholera, which has killed as many people in India as smallpox has. On the other hand, the O allele may protect against syphilis, which originated in the New World. Frequencies of type O blood are very high among the native populations of Central and South America. The distribution of human blood groups appears to represent a compromise among the selective effects of many diseases.

In the case of diseases for which there are no known cures, genetic resistance maintains its significance (see Hartigan 2013). There is genetic variation in susceptibility to the HIV virus, for example. Longitudinal studies have shown that people exposed to HIV vary in their risk of developing AIDS and in the rate at which the disease progresses.

As an interesting case of what we might call fortuitous preadaptation or preselection, consider the *CCR5* gene. This gene, which codes for a chemical receptor protein on the surface of white blood cells, is involved in the human immune system. The viral infection HIV uses the *CCR5* receptor to invade and infect cells. But individuals who are homozygous for an allele known as *CCR5-Δ32* (*delta 32*) are resistant to this invasion. This HIV immunity illustrates preadaptation or preselection, because the original selection for the allele had nothing to do with HIV. The allele was adaptive and spread because of the resistance it offered against deadly epidemics that occurred much earlier in European history.

The *CCR5-Δ32* allele is found in between 3 and 14 percent of Europeans, but it is absent in Africans, East Asians, and Native Americans. Among Europeans, the allele is most common in Scandinavia and Russia and least common near the Mediterranean. Susan Scott and Christopher Duncan (2004) argue that most of the lethal epidemics that ravaged Europe between 1347 and 1660 were not bubonic plague (a bacterial infection), as is commonly thought. Instead, they involved a lethal, viral, hemorrhagic fever that used the *CCR5* receptor gene to invade (and usually kill) its human hosts. Hemorrhagic fever disappeared from England after London's Great Plague of 1665–1666, but it continued through 1800 in Sweden, Denmark, Russia, Poland, and Hungary. Given the persistent hemorrhagic plague threat, selection for *CCR5-Δ32* continued in those countries, where it has its highest frequencies (see Relethford 2012, p. 368). Others have suggested a link between the spread of *CCR5-Δ32* and resistance to smallpox. Whatever the disease may have been that favored this allele to begin with, it is clear that it is merely by lucky chance that *CCR5-Δ32* also confers resistance to HIV and AIDS.

Genetic variation no doubt will help determine differential resistance and susceptibility to microbes that may emerge or mutate in the future. (This chapter's "Focus on Globalization" discusses the global spread of infectious diseases.)

Lactose Tolerance

Many biological traits that illustrate human adaptation are not under simple genetic control. Genetic determination of such traits may be only partial, or several genes may work or interact to influence the trait in question. Sometimes there is a known genetic component but the trait also responds to stresses encountered during growth. We speak of **phenotypical adaptation** when adaptive changes occur during an individual's lifetime. Phenotypical adaptation is made possible by biological plasticity—our ability to change in response to the environments we encounter as we grow (see Cameron and Bogin 2012).

One genetically determined biochemical difference among human groups involves the ability to digest large amounts of milk—an adaptive advantage when other foods are scarce and milk is available, as it is in dairying societies. Milk contains a complex sugar called *lactose,* and the digestion of milk depends on an enzyme called *lactase,* which works in the small intestine. Among all mammals except humans and some of their pets, lactase production ceases after weaning, so that these animals can no longer digest milk.

Lactase production and the ability to tolerate milk vary between populations. About 90 percent of northern Europeans and their descendants are lactose tolerant; they can digest several glasses of milk with no difficulty. Similarly, about 80 percent of two African populations, the Tutsi of Rwanda and Burundi in East Africa and the Fulani of Nigeria in West Africa, produce lactase and digest milk easily. Both of these groups traditionally have been herders. However, such nonherders as the Yoruba and the Igbo in Nigeria, the Baganda in Uganda, the Japanese and other Asians, Inuit, South American Indians, and many Israelis cannot digest lactose (Kretchmer 1972/1975).

Recent genetic studies have helped clarify when and how humans developed lactose tolerance (see Mielke, Konigsberg, and Relethford 2011). An allele known to favor adult lactose tolerance existed, but still was uncommon, in central and eastern Europe as recently as 3,800 years ago (Burger et al. 2007). Sarah Tishkoff and her associates found that the alleles behind lactose tolerance in East Africans differ from those of lactose-tolerant Europeans. Her genetic studies of 43 East African groups suggested that three different mutations favoring lactose tolerance arose in Africa between 6,800 and 2,700 years ago (Tishkoff et al. 2007). Again we see that the same phenotype—in this case, lactose tolerance—can be produced by different genotypes. It also should be noted that the variable human ability to digest milk seems to be a difference of degree. Some populations can tolerate very little or no milk, but others arc able to metabolize much greater quantities. People who move from no-milk or low-milk diets to high-milk diets can increase their lactose tolerance; this suggests some phenotypical adaptation.

Human biology changes constantly, even without genetic change. In this chapter, we've considered several ways in which humans adapt biologically to their environments, and the effects of such adaptation on human biological diversity. Modern biological anthropology seeks to explain specific aspects of human biological variation. The explanatory framework encompasses the same mechanisms—selection, mutation, drift, gene flow, and plasticity—that govern adaptation, variation, and evolution among other life forms.

phenotypical adaptation
Adaptive biological changes during an individual's lifetime.

for REVIEW

1. Humans have access to varied ways—biological and cultural—of adapting to environmental stresses, such as disease, heat, cold, humidity, sunlight, and altitude. Biological diversity among contemporary and prehistoric humans has many causes. This chapter examines those causes, while rejecting attempts to pigeonhole humans into discrete biological categories called races.

summary

2. How do scientists approach the study of human biological diversity? Because of a range of problems involved in classifying humans into racial categories, contemporary biologists focus on specific differences and try to explain them. Because of extensive gene flow and interbreeding, *Homo sapiens* has not evolved subspecies, or distinct races. The genetic breaks that do exist among human populations have not led to the formation of discrete races.

3. Biological similarities between groups may reflect—rather than common ancestry—similar but independent adaptations to similar natural selective forces, such as degrees of ultraviolet radiation from the sun in the case of skin color.

4. Differential resistance to infectious diseases such as smallpox has influenced the distribution of human blood groups. There are genetic anti-malarials, such as the sickle-cell allele. Natural selection also has operated on facial features and body size and shape.

5. *Phenotypical adaptation* refers to adaptive changes that occur in an individual's lifetime in response to the environment the organism encounters as it grows. Biological similarities between geographically distant populations may be due to similar but independent genetic changes, rather than to common ancestry. Alternatively, they may reflect similar physiological responses to common stresses during growth. In addition, human populations have developed different but equally effective ways of adapting to environmental conditions such as heat, cold, and UV radiation.

key terms

Allen's rule 100

Bergmann's rule 100

cline 91

haplogroup 94

melanin 95

phenotypical adaptation 103

racial classification 90

rickets 98

Thomson's nose rule 99

tropics 95

critical thinking

1. Describe three problems with human racial classification.

2. What explains skin color in humans? Are the processes that determined skin color in humans still continuing today? If so, what are some examples of this?

3. Consider the "American Anthropological Association Statement on Race" (http://www.aaanet.org/stmts/racepp.htm). (This chapter's "Appreciating Anthropology" offers an abridged version of that statement.) What is its main argument? Why was such a public statement by this institution necessary?

4. If "race" is a discredited concept when applied to humans, what has replaced it?

5. Choose five people in your classroom who illustrate a range of phenotypical diversity. Which of their features vary most evidently? How do you explain this variation? Is some of the variation due to culture rather than to biology?

The Primates

- ▶ How closely are the main primate groups related to one another and to humans?

- ▶ Why should the study of monkeys and apes be of interest to anthropologists?

- ▶ When, where, and how did the first primates, monkeys, apes, and hominins evolve?

© C.O. Mercial/Alamy Stock Photo

In the Muenster, Germany zoo, a gorilla mother holds her nine-week-old baby, while Dad looks on.

understanding OURSELVES

Think about our senses—vision, hearing, touch, taste, and smell. Which are you using right now? Which do you most depend upon to navigate the world? Like almost all other anthropoids (humanlike primates)—a group that includes monkeys, humans, and apes—humans are diurnal, or active during the day. As animals, we are programmed to rise at dawn and to sleep when the sun goes down. As cultural creatures, we venture into the night with torches, lanterns, and flashlights and shut the dark out of our dwellings with artificial light. If we were night animals, we'd sense things differently. Our eyes might be bigger, like those of an owl or a tarsier. Maybe we'd have biological radar systems, as bats do. Perhaps we'd develop a more acute sense of hearing or smell to penetrate the dark.

Many animals rely upon scents and odors to help them interpret the world. Humans, by contrast, use an array of products to cover up or eliminate even the faint odors our limited olfactory apparatus permits us to smell. *Blindness* and *deafness* are common words that indicate the senses whose loss we deem most significant. The rarity of the word *anosmia,* the inability to smell, tells us something about our senses and our values. The sensory shifts that occurred in primate evolution, especially the one from smell to sight, explain something fundamental about ourselves.

How different are we from other primates? No human looks much like a lemur or a tarsier. That's understandable; our ancestries diverged more than 50 million years ago. We're much more closely related to, and look more like, our fellow anthropoids—monkeys and apes. Within this group, we are much more similar to apes than to monkeys. Likewise, apes are more similar to humans than to monkeys. Still, in the popular imagination, humans associate apes with monkeys, rather than with themselves. At zoos, human parents say to their kids, "Look at the monkey," when they are seeing a chimp, a gorilla, or an orangutan. The national tabloids use phrases like "monkeying around" or "monkey see, monkey do" when reporting on stories that involve apes. We easily appreciate the monkey in the ape but not the ape in ourselves.

Still, the apes do fascinate us to some degree because of their humanlike qualities. Zoo gorillas are especially popular when they are displayed in "family" groups. The antics of orangutans and especially of chimps have been featured in movies and TV shows. The *Planet of the Apes* movies recognize both that apes are not monkeys and that apes are quite similar to us. Imagine a live-action film called *Planet of the Monkeys.* Where could a director find human actors who could locomote on four legs for an entire movie?

Primatology is the study of nonhuman primates—fossil and living apes, monkeys, tarsiers, lemurs, and lorises—including behavior and social life (see Campbell 2011; Strier 2014). Fascinating in itself, primatology also helps anthropologists make inferences about the early social organization and adaptive strategies of *hominids* (members of the family that includes fossil and living humans). Of particular relevance are two kinds of primates:

1. Those whose ecological adaptations are similar to our own: **terrestrial** monkeys and apes—that is, primates that live on the ground rather than in the trees.

2. Those that are most closely related to us: the great apes, specifically the chimpanzees and gorillas (see Schaik 2015).

OUR PLACE AMONG PRIMATES

Similarities between humans and apes are evident in anatomy, brain structure, genetics, and biochemistry. The physical similarities between humans and apes are recognized in zoological **taxonomy**—the assignment of organisms to categories (*taxa*; singular, *taxon*) according to their relationship and resemblance. Taxonomy is an important way of conceptualizing evolutionary, or phylogenetic, relationships. Many similarities between organisms reflect their common *phylogeny*—their genetic relatedness based on common ancestry. In other words, organisms share features they have inherited from the same ancestor. Humans and apes belong to the same taxonomic superfamily Hominoidea (hominoids). Monkeys are placed in two others (Ceboidea and Cercopithecoidea). Humans are placed in the same taxon as apes because humans and apes share a more recent common ancestry with each other than either does with monkeys.

Figure 7.1 summarizes the various levels of classification used in zoological taxonomy. Each lower-level unit belongs to the higher-level unit above it. Thus, toward the bottom of Figure 7.1, similar species belong to the same genus (plural, *genera*). Similar genera make up the same family, and so on through the top of Figure 7.1, where similar phyla (plural of *phylum*) are included in the same kingdom. The highest (most inclusive) taxonomic level is the *kingdom*. At that level, animals are distinguished from plants.

At the lowest level of taxonomy, a species may have subspecies. These are more or less—but not yet totally—isolated subgroups. Subspecies can coexist in time and space. For example, the Neandertals, who lived between 130,000 and 28,000 years ago, may have belonged not to a separate species but merely to a different subspecies of *Homo sapiens*. Just one subspecies of *Homo sapiens* survives today.

The similarities used to assign organisms to the same taxon are called **homologies,** similarities they have jointly inherited from a common ancestor. Table 7.1 summarizes the place of humans in zoological taxonomy. We see in Table 7.1 that we are mammals, members of the class Mammalia. This is a major subdivision of the kingdom Animalia. Mammals share certain traits, including mammary glands, that set them apart from other taxa, such as birds, reptiles, amphibians, and insects. Mammalian homologies indicate that all mammals share more recent common ancestry with each other than they do with any bird, reptile, or insect.

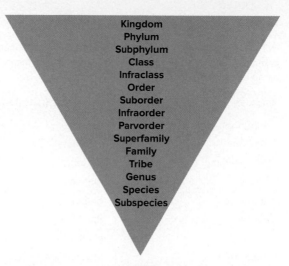

Kingdom
Phylum
Subphylum
Class
Infraclass
Order
Suborder
Infraorder
Parvorder
Superfamily
Family
Tribe
Genus
Species
Subspecies

FIGURE 7.1   The Principal Classificatory Units of Zoological Taxonomy.
Moving down the figure, the classificatory units become more exclusive, so that "Kingdom" at the top is the most inclusive unit and "Subspecies" at the bottom is the most exclusive.

Humans are mammals that, at a lower taxonomic level, belong to the *order* Primates. Another mammalian order is Carnivora: the carnivores (dogs, cats, foxes, wolves, badgers, weasels). Rodentia (rats, mice, beavers, squirrels) form yet another mammalian order. The primates share structural and biochemical homologies that distinguish them from other mammals. These resemblances were inherited from their common early primate ancestors after those early primates became reproductively isolated from the ancestors of the other mammals.

HOMOLOGIES AND ANALOGIES

Organisms are assigned to the same taxon on the basis of homologies. The extensive biochemical homologies between apes and humans confirm our common ancestry and support our traditional joint classification as hominoids (see Figure 7.2). For example, it is estimated that humans, chimpanzees, and gorillas have more than 98 percent of their DNA in common.

However, common ancestry isn't the only reason for similarities between species. Similar traits also can arise if species experience similar selective forces and adapt to them in similar ways. We call such similarities **analogies.** The process by which analogies are produced is called **convergent evolution.** For example, fish and porpoises share many analogies resulting from convergent evolution to life in the water. Like fish, porpoises, which are mammals, have fins. They also are hairless and streamlined for efficient locomotion. Analogies between birds and bats (wings, small

primatology
The study of apes, monkeys, tarsiers, lemurs, and lorises.

terrestrial
Ground-dwelling.

taxonomy
Classification scheme; assignment to categories (*taxa*; singular, *taxon*).

homologies
Traits inherited from a common ancestor.

analogies
Adaptive traits due to convergent evolution.

convergent evolution
Similar selective forces produce similar adaptive traits.

TABLE 7.1 The Place of Humans (*Homo sapiens*) in Zoological Taxonomy

Homo sapiens can be classified using these common names: *animal, chordate, vertebrate, mammal, eutherian, primate, haplorrhine, simian, catarrhine, hominoid, hominid, and hominin. (Figure 7.2 shows the taxonomic placement of the other primates.)*

TAXON	SCIENTIFIC (LATIN) NAME	COMMON (ENGLISH) NAME
Kingdom	Animalia	Animals
Phylum	Chordata	Chordates
Subphylum	Vertebrata	Vertebrates
Class	Mammalia	Mammals
Infraclass	Eutheria	Eutherians
Order	Primates	Primates
Suborder	Haplorrhini	Haplorrhines
Infraorder	Simiiformes	Simians ("Anthropoids")
Parvorder	Catarrhini	Catarrhines
Superfamily	Hominoidea	Hominoids
Family	Hominidae	Hominids
Tribe	Hominini	Hominins
Genus	*Homo*	Humans
Species	*Homo sapiens*	Recent humans
Subspecies	*Homo sapiens sapiens*	Anatomically modern humans

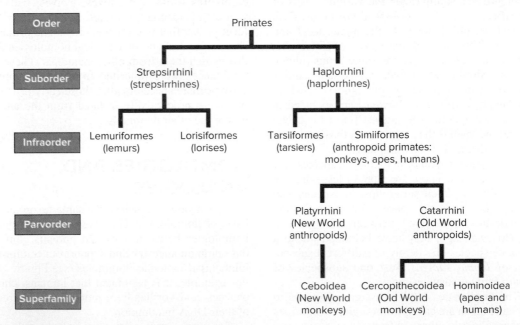

FIGURE 7.2 Classification of Primates.
Names within parentheses are common names.

size, light bones) illustrate convergent evolution to flying.

In theory, only homologies should be used in taxonomy. In the past, a reluctance to lump apes and humans too closely together resulted in placing chimps, gorillas, and orangs all together in the family *Pongidae* (the pongids). This placement, however, violates the rule that taxonomy should be based on recent common ancestry. There is absolutely no doubt that humans, gorillas, and chimpanzees are more closely related to each other than any of the three is to orangutans, which are Asiatic apes. *Hominidae* is the name of the zoological family that includes hominids—fossil and living humans. Because chimps and gorillas share a more recent common ancestor with humans than they do with the orangutan, most scientists now also place gorillas and chimps in the hominid family. *Hominid,* then, refers to the zoological family that includes fossil and living humans, chimpanzees, gorillas, and their common ancestors. This leaves the orangutan (genus *Pongo*) as the only member of the pongid family (*Pongidae*). If chimps and gorillas are classified as hominids, what do we call the group that leads to humans but not to chimps and gorillas? For that, some scientists insert a taxonomic level called *tribe* between family and genus. The tribe *hominini* describes all the human species that ever have existed (including the extinct ones) and excludes chimps and gorillas. When scientists use the word *hominin* today, they mean pretty much the same thing as when they used the word *hominid* 20 years ago. Figure 7.2 summarizes primate taxonomy, and Figure 7.3 illustrates our degree of relatedness to the living great apes.

PRIMATE ADAPTATIONS

Primates have adapted to diverse ecological niches (see Fleagle 2013). Some primates are active during the day; others, at night. Some eat insects; others, fruits; others, shoots, leaves, and bulk vegetation; and others, seeds or roots. *Terrestrial* primates live on the ground; **arboreal** primates live in trees, and there are intermediate adaptations.

Many trends in primate evolution are best exemplified by monkeys, apes, and humans, and those trends can be summarized briefly. Together they constitute an anthropoid heritage that humans share with monkeys and apes.

1. **Grasping.** Primates have five-digited feet and hands that are suited for grasping (e.g., of tree branches) and manipulating objects (e.g., food items). Facilitating manual dexterity is the fact that humans and many other primates have **opposable thumbs:** The thumb can touch the other fingers. Some primates also have grasping feet. Grasping ability was an adaptive advantage in the arboreal niches in which many primates live. However, in adapting to **bipedal** (two-footed) locomotion, humans eliminated most of the foot's grasping ability.

2. **Smell to sight.** Several anatomical changes reflect the shift from smell to sight as the primates' most important means of obtaining information. Primates have excellent *stereoscopic* (able to see in depth) and color vision. The portion of the brain devoted to vision expanded, while the area concerned with smell shrank.

3. **Nose to hand.** Sensations of touch, conveyed by *tactile organs,* also provide information.

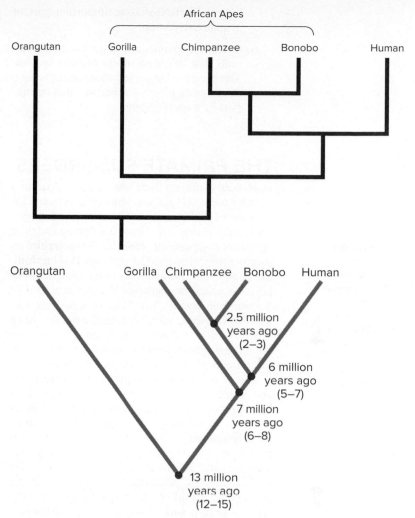

FIGURE 7.3 Humans and the Apes.

The top drawing shows the evolutionary (phylogenetic) relationships among the living great apes and humans. Note that humans and the African apes are more closely related to each other (as hominids) than either is to the orangutan (a pongid). The bottom drawing shows the same phylogeny, along with estimated dates of divergence and last common ancestor (represented by dots). It is based on the extent of shared DNA among these groups.

The tactile skin on a dog's or cat's nose transmits information. Cats' tactile hairs, or whiskers, also serve this function. In primates, however, the main touch organ is the hand, specifically the sensitive pads of the "fingerprint" region.

4. **Brain complexity.** The proportion of brain tissue concerned with memory, thought, and association has increased in primates. The primate ratio of brain size to body size exceeds that of most mammals.

5. **Parental investment.** Most primates give birth to a single offspring rather than a litter. Because of this, growing primates receive more attention and have more learning opportunities than do other mammals.

arboreal
Living in the trees.

opposable thumb
A thumb that can touch all the other fingers.

bipedal
Two-footed; upright locomotion (of hominins).

Learned behavior is an important part of primate adaptation.

6. **Sociality.** Primates tend to be social animals that live with others of their species. The need for longer and more attentive care of offspring places a selective value on support by a social group.

THE PRIMATE SUBORDERS

In primate evolution there was an early separation of two groups: (1) the ancestors of lemurs and lorises and (2) the ancestors of tarsiers, monkeys, apes, and humans. The lemur-loris group and their ancestors compose the suborder **Strepsirrhini** or strepsirrhine primates. The suborder **Haplorrhini**, the haplorrhine primates, includes tarsiers, monkeys, apes, and humans (see Masters et al. 2013). Strepsirrhine nostrils, like those of a dog, are surrounded by moist, naked skin, unlike the dry, hairy skin that surrounds haplorrhine nostrils. Another distinguishing strepsirrhine feature is a layer of the eye that reflects lights and provides better night vision.

Based on certain analogies in the appearance and adaptation of these primates, scientists used to lump together tarsiers, lemurs, and lorises as *prosimians*, meaning "pre-monkeys," in contrast to *anthropoids,* meaning "humanlike" (and also encompassing monkeys and apes). Some researchers still use the term *prosimian* colloquially to refer to these primates, but it does not reflect phylogeny. Based on their evolutionary history, tarsiers belong with monkeys, apes, and humans rather than with the lemurs.

The split between haplorrhines and strepsirrhines took place over 60 million years ago. The early history of the primates is limited to lemurlike and tarsierlike animals known through the fossil record. By 50 million years ago, several genera of tarsierlike primates were living in Asia, North America, and Europe, which were much warmer than they are now. Tarsiers survive today only in Indonesia, Malaysia, and the Philippines. The lone surviving genus of tarsier is nocturnal. Active at night, tarsiers do not compete directly with monkeys, apes, and humans, which are diurnal. Lorises also survive as nocturnal primates in parts of Asia.

The lemurs of Madagascar are the best known nonhuman primates other than monkeys and apes. Ancestral lemurs were able to survive, multiply, and diversify on the isolated island of Madagascar, where they had no primate competitors until humans arrived on that island around 2,000 years ago. In their behavior and biology, Madagascar's lemurs, which include some 50 species, show adaptations to an array of environments. Their diets and times of activity differ. Lemurs eat fruits, other plant foods, eggs, and insects. Some are nocturnal;

Strepsirrhini
The primate suborder that includes lemurs, lorises, and their ancestors.

Haplorrhini
The primate suborder that includes tarsiers, monkeys, apes, and humans.

anthropoids
Monkeys, apes, and humans.

Compare this line drawing reconstruction of Shoshonius, a tarsierlike Eocene primate, with a modern tarsier from Mindanao in the Philippines. What similarities and differences do you notice?

Top: © All Rights Reserved, Image Archives, Denver Museum of Nature & Science. bottom: © Tom McHugh/Science Source

others are active during the day. Some are totally arboreal; others spend some time in the trees and some on the ground. Like all nonhuman primates, they are endangered today, primarily as a result of human activity.

MONKEYS

The haplorrhine suborder has two infraorders, one consisting of living and fossil tarsiers; the other includes all the anthropoid, or humanlike, primates. The term **anthropoid** refers to monkeys, apes, and humans, as distinct from tarsiers and all other primates.

There are two groups of monkeys—New World monkeys (platyrrhines) and Old World Monkeys

FIGURE 7.4 Nostril Structure of Catarrhines and Platyrrhines.

Above: narrow septum and "sharp nose" of a guenon, a catarrhine (Old World monkey). Below: broad septum and "flat nose" of Humboldt's woolly monkey, a platyrrhine (New World monkey). Which nose is more like your own? What does that similarity suggest?

monkeys, apes, and humans. This is why New World monkeys belong to a different taxon.

All New World monkeys and many Old World monkeys are arboreal. Whether in the trees or on the ground, however, monkeys move differently than apes and humans. Their arms and legs move parallel to one another, as dogs' legs do. This contrasts with the tendency toward *orthograde posture,* the straight and upright stance of apes and humans. Unlike apes, which have longer arms than legs, and humans, who have longer legs than arms, monkeys have arms and legs of about the same length. Most monkeys also have tails, which help them maintain balance in the trees. Apes and humans lack tails. The apes' tendency toward orthograde posture is most evident when they sit down. When they move about, chimps, gorillas, and orangutans habitually use all four limbs.

New World Monkeys

New World monkeys live in the forests of Central and South America. Unlike Old World monkeys, many New World monkeys have *prehensile,* or grasping, tails. Sometimes the prehensile tail has tactile skin, which permits it to work like a hand, for instance, in conveying food to the mouth. Old World monkeys, however, have developed their own characteristic anatomical specializations. They have rough patches of skin on the buttocks, adapted to sitting on hard, rocky ground and rough branches. If the primate you see in the zoo has such patches, it's from the Old World. If it has a prehensile tail, it's a New World monkey. There's only one nocturnal monkey, a New World monkey appropriately called the night monkey or owl monkey. All other monkeys and apes, and humans, too, of course, are diurnal—active during the day.

(catarrhines). The catarrhines also include apes and humans, all of which originated in the Old World. *Catarrhine* means sharp-nosed, and *platyrrhine* means flat-nosed. These names come from Latin terms that describe the placement of the nostrils (see Figure 7.4).

Catarrhines (Latin, *Catarrhini*) is the taxonomic name for the group that includes all Old World monkeys, apes, and humans. Because taxonomy reflects phylogeny, this placement together means that Old World monkeys, apes, and humans are more closely related to each other than they are to New World monkeys. In other words, one kind of monkey (Old World) is more like a human than it is like another kind of monkey (New World). The New World monkeys were reproductively isolated from the catarrhines before the latter diverged into the Old World

Shown here in Brazil's Atlantic rainforest is a muriqui (or wooly spider monkey)—the largest New World monkey. Note the prehensile tail.

© Jose Caldas/Brazil Photos/LightRocket via Getty Images

Old World Monkeys

The Old World monkeys have both terrestrial and arboreal species. Baboons and many macaques are terrestrial monkeys. Certain traits differentiate terrestrial and arboreal primates. Arboreal primates tend to be smaller. Smaller animals can reach a greater variety of foods in shrubs and trees, where the most abundant foods are located at the ends of branches. Arboreal monkeys typically are lithe and agile. They escape from the few predators in their environment—snakes and monkey-eating eagles—through alertness and speed. Large size, by contrast, is advantageous for terrestrial primates in dealing with their predators, which are more numerous on the ground.

Another contrast between arboreal and terrestrial primates is in **sexual dimorphism**—marked differences in male and female anatomy and temperament. Sexual dimorphism tends to be more marked in terrestrial than in arboreal species. Baboon and macaque males are larger and fiercer than are females of the same species. However, it's hard to tell, without close inspection, the sex of an arboreal monkey.

Of the terrestrial monkeys, the baboons of Africa and the (mainly Asiatic) macaques have been the subjects of many studies. Terrestrial monkeys have specializations in anatomy, psychology, and social behavior that enable them to cope with terrestrial life. Adult male baboons, for example, are fierce-looking animals that can weigh 100 pounds (45 kilograms). They display their long, projecting canines to intimidate predators and when confronting other baboons. Faced with a predator, a male baboon can puff up his ample mane of shoulder hair, so that the would-be aggressor perceives the baboon as larger than he actually is.

Longitudinal field research shows that, near the time of puberty, baboon and macaque males typically leave their home troop for another. Because males move in and out, females form the stable core of the terrestrial monkey troop (Cheney and Seyfarth 1990). By contrast, among chimpanzees and gorillas, females are more likely to emigrate and seek mates outside their natal social groups (Bradley et al. 2004; Matsuzawa 2011; Nishida 2012; Wilson and Wrangham 2003). Among terrestrial monkeys, then, the core group consists of females; among apes it is made up of males.

APES

The Old World monkeys have their own separate superfamily (Cercopithecoidea), while humans and the apes together compose the hominoid superfamily (Hominoidea). Among the hominoids, the so-called great apes are orangutans, gorillas, and chimpanzees (see Raffaele 2010). Humans could be included here, too; sometimes we are called "the third African ape." The lesser (smaller) apes are the gibbons and siamangs of Southeast Asia and Indonesia.

Several traits are shared by apes (and humans) as distinct from monkeys and other primates. Body size tends to be larger. The life span is longer. There is a longer interval between births of infants, which depend on their parent(s). There is a tendency toward upright posture, although habitual upright bipedalism is characteristic only of hominins. The brain is larger, the muzzle or face is shorter and less projecting, and no hominoid has a tail.

Apes live in forests and woodlands, and almost all apes are threatened or endangered today because of human encroachment. The light and agile **gibbons,** which are skilled brachiators, are completely arboreal. (**Brachiation** is hand-over-hand movement through the trees.) The heavier gorillas, chimpanzees, and adult male orangutans spend considerable time on the ground. Nevertheless, ape behavior and anatomy reveal past and present adaptation to arboreal life. For example, apes still build nests to sleep in trees. Apes have longer arms than legs, which is adaptive for brachiation (see Figure 7.5). The structure of the shoulder and clavicle (collarbone) of the apes and humans suggests that we had a brachiating ancestor. In fact, young apes still do brachiate. Adult apes (except gibbons) tend to be too heavy to brachiate safely. Their weight is more than many branches can withstand. Gorillas and chimps now use the long arms they have inherited from their more arboreal ancestors for life on the ground. The terrestrial locomotion of chimps and gorillas is called *knuckle-walking*. In it, long arms and callused knuckles support the trunk as the apes amble around, leaning forward.

Gibbons

Gibbons are found in the forests of Southeast Asia, especially in Malaysia.

sexual dimorphism
Marked differences in male and female anatomy and temperament.

gibbons
Small, arboreal, Asiatic apes.

brachiation
Under-the-branch swinging.

Mandrills (*Papio sphinx*) are terrestrial Old World monkeys. Related to baboons, mandrills live in groups consisting of an adult male, several females, and their young. What kind of sexual dimorphism is shown in this photo?

© blickwinkel/Alamy Stock Photo

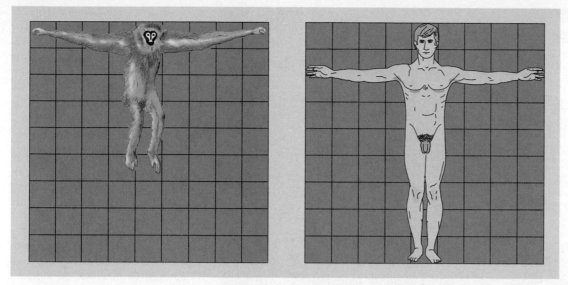

FIGURE 7.5 The Limb Ratio of the Arboreal Gibbon and Terrestrial *Homo*.
How does this anatomical difference fit the modes of locomotion used by gibbons and humans?

Smallest of the apes, male and female gibbons have about the same average height (3 feet, or 1 meter) and weight (12–25 pounds, or 5–10 kilograms). Gibbons spend most of their time just below the forest canopy (treetops). For efficient brachiation, gibbons have long arms and fingers, with short thumbs. Slenderly built, gibbons are the most agile apes. They use their long arms for balance when they occasionally walk erect on the ground or along a branch. Gibbons are the preeminent arboreal specialists among the apes. They subsist on a diet mainly of fruits, with occasional insects and small animals. Gibbons and siamangs, their slightly larger relatives, tend to live in *primary groups,* which are composed of a permanently bonded male and female and their preadolescent offspring.

Orangutans

There are two surviving species of orangutan, Asiatic apes that belong to the genus *Pongo.* Orangutans once were found throughout Southeast Asia, but today they are confined to two Indonesian islands—Borneo and Sumatra. Bornean orangutan populations have declined by more than 50 percent over the past 60 years, and their habitat has been reduced by at least 55 percent over the past 20 years. Borneo now has fewer than 40,000 orangutans, while no more than 7,000 survive on Sumatra (Isaacson 2012). Historically, orangutans existed throughout Sumatra, but today they are restricted to the north of the island. Only seven existing populations of Sumatran orangs have prospects of long-term viability. Only three populations contain more than 1,000 orangutans.

The degree of sexual dimorphism in orangs is striking. Adult males weigh more than twice as much as females. The orangutan male, like his

With long arms and fingers, the gibbon is the most agile of the apes. As we see here, gibbons occasionally walk upright on the ground, using their long arms as balancers.
© Holger Ehlers/Alamy Stock Photo

human counterpart, is intermediate in size between chimps and gorillas. Orang males can weigh up to 300 pounds (135 kilograms), but usually they weigh around 200 pounds (90 kilograms). Less bulky than gorillas, male orangs can be more arboreal than male gorillas, although they

Dr. Biruté Galdikas has studied orangutans in Indonesia for decades. Here she carries an orangutan named Isabel, soon to be released (from a rehabilitation center) into the wild at Tanjung Puting National Park on the Indonesian island of Borneo.

© Irwin Fedriansyah/AP Images

however, is a large, populous country with millions of poor people. The temptation to exploit natural resources to feed people, and to expand the economy, is great. Is there a realistic chance that the orangutan will survive in the wild?

Gorillas

With just one species, *Gorilla gorilla,* there are three subspecies of gorillas. The western lowland gorilla is the animal you normally see in zoos. This, the smallest subspecies, lives mainly in forests in the Central African Republic, Congo, Cameroon, Gabon, Nigeria, and Equatorial Guinea (see Matsuzawa 2011). The eastern lowland gorilla, of which there are only four in captivity, is slightly larger and lives in eastern Congo. There are no mountain gorillas, the third subspecies, in captivity, and it's estimated that no more than 650 of these animals survive in the wild. These are the largest gorillas, with the longest hair (to keep them warm in their mountainous habitat). They also are the rarest gorillas, which Dian Fossey (1983) and other scientists have studied in Rwanda, Uganda, and eastern Congo.

Full-grown male gorillas may weigh 400 pounds (180 kilograms) and stand 6 feet tall (183 centimeters). Like most terrestrial primates, gorillas show marked sexual dimorphism. The average adult female weighs half as much as the male. Gorillas spend little time in the trees. It's hard for an adult male to move his bulk about in a tree. When gorillas sleep in trees, they build nests, which usually are no more than 10 feet (3 meters) off the ground. By contrast, the nests of chimps and female orangs may be 100 feet (30 meters) above the ground.

Most of the gorilla's day is spent feeding. Gorillas move through jungle undergrowth eating ground plants, leaves, bark, fruits, and other vegetation (see Rothman, Raubenheimer, and Chapman 2011). Like most primates, gorillas live in social groups. The *troop* is a common unit of primate social organization, consisting of multiple males and females and their offspring. Although troops with up to 30 gorillas have been observed, most gorillas live in groups of from 10 to 20. Gorilla troops tend to have fairly stable memberships, with little shifting between troops (Fossey 1983). Each troop has a silverback male, so designated because of the strip of white hair that extends down his back. This is the physical sign of full maturity among male gorillas. The silverback is usually the only breeding male in the troop, which is why gorilla troops are sometimes called "one-male groups." However, a few younger, subordinate males may also adhere to such a one-male group.

typically climb, rather than swing through, the trees. The smaller size of females and young permits them to make fuller use of the trees. Orangutans have a varied diet of fruits, bark, leaves, and insects. Because orangutans live in jungles and feed in trees, they are especially difficult to study. However, field reports about orangutans in their natural setting (Schaik 2004) have clarified their behavior and social organization. Orangs are the least sociable of the great apes (see Isaacson 2012; Schaik 2004). Often they are solitary, with their tightest social units formed by females and preadolescent young, and males foraging alone.

Since 1971 Biruté Mary Galdikas has studied wild orangutans in central Borneo. She is one of three prominent primatologists—all women—encouraged by famed paleoanthropologist Louis B. Leakey to study and protect the great apes. Leakey sent those three researchers to study apes specifically because he felt such studies would offer some insight into ourselves and our extinct ancestors (as indeed they have). The others are Jane Goodall (working with chimpanzees) and the late Dian Fossey (who worked with mountain gorillas). As Galdikas (2007) reports, economic globalization has fueled worldwide demand for pulp, paper, palm oil, and precious metals, leading to the destruction of Indonesia's tropical forests and endangering the orang. About 80 percent of the orang habitat has been either depopulated or totally destroyed (Galdikas 2007). Galdikas has urged Indonesia to impose a tax on multinational companies that profit from rain forest destruction and to use the revenues for forest and orangutan conservation. Indonesia,

Mountain gorillas are the rarest and most endangered kind of gorilla. Dian Fossey (shown here) and other scientists have studied them in Rwanda, Uganda, and eastern Congo. Here, Fossey (now deceased) observes a young gorilla in Rwanda's Virunga Mountains.
© Liam White/Alamy Stock Photo

Chimpanzees

Chimpanzees belong to the genus *Pan*, which has two species: *Pan troglodytes* (the common chimpanzee) and *Pan paniscus* (the bonobo, or "pygmy," chimpanzee). Like humans, chimps are closely related to the gorilla, although there are some obvious differences. Like gorillas, chimps live in tropical Africa, but they range over a larger area and more varied environments than gorillas do. The common chimp, *Pan troglodytes,* lives in western central Africa (Gabon, Congo, Cameroon), as well as in western Africa (Ivory Coast, Sierra Leone, Liberia, Gambia) and eastern Africa (Uganda and Tanzania). Bonobos live in remote and densely forested areas of just one country—the Democratic Republic of

Chimpanzees live mainly in tropical rain forests but also in woodlands and mixed forest–woodland–grassland areas, such as the Gombe Stream National Park, Tanzania, where Jane Goodall began to study them in 1960. Shown here 30 years after her first visit to Gombe, Goodall continues her lifelong commitment to these endangered animals.
© Michael Nichols/ National Geographic/ Getty Images

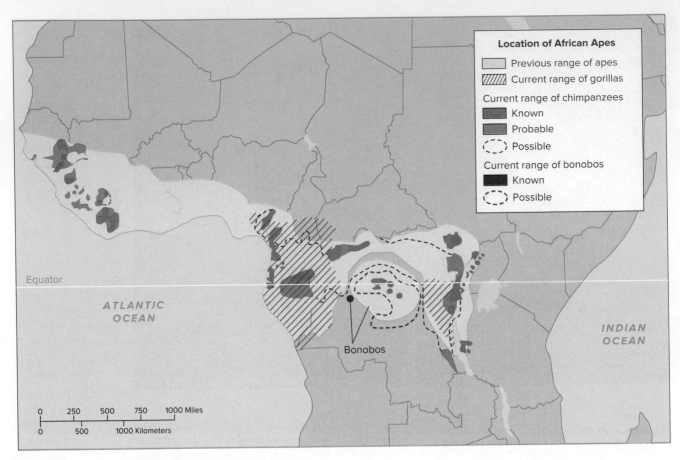

FIGURE 7.6 Distribution of the African Apes.

Shows the known, probable, and possible current distributions of chimps, bonobos, and gorillas, along with their previous range.

Congo. (Figure 7.6 maps the distribution of chimps, bonobos, and gorillas.) Common chimps live mainly in tropical rain forests but also in woodlands and mixed forest–woodland–grassland areas, such as the Gombe Stream National Park, Tanzania, where Jane Goodall and other researchers began to study them in 1960 (see Goodall 2009, 2010).

There are dietary differences between chimps and gorillas. Gorillas eat large quantities of green bulk vegetation, but chimps, like orangutans and gibbons, prefer fruits. Chimps actually are omnivorous, adding animal protein to their diet by hunting small mammals (especially monkeys), birds' eggs, and insects.

Chimps are lighter and more arboreal than gorillas are. The adult male's weight—between 100 and 200 pounds (45–90 kilograms)—is about a third that of the male gorilla. There is much less sexual dimorphism among chimps than among gorillas. Females approximate 88 percent of the average male height. This is similar to the ratio of sexual dimorphism in *Homo sapiens*.

Several scientists have studied wild chimps, and we know more about the full range of their behavior and social organization than we do about the other apes (see Goodall 2009; Matsuzawa 2011; Nishida 2012). The long-term research of

Jane Goodall (2010) and others at Gombe provides especially useful information. Approximately 150 chimpanzees range over Gombe's 30 square miles (80 square kilometers). Goodall (2009, 2010) has described communities of about 50 chimps, all of which know one another and interact from time to time. Communities regularly split up into smaller groups: a mother and her offspring; a few males; males, females, and young; and occasionally solitary animals. The social networks of males are more closed than are those of females, which are more likely to migrate and mate outside their natal group than males are (Wrangham et al. 1994).

When chimps, which are very vocal, meet, they greet one another with gestures, facial expressions, and calls. They hoot to maintain contact during their daily rounds. Like baboons and macaques, chimps exhibit dominance relationships through attacks and displacement. Some adult females outrank younger males, although females do not display as strong dominance relationships among themselves as males do. Males occasionally cooperate in hunting parties (see Nishida 2012). Because apes, especially chimps, are such close kin of humans, both scientists and animal rights activists have questioned whether it is ethical to use them as research animals. This chapter's "Appreciating

Should Apes Have Human Rights?

In Africa and Asia, the dwindling populations of great apes face extinction due to human warfare, oil exploration, deforestation, deliberate hunting, and other threats. Continents away, animal rights activists work to conserve apes, even to grant them legal rights. In 2000, the U.S. Congress enacted the Great Apes Conservation Act, which authorized $5 million annually over five years to protect apes in the wild. In 2005, Congress reauthorized that act, which matched public with private funding, for another five years. The money would help protect habitats, battle poachers, and educate local populations about the importance of the apes.

In Indonesia, for example, funding has slowed the conversion of forests to commercial plantations. In Congo, one of the few countries in which the mountain gorilla survives, promotion of alternative fuels has helped reduce deforestation for charcoal production. By 2010, when it ended, the Great Apes Conservation Fund had helped fund more than 50 programs in 7 Asian and 12 African countries.

The humanlike characteristics of the great apes is evident to anyone who has seen the various *Planet of the Apes* movies, especially the most recent ones, featuring the intelligent, speaking chimpanzee named Caesar and his companions. Scientific knowledge confirms that apes are close to humans in their cognitive abilities and emotional states. Experiments teaching sign language to chimps and gorillas, described in Chapter 14 ("Language and Communication"), demonstrate that apes are capable of learning hundreds of meaningful signs and of communicating with humans and other signing apes. DNA confirms the close relationship among humans, chimps, and gorillas.

Scientists know that the great apes have complex mental abilities, which elevate their capability for suffering. On that basis alone, say rights advocates, apes deserve basic protections from the pain, isolation, and arbitrary imprisonment inflicted by medical experiments or captivity in zoos. In 1993, philosophers Peter Singer and Paola Cavalieri published *The Great Ape Project,* a book that argued that chimpanzees, gorillas, bonobos, and orangutans should have the same basic rights as human beings. In fact, in December 2014, an Argentine court did extend legal rights to a 28-year-old orangutan named Sandra, a captive ape born in Germany and taken to the Buenos Aires zoo, where she lived for 20 years. As the world's first animal legally recognized as a "nonhuman person," Sandra's new status facilitated her transfer to a sanctuary in Brazil. A month earlier, in North America, a New York state court had denied an appeal put forth on behalf of a pet chimp named Tommy. The court argued that, regardless of their intelligence or feelings, chimpanzees cannot fulfill the social obligations expected of a person with rights.

In addition to promoting legal rights for apes, advocates have urged governments and the United Nations to ban ape captivity in zoos and circuses and their use in scientific research, especially medical testing. Several nations, including New Zealand, the United Kingdom, Sweden, Austria, Belgium, and the Netherlands have banned research on apes for ethical reasons. In January 2013, the U.S. National Institutes of Health (NIH) accepted a committee recommendation to curtail the use of chimpanzees in research. Of the 450 chimpanzees then under NIH control, 400 would be retired and moved to sanctuaries. NIH did retain 50 chimps for possible future research use, but they, too, were transferred to a sanctuary in November 2015. Today, NIH no longer uses chimps for research; its former research chimps are enjoying their freedom in animal sanctuaries. Most of them now live in the federally run Chimp Haven in Shreveport, Louisiana, home to more than 150 chimps living in large social groups on 200 acres of parkland.

How do you feel about animal rights in general and ape rights in particular? Because the great apes are so close to humans genetically, physically, and temperamentally, do they merit special treatment among the animals? Should some apes be more equal than others?

SOURCE: Becker (2013), Eldred (2013), Kahn (2011), Keim (2014), Mitani (2011), *The Week* (2013), and 2015 news accounts.

Diversity" considers the issue of chimps in research and asks an even more contentious question—whether apes should have human rights.

Bonobos

Ancestral chimps, and especially hominins, eventually spread out of the forests and into woodlands and more open habitats (see Choi 2011). Bonobos, which belong to the species *Pan paniscus,* apparently never left the protection of the trees. Up to 10,000 bonobos survive in the humid forests south of the Zaire River, in the Democratic Republic of Congo (see Furuichi and Thompson 2008). Despite their common name of *pygmy* chimpanzee, bonobos aren't necessarily smaller than chimps. Bonobos are about the same size as members of the smallest subspecies of common chimpanzee—95 pounds (43 kilograms) for males and 73 pounds (33 kilograms) for females.

Although much smaller than the males, female bonobos seem to rule. de Waal (1995, 1997) characterizes bonobo communities as female-centered,

This photo was taken at a bonobo sanctuary in the Democratic Republic of Congo. Are bonobos (pygmy chimpanzees) smaller than chimps?
© Purestock/Getty Images RF

peace-loving, and egalitarian. The strongest social bonds are among females, although females also bond with males. The male bonobo's status reflects that of his mother, to which he remains closely bonded for life.

The frequency with which bonobos have sex—and use it to avoid conflict—makes them exceptional among the primates (de Waal 1997). Despite frequent sex, the bonobo reproductive rate doesn't exceed that of the chimpanzee. A female bonobo gives birth every 5 or 6 years. Then, like chimps, female bonobos nurse and carry around their young for up to 5 years. Bonobos reach adolescence around 7 years of age. Females, which first give birth at age 13 or 14, are full grown by 15 years.

BEHAVIORAL ECOLOGY AND FITNESS

Behavioral ecology studies the evolutionary basis of animal behavior—how certain behaviors may be related to differential reproductive success. Remember that natural selection is based on differential fitness, with some members of a population transmitting more of their genes to future generations than others do. Individuals within a species may compete to maximize their *reproductive fitness*—their genetic contribution to future generations. *Individual fitness* is measured by the number of direct descendants an individual has. Illustrating

a primate strategy that may enhance individual fitness are cases in which male monkeys kill infants after entering a new troop. Destroying the offspring of other males, they clear a place for their own progeny (Hausfater and Hrdy 2008).

Besides competition, an individual's genetic contribution to future generations also can be enhanced by cooperation, sharing, and other apparently unselfish behaviors. This is because of *inclusive fitness*—reproductive success measured by the genes one shares with relatives. By sacrificing for their close kin—even if this means limiting their own direct reproduction—individuals actually may increase their genetic contributions (their shared genes) to the future. Inclusive fitness helps us understand why a female might invest in her sister's offspring, or why a male might risk his life to defend his brothers. If self-sacrifice perpetuates more of their genes than direct reproduction does, it makes sense in terms of differential reproduction (see Marshall 2015).

Maternal care always makes sense in terms of reproductive fitness, because females know their offspring are their own. It's more difficult, however, for males to be sure about paternity. Inclusive fitness theory predicts that males will invest most in offspring when they are surest the offspring are their own. Most gibbons, for example, have strict male–female pair bonding, which makes it likely that the offspring are those of both members of the pair. When primates form pair bonds, we expect both males and females to offer care and protection to their young, as gibbons do. However, among species and in situations in which a male can't be sure about his paternity, it may make more sense for him to invest in his sister's offspring than in his mate's, because his nieces and nephews definitely share some of his genes. (For application of inclusive fitness theory to humans, see Chapais 2008 and Hill et al. 2011).

PRIMATE EVOLUTION

The fossil record gives us only a glimpse of the diverse bioforms—living beings—that have existed on Earth, including only a small fraction of all the extinct types of primates. With reference to the primate fossil record, we'll see that different geographic areas provide more abundant fossil evidence for different time periods. This doesn't necessarily mean that primates were not living elsewhere at the same time. Discussions of primate and human evolution must be tentative, because the fossil record is limited and spotty (see Ciochon and Fleagle 2012). Much is subject to change as knowledge increases. A key feature of science is to recognize the tentativeness and uncertainty of knowledge. Scientists, including fossil hunters, constantly seek out new evidence and devise new methods, such as DNA comparison, to improve their understanding, in this case of primate and human evolution.

CHRONOLOGY

Based on fossils found in stratigraphic sequences, the history of vertebrate life has been divided into three main eras. The *Paleozoic* (544–245 **m.y.a.**—million years ago) was the era of ancient life—fishes, amphibians, and primitive reptiles. The *Mesozoic* (245–65 m.y.a.) was the era of middle life—reptiles, including the dinosaurs. The *Cenozoic* (65 m.y.a.–present) is the era of recent life—birds and mammals. Each era is divided into periods; the periods, into epochs.

Anthropologists are concerned with the Cenozoic *era* (Figure 7.7), which includes two *periods:* Tertiary and Quaternary. Each of these periods is subdivided into *epochs.* The Tertiary had five epochs: Paleocene, Eocene, Oligocene, Miocene, and Pliocene. The Quaternary includes just two epochs: Pleistocene and Holocene, or Recent. Figure 7.7 gives the approximate dates of these epochs. Sediments from the Paleocene epoch (65–54 m.y.a.) have yielded fossil remains of diverse small mammals, including, by the late Paleocene, the earliest known primate. Lemurlike and tarsierlike fossils abound in strata dating from the Eocene (54–34 m.y.a.). Haplorrhine fossils date to the Eocene and become more abundant (as proto-monkeys) during the ensuing Oligocene (34–23 m.y.a.). Hominoids (proto-apes) became widespread during the Miocene (23–5 m.y.a.). Hominins first appeared in the late Miocene, just before the Pliocene (5–2.6 m.y.a.).

EARLY PRIMATES

When the Mesozoic era ended, and the Cenozoic era began, around 65 m.y.a., North America was connected to Europe but not to South America. (The Americas joined around 3 m.y.a.) Over millions of years, the continents have "drifted" to their present locations, carried along by the gradually shifting plates of the Earth's surface (Figure 7.8).

The Mesozoic era had ended with a massive worldwide extinction of plants and animals, including the dinosaurs. Thereafter, mammals eventually replaced reptiles as the dominant large land animals. A rich new ecological niche that early primates could exploit was created by the spread of angiosperms (flowering plants) during the Cenozoic era (see Sussman, Rasmussen, and Raven 2013). Primates evolved—spreading and diversifying—along with the expansion of flowering plants during a long period of global warming

m.y.a.
Million years ago.

Era	Period	Epoch	Climate and Life Forms
Cenozoic	Quaternary	Holocene 10,000 B.P.	Transition to agriculture; emergence of states
		Pleistocene 2.6 m.y.a.	Climatic fluctuations, glaciation; spread of *Homo*, extinction of (hyper)robust australopiths
	Tertiary	Pliocene 5 m.y.a.	*Au. africanus, Au. afarensis, Au. anamensis, Ardipithecus*
		Miocene 23 m.y.a.	Cooler and drier grasslands spread in middle latitudes; Africa collides with Eurasia (16 m.y.a.); proto-apes (ape precursors) diverse and abundant
		Oligocene 34 m.y.a.	Cooler and drier in the north; proto-monkeys (monkey precursors) in Africa (Fayum); separation of catarrhines and platyrrhines; separation of hylobatids (gibbons) from pongids and hominids
		Eocene 54 m.y.a	Warm tropical climates become widespread; modern orders of mammals appear; strepsirrhine and tarsierlike primates are abundant; simians appear later
		Paleocene 65 m.y.a	First major mammal radiation; first primates; separation of strepsirrhines and haplorrhines

FIGURE 7.7 Periods and Epochs of the Cenozoic Era.
The geological time scale is based on stratigraphy. Eras are subdivided into periods, and periods into epochs. In what era, period, and epoch did *Homo* originate?

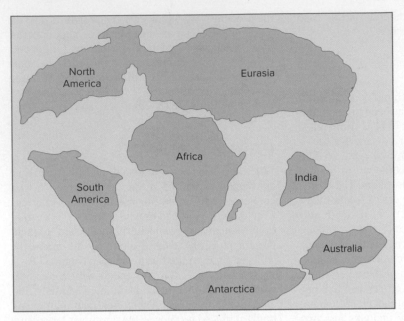

FIGURE 7.8 Placement of Continents at the End of the Mesozoic.

When the Mesozoic era ended and the Cenozoic began, some 65 m.y.a., North America was connected to Europe but not to South America.

that began around 56 m.y.a. With the rising temperatures, tropical forests spread throughout North America, Europe, and Asia. (Africa and South America were island continents at that time.) Primates adapted to this expanding niche—widespread tropical forests and the flowering trees within them. Manual dexterity, including a good grasping ability, would have helped early primates reach, and feed near, the ends of delicate tree branches. This is where the most abundant fruits, flowers, gums, and nectars were located, along with the insects that pollinate flowering plants.

One early proto-primate, *Carpolestes simpsoni*, whose remains come from Wyoming and date back 56 million years, had the hands and feet of a good grasper. It had an opposable big toe and nails rather than claws. Its flattened teeth suggest a diet that included grinding of fruits, nuts, and other plant parts. *Carpolestes* did not, however, have eyes that faced completely forward, so it would have lacked depth perception. All the key primate features did not appear at once. Enhanced vision seems to have come later. Color and depth perception would eventually help primates to judge distances; identify foods and other objects; and see through their cluttered, leafy tropical forest environment (Wayman 2012).

Early Cenozoic Primates

A tiny, complete skeleton from China, first described in 2013, is the earliest definite primate so far discovered (*Carpolestes* is classified as a proto-primate, a primate precursor or early relative, but not an actual primate). Named

Archicebus achilles because of its prominent (and monkeylike) ankle and heel, this early Chinese primate has been tentatively assigned to the tarsier lineage, but it is dated very close to the time when the ancestors of tarsiers separated from those of the monkeys. *Archicebus achilles* weighed no more than 1 ounce, and it had a 5-inch tail that was longer than its 4-inch body. It lived 55 m.y.a., when Earth was a natural greenhouse, with rain forests everywhere and palm trees growing in what is now Alaska. This finding supports the view that the first primates evolved in Asia—not too long after the dinosaurs went extinct (66 m.y.a.). Somehow primates crossed open water to reach Africa by 38 m.y.a. (Africa remained an island continent until 16 m.y.a.). *Archicebus* had the feet of a small monkey; the arms, legs, and teeth of a very primitive primate; and a primitive skull with very small eyes. If it was indeed an early tarsier, its heel and ankle still suggest a close connection to the monkey line. Unlike today's tarsiers, *Archicebus achilles* was not nocturnal. Being so small and metabolically active, it probably spent its days frantically leaping around in the humid tropical forest it inhabited (Ni et al. 2013; Wilford 2013).

Like *Carpolestes, Archicebus achilles* lived late in the Paleocene (65–54 m.y.a.), the first epoch of the Cenozoic era. A variety of primate species inhabited Europe and North America during the Cenozoic's second epoch, the Eocene (54–34 m.y.a.). The primates of the Eocene were early strepsirrhines and tarsierlike haplorrhines, with at least 60 genera living in Asia, North America, and Europe, and reaching Africa by the late Eocene. By the end of the Eocene, ancestral lemurs had reached Madagascar. They must have traveled from East Africa across the Mozambique Channel—narrower then than now—on thick mats of vegetation. Such naturally formed "rafts" have been observed forming in East African rivers, then floating out to sea.

It was also during the Eocene that, ancestral simians (proto-monkeys) branched off from the tarsier line. These proto-monkeys (monkey precursors) were diurnal (active during the day) (see Schultz, Opie, and Atkinson 2011). In this diurnal niche, vision was favored over smell. The eyes and brain got bigger, and the snout was reduced. Haplorrhine eyes are rotated more forward than

Smilodectes was a lemurlike primate that lived during the Eocene. Compare the painting reconstructing a *Smilodectes* from Wyoming (left) with this pair of modern black lemurs (*Eulemur macaco*) from Madagascar.

Left: © Tom McHugh/Science Source; right: © Arco Images GmbH/Alamy Stock Photo

are those of strepsirrhines. Also, haplorrhines have a fully enclosed bony eye socket, but lemurs and lorises do not have this feature. The strepsirrhines also have a rhinarium, a moist nose continuous with the upper lip. Haplorrhines have a dry nose, separate from the upper lip which strepsirrhines lack. By the end of the Eocene, most strepsirrhine species had become extinct in areas where they had to compete with the proto-monkeys. Some strepsirrhines did manage to survive by becoming nocturnal. Another strepsirrhine group, the lemurs of Madagascar not only survived but thrived on that large island, where they could adapt and diversify without any haplorrhine competition until the first humans reached Madagascar around 2,000 years ago.

Oligocene Proto-monkeys

The Oligocene epoch (34-23 m.y.a.) was a time of major geological and climatic change. The Great Rift Valley formed in East Africa, and India drifted into Asia. A cooling trend began, especially in the Northern Hemisphere, leading to the extinction of many primate species.

Proto-monkeys were the most common primates of the Oligocene. Most of our knowledge of those proto-monkeys comes from fossils discovered in Egypt's Fayum region. This area is a desert

today, but 34–31 m.y.a. it was a swampy area, where conditions were favorable for fossilization. The Fayum proto-monkeys lived in trees and ate fruits and seeds. Compared with earlier primates, they had larger brains, reduced snouts, and more forward-looking eyes.

These Fayum fossils illustrate that the split between New World monkeys and Old World monkeys was already under way. One group of the Fayum proto-monkeys was plausibly ancestral to the New World monkeys. Members of this group were small (2–3 pounds, or 0.9–1.4 kilograms), with similarities to living marmosets and tamarins, which are small South American monkeys. Like living New World monkeys, members of this group retained the dental formula of earlier primates. That formula, also shared with lemurs, lorises, and tarsiers, is 2.1.3.3, meaning two incisors, one canine, three premolars, and three molars. (The formula is based on one-fourth of the mouth, either the right or left side of the upper or lower jaw.)

The other group of Fayum proto-monkeys had a new and different dental formula (2.1.2.3), indicating the loss of a premolar, and a total of 32 teeth, versus 36 in the other primates. This formula is shared by all later Old World monkeys, apes, and humans. This group of Fayum fossils is plausibly ancestral to the catarrhines—Old World monkeys, apes, and humans.

Evidence for another important evolutionary split comes from Tanzania's Rukwa Rift Basin. In 2013, researchers working there reported their discovery of two late Oligocene finds, dated to 25.2 m.y.a. One find seems to be a hominoid (a *proto-ape*, plausibly ancestral to apes and humans), while the other is an Old World monkey. The proto-ape fossil is a lower right jaw with teeth, and the Old World monkey find is a jaw fragment with a single tooth (Bower 2013; Stevens et al. 2013). Proto-apes became the most common primate during the Miocene epoch, which followed the Oligocene. But exactly when did the hominoid line diverge from the Old World monkeys? Molecular dating based on DNA comparisons suggests that proto-apes split from the Old World monkey line between 25 and 30 m.y.a. The fact that these Tanzanian fossils date back 25.2 m.y.a. suggests that the split occurred earlier in that range of dates—perhaps 30 m.y.a. In addition to Egypt and Tanzania, primate bones have been found in Oligocene deposits in other parts of North Africa, West Africa, southern Arabia, China, Southeast Asia, and North and South America.

between Africa, Europe, and Asia. Migrating both ways—out of and into Africa—after 16 m.y.a. were various animals, including hominoids. Proto-apes were the most common primates of the middle Miocene (16–10 m.y.a.). Over 20 species have been discovered in Europe, Africa, and Asia.

The most remarkable Miocene ape was *Gigantopithecus*—almost certainly the largest primate that ever lived. Confined to Asia, it persisted for millions of years, from the Miocene until 400,000 years ago, when it coexisted with members of our own genus, *Homo erectus*. Some people think *Gigantopithecus* is not extinct yet, that we know it today as the yeti and Bigfoot (Sasquatch).

With a fossil record consisting of nothing more than jawbones and teeth, it is difficult to say for sure just how big *Gigantopithecus* was. Based on ratios of jaw and tooth size to body size in other apes, various reconstructions have been made. One has *Gigantopithecus* weighing 1,200 pounds (544 kilograms) and standing 10 feet (3 meters) tall (Ciochon, Olsen, and James 1990). Another puts the height at 9 feet (2.7 meters) and cuts the weight in half (Simons and Ettel 1970). All reconstructions agree, however, that *Gigantopithecus* was the

MIOCENE HOMINOIDS

Hominoid fossils become abundant during the Miocene epoch (23–5 m.y.a.), which is divided into three parts: lower, middle, and upper or late. The early or lower Miocene (23–16 m.y.a.) was a warm and wet period, when forests covered East Africa. Recall that Hominoidea is the superfamily that includes fossil and living apes and humans. For simplicity's sake, the earliest **hominoids** are here called proto-apes, or simply *apes*. Although some of these may be ancestral to living apes, none is identical, or often even very similar, to modern apes.

Proconsul is the name of a group (three known species) of early Miocene proto-apes. These ancient African apes had teeth with similarities to those of living apes. Below the neck, however, their skeleton was more monkeylike. The *Proconsul* species ranged in size from that of a small monkey to that of a chimpanzee, usually with marked sexual dimorphism. Their dentition suggests they ate fruits and leaves. By the middle Miocene, *Proconsul* had been replaced by other apes.

hominoid

The zoological superfamily that includes extinct and living apes and hominins.

Later Miocene Apes

During the early (lower) Miocene (23–16 m.y.a.), water had separated Africa from Europe and Asia. But during the middle Miocene, Arabia drifted into Eurasia, providing a land connection

A model of Gigantopithecus, the largest ape ever to have lived, in the San Diego Museum of Man. What would be the likely environmental effects of a population of such large apes?

Daderot /CC0 1.0 Universal (CC0 1.0) Public Domain Dedication /https:// commons.wikimedia.org/wiki/File%3AGigantopithecus_blacki%2C_model_-_ San_Diego_Museum_of_Man_-_DSC06889_01.JPG/3/26/2016

largest ape that ever lived. There were at least two species of *Gigantopithecus:* One coexisted with *H. erectus* in China and Vietnam, and the other, much earlier (5 m.y.a.), lived in northern India.

Pierolapithecus catalaunicus

An ancient ape species known as *Pierolapithecus catalaunicus* has been proposed as the last common ancestor of humans, chimps, gorillas, and orangs (Moyá-Solá et al. 2004). *Pierolapithecus* lived around 13 m.y.a., during the middle Miocene. The find includes much of the skull, hand and foot bones, three vertebrae, two complete ribs, and large pieces of a dozen other bones. *Pierolapithecus* was an adult male that weighed about 75 pounds (34 kilograms). Like chimps and gorillas, this ape was well adapted for tree climbing and knuckle-walking on the ground. Based on the shape of the single surviving tooth, it probably was a fruit eater. Several features distinguished *Pierolapithecus* from the lesser apes (gibbons and siamangs) and monkeys. Its rib cage, lower spine, and wrist suggest it climbed the way modern great apes do. The ape's chest, or thorax, is wider and flatter than that of monkeys and is the earliest modern apelike thorax yet found in the fossil record.

In the current timetable of primate evolution, the lineage of Old World monkeys diverged from the hominoid line around 30 m.y.a. The ancestors of the lesser apes separated from those of the great apes some 16–14 m.y.a. Then, by 11–10 m.y.a., the orangutan line had diverged from that leading to the African apes and humans. Yet another split took place when the gorilla line branched off from the line leading to chimpanzees and hominins. Around 7–6 m.y.a., another split in the lineage led to the various early hominins. Some intriguing fossils dating from that critical time period have been discovered recently.

We construct such evolutionary timetables based on a combination of comparative DNA and fossil evidence. We know that chimps, bonobos,

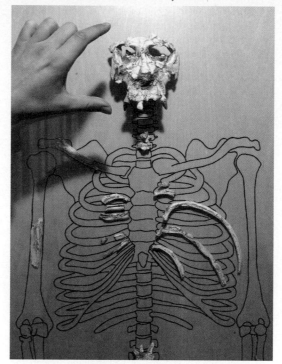

Pierolapithecus catalaunicus. The *Pierolapithecus* bones discovered so far include much of the skull, hand and foot bones, including toe and finger fragments, three vertebrae, two complete ribs, and large pieces of a dozen others. This Miocene ape, first described in 2004, may be the last common ancestor of all the world's living great apes, including the human family.

© Luis Gene/AFP/Getty Images

and gorillas are our closest surviving cousin species. We do not, however, know much about the specific ancestry of gorillas and chimps. This is primarily because those apes tend to live in humid forests, where conditions are not favorable to preservation and fossilization. Ancient hominins, however, tended to live in less humid environments, so we are fortunate to have a larger, and constantly growing, hominin fossil record.

for REVIEW

1. Humans, apes, monkeys, tarsiers, lemurs, and lorises are primates. The primate order is subdivided into suborders, infraorders, parvaorders, superfamilies, families, tribes, genera, species, and subspecies. Organisms in any subdivision (taxon) of a taxonomy are assumed to share more recent ancestry with each other than they do with organisms in other taxa. But it's sometimes hard to tell the difference between homologies, which reflect common ancestry, and analogies, biological similarities that develop through convergent evolution.

2. The primate order has two suborders: Strepsirrhini (lemurs and lorises) and Haplorrhini (tarsiers, monkeys, apes, and humans). The strepsirrhine and haplorrhine lines had split by 60 m.y.a. By the end of the Eocene, early simians

summary

(proto-monkeys) had adapted to a diurnal (daytime) ecological niche. Tarsiers and lorises survived by adapting to nocturnal life. Lemurs survived on the island of Madagascar.

3. The infraorder Simiiformes includes the anthropoid or "humanlike" primates—monkeys, apes, and humans. All share a common dental formula (2.1.2.3) and fully developed primate features, such as depth and color vision, and a shift in tactile areas to the fingers. All New World monkeys are arboreal. Old World monkeys include both terrestrial species (e.g., baboons and macaques) and arboreal ones. The great apes are orangutans, gorillas, chimpanzees, and bonobos. The lesser apes are gibbons and siamangs.

4. Gibbons and siamangs live in Southeast Asian forests. Smallest of the apes, these "lesser apes" are arboreal animals whose mode of locomotion is brachiation. Sexual dimorphism, slight among gibbons, is marked among orangutans, which are confined to two Indonesian islands. Sexually dimorphic gorillas, the most terrestrial apes, are vegetarians confined to equatorial Africa. Two species of chimpanzee live in the forests and woodlands of tropical Africa. Chimps are less sexually dimorphic, more numerous, and more omnivorous than gorillas.

5. From the perspective of behavioral ecology, individuals in a population compete to increase their genetic contribution to future generations. Maternal care makes sense from this perspective, because females can be sure their offspring are their own. Because it's harder for males to be sure about paternity, evolutionary theory predicts they will invest most in offspring when they are surest the offspring are theirs.

6. Primates have lived during the past 65 million years, the Cenozoic era, with seven epochs: Paleocene, Eocene, Oligocene, Miocene, Pliocene, Pleistocene, and Holocene, or Recent. Early primates adapted to niches created by the proliferation of flowering plants during the Cenozoic.

7. The earliest known primate, discovered in China 55 m.y.a., dates to the late Paleocene epoch (65–54 m.y.a.). Thereafter, lemurlike and tarsierlike primates proliferated during the Eocene (54–34 m.y.a.). During the Oligocene (34–23 m.y.a.), proto-monkeys became the most common primates. The split between ancestral platyrrhines (New World monkeys) and catarrhines (Old World monkeys, apes, and humans) occurred during the Oligocene, as did the split between Old World monkeys and hominoids.

8. The earliest known hominoid (proto-ape) dates to 25.2 m.y.a., just before the Miocene (23–5 m.y.a.). Proto-apes proliferated during the middle and late Miocene. Since the middle Miocene (16–10 m.y.a.), Africa, Europe, and Asia have been connected. Proto-apes spread to all three continents and became the most common primates of the middle Miocene. Asia's *Gigantopithecus,* the largest primate ever to live, persisted for millions of years, finally coexisting with *Homo erectus. Pierolapithecus catalaunicus,* which lived around 13 m.y.a., could be the last common ancestor of humans, chimpanzees, gorillas, and orangutans.

key terms

analogies 107	hominoid 122
anthropoids 110	homologies 107
arboreal 109	m.y.a. 119
behavioral ecology 118	opposable thumb 109
bipedal 109	primatology 107
brachiation 112	sexual dimorphism 112
convergent evolution 107	Strepsirrhini 110
gibbons 112	taxonomy 107
Haplorrhini 110	terrestrial 107

critical thinking

1. How does social organization vary among primates?
2. What is behavioral ecology? How would a behavioral ecologist explain parental investment in offspring? Can you think of any other theoretical frameworks that could be used to explain these cases?
3. What are some unanswered questions about early primate evolution? What kinds of information would help provide answers? What are some of the difficulties that investigators face in solving these questions?
4. There have been reported sightings of Bigfoot in the Pacific Northwest of North America and of the yeti (abominable snowman) in the Himalayas. What facts about apes might lead you to question such reports?
5. Our cultural background affects the ways in which we perceive nature, human nature, and "the natural." Can you think of aspects of your culture that have affected the way you think about humans' relationship to other primates?

Early Hominins

© Kenneth Garrett

- ▶ What key traits make us human, and when and how are they revealed in the fossil record?

- ▶ Who were the australopiths, and what role did they play in human evolution?

- ▶ When and where did hominins first make tools?

Paleoanthropologist Meave Leakey excavates at Kanapoi in northern Kenya. Remains of *Australopithecus anamensis* (4.2–3.9 m.y.a.) have been found at this site.

understanding OURSELVES

I n 1924, the Australian anatomist Raymond Dart, working in South Africa, announced the discovery of *Australopithecus africanus* as an early *bipedal* human ancestor. Dart's fellow scientists, however, found it hard to accept this small-brained, primitive creature as a hominin. It looked too apelike, and besides, it came from Africa. The ethnocentrism associated with colonialism dismissed Africa as a proper place to look for human origins. Furthermore, scientists back then assumed erroneously that a key early hominin marker would be a large brain—certainly not the ape-sized cranium of Dart's South African fossil.

"Piltdown man," ostensibly found in a gravel pit in Piltdown, East Sussex, England, in 1912, seemed a more proper human ancestor. It had a large, modern-looking skull, and it came from Europe. Its apelike jaw, however, was hard to explain. What was one to make of this unusual and perplexing mixture? Amazingly, it took over 40 years for Piltdown man to be debunked as a forgery. Fluorine absorption analysis applied to the skull and jaw in 1953 turned Piltdown man into the now infamous "Piltdown hoax." The skull had much more fluorine than the jaw—impossible if they had come from the same individual and had been deposited in the same ground at the same time. Someone had attached the jaw of a young orangutan to the skull of a modern human, then buried the "fossil" in an attempt to muddle the interpretation of the fossil record. The hoax survived longer than its perpetrator probably imagined. Even big-brained scientists can be fooled by the biases of their time.

We know now that bipedalism, rather than a big brain, is the key attribute that distinguishes early hominins from the apes, and upright bipedal locomotion remains fundamental to human existence. Only when we lose it do we fully appreciate the supreme significance of bipedalism. I know this from personal experience. On the day before her 99th birthday, my mother broke her hip. She survived hip replacement surgery, spent a week in the hospital, then entered a rehab center, where she had to rely on staff for much of what she previously had done on her own. She couldn't climb in and out of bed, nor could she bathe herself or attend to personal functions.

Younger people with greater upper body strength often can move about independently without using their legs. Not so a very old woman who over the years had developed osteoporosis and suffered several fractures affecting wrists, arms, and shoulders. All those had been painful reminders of the aging process. None, however, was as devastating as her hip break. Unable to walk and debilitated by an infection she picked up in the hospital, my mother gradually lost her will to live; she died less than two months after her fall.

My mother's longevity illustrates how cultural advances (e.g., medicine, nutrition, operations) have extended the human lifespan—but only to a point. Certainly no ancient hominin lived for a century; however, humans today are no less bipedal than our ancestors were five million years ago. Bipedalism is an integral and enduring feature of human adaptation.

WHAT MAKES US HUMAN?

In trying to determine whether a fossil is a human ancestor, should we look for traits that make us human today? Sometimes yes; sometimes no. We do look for similarities in DNA, including mutations shared by certain lineages but not others. But what about such key human attributes as bipedal locomotion, a long period of childhood dependency, big brains, and the use of tools and language? Some of these key markers of humanity are fairly recent—or have origins that are difficult to date. And ironically, some of the physical markers that have led scientists to identify certain fossils as early hominins rather than apes are features that have receded during subsequent human evolution.

Recall that the term *hominin* is used to designate the human line after its split from ancestral chimps. *Hominid* refers to the taxonomic family that includes humans and the African apes and their immediate ancestors. In this book, *hominid* is used when there is doubt about the hominin status of the fossil.

Bipedalism

Postcranial material from **Ardipithecus,** the earliest widely accepted hominin genus (5.8–4.4 m.y.a.), indicates a capacity—albeit an imperfect one—for upright bipedal locomotion. The *Ardipithecus* pelvis appears to be transitional between one suited for arboreal climbing and one modified for bipedalism. Reliance on *bipedalism*—upright, two-legged locomotion—is the key feature differentiating early hominins from the apes. Based on African fossil discoveries, such as Ethiopia's *Ardipithecus,* hominin bipedalism is more than five million years old. Some scientists see even earlier evidence of bipedalism in two other fossil finds, described below—one from Chad (*Sahelanthropus tchadensis*) and one from Kenya (*Orrorin tugenensis*).

Bipedalism traditionally has been viewed as an adaptation to open grassland or savanna country, although *Ardipithecus* lived in a humid woodland habitat. Perhaps bipedalism developed in the woodlands but became even more adaptive in a savanna habitat (see Choi 2011). Scientists have suggested several advantages of bipedalism: the abilities to see over long grass and scrub vegetation, to carry items back to a home base, and to reduce the body's exposure to solar radiation. Quadrupedalism exposes the body to 60 percent more solar radiation than does bipedalism. Based on the fossil and archaeological records, upright, bipedal locomotion preceded stone tool manufacture and the expansion of the hominin brain. However, although early hominins could move bipedally on the ground, they also preserved enough of an apelike anatomy to make them good climbers (see the section on *Ardipithecus*). They could take to the trees to sleep and to escape terrestrial predators.

Brains, Skulls, and Childhood Dependency

Compared with contemporary humans, early hominins had very small brains. *Australopithecus afarensis,* a bipedal hominin that lived more than three million years ago, had a cranial capacity (430 cm^3—cubic centimeters) that barely surpassed the chimp average (390 cm^3). The form of the *afarensis* skull also is like that of the chimpanzee, although the brain-to-body size ratio may have been larger. Brain size has increased during hominin evolution, especially with the advent of the genus *Homo*. But this increase had to overcome some obstacles. Compared with the young of other primates, human children have a long period of childhood dependency, during which their brains and skulls grow dramatically. Larger skulls demand larger birth canals, but the requirements of upright bipedalism impose limits on the expansion of the human pelvic opening. If the opening is too large, the pelvis doesn't provide sufficient support for the trunk. Locomotion suffers, and posture problems develop. If, by contrast, the birth canal is too narrow, mother and child (without the modern option of Caesarean section) may die. Natural selection has struck a balance between the structural demands of upright posture and the tendency toward increased brain size—the

Ardipithecus
Earliest recognized hominin genus (5.8–4.4 m.y.a.), Ethiopia.

Australopithecus afarensis

40 cm

12 inches

Australopithecus afarensis (3.8–3.0 m.y.a.) striding bipedally. A key part of being human, bipedalism evolved among hominins long before the big brain.

© Encyclopaedia Britannica/UIG/Getty Images

birth of immature and dependent children whose brains and skulls grow dramatically after birth.

Tools

Given what is known about tool use and manufacture by the great apes, it is likely that early hominins shared this ability as a homology with the apes. We'll see later that the first evidence for hominin stone tool manufacture is dated to 3.3 m.y.a. Upright bipedalism would have facilitated the use of tools and weapons. Bipedal locomotion also allowed early hominins to carry things, including scavenged parts of carnivore kills, back to a home base (see Ferraro et al. 2013). We know that primates have generalized abilities to adapt through learning. Early hominins surely had greater cultural abilities than those of modern apes.

Teeth

One example of a hominin trait that has been reduced during subsequent human evolution is big back teeth. (Indeed, a pattern of overall dental reduction characterizes human evolution.) Once they adapted to the savanna, with its gritty, tough, and fibrous vegetation, it was adaptively advantageous for early hominins to have large back teeth and thick tooth enamel. This permitted thorough chewing and mixture with salivary enzymes to permit digestion of foods that otherwise would not have been digestible. The churning, rotary motion associated with such chewing also favored reduction of the canines and first premolars (bicuspids). These front teeth are much sharper and longer in the apes than in early hominins. The apes use their sharp, self-honing teeth to pierce fruits. Males also flash their big, sharp canines to intimidate and impress others, including potential mates and competitors for those mates. Although bipedalism seems to have characterized the human lineage since it split from the line leading to the African apes, many other "human" features came later. Yet other hominin features, such as large back teeth and thick enamel—which are much less characteristic now—offer clues about who was a human ancestor back then.

CHRONOLOGY OF HOMININ EVOLUTION

Although recent fossil discoveries have pushed the hominin lineage back to almost six million years ago, humans actually haven't been around too long when the age of the Earth is considered. If we compare Earth's history to a 24-hour day (with one second equaling 50,000 years),

Earth originated at midnight.

The earliest fossils were deposited at 5:45 A.M.

The first vertebrates appeared at 9:02 P.M.

The earliest mammals, at 10:45 P.M.

The earliest primates, at 11:42 P.M.

The earliest hominins, at 11:56 P.M.

And *Homo sapiens* arrived 36 seconds before midnight. (Wolpoff 1999, p. 10)

Although the first hominins appeared late in the Miocene epoch, for the study of hominin evolution, the Pliocene (5–2.6 m.y.a.), Pleistocene (2.6 m.y.a.–10,000 B.P.), and Recent (10,000 B.P.–present) epochs are most important.

WHO WERE THE EARLIEST HOMININS?

Decades of important, and continuing, discoveries of fossils and tools have increased our knowledge of hominid and hominin evolution. The most significant recent discoveries have been made in Africa—Kenya, Tanzania, Ethiopia, South Africa, and Chad. These finds come from different sites and may be the remains of individuals that lived hundreds of thousands of years apart. Furthermore, geological processes operating over thousands or millions of years inevitably distort fossil remains. Table 8.1 summarizes the major events in hominid and hominin evolution. You should consult it throughout this chapter and the next one.

Sahelanthropus tchadensis

In July 2001 anthropologists working in Central Africa—in northern Chad—unearthed the six- to seven-million-year-old skull of the oldest possible human ancestor yet found. This discovery consists of a nearly complete skull, two lower jaw fragments, and three teeth. It dates to the time period when humans and chimps would have been diverging from a common ancestor. The discovery was made by a 40-member multinational team led by the French paleoanthropologist Michel Brunet. The actual discoverer was the university undergraduate Ahounta Djimdoumalbaye, who spied the skull embedded in sandstone. The new fossil was dubbed *Sahelanthropus tchadensis,* referring to the northern Sahel region of Chad, where it was found. The fossil also is known as "Toumai," a local name meaning "hope of life."

The discovery team identified the skull as that of an adult male with a chimp-sized brain (320–380 cm^3), heavy brow ridges, and a relatively flat, humanlike face. Toumai's habitat included savanna, forests, rivers, and lakes—and abundant animal life such as elephants, antelope, horses, giraffes, hyenas, hippopotamuses, wild boars, crocodiles, fish, and rodents. The associated animal species enabled the team to date the site where Toumai was found (by comparison with radiometrically dated sites with similar fauna).

TABLE 8.1 Dates and Geographic Distribution of Major Hominoid, Hominid, and Hominin Fossil Groups

FOSSIL GROUP	DATES, m.y.a.	KNOWN DISTRIBUTION
Hominoid		
Pierolapithecus catalaunicus	13	Spain
Hominid		
Common ancestor of hominids	8?	East Africa
Sahelanthropus tchadensis	7–6	Chad
Orrorin tugenensis	6	Kenya
Hominins		
Ardipithecus kadabba	5.8–5.5	Ethiopia
Ardipithecus ramidus	4.4	Ethiopia
Kenyanthropus platyops	3.5	Kenya
Gracile australopiths (*Australopithecus*)		
Au. anamensis	4.2–3.9	Kenya
Au. afarensis	3.8–3.0	East Africa (Laetoli, Hadar)
Au. garhi	2.6–2.5	Ethiopia
Au. africanus	3.5–2.5	South Africa
Au. sediba	1.98–1.78	South Africa
Robust australopiths (*Paranthropus*)	2.6–1.0	East and South Africa
Paranthropus aethiopicus	2.6	Kenya
Paranthropus robustus	1.9–1.0	South Africa
Paranthropus boisei	2.3–1.4	East Africa
Homo		
H. rudolfensis	2.03–1.78	East Africa
H. habilis	1.9–1.44	East Africa
H. erectus	1.9–0.44?	Africa, Asia, Europe
H. heidelbergensis	0.8–0.2	Africa, Asia, Europe
Neandertals	0.13–0.028 (130,000–28,000)	Europe, Middle East, Central Asia, Siberia
Anatomically modern humans	0.195–present (95,000–present)	Worldwide (after 20,000 B.P.)

A skull found in 2001 in northern Chad, dated at six to seven million years old, officially named *Sahelanthropus tchadensis*, more commonly called "Toumai," may or may not be the earliest hominin yet known. On the left, French paleontologist Michel Brunet holds Toumai's skull, a cast of which is shown on the right.

Left: © Patrick Robert/Corbis; right: © Acques Demarthon/AFP/Getty Images

The discovery of Toumai moves scientists close to the time when humans and the African apes diverged from a common ancestor (see Weiss 2005; Wood 2011). As we would expect in a fossil so close to the common ancestor, Toumai blends apelike and human characteristics. Although the brain was chimp-sized, the tooth enamel was thicker than a chimp's enamel, suggesting a diet that included not just fruits but also tougher vegetation. Also, Toumai's snout did not protrude as far as a chimp's, making it more humanlike, and the canine tooth was shorter than that of other apes. "The fossil is showing the first glimmerings of evolution in our direction," according to University of California at Berkeley anthropologist Tim White (quoted in Gugliotta 2002).

Toumai is a nearly complete, although distorted, skull. The placement of its *foramen magnum* (the "big hole" through which the spinal cord joins the brain) farther forward than in apes suggests that *Sahelanthropus* moved bipedally. Its discovery in Chad indicates that early hominin evolution was not confined to East Africa's Rift Valley. The abundant fossil record that has come out of the Rift Valley may well reflect geology, preservation, and modern exposure of fossils rather than the actual geographic distribution of species in the past. If *Sahelanthropus* was indeed a hominin, its discovery in Chad is the first proof of a more widespread distribution of early hominins.

Orrorin tugenensis

In January 2001 Brigitte Senut, Martin Pickford, and others reported the discovery, near the village of Tugen in Kenya, of possible early hominin fossils they called *Orrorin tugenensis* (Aiello and Collard 2001; Senut et al. 2001). The find consisted of 13 fossils from at least five individuals. The fossils include pieces of jaw with teeth, isolated upper and lower teeth, arm bones, and a finger bone. *Orrorin* appears to have been a chimp-sized or smaller creature that climbed easily and walked on two legs when on the ground. Its date of six million years ago is close to the time of the common ancestor of humans and chimps. The fossilized left femur (thigh bone) suggests upright bipedalism, while the thick right humerus (upper arm bone) suggests tree-climbing skills. Animal fossils found in the same rocks indicate *Orrorin* lived in a wooded environment.

Orrorin's upper incisor, upper canine, and lower premolar are more like the teeth of a female

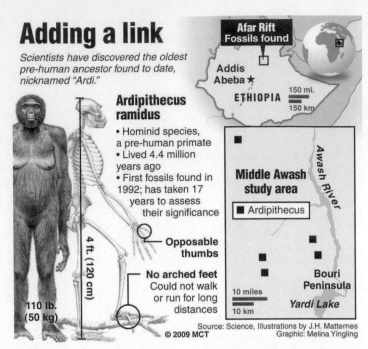

Adding a link

Scientists have discovered the oldest pre-human ancestor found to date, nicknamed "Ardi."

Afar Rift Fossils found

Addis Abeba ★ ETHIOPIA
150 mi.
150 km

Ardipithecus ramidus
• Hominid species, a pre-human primate
• Lived 4.4 million years ago
• First fossils found in 1992; has taken 17 years to assess their significance

4 ft. (120 cm)

110 lb. (50 kg)

— Opposable thumbs

— No arched feet
Could not walk or run for long distances

Middle Awash study area
■ Ardipithecus

Awash River

Bouri Peninsula

Yardi Lake

10 miles
10 km

Source: Science, Illustrations by J.H. Matternes
Graphic: Melina Yingling
© 2009 MCT

Ardipithecus ramidus: Representations of "Ardi," including its skeleton and a map of the discovery area. Living 4.4 million years ago, Ardi was both a hominid and a hominin. What's the difference between those terms?
© Yingling/MCT/Newscom

chimpanzee than like human teeth. But other dental and skeletal features, especially bipedalism, led the discoverers to assign *Orrorin* to the hominin lineage. *Orrorin* lived after *Sahelanthropus tchadensis* but before *Ardipithecus kadabba*, discovered in Ethiopia, also in 2001, and dated to 5.8–5.5 m.y.a. The hominin status of *Ardipithecus* is more generally accepted than is that of either *Sahelanthropus* or *Orrorin*.

Ardipithecus

Ardipithecus had two known species—*Ardipithecus kadabba* (5.8–5.5 m.y.a.) and *Ardipithecus ramidus* (4.4 m.y.a.). The later (*ramidus*) fossils were discovered first, in 1992–1994 in Ethiopia by Berhane Asfaw, Gen Suwa, and Tim White. Dating to 4.4 m.y.a. those ramidus fossils are the remains of some 17 individuals, with cranial, facial, dental, and upper limb bones. Subsequently, much older *Ardipithecus* (*kadabba*) fossils, dating back to the Miocene epoch, were found in Ethiopia. The *kadabba* find consists of 11 specimens, including a jawbone with teeth, hand and foot bones, fragments of arm bones, and a piece of collarbone. At least five individuals are represented. These creatures were apelike in size and anatomy. Their habitat was a mixture of woods and grasslands, and they had ample access to water in springs and lakes. As of this writing, because of its likely bipedalism, *Ardipithecus kadabba* is recognized as the earliest known hominin, with the *Sahelanthropus tchadensis* find from Chad, dated

The Ethiopian paleoanthropologist Yohannes Haile-Selassie was a key member of the multinational, multidisciplinary team responsible for the "Ardi" discovery and analysis.

© Lea-Lisa Westerhoff/AFP/Getty Images

to 7–6 m.y.a., and *Orrorin tugenensis* from Kenya, dated to 6 m.y.a., as possibly even older hominins.

In 2009, a newly reported find—a fairly complete skeleton dubbed "Ardi"—was heralded on the front page of the *New York Times* and throughout the media (Wilford 2009a). Ardi (4.4 m.y.a.), a member of the species *Ardipethicus ramidus,* replaces Lucy (3.2 m.y.a.—see the section on *Austrolapithecus afarensis*) as the earliest known hominin skeleton. Ardi's Ethiopian discovery site lies 45 miles south of Hadar, where Lucy was found. Scientists infer that Ardi was female, based on its small and lightly built (gracile) skull and its small canine teeth compared with others at the site. At 4 feet (1.2 meters) tall and 120 pounds (54 kg), Ardi stood about a foot taller than and weighed twice as much as Lucy.

Ardi's pelvis appears to be transitional between one suited for arboreal climbing and one modified for bipedal locomotion. The pelvis of later hominins such as Lucy shows nearly all the adaptations needed for full bipedalism. Although Ardi's lower pelvis remains primitive, the structure of her upper pelvis allowed her to walk on two legs with a straightened hip. Still, she probably could neither walk nor run as well as Lucy and later hominins. Her feet lacked the archlike structure of later hominin feet, and she had a divergent big toe, like an ape (see Ward, Kimbel, and Johanson 2011). Ardi's apelike lower pelvis indicates retention of powerful hamstring muscles for

climbing. Her hands, very long arms, and short legs all recall those of extinct apes, and her brain was no larger than that of a modern chimp.

Based on associated animal and plant remains, *Ardipithecus* lived in a humid woodland habitat. In this environment, *ramidus* did not need, or have, the heavy chewing specializations of later australopiths. The size, shape, and wear patterns of *ramidus* teeth suggest an omnivorous diet of plants, nuts, and small mammals. Although *Ardipithecus* probably fed both in trees and on the ground, the canines suggest less of a fruit diet than is characteristic of living apes. *Ardipithecus* canines resemble modern human canines more than the tusklike, piercing upper canines of chimps and gorillas.

The first comprehensive reports describing Ardi and related findings, the result of 17 years of study, were published on October 2, 2009, in the journal *Science,* including 11 papers by 47 authors from 10 countries. They analyzed more than 110 *Ardipithecus* specimens from at least 36 different individuals, including Ardi. The ancestral relationship of *Ardipithecus* to *Australopithecus* has not been determined, but Ardi has been called a plausible ancestor for *Australopithecus* (see Wilford 2009a).

AUSTRALOPITHS AND OTHER PLIOCENE HOMININS

Some Miocene hominins evolved into a varied group of Pliocene–Pleistocene hominins known collectively as the **australopiths**—for which we have an abundant fossil record. Two genera are generally recognized within the australopiths: *Australopithecus* (*Au.*) and *Paranthropus.* The various species (with the oldest at the bottom of each group) are as follows:

Genus *Australopithecus*

Au. sediba (1.98–1.78 m.y.a.)

Au. garhi (2.6–2.5 m.y.a.)

Au. africanus (3.5–2.5 m.y.a.)

Au. afarensis (3.8–3.0 m.y.a.)

Au. anamensis (4.2–3.9 m.y.a.)

Genus *Paranthropus*

Paranthropus robustus (1.9–1.0 m.y.a.)

Paranthropus boisei (2.3–1.4 m.y.a.)

Paranthropus aethiopicus (2.6 m.y.a.)

The date ranges given for these species are approximate, because an organism isn't a member of one species one day and a member of another species the next day. Nor could the same dating techniques be used for all the finds. The earliest South African australopith fossils (*Au. africanus* and *Paranthropus robustus*), for example, were found

australopith

Common term for all members of the *Australopithecus* and *Paranthropus* genera.

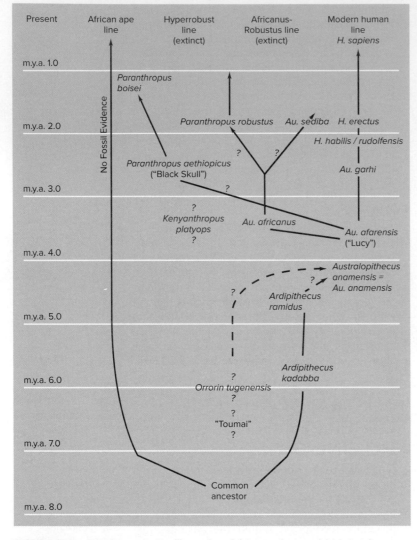

FIGURE 8.1 Phylogenetic Tree for African Apes, Hominids, and Hominins.

The presumed divergence date for ancestral chimps and hominins was between 6 and 8 m.y.a. Branching in later hominin evolution is also shown. For more exact dates, see the text and Table 8.1.

in a nonvolcanic area where radiometric dating could not be done until recently. The hominin fossils from the volcanic regions of East Africa usually have radiometric dates.

Australopithecus anamensis

Ardipithecus may (or may not) have evolved into *Au. anamensis*, a bipedal hominin from northern Kenya, whose fossil remains were reported first by Maeve Leakey and Alan Walker in 1995 (Leakey et al. 1995; Rice 2002). *Au. anamensis* consists of 78 fragments from two sites: Kanapoi and Allia Bay. The fossils include upper and lower jaws, cranial fragments, and parts of a leg bone (tibia, or shinbone). The Kanapoi fossils date to 4.2 m.y.a., and those at Allia Bay to 3.9 m.y.a. Members of this species had apelike canines, along with strong jaws and heavily enameled teeth, suggesting they may at times have eaten

hard, abrasive foods. They probably preferred the fruits and nuts available in their habitat—one of lakes surrounded by forests and woodlands. Based on the tibia, *anamensis* weighed about 110 pounds (50 kg). This would have made it larger than either the earlier *Ardipithecus* or the later *Au. afarensis*. Because of its date and its location in the East African Rift Valley, *Au. anamensis* may be ancestral to *Au. afarensis* (3.8–3.0 m.y.a.), which usually is considered ancestral to all the later australopiths, as well as to *Homo* (Figure 8.1)

Australopithecus afarensis

Au. afarensis includes fossils found at two sites, Laetoli in northern Tanzania and Hadar in the Afar region of Ethiopia. Laetoli is earlier (3.8–3.6 m.y.a.). The Hadar fossils date to between 3.3 and 3.0 m.y.a. All told, *Au. afarensis* existed for about 800,000 years, from 3.8 to 3.0 m.y.a. Mary Leakey (Meave's mother-in-law) directed the research that led to the Laetoli finds. D. C. Johanson and M. Taieb led the international expedition that made the discoveries at Hadar. The two sites have yielded significant samples of early hominin fossils. From Laetoli we have two dozen specimens; and from Hadar, between 35 and 65 individuals. The Laetoli remains are mainly teeth and jaw fragments, along with some very informative fossilized footprints. The Hadar sample includes skull fragments and postcranial material, most notably 40 percent of the skeleton of a tiny hominin female, dubbed "Lucy," who lived around 3 m.y.a. Figure 8.2 is a map showing the major fossil sites discussed so far in this chapter.

Although the hominin remains at Laetoli and Hadar were deposited half a million years apart, their many resemblances explain their placement in the same species. *Au. afarensis,* although clearly a hominin, was similar in many ways to chimps and gorillas (*Ardipithecus* and *Au. anamensis* were even more apelike).

From the same general area of northern Ethiopia as Lucy comes another important member of *Au. afarensis* (Owen 2006, 2012). This toddler, the world's oldest fossil child, soon was dubbed "Lucy's Baby"—despite having lived a hundred thousand years before Lucy (3.3 m.y.a. for the child versus 3.2 for Lucy). The child is an amazingly complete find, with a more intact skull and much more skeletal material than exists for Lucy. Not surprisingly, given what we already know about *Au. afarensis,* the skull and upper body are apelike, while the lower body confirms bipedalism. Despite bipedalism, the skeleton's upper body includes two complete shoulder blades similar to a gorilla's, so it probably was better at climbing than humans are (see Owen 2012).

Unearthed in 2000, the child probably was female and about 3 years old when she died. The

Au. anamensis
Earliest known *Australopithecus* species (4.2–3.9 m.y.a.), Kenya.

Au. afarensis
Early *Australopithecus* species (3.8–3.0 m.y.a.), Ethiopia ("Lucy"), Tanzania.

remains include a well-preserved skull, baby teeth, tiny fingers, a torso, a foot, and a kneecap. Although Lucy doesn't have much of a head, her "baby" has a complete skull, a mandible (jawbone), and a monkey-sized face with a smooth brow.

If Lucy's Baby had lived, she would have developed rapidly, reaching adulthood earlier than modern humans, and her lifespan would have been much shorter than ours. The *afarensis* growth cycle was more similar to the chimpanzee pattern than to the modern human pattern. The shorter growth period would have allowed less time for guidance and socialization.

How did the dentition of *Au. afarensis* compare with ape and human dentitions? The *afarensis* canines were longer and sharper than in *Homo* and projected beyond the other teeth. Compared with an ape's tusklike canines, however, the *afarensis* canines were reduced. More like an ape's than a human's premolar, the *afarensis* lower premolar was pointed and projecting. It had one long cusp and only a tiny bump that hints at the bicuspid premolar that eventually developed in hominin evolution (see Figure 8.3).

The *afarensis* diet was mainly vegetarian, including leaves, seeds, fruits, and nuts. Lucy and her kind probably also ate insects and small vertebrates, such as lizards. Dental microwear studies show that *afarensis* ate soft, sugar-rich foods (such as fruits), but their tooth size and shape confirm that they could also process hard, brittle foods. These may have been fallback foods, which they ate when more desirable foods were unavailable. *Au. afarensis* molars are large. The lower jaw (mandible) is thick and is buttressed with a bony ridge behind the front teeth. The cheekbones are large and flare out to the side for the attachment of chewing muscles.

The small *Au. afarensis* skull contrasts with those of later hominins. Its cranial capacity (430 cm^3) barely surpasses the chimp average (390 cm^3).

Although bidepal, *Au. afarensis* still contrasts in many ways with later hominins. For example, sexual dimorphism is marked. *Au. afarensis* females, such as Lucy, stood between 3 and 4 feet (0.9 and 1.2 meters) tall; males might have reached 5 feet (1.5 meters). Adult males may have weighed almost twice as much as the females did. Recap 8.1 summarizes data on the various australopiths, including dates, locations, average weight, and brain size. Mid-sex means midway between the male average and the female average.

Lucy and her kind were far from dainty. Her muscle-engraved bones are much more robust than ours are. With only rudimentary tools and weapons, early hominins needed powerful and resistant bones and muscles. Lucy's apelike arms are longer relative to her legs than are those of later hominins; she probably spent some of her time in the trees.

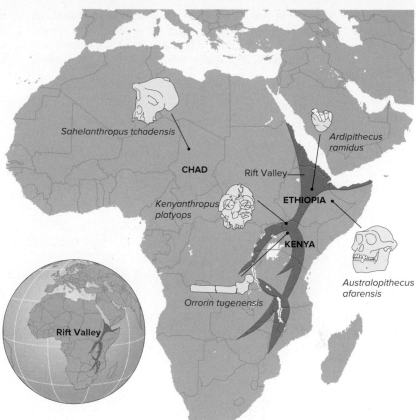

FIGURE 8.2 The East African Rift Valley and Early Fossil Hominins. Early fossil hominins have been found throughout the valley as well as in Chad in north-central Africa.

An ancient trail of hominin footprints fossilized in volcanic ash. Mary Leakey found this 230-foot (70-meter) trail at Laetoli, Tanzania, in 1979. It dates from 3.6 m.y.a. and confirms that *Au. afarensis* was a striding biped.

© John Reader/Science Photo Library/Science Source

The *Au. afarensis* fossils show that as recently as three million years ago, our ancestors had a mixture of apelike and hominin features. Canines, premolars, and skulls were apelike, but the molars, chewing apparatus, and cheekbones foreshadowed later hominin trends, and the pelvic and limb bones were indisputably hominin (Figure 8.4). The hominin pattern was being built from the ground up.

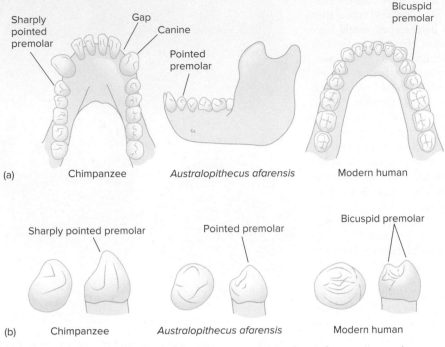

(a) Chimpanzee | *Australopithecus afarensis* | Modern human

(b) Chimpanzee | *Australopithecus afarensis* | Modern human

FIGURE 8.3 Comparison of Dentition in Ape, *Au. afarensis,* and Human Palates.

Teeth of chimpanzee, *Australopithecus afarensis,* and modern human. In (a), note the parallel tooth rows in the chimpanzee, as compared to those of the modern human. In (b), note the sharply pointed premolar of the chimpanzee, the pointed premolar of *Au. afarensis,* and the bicuspid premolar of the modern human.

RECAP 8.1   Facts about the Australopiths Compared with Chimps and *Homo*

SPECIES	DATES (m.y.a.)	KNOWN DISTRIBUTION	IMPORTANT SITES	BODY WEIGHT (MID-SEX)	BRAIN SIZE (MID-SEX) (cm³)
Anatomically modern humans	195,000–present			132 lb/60 kg	1,350
Pan troglodytes (chimpanzee)	Modern			93 lb/42 kg	390
Au. sediba	1.98–1.78	S. Africa	Malapa	Insufficient data	420
Paranthropus boisei	2.3–1.4	E. Africa	Olduvai, East Turkana	86 lb/39 kg	490
Paranthropus robustus	1.9–1.0	S. Africa	Kromdraai, Swartkrans	81 lb/37 kg	540
Au. africanus	3.5–2.5	S. Africa	Taung, Sterkfontein, Makapansqat	79 lb/36 kg	490
Au. afarensis	3.8–3.0	E. Africa	Hadar, Laetoli	77 lb/35 kg	430
Au. anamensis	4.2–3.9	Kenya	Kanapoi, Allia Bay	Insufficient data	No published skulls
Ardipithecus	5.8–4.4	Ethiopia	Aramis	Insufficient data	No published skulls

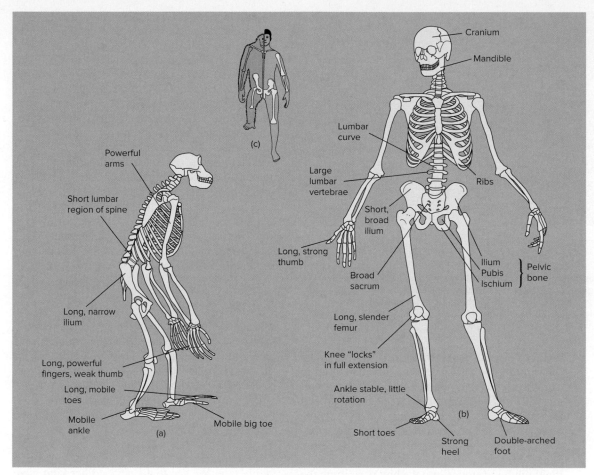

FIGURE 8.4 Comparison of *Homo sapiens* and *Pan troglodytes* (the Common Chimp). (a) Skeleton of chimpanzee in bipedal position; (b) skeleton of modern human; (c) chimpanzee and human "bisected" and drawn to the same trunk length for comparison of limb proportions. The contrast in leg length is largely responsible for the proportional difference between humans and apes.

Important evidence of striding bipedalism by *Au. afarensis* comes from Laetoli. Volcanic ash, which can be directly dated by the K/A (potassium/argon) technique, covered a trail of footprints of two or three hominins walking to a water hole. These prints leave no doubt that a striding biped lived in Tanzania by 3.6 m.y.a. The structure of the pelvic, hip, leg, and foot bones leaves no doubt that upright bipedalism was *Au. afarensis*'s mode of locomotion (see Choi 2012; Ward et al. 2011). Accordingly, australopith (*afarensis* and later) pelvises are much more similar to the human pelvis than to an ape pelvis (Figure 8.5). The blades of the *afarensis* pelvis (iliac blades) are shorter and broader than those of the ape. The sacrum, which anchors the pelvis's two side bones, is larger, as in *Homo*. With bipedalism, the pelvis forms a sort of bowl that balances the weight of the trunk and supports that weight with less stress. The *afarensis* spine had the lower spine (lumbar) curve characteristic of *Homo*. This curvature helps transmit the weight of the upper body to the pelvis and the legs. Placement of the *foramen magnum*

Illustration of female *Australopithecus afarensis* "Lucy," discovered in Ethiopia's Omo Valley in 1974.

© Lionel Bret/Science Source

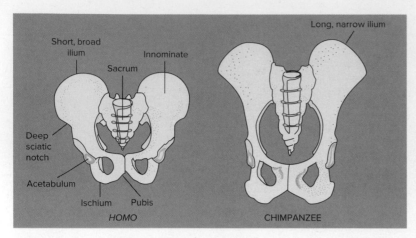

FIGURE 8.5 A Comparison of Human and Chimpanzee Pelvises.

The human pelvis has been modified to meet the demands of upright bipedalism. The blades (*ilia; singular, ilium*) of the human pelvis are shorter and broader than those of the ape. The sacrum, which anchors the side bones, is wider. The australopith pelvis is far more similar to that of *Homo* than to that of the chimpanzee, as we would expect in an upright biped.

farther forward in *Australopithecus* and *Homo* than in the ape also represents an adaptation to upright bipedalism (Figure 8.6). The head balances directly on top of the neck if the hole is right underneath the skull rather than at the back, as in a quadruped. In apes, the thigh bone (femur) extends straight down from the hip to the knees. In *Australopithecus* and *Homo,* however, the thigh bone angles into the hip, permitting the space between the knees to be narrower than the pelvis during walking.

Although the pelvises of the australopiths (*afarensis* and later) were similar to those of *Homo*, they were not identical. The most significant contrast is a narrower australopith birth canal. Expansion of the birth canal is a trend in hominin evolution. Undoubtedly, their skulls grew after birth to accommodate a growing brain, as ours do (much more). However, the brains of the australopiths expanded less than ours do. The cranial sutures (the lines where the bones of the skull eventually come together) fused earlier for australopiths than for humans. Nevertheless, young australopiths must have depended on their parents and kin for nurturance and protection. Those years of childhood dependency would have provided time for observation, teaching, and learning. This may provide indirect evidence for a rudimentary cultural life.

Kenyanthropus

Adding to the complexity of the early hominin family tree is yet another discovery, which Meave Leakey has named *Kenyanthropus platyops,* or flat-faced "man" of Kenya. (Actually, the sex hasn't been determined.) This 1999 fossil find—of a nearly complete skull and partial jawbone—was made by a research team led by Leakey, excavating in northern Kenya. The researchers consider this 3.5-million-year-old find to represent an entirely new branch of the early hominin family tree. We see that Lucy and her kind were not the only early hominins to inhabit Africa's Great Rift Valley. Recent fossil discoveries have

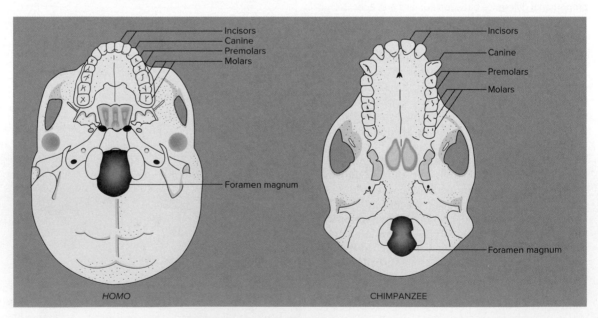

FIGURE 8.6 A Comparison of the Skull and Dentition (Upper Jaw) of *Homo* and the Chimpanzee.

The foramen magnum, through which the spinal cord joins the brain, is located farther forward in *Homo* than in the ape. This permits the head to balance atop the spine with upright bipedalism. The molars and premolars of the ape form parallel rows. Human teeth, by contrast, are arranged in rounded, parabolic form. What differences do you note between human and ape canines? Canine reduction has been an important trend in hominin evolution.

made it increasingly apparent that the hominin family tree, once drawn with a straight trunk, now looks more like a bush, with branches leading in many directions. (Such bushlike, rather than straight-line, evolutionary trees tend to be the rule in nature.)

Gracile and Robust Australopiths

In 1924, the anatomist Raymond Dart coined the term *Australopithecus africanus* to describe the first fossil representative of this species, the skull of a juvenile that was found accidentally in a quarry at Taung, South Africa. The many australopith fossils found subsequently in South Africa appear to have lived between 3.5 and 1 m.y.a. The most recent South African *Australopithecus* find, *Au. sediba,* described in this chapter's "Appreciating Anthropology," has been dated to 1.98 m.y.a.

The South African australopiths fall into two groups: **gracile** (*Au. africanus* and *Au. sediba*) and **robust** (*Paranthropus robustus*). Based on recent advances in dating techniques, **Au. africanus** appears to have lived between 3.5 and 2.5 m.y.a. *Au. sediba,* also gracile and a likely descendant of *africanus,* is more recent, having lived just under 2 m.y.a. "Gracile" indicates that the australopiths in that category were slighter, less rugged and robust, with smaller teeth and faces, than were members of *Paranthropus robustus*. Recap 1 summarizes the average weight of the different australopith species. We see, perhaps surprisingly, that *Au. afarensis* was actually larger, on average, than the later australopiths.

The current dating for **Paranthropus robustus** is 1.9–1.0 m.y.a. A related hominin is the somewhat older and even more robust, or *hyperrobust,* **Paranthropus boisei** of East Africa, whose dates are 2.3–1.4 m.y.a. Both *Au. africanus* and *Paranthropus* probably descend from *Au. afarensis,* which itself was gracile in form, or from a South African version of *Au. afarensis.*

In 1985 the paleoanthropologist Alan Walker made a significant fossil find near Lake Turkana in northern Kenya. This discovery is commonly called the "black skull" because of the blue-black sheen it bore from the minerals surrounding it. The jaw was apelike and the brain was small (as in *Au. afarensis*), but there was a massive bony crest atop the skull (as in *Paranthropus boisei*). Walker and Richard Leakey (Meave's husband, and Walker's associate on the 1985 expedition) view the black skull (dated to 2.6 m.y.a.) as a very early hyperrobust *Paranthropus boisei*. Others assign the black skull to its own species, *Paranthropus aethiopicus*. The black skull shows that some of the anatomical features of the genus *Paranthropus* (2.6–1.0 m.y.a.) did not change very much during about 1.5 million years.

Like earlier hominins, the South African australopiths still had skulls that were more ape-sized

Meave Leakey and *Kenyanthropus platyops,* which she discovered in 1999 by Lake Turkana.

© Kenneth Garrett/National Geographic Creative

than human. The average brain size of *Au. africanus* was 490 cm³, compared with 540 cm³ for *Paranthropus robustus*. These figures can be compared with an average cranial capacity of 430 cm³ in *Au. afarensis* and 1,350 cm³ in *Homo sapiens*. The cranial capacity of chimps (*Pan troglodytes*) averages 390 cm³ (see Recap 8.1). The brains of gorillas *(Gorilla gorilla)* average around 500 cm³, which is within the australopith range, but gorilla body size is much greater.

Also as in earlier hominins, sexual dimorphism within each South African species remained much more pronounced than it is in *Homo sapiens*. Australopith females, whether gracile or robust, were shorter, weighed much less, and had smaller canines than males of the same species. The dimorphism in body size exceeded that in chimpanzees but probably was less than in gorillas.

The teeth, jaws, and skulls of these australopiths leave no doubt that their diet was mainly vegetarian, although they did eat meat from time to time. They captured small and slow-moving game, and they scavenged, bringing home parts of kills made by large cats and other carnivores. Natural selection modifies the teeth and surrounding structures to conform to the stresses associated with a particular diet. Large back teeth, jaws, and associated facial and cranial structures confirm a diet requiring extensive grinding and crushing. The cheekbones of the South African australopiths (especially *Paranthropus*) were elongated structures (Figure 8.7) that anchored large chewing muscles running up the jaw. Another set of robust chewing muscles extended from the back of the jaw to the sides of the skull. Their canines, however, are reduced, and their premolars are fully bicuspid.

Au. africanus
Gracile *Australopithecus* species (3.5–2.5 m.y.a.), South Africa.

gracile
e.g., *Au. afarensis; Au. africanus; Au. sediba;* less robust, i.e., slighter than *Paranthropus.*

robust
e.g., *Paranthropus robustus* and *Paranthropus boisei;* having large, strong, sturdy bones, muscles, and teeth.

Paranthropus robustus
Robust South African australopiths (1.9–1.0 m.y.a.).

Paranthropus boisei
Late, hyperrobust East African australopiths (2.3–1.4 m.y.a.).

appreciating ANTHROPOLOGY

Au. sediba: Ancestor or Fascinating Sideline?

Named by *Smithsonian* magazine as the number one hominid (and hominin) fossil discovery of 2011, *Australopithecus sediba* (actually discovered between 2008 and 2010 but described in 2011) initially generated a new debate about human origins. The original find is an almost complete skull and partial skeleton of an 11- to 12-year-old boy who stood 4'3" (1.3 m.) tall. Its discoverer, paleoanthropologist Lee Berger, originally viewed *Au. sediba* as a possible human ancestor. Most experts rejected that view, while appreciating the fossil for its unique blend of hominin features. *Au. sediba* dates to 1.98–1.78 m.y.a. This is well after the human line (genus *Homo*) diverged from the australopith line. The earliest known fossil member of the genus *Homo,* reported in 2015, lived 2.8 m.y.a.—a million years before *Au. sediba.* Anthropologists now view *Au. sediba* as another one of the many divergent branches of the bushy tree of hominin evolution.

With long arms . . . and powerful fingers, the ancient creatures were built for climbing trees. But they also had long lower limbs, flat feet and a flexible lumbar spine that [allowed them to] . . . cover long distances by walking upright on two legs.

After four years of intense analysis, a team of paleoanthropologists is making its most detailed case yet that a pair of ancient skeletons discovered in a grassy South African valley could represent the direct evolutionary link between modern humans and the family of human ancestors that includes the *Australopithecus* known as Lucy.

In a series of papers published in . . . the journal *Science* [on April 12, 2013], the researchers argue that the "mosaic nature" of the *Australopithecus sediba* specimens makes them a strong candidate to be the . . . "branch of *Australopithecus* that ultimately gave rise to the genus *Homo,* which includes *Homo sapiens.*"

The skeleton fossils have so many human-like features "across the whole of the body that it must be considered, at the very least, a possible ancestor," said Lee R. Berger, a paleoanthropologist at the University of Witwatersrand in Johannesburg, South Africa, who discovered the fossils in 2008. . . . But not everyone accepts this view. Critics say the skeletons are not old enough to be the precursors to *Homo.* Others say the similarities can be chalked up to the diversity of early hominids.

At a minimum, the new details . . . are causing scientists to revise . . . some long-held assumptions about the anatomical makeup of our extended evolutionary family. For example, though it was long believed that Australopiths had six lower vertebrae, "one more than humans and at least two more than apes," it is now clear that they had the same number as humans: five. The ape-like boy and older woman who tumbled through a sinkhole and lay buried in a deep underground cave for nearly 2 million years have also given scientists a better view of how our early relatives walked. . . .

By examining bone grooves and muscle attachments in the kneecap, thigh and lower leg bones and comparing them with those in humans and apes, the scientists were able to figure out that the roughly 4-foot-tall [female] walked upright. But she probably did so with a peculiar

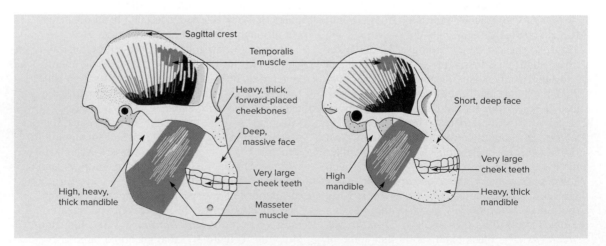

FIGURE 8.7 Skulls of Robust (Left) and Gracile (Right) Australopiths, Showing Chewing Muscles.
Flaring cheek arches and, most typically in robusts, a sagittal crest supported this massive musculature. A diet of coarse, gritty vegetation led to such structures. These features were most pronounced in *Paranthropus,* especially in the hyperrobust *Paranthropus boisei.*

gait marked by an inward rotation of the knee and hip, causing her narrow-heeled feet to twist slightly. . . . The team wrote that it would need to examine more fossils before it could say whether the entire species walked the same way. Berger said that if modern humans were to observe an *Au. sediba* walking by, their attention would probably not be drawn to its legs. "What would be a great difference would be how it swung its long upper limbs during that walk and the shrugged-shoulder appearance of its upper body," he said. The researchers speculated that the animals spent their lives both in trees and walking on the ground. In other aspects of the research, scientists reported that these specimens had jaws and teeth that are recognizably human. In earlier studies, researchers concluded too that the creature's hands were capable of precise gripping. The presence of several human-like features has led Berger and others to suggest that *Au. sediba*, which lived an estimated 1.78 million to 1.95 million years ago, may have been the species that evolved into the earliest members of the *Homo* genus. But other paleoanthropologists have pointed out several problems with that thesis.

Lee Berger and his son, Matthew, announce the discovery of *Australopithecus sediba*. Matthew found one of the fossils while chasing his dog.
© Foto24/Gallo Images/Getty Images

Donald Johanson, the Arizona State University paleoanthropologist who discovered Lucy in 1974, said the first *Homo* species appeared 2.4 million years ago in eastern Africa. Instead of giving rise to the genus *Homo*, *Au. sediba* would have been a contemporary. "Sediba abundantly demonstrates a unique set of anatomical features of an *Australopithecus* species that was most likely a dead-end branch on our tree," said Johanson, who was not involved in the new studies. . . .

SOURCE: Monte Morin, "Evidence Points toward Solving Evolutionary 'Missing Link.'" *Los Angeles Times,* April 11, 2013. Copyright © 2013 Los Angeles Times. Reprinted with permission.

(Left) Profile view of *Paranthropus boisei* skull—Olduvai Hominid (OH) 5, originally called *Zinjanthropus boisei*. This skull of a young male, discovered by Mary Leakey in 1959 at Olduvai Gorge, Tanzania, dates back 1.8 million years. (Right) Profile view of an *Au. africanus* (gracile) skull (Sterkfontein 5). The cranium, discovered by Dr. Robert Broom and J. T. Robinson in April 1947, dates back to 3.5–2.5 m.y.a.

Left: © The Natural History Museum/Alamy Stock Photo; right: © The Natural History Museum/Alamy Stock Photo

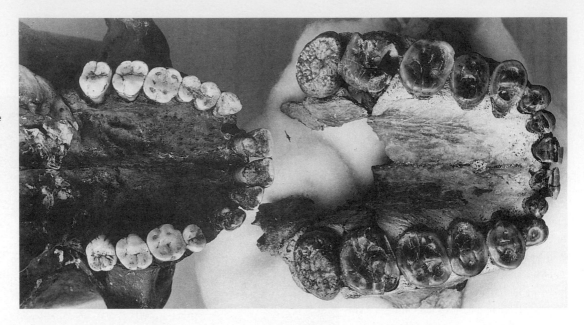

Palates of *Homo sapiens* (left) and *Paranthropus boisei* (right), a late, hyperrobust australopith. In comparing them, note the australopith's huge molars and premolars. The large back teeth represent an extreme adaptation to a diet based on coarse, gritty savanna vegetation.

© Des Bartlett/Science Source

Oldowan

Earliest (2.6–1.2 m.y.a.) stone tools; sharp flakes struck from cores (choppers).

Compared with the graciles, *Paranthropus* had larger skulls and back teeth. They also had thicker faces and more rugged skull features and muscle markings on the skeleton. Their front teeth, however, were about the same size as those of the graciles. *Paranthropus* had chewing muscles that were strong enough to produce a *sagittal crest,* a bony ridge on the top of the skull. Such a crest forms as the bone grows. It develops from the pull of the chewing muscles as they meet at the midline of the skull and serves to anchor those muscles.

Members of *Paranthropus boisei* had mammoth back teeth. Their females had bigger back teeth than did earlier australopith males. The destiny of the *Paranthropus* branch of the hominin family tree was to adapt to arid areas and become ever more specialized with respect to one part of the traditional australopith diet. The need to process vegetation that was harder to chew than for any previous hominin would explain the hyperrobusts' huge back teeth, jaws, and associated areas of the face and skull. *Paranthropus boisei* persisted in East Africa until about 1.4 m.y.a., when it finally became extinct, as did *Paranthropus robustus* in South Africa around 1 m.y.a. Figure 8.8 is a drawing of the skulls of four species of australopithecus.

EARLY STONE TOOLS

The simplest obviously manufactured tools were discovered in 1931 by L. S. B. and Mary Leakey at Olduvai Gorge, Tanzania. That locale gave the tools their name—**Oldowan** pebble tools. The oldest tools from Olduvai are about 1.8 million years old, but older Oldowan tools (2.6–2.0 m.y.a.) have been found in other parts of Africa.

Stone tools consist of flakes and cores. The *core* is the piece of rock, in the Oldowan case about the size of a tennis ball, from which flakes are struck. Once flakes are removed, the core can become a tool itself. A *chopper* is a tool made by flaking the edge of such a core on one side and thus forming a cutting edge.

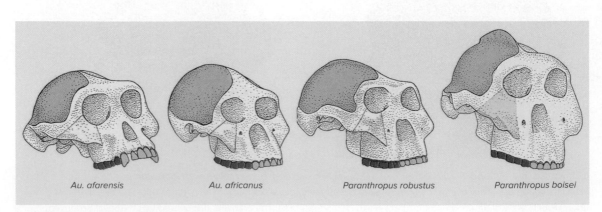

| Au. afarensis | Au. africanus | Paranthropus robustus | Paranthropus boisei |

FIGURE 8.8 Four Types of Australopith.
What are the main differences you notice among these four types of early hominins?

The purpose of flaking stone in the Oldowan tradition was not so much to make pebble tools or choppers as to create the sharp stone flakes that were the mainstay of the Oldowan tool kit (Figure 8.9). Choppers were a convenient by-product of flaking and were used as well, probably for food processing—by pounding, breaking, or bashing. Flakes probably were used mainly as cutters, for example, to dismember game carcasses. Crushed fossil animal bones indicate that stones were used to break open marrow cavities. Also, Oldowan deposits include pieces of bone or horn with scratch marks suggesting they were used to dig up tubers or insects.

Surpisingly Early Stone Tools

In 1999 an international team reported the discovery, in Ethiopia, of a new australopith species, dated to 2.6–2.5 m.y.a. Surprised by the combination of skeletal and dental features in this new hominin, they named it *Australopithecus garhi* (***Au. garhi***). The word *garhi* means "surprise" in the Afar language. Associated with these hominin fossils is evidence, the earliest yet found, of animal butchery (Asfaw, White, and Lovejoy 1999). *Au. garhi* (or whoever did the butchering) must have used early stone tools to butcher, and extract marrow from, the bones of the antelopes and horses found at the site.

In 1997 the Ethiopian archaeologist Sileshi Semaw had found stone tools dating to 2.6 m.y.a. at the nearby Ethiopian site of Gona. Did *Au. garhi* make these tools, and what were they used for? If not, who did? Based on what we know about chimpanzee stone tool use, combined with discoveries of increasingly older stone tools, it becomes increasingly likely that the australopiths were toolmakers, with some capacity for culture.

The year 2015 was an important one for announcements about hominin evolution. A hard-to-reach cave in South Africa yielded a treasure trove of fossils (see Chapter 9). The earliest member of the genus *Homo*, dated to 2.8 m.y.a., was found in Ethiopia, and the earliest stone tools were discovered in Kenya. Dated to 3.3 m.y.a., these tools are 700,000 years older than the previously recognized earliest stone tools. Sonia Harmand of Stony Brook University led the team that discovered these tools, scattered in a dry river bed near the western shore of Kenya's Lake Turkana. At this site, Lomekwi 3, the ancient toolmakers had knapped stone intentionally, breaking off sharp pieces from a core with quick, hard strikes. Much larger and cruder than the Oldowan tools that came later, the Lomekwi tools bear scars from the rudimentary techniques used to make them. The toolmakers probably used two hands and rested the stone core on an anvil when hitting it with a hammer stone, as wild chimps still do today when cracking open nuts.

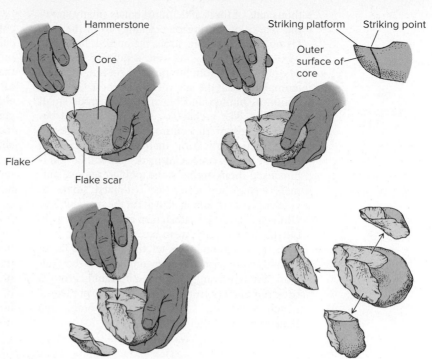

FIGURE 8.9 *Making Oldowan Tools.*
The toolmaker strikes a hard stone (the core) in just the right place to remove thin, sharp flakes.

Oldowan Hominins at the Kanjera Site

Comparisons with chimps and bonobos suggest that hominins always have lived in social groups composed of multiple males and females. In such a group, a chimp female in estrus will mate with multiple males, and males mate with multiple females. Hominins, which are even more social than chimps and bonobos, have continued to live in groups with multiple adult males and females. At some point in their evolution, however, hominins developed pair bonding (Lukas and Clutton-Brock 2013; Opie et al. 2013; Zimmer 2013). A male and a female would pair off, bond, and mate exclusively or mainly with each other for a significant period of time. Such a bond would increase the likelihood that the offspring of the female were also those of the male. Both parents would do all they could to ensure the child's survival and well-being. At some point, especially as hominins became dependent on hunting, a gender-based division of labor developed. Men who hunted took meat home to share with their mates, their children, and other members of their social group.

Anthropologists have found excellent evidence for hunting around two million years ago at a very rich site in Kenya—the Kanjera South, or KJS, site, located on the shores of Lake Victoria (Ferraro et al. 2013). The archaeologists analyzed

Au. garhi
Toolmaking *Australopithecus* species (2.6–2.5 m.y.a.), Ethiopia.

thousands of tools and animal bones (many showing marks of cutting or cracking) from the site. Using Oldowan stone tools, the ancient hominins who occupied the site were acquiring and processing meat—from hunting and scavenging. The animal bones at the site reveal that these Oldowan hominins hunted and butchered numerous small antelopes. The archaeologists could tell this because bones of the entire animal were present at the site—indicating that carcasses had been brought back whole. Cut marks show that hominins used their simple stone tools to remove animal flesh. They also used fist-sized stones to crack open animal bones to get at the marrow. The Oldowan hominins ate larger antelopes as well, but these typically were scavenged rather than hunted. Again the bones tell the story: The larger animals were represented by only part of the skeleton and skull, suggesting that hominins brought back remainders from the kills of other predators, which could not as easily get at the brains and bone marrow of their prey.

The Kanjera site provides the earliest, and very complete, evidence for what the anthropologists call "persistent" reliance on meat within the hominin diet. We don't know the genus or species of these hominins, but we do know the significance of a meat-laden diet. Among the likely social changes associated with such a diet were a gender-based division of labor, pair bonding, and increased parental (especially male) investment in children. Meat supported population increase and territorial expansion among hominins. We hear so much today about the dangers of too much red meat that we forget that meat is an excellent and concentrated source of calories, protein, and fat. Its inclusion in the ancient hominin diet supported an increase in the size of the human body and brain, which is a very expensive organ in terms of its energy needs. To summarize, a regular diet of red meat was a key factor allowing the growth of the hominin body and brain and the spread of hominins within and beyond Africa, a story told in the next chapter.

for REVIEW

summary

1. A skull found in 2001 in northern Chad, dated at 6–7 million years old, officially named *Sahelanthropus tchadensis,* more commonly called "Toumai," may or may not be the earliest hominin yet known, as may the somewhat less ancient *Orrorin tugenensis,* found in Kenya in 2001.

2. Hominins have lived during the late Miocene, Pliocene (5.0–2.6 m.y.a.), and Pleistocene (2.6 m.y.a–10,000 B.P.) epochs. The australopiths had appeared by 4.2 m.y.a. (as *Au. anamensis*). The australopiths include two genera: *Australopithecus* and *Paranthropus.* The known species of *Australopithecus* are as follows: *Au. anamensis* (4.2–3.9 m.y.a.), *Au. afarensis* (3.8–3.0 m.y.a.), *Au. africanus* (3.5–2.5 m.y.a.), *Au. garhi* (2.6–2.5 m.y.a.), and *Au. sediba* (1.98–1.78 m.y.a.). The species of *Paranthropus are as follows: Paranthropus robustus* (1.9–1.0 m.y.a.), *Paranthropus boisei* (2.3–1.4 m.y.a.), and *Paranthropus aethiopicus* (2.6 m.y.a.). The earliest definite hominin remains, from Ethiopia, are classified as *Ardipithecus kadabba* (5.8–5.5 m.y.a.) and *ramidus* (4.4 m.y.a.). Next comes *Au. anamensis,* then a group of fossils from Hadar, Ethiopia, and Laetoli, Tanzania, classified as *Au. afarensis.*

3. These earliest hominins shared many primitive (apelike) features, including upper bodies adapted for climbing; elongated premolars; a small, apelike skull; and marked sexual dimorphism. Still, *Au. afarensis* and its predecessors were definite hominins. In *Au. afarensis* this is confirmed by abundant skeletal evidence for upright bipedalism.

4. Remains of two later groups, *Au. africanus* (graciles) and *Paranthropus robustus* (robusts), were found in South Africa. Both groups show the australopith trend toward a powerful chewing apparatus. They had large molars and premolars and large and robust faces, skulls, and muscle markings. All these features are more pronounced in the robusts than they are in the graciles. The basis of the australopith diet was savanna vegetation.

5. *Paranthropus boisei,* the hyperrobust australopiths, became extinct around 1.4 m.y.a., as did *Paranthropus robustus* around 1 m.y.a. *Paranthropus* became increasingly specialized, dependent on tough, coarse, gritty, fibrous savanna vegetation.

6. Oldowan tools (flakes and choppers) dated to 1.8 m.y.a. were first found at Olduvai Gorge in Tanzania, hence, their name. Earlier Oldowan tools (some as old as 2.6 m.y.a.) have been found subsequently at other African sites. Even earlier stone tools (3.3 m.y.a.) come from a recent discovery at the Lomekwi 3 site in Kenya.

A regular diet of red meat was a key factor allowing the growth of the hominin body and brain and the spread of hominins within and beyond Africa. Among the likely social changes associated with the new diet were a gender-based division of labor, pair bonding, and increased parental (especially male) investment in children.

key terms

critical thinking

1. If you found a new hominid fossil in East Africa, dated to five million years ago, would it most likely be an ape ancestor or a human ancestor? How would you tell the difference?
2. In trying to determine whether a fossil is a human ancestor, researchers sometimes look for traits that have receded during subsequent human evolution. What is an example of this? What early hominin traits have persisted in humans, and which ones have changed significantly?
3. In human evolution, what is the relationship between brains, skulls, and childhood dependency? Thinking back to Chapter 1, how does the study of this relationship illustrate anthropology's biocultural approach?
4. What new light did the fossil known as "Ardi" shed on the understanding of human evolution?
5. Compare the significance of the *Ardipithecus* and *Au. afarensis* finds (i.e., Ardi and Lucy, respectively). Which do you consider to be more important, and why?

CHAPTER 9

The Genus *Homo*

▶ What were the earliest forms of *Homo,* and where did they originate and eventually migrate?

▶ What were the major toolmaking traditions and adaptive strategies of *Homo erectus* and its successors?

▶ What were the Neandertals like, and how did they differ from earlier and later forms of *Homo*?

A Neandertal skeleton (right) and a modern human skeleton (left and behind) displayed at New York's American Museum of Natural History. The Neandertal skeleton, reconstructed from casts of more than 200 fossil bones, was part of an exhibit titled "The First Europeans: Treasures from the Hills of Atapuerca" (Spain).

chapter outline

understanding OURSELVES

Fred Flintstone was the only caveman (the only cave person, for that matter) to appear on a VH1 list of the "200 Greatest Pop Culture Icons." He ranked number 42, between Cher and Martha Stewart. The Flintstones and their neighbors, the Rubbles, don't look much like Neanderthals (which anthropologists spell Neandertal, without the *h*). Real Neandertals had heavy brow ridges and slanting foreheads, and they lacked chins. *The Flintstones* transposed a 20th-century American blue-collar lifestyle back to prehistoric times—Fred and Barney worked in factories, "drove" stone cars, and used dinosaurs as construction cranes and can openers. While it is clearly ridiculous to imagine that Neandertals used dinosaurs as tools, it is equally outlandish to think that dinosaurs and Neandertals might have coexisted. Dinosaurs were extinct long before humans, hominins, or hominids ever walked the Earth. Just as American popular culture never tires of calling apes "monkeys," it can't seem to resist mixing dinosaurs and cave people.

Decades after Fred first appeared on TV, Geico commercials introduced new cavemen, along with the slogan "So easy a caveman can do it." The 21st-century world of Geico's cavemen included cell phones, airports, and tennis courts. Geico's cavemen shared another modern trait—a sense of outrage over the insult implied in their sponsor's slogan. Should it be insulting to call someone a "caveman" or a "Neandertal"? Consider that the average Neandertal brain was larger than the average human brain, although what that says about intelligence isn't clear. One fossil in particular helped create the enduring popular stereotype of the slouching, inferior Neandertal caveman. This was a skeleton discovered a century ago at La Chapelle-aux-Saints in southwestern France. The original assessment of this fossil created an inaccurate image of Neandertals as apelike brutes who had trouble walking upright. Closer analysis revealed that La Chapelle was an aging man with arthritic bones. This illustrates the danger of attempting to reach broad conclusions based upon a small sample size.

Actually, as one would expect, Neandertals were a variable population. Some fossil hominins even combine Neandertal robustness with modern features. For example, the remains of a 4-year-old boy found in Portugal, dating back some 24,000 years, show mixed Neandertal and modern features. This find and others have raised the question as to whether Neandertals and anatomically modern humans could have mated. Another modern activity in which the Geico cavemen engage is dating anatomically modern women. The extent to which similar attractions are part of history is one more subject for scientific debate.

EARLY *HOMO*

This chapter surveys the biological and cultural features associated with the various species of early *Homo* known through the fossil record: *H. rudolfensis, H. habilis, H. erectus, H. heidelbergeneis*, the Neandertals, and their cousins the Denisovans. The chapter concludes with a look at a primitive form of *Homo* that somehow managed to survive until relatively recent times on the Indonesian island of Flores.

2015 Discoveries

Chapter 8 reported on the discovery of the earliest stone tools (dated to 3.3 m.y.a.) in Lomekwi, Kenya. This was one of three very important early hominin discoveries in Africa announced in 2015. The second is the discovery in Ethiopia of a hominin jawbone fragment with five teeth dated to 2.8 m.y.a.—close to the end of the *Au. afarensis* time span (3 m.y.a.) The fossil, found by a multinational team, is now evidence of the earliest known member of the *Homo* lineage (Villamoare et al. 2015). The human lineage had already started diverging from other hominin lines by that time. The team member who found the fossil was Chalachew Seyoum, a graduate student at Arizona State University and an Ethiopian national. Working in the Afar region, about a dozen miles from where Lucy was found, he spied a tooth sticking out of the ground, which led the researchers to unearth the jawbone. It's unclear whether this fossil, known as LD 350-1, belongs to a known early species of *Homo*, or whether it deserves its own species name. Linking the fossil to *Homo* are its slim molar teeth, its cusp pattern, and the shape of the mandible. The front of the jaw, however, has a more primitive look, including a receding chin line, like *Au. afarensis*.

The third key 2015 announcement was one of the most exciting fossil finds of the 21st century. The discovery site was South Africa's Rising Star cave, located in an area known as the "Cradle of Humankind," because of the important hominin fossil discoveries made there during the first half of the 20th century. So far, the Rising Star cave has yielded the remains of at least 15 individuals, ranging in age from infants and juveniles to older adults. Paleoanthropologist Lee Berger, the leader of the discovery team, dubbed the fossils *Homo naledi*, after the word (*naledi*) for "star" in the local Sotho language. Based on their mix of primitive and modern features, these fossils could have lived between 3 and 2 m.y.a., when *Homo* was just branching off from *Au. afarensis*. Unfortunately, the fossils have not yet been dated.

Among their primitive, apelike features are curved fingers on an otherwise humanlike hand, apelike shoulders adapted to climbing, and flaring iliac blades in the upper pelvis. As in other early hominins, the skeleton gets more human as it gets closer to the ground, reflecting bipedalism. The lower pelvis, lower legs, and feet are very human. The teeth, too, especially the reduced molars, are more modern, and belong with *H. erectus*, Neandertals, and modern humans rather than with australopiths.

One of *H. naledi*'s most noticeable primitive characteristics is its tiny brain. The remains include four skulls, two males and two females. Cranial capacity was small in both sexes, averaging just 560 cm^3 for the males and 465 cm^3 for the females (compared with an average of 1,350 cm^3 for modern humans). As expected, sexual dimorphism shows up not only in the skulls but also in body size. The males were about 5 feet (1.5 meters) tall, weighing about 100 pounds (45 kg); females were somewhat shorter and lighter.

The members of Berger's team who did the actual work of collecting and excavating the bones were all young, slender women (see this chapter's "Appreciating Anthropology"). Such a body frame was necessary to navigate the extremely narrow passages leading to the chamber where the fossils were located. Many of the bones were simply lying on the cave floor; others had to be dug out. The researchers removed more than 1,500 bones during an initial three weeks of intensive work. These fossils, which include bones, teeth, and skulls, provide an unusually complete picture of the hominins buried there. The bones range from skulls, ribs, and long bones, to remains as tiny as the bones of the inner ear. There also are complete hands and feet. The range of ages present—from infants and juveniles to aged adults—exposes the entire length of the *H. naledi* life cycle.

Some paleoanthropologists, while recognizing the importance of this find, doubt that *H. naledi* represents a new species. Tim White, a member of the Ardi team, considers *H. naledi* a probable early *H. erectus*. Watch the news for further developments on *H. naledi* and the Rising Star cave.

H. rudolfensis

In 1972, in an expedition led by Richard Leakey, Bernard Ngeneo unearthed a skull designated KNM-ER 1470. The name comes from its catalog number in the Kenya National Museum (KNM) and its discovery location (East Rudolph—ER)—east of Lake Rudolph, at a site called Koobi Fora, in Kenya. The 1470 skull attracted immediate attention because of its unusual combination of a large brain (775 cm^3) and very large molars. Its brain size was more human than that of the australopiths, but its molars recalled those of the hyperrobust australopiths. Some paleoanthropologists attributed the large skull and teeth to a very large body, assuming that this had been one *really big* hominin. But no postcranial remains were found with 1470, nor have they been found with any later discovery of a 1470-like specimen.

How to interpret 1470 when its brain size suggested *Homo,* while its back teeth resembled those of an australopith? Dating estimates ranged from 1.8 m.y.a. to as far back as 2.4 m.y.a. In 1986, it received its own species name, *H. rudolfensis,* from the lake near which it was found. This label has stuck. Note the contrasts in the two skulls in the photo on the next page. KNM-ER 1470, on the right, is *H. rudolfensis*; KNM-ER 1813, on the left, is a skull of *H. habilis*. (*H. habilis*, discussed in the next section, is a species of early *Homo*

Meet two kinds of early *Homo:* on the left, KNM-ER 1813; on the right, KNM-ER 1470. The latter (1470) has been classified as *H. rudolfensis.* What's the classification of 1813?

© Kenneth Garrett

discovered and named in 1960 by L. S. B. and Mary Leakey, parents of Richard). The *habilis* skull has a more marked brow ridge and a depression behind it, whereas 1470 has a less pronounced brow ridge and a longer, flatter face.

For almost 40 years after finding 1470, the Leakey family and others scoured deposits near Lake Turkana for fossils similar to 1470. Between 2007 and 2009 they found them (see Gibbons 2012; Leakey et al. 2012). In 2012 Meave Leakey and her associates announced the discovery at Koobi Fora of a face and two jawbones, showing that 1470 was not unique. These new fossils, dating to 2.03–1.78 m.y.a., confirmed that *H. rudolfensis* lived in the same area and at the same time as at least two other species of *Homo*—*habilis* and *erectus*. Note that *Paranthropus* also existed at this time. The bushy tree of hominin evolution had produced at least four species living in Africa at the same time, but no doubt separated in space or by adaptation to different ecological niches.

The face of the newly discovered *H. rudolfensis* skull—that of a juvenile—was well preserved and included upper teeth. It was a smaller version of the 1470 skull, both featuring an unusually flat face that contrasts with the more jutting upper jaw of *H. habilis*. The lower jawbones, one of which was remarkably complete, gave new information, because the 1470 fossil had no lower jaw. The new jaw and face showed that *H. rudolfensis* had an unusual U-shaped palate, with canines facing the front of the jaw rather than placed on the sides in a V-shaped palate, as in *H. habilis*. The new jaws also had smaller molars than expected, based on those of 1470. The new fossils were found within 10 kilometers of the 1470 discovery site, and within the same region where fossils of *H. habilis* and *H. erectus* have been discovered. (Table 9.1 lists the cranial capacities of various

members of the genus Homo, from H. habilis to AMHs.)

H. habilis and *H. erectus*

A team headed by L. S. B. and Mary Leakey discovered the first representative of *H. habilis* (OH7—Olduvai Hominid 7) at Olduvai Gorge in Tanzania in 1960. Olduvai's oldest layer, Bed I, dates to 1.8 m.y.a. This layer has yielded both small-brained *Paranthropus boisei* fossils (average 490 cm³) and *H. habilis* skulls, with cranial capacities between 600 and 700 cm³. (Table 9.1 gives cranial capacities for the various forms of *Homo* discussed in this chapter.) The Leakeys named their new find Homo habilis (which means "*able* man" in Latin), because they assumed that *H. habilis* had toolmaking *ability* and was responsible for the Oldowan tools also found in Bed I. We now know, however, that toolmaking preceded *H. habilis* and may be as old as 3.3 m.y.a.

Another important *habilis* find is OH62, the partial skeleton of a female *H. habilis* from Olduvai Bed I. This was the first find of an *H. habilis* skull with a significant amount of skeletal material. OH62, dating to 1.8 m.y.a., consists of parts of the skull, the right arm, and both legs. The fossil, found by Tim White in 1986, was surprising because of its small size and apelike limb bones. Not only was OH62 just as tiny as Lucy (3 feet, or 0.9 meter), but also its arms were longer than expected. The limb proportions suggested greater tree-climbing ability, compared with later hominins. *H. habilis* may still have sought occasional refuge in the trees.

The small size and primitive proportions of *H. habilis* were unexpected, given what was known about early *H. erectus* in East Africa. In deposits near Lake Turkana, Kenya, Richard Leakey had uncovered two *H. erectus* skulls

H. habilis

Term coined by L. S. B. and Mary Leakey; early form of *Homo* (1.9–1.44 m.y.a.); co-existed in East Africa with *I l. erectus*.

TABLE 9.1   Cranial Capacities in Different Forms of *Homo*

SPECIES/ TYPE	SPECIMEN	SITE	CRANIAL CAPACITY (CUBIC CENTIMETERS)
Homo habilis	OH 7	Olduvai Gorge	674
Homo habilis	OH 24	Olduvai Gorge	594
Homo habilis	KNM-ER 1813	East Lake Turkana	509
Homo rudolfensis	KNM-ER 1470	East Lake Turkana	752
Homo erectus	KNM-ER 3733	East Lake Turkana	850
Homo erectus	WT 15000	West Lake Turkana	900
Homo erectus	OH 9	Olduvai Gorge	1067
Homo erectus	BOU-VP-2/66	Bouri (Middle Awash)	995
Homo erectus	Skull III	Zhoukoudian	918
Homo erectus	Skull X	Zhoukoudian	1225
Homo heidelbergensis	Kabwe	Kabwe	1285
Homo heidelbergensis	Steinheim	Steinheim	1100
Homo heidelbergensis	Swanscombe	Swanscombe	1325
Neandertal	Neandertal	Neander Valley	1525
Neandertal	La Chapelle	La Chapelle-aux-Saints	1625
AMH	Cro-Magnon	Cro-Magnon	1600

SOURCE: Adapted from Philip L. Stein and Bruce M. Rowe, *Physical Anthropology*, 11th ed., p. 325. McGraw-Hill Education, 2014.

H. erectus

Highly successful form of early human; expanded from Africa into Eurasia by 1.77 m.y.a. (1.9–0.4 m.y.a.).

dating to 1.6 m.y.a. By that date, **H. erectus** (males, at least) had already attained a cranial capacity of 900 cm³, along with a modern body shape and height. An amazingly complete young male *H. erectus* fossil (WT15,000) found at West Turkana in 1984 by Kimoya Kimeu, a collaborator of the Leakeys, has confirmed this. WT15,000, also known as the Nariokotome boy, was a 12-year-old male who had already reached

5 feet 5 inches (1.67 meters). He might have grown to 6 feet had he lived.

Sister Species

Two recent hominin fossil finds from Ileret, Kenya (east of Lake Turkana), are very significant, mainly for two reasons: They show that (1) *H. habilis* and *H. erectus* overlapped in time rather than being ancestor and descendant, as had been thought, and (2) sexual dimorphism in *H. erectus* was much greater than expected (see Spoor et al. 2007; Wilford 2007*a*).

One of these finds (KNM-ER 42703) is the upper jawbone of a 1.44 million-year-old *H. habilis*. The other (KNM-ER 42700) is the almost complete but faceless skull of a 1.55 million-year-old *H. erectus*. These finds negated the conventional view (held since the Leakeys described the first *habilis* in 1960) that *habilis* and then *erectus* evolved, one after the other. Instead, they apparently split from a common ancestor prior to 2 m.y.a. Then they lived side by side in eastern Africa for perhaps half a million years. According to Meave Leakey, one of the authors of the report (Spoor et al. 2007), the fact that they remained separate species for so long "suggests that they had their own ecological niche, thus avoiding direct competition" (quoted in Wilford 2007*a*, p. A6). They coexisted in the same general area (an ancient lake basin), much as gorillas and chimpanzees do today.

Given these finds, the fossil record for early *Homo* in East Africa must be revised as follows:

Paranthropus boisei (left) and *H. habilis* (right). Both OH5 (L) and OH24 (R) were found in Bed I at Olduvai Gorge, Tanzania, and were probable contemporaries.
© The Natural History Museum/Alamy Stock Photo

H. rudolfensis (2.03–1.78 m.y.a.), *H. habilis* (1.9–1.44 m.y.a), and *H. erectus* (1.9–0.4? m.y.a.). The oldest definite *H. habilis* (OH24) dates to 1.9 m.y.a., as does the oldest *erectus*.

What about sexual dimorphism in *H. erectus*? As the smallest *erectus* find ever, KNM-ER 42700 also may be the first female *erectus* yet found, most probably a young adult or late subadult. Its small skull suggests that the range in overall body size among *H. erectus* may have been greater than previously thought, with greater sexual dimorphism than among chimps or contemporary humans. Another possibility is that the (as yet undiscovered) *H. erectus* males that lived in this area along with the female also were smaller than the typical *erectus* male.

Hunting, Tools, and Teeth

The ecological niche that separated *H. erectus* from earlier hominins involved greater reliance on hunting, along with improved cultural means of adaptation. Significant changes in technology occurred during the 200,000-year period between Bed I (1.8 m.y.a.) and Lower Bed II (1.6 m.y.a) at Olduvai. Out of the crude Oldowan tools in Bed I evolved more varied tools. The earliest (1.76 m.y.a.) tools of the *Acheulean* type (see the following section) associated with *H. erectus* come from the site of Kokiselei near Lake Turkana in Kenya (Wilford 2011c). These tools show signs of symmetry, uniformity, and functional differentiation. *H. erectus* was making and using tools for different jobs, such as smashing bones or digging for tubers. The new technology allowed *H. erectus* to acquire meat more reliably and to dig and process tubers, roots, nuts, and seeds more efficiently. New tools that could batter, crush, and pulp coarse vegetation also reduced chewing demands.

Dietary changes eased the burden on the chewing apparatus, so that chewing muscles developed less. Supporting structures, such as jaws and cranial crests, also were reduced. Smaller jaws had less room to fit large teeth. The size of teeth, which form before they erupt, is under stricter genetic control than jaw size and bone size are (see von Cramon-Taubadel 2011). Natural selection began to operate against the genes that produced large teeth, which now caused dental crowding, impaction, pain, sickness, fever, and sometimes death (there were no dentists). *H. erectus* back teeth are smaller, and the front teeth are relatively larger, than australopith teeth. *H. erectus* used those front teeth to pull, twist, and grip objects.

OUT OF AFRICA I: *H. ERECTUS*

Hominins migrated out of Africa in multiple waves. First to expand was *H. erectus,* whose spread occurred between 2 and 1 m.y.a. Much later, populations of anatomically modern humans (**AMHs**) certainly left Africa, maybe more than once, as early perhaps as 110,000 B.P., but mainly around and after 70,000 B.P. That last wave included the ancestors of all humans on Earth today.

H. erectus initiated the expansion of hominins beyond Africa—to Asia and Europe. Small groups broke off from larger ones and moved a few miles away. They foraged new tracts of edible vegetation and carved out new hunting territories. Through population growth and dispersal, *H. erectus* gradually spread and changed. Fueling this expansion was commitment to an essentially human lifestyle based on hunting and gathering. This basic pattern survived until recently in certain parts of the world, although it now is fading rapidly. We focus in this chapter on the biological and cultural changes that led from early *Homo,* through intermediate forms, to anatomically modern humans.

Paleolithic Tools

The stone toolmaking techniques that evolved out of the Oldowan tradition, and that lasted until about 15,000 years ago, are described by the term **Paleolithic** (from Greek roots meaning "old" and "stone"). The Paleolithic, or Old Stone Age, has three divisions: Lower (early), Middle, and Upper (late). Stone tools were made from rocks, such as flint, that fracture sharply and in predictable ways when hammered. Quartz, quartzite, chert, and obsidian also are suitable. Each of the three main divisions of the Paleolithic had its typical *toolmaking traditions*—coherent patterns of tool manufacture. The main Lower Paleolithic toolmaking tradition used by *H. erectus* was the **Acheulean,** named after

AMHs
Anatomically modern humans.

Paleolithic
Old Stone Age, including Lower (early), Middle, and Upper (late).

Acheulean
Lower Paleolithic tool tradition associated with *H. erectus.*

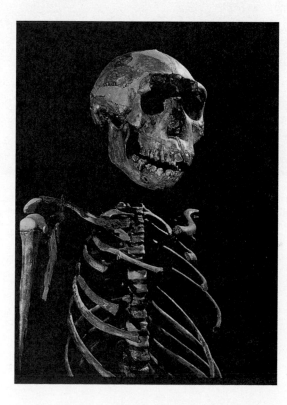

This photo shows the early (1.6 m.y.a.) *Homo erectus* WT 15,000, or Nariokotome boy, found in 1984 near Lake Turkana, Kenya. This is the most complete *Homo erectus* ever found.
© Kenneth Garrett/ National Geographic Creative

appreciating ANTHROPOLOGY

The Rising Stars of a South African Cave

Lee Berger is an American paleoanthropologist who has worked at South Africa's Witwatersrand University since the 1990s. Prior to the discovery of *H. naledi*, as described here, Berger was known for the discovery of *Au. sediba,* another important recent find, as described in the "Appreciating Anthropology" in Chapter 8.

Cavers Rick Hunter and Steve Tucker first drew Berger's attention to the Rising Star cave, located about 30 miles northwest of Johannesburg. When Hunter and Tucker entered that cave in October 2013, they weren't expecting to make a new discovery. Cavers had explored there for decades. Tucker made the discovery by accident when, after wedging himself into a crevice, he found that his feet didn't touch the bottom. That crevice, it turned out, led to a very narrow shaft, which descended for 40 feet (12 meters) before opening into a chamber. Tucker and Hunter dropped into that chamber and found its floor

covered with bones. Tucker took snapshots to show Berger, who had asked Tucker and Hunter to look out for bones during their caving.

Once he saw the photos, Berger knew he was dealing with a hominin site. As a National Geographic explorer-in-residence, he persuaded that organization to fund a research expedition. His most immediate need was for researchers who could navigate the cave's ups, downs, and narrow passages to reach the floor where the bones were located. Berger used social media to recruit his ideal candidates: researchers who had a slim or thin build, a background in paleoanthropology or archaeology, and some caving and climbing experience. In response to his October 2013 Facebook post, he received 57 applications and chose six young, fit, well-trained women—Canadian Marina Elliott; Australian Elen Feuerriegel; and Americans Lindsay Eaves, Alia Gurtov, Hannah Morris, and Becca Peixotto.

The fossil chamber containing the bones lies just 100 yards from the cave entrance, but that distance is a tortuous one, with three daunting obstacles. The first is a narrow space, a mere 10 inches wide, called "Superman's Crawl," because one can best squeeze through it by extending one arm in front while holding the other arm tightly against one's side, like Superman in flight. The next challenge is to climb a sharp ridge called the Dragon's Back, with steep falls on either side. The final obstacle is the 40 foot chute, barely 8 inches wide. (Tucker and Hunter were wiry enough to make the descent; Berger and most of his male associates were not.) At the bottom of the chute lies the Landing Zone (as the team members dubbed it), which leads into the Dinaledi ("many stars") chamber where the fossils were located.

For three weeks, the six young women, whom Berger described as "underground astronauts," went to and fro along this daunting route each

Left: An elaborate wiring setup allows Lindsay Eaves to enter data into a laptop computer in South Africa's Rising Star cave. *Center:* The six "underground astronauts" who excavated the fossil trove known as Homo naledi from the inner recesses of South Africa's Rising Star Cave. From left to right: Becca Peixoto, Alia Gurtov, Elen Feuerrigel, Marina Elliott, Lindsay Eaves, and Hannah Morris. *Right:* Alia Gurtov emerges from excavating at the Rising Star Cave, South Africa.

Left: © University Of The Witwatersrand/Barcroft Media via Getty Images; center: Courtesy of Dr. John Hawks, University of Wisconsin-Madison; right: © Herman Verwey/Foto24/Gallo Images/Getty Images

the French village of St. Acheul, where it was first identified. Recent finds in Kenya date the oldest Acheulean hand axes to 1.76 m.y.a.

Previously, with Oldowan tools, flaking was done simply to produce sharp flakes. A fundamental difference shows up in the Acheulean tradition, which involved chipping the core bilaterally and symmetrically. That core was converted from a round piece of rock into a flattish, oval hand ax about 6 inches (15 centimeters) long. The Acheulean

day, working in teams of three for alternating shifts. They wore hat torches to light their way. Prior to their arrival, cavers had threaded communication cables down to the fossil chamber. Their mission was to collect the bones scattered on the cave floor and to excavate fossils embedded in that floor. In 21 days, they brought up more than 1,500 bones, representing at least 15 individuals—a treasure trove of hominin fossils unsurpassed in the history of paleoanthropology.

While the six underground astronauts worked below the surface, other team members were busy examining and analyzing the bones being brought out of the cave. Eventually, Berger would host an analytic workshop at Witwatersrand University, attended not only by members of his *Au. sediba* team but also by young paleoanthropologists from around the world invited to help interpret this enigmatic new hominin.

Berger's approach to analyzing and publicizing the *H. naledi* fossils posed a sharp contrast to what was usual in paleoanthropology. Typically a discovery team spends years working on its analysis before announcing the discovery and its presumed significance. Berger's team immediately made the information widely available in the media, including a 2015 PBS program based on filming done during the excavation and analysis. The team also made images of the fossils available worldwide for study by other scientists and their students. Some paleoanthropologists were peeved (or worse) at Berger's departure from tradition and, particularly, his release of information about the *naledi* find before dating was established for the fossils. Berger's initial description of the find as a possible burial site drew specific criticism. Most scientists doubted that such small-brained hominins would have been capable of that type of behavior. The fossils themselves are described more fully in the text. It is likely that additional information on this find will be available by the time you read this.

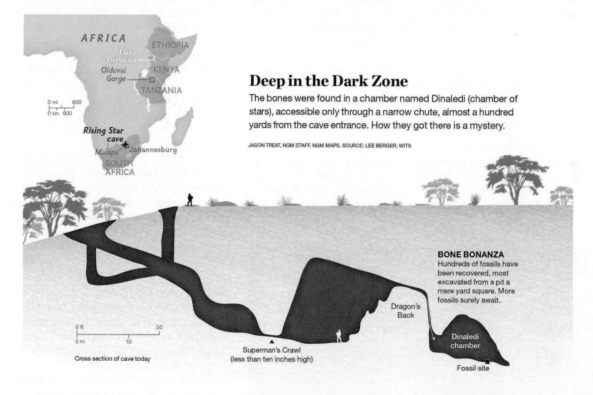

Deep in the Dark Zone

The bones were found in a chamber named Dinaledi (chamber of stars), accessible only through a narrow chute, almost a hundred yards from the cave entrance. How they got there is a mystery.

JASON TREAT, NGM STAFF. NGM MAPS. SOURCE: LEE BERGER, WITS

BONE BONANZA
Hundreds of fossils have been recovered, most excavated from a pit a mere yard square. More fossils surely await.

Location of the Rising Star cave in South Africa, and a cross-section showing the Dinaledi chamber within that cave and the tortuous path leading to that chamber—the fossil site.

hand ax embodies a predetermined shape created from a template in the toolmaker's mind. Archaeological evidence for tools illustrating such a mental template confirms a cognitive leap between earlier hominins and *H. erectus*.

Analysis of their wear patterns suggests that hand axes were versatile tools used for many tasks, from butchering and cutting to woodworking and vegetable preparation. Cleavers—core tools with a straight edge at one end—were used for heavy

A cast of H. erectus skullcap number 1, discovered at Zhoukoudian cave near Beijing, China. Formerly known as "Peking Man," the Zhoukoudian fossils may be as old as 780,000 B.P. and as young as 400,000 B.P. The two other skulls are much older. Sangiran 2 from Java (middle photo) may be as old as 1.6 m.y.a., while OH9 from Olduvai Gorge, Tanzania (right), may date back 1.4 million years. What similarities do you note among the three skulls?

Left: © DEA/L. DE MASI/De Agostini/Getty Images; center: © John Reader/Science Source; right: © The Natural History Museum/Alamy Stock Photo

chopping and hacking at the sinews of larger animals. Stone picks probably were used for digging. Acheulean toolmakers also used flakes, with finer edges, for light-duty tools—to make incisions and for finer work. Flakes became progressively more important in human evolution, particularly in Middle and Upper Paleolithic toolmaking.

Dating back at least 1.76 m.y.a., the Acheulean tradition illustrates trends in the evolution of technology: the manufacture of more varied tools with predetermined forms, designed for specific tasks.

Adaptive Strategies of *H. erectus*

Interrelated changes in biology and culture have increased human adaptability—the capacity to live in and modify an ever-wider range of environments. More sophisticated tools helped *H. erectus* expand its range. Biological changes also increased

An Acheulean hand ax from Gesher Benot Ya'aqov, Israel, Jordan River. This site, shown here under excavation, dates back to 750,000 B.P. Which hominin might have made the ax?

© Kenneth Garrett/National Geographic Creative

hunting efficiency. *H. erectus* had a rugged but essentially modern skeleton that permitted long-distance stalking and endurance during the hunt. The *H. erectus* body was much larger and longer-legged than those of previous hominins, permitting longer-distance hunting of large prey. There is archaeological evidence of *H. erectus*'s success in hunting elephants, horses, rhinos, and giant baboons.

Increased cranial capacity has been a trend in human evolution. The average *H. erectus* brain (about 1,000 cm^3) doubled the australopith average. The capacities of *H. erectus* skulls range from 800 to 1,250 cm^3, well above the modern minimum.

H. erectus had an essentially modern, though very robust, skeleton with a brain and body closer in size to *H. sapiens* than to the australopith. Still, several anatomical contrasts, particularly in the cranium, do distinguish *H. erectus* from modern humans. *H. erectus* had a lower and more sloping forehead accentuated by a large brow ridge above the eyes. Skull bones were thicker, and the braincase was lower and flatter than in *H. sapiens,* with spongy bone development at the lower rear of the skull. Seen from behind, the *H. erectus* skull has been compared to a half-inflated football and to a hamburger bun. The face, teeth, and jaws were larger than those of contemporary humans but smaller than those of the australopiths. The front teeth were especially large, but molar size was well below the australopith average.

Archaeologists have found and studied several sites of *H. erectus* activity, including cooperative hunting. Hearths at various sites confirm that fire was part of the adaptive kit controlled by *H. erectus*. Evidence for human control over fire has been found in Israel, dating back to almost 800,000 years ago. The newest evidence of fire, dated at 1 m.y.a., comes from Wonderwerk Cave (South Africa), where microscopic plant ashes and burned bits of bone have been found in soil that previously yielded dozens of stone tools (Berna et al. 2012). However, no remains of a hearth or campfire area, where fires would have been lit repeatedly, have been found in Wonderwerk Cave. The first hearths date back only 400,000 years (Rice 2012). Fire provided protection against predators. It permitted *H. erectus* to occupy cave sites, including Zhoukoudian, near Beijing, China, which has yielded the remains of more than 40 specimens of *H. erectus*. Fire widened the range of climates open to human colonization. Its warmth enabled people to survive winter cold in temperate regions. Cooking breaks down vegetable fibers and tenderizes meat. Cooking also kills parasites and makes meat more digestible, thus reducing strain on the chewing apparatus.

Could language (fireside chats, perhaps) have been an additional advantage available to *H. erectus*? Archaeological evidence confirms the cooperative hunting of large animals and the manufacture of complicated tools. These activities may well have been too complex to proceed without some kind of language. Speech would

have aided coordination, cooperation, and the learning of traditions. Words, of course, aren't preserved until the advent of writing. However, given the fact that even apes have been shown to have some potential for language-based communication, and given the brain size within the low *H. sapiens* range, it seems plausible to assume that *H. erectus* had rudimentary speech.

The Evolution and Expansion of *H. erectus*

Let's review now some of the *H. erectus* fossil finds, whose geographic distribution is mapped in Figure 9.1. The most important early out-of-Africa site is Dmanisi in the former Soviet Republic of Georgia, at the easternmost edge of Europe. Discoveries there include one fairly complete skull, one large mandible, and two partial skulls—

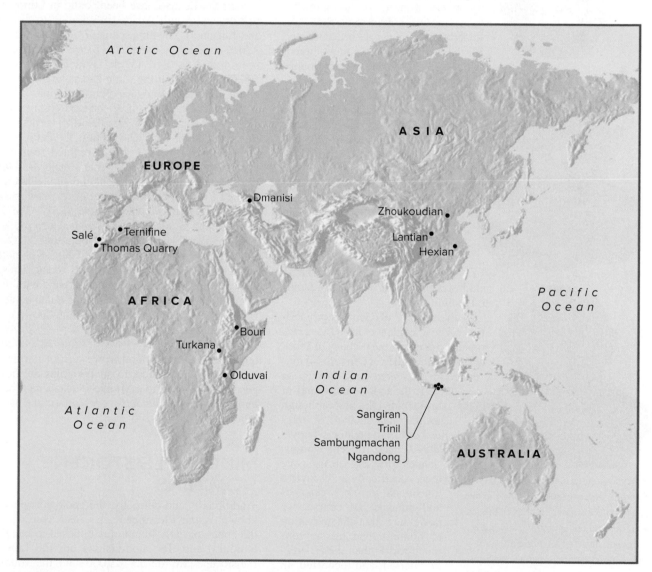

FIGURE 9.1 Location of Some Major *Homo erectus* Sites.

one of a young adult male (780 cm^3) and one of an adolescent female (650 cm^3). Note the small cranial capacities, at the lower end of the *H. erectus* range of variation. These fossils are dated to 1.77–1.7 m.y.a. There are notable similarities between the two partial skulls and that of the Nariokotome boy from Kenya (1.6 m.y.a.). Tools of comparable age associated with the Kenyan and Georgian fossils also are similar (see Vekua, Lordkipanidze, and Rightmire 2002). The Dmanisi finds suggest a rapid spread, by 1.77 m.y.a., of early *Homo* out of Africa and into Eurasia.

The Dmanisi fossils are the most ancient undisputed hominin finds outside Africa. How did they get to Georgia? The most probable answer is "in pursuit of meat." As hominins became more carnivorous, they expanded their home ranges in accordance with those of the animals they hunted. Meat-rich diets provided higher-quality protein and fat as fuel. Once hominins developed stronger bodies and high-protein meat diets, they could—indeed had to—spread out. They ranged farther to find meat, and this expansion eventually led them out of Africa, into Eurasia (Georgia) and eventually Asia.

More recent skeletal finds from Dmanisi suggest how this expansion might have taken place (Wilford 2007b). (Previously only skulls had been found there.) Four new fossil skeletons revealed an advanced spine and lower limbs that would have facilitated mobility.

If the country of Georgia provides the earliest evidence for *H. erectus* outside of Africa, the country of Indonesia provided the very first fossil evidence for *H. erectus* as a species. In 1891, the Indonesian island of Java yielded the first (although not the most ancient) *H. erectus* fossil find, popularly known as "Java man." Eugene Dubois, a Dutch army surgeon, had gone there specifically to discover a transitional form between apes and humans. Of course, we now know that the transition to hominin had taken place much earlier than the *H. erectus* period and occurred in Africa. However, Dubois's good luck did lead him to the most ancient human fossils

then known—parts of an *H. erectus* skull and a thigh bone. Later excavations in Java uncovered additional remains. The various Indonesian *H. erectus* fossils date back at least 700,000, and perhaps as much as 1.6 million, years. The four-stage photo spread at the left shows a reconstruction of *H. erectus* based on the Javanese find Sangiran 17, the most complete *H. erectus* skull from Indonesia.

Fragments of a skull and a lower jaw found in northern China at Lantian may be as old as the oldest Indonesian fossils. Other *H. erectus* remains, of uncertain date, have been found in Algeria and Morocco in North Africa. *H. erectus* remains also have been found in Upper Bed II at Olduvai, Tanzania, in association with Acheulean tools. On p. 152, you will find a photo of one such find, OH9, which dates back perhaps 1.4 million years, along with a photo of a Javanese find, Sangiran 2, which may be a bit older. African *H. erectus* fossils also have been found in Ethiopia, Eritrea, and South Africa (in addition to Kenya and Tanzania). The time span of *H. erectus* in East Africa was long. Later *H. erectus* fossils have been found in Bed IV at Olduvai, dating to 500,000 B.P., about the same age as an important group of fossils found near Beijing, China.

The largest group of *H. erectus* fossils ever found comes from the Zhoukoudian cave, near Beijing, China. The Zhoukoudian ("Peking"—now Beijing—"man") site, excavated from the late 1920s to the late 1930s, was a major find for the human fossil record. Zhoukoudian yielded remains of tools, hearths, animal bones, and more than 40 hominins, including five skulls. One of these Beijing fossils, Skull XII, is shown on p. 152. The Zhoukoudian group lived between 780,000 and 400,000 years ago, when the Chinese climate was colder and moister than it is today. These dates are based on animal remains found with the human fossils. The people at Zhoukoudian hunted venison; seed and plant remains show they gathered as well as hunted.

What about Europe? No definite *H. erectus* remains have been found in western or northern Europe, whose earliest fossil hominins are now generally assigned to a Middle Pleistocene group known as *Homo heidelbergensis* (see the next section).

MIDDLE PLEISTOCENE HOMININS

Traditionally and correctly, the geological epoch known as the **Pleistocene** has been considered the epoch of early human (as opposed to merely hominin) life. Its subdivisions are the Lower Pleistocene (2.6 m.y.a.–781,000 B.P.), the Middle Pleistocene (781,000–126,000 B.P.), and the Upper Pleistocene (126,000–10,000 B.P.). These subdivisions refer to the placement of geological

(a)

(b)

(c)

(d)

Meet *Homo erectus*. Sangiran 17 is the most complete *H. erectus* skull from Java. In this process of reconstruction, a cast of the fossil (a) was rounded out with teeth, lower jaw, and chewing muscles (b). Additional soft tissues (c) and then the skin (d) were added. Given the robust features of this fossil, it is assumed to be male.

Courtesy Hisao Baba

strata containing, respectively, older, intermediate, and younger fossils. The Lower Pleistocene extends from the start of the Pleistocene through the advent of the ice ages in the Northern Hemisphere.

Ice Ages of the Pleistocene

Europe and North America experienced several ice ages, or **glacials**, major advances of continental ice sheets. These periods were separated by **interglacials**, long warm periods. With each glacial advance, the world climate cooled and continental ice sheets—massive glaciers—covered the northern parts of Europe and North America. Climates that are temperate today were arctic during the glacials.

The ice sheets advanced and receded several times during the last glacial period, the *Würm* (75,000–12,000 B.P.). Brief periods of relative warmth during the Würm (and other glacials) are called *interstadials,* in contrast to the longer interglacials. Hominin fossils found in association with animals known to occur in cold or warm climates, respectively, permit us to date them to glacial or interglacial (or interstadial) periods.

H. heidelbergensis

Africa, which was center stage before and during the australopith period, is joined by Asia and Europe during later hominin evolution. In fact, European fossils and tools have contributed disproportionately to our knowledge and interpretation of later hominin evolution. This doesn't mean that our own species, *H. sapiens,* evolved in Europe. Far from it! There is no doubt that *H. sapiens,* like *H. erectus* before it, originated in Africa. Anatomically modern *H. sapiens* lived in Africa for perhaps 150,000 years before reaching Europe around 45,000 years ago (Benazzi et al. 2011; Higham et al. 2011). There probably were many more AMHs in the tropics than in Europe during the ice ages. We merely *know more* about recent human evolution in Europe because archaeology and fossil hunting—not human evolution—have been going on longer there than in Africa and Asia.

Recent discoveries, along with reinterpretation of the dating and the anatomical relevance of some earlier finds, are filling in the gap between *H. erectus* and later forms of *Homo.* (See Recap 9.1 and Figure 9.2 for a summary and timeline of species within the genus *Homo.*) The human skull and brain continued to increase after *H. erectus* and eventually overlapped with the modern range. (The modern average, remember, is about 1,350 cm^3.) A rounding out of the braincase was associated with the increased brain size. As Jolly and White (1995) put it, evolution was pumping more brain into the cranium—like filling a football with air.

A massive hominin jaw was discovered in 1907 in a gravel pit at Mauer, near Heidelberg, Germany. Dubbed "Heidelberg man," or *Homo heidelbergensis,* the jaw appears to be around 500,000 years old. The deposits that yielded this jaw also contained fossil remains of several animals, including bear, bison, deer, elephant, horse, and rhinoceros. The species name *H. heidelbergensis* is now commonly used to refer to the Middle Pleistocene hominins that lived between *H. erectus* and the Neandertals. This group includes fossil hominins that lived in Europe, Asia, and Africa between (very roughly) 850,000 and 200,000 B.P. (see Mounier, Condemi, and Manzi 2011).

A hominin jaw that is more than one million years old, found in Spain, is the oldest known hominin fossil in Europe and may be ancestral to *H. heidelbergensis.* Some of the earliest likely

Pleistocene
Main epoch (2 m.y.a.–10,000 B.P.) of evolution of *Homo.*

glacials
Major advances of continental ice sheets in Europe and North America.

interglacials
Extended warm periods between glacials.

H. heidelbergensis
Hominin group that lived in Europe, Africa, and Asia from about 850,000 to about 200,000 B.P.

RECAP 9.1	Summary of Data on *Homo* Fossil Groups

Fossil representatives of the genus Homo, *compared with anatomically modern humans (AMHs) and chimps* (Pan troglodytes).

SPECIES	DATES	KNOWN DISTRIBUTION	IMPORTANT SITES	BRAIN SIZE (cm^3)
Anatomically modern humans (AMHs)	195,000 B.P. to present	Worldwide	Omo Kibish, Herto, Border Cave, Klasies River, Skhūl, Qafzeh, Cro-Magnon	1,350
Neandertals	130,000 to 28,000 B.P.	Europe, southwestern Asia	La Chapelle-aux-Saints	1,430
H. heidelbergensis	850,000? to 200,000 B.P.	Africa, Europe, Asia	Kabwe, Petralona, Dali, Mount Carmel caves	1,135
Homo erectus	1.9 m.y.a. to 400,000 B.P.	Africa, Asia, Europe	East, West Turkana, Olduvai, Ileret, Dmanisi, Zhoukoudian, Java, Ceprano	900
Pan troglodytes	Modern	Central Africa	Gombe, Mahale	390

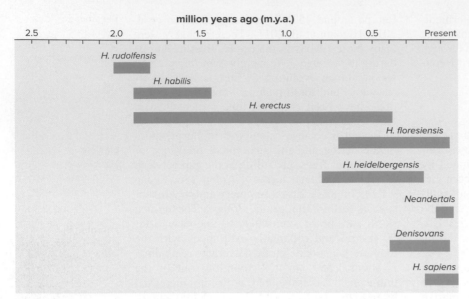

FIGURE 9.2 Timeline of Species within the Genus *Homo* in Increments of 100,000 Years, from 2.5 m.y.a. through the Present.

H. heidelbergensis lived during the *Mindel* (second) glacial, the interglacial that followed it, and the following *Riss* (third) glacial. Humans (probably late members of *H. heidelbergensis*) occupied the Arago cave in southeastern France during the Riss glacial—a time when Europe was bitterly cold. Arago is the only Riss glacial site with hominin facial material. The fossils from this cave consist of a partially intact skull, two jawbones, and teeth from a dozen individuals, with an apparent date of about 200,000 B.P. The geographic distribution of *H. heidelbergensis* extended well beyond Europe. African representatives have been found in Ethiopia (at Bodo), Tanzania (at Ndutu), and Zambia (at Broken Hill/Kabwe). Figure 9.3 shows various sites of *H. heidelbergensis*. Asian representatives have been found at the Chinese sites of Dali and Maba. An African version of *H. heidelbergensis* gave rise to AMHs by 195,000 years ago.

members of *H. heidelbergensis* come from northern Spain's Atapuerca Mountains, where the site of Gran Dolina has yielded the remains of 780,000-year-old hominins. The Spanish researchers who excavated them call this group *Homo antecessor*, but others include them in *H. heidelbergensis*. The nearby Spanish cave of Sima de los Huesos has yielded thousands of fossils representing at least 33 hominins, dated considerably later, at about 300,000 years B.P. Another early possible *H. heidelbergensis* fossil is a cranial fragment found at Ceprano, near Rome, Italy, dated to 850,000 B.P. (see Mounier et al. 2011). Other European fossils now assigned to *H. heidelbergensis* have been found in England (at Swanscombe), Germany (at Steinheim and Mauer), and Greece (at Petralona).

In addition to the fossil record, there also is ample archaeological evidence for the presence and behavior of Middle Pleistocene hominins in Europe. A chance discovery on England's Suffolk seacoast shows that humans had reached northern Europe by 700,000 years ago (Gugliotta 2005). Several stone flakes were recovered from seashore sediment bordering the North Sea. These early human colonists reached northern Europe more than 200,000 years earlier than previously imagined—during an interglacial period. At that time, the fertile lowlands they inhabited were part of a land bridge connecting what is now Britain to the rest of Europe. They lived in a large delta with several rivers and a dry, mild Mediterranean climate. Various animals were among its abundant resources. It is not

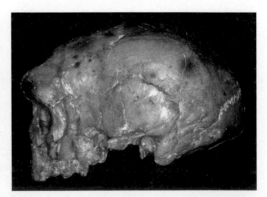

H. heidelbergensis Hominin group that lived in Europe, Africa, and Asia between ca. 850,000 and ca. 200,000 B.P. *Left:* The Broken Hill skull, from Kabwe, Zambia—an African example of *H. heidelbergensis*. *Center:* The Petralona skull, from Greece—a European example of *H. heidelbergensis*. *Right:* The Dali skull from Dali county, China—an Asian example of *H. heidelbergensis*.

Left: © The Natural History Museum/Alamy Stock Photo; center: © DEA/A. DAGLI ORTI/De Agostini Picture Library/Getty Images; right: Courtesy of Dr. Milford H. Wolpoff, The University of Michigan, Ann Arbor

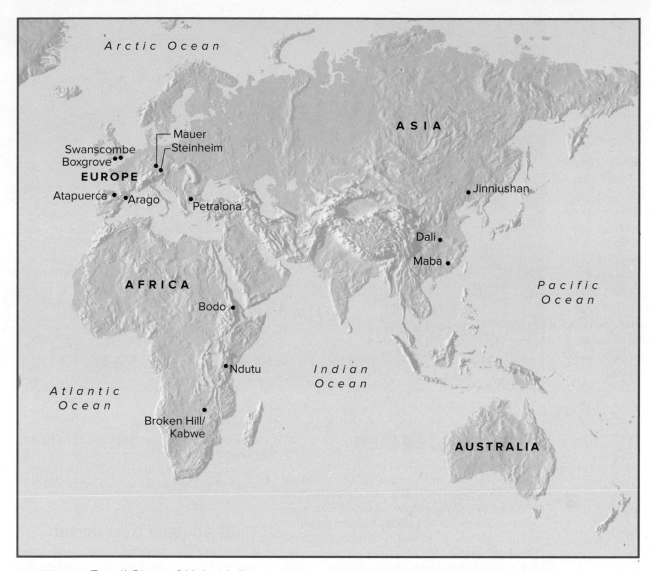

FIGURE 9.3 Fossil Sites of *H. heidelbergensis*.

SOURCE: Relethford, John. *The Human Species: An Introduction to Biological Anthropology*, 9th ed., p. 289. Copyright © 2013 by McGraw-Hill Education, LLC. All rights reserved. Used with permission.

known whether the descendants of these settlers remained in England. The next glacial period may have been too extreme for human habitation so far back.

At the site of Terra Amata, overlooking Nice in southern France, archaeologists have documented human activity dating back 300,000 years. Small bands of hunter-gatherers (15–25 people) made annual visits, during late spring–early summer, to Terra Amata, then a sandy cove on the Mediterranean coast. There is evidence for 21 such visits. Four groups camped on a sand bar, six on the beach, and 11 on a sand dune. Archaeologists surmise that the 11 dune sites represent that number of annual visits by the same band (deLumley 1969/1976).

From a camp atop the dune, these people looked down on a river valley where animals were abundant. Bones found at Terra Amata show that their diet included red deer, young elephants, wild boars, wild mountain goats, an extinct variety of rhinoceros, and wild oxen. The Terra Amata people also hunted turtles and birds, fished, and collected oysters and mussels. The arrangement of postholes shows that these people used saplings to support temporary huts. There were hearths within the shelters. Tools were made from locally available rocks and beach pebbles. Thus, at Terra Amata, hundreds of thousands of years ago, people were already pursuing a lifestyle that survived in certain coastal regions until very recently.

Reconstruction of a hut made from saplings about 300,000 years ago at the Terra Amata site in Nice, France. The Terra Amata Museum, whose diorama is shown here, was built on the archaeological site, which was visited annually by ancient foragers. What foods did they eat?
© Conrad P. Kottak

THE NEANDERTALS

Neandertals were first discovered in western Europe. The first one was found in 1856 in a German valley called Neander Valley—*tal* is the German word for "valley." Scientists had trouble interpreting the discovery. It was clearly human, yet different enough from modern Europeans to be considered strange and abnormal. This was, after all, 35 years before Dubois found the first *H. erectus* fossils in Java and almost 70 years before the first australopith was found in South Africa. Darwin's *On the Origin of Species,* published in 1859, had not yet appeared to offer a theory of evolution through natural selection. There was no framework for understanding human evolution. Over time, the fossil record filled in, along with evolutionary theory. There have been numerous subsequent discoveries of **Neandertals** in Europe and the Middle East, and extending eastward to central Asia and even Siberia. (Figure 9.4 shows the geographic distribution of Neandertal fossils.)

In 2007 Svante Pääbo and his colleagues at Germany's Max Planck Institute for Evolutionary Anthropology announced their identification of Neandertal mitochondrial DNA (mtDNA) in bones found at two sites in central Asia and Siberia. One of them, Teshik-Tash, in Uzbekistan, previously had been seen as the easternmost limit of Neandertal territory. However, bones from the second site, the Okladnikov cave in the Altai Mountains, place the Neandertals much farther (1,250 miles) east, in southern Siberia. The mtDNA sequence at these sites differs only slightly

from that of European Neandertals. The Neandertals may have reached these areas around 127,000 years ago, when a warm period made Siberia more accessible than it is today (see Wade 2007).

Cold-Adapted Neandertals

By 75,000 B.P., after an interglacial interlude, western Europe's hominins (Neandertals, by then) again faced extreme cold as the Würm glacial began. To deal with this environment, they wore clothes, made more elaborate tools and hunted reindeer, mammoths, and woolly rhinos (see Conard 2011).

The Neandertals were stocky, with large trunks relative to limb length—a phenotype that minimizes surface area and thus conserves heat. Another adaptation to extreme cold was the Neandertal face, which has been likened to an *H. erectus* face that has been pulled forward by the nose. Illustrating Thomson's rule, this extension increased the distance between outside air and the arteries that carry blood to the brain and was adaptive in a cold climate. The brain is sensitive to temperature changes and must be kept warm. The massive nasal cavities of Neandertal fossils suggest long, broad noses. This would expand the area for warming and moistening air.

Neandertal characteristics also include huge front teeth, broad faces, large brow ridges, and ruggedness of the skeleton and musculature. What activities were associated with these anatomical traits? Neandertal teeth probably did many jobs

Neandertals
Important hominin group (130,000–28,000 B.P.) found mainly in Europe and the Middle East, but also extending eastward to central Asia and even Siberia; coexisted for a time with AMHs in Europe and perhaps elsewhere.

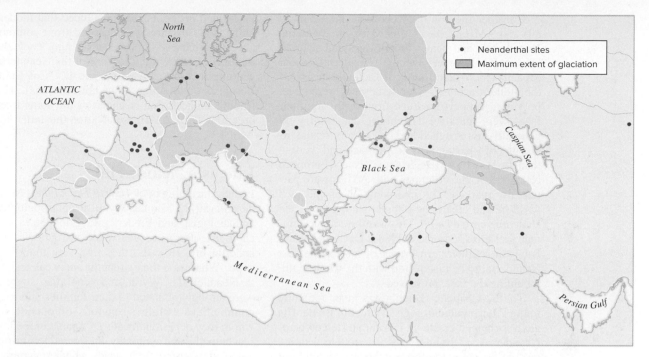

FIGURE 9.4 Geographic Distribution of Neandertal Fossils.

Also shown is maximum extent of glaciation. Neandertals were well adapted to live in the cold climates of Europe at the end of the Pleistocene.

later done by tools. The front teeth show heavy wear, suggesting that they were used for varied purposes, including chewing animal hides to make soft winter clothing out of them. The massive Neandertal face showed the stresses of constantly using the front teeth for holding and pulling.

Neandertal technology, a Middle Paleolithic tradition called **Mousterian**, included a variety of tools designed for different jobs. The Neandertals elaborated on a revolutionary technique of flake-tool manufacture (the *Levallois* technique) invented in southern Africa around 200,000 years ago, which spread widely throughout the Old World. Uniform flakes were chipped off a specially prepared core of rock. Additional work on the flakes produced the special-purpose tools shown in Figure 9.5. Scrapers were used to prepare animal hides for clothing. Larger points were attached to spears. Other special tools were designed for sawing, gouging, and piercing (Conard 2011).

The Neandertals and Modern People

Generations of scientists have debated whether and to what extent the Neandertals may have been ancestral to anatomically modern humans especially those of the Middle East and Europe, where fossils of both groups have been found. The current prevailing view proposes that *H. erectus* split into separate groups: one ancestral to the Neandertals, the other ancestral to AMHs, who first reached Europe around 45,000 B.P. Current evidence leaves little doubt that modern humans evolved in Africa and eventually colonized Europe, displacing, or at least replacing, the Neandertals there.

Mousterian
Middle Paleolithic toolmaking tradition associated with Neandertals.

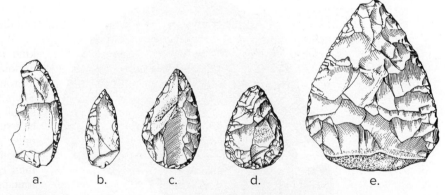

FIGURE 9.5 Examples of Mousterian Tools: (a) Scraper, (b) Point, (c) Scraper, (d) Point, (e) Hand Ax.

The Neandertals manufacture of diverse tool types for special purposes confirms Neandertal sophistication.

Consider the contrasts between the Neandertals and AMHs. Like *H. erectus* before them, the Neandertals had heavy brow ridges and slanting foreheads. However, average Neandertal cranial capacity (more than 1,400 cm^3) actually surpassed the modern average. Neandertal jaws were large, providing support for huge front teeth, and their faces were massive. The bones and skull were generally more rugged and had greater sexual dimorphism—particularly in the face and skull—than do those of AMHs. In some western European Neandertals, the contrasts with AMHs were particularly marked. The interpretation of one such fossil helped create the popular stereotype of the slouching cave dweller. This was the complete human skeleton discovered in 1908 at La Chapelle-aux-Saints in southwestern France. This was the first Neandertal to be discovered with the whole skull, including the face, preserved.

The La Chapelle skeleton was given for study to the French paleontologist Marcellin Boule. His analysis helped create an inaccurate stereotype of Neandertals as brutes who had trouble walking upright. Boule suggested that the Neandertal head was slung forward like an ape's. To round out the primitive image, Boule proclaimed that the Neandertals were incapable of straightening their legs for fully erect locomotion. However, a series of subsequent fossil discoveries show that the La Chapelle fossil wasn't a typical Neandertal but an extreme one. Also, this much-publicized Neandertal "cave man" turned out to be an aging man whose skeleton had been distorted by osteoarthritis. Hominins, after all, have been erect bipeds for millions of years. European Neandertals were a variable population. Other Neandertal finds lack La Chapelle's combination of extreme features.

Based on his reconstruction (announced in 2010) of the complete Neandertal genome, Svante

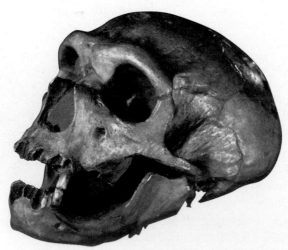

A cast of the anatomically extreme classic Neandertal skull found at La Chapelle-aux-Saints, France.

© Philippe Plailly/Science Source

Pääbo and his colleagues concluded that modern humans and Neandertals descend from common ancestors that lived 600,000 years ago. They also found between 1 and 4 percent of the Neandertal genome incorporated within the DNA of living Europeans and Asians (but not Africans). This finding suggests that Neandertals did some interbreeding with AMHs soon after the latter left Africa.

Life as a Neandertal

In their intriguing book *How to Think Like a Neanderthal* (2011), Thomas Wynn, an anthropological archaeologist, and Frederick L. Coolidge, a psychologist, offer a speculative reconstruction of Neandertal life. How did they live, feel, think, and cope? What were their strengths and weaknesses?

Neandertals, Wynn and Coolidge suggest, were strongly attached to their families and local communities (while suspicious of outsiders—whom they occasionally ate!). Capable of feelings like empathy and sympathy, they cared for the disabled and buried their dead, whether symbolically, as an expression of grief, or practically, as a way to dispose of a decaying body. They used some form of language, maybe tones or whistles (see Viegas 2013), which allowed them to communicate, coordinate, and plan ahead.

They were very strong and had excellent mechanical skills. If alive today, they might work effectively as commercial fishermen or mechanics, Wynn and Coolidge speculate. One illustration of their mechanical skills is the Levallois spear head, an intricately faceted point that could maim or kill an animal as large as a mammoth. The Neandertals learned how to fasten this point securely to a wooden shaft, so that it would not dislodge. They may have used bitumen as an adhesive or lashed the point to the spear. But they lacked the spear thrower, an artificial extension of the hunter's arm invented by AMHs, which put human hunters farther from their prey. Neandertal hunting was close range, dangerous, and sometimes lethal—a pursuit that left behind few elders.

At times they even hunted down their own kind. Important remains of 50,000-year-old Neandertal bones and stone tools discovered in El Sidrón Cave, a rich Neandertal site in northern Spain, have given scientists a glimpse of ancient social structure and behavior—including cannibalism. This discovery illustrates how anthropologists combine fossil, archaeological, and DNA evidence to reconstruct the hominin past. More than 1,800 Neandertal bone fragments have been found in the "Tunnel of the Bones" at El Sidrón; scientists were able to extract snippets of DNA from some of them (Zimmer 2010).

The remains appear to represent a dozen members of an extended family. How did they die? When the discovery team closely examined the bones, they found cut marks—signs that the stone blades had been used to slice muscle from bone. The long bones had been snapped open, presumably to get at their marrow. The scientists concluded that the El Sidrón Neandertals were victims of cannibalism. This find almost certainly predates the arrival of AMHs in this area, supporting the conclusion that, on occasion, Neandertals ate members of their own species.

The shape of the bones allowed the scientists to estimate the age and sex of the victims. The bones came from three men, three women, three teenage boys, and three children, including one infant. DNA analysis helped confirm the conclusions based on the bones. From four specimens, scientists extracted a Y chromosome, confirming their initial assessment that those four were males. El Sidrón turned out to be an excellent storehouse for ancient DNA because of its cold, dark, and damp environment. DNA even provided a clue about physical appearance: Two individuals shared an allele (gene variant) that likely gave them red hair (Zimmer 2010).

The Neandertals moved about within a particular territory—their home range. Their contacts with outsiders were limited (and, as we just saw, potentially hostile). There is no evidence that Neandertals engaged in long-distance trade. By contrast, we know that AMHs living far inland in Europe used shells imported from the Mediterranean and Atlantic coasts. Unlike Neandertals, AMHs were tied into regional social networks; they had relatives, trade partners, in-laws, and allies in other groups. The expanded, regional network and the alliances and social support it offered were key differences between AMHs and Neandertals.

Wynn and Coolidge (2011) interpret the archaeological and fossil evidence as indicating that Neandertals were suspicious of both outsiders and change. Their limited imagination is shown in their unchanging tool designs. Their tools, found across Eurasia, varied little in form or function over thousands of years, and miles. Neandertals no doubt were eventually exposed to the far more effective spears and spear throwers made by their AMH contemporaries, but they borrowed none of those techniques.

Their unwillingness or inability to borrow or innovate put them at a disadvantage in competing with AMHs for shrinking resources in Ice Age Europe around 30,000 years ago. AMHs lived in larger, regionally connected communities (see "Appreciating Anthropology" in Chapter 10) that encouraged innovation, social thinking, and mental processing of complex information. Twin lacks—of allies and of innovation—helped doom the Neandertals.

THE DENISOVANS

In late 2010, scientists identified the Denisovan hominin group as distant cousins to Neandertals (Callaway 2011; Zimmer 2010). Once again, the

The Denisova Cave research site.
© RIA Novosti/Science Source

ancient DNA research was led by Svante Pääbo, who earlier that year had published a complete Neandertal genome.

The Denisovans get their name from Denisova, a cave in southern Siberia where their traces (so far only a finger fragment and a wisdom tooth) were found. The Denisovans apparently lived in Asia from roughly 400,000 to 50,000 years ago. Remarkably, scientists have managed to extract the entire Denisovan genome from the finger and the tooth (see "Appreciating Anthropology" in Chapter 4). The DNA suggests that the split between ancestral Neandertals and Denisovans happened around 400,000 years ago. The Neandertals spread to the west, eventually reaching the Middle East and Europe. The Denisovans headed east (while AMHs remained for a time in Africa).

The distinctive Denisovan wisdom tooth resembles the teeth of neither AMHs nor Neandertals. It has bulging sides and large, flaring roots. Only when someone finds the same kind of tooth in a fossil skull, or perhaps even a complete skeleton, will we be able to see what the Denisovans really looked like. The genome sequencing done of a Denisovan girl does, however, suggest that the phenotype included brown skin, hair, and eyes.

Comparison of the Denisovan genome with modern humans revealed a striking relationship. Melanesians, who inhabit Papua New Guinea and islands northeast of Australia, have inherited about 5 percent of their DNA from the Denisovans. This suggests that after the ancestors of today's Papuans split from other AMHs and migrated east, they interbred with Denisovans (see Callaway 2011). Precisely when and where is unclear. The oldest AMH remains in Southeast Asia, from a cave in northern Laos, date to at least 46,000 years ago (Demeter et al. 2012). If the Denisovan range extended from Siberia to Southeast Asia, they must have been a very successful kind of hominin.

HOMO FLORESIENSIS

A decade or so ago, news reports trumpeted the discovery of bones and tools of a group of tiny humans who inhabited Flores, an Indonesian island 370 miles east of Bali, until fairly recent times (see Roach 2007; Wade 2004). Early in hominin evolution, as we saw in the last chapter, it wasn't unusual for different species, even genera, of hominins, to live at the same time. But until the 2003–2004 discoveries on Flores, few scientists imagined that a previously undiscovered archaic human species had survived through 50,000 B.P., and possibly even later. These tiny people lived, hunted, and gathered on Flores until at least 50,000 B.P. One of their most surprising features is a very small skull, about 370 cm^3—slightly smaller than the chimpanzee average.

A skull and several skeletons of these miniature people were found in a limestone cave on Flores by a team of Australian and Indonesian archaeologists, who assigned them to a new human species, *H. floresiensis.* (As described in 2016, much older H. floresiensis remains, apparently dating back some 700,000 years, have been found in another cave on Flores. Amazingly, this tiny hominin species appears to have survived on Flores for more than half a million years—from 700,000 through 50,000 B.P.) The discovery of *H. floresiensis,* described as a downsized version of *H. erectus,* shows that archaic humans survived much later than had been thought. Before modern people reached Flores, which is very isolated, the island was inhabited only by a select group of animals that had managed to reach it. These animals, including *H. floresiensis,* faced unusual evolutionary forces that pushed some toward gigantism and some toward dwarfism. The carnivorous lizards that reached Flores, perhaps on natural rafts, became giants. These Komodo dragons now are confined mainly to the nearby island of Komodo. Elephants, which are excellent swimmers, reached Flores, where they evolved to a dwarf form the size of an ox.

Previous excavations by Michael Morwood, one of the discoverers of *H. floresiensis,* estimated that *H. erectus* had reached Flores by 840,000 years ago, based on crude stone tools found there. This *H. erectus* population and its descendants are assumed to have been influenced by the same evolutionary forces that reduced the size of the elephants. The first specimen of *H. floresiensis,* an adult female, was uncovered in 2003 from a cave floor. Paleoanthropologists identified her as a very small but otherwise normal individual—a diminutive version of *H. erectus.* Because the downsizing was so extreme, smaller than that in modern human pygmies, she and her fellows were assigned to a new species. Remains of six additional individuals found in that cave date from 95,000 to 50,000 B.P. The cave also has yielded bones of giant lizards, giant rats, pygmy elephants, fish, and birds.

H. floresiensis apparently controlled fire, and by 95,000 B.P., stone tools found with them appear more sophisticated than any known to have been made by *H. erectus.* Among the tools were small blades that might have been mounted on wooden shafts and used to hunt elephants. The small cranium has raised some doubt that *H. floresiensis* actually made the tools. The ancestors of the anatomically modern people who colonized Australia might have traveled through this area, and it is possible that they made the stone tools. On the other hand, there is no evidence that modern humans reached Flores prior to 11,000 years ago.

This *H. floresiensis* population appears to have been wiped out by a volcanic eruption around 50,000 B.P., but they may have survived until much later elsewhere on Flores. The Ngadha people of central Flores and the Manggarai people of west Flores still tell stories about little people who lived in caves until the arrival of the Dutch traders in the 16th century (Wade 2004).

An analysis of the lower limbs and especially an almost complete left foot and parts of the right foot shows that *H. floresiensis* walked upright but possessed apelike features (Wilford 2009*b*). The big toe, for example, was stubby, like a chimp's. The feet were large, more than 7.5 inches (20 cm.) long, out of proportion to the short lower limbs. These proportions, similar to those of some African apes, have never before been seen in hominins. The feet were flat. The bone that helps form the arch in modern human feet was more apelike than human. Without a strong arch, *H. floresiensis* could have walked but not run like humans (see Wilford 2009*b*).

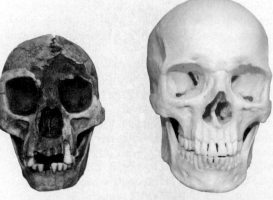

The skull of *Homo floresiensis* (left; modern human, right), a miniature hominin that inhabited Middle Earth, or at least the Indonesian island of Flores, between 700,000 and 50,000 years ago.

© Sabena Jane Blackbird/Alamy Stock Photo

THE RED DEER CAVE PEOPLE

As with *H. floresiensis,* hominin fossils found in two Chinese caves are notable because of their recent date (14,300–11,500 B.P.) and their unexpected inclusion of very primitive features. The fossils, representing at least four individuals, consist of partial skulls and other bone fragments (Sample 2012). Specifically, they come from two caves in southwestern China—Longlin Cave and Maludong, or "Red Deer," Cave. The fossils have been labeled the "Red Deer Cave people" based on the cave name and on evidence that they cooked giant red deer (now extinct) there. The Longlin Cave fossils, unearthed in 1979, lay unnoticed in the basement of a Chinese scientific institute for 30 years until their rediscovery. The Red Deer Cave fossils, discovered 10 years later, also remained barely studied in another Chinese institute. Darren Curnoe and Ji Xueping began their study and analysis of both sets of fossils in 2008 (see Bhanoo 2015; Curnoe et al. 2012).

The skulls of the Red Deer Cave people differ from those of modern humans in their thickness, jutting jaws, large molar teeth, prominent brows, broad noses, flat faces, and lack of a chin. Curnoe contends that a partial femur from the Red Deer Cave resembles *H. erectus* and *H. habilis* as much as *H. sapiens* (Bhanoo 2015). Scientists currently are debating the evolutionary status of these fossils. Could they be late Denisovans, or perhaps a product of interbreeding between Denisovans and anatomically modern humans? Confirmation awaits the eventual analysis of DNA extracted from the Red Deer Cave bones—a task that so far has been unsuccessful.

The Red Deer Cave fossils also help fill a geographic gap: Very few post–Ice Age human fossils from Asia have been well described and reliably dated (Sample 2012). Our picture of recent human evolutionary history in Asia has grown more complex. We know now that multiple human populations, including *H. floresiensis* and the Red Deer Cave people, lived in the area, apparently representing different evolutionary lines.

for REVIEW

summary

1. Key hominin fossil discoveries announced in 2015 included (a) a jaw fragment found in Ethiopia, dating to 2.8 m.y.a., that appears to be the earliest known member of the genus *Homo,* and (b) finds at South Africa's Rising Star cave of more than 1,500 bones, representing at least 15 individuals, which have been assigned to a new species, *H. naledi.* As yet undated, the *naledi* finds show a mixture of apelike and human characteristics, suggesting they lived after *Au. afarensis* and before *H. erectus.*

2. Four hominin species coexisted in Africa around 2 m.y.a. They were *Paranthropus* (2.4–1.0 m.y.a.), *H. rudolfensis* (2.03–1.78 m.y.a.), *H. habilis* (1.9–1.44 m.y.a.), and *H. erectus* (1.9–0.4 m.y.a.). Compared with the australopiths, dental, facial, and cranial robustness was reduced in early *Homo habilis* (1.9–1.44 m.y.a.) and *erectus* (1.9?–0.3? m.y.a.). *H. erectus* extended the hominin food quest to the hunting of large animals. *H. erectus* was the first hominin to achieve modern body size and form. *H. erectus*'s average cranial capacity doubled the australopith average. Tool complexity and archaeological evidence for cooperative hunting suggest a long period of enculturation and learning. *H. erectus* extended the hominin range beyond Africa to Asia and Europe.

3. Ancient *H. erectus* skulls have been found in Kenya and Georgia (in Eurasia), dating back some 1.77–1.6 million years. *H. erectus* persisted for more than a million years, evolving into *H. heidelbergensis* by the Middle Pleistocene. Fire allowed *H. erectus* to expand into cooler areas, to cook, and to live in caves.

4. *H. heidelbergensis* lived in Europe, Africa, and Asia between about 850,000 and 200,000 years ago. An African version of *H. heidelbergensis* gave rise to anatomically modern humans (AMHs) by 195,000 years ago.

5. The Neandertals, who inhabited western Europe during the early part of the Würm glacial, were among the first hominin fossils found. With no examples of the australopiths or *H. erectus* yet discovered, the differences between them and modern humans were accentuated. The last common ancestors of Neandertals and AMHs lived about 600,000 years ago.

6. The Neandertals adapted physically and culturally to bitter cold. Their front teeth were among the largest to appear in human evolution. They manufactured a diverse inventory of Mousterian flake tools. Neandertals may have persisted in western Europe, where they did some interbreeding with AMHs, through 28,000 B.P. Compared with

AMHs, Neandertals were suspicious of outsiders and reluctant to innovate. Their narrow social networks, lack of regional alliances, and limited imaginations help explain their eventual extinction.

7. The Denisovans were cousins of the Neandertals who lived in Asia between about 400,000 and 50,000 years ago. After their split around 400,000 B.P., the ancestral Neandertals spread westward, to the Middle East and Europe, while the Denisovans headed east.

8. *H. floresiensis* is the name of a species of tiny humans that lived on the isolated island of Flores in Indonesia. A probable descendant of *H. erectus,* which had settled Flores by 840,000 B.P., *H. floresiensis* is marked by the unusually small size of its body and its chimp-sized skull. There is debate about whether *H. floresiensis* was smart enough to have made the stone tools found in association with the skeletal remains, though there is no evidence that AMHs reached Flores before 11,000 B.P. The *H. floresiensis* remains have been assigned dates ranging from 95,000 to 50,000 B.P. The Red Deer Cave people lived in southwestern China fairly recently (14,300–11,500 B.P.), but they contrast significantly with AMHs because of their thick skulls, jutting jaws, large molar teeth, prominent brows, broad noses, flat faces, and lack of a chin.

key terms

Acheulean 149
AMHs 149
glacials 155
H. erectus 148
H. habilis 147
H. heidelbergensis 155

interglacials 155
Mousterian 159
Neandertals 158
Paleolithic 149
Pleistocene 155

critical thinking

1. As anatomically modern humans, we make up a variable population, yet we are all one species. When looking at the fossil record, how have scientists confronted the issue of variability and speciation? Consider the Neandertals and AMHs. Remembering the definition of species given in Chapter 5, should these hominins be placed in the same or different species?

2. *H. erectus* persisted for more than a million years. What were its key strategies of adaptation? In particular, what do its toolmaking abilities and hunting strategies suggest about its evolving cognitive capacities?

3. The Neandertals who inhabited western Europe during the early part of the Würm glacial were among the first hominin fossils found. Why did scientists have trouble interpreting these early discoveries? How have early misinterpretations of Neandertals persisted in our culture? Do these persistent misinterpretations matter?

4. Paleoanthropology is an exciting and constantly changing field! Pick two 21st-century fossil finds discussed in this chapter and explain their significance.

The Origin and Spread of Modern Humans

▸ When and where did modern human anatomy and behavior originate?

▸ What major changes took place in human lifestyles and adaptive strategies as the Ice Age ended?

▸ When and how did modern humans settle Australia, the Americas, and the Pacific?

© Bill Brooks/Alamy Stock Photo

Outrigger canoes in the morning near the island of Maui, Hawaii, which is in Polynesia.

understanding OURSELVES

O ur choices about how, and to whom, we display aspects of ourselves say something about us not only as individuals but also as social and cultural beings. Think about your appearance right now. What does your clothing say about you—implicitly or explicitly, intentionally or unintentionally? Does your cap, shirt, or jacket display the name of your school, a brand, or a favorite sports team? Why do or don't you have tattoos or piercings? What does facial hair, or its absence, say about you or someone else? Why is your hair long or short? Why did you choose any makeup you are wearing? How about any jewelry? If you're male, why are you, or are you not, circumcised? The way that we present our bodies reflects both (1) who and what we're trying to look like and (2) what sort of person we're trying *not* to resemble.

Body decoration is a cultural universal, as are other forms of creative expression, including the arts and language, and all say something about us. Expressive culture rests on symbolic thought. As is true generally of symbols (remember Chapter 2), the relation between a symbol and what it stands for is arbitrary.

Intrinsically, Nike shoes are no more swooshlike than Adidas are. Michigan Wolverines are no more like wolverines than Florida Gators are, and vice versa. For archaeologists,

evidence for symbolic thought, as manifested materially in patterned or decorated artifacts, strongly suggests modern behavior. Consider the pigment red ocher, a natural iron oxide that modern hunter-gatherers use to create body paint for ritual occasions. Archaeologists are pretty sure that ocher was used similarly in the past. Evidence for the manufacture of red ocher dates back 100,000 years, at South Africa's Blombos Cave. An artifact also discovered in that cave has a carved crosshatch design— three straight lines with another set of three at a diagonal to them—offering the world's earliest evidence for intentional patterning with symbolic meaning. There is abundant evidence for expressive culture, including art and music, in Europe by 35,000 years ago. At that point, humans were decorating themselves with paints and jewelry and making flutes and figurines. They would not have done all that without language. Linguist Merritt Ruhlen (1994) speculates that all the world's languages descend from a common one spoken 40,000 to 50,000 years ago by anatomically modern humans who originated in Africa. Did a "creative" gene emerge in Africa and fuel human colonization of the rest of the world? Although anthropologists don't have a definitive answer to this question, we do agree about the key role that expressive culture plays in human life.

MODERN HUMANS

Anatomically modern humans (AMHs) evolved from an African version of *H. heidelbergensis* by 195,000 years ago. Eventually, AMHs spread to other areas, including Europe, where they replaced the Neandertals, whose robust traits eventually disappeared (see Barton et al. 2011).

Out of Africa: AMH Edition
Recent Fossil and Archaeological Evidence

Fossil and archaeological evidence has been accumulating to support the African origin of AMHs. A major find was announced in 2003: the 1997 discovery in an Ethiopian valley of three anatomically modern skulls—those of two adults and a child. When found, the fossils had been fragmented so badly that their reconstruction took several years. Tim White and Berhane Asfaw were coleaders of the international team that made the find near the village of Herto, 140 miles northeast of Addis Ababa. All three skulls were missing the lower jaw. The skulls showed evidence of cutting and handling, suggesting they had been detached from their bodies and used—perhaps ritually—after death. A few teeth, but no other bones, were found with the skulls, again suggesting their deliberate removal from the body. Layers of volcanic ash allowed geologists to date them to 154,000–160,000 B.P. The people represented by the skulls lived on the shore of an ancient lake, where they hunted and fished. The skulls were found along with hippopotamus and antelope bones and some 600 tools, including blades and hand axes.

Except for a few primitive characteristics, the **Herto** skulls are anatomically modern—long with broad midfaces, featuring tall, narrow nasal bones. The cranial vaults are high, falling within modern dimensions. These finds offered important support for the view that modern humans originated in Africa.

Omo Kibish is one of several sites along the Omo River in southwestern Ethiopia. Between 1967 and 1974, Richard Leakey and his colleagues from the Kenya National Museum recovered AMH remains originally considered to be about 125,000 years old. The specimens now appear to be much older. Indeed, with an estimated date of 195,000 B.P., they appear to be the earliest AMH fossils yet found (McDougall, Brown, and Fleagle 2005). The Omo remains include two partial skulls (Omo 1 and Omo 2), four jaws, a leg bone, about 200 teeth, and several other parts. One site, Omo Kibish I, contained a nearly complete skeleton of an adult male. Middle Stone Age tools have been found in the same stratigraphic layers. The Omo 1 skull (see photo) and the skeleton are modern overall, with a few primitive features. The Omo 2 skull is more primitive.

From sites in South Africa comes further evidence of early African AMHs. At Border Cave, a remote rock shelter in South Africa, fossil remains dating back at least 100,000 years are believed to be those of early modern humans. The remains of at least five AMHs have been discovered (see the photo for one of them), including the nearly complete skeleton of a 4- to 6-month-old infant buried in a shallow grave. Excavations at Border Cave also have produced some 70,000 stone tools, along with the remains of several mammal species, including elephants, believed to have been hunted by the ancient people who lived there. Middle Stone Age tools and considerable evidence for behavioral modernity have been found at two other South African caves: Pinnacle Point (164,000 B.P.) and Blombos Cave (100,000 B.P.).

A complex of South African caves near the Klasies River Mouth was occupied by a group of hunter-gatherers some 120,000 years ago. Fragmentary bones suggest how those people looked. A forehead fragment has a modern brow ridge. There is a thin-boned cranial fragment and a piece of jaw with a modern chin. The archaeological evidence suggests that these cave dwellers did coastal gathering and used Middle Stone Age stone tools.

Anatomically modern specimens, including an intact skull (see photo of Skhul skull on p. 168) have been found at Skhūl, a site on Mount Carmel in Israel. The Skhūl fossils date to 100,000 B.P. Other modern-looking and similarly dated (92,000 B.P.) skulls come from the Israeli site of Qafzeh. All these skulls have a modern shape; their braincases are higher and rounder than those of Neandertals. There is a more filled-out fore-

Herto
Very early (160,000–154,000 B.P.) AMHs found in Ethiopia.

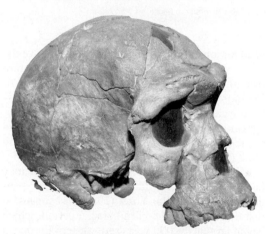

Herto skull BOU-VP-16/1, an early AMH cranium from the Middle Awash area of Ethiopia (160,000–154,000 B.P.).

© age fotostock/Alamy Stock Photo

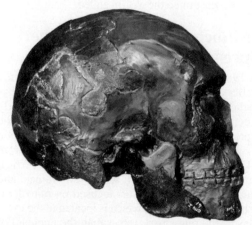

The Omo 1 skull from Omo, Ethiopia. This skull shows modern human characteristics such as a high, well-rounded cranium and a chin. The Omo site dates to 195,000 years ago, making this specimen the earliest example of an AMH.

© The Natural History Museum/Alamy Stock Photo

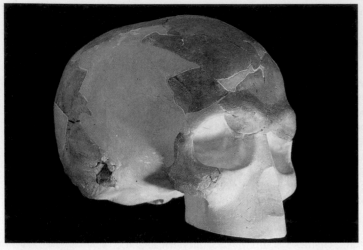

The Border Cave skull, South Africa. The fragmentary remains are clearly those of an AMH (note the vertical forehead). Its age is estimated at more than 100,000 years ago.

Courtesy of Dr. Milford H. Wolpoff, The University of Michigan, Ann Arbor

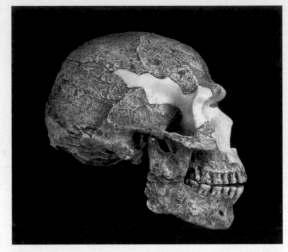

This early AMH skull dates to 100,000 B.P. This is one of several fossils found at Skhūl, Israel.

© The Natural History Museum/Alamy Stock Photo

head region, which rises more vertically above the brows. A marked chin is another modern feature (see the photo on p. 169 of the original Cro Magnon find). Early AMHs in western Europe often are called **Cro Magnons,** after the earliest fossil find of an anatomically modern human, in France's Les Eyzies region, Dordogne Valley, in 1868 (see Fagan 2010).

Given these early dates from Israel, AMHs may have inhabited the Middle East before the Neandertals did. Ofer Bar-Yosef (1987) has suggested that during the last (Würm) glacial period, which began around 75,000 years ago, western European Neandertals spread into the Middle East as part of a general southward expansion of cold-adapted fauna. AMHs, in turn, may have followed warmer-climate fauna south into Africa, returning to the Middle East once the Würm ended.

"Mitochondrial Eve" and the Spread of AMHs

In 1987 geneticists at the University of California at Berkeley gathered evidence supporting the hypothesis that modern humans (AMHs) arose fairly recently in Africa, then spread to the rest of the world. Rebecca Cann, Mark Stoneking, and Allan C. Wilson (1987) analyzed genetic samples from 147 women whose ancestors came from Africa, Europe, the Middle East, Asia, New Guinea, and Australia. The researchers focused on mitochondrial DNA (mtDNA), which is located in the cytoplasm (the outer part, rather than the nucleus) of cells. Ordinary DNA, which makes up the genes that determine most physical traits, is found in the nucleus and comes from both parents. Only the mother, however, can transmit mitochondrial DNA to her offspring. The father plays no part in mtDNA transmission, just as the mother has

Cro Magnon
The first fossil find (1868) of an AMH, from France's Dordogne Valley.

nothing to do with the transmission of the Y chromosome, which comes from the father (and determines the sex of the child).

The Berkeley researchers counted, then compared, the number of mutations in the mtDNA in each of their 147 tissue samples. Based on the number of mutations shared, the researchers drew an evolutionary, or phylogenetic, tree. That tree started in Africa, then branched in two. One group remained in Africa, while the other one split off, carrying its mtDNA to the rest of the world. The variation in mtDNA was greatest among Africans. This suggests they have been evolving the longest. The Berkeley researchers concluded that everyone alive today has mtDNA that descends from a woman (they called her "Mitochondrial Eve") who lived in sub-Saharan Africa around 200,000 years ago. Eve was not the only woman alive then; she was just the only one whose descendants have included a daughter in each generation up to the present. Because mtDNA passes exclusively through females, mtDNA lines disappear whenever a woman has no children or has only sons. The nature of the branches in the phylogenetic tree suggests that Eve's descendants left Africa no more than 135,000 years ago. (Other evidence suggests a major migration out of Africa between 70,000 and 50,000 years ago.) Eve's descendants eventually displaced the Neandertals in Europe, as they colonized the rest of the world—a story told in this chapter.

In 1997 Svante Pääbo succeeded in extracting ancient DNA from a Neandertal bone (an upper arm or humerus) originally found in Germany's Neander Valley in 1856. This was the first time that DNA of a premodern human had been recovered. When Pääbo compared this Neandertal DNA with a reference sample of modern human DNA, he found 27 differences. By contrast,

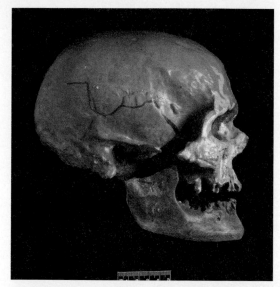

Cro Magnon I, the skull of a 45-year-old anatomically modern human, discovered in 1868 near Les Eyzies in France's Dordogne region. Note the distinct chin.
© The Natural History Museum/Alamy Stock Photo

The Cro Magnon rock shelter near Les Eyzies, Dordogne, France. Remains of anatomically modern humans, such as the famous fossil found here in 1868, have been found in rock shelters from France to South Africa. The Cro Magnon people lived here around 31,000 years ago.
© Richard Wadey/Alamy Stock Photo

samples of DNA from modern populations worldwide show only five to eight differences with that reference sample. Based on these genetic contrasts, Pääbo calculated that the common ancestor of Neandertals and AMHs probably lived around 600,000 years ago.

The Neandertals may (or may not) have coexisted with modern humans in the Middle East for thousands of years. The overlap in Europe apparently spanned the period between around 45,000 B.P. and Neandertal extinction around 28,000 B.P. The recent redatings of a piece of modern jawbone with three teeth from England and of two baby teeth from Italy provide the oldest known skeletal evidence for AMHs in Europe (Wilford 2011a).

The baby teeth from Italy were dated at 43,000 to 45,000 years old (Benazzi et al. 2011). The jawbone, from Kents Cavern in Devon, was 41,500 to 44,200 years old—the oldest known AMH fossil from northwestern Europe. Also significant is the fact that the English jawbone was found in cave layers associated with Upper Paleolithic tools (Higham et al. 2011). Prior to these dates, the earliest reliably dated European AMH came from Romania (42,000–37,800 B.P.).

The English jawbone might represent an early dispersal of AMHs through central Europe that crossed into Britain on a land bridge where the North Sea now stands. The southern Italian remains might represent an even earlier migration along the southern European coasts (Wilford 2011a).

THE ADVENT OF BEHAVIORAL MODERNITY

Scientists agree that (1) around six million years ago, our hominin ancestors originated in Africa, and as apelike creatures they became habitual bipeds; (2) by 3.3 million years ago, still in Africa, hominins were making crude stone tools; (3) by 1.7 million years ago, hominins had spread from Africa to Asia and eventually Europe; and (4) sometime around 200,000 years ago, anatomically modern humans (AMHs) evolved from ancestors who had remained in Africa. Like earlier hominins (*H. erectus*), AMHs spread out from Africa. Eventually, they replaced nonmodern human types, such as the Neandertals in Europe and the successors of *H. erectus* in the Far East.

There is disagreement, however, about when, where, and how early AMHs achieved **behavioral modernity**—relying on symbolic thought, elaborating cultural creativity, and as a result becoming fully human in behavior as well as in anatomy. Was it as much as 165,000 or as little as 45,000 years ago? Was it in Africa, the Middle East, or Europe? What triggered the change: a genetic mutation, population increase, competition with nonmodern humans, or some other cause? The traditional view has been that modern behavior originated fairly recently, perhaps 45,000 years ago, and only after *Homo sapiens* pushed into Europe. This theory of a "creative explosion" is based on finds such as the impressive cave paintings at Lascaux, Chauvet Cave, and other sites in France, Spain, and most recently Romania (Balter 2010). However, recent discoveries outside Europe raise the possibility of a much older, more gradual evolution of modern behavior.

Anthropologist Richard G. Klein of Stanford University is a leading advocate for the idea that human creativity dawned suddenly, in Europe around 45,000 years ago. Klein thinks that, prior to then, *Homo* had changed very slowly in anatomy and behavior. After this "dawn of culture,"

behavioral modernity
Fully human behavior based on symbolic thought and cultural creativity.

human anatomy changed little, but behavior started changing dramatically (Klein with Edgar 2002). Indeed, by 40,000 years ago, AMHs in Europe were making varied tools that display a pattern of abstract and symbolic thought. Their modern behavior included burying their dead with ceremonies, adorning their bodies with paints and jewelry, and making musical instruments and figurine images of fertile females. Their cave paintings displayed images from their minds, as they remembered the hunt, and events and symbols associated with it.

To explain such a flowering of creativity, Klein proposes a neurological hypothesis. Perhaps around 50,000 years ago, he thinks, a genetic mutation acted to rewire the human brain, possibly allowing for an advance in language. Improved communication, in Klein's view, could have given people "the fully modern ability to invent and manipulate culture" (quoted in Wilford 2002*b*). Klein thinks this genetic change probably happened in Africa and then allowed "human populations to colonize new and challenging environments" (quoted in Wilford 2002*b*). Reaching Europe, the rewired modern humans met and replaced the resident Neandertals. Klein recognizes that his genetic hypothesis "fails one important measure of a proper scientific hypothesis—it cannot be tested or falsified by experiment or by examination of relevant human fossils" (quoted in Wilford 2002*b*). AMH skulls from the time period in question show no change at all in brain size or function.

Challenging Klein's views are discoveries made in Africa and the Middle East that provide substantial evidence for earlier (than in Europe) modern behavior. These finds include finely made stone and bone tools, self-ornamentation, and abstract carvings. Surveying African archaeological sites dating to between 300,000 and 30,000 years ago, Sally McBrearty and Alison Brooks (2000) conclude that what might appear to be a sudden event in Europe actually rested on a slow process of cultural accumulation within Africa, where *Homo sapiens* became fully human long before 45,000 years ago. At South Africa's Blombos Cave, for example, an archaeological team led by Christopher Henshilwood found evidence that AMHs were making bone awls and weapon points more than 70,000 years ago. Three points had been shaped with a stone blade and then polished. Henshilwood thinks these artifacts indicate symbolic behavior and artistic creativity; their makers were trying to create beautiful objects (Wilford 2002*b*).

Representing an even earlier occupation of Blombos Cave, Henshilwood's team excavated a 100,000-year-old workshop where early AMHs mixed the world's earliest known paint. They used stones to grind colorful chunks of dirt, transported to Blombos from several miles away, into a red powder, known as ocher. This was blended with

An engraved stone fragment of red ocher from Blombos Cave, South Africa. The fragment, which is 77,000 years old, suggests early human creativity and symbolic thought.

© Anna Zieminski/AFP/Getty Images

charcoal and binding fat from animal bone marrow, to make it stick to the body or other surfaces. The Blombos people mixed their ocher in large abalone shells, where they liquefied and stirred it, then scooped it out as paint using a bone spatula (Wilford 2011*b*). They may have applied the mixture to their skin, perhaps as decoration for some special event.

What, if anything special, did the color red mean to these ancient people? Did they associate it with blood as a sign of life or death, or with menstruation as a sign of fertility? Could they have used red ocher to inspire anger in others? The ocher makers apparently used Blombos Cave only as a work site. Archaeologists found no associated evidence of living quarters, such as hearths (Wilford 2011*b*). What they did the rest of the time remains a mystery. Surely, they hunted, gathered, and fished, most likely eating the abalone and other sea products whose shells also could be used as tools.

Excavations in Congo's Katanda region have uncovered bone harpoon points dating back 90,000 to 80,000 years (Yellen, Brooks, and Cornelissen 1995). Anthropologists Alison Brooks and John Yellen contend that these ancient people "not only possessed considerable technological capabilities at this time, but also incorporated symbolic or stylistic content into their projectile forms" (quoted in Wilford 2002*b*).

In 2007 anthropologists reported the discovery of even earlier evidence (dating back to 164,000 B.P.) for behavioral modernity in a cave site at Pinnacle Point, South Africa. The cave yielded small stone bladelets, which could be attached to wood to make spears, as well as red ocher. Also significant is the ancient diet revealed by remains from this seaside site. For the first time, we see early representatives of *H. sapiens* subsisting on a variety of shellfish and other marine resources. According to paleoanthropologist Curtis Marean (Marean et al. 2007), who led the discovery

Body ornamentation is a sign of behavioral modernity. On the left is a decorated Munjika man from Papua New Guinea. The photo on the right also shows body piercing and a necklace, plus distinctive eyeglasses and body tattoos. What are the social functions of such ornamentation?

Left: © John W. Banagan/ Lonely Planet Images/ Getty Images; right: © druvo/Vetta/Getty Images RF

team, once early humans knew how to make a living from the sea, they could use coastlines as productive home ranges and move long distances

Four Venus figurines, dated between 30,000 and 22,000 B.P. Left to right, they are: (a) a fired clay statuette from Moravia, (b) a figure from France carved in mammoth ivory, (c) the Willendorf Venus in limestone from Austria, and (d) a figure carved in mammoth ivory from Ukraine. Notice the apparent fertility symbolism.

© The Natural History Museum/Alamy Stock Photo

(see also Guyot and Hughes 2007; McBrearty and Stringer 2007).

Cultural advances would have facilitated the spread of AMHs out of Africa. Such advances had reached the Middle East by 43,000 years ago, where, in Turkey and Lebanon, Steven Kuhn, Mary Stiner, and David Reese (2001) found evidence that coastal people made and wore beads and shell ornaments (see also Mayell 2004). Some of the shells were rare varieties, white or brightly colored. These authors suggest that population increase could have caused changes in the living conditions of these AMHs—putting pressure on their resources and forcing experimentation with new strategies for survival (Kuhn et al. 2001).

Even a modest increase in the population growth rate could double or triple the numbers and populations of small AMH bands (see this chapter's "Appreciating Anthropology"). People would be living nearer to one another with more opportunities to interact. Body ornaments could have been part of a system of communication, signaling group identity and social status. Such communication through ornamentation implies "the existence of certain [modern] cognitive capacities" (Stiner and Kuhn, quoted in Wilford 2002b; Kuhn et al. 2001).

Clive Gamble attributes the rise of modern human behavior more to increasing social competition than to population increase. Competition

In with the Old: The Evolutionary Importance of Grandparents

How do people transmit their knowledge, memories, and personal experience to others? Today we rely on the cloud of cyberspace (how often do you post on Instragram?) and the growing arsenal of audiovisual and digital means of storing, processing, and transmitting information orally, visually, and in writing. Before the advent of writing (which has been around only 6,000 years), humans could pass on their experience through enculturation (the process by which culture is learned and transmitted across the generations), but oral tradition preserves knowledge less effectively than writing does. Inevitably, and still today, information is lost, social bonds are severed, and people become mere memories whenever someone dies.

The extent of information transfer between generations increased during hominin evolution, particularly in Upper Paleolithic times, when human behavioral modernity began to flower. People started living longer. They couldn't write down lessons of the past, but they could share their memories orally over a longer lifespan and with more people, including their grandchildren. An evolutionary leap forward occurred when humans started benefiting from the coresidence and consistent association of three generations. In this situation, adults interacted with their beloved parents longer, and their children could thrive in a larger kinship network that included grandparents.

Experience counts in child rearing. Among nonhuman primates, infant survival rates are higher when the mother is experienced (Hrdy 2009; Rilling 2013). Among baboons, for example, infants of experienced mothers had a 63 percent survival rate, versus only 29 percent for infants of first-time mothers (Altmann, Hausfater, and Altmann 1988). Having a grandmother around

means that experience is available, and greater infant survival is one likely reason for the population burst associated with the Upper Paleolithic.

Underlying the cultural advances of the Upper Paleolithic was a fundamental change in human biology—the lengthening of the human lifespan. We have evidence for this change in hard materials that fossilize, specifically in teeth; the older you are, the more dental wear you exhibit. Biological anthropologists Rachel Caspari and Sang-Hee Lee (2004) examined the teeth of 768 hominins representing four fossil groups: later australopiths (including gracile and robusts); Early and Middle Pleistocene *Homo* (including *erectus* and *H. heidelbergensis,* but not *habilis* or *rudolfensis*); Neandertals; and AMHs—early Upper Paleolithic Europeans. These groups were chosen because they provided large samples, whose teeth could be studied for wear and age estimation.

Caspari and Lee classified their specimens as older or younger adults based on patterns of molar eruption and degree of wear on the teeth. Any individual whose wisdom teeth (third molars) had come in was classified as an adult. More dental wear thereafter indicated greater age. The appearance of wisdom teeth is associated with physiological maturation, including reproductive maturity, in primates. For their sample, Caspari and Lee assumed that wisdom teeth appeared at age 15, and that it would be at this age that females could become mothers. (Age 15 is not unusual for current-day first-time mothers among the Inuit and some Australian populations.) A woman could become a grandmother by age 30 if she and her daughter both had had their first child at 15.

Using their sample of 768 specimens, Caspari and Lee calculated a ratio of older (age 30

and older) to younger (age 15–29) adults (the OY ratio) in each of the four hominin groups. They found a steady increase in that ratio during human evolution—rising from late australopiths, through early *Homo* and the Neandertals, to a real leap after 45,000 years ago, with the advent of the Upper Paleolithic. With that jump, for the first time in human history more adults—and significantly more—were dying after age 30 than before it.

This increase in lifespan created a reliable three-generation social structure, which had substantial evolutionary impact. Social groups with three generations could store, process, and transmit more information and experience. The increase in the number of older people facilitated the transmission of specialized knowledge, illustrated by the sophisticated tools and art of the Upper Paleolithic, compared with what came before, when elders were scarce.

Increased longevity also favored population growth, for two reasons. First, someone who lives longer (up to a point) can have more children. Second, elders typically assist their children's families. Having supportive grandparents enhances child survival (see Strassmann and Garrard 2011), which also favors population growth. Population increase likely spurred the many advances known through archaeology to have occurred during the Upper Paleolithic. Among those advances were increased mobility, long-distance trade (including of ornamental objects), and new forms of cooperation and competition between groups (Caspari and Lee 2004; Sussman and Cloninger 2011). All things considered, Caspari and Lee (2004) reasonably conclude that the extended human lifespan may be the most important biological factor underlying the flowering of behavioral modernity.

with neighboring populations, including the Ne-andertals, could have produced new subsistence strategies along with new ways of sharing ideas and organizing society. Such innovations would have advantaged AMH bands as they occupied new lands and faced new circumstances (see Barton et al. 2011).

According to archaeologist Randall White, early personal adornment in Africa and the Middle East shows that a creative capacity existed among AMHs long before they reached Europe (Wilford 2002b). Facing new circumstances, including competition, AMHs honed their cultural abilities, which enabled them to maintain a common identity, communicate ideas, and organize their societies into "stable, enduring regional groups" (quoted in Wilford 2002b). Symbolic thought and cultural advances, expressed most enduringly in artifacts, ornamentation, and art, gave them the edge over the Neandertals, whom they eventually replaced in Europe.

The origin of behavioral modernity continues to be debated. We see, however, that archaeological work in many world areas suggests strongly that neither anatomical modernity nor behavioral modernity was a European invention. Africa's role in the origin and development of humanity has been prominent for millions of years of hominin evolution (see also Stringer 2012a and Wilford 2012; for a contrary view, see Klein 2013).

ADVANCES IN TECHNOLOGY

In Europe, Upper Paleolithic toolmaking is associated with AMHs. In Africa, earlier AMHs made varied tools. The terms *Lower, Middle,* and *Upper Paleolithic* are applied to stone tools from Europe. The terms *Early, Middle,* and *Late Stone Age* are applied to tools from Africa. The AMHs who lived at the Klasies River Mouth cave sites in South Africa made Middle Stone Age tools. However, some of the early tool finds at Blombos Cave and elsewhere in Africa are reminiscent of the European Upper Paleolithic. AMHs in Europe made tools in a variety of traditions, collectively known as Upper Paleolithic because of the tools' location in the upper, or more recent, layers of sedimentary deposits. Some European cave deposits have Middle Paleolithic Mousterian tools (made by Neandertals) at lower levels and increasing numbers of Upper Paleolithic tools at higher levels (Hublin 2012).

The **Upper Paleolithic** traditions all emphasized **blade tools.** Blades were hammered off a prepared core, as in Mousterian technology, but a blade is longer than a Mousterian flake—its length is more than twice its width. Blades were chipped off cores 4 to 6 inches (10 to 15 centime-

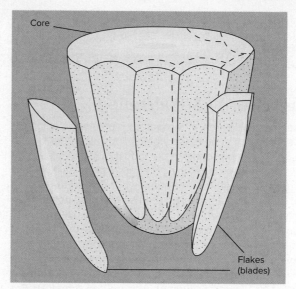

FIGURE 10.1 Upper Paleolithic Blade-Toolmaking.

Blades are flakes that are detached from a specially prepared core. A punch (usually a piece of bone or antler) and a hammerstone (not shown here) were used to knock the blade off the core.

ters) high by hitting a punch made of bone or antler with a hammerstone (Figure 10.1). Blades were then modified to produce a variety of special-purpose implements. Some were composite tools that were made by joining reworked blades to other materials.

The blade-core method was faster than the Mousterian and produced 15 times as much cutting edge from the same amount of material. More efficient tool production might have been especially valued by people whose economy depended on cooperative hunting of mammoths, woolly rhinoceroses, bison, wild horses, bears, wild cattle, wild boars, and—principally—reindeer. It has been estimated that approximately 90 percent of the meat eaten by western Europeans between 25,000 and 15,000 B.P. came from reindeer.

We see certain trends when we compare Upper Paleolithic tools with the earlier Mousterian tradition. First, the number of distinct tool types increased. This trend reflected functional specialization—the manufacture of special tools for particular jobs. A second trend was increasing standardization in tool manufacture. The form and inventory of tools reflect several factors: the jobs tools are intended to perform, the physical properties of the raw materials, and distinctive cultural traditions about how to make tools (Isaac 1972).

Other trends include growth in *Homo*'s total population and geographic range and increasing local cultural diversity as people specialized in particular economic activities. Illustrating increasing economic diversity are the varied special-purpose tools made by Upper Paleolithic

Upper Paleolithic
Blade-toolmaking traditions of early AMHs.

blade tool
Basic Upper Paleolithic tool, hammered off a prepared core.

Giant Steps toward Globalization

Among academic disciplines, anthropology is uniquely qualified to study the succession of necessary giant steps along the road to globalization. Those prerequisites to globalization may be summarized as follows: (1) settlement of the six continents by anatomically modern humans; (2) the Neolithic Revolution, which fueled the growth and expansion of human populations; (3) the rise of cities, states, civilizations, and empires; (4) the European Age of Discovery, which established the Columbian exchange and gave rise to (5) the world capitalist economy, the Industrial Revolution, and the modern world system.

For a global system to form, humans needed to settle all the habitable continents, and the hemispheres needed to be linked. The latter didn't happen until 1492, when Columbus reached the Americas. But global forces—most notably an early form of global climate change known as the Ice Age—did influence the human migrations that led to the settlement of the six continents. The Ice Age, with its ebb and flow of continental glaciers, had a strong impact on Paleolithic humans, influencing their livelihoods, settlement patterns, and opportunities to spread out. During the major glacial phases, with so much water frozen in ice, land bridges over areas that now are under water aided human colonization of vast new areas, especially Australia and North America.

Scientists can follow human migrations of the past by constructing global phylogenetic trees (as well as through fossil and archaeological evidence). Branches of such trees—human genetic lineages, or haplogroups—show how the peoples of today's world are related to one another. One key global genetic tree is based on mtDNA—mitochondrial DNA, which is transmitted only through the female line. (A son cannot transmit his mother's mtDNA; only daughters can.) Another tree, based on the Y chromosome tree, is based on transmission from fathers to sons. Only sons receive their father's Y chromosome and pass it on. (Girls get their dad's X chromosome.) The global phylogenetic tree based on mtDNA and the one based on the Y chromosome each have known branches whose global distribution can be plotted to show relationships and human migratory paths. Certain branches, for example, are known to be associated with the spread of modern humans out of Africa between 70,000 and 50,000 B.P. Other (smaller) branches show that the Americas were settled not by a single ancestral population but by multiple haplogroups. In other words, there were waves of migration into North, and eventually South, America.

This chapter examines the human settlement of most of the globe, as anatomically modern humans spread from Africa into Australia, Europe, Asia, the Americas, and the Pacific. Chapter 11 focuses on a major economic transformation—the emergence of food production (i.e., farming and animal domestication)—sometimes called the Neolithic Revolution. Neolithic economies spread rapidly, because they were more productive and reliable than Paleolithic economies based on hunting, gathering, and collecting. The eventual rise of ancient cities and states was fueled by the population growth and economic complexity associated with food production. For thousands of years after the first cities and states appeared (see Chapter 12), empires rose and fell. None of them, however, was an empire on which "the sun never set." What was necessary before such an empire (of which the British empire is the best-known example) could form?

people. Scrapers were used to hollow out wood and bone, scrape animal hides, and remove bark from trees. Burins, the first chisels, were used to make slots in bone and wood and to engrave designs on bone. Awls, which were drills with sharp points, were used to make holes in wood, bone, shell, and skin.

Upper Paleolithic bone tools included knives, pins, needles with eyes, and fishhooks. The needles suggest clothing sewn with thread, probably from the sinews of animals. Fishhooks and harpoons confirm an increased emphasis on fishing. (As described by Marean et al. [2007], South Africa's Pinnacle Point Cave provides the earliest evidence, at 164,000 B.P., for a diet based on marine resources, along with small stone blade tools.)

Different tool groups (assemblages) may represent culturally distinct populations, or they may reflect different activities carried out by a single population for particular purposes. Some sites, for example, are obviously butchering stations, where prehistoric people hunted, made their kills, and carved them up. Others are residential sites, where a wider range of activities was carried out.

With increasing technological differentiation, specialization, and efficiency, humans have become increasingly adaptable. Through heavy reliance on cultural means of adaptation, *Homo* has become (in numbers and range) the most successful primate by far. The hominin range expanded significantly in Upper Paleolithic times (see "Focus on Globalization").

GLACIAL RETREAT

Consider now one regional example, western Europe, of the consequences of glacial retreat. The Würm glacial ended in Europe between 17,000 and 12,000 years ago, with the melting of the ice sheet in northern Europe (Scotland, Scandinavia, northern Germany, and Russia). As the ice retreated, the tundra and steppe vegetation grazed by reindeer and other large herbivores gradually moved north. Some people moved north, too, following their prey.

Shrubs, forests, and more solitary animals appeared in southwestern Europe. With most of the big-game animals gone, western Europeans were forced to use a greater variety of foods. To replace specialized economies based on big game, more generalized adaptations developed during the 5,000 years of glacial retreat.

As water flowed from melting glacial ice, sea levels all over the world started rising. Today, off most coasts, there is a shallow-water zone called the *continental shelf,* over which the sea gradually deepens until the abrupt fall to deep water, which is known as the *continental slope.* During the Ice Ages, so much water was frozen in glaciers that most continental shelves were exposed. Dry land extended right up to the slope's edge. The waters right offshore were deep, cold, and dark. Few species of marine life could thrive in this environment.

As the sea level rose, conditions became more favorable to marine life in the shallower, warmer offshore waters. The quantity and variety of edible species increased tremendously in waters over the shelf. Furthermore, because rivers now flowed more gently into the oceans, fish such as salmon could ascend rivers to spawn. Flocks of birds that nested in seaside marshes migrated across Europe during the winter. Even inland Europeans could take advantage of new resources, such as migratory birds and springtime fish runs.

Although hunting remained important, southwestern European economies became less specialized. A wider range, or broader spectrum, of plant and animal life was being hunted, gathered, collected, caught, and fished. This was the beginning of what anthropologist Kent Flannery (1969) has called the *broad-spectrum revolution*. It was revolutionary because, in the Middle East, it led to human control over the reproduction of plants and animals, a "Neolithic Revolution" to be examined in Chapter 11. In a mere 10,000 years—after millions of years during which hominins had subsisted by foraging for natural resources—plant cultivation and animal domestication replaced hunting and gathering in most areas.

CAVE ART

It isn't the tools or the skeletons of Upper Paleolithic people but their art that has made them most familiar to us. Most extraordinary are the cave paintings, the earliest of which dates back some 36,000 years. More than a hundred cave painting sites are known, mainly from a limited area of southwestern France and adjacent northeastern Spain. The most famous site is Lascaux, found in 1940 in southwestern France by a dog and his young human companions.

The paintings adorn limestone walls of caves located deep in the Earth. Over time, the paintings have been absorbed by the limestone and thus preserved. Prehistoric big-game hunters painted their prey: woolly mammoths, wild cattle and horses, deer, and reindeer. The largest animal image is 18 feet (5.5 meters) long.

Most interpretations associate cave painting with magic and ritual surrounding the hunt. For example, because animals sometimes are depicted with spears in their bodies, the paintings might have been attempts to ensure success in hunting. Artists might have believed that by capturing the animal's image in paint and predicting the kill, they could influence the hunt's outcome.

Another interpretation sees cave painting as a magical human attempt to control animal reproduction. Something analogous was done by Native Australian (Australian aboriginal) hunters and gatherers, who held annual *ceremonies of increase* to honor and to promote, magically, the fertility of the plants and animals that shared their homeland. Australians believed that ceremonies were necessary to perpetuate the species on which humans depended. Similarly, cave paintings might have been part of annual ceremonies of increase. Some of the animals in the cave murals are

Vivid Upper Paleolithic cave paintings from Lascaux, Dordogne, France. How might you explain what you see depicted here?
© JM Labat/Science Source

pregnant, and some are copulating. Did Upper Paleolithic people believe they could influence the mating behavior and reproduction of their prey by drawing them? Or did they perhaps think that animals would return each year to the place where their souls had been captured pictorially?

Paintings often occur in clusters. In some caves, as many as three paintings have been drawn over the original, yet next to these superimposed paintings stand blank walls never used for painting. It seems reasonable to speculate that an event in the outside world sometimes reinforced a painter's choice of a given spot. Perhaps there was an especially successful hunt soon after the painting had been done. Perhaps members of a social subdivision significant in Upper Paleolithic society customarily used a given area of wall for their drawings.

Cave paintings also might have been a kind of pictorial history. Perhaps Upper Paleolithic people, through their drawings, were reenacting the hunt after it took place, as hunters of the Kalahari Desert in southern Africa still do today. Designs and markings on animal bones may indicate that Upper Paleolithic people had developed a calendar based on the phases of the moon (Marshack 1972). If this is so, it seems possible that Upper Paleolithic hunters, who were certainly as intelligent as we are, would have been interested in recording important events in their lives.

It is worth noting that the *late* Upper Paleolithic, when many of the most spectacular multicolored cave paintings were done and Paleolithic artistic techniques were perfected, coincides with the period of glacial retreat. An intensification of cave painting for any of the reasons connected with hunting magic could have been caused by concern about decreases in herds as the open lands of southwestern Europe were being replaced by forests.

SETTLING AUSTRALIA

As continental glaciers ebbed and flowed, modern humans took advantage of global climate change to expand their range. During the major glacial phases, with so much water frozen in ice, land bridges formed, aiding human colonization of new areas. People spread from Africa into Europe and Asia, eventually reaching Australia and, much later, the Americas and the Pacific islands.

When and how was Australia settled? At times of major glacial advance, such as 50,000 years ago, dry land connected Australia, New Guinea, and Tasmania.

Sahul is the name for the larger continent thus formed (O'Connell and Allen 2004). At its largest, Sahul was separated from Asia only by narrow straits (Figure 10.2). Humans somehow made the crossing, perhaps in primitive watercraft, from Asia into Sahul, perhaps around 50,000 B.P. Genetic markers, fossils, and archaeological sites help us understand that settlement process.

Georgi Hudjashov and his colleagues (2007) analyzed genetic samples from Native Australians and New Guineans/Melanesians. They looked at both mitochondrial DNA (mtDNA) (n = 172 samples) and Y chromosomes (n = 522). They compared those samples with known branches of global phylogenetic trees. The global mtDNA tree includes branches known as M and N (among others). The Y chromosome tree includes branches known as C and F (among others). All the Australian/New Guinean samples fit into one of those four branches (either M or N for mtDNA and either C or F for the Y chromosome). Those four branches are known to be associated with the spread of modern humans out of Africa between 70,000 and 50,000 B.P.

The earliest Australian skeletons, including the one being excavated here in 1974, come from Lake Mungo in New South Wales. The world's oldest modern human mtDNA (dating back 46,000 years) has been extracted from one of these Lake Mungo finds. When was Australia first settled?

© J.M.Bowler, University of Melbourne

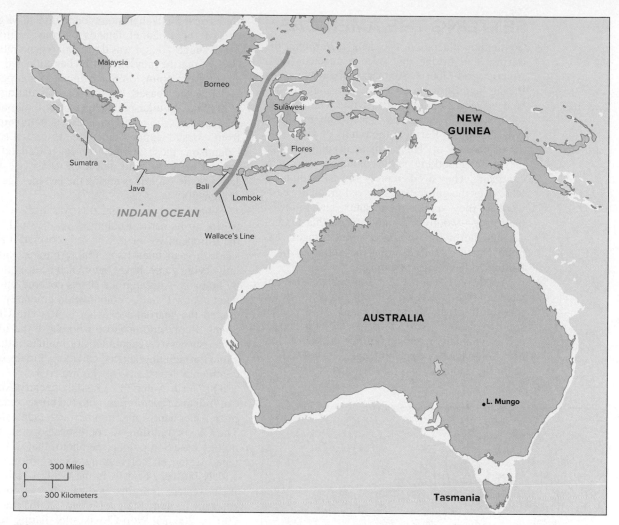

FIGURE 10.2

At times of major glacial advance, such as 50,000 years ago, Australia, New Guinea, and Tasmania were connected by dry land. Sahul was the name of that larger continent. The straits between Bali and Lombok were open water even when sea levels fell during the Ice Ages. Animals to the west of the Wallace line were Asiatic forms, while those to the east resembled the animals of Sahul—that is, Australia and New Guinea.

Not surprisingly (given their geographic proximity), Native Australians are closely related to New Guineans and Melanesians. This close genetic relationship suggested that there was only one initial colonization of Sahul. Genetic dating (ca. 50,000 B.P.) agrees more or less with archaeological evidence for early Australian settlement by 46,000 B.P. After that, gene flow continued between people living in Australia and the islands to the north until the land bridge connecting those areas was submerged around 8000 B.P.

In terms of the fossil record, Australia has given us a few of the oldest (ca. 46,000 B.P.) modern human skeletons known outside Africa. The earliest Australian skeletons come from Lake Mungo in New South Wales (Figure 10.2). One of these finds (Mungo III) is of the world's oldest

ritual ocher burial. The body was intentionally buried and decorated with ocher (Bowler et al. 2003). The world's oldest AMH mtDNA was extracted from this fossil. The same stratum at Mungo contains evidence for the first recorded cremation of a human being (Mungo I). Radiometric dating places humans, including these specimens, at Lake Mungo by 46,000 B.P. O'Connell and Allen (2004) reviewed data from more than 30 Australian archaeological sites older than 20,000 B.P. They concluded that Australia was occupied by 46,000 B.P.—but not much earlier. Dating based on genetic markers, on the other hand, has not ruled out earlier colonization. Northern and western Australia, closer to the rest of Sahul, may have been settled by 50,000 years ago.

SETTLING THE AMERICAS

Continental glaciation also created *Beringia,* the Bering land bridge that once connected North America and Siberia. Submerged today under the Bering Sea, Beringia once was a vast area of dry land, several hundred miles wide. The original settlers of the Americas came from northeast Asia. Living in Beringia thousands of years ago, these ancestors of Native Americans didn't realize they were embarking on the colonization of a new continent. They were merely big-game hunters who, over the generations, moved gradually eastward as they spread their camps and followed their prey—woolly mammoths and other tundra-adapted herbivores. Other ancient foragers entered North America along the shore by boat, fishing and hunting sea animals.

Archaeologist Jon Erlandson believes that ancient mariners traveled a "kelp highway" down the south coast of Beringia and Alaska, then southward down North America's North Pacific coast, eventually reaching California. Such a "forest" would have been rich in seals, sea otters, fish, seabirds, and shellfish (see Jenkins et al. 2012).

Clovis

Early American tool tradition; projectile point attached to hunting spear.

Barbs on a small chert point found on San Miguel, one of the Channel Islands off the California coast, suggest that it was designed to penetrate the flesh of marine prey. Erlandson has collected dozens of these points on San Miguel, which people had reached, based on radiocarbon dating, by 12,000 B.P. Similar points have been found along the North Pacific rim. The oldest such implement, from coastal Japan, dates to 15,600 B.P. To Erlandson, these artifacts reveal a trail left by ancient mariners who journeyed coastwise from Japan to the Americas during the last Ice Age (see Pringle 2008).

Whatever their origin, this was truly a "new world" to its earliest colonists, as it would be to the European voyagers who rediscovered it thousands of years later. Its natural resources, particularly its big game, never before had been exploited by humans. Although ice sheets covered most of what is now Canada, colonization gradually penetrated the heartland of what is now the United States. Representing those who chose the inland route, successive generations of hunters followed game through unglaciated corridors, breaks in the continental ice sheets (see Figure 10.3).

On North America's grasslands, early American Indians, *Paleoindians,* hunted horses, camels, bison, elephants, mammoths, and giant sloths. The **Clovis** tradition—a sophisticated stone technology based on points (see photo) that were fastened to the end of hunting spears—flourished, widely but very briefly, in the Central Plains, on their western margins, and in what is now the eastern United States (Green 2006; Largent 2007*a,* 2007*b*). Non-Clovis sites dating to the Clovis period also exist, in both North and South America.

Using C^{14} (radiocarbon) dates, where available, for all known Clovis sites, Michael Waters and Thomas Stafford (2007) concluded that the Clovis tradition lasted no more than 450 years (13,250–12,800 B.P.). During this short time span, Clovis technology originated and spread throughout North America. Unknown is whether its spread involved the actual movement of big-game hunters or the very rapid diffusion of a superior technology from group to group (Largent 2007*b*). Waters and Stafford (2007) also calculate that it would have taken from 600 to 1,000 years for the first Americans and their descendants to spread by land from the southern part of the Canadian ice-free corridor to Tierra del Fuego at the southern tip of South America—a distance of more than 8,680 miles (14,000 km). At least four sites in southern South America have C^{14} dates that are roughly the same as the Clovis C^{14} dates.

Waters and Stafford conclude there must have been people in the Americas before Clovis. Indeed, an emerging archaeological record supports a pre-Clovis occupation of the New World. One pre-Clovis find is a bone projectile point found embedded in a mastodon rib at the Manis site in

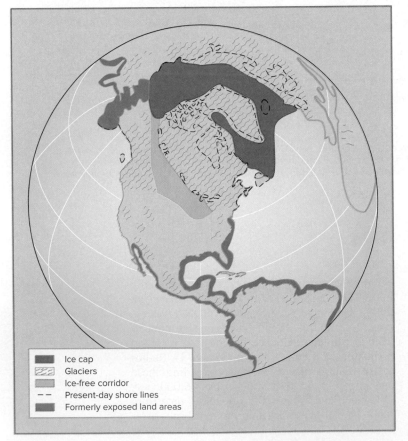

Ice cap
Glaciers
Ice-free corridor
Present-day shore lines
Formerly exposed land areas

FIGURE 10.3 The Ancestors of Native Americans Came to North America as Migrants from Asia.

They followed big-game herds across Beringia, an immense stretch of land exposed during the Ice Ages. Was their settlement of the Americas intentional? When did it probably happen? Other migrants reached North America along the shore by boat, fishing and hunting sea animals.

Washington State, dated to 13,800 B.P. (Waters et al. 2011). Non-Clovis tools and butchered mammoth remains dating to 13,500 B.P. and 12,500 B.P. have been found at sites in Wisconsin. The oldest pre-Clovis site is in South America, at the northern Patagonia settlement of Monte Verde, Chile, dating to 14,800 B.P.

In Oregon's Paisley Caves, scientists have uncovered 13,200-year-old tools (Western Stemmed projectile points) and human *coprolites* (fossilized

Clovis points, such as these from sites in Arizona, were attached to spears used by Paleoindians of the North American plains between 13,250 and 12,800 B.P. Are there sites with comparable ages or older elsewhere in the Americas?
Arizona State Museum/ University of Arizona, Helga Teiwes, Photographer

Woolly-mammoth hunters in Beringia, the vast stretch of land between Siberia and North America that was exposed during the Ice Ages.
© North Wind Picture Archives/Alamy Stock Photo

feces), from which DNA has been extracted (Jenkins et al. 2012). These non-Clovis points date to a time during or before the Clovis tradition. The Western Stemmed tradition appears to have developed separately from Clovis, which may have arisen in the southeastern United States and moved west. The Western Stemmed tradition began, perhaps earlier, in the West and moved east.

The DNA from the Paisley coprolites provides the oldest direct evidence for humans in the Americas. It represents haplogroup A, which is common in Siberia and found, along with haplogroup B, in contemporary Native Americans (see Jenkins et al. 2012). A haplogroup is a lineage marked by one or more specific genetic mutations. Analysis of DNA—bolstered, some anthropologists believe, by anatomical evidence—suggests that the Americas were settled by more than one haplogroup. The Clovis people were not the first or only early settlers of the Americas. Migration(s) of people into the Americas may date back as far as 18,000 years. Those early set-

tlers came at different times and by different routes (see Wade 2012).

PEOPLING THE PACIFIC

Who settled the vast Pacific and when? As we saw in the section "Settling Australia," people may have reached Sahul (Australia and New Guinea) by 50,000 years ago. The Solomon Islands (just east of New Guinea) were settled by 30,000 B.P. (Terrell 1998). (Consult the map in Figure 10.4 throughout this discussion.) From 30,000 B.P. until 3000 B.P., the Solomon Islands formed the eastern edge of the inhabited Pacific. People did not start sailing further east until around 3000 B.P., when a period of deep-sea crossings and island settlement began. This colonization of the Pacific was accompanied by the rapid spread of the earliest pottery found in Oceania, an ornately decorated ware with geometric designs called Lapita.

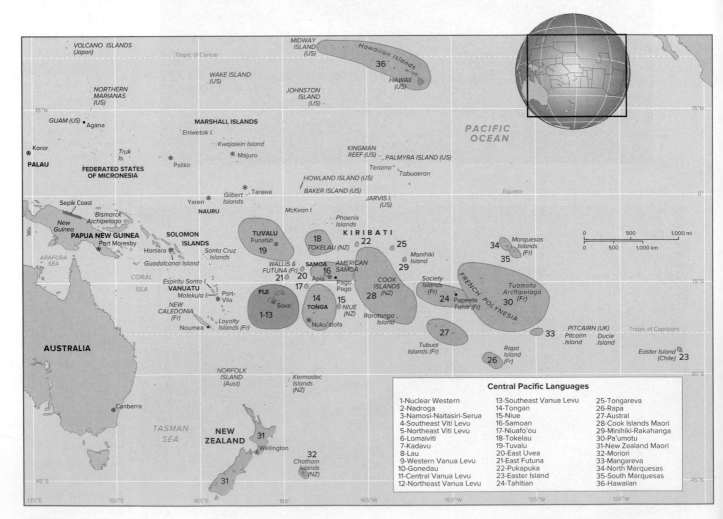

FIGURE 10.4 Oceania.

Polynesian islands are shaded khaki. Other Central Pacific languages outside of Polynesia are spoken in the area shaded orange, which includes Fiji.

On the left, an archaeologist holding a freshly scrubbed piece of Lapita pottery from the Teouma Lapita site, Republic of Vanuatu. On the right, a newly reconstructed stamped Lapita pot displayed in a Vanuatu museum.

© Stephen Alvarez/National Geographic Creative

The first Lapita potsherds were excavated in 1952. The name comes from the discovery site on the Melanesian island of New Caledonia. (Locate New Caledonia on the map in Figure 10.4.) Many scholars see this pottery as the creation of a distinct ethnic group (the Laptia—newcomers from Asia) who spread their pottery, along with distinctive stone tools, beads, rings, and shell ornaments, across the Pacific. The Lapita people eventually became the Polynesians.

No one knows why the Lapita people left home and risked sailing in deeper waters. Was it for reasons of wanderlust, a pioneering spirit, or improvements in canoe building and navigation? Some experts think the domestication of certain plants and animals thought to be of Asian origin—such as dogs, pigs, and chickens—fueled the Lapita expansion (Terrell 1998).

Archaeologist David Burley uncovered early Lapita shards (potsherds) at a lagoon site on the island of Tongatapu in the Polynesian kingdom of Tonga. Early outrigger canoes reached that lagoon after traveling hundreds, and perhaps more than a thousand, miles from the west. Radiocarbon dating of charcoal among the shards showed that seafarers reached Tonga between 2,950 and 2,850 years ago. *This is the earliest known settlement in Polynesia.* Burley thinks that Tongatapu "probably served as the initial staging point for population expansion" to other islands of Tonga, then to Samoa, and then on to the rest of Polynesia (quoted in Wilford 2002*a*).

Improvements in their outrigger canoes allowed these early Polynesian navigators to sail across large stretches of open sea, thus propelling the Polynesian diaspora. The larger canoes could carry dozens of people, plus pigs and other cargo. These seafarers (and their Lapita pottery) eventu-ally reached Tahiti to the east, as well as Hawaii—located more than 2,500 miles northeast of Tonga and Samoa. Later voyages carried the Polynesian diaspora south to New Zealand and farther east to Easter Island. Covering one-fourth of the Pacific, Polynesia became the last large area of the world to be settled by humans.

The Lapita pottery found at Tongatapu offered clues about where the seafarers originated and the connections between Polynesians and Melanesians. Analyzing bits of the shards, William Dickinson, a University of Arizona geologist, found sandy minerals from outside Tonga. Some of the pots had been brought there from elsewhere. It turned out that the artifacts were made of minerals found only on the Santa Cruz Islands in Melanesia, located 1,200 miles to the west of Tonga, and just east of the Solomon Islands (Burley and Dickinson 2001). The Tongatapu shards provided the first physical evidence linking the voyages of the Lapita people between the western and eastern parts of the Pacific. Tonga's first settlers may have come there directly from central Melanesia (Wilford 2002*a*).

The indigenous peoples of New Guinea and Melanesia tend to be dark-skinned; Polynesians are lighter-skinned (see photos). Remember that Lapita pottery was first found on a Melanesian island. Were its creators indigenous, dark-skinned Melanesians, or was Lapita pottery introduced to Melanesia by new, lighter-skinned immigrants from Southeast Asia? Did Melanesians and the Asian immigrants intermarry in Melanesia, forming a hybrid population that created the Lapita complex and eventually colonized Polynesia?

Until recently, anthropologists supposed that the ancestors of the Polynesians originated in

This print from 1811 shows a traditional (New Zealand) Maori war canoe. Earlier, the Lapita people had reached and colonized vast areas of the Pacific, including New Zealand, in their outrigger canoes.
© Gianni Dagli Orti/Corbis

southern China and/or Taiwan, which they left between 3,600 and 6,000 years ago. They were seen as spreading rapidly through the Pacific, largely bypassing Melanesia. This would explain why the Polynesians are not dark-skinned and why they speak Austronesian languages, rooted in Taiwan, rather than Papuan languages, spoken in parts of Melanesia. This view now seems discredited by the fact that nothing resembling Lapita pottery has ever been found in Taiwan or southern China. Lapita features first show up in Melanesia. Recent genetic studies also suggest that ancestral Polynesians stopped off in Melanesia. Interbreeding between early Polynesians and Melanesians has left clear genetic markers in today's Polynesians. DNA evidence has convinced Mark Stoneking, a molecular anthropologist, that ancestral Polynesians left Southeast Asia and sailed to, then expanded along, the coast of New Guinea and nearby islands. They intermingled with Melanesians there and then started voyaging eastward into the Pacific. (Gibbons 2001; Wilford 2002a).

Excavating in Melanesia's Bismarck Archipelago, archaeologist Patrick Kirch found evidence that newcomers from the islands of Southeast Asia had reached Melanesia by 3500 B.P. (see also Valentin et al. 2015). They built their homes on stilts, as in houses still found in Southeast Asia. They sailed in outrigger canoes and carried agricultural plants along with them. There was mixing between the newcomers and the Melanesians. *Out of their contact and interaction emerged the Lapita pottery style* (see Kirch 2000, 2016).

How can we explain the phenotypical differences between Polynesians and Melanesians? One possibility is that the Polynesian population originated in what geneticists call a *founder effect*. In such an event, just a few people, whose physical traits do not randomly sample the larger population from which they came, happen to give rise to a very large diaspora. A very small number of people—say, a few canoeloads who settled the Tongatapu lagoon—may have given rise to the entire, geographically dispersed Polynesian population. The physical traits of such a small founding group could not fully represent the population from which they had come. Whatever traits the founders happened to have, such as light skin color, would be transmitted to their descendants. This may explain why the Polynesians look so different from Melanesians, even though they have DNA in common.

By 2000 B.P., according to Patrick Kirch (2000, 2016), the people of Tonga had developed a significant new technology: the double-hull sailing canoe.

Even though they could not spot other islands on the distant horizon, as their ancestors had been able to do in the southwestern Pacific, the notion that the ocean was full of islands endured. Once they could more securely travel long distances—with the new canoe—they set forth. These weren't all accidental voyages and discoveries, as once was thought. These ancient sailors tacked against the prevailing east-to-west winds, knowing that, if necessary, they could ride a following wind back home.

Long ago, the anthropologist Alexander Lesser disputed what he saw as the "myth of the primitive isolate" (quoted in Terrell 1998)—the idea that ancient peoples lived in closed societies, each one out of contact with others. Behavioral modernity is incompatible with sealed cultures and social isolation. Even the small islands and atolls of the vast Pacific Ocean were inhabited by people who had regular contact with outsiders. The adventurous and interconnected peoples of the Pacific and their prehistoric past reveal that human diversity is as much a product of contact as of isolation (Terrell 1998).

On the left, a Polynesian woman from Tahiti, Society Islands, French Polynesia. On the right, a Melanesian woman from Madang, Papua New Guinea. What differences and similarities do you notice between these two women?

Left: © Gonzalez/Laif/Aurora Photos; right: © Albrecht G. Schaefer/Corbis

for REVIEW

summary

1. An African version of *H. heidelbergensis* gave rise to anatomically modern humans (AMHs) by 195,000 years ago. The earliest AMH fossil finds include Omo Kibish (195,000 B.P.), Herto (160,000–154,000 B.P.), and various South African sites, along with Skhūl (100,000 B.P.) and Qafzeh (92,000 B.P.). The Neandertals (130,000–28,000 B.P.) and AMHs were contemporaries, rather than ancestor and descendant. AMHs made Upper Paleolithic blade tools in Europe and Middle and Late Stone Age flake tools in Africa.

2. Scientists continue to debate whether human behavioral modernity originated in Africa as early as 100,000 years ago or in Europe around 45,000 years ago. Mounting evidence now tends to favor an African origin. As glacial ice melted and the Upper Paleolithic ended, foraging patterns became generalized. Fish, fowl, and plant foods supplemented, then replaced, the diminishing big-game supply. The beginning of a broad-spectrum economy in western Europe coincided with an intensification of Upper Paleolithic cave art. On limestone cave walls, prehistoric hunters painted images of animals important in their lives. Explanations of cave paintings (a prime example of human behavioral modernity) link them to hunting magic, ceremonies of increase, and initiation rites.

3. During the major glacial advances, land bridges formed, aiding human colonization of new areas, including Australia and the Americas. Around 50,000 years ago, dry land connected Australia, New Guinea, and Tasmania, forming the large continent of Sahul, separated from Asia only by narrow straits, which humans somehow crossed. The close genetic relationship between Native Australians, New Guineans, and Melanesians suggests a single initial colonization of Sahul from Asia. Genetic dating (ca. 50,000 B.P.) agrees more or less with archaeological evidence for early Australian settlement by 46,000 B.P. Australia has yielded a few of the oldest (ca. 46,000 B.P.) modern human skeletons known outside Africa, including the Lake Mungo finds.

4. Humans probably entered the Americas no more than 18,000 years ago. Pursuing big game or moving by boat along the North Pacific coast, they gradually settled the Americas. Adapting to different environments, Native Americans developed a variety of cultures.

5. New Guinea and the neighboring smaller islands of the southwestern Pacific (the Melanesian islands) have been settled for at least 30,000 years. Only around 3000 B.P. did people start sailing farther eastward, carrying the earliest

Oceanian pottery, called Lapita. Seafarers reached Tonga between 2,950 and 2,850 years ago—the earliest known settlement in Polynesia. Tonga appears to have served as the initial point of expansion, via outrigger canoe, to Samoa and eventually to Tahiti, Hawaii, New Zealand, and Easter Island. The ancestral Polynesians probably left Southeast Asia, sailed to, and then expanded along the coast of New Guinea and the adjacent islands. They intermingled with Melanesians there, then started voyaging eastward. The light skin color of Polynesians, which contrasts with the darker skin color of Melanesians, may have originated as an instance of the founder effect.

key terms

behavioral modernity 169

blade tool 173

Clovis 178

Cro Magnon 168

Herto 167

Upper Paleolithic 173

critical thinking

1. In 1997, ancient DNA was extracted from one of the Neandertal bones originally found in Germany in 1856. This was the first time that DNA of a premodern human had been recovered. What does the analysis of this DNA suggest about Neandertals' relation to AMHs?

2. What does *behavioral modernity* mean? What are the competing theories that attempt to explain the advent of behavioral modernity in AMHs? Is behavioral modernity a quality of individual humans or of humans as part of a social group? (Perhaps the answer is not one or the other but an interaction between the two, which some anthropologists might argue are inseparable.)

3. What cultural advances facilitated the spread of AMHs out of Africa?

4. What cultural changes accompanied glacial retreat in Europe during the late Upper Paleolithic?

5. It isn't the tools or the skeletons of Upper Paleolithic people but their art that has made them most familiar to us. What are some of the interpretations of cave art that researchers have proposed?

CHAPTER 11

The First Farmers

- ▶ When and where did the Neolithic originate, and what were its main features?

- ▶ What similarities and differences marked the Neolithic economies of the Old World and the New World?

- ▶ What costs and benefits are associated with food production?

© Philippe Lissac/Godong/Corbis

A farmer holds rice stalks on Mindanao Island, the Philippines. Rice was domesticated in southern China around 10,000 years ago.

understanding OURSELVES

What could be more American than McDonald's, hamburgers, hot dogs, or apple pie—more American, in other words, than a now global fast-food chain, a sandwich and sausage named for German cities, or a fruit first grown in the Middle East baked in a pastry crust from wheat, domesticated there as well. What we think of as truly American usually has foreign roots. Consider just McDonald's Big Mac as a world system in miniature. It consists of two all-beef patties (from cattle, an Old World domesticate), special sauce (similar to mayonnaise, invented in France), lettuce (Egypt), cheese (from cow's milk—Old World), pickles (India), and onions (Iran and West Pakistan), and it comes on a sesame-seed (India) bun (wheat—the Middle East). The Breakfast Egg McMuffin is only slightly less cosmopolitan. Eggs are from chickens, domesticated in Southeast Asia. Cheese comes from cow's milk (cows were domesticated in India, the Middle East, and Africa's eastern Sahara). Canadian bacon is from pork (western Asia), and the muffin is made of wheat (the Middle East). If you crave "real American" food—that is, food of New World origin—have some turkey or beans on a taco or tortilla (from maize or corn) and chocolate for dessert.

The first domesticated food crops appeared about 11,000 years ago in both the Old World and the Americas. Such crops as wheat, barley, rice, and millet became key caloric staples in the Old World, just as maize (corn), manioc (cassava), and potatoes did in the Americas. Animal domestication, however, was to become significantly more important in the Old World than in the New World, where the Peruvian llama was the only large domesticated animal. A mutually supportive relationship developed between farming and herding in the Old World, where crops sustained sheep, goats, and eventually cattle, pigs, horses, and donkeys. No such relationship developed in the pre-Columbian Americas.

This leads to a second (deceptive) question: What could be more American than the habit of using your own wheels to get to your favorite restaurant? Wheels? Only in Old World prehistory were animals harnessed to wheeled vehicles. Ancient Mexicans did also invent the wheel, but only for toys. Their homeland lacked the appropriate animals to pull plows, oxcarts, chariots, and carriages. How could a dog, turkey, or duck match a horse, a donkey, or an ox as a beast of burden? The absence of large-animal domestication in ancient Mexico is a key factor in world history, helping us understand the divergent development of societies on different sides of the oceans. Wheels fueled the growth of transport, trade, and travel in the Old World. Thousands of years after the origin of food production, advantages in transport would fuel an "Age of Discovery" and enable the European conquest of the Americas. Again, a key feature of contemporary American life turns out to have foreign roots.

As the Ice Age ended and glaciers retreated in Europe, foragers pursued a more generalized economy, focusing less on large animals. This was the beginning of what Kent Flannery (1969) has called the **broad-spectrum revolution.** This refers to the period beginning around 15,000 B.P. in the Middle East and 12,000 B.P. in Europe, during which a wider range, or broader spectrum, of plant and animal life was hunted, gathered, collected, caught, and fished. It was revolutionary because in the Middle East it led to food production—human control over the reproduction of plants and animals.

THE MESOLITHIC

The broad-spectrum revolution in Europe includes the late Upper Paleolithic and the **Mesolithic,** which followed it. Again, because of the long history of European archaeology, our knowledge of the Mesolithic (particularly in southwestern Europe and the British Isles) is extensive. The Mesolithic had a characteristic tool type—the *microlith* (Greek for "small stone"). Of interest to us is what an abundant inventory of small and delicately shaped tools can tell us about the total economy and way of life of the people who made them (see Bailey and Spikins 2008; Cummings et al. 2014; Renfrew and Bahn 2014).

By 10,000 B.P. the glaciers had retreated to such an extent that foragers now lived in the formerly glaciated British Isles and Scandinavia. People still hunted, but their prey were solitary forest animals, such as the roe deer, wild ox, and wild pig, rather than herd species. This led to new hunting techniques: solitary stalking and trapping. The coasts and lakes of Europe, the Middle East, and Japan were fished intensively. Some important Mesolithic sites are Scandinavian shell mounds—the garbage dumps of prehistoric oyster collectors. Microliths were used as fishhooks and in harpoons. Dugout canoes facilitated fishing and travel. For woodworking, Mesolithic carpenters used new kinds of axes, chisels, and gouges. The process of preserving meat and fish by smoking and salting grew increasingly important. (Meat preservation had been less of an issue when the climate was colder, because winter snow and ice, often on the ground nine months of the year, offered convenient refrigeration.) The bow and arrow became essential for hunting waterfowl in swamps and marshes. Dogs were used as retrievers.

A recent analysis of mitochondrial DNA in dogs and wolves suggests that there were two phases of domestication leading to contemporary dogs (see Arnold 2015). The first phase began in China around 33,000 years ago. The second phase began around 15,000 years ago, when dogs started spreading around the world. Compared with other dog populations, Asian dogs are genetically closest to the (grey) wolf. They also display the greatest genetic diversity, which we would expect if Asia was indeed the site of their first domestication. Dogs did not begin to spread beyond Asia until around 15,000 years ago. The first dogs may have arrived in Europe no more than 10,000 years ago, where they would have been useful as retrievers in the Mesolithic economy. Broad-spectrum economies lasted about 5,000 years longer in Europe than in the Middle East. Whereas Middle Easterners had begun to cultivate plants and breed animals by 10,000 B.P., farming and herding reached western

Europe only around 5000 B.P. (3000 B.C.E.) and northern Europe 500 years later.

As the big-game supply dwindled after 15,000 B.P., foragers had to pursue new resources. Their attention shifted from large-bodied, slow reproducers (such as mammoths) to species such as fish, mollusks, and rabbits, which reproduce quickly and prolifically. This happened with the European Mesolithic. It also happened at the Japanese site of Nittano, located on an inlet near Tokyo. Nittano was occupied several times between 6000 and 5000 B.P. by members of the *Jomon* culture (16,000–2500 B.P.), for which more than 30,000 sites are known in Japan. The Jomon people made stone and bone tools, and some of the world's earliest pottery—beginning as early as 15,500 B.P. They hunted deer, pigs, bears, and antelope, gathered plants and nuts, and ate fish and shellfish. Their sites have yielded the remains of more than 300 species of shellfish and 180 species of edible plants, including berries, nuts, and tubers (Akazawa and Aikens 1986; Habu et al. 2011).

Jomon foragers used their pottery to cook and serve stews of salmon and shellfish. In burnt fragments of clay pots dating back 15,300 years, scientists have found traces of fat from marine and freshwater fish and shellfish (Craig 2013; Subbaraman 2013). Whether in the form of a family meal, a potluck dinner, or a lavish feast, eating tends to be a social activity, just as it appears to have been in the Jomon culture. Not only did the Jomon people stew their fish, they feasted on it in groups. Their large clay pots weren't just utilitarian cooking vessels; they also brought people together to socialize (Craig 2013; Subbaraman 2013).

Even earlier than Jomon, the world's oldest known pottery has been found recently in Jiangxi Province, southern China (Wu et al. 2012). Dated to 20,000 B.P., these pots were simple vessels used

Visualization of life in a Mesolithic settlement by the sea at Nab Head, Wales, United Kingdom. Dugout canoes facilitated fishing and travel. For woodworking, Mesolithic carpenters used new kinds of axes, chisels, and gouges. The process of preserving meat and fish by smoking and salting grew increasingly important.
© National Museum of Wales

broad-spectrum revolution
Foraging of varied plant and animal foods at end of Ice Age; prelude to Neolithic.

Mesolithic
Stone toolmaking, emphasizing microliths within broad-spectrum economies.

A group of Mesolithic tools; note the small, delicately shaped tools, known as microliths. For what activities were such tools used?

Vaneiles/Creative Commons Attribution-Share Alike 3.0 Unported/https://commons.wikimedia.org/wiki/ File:OpgravingStevoort.jpg/5/5/2016

for cooking food. It appears that pottery making began in China 20,000 years ago and never stopped. The Chinese kitchen always has been based on cooking and steaming, which ceramics facilitate. Unlike other parts of Asia and the Middle East, breads never have been prominent in Chinese cuisine. According to Harvard professor Ofer Bar-Yosef, a member of the discovery team, these early Chinese pots were made by a group of mobile hunter-gatherers (see Wu et al. 2012). Plant cultivation did not reach China for another 10,000 years.

In the Middle East, the first pottery appeared 3,000–2,000 years after, rather than before, the turn to farming. Bar-Yosef suggests that the earliest farmers/herders in the Middle East had a diet based on barbecued meats and pita breads and didn't need pottery. In their cooking style, one simply grinds the seeds, mixes them with water, then cooks the dough right on the fire. Chinese cooking, by contrast, needed pots to cook and steam foods thousands of years earlier (see Wu et al. 2012).

THE NEOLITHIC

The Neolithic Revolution, sometimes called the Agricultural Revolution, was the widespread transition, beginning about 12,000 years ago, of human societies from lifestyles based on foraging to lifestyles based on farming and herding. The **Neolithic** is considered revolutionary because, in just a few thousand years—after millions of years of foraging as the sole human subsistence strategy—it would transform small, mobile groups into societies living in permanent settlements—villages, towns, and eventually cities. (see Renfrew and Bahn 2014; Whittle and Bickle 2014).

The transition from Mesolithic to Neolithic occurs when groups become dependent

Neolithic
Term used to describe economies based on food production (cultivated crops and domesticated animals).

on domesticated plants, animals, and animal products for more than 50 percent of their diet. Usually, this happens after a very long period of experimenting with and using domesticates as supplements to broad-spectrum foraging (see Bellwood 2005; Simmons 2007). More productive and reliable than foraging, Neolithic economies fueled population growth and expansion, as well as the settlement of new environments.

The archaeological signature of Neolithic cultures (which are called *Formative* in the Americas) includes dependence on cultivation, sedentary (settled) life, and the use of ceramic vessels. The term *Neolithic* originally was coined to refer to new techniques of grinding and polishing stone tools (see Saville 2012). However, the primary significance of the Neolithic was the new total economy rather than just its characteristic artifacts (see Simmons 2007).

THE FIRST FARMERS AND HERDERS IN THE MIDDLE EAST

Early economies based on food production were associated with substantial changes in human lifestyles. By 12,000 B.P., the shift toward the Neolithic was under way in the Middle East (Turkey, Iraq, Iran, Syria, Jordan, and Israel). People started intervening in the reproductive cycles of plants and animals. No longer simply hunting, gathering, and fishing, people started modifying the biological characteristics of plants and animals as they began to grow their own food. By 10,000 B.P., domesticated plants and animals were part of the broad spectrum of resources used by Middle Easterners. By 7500 B.P., most Middle Easterners had abandoned broad-spectrum foraging for more

Neolithic was coined to refer to techniques of grinding and polishing stone tools, such as this hammer head and two polished axes, found in England. Was the new toolmaking style the most significant thing about the Neolithic?

© CM Dixon/age fotostock

specialized, Neolithic economies based on fewer species, which were domesticates. They had become committed farmers and herders.

Kent Flannery (1969) laid out a series of eras during which the Middle Eastern transition to farming and herding took place. The era of seminomadic hunting and gathering (12,000–10,000 B.P.) encompasses the last stages of broad-spectrum foraging. By the end of this period, some early domesticates had been added to the diet. Next came the era of early dry farming (of wheat and barley) and caprine domestication (10,000–7500 B.P.). *Dry farming* refers to farming without irrigation; such farming depended on rainfall. *Caprine* (from *capra,* Latin for "goat") refers to goats and sheep, which were domesticated during this era.

During the era of increased specialization in food production (7500–5500 B.P.), new crops were added to the diet, along with more productive varieties of wheat and barley. Cattle and pigs were domesticated. By 5500 B.P., agriculture had extended to the alluvial plain of the Tigris and Euphrates Rivers (Figure 11.1), where early Mesopotamians lived in walled towns, some of which grew into cities. (Recap 11.1 highlights these stages, or eras, in the transition to food production in the ancient Middle East.) After two million years of stone-toolmaking, *H. sapiens* was living in the Bronze Age, when metallurgy and the wheel were invented.

Middle Eastern food production arose in the context of four environmental zones. From highest to lowest, they are high plateau (5,000 feet, or 1,500 meters), hilly flanks, piedmont steppe (treeless plain), and alluvial desert. The last zone is the area watered by the Tigris and Euphrates Rivers (100–500 feet, or 30–150 meters). The **hilly flanks** is a subtropical woodland zone that flanks those rivers to the north (see Figure 11.1).

It once was speculated that food production might have begun in oases in the alluvial desert, places where water would have been available for humans, plants, and animals. (*Alluvial* describes rich, fertile soil deposited by rivers and streams.) Today, we know that although the world's first civilization (Mesopotamian) did indeed develop in this arid zone, irrigation, a late invention (7000 B.P.), was necessary to farm the alluvial desert. Plant cultivation and animal domestication started not in the dry river zone but in areas with reliable rainfall.

The archaeologist Robert J. Braidwood (1975) proposed that food production started in the hilly

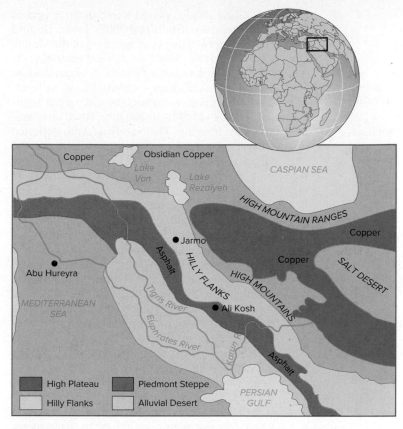

FIGURE 11.1 The Vertical Economy of the Ancient Middle East.

Geographically close but contrasting environments were linked by seasonal movements and trade among broad-spectrum foragers. As people traveled and traded, they removed plants from the zones where they grew wild in the hilly flanks into adjacent zones where humans became agents of selection. Food production emerged on the margins of the hilly flanks, at places such as Ali Kosh, rather than within that area, at places such as Jarmo.

flanks, or subtropical woodland zone, where wild wheat and barley would have been most abundant (see Figure 11.1). In 1948, a team headed by Braidwood started excavations at Jarmo, an early farming village inhabited between 9000 and 8500 B.P., located in the hilly flanks. We now know that there were farming villages earlier than Jarmo in zones adjacent to the hilly flanks. One example is Ali Kosh (see Figure 11.1), a village in the foothills (piedmont steppe) of the Zagros Mountains. By 9000 B.P., the people of Ali Kosh were herding goats, intensively collecting various wild plants, and harvesting wheat during the late winter and early spring (Hole, Flannery, and Neely 1969).

hilly flanks
Woodland zone just north of Tigris and Euphrates Rivers.

RECAP 11.1	The Transition to Food Production in the Middle East

ERA	DATES
Origin of state (Sumer)	5500 B.P.
Increased specialization in food production	7500–5500 B.P.
Early dry farming and caprine domestication	10,000–7500 B.P.
Seminomadic hunting and gathering (e.g., Natufians)	12,000–10,000 B.P.

Climate change played a role in the origin of food production (Bellwood 2005). Lewis Binford (1968) proposed that in certain areas of the Middle East (such as the hilly flanks), local environments were so rich in resources that foragers could adopt **sedentism**—sedentary (settled) life in villages. Binford's prime example is the widespread Natufian culture (12,800–10,200 B.P.), based on broad-spectrum foraging. The **Natufians**, who collected wild cereals and hunted gazelles, had year-round villages. They could stay in the same place (early villages) because they could harvest nearby wild cereals for six months (see Simmons 2007).

The climate became warmer and more humid just before the Natufian period. This expanded the altitude range of wild wheat and barley, thus enlarging the available foraging area and allowing a longer harvest season. Wheat and barley ripened in the spring at low altitudes, in the summer at middle altitudes, and in the fall at high altitudes. As locations for their villages, the Natufians chose central places where they could harvest wild cereals in all three zones.

Around 11,000 B.P., this favorable foraging pattern was threatened by a shift to drier conditions. Many wild cereal habitats dried up, and the optimal zone for foraging shrank. Natufian villages were now restricted to areas with permanent water. As population continued to grow, some Natufians attempted to maintain productivity by transferring wild cereals to well-watered areas, where they started cultivating those cereals.

In the view of many scholars, the people most likely to adopt a new subsistence strategy, such as cultivation, would be those having the most trouble in following their traditional subsistence strategy (Binford 1968; Flannery 1973; Wenke and Olszewski 2007). Thus, those ancient Middle Easterners living outside the area where wild foods were most abundant would be the most likely to experiment and to adopt new subsistence strategies. Recent archaeological finds support this hypothesis that food production began in *marginal areas,* such as the piedmont steppe, rather than in the optimal zones, such as the hilly flanks, where traditional foods were most abundant.

Wild wheat still grows so densely in areas of the hilly flanks that one person working just an hour with Neolithic tools can easily harvest a kilogram of wheat (Harlan and Zohary 1966). People would have had no reason to invent cultivation when wild grain was ample to feed them. Wild wheat ripens rapidly and can be harvested over a three-week period. According to Flannery, over that time period, a family of experienced plant collectors could harvest enough grain—2,200 pounds (1,000 kilograms)—to feed themselves for a year. But after harvesting all that wheat, they'd need a place to put it. They could no longer maintain a nomadic lifestyle: They'd need to stay close to their wheat.

Sedentary village life thus developed before farming and herding in the Middle East. The Natufians

and other hilly flanks foragers had no choice but to build villages near the densest stands of wild grains. They needed a place to keep their grain. Furthermore, sheep and goats came to graze on the stubble that remained after humans had harvested the grain. The fact that basic plants and animals were available in the same area also favored village life. Hilly flanks foragers built houses, dug storage pits for grain, and made ovens to roast it.

Natufian settlements, occupied year round, show permanent architectural features and evidence for the processing and storage of wild grains. One such site is Abu Hureyra, Syria (see Figure 11.1), which was initially occupied by Natufian foragers around 11,000 to 10,500 B.P. Then it was abandoned—to be reoccupied later by farmer-herders, between 9500 and 8000 B.P.

Prior to domestication, the favored hilly flanks zone had the densest human population. Approaching *carrying capacity* (the maximum number of people who could be supported by a given subsistence base), that population began to spill over into adjacent, more marginal areas. Colonists from the flanks tried to maintain their traditional broad-spectrum foraging in these marginal zones. But with sparser wild foods available, they had to experiment with new subsistence strategies, including cultivation (Binford 1968; Bocquet-Appel and Bar-Yosef 2008; Flannery 1969). *Early cultivation began as an attempt to copy, in a less favorable environment, the dense stands of wheat and barley that grew wild in the hilly flanks.*

The Middle East, along with certain other world areas where food production originated, is a region that for thousands of years has had a *vertical economy.* (Other examples include Peru and **Mesoamerica**—Middle America, including Mexico, Guatemala, and Belize.) A vertical economy exploits environmental zones that, although close together in space, contrast with one another in altitude, rainfall, overall climate, and vegetation (see Figure 11.1). Such a close juxtaposition of varied environments allowed broad-spectrum foragers to use different resources in different seasons.

Early seminomadic foragers in the Middle East had followed game from zone to zone. In winter they hunted in the piedmont steppe region, which had winter rains rather than snow and provided winter pasture for game animals 12,000 years ago. (Indeed, it still is used for winter grazing by herders today.) When winter ended, the steppe dried up. Game moved up to the hilly flanks and high plateau country as the snow melted. Pastureland became available at higher elevations. Foragers gathered as they climbed, harvesting wild grains that ripened later at higher altitudes. Sheep and goats followed the stubble in the wheat and barley fields after people had harvested the grain.

The four Middle Eastern environmental zones shown in Figure 11.1 also were tied together through trade. Certain resources were confined to specific zones. Asphalt, used as an adhesive in the manufacture of sickles, came from the steppe. Copper and turquoise sources were located in the high plateau. Contrasting environments were linked in two ways: by foragers' seasonal migration and by trade.

The movement of people, animals, and products between zones—plus population increase supported by highly productive broad-spectrum foraging—was a precondition for the emergence of food production (Bocquet-Appel and Bar-Yosef 2008). As they traveled between zones, people carried seeds into new habitats. Mutations, genetic recombinations, and human selection led to new kinds of wheat and barley. Some of the new varieties were better adapted to the steppe and, eventually, the alluvial desert than the wild forms had been.

Genetic Changes and Domestication

What are the main differences between wild and domesticated plants? The seeds of domesticated cereals, and often the entire plant, are larger. Compared with wild plants, crops produce a higher yield per unit of area. Domesticated plants also lose their natural seed-dispersal mechanisms. Cultivated beans, for example, have pods that hold together, rather than shattering as they do in the wild. Domesticated cereals have tougher connective tissue holding the seedpods to the stem.

Grains of wheat, barley, and other cereals occur in bunches at the end of a stalk (Figure 11.2). The grains are attached to the stalk by an *axis* (plural, *axes*). In wild cereals, this axis is brittle. Sections of the axis break off one by one, and a seed attached to each section falls to the ground. This is how wild

cereals spread their seeds and propagate their species. But a brittle axis is a problem for people. Imagine the annoyance experienced by broad-spectrum foragers as they tried to harvest wild wheat, only to have the grain fall off or be blown away.

In very dry weather, wild wheat and barley ripen—their axes totally disintegrating—in just three days (Flannery 1973). The brittle axis must have been even more irritating to people who planted the seeds and waited for the harvest. But fortunately, certain stalks of wild wheat and barley happened to have tough axes. These were the ones whose seeds people saved to plant the following year.

Another problem with wild cereals is that the edible portion is enclosed in a tough husk. This husk was too tough to remove with a pounding stone. Foragers had to roast the grain to make the husk brittle enough to come off. However, some wild plants happened to have genes for brittle husks. Humans chose the seeds of these plants (which would have germinated prematurely in nature), because they could be more effectively prepared for eating.

People also selected certain features in animals (Miller, Zeder, and Arter 2009). Some time after sheep were domesticated, advantageous new phenotypes arose. Wild sheep aren't woolly; wool coats were products of domestication. Although it's hard to imagine, a wool coat offers protection against extreme heat. Skin temperatures of sheep living in very hot areas are much lower than temperatures on

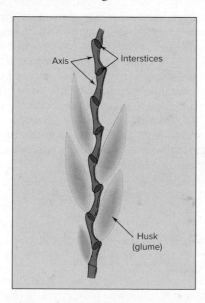

FIGURE 11.2 A Head of Wheat or Barley.
In the wild, the axis comes apart as its parts fall off one by one. The connecting parts (interstices) are tough and don't come apart in domesticated grains. In wild grains, the husks are hard. In domestic plants, they are brittle, which permits easy access to the grain. How did people deal with hard husks before domestication?

Between 12,000 and 10,000 years ago, foragers in the Middle East followed the availability of plants and animals from lower to higher zones. This pattern evolved into the nomadic herding of domesticated sheep and goats. Here we see a contemporary (2013) herder, a shepherd in Rajasthan, India.

© Stanford Ullner

the surface of their wool. Woolly sheep, but not their wild ancestors, could survive in hot, dry alluvial lowlands.

Plants got larger with domestication, while animals got smaller, probably because smaller animals are easier to control. Middle Eastern sites reveal changes in the horn shape of domesticated goats. Such a change, which in itself seems unlikely to have offered any particular advantage to domesticators, may have been genetically linked to some other desirable trait that has left no skeletal evidence behind.

Archaeological evidence for herd management (from Iraq and Iran) predates anatomical evidence (e.g, changes in size or horns) for full animal domestication. For example, certain sites show a large number of bones from 2- to 3-year-old males. This suggests a concern with preserving female breeding stock. Those ancient herd managers realized that a steady stream of young immigrant males from surrounding territories would replace slaughtered local males. Herd management also involved moving animals (goats, sheep, cattle, and pigs) from their natural habitats to lower altitudes, where they adapted to hotter, drier climates by becoming smaller. By managing (e.g., selectively culling) wild animal populations, ancient Middle Easterners were gradually converting their prey animals into herd animals. In doing so, in a process that lasted more than a thousand years, they also were transforming themselves from hunters into herders (Zeder 2008).

Food Production and the State

The shift from foraging to food production was gradual (see Olszewski 2016; Pandika 2013). Knowing how to grow crops and breed livestock didn't immediately convert Middle Easterners into full-time farmers and herders. Domesticated plants and animals began as minor parts of a broad-spectrum economy. Foraging for fruits, nuts, grasses, grains, snails, and insects continued (see Simmons 2007).

Over time, Middle Eastern economies grew more specialized, geared more exclusively toward crops and herds. The former marginal zones became centers of the new economy and of population increase and emigration. Some of the increasing population spilled back into the hilly flanks, where people eventually had to intensify production by cultivating. Domesticated crops could now provide a bigger harvest than could the grains that grew wild there. Thus, in the hilly flanks, too, farming eventually replaced foraging as the economic mainstay.

Farming colonies spread down into drier areas. By 7000 B.P., simple irrigation systems had developed, tapping springs in the foothills. By 6000 B.P., more complex irrigation techniques made

Simple irrigation systems, like this one in rural Bangladesh, were being used in the Middle East by 7000 B.P. More complex systems were supporting irrigated agriculture in the arid lowlands of southern Mesopotamia by 6000 B.P.
© Rehman Asad/Demotix/Corbis

agriculture possible in the arid lowlands of southern Mesopotamia. In the alluvial desert plain of the Tigris and Euphrates Rivers, a new economy based on irrigation and trade fueled the growth of an entirely new form of society. This was the *state,* a social and political unit featuring a central government, extreme contrasts of wealth, and social classes (see Olszewski 2016).

As discussed, we now understand why the first farmers lived neither in the alluvial lowlands, where the Mesopotamian state arose around 5500 B.P., nor in the hilly flanks, where wild plants and animals abounded. Food production began in marginal zones, such as the piedmont steppe, where people experimented at reproducing, artificially, the dense grain stands that grew wild in the hilly flanks. As seeds were taken to new environments, new phenotypes were favored by a combination of natural and human selection. The spread of cereal grains outside their natural habitats was part of a system of migration and trade between zones, which had developed in the Middle East during the broad-spectrum period. Food production also owed its origin to the need to intensify production to feed an increasing human population—the legacy of thousands of years of productive foraging (see Bocquet-Appel and Bar-Yosef 2008).

OTHER OLD WORLD FOOD PRODUCERS

The path from foraging to food production was one that people followed independently in at least seven world areas: the Middle East, northern China, southern China, sub-Saharan Africa, central Mexico, the south central Andes, and the eastern United States. We see that three of these locations were in the Americas, with four in the Old World. In each of these centers, people

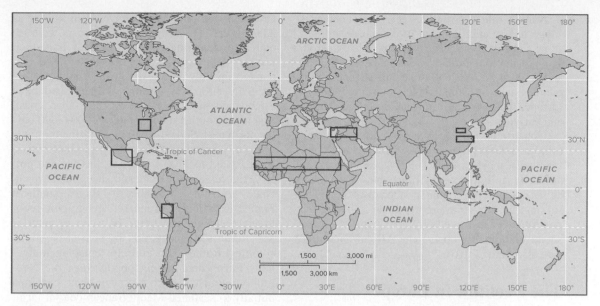

FIGURE 11.3 Seven World Areas Where Food Production Was Invented Independently.
Do any of these areas surprise you?

SOURCE: Bruce D. Smith, *The Emergence of Agriculture* (New York: Scientific American Library, 1995), p. 12. Reprinted by permission of the author. smith.bruce@nmnh.si.edu

independently invented domestication, although of different sets of crops and animals. (Figure 11.3 is a map highlighting those seven areas.)

In the Old World, food production soon began to spread out from the Middle East. This happened through trade; through the diffusion of plants, animals, products, and information; and through the actual migration of farmers. Middle Eastern domesticates spread westward to northern Africa, including Egypt's Nile Valley, and eventually into Europe (Zeder 2008). Trade also extended eastward to India and Pakistan. In Egypt, an agricultural economy based on plants and animals originally domesticated in the Middle East led to a pharaonic civilization.

The Neolithic in Africa

Excavations in southern Egypt have revealed considerable complexity in its Neolithic economy and social system, along with very early pottery and cattle, which may have been domesticated locally. Located in southern Egypt, Nabta Playa is a basin in the eastern Sahara Desert that, during prehistoric summers, filled with water. Over several millennia this temporary lake attracted people, who used it for social and ceremonial activities (Wendorf and Schild 2000). Nabta Playa was first occupied around 12,000 B.P., as Africa's summer rains moved northward, providing moisture for grasses, trees, bushes, hares, and gazelle, along with humans. The earliest settlements (11,000–9300 B.P.) at Nabta were small, seasonal camps of herders of domesticated cattle. (Note the very early, and perhaps independent, domestication of cattle here.) According to Wendorf and

Schild (2000), Nabta Playa provides early evidence for what anthropologists have called the "African cattle complex," in which cattle are used economically for their milk and blood, rather than killed for their meat (except on ceremonial occasions). Nabta was occupied only seasonally, as people came over from the Nile or from better-watered areas to the south. They returned to those areas in the fall.

By 9000 B.P., people were living at Nabta Playa year round. To survive in the desert, they dug large, deep wells and lived in well-organized villages, with small huts arranged in straight lines. Plant remains show they collected sorghum, millet, legumes (peas and beans), tubers, and fruits. These were wild plants, and so the economy was not fully Neolithic. By 8800 B.P., these people were making their own pottery, possibly the earliest pottery in Egypt. By 8100 B.P., sheep and goats had arrived from the Middle East.

Around 7500 B.P., new settlers occupied Nabta, whose previous inhabitants had been forced away by a major drought. The newcomers brought a more sophisticated social and ceremonial system. They sacrificed young cattle, which they buried in clay-lined chambers covered with stone slabs. They also built Egypt's earliest astronomical measuring device: a "calendar circle" used to mark the summer solstice. Nabta Playa had become a regional ceremonial center: a place where various groups gathered seasonally or occasionally to conduct ceremonies and to socialize. The existence of such centers, as well as their religious, political, and social functions, is familiar to ethnographers who have worked in Africa.

Nabta's role as a regional ceremonial center is suggested by an alignment of nine large, upright stone slabs near the place where people gathered. This formation, probably dating between 7500 and 5500 B.P., recalls similar large stone alignments, such as Stonehenge, found in western Europe, that were built during the late Neolithic and early Bronze Age.

Construction of such large, complex megalithic structures requires well-organized work parties and a major effort. This suggests that some authority (religious or civil) may have been managing resources and human labor over time. The findings at Nabta Playa represent an elaborate and previously unsuspected ceremonialism, as well as social complexity, during the African Neolithic (see also Sadig 2010).

The Neolithic in Europe

How did the Neolithic and its farming techniques spread to Europe? Did Middle Eastern farmers colonize Europe, or did their ideas and techniques spread there without any actual migration? We have good evidence now that the Neolithic was spread by the actual migration of farmers. Scandinavian scientists recently have found evidence for this migration. They compared DNA from two sets of Swedish burials, both 5,000 years old. One burial represented a hunter-gatherer group; the other, a farmer group about 250 miles (400 kilometers) away. The ancient hunter-gatherer DNA linked them to living northern Europeans, especially Finns, while the farmer genome resembled that of contemporary southeastern Europeans. The researchers concluded that migrating farmers spread their crops and techniques across Europe from the Mediterranean beginning around 8,500 years ago. It took them about 3,000 years to reach northwestern Europe (Skoglund et al. 2012).

Excavations on Cyprus show that the island had been colonized by 10,600 B.P.—the early Neolithic—with village life and farming well underway. This confirms that migration from the mainland Middle East began—by boat—shortly after the beginning of farming (Vigne et al. 2012). Sailing about 40 miles (60 kilometers) from the mainland to Cyprus, Neolithic colonists carried with them all four major livestock species (sheep, goats, cattle, and pigs). To Cyprus they introduced the full Neolithic package: farming and herding, technologies, and, most likely, the social networks and belief systems they brought from their original homeland. The colonization of Cyprus can serve as a model of how the Neolithic spread across the rest of the Mediterranean basin—by boat and seafaring colonists (Zeder 2008).

The Mediterranean basin experienced a diaspora—slowly at first, then more rapidly—of Neolithic people and their lifestyle westward from the Middle East and Cyprus to the shores of the Atlantic (Zeder 2008). Expansion from Cyprus to Greece and its islands may have taken as long as 2,000 years. Thereafter, only 500 years were required for seafaring colonists to reach Italy, then just 500–600 years to travel the much greater distance from Italy to the Atlantic. To be more specific, by 8000 B.P., farming villages had been established in Greece and on the Italian coast, first in the southeast and then, by 7800–7600 B.P., the northwest. Soon thereafter, seafaring migrants from Italy began to settle southern France, where a site, dated to 7700–7600 B.P., has yielded pottery, the remains of domestic sheep, and wheat. Once the Neolithic reached its shores, southern France experienced a marked geographic, ecological, and cultural break between its interior Mesolithic settlements and its coastal Neolithic colonies. Rather than entirely replacing indigenous European foraging populations, the Neolithic colonists seem to have been confined initially to scattered Mediterranean coastal farming communities (Zeder 2008). By 6000 B.P., however, Europe had thousands of farming villages, from as far east as Russia to as far west as northern France (see Fowler 2015).

Recent studies confirm that modern Europeans get their DNA from three main sources (Zimmer 2015). First is that of the pre-Neolithic hunter-gatherers of the Upper Paleolithic and Mesolithic periods. Second was a wave of farmers who started arriving from Anatolia (in what is now Turkey) around 8500 B.P. They share DNA with contemporary Middle Easterners. The third source, reaching Europe around 4500 B.P., was a population of nomads from the Russian steppes known as the Yamnaya.

The DNA of Europeans changed significantly after the introduction of farming (Zimmer 2015). Those changes affected digestion, skin color, and height. A team led by David Reich, a geneticist at Harvard Medical School, analyzed the genomes of 230 Europeans who lived between 8,500 and 2,300 years ago. Reich's team observed specific genetic changes that were adaptations to the new diet based on farming and herding. One genetic change made it easier to absorb nutrients from wheat and other crops. Another involved a gene that aids milk digestion, useful among herders, which became increasingly common after 4500 B.P.

Reich's team also identified changes in Europeans' skin color. Europe's original hunter-gatherers, as descendants of people who had come from Africa, retained dark skin as recently as 9,000 years ago. Apparently they did not need to reduce the melanin in their skin because their meat-rich diet was a sufficient source of vitamin D. The Anatolian farmers who colonized Europe after 8500 B.P. had lighter skin, and a new gene variant that emerged later lightened European skin even more. The widespread shift to farming, which reduced the intake of vitamin D compared with a meat diet, may have triggered the reduction in epidermal melanin.

Finally, the DNA of the Anatolian farmers made them relatively tall, with the Yamnaya even taller. Northern Europeans have inherited a larger amount of Yamnaya DNA, making them taller, too. The average height of southern Europeans, however, declined after the advent of farming, probably because of reduced animal protein in their diet (Zimmer 2015).

The Neolithic in Asia

Archaeological research confirms the early presence of domesticated goats, sheep, cattle, wheat, and barley in Pakistan by 8000 B.P.. In that country's Indus River Valley, ancient cities (Harappa and Mohenjo-daro) emerged slightly later than did the first Mesopotamian city-states. Domestication and state formation in the Indus Valley were influenced by developments in, and trade with, the Middle East.

China was also one of the first world areas to develop farming, based on millet and rice. Millet is a tall, small-seeded cereal still grown in northern China. This grain, which today feeds a third of the world's population, is used in contemporary North America mainly as birdseed. Millet was first domesticated in northern China around 10,000 B.P. By 7500 B.P., two varieties of millet supported early farming communities in northern China, along the Yellow River. Millet cultivation paved the way for widespread village life and eventually for Shang dynasty civilization, based on irrigated agriculture, between 3600 and 3100 B.P. The northern Chinese also had domesticated dogs, pigs, and possibly cattle, goats, and sheep by 7000 B.P.

Combining radiocarbon dating of sites with genetic analysis of grain, researchers have traced the spread of domesticated millet from its origin point in northern China westward into Europe via the foothills of Eurasia (Cambridge 2015). Millet was an ideal crop to bridge the transition from nomadic foraging to village farming in Neolithic Eurasia. Because of millet's rapid growing season (only 45 days, versus 100 for rice), ancient hunter-gatherers (and eventually herders) could cultivate that grain while maintaining a nomadic lifestyle. People could plant and harvest quickly, then move on. Millet, which grows best in uphill locations and needs little water, spread readily along the hilly corridor provided by the foothills of Eurasia.

Between 4500 and 3600 B.P., nomadic tribes in those foothills combined millet cultivation with hunting and gathering. Eventually they added other cereal grains, such as wheat and barley. This multicropping allowed those early farmers to expand their growing season and provided a more reliable source of food. As in the Middle East, the era of seminomadic hunting and gathering gave way to one of settled village life.

Rice appears to have been domesticated in southern China at about the same time that millet

Nepalese women harvest in a millet field at sunset. Millet was grown in China's Hwang-He (Yellow River) Valley by 10,000 B.P. This grain eventually supported early farming communities in northern China. What was being grown in southern China at the same time?
© Chad Ehlers/Alamy Stock Photo

was domesticated in northern China—around 10,000 B.P. (Cambridge 2015). Rice was being cultivated in the Yangtze River corridor of southern China by 8400 B.P. (Jiao 2007).

China thus seems to have been the scene of two independent transitions to food production, based on different crops grown in strikingly different climates. Southern Chinese farming was rice aquaculture in rich subtropical wetlands. Southern winters were mild and summer rains reliable. Northern China, by contrast, had harsh winters, with unreliable rainfall during the summer growing season. This was an area of grasslands and temperate forests. Still, in both areas by 7500 B.P., food production was supporting large and stable villages. Based on the archaeological evidence, early Chinese villagers lived in substantial houses, made elaborate ceramic vessels, and had rich burials.

Northern and southern China are two of the seven areas where food production was invented independently. (The others, recall, were the Middle East, Africa, and three areas of the New World—see the next section.) A different set of major foods was domesticated, at different times, in each area, as is shown in Recap 11.2. Some grains, such as millet and rice, were domesticated more than once. Millet grows wild in China and Africa, where it became an important food crop, as well as in Mexico, where it did not. Indigenous African rice, grown only in West Africa, belongs to the same genus as Asian rice. Pigs and probably cattle were domesticated independently in the Middle East, China, and sub-Saharan Africa. We turn now to archaeological sequences in the Americas.

WORLD AREA	MAJOR DOMESTICATE	DATE OF EARLIEST DOMESTICATES (B.P.)
Middle East	Wheat, barley Sheep, goats, cattle, pigs	11,000–10,000
Northern China (Yellow River)	Millet Dogs, pigs, chickens	10,000
Southern China (Yangtze River corridor)	Rice Water buffalo, dogs, pigs	10,000–6500
Sub-Saharan Africa	Cattle Sorghum, pearl millet, African rice	10,000–4000
Andean Region	Squash, potato, quinoa, beans Camelids (llama, alpaca), guinea pigs	10,000–5000
Mesoamerica	Maize, beans, squash Dogs, turkeys, guinea fowl	8000–4700
Eastern United States	Goosefoot, marsh elder, sunflower, squash	4500

THE FIRST AMERICAN FARMERS

Benefiting from an abundance of game, human foragers gradually occupied the Americas, learning to cope with a great diversity of environments. Their descendants would eventually turn to farming, paving the way for the emergence of states based on agriculture and trade in Mexico and Peru.

The most significant contrast between Old and New World food production involved animal domestication, which was much more important in the Old World. The animals that had been hunted during the early American big-game tradition either became extinct before people could domesticate them or were not domesticable. The largest animal ever tamed in the New World (in Peru, around 4500 B.P.) was the llama. Ancient Peruvians and Bolivians ate llama meat and used that animal as a beast of burden (Flannery, Marcus, and Reynolds 1989). They bred the llama's relative, the alpaca, for its wool. Peruvians also added animal protein to their diet by raising and eating guinea pigs and ducks.

Early Peruvians and Bolivians ate llama meat, harnessed llamas as beasts of burden, and used llama dung to fertilize their fields. What was the largest animal domesticated in the New World?

© Craig Lovell/Corbis

The turkey was domesticated in Mesoamerica and in the southwestern United States. Lowland South Americans domesticated a type of duck. Domesticated dogs were widespread in the New World. There were no cattle, sheep, or goats in the areas of the Americas where farming arose. Neither herding nor the kinds of relationships that linked Old World farmers and herders developed in the precolonial Americas.

Three key caloric staples, major sources of carbohydrates, were domesticated by Native Americans. **Maize,** or corn, first domesticated in the tropical lowlands of southwestern Mexico, became the caloric staple in Mesoamerica and Central America and eventually reached coastal Peru. The other two staples were root crops: white ("Irish") potatoes, first domesticated in the Andes, and **manioc,** or cassava, a tuber first cultivated in the South American lowlands, where other root crops such as yams and sweet potatoes also were important. Other crops added variety to New World diets and made them nutritious. Beans and squash provided essential proteins, vitamins, and minerals. Maize, beans, and squash were the basis of the Mesoamerican diet. Anthropologists recently have confirmed that the earliest domesticates in the Americas are about as early as the first Old World domesticates.

Spreading across oceans and continents, manioc or cassava, originally domesticated in lowland South America, has become a caloric staple throughout the tropics, including Ghana, shown here.

© Universal Images Group/DeAgostini/Alamy Stock Photo

Food production was independently invented in at least three areas of the Americas: Mesoamerica, the eastern United States, and the south central Andes. (Mesoamerica is discussed in detail below.) Food plants known as goosefoot and marsh elder, along with the sunflower and a squash, had been domesticated in the eastern United States by 4500 B.P. Those crops supplemented a diet based mainly on hunting and gathering. They never became caloric staples like maize, wheat, rice, millet, manioc, and potatoes. Eventually, maize diffused from Mesoamerica into what is now the United States, reaching both the Southwest and the eastern area just mentioned. Maize provided a more reliable caloric staple for native North American farming. Domestication of several food species was under way in the south central Andes of Peru and Bolivia by 5000 B.P. They were the potato, quinoa, beans, llamas, alpacas, and guinea pigs. Anthropologists also have confirmed the (very early) domestication of squash, cotton, and peanuts in Peru.

The Tropical Origins of New World Domestication

Based on current evidence, New World farming began in the South American lowlands, spreading eventually to Central America, Mexico, and the Caribbean Islands. Archaeologists and botanists have recovered and analyzed microscopic evidence from pollens, starch grains, and phytoliths (plant crystals). This evidence has forced revision of the old assumption that New World farming originated in upland areas, such as the highlands of Mexico and Peru. Domesticated squash seeds from Peru date back 10,000 years. Although found in the highlands (western Andes), those seeds, along with other early domesticates from the same site, were not domesticated there originally. Domestication must have occurred even earlier, most probably in South America's tropical lowlands.

By 10,000 B.P., people in Panama, Peru, Ecuador, and Colombia were cultivating plants such as squash and gourds in garden plots near their homes (Piperno and Pearsall 1998). Between 9000 and 8000 B.P., changes in seed form and phytolith size suggest that farmers were selecting certain characteristics in their cultivated plants. By 7,000 years ago, farmers had expanded their plots into nearby forests, which they cleared using slash-and-burn techniques. By that time, early farming techniques were diffusing from tropical lowlands into drier regions at higher elevations (Bryant 1999, 2003).

Recent molecular and genetic studies indicate that maize domestication actually took place in the tropical lowlands of southwestern Mexico. The wild ancestor of maize is a species of **teosinte,** which is native to the Rio Balsas watershed of

maize
Corn; first domesticated in tropical southwestern Mexico around 8000 B.P.

manioc
Cassava; tuber domesticated in the South American lowlands.

teosinte
Wild ancestor of maize; grows wild in southwestern Mexico.

Two different types of corn (maize) from among the many varieties grown in Oaxaca, Mexico, where archaeologists have studied early highland maize cultivation. Do the earliest Mesoamerican domesticates come from the Mexican highlands?

© Marco Ugarte/AP Images

tropical southwestern Mexico (Holst, Moreno, and Piperno 2007). Evidence for the evolution of maize from its wild ancestor has yet to be found in that poorly studied region. Still, we can infer some of the likely steps in maize domestication.

Such a process would have included increases in the number of kernels per cob, the cob size, and the number of cobs per stalk. These changes would make it increasingly profitable to collect wild teosinte and eventually to plant maize. Once people started harvesting wild maize intensively, they became selective agents, taking back to camp a greater proportion of plants with tough axes and cobs. These were the plants most likely to hold together during harvesting and least likely to disintegrate on the way back home. Eventually, teosinte became dependent on humans for its survival, because maize lacks a natural means of dispersal—a brittle axis or cob. If humans chose plants with tough axes inadvertently, their selection of plants with soft husks must have been intentional, as was their selection of larger cobs, more kernels per cob, and more cobs per plant.

Maize spread rapidly from its domestication cradle in tropical southwestern Mexico during the

eighth millennium B.P. (8000–7000) (Bryant 2007b; Piperno 2001; Pohl et al. 2007). For example, analysis of starch grains from stone tools in Panama's tropical lowlands confirms that maize was grown there by 7800–7000 B.P. (Dickau, Ranere, and Cooke 2007). Maize cultivation had spread eastward to the Mexican Gulf Coast by 7300 B.P.

Before these lowland discoveries, archaeologists had excavated extensively in the Mexican highlands, which have caves and rock shelters with preserved plant remains and are located near the centers of the civilizations that eventually developed in the Mexican highlands. Decades ago, excavations in the Valleys of Tehuacan and Oaxaca (see the next section) yielded well-preserved seeds and fruits, along with maize kernels and cobs. Until recently, few archaeologists sought the origin of domestication in lowland and jungle regions, which were wrongly assumed to be infertile and where plants did not preserve well (Bryant 2003). Today, the microscopic evidence says otherwise and reveals the key role of tropical lowland regions in early New World farming.

The Mexican Highlands

Long before Mexican highlanders developed a taste for maize, beans, and squash, they hunted as part of a pattern of broad-spectrum foraging. Mammoth remains dated to 11,000 B.P. have been found along with spear points in the basin that surrounds Mexico City. However, small animals were more important than big game, as were the grains, pods, fruits, and leaves of wild plants.

In the Valley of Oaxaca, in Mexico's southern highlands, between 10,000 and 4000 B.P., foragers concentrated on certain wild animals—deer and rabbits—and plants—cactus leaves and fruits and tree pods, especially mesquite (Flannery 1986). Those early Oaxacans dispersed to hunt and gather in fall and winter. But they came together in late spring and summer, forming larger groups to harvest seasonally available plants. Cactus fruits appeared in the spring. Since summer rains would reduce the fruits to mush and since birds, bats, and rodents competed for them, cactus collection required hard work by large groups of people. The edible pods of the mesquite, available in June, also required intensive gathering.

Eventually, people started planting maize in the alluvial soils of valley floors. This was the zone where foragers traditionally had congregated for the annual spring/summer harvest of cactus fruits and mesquite pods. By 4000 B.P., a type of maize was available that provided more food than the mesquite pods did. Once that happened, people started cutting down mesquite trees and replacing them with cornfields.

By 3500 B.P. in the Valley of Oaxaca, where winter frosts are absent, simple irrigation permitted the establishment of permanent villages based on maize farming. Water close to the surface allowed early farmers to dig wells right in their cornfields. Using pots, they dipped water out of these wells and poured it on their growing plants, a technique known as pot irrigation. Early permanent villages supported by farming appeared in areas of Mesoamerica where there was reliable rainfall, pot irrigation, or access to humid river bottomlands.

The spread of maize farming resulted in further genetic changes, higher yields, higher human populations, and more intensive farming. Pressures to intensify cultivation led to improvements in water-control systems. New varieties of fast-growing maize eventually appeared, expanding the range of areas that could be cultivated. Increasing population and irrigation also helped spread maize farming. The advent of intensive cultivation laid the foundation for the emergence of the state in Mesoamerica—some 3,000 years later than in the Middle East (see Chapter 12).

EXPLAINING THE NEOLITHIC

This section examines the factors that influenced the origin and spread of Neolithic economies in various world areas. (Much of this section is based on observations in Chapters 8 through 10 of Jared Diamond's influential book *Guns, Germs, and Steel: The Fates of Human Societies* [2005].)

Several factors had to converge to make domestication happen and to promote its spread. Most plants, and especially animals, aren't easy—or particularly valuable—to domesticate. Thus, of some 148 large animal species that seem potentially domesticable, only 14 actually have been domesticated. And a mere dozen out of 200,000 known plant species account for 80 percent of the world's farm production. That dozen consists of wheat, corn (maize), rice, barley, sorghum (millet), soybeans, potatoes, cassava (manioc), sweet potatoes, sugarcane, sugar beets, and bananas.

Domestication resulted from a combination of factors that had not come together previously. The development of a full-fledged Neolithic economy required settling down. Sedentism, such as that adopted by ancient Natufian hunter-gatherers, was especially attractive when several species of plants and animals were available locally for foraging and eventual domestication. The Fertile Crescent area of the Middle East had such species, along with a Mediterranean climate favorable to a Neolithic economy. Among those species were several self-pollinating plants, the easiest wild plants to domesticate, including wheat, which required few genetic changes for domestication. We've seen that the Natufians adopted sedentism prior to farming. They lived off abundant wild grain and the animals attracted to the stubble left after the harvest. Eventually, with

As maize cultivation spread, genetic changes led to higher yields and more productive farming, eventually supporting state-level societies, such as that of the Aztecs. This mural in the National Palace, Mexico City, depicts everyday Aztec life, including growing corn and making flour and bread.
© Travelpix/Alamy Stock Photo

climate change, population growth, and the need for people to sustain themselves in the marginal zones, hunter-gatherers started cultivating (see Bocquet-Appel and Bar-Yosef 2008). (See this chapter's "Appreciating Anthropology" for a discussion of contemporary climate change and some of the dangers it poses to archaeological sites.)

Compared with other world areas, the Fertile Crescent region had the largest area with a Mediterranean climate, and the highest species diversity. As we saw previously, this was an area of vertical economy and closely packed microenvironments. Such diverse terrains and habitats concentrated in a limited area offered a multiplicity of plant species, as well as goats, sheep, pigs, and cattle. As in Mesoamerica, where corn (supplying carbohydrate) was supplemented by squash and beans (supplying protein), the Middle Eastern diet combined caloric staples such as wheat and barley

Global Climate Change and Political Threats to Sites

Global climate change (GCC) involves not only global warming but also the fact that weather patterns are becoming more extreme and less predictable. GCC threatens archaeological sites, and Andrew Curry (2009) highlights some of those threats, which are summarized here, in locales as diverse as coastal Peru, Greenland, the Eurasian steppes, California's Channel Islands, and Africa's Sahara Desert.

Coastal Peru. When Spanish conquistadors arrived in Peru, they noticed a weather phenomenon that occasionally occurred around Christmas. They called it El Niño, or little boy, after the Christ child. El Niño occurs every 3 to 10 years, as currents in the Pacific Ocean shift, changing global weather patterns. In Peru, El Niño brings warmer water and heavy rainfall along the coast. Peru's deserts typically get just over an inch of rain annually. In 1998, a particularly severe El Niño season, the region was seriously flooded with 120 inches of rain. Excess water can threaten archaeological sites, many of which are located along rivers or on easily eroded slopes (Curry 2009). Severe flooding in 2010 closed Machu Picchu, Peru's most famous ancient site, to tourism. If GCC leads to more frequent El Niño years, Peru's archaeological treasures may be further damaged.

Greenland. Violent wave action linked to GCC is destroying early coastal sites. Traditionally in summer, Greenland's coasts have been surrounded by an ice belt 30 to 40 miles wide. This drifting ice serves as a shock absorber, dampening the strength of the North Atlantic. In the past decade, however, this ice shield has virtually vanished, and Greenland's coasts are being pounded by huge waves. Most threatened are sites associated with the Thule culture, likely ancestors of the Inuit, whose members reached Greenland about 2,000 years ago. Supported by hunting and fishing, Thule villages were built close to the shore. Today, their ancient homes are disappearing, along with buried tools and artifacts (Curry 2009).

Scythian Tombs. Between 3,000 and 2,200 years ago, Scythian nomads dominated the Eurasian steppes from the Black Sea in the west to China in the east. Huge Scythian burial mounds, called kurgans, have been rich resources for archaeologists. Found from Ukraine to Kazakhstan, some of the best-preserved kurgans are located in the Altai Mountains, near Siberian permafrost, where the cold has protected the graves for millennia. The tombs have yielded well-preserved mummies, often with clothing, burial goods, horses, and even stomach contents intact. With GCC, as the mountains warm up and the permafrost melts, the tombs are in danger of thawing and rotting away (Curry 2009).

California's Channel Islands. Some of the early settlers of the Americas came by boat, island-hopping from Siberia down to the California coast. Some of the best evidence for this comes from the Channel Islands, which were occupied at least 13,000 years ago by settlers who hunted pygmy mammoths, elephant seals, and sea lions. Human bones found on Santa Rosa Island, radiocarbon-dated to 13,000 B.P., are the oldest human bones yet found in the Americas. At that time, the world was much colder, and the oceans much lower, than today. Rising sea levels now threaten shell middens and coastal rock shelters. As well, coastal winds, waves, storm surges, and even seals can damage coastal sites. GCC now threatens to wipe out clues about how early humans settled the Americas just as researchers have begun to focus on the likelihood of coastal migration (Curry 2009).

Desertification in Sudan. Encroaching desert sands increasingly threaten historic artwork at Musawwarat es-Sufra, Sudan. More than 2,000 years ago, the rulers of Meroe—a desert kingdom linked to ancient Egypt—constructed a temple complex and pilgrimage site 20 miles

with protein-rich pulses such as lentils, peas, and chickpeas (garbanzo beans).

There have been changes in anthropological thought about the process of domestication in the Neolithic. Anthropologists once thought, erroneously, that domestication would happen almost automatically once people gained sufficient knowledge of plants and animals and their reproductive habits to figure out how to make domestication work. Anthropologists now realize that foragers have an excellent knowledge of plant and animal reproduction, and that some other trigger is needed to start and sustain the process of domestication. A full-fledged Neolithic economy requires a combination of favorable factors, as has been discussed for the Middle East, including an adequate inventory of nutritious domesticates. Some world areas—for example, North America (north of Mesoamerica)—managed independently to invent domestication, but the inventory of available plants and animals was too meager to sustain a Neolithic economy. The early North American domesticates—squash, sunflower, marsh elder, and goosefoot—had to be supplemented by hunting and gathering. A full Neolithic economy and sedentism did not develop in the east, southeast, and southwest of what is now the United States until maize diffused in from Mesoamerica.

east of the Nile. Built of soft yellow sandstone, the walls and columns of the complex featured hieroglyphs and elaborate painted reliefs. Dominating the site was the 50-foot-long Temple of the Lion God, decorated with reliefs dedicated to the Meroitic god of fertility. Rising temperatures and overuse have killed off the area's vegetation, and Saharan sands creep ever closer. The reliefs suffer heavily from wind erosion, because the soft sandstone abrades easily (Curry 2009).

GCC is not, of course, the only current threat to archaeological sites and research. Political events also pose risks. In 2001 in Afghanistan, the Taliban destroyed a series of pre-Islamic figures, including two monumental stone Buddhas, in an attempt to stop the worship of false idols. In 2013, a group of ancient Islamic manuscripts in Mali's historic city of Timbuktu were threatened by a fire caused by fighting between Islamist militants and French troops. More recently, in Syria and Iraq, the entity known as ISIS, ISIL, the Islamic state, or Daesh has defaced or destroyed various archaeological sites, while also relying on trade in pilfered antiquities as its second source of financial support after oil.

Politics and regime change also can limit archaeological research. Iran and Iraq have been dangerous or off limits for decades. For on-site investigation of emerging food production and

The Peruvian village of Aguas Calientes is flooded by the Vilcanota River in January 2010. Heavy rains and mudslides that year blocked the train route to the nearby ancient Inca citadel of Machu Picchu, leaving nearly 2,000 tourists stranded.
© AFP/Getty Images

state formation in the Middle East, archaeologists turned increasingly to Syria and Turkey. Syria, too, is now off limits because of political unrest. Fortunately, previously assembled museum collections of human and animal remains outside those countries allow continuing analysis and new insights (e.g., Zeder 2008), even when national borders are closed to new field-work. However, archaeologists who manage museum collections increasingly must deal with nations and cultural groups that wish to repatriate remains collected, often a century ago or more and sometimes without proper legal authorization. Can you think of other threats to archaeological sites and research?

This happened more than 3,000 years after the first domestication of other plants in the eastern United States.

We've seen how the presence or absence of large domesticable animals helps explain the divergent trajectories of the Eastern and Western Hemispheres in that the mixed economies that developed in Eurasia and Africa never emerged in Mesoamerica. Of the world's 14 large, domesticated animal species, 13 are from Eurasia, and only one (the llama) is from South America. Ancient Mexicans had dogs and domesticated turkeys and created toy wheels, but they lacked sheep, goats, and pigs as well as the oxen or horses

needed to make the wheel a viable transport option. Once the big five Eurasian animal domesticates (cow, sheep, goat, pig, horse) were introduced into Africa and the Americas, they spread rapidly.

Just as some plants (e.g., self-pollinating annuals) are easier to domesticate than others are, so are some animals. Cattle and pigs were so easy to domesticate that they were domesticated independently in multiple world areas. A key factor in animal domestication is their social structure. The easiest wild animals to domesticate are those that live in hierarchical herds. Accustomed to dominance relations, they allow humans to assume superior positions in the hierarchy. Herd animals are easier to domesticate than solitary ones are. Among the latter, only cats and ferrets have been domesticated, and there's some question about the completeness of domestication of those animals (hence the expression "It's like herding cats").

Geography and the Spread of Food Production

As Jared Diamond (2005, Chapter 10) emphasizes, the geography of the Old World facilitated the diffusion of plants, animals, technology (e.g., wheels and vehicles), and information (e.g., writing) (see also Ramachandran and Rosenberg 2011). Most crops in Eurasia were domesticated just once and spread rapidly in an east–west direction. The first domesticates spread from the Middle East to Egypt, northern Africa, Europe, India, and eventually China (which, however, also had its own domesticates, as we have seen). By contrast, there was less diffusion of American domesticates.

Figure 11.4 shows that Eurasia has a much broader east–west spread than does Africa or either of the Americas, which are arranged north–south. This is important because climates are more likely to be similar moving across thousands of miles east–west than doing so north–south. In Eurasia, plants and animals could spread more easily east–west than north–south because of common day lengths and similar growing seasons.

More radical climatic contrasts have hindered north–south diffusion. In the Americas, for example, although the distance between the cool Mexican highlands and the South American highlands is just 1,200 miles, those two similar zones are separated by a low, hot, tropical region, which supports very different plant species than the highlands. Such environmental barriers to diffusion kept the Neolithic societies of Mesoamerica and South America more separate and independent than they were in Eurasia. It took some 3,000 years for maize to reach what is now the United States, where productive Neolithic economies eventually did develop. They were based on the cultivation of new varieties of maize adapted to a colder climate and different day lengths.

In the Old World, the spread of Middle Eastern crops southward into Africa eventually was halted by climatic contrasts as well. Certain tropical crops did spread west–east in Africa, but they did not reach southern Africa because of climatic barriers. Again and again, the geographic and climatic barriers posed by high mountains and broad deserts have slowed the spread of domesticates. In what is now the United States, for example, the east–west spread of farming from the Southeast to the Southwest was slowed by the dry climates of Texas and the southern Great Plains.

This section has examined the factors that favored or hindered the origin and spread of Neolithic economies in various world areas. Several

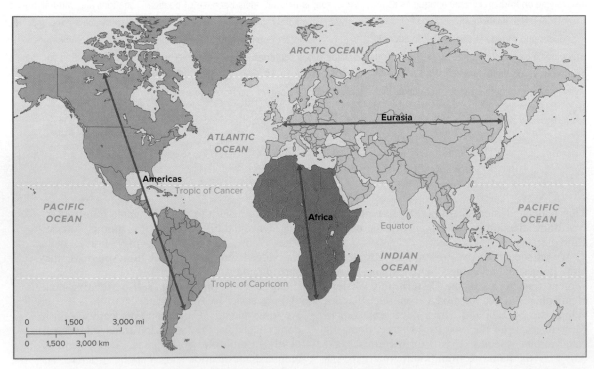

FIGURE 11.4 Major Axes of the Continents.
Note the breadth of the east–west axis in Eurasia, compared with the much narrower east–west spreads in Africa, North America, and South America. Those three continents have north–south as their major axes.

factors combined to promote early domestication in the ancient Middle East. The first domesticates spread rapidly across Eurasia, facilitated by climatic similarities across a broad territorial expanse. In the Americas, food production spread less rapidly because of north–south contrasts. Another factor that slowed the Neolithic transition in the Americas was the lack of large animals suitable for domestication. Factors that explain the process of domestication in the Neolithic involve climate, economic adaptation, demography, and the specific attributes of plants and animals.

COSTS AND BENEFITS

Food production brought advantages and disadvantages. Among the advantages were discoveries and inventions. People eventually learned to spin and weave; to make pottery, bricks, and arched masonry; and to smelt and cast metals. They developed trade and commerce by land and sea. By 5500 B.P., Middle Easterners were living in vibrant cities with markets, streets, temples, and palaces. They created sculpture, mural art, writing systems, weights, measures, mathematics, and new forms of political and social organization.

Because it increased economic production and led to new social, scientific, and creative forms, food production often is considered an evolutionary advance. But the new economy also brought hardships. For example, food producers typically work harder than foragers do—and for a less adequate diet.

Herds, fields, and irrigation systems need care. Weeding can require hours of arduous bending.

Pens and corrals must be built and maintained for livestock. Trade takes men, and sometimes women, away from home, leaving burdens for those who stay behind. For several reasons, food producers tend to have more children than foragers do. This means greater child care demands, but child labor also tends to be more needed and valued than it is among foragers. Many tasks in farming and herding can be done by children. The division of economic labor grows more complex, so that children and older people have assigned economic roles.

Compared with Paleolithic and Mesolithic foraging, public health declined in food-producing societies. Diets based on crops and dairy products tend to be less varied, less nutritious, and less healthful than foragers' diets, which usually are higher in proteins and lower in fats and carbohydrates. With the shift to food production, the physical well-being of the population often declines. Communicable diseases, protein deficiency, and dental caries increase (Cohen and Armelagos 2013).

Compared with nomadic or seminomadic foragers, food producers tend to be sedentary. Their populations are denser, which makes it easier to transmit and maintain diseases. Malaria, sickle-cell anemia, and smallpox all spread along with food production. Population concentrations, especially cities, are breeding grounds for epidemic diseases. People live nearer to other people and animals and their wastes, which also affect public health (Diamond 2005). Compared with farmers, herders, and city dwellers, foragers were relatively disease free, stress free, and well nourished.

The labor demands of food production far exceed those associated with foraging. Here, in Timbuktu, Mali, a Songhai family pounds grain. Such processing of food is just one step in getting the grain from the fields into people's mouths. What are some of the other steps?

© Frans Lemmens/Lonely Planet Images/Getty Images

Other hardships and stresses accompanied food production. Social inequality and poverty increased (see Flannery and Marcus 2012). Elaborate systems of social stratification eventually replaced the egalitarianism of the past. Resources were no longer common goods, open to all, as they tend to be among foragers. Property distinctions proliferated. Slavery and other forms of human bondage eventually were invented. Crime, war, and human sacrifice became widespread.

The rate at which human beings degrade their environments also increased with food production. Population increase and the need to expand farming led to deforestation in the Middle East. Even today, many farmers think of trees as giant weeds to be cut down to make way for productive fields. Previously, we saw how early Mesoamerican farmers cut down mesquite trees for maize cultivation in the Valley of Oaxaca.

Many farmers and herders burn trees, brush, and pasture. Farmers burn to remove weeds; they also use the ashes for fertilizer. Herders burn to promote the growth of new, tender shoots for their livestock. But such practices do have environmental costs, including air pollution. The by-products of smelting and other chemical processes basic to the manufacture of metal tools also have environmental costs. As modern industrial pollution has harmful effluents, early chemical processes had by-products that polluted air, soils, and waters. Salts, chemicals, and microorganisms accumulate in irrigated fields. Pathogens and pollutants that were nonissues during the Paleolithic endanger growing human populations. To be sure, food production has benefits. But its costs are just as evident. Recap 11.3 summarizes the costs and benefits of food production. We see that *progress* is much too optimistic a word to describe food production, the state, and many other aspects of the evolution of society.

RECAP 11.3	The Benefits and Costs of Food Production (Compared with Foraging)

DO THE COSTS OUTWEIGH THE BENEFITS?	
BENEFITS	**COSTS**
Discoveries and inventions	Harder work
New social, political, scientific, and creative forms (e.g., spinning, weaving, pottery, bricks, metallurgy)	Less nutritious diets
	Child labor and child care demands
Monumental architecture, arched masonry, and sculpture	Taxes and military drafts
	Public health declines (e.g., more exposure to pathogens, including communicable and epidemic diseases)
Writing	Rise in protein deficiency and dental caries
Mathematics, weights, and measures	Greater stress
Trade and markets	Social inequality and poverty
Urban life	Slavery and other forms of human bondage
Increased economic production	Rise in crime, war, and human sacrifice
More reliable crop yields	Increased environmental degradation (e.g., air and water pollution, deforestation)

for REVIEW

summary

1. By 10,000 B.P., people were pursuing broad-spectrum economies in western Europe. Tool kits adapted to a forested environment included small, delicately shaped stone tools called microliths. The Mesolithic had begun. The broad-spectrum revolution, based on a wide variety of dietary resources, began in the Middle East somewhat earlier than in Europe. It culminated in the first food-producing economies in the Middle East by 10,000 B.P.

2. By 10,000 B.P., domesticated plants and animals were part of a broad spectrum of resources used by Middle Easterners. By 7500 B.P., most Middle Easterners were moving away from broad-spectrum foraging toward more specialized

food-producing economies. *Neolithic* refers to the period when the first signs of domestication appeared.

3. Braidwood proposed that food production started in the hilly flanks zone, where wheat and barley grew wild. Others questioned this: The wild grain supply in that zone already provided an excellent diet for the Natufians and other ancient Middle Easterners. There would have been no incentive to domesticate. Other scholars view the origin of food production in the context of increasing population and climate changes.

4. Ancient Middle Eastern foragers migrated seasonally in pursuit of game. They also collected wild plant foods as the plants ripened at different altitudes. As they moved about, these foragers took grains from the hilly flanks zone, where they grew wild, to adjacent areas. Population spilled over from the hilly flanks into areas like the piedmont steppe. In such marginal zones, people started cultivating plants. They were trying to duplicate the dense wild grains of the hilly flanks.

5. After the harvest, sheep and goats fed off the stubble of these wild plants. Animal domestication occurred as people started selecting certain features and behavior and guiding the reproduction of goats, sheep, cattle, and pigs. Gradually, food production spread into the hilly flanks. Later, with irrigation it spread down into Mesopotamia's alluvial desert, where the first cities, states, and civilizations developed by 5500 B.P. Food production then spread west from the Middle East into North Africa and Europe and east to India and Pakistan.

6. There were at least seven independent inventions of food production: in the Middle East, sub-Saharan Africa, northern and southern China, Mesoamerica, the south central Andes, and the eastern United States. Millet was domesticated by 10,000 B.P. in northern China; rice, by 10,000 B.P. in southern China.

7. In the New World the most important domesticates were maize, potatoes, and manioc. The llama of the central Andes was the largest animal domesticated in the New World, where herding traditions analogous to those of the Old World did not develop. Economic similarities between the hemispheres must be sought in foraging and farming.

8. New World farming started in the lowlands of South America, then spread to Central America, Mexico, and the Caribbean Islands. Tropical lowland cultivation in Central and South America began at about the same time as food production arose in the Middle East—around 10,000 years ago. By 7000 B.P., farming was diffusing from tropical lowlands into drier regions at higher elevations. The ancestor of maize, teosinte, grows wild in tropical southwestern Mexico, where maize probably was domesticated around 8000 B.P. At Oaxaca, in Mexico's southern highlands, maize was gradually added to a broad-spectrum diet by 4000 B.P.

9. Several factors, including a diversity of useful plant and animal species and early sedentism, combined to promote domestication in the ancient Middle East. Domesticates spread rapidly across Eurasia, facilitated by climatic similarities across a broad territorial expanse. In the Americas, food production spread less rapidly because of north–south contrasts. Another factor that slowed the Neolithic transition in the Americas was the lack of large animals suitable for domestication. Factors that explain the origin and diffusion of food production involve climate, economic adaptation, demography, and the specific attributes of plants and animals.

10. Food production and the social and political system it supported brought advantages and disadvantages. The advantages included discoveries and inventions. The disadvantages included harder work, poorer health, crime, war, social inequality, and environmental degradation.

key terms

critical thinking

1. What is revolutionary about what Kent Flannery called the "broad-spectrum revolution"? What other or more recent events in history do you consider revolutionary? Why?

2. Why is the lack of animal domestication in Mesoamerica considered a key factor in world history?

3. Previously, anthropologists had believed that Old World (Middle Eastern) farming predated the earliest cultivation in the Americas by three or four millennia. Is this still the case? If not, what has changed?

4. In this chapter, what are some examples of the role geography plays in key events in human history? Geography also affects how we come to know about the past. How so?

5. Was the origin of food production good or bad? Why?

The First Cities and States

▶ When, where, and why did early states originate, and what were their key attributes?

▶ How do archaeologists distinguish between chiefdoms and states?

▶ What similarities and differences marked the origin of early states in the Old World and the New World?

© Massimo Pizzotti/Photographer's Choice/Getty Images

The ruins of the Throne Hall at Persepolis in what is now Iran. Persepolis, which means "the Persian city," was an important center of the Achaemenid empire, which thrived between 550 and 330 B.C.E.

understanding OURSELVES

"You're not the boss of me": Have you ever heard or uttered those words? Who might say them to whom? Certainly, you would not be likely to say this to an employer, or to a police officer who had just pulled you over, or to someone judging you in a court of law. We resent it when our siblings, cousins, or friends tell us what to do. But we learn to call judges "Your Honor"; police officers "Officer," "Detective," "Lieutenant," "Captain," or "Chief"; and employers "Ms." or "Mr." (as in "Mr. Carson"). Such titles (honorifics) mark differences in status and authority. Generally, we learn to respect and obey such people ("the authorities"). That is, we follow their orders or instructions, as people in the military routinely do with their superiors.

Marked contrasts in status, power, wealth, and privilege distinguish cities and states from the societies that came before them. Everyone reading this book lives in a state-organized society. Our lives differ dramatically from those of our Paleolithic ancestors, or those of more recent foragers. The state has a lot to do with these differences. The demand for labor (human, animal, etc.) increased in Neolithic economies compared with Paleolithic times. This trend continued in states, whose economies and political systems have placed even greater demands on ordinary people.

Perhaps you've seen a museum display depicting an early state society (e.g., Egypt, Mesopotamia, Maya). Such exhibits tend to highlight the artistic, architectural, literary, and scientific achievements of those civilizations. Ancient Sumerians (in Mesopotamia), Egyptians, Mexicans, and Peruvians had their artists, architects, mathematicians, astronomers, priests, and rulers—just as we do. However (but depicted more rarely), their ordinary citizens had to sweat in the fields to grow food for landlords, specialists, and elites. Unlike hunter-gatherers, residents of states must deal with bosses, despots, and commanders. The elites of ancient states could summon involuntary labor to build temples and pyramids, and to move stone for enduring monuments. In all states, people must pay taxes; in many states, citizens are drafted for work or war. Ordinary people no longer set their own priorities.

How do modern state-organized societies mirror those of the past? Ordinary people no longer may be drafted for work or war, but we do have to work to pay the taxes that pay for wars and public works. Our society is still stratified. Perks still go with wealth, fame, and power. Most of us still work much harder (usually for bosses) than foragers ever did. It's a myth that leisure time has increased with civilization. For a few, there is leisure and privilege; for most, there is work and obligation. And that's not because of human nature; it's because of the state.

STATE FORMATION

As Neolithic economies spread, diversified, and became more productive, new political entities, or **polities** (singular, *polity*), developed to manage them. The major new political forms were chiefdoms and states.

A **chiefdom** is a polity with hereditary leaders and a permanent political structure. Some of its people and some of its settlements are ranked above others, and people with higher rank are favored in their access to resources. Often in chiefdoms, individuals are ranked in terms of their genealogical distance from the chief. The closer one is to the chief, the greater one's social importance, but the status distinctions are of degree rather than of kind. Chiefdoms are not divided into clearly defined social classes. Such social *stratification* is, however, a key feature of the state.

A **state** is a polity that has a formal, central government and *social stratification*—a division of society into classes. The first states had formed in Mesopotamia by 5500 B.P. and in Mesoamerica about 3,000 years later. Chiefdoms were precursors to states, with privileged and effective leaders—chiefs—but lacking the sharp class divisions that characterize states. By 7000 B.P. in the Middle East and 3200 B.P. in Mesoamerica, there is evidence for what archaeologists call the *elite level* of social and political organization, indicating a chiefdom or a state.

How and why did these new polities originate? The development and spread of Neolithic economies fueled population growth and established large group settlements. New tasks, activities, and functions emerged in the larger and denser populations. Systems of political authority and control typically develop to handle regulatory problems that arise as the population grows, social groups proliferate, and the economy increases in scale and diversity.

Primary states are states that formed on their own, rather than through contact with already-established state societies (Wright 1994). Primary states are also known as archaic states or first-generation states. They formed in the context of competition among chiefdoms, as one chiefdom managed to conquer its neighbors and make them part of a larger political unit (Stanish and Levine 2011). Scholars have documented the process of state formation in at least six areas where first-generation states are known to have developed: Egypt, Mesopotamia, the Indus River Valley, northern China, Mesoamerica, and the Andes (Millaire 2010).

A systemic, regional perspective is necessary to understand any case of state formation. Primary states emerge from a regional process that requires a long period (generations) of interaction among competing polities (Stanish and Levine 2011). Furthermore, multiple factors always contribute to state formation, with the effects of one magnifying those of the others.

Regulation of Hydraulic Economies

Many factors have played a role in state formation. One such factor has been the need to regulate hydraulic (water-based, e.g., irrigation) systems in societies with agricultural economies (Wittfogel 1957). In arid areas, such as ancient Egypt and Mesopotamia, a key role of state officials was to manage systems of irrigation, drainage, and flood control (see Scarre and Fagan 2016). Hydraulic agriculture spurs state formation because it has certain implications. Because it can feed more people, while requiring more labor, irrigated agriculture sustains and fuels population growth, which in turn promotes expansion of the system. With larger and denser concentrations of people, the potential grows for conflict over access to water and irrigated land. Political authorities typically arise to regulate production, as well as to manage interpersonal and intergroup relations. Regulators protect the economy by mobilizing crews to maintain and repair the hydraulic system, and they settle disputes about access to water. These life-and-death functions enhance the authority of state officials. Thus, growth in hydraulic systems is often (as in Mesopotamia, Egypt, and the Valley of Mexico) but not always associated with state formation.

Regional Trade

All states have well-developed trade networks, and regional trade is a key factor that contributes to primary state formation (Stanish and Levine 2011). States may arise to control and regulate key nodes in regional trade networks. Examples include crossroads of caravan routes and places (e.g., mountain passes and river narrows) situated to threaten trade between centers. Long-distance trade has been important in the formation of many states, including those of Mesopotamia, Mesoamerica, and Peru (Hirth and Pillsbury 2013). Long-distance trade also exists, however, in areas where no primary states developed, such as in Papua New Guinea.

Population, War, and Circumscription

Robert Carneiro (1970) saw three key factors as interacting to promote state formation: environmental circumscription, population increase, and warfare (see Figure 12.1). An environment is *circumscribed* when it has definite boundaries that cut it off from surrounding areas and confine it. Environmental circumscription may be physical or social. Physically circumscribed environments include small islands and, in arid areas, river plains, oases, and valleys with streams—areas surrounded by some sort of physical or geographic boundary. Social circumscription exists when neighboring societies block expansion, emigration, or access to resources. When strategic resources are concentrated in limited areas—even when no obstacles to migration exist—the effects are similar to those of circumscription.

Coastal Peru, usually one of the world's most arid areas, illustrates the interaction of environmental circumscription, warfare, and population increase. The earliest cultivation there was limited to valleys with springs. Each valley was circumscribed

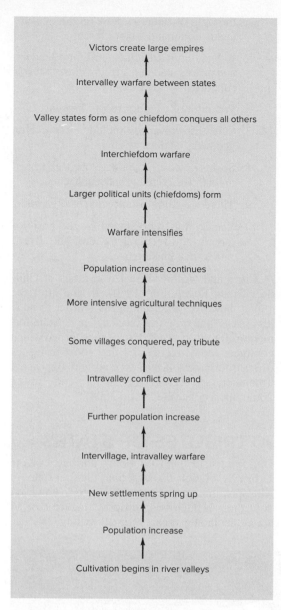

FIGURE 12.1 Carneiro's Approach to the Origin of the State as Applied to Coastal Peru.

In this very arid area, food production developed in narrow river valleys where water for cultivation was available (resource concentration). With cultivation, the population increased. Population pressure on land led to warfare, and some villages conquered others. Physical circumscription meant that the losers had no way to escape. The process accelerated as the population grew and as warfare and cultivation intensified. Chiefdoms, states, and empires eventually developed.

by the Andes Mountains to the east, the Pacific Ocean to the west, and desert regions to the north and south (see Millaire 2010). The advent of food production triggered population increase, leading to bigger villages in each valley. Colonists split off from the old villages and founded new ones. With more villages and people, a scarcity of land developed. Rivalries and raiding developed among villages in the same valley.

Because the valleys were circumscribed, when one village conquered another, the losers had to submit to the winners—they had nowhere else to go. Conquered villagers were allowed to keep their land only by paying tribute to their conquerors. To do this, they had to intensify production, using new techniques to produce more food. By working harder, they managed to pay tribute while meeting their own subsistence needs. Villagers brought new areas under cultivation by means of irrigation and terracing.

Those early Peruvians didn't work harder because they chose to do so. They were forced to pay tribute, accept political domination, and intensify production by factors beyond their control. Once established, all these trends accelerated. Population continued to grow, warfare intensified, and villages eventually were incorporated into chiefdoms. Remember that primary states emerge in the context of competition among chiefdoms. State formation occurred when one chiefdom in a valley succeeded in conquering and incorporating the others (Carneiro 1990; Stanish and Levine 2011). Eventually, the states based in different valleys began to fight. The winners brought the losers into growing states and empires, which eventually expanded from the coast to the highlands. (An **empire** is a mature state that is large, multiethnic, militaristic, and expansive.) By the 16th century, from their capital, Cuzco, in the high Andes, the Inca ruled one of the major empires of the tropics.

We should note, however, that the combination of population increase, warfare, and circumscription does not always lead to state formation. In highland Papua New Guinea, for example, valleys that were socially or physically circumscribed had population densities close to those of many states. Warfare also was present, but no states emerged. Whether states would have formed eventually will never be known, because European conquest truncated autonomous development there.

Whenever state formation occurred, the interacting causes, such as irrigation, population increase, or regional trade, magnified each other's effects. Key factors in state formation are changes in patterns of control over resources, resulting in social stratification, and increasing regulatory concerns, fostering management by state machinery. Different agencies arise to handle particular tasks and concerns. We must remember, as well, that food production did not always lead to the formation of chiefdoms and states. Many societies with Neolithic economies did not develop into chiefdoms or states. Similarly, there are chiefdoms that never developed into states, just as certain foragers never adopted food production, even when they knew about it.

empire
A mature state that is large, multiethnic, militaristic, and expansive.

THE URBAN REVOLUTION

It was V. Gordon Childe (1951), one of the most influential archaeologists of the 20th century, who coined the phrase "Neolithic Revolution" to describe the origin and impact of food production, which was examined in Chapter 11. Childe chose the term *revolution* deliberately, because he wanted to compare the major social transformations of prehistory (food production and the state) to the Industrial Revolution (Smith 2009). He used the phrase "Urban Revolution" (1950) to describe the major transformation of human life and social institutions examined in this chapter. A key feature was that institutions of government, including rulers with real power, emerged for the first time, along with social stratification. As a result of the Urban Revolution, economic activity of all sorts expanded greatly, and the first cities were built. On the downside, former freedoms and independence were replaced by an array of rules and regulations, along with taxes, inequality, servitude and slavery (Flannery and Marcus 2012; Jennings 2016; Smith 2009).

Childe listed 10 key attributes of early cities and states—all supported by archaeological evidence. They may be paraphrased as follows:

1. The first cities were larger and more densely populated than previous settlements.

2. Within the city were full-time specialists, including artisans, transport workers, merchants, officials, and priests.

3. Each primary producer (e.g., farmer) had to pay a tithe or tax; those contributions were stored in a central place, such as a temple or treasury.

4. Monumental buildings distinguished cities from villages while also symbolizing the right of rulers to draw on the treasury and to command a labor force.

5. Rulers, civil officials, military leaders, and priests made up a ruling class that was supported by the treasury.

6. Writing was used for record keeping.

7. Scientific advances included arithmetic, geometry, and astronomy.

8. Sophisticated art styles developed, expressed in sculpture, painting, and architecture.

9. There was long-distance and foreign trade.

10. Society was reorganized on the basis of territorial divisions (where one lived) rather than kinship groups.

Cities and writing were key features of Childe's Urban Revolution (1950). In and after the 1960s, however, anthropologists shifted to such phrases as "the origin of the state" and "state formation" for this process. Use of such terms, which continues today, recognizes that some instances of state formation lacked writing and significant urbanism (see Peregrine, Ember, and Ember 2007; Spencer and Redmond 2004).

ATTRIBUTES OF STATES

Childe's list of the 10 defining attributes of the Urban Revolution also describes the first states in Mesopotamia and Egypt. We need, however, something a bit less specific to characterize all states, including those without writing. We can

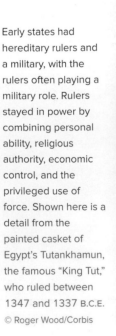

Early states had hereditary rulers and a military, with the rulers often playing a military role. Rulers stayed in power by combining personal ability, religious authority, economic control, and the privileged use of force. Shown here is a detail from the painted casket of Egypt's Tutankhamun, the famous "King Tut," who ruled between 1347 and 1337 B.C.E.
© Roger Wood/Corbis

use the following six attributes (suggested by Fagan 1996) to distinguish states from earlier forms of society:

1. A state controls a specific regional territory, such as the Nile Valley or the Valley of Mexico. The regional expanse of a state contrasts with the much smaller territories controlled by kin groups and villages in pre-estate societies. Early states were expansionist; they arose from competition among chiefdoms, as the most powerful chiefdom conquered the others, extended its rule over a larger territory, and managed to hold on to, and rule, the land and people acquired through conquest.

2. Early states had productive agricultural economies, supporting dense populations, often in cities. Those economies usually featured some form of water control or irrigation.

3. Early states used tribute and taxation to accumulate, at a central place, resources needed to support hundreds, or thousands, of specialists. These states had rulers, a military, and control over human labor.

4. States are stratified into social classes. In early states, the non-food-producing population consisted of a small elite group, plus artisans, officials, priests, and other specialists. Most people were commoners. Slaves and prisoners constituted the lowest rung of the social ladder. Rulers stayed in power by combining personal ability, religious authority, economic control, and force.

5. Early states had imposing public buildings and monumental architecture, including temples, palaces, and storehouses. (See this chapter's "Focus on Globalization" for some of the most impressive examples of monumental architecture.)

6. Early states developed some form of record-keeping system, usually a written script.

STATE FORMATION IN THE MIDDLE EAST

In the last chapter we saw that Neolithic economies emerged in the ancient Middle East around 10,000 B.P. In the ensuing process of change, the center of population growth shifted from the zone where wheat and barley grew wild to adjacent areas where those grains were first domesticated. By 6000 B.P., population was increasing most rapidly in the alluvial plain of southern Mesopotamia. (**Mesopotamia** refers to the area between the Tigris and Euphrates Rivers in what is now southern Iraq and southwestern Iran.) This growing population supported itself through irrigation and intensive river valley agriculture. By 5500 B.P.,

The world's earliest known town is Jericho, located in what now is Israel. Jericho was first settled by Natufian foragers around 11,000 B.P. The round tower in this photo dates back 8,000 years.

© www.BibleLandPictures.com/Alamy Stock Photo

towns had grown into cities. The earliest city-states were Sumer (southern Iraq) and Elam (southwestern Iran), with their capitals at Uruk (Warka) and Susa, respectively (see Potts 2015).

Urban Life

The first towns arose around 10,000 years ago in the Middle East. Over the generations, houses of mud brick were built and rebuilt in the same place. Substantial *tells,* or mounds, arose from the debris of a succession of such houses. These sites have yielded remains of ancient community life, including streets, buildings, terraces, courtyards, wells, and other artifacts. The earliest known town was Jericho, located in what is now Israel, at a well-watered oasis near the Dead Sea (Figure 12.2). From the lowest (oldest) level, we know that around 11,000 years ago Jericho was first settled by Natufian foragers. Occupation continued thereafter, through and beyond biblical times, when "Joshua fit the battle of Jericho, and the walls came tumbling down" (Laughlin 2006).

During the phase just after the Natufians, the earliest known town appeared. It was an un-planned, densely populated settlement with round houses and about 2,000 people. The town was surrounded by a sturdy wall with a massive tower. The wall may have been built initially as a flood barrier rather than for defense. Around 9000 B.P., Jericho was destroyed, to be rebuilt later. The new occupants lived in square houses with finished plaster floors. They buried their dead beneath their homes, a pattern seen at other sites, such as Çatalhöyük in Turkey (see the following paragraph). Pottery reached Jericho around 8000 B.P..

Mesopotamia The area where the earliest states developed, between the Tigris and Euphrates Rivers.

focus on GLOBALIZATION

The Seven Wonders of the World

States are precursors to empires, which are precursors to the world system and globalization. The state is an expansive form of human social organization that wields considerable power. Many states have developed into empires that cover huge territories and rule large numbers of people. Some historic examples include the Persian empire, the empire created by Alexander the Great, the Roman and Byzantine empires, the Ottoman empire, and more recently the British and French empires. The Inca (Peru) and Aztec (Mexico) empires are New World examples.

States clearly mark their environments. They build; they create a "built environment"—architecture that lasts and that archaeologists can study to determine the spread and influence of ancient states. Early states erected imposing public buildings and monumental architecture, including temples, palaces, and storehouses.

Occasionally, a feature of a state's "built environment" is impressive enough to earn it the status of "wonder of the world." The "Seven Wonders of the Ancient World" were renowned among ancient Greeks and other Mediterranean tourists, particularly in the first and second centuries B.C.E. Those sites worth seeing were close to, or on, the eastern rim of the Mediterranean Sea. Of them, only the Great Pyramid of Giza, the oldest of the seven wonders, is still standing after all those years.

Listed in order from oldest to youngest, the seven wonders of the ancient world are as follows: the Great Pyramid of Giza (constructed by ancient Egyptians), the Hanging Gardens of Babylon (Babylonians), the Temple of Artemis at Ephesus (Lydians, Persians, Greeks), the Statue of Zeus at Olympia (Greeks), the Mausoleum of Halicarnassus (Carians, Persians, Greeks), the Colossus of Rhodes (Greeks), and the Lighthouse of Alexandria (Ptolemaic Egyptians, Greeks).

Today's world has its own seven wonders, selected through a worldwide popular vote and announced in 2007. The New Seven Wonders of the World (2001–2007) was an initiative launched in 2001 by a Swiss corporation to choose new wonders from a selection of 200 existing monuments through a popularity poll. The winners—from oldest to youngest, based on when construction began—were Petra (Jordan), the Great Wall of China (Beijing), the Colosseum (Rome, Italy), Chichén Itzá (Yucatan, Mexico), Machu Picchu (Peru), the Taj Mahal (Agra, India), and the Christ the Redeemer statue (Corcovado) (Rio de Janeiro, Brazil). Common to all these wonders—ancient and modern—is that they were erected by states, often for political or religious reasons, and eventually they became sites that people wanted to visit to marvel at these creations. Sightseeing tourism certainly existed in the ancient world, but on a much more limited scale than today. Nowadays, in the context of global tourism, the world's most popular attractions still include monuments named for people (e.g., Washington, Lincoln, Eiffel, Disney) and structures built for religious reasons (e.g., St. Peter's in Rome, Notre Dame de Paris, Hagia Sophia in Istanbul). No doubt the seven wonders of today's world are "must sees" for anyone doing tourism in a given country. I've seen five of the seven. How about you?

The Taj Mahal, in Agra, India, is considered one of the seven wonders of today's world.
© Conrad P. Kottak

Long-distance trade, especially of obsidian, a volcanic glass used to make tools and ornaments, became important in the Middle East between 9500 and 7000 B.P. One town that prospered from this trade was Çatalhöyük in Anatolia, Turkey (Fowler 2011; Hodder 2013). A grassy mound 65 feet high holds the remains of this 9,000-year-old town, probably the largest settlement of the Neolithic age. Çatalhöyük was located on a river, which deposited rich soil for crops, created a lush environment for animals, and was harnessed for irrigation by 7000 B.P. Over the mound's 32 acres (12.9 hectares), up to 10,000 people once lived in crowded mud-brick houses packed so tightly that residents entered from their roofs.

Shielded by a defensive wall, Çatalhöyük flourished between 8000 and 7000 B.P. Its mud-brick dwellings, rarely larger than an American bedroom, had separate areas reserved for ritual and secular uses. In a given house, the ritual images (wall paintings) were placed along the walls that faced north, east, or west, but never south. That area was reserved for cooking and other domestic tasks.

The ritual spaces were decorated with wall paintings, sculpted ox heads, bull horns, and relief models of bulls and rams. The paintings showed bulls surrounded by stick figures running, dancing, and sometimes throwing stones. Vultures attacked headless humans. One frieze had human

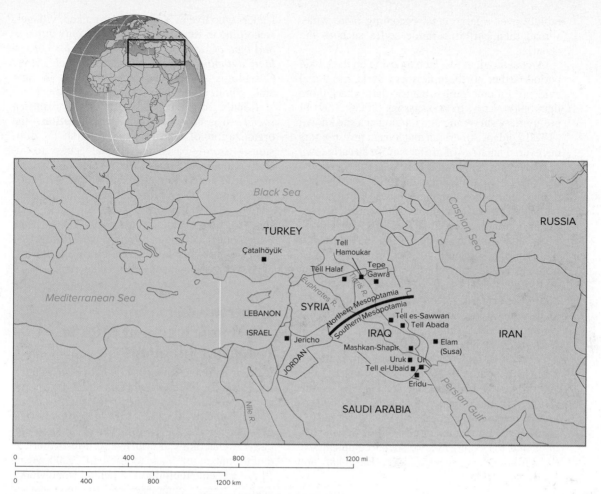

FIGURE 12.2 Sites in Middle Eastern State Formation.

handprints painted below mounted bull horns. These images and their placement are reminiscent of Paleolithic cave art. The dwellings at Çatalhöyük were entered through the roof, and people had to crawl through holes from room to room, somewhat like moving between chambers in a cave. The deeper down one went, the richer the art became. The town's spiritual life seems to have revolved around a preoccupation with animals, danger, and death, perhaps related to the site's hunter-gatherer past.

Two or three generations of a family were buried beneath their homes. In one dwelling, archaeologists found remains of 17 individuals, mostly children. After two or three generations of family burials, the dwelling was burned. The site was then covered with fine dirt and a floor laid for a new dwelling.

Çatalhöyük's residents, although they lived in a town, acted independently in family groups without any apparent control by a priestly or political elite. The town never became a full-fledged city with centralized organization. Just as it lacked priests, Çatalhöyük never had leaders who controlled or managed trade and production. Food was stored and processed not collectively but on a smaller, domestic scale (Fowler 2011; Hodder 2013).

The Elite Level

The first Middle Eastern pottery dates back a bit more than 8,000 years. By 7000 B.P., pottery had become widespread in the Middle East. Archaeologists consider pottery shape, finishing, decoration, and type of clay as features used for dating. The geographic distribution of a given pottery style may indicate trade or an alliance spanning a large area at a particular time.

An early and widespread pottery style, the **Halafian,** was first found at Tell Halaf in the mountains of northern Syria. *Halafian* (7500–6500 B.P.) refers to a delicate ceramic style. It also describes the period during which the elite level and the first chiefdoms emerged (by 7000 B.P.). The low number of Halafian ceramics suggests they were luxury goods associated with a social hierarchy.

The Ubaid period (7000–6000 B.P.) is named for a southern Mesopotamian pottery type first discovered at a small site, Tell el-Ubaid, located near the major city of Ur in southern Iraq. Similar pottery has been discovered in the deep levels of the Mesopotamian cities of Ur, Uruk, and Eridu. Ubaid pottery is associated with advanced chiefdoms and perhaps the earliest states. It diffused

Halafian

Early (7500–6500 B.P.), widespread Mesopotamian pottery style.

rapidly over a large area, becoming more widespread than earlier ceramic styles such as the Halafian.

Archaeological research focusing on the Ubaid period farther north, in northern Syria, has found evidence for emerging urbanism dating back more than 6,000 years. In two seasons (2008, 2009) of preliminary surveying and digging at a site known as Tell Zeidan, American and Syrian investigators uncovered an array of artifacts from an early town on the upper Euphrates River. People occupied this site for two millennia, until 6000 B.P. The site, dominated by three large mounds, featured houses with mud-brick walls, floors with hearths, painted pottery, stone seals, kilns, and obsidian blades. There also is evidence suggesting the emergence of irrigated agriculture, long-distance trade, political leadership, and social differentiation (Wilford 2010).

Blocked by war from Iraq (with its prime sites of Mesopotamian antiquity), archaeologists, including the Tell Zeidan researchers, could still work in Syria. They turned their attention to the upper river valleys, across the border from Iraq in Syria and southern Turkey (see Hodder 2006; Wilford 2010). Unfortunately, recent political unrest in Syria has impeded continuation of archaeological research there, leaving Turkey as today's prime locus for research on Neolithic transformations and the emergence of social complexity in the Middle East (see Özdoğan, Başgelen, and Kuniholm 2011).

Social Ranking and Chiefdoms

The anthropologist Morton Fried (1960) defined three kinds of societies, based on the degree of status differentiation within each type. The **egalitarian society** is most typically found among foragers and has few status distinctions. It makes status distinctions based only on age, gender, and individual talents or achievements. Thus, depending on the society, adult men, elder women, talented musicians, or ritual specialists might have somewhat higher status because of their activities or knowledge. In egalitarian societies, status distinctions are not usually inherited. Children of a respected person get no special recognition because of their parent; they have to earn it on their own.

Fried's second type of society, the **ranked society,** does have hereditary inequality, but it lacks stratification—clearly defined social classes. In a ranked society, individuals often are ranked according to their genealogical distance from the chief. Refining Fried's typology, Carneiro (1991) points out that we should distinguish between *two kinds of ranked society*. In type 1, individuals are ranked, but villages are independent (autonomous) of one another. In type 2, both individuals and villages are ranked, and there is loss of village autonomy. Smaller villages, no longer independent, have come under the authority of

leaders who live in larger, higher-ranked, villages. According to Kent Flannery (1999), *only this second type of ranked society, featuring loss of village autonomy, should be called a chiefdom.* Chiefdoms are marked by differences in rank among both individuals and communities.

Fried's third type of society is the *stratified society*. It is based on social **stratification**—the organization of society into sharp social divisions—*strata*—based on unequal access to socially valued resources. The upper classes have privileged access to wealth and power, while the lower classes have inferior access. In stratified societies, class status often is hereditary. In early state-organized societies, the social classes were often nobles, commoners, and slaves. Recap 12.1 lists key features and examples of egalitarian, ranked (two types), and stratified societies.

Contrasts between Mesoamerican and Middle Eastern Chiefdoms

It's easy for archaeologists to identify early states. Evidence for state organization includes monumental architecture, aqueducts, central storehouses, and written records. In Mesoamerica, even chiefdoms are easy to detect archaeologically. Archaeological evidence for Mesoamerican chiefdoms dates back more than 3,000 years. Those ancient chiefdoms left behind stone works, such as temple complexes and the huge carved Olmec heads (see the photo on p. 221). Mesoamericans also liked to bury chiefs and their families with durable ornaments and prestige goods. High-status families distinguished their infants by deforming their heads. When they died, high-status infants were buried with special symbols and grave goods (Flannery 1999).

Early Middle Eastern chiefs, by contrast, were much less ostentatious in their use of durable markers of prestige. This makes it harder for archaeologists to detect their chiefdoms from material remains (Flannery 1999). In the Middle East, the first chiefdoms developed between 7500 and 7000 B.P. (The first states emerged in the Middle East about 1,500 years later—between 6000 and 5500 B.P.) The Middle Eastern archaeological record after 7300 B.P. reveals behavior typical of chiefdoms, including exotic goods used as markers of status, along with raiding and political instability. Early chiefdoms included both the Halafian culture of northern Iraq and the Ubaid culture of southern Iraq, which spread north.

As in Mesoamerica, ancient Middle Eastern chiefdoms had cemeteries where high-status people were buried with distinctive items: vessels, statuettes, necklaces, and high-quality ceramics. Such goods were buried with children too young to have earned prestige on their own, who happened to be born into elite families. In the ancient

egalitarian society
A society with rudimentary status distinctions.

ranked society
A society with hereditary inequality but lacking social stratification.

stratification
The presence of social divisions—*strata*—with unequal wealth and power.

Unlike states such as Cameroon, whose Sultan Njoya is shown here, egalitarian societies lack inherited wealth and status and succession to political office. How are inherited status distinctions marked in your society?

© Heiner Heine/age fotostock

RECAP 12.1	Egalitarian, Ranked, and Stratified Societies			
KIND OF STATUS DISTINCTION	**NATURE OF STATUS**	**COMMON FORM OF SUBSISTENCE ECONOMY**	**COMMON FORMS OF SOCIAL ORGANIZATION**	**EXAMPLES**
Egalitarian	Status distinctions are not inherited. Status is based on age, gender, and individual qualities, talents, and achievements.	Foraging	Bands and tribes	Inuit, Ju/'hoansi San, and Yanomami
Ranked		Horticulture, pastoralism, and some foraging groups	Chiefdoms and some states	
Type 1	Status distinctions are distributed along a continuum and inherited; independent villages.			Salish, Kwakiutl (Pacific Northwest)
Type 2	Status distinctions are distributed along a continuum and inherited; loss of village autonomy, ranked villages.			Halaf and Ubaid period polities, Olmec, Cauca (Colombia), Natchez (eastern U.S.)
Stratified	Status distinctions are inherited and divided sharply between classes.	Agriculture	States	Teotihuacán, Uruk period states, Inca, Shang dynasty, Rome, United States, Great Britain

Archaeologists studying chiefdoms and states infer social status based on objects (grave goods) found in human burials. The clay crocks in this burial suggest a young woman of medium social status. She was buried within the tomb of a higher-status woman—a priestess of the Moche culture, which thrived between 200 and 700 C.E. In the second photo, an archaeology student draws to scale the same skeleton.

© STR/AFP/Getty Images

village of Tell es-Sawwan, infant graves show a continuum of richness from six statuettes, to three statuettes, to one statuette, to none. Such signs of slight gradations in social status are exactly what one expects in ranked societies.

Such burials demonstrate that hereditary status distinctions were present in the Middle East by 7000 B.P. But had chiefdoms (as opposed to type 1 ranked societies) formed? Had the leaders of large villages extended their authority to the smaller villages nearby? One line of evidence for such loss of village autonomy is that a common canal was used to irrigate several villages. This suggests a way of resolving disputes among farmers over access to water, for example, by appeal to a strong leader—a chief. Further evidence for the loss of village autonomy is the emergence of a two-tier settlement hierarchy, with small villages clustering around a large village, especially one with public buildings. This settlement pattern was present in northern Mesopotamia during the Halafian period.

Advanced Chiefdoms

In northeastern Syria, near the border with Iraq, archaeologists have excavated an ancient settlement that once lay on a major trade route. This large site, Tell Hamoukar, dates back more than 5,500 years (Wilford 2000). Its remains suggest that advanced chiefdoms arose in northern areas of the Middle East independently of the better-known Mesopotamian city-states of southern Iraq.

By 5700 B.P., Tell Hamoukar was a prosperous town of 32 acres, enclosed by a defensive wall. The site had fine pottery and large ovens—evidence of food preparation on an institutional scale. The site has yielded pieces of large cooking pots, animal bones, and traces of wheat, barley, and oats for baking and brewing. The archaeologist McGuire Gibson, one of the excavators, believes that food

preparation on this scale is evidence of a ranked society in which elites were organizing people and resources (Wilford 2000). Most likely they were hosting and entertaining in a chiefly manner.

Providing further evidence for social ranking are the seals used to mark containers of food and other goods. Some of the seals are small, with only simple incisions or cross-hatching. Others are larger and more elaborate, presumably for higher officials to stamp more valuable goods. Gibson suspects the larger seals with figurative scenes were held by the few people who had greater authority. The smaller, simply incised seals were used by many more people with less authority (Wilford 2000).

A huge battle destroyed Tell Hamoukar around 5500 B.P. This site provides the earliest evidence for large-scale organized warfare in the Middle East. The archaeologists found extensive destruction, with collapsed walls, which had undergone heavy bombardment by sling bullets and eventually collapsed in an ensuing fire. The excavators retrieved more than 1,200 small oval-shaped bullets and some 120 larger round clay balls used during the siege. Sadly and ironically, archaeological excavation at Tell Hamoukar and most other sites in Syria and Iraq has been halted by warfare proceeding there today. (Visit the Tell Hamoukar project website at https://oi.uchicago.edu/research/projects/ham/.)

The Rise of the State

In southern Mesopotamia at this time (5700 B.P.), an expanding population and increased food production from irrigation were changing the social landscape even more drastically than in the north. Irrigation had allowed Ubaid communities to spread along the Euphrates River. Travel and trade were expanding, with water serving as the highway system. Such raw materials as hardwood and stone, which southern Mesopotamia lacked,

DATES	PERIOD	AGE
3000–2539 B.P.	Neo-Babylonian	Iron Age
3600–3000 B.P.	Kassite	
4000–3600 B.P.	Old Babylonian	Bronze Age
4150–4000 B.P.	Third Dynasty of Ur	
4350–4150 B.P.	Akkadian	
4600–4350 B.P.	Early Dynastic III	
4750–4600 B.P.	Early Dynastic II	
5000–4750 B.P.	Early Dynastic I	
5200–5000 B.P.	Jemdet Nasr	
6000–5200 B.P.	Uruk	Chalcolithic (Copper/Stone)
7500–6000 B.P.	Ubaid (southern Mesopotamia)–Halaf (northern Mesopotamia)	
10,000–7000 B.P.		Neolithic

were imported via river routes. Social and economic networks now linked communities on the rivers in the south and in the foothills to the north. Social differentials also increased. Priests and political leaders joined expert potters and other specialists. These non-food-producers were supported by the larger population of farmers and herders.

Economies were being managed by central leadership. Agricultural villages had grown into cities, some of which were ruled by local kings. The Uruk period (6000–5200 B.P.), which succeeded the Ubaid period, takes its name from a prominent southern city-state located more than 400 miles south of Tell Hamoukar. The Uruk period established Mesopotamia as "the cradle of civilization." Recap 12.2 highlights archaeological periods in the process of state formation in the ancient Middle East.

There is no evidence of Uruk influence at Tell Hamoukar in Syria until 5200 B.P., when some Uruk pottery showed up. When southern Mesopotamians expanded north, they found advanced chiefdoms, which were not yet states. The fact that writing originated in Sumer, in southern Mesopotamia, indicates a more advanced, state-organized society there. The first writing presumably developed to handle record keeping for a centralized economy.

Initially, writing was used to keep accounts, reflecting the needs of trade. Rulers, nobles, priests, and merchants were the first to benefit from it. Writing had reached Egypt by 5200 B.P., probably from Mesopotamia. The earliest writing was pictographic, for example, with pictorial symbols of horses used to represent them.

Early Mesopotamian scribes used a stylus (writing implement) to scrawl symbols on raw clay. This writing, called **cuneiform** writing, from the Latin word for "wedge," left a wedge-shaped impression on the clay. Both the Sumerian (southern Mesopotamia) and the Akkadian (northern

Pictographic writing on a Mesopotamian clay tablet, inscribed between 3100 and 2900 B.C.E. The earliest of such tablets represent the work of administrators, perhaps of large temple institutions.

© Ann Ronan Pictures/Print Collector/Hulton Archive/Getty Images

Mesopotamia) languages were written in cuneiform (Gowlett 1993).

Writing and temples played key roles in the Mesopotamian economy. For the historic period after 5600 B.P., when writing was invented, there are temple records of economic activities. States can exist without writing, but literacy facilitates the flow and storage of information. We know that Mesopotamian priests managed herding, farming, manufacture, and trade. Temple officials allotted fodder and pastureland for cattle and donkeys, which were used as plow and cart animals. As the economy expanded, trade, manufacture, and grain storage were centrally managed. Temples

cuneiform
Early Mesopotamian wedge-shaped writing, using stylus on clay.

metallurgy
The extraction and processing of metals to make tools.

smelting
The high temperature extraction of metal from ore.

bronze
An alloy of copper and arsenic or copper and tin.

collected and distributed meat, dairy products, crops, fish, clothing, tools, and trade items. Potters, metalworkers, weavers, sculptors, and other artisans perfected their crafts.

Prior to the invention of **metallurgy** (knowledge of the properties of metals, including their extraction and processing and the manufacture of metal tools), raw copper was shaped by hammering. If copper is hammered too long, it hardens and becomes brittle, with a risk of cracking. But once heated (annealed) in a fire, copper becomes malleable again. Such annealing of copper was an early form of metallurgy. A vital step for metallurgy was the discovery of **smelting,** the high-temperature process by which pure metal is produced from an ore. Ores, including copper ore, have a much wider distribution than does native copper, which was initially traded as a luxury good because of its rarity.

When and how smelting was discovered is unknown. But after 5000 B.P., metallurgy evolved rapidly. The Bronze Age began when alloys of arsenic and copper, or tin and copper (in both cases known as **bronze**), became common and greatly extended the use of metals. Bronze flows more easily than copper does when heated to a similar temperature, so bronze was more convenient for metal casting. Early molds were carved in stone, as shaped depressions to be filled with molten metal. A copper ax cast from such a mold has been found in northern Mesopotamia and predates 5000 B.P. Thereafter, other metals came into common use. By 4500 B.P., golden objects were found in royal burials at Ur.

Iron ore is distributed more widely than is copper ore. Iron, when smelted, can be used on its own; there is no need for tin or arsenic to make a metal alloy (bronze). The Iron Age began once high-temperature iron smelting was mastered. In the Old World after 3200 B.P., iron spread rapidly.

Formerly valued as highly as gold, iron crashed in value when it became plentiful (Gowlett 1993).

The Mesopotamian economy, based on intensive agriculture, craft production, and trade, spurred population growth and increased urbanism. Sumerian cities were protected by a fortress wall and surrounded by a farming area. By 4800 B.P., Uruk, the largest early Mesopotamian city, had a population of 50,000. As irrigation and the population expanded, communities fought over water. People sought protection in the fortified cities (Adams 2008) when neighbors or invaders threatened.

By 4600 B.P., secular authority had replaced temple rule. The office of military coordinator developed into kingship. This change shows up architecturally in palaces and royal tombs. The palace raised armies and supplied them with armor, chariots, and metal armaments. At Ur's royal cemetery, by 4600 B.P. monarchs were being buried with soldiers, charioteers, and ladies in waiting. These subordinates were killed at the time of a royal burial to accompany the monarch to the afterworld.

Agricultural intensification made it possible for the number of people supported by a given area to increase. Population pressure on irrigated fields helped create a stratified society. Land became private property that was bought and sold. The wealth of people with large estates set them off from ordinary farmers. Those landlords joined the urban elite, while sharecroppers and serfs toiled in the fields. By 4600 B.P., Mesopotamia had a well-defined class structure, with complex stratification into nobles, commoners, and slaves.

OTHER EARLY STATES

The Indus River Valley state takes its name from the river valley along which it extended. Located in what is today northwestern India and adjacent Pakistan, the major cities of the Indus River Valley state were Harappa and Mohenjo-daro. (Figure 12.3 maps the four great early river valley states of the Old World: Mesopotamia, Egypt, India/Pakistan, and northern China.) Trade and the spread of writing from Mesopotamia may have played a role in the emergence of the Indus River Valley state around 4600 B.P. The ruins of the ancient city of Harappa, located in Pakistan's Punjab Province, were the first to be identified as part of the Indus River Valley civilization. At its peak, the Indus River Valley state incorporated 1,000 cities, towns, and villages, spanning 280,000 square miles (725,000 square kilometers). This state, which flourished between 4600 and 3900 B.P., featured urban planning, social stratification, and an early writing system, which remains undeciphered.

In *cuneiform,* another early Mesopotamian script, a stylus was used to scrawl wedge-shaped symbols on raw clay. What languages were written in cuneiform?

© imageBROKER/Alamy Stock Photo

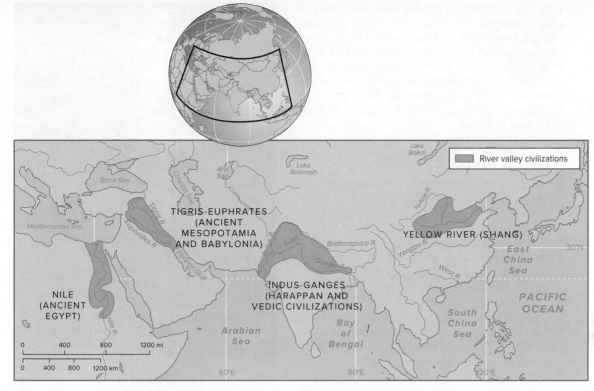

FIGURE 12.3 The Four Great Early River Valley States of the Old World.

By approximately 4000 B.P., urban life had been established along the Tigris and Euphrates Rivers in Mesopotamia, the Nile River in Egypt, the Indus and Ganges Rivers in India/Pakistan, and the Yellow River in China.

SOURCE: Based on Map 1-1 from Craig, Albert M.; Graham, William A.; Kagan, Donald; Ozment, Steven; Turner, Frank M., *Heritage of World Civilizations: Volume I to 1650,* 4th ed. © 1997. Reprinted and electronically reproduced by permission of Pearson Education, Inc., Upper Saddle River, New Jersey.

This state maintained a uniform system of weights. Its cities had carefully planned residential areas with waste-water systems. Sophisticated craft industries produced an array of products including ceramic vessels made on potter's wheels (Meadow and Kenoyer 2000).

The Indus River Valley state collapsed, apparently because of warfare, around 3900 B.P. Its cities were destroyed and abandoned. Skeletons of massacre victims have been found in the streets of Mohenjo-daro. Harappa continued to be occupied, but on a much smaller scale than previously (Meadow and Kenoyer 2000). (For more on the Harappa Archaeological Research Project, visit http://www.harappa.com.)

The first Chinese state, dating to 3750 B.P., was that of the Shang dynasty. It arose in the Huang He (Yellow) River area of northern China, with wheat as its dietary staple. This state was characterized by urbanism, palatial (as well as domestic) architecture, human sacrifice, and a sharp division between social classes. Burials of the aristocracy were marked by ornaments of stone, including jade. The Shang had bronze metallurgy and an elaborate writing system. In warfare they used chariots and took prisoners.

Like Mesopotamia and China, many early civilizations came to rely on metallurgy. At Nok Nok Tha in northern Thailand, metalworking goes back 6,000 years. In Peru's Andes, metalworking appeared around 4000 B.P. Ancient Andeans were skilled in working with bronze, copper, and gold.

This ziggurat, or temple tower, at Ur, Iraq, dates back to 4100 B.P. (2100 B.C.E.). Temples and their officials played key roles in the Mesopotamian economy. Who handles such duties in our society?

© Georg Gerster/Science Source

They are well known, too, for their techniques of pottery manufacture. Their arts, crafts, and agricultural knowledge compared well with those of Mesoamerica at its height, to which we turn after a discussion of African states. Note that both Mesoamerican and Andean state formation were truncated by Spanish conquest. The Aztecs of Mexico were conquered in 1519 C.E., and the Inca of Peru in 1532 C.E.

African States

Egypt, a major ancient civilization, developed in northern Africa, as one of the world's first states (Morkot 2005). Egyptian influence extended southward along the Nile into what is now Sudan. Sub-Saharan Africa witnessed the emergence of several states, only a few of which will be described here.

As in the states just discussed, metallurgy (especially iron and gold) played a role in the eventual rise of African states (Connah 2016). About 2,000 years ago, iron smelting began to diffuse rapidly throughout Africa. That spread was aided by the migrations of Bantu speakers. (Bantu is Africa's largest linguistic family.) The Bantu migrations, launched from north central Africa around 2100 B.P., continued for more than a thousand years. Bantu speakers migrated south into the rain forests of the Congo River and east into the African highlands. Along with their language and iron-smelting techniques, they also spread farming, particularly of high-yielding crops such as yams, bananas, and plantains.

One crowning achievement of the Bantu migrations was the Mwenemutapa empire. The southeast-moving ancestors of the Mwenemutapa took iron smelting and farming to the region called Zimbabwe, south of the Zambezi River and located within the contemporary nation of the same name. This area was rich in gold, which the Mwenemutapa mined and traded with cities on the Indian Ocean, starting around 1000 C.E. (1000 B.P.). The Mwenemutapa developed a powerful kingdom based on trade. The first centralized state there was Great Zimbabwe (*zimbabwe* means "stone enclosure"—the capital was protected by huge stone walls), which arose around 1300 C.E. By 1500, Great Zimbabwe dominated the Zambezi Valley militarily and commercially as the seat of the Mwenemutapa empire.

Another African region where states arose, also abetted by trade, was the Sahel, the area just south of the Sahara in western Africa. Farming towns started appearing in the Sahel around 2600 B.P. One such town, Kumbi Saleh, eventually became the capital of the ancient kingdom of Ghana. West Africa was rich in gold, precious metals, ivory, and other resources, which after 750 C.E. (1250 B.P.) were traded (thanks to the

A 16th-century bronze statue of a royal messenger from Benin. An important precolonial state in what is now southern Nigeria, Benin, which thrived in the 15th–16th centuries C.E., is known for its artistic creativity. Benin art became one of the most influential African art traditions.
© AAAC /TopFoto/The Image Works

camel) across the Sahara to North Africa, Egypt, and the Middle East. Cities in the Sahel served as southern terminal points for the trans-Saharan trade (e.g., of gold for salt). Several kingdoms developed in this area: Ghana, Mali, Songhay, and Kanem-Bornu, together known as the Sahelian kingdoms, of which Ghana was the first. By 1000 C.E., Ghana's economic vitality, based on the trans-Saharan trade, was supporting an empire formed through the conquest of local chiefdoms, from which tribute was extracted.

States also arose in the forested region of western Africa south of the Sahel. Between 1000 and 1500 C.E., local farming villages started consolidating into larger units, which eventually became centralized states. The largest and most enduring of these states was Benin, in what is now southern Nigeria. Benin, which thrived in the 15th century C.E., is known for its artistic creativity, expressed in terra-cotta, ivory, and brass sculpture. Benin art became one of the most influential African art traditions.

STATE FORMATION IN MESOAMERICA

In Chapter 11, we examined the independent inventions of farming in the Middle East and Mesoamerica. The processes of state formation that took place in these areas also were comparable, beginning with ranked societies and chiefdoms, and ending with fully formed states and empires.

The first monumental buildings (temple complexes) in the Western Hemisphere were constructed by Mesoamerican chiefdoms in many areas, from the Valley of Mexico to Guatemala. Those chiefdoms influenced one another as they traded materials, such as obsidian, shells, jade, and pottery. (Figure 12.4 maps major sites in the emergence of Mesoamerican food production, chiefdoms, and states.)

Early Chiefdoms and Elites

The Olmec built a series of ritual centers on Mexico's southern Gulf Coast between 3200 and 2500 B.P. There were at least three of these centers, each from a different century. All had earthen mounds grouped into plaza complexes, presumably for religious use. Such centers show that Olmec chiefs could marshal human labor to construct such mounds. The Olmec were also master sculptors; they carved massive stone heads, perhaps as images of their chiefs or their ancestors.

There is evidence, too, that trade routes linked the Olmec with other parts of Mesoamerica, such as the Oaxaca Valley in the southern highlands and the Valley of Mexico (see Figure 12.4). By 3000 B.P. (1000 B.C.E.—formerly B.C.), a ruling elite had emerged in Oaxaca. The items traded at that time between Oaxaca and the Olmec were for elite consumption. High-status Oaxacans wore mussel-shell ornaments from the coast. In return the Olmec elites got mirrors and jade made by Oaxacan artisans. Oaxacan chiefdoms developed irrigation systems, exported magnetite mirrors, and were precocious in their use of adobes (mud bricks), stucco, stone masonry, and architecture. Olmec chiefdoms farmed river levees, built mounds of earth, and carved those colossal stone heads. Other early Mexican chiefdoms also had skilled artists and builders, using adobes and lime plaster and constructing stone buildings, precisely oriented 8 degrees north of east.

The period between 3200 and 3000 B.P. (1200–1000 B.C.E.) was one of rapid social change. Mesoamerica's many chiefdoms were linked by trade and exchange. Chiefly centers were concentrating labor power, intensifying agriculture, exchanging trade goods, and borrowing ideas, including art motifs and styles, from each other. Archaeologists now believe it was the *intensity of competitive*

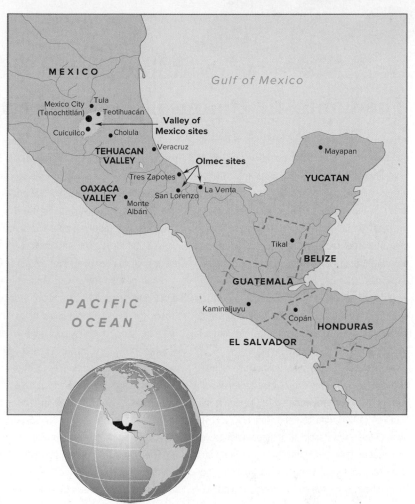

FIGURE 12.4 Major Sites in the Emergence of Food Production and the State in Mesoamerica.

FROM CLIFFORD J. JOLLY AND FRED PLOG, *PHYSICAL ANTHROPOLOGY AND ARCHAEOLOGY*, 4TH ED., P. 115. COPYRIGHT © 1986 BY THE MCGRAW-HILL COMPANIES, INC. REPRINTED WITH PERMISSION.

A colossal Olmec head, carved from basalt, is displayed at the Jalapa Museum of Archaeology in Veracruz, Mexico, in a setting designed to recall its original site. Such heads, often weighing many tons, are thought to represent individual chiefs.

© Heritage Image Partnership Ltd/Alamy Stock Photo

The Fantastic Claims of Pseudo-Archaeology

Interest in prehistory has spawned numerous popular-culture creations, including movies, TV programs, and books. In fictional works, the anthropologists don't bear much resemblance to their real-life counterparts. Unlike Indiana Jones, the most famous pop-culture archaeologist, normal and reputable archaeologists don't go around fighting Nazis, lashing whips, or seizing antiquities. The archaeologist's profession isn't a matter of raiding lost arks, going on crusades, or finding crystal skulls but rather of reconstructing ancient lifeways through the careful and systematic analysis of material remains.

Over the generations, the media have exposed us to the pseudoscientific theories of such popular writers as Thor Heyerdahl (1971), Erich von Däniken (1971), and Graham Hancock (2015)—none of them a professional archaeologist. Heyerdahl argued that developments in one world area (e.g., Mesoamerica) were based on ideas borrowed from somewhere else (e.g., Egypt). Von Daniken carried diffusionism several steps further, proposing that major human achievements were created or assisted by extraterrestrials. These writers share a degree of contempt for human inventiveness. They assume that major features of the ancient human landscape were beyond the capabilities of people actually living in the places where the achievements occurred.

In *The Ra Expeditions,* world traveler and adventurer Heyerdahl (1971) argued that his voyage in a papyrus boat from the Mediterranean to the Caribbean demonstrated that ancient Egyptians could have navigated to the New World. (The boat was modeled on an ancient Egyptian vessel, but Heyerdahl and his crew had with them such modern conveniences as a radio and canned goods.) Heyerdahl maintained that, given the possibility of ancient trans-Atlantic travel, Old World people could have influenced the emergence of civilization in the Americas. In *Fingerprints of the Gods* (2011) and other books aimed at popular audiences, writer–journalist Graham Hancock has advanced a series of fantastic claims, including that Africans influenced the Olmec (because of, in his opinion, African-looking faces in Olmec sculpture).

The University of Michigan offers a popular undergraduate class titled Frauds and Fantastic Claims in Archaeology. The course examines and debunks popular media theories that archaeologists view as fringe, or "pseudoscientific." Especially problematic are claims that cultural achievements by indigenous peoples result from contact with superior beings. The course exposes the logical flaws and questionable evidence used to support such claims. The course textbook is Kenneth L. Feder's *Frauds, Myths, and Mysteries: Science and Pseudoscience in Archaeology* (2014)—a must for any reader wanting to pursue this topic further.

Pseudo-archaeologists often have trouble with chronology. We've seen in this chapter that around 2,000 years ago states fully comparable to those of Mesopotamia and Egypt began to rise and fall in the Mexican highlands. This occurred about 1,500 years after the major period of Egyptian pyramid building. If Egypt did contribute to Mesoamerican civilization, we would expect this influence to have been exerted during Egypt's heyday as an ancient power—not 1,500 years later. There is, however, no archaeological evidence for trans-Atlantic contact at either time.

There is, on the other hand, abundant archaeological evidence for the gradual emergence of food production and the state in the Middle East, in Mesoamerica, and in Peru. This evidence effectively counters the diffusionist theories and other fantastic claims about how and why human achievements, including farming and the state, began. Popular theories to the contrary, changes, advances, and setbacks in ancient American social life were the products of the ideas and activities of Native Americans themselves.

---

interaction—rather than the supremacy of any one chiefdom—that made social change so rapid. The social and political landscape of Mexico around 3000 B.P. (1000 B.C.E.) was one in which 25 or so chiefly centers were (1) sufficiently separate and autonomous to adapt to local zones and conditions and (2) sufficiently interactive and competitive to borrow and incorporate new ideas and innovations as they arose in other regions (Flannery and Marcus 2000).

It used to be thought that a single chiefdom could become a state on its own. Archaeologists know now that state formation involves one chiefdom's incorporating several others into the emerging state it controls, and making changes in its own infrastructure as it acquires and holds on to new territories, followers, and goods. Waging warfare and attracting followers are two key elements in state formation. (This chapter's "Appreciating Anthropology" debunks popular pseudo-archaeological theories about the origin of Mesoamerican civilization.)

Many chiefdoms had dense populations, intensive agriculture, and settlement hierarchies that included hamlets, villages, and perhaps towns. These factors paved the way for greater social and political complexity. Political leaders emerged, and military success often solidified their position.

Neither Mexico nor Peru has yielded a shred of accepted archaeological evidence for Old World interference prior to the European Age of Discovery, which began late in the 15th century. Francisco Pizarro conquered Peru's Inca state in 1532, 11 years after its Mesoamerican counterpart, Tenochtitlán, the Aztec capital, fell to Spanish conquistadores. (We do have abundant archaeological, as well as written, evidence for this contact between Europeans and Native Americans.)

The archaeological record also casts doubt on contentions that the advances of earthlings came with extraterrestrial help. Abundant, well-analyzed archaeological data from the Middle East, Mesoamerica, and Peru tell a clear story. Food production and the state were not brilliant secrets, discoveries, or inventions that humans needed to learn or borrow from outsiders. They were long-term developments, gradual processes with down-to-earth causes and effects. They required thousands of years of orderly change, not a chance meeting in the high Andes between an ancient Inca chief and a beneficent Johnny Appleseed from Aldebaran.

Occasionally, fantastic claims about prehistory exaggerate, rather than deny, the abilities of ancient humans. One example is when pseudo-archaeologists claim that Paleolithic societies could have constructed monumental structures. Graham Hancock, for example, has suggested that an Upper Paleolithic civilization, rather than ancient Egyptians, built Egypt's great Sphinx, some 7,000 years earlier than its actual construction date (Hancock 2015).

Semir Osmanagic is a Bosnian amateur archaeologist who has been dubbed the Indiana Jones of the Balkans because of his flat-crowned Navajo hat. Osmanagic claims to have identified in Bosnia the world's largest ancient pyramid, which he thinks is "older than the last ice age" (Smith 2006). Archaeologists and geologists, however, say that his "pyramid" is actually a large, symmetrical hill formed by buckling of the Earth's crust millions of years ago. Zilka Kujundzic-Vejzagic, a trained prehistoric archaeologist at Bosnia's National Museum, points out the lack of any evidence whatsoever for a Paleolithic civilization in Bosnia. (Were there Paleolithic civilizations anywhere in the world?) Indeed, archaeologists working in Bosnia have found little more than flint tools from the end of the last Ice Age and only simple Neolithic settlements that appeared thousands of years after that. The country's most substantial ancient monument is a modest stone city in southern Bosnia built during the third century B.C.E. Nevertheless, uncritical media coverage has popularized Osmanagic's theories, and volunteers have flocked to the site to help him excavate (Smith 2006). Responding to his claims, the European Association of Archaeologists issued an official statement signed by the heads of the official archaeological organizations of seven European countries (Parzinger et al. 2006). Their statement called Osmanagic's so-called pyramid project "a cruel hoax on an unsuspecting public" that "has no place in the world of genuine science" (Parzinger et al. 2006). When and where have you heard a fantastic claim about prehistory?

Sarajevo-born American Semir Osmanagic claims to have discovered a giant pyramid built by an ancient civilization under Visocica Hill, Bosnia. Most scientists doubt his claim.
© Fehim Demir/epa/Corbis

Such figures attracted lots of followers, loyal to their leader. Conquest warfare brought in new territories and subjects. States, in contrast to chiefdoms, can acquire labor and land and hold on to them. States have armies, warfare, developed political hierarchies, law codes, and military force, which can be used in fact or as a threat.

Olmec and Oaxaca were just two among many flamboyant early Mexican chiefdoms that once thrived in the area from the Valley of Mexico to Guatemala. Oaxaca went on to develop a state a bit earlier than the Teotihuacán state of the Valley of Mexico. Oaxaca and other highland areas came to overshadow the Olmec area and the Mesoamerican lowlands in general. By 2500 B.P. (500 B.C.E.), Oaxaca's Zapotec people had developed a distinctive art style, perfected at their capital city of Monte Albán (see Blanton 1999; Marcus and Flannery 1996).

Warfare and State Formation: The Zapotec Case

The first Mesoamerican state, the **Zapotec state,** arose in the Valley of Oaxaca. The city of Monte Albán served as capital of this Zapotec polity for *1,200 years,* between 500 B.C.E. and 700 C.E. The

Zapotec state

The first Mesoamerican state, in the Valley of Oaxaca.

Three of more than 300 carved stones depicting slain war captives at the important archaeological site of Monte Albán, Oaxaca, Mexico. Dated to 500–400 B.C.E., these images originally were set in the Prisoner Gallery of Monte Albán's Building L. This huge display of slain enemies was a form of political and military propaganda. The carved stones warned potential rivals what would happen if they defied Monte Albán.

© DEA/G. Dagliorti/Getty Images

Zapotec polity was a chiefdom from about 500 B.C.E. to 100 B.C.E., and after that a state that lasted 800 years—from 100 B.C.E. to 700 C.E.

As has been noted previously, *warfare* plays a key role in primary state formation. In the Valley of Oaxaca, armed conflict began as village-on-village raiding, with killing, burning, and captive taking but no permanent acquisition of territory (Flannery and Marcus 2003*b*). A monument from the site of San José Mogote, erected no later than 500 B.C.E., is the earliest reliably dated monument with writing in Mesoamerica. It depicts a named, sacrificed captive, likely a rival chief. The first evidence for organized conquest warfare in Oaxaca occurs four centuries later, simultaneously with evidence for state formation. This co-occurrence supports the idea of a causal link between conquest warfare and state formation (Spencer 2003).

As states emerge and grow, they develop an internally specialized, administrative organization—a bureaucracy. Chiefdoms, by contrast, lack this kind of administrative specialization. States have at least four levels of decision making (Wright 1977). The center, or capital, establishes subsidiary administrative centers (Elson 2007). The result is a nested structure of secondary, tertiary, and even quaternary centers. Population size tends to follow this administrative structure. A key difference between chiefdoms and states is that states typically have at least a *four-level* hierarchy of settlements according to both administrative

functions and population size. Chiefdoms have no more than *three levels* (Spencer 2003).

Conquest warfare helps the state build its bureaucracy. An expansive state must send delegates, such as soldiers, governors, and other officials, to subjugate and rule in distant territories. Lacking such bureaucrats, chiefdoms can't do this, which means that the geographic range of chiefly authority is smaller than in a state. According to Spencer (2003), the limit of a chiefdom's range is half a day's travel from its center. States, however, can transcend such limits and carry out long-distance conquests. Archaeological evidence for conquest warfare includes burned and abandoned villages, specialized forts and administrative outposts, and forced changes in the economic, social, and religious behaviors of subjugated peoples.

The conquest of polities in distant regions, coupled with regularized tribute exaction, can bring about a transition from chiefdom to state (Spencer 2003). For such a strategy to succeed (especially when the conquered polities lie more than a half-day's trip away), the conquering state has to send agents to the subjugated areas. Generals and bureaucrats are needed not only to carry out the subjugation but also to maintain long-term control and to manage tribute collection. Given its need to rely on distant representatives, the state's central leadership promotes internal administrative specialization and loyalty. Tribute provides new resources to support this administrative transformation. The conquest of distant polities and bureaucratic growth were integral parts of the process of Zapotec state formation.

Typically, state bureaucracies occupy a group of administrative buildings, especially at the capital. Thus, surrounding the Main Plaza at Monte Albán were specialized buildings, including palaces, temples, and ball courts. Hieroglyphs on one building in Monte Albán's Main Plaza record how outlying areas were acquired. We learn that while the Zapotec state had managed to conquer distant regions to the north, west, and southwest, certain areas to the east and south managed to resist for centuries.

By 30–20 B.C.E., the Zapotec state, from its capital at Monte Albán, presided over a fully developed four-tier settlement hierarchy (see Elson 2007), which it maintained for several hundred years. Eventually, Monte Albán lost its prominence, as other Zapotec centers successfully challenged its authority. After 700 C.E. (formerly A.D. 700), the Zapotec state fragmented into a series of smaller centers, or principalities, alternately vying for supremacy through continued warfare and peaceful alliances through marriage (Flannery and Marcus 2003*a*; Marcus 1989).

States in the Valley of Mexico

During the first century C.E., the Valley (Basin) of Mexico, located in the highlands where Mexico

City now stands, rose to prominence in Meso-american state formation. In this large valley, **Teotihuacán** flourished between 100 and 700 C.E.

The valley is actually a large basin surrounded by mountains; it has rich volcanic soils, but rainfall isn't always reliable. The northern valley, where the huge city and state of Teotihuacán eventually arose, is colder and drier than the south. Frosts limited farming in that northern valley until quick-growing varieties of maize were developed. Until 500 B.C.E., most people lived in the warmer and wetter southern part of the valley, where rainfall made farming possible. After 500 B.C.E., new maize varieties and small-scale irrigation appeared. The population increased and began to spread north (see Carballo 2016).

By 1 C.E., Teotihuacán was a town of 10,000 people. It governed a territory of a few thousand square kilometers and perhaps 50,000 people (Parsons 1974). Teotihuacán's growth reflected its agricultural potential. Perpetual springs permitted irrigation of a large alluvial plain. Rural farmers supplied food for the growing urban population (Clayton 2013).

By this time, a clear **settlement hierarchy** had emerged. This is a ranked series of communities that differ in size, function, and building types. The settlements at the top of the hierarchy were political and religious centers. Those at the bottom were rural villages. We have seen that a four-level settlement hierarchy provides archaeological evidence for state organization.

Along with state organization at Teotihuacán went large-scale irrigation, status differentiation, and complex architecture. Teotihuacán thrived between 100 and 700 C.E. It grew as a planned city built on a grid pattern, with the Pyramid of the Sun at its center. By 500 C.E., the population of Teotihuacán may have reached 125,000, making it larger than imperial Rome. Farmers were one of its diverse specialized groups, along with artisans, merchants, and political, religious, and military personnel (see Clayton 2013; Cowgill 2008).

After 700 C.E., Teotihuacán declined in size and power. By 900 C.E., its population had shrunk to 30,000. Between 900 and 1200 C.E., the Toltec period, the population scattered, and small cities and towns sprang up throughout the valley (see Cowgill 2013). People also left the Valley of Mexico to live in larger cities—like Tula, the Toltec capital—on its edge (see Figure 12.4).

Population increase (including immigration by the ancestors of the Aztecs) and urban growth returned to the Valley of Mexico between 1200 and 1520 C.E. During the **Aztec** period (1325–1520 C.E.) there were several cities, the largest of which—Tenochtitlán, the capital—may have surpassed Teotihuacán at its height (Gonlin and French 2015; Rojas and Smith 2012). A dozen Aztec towns had more than 10,000 people. Fueling this population growth was intensification of agriculture, particularly in the southern part

Teotihuacán is one of the most important archaeological sites in the Americas. In the photo we see the Pyramid of the Sun (back left), Teotihuacán's largest structure, along with the Avenue of the Dead (foreground leading back). At its height around 500 C.E., Teotihuacán was larger than imperial Rome. The mobilization of manual labor to build such a city is one of the costs of state organization.
© Prisma Bildagentur AG/Alamy Stock Photo

of the valley, where the drainage of lake bottoms and swamps added new cultivable land (see Berdan 2013).

Another factor in the renaissance of the Valley of Mexico was trade. The major towns and markets were located on the lakeshores, with easy access to canoe traffic (see Hirth 2016). The Aztec capital stood on an island in the lake. In Tenochtitlán, the production of luxury goods was more prestigious and more highly organized than that of pottery making, basket making, and weaving. Luxury producers, such as stone workers, feather workers, and gold- and silversmiths, occupied a special position in Aztec society. The manufacture of luxury goods for export was an important part of the economy of the Aztec capital (see Garraty 2013).

WHY STATES COLLAPSE

States can disintegrate along the same cleavage lines (e.g., regional political units) that were originally forged together to form the state. Various factors, such as invasion, disease, famine, or prolonged drought, can threaten their economies and political institutions. Citizens might degrade the environment, usually with economic costs (see Jannone 2013). For example, farmers and smelters might cut down trees. Such deforestation promotes erosion and leads to a decline in the water supply. Overuse of land may deplete the soil of the nutrients needed to grow crops.

If factors such as irrigation help create states to begin with, does their decline or failure explain the fall of the state? Irrigation does have costs as well as benefits. In ancient Mesopotamia, irrigation water came from the Tigris and

Teotihuacán
The first Valley of Mexico state (100–700 C.E.); earliest Mesoamerican empire.

settlement hierarchy
Communities with varying size, function, and building types.

Aztec
The last independent Valley of Mexico state (thrived between 1325 and the Spanish Conquest in 1520).

Ruins at Copán, a center of classic Maya royalty in western Honduras.

© DreamPictures/The Image Bank/Getty Images

Euphrates Rivers. Because sediment (silt) had accumulated in those rivers, their beds were higher than the alluvial plain and fields they irrigated. Canals channeled river water as it flowed down into the fields by gravity. As the water evaporated, water-borne mineral salts remained in the fields. This accumulation eventually created a poisonous environment for crops, forcing abandonment of the fields.

The Maya Decline

Generations of scholars have debated the decline of classic Maya civilization around 900 C.E. Classic Maya culture, featuring several competing states, flourished between 300 and 900 C.E. in parts of what are now Mexico, Honduras, El Salvador, Guatemala, and Belize. The ancient Maya are known for their monuments (temples and pyramids), calendars, mathematics, and hieroglyphic writing.

Archaeological clues to Maya decline have been found at Copán, in western Honduras. This classic Maya royal center, the largest site in the southeastern part of the Maya area, covered 29 acres (11.7 hectares). It was built on an artificial terrace overlooking the Copán River. Its rulers inscribed their monuments with accounts of their coronation, their lineage history, and reports of important battles. The Maya dated their monuments with the names of kings and the dates of their reign. One monument at

Copán was intended to be the ruler's throne platform, but only one side had been finished. The monument bears a date, 822 C.E., in a section of unfinished text. Copán has no monuments with later dates. The site probably had been abandoned by 830 C.E.

The environmental factors behind Copán's collapse may have included deforestation, erosion, and soil exhaustion due to overpopulation and overfarming. Hillside farmhouses, in particular, had debris from erosion—probably caused by overfarming of the hillsides. This erosion began as early as 750 C.E.—until these farm sites were abandoned, with some eventually buried by erosion debris (see Jannone 2013).

Food stress and malnutrition were clearly present at Copán, where 80 percent of the buried skeletons display signs of anemia, due to iron deficiency. One skull shows anemia severe enough to have been the cause of death. Even the nobles were malnourished. The skull of one member of the nobility, known to be such from its carved teeth and cosmetic deformation, also has telltale signs of anemia: spongy areas at its rear (Annenberg/CPB Exhibits 2000).

Just as the origins of states, and their causes, are diverse, so are the reasons for state decline. The Maya state was not as powerful as was once assumed; it was fragile and vulnerable. Increased warfare and political competition destabilized many of its dynasties and governments. Archaeologists now stress the role of warfare in Maya state decline. Hieroglyphic texts document increased warfare among many Maya cities. From the period just before the collapse, there is archaeological evidence for increased concern with fortifications and relocation to defensible locations. Archaeologists have evidence of the burning of structures, the projectile points from spears, and some of the bodies of those killed. Some sites were abandoned, with the people fleeing into the forests to occupy perishable huts. (Copán, as we have seen, was depopulated after 822 C.E.) Archaeologists now believe that social, political, and military upheaval and competition had as much as or more to do with the Maya decline and abandonment of cities as did natural environmental factors (Marcus, personal communication).

Formerly, archaeologists tended to explain state origin and decline mainly in terms of natural environmental factors, such as climate change, habitat destruction, and demographic pressure (see Weiss 2005). Archaeologists now see state origins and declines more fully—in social and political terms—because they can read the texts. And the Maya texts document competition and warfare between dynasties jockeying for position and power. Warfare was indeed a creator and a destroyer of ancient chiefdoms and states. What is its role in our own?

for REVIEW

1. States develop to handle regulatory problems as the population grows, social groups proliferate, and the economy gets more complex. Important factors that contribute to state formation include irrigation, warfare, and regional trade. Coastal Peru, a very arid area, illustrates how environmental circumscription, population growth, and warfare may contribute to state formation.

2. A state is a society with a formal, central government and a division of society into classes. The first cities and states, supported by irrigated farming, developed in southern Mesopotamia between 6000 and 5500 B.P. Evidence for early state organization includes monumental architecture, central storehouses, irrigation systems, and written records.

3. The first Middle Eastern towns grew up 10,000 to 9,000 years ago. The first pottery dates back just over 8,000 years. Halafian (7500–6500 B.P.) is a pottery style and the period when the first chiefdoms emerged. Ubaid pottery (7000–6000 B.P.) is associated with advanced chiefdoms and perhaps the earliest states. Most state formation occurred during the Uruk period (6100–5100 B.P.).

4. Based on the status distinctions they include, societies may be divided into egalitarian, ranked, and stratified types. In egalitarian societies, status distinctions are not usually inherited. Ranked societies have hereditary inequality, but they lack stratification. Stratified societies have sharp social divisions—social classes, or *strata*—based on unequal access to wealth and power. Ranked societies with loss of village autonomy are chiefdoms.

5. Mesopotamia's economy was based on craft production, trade, and intensive agriculture. Writing, invented by 5600 B.P., was first used to keep accounts for trade. With the invention of smelting, the Bronze Age began just after 5000 B.P.

6. In northwestern India and Pakistan, the Indus River Valley state flourished from 4600 to 3900 B.P. The first Chinese state, dating to 3750 B.P., was that of the Shang dynasty in northern China. Various states developed in sub-Saharan Africa. The major early states of the Western Hemisphere were in Mesoamerica and Peru.

7. Between 3200 and 3000 B.P. (1200–1000 B.C.E.—formerly B.C.), intense competitive interaction among many chiefdoms in Mesoamerica fueled rapid social change. Some chiefdoms would develop into states (e.g., Oaxaca, Valley of Mexico). Others (e.g., Olmec) would not. In the Valley of Oaxaca, changing military patterns—from village raiding to conquest warfare—played a prominent role in the formation of Mesoamerica's earliest state, the Zapotec state, whose capital was Monte Albán. This city served as the Zapotec capital for 1,200 years, from 500 B.C.E. to 700 C.E. (formerly A.D.). After that, the Zapotec state continued, but in the form of small principalities that fought among themselves until Spanish conquest in the early 16th century C.E. By 1 C.E., the Valley of Mexico had come to prominence. In this large valley in the highlands, Teotihuacán thrived between 100 and 700 C.E. Tenochtitlán, the capital of the Aztec state (1325–1520 C.E.), may have surpassed Teotihuacán at its height.

8. Early states faced various threats: invasion, disease, famine, drought, soil exhaustion, erosion, and the buildup of irrigation salts. States may collapse when they fail to keep social and economic order or to protect themselves against outsiders. The Maya state fell in the face of increased warfare among competing dynasties.

Aztec 225

bronze 218

chiefdom 207

cuneiform 217

egalitarian society 214

empire 209

Halafian 213

Mesopotamia 211

metallurgy 218

polity 208

primary states 208

ranked society 214

settlement hierarchy 225

smelting 218

state 208

stratification 214

Teotihuacán 225

Zapotec state 223

critical thinking

1. This chapter discusses Robert Carneiros's theory of state formation, with special reference to Peru. Do the explanatory factors (e.g., population increase) he identifies always lead to state formation? Discuss those explanatory factors.

2. Imagine yourself an archaeologist trying to identify ancient chiefdoms in the Middle East after excavating Mesoamerican chiefdom sites. What similar and different lines of evidence for ranking and political alliance might you find in the two contexts?

3. How could reviewing the history of state formation prompt us to reexamine our assumptions about what is natural or universal about social organization?

4. Only those ranked societies with loss of village autonomy should be called chiefdoms. What kinds of evidence could archaeologists search for as clues to this loss of autonomy?

5. Based on the evidence from coastal Peru (near the beginning of this chapter) and Oaxaca (near the end of this chapter), what role did warfare play in early state formation?

Method and Theory in Cultural Anthropology

▶ Where and how do cultural anthropologists do fieldwork?

▶ What are some ways of studying modern societies?

▶ What theories have guided anthropologists over the years?

Courtesy of Dr. Priscilla Magrath

Anthropologist Priscilla Magrath of the University of Arizona does ethnographic fieldwork in Indonesia.

understanding OURSELVES

To many, the word *anthropology* may evoke an image of archaeological digs. Remember, however, that anthropology has four subfields, only two of which (archaeology and biological anthropology) require much digging—in the ground, at least. To be sure, cultural anthropologists "dig out" information about lifestyles, just as linguistic anthropologists do about the features of unwritten languages. Traditionally, cultural anthropologists have done a variant on the *Star Trek* theme of seeking out if not new, at least different "life" and "civilizations," sometimes boldly going where no scientist has gone before.

Despite globalization, the cultural diversity under anthropological scrutiny right now may be as great as ever before, because the anthropological universe has expanded to modern nations. Today's cultural anthropologists are as likely to be studying artists in Miami or bankers in Beirut as Trobriand sailors in the South Pacific. Still, we can't forget that anthropology did originate in non-Western, nonindustrial societies. Its research techniques,

especially those subsumed under the label *ethnography,* were developed to deal with small populations. Even when working in modern nations, anthropologists still consider ethnography with small groups to be an excellent way of learning about how people live their lives and make decisions.

For the general public, biological anthropologists and archaeologists tend to be better known than cultural anthropologists because of what they study. One cultural anthropologist was an extremely important public figure when (and before and after) I was in college. Margaret Mead, famed for her work on teen sexuality in Samoa and gender roles in New Guinea, may well be the most famous anthropologist who ever lived. Mead, one of my own professors at Columbia University, appeared regularly on NBC's *The Tonight Show*. In all her venues, including teaching, museum work, TV, anthropological films, popular books, and magazines, Mead helped Americans appreciate the relevance of anthropology to understanding their daily lives. Her work is featured here and elsewhere in this book.

ETHNOGRAPHY: ANTHROPOLOGY'S DISTINCTIVE STRATEGY

Anthropology emerged as a distinctive field of inquiry as its early scholars focused on Native Americans or traveled to distant lands to study small groups of foragers (hunters and gatherers) and cultivators. Traditionally, the process of becoming a cultural anthropologist has required a field experience in another society. Early ethnographers studied small-scale, relatively isolated societies with simple technologies and economies.

Ethnography thus emerged as a research strategy in societies with less social

differentiation than is found in large, modern, industrial nations (see Konopinski 2014; Moore 2012). Traditionally, ethnographers have tried to understand the whole of a particular culture (or, more realistically, as much as they can, given limitations of time and perception). To pursue this goal, ethnographers adopt a free-ranging strategy. The ethnographer moves from setting to setting, place to place, and subject to subject to discover the totality and interconnectedness of social life. Ethnographers draw on varied techniques to piece together a picture of otherwise alien lifestyles. Anthropologists usually employ several (but rarely all) of the techniques discussed next (see also Bernard 2011; Wolcott 2010).

ETHNOGRAPHIC TECHNIQUES

The characteristic *field techniques* of the ethnographer include the following:

1. Direct, firsthand observation of behavior, including *participant observation.*

2. Conversation with varying degrees of formality, from the daily chitchat that helps maintain rapport and provides knowledge about what is going on to prolonged *interviews,* which can be unstructured or structured.

3. The *genealogical method.*

4. Detailed work with *key consultants,* or *informants,* about particular areas of community life.

5. In-depth interviewing, often leading to the collection of *life histories* of particular people (narrators).

6. Problem-oriented research of many sorts.

7. Longitudinal research—the continuous long-term study of an area or a site.

8. Team research—coordinated research by multiple ethnographers.

Observation and Participant Observation

Ethnographers must pay attention to hundreds of details of daily life, seasonal events, and unusual happenings. They should record what they see as they see it. Things never again will seem quite as strange as they do during the first few weeks in the field. Often anthropologists experience culture shock—a creepy and profound feeling of alienation—on arrival at a new field site (see Cohen 2015). Although anthropologists study human diversity, the actual field experience of diversity takes some getting used to, as we see in this chapter's "Appreciating Diversity." The ethnographer eventually grows accustomed to, and accepts as normal, cultural patterns that initially were alien. Staying a bit more than a year in the field allows the ethnographer to repeat the season of his or her arrival, when certain events and processes may have been missed because of initial unfamiliarity and culture shock.

Many ethnographers record their impressions in a personal *diary,* which is kept separate from more formal *field notes.* Later, this record of early impressions will help point out some of the most basic aspects of cultural diversity. Such aspects include distinctive smells, noises people make, how they cover their mouths when they eat, and how they gaze at others. These patterns, which are so basic as to seem almost trivial, are part of what Bronislaw Malinowski called "the imponderabilia

of native life and of typical behavior" (Malinowski 1922/1961, p. 20). These aspects of culture are so fundamental that people take them for granted. They are too basic even to talk about, but the unaccustomed eye of the fledgling ethnographer picks them up. Thereafter, becoming familiar, they fade to the edge of consciousness. I mention my initial impressions of some such imponderabilia of northeastern Brazilian culture in this chapter's "Appreciating Diversity."

Ethnographers strive to establish *rapport,* a good, friendly working relationship based on personal contact, with their hosts. One of ethnography's most characteristic procedures is participant observation, which means that we take part in community life as we study it. As human beings living among others, we cannot be totally impartial and detached observers. We take part in many events and processes we are observing and trying to comprehend. By participating, we may learn why people find such events meaningful, as we see how they are organized and conducted.

In Arembepe, Brazil, I learned about fishing by sailing on the Atlantic with local fishers. I gave Jeep rides to malnourished babies, to pregnant mothers, and once to a teenage girl possessed by a spirit. All those people needed to consult specialists outside the village. I danced on Arembepe's festive occasions, drank libations commemorating new births, and became a godfather to a village girl. Most anthropologists have similar field experiences. The common humanity of the student and the studied, the ethnographer and the research community, makes participant observation inevitable.

Conversation, Interviewing, and Interview Schedules

Participating in local life means that ethnographers constantly talk to people and ask questions. As their knowledge of the local language and culture increases, they understand more. There are several stages in learning a field language. First is the naming phase—asking name after name of the objects around us. Later we are able to pose more complex questions and understand the replies. We begin to understand simple conversations between two villagers. If our language expertise proceeds far enough, we eventually become able to comprehend rapid-fire public discussions and group conversations.

One data-gathering technique I have used in both Arembepe and Madagascar involves an ethnographic survey that includes an interview schedule. During my second summer of fieldwork in Arembepe, my fellow field workers and I attempted to complete an interview schedule in each of that community's 160 households. We entered almost every household (fewer than 5 percent refused to participate) to ask a set of questions on a printed form. Our results provided us with a census and basic information about the village.

Even Anthropologists Get Culture Shock

My first field experience in Arembepe (Brazil) took place between my junior and senior years at New York City's Columbia College, where I was majoring in anthropology. I went to Arembepe as a participant in a now defunct program designed to provide undergraduates with experience doing ethnography—firsthand study of an alien society's culture and social life.

Brought up in one culture, intensely curious about others, anthropologists nevertheless experience culture shock, particularly on their first field trip. *Culture shock* refers to the whole set of feelings about being in an alien setting, and the ensuing reactions. It is a chilly, creepy feeling of alienation, of being without some of the most ordinary, trivial (and therefore basic) cues of one's culture of origin.

As I planned my departure for Brazil that year, I could not know just how naked I would feel without the cloak of my own language and culture. My sojourn in Arembepe would be my first trip outside the United States. I was an urban boy who had grown up in Atlanta, Georgia, and New York City. I had little experience with rural life in my own country, none with Latin America, and I had received only minimal training in the Portuguese language.

New York City direct to Salvador, Bahia, Brazil. Just a brief stopover in Rio de Janeiro; a longer visit would be a reward at the end of fieldwork. As our prop jet approached tropical Salvador, I couldn't believe the whiteness of the sand. "That's not snow, is it?" I remarked to a fellow field team member. . . .

My first impressions of Bahia were of smells— alien odors of ripe and decaying mangoes, bananas, and passion fruit—and of swatting the ubiquitous fruit flies I had never seen before, although I had read extensively about their reproductive behavior in genetics classes. There were strange concoctions of rice, black beans, and gelatinous gobs of unidentifiable meats and floating pieces of skin. Coffee was strong and

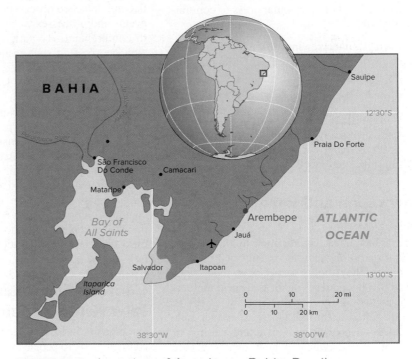

FIGURE 13.1   Location of Arembepe, Bahia, Brazil.

---

interview schedule
A form (guide) used to structure a formal, but personal, interview.

questionnaire
A form used by sociologists to obtain comparable information from respondents.

We wrote down the name, age, and gender of each household member. We gathered data on family type, religion, present and previous jobs, income, expenditures, diet, possessions, and many other items on our eight-page form.

Although we were doing a survey, our approach differed from the survey research done by sociologists and other social scientists working in large, industrial nations. That survey research, discussed on pp. 238–239, involves *sampling* (choosing a small, manageable study group from a larger population). We did not select a partial sample from Arembepe's total population. Instead, we tried to interview in all households

(i.e., to have a total sample). We used an interview schedule rather than a questionnaire. With the **interview schedule,** the ethnographer talks face-to-face with people, asks the questions, and writes down the answers. **Questionnaire** procedures tend to be more impersonal; often the respondent fills in the form. Think of how many times in the past month you have been asked to fill out some kind of the survey, usually online, frequently using a service known as Survey Monkey. Calls to customer service frequently lead to a request that a survey be completed at the end of the call. The ostensible purpose of such surveys is to improve customer service.

sugar crude, and every tabletop had containers for toothpicks and for manioc (cassava) flour to sprinkle, like Parmesan cheese, on anything one might eat. I remember oatmeal soup and a slimy stew of beef tongue in tomatoes. At one meal a disintegrating fish head, eyes still attached, but barely, stared up at me as the rest of its body floated in a bowl of bright orange palm oil. . . .

I only vaguely remember my first day in Arembepe [Figure 13.1]. Unlike ethnographers who have studied remote tribes in the tropical forests of interior South America or the highlands of Papua New Guinea, I did not have to hike or ride a canoe for days to arrive at my field site. Arembepe was not isolated relative to such places, only relative to every other place I had ever been. . . .

I do recall what happened when we arrived. There was no formal road into the village. Entering through southern Arembepe, vehicles simply threaded their way around coconut trees, following tracks left by automobiles that had passed previously. A crowd of children had heard us coming, and they pursued our car through the village streets until we parked in front of our house, near the central square. Our first few days in Arembepe were spent with children following us everywhere. For weeks we had few moments of privacy. Children watched our every move through our living room window. Occasionally one made an incomprehensible remark. Usually they just stood there. . . .

The sounds, sensations, sights, smells, and tastes of life in northeastern Brazil, and in Arembepe, slowly grew familiar. . . . I grew accustomed to this world without Kleenex, in which globs of mucus habitually drooped from the noses of village children whenever a cold passed through Arembepe. A world where, seemingly without effort, women . . . carried 18-liter kerosene cans of water on their heads, where boys sailed kites and sported at catching houseflies in their bare hands, where old women smoked pipes, storekeepers offered cachaça (common rum) at nine in the morning, and men played dominoes on lazy afternoons when there was no fishing. I was visiting a world where human life was oriented toward water—the sea, where men fished, and the lagoon, where women communally washed clothing, dishes, and their own bodies.

Conrad Kottak, with his Brazilian nephew, Guilherme Roxo, on a revisit to Arembepe in 2004.
© Conrad P. Kottak

This description is adapted from my ethnographic study *Assault on Paradise: The Globalization of a Little Community in Brazil,* 4th ed. (New York: McGraw-Hill, 2006).

During the survey process, however, no one ever sees another human being.

In contrast, our goal as ethnographers to obtain a total sample allowed us to meet almost everyone in the village and helped us establish rapport. Decades later, Arembepeiros still talk warmly about how we were interested enough in them to visit their homes and ask them questions. We stood in sharp contrast to the other outsiders the villagers had known, who considered them too poor and backward to be taken seriously.

Like other survey research, however, our interview schedule did gather comparable quantifiable information. It gave us a basis for assessing patterns and exceptions in village life. Our schedules included a core set of questions that were posed to everyone. However, some interesting side issues often came up during the interview, which we would pursue then or later. We followed such leads into many dimensions of village life. One woman, for instance, a midwife, became the key cultural consultant we sought out later when we wanted detailed information about local childbirth. Another woman had done an internship in an Afro-Brazilian cult (*candomblé*) in the city. She still went there regularly to study, dance, and get possessed. She became our candomblé expert.

Kinship and descent are vital social building blocks in nonindustrial cultures. Without writing, genealogical information may be preserved in material culture, such as this totem pole being raised in Metlakatla, Alaska.

© Lawrence Migdale/Science Source

genealogical method
The use of diagrams and symbols to record kin connections.

cultural consultants
People who teach an ethnographer about their culture.

key cultural consultants
Experts on a particular aspect of local life.

Thus, our interview schedule provided a structure that *directed but did not confine* us as researchers. It enabled our ethnography to be both quantitative and qualitative. The quantitative part consisted of the basic information we gathered and later analyzed statistically. The qualitative dimension came from our follow-up questions, open-ended discussions, pauses for gossip, and work with key consultants.

The Genealogical Method

Many of us learn about our ancestry and relatives by tracing our genealogies. Computer programs

Anthropologists such as Christie Kiefer typically form personal relationships with their cultural consultants, such as this Guatemalan weaver.

© Yoram Kahana/Shooting Star

and websites allow us to fill in our "family trees." The **genealogical method** is a well-established ethnographic technique. Kinship is a prominent building block in the social organization of nonindustrial societies, where people live and work each day with their close kin. Anthropologists need to collect genealogical data to understand current social relations and to reconstruct history. In many nonindustrial societies, links through kinship and marriage form the core of social life. Anthropologists even call such cultures "kin-based societies." Everyone is related and spends most of his or her time with relatives. Rules of behavior associated with particular kin relations are basic to everyday life. Marriage also is crucial in organizing such societies, because strategic marriages between villages, tribes, and clans create political alliances.

Key Cultural Consultants

The term **cultural consultants,** or *informants,* refers to individuals the ethnographer gets to know in the field, the people who teach him or her about their culture. Every community has people who by accident, experience, talent, or training can provide the most complete or useful information about particular aspects of life. These people are **key cultural consultants,** also called *key informants.* In Ivato, the Betsileo village in Madagascar where I spent most of my time, a man named Rakoto was particularly knowledgeable about village history. However, when I asked him to work with me on a genealogy of the 50 to 60 people buried in the village tomb, he called in his cousin Tuesdaysfather, who knew more about that subject. Tuesdaysfather had survived an epidemic of influenza that ravaged Madagascar, along with much of the world, around 1919. Immune to the disease himself, Tuesdaysfather had the grim job of burying his kin as they died. He kept track of everyone buried in the tomb. Tuesdaysfather helped me with the tomb genealogy. Rakoto joined him in telling me personal details about the deceased villagers.

Life Histories

In nonindustrial societies as in our own, individual personalities, interests, and abilities vary. Some villagers prove to be more interested in the ethnographer's work and are more helpful, interesting, and pleasant than others are. Anthropologists develop likes and dislikes in the field as we do at home. Often, when we find someone unusually interesting, we collect his or her **life history.** This recollection of a lifetime of experiences provides a more intimate and personal cultural portrait than would be possible otherwise. Life histories, which may be audio or video recorded for later review and analysis, reveal how specific people perceive, react to, and contribute to changes that affect their lives. Such accounts can illustrate diversity, which exists within any community, because the focus is on how different people interpret and deal with some of the same problems. Many ethnographers include the collection of life histories as an important part of their research strategy.

Problem-Oriented Ethnography

Although anthropologists remain interested in the totality of people's lives in a particular community or society, it is impossible to study everything. As a result, contemporary ethnographic fieldwork generally is aimed at investigating one or more specific topics or problems (see Murchison 2010; Sunstein and Chiseri-Strater 2012). Topics that an ethnographer might choose to investigate include marriage practices, gender roles, religion, and economic change. Examples of problem-oriented research include various impact studies done by anthropologists, such as the impact on a particular community or society of television, the Internet, education, drought, a hurricane, or a change in government.

In researching a specific problem, today's anthropologists often need to look beyond local people for relevant data. Government agencies or international organizations may have gathered information on such matters as climate and weather conditions, population density, and settlement patterns. Often, however, depending on the problem they are investigating, anthropologists have to do their own measurements of such variables as field size, yields, dietary quantities, or time allocation. Information of interest to ethnographers extends well beyond what local people can and do tell us. In an increasingly interconnected and complicated world, local people lack knowledge about many factors that may affect their lives— for example, international terrorism, warfare, or the exercise of power from regional, national, and international centers (see Sanjek 2014).

Longitudinal Research

Geography limits anthropologists much less now than in the past, when it could take months to reach a field site and return visits were rare. Airplanes are a lot faster than boats and ships. Modern transportation networks have allowed anthropologists to widen the area of their research and to return repeatedly. Ethnographic reports now routinely include data from two or more field stays. **Longitudinal research** is the long-term study of a community, region, society, culture, or other unit.

One of the best examples of longitudinal research is the study of Gwembe District, Zambia (see Figure 13.2). Planned in 1956 to be a longitudinal project by Elizabeth Colson and Thayer Scudder, research at Gwembe has continued over the years with fieldwork by Colson, Scudder, and their associates of various nationalities. Thus, as is often the case with longitudinal research, the Gwembe study also illustrates team research—coordinated research by multiple ethnographers (Colson and Scudder 1975; Scudder and Colson 1980). The researchers have studied four villages, in different areas, for over 60 years. Periodic village censuses have provided basic data on population, economy, kinship, and religious behavior. Censused people who have moved are traced and interviewed to see how their lives compare with those of people who have stayed in the villages.

An early focus of research was the impact of a large hydroelectric dam, which led to the forced resettlement of many Gwembe residents. That dam also spurred road building and other activities that brought the people of Gwembe in closer touch with the rest of Zambia. In their subsequent research Scudder and Colson (1980) examined how education provided access to new opportunities as it also widened a social gap between people

life history
Of a key consultant; a personal portrait of someone's life in a culture.

longitudinal research
Long-term study, usually based on repeated visits.

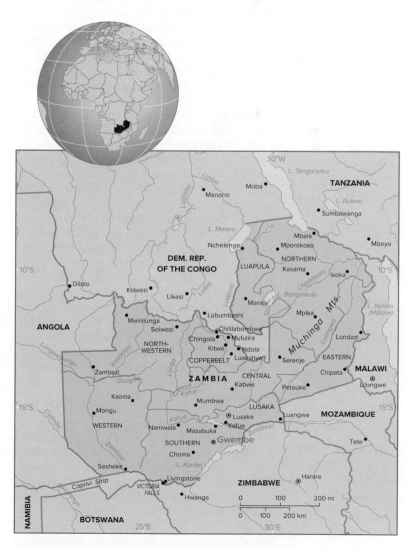

FIGURE 13.2 Location of Gwembe in Zambia.

with different educational levels. A third study examined a change in brewing and drinking patterns, including a rise in alcoholism, in relation to changing markets, transportation, and exposure to town values (Colson and Scudder 1988). Colson, now in her nineties and retired from the University of California at Berkeley, where she holds the title of Professor Emerita, has moved to the Gwembe district, where this remarkable project continues.

Team Research

My own field site of Arembepe, Bahia, Brazil, where research began in 1962, provides another example of longitudinal research, which, as mentioned, is frequently team research as well. Arembepe first entered the world of anthropology as a field-team village in the 1960s. It was one of four sites for the now defunct Columbia-Cornell-Harvard-Illinois Summer Field Studies Program in Anthropology. For at least three years, that program sent a total of about 20 undergraduates annually, the author included, to do summer research abroad. We were stationed in rural communities in four countries: Brazil, Ecuador, Mexico, and Peru. See this chapter's "Appreciating Diversity" for information on how a novice undergraduate ethnographer perceived Arembepe.

Since my wife, Isabel Wagley Kottak, and I first studied Arembepe in the 1960s, it has become a longitudinal field site, where many researchers have monitored various aspects of change and development. Arembepe, now a small city, illustrates the process of globalization at the local level. Its economy, religion, and social life have been transformed (see Kottak 2006).

Brazilian and American researchers worked with us on team research projects during the 1980s (on the impact of television) and the 1990s (on ecological awareness and environmental risk perception). Students from various universities have drawn on our baseline information from the 1960s in their recent studies in Arembepe. Their topics have included standards of physical attractiveness, family planning and changing female reproductive strategies, conversion to Protestantism, and changing food habits in relation to globalization. Arembepe is thus a site where various field workers have worked as members of a longitudinal, multigenerational team. The more recent researchers have built on prior contacts and findings to increase knowledge about how local people meet and manage new circumstances. Most recently, in 2013–2014, researchers gathered information to update our 1980s research on media. Our original focus was on television, but the project has expanded to include the Internet and other new media, including the impact of social media.

emic
A research strategy focusing on local explanations and meanings.

etic
A research strategy emphasizing the ethnographer's explanations and categories.

ETHNOGRAPHIC PERSPECTIVES

Emic and Etic

One goal of ethnography is to discover local (native) views, beliefs, and perceptions, which may be compared with the ethnographer's own observations and conclusions. In the field, ethnographers typically combine two perspectives, the emic (native-oriented) and the etic (scientist-oriented). These terms, derived from linguistics, have been applied to ethnography by various anthropologists. Marvin Harris (1968/2001*b*) popularized the following meanings of the terms: An **emic** perspective is concerned with how local people think. How do they perceive, categorize, and explain things? What are their rules for behavior? What has meaning for them? The ethnographer seeks to understand the "native viewpoint," relying on local people to explain things and to say whether something is significant or not.

With the **etic** perspective, the focus shifts from local observations, categories, explanations, and interpretations to those of the anthropologist. Members of a culture often are too involved in what they are doing to interpret their culture impartially. Operating etically, the ethnographer emphasizes what he or she (the observer) notices and considers important. As a trained scientist, the ethnographer should try to bring an objective and comprehensive viewpoint to the study of other cultures. Of course, the ethnographer, like any other scientist, is also a human being with cultural blinders that prevent complete objectivity. As in

Janet Dunn, one of many anthropologists who have worked in Arembepe. Her study focused on family planning and female reproductive strategies. Where is Arembepe, and what kinds of research have been done there?
© Christopher M. O'Leary

other sciences, proper training can reduce, but not totally eliminate, the observer's bias. But anthropologists do have special training to compare behavior in different societies.

What are some examples of emic versus etic perspectives? Consider our holidays. For North Americans, Thanksgiving Day has special significance. In our view (emically) it is a unique cultural celebration that commemorates particular historical themes. But a wider, etic, perspective sees Thanksgiving as just one more example of the postharvest festivals held in many societies. Another example: Local people (including many Americans) may believe that chills and drafts cause colds, which scientists know are caused by germs. In cultures that lack the germ theory of disease, illnesses are emically explained by various causes, ranging from spirits to ancestors to witches. *Illness* refers to a culture's (emic) perception and explanation of bad health, whereas *disease* refers to the scientific (etic) explanation of poor health, involving known pathogens.

Ethnographers typically combine emic and etic perspectives in their fieldwork. The statements, perceptions, categories, and opinions of local people help ethnographers understand how cultures work. Local beliefs also are interesting and valuable in themselves. However, people often fail to admit, or even recognize, certain causes and consequences of their behavior. This is as true of North Americans as it is of people in other societies.

Expansion in Analytic Scale

The previous sections on longitudinal and team research illustrate an important shift in cultural anthropology. Traditional ethnographic research focused on a single community or "culture," which was treated as more or less isolated and unique in time and space. The shift has been toward a wider and larger scale of analysis that includes flows (now global in scope) of people, technology, images, and information. The study of such flows and linkages is now an important part of anthropological analysis. And reflecting today's world—in which people, images, and information move about as never before—fieldwork must be more flexible and on a larger scale. Ethnography is increasingly multitimed and multisited (see Howell and Talle 2012). Malinowski could focus on Trobriand culture and spend most of his field time in a particular community. Nowadays we cannot afford to ignore, as Malinowski did, the "outsiders" who increasingly impinge on the places we study (e.g., migrants, refugees, terrorists, warriors, tourists, developers). Integral to our analyses now are the external organizations and forces (e.g., governments, businesses, nongovernmental organizations) laying claim to land, people, and resources throughout the world.

Anthropologists increasingly study people in motion. Examples include people living on or near national borders, nomads, seasonal migrants, homeless and displaced people, immigrants, and refugees (see DeLeon 2015; Lugo 1997, 2008). As fieldwork changes, with less and less of a spatially set field, what can we take from traditional ethnography? Gupta and Ferguson correctly cite the "characteristically anthropological emphasis on daily routine and lived experience" (1997*a*, p. 5). The treatment of communities as discrete entities may be a thing of the past. However, "anthropology's traditional attention to the close observation of particular lives in particular places" has an enduring importance (Gupta and Ferguson 1997*b*, p. 25). The method of close observation helps distinguish cultural anthropology from sociology and survey research (see pp. 238–239).

Online Ethnography

The relatively recent creation of virtual worlds has attracted contemporary ethnographers to venture into online communities. Tom Boellstorff, Bonnie Nardi, Celia Pearce, and T. L. Taylor offer a handbook for fieldwork in virtual worlds (2012). All four have researched gaming-oriented online environments, including *Second Life, World of Warcraft, Dreamscape, There.com,* and *Myst Online: Uru Live.* Ethnographers used various techniques in studying these virtual worlds. Most important has been participant observation; the ethnographic researchers became skilled players as they observed the online environment and the interactions within it.

Each virtual world has developed its own culture, which includes rules and governance, customary practices and events, social roles and modes of interaction, and power differentials. When *Uru Live* was discontinued in 2008, Uru refugees moved on to other virtual worlds, where they have created and retain a strong ethnic Uru identity. Although virtual environments are created by software designers, those who enter and thrive in these worlds can innovate within the constraints set by "the system"—either the software program or other participants. Within these worlds, the online ethnographers have observed and described various forms of play, performance, creativity, and ritual.

Virtual worlds have been heavily influenced by works of science fiction and fantasy. Early games owed a debt to the imaginary world of Middle Earth created by J. R. R. Tolkien, of *The Hobbit* and *The Lord of the Rings* fame. Online worlds are sophisticated places of imagination with their own species, artifacts, characters, and customs. The avatar is the representation of self in a virtual world. People in cyberspace can have multiple identities, which often contrast—in gender, for example—with their real-world identities. A person's multiple avatars are known as alts—alternative identities or personalities.

An online community: Visitors play World of Warcraft, a popular multiplayer online role-playing game, at the 2014 Gamescom trade fair in Cologne, Germany. Gamescom, held annually, is the world's largest gaming convention.

© Sascha Steinbach/Getty Images News/Getty Images

survey research
The study of society through sampling, statistical analysis, and impersonal data collection.

sample
A smaller study group chosen to represent a larger population.

random sample
A sample in which all population members have an equal statistical chance of inclusion.

variables
Attributes that differ from one person or case to the next.

The online ethnographer sometimes moves offline to visit players in their real-world setting (e.g., a home or an Internet café). In some cases, ethnographers have traveled abroad to see how a given game is played in different countries and how real-world culture influences participation in the virtual world. There are virtual world fan conventions, which the ethnographer may attend. Interviews can be conducted online and/or offline in a participant's virtual or real-world home. Informal conversations online reveal what players are thinking about as they play. To understand the social organization of their virtual field site, ethnographers may draw diagrams of social relations, similar to genealogies drawn during real-world fieldwork. Timelines are useful for understanding

the succession of virtual events such as dances, festivals, or auctions. Brief site drop-ins can be used to respond to instant messages, keep up with announcements, and find out when players typically log in. Virtual research offers various means of record keeping, note taking, and recording typical of the online environment. These include chat logs and screenshots, as well as audio and video recording.

This section has summarized some features of online research as discussed by Boellstorff and his coauthors (2012). Readers interested in doing virtual world fieldwork should consult that handbook.

SURVEY RESEARCH

As anthropologists work increasingly in large-scale societies, they have developed innovative ways of blending ethnography and survey research (Fricke 1994). Before examining such combinations of field methods, let's consider survey research and the main differences between survey research and ethnography. Working mainly in large, populous nations, sociologists, political scientists, and economists have developed and refined the **survey research** design, which involves sampling, impersonal data collection, and statistical analysis. Survey research usually draws a **sample** (a manageable study group) from a much larger population. By studying a properly selected and representative sample, social scientists can make accurate inferences, or at least good guesses, about the larger population.

In smaller-scale societies and communities, ethnographers get to know most of the people. Given the greater size and complexity of nations, survey research can't help being more impersonal. Survey researchers call the people they study *respondents*. These are people who respond to questions during a survey. Sometimes survey researchers interview their respondents directly—in person or by phone. Respondents may be asked to fill out a questionnaire, written or online. A survey may be mailed or e-mailed to randomly selected sample members. In a **random sample,** all members of the population have an equal statistical chance of being chosen for inclusion. A random sample is selected by randomizing procedures, such as tables of random numbers, which are found in many statistics textbooks.

Probably the most familiar example of sampling is political polling. An ever increasing number of organizations now gather information designed to estimate outcomes and to determine what kinds of people voted for which candidates. During sampling, researchers gather information about age, gender, education, religion, occupation, income, and political party preference. These characteristics (**variables**—attributes that vary among members of a sample or population) are known to influence political decisions.

On November 1, 2010, in China's Shandong Province, census takers gathered personal information from a family during the Sixth National Population Census. From November 1 to November 10, more than six million census takers visited over 400 million households across the country.

© Imaginechina/Corbis

ETHNOGRAPHY (TRADITIONAL)	SURVEY RESEARCH
Studies whole, functioning communities	Studies a small sample of a larger population
Usually is based on firsthand fieldwork, during which information is collected after rapport, based on personal contact, is established	Often is conducted with little or no personal contact between study subjects and researchers, as interviews are frequently conducted in printed form, over the phone, or online
Traditionally is interested in all aspects of local life (holistic)	Usually focuses on a small number of variables (e.g., factors that influence voting) rather than on the totality of people's lives
Traditionally has been conducted in nonindustrial, small-scale societies, where people often do not read and write	Typically is carried out in modern nations, where most people are literate, permitting respondents to fill in their own questionnaires
Makes little use of statistics, because the communities being studied tend to be small, with little diversity besides that based on age, gender, and individual personality variation	Depends heavily on statistical analyses to make inferences regarding a large and diverse population, based on data collected from a small subset of that population

Many more variables affect social identities, experiences, and activities in a modern nation than in the small communities where ethnography grew up. In contemporary North America, hundreds of factors influence our behavior and attitudes. These social predictors include our religion; where we grew up; and our parents' professions, ethnic origins, political leanings, and income levels.

Ethnography can be used to supplement and fine-tune survey research. Anthropologists can transfer the personal, firsthand techniques of ethnography to a variety of settings. A combination of survey research and ethnography can provide new perspectives on life in **complex societies** (large and populous societies with social stratification and central governments). Preliminary ethnography also can help develop culturally appropriate questions for inclusion in surveys. Recap 13.1 contrasts traditional ethnography with elements of survey research.

In any complex society, many predictor variables (*social indicators*) influence behavior and opinions. Because we must be able to detect, measure, and compare the influence of social indicators, many contemporary anthropological studies have a statistical foundation. Even in rural fieldwork, anthropologists increasingly use samples, gather quantitative data, and use statistics to interpret them (see Bernard 2011, 2013). Quantifiable information may permit a more precise assessment of similarities and differences among communities. Statistical analysis can support and round out an ethnographic account of local social life.

However, in the best studies, the hallmark of ethnography remains: Anthropologists enter the community and get to know the people. They participate in local activities, networks, and associations. They watch the effects of national and international policies on local life.

The ethnographic method and the emphasis on personal relationships in social research are valuable gifts that cultural anthropology brings to the study of any society.

DOING ANTHROPOLOGY RIGHT AND WRONG: ETHICAL ISSUES

The anthropologist Clyde Kluckhohn (1944) saw a key public service role for anthropology. It could provide a "scientific basis for dealing with the crucial dilemma of the world today: how can peoples of different appearance, mutually unintelligible languages, and dissimilar ways of life get along peaceably together?" Many anthropologists never would have chosen their profession had they doubted that anthropology had the capacity to enhance human welfare. Because we live in a world full of failed states, unrest, war, and terrorism, we must consider the proper role of anthropologists in studying such phenomena.

Anthropologists can't study things simply because they happen to be interesting or of value to science—or even because they may benefit the public. Ethical issues must also be a prime consideration. Working internationally and in the context of cultural diversity, different ethical codes and value systems will meet, and often challenge one another (see Fluehr-Loban 2013; Whiteford and Trotter 2008).

Anthropologists must be sensitive to cultural differences and aware of procedures and standards in the host country (the place where the research takes place). Researchers must *inform* officials and colleagues about the purpose, funding, and likely results of their research. **Informed consent**

complex societies
Large, populous societies (e.g., nations) with social stratification and central governments.

informed consent
An agreement to take part in research—after having been informed about its purpose, nature, procedures, and possible impacts.

should be obtained from anyone who provides information or who might be affected by the research.

Anthropologists should try to (1) include host country colleagues in their research planning, (2) establish collaborative relationships with host country institutions, (3) include host country colleagues in dissemination, including publication, of the research results, and (4) ensure that something is "given back" to the host country. For example, research equipment stays in the host country, or funding is sought for host country colleagues to do research, attend international meetings, or visit foreign institutions.

The Code of Ethics

The Code of Ethics of the American Anthropological Association (AAA) recognizes that anthropologists have obligations to their scholarly field, to the wider society, and to the human species, other species, and the environment (see Piemmons and Barker 2015). The anthropologist's primary obligation is to *do no harm* to the people being studied (see Borofsky and Hutson 2016). The stated aim of the AAA code is to offer guidelines and to promote discussion and education, rather than to investigate possible misconduct. Two of the code's key points are as follows: (1) anthropologists should inform all parties affected by their research about its nature, goals, procedures, potential impacts, and source(s) of funding (and obtain their consent based on the information provided), and (2) researchers should establish proper relationships with the countries and communities where they work. The full AAA Code of Ethics, as revised in 2012, can be found at the following website: http://ethics.aaanet.org/category/statement/.

Anthropologists and Terrorism

The AAA has deemed it of "paramount importance" that anthropologists study the roots of terrorism and violence. How should such studies be conducted? What ethical issues might arise?

Consider a Pentagon program, Project Minerva, initiated late in the (George W.) Bush administration, designed to draw on social science expertise in dealing with national security threats. Project Minerva sought scholars to translate original documents captured in Iraq, study political shifts in China, and explain the resurgence of the Taliban in Afghanistan (Cohen 2008). Project Minerva and related programs raised concerns that governments might use anthropological knowledge in ethically problematic ways. Government policies and military operations have the potential to harm the people anthropologists study.

More recently, anthropologists have been especially critical of the Pentagon's Human Terrain System (HTS) program. Launched in February 2007, HTS has embedded anthropologists and other social scientists in military teams in Iraq and Afghanistan. On October 31, 2007, the AAA Executive Board issued a statement of disapproval of HTS—outlining how HTS violates the AAA Code of Ethics. (See http://www.aaanet.org/about/policies/statements/human-terrain-system-statement.cfm.) The board noted that HTS places

A member of a U.S. Army Human Terrain Team, left, talks (through an interpreter) to local people at a market in Basra, Iraq, in June 2009. What's problematic about anthropologists' participation in such projects?
U.S. Air Force photo by Staff Sgt. Chrissy Best/Released

anthropologists, as contractors with the U.S. military, in war zones, where they are charged with collecting cultural and social data for use by the military. The ethical concerns raised by these activities include the following:

1. It may be impossible for anthropologists in war zones to identify themselves as anthropologists, as distinct from military personnel. This constrains their ethical responsibility as anthropologists to disclose who they are and what they are doing.

2. HTS anthropologists are asked to negotiate relations among several groups, including local populations and the military units in which they are embedded. Their responsibilities to their units may conflict with their obligations to the local people they study or consult. This may interfere with the obligation, stipulated in the AAA Code of Ethics, to do no harm.

3. In an active war zone, it is difficult for local people to give informed consent without feeling coerced to provide information. As a result, "voluntary informed consent" (as stipulated in the AAA Code of Ethics) is compromised.

4. Information supplied by HTS anthropologists to military field commanders could help target specific groups for military action. Such use of fieldwork-derived information would violate the AAA Code of Ethics stipulation to do no harm to people.

5. The identification of anthropology and anthropologists with the U.S. military may indirectly (through suspicion of guilt by association) endanger the research, and even the personal safety, of other anthropologists and their consultants throughout the world.

What do you think about anthropologists' proper role in studying terrorism and war?

THEORY IN ANTHROPOLOGY OVER TIME

Anthropology has various fathers and mothers. The fathers include Lewis Henry Morgan, Sir Edward Burnett Tylor, Franz Boas, and Bronislaw Malinowski. The mothers include Ruth Benedict and Margaret Mead. Some of the fathers might be classified better as grandfathers, since one, Franz Boas, was the intellectual father of Mead and Benedict, and since what is known now as Boasian anthropology arose mainly in opposition to the 19th-century evolutionism of Morgan and Tylor.

My goal in the remainder of this chapter is to survey the major theoretical perspectives that have characterized anthropology since its emergence in the second half of the 19th century (see also Erickson and Murphy 2013; McGee and Warms 2012; Moberg 2013; Moore 2012). Evolutionary perspectives, especially those associated with Morgan and Tylor, dominated 19th-century anthropology. The early 20th century witnessed various reactions to 19th-century evolutionism. In Great Britain, functionalists such as Malinowski and Alfred Reginald Radcliffe-Brown abandoned the speculative historicism of the evolutionists and instead did studies of living societies. In the United States, Boas and his followers rejected the search for evolutionary stages in favor of a historical approach that traced borrowing and the spread of culture traits across geographic areas. Functionalists and Boasians alike saw cultures as integrated and patterned.

Nineteenth-Century Evolutionism

Let's begin this survey of anthropology's history with Morgan (United States) and Tylor (Great Britain), both of whom wrote classic books during the 19th century. Lewis Henry Morgan, although an important founder of anthropology, was not himself a professionally trained anthropologist. Rather, he was a lawyer in upper New York state who was fond of visiting a nearby Seneca reservation and learning about the tribe's history and customs. He wrote about the Seneca and other Iroquois tribes in his book *League of the Ho-dé-no-sau-nee or Iroquois* (1851/1966). This work, anthropology's earliest ethnography, was based on occasional rather than protracted fieldwork. Through his fieldwork, and his friendship with Ely Parker, an educated Iroquois man, Morgan was able to describe the social, political, religious, and economic principles of Iroquois life, including the history of their confederation. He laid out the structural principles on which Iroquois society was based. Morgan also used his skills as a lawyer to help the Iroquois in their fight with the Ogden Land Company, which was attempting to seize their lands.

Morgan's second influential book, *Ancient Society* (1877/1963), was a theoretical treatise rather than an ethnography. *Ancient Society* is a key example of 19th-century evolutionism applied to society. Morgan assumed that human society had evolved through a series of stages, which he called savagery, barbarism, and civilization. He subdivided savagery and barbarism into three substages each: lower, middle, and upper savagery and lower, middle, and upper barbarism. In Morgan's scheme, the earliest humans lived in lower savagery, with a subsistence based on fruits and nuts. In middle savagery, people started fishing and gained control over fire. Upper savagery was marked by the invention of the bow and arrow. Lower barbarism began when humans started making pottery. Middle barbarism in the Old World depended on the domestication of plants and animals, and in the Americas on irrigated

The early American anthropologist Lewis Henry Morgan described lacrosse (shown here) as one of the six games played by the tribes of the Iroquois nation, whose League he described in a famous book (1851/1966).
© Bettmann/Corbis

In his two-volume work, *Primitive Culture* (1871/1958), Tylor offered an influential and enduring definition of culture (see the chapter "Culture" in this book) and proposed it as a topic to be studied scientifically. The second volume of *Primitive Culture*, titled *Primitive Religion*, offered an evolutionary approach to the anthropology of religion. Like Morgan, Tylor proposed a unilinear path—from animism to polytheism, then monotheism, and finally science. In Tylor's view, religion would retreat when science provided better explanations. Both Tylor and Morgan were interested in *survivals*, practices that survive in contemporary society from earlier evolutionary stages. The belief in ghosts today, for example, would represent a survival from the stage of animism—the belief in spiritual beings. Survivals were taken as evidence that a particular society had passed through earlier evolutionary stages.

Historical Particularism

Franz Boas is the founder of American four-field anthropology. His book *Race, Language, and Culture* (1940/1966) is a collection of essays on those key topics. Boas contributed to cultural, biological, and linguistic anthropology. His biological studies of European immigrants to the United States revealed and measured phenotypical plasticity. The children of immigrants differed physically from their parents not because of genetic change but because they had grown up in a different environment. Boas showed that human biology was plastic. It could be changed by the environment, including cultural forces. Boas and his students worked hard to demonstrate that biology (including race) did not determine culture. In her important book, *Race, Science, and Politics,* Ruth Benedict (1940) stressed the idea that people of many races have contributed to major historical advances.

In his ethnographic fieldwork, Boas studied language and culture among Native Americans, most notably the Kwakiutl of the North Pacific coast of North America. Boas and his many influential students at New York's Columbia University took issue with 19th-century evolutionism on many counts, including the idea of a single, preordained evolutionary path. The Boasians argued that a particular cultural feature, for example, totemism, did not follow a single path of development but could arise for many reasons. Their position was one of **historical particularism.** Because the particular histories of totemism in societies A, B, and C had all been different, those forms of totemism had different causes. Totemism might look the same in all these cases, but each case was actually unique, because it had its own, separate and distinct, history. Any cultural form, from totemism to clan organization, could develop, the Boasians believed, for all sorts of reasons.

unilinear evolutionism

The (19th-century) idea of a single line or path of cultural development.

agriculture. Iron smelting and the use of iron tools ushered in upper barbarism. Civilization, finally, came about with the invention of writing.

Morgan's evolutionism is known as **unilinear evolutionism,** because he assumed there was one line or path along which all societies evolved. Any society in upper barbarism, for example, had to include in its history, in order, periods of lower, middle, and upper savagery, and then lower and middle barbarism. Furthermore, Morgan believed that the indigenous societies that had managed to survive into the 19th century could be viewed as, in a sense, "living fossils," which could be placed in the various stages. Some had not advanced beyond upper savagery. Others had made it to middle barbarism, while others had attained civilization.

Morgan's critics have disputed various elements of his scheme, including such loaded terms as "savagery" and "barbarism," and the particular criteria he used for each stage. Also, Morgan erred in assuming that societies could follow only one evolutionary path. In fact, societies have followed multiple developmental paths.

Like Morgan, Sir Edward Burnett Tylor came to anthropology through personal experience rather than through formal training. In 1855, he left England to travel to Mexico and Central America, where he began what turned out to be a lifelong investigation of unfamiliar cultures. Returning to England, Tylor continued his study of the customs and beliefs of non-Western peoples—both contemporary and prehistoric. He wrote a series of books that established his reputation, leading to his eventual appointment as the first professor of anthropology at Oxford University.

historical particularism

(Boas) The idea that histories are not comparable; diverse paths can lead to the same cultural result.

Franz Boas, founder of American four-field anthropology, studied the Kwakwaka'wakw, or Kwakiutl, in British Columbia (BC), Canada. The photo above shows Boas posing for a museum model of a Kwakiutl dancer. The photo on the right is a still from a film by anthropologist Aaron Glass titled In *Search of the Hamat'sa: A Tale of Headhunting* (DER distributor). It shows a real Kwakiutl dancer, Marcus Alfred, performing the same Hamat'sa (or "Cannibal Dance"), which is a vital part of an important Kwakiutl ceremony. The U'mista Cultural Centre in Alert Bay, BC (www.umista.org) owns the rights to the video clip of the Hamat'sa featuring Marcus Alfred.

Left: © Science Source; right: Used with permission of Dr. Aaron Glass and U'mista Cultural Centre in Alert Bay, BC

To explain *cultural generalities* (cultural traits that are shared by some but not all societies), 19th-century evolutionists had stressed independent invention: People in many areas had come up with the same cultural solution to a common problem. Agriculture, for example, was invented several times. The Boasians, while not denying independent invention, stressed the importance of diffusion, or borrowing, among cultures. The analytic units they used to study diffusion were the culture trait, the trait complex, and the culture area. A culture trait was something like a bow and arrow. A trait complex was the hunting pattern that went along with it. A culture area was based on the diffusion of traits and trait complexes across a particular geographic area, such as the Plains, the Southwest, or the North Pacific coast of North America. Such areas often had environmental boundaries that limited the spread of culture traits beyond that area. For the Boasians, historical particularism and diffusion were complementary. As culture traits diffused, they developed their particular histories as they entered and moved through particular societies.

Historical particularism was based on the idea that each element of culture, such as the culture trait or trait complex, had its own distinctive history and that social forms (such as totemism in different societies) that might look similar were far from identical because of their different histories. Historical particularism rejected comparison and generalization in favor of an individuating historical approach. In this rejection, historical particularism stands in contrast to most of the approaches that have followed it (see Salzman 2012).

Functionalism

Another challenge to evolutionism (as well as to historical particularism) came from Great Britain. *Functionalism* postponed the search for origins (whether through evolution or through diffusion) and instead focused on the role of culture traits and practices in contemporary society. The two main strands of **functionalism** are associated, respectively, with Bronislaw Malinowski, a Polish anthropologist who taught mainly in Great Britain, and the British anthropologist Alfred Reginald Radcliffe-Brown.

functionalism
An approach that focuses on the role (function) of sociocultural practices in social systems.

Malinowski
Both Malinowski and Radcliffe-Brown focused on the present rather than on historical reconstruction. Malinowski did pioneering fieldwork among living people. Usually considered the father of ethnography by virtue of his years of fieldwork in the Trobriand Islands, Malinowski was a functionalist in two senses. In the first, rooted in his ethnography, he believed that all customs and institutions in society were integrated and interrelated, so that if one changed, others would change as well. Each, then, was a *function* of the others. A corollary of this belief was that an ethnographer could begin anywhere and eventually

get at the rest of the culture. Thus, a study of Trobriand fishing eventually would lead the ethnographer to study the entire economic system, the role of magic and religion, myth, trade, and kinship. The second strand of Malinowski's functionalism is known as *needs functionalism*. Malinowski (1944) believed that humans had a set of universal biological needs, and that customs developed to fulfill those needs. The function of any practice was the role it played in satisfying those universal biological needs, such as the need for food, sex, shelter, and so on.

Radcliffe-Brown and Structural Functionalism

According to Radcliffe-Brown (1962/1965), although history is important, anthropologists could never hope to discover the histories of people without writing. He trusted neither evolutionary nor diffusionist reconstructions. Viewing all historical statements about nonliterate peoples as merely conjectural, Radcliffe-Brown urged anthropologists to focus on the role that particular practices play in the life of societies today. For example, in a famous essay Radcliffe-Brown (1962/1965) examined the prominent role of the mother's brother among the Ba Thonga of Mozambique. An evolutionist priest previously had explained the special role of the mother's brother in this patrilineal society as a survival from a time when the descent rule had been matrilineal. (In a patrilineal society, people belong to their father's group, whereas in a matrilineal society they belong to their mother's group. The unilinear evolutionists believed that all human societies had passed through a matrilineal stage before becoming patrilineal.) Because Radcliffe-Brown believed that the history of the Ba Thonga could only be conjectural, he explained the special role

of the mother's brother with reference to the institutions of present rather than past Ba Thonga society. Radcliffe-Brown advocated that anthropology be a **synchronic** rather than a **diachronic** science, that is, that it study societies as they exist today (synchronic, at one time) rather than across time (diachronic).

The term *structural functionalism* is associated with Radcliffe-Brown and Edward Evan Evans-Pritchard, another prominent British social anthropologist. The latter is famous for many books, including *The Nuer* (1940), an ethnographic classic that laid out very clearly the structural principles that organized Nuer society in what is now South Sudan. According to structural functionalism, customs (social practices) function to preserve the social structure. In Radcliffe-Brown's view, the *function* of any practice is the role it plays in maintaining the system of which it is a part. That system has a structure whose parts work (function) to maintain the whole. Radcliffe-Brown saw social systems as comparable to anatomical and physiological systems. The function of organs and physiological processes is their role in keeping the body running smoothly. So, too, he thought, did customs, practices, social roles, and behavior function to keep the social system running smoothly. Given this suggestion of harmony, some functionalist models have been criticized as Panglossian, after Dr. Pangloss, a character in Voltaire's *Candide* who was fond of proclaiming, in response to any mentions of suffering or unfairness in life, that this was "the best of all possible worlds." Panglossian functionalism refers to a tendency to see things as functioning not just to maintain the system but to do so in the most optimal way possible, so that any deviation from the norm is viewed as detrimental.

The Manchester School

A group of British anthropologists working at the University of Manchester, dubbed the Manchester school, are well known for their research in African societies and their departure from a Panglossian view of social harmony. Manchester anthropologist Max Gluckman, for example, made conflict an important part of his analysis by focusing on rituals of rebellion and other expressions of discontent. However, Gluckman and his colleagues did not abandon functionalism totally. The Manchester anthropologists examined how rebellion and conflict were regulated and dissipated, thus maintaining the system.

Contemporary Functionalism

A form of functionalism persists today in the widely accepted view that there are social and cultural systems and that their elements, or constituent parts, are functionally related (are functions of each other) so that they covary: When one part changes, others also change. Also enduring is the idea that some elements—often the economic

Bronislaw Malinowski (1884–1942), who was born in Poland but spent most of his professional life in England, did fieldwork in the Trobriand Islands from 1914 to 1918. Malinowski is generally considered to be the father of ethnography. Does this photo suggest anything about his relationship with Trobriand villagers?

© Mary Evans Picture Library/ The Image Works

ones—are more important than others are. Few would deny, for example, that significant economic changes, such as the increasing cash employment of women, have led to changes in family and household organization and in related variables such as age at marriage and frequency of divorce. Changes in work and family arrangements then affect other variables, such as frequency of church attendance, which has declined in the United States and Canada.

Configurationalism

Two of Boas's best-known students, Benedict and Mead, developed an approach to culture that has been called **configurationalism.** This is related to functionalism in the sense that culture is seen as integrated. We've seen that the Boasians traced the geographic distribution of culture traits. But Boas recognized that diffusion wasn't automatic. Traits might not spread if they met environmental barriers, or if they were not accepted by a particular culture. There had to be a fit between the culture and the trait diffusing in, and borrowed traits would be *indigenized*—modified to fit the culture adopting them. Although traits can diffuse in from various directions, Benedict stressed that culture traits—indeed, whole cultures—are uniquely patterned or integrated. Her best-selling book *Patterns of Culture* (1934/1959) described such culture patterns.

Mead, who is best known for her focus on child-rearing practices, also found patterns in the cultures she studied, including Samoa, Bali, and Papua New Guinea. Mead was particularly interested in different patterns of enculturation. Stressing the plasticity of human nature, she saw culture as a powerful force that created almost endless possibilities. Even among neighboring societies, different patterns of enculturation could mold children into very different kinds of adults. Neighboring cultures could therefore have very different personality types and cultural configurations. Mead's best-known—albeit controversial—book is *Coming of Age in Samoa* (1928/1961). As a young woman, she traveled to Samoa to study female adolescence there in order to compare it with the same period of life in the United States. Suspicious of biologically determined universals, she assumed that Samoan adolescence would differ from the same period in the United States and that this would affect adult personality. Using her Samoan ethnographic findings, Mead contrasted the apparent sexual freedom there with the repression of adolescent sexuality in the United States. Her findings supported the Boasian view that culture, not biology, determines variation in human behavior and personality. Mead's later fieldwork among the Arapesh, Mundugumor, and Tchambuli of New Guinea resulted in *Sex and Temperament in Three Primitive Societies* (1935/1950). She offered that book, which documented significant variation in male and female personality traits and behavior in three nearby societies, as further support for cultural determinism.

Evolutionism Returns

Around 1950, with the end of World War II and a growing anticolonial movement, anthropologists renewed their interest in culture change and even

configurationalism
The view of culture as integrated and patterned.

Two U.S. stamps commemorating anthropologists. The 46-cent stamp, issued in 1995, honors Ruth Fulton Benedict (1887–1948), best known for her widely read book *Patterns of Culture*. In 1998, the U.S. Postal Service issued this 32-cent Margaret Mead (1901–1978) stamp as part of its "Celebrate the Century" commemorative series. The stamp shows a young Dr. Mead against a Samoan background.
Left: © Solodov Alexey/Shutterstock.com RF; right: © catwalker/Shutterstock.com RF

evolution. The American anthropologists Leslie White and Julian Steward complained that the Boasians had inappropriately thrown the baby (evolution) out with the bath water (the particular flaws of 19th-century evolutionary schemes). In his book *The Evolution of Culture* (1959), White claimed to be returning to the same concept of cultural evolution used by Tylor and Morgan, now better informed by a century of archaeological discoveries and a much larger ethnographic record. White's approach has been called *general evolution,* the idea that over time and through the archaeological, historical, and ethnographic records, we can see the evolution of culture as a whole. For example, human economies have evolved from Paleolithic foraging, through early farming and herding, to intensive forms of agriculture, to industrialism. Sociopolitically, too, there has been evolution, from bands and tribes to chiefdoms and states. There can be no doubt, White argued, that culture has evolved. But unlike the unilinear evolutionists of the 19th century, White realized that particular cultures might not evolve in the same direction.

White considered energy capture to be the main engine of cultural evolution. Cultural advance, he thought, could be measured by the amount of energy harnessed per capita per year in a society. In this view, Canada and the United States would rank among the world's most advanced nations because of the amount of energy they use per capita. White's notion that social advance can be measured by energy expenditure seems strange today, because it views societies that use the most fossil fuel per capita as being more advanced than those that have taken measures to reduce their dependence on finite energy sources.

Marvin Harris (1927–2001), chief advocate of the approach known as cultural materialism. Harris taught anthropology at Columbia University and the University of Florida.
Courtesy University of Florida

Julian Steward, in his influential book *Theory of Culture Change* (1955), proposed a different evolutionary model, which he called *multilinear evolution.* He showed how cultures have followed several different evolutionary paths. For example, he recognized different paths to statehood (e.g., those followed by irrigated versus nonirrigated societies). Steward also was a pioneer in a field of anthropology he called *cultural ecology,* today generally known as *ecological anthropology,* which pays particular attention to the relationships between cultures and their environments. Steward looked to technology and the environment as the main causes of culture change. The environment and the technology available to exploit it were seen as part of what he called the *culture core*—the combination of environmental and economic factors that determined the overall configuration of any society.

Cultural Materialism

In proposing **cultural materialism** as a theoretical paradigm, Marvin Harris drew on models of determinism associated with White and Steward. Harris (1979/2001a) thought that any society had three parts: infrastructure, structure, and superstructure. The *infrastructure,* similar to Steward's culture core, consisted of technology, economics, and demography—the systems of production and reproduction without which societies could not survive. Growing out of infrastructure was *structure*—social relations, forms of kinship and descent, patterns of distribution and consumption. The third layer was *superstructure:* religion, ideology, play—aspects of culture farthest away

cultural materialism (Harris) The idea that cultural infrastructure determines structure and superstructure.

Margaret Mead in the field in Bali, Indonesia, in 1957.
© AP Images

from the meat and bones that enable cultures to survive. Harris's key belief, shared with White, Steward, and Karl Marx, was that in the final analysis infrastructure determines structure and superstructure. Harris therefore took issue with theorists (he called them "idealists"), such as Max Weber (see the chapter, "Religion"), who argued for the prominent role of religion (an aspect of superstructure) in changing society. Like most of the anthropologists discussed so far, Harris insisted that anthropology is a *science*. For Harris, as for White and Steward, the primary goal of anthropology, as a science, is to seek explanations—relations of cause and effect.

Cultural Determinism: Culturology, the Superorganic, and Social Facts

In this section we consider three prominent early anthropologists (White, Kroeber, and Durkheim) who stressed the importance of culture and the role it plays in determining individual behavior. Leslie White, although an avowed evolutionist, was also a strong believer in the power of culture. White saw cultural anthropology as a distinctive science, which he named *culturology*. The cultural forces studied by that science were so powerful, White believed, that individuals made little difference. White disputed what was then called the "great man theory of history," the idea that particular individuals were responsible for great discoveries and epochal changes. White looked instead to the constellation of cultural forces that produced great individuals. During certain historical periods, such as the Renaissance, conditions were right for the expression of creativity and greatness, and individual genius blossomed. At other times and places, there may have been just as many great minds, but the culture did not encourage their expression. As proof of this theory, White pointed to the simultaneity of discovery. Several times in human history, when culture was ready, people working independently in different places have come up with the same revolutionary idea or achievement at the same time. Examples include the formulation of the theory of evolution through natural selection by Charles Darwin and Alfred Russel Wallace, the independent rediscovery of Mendelian genetics by three scientists in 1917, and the independent invention of flight by the Wright brothers in the United States and Santos Dumont in Brazil.

The prolific Boasian anthropologist Alfred Kroeber (1952) also stressed the need for a new and distinctive science focusing on culture, perceived as a distinctive realm, which he called the **superorganic.** Its study, he thought, was just as important as the study of the organic (biology) and the inorganic (chemistry and physics). In his studies of fashion, such as variations in women's

hemlines from year to year, Kroeber (1944) attempted to show the power of culture over the individual. People had little choice, he thought, but to follow the styles and trends of their times.

In France, Émile Durkheim had taken a similar approach, calling for a new social science to be based in what he called, in French, the *conscience collectif*. The usual translation of this as "collective consciousness" does not convey adequately the similarity of this notion to Kroeber's superorganic and White's culturology. This new science, Durkheim proposed, would be based on the study of *social facts,* which were analytically distinct from facts about individuals. Psychologists study individuals; anthropologists study individuals as representative of something more. It is those larger systems, which consist of social positions—statuses and roles—and which are perpetuated across the generations through enculturation, that anthropologists should study.

Of course, sociologists also study such social systems, and Durkheim was a prominent early figure in both anthropology and sociology. He wrote about religion in Native Australia as readily as about suicide rates in modern societies. As analyzed by Durkheim, suicide rates (1897/1951) and religion (1912/2001) are collective phenomena. Individuals commit suicide for all sorts of reasons, but the variation in rates (which apply only to collectivities) can and should be linked to social phenomena, such as a sense of anomie, malaise, or alienation at particular times and in particular places.

Symbolic and Interpretive Anthropology

Victor Turner was originally a colleague of Max Gluckman in the Department of Social Anthropology at the University of Manchester, and thus a member of the Manchester school, previously described, before moving to the United States, where he taught at the University of Chicago and the University of Virginia. Turner wrote several important works on ritual and symbols. *The Forest of Symbols* (1967) is a collection of essays about symbols and rituals among the Nbembu of Zambia, where Turner did his major fieldwork. In *The Forest of Symbols,* Turner examines how symbols and rituals are used to regulate, anticipate, and avoid conflict. He also examines a hierarchy of meanings of symbols, from their social meanings and functions to their internalization within individuals.

Turner recognized links between **symbolic anthropology** (the study of symbols in their social and cultural context), a school he pioneered along with Mary Douglas (1970a), and such other fields as social psychology, psychology, and psychoanalysis. The study of symbols is all-important in psychoanalysis, whose founder, Sigmund Freud, also

superorganic
(Kroeber) The special domain of culture, beyond the organic and inorganic realms.

symbolic anthropology
The study of symbols in their social and cultural context.

recognized a hierarchy of symbols, from potentially universal ones to those that had meaning for particular individuals and emerged during the analysis and interpretation of their dreams. Turner's symbolic anthropology flourished at the University of Chicago, where another major advocate, David Schneider (1968), developed a symbolic approach to American culture in his book *American Kinship: A Cultural Account.*

Related to symbolic anthropology, and also associated with the University of Chicago (and later with Princeton University), is **interpretive anthropology.** The primary advocate of this approach was Clifford Geertz (1973, 1983), who defined culture as ideas based on cultural learning and symbols. During enculturation, individuals internalize a previously established system of meanings and symbols. They use this cultural system to define their world, express their feelings, and make their judgments.

Interpretive anthropology (Geertz 1973, 1983) approaches cultures as texts whose meanings must be deciphered in particular cultural and historical settings. Geertz's approach recalls Malinowski's belief that the ethnographer's primary task is "to grasp the native's point of view, his relation to life, to realize *his* vision of *his* world" (1922/1961, p. 25—Malinowski's italics). Since the 1970s, interpretive anthropology has considered the task of describing and interpreting that which is meaningful to natives. According to Geertz (1973), anthropologists may choose anything in a culture that interests or engages them (such as a Balinese cockfight he interprets in a famous essay), fill in details, and elaborate to inform their readers about meanings in that culture. Meanings are carried by and expressed in public symbolic forms, including words, rituals, and customs.

Mary Douglas (1921–2007), a prominent symbolic anthropologist, who taught at University College, London, England, and Northwestern University, Evanston, Illinois. This photo shows her at an awards ceremony celebrating her receipt in 2003 of an honorary degree from Oxford.
© Rob Judges

interpretive anthropology
(Geertz) The study of a culture as a system of meaning.

Structuralism

In anthropology, structuralism mainly is associated with Claude Lévi-Strauss, a renowned and prolific

Anthropologist Clifford Geertz (1926-2006), who taught for many years at Princeton University.
© Laura Pedrick/Redux Pictures

French anthropologist, who died in 2009 at the age of 100. Lévi-Strauss's structuralism evolved over time, from his early interest in the structures of kinship and marriage systems to his later interest in the structure of the human mind. In this latter sense, Lévi-Straussian structuralism (1967) aims not at explaining relations, themes, and connections among aspects of culture but at discovering them.

Structuralism rests on Lévi-Strauss's belief that human minds have certain universal characteristics, which originate in common features of the *Homo sapiens* brain. These common mental structures lead people everywhere to think similarly regardless of their society or cultural background. Among these universal mental characteristics are the need to classify: to impose order on aspects of nature, on people's relation to nature, and on relations between people.

According to Lévi-Strauss, a universal aspect of classification is opposition, or contrast. Although many phenomena are continuous rather than discrete, the mind, because of its need to impose order, treats them as being more different than they are. One of the most common means of classifying is by using binary opposition. Good and evil, white and black, old and young, high and low are oppositions that, according to Lévi-Strauss, reflect the universal human need to convert differences of degree into differences of kind.

Lévi-Strauss applied his assumptions about classification and binary opposition to myths and folk tales. He showed that these narratives have simple building blocks—elementary structures or "mythemes." Examining the myths of different cultures, Lévi-Strauss shows that one tale can be converted into another through a series of simple operations—for example, by doing the following:

1. Converting the positive element of a myth into its negative.

2. Reversing the order of the elements.

3. Replacing a male hero with a female hero.

4. Preserving or repeating certain key elements.

Through such operations, two apparently dissimilar myths can be shown to be variations on a common structure—that is, to be transformations of each other. One example is Lévi-Strauss's (1967) analysis of "Cinderella," a widespread tale whose elements vary between neighboring cultures. Through reversals, oppositions, and negations, as the tale is told, retold, diffused, and incorporated within the traditions of successive societies, "Cinderella" becomes "Ash Boy," along with a series of other oppositions (e.g., stepfather versus stepmother) related to the change in gender from female to male.

Processual Approaches

Agency

Anthropologists traditionally have viewed culture as a kind of social glue transmitted across the generations, binding people through their common past–cultural traditions. More recently, anthropologists have come to see culture as something that is continually created and reworked in the present. Contemporary anthropologists now emphasize how the day-to-day actions of individuals can make and remake culture (Gupta and Ferguson 1997). **Agency** refers to the actions that individuals take, both alone and in groups, in forming and transforming culture.

Practice Theory

The approach to culture known as *practice theory* (Ortner 1984) recognizes that individuals within a society vary in their motives and intentions and in the amount of power and influence they have. Such contrasts may be associated with gender, age, ethnicity, class, and other social variables. Practice theory focuses on how these varied individuals—through their actions and practices—influence and transform the world they live in. Practice theory appropriately recognizes a reciprocal relation between culture and the individual. Culture shapes how individuals experience and respond to events, but individuals also play an active role in how society functions and changes. Practice theory recognizes both constraints on individuals and the flexibility and changeability of cultures and social systems. Well-known practice theorists include Sherry Ortner, an American anthropologist, and Pierre Bourdieu and Anthony Giddens, French and British social theorists, respectively.

Edmund Leach

Some of the germs of practice theory, sometimes also called action theory (Vincent 1990), can be traced to the British anthropologist Edmund Leach, who wrote the influential book *Political Systems of Highland Burma* (1954/1970). Leach focused on how individuals work to achieve power and how their actions can transform society. In the Kachin Hills of Burma, now Myanmar, Leach identified three forms of sociopolitical organization, which he called *gumlao, gumsa,* and Shan. Leach made a tremendously important point by taking a regional rather than a local perspective. The Kachins participated in a regional system that included all three forms of organization. Leach showed how the three coexist and interact, as forms and possibilities known to everyone, in the same region. He also showed how Kachins creatively use power struggles—for example, to convert *gumlao* into *gumsa* organization—and how they negotiate their own identities within the regional system. Leach brought process into the formal models of structural functionalism. By focusing on power and how individuals get and use it, he showed the creative role of the individual in transforming culture.

World-System Theory and Political Economy

Leach's regional perspective and interest in power was not all that different from another development at the same time. Julian Steward, discussed previously for his work on multilinear evolution and cultural ecology, joined the faculty of Columbia University in 1946. He worked there with a group of graduate students including Eric Wolf and Sidney Mintz, who would go on to become prominent anthropologists themselves. Steward and his students planned and conducted a team research project in Puerto Rico, described in Steward's volume *The People of Puerto Rico* (1956). This project exemplified a post–World War II turn of anthropology away from "primitive" and nonindustrial societies, assumed to be somewhat isolated and autonomous, to contemporary societies recognized as forged by colonialism and participating fully in

Eric Wolf (1923–1999) with his son David in the Italian Alps, one of Eric Wolf's research sites; he also worked in and wrote about Mexico and Puerto Rico.
Courtesy of Sydel Silverman

agency
The actions of individuals, alone and in groups, that create and transform culture.

THEORETICAL APPROACH	KEY AUTHORS AND WORKS
Culture, history, power	Ann Stoler, *Carnal Knowledge and Imperial Power* (2002); Frederick Cooper and Ann Stoler, *Tensions of Empire* (1997)
Crisis of representation/ postmodernism	Jean-François Lyotard, *The Postmodern Explained* (1993); George Marcus and Michael Fischer, *Anthropology as Cultural Critique* (1986)
Practice theory	Sherry Ortner, "Theory in Anthropology since the Sixties" (1984); Pierre Bourdieu, *Outline of a Theory of Practice* (1977)
World-system theory/ political economy	Sidney Mintz, *Sweetness and Power* (1985); Eric Wolf, *Europe and the People without History* (1982)
Feminist anthropology (see the chapter on "Gender")	Rayna Reiter, *Toward an Anthropology of Women* (1975); Michelle Rosaldo and Louise Lamphere, *Women, Culture, and Society* (1974)
Cultural materialism	Marvin Harris, *Cultural Materialism* (1979), *The Rise of Anthropological Theory* (1968)
Interpretive anthropology	Clifford Geertz, *The Interpretation of Cultures* (1973)*
Symbolic anthropology	Mary Douglas, *Purity and Danger* (1970b); Victor Turner, *The Forest of Symbols* (1967)*
Structuralism	Claude Lévi-Strauss, *Structural Anthropology* (1967)*
Twentieth-century evolutionism	Leslie White, *The Evolution of Culture* (1959); Julian Steward, *Theory of Culture Change* (1955)
Manchester school and Leach	Victor Turner, *Schism and Continuity in an African Society* (1957); Edmund Leach, *Political Systems of Highland Burma* (1954)
Culturology	Leslie White, *The Science of Culture* (1949)*
Configurationalism	Alfred Kroeber, *Configurations of Cultural Growth* (1944); Margaret Mead, *Sex and Temperament in Three Primitive Societies* (1935); Ruth Benedict, *Patterns of Culture* (1934)
Structural functionalism	A. R. Radcliffe-Brown, *Structure and Function in Primitive Society* (1962)*; E. E. Evans-Pritchard, *The Nuer* (1940)
Functionalism	Bronislaw Malinowski, *A Scientific Theory of Culture* (1944)*, *Argonauts of the Western Pacific* (1922)
Historical particularism	Franz Boas, *Race, Language, and Culture* (1940)*
Nineteenth-century evolutionism	Lewis Henry Morgan, *Ancient Society* (1877); Sir Edward Burnett Tylor, *Primitive Culture* (1871)

*Includes essays written at earlier dates.

political economy
The web of interrelated economic and power relations in society.

the modern world system. The team, which included Mintz and Wolf, studied communities in different parts of Puerto Rico. The field sites were chosen to sample major events and adaptations, such as the sugar plantation, in the island's history. The approach emphasized economics, politics, and history.

Wolf and Mintz retained their interest in history throughout their careers. Wolf wrote the modern classic *Europe and the People without History* (1982), which viewed local people, such as Native Americans, in the context of world-system events, such as the fur trade. Wolf focused on how such "people without history"—that is, nonliterate people, those who lacked written histories of their own—participated in and were transformed by the world system and the spread

of capitalism. Mintz's *Sweetness and Power* (1985) is another example of historical anthropology that focuses on **political economy** (the web of interrelated economic and power relations). Mintz traces the domestication and spread of sugar, its transformative role in England, and its impact on the New World, where it became the basis for slave-based plantation economies in the Caribbean and Brazil. Such works in political economy illustrate a movement of anthropology toward interdisciplinarity, drawing on other academic fields, most notably history. Such approaches have been criticized, however, for overstressing the influence of outsiders, and for paying insufficient attention to the transformative actions of "the people without history" themselves. Recap 13.2 summarizes

Sidney Mintz (1922-2015) at his office at Johns Hopkins University. Mintz, who died in 2015 at the age of 93, was an anthropologist known best for his studies of Caribbean, the anthropology of food, and Afro-Caribbean traditions.

© Jay VanRensselaer/homewoodphoto.jhu.edu

anthropology's major theoretical perspectives and key works associated with them.

Culture, History, Power

More recent approaches in historical anthropology, while sharing an interest in power and inequality with the world-system theorists, have focused more on local agency, the transformative actions of individuals and groups within colonized societies. Archival work has been prominent in recent historical anthropology, particularly in areas, such as Indonesia, for which colonial and postcolonial archives contain valuable information on relations between colonizers and colonized (see Roque and Wagner 2011). Studies of culture, history, and power have drawn heavily on the work of European social theorists such as Antonio Gramsci and Michel Foucault.

Gramsci (1971) developed the concept of *hegemony* to describe a stratified social order in which subordinates comply with domination by internalizing their rulers' values and accepting domination as "natural." Both Pierre Bourdieu (1977) and Foucault (1979) contend that it is easier to dominate people in their minds than to try to control their bodies. Contemporary societies have devised various forms of social control in addition to physical violence. These include techniques of persuading, coercing, and managing people and of monitoring and recording their beliefs, behavior, movements, and contacts. Anthropologists interested in culture, history, and power, such as Ann Stoler (1995, 2002, 2009),

have examined systems of power, domination, accommodation, and resistance in various contexts, including colonies, postcolonies, and other stratified contexts.

ANTHROPOLOGY TODAY

Early American anthropologists typically contributed to more than one of the four subfields. If there has been a single dominant trend in anthropology since the 1960s, it has been one of increasing specialization. During the 1960s, when I attended graduate school at Columbia University, graduate students had to study and take qualifying exams in all four subfields. This has changed. There are still strong four-field anthropology departments, but many excellent departments lack one or more of the subfields. Even in four-field departments, graduate students are expected to specialize in a particular subfield. In Boasian anthropology, all four subfields shared a single theoretical assumption about human plasticity. Today, following specialization, the theories that guide the subfields differ. Evolutionary paradigms of various sorts still dominate biological anthropology and remain strong in archaeology as well. Within cultural anthropology, it has been many decades since evolutionary approaches dominated.

Ethnography, too, has grown more specialized. Cultural anthropologists now head for the field with a specific problem in mind, rather than with the goal of producing a holistic ethnography—a complete account of a given culture—as Morgan and Malinowski intended when they studied, respectively, the Iroquois and the Trobriand Islanders. Boas, Malinowski, and Mead went somewhere and stayed there for a while, studying the local culture. Today "the field" that anthropologists study has expanded—inevitably and appropriately—to include regional and national systems and the movement of people, such as immigrants and diasporas, across national boundaries. Border theory (see Lugo 1997) is an emerging field that examines social relations at the margins of a society, contexts in which members of different groups increasingly meet and interact. Border research can occur on the boundaries of nation-states, such as the U.S–Mexican border (DeLeon 2015; Lugo 2008), as well as in places within a nation where diverse groups come into regular contact. Many anthropologists now follow the flows of people, information, finance, and media to multiple sites. Such movement—and the anthropologist's ability to study it—has been made possible by advances in transportation and communication.

Reflecting the trend toward specialization, the American Anthropological Association now has all sorts of active and vital subgroups. In its early years, there were just anthropologists within the AAA. Now there are groups based on specialization in biological anthropology, archaeology, and linguistic, cultural, and applied anthropology. The AAA also includes dozens of groups formed around particular interests (e.g., psychological anthropology, urban anthropology, culture and agriculture) and identities (e.g., midwestern or southeastern anthropologists, anthropologists in community colleges or small programs). The AAA also includes units representing senior anthropologists, LGBT anthropologists, Latino and Latina anthropologists, and so on.

Anthropology also has witnessed a crisis in representation, including questions about the ethnographer's impartiality and the validity of ethnographic accounts. The value of science itself may be challenged, by pointing out that all scientists come from particular individual and cultural backgrounds, which interfere with objectivity. What are we to do if we, as I do, continue to share Margaret Mead's view of anthropology as a humanistic science of unique value in understanding and improving the human condition? We must try, I think, to stay aware of our biases and our inability totally to escape them. The best scientific choice would seem to be to combine the perpetual goal of objectivity with skepticism about our capacity to achieve it.

for REVIEW

summary

1. Ethnographic methods include observation, rapport building, participant observation, interviewing, genealogies, work with key consultants, life histories, problem-oriented research, longitudinal research, and team research. Ethnographers do not systematically manipulate their subjects or conduct experiments. Rather, they work in actual communities and form personal relationships with local people as they study their lives.

2. An interview schedule is a form that an ethnographer completes as he or she visits a series of households. The schedule organizes and guides each interview, ensuring that comparable information is collected from everyone. Key cultural consultants teach about particular areas of local life. Life histories dramatize the fact that culture bearers are individuals. Such case studies document personal experiences with culture and culture change. Genealogical information is particularly useful in societies in which principles of kinship and marriage organize social and political life. Emic approaches focus on native perceptions and explanations. Etic approaches give priority to the ethnographer's own observations and conclusions. Longitudinal research is the systematic study of an area or a site over time. Anthropological research may be done by teams and at multiple sites. Outsiders, flows, linkages, and people in motion are now included in ethnographic analyses. Anthropologists also have developed techniques of doing online ethnography in studying virtual worlds.

3. Traditionally, anthropologists worked in small-scale societies; sociologists, in modern nations.

Different techniques were developed to study such different kinds of societies. Social scientists working in complex societies use survey research to sample variation. Anthropologists do their fieldwork in communities and study the totality of social life. Sociologists study samples to make inferences about a larger population. The diversity of social life in modern nations and cities requires survey procedures. However, anthropologists add the intimacy and direct investigation characteristic of ethnography.

4. Because science exists in society, and in the context of law and ethics, anthropologists can't study things simply because they happen to be interesting or of scientific value. Anthropologists have obligations to their scholarly field, to the wider society and culture (including that of the host country), and to the human species, other species, and the environment. The AAA Code of Ethics offers ethical guidelines for anthropologists. Ethical problems often arise when anthropologists work for governments, especially the military.

5. Evolutionary perspectives, especially those of Morgan and Tylor, dominated early anthropology, which emerged during the latter half of the 19th century. The early 20th century witnessed various reactions to 19th-century evolutionism. In the United States, Boas and his followers rejected the search for evolutionary stages in favor of a historical approach that traced borrowing between cultures and the spread of culture traits across geographic areas. In Great Britain, functionalists such as Malinowski and Radcliffe-Brown abandoned conjectural history in favor of studies of present-day living societies.

Functionalists and Boasians alike saw cultures as integrated and patterned. The functionalists especially viewed societies as systems in which various parts worked together to maintain the whole. A form of functionalism persists in the widely accepted view that there are social and cultural systems whose constituent parts are functionally related, so that when one part changes, others change as well.

6. In the mid-20th century, following World War II and as colonialism was ending, there was a revived interest in change, including evolutionary approaches. Some anthropologists developed symbolic and interpretive approaches to uncover patterned symbols and meanings within cultures. By the 1980s, anthropologists had grown more interested in the relation between culture and the individual, as well as the role of human action (agency) in transforming culture. There also was a resurgence of historical approaches, including those that viewed local cultures in relation to colonialism and the world system.

7. Contemporary anthropology is marked by increasing specialization, based on special topics and identities. Reflecting this specialization, some universities have moved away from the holistic, biocultural view of anthropology that is reflected in this book. However, this Boasian view of anthropology as a four-subfield discipline—including biological, archaeological, cultural, and linguistic anthropology—continues to thrive at many universities as well.

key terms

agency 249

complex societies 239

configurationalism 245

cultural materialism 246

cultural consultants 234

diachronic 244

emic 236

etic 236

functionalism 243

genealogical method 234

historical particularism 242

informed consent 239

interpretive anthropology 248

interview schedule 232

key cultural consultants 234

life history 235

longitudinal research 235

political economy 250

questionnaire 232

random sample 238

sample 238

superorganic 247

survey research 238

symbolic anthropology 247

synchronic 244

unilinear evolutionism 242

variables 238

critical thinking

1. What do you see as the strengths and weaknesses of ethnography compared with survey research? Which provides more accurate data? Might one be better for finding questions, while the other is better for finding answers? Or does it depend on the context of research?

2. In what sense is anthropological research comparative? How have anthropologists approached the issue of comparison? What do they compare (what are their units of analysis)?

3. In your view, is anthropology a science? How have anthropologists historically addressed this question? Should anthropology be a science?

4. Historically, how have anthropologists studied culture? What are some contemporary trends in the study of culture, and how have they changed the way anthropologists carry out their research?

5. Do the theories examined in this chapter relate to ones you have studied in other courses? Which courses and theories? Are those theories more scientific or humanistic, or somewhere in between?

Language and Communication

▸ What makes language different from other forms of communication?

▸ How do anthropologists and linguists study language in general and specific languages in particular?

▸ How does language change over short and long time periods?

© Raminder Pal Singh/epa/Corbis

Schoolgirls wearing traditional Punjabi attire laugh as they wait to take part in a national celebration in the northern Indian city of Amritsar. Republic Day, celebrated annually on January 26, commemorates the transition of India from British domination to a republic on January 26, 1950.

understanding OURSELVES

chapter outline

Can you appreciate anything distinctive or unusual in the way you talk? If you're from Canada, Virginia, or Savannah, you may say "oot" instead of "out." A southerner may request a "soft drink" rather than the New Yorker's "soda." How might a "Valley girl" or "surfer dude" talk? Usually when we pay attention to how we talk, it's because someone comments on our speech. It may be only when students move from one state or region to another that they appreciate how much of a regional accent they have. I moved as a teenager from Atlanta to New York City. Previously I hadn't realized I had a southern accent, but teachers in my new high school did. They put me in a speech class, pointing out linguistic flaws I never knew I had. One was my "dull s," particularly in terminal consonant clusters, as in the words "tusks" and "breakfasts." Apparently I didn't pronounce all three consonants at the ends of those words. Later it occurred to me that these weren't words I used very often. As far as I know, I've never conversed about tusks or proclaimed, "I ate seven breakfasts last week."

Unlike grammarians, linguists and anthropologists are interested in what people do say, rather than what they should say. Speech differences are associated with, and tell us a lot about, social variation, such as region, education, ethnic background, and gender. Men and women talk differently. I'm sure you can think of examples based on your own experience, although you probably never realized that women tend to peripheralize their vowels (think of "aiiee"), whereas men tend to centralize them (think of "uh"). Men are more likely to speak "ungrammatically" than women are. Men and women also show differences in their sports and color terminologies. Men typically know more terms related to sports, make more distinctions among them (e.g., "runs" versus "points"), and try to use the terms more precisely than women do.

Correspondingly, women use more color terms and attempt to use them more specifically than men do. To make this point when I lecture, I bring an off-purple shirt to class. Holding it up, I first ask women to say aloud what color the shirt is. The women rarely answer with a uniform voice, as they try to distinguish the actual shade (mauve, lilac, lavender, wisteria, or some other purplish hue). I then ask the men, who consistently answer as one, "PURPLE." Rare is the man who on the spur of the moment can imagine the difference between fuchsia and magenta or grape and aubergine.

WHAT IS LANGUAGE?

Language, which may be spoken (*speech*) or written (*writing*), is our primary means of communication. Writing has existed for less than 6,000 years. Language originated thousands of years before that, but no one can say exactly when. Like culture in general, of which language is a part, language is transmitted through learning, as part of enculturation. Language is based on arbitrary, learned associations between words and the things for which they stand. The complexity of language—absent in the communication systems of other animals—allows humans to conjure up elaborate images, to discuss the past and the future, to share our experiences with others, and to benefit from their experiences.

Anthropologists study language in its social and cultural context (see Bonvillain 2012; Salzmann, Stanlaw, and Adachi 2015). Linguistic anthropology illustrates anthropology's characteristic interest in comparison, variation, and change—but here the focus is on language (see Bonvillain 2016; Duranti 2009; Salzmann 2012). A key feature of language is that it is always changing. Some linguistic anthropologists reconstruct ancient languages by comparing their contemporary descendants and in so doing make discoveries about history. Others study linguistic differences to discover the varied worldviews and patterns of thought in a multitude of cultures. Sociolinguists examine linguistic diversity in nation-states, ranging from multilingualism to the varied dialects and styles used in a single language, to show how speech reflects social differences (Fasold and Connor-Linton 2014; Labov 1972a, 2006). Linguistic anthropologists also explore the role of language in colonization and in the expansion of the world economy (Geis 1987; Trudgill 2010).

NONHUMAN PRIMATE COMMUNICATION

Call Systems

Only humans speak. No other animal has anything approaching the complexity of language. The natural communication systems of other primates (monkeys and apes) are **call systems.** These vocal systems consist of a limited number of sounds—*calls*—that are produced only when particular environmental stimuli are encountered. Such calls may be varied in intensity and duration, but they are much less flexible than language because they are automatic and can't be combined. When primates encounter food and danger simultaneously, they can make only one call. They can't combine the calls for food and danger into a single utterance, indicating that both are present (for example, "There are lots of bananas here, but also snakes."). At some point in human evolution, however, our ancestors began to combine calls and to understand the combinations. The number of calls also expanded, eventually becoming too great to be transmitted even partly through the genes. Communication came to rely almost totally on learning.

Although wild primates use call systems, the vocal tract of apes is not suitable for speech. Until the 1960s, attempts to teach spoken language to apes suggested that they lack linguistic abilities. In the 1950s, a couple raised a chimpanzee, Viki, as a member of their family and systematically tried to teach her to speak. However, Viki learned only four words ("mama," "papa," "up," and "cup").

Sign Language

More recent experiments have shown that apes can learn to use, if not speak, true language. Several apes have learned to converse with people

Apes, such as these chimpanzees, use call systems to communicate in the wild. Their vocal systems consist of a limited number of sounds—*calls*—that are produced only when particular environmental stimuli are encountered. What might they be signaling here?
© Michael Nichols/National Geographic/Getty Images

through means other than speech. One such communication system is American Sign Language, or ASL, which is widely used by deaf Americans. ASL employs a limited number of basic gesture units that are analogous to sounds in spoken language. These units combine to form words and larger units of meaning.

The first chimpanzee to learn ASL was Washoe, a female who died in 2007 at the age of 42. Captured in West Africa, Washoe was acquired by R. Allen Gardner and Beatrice Gardner, scientists at the University of Nevada in Reno, in 1966, when she was a year old. Four years later, she moved to Norman, Oklahoma, to a converted farm that had become the Institute for Primate Studies. Washoe revolutionized the discussion of the language-learning abilities of apes (Carey 2007). At first she lived in a trailer and heard no spoken language. The researchers always used ASL to communicate with each other in her presence. The chimp gradually acquired a vocabulary of more than 100 signs representing English words (Gardner, Gardner, and Van Cantfort 1989). At the age of 2, Washoe began to combine as many as five signs into rudimentary sentences such as "you, me, go out, hurry."

The second chimp to learn ASL was Lucy, Washoe's junior by one year. Lucy died, or was murdered by poachers, in 1986, after having been introduced to "the wild" in Africa in 1979 (Carter 1988). From her second day of life until her move to Africa, Lucy lived with a family in Norman, Oklahoma. Roger Fouts, a researcher from the nearby Institute for Primate Studies, came two days a week to test and improve Lucy's knowledge of ASL. During the rest of the week, Lucy used ASL to converse with her foster parents. After acquiring language, Washoe and Lucy exhibited several human traits: swearing, joking, telling lies, and trying to teach language to others (Fouts 1997).

When irritated, Washoe called her monkey neighbors at the institute "dirty monkeys." Lucy insulted her "dirty cat." On arrival at Lucy's place, Fouts once found a pile of excrement on the floor. When he asked the chimp what it was, she replied, "dirty, dirty," her expression for feces. Asked whose "dirty, dirty" it was, Lucy named Fouts's coworker, Sue. When Fouts refused to believe her about Sue, the chimp blamed the excrement on Fouts himself.

A fundamental attribute of language is its **cultural transmission** through learning. People talk to you and around you, and you learn. Washoe, Lucy, and other chimps have tried to teach ASL to other animals. Washoe taught gestures to other institute chimps, including her son Sequoia, who died in infancy (Gardner, Gardner, and Van Cantfort 1989).

Because of their size and strength as adults, gorillas are less likely subjects than chimps for such experiments. Lean adult male gorillas in the wild weigh 400 pounds (180 kilograms), and full-grown females can easily reach 250 pounds (110 kilograms). Because of this, psychologist Penny Patterson's work with gorillas at Stanford University seems more daring than the chimp experiments. Patterson raised the now full-grown female gorilla, Koko, in a trailer next to a Stanford museum. Koko's vocabulary surpasses that of any chimp. She regularly employs 400 ASL signs and has used about 700 at least once.

Koko and the chimps also show that apes share still another linguistic ability with humans: **productivity.** Speakers routinely use the rules of their language to produce entirely new expressions that are comprehensible to other native speakers. I can, for example, create "baboonlet" to refer to a baboon infant. I do this by analogy with English words in which the suffix -*let* designates the young of a species. Anyone who speaks English immediately understands the meaning of my new word. Koko, Washoe, Lucy, and others have shown that apes also are able to use language productively. Lucy used gestures she already knew to create "drinkfruit" for watermelon. Washoe, seeing a swan for the first time, coined "waterbird." Koko, who knew the gestures for "finger" and "bracelet," formed "finger bracelet" when she was given a ring.

Kanzi, a male bonobo, identifies an object he has just heard named through headphone speakers. At a young age, Kanzi learned to understand simple human speech and to communicate by using lexigrams, abstract symbols that represent objects and actions. A keyboard of lexigrams is pictured in the background.
© Michael Nichols/National Geographic Creative

Chimps and gorillas have a rudimentary capacity for language. They may never have invented a meaningful gesture system in the wild. However, given such a system, they can learn and use it. Of course, language use by apes is a product of human intervention and teaching. The experiments mentioned here do not suggest that apes can invent language (nor are human children ever faced with that task). However, young apes have managed to learn the basics of gestural language. They can employ it productively and creatively, although not with the sophistication of human ASL users.

Apes also have demonstrated linguistic **displacement.** Absent in call systems, this is a key ingredient in language. Normally, a call is tied to a particular environmental stimulus and is uttered only when that stimulus is present. Displacement means that humans can talk about things that are not present. We can discuss the past and future, share our experiences with others, and benefit from theirs.

Patterson has described several examples of Koko's capacity for displacement (Patterson 1978, 1999). The gorilla once expressed sorrow about having bitten Penny three days earlier. Koko has used the sign "later" to postpone doing things she doesn't want to do. Recap 14.1 summarizes the contrasts between language, whether sign or spoken, and the call systems that primates use in the wild.

Certain scholars doubt the linguistic abilities of chimps and gorillas (Hess 2008; Sebeok and Umiker-Sebeok 1980; Terrace 1979). These people contend that Koko and the chimps are comparable to trained circus animals and don't really have linguistic ability. However, in defense of Patterson and the other researchers (Hill 1978;

cultural transmission
Transmission through learning, basic to language.

displacement
Describing things and events that are not present; basic to language.

productivity
Creating new expressions that are comprehensible to other speakers.

HUMAN LANGUAGE	PRIMATE CALL SYSTEMS
Has the capacity to speak of things and events that are not present (displacement)	Are stimuli dependent; the food call will be made only in the presence of food; it cannot be faked
Has the capacity to generate new expressions by combining other expressions (productivity)	Consist of a limited number of calls that cannot be combined to produce new calls
Is group specific in that all humans have the capacity for language, but each linguistic community has its own language, which is culturally transmitted	Tend to be species specific, with little variation among communities of the same species for each call

Van Cantfort and Rimpau 1982), only one of their critics has worked with an ape. This was Herbert Terrace, whose experience teaching a chimp sign language lacked the continuity and personal involvement that have contributed so much to Patterson's success with Koko. (For more on Terrace and his ill-fated chimp, Nim Chimpsky, see Hess [2008] and the acclaimed 2011 documentary film *Project Nim*.)

No one denies the huge difference between human language and gorilla signs. There is a major gap between the ability to write a book or say a prayer and the few hundred gestures employed by a well-trained chimp. Apes aren't people, but they aren't just animals, either. Let Koko express it: When asked by a reporter whether she was a person or an animal, Koko chose neither. Instead, she signed "fine animal gorilla" (Patterson 1978).

The Origin of Language

Although the capacity to remember and combine linguistic symbols may be latent in the apes, human evolution was needed for this seed to flower into language. A mutated gene known as *FOXP2* helps explain why humans speak and chimps don't (Paulson 2005). The key role of *FOXP2* in speech came to light in a study of a British family, identified only as KE, half of whose members had an inherited, severe deficit in speech (Trivedi 2001). The same variant form of *FOXP2* that is found in chimpanzees causes this disorder. Those who have the nonspeech version of the gene cannot make the fine tongue and lip movements that are necessary for clear speech, and their speech is unintelligible—even to other members of their family (Trivedi 2001). Chimps have the same (genetic) sequence as the KE family members with the speech deficit. Comparing chimp and human genomes, it appears that the speech-friendly form of *FOXP2* took hold in humans around 150,000 years ago. (Paulson 2005). What role did this mutation play in the origin of language? We know now that other genes and a series of anatomical changes were necessary for fully evolved human speech. It would be an oversimplification to call

FOXP2 "the language gene," as was done initially in the popular press, because other genes also determine language development.

Whatever its genetic underpinnings, language confers a tremendous adaptive advantage on *Homo sapiens*. Language permits the information stored by a human society to exceed by far that of any nonhuman group. Language is a uniquely effective vehicle for learning. Because we can speak of things we have never experienced, we can anticipate responses before we encounter the stimuli. Adaptation can occur more rapidly in *Homo* than in the other primates because our adaptive means are much more flexible.

NONVERBAL COMMUNICATION

Language is our principal means of communicating, but it isn't the only one we use. We communicate when we transmit information about ourselves to others and receive such information from them. Our facial expressions, bodily stances, gestures, and movements, even if unconscious, convey information. Deborah Tannen (1990) discusses differences in the communication styles of American men and women. She notes that American girls and women tend to look directly at each other when they talk, whereas American boys and men do not. Males are more likely to look straight ahead rather than turn and make eye contact with someone, especially another man, seated beside them. Also, in conversational groups, American men tend to relax and sprawl out. Consider the phenomenon known as "manspreading"—the tendency for men using public transportation to open their legs and thus take up more than one place. American women may relax their posture in all-female groups, but when they are with men, they tend to draw in their limbs and assume a tighter stance.

Kinesics is the study of communication through body movements, stances, gestures, and facial expressions. Linguists pay attention not only to what is said but to how it is said, and to

kinesics
The study of communication through body movements and facial expressions.

Compare the communication style of these women in a café with that of the two men conversing as they walk. Do you think the men would use the same communication style as the women if they were in a café setting?

Left: © Dana Neely/Digital Vision/Getty Images RF; right: © Susan Chiang/iStock/Getty Images Plus RF

features besides language itself that convey meaning. A speaker's enthusiasm is conveyed not only through words but also through facial expressions, gestures, and other signs of animation. We use gestures, such as a jab of the hand, for emphasis. We use verbal and nonverbal ways of communicating our moods: enthusiasm, sadness, joy, regret. We vary our intonation and the pitch or loudness of our voices. We communicate through strategic pauses, and even by being silent. An effective communication strategy may be to alter pitch, voice level, and grammatical forms, such as declaratives ("I am . . ."), imperatives ("Go forth . . ."), and questions ("Are you . . . ?"). Culture teaches us that certain manners and styles should accompany certain kinds of speech. Our demeanor, verbal and nonverbal, when our favorite team is winning would be out of place at a funeral.

Much of what we communicate is nonverbal and reflects our emotional states and intentions. This can create problems when we use rapid means of communication such as texting and online messaging. People can use emoticons (coined from *emotion* and *icon*) to suggest what otherwise would be communicated by tone of voice, laughter, or facial expressions (see Baron 2009; Tannen and Trester 2012). Examples of emoticons are the following: (☺, ☹, :~/ [confused], :~0 ["hah!" no way!]) and abbreviations (lol—laugh out loud; lmao—laugh my a** off; wtf—what the f***; omg—oh my gosh). This chapter's "Appreciating Diversity" considers the growing role of emojis in digital communication. An *emoji* is a digital image or pictograph, widely available on smartphones and tablets, used to express an idea or emotion, such as happiness or sadness.

Culture always plays a role in shaping how people communicate. Cross-culturally, nodding does not always mean affirmative, nor does head shaking from side to side always mean negative. Brazilians wag a finger to mean no. Americans say "uh huh" to affirm; in Madagascar a similar sound is used to deny. Americans point with their fingers; the people of Madagascar point with their lips.

Body movements communicate social differences. In Japan, bowing is a regular part of social interaction, but different bows are used depending on the social status of the people who are interacting. In Madagascar and Polynesia, people of lower status should not hold their heads above those of people of higher status. When one approaches someone older or of higher status, one bends one's knees and lowers one's head as a sign of respect. In Madagascar, one always does this, for politeness, when passing between two people. Although our gestures, facial expressions, and body stances have roots in our primate heritage, they have not escaped cultural shaping. Language, which is so highly dependent on the use of symbols, is the domain of communication, in which culture plays the strongest role.

THE STRUCTURE OF LANGUAGE

The scientific study of a spoken language (*descriptive linguistics*) involves several interrelated areas of analysis: phonology, morphology, lexicon, and syntax (see McGregor 2015). **Phonology,** the study of speech sounds, considers which sounds are present and significant in a given language. **Morphology** studies how sounds combine to form *morphemes*—words and their meaningful parts. Thus, the word *cats* would be analyzed as containing two morphemes: *cat,* the name for a

phonology
The study of sounds used in speech in a particular language.

morphology
The (linguistic) study of morphemes and word construction.

lexicon
Vocabulary; all the morphemes in a language and their meanings.

syntax
The arrangement and order of words in phrases and sentences.

phoneme
The smallest sound contrast that distinguishes meaning.

phonemics
The study of significant sound contrasts (phonemes) in a language.

phonetics
The study of speech sounds—what people actually say.

kind of animal, and *-s,* a morpheme indicating plurality. A language's **lexicon** is a dictionary containing all its morphemes and their meanings. **Syntax** refers to the arrangement and order of words in phrases and sentences. Syntactic questions include whether nouns usually come before or after verbs, and whether adjectives normally precede or follow the nouns they modify.

From the media, and from actually meeting foreigners, we know something about foreign accents and mispronunciations. We know that someone with a marked French accent doesn't pronounce *r* the same way an American does. But at least someone from France can distinguish between "craw" and "claw," which someone from Japan may not be able to do. The difference between *r* and *l* makes a difference in English and in French, but it doesn't in Japanese. In linguistics, we say that the difference between *r* and *l* is *phonemic* in English and French but not in Japanese; that is, *r* and *l* are phonemes in English and French but not in Japanese. A **phoneme** is a sound contrast that makes a difference, that differentiates meaning.

We find the phonemes in a given language by comparing *minimal pairs,* words that resemble each other in all but one sound. The words have totally different meanings, but they differ in just one sound. The contrasting sounds are therefore phonemes in that language. An example in English is the minimal pair *pit/bit.* These two words are distinguished by a single sound contrast between /p/ and /b/ (we enclose phonemes in slashes). Thus /p/ and /b/ are phonemes in English. Another example is the different vowel sounds of *bit* and *beat* (see Figure 14.1). This contrast serves to distinguish these two words and the two vowel phonemes written /I/ and /i/ in English.

Standard (American) English, the "region-free" dialect of TV network newscasters, has about 35 phonemes: at least 11 vowels and 24 consonants. The number of phonemes varies from language to language—from 15 to 60, averaging between 30 and 40. The number of phonemes also varies between dialects of a given language. In American English, for example, vowel phonemes vary noticeably from dialect to dialect. Readers should pronounce the words in Figure 14.1, paying attention to (or asking someone else) whether they distinguish each of the vowel sounds. Most Americans don't pronounce them all. My grandson Lucas thinks it's funny that I make a phonemic distinction he doesn't make. I pronounce words beginning with *wh* as though they began with *hw.* My personal set of phonemes includes both /hw/ and /w/. This enables me to distinguish between *white* and *Wight* (as in the Isle of Wight) and between *where* and *wear.* Lucas pronounces all four of those words as though they begin with [w], so that he does not distinguish between *white* and *Wight* or between *where* and *wear.* How about you?

Phonetics is the study of speech sounds in general, what people actually say in various

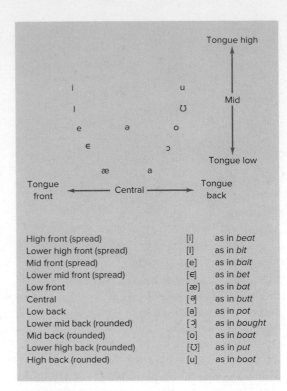

FIGURE 14.1 Vowel Phonemes in Standard American English.
The phonemes are shown according to height of tongue and tongue position at front, center, or back of mouth. Phonetic symbols are identified by English words that include them; note that most are minimal pairs.

SOURCE: Adaptation of excerpt and Figure 2-1 from Dwight Bolinger and Donald A. Sears, *Aspects of Language,* 3rd ed., Cengage Learning, 1981.

languages. **Phonemics** studies only the *significant* sound contrasts (phonemes) of a given language. In English, like /r/ and /l/ (remember *craw* and *claw*), /b/ and /v/ are also phonemes, occurring in minimal pairs like *bat* and *vat.* In Spanish, however, the contrast between [b] and [v] doesn't distinguish meaning, and they therefore are not phonemes (we enclose sounds that are not phonemic in brackets). Spanish speakers normally use the [b] sound to pronounce words spelled with either *b* or *v.*

In any language, a given phoneme extends over a phonetic range. In English, the phoneme /p/ ignores the phonetic contrast between the [pʰ] in *pin* and the [p] in *spin.* Most English speakers don't even notice that there is a phonetic difference: [pʰ] is aspirated, so that a puff of air follows the [p]; the [p] in *spin* is not. (To see the difference, light a match, hold it in front of your mouth, and watch the flame as you pronounce the two words.) The contrast between [pʰ] and [p] is phonemic in some languages, such as Hindi (spoken in India). That is, there are words whose meaning is distinguished only by the contrast between an aspirated and an unaspirated [p].

Native speakers vary in their pronunciation of certain phonemes. This variation is important in the evolution of language. With no shifts in pronunciation, there can be no linguistic change. The section on sociolinguistics later in this chapter considers phonetic variation and its relationship to social divisions and the evolution of language.

LANGUAGE, THOUGHT, AND CULTURE

The well-known linguist Noam Chomsky (1957) has argued that the human brain contains a limited set of rules for organizing language, so that all languages have a common structural basis. (Chomsky calls this set of rules *universal grammar*.) The fact that people can learn foreign languages and that words and ideas can be translated from one language into another tends to support Chomsky's position that all humans have similar linguistic abilities and thought processes. Another line of support comes from creole languages. Such languages develop from pidgins, languages that form in situations of acculturation, when different societies come into contact and must devise a system of communication (see Lim and Ansaldo 2016). Pidgins based on English and native languages developed in the context of trade and colonialism in China, Papua New Guinea, and West Africa (see Gu 2012). Eventually, after generations of being spoken, pidgins may develop into *creole languages.* These are more mature languages, with developed grammatical rules and native speakers (i.e., people who learn the language as their primary means of communication during enculturation). Creoles are spoken in several Caribbean societies. Gullah, which is spoken by African Americans on coastal islands in South Carolina and Georgia, is a creole language. Supporting the idea that creoles are based on universal grammar is the fact that they all share certain features. Syntactically, all creole languages use participles (e.g., *will, was*) to form future and past tenses, and multiple negation to deny or negate (e.g., "he don't got none"). Also, all form questions by changing inflection rather than by changing word order—for example, "You're going home for the holidays?" (with a rising tone at the end) rather than "Are you going home for the holidays?"

The Sapir-Whorf Hypothesis

Other linguists and anthropologists take a different approach to the relation between language and thought. Rather than seeking universal linguistic structures and processes, they believe that different languages produce different ways of thinking. This position is sometimes known as the **Sapir-Whorf hypothesis** after Edward Sapir (1931) and

At the top, Lee Wayne Lomayestewa of the Hopi Cultural Preservation Office points out the site of the ancient Tutuveni petroglyphs near Tuba City, Arizona. This site, whose name means "newspaper rock," contains some 5,000 petroglyphs of Hopi clan symbols. The photo on the bottom shows the petroglyphs (rock engravings) up close.
© Pauline Arrillaga/AP Images

his student Benjamin Lee Whorf (1956), its prominent early advocates. Sapir and Whorf argued that the grammatical categories of different languages lead their speakers to think about things in particular ways. For example, the third-person singular pronouns of English (*he, she; him, her; his, hers*) distinguish gender, whereas those of the Palaung, a small tribe in Burma, do not (Burling 1970). Gender exists in English, although a fully developed noun-gender and adjective-agreement system, as in French and other Romance languages (*la belle fille, le beau fils*), does not. The Sapir-Whorf hypothesis therefore might suggest that English speakers can't help paying more attention to differences between males and females than do the Palaung and less than do French or Spanish speakers.

English divides time into past, present, and future. Hopi, a language of the Pueblo region of the Native American Southwest, does not. Rather, Hopi distinguishes between events that exist or have existed (what we use present and past to discuss) and those that don't or don't yet (our future events, along with imaginary and hypothetical

Sapir-Whorf hypothesis
The theory that different languages produce different patterns of thought.

events). Whorf argued that this difference causes Hopi speakers to think about time and reality in different ways than English speakers do. A similar example comes from Portuguese, which employs a future subjunctive verb form, introducing a degree of uncertainty into discussions of the future. In English, we routinely use the future tense to talk about something we think will happen. We don't feel the need to qualify "The sun'll come out tomorrow" by adding "if it doesn't go supernova." We don't hesitate to proclaim "I'll see you next year," even when we can't be absolutely sure we will. The Portuguese future subjunctive qualifies the future event, recognizing that the future can't be certain. Our way of expressing the future as certain is so ingrained that we don't even think about it, just as the Hopi don't see the need to distinguish between present and past, both of which are real, while the future remains hypothetical. It would seem, however, that language does not tightly restrict thought, because cultural changes can produce changes in thought and in language, as we shall see in the next section.

Focal Vocabulary

A *lexicon* (vocabulary) is a language's dictionary, its set of names for things, events, actions, and qualities. Lexicon influences perception. Thus, Eskimos recognize, and have several distinct words for, types of snow that in English are all called *snow*. Most English speakers never notice the differences between these types of snow and might have trouble seeing them even if someone pointed them out. Similarly, the Nuer of South Sudan have an elaborate vocabulary to describe cattle. Eskimos have several words for snow and Nuer have dozens for cattle because of their

particular histories, economies, and environments (Robson 2013). When the need arises, English speakers also can elaborate their snow and cattle vocabularies. For example, skiers name varieties of snow with words that are missing from the lexicons of Florida retirees. Similarly, the cattle vocabulary of a Texas rancher is much ampler than that of a salesperson in a New York City department store. Such specialized sets of terms and distinctions that are particularly important to certain groups (those with particular foci of experience or activity) are known as **focal vocabulary.**

Vocabulary is the area of language that changes most readily. New words and distinctions, when needed, appear and spread. For example, who would have "texted" or "e-mailed" anything a generation ago? Names for items get simpler as they become common and important. A television has become a *TV*, an automobile a *car,* and a digital video disc a *DVD* (see this chapter's "Appreciating Diversity" for a discussion of recent changes in word use in English).

Language, culture, and thought are interrelated. However, and in opposition to the Sapir-Whorf hypothesis, it might be more reasonable to say that changes in culture produce changes in language and thought than the reverse. Consider differences between female and male Americans in regard to the color terms they use (Lakoff 2004). Distinctions implied by such terms as *salmon, rust, peach, beige, teal, mauve, cranberry,* and *dusky orange* aren't in the vocabularies of most American men. However, many of them weren't even in American women's lexicons 70 years ago. Color terms and distinctions have increased with the growth of the fashion and cosmetic industries. A similar contrast (and growth) in Americans' lexicons shows up in football, baseball, basketball, and hockey vocabularies. Sports fans, more often males than females, use more terms in reference to, and make more elaborate distinctions involving the games they watch. Cultural contrasts and changes affect lexical distinctions (for instance, "peach" versus "salmon") within semantic domains (for instance, color terminology). **Semantics** refers to a language's meaning system.

Meaning

Speakers of particular languages use sets of terms to organize, or categorize, their experiences and perceptions. Linguistic terms and contrasts encode (embody) differences in meaning that people perceive. **Ethnosemantics** studies such classification systems in various languages. Well-studied ethnosemantic *domains* (sets of related things, perceptions, or concepts named in a language) include kinship terminology and color terminology. When we study such domains, we are examining

focal vocabulary
A set of words describing particular domains (foci) of experience.

semantics
A language's meaning system.

ethnosemantics
The study of lexical (vocabulary) categories and contrasts.

Spices galore, but what kinds? Merchants at this spice market in Istanbul, Turkey, have a much more elaborate focal vocabulary for what they sell than you or I do.

© Conrad P. Kottak

Words of the Year

Annual lists of "words of the year" provide an excellent illustration of how vocabulary shifts in response to cultural changes. Organizations in various countries routinely publish such lists, which usually choose one increasingly common word as the winner—the "word of the year." According to various lists, the 2015 winners in English included single words, words in combination (such as "binge watch"), and even, in one case, a pictograph, known as the "Face with Tears of Joy" emoji. Among the 2015 words of the year listed by the American Dialect Society were *they* (as a *singular* pronoun), *binge watch, sharing economy, identity, austerity, content marketing, microaggression, refugee, feardom,* and *ammosexual.* These words are viewed as reflecting the ethos, mood, and preoccupations of 2015 (Northover 2016). Let's consider two of the more interesting choices, the singular *they* and the "Face with Tears of Joy" emoji.

Several organizations chose singular *they* as their word of the year (Baron 2015). *They* is a third-person pronoun that is gender neutral; it includes males and females. For centuries it also has been used informally in speech and writing as a singular pronoun. Someone can use *they* when they want to avoid having to use "he or she" in a sentence—as I just did. Historical documents show that *they* has been used as a singular pronoun for over 600 years (Baron 2015). The popularity of the singular *they* has been growing recently because it fills an important linguistic niche—the need for a gender-neutral third-person singular pronoun.

The word *they* itself was introduced into the English language by Danish immigrants in the ninth century. It gradually replaced the then-existing English third-person plural pronoun. For centuries thereafter, English writers and speakers commonly used both the singular and the plural *they.* Its use as a singular pronoun began to meet resistance around 1800. Grammarians discouraged the use of the singular *they* because of lack of agreement between an apparently plural pronoun and a singular verb (e.g., "They eats dinner."). Those grammatical purists who continue to resist the singular *they* might be reminded that the singular pronoun *you* in English began as a plural pronoun, which eventually replaced *thou* and *thee* as a singular pronoun. According to various "word of the year" lists, the time has come for a similar shift to using *they* instead of the more unwieldy "he or she." If someone wants to do that, they won't get any flak from me.

Another illustration of lexical change in progress today is Oxford Dictionaries' first-ever choice of an emoji as 2015's word of the year (Oxford University Press 2015). An *emoji* is a digital image used to express an idea or emotion in electronic communication. Despite its similarity to the English word *emoticon* (coined from *emotion* and *icon*), the word *emoji* actually comes from Japanese. Emojis have been around since the late 1990s, but their use, along with the use of the term *emoji* itself, have increased substantially. No doubt, this reflects the growing availability of these pictographs on smartphones, tablets, computers, and other devices we use to communicate

The Face with Tears of Joy emoji—one of 2015's "words" of the year. Have you ever used this, or a similar, emoji?
© Maksym Chechel/Shutterstock.com RF

on a daily basis. Between 2014 and 2015, use of the word *emoji* tripled in the United States and the United Kingdom (Northover 2016). According to a study done by Oxford University Press and the mobile technology company SwiftKey, the most popular emoji—the "Face with Tears of Joy"—represented 20 percent of all emojis used in the United Kingdom, and 17 percent of those used in the United States, in 2015 (Northover 2016). The growing role of digital transmission in our everyday lives, including reliance on emojis, illustrates once again how language and communication continue to evolve in our globalizing world.

how those people perceive and distinguish between kin relationships or colors. Other such domains include ethnomedicine—the terminology for the causes, symptoms, and cures of disease; ethnobotany—native classification of plant life; and ethnoastronomy.

Anthropologists have discovered that certain lexical domains and vocabulary items evolve in a determined order. For example, after studying color terminology in more than 100 languages, Berlin and Kay (1991, 1999) discovered 10 basic color terms: *white, black, red, yellow, blue, green, brown, pink, orange,* and *purple* (they evolved in more or less that order). The number of terms varied with cultural complexity. Representing one extreme were Papua New Guinea cultivators and Australian hunters and gatherers, who used only two basic terms, which translate as *black* and *white* or *dark* and *light.* At the other end of the continuum were European and Asian languages with all the color terms. Color terminology was most developed in areas with a history of using dyes and artificial coloring.

SOCIOLINGUISTICS

No language is a uniform system in which everyone talks just like everyone else. The field of sociolinguistics investigates relationships between social and linguistic variation (Edwards 2013; Spencer 2010; Wardhaugh and Fuller 2015). How do different speakers use a given language? How do linguistic features correlate with social diversity and stratification, including class, ethnic, and gender differences (Eckert and McConnell-Ginet 2013; McConnell-Ginet 2010; Tannen 1990, 1993)? How is language used to gain, express, reinforce, or resist power (Fairclough 2015; Mesthrie 2011; Mooney 2011; Trudgill 2010)?

Sociolinguists focus on features that vary systematically with social position and situation. To study variation, sociolinguists must observe, define, and measure variable use of language in real-world situations. In his book *The Language of Food,* linguist Dan Jurafsky (2014) describes a recent study based on measurement of sociolinguistic variation. Jurafsky and his colleagues analyzed the menus of 6,500 contemporary American restaurants. One of their goals was to see how the food vocabularies of upscale restaurants differed from those of cheaper establishments. One key difference they found was that upscale menus paid much more attention to the sources of the foods they served. They named specific farms, gardens, ranches, pastures, woodlands, and farmers' markets. They were careful to mention, if the season was right, that their tomatoes or peas were heirloom varieties. Very expensive restaurants mentioned the origin of food more than 15 times as often as inexpensive restaurants. Another key difference was that the cheaper restaurants offered about twice as many menu choices as the expensive ones.

Word length was another differentiator. Upscale menu words averaged half a letter longer than in the cheaper restaurants. Cheaper eateries, for instance, were more likely to use *decaf,* rather than *decaffeinated,* and *sides* rather than *accompaniments.* Diners had to pay higher prices for those longer words: Every increase of one letter in the average length of words describing a dish meant an average increase of $0.18 in the price of that dish.

Cheaper restaurants were more apt to use linguistic fillers. These included positive but vague words like *delicious, tasty, mouthwatering,* and *flavorful,* or other positive, but impossible to measure, adjectives such as *terrific, wonderful, delightful,* and *sublime.* Each positive vague word for a dish in a modest restaurant reduced its average price by 9 percent. Downscale restaurants also were more likely to assure their diners that their offerings were *fresh,* as though there might be some reason to doubt that freshness. Expensive restaurants expect their patrons to assume that their offerings are fresh, without having to say it.

Jurafsky and his associates also analyzed vocabulary used in one million online Yelp restaurant reviews, representing seven American cities—Boston, Chicago, Los Angeles, New York, Philadelphia, San Francisco, and Washington, D.C. The researchers found that good and bad reviews differed linguistically. Reviewers used a greater variety of words, with more differentiated meanings, to express negative than positive opinions. This tendency, known as negative differentiation, extends to other linguistic domains in English, and even to other languages. People seem to need more varied and elaborate ways of being negative than positive. Yelp reviews are actually brief stories that people tell about their experiences. Bad reviews are stories about bad things that restaurant personnel have done to the reviewer and his or her party. Negative reviewers wanted to comment on the restaurant's failings as fully as possible and as a shared experience. Bad reviews were much more likely than good ones to use the inclusive pronouns *we* and *us.* Psychologists know that traumatized people seek comfort in groups by emphasizing their belonging, using the words *we* and *us* with high frequency when reporting about negative experiences. Next time you eat out and/or are tempted to write a review, pay attention to these findings about "the language of food."

Study these menus from two restaurants, one more upscale than the other. Note the use of names of farms (food origin) in one menu and the use of adjectives such as "delicious," "fresh," and "premium" in the other. Which menu is from the more upscale restaurant?

© McGraw-Hill Education. Mark Dierker, photographer RF

Variation within a language at a given time is historic change in progress. The same forces that, working gradually, have produced large-scale linguistic change over the centuries are still at work today. Linguistic change occurs not in a vacuum but in society. When new ways of speaking are associated with social factors, they are imitated, and they spread. In this way, a language changes.

Linguistic Diversity within Nations

As an illustration of the linguistic variation that is encountered in all nations, consider the contemporary United States. Ethnic diversity is revealed by the fact that millions of Americans learn first languages other than English. Spanish is the most common. Most of those people eventually become bilinguals, adding English as a second language. In many multilingual (including colonized) nations, people use two or more languages on different occasions: one in the home, for example, and the other on the job or in public. In India, where some 22 languages are spoken, a person may need to use three different languages when talking, respectively, with a boss, a spouse, and a parent. Only about one-tenth of India's population speaks English, the colonial language. As they interact today with one of the key instruments of globalization—the Internet—even those English speakers appreciate being able to read, and to find Internet content in, their own regional languages.

Whether bilingual or not, we all vary our speech depending on context; we engage in **style shifts.** In 2013, I traveled to India with a friend, an India-born American who speaks perfectly good standard American English. During the time we spent in India, it was fascinating to watch as he shifted back and forth between Hindi, English with a strong Indian accent (when speaking to Indians in English), and American English (when speaking to his American fellow travelers). In certain parts of Europe, people regularly switch dialects. This phenomenon, known as **diglossia,** applies to "high" and "low" variants of the same language, for example, in German and Dutch. People employ the "high" variant at universities and in writing, professions, and the mass media. They use the "low" variant for ordinary conversation with family members and friends.

Just as social situations influence our speech, so do geographic, cultural, and socioeconomic differences. Many dialects coexist in the United States with Standard (American) English, which itself is a dialect that differs, say, from "BBC English," the preferred dialect in Great Britain. According to the principle of *linguistic relativity,* all dialects are equally effective as systems of communication, which is language's main job. Our tendency to think of particular dialects as cruder or more sophisticated than others is a social rather than a linguistic judgment. We rank certain speech patterns as better or worse because we recognize that they are used by groups that we also rank. People who say *dese, dem,* and *dere* instead of *these, them,* and *there* communicate perfectly well with anyone who recognizes that the *d* sound systematically replaces the *th* sound in their speech. However, this form of speech is stigmatized; it has become an indicator of low social rank. We call it, like the use of *ain't,* "uneducated speech." The use of *dem, dese,* and *dere* is one of many phonological differences that Americans recognize and look down on (see Labov 2012).

Gender Speech Contrasts

Comparing men and women, there are differences in phonology, grammar, and vocabulary as well as in the body stances and movements that accompany speech (Eckert and McConnell-Ginet 2013; Lakoff 2004; McConnell-Ginet 2010; Tannen 1990). In public contexts, traditional Japanese women tend to adopt an artificially high voice, for the sake of politeness. In North America and Great Britain, women's speech tends to be more similar to the standard dialect than men's speech. Consider the data in Table 14.1, gathered in Detroit. In all social classes, but particularly in the working class, men were more apt to use double negatives (e.g., "I don't want none"). Women tend to be more careful about "uneducated speech." Men may adopt working-class speech because they associate it with masculinity. Perhaps women pay more attention to the media, where standard dialects are employed.

According to Robin Lakoff (2004), the use of certain types of words and expressions has been associated with women's traditional lesser power

style shifts
Varying one's speech in different social contexts.

diglossia
A language with "high" (formal) and "low" (informal, familial) dialects.

TABLE 14.1 Multiple Negation ("I don't want none") According to Gender and Class (in Percentages)

	UPPER MIDDLE CLASS	LOWER MIDDLE CLASS	UPPER WORKING CLASS	LOWER WORKING CLASS
Male	6.3	32.4	40.0	90.1
Female	0.0	1.4	35.6	58.9

SOURCE: Peter Trudgill, *Sociolinguistics: An Introduction to Language and Society,* 5th ed. (London: Penguin Books, 1974, revised editions 1983, 1995, 2000), p. 70.

in American society (see also Tannen 1990). For example, *Oh dear, Oh fudge,* and *Goodness!* are less forceful than *Hell* and *Damn.* Watch the lips of a disgruntled player in a football game. What's the likelihood he's saying "Phooey on you"? Women are more likely to use such adjectives as *adorable, charming, sweet, cute, lovely,* and *divine* than men are.

Language and Status Position

Honorifics are terms used with people, often by being added to their names, to "honor" them. Such terms may convey or imply a status difference between the speaker and the person being referred to ("the good doctor") or addressed ("Professor Dumbledore"). Although Americans tend to be less formal than other nationalities, American English still has its honorifics. They include such terms as *Mr., Mrs., Ms., Dr., Professor, Dean, Senator, Reverend, Honorable,* and *President.* Often these terms are attached to names, as in "Dr. Wilson," "President Clinton," and "Senator Klobuchar," but some of them can be used to address someone without using his or her name, such as "Dr.," "Mr. President," "Senator," and "Miss." The British have a more developed set of honorifics, corresponding to status distinctions based on class, nobility (e.g., "Lord and Lady Trumble"), and special recognition (e.g., knighthood—"Sir Elton" or "Dame Judi").

In Japanese, several honorifics convey different degrees of respect. The suffix *-sama* (added to a name), showing great respect, is used to address someone of higher social status, such as a lord or a respected teacher. Women can use it to demonstrate love or respect for their husbands. The most common Japanese honorific, *-san,* attached to the last name, is respectful, but it is less formal than "Mr.," "Mrs.," or "Ms." in American English. Attached to a first name, *-san* denotes more familiarity (*Free Dictionary* 2004; Loveday 1986, 2001).

Kin terms, too, can be associated with gradations in age, rank, and status. *Dad* is a more familiar, less formal kin term than *Father,* but it still shows more respect than would using the father's first name. Outranking their children, parents routinely use their kids' first names, nicknames, or baby names, rather than addressing them as "son" and "daughter." Southerners up to (and sometimes long past) a certain age routinely use "ma'am" and "sir" for older or higher-status women and men.

Stratification

We use and evaluate speech in the context of *extralinguistic* forces—social, political, and economic. Mainstream Americans evaluate the speech of low-status groups negatively, calling it "uneducated." This is not because these ways of speaking are bad in themselves but because they have come to symbolize low status. Consider variation in the pronunciation of *r.* In some parts of the United States, *r* is regularly pronounced, and in other (*r*less) areas, it is not. Originally, American *r*less speech was modeled on the fashionable speech of England. Because of its prestige, *r*lessness was adopted in many areas and continues as the norm around Boston and in the South.

New Yorkers sought prestige by dropping their *r*'s in the 19th century, after having pronounced them in the 18th. However, contemporary New Yorkers are going back to the 18th-century pattern of pronouncing *r*'s. What matters, and what governs linguistic change, is not the reverberation of a strong midwestern *r* but *social* evaluation, whether *r*'s happen to be "in" or "out."

Studies of *r* pronunciation in New York City have clarified the mechanisms of phonological change. William Labov (1972*b*) focused on whether *r* was pronounced after vowels in such words as *car, floor, card,* and *fourth.* To get data on how this linguistic variation correlated with social class, he used a series of rapid encounters with employees in three New York City department stores, each of whose prices and locations attracted a different socioeconomic group. Saks Fifth Avenue (68 encounters) catered to the upper middle class, Macy's (125) attracted middle-class shoppers, and S. Klein's (71) had predominantly lower-middle-class and working-class customers. The class origins of store personnel tended to reflect those of their customers.

Having already determined that a certain department was on the fourth floor, Labov approached ground-floor salespeople and asked where that department was. After the salesperson had answered, "Fourth floor," Labov repeated his "Where?" in order to get a second response. The second reply was more formal and emphatic, the salesperson presumably thinking that Labov hadn't heard or understood the first answer. For each salesperson, therefore, Labov had two samples of /r/ pronunciation in two words.

Labov calculated the percentages of workers who pronounced /r/ at least once during the interview. These were 62 percent at Saks, 51 percent at Macy's, but only 20 percent at S. Klein's. He also found that personnel on upper floors, where he asked "What floor is this?" (and where more expensive items were sold), pronounced /r/ more often than ground-floor salespeople did (see also Labov 2006).

In Labov's study, summarized in Table 14.2, /r/ pronunciation was clearly associated with prestige. Certainly the job interviewers who had hired the salespeople never counted *r*'s before offering employment. However, they did use speech evaluations to make judgments about how effective certain people would be in selling particular kinds of merchandise. In other words, they practiced sociolinguistic discrimination, using linguistic features in deciding who got certain jobs.

Americans have stereotypes about how people from certain regions talk, and some stereotypes are more widespread than others are (see this

---

honorifics
Terms of respect; used to honor people.

TABLE 14.2 Pronunciation of *r* in New York City Department Stores

STORE	NUMBER OF ENCOUNTERS	% *r* PRONUNCIATION
Saks Fifth Avenue	68	62
Macy's	125	51
S. Klein's	71	20

Certain dialects are stigmatized, not because of actual linguistic deficiencies but because of a symbolic association between a certain way of talking and low social status. In this scene from the movie *My Fair Lady,* Professor Henry Higgins (Rex Harrison) teaches Eliza Doolittle (Audrey Hepburn), formerly a Cockney flower girl, how to speak "proper English."

© Warner Brothers/Album/Newscom

chapter's "Appreciating Anthropology" for stereotypes about, and the reality of, California speech patterns). Most Americans think they can imitate a "southern accent," and southern speech tends to be devalued outside the South. Americans also stereotype, without necessarily stigmatizing, speech in New York City (the pronunciation of *coffee,* for example), Boston ("I pahked the kah in Hahvahd Yahd"), and Canada ("oot" for "out").

It's sometimes asserted that midwestern Americans don't have accents. This belief stems from the fact that midwestern dialects don't have many stigmatized linguistic variants—speech patterns that people in other regions recognize and look down on, such as *r*lessness and *dem, dese,* and *dere* (instead of *them, these,* and *there*).

Far from having no accents, midwesterners, even in the same high school, exhibit linguistic diversity (see Eckert 1989, 2000). One of the best examples of variable midwestern speech, involving vowels, is pronunciation of the *e* sound (the /e/ phoneme) in such words as *ten, rent, section, lecture, effect, best,* and *test.* In southeastern Michigan, there are four different ways of pronouncing this *e* sound. Speakers of African American English and immigrants from Appalachia often pronounce *ten* as "tin," just as southerners habitually do. Some Michiganders say "ten," the correct pronunciation in Standard English. However, two other pronunciations also are common. Instead of "ten," many Michiganders say "tan," or "tun" (as though they were using the word *ton,* a unit of weight).

My students often astound me with their pronunciation. One day I met a Michigan-raised graduate student instructor in the hall. She was deliriously happy. When I asked why, she replied, "I've just had the best suction."

"What?" I said.

She finally spoke more precisely. "I've just had the best saction." She considered this a clearer pronunciation of the word *section.*

In another example of such speech, one of my students lamented, after an exam, that she had not done her "bust on the tust" (i.e., best on the test). The truth is, regional patterns affect the way we all speak.

Our speech habits help determine how others evaluate us and thus our access to employment and other material resources. Because of this,

Use of language can be a strategic resource, correlated with wealth, prestige, and power. Shown here is a recent graduate of an ESL (English as a Second Language) class in Modesto, California. How necessary is it for Spanish speakers in the United States to learn English?

© ZUMA Press Inc /Alamy Stock Photo

I Wish They All Could Be California Vowels

Is there a "California accent"? Popular stereotypes of how Californians talk reflect exposure to media images of blond surfer boys who say things like "dude" and "gnarly" and white Valley girls who intone "Like, totally!" and "Gag me with a spoon!" Such stereotypes have some accuracy, as we'll see. Just as striking, however, is the linguistic diversity that also marks contemporary California.

To document this diversity, Professor Penelope Eckert, a sociolinguist at Stanford University, and her graduate students are engaged in an ongoing, multiyear research project called Voices of California (see http://www.stanford.edu/dept/linguistics/VoCal/). Eckert's team of 10–15 researchers visits a new site each fall, spending about 10 days interviewing residents who grew up in the area. Recently, their focus has been on inland California, which has been less studied than have the main coastal cities. The group has studied Merced, Redding, and Bakersfield. The researchers always test certain words that elicit specific pronunciations. These words include *wash,* sometimes pronounced "warsh," *greasy* ("greezy"), and *pin* and *pen,* which some people pronounce the same. Interviews in Merced and Shasta Counties have revealed ways that Depression-era migrants from Oklahoma's Dust Bowl left their mark on California speech, such as their pronunciation of *wash* and *greasy* (see King 2012).

We see, then, that one factor in determining how people speak is where their ancestors came from. Another factor is their own attitudes and feelings about the people around them and about the outside world. For example, in California's Central Valley, which is economically depressed, young people must choose whether to stay put or to move elsewhere, seeking work. When people are, and want to stay, involved in their home community, they tend to talk like locals. A desire not to be perceived as being from a particular place also affects how people talk (King 2012).

I know this feeling well, having abandoned my original southern accent when I was an adolescent. In fact, my own speech shift wasn't totally voluntary: as mentioned previously, I was placed in a speech class when I moved from Atlanta to New York City at the age of 13. The same thing happened to my college roommate, from Baton Rouge, Louisiana, when he enrolled at Columbia University in New York City. By then, my own speech had become sufficiently accent free to avoid further speech indoctrination.

In addition to regional diversity, the speech of Californians also reflects ethnic contrasts. Non-Hispanic whites now represent under 40 percent of the state's total population, while Latinos (Hispanics) constitute 38 percent. California also has a large and diverse Asian American population and a sizable group of African Americans.

Representing California's largest minority, as well as its earliest nonindigenous settlers, Chicanos (Mexican Americans) display interesting speech patterns. California's Mexican-derived populations can claim the longest continuous (nonindigenous) linguistic history in the state, including Spanish/English bilingualism and the source of most important place names. So strong is the Spanish heritage that Spanish-like vowels even influence the way English is spoken by Hispanics who learn English as their first, or native, language. For example, among Chicano speakers in northern California the vowel in the second syllable of *nothing* has come to resemble the Spanish "ee" sound. Not all innovations in Chicano English come from Spanish. One widespread speech innovation in Los Angeles has been the lowering of the vowel in the first syllable of *elevator,* so that it rhymes with the first syllable of *alligator.* That shift owes nothing to Spanish (see Eckert and Mendoza-Denton 2002).

Despite the well-documented diversity in California speech, linguists have detected trends toward uniformity as well, particularly among coastal whites. Since the 1940s, a distinctive "California accent" has been developing, and some of its features were indeed highlighted in Moon Unit Zappa's 1982 recording of "Valley Girl."

The accent is most evident in vowels, as we see in the following examples. First, the vowels in *hock* and *hawk,* or *cot* and *caught,* are pronounced the same, so that *awesome* rhymes with *possum.* Second, the vowel sound in *boot* and *dude* has shifted and now is pronounced as in *cute* or *pure* (thus, *boot* becomes "beaut," and *dude* becomes "dewed," rather than "dood").

"proper language" itself becomes a strategic resource—and a path to wealth, prestige, and power (Gal 1989; Mooney 2011). Illustrating this, many ethnographers have described the importance of verbal skill and oratory in politics (Beeman 1986; Brenneis 1988; Geis 1987). Ronald Reagan, known as a "great communicator," dominated American society in the 1980s as a two-term president. Another twice-elected president, Bill Clinton, despite his Arkansas accent, is known for his verbal skills. Communications flaws may have helped doom the presidencies of Gerald Ford, Jimmy Carter, and George Bush (the elder). How do you evaluate the linguistic skills of the current leader of your country?

The French anthropologist Pierre Bourdieu views linguistic practices as *symbolic capital* that people, if trained properly, can convert into economic and social capital. The value of a dialect—its standing in a "linguistic market"—depends on the extent to which it provides access to desired positions in society. In turn, this reflects its

Third, the vowel sound in *but* and *cut* is shifting, so that those words sound more like *bet* and *ket*. Finally, *black* is being pronounced more like *block;* and *bet,* like *bat* (see Eckert and Mendoza-Denton 2002).

Such coordinated phonological changes are known as chain shifts. The most extreme ver-sions of these chain-shifted vowel sounds are found in the speech of young white Californians. Young people tend to be leaders in speech in-novations, which is why linguists spend a lot of time studying them. California's communities bring together adolescents from varied back-grounds. Their linguistic styles, like their clothing and behavioral styles, influence one another. Hostility may cause people to differentiate and diversify their styles, while curiosity or admira-tion may cause people to copy, or adopt ele-ments from, other styles. Whose styles, linguistic or otherwise, might you have copied—or avoided?

Stereotypes about regional speech styles show up in mass media, which then reinforce and help spread those stereotypes. Linguistic stereotypes abound in the movies, *Clueless* and *Bill and Ted's Excellent Adventure.*
Left: © Buyenlarge/Moviepix/Getty Images; right: © Everett Collection/Alamy Stock Photo

legitimation by formal institutions: educational institutions, state, church, and prestige media. Even people who don't use the prestige dialect accept its authority and correctness, its "sym-bolic domination" (Bourdieu 1982, 1984; Labov 2012). Thus, linguistic forms, which lack power in themselves, take on the power of the groups they symbolize (see Mooney and Evans 2015). The ed-ucation system, however (defending its own worth), denies linguistic relativity, misrepresent-ing prestige speech as being inherently better. The linguistic insecurity often felt by lower-class and minority speakers is a result of this symbolic domination.

African American Vernacular English (AAVE)

No one pays much attention when someone says "saction" instead of "section." But some nonstan-dard speech carries more of a stigma. Sometimes stigmatized speech is linked to region, class, or

African American
Vernacular English
(AAVE)
The rule-governed
dialect spoken by some
African Americans.

educational background; sometimes it is associated with ethnicity or "race."

Sociolinguists have conducted detailed studies of what they call **African American Vernacular English (AAVE).** (*Vernacular* means ordinary, casual speech.) AAVE is the "relatively uniform dialect spoken by the majority of black youth in most parts of the United States . . . , especially in the inner city areas of New York, Boston, Detroit, Philadelphia, Washington, Cleveland, . . . and other urban centers. It is also spoken in most rural areas and used in the casual, intimate speech of many adults" (Labov 1972*a*, p. xiii). This does not imply that all, or even most, African Americans speak AAVE.

AAVE may be a nonstandard dialect, but it is not an ungrammatical hodgepodge. Rather, AAVE is a complex linguistic system with its own rules, which linguists have described. The phonology and syntax of AAVE are similar to those of southern dialects. This reflects generations of contact between southern whites and blacks, with mutual influence on each other's speech patterns. Many features that distinguish AAVE from Standard English (SE) also show up in southern white speech, but less frequently than in AAVE.

Linguists disagree about exactly how AAVE originated (Rickford 1997; Rickford and Rickford 2000). Smitherman (1986) notes certain structural similarities between West African languages and AAVE. African linguistic backgrounds no doubt influenced how early African Americans learned English. Did they restructure English to fit African linguistic patterns? Or, possibly, in acquiring English, did African slaves fuse English with African languages to make a pidgin or creole, which influenced the subsequent development of AAVE? Creole speech may have been brought to the American colonies by the many slaves who were brought in from the Caribbean during the 17th and 18th centuries (Rickford 1997).

Origins aside, there are phonological and grammatical differences between AAVE and SE. One phonological difference is that AAVE speakers are less likely to pronounce *r* than SE speakers are. Actually, many SE speakers don't pronounce *r*'s that come right before a consonant (ca*r*d) or at the end of a word (ca*r*). But SE speakers do usually pronounce an *r* that comes right before a vowel, either at the end of a word (fou*r* o'clock) or within a word (Ca*r*ol). AAVE speakers, by contrast, are much more likely to omit such intervocalic (between vowels) *r*'s. The result is that speakers of the two dialects have different *homonyms* (words that sound the same but have different meanings). AAVE speakers who don't pronounce intervocalic *r*'s have the following homonyms: Carol/Cal; Paris/pass.

Observing different phonological rules, AAVE speakers pronounce certain words differently than SE speakers do. Particularly in the elementary school context, the homonyms of AAVE-speaking students typically differ from those of their SE-speaking teachers. To evaluate reading accu-racy, teachers should determine whether students are recognizing the different meanings of such AAVE homonyms as *passed, past,* and *pass.* Teachers need to make sure students understand what they are reading, which is probably more important than whether they are pronouncing words correctly according to the SE norm.

The phonological contrasts between AAVE and SE speakers often have grammatical consequences. One of these involves *copula deletion,* which means the absence of SE forms of the copula—the verb *to be.* SE habitually uses contractions, as in "you're tired" instead of "you are tired." Where SE shortens with contractions, AAVE goes one step further and deletes the copular altogether—thus "you tired." AAVE's copula deletion is a grammatical result of its phonological rules, which dictate that *r*'s (as in *you're, we're,* and *they're*) and word-final *s*'s (as in *he's*) be dropped. However, AAVE speakers do pronounce *m,* so that the AAVE first-person singular is "I'm tired," just as in SE. In its deletion of the present tense of the verb *to be,* AAVE is similar to many languages, including Russian, Hungarian, and Hebrew.

SE	SE CONTRACTION	AAVE
you are tired	you're tired	you tired
he is tired	he's tired	he tired
we are tired	we're tired	we tired
they are tired	they're tired	they tired

Also, phonological rules may lead AAVE speakers to omit *-ed* as a past-tense marker and *-s* as a marker of plurality. However, other speech contexts demonstrate that AAVE speakers do understand the difference between past and present verbs, and between singular and plural nouns. Confirming this are irregular verbs (e.g., *tell, told*) and irregular plurals (e.g., *child, children*), in which AAVE works the same as SE.

SE is not superior to AAVE as a linguistic system, but it does happen to be the prestige dialect—the one used in the mass media, in writing, and in most public and professional contexts. SE is the dialect that has the most "symbolic capital." In areas of Germany where there is diglossia, speakers of Plattdeusch (Low German) learn the High German dialect (originally spoken in the highlands of southern Germany) to communicate appropriately in the national context. High German is the standard literary and spoken form of German. Similarly, upwardly mobile AAVE-speaking students learn SE.

HISTORICAL LINGUISTICS

Sociolinguists study contemporary variation in speech—language change in progress. **Historical linguistics** deals with longer-term change. Language changes over time. It evolves—varies,

Rapper Kendrick Lamar (center) performs on the 2016 GRAMMY Awards show at Staples Center in Los Angeles, California. How does contemporary music reflect and express ideas about race, ethnicity, and gender?

© Kevork Djansezian/Getty Images Entertainment/Getty Images

spreads, divides into dialects and eventually into **subgroups** (languages within a taxonomy of related languages that are most closely related). Historical linguists can reconstruct many features of past languages by studying contemporary **daughter languages.** These are languages that descend from the same parent language and that have been changing for hundreds or even thousands of years. We call the original language from which they diverge the **protolanguage.** Romance languages such as French and Spanish, for example, are daughter languages of Latin, their common protolanguage. German, English, Dutch, and the Scandinavian languages are daughter languages of proto-Germanic. Latin and proto-Germanic were both Indo-European (IE) languages (see Figure 14.2). Proto-Indo-European (PIE), spoken in the more distant past, was the common protolanguage of Latin, proto-Germanic, and many other ancient languages.

According to one theory, PIE was introduced by chariot-driving pastoralists who spread out from the Eurasian steppes above the Black Sea about 4,000 years ago and conquered Europe and Asia (see Wade 2012). The main line of evidence for this view is linguistic: PIE had a vocabulary for chariots and wagons that included words for "wheel," "axle," "harness-pole," and "to go or convey in a vehicle." These PIE words (as reconstructed by historical linguists) have recognizable descendant words in many IE languages. This

suggests that wheeled vehicles must have been invented before PIE started diverging (Wade 2012). The earliest such vehicles date to 3500 B.C.E.

The main rival theory, first proposed by archaeologist Colin Renfrew (1987), is that PIE was spoken and spread by peaceful farmers who lived in Anatolia, now Turkey, about 9,000 years ago. Recent studies by the evolutionary biologist Quentin Atkinson and his colleagues in New Zealand support the Anatolian origin of PIE (see Bouckaert et al. 2012). Atkinson's team focused on a set of vocabulary items known to be resistant to linguistic change. These include pronouns, parts of the body, and family relations. For 103 IE languages, the researchers compared those words with the PIE ancestral word (as reconstructed by historical linguists). Words that clearly descend from the same ancestral word are known as *cognates*. For example, *mother* (English) is cognate with all these words for the same relative: *mutter* (German), *mat* (Russian), *madar* (Persian), *matka* (Polish) and *mater* (Latin). All are descendants of the PIE word *mehter*.

For each language, when the word was a cognate the researchers scored it 1; when it was not (having been replaced by an unrelated word), it was scored 0. With each language represented by a string of 1s and 0s, the researchers could establish a family tree showing the relationships among the 103 languages. Based on those relationships and the geographic areas where the daughter

subgroups
(Linguistic) closely related languages.

daughter languages
The languages sharing a common parent language, e.g., Latin.

protolanguage
A language ancestral to several daughter languages.

FIGURE 14.2 PIE Family Tree.

This is a family tree of the Indo-European languages. All can be traced back to a protolanguage, Proto-Indo-European (PIE). PIE split into dialects that eventually evolved into separate daughter languages, which, in turn, evolved into granddaughter languages such as Latin and proto-Germanic, which are ancestral to dozens of modern languages.

languages are spoken, the computer determined the likeliest routes of movement from an origin. The calculation pointed to Anatolia, southern Turkey. This is precisely the region originally proposed by Renfrew, because it was the area from which farming spread to Europe. Atkinson also ran a computer simulation on a grammar-based IE tree—once again finding Anatolia to be the most likely origin point for PIE (Wade 2012). Although many linguists still support the chariot/steppe origin theory, several lines of biological and archaeological evidence now indicate that the Neolithic economy spread more through the actual migration of farmers than through the diffusion of crops and ideas. This would seem to offer support to the Renfrew–Atkinson model of PIE origin and dispersal of Neolithic farmers.

Historically oriented linguists suspect that a very remote protolanguage, spoken perhaps 50,000 years ago in Africa, gave rise to all contemporary languages. Murray Gell-Mann and Merritt Ruhlen (2011), who co-direct the Program on the Evolution of Human Languages at the Sante Fe Institute, have reconstructed the syntax (word ordering) of this ancient protolanguage. Their study focused on how subject (S), object (O), and verb (V) are arranged in phrases and sentences in some 2,000 contemporary languages. There are six possible word orders: SOV, SVO, OSV, OVS, VSO, and VOS. Most common is SOV ("I you like," e.g., Latin), present in more than half of all languages. Next comes SVO ("I like you," e.g., English). Much rarer are OSV, OVS, VOS, and VSO. Gell-Mann and Ruhlen constructed a family tree of relationships among 2,000 contemporary languages. The directions of change involving the six word orders were clear. All the languages that were SVO, OVS, and OSV

Modern technology can be a valuable tool for language preservation. Two centuries after a Cherokee silversmith named Sequoyah developed a system of symbols for Cherokee syllables, students at the Cherokee Nation Immersion School in Oklahoma use computers, tablets, iPhones, and iPods to learn to read and write the Cherokee language.

© Sue Ogrocki/AP Images

derived from SOV languages—never the other way around. Furthermore, any language with VSO or VOS word order always came from an SVO language (see Figure 14.3). The fact that SVO always comes from SOV confirms SOV as the original, ancestral word order.

Language, Culture, and History

A close relationship between languages does not necessarily mean that their speakers are closely related biologically or culturally, because people can adopt new languages. In the equatorial forests of Africa, "pygmy" hunters have discarded their ancestral languages and now speak those of the cultivators who have migrated to the area. Immigrants to the United States and Canada spoke many different languages on arrival, but their descendants now speak fluent English.

Knowledge of linguistic relationships is often valuable to anthropologists interested in history, particularly events during the past 5,000 years. Cultural features may (or may not) correlate with the distribution of language families. Groups that speak related languages may (or may not) be more culturally similar to each other than they are to groups whose speech derives from different linguistic ancestors. Of course, cultural similarities aren't limited to speakers of related languages. Even groups whose members speak unrelated languages have contact through trade, intermarriage, and warfare. Ideas and inventions diffuse widely among human groups. Many items of vocabulary in contemporary English come from French. Even without written documentation of France's influence after the Norman Conquest of England in 1066, linguistic evidence in contemporary English would reveal a long period of important firsthand contact with France. Similar linguistic evidence may confirm cultural contact and borrowing when written history is lacking. By considering which words have been borrowed, we also can make inferences about the nature of the contact.

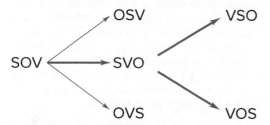

FIGURE 14.3 Evolution of Word Order from Original SOV (Subject, Object, Verb) in Ancient Ancestral Protolanguage.

Language Loss

One aspect of linguistic history is language loss. When languages disappear, cultural diversity is reduced as well. According to linguist K. David Harrison, "When we lose a language, we lose centuries of thinking about time, seasons, sea creatures, reindeer, edible flowers, mathematics, landscapes, myths, music, the unknown and the everyday" (quoted in Maugh 2007). Harrison's book *When Languages Die* (2007), notes that an indigenous language goes extinct every two weeks, as its last speakers die. The world's linguistic diversity has been cut in half (measured by number of distinct languages) in the past 500 years, and half of the remaining languages are predicted to disappear during this century. Colonial languages (e.g., English, Spanish, Portuguese, French, Dutch, Russian) have expanded at the expense of indigenous ones. Of approximately 7,000 remaining languages, about 20 percent are endangered, compared with 18 percent of mammals, 8 percent of plants, and 5 percent of birds (Harrison 2010; Maugh 2007). National

Geographic's Enduring Voices Project (http://www.nationalgeographic.com/mission/enduringvoices/about-the-project.html) strives to preserve endangered languages by identifying the geographic areas with unique, poorly understood, or threatened languages and by documenting those languages and cultures. The website shows various language hot spots where the endangerment rate ranges from low to severe. The rate is high in an area encompassing Oklahoma, Texas, and New Mexico, where 40 Native American languages are at risk (see Coronel-Molina and McCarty 2016). The top hot spot is northern Australia, where 153 Aboriginal languages are endangered (Maugh 2007). Other hot spots are in central South America, the Pacific Northwest of North America, and eastern Siberia. In all these areas indigenous tongues have yielded, either voluntarily or through coercion, to a colonial language (see Harrison 2010).

for REVIEW

summary

1. Wild primates use call systems to communicate. Environmental stimuli trigger calls, which cannot be combined when multiple stimuli are present. Contrasts between language and call systems include displacement, productivity, and cultural transmission. Over time, our ancestral call systems grew too complex for genetic transmission, and hominid communication began to rely on learning. Humans still use nonverbal communication, such as facial expressions, gestures, and body stances and movements. But language is the main system humans use to communicate. Chimps and gorillas can understand and manipulate nonverbal symbols based on language.

2. No language uses all the sounds the human vocal tract can make. Phonology—the study of speech sounds—focuses on sound contrasts (phonemes) that distinguish meaning. The grammars and lexicons of particular languages can lead their speakers to perceive and think in certain ways. Studies of domains such as kinship, color terminologies, and pronouns show that speakers of different languages categorize their experiences differently.

3. Linguistic anthropologists share anthropology's general interest in diversity in time and space. Sociolinguistics investigates relationships between social and linguistic variation by focusing on the actual use of language. Only when features of speech acquire social meaning are

they imitated. If they are valued, they will spread. People vary their speech, shifting styles, dialects, and languages. As linguistic systems, all languages and dialects are equally complex, rule-governed, and effective for communication. However, speech is used, is evaluated, and changes in the context of political, economic, and social forces. Often the linguistic traits of a low-status group are negatively evaluated. This devaluation is not because of *linguistic* features per se. Rather, it reflects the association of such features with low *social* status. One dialect, supported by the dominant institutions of the state, exercises symbolic domination over the others.

4. Historical linguistics is useful for anthropologists interested in historic relationships among populations. Cultural similarities and differences often correlate with linguistic ones. Linguistic clues can suggest past contacts between cultures. Related languages—members of the same language family—descend from an original protolanguage. Relationships between languages don't necessarily mean that there are biological ties between their speakers, because people can learn new languages.

5. One aspect of linguistic history is language loss. The world's linguistic diversity has been cut in half in the past 500 years, and half of the remaining 7,000 languages are predicted to disappear during this century.

key terms

critical thinking

1. What dialects and languages do you speak? Do you tend to use different dialects, languages, or speech styles in different contexts? Why or why not?

2. Culture always plays a role in shaping what we understand as "natural." What does this mean? Provide three examples of the relevance of this fact in the context of human language and communication.

3. Consider how changing technologies are altering the ways you communicate with family, friends, and even strangers. Suppose your best friend decides to study sociolinguistics in graduate school. What ideas about the relationship among changing technologies, language, and social relations could you suggest to him or her as worth studying?

4. List some stereotypes about how different people speak. Are those real differences, or just stereotypes? Are the stereotypes positive or negative? Why do you think those stereotypes exist?

5. What is language loss? Why are some researchers and communities worldwide so concerned by this growing phenomenon?

Ethnicity and Race

▸ What is social status, and how does it relate to ethnicity?

▸ How are race and ethnicity socially constructed in various societies?

▸ What are the positive and negative aspects of ethnicity?

© David Grossman/Alamy Stock Photo

Racial/ethnic diversity in today's United States. Might this photo have been taken in your neighborhood?

understanding OURSELVES

When asked "Who are you?" what first comes to mind? Think of the last person you met, or the person sitting nearest you. What labels pop into your head to describe that person? What kinds of identity cues and clues do people use to figure out the kinds of people they are dealing with, and how to act in various social situations? Part of human adaptive flexibility is our ability to shift self-presentation in response to context. Italians, for example, maintain separate sets of clothing to be worn inside and outside the home. They invest much more in their outside wardrobe (thus supporting a vibrant Italian fashion industry)—and what it says about their public persona—than in indoor garb, which is for family and intimates to see. Identities and behavior change with context: "I may be a Neandertal at the office, but I'm all *Homo sapiens* at home." Many of the social statuses we occupy, the "hats" we wear, depend on the situation. A person can be both black and Hispanic, or both a father and a ballplayer. One identity is claimed or perceived in certain settings, another in different ones. Among African Americans a "Hispanic" baseball player might be black; among Hispanics, Hispanic.

When our claimed or perceived identity varies depending on the context, this is called the *situational negotiation of social identity*. Depending on the situation, the same woman might declare: "I'm Jimmy's mother." "I'm your boss." "I'm African American." "I'm your professor." In face-to-face encounters, other people see who we are—actually, who they perceive us to be. They may expect us to think and act in certain (stereotypical) ways based on their perception of our identity (e.g., Latina woman, older white male golfer). Although we can't know which aspect of identity they'll focus on (e.g., ethnicity, gender, age, or political affiliation), face to face it's hard to be anonymous or to be someone else entirely. That's what masks, costumes, disguises, and hiding are for. Who's that little man behind the curtain?

Unlike our early ancestors, people today don't just interact face to face. We routinely give our money and our trust to individuals and institutions we've never laid eyes on. We phone, text, write, and—more than ever—use the Internet, where we must choose which aspects of ourselves to reveal. The Internet allows myriad forms of cybersocial interaction, and people can create new personas by using different "handles," including fictitious names and identities. In anonymous regions of cyberspace, people can manipulate ("lie about") their ages, genders, and physical attributes and create their own cyberfantasies. In psychology, multiple personalities are abnormal, but for anthropologists, multiple identities are more and more the norm.

Ethnicity is based on cultural similarities (with members of the same ethnic group) and differences (between that group and others). Ethnic groups must deal with other such groups in the nation or region they inhabit. Interethnic relations are important in the study of any nation or region—especially so because of the ongoing transnational movement of migrants and refugees (see Marger 2015; Parrillo 2016).

chapter outline

ETHNIC GROUPS AND ETHNICITY

ethnic group
One among several culturally distinct groups in a society or region.

achieved status
Social status based on choices or accomplishments.

ethnicity
Identification with an ethnic group.

Members of an **ethnic group** *share* certain beliefs, values, habits, customs, and norms because of their common background. They define themselves as different and special because of cultural features. This distinction may arise from language, religion, historical experience, geographic placement, kinship, or "race" (see Spickard 2004, 2012a). Markers of an ethnic group may include a collective name, belief in common descent, a sense of solidarity, and an association with a specific territory, which the group may or may not hold (Ryan 1990, pp. xiii, xiv).

Ethnicity means identification with, and feeling part of, an ethnic group and exclusion from certain other groups because of this affiliation. Issues of ethnicity can be complex. Ethnic feelings and associated behavior vary in intensity within ethnic groups and countries and over time. A change in the degree of importance attached to an ethnic identity may reflect political changes (Soviet rule ends—ethnic feeling rises) or individual life-cycle changes (old people relinquish, or young people reclaim, an ethnic background).

Status and Identity

Ethnicity is only one basis for group identity. Cultural differences also are associated with class, region, religion, and other social variables (see Warne 2015). Individuals often have more than one group identity. In a complex society such as the United States or Canada, people negotiate their social identities continually. All of us "wear different hats," presenting ourselves sometimes as one thing, sometimes as another.

status
Any position that determines where someone fits in society.

These different social identities are known as statuses. In daily conversation, we hear the term *status* used as a synonym for *prestige*. In this context, "She's got a lot of status" means she's got a lot of prestige; people look up to her. Among social scientists, that's not the primary meaning of *status*. Social scientists use *status* more neutrally—for any position, no matter what the prestige, that someone occupies in society. Parent is a social status. So are professor, student, factory worker, Republican, salesperson, homeless person, labor leader, ethnic-group member, and thousands of others. People always occupy multiple statuses (e.g., Hispanic, Catholic, infant, brother). Among the statuses we occupy, particular ones dominate in particular settings, such as son or daughter at home and student in the classroom.

ascribed status
Social status based on limited choice.

Some statuses are **ascribed:** People have limited choice about occupying them. Age is an ascribed status. We can't choose not to age, although many people, especially wealthy ones, use cultural means, such as plastic surgery, to try to disguise the biological aging process. Race and gender usually are ascribed; most people are born members of a given race or gender and remain so all their lives. **Achieved statuses,** by contrast, aren't automatic; they come through choices, actions, efforts, talents, or accomplishments and may be positive or negative. Examples of achieved statuses include physician, senator, convicted felon, salesperson, union member, father, and college student.

From the media, you will be familiar with recent cases in which gender and race have become achieved rather than ascribed statuses. Transgender individuals, including the widely reported media figure Caitlyn Jenner, modify the gender status they were assigned at birth or during childhood. People who were born members of one race have chosen to adopt another. In some cases, individuals who were born African American have passed as white, Hispanic, or Native American. In a case widely reported in 2015, a woman known as Rachel Dolezal, who was born white, changed her racial identity to black or African American as an adult. In doing this, she modified her phenotype by changing her hairstyle to better fit her new identity. Given what culture can do to biology, few statuses are absolutely ascribed.

Often status is contextual: One identity is used in certain settings, another in different ones. We call this the *situational negotiation of social identity* (Leman 2001; Spickard 2013; Warne 2015). Members of an ethnic group may shift their ethnic identities. Hispanics, for example, may use different ethnic labels (e.g., "Cuban" or "Latino") to describe themselves depending on context. In a recent study, half (51 percent) of American Hispanics surveyed preferred to identify using their family's country of origin (as in "Mexican," "Cuban," or "Dominican") rather than "Hispanic" or "Latino." Just one-quarter (24 percent) chose one of those two pan-ethnic terms, while 21 percent said they use the term "American" most often (Taylor et al. 2012).

Latinos who have different national origins may mobilize around issues of general interest to Hispanics, such as a path to citizenship for undocumented immigrants, while acting as separate interest groups in other contexts. Among Hispanics, Cuban Americans are older and richer on average than Mexican Americans and Puerto Ricans, and their class interests and voting patterns differ. Cuban Americans are more likely to vote Republican than are Puerto Ricans and Mexican Americans. Some Mexican Americans whose families have lived in the United States for generations have little in common with new Hispanic immigrants, such as those from Central America.

Hispanics are the fastest-growing ethnic group in the United States, increasing by 57 percent between 2000 and 2014—from 35.3 million to 55.5 million. "Hispanic" is a category based mainly on language. It includes whites, blacks, and "racially" mixed Spanish speakers and their ethnically conscious descendants. (There also are

TABLE 15.1   Racial/Ethnic Identification in the United States, 2014

CLAIMED IDENTITY	NUMBER (MILLIONS)	PERCENTAGE
White (non-Hispanic)	198.0	62.1%
Hispanic	55.5	17.4
Black	42.1	13.2
Asian	17.2	5.4
Other	6.1	1.9
Total population	318.9	100.0%

SOURCE: U.S. Census Bureau. QuickFacts. http://www.census.gov/quickfacts/table/PST045215/00.

Native American and even Asian Hispanics.) The label "Hispanic" lumps together people of diverse geographic origin—Mexico, Puerto Rico, El Salvador, Cuba, the Dominican Republic, Guatemala, and other Spanish-speaking countries of Central and South America and the Caribbean. "Latino" is a broader category, which also can include Brazilians (who speak Portuguese). Mexicans constitute about two-thirds of American Hispanics. Next come Puerto Ricans at around 9 percent. Salvadorans, Cubans, Dominicans, and Guatemalans living in the United States all number more than one million people per nationality. Of the major racial and ethnic groups in the United States, Hispanics are by far the youngest. At 27 years, their median age is a decade lower than that of the U.S. overall (Krogstad 2014). (Table 15.1 lists American ethnic groups, based on 2014 figures.)

Minority Groups and Stratification

Minority groups are so called because they occupy subordinate (lower) positions within a social hierarchy. They have inferior power and less secure access to resources than do *majority groups*. Minority groups are obvious features of stratification in the United States. The 2014 poverty rate was 10.1 percent for non-Hispanic whites, 12.0 percent for Asian Americans, 23.6 percent for Hispanics, and 26.2 percent for

African Americans (DeNavas-Walt and Proctor 2015). Inequality shows up consistently in unemployment figures as well as in income and wealth. Median household incomes in 2014 were as follows: $74,297 for Asian Americans, $60,256 for non-Hispanic whites, $42,491 for Hispanics, and $35,398 for African Americans (DeNavas-Walt and Proctor 2015). The median wealth of white households in 2013 was 13 times that of black households and more than 10 times that of Hispanic households. The gap in household wealth between blacks and whites has reached its highest point since 1989, when whites had 17 times the wealth of black households and 14 times that of Hispanics (Kochhar and Fry 2015). (These measures of stratification are summarized in Recap 15.1.)

RACE AND ETHNICITY

When an ethnic group is assumed to have a biological basis (distinctively shared "blood" or genes), it is called a **race** (see Mukhopadhyay et al. 2014; Wade 2015). Discrimination against such a group is called **racism** (Gotkowitz 2011; Scupin 2012). However, race, like ethnicity in general, actually is a *cultural* category rather than a biological reality. That is, "races" are defined through contrasts perceived and perpetuated in particular societies, rather than from scientific classifications based on common genes.

race
An ethnic group assumed to have a biological basis.

racism
Discrimination against an ethnic group assumed to have a biological basis.

| RECAP 15.1 | Measures of Stratification Involving Minority Groups | |

GROUP	POVERTY RATE	MEDIAN HOUSEHOLD INCOME
Non-Hispanic whites	10.1%	$60,256
Asian Americans	12.0%	$74,297
Hispanic Americans	23.6%	$42,491
African Americans	26.2%	$35,398
Overall	14.8%	$53,657

SOURCE: 2014 data from U.S. Census Bureau.

"Hispanic" and "Latino" are ethnic categories that crosscut "racial" contrasts such as that between "black" and "white." Note the physical diversity among these children in Old Havana, Cuba.
© Kumar Sriskandan/ Alamy Stock Photo

In American culture, we hear the words *ethnicity* and *race* frequently, without clear distinctions made between them. For example, the term *race* often is used inappropriately to refer to Hispanics, who, in fact, can be of any race. The following example provides one illustration of the popular confusion about ethnicity and race in American culture. Eight years prior to her appointment to the U.S. Supreme Court, Sonia Sotomayor, then an appeals court judge, gave a talk titled "A Latina Judge's Voice," at the University of California, Berkeley, School of Law. As part of a much longer speech, Sotomayor declared:

> I would hope that a wise Latina woman with the richness of her experiences would more often than not reach a better conclusion than a white male who hasn't lived that life (Sotomayor 2001/2009).

On hearing about that speech, conservatives, including former House Speaker Newt Gingrich and radio talk show host Rush Limbaugh, seized on this declaration as evidence that Sotomayor was a "racist" or a "reverse racist." Her critics ignored the fact that "Latina" is an ethnic (and gendered-female) rather than a racial category. I suspect that Sotomayor also was using "white male" as an ethnic-gender category, to refer to nonminority men. Our popular culture does not consistently distinguish between ethnicity and race (see Ansell 2013; Banton 2015).

descent
Social identity based on ancestry.

THE SOCIAL CONSTRUCTION OF RACE

Most Americans believe (incorrectly) that their population includes *biologically based* races to which various labels are applied. Such *racial terms* include "white," "black," "yellow," "red," "Caucasoid," "Negroid," "Mongoloid," "Amerindian," "Euro-American," "African American," "Asian American," and "Native American."

We have seen that races, while assumed to have a biological basis, actually are socially constructed in particular societies. Let's consider now several examples of the social construction of race, beginning with the United States.

Hypodescent: Race in the United States

Most Americans acquire their racial identity at birth, but race isn't based on biology or on simple ancestry. Take the case of the child of a "racially mixed" marriage involving one black and one white parent. We know that 50 percent of the child's genes come from one parent and 50 percent from the other. Still, American culture overlooks heredity and classifies this child as black. This classificatory rule is arbitrary. On the basis of genotype (genetic composition), it would be just as logical to classify the child as white. Operating here is a rule of **descent** (it assigns social identity on the basis of ancestry), but of a sort that

appreciating DIVERSITY

Why Are the Greens So White?

How do race and ethnicity figure in the world of golf, a sport whose popularity has been growing not only in the United States but also in Europe, Asia, and Australia? More than 20 million Americans play golf, an industry that also supports about 400,000 workers. For decades, golf has been the preferred sport of business tycoons and politicians—mainly white. President Dwight D. Eisenhower (1953–1960), whose love for golf was well known, etched a lasting (and accurate) image of golf as a Republican sport (despite the fact that Presidents Bill Clinton and Barack Obama also play the game). A recent survey found that only 2 of the top 125 PGA touring pros identified as Democrats.

A glance at golfers in any televised game reveals a remarkable lack of variation in skin color. American golf was the nation's last major sport to desegregate, and minorities traditionally have been relegated to supporting roles. Latinos maintain the game's greens and physical infrastructure. Until the motorized golf cart replaced them, African Americans had significant opportunities to observe and learn the game by caddying. Indeed, there once was a tradition of African American caddies becoming excellent golfers.

The best example of this trajectory is Dr. Charlie Sifford (1922–2015), who, in 1961, broke the color barrier in American professional golf. Sifford began his golf career as a caddie for white golfers. He went on to dominate the all-black United Golf Association, winning five straight national titles, but he wanted to play with the world's best golfers. At the age of 39, Sifford successfully challenged—and ended— the white-only policy of the Professional Golfers' Association of America (PGA), becoming its first African American member.

Sifford, who had to endure phone threats, racial slurs, and other indignities at the beginning of his PGA career, went on to win the Greater Hartford Open in 1967, the Los Angeles Open in 1969, and the 1975 Senior PGA Championship. In 2004, he became the first African American inducted into the World Golf Hall of Fame. His major regret was that he never got to play in a Masters Tournament. That event, held annually in Augusta, Georgia, did not invite its first black player until Lee Elder in 1975. Sifford's bitterness about his own exclusion from the Masters was tempered somewhat by his pleasure when Tiger Woods, another African American golfer, won the first of his four green Masters jackets in 1997.

In terms of diversity, golf has actually regressed since the 1970s, when 11 African Americans played on the PGA tour. If we consider multiracial players to be African American, there currently is only one African American (Tiger Woods) among the 125 top players on the PGA tour. In Britain, only 2 percent of an estimated 850,000 regular golfers are non-white. Economic factors continue to limit minority access to golf. Prospective golfers need money for instruction, equipment, access to top-notch courses, and travel to tournaments. Asian Americans, who enjoy a relatively high socioeconomic status, are the only minority group in the United States with a growing representation in golf, for both men and women.

Tiger Woods is currently the single exceptional non-white individual in this mainly white, affluent, Republican sport. Woods became one of America's most celebrated and popular athletes by combining golfing success with a carefully cultivated reputation as a family man. He presented himself as the hard-working and achievement-oriented son of an Asian mother and an African American father, and as the devoted husband and father of his Scandinavian wife and two photogenic children. Woods's fall from grace began late in 2009, as a flood of media reports converted his image from family man into serial philanderer. Although his marriage did not survive his transgressions, his golfing career did. Woods reintegrated gradually into the world of golf, even receiving the 2013 PGA Tour Player of the Year Award. He had won 5 of the 16 tournaments he played that year and placed in the top 10 in three others. Tiger Woods remains the world's most prominent and celebrated African American golfer. No longer, however, is he the untarnished hero of yesteryear. What role, if any, do you think race, ethnicity, racism, and racial stereotyping have played in the rise, fall, and reintegration of Tiger Woods?

SOURCE: Ferguson (2015); Riach (2013); and Starn (2011).

---

is rare outside the contemporary United States. It is called **hypodescent** (Harris and Kottak 1963) because it automatically places children of mixed unions in the group of their minority parent (*hypo* means "lower"). Hypodescent divides American society into groups that have been unequal in their access to wealth, power, and prestige.

The hypodescent rule may be arbitrary, but it is very strong. How else can we explain the common assertion that Barack Obama is the first black president, rather than the first biracial president, of the United States? (This chapter's "Appreciating Diversity" focuses on another successful biracial or multiracial American, Tiger Woods, in a discussion of the lack of racial diversity in golf.) American rules for assigning racial status can be even more arbitrary. In some states, anyone known to have any black ancestor, no matter how remote,

hypodescent
Children of mixed unions assigned to the same group as their minority parent.

An international and multiethnic American family. Joakim Noah, center, is an All-Star professional basketball player, who played in college for the Florida Gators. Also shown are his mother, a former Miss Sweden, and father, a French singer and tennis player who won the French open in 1983. Joakim's grandfather, Zacharie Noah, was a professional soccer player from the African nation of Cameroon. What is Joakim Noah's race?

© Matt Marton/AP Images

can be classified as a member of the black race. The following case from Louisiana is an excellent illustration of the arbitrariness of the hypodescent rule and of the role that governments (federal or, in this case, state) play in legalizing, inventing, or eradicating race and ethnicity (see Mullaney 2011). Susie Guillory Phipps, a light-skinned woman with Caucasian features and straight black hair, discovered as an adult that she was black. When Phipps ordered a copy of her birth certificate, she found her race listed as "colored." Since she had been "brought up white and married white twice," Phipps challenged a 1970 Louisiana law declaring anyone with at least one-thirty-second "Negro blood" to be legally black. Although the state's lawyer admitted that Phipps "looks like a white person," the state of Louisiana insisted that her racial classification was proper (Yetman 1991, pp. 3–4).

Cases like Phipps's are rare because racial identity usually is set at birth and doesn't change. The rule of hypodescent affects blacks, Asians, Native Americans, and Hispanics differently. It's easier to negotiate Native American or Hispanic identity than black identity perhaps because the assumption of a biological basis isn't as strong.

To be considered Native American, one ancestor out of eight (great-grandparents) or out of four (grandparents) may suffice. This depends on whether the assignment is by federal or state law or by a Native American tribal council. The child of a Hispanic may (or may not, depending on context)

claim Hispanic identity. Many Americans with a Native American or Latino grandparent consider themselves white and lay no claim to minority group status.

Race in the Census

The U.S. Census Bureau has gathered data by race since 1790. Figure 15.1 shows that the most recent (2010) census asked about both race and Hispanic origin. What do you think of the racial categories included?

Racial classification in the census is a political issue involving access to resources, including jobs, voting districts, and programs aimed at minorities. The hypodescent rule results in all the population growth being attributed to the minority category. Attempts to add a "multiracial" category to the U.S. Census have been opposed by the National Association for the Advancement of Colored People (NAACP) and the National Council of La Raza (a Hispanic advocacy group). Minorities fear their political clout will decline if their numbers go down.

But things are changing. Choice of "some other race" in the U.S. Census tripled from 1980 (6.8 million) to 2010 (over 19 million)—suggesting imprecision in and dissatisfaction with the existing categories. In the 2000 census, 2.4 percent of Americans chose a first-ever option of identifying themselves as belonging to more than one race. That figure rose to 2.9 percent in the 2010 census. The number of interracial marriages and children is increasing, with implications for the traditional system of American racial classification. "Interracial," "biracial," or "multiracial" children undoubtedly identify with qualities of both parents. It is troubling for many of them to have so important an identity as race dictated by the arbitrary rule of hypodescent. It may be especially discordant when racial identity doesn't parallel gender identity, for instance, a boy with a white father and a black mother, or a girl with a white mother and a black father.

Rather than race, the Canadian census asks about "visible minorities." That country's Employment Equity Act defines such groups as "persons, other than Aboriginal peoples [First Nations in Canada], who are non-Caucasian in race or non-white in colour" (Statistics Canada 2001). "South Asian" and "Chinese" are Canada's largest visible minorities (see Figure 15.2). Canada's visible minority population of 19.1 percent in 2011 (up from 11.2 percent in 1996) contrasts with a figure of 38 percent for the United States (in 2014, up from 25 percent in 2000).

As in the United States, Canada's visible minority population has been growing much faster than the country's overall population. In 1981, visible minorities accounted for just 4.7 percent of the Canadian population, versus 19.1 percent in 2011 (the most recent data available as of this writing). Between 2006 and 2011, Canada's total population increased 5 percent, while visible minorities rose 24 percent. If recent immigration trends continue, by 2031 visible minorities will comprise almost one-third (31 percent) of the Canadian population (Statistics Canada 2010).

Not Us: Race in Japan

Japan presents itself and is commonly viewed as a nation that is homogeneous in race, ethnicity, language, and culture.

Although Japan's population is in fact less diverse than those of most nations, it does contain significant minority groups (see Graburn 2008; Weiner 2009). Constituting about 10 percent of Japan's total population, those groups include aboriginal Ainu, annexed Okinawans, outcast *burakumin,* children of mixed marriages, and immigrant nationalities, especially Koreans, who number more than 700,000 (Lie 2001; Ryang and Lie 2009). The (majority) Japanese define themselves by opposition to others, whether minority groups in their own nation or outsiders—anyone who is "not us." The "not us" should stay that way; assimilation generally is discouraged. Cultural mechanisms, especially residential segregation and taboos on "interracial" marriage, work to keep minorities "in their place."

To describe racial attitudes in Japan, Jennifer Robertson (1992) used Kwame Anthony Appiah's (1990) term "intrinsic racism"—the belief that a (perceived) racial difference is a sufficient reason to value one person less than another. In Japan the valued group is majority ("pure") Japanese, who are believed to share "the same blood." Thus, the caption to a printed photo of a Japanese American model reads: "She was born in Japan but raised in Hawaii. Her nationality is American but no foreign blood flows in her veins" (Robertson 1992, p. 5). Something like hypodescent also operates in Japan, but less precisely than in the United States, where mixed offspring automatically become members of the minority group. The children of mixed marriages between majority Japanese and others (including Euro-Americans) may not get the same "racial" label as their minority parent, but they are still stigmatized for their non-Japanese ancestry (De Vos and Wagatsuma 1966).

In its construction of race, Japanese culture regards certain ethnic groups as having a biological basis, when there is no evidence that they do. The best example is the burakumin, a stigmatized group of some three million outcasts, sometimes compared to India's untouchables. The burakumin are physically and genetically indistinguishable from other Japanese. Many of them "pass" as (and marry) majority Japanese, but a deceptive marriage can end in divorce if burakumin identity is discovered (Amos 2011).

Burakumin are perceived as standing apart from majority Japanese. Based on their ancestry (and thus, it is assumed, their "blood," or genetics), burakumin are considered "not us." Majority Japanese try to keep their lineage pure by discouraging mixing. The burakumin are residentially segregated in neighborhoods (rural or urban) called *buraku,* from which the racial label is derived. Compared with majority Japanese, the burakumin are less likely to attend high school and college. When burakumin attend the same schools as majority Japanese, they face discrimination. Majority children and teachers may refuse to eat with them because burakumin are considered unclean.

5. Is this person of Hispanic, Latino, or Spanish origin?

- ☐ No, not of Hispanic, Latino, or Spanish origin
- ☐ Yes, Mexican, Mexican Am., Chicano
- ☐ Yes, Puerto Rican
- ☐ Yes, Cuban
- ☐ Yes, another Hispanic, Latino, or Spanish origin — *Print origin, for example, Argentinean, Colombian, Dominican, Nicaraguan, Salvadoran, Spaniard, and so on.*

6. What is this person's race? *Mark* ☒ *one or more boxes.*

- ☐ White
- ☐ Black, African Am., or Negro
- ☐ American Indian or Alaska Native — *Print name of enrolled or principal tribe.*
- ☐ Asian Indian
- ☐ Chinese
- ☐ Filipino
- ☐ Other Asian — *Print race, for example, Hmong, Laotian, Thai, Pakistani, Cambodian, and so on.*
- ☐ Japanese
- ☐ Korean
- ☐ Vietnamese
- ☐ Native Hawaiian
- ☐ Guamanian or Chamorro
- ☐ Samoan
- ☐ Other Pacific Islander — *Print race, for example, Fijian, Tongan, and so on.*
- ☐ Some other race — *Print race.*

FIGURE 15.1 Reproduction of Questions on Race and Hispanic Origin from Census 2010.

SOURCE: U.S. Census Bureau, Census 2010 questionnaire.

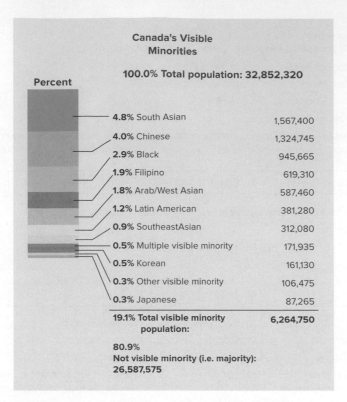

Canada's Visible Minorities

100.0% Total population: 32,852,320

Percent

4.8% South Asian	1,567,400
4.0% Chinese	1,324,745
2.9% Black	945,665
1.9% Filipino	619,310
1.8% Arab/West Asian	587,460
1.2% Latin American	381,280
0.9% SoutheastAsian	312,080
0.5% Multiple visible minority	171,935
0.5% Korean	161,130
0.3% Other visible minority	106,475
0.3% Japanese	87,265
19.1% Total visible minority population:	6,264,750

80.9%
Not visible minority (i.e. majority):
26,587,575

FIGURE 15.2 Visible Minority Population of Canada, 2011 National Household Survey.

SOURCE: From Statistics Canada, 2011 National Household Survey. http://www12. statcan.gc.ca/nhs-enm/2011/as-sa/99-010-x/99-010-x2011001-eng.cfm#a4

Ariana Miyamoto, the daughter of a Japanese woman and an African American man, was crowned Miss Universe Japan in March 2015. Soon thereafter, complaints emerged on social media that she did not look "Japanese enough" to represent Japan in an international beauty competition. Over 3 percent of new marriages in Japan each year are now international, and almost 2 percent of children born in Japan are biracial.

© Kyodo via AP Images

In applying for university admission or a job and in dealing with the government, Japanese must list their address, which becomes part of a household or family registry. This list makes residence in a buraku, and likely burakumin social status, evident. Schools and companies use this information to discriminate. (The best way to pass is to move so often that the buraku address eventually disappears from the registry.) Majority Japanese also limit "race" mixture by hiring marriage mediators to check out the family histories of prospective spouses. They are especially careful to check for burakumin ancestry (Amos 2011).

The origin of the burakumin lies in a historical tiered system of stratification (from the Tokugawa period, 1603–1868). The top four ranked categories were warrior-administrators (*samurai*), farmers, artisans, and merchants. The ancestors of the burakumin were below this hierarchy. They did "unclean" jobs such as animal slaughter and disposal of the dead. Burakumin still do similar jobs, including work with leather and other animal products. They are more likely than majority Japanese to do manual labor (including farm work) and to belong to the national lower class. Burakumin and other Japanese minorities also are more likely to have careers in crime, prostitution, entertainment, and sports.

Like blacks in the United States, the burakumin are internally **stratified.** In other words, there are class contrasts within the group. Because certain jobs are reserved for the burakumin, people who are successful in those occupations (e.g., shoe factory owners) can be wealthy. Burakumin also have found jobs as government bureaucrats. Financially successful burakumin can temporarily escape their stigmatized status by travel, including foreign travel.

Discrimination against the burakumin is strikingly like the discrimination that blacks have experienced in the United States. The burakumin often live in villages and neighborhoods with poor housing and sanitation. They have limited access to education, jobs, amenities, and health facilities. In response to burakumin political mobilization, Japan has dismantled the legal structure of discrimination against burakumin and has worked to improve conditions in the buraku. (The website http://www.blhrri.org/old/blhrri_e/blhrri/about.htm is sponsored by the Buraku Liberation and Human Rights Research Institute and includes the most recent information about the burakumin liberation movement.) However, discrimination against nonmajority Japanese is still the rule in companies. Some employers say that hiring burakumin would give their company an unclean image and thus create a disadvantage in competing with other businesses.

Phenotype and Fluidity: Race in Brazil

There are more flexible, less exclusionary ways of socially constructing race than those used in the United States and Japan. Consider Brazil, which shares a history of slavery with the United States but lacks the hypodescent rule. Nor does Brazil have racial aversion of the sort found in Japan.

Brazilians use many more racial labels—over 500 were once reported (Harris 1970)—than Americans or Japanese do. In northeastern Brazil, I found 40 different racial terms in use in Arembepe, a village of only 750 people (Kottak 2006). Through their traditional classification system, Brazilians recognize and attempt to describe the physical variation that exists within their population. The system used in the United States, by recognizing relatively few races, blinds Americans to an equivalent range of evident physical contrasts. The system Brazilians use to construct social race has other special features. In the United States, one's race is assigned automatically by hypodescent and usually doesn't change. In Brazil, racial identity is more flexible, more of an achieved status.

Brazilian racial classification pays attention to **phenotype.** Scientists distinguish between *genotype,* or hereditary makeup, and *phenotype*—expressed physical characteristics. Genotype is what you are genetically; phenotype is what you appear as. Identical twins and clones have the same genotype, but their phenotypes vary if they have been raised in different environments. *Phenotype* describes an organism's evident traits, its "manifest biology"—physiology and anatomy, including skin color, hair form, facial features, and eye color. A Brazilian's phenotype and racial label may change because of environmental factors, such as the tanning rays of the sun or the effects of humidity on the hair.

A Brazilian can change his or her "race" (say from "Indian" to "mixed") by changing his or her manner of dress, language, location (e.g., rural to urban), and even attitude (e.g., by adopting urban behavior). Two racial/ethnic labels used in Brazil are *indio* (indigenous, Native American) and *cabôclo* (someone who "looks *indio*" but wears modern clothing and participates in Brazilian culture, rather than living in an indigenous community). Similar shifts in racial/ethnic classification occur in other parts of Latin America, for example, Guatemala (see Wade 2010). The perception of biological race is influenced not just by the physical phenotype but by how one dresses and behaves.

Furthermore, racial differences in Brazil may be so insignificant in structuring community life that people may forget the terms they have applied to others. Sometimes they even forget the ones

stratified
Class structured, with differences in wealth, prestige, and power.

phenotype
The expressed physical characteristics of an organism.

These photos, taken in Brazil by the author, give just a glimpse of the spectrum of phenotypical diversity encountered among contemporary Brazilians.

© Conrad P. Kottak

state
A stratified society with formal, central government.

nation-state
An autonomous political entity; a country.

they've used for themselves. In Arembepe, I made it a habit to ask the same person on different days to tell me the races of others in the village (and my own). In the United States, I am always "white" or "Euro-American," but in Arembepe I got lots of terms besides *branco* ("white"). I could be *claro* ("light"), *louro* ("blond"), *sarará* ("light-skinned redhead"), *mulato claro* ("light mulatto"), or *mulato* ("mulatto"). The racial term used to describe me or anyone else varied from person to person, week to week, even day to day. My best informant, a man with very dark skin color, changed the term he used for himself all the time—from *escuro* ("dark") to *preto* ("black") to *moreno escuro* ("dark brunet").

For centuries the United States and Brazil have had mixed populations, with ancestors from Native America, Europe, Africa, and Asia. Although races have mixed in both countries, Brazilian and American cultures have constructed the results differently. The historical reasons for this contrast lie mainly in the different characteristics of the settlers of the two countries. The mainly English early settlers of the United States came as women, men, and families, but Brazil's Portuguese colonizers were mainly men—merchants and adventurers. Many of these Portuguese men married indigenous women and recognized their racially mixed children as their heirs. Like their North American counterparts, Brazilian plantation owners had sexual relations with their slaves. But the Brazilian landlords more often freed the children that resulted. (Sometimes these were their only children.) Freed offspring became plantation overseers and foremen and filled many intermediate positions in the emerging Brazilian economy. They were not classed with the slaves but were allowed to join a new intermediate category. No hypodescent rule developed in Brazil to ensure that whites and blacks remained separate (see Degler 1970; Harris 1964).

In today's world system, Brazil's system of racial classification is changing in the context of international identity politics and rights movements. Just as more and more Brazilians claim indigenous identities, an increasing number now assert their blackness and self-conscious membership in the African diaspora. Particularly in such northeastern Brazilian states as Bahia, where African demographic and cultural influence is strong, public universities have instituted affirmative action programs aimed at indigenous peoples and especially at blacks. Racial identities firm up in the context of international (e.g., pan-African and pan–Native American) mobilization and access to strategic resources based on race.

ETHNIC GROUPS, NATIONS, AND NATIONALITIES

nation
A society that shares a language, religion, history, territory, ancestry, and kinship.

The term **nation** once was synonymous with *tribe* or *ethnic group*. All three of these terms have been used to refer to a single culture sharing a single language, religion, history, territory, ancestry, and kinship. Thus, one could speak interchangeably of the Seneca (Native American) nation, tribe, or ethnic group. Now *nation* has come to mean **state**—an independent, centrally organized political unit, or a government. *Nation* and *state* have become synonymous. Combined in **nation-state** they refer to an autonomous political entity, a country.

Because of migration, conquest, and colonialism, most nation-states aren't ethnically homogeneous. A 2003 study by James Fearon found that about 70 percent of all countries have an ethnic group that forms an absolute majority of the population; the average population share of such a group is 65 percent. The average size of the second-largest group, or largest ethnic minority, is 17 percent. Only 18 percent of all countries, including Japan, have a single ethnic group accounting for 90 percent or more of the population.

Ethnic Diversity by Region

There is substantial regional variation in countries' ethnic structures. Strong states, particularly in Europe (e.g., France), have deliberately and actively worked to homogenize their diverse premodern populations to a common national identity and culture (see Beriss 2004). Although countries with no ethnic majority are fairly rare in the rest of the world, this is the norm in Africa. The average African country has a plurality group of about 22 percent, with the second largest slightly less than this. Rwanda, Burundi, Lesotho, Swaziland, and Zimbabwe are exceptions; each has a large majority group and a minority that makes up almost all the rest of the population. Botswana has a large majority (the Tswana) and a set of smaller minorities (Fearon 2003).

Most Latin American and Caribbean countries have a majority group (speaking a European language, such as Portuguese in Brazil, Spanish in Argentina) and a single minority group—"indigenous peoples." The latter is a catch-all category encompassing several small Native American tribes or remnants. Exceptions are Guatemala and the Andean countries of Bolivia, Peru, and Ecuador, with large indigenous populations (see Gotkowitz 2011; Wade 2010).

Most countries in Asia and the Middle East/North Africa have ethnic majorities. The Asian countries of Myanmar, Laos, Vietnam, and Thailand contain a large lowland majority edged by more fragmented mountain folk. Several oil-producing countries in the Middle East, including Saudi Arabia, Bahrain, United Arab Emirates, Oman, and Kuwait, contain an ethnically homogeneous group of citizens who form either a plurality or a bare majority; the rest of the population consists of ethnically diverse noncitizen workers. Other countries in the Middle East/North Africa contain two principal ethnic or ethnoreligious groups: Arabs and Berbers in Morocco, Algeria,

Libya, and Tunisia; Muslims and Copts in Egypt; Turks and Kurds in Turkey; Greeks and Turks in Cyprus; and Palestinians and Transjordan Arabs in Jordan (Fearon 2003).

Nationalities without Nations

Benedict Anderson (1991/2006) traces Western European *nationalism* (the feeling of belonging to a nation), back to the 18th century. He stresses that spoken language and the printed word played a crucial role in the growth of national consciousness in places such as England, France, and Spain. The novel and the newspaper were "two forms of imagining" communities (consisting of all the people who read the same sources and thus witnessed the same events) that flowered in the 18th century (Anderson 1991/2006, pp. 24–25). Groups that have, once had, or wish to have or regain, autonomous political status (their own country) are called **nationalities.** As a result of political upheavals, wars, and migration, many nationalities have been split up and placed in separate nation-states. For example, the German and Korean homelands were artificially divided after wars, according to communist and capitalist ideologies. World War I dispersed the Kurds, who form a majority in no state, but exist as minority groups in Turkey, Iran, Iraq, and Syria.

Colonialism—the foreign domination of a territory—established a series of multitribal and multiethnic states. The new national boundaries that were created under colonialism often corresponded poorly with preexisting cultural divisions. However, colonial institutions also helped forge new identities that extended beyond nations and nationalities. A good example is the idea of *négritude* ("black identity") developed by African intellectuals in Francophone (French-speaking) West Africa. Négritude can be traced to the association and common experience in colonial times of youths from Guinea, Mali, the Ivory Coast, and Senegal at the William Ponty School in Dakar, Senegal (Anderson 1991/2006, pp. 123–124).

ETHNIC TOLERANCE AND ACCOMMODATION

Ethnic diversity may be associated with either positive group interaction and coexistence or with conflict (to be discussed shortly). There are nation-states in which multiple ethnic groups live together in reasonable harmony, including some less-developed countries.

Assimilation

Assimilation describes the process of change that ethnic groups may experience when they move to a country where another culture dominates. In assimilating, the immigrant group adopts the patterns and norms of its host culture. It is incorporated

nationalities
Ethnic groups that have, once had, or want their own country.

colonialism
Long-term foreign domination of a territory and its people.

assimilation
Absorption of minorities within a dominant culture.

German, Italian, Japanese, Middle Eastern, and Eastern European immigrants have assimilated, culturally and linguistically, to a common Brazilian culture. More than 220,000 people of Japanese descent live in Brazil, mostly in and around the city of São Paulo, Brazil's largest. Shown here, a Sunday morning street scene in São Paulo's Liberdade district, home to many of that city's assimilated Japanese Brazilians.
© Pierre Merimee/Corbis

into the dominant culture to the point that it no longer exists as a separate cultural unit. Some countries, such as Brazil, are more assimilationist than others. Germans, Italians, Japanese, Middle Easterners, and Eastern Europeans started migrating to Brazil late in the 19th century. These immigrants have assimilated to a common Brazilian culture, which has Portuguese, African, and Native American roots. The descendants of these immigrants speak the national language (Portuguese) and participate in the national culture. (During World War II, Brazil, which was on the Allied side, forced assimilation by banning instruction in any language other than Portuguese—especially in German.) The United States was much more assimilationist during the early 20th century than it is today, as the multicultural model has become more prominent (see the section "Multiculturalism").

The Plural Society

Assimilation isn't inevitable, and there can be ethnic harmony without it. Ethnic distinctions can persist despite generations of interethnic contact. Through a study of three ethnic groups in Swat, Pakistan, Fredrik Barth (1958/1968) challenged an old idea that interaction always leads to assimilation. He showed that ethnic groups can be in contact for generations without assimilating and can live in peaceful coexistence.

Barth (1958/1968, p. 324) defines **plural society** (an idea he extended from Pakistan to the entire Middle East) as a society combining ethnic contrasts, ecological specialization (i.e., use of different environmental resources by each ethnic group), and the economic interdependence of those groups. In Barth's view, ethnic boundaries are most stable and enduring when the groups occupy different ecological niches. That is, they make their living in different ways and don't compete. Ideally, they should depend on one another's activities and exchange with one another. When different ethnic groups exploit the *same* ecological niche, the militarily more powerful group usually will replace the weaker one. If they exploit more or less the same niche, but the weaker group is better able to use marginal environments, they also may coexist (Barth 1958/1968, p. 331). Given niche specialization, ethnic boundaries and interdependence can be maintained, although the specific cultural features of each group may change. By shifting the analytic focus from individual cultures or ethnic groups to *relationships* between cultures or ethnic groups, Barth (1958/1968, 1969) made important contributions to ethnic studies (see also Kamrava 2013).

Multiculturalism

The view of cultural diversity in a country as something good and desirable is called **multiculturalism** (see Kottak and Kozaitis 2012). The multicultural model is the opposite of the assimilationist model, in which minorities are expected to abandon their cultural traditions and values, replacing them with those of the majority population. The multicultural view encourages the practice of cultural–ethnic traditions. A multicultural society socializes individuals not only into the dominant (national) culture but also into an ethnic culture. Thus, in the United States millions of people speak both English and another language, eat both "American" foods (apple pie, steak, hamburgers) and "ethnic" dishes, and celebrate both national (July 4, Thanksgiving) and ethnic–religious holidays.

Multiculturalism seeks ways for people to understand and interact that depend not on sameness but rather on respect for differences. Multiculturalism stresses the interaction of ethnic groups and their contribution to the country. It assumes that each group has something to offer to and learn from the others. The United States and Canada have become increasingly multicultural, focusing on their internal diversity. Rather than as "melting pots," they are better described as ethnic "salads" (each ingredient remains distinct, although in the same bowl, with the same dressing).

Several forces have propelled North America away from the assimilationist model toward multiculturalism. First, multiculturalism reflects the fact of recent large-scale migration, particularly from the "less-developed" countries to the "developed" nations of North America, as well as Western Europe. The global scale of modern migration introduces unparalleled ethnic variety to host nations (see Marger 2015; Parrillo 2016). Multiculturalism is related to globalization: People use modern means of transportation to migrate to nations whose lifestyles they learn about through the media and from tourists who increasingly visit their own countries.

Migration also is fueled by rapid population growth, coupled with insufficient jobs (for both educated and uneducated people), in the less-developed countries. As traditional rural economies decline or mechanize, displaced farmers move to cities, where they and their children often are unable to find jobs. As people in the less-developed countries get better educations, they seek more skilled employment. They hope to partake of an international culture of consumption that includes such modern amenities as refrigerators, televisions, computers, and automobiles (Ahmed 2004).

Changing Demographics

The multicultural model has become increasingly prominent in the United States and Canada. This reflects an awareness that ethnic diversity has increased dramatically in recent years. This trend will continue, and the minority proportion of the American population will exceed 50 percent by 2050 (see Figure 15.3).

plural society
A society with economically interdependent ethnic groups.

multiculturalism
The view of cultural diversity as valuable and worth maintaining.

In October 2006, the population of the United States reached 300 million people, just 39 years after reaching 200 million (in 1967) and 91 years after reaching the 100 million mark (in 1915). The country's ethnic composition has changed dramatically in the past 50 years. The 1970 census, the first to attempt an official count of Hispanics, found they represented no more than 4.7 percent of the American population. By 2014, this figure had risen to 17.4 percent—over 55 million Hispanics. The percentage of African Americans grew from 11.1 percent in 1967 to 13.2 percent in 2014, while (non-Hispanic) whites ("Anglos") declined from 83 to 62.1 percent (DeNavas-Walt and Proctor 2015).

In 1967, fewer than 10 million people in the United States (5 percent of the population) had been born elsewhere, compared with about 41 million foreign born today (12.9 percent) (all data from U.S. Census Bureau). In 2011, for the first time in American history, minorities (including Hispanics, blacks, Asians, Native Americans, and those of mixed race) accounted for more than half (50.4 percent) of all births in the United States (Tavernise 2012).

In 1973, 78 percent of the students in American public schools were white, and 22 percent were minorities. By 2004, only 57 percent of public school students were white. In fall 2014, for the first time, the overall number of Latino, African American, and Asian students in public K–12 classrooms surpassed the number of non-Hispanic whites (see this chapter's "Focus on Globalization").

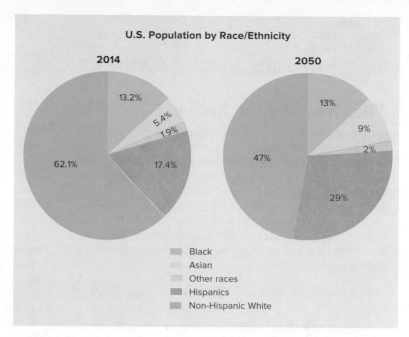

FIGURE 15.3 Ethnic Composition of the United States.
The proportion of the American population that is white and non-Hispanic is declining. The projection for 2050 shown here comes from a 2008 report. Note especially the dramatic rise in the Hispanic portion of the American population between 2014 and 2050.

SOURCE: 2014 data from U.S. Census Bureau, QuickFacts. http://www.census.gov/quickfacts/table/PST045215/00; 2050 projection from a 2008 projection by the U.S. Census Bureau, http://www.census.gov/population/www/ projections/analytical-document09.pdf, Table 1, p. 17.

The Backlash to Multiculturalism: Ethno-nationalism

When Barack Obama was elected president of the United States in 2008, it seemed to many commentators that the United States had entered a postracial era. It was taken as a sign of progress in racial and ethnic relations that an African American man could be elected to the highest office in the land. The backlash began soon after Obama's election. The period between 2008 and 2010 saw the growth of the Tea Party wing of the Republican Party and a dramatic reduction in the power of Democrats after the 2010 election. The same coalition of young people, women, and minorities who had backed Obama in 2008 came together again to ensure his reelection in 2012. Again, however, Republican opposition culminated in an even more substantial congressional defeat for Obama's party in the 2014 midterm elections. The Obama coalition simply did not turn out for the midterm elections. The gray—that is, older, predominately white, Americans—were more reliable voters than the brown (see this chapter's "Focus on Globalization").

In the United States, Canada, and western Europe, multiculturalism is of growing importance, as is suggested by this contemporary scene from London, England. Can you find evidence for both multiculturalism and globalization in this photo?

© LOOK Die Bildagentur der Fotografen GmbH/Alamy Stock Photo

The Gray and the Brown

International migration, a key feature of globalization, has transformed the demographic composition of the United States, Canada, and Western Europe. Drawing on a 2010 Brookings Institution report titled "State of Metropolitan America: On the Front Lines of Demographic Transformation," Ronald Brownstein (2010) analyzes an intensifying confrontation between groups he describes as "the gray and the brown." Brownstein and demographer William Frey, an author of the Brookings report, focus on two key U.S. demographic trends:

(1) Minorities now constitute 50.2 percent of American children under age 5. The U.S. Census Bureau projects that by 2020 the minority proportion of all American children under age 18 will exceed 50 percent. (2) The country is aging, and about 80 percent of the senior population is white.

The under-18 share of the U.S. population is projected eventually to stabilize at around 23 percent, as the senior share rises steadily from about 12 percent today to 20 percent by 2040. The U.S. working-age population is projected to shrink from about 63 percent today to 57 percent in two to three decades. Frey (in Brookings Institution 2010, pp. 26, 63) sees these trends as creating a "cultural generation gap"—a sharp contrast in the attitudes, priorities, and political leanings of younger and older Americans.

Politically the two groups—the gray (older) and the brown (younger)—are poles apart. Older whites, the most reliable voters, tend to oppose taxes and public spending, while younger people and minorities value government support of education, health, and social welfare. In the 2008 and 2012 elections, young people, especially minorities, strongly supported Democrat Barack Obama. Seniors, especially white ones, voted solidly for Republicans John McCain and Mitt Romney. These differences persisted post-election in measures of approval for President Obama's job performance—consistently highest among nonwhites and young people.

The gray and the brown are actually more interdependent economically than either usually realizes. If minority children benefit disproportionately from public education today, minority workers will pay a growing share of the payroll

taxes needed to sustain Social Security and Medicare—programs that most directly benefit older white people.

The history of national immigration policy helps us understand how the gap between the gray and the brown arose. Federal policies established in the 1920s had severely curtailed immigration from areas other than northern Europe. In 1965, Congress loosened restrictions—resulting in an eventual influx of immigrants from southern Europe, Asia, Africa, the Caribbean, and Latin America (see Vigil 2012).

Non-Hispanic whites comprised the overwhelming majority of Americans through the mid-20th century, including the post–World War II baby boom (1946–1964). Most baby boomers grew up and have lived much of their lives in white suburbs, residentially isolated from minorities (Brownstein 2010). As they age and retire, many older white Americans are reconstituting such communities in racially homogeneous enclaves in the Southeast and Southwest.

In such communities, except for their yard and construction workers and house cleaners, older white Americans live apart from the minorities who represent a growing share of the national population. Since 1965, expanded immigration and higher fertility rates among minorities have transformed American society. As recently as 1980, minorities made up only 20 percent of the total population (versus 38 percent today), and 25 percent of children under 18 (versus more than 45 percent today, expected to exceed 50 percent by 2020). Similar trends are evident in Western Europe and are everyday expressions of globalization.

© James Marshall/Corbis

One of the rallying cries of Tea Party voters has been to "take our country back." A similar sentiment was prominent in the 2016 presidential campaign. Businessman and reality TV star Donald J. Trump rose to prominence in 2015 as a Republican presidential candidate by promising to "make our country great again." Cynics wondered whether the hidden agenda behind that slogan might actually be "make our country white again." Prominent in Trump's campaign was open *ethno-nationalism,* the idea of an association between ethnicity—traditionally and predominantly European derived and Christian—and the right to rule the United States. Trump advocated deportation of undocumented immigrants, focusing on Mexicans. He also proposed a temporary ban on admission of Muslims to the United States, initially in response to a shooting by jihadist terrorists in San Bernardino, California, and supposed threats from ISIS and Syrian refugees. (As of this writing, fewer than 10,000 Syrian refugees have been admitted to the United States.) Trump was promising to purge the United States of ethnic groups here illegally and to protect the country from members of what is in the United States a minority religion.

Other Republican presidential candidates joined Trump in urging deportation but did not support his call for a ban on Muslims. All, however, faulted President Obama, like President George W. Bush before him, for avoiding the word *Radical Islam* when he spoke of terrorists and enemies. The Republican presidential candidates also railed against "political correctness," which they saw as excessive caution about using language and labels that might offend particular groups. Trump, in particular, used the claim of hyper-political correctness to justify his stereotyping of Mexicans, Muslims, and Syrian refugees. Anyone who complained about insults was "overreacting"—just being hyper-politically correct. Trump's candidacy harnessed and expressed the backlash against the multicultural model of ethnic relations that has been gaining ground in the United States for the past few decades. Rarely, if ever, does cultural change occur without opposition. Those who hold power and privilege do not give it up readily.

ETHNIC CONFLICT

Ethnic differences can exist harmoniously, for example, in plural societies or through multiculturalism. However, ethnic differences can also lead to interethnic confrontation and discrimination. The perception of cultural differences can have disastrous effects on social interaction. Why are ethnic differences often associated with conflict and violence? Ethnic groups may compete economically and/or politically. An ethnic group may react if it perceives prejudice or discrimination by another group or society as a whole, or if it feels otherwise devalued or disadvantaged (see the section "Black Lives Matter"). An ethnic group can

Two Nevada women take a selfie with a Donald Trump campaign sign at a rally held in Las Vegas just before the February 2016 Republican caucuses. How might a sociocultural anthropologist cite features of language, ethnicity, race, and gender to explain Trump's rise to political prominence?
© Ethan Miller/Getty Images News/Getty Images

resent the actual or perceived privileges of other groups (see Donham 2011; Friedman 2003).

The roots of ethnic differentiation can be linguistic, cultural, religious, or racial. Much of the ethnic unrest in today's world has a religious component—whether between Christians and Muslims, Muslims and Jews, or different sects within one of the major religions. The Iraqi dictator Saddam Hussein, who was deposed in 2003, favored his own Sunni Muslim sect while fostering discrimination against others (Shiites and

Fleeing bombing from Russian airstrikes in Aleppo, Syria, refugees from that city line up for food in a tent city near the Turkish-Syrian border (February 2016).
© Fatih Aktas/Anadolu Agency/Getty Images

Kurds). Sunnis, although a numeric minority within Iraq's population, enjoyed privileged access to power, prestige, and position. After the elections of 2005, which many Sunnis chose to boycott, Shiites gained political control over Iraq and retaliated quickly against prior Sunni favoritism. A civil war soon developed out of "sectarian violence" (conflicts among sects of the same religion) as Sunnis (and their foreign supporters) fueled an insurgency against the new government and its foreign supporters, including the United States. Shiites then retaliated further against Sunni attacks and a history of Sunni privilege and perceived discrimination against Shiites. The Sunnis, lacking power in the new Iraqi government, eventually helped form the so-called Islamic state (IS), also known as ISIS, ISIL, and Daesh, which, as of this writing, controls portions of Iraq and adjacent areas of Syria.

Iraq and Syria each contain substantial Muslim populations of Shiites, Sunnis, and Kurds (along with various ethno-religious minorities). Syria's president, Bashar al-Assad, like his father and predecessor in office, Hafez al-Assad (who ruled from 1971 to 2000), has favored his own minority Muslim group (Alawites—allied with the Shiites) over his country's Sunni majority. Syria has witnessed escalating internal warfare since 2011, when, as in other parts of the Middle East, a series of uprisings known collectively as the Arab Spring arose in opposition to authoritarian governments. The Assad regime fanned the flames of civil war by its violent repression of the protesters and eventual rebels.

The parties to the ongoing conflict in Syria include (among others) the Assad government and its foreign allies, including Russia, Shiite Iran, and the Lebanese militia Hezbollah. Sunni-led ISIS maintains a significant presence in northern and eastern Syria, adjacent to and extending into Iraq. A third group consists of "moderate" rebels, presumably including Sunnis opposed to both Assad and ISIS. These rebels, whose numbers and effectiveness are currently unclear, are supported by the United States and other Sunni-majority countries of the Middle East. Finally, the Kurds, also supported by the United States, are assisting in the war against ISIS.

The conflict in Syria has displaced about half of Syria's population of 23 million. Some 6.6 million people have been displaced internally, while about 4.6 million others have fled Syria as refugees. The latter have sought refuge primarily in other Middle Eastern countries, including Turkey, Lebanon, Jordan, Iraq, and Egypt. Others have traveled by boat across the Aegean Sea to the Greek islands and mainland, and from there into Europe via the Balkans. Others have crossed the Mediterranean into Italy, and some have crossed from North Africa to Spain. Sweden and, particularly, Germany have been the most welcoming European countries, with Germany pledging eventually to accept up to 800,000 Syrian refugees. In Syria itself, if Assad eventually vacates the presidency, Sunni reprisals are likely against Alawites and other religious minorities, including Christians and Shiite Muslims (see Adams 2012).

Prejudice and Discrimination

Members of an ethnic group may be the targets of prejudice (negative attitudes and judgments) or discrimination (punitive action). **Prejudice** means devaluing (looking down on) a group because of its assumed behavior, values, capabilities, or attributes. People are prejudiced when they hold stereotypes about groups and apply them to individuals. (**Stereotypes** are fixed ideas—often unfavorable—about what the members of a group are like.) Prejudiced people assume that members of the group will act as they are "supposed to act" (according to the stereotype) and interpret a wide range of individual behaviors as evidence of the stereotype. They use this behavior to confirm their stereotype (and low opinion) of the group.

Discrimination refers to policies and practices that harm a group and its members. Discrimination may be legally sanctioned—*de jure* (part of the law), or it may be *de facto* (practiced, but not legally sanctioned). Segregation in the southern United States and *apartheid* in South Africa provide two historical examples of de jure discrimination. In both systems, by law, blacks and whites had different rights and privileges. Also, their social interaction ("mixing") was legally curtailed. An example of de facto discrimination is the harsher treatment that American minorities (compared with other Americans) tend to get from the police and the judicial system. This unequal treatment isn't legal, but it happens anyway, as the following section documents.

Black Lives Matter

Anyone who follows the news regularly will be familiar with a series of cases in which young African American men have been shot dead by white police officers. The "Black Lives Matter" movement has arisen in the United States in response to these and other incidents in which black lives have not seemed to matter much to local officials. As described by Elizabeth Day (2015), the movement originated in July 2013, when an African American woman named Alicia Garza reacted to the acquittal of George Zimmerman, a neighborhood watch volunteer, in the shooting of Trayvon Martin, an unarmed black teenager, in Sanford, Florida. Stunned by Zimmerman's acquittal on charges of second-degree murder and manslaughter, Garza posted the following message on Facebook "Black people. I love you. I love us. Our lives matter."

prejudice
Devaluing a group because of its assumed attributes.

stereotypes
Fixed ideas—often unfavorable—about what members of a group are like.

discrimination
Policies and practices that harm a group and its members.

Garza's friend, Patrisse Cullors, adopted Garza's words and began to post them online using the hashtag #blacklivesmatter. The two women wanted to raise public awareness about the apparent devaluation of black lives in the American judicial and enforcement systems. Using Facebook, Tumblr, and Twitter, Garza and Cullors encouraged users to share stories of why #blacklivesmatter. In August 2014, another unarmed African American teenager, 18-year-old Michael Brown, was killed by 12 rounds of ammunition from the gun of a white police officer in Ferguson, Missouri. Garza helped organize a "Freedom Ride" to Ferguson that brought some 500 people to the St. Louis suburb. On arrival, she was astonished to see her own phrase being shouted by protesters and written on their banners. There were additional protests in Ferguson after a grand jury failed to indict the white police officer. Thereafter, with a series of additional cases in which unarmed black men were shot by white police officers, the slogan "Black Lives Matter" rose to national prominence. The American Dialect Society even named #blacklivesmatter as their word of the year for 2015. By 2016, Black Lives Matter chapters had opened throughout the country (Day 2015).

The movement has grown not only in response to police shootings and brutality but also following the mass murder on June 17, 2015, of nine African American churchgoers in Charleston, South Carolina, by a white supremacist domestic terrorist. That tragic event prompted the governor to call for and achieve the removal of a contentious and racially charged symbol, the Confederate battle flag, from prominent display in the state capital, Columbia.

Social media continue to be prominent in linking and organizing the #blacklivesmatter movement. Activists have been able to respond quickly to an ongoing series of widely reported incidents (e.g., in Baltimore, Baton Rouge, Chicago, Cleveland, North Charleston, and St. Paul) in which black people have been killed by police or died in police custody. Critics of the movement contend that not only "black lives" but "all lives" should matter, as indeed they should. However, this criticism ignores, and would diminish needed attention to, the disproportionate likelihood of arrest, incarceration, and mistreatment by police that African Americans, in particular, face. Americans have not heard in recent years a series of reports about unarmed white men being shot to death by police officers. Discrimination against American minorities may no longer be *de jure*, but it certainly remains *de facto*.

Anti-ethnic Discrimination

This section considers some of the more extreme forms of anti-ethnic discrimination, including genocide, forced assimilation, ethnocide, ethnic expulsion, and cultural colonialism. The most extreme form is **genocide,** the deliberate elimination

Top: People gather outside the Emanuel AME Church prior to the first service following the mass murder (on June 21, 2015) of nine unarmed African American congregants by an avowed white supremacist. *Bottom:* A Black Lives Matter protest on Black Friday (November 27, 2015) in Seattle, Washington. What events spurred the Black Lives Matter movement?

Top: © Cem Ozdel/Anadolu Agency/Getty Images; bottom: © Jason Redmond/AFP/Getty Images

of a group (such as Jews in Nazi Germany, Muslims in Bosnia, or Tutsi in Rwanda) through mass murder (see Hinton and O'Neill 2009). More recently, in the Darfur region of western Sudan, government-supported Arab militias, called the *Janjaweed,* have forced black Africans off their land. The militias are accused of genocide, of killing up to 30,000 darker-skinned Africans.

Ethnocide is the deliberate suppression or destruction of an ethnic culture by a dominant group. One way of implementing a policy of ethnocide is through *forced assimilation*, in which the dominant group forces an ethnic group to adopt the dominant culture. Many countries have penalized or banned the language and customs of an ethnic

genocide
The deliberate elimination of a group through mass murder.

ethnocide
The deliberate suppression or destruction of an ethnic culture by a dominant group.

group (including its religious observances). One example of forced assimilation is the anti-Basque campaign that the dictator Francisco Franco (who ruled between 1939 and 1975) waged in Spain. Franco banned Basque books, journals, newspapers, signs, sermons, and tombstones and imposed fines for using the Basque language in schools. In reaction to his policies, nationalist sentiment strengthened in the Basque region, and a Basque terrorist group took shape.

A policy of *ethnic expulsion* aims at removing groups that are culturally different from a country. There are many examples, including Bosnia-Herzegovina in the 1990s. Uganda expelled 74,000 Asians in 1972. The neofascist parties of contemporary Western Europe advocate repatriation (expulsion) of immigrant workers, such as Algerians in France and Turks in Germany. As of this writing (2016), the United States contains approximately 11 million undocumented immigrants. They are here without documents because they overstayed their visas or work permits, entered unofficially, or were smuggled in. Millions of them work, pay taxes, and have children born in the United States, who are American citizens. What are their prospects? The future of undocumented immigrants became a particularly contentious political issue during the 2016 presidential election. More than one of the Republican candidates for president advocated their mass deportation. No one explained the logistics of deporting 11 million people. Such deportation would be a form of forced expulsion, although America's undocumented immigrants come from many countries and lack legal documents granting them the right to remain in the United States.

When members of an ethnic group are expelled, they often become **refugees**—people who have been forced (involuntary refugees) or who have chosen (voluntary refugees) to flee a country, to escape persecution or war. A government policy of ethnic expulsion is only one source of refugees. The Syrian refugees who dominated the news in 2015 and 2016 were driven from their homes by civil war and reprisals by various factions and their foreign allies. They were not, by and large, voluntary refugees, but they were not forced out by a government policy of ethnic expulsion.

Cultural colonialism refers to the internal domination by one group and its culture or ideology over others. One example is how the Russian people, language, and culture and the communist ideology dominated the former Soviet empire. In cultural colonialism, the dominant culture makes itself the official culture. This is reflected in schools, the media, and public interaction. Under Soviet rule, ethnic minorities had very limited self-rule in republics and regions controlled by Moscow. All the republics and their peoples were to be united by the oneness of "socialist internationalism." A common technique in cultural colonialism is to flood ethnic areas with members of the dominant ethnic group. In the former Soviet Union, ethnic Russian colonists were sent to many areas, to diminish the cohesion and clout of the local people.

For example, when Ukraine belonged to the Soviet Union, Moscow promoted a policy of Russian in-migration and Ukrainian out-migration, so that ethnic Ukrainians' share of the population of Ukraine declined from 77 percent in 1959 to 73 percent in 1991. That trend reversed after Ukraine gained independence, so that, by the turn of the 21st century, ethnic Ukrainians made up more than three-fourths of their country's population. Russians still constitute Ukraine's largest minority, but they now represent less than one-fifth of the population. They are concentrated in eastern

cultural colonialism
The internal domination by one group and its culture or ideology over others.

refugees
People who flee a country to escape persecution or war.

Faces of ethnic difference in the former Soviet empire. The propaganda poster on the left depicts a happy mix of nationalities representing the populace of Kyrgyzstan, Central Asia. In the photo on the right, taken on February 18, 2016, Ukrainians in Kiev (the Ukrainian capital) protest Russian "economic aggression" and incursions into eastern Ukraine.

Left: © Bradley Mayhew/Lonely Planet Images/Getty Images; right: © Vladimir Shtanko/Anadolu Agency/Getty Images

TYPE	NATURE OF INTERACTION	EXAMPLES
POSITIVE		
Assimilation	Ethnic groups absorbed within dominant culture	Brazil; United States in early, mid-20th century
Plural society	Society or region contains economically interdependent ethnic groups	Areas of Middle East with farmers/herders; Swat, Pakistan
Multiculturalism	Cultural diversity valued; ethnic cultures coexist with dominant culture	Canada; United States in 21st century
NEGATIVE		
Prejudice	Devaluing a group based on assumed attributes	Worldwide
Discrimination de jure	Legal policies and practices harm ethnic group	South African apartheid; former segregation in southern United States.
Discrimination de facto	Not legally sanctioned but practiced	Worldwide
Genocide	Deliberate elimination of ethnic group through mass murder	Nazi Germany; Bosnia; Rwanda; Cambodia; Darfur
Ethnocide	Cultural practices attacked by dominant culture or colonial power	Spanish Basques under Franco
Ethnic expulsion	Forcing ethnic group(s) out of a country or region	Ugandan Asians; Serbia; Bosnia; Kosovo

Ukraine, where ethnic Russians have rebelled against Ukraine's pro-Western government. Eastern Ukraine, especially those provinces dominated by the Russian language and ethnicity, is considered a potential target of Russian annexation. In 2014, Russia did annex Crimea, where ethnic Russians (composing over 60 percent of the Crimean population) and the Russian language dominate. Recap 15.2 summarizes the various types of ethnic interaction—positive and negative—that have been discussed.

The fall of the Soviet Union in 1991 was accompanied by a resurgence of ethnic feeling among formally dominated groups. The ethnic groups and nationalities once controlled by Moscow have sought, and continue to seek, to forge their own separate and viable nation-states. This celebration of ethnic autonomy is part of an ethnic florescence that—as surely as globalization and transnationalism—is a trend of the late 20th and early 21st centuries. The new assertiveness of long-resident ethnic groups extends to the Welsh and Scots in the United Kingdom, Bretons and Corsicans in France, and Basques and Catalans in Spain.

for REVIEW

summary

1. *Ethnic group* refers to members of a particular culture in a nation or region that contains others. Ethnicity is based on cultural similarities (among members of the same ethnic group) and differences (between that group and others). A race is an ethnic group assumed to have a biological basis.

2. Human races are cultural (rather than biological) categories that derive from contrasts perceived in particular societies. Racial labels such as "white" and "black" designate socially constructed races—categories defined by American culture. In American racial classification, governed by the rule of hypodescent,

children of mixed unions, no matter what their appearance, are classified with the minority group parent.

3. Racial attitudes in Japan illustrate intrinsic racism—the belief that a perceived racial difference is a sufficient reason to value one person less than another. The valued group is majority (pure) Japanese, who define themselves in opposition to others, anyone who is "not us." In Brazil, racial identity is more of an achieved status, which can change during someone's lifetime, reflecting phenotypical changes.

4. The term *nation,* which once was synonymous with *ethnic group,* now means a state—a centrally organized political unit. Most nation-states are not ethnically homogeneous. Ethnic groups that seek autonomous political status are nationalities.

5. An ethnic group may undergo assimilation when it moves to a country where another culture dominates. It adopts the patterns and norms of its host culture. A plural society combines ethnic contrasts and economic interdependence between ethnic groups. Multiculturalism socializes individuals not only into the dominant (national) culture but also into an ethnic one.

6. Ethnic conflict often arises in reaction to prejudice (attitudes and judgments) or discrimination (action). The most extreme form of ethnic discrimination is genocide, the deliberate elimination of a group through mass murder. A dominant group may try to destroy certain ethnic practices (ethnocide), or to force ethnic group members to adopt the dominant culture (forced assimilation). *Cultural colonialism* refers to internal domination by one group and its culture or ideology over others.

key terms

achieved status 278
ascribed status 278
assimilation 287
colonialism 287
cultural colonialism 294
descent 280
discrimination 292
ethnic group 278
ethnicity 278
ethnocide 293
genocide 293
hypodescent 281
multiculturalism 288

nation 286
nationalities 287
nation-state 286
phenotype 285
plural society 288
prejudice 292
race 279
racism 279
refugees 294
state 286
status 278
stereotypes 292
stratified 285

critical thinking

1. What's the difference between a culture and an ethnic group? In what culture(s) do you participate? To what ethnic group(s) do you belong? What is the basis of your primary cultural identity? Do others readily recognize this basis and identity? Why or why not?

2. Name five social statuses you currently occupy. To what extent are these statuses achieved? Are any of them mutually exclusive? Which are contextual?

3. In describing the recent history of the census in the United States, this chapter notes how the National Association for the Advancement of Colored People and the National Council of La Raza (a Hispanic advocacy group) have opposed adding a "multiracial" census category. What does this suggest about racial categories?

4. Would "All Lives Matter" be a useful slogan for a civil rights movement? How might social media function in organizing social and political movements?

5. This chapter describes different types of ethnic interaction. What are they? Are they positive or negative? Anthropologists have made and continue to make important contributions to understanding past and ongoing cases of ethnic conflict. What are some examples of this?

CHAPTER 16

Making a Living

▶ How do people make a living in different types of society?

▶ What is an economy, and what is economizing behavior?

▶ What principles regulate the exchange of goods and services in various societies?

© Nicholas Pitt/Photodisc/Getty Images RF

Thailand's Damnoen Saduak floating market, located about 60 miles (100 kilometers) south of Bangkok. What's being sold here, and by whom?

understanding OURSELVES

The necessities of work, marriage, and raising children are fundamental. However, in the non-Western societies where the study of anthropology originated, the need to balance work (economy) and family (society) wasn't as stark as it is for us. In traditional societies, one's workmates usually were also one's kin. There was no need for a "take your child to work" day, because most women did that every day. People didn't work with strangers. Home and office, society and economy, were intertwined.

The fact that subsistence and sociality are both basic human needs creates conflicts in modern society. People have to make choices about allocating their time and energy between work and family. Parents in dual-earner and single-parent households always have faced a work–family time bind, and the number of Americans living in such households has almost doubled in recent decades. Fewer than one-third of American wives worked outside the home in 1960, compared with about two-thirds today. That same year, only one-fifth of married women with children under age 6 were in the workforce, versus three-fifths today.

Think about the choices your parents have made in terms of economic versus social goals. Have their decisions maximized their incomes, their lifestyles, their individual happiness, family benefits, or what? What about you? What factors motivated you when you chose to apply to and attend college? Did you want to stay close to home, to attend college with friends, or to maintain a romantic attachment (all social reasons)? Did you seek the lowest tuition and college costs—or get a generous scholarship (economic decisions)? Did you choose prestige, or perhaps the likelihood that one day you would earn more money because of the reputation of your alma mater (maximizing prestige and future wealth)? Economists tend to assume that the profit motive rules in contemporary society. However, different individuals, like different cultures, may choose to pursue goals other than monetary gain.

Studies show that most American women now expect to join the paid labor force, just as men do. But the family remains attractive. Many young women also plan to stay home with small children and return to the workforce once their children enter school. How about you? If you have definite career plans, how do you imagine your work will fit in with your future family life—if you have one planned? What do your parents want most for you—a successful career or a happy family life with children? Probably both. Will it be easy to fulfill such expectations?

In today's globalizing world, communities and societies are being incorporated, at an accelerating rate, into larger systems. The first major acceleration in the growth of human social systems can be traced back to around 12,000–10,000 years ago, when humans started intervening in the reproductive cycles of plants and animals. *Food production* refers to human control over the reproduction of plants and animals, and it contrasts with the foraging economies that preceded it and that still persist in some parts of the world today. To make their living, foragers hunt, gather, and collect what nature has to offer. Foragers may harvest, but they don't plant. They may hunt animals, but (except for the dog) they don't domesticate them. Only food producers systematically select and breed for desirable traits in plants and animals. With the advent of **food production,** which includes plant cultivation and animal domestication, people, rather than nature, become selective agents. Human selection replaced natural selection as food collectors became food producers.

The origin and spread of food production (plant cultivation and animal domestication) accelerated human population growth and led to the formation of larger and more powerful social and political systems. The pace of cultural transformation increased enormously. This chapter provides a framework for understanding a variety of human adaptive strategies and economic systems.

ADAPTIVE STRATEGIES

The anthropologist Yehudi Cohen (1974) used the term **adaptive strategy** to describe a group's main system of economic production—its way of making a living. Cohen argued that the most important reason for similarities between two (or more) unrelated societies is their possession of a similar adaptive strategy. For example, there are clear similarities among societies that have a foraging (hunting-and-gathering) strategy. Cohen developed a typology of societies based on correlations between their economies and their social features. His typology includes these five adaptive strategies: foraging, horticulture, agriculture, pastoralism, and industrialism. This chapter focuses on the first four adaptive strategies. Industrialism is examined in the last two chapters of this book.

FORAGING

Foraging—an economy and way of life based on hunting and gathering—was humans' only way of making a living until about 12,000 years ago, when people began experimenting with food production. To be sure, environmental differences did create substantial contrasts among foragers living in different parts of the world. Some, like the people who lived in Europe during the Ice Ages, were big-game hunters. Today, hunters in the Arctic still focus on large animals. Those far northern foragers have much less vegetation and variety in their diets than do tropical foragers. Moving from colder to hotter areas, the number of species increases. The tropics contain tremendous biodiversity, and tropical foragers typically hunt and gather a wide range of plant and animal species. Some temperate areas also offer abundant and varied species. For example, on the North Pacific Coast of North America, foragers could draw on varied sea, river, and land species, such as salmon and other fish, sea mammals, berries, and mountain goats. Despite differences caused

by such environmental variation, all foraging economies have shared one essential feature: People rely on nature to make their living. They don't grow crops or breed and or tend animals.

Animal domestication (initially of sheep and goats) and plant cultivation (of wheat and barley) began 12,000 to 10,000 years ago in the Middle East. Cultivation based on different crops, such as corn (maize), manioc (cassava), and potatoes, arose independently in the Americas. In both hemispheres, most societies eventually turned from foraging to food production. Today most foragers have at least some dependence on food production or on food producers (Kent 1992, 2002).

Foraging economies survived into modern times in certain forests, deserts, islands, and very cold areas—places where cultivation was not practicable with simple technology (see Lee and Daly 1999). Figure 16.1 presents a partial distribution of recent foragers. Their habitats tend to have one thing in common—their marginality. Posing major obstacles to food production, these environments did not attract farmers or herders. The difficulties of cultivating at the North Pole are obvious. In southern Africa, the Dobe Ju/'hoansi San area studied by Richard Lee and others is surrounded by a huge waterless belt (Solway and Lee 1990). Farming could not exist in much of California without irrigation, which is why its native populations were foragers.

We should not assume that foragers will inevitably turn to food production once they learn of its existence. In fact, foragers in many areas have been—and still are—in contact with farmers or herders, but they have chosen to maintain their

---

food production
Plant cultivation and animal domestication.

adaptive strategy
Means of making a living; productive system.

foraging
An economy and a way of life based on hunting and gathering.

In southwestern Madagascar, two young Vezo girls (members of a maritime ethnic group) fish in the coastal waters of the Mozambique Channel, which separates Madagascar from Africa.
© Cristina Mittermeier/National Geographic Creative

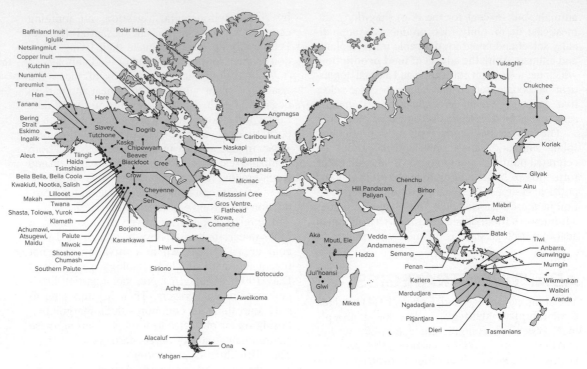

FIGURE 16.1 Worldwide Distribution of Selected Hunter-Gatherers.

Source: Kelly, Robert L. *The Foraging Spectrum: Diversity in Forager Lifeways,* fig. 1.1. Copyright © 2007 by Eliot Werner Publications, Inc. All rights reserved. Used with permission of the publisher.

foraging lifestyle. Their traditional economy supported them well enough, lacked the labor requirements associated with farming and herding, and provided an adequate and nutritious diet. In some places, people tried food production, only to abandon it eventually and return to foraging.

All contemporary foragers live in nation-states. Typically, they are in contact with food-producing neighbors as well as with missionaries and other outsiders. We should not view contemporary foragers as isolated or pristine survivors of the Stone Age. Modern foragers are influenced by national and international policies and political and economic events in the world system.

Geographic Distribution of Foragers

It will be helpful to refer to Figure 16.1 throughout this section. Africa contains two broad belts of contemporary or recent foraging. One is the Kalahari Desert of southern Africa. This is the home of the San ("Bushmen"), who include the Ju/'hoansi (see Kent 1996; Lee 2003, 2012). The other main African foraging area is the equatorial forest of central and eastern Africa, home of the Mbuti, Efe, and other "pygmies" (Bailey et al. 1989; Turnbull 1965).

People still do, or until recently did, subsistence foraging in certain remote forests in Madagascar, South and Southeast Asia, Malaysia, and the

Philippines and on certain islands off the Indian coast. In addition, some of the best-known recent foragers are the aborigines of Australia. Those Native Australians lived on their island continent for perhaps 50,000 years without developing food production.

The Western Hemisphere also had recent foragers. The Eskimos, or Inuit, of Alaska and Canada are well-known hunters. These (and other) northern foragers now use modern technology, including rifles and snowmobiles, in their subsistence activities. The native populations of the North Pacific Coast of North America (northern California, Oregon, Washington, British Columbia, and southern Alaska) all were foragers, as were those of inland subarctic Canada and the Great Lakes. For many Native Americans, fishing, hunting, and gathering remain important subsistence (and sometimes commercial) activities. Considering South America, there were coastal foragers along that continent's southern tip, in Patagonia. Additional foragers inhabited the grassy plains of Argentina, southern Brazil, Uruguay, and Paraguay.

Jana Fortier (2009) summarizes key attributes of foragers in South Asia, which today is home to more full- and part-time hunter-gatherers than any other world area. In India, Nepal, and Sri Lanka, about 40 societies and an estimated 150,000 people continue to derive their subsistence from full- or part-time foraging. Hill Kharias and Yanadis are the largest contemporary South Asian foraging populations, with about 20,000 members each. Several other ethnic groups are highly endangered, with fewer than 350 members still doing subsistence foraging.

Surviving South Asian foraging societies are those whose members, despite having lost many of their natural resources to deforestation and spreading farming populations, have been unwilling to adopt food cultivation and its cultural correlates. These hunter-gatherers share features with other foragers worldwide: small social groups, mobile settlement patterns, sharing of resources, immediate food consumption, egalitarianism, and decision making by mutual consent (Fortier 2009).

As is true elsewhere, specific foraging techniques reflect variations in environment and resource distribution. Hill and mountain South Asian foragers favor focused hunting of medium-sized prey (langur monkey, macaque, porcupine). Other groups pursue several small species or practice broad-spectrum foraging of bats, porcupines, and deer. Larger groups use communal hunting techniques, such as spreading nets over large fig trees to entangle sleeping bats. Some South Indian foragers focus on such wild plant resources as yams, palms, and taro, in addition to 100+ locally available plants. Harvesting honey and beeswax has been prominent in many South Asian foraging societies (Fortier 2009).

Their members cherish their identities as people who forage for a living in biologically rich and diverse environments. They stress their need for ongoing access to rich forest resources to continue their lifestyles, yet many have been evicted from their traditional habitats. Their best chances for cultural survival depend on national governments that maintain healthy forests, allow foragers access to their traditional natural resources, and foster cultural survival rather than assimilation (Fortier 2009).

Some governments have done quite the opposite. For example, between 1997 and 2002, the government of Botswana (in southern Africa) carried out a relocation scheme affecting about 3,000 Basarwa San Bushmen (Motseta 2006). The government forced these people to leave their ancestral territory, which became a wildlife reserve. After some of them sued, Botswana's High Court eventually ruled that the Basarwa had been wrongly evicted, and issued a court order allowing them to return, but under very restrictive conditions. Although 3,000 people had been relocated, only the 189 people who actually filed the lawsuit were granted an automatic right of return with their children. The many other Basarwa San who wanted to return to their ancestral territory would need to apply for special permits. Even the 189 favored people would be allowed to build only temporary structures and to use only enough water for subsistence needs. Water would be a major obstacle, because the government had shut down the main well. Furthermore, anyone wishing to hunt would have to apply for a permit. This case illustrates how contemporary governments can limit the independence of indigenous peoples and restrict their traditional lifestyle.

Correlates of Foraging

Typologies, such as Cohen's adaptive strategies, are useful because they suggest **correlations**—that is, association or covariation between two or more variables. (Correlated variables are factors that are linked and interrelated, such as food intake and body weight, such that when one increases or decreases, the other changes as well.) Ethnographic studies in hundreds of societies have revealed many correlations between the economy and social life. Associated (correlated) with each adaptive strategy is a bundle of particular sociocultural features. Correlations, however, rarely are perfect. Some foragers lack cultural features usually associated with foraging, and some of those features are found in groups with other adaptive strategies.

correlation
An association; when one variable changes, another does, too.

On December 13, 2006, Roy Sesana (left), lead representative of the Basarwa San, listens to an attorney (tallest man) explain the verdict of the High Court in Lobatse, Botswana: The plaintiffs could resume living and hunting on their ancestral lands, which had been wrongly enclosed within a game reserve. Six years later, in 2012, Basarwa workers and a member of a US-based aid group install a pump for a water well in the Kalahari. A series of new wells will permit more San to return to their ancestral lands.

Left: © Gianluigi Guercia/AFP/Getty Images; right: © Stephane De Sakutin/AFP/Getty Images

What, then, are some correlates of foraging? People who subsisted by hunting and gathering often, but not always, lived in band-organized societies. Their basic social unit, the **band,** was a small group of fewer than a hundred people, all related by kinship or marriage. Among some foragers, band size stayed about the same year-round. In others, the band split up for part of the year. Families left to gather resources that were better exploited by just a few people. Later, they regrouped for cooperative work and ceremonies.

Typical characteristics of the foraging life are flexibility and mobility. In many San groups, as among the Mbuti of Congo, people shifted band membership several times in a lifetime. One might be born, for example, in a band in which one's mother had kin. Later, one's family might move to a band in which the father had relatives. Because bands were exogamous (people married outside their own band), one's parents came from two different bands, and one's grandparents might have come from four. People could join any band to which they had kin or marital links. A couple could live in, or shift between, the husband's band and the wife's band.

Foraging societies tend to be *egalitarian*. That is, they make few status distinctions, and the ones they make are mainly based on age, gender, and personal qualities or achievements. For example, old people—elders—may receive respect as guardians of myths, legends, stories, and traditions. Younger people may value the elders' special knowledge of ritual and practical matters. A good hunter, an especially productive gatherer, or a skilled midwife or shaman may be recognized as such. But foragers are known for sharing rather than bragging. Their status distinctions are not associated with differences in wealth and power, nor are they inherited. When considering issues of "human nature," we should remember that the egalitarian society associated with foraging was a basic form of human social life for most of our history. Food production has existed less than 1 percent of the time *Homo* has spent on Earth. However, it has produced huge social differences. We now consider the main economic features of food-producing strategies.

ADAPTIVE STRATEGIES BASED ON FOOD PRODUCTION

In Cohen's typology, the three adaptive strategies based on food production in nonindustrial societies are horticulture, agriculture, and pastoralism. With horticulture and agriculture, plant cultivation is the mainstay of the economy, while with

In slash-and-burn horticulture, the land is cleared by cutting down (slashing) and burning trees and brush, using simple technology, as is done here among mountain rice farmers in the hills of Thailand.
© UniversalImagesGroup/Universal Images Group via Getty Images

pastoralism, herding is key. All three strategies originated in nonindustrial societies, although they may persist as ways of making a living even after some degree of industrialization reaches the nation-states that include them. In fully industrial societies, such as the United States and Canada, most cultivation has become large-scale, commercial, mechanized, agrochemical-dependent farming. Rather than simple pastoralism, industrial societies use technologically sophisticated systems of ranch and livestock management.

Food producers typically carry out a variety of economic activities. In Cohen's typology, each adaptive strategy refers to the main economic activity. Pastoralists (herders), for example, consume milk, blood, and meat from their animals as mainstays of their diet. However, they also add grain to their diet by doing some cultivating or by trading with neighbors.

Horticulture

The two types of plant cultivation found in nonindustrial societies are **horticulture** (nonintensive, shifting cultivation) and **agriculture** (intensive, continuous cultivation). Both differ from the commercially oriented farming systems of industrial nations, which use large land areas and rely on machinery and petrochemicals.

When food production arose, both in the Middle East and in Mexico, the earliest cultivators were rainfall-dependent horticulturalists. More recently, horticulture has been—and in many cases still is—the primary form of cultivation in parts of Africa, Southeast Asia, the Pacific islands, Mexico, Central America, and the South American tropical forest.

Horticulturalists use simple tools such as hoes and digging sticks to grow their crops. Horticulturalists preserve their ecosystems by allowing their fields to lie fallow for varying lengths of time. Horticulturalists typically rely on *slash-and-burn* techniques. Farmers clear land by cutting down (slashing) trees, saplings, and brush. Then they burn that vegetation. They also may set fire directly to grasses and weeds on their farm plots before planting. Slashing and burning not only gets rid of unwanted vegetation, but it also kills pests and provides ashes that help fertilize the soil. The farmers then sow, tend, and harvest their crops on the cleared plot. They do not use that plot continuously; often they farm it for only a year or two.

Horticulture also is known as *shifting cultivation*, because farmers shift back and forth between plots, rather than using any one of those plots continuously. With shifting cultivation, horticulturalists farm a plot for a year or two, then abandon it, clear another plot, cultivate it for a year or two, then abandon it, and so on. After the original plot lies fallow for several years (the duration varies in different societies), it can be farmed again.

Shifting cultivation doesn't mean that whole villages must move when plots are abandoned. Horticulture can support large, permanent villages. Among the Kuikuru of the South American tropical forest, for example, one village of 150 people remained in the same place for 90 years (Carneiro 1956). Kuikuru houses are large and well made. Because the work involved in building them is great, the Kuikuru preferred to walk farther to their fields, rather than construct a new village. They chose to shift their plots rather than their villages. By contrast, other horticulturalists in the montaña (Andean foothills) of Peru maintained small villages of about thirty people (Carneiro 1961/1968). Their houses were small, simple, and easy to rebuild, so that they would stay a few years in one place, then move on to a different site near their fields where they would build new homes. They preferred rebuilding to walking even a half-mile to their fields.

Agriculture

The greater labor demands associated with agriculture, as compared with horticulture, reflect its common use of domesticated animals, irrigation, or terracing.

Domesticated Animals

Many agriculturalists use animals as means of production—for transport, as cultivating machines, and for their manure. Asian farmers typically incorporate cattle and/or water buffalo into agricultural economies based on rice production. Rice farmers may use cattle to trample pretilled flooded fields, thus mixing soil and water, prior to transplanting. Many agriculturalists attach animals to plows and harrows for field preparation before planting or transplanting. Also, agriculturalists typically collect manure from their animals,

using it to fertilize their plots, thus increasing yields. Animals are attached to carts for transport as well as to implements of cultivation.

Irrigation

While horticulturalists must await the rainy season, agriculturalists can schedule their planting in advance, because they control water. Like other irrigation experts in the Philippines, the Ifugao (Figure 16.2) irrigate their fields with canals from rivers, streams, springs, and ponds. Irrigation makes it possible to cultivate a plot year after year. Irrigation enriches the soil, because the irrigated field is a unique ecosystem with several species of plants and animals, many of them minute organisms, whose wastes fertilize the land.

An irrigated field is a capital investment that usually increases in value. It takes time for a field to start yielding; it reaches full productivity only after several years of cultivation. The Ifugao, like other irrigators, have farmed the same fields for generations. In some agricultural areas, including the Middle East, however, salts carried in the irrigation water can make fields unusable after 50 or 60 years.

Terracing

Terracing is another agricultural technique the Ifugao have mastered. Their homeland has small valleys separated by steep hillsides. Because the population is dense, people need to farm the hills. However, if they simply planted on the steep hillsides, fertile soil and crops would be washed away during the rainy season. To prevent this, the Ifugao cut into the hillside and build stage after

FIGURE 16.2 Location of the Ifugao.

stage of terraced fields rising above the valley floor. Springs located above the terraces supply their irrigation water. The labor necessary to build and maintain a system of terraces is great. Terrace walls crumble each year and must be partially rebuilt. The canals that bring water down through the terraces also demand attention.

Costs and Benefits of Agriculture

Agriculture requires human labor to build and maintain irrigation systems, terraces, and other works. People must feed, water, and care for their animals. Given sufficient labor input and management, agricultural land can yield one or two crops annually for years or even generations. An agricultural field does not necessarily produce a higher single-year yield than does a horticultural plot. The first crop grown by horticulturalists on long-idle land may be larger than that from an agricultural plot of the same size. Furthermore, because agriculturalists have to work more hours than horticulturalists do, agriculture's yield relative to the labor time invested also is lower. Agriculture's main advantage is that the long-term yield per area is far greater and more dependable. Because a single field sustains its owners year after year, there is no need to maintain a reserve of uncultivated land as horticulturalists do. This is why agricultural societies tend to be more densely populated than are horticultural ones.

The Cultivation Continuum

Because nonindustrial economies can have features of both horticulture and agriculture, it is useful to discuss cultivators as being arranged along a **cultivation continuum.** Horticultural systems stand at one end—the "low-labor, shifting-plot" end. Agriculturalists are at the other—the "labor-intensive, permanent-plot" end.

We speak of a continuum because there are intermediate economies, which combine horticultural and agricultural features. In such economies, cultivation is more intensive than with annually shifting horticulture, but less so than with permanent agriculture. The South American Kuikuru, for example, grow two or three crops of *manioc,* or cassava—an edible tuber—before abandoning their plots. Cultivation is even more intensive in certain densely populated areas of Papua New Guinea, where plots are planted for two or three years, allowed to rest for three to five, and then recultivated. After several of these cycles, the plots are abandoned for a longer fallow period. These intermediate economies, which support denser populations than does simple horticulture, also are found in parts of West Africa, and in the highlands of Mexico, Peru, and Bolivia.

The one key difference between horticulture and agriculture is that *horticulture always has a fallow period,* whereas agriculture does not.

Intensification: People and the Environment

The range of environments available for cultivation has widened as people have increased their control over nature. Agriculturalists have been able to colonize many areas that are too arid for nonirrigators or too hilly for nonterracers. Agriculture's increased labor intensity and permanent land use have major demographic, social, political, and environmental consequences.

How, specifically, does agriculture affect society and environment? Because of their permanent fields, agriculturalists tend to be sedentary. People live in larger and more permanent communities located closer to other settlements. Growth in population size and density increases contact between individuals and groups. There is more need to regulate interpersonal relations, including conflicts of interest. Economies that support more people usually require more coordination in the use of land, labor, and other resources.

Intensive agriculture has significant environmental effects. Irrigation ditches and paddies (fields with irrigated rice) become repositories for organic wastes, chemicals (such as salts), and disease microorganisms. Intensive agriculture typically spreads at the expense of trees and forests, which are cut down to be replaced by fields. Accompanying such deforestation is loss of environmental diversity (see Srivastava, Smith, and Forno 1999). Compared with horticulture, agricultural economies are specialized. They focus on one or a few caloric staples, such as rice, and on the

Agriculture requires longer hours than horticulture does and uses land intensively and continuously. Labor demands associated with agriculture reflect its use of domesticated animals, irrigation, and terracing. Shown here, irrigated terraces surround the Ifugao village of Banaue on Luzon Island in the Philippines.
© Michele Falzone/JAI/Corbis RF

animals that are raised and tended to aid the agricultural economy. Because tropical horticulturalists typically cultivate dozens of plant species simultaneously, a horticultural plot tends to mirror the botanical diversity that is found in a tropical forest. Agricultural plots, by contrast, reduce ecological diversity by cutting down trees and concentrating on just a few staple foods.

Agriculturalists attempt to reduce risk by favoring stability in the form of a reliable annual harvest and long-term production. Tropical foragers and horticulturalists, by contrast, attempt to reduce risk by relying on multiple species and benefiting from ecological diversity. The agricultural strategy is to put all one's eggs in one big and dependable basket. Of course, even with agriculture, there is a possibility that the single staple crop may fail, and famine may result. The strategy of horticulturalists is to have several, smaller baskets, a few of which may fail without endangering subsistence. The agricultural strategy makes sense when there are lots of children to raise and adults to be fed. Horticulture, like foraging, is associated with smaller, sparser, and more mobile populations.

Many indigenous groups, especially foragers and horticulturalists, have done a reasonable job of managing their resources and preserving their ecosystems (see also Menzies 2006). Such societies had traditional ways of categorizing resources and regulating their use. Increasingly, however, these traditional management systems have been challenged by national and international incentives to exploit and degrade the environment (see Dove, Sajise, and Doolittle 2011).

Pastoralism

Herders, or **pastoralists,** are people whose activities focus on such domesticated animals as cattle, sheep, goats, camels, yak, and reindeer. They live in northern and sub-Saharan Africa, the Middle East, Europe, and Asia. East African pastoralists, like many others, live in symbiosis with their herds. (*Symbiosis* is an obligatory interaction between groups—here, humans and animals—that is beneficial to each.) Herders attempt to protect their animals and to ensure their reproduction in return for food (dairy products and meat) and other products, such as leather.

People use livestock in various ways. Natives of North America's Great Plains, for example, didn't eat, but only rode, their horses. (They got those horses after Europeans reintroduced them to the Western Hemisphere; the native American horse had become extinct thousands of years earlier.) For Plains Indians, horses served as "tools of the trade," means of production used to hunt buffalo, the main target of their economies. So the

pastoralists
Herders of domesticated animals.

Pastoralists may be nomadic or transhumant, but they don't typically live off their herds alone. They either trade or cultivate. Above, a nomadic Afghan Koochi (also spelled Kuchi) woman, with her herd and belongings, returns to Afghanistan from a tribal area of neighboring Pakistan. Nomadic caravans like this one have followed this route for thousands of years. Below, in spring 2011, a transhumant shepherd guides sheep along a country road in Altlandsberg, Germany.

Top: © B.K.Bangash/AP Images; bottom: © Patrick Pleul/dpa/Corbis

ADAPTIVE STRATEGY	ALSO KNOWN AS	KEY FEATURES/VARIETIES
Foraging	Hunting-gathering	Mobility, use of nature's resources
Horticulture	Slash-and-burn, shifting cultivation, swiddening, dry farming	Fallow period
Agriculture	Intensive farming	Continuous use of land, intensive use of labor
Pastoralism	Herding	Nomadism and transhumance
Industrialism	Industrial production	Factory production, capitalism, socialist production

nomadism (pastoral)
The annual movement of entire pastoral group with herds.

Plains Indians were not true pastoralists but hunters who used horses—as many agriculturalists use animals—as means of production.

Pastoralists, by contrast, typically use their herds for food. They consume their meat, blood, and milk, from which they make yogurt, butter, and cheese. Although some pastoralists rely on their herds more completely than others do, it is impossible to base subsistence solely on animals. Most pastoralists therefore supplement their diet by hunting, gathering, fishing, cultivating, or trading.

transhumance
A system in which only part of a population moves seasonally with herds.

The Samis (also known as Lapps or Laplanders) of Norway, Sweden, and Finland domesticated the reindeer, which their ancestors once hunted, in the 16th century. Like other herders, they follow their animals as they make an annual trek, in this case from coast to interior. Today's Samis use modern technology, such as snowmobiles and four-wheel-drive vehicles, to accompany their herds on their annual nomadic trek. Some of them probably use reindeer management software on their laptops, tablets, PDAs, or smartphones. Although their environment is harsher, the Samis, like other herders, live in nation-states and must deal with outsiders, including government officials, as they follow their herds and make their living through animal husbandry, trade, and sales (Paine 2009).

economy
A system of resource production, distribution, and consumption.

Unlike foraging and cultivation, which existed throughout the world before the Industrial Revolution, herding was confined almost totally to the Old World. Before European conquest, the only herders in the Americas lived in the Andean region of South America. They used their llamas and alpacas for food and wool and in agriculture and transport. Much more recently, the Navajo of the southwestern United States developed a pastoral economy based on sheep, which were brought to North America by Europeans. The populous Navajo became the major pastoral population in the Western Hemisphere.

mode of production
Specific set of social relations that organizes labor.

Two patterns of movement occur with pastoralism: nomadism and transhumance. Both are based on the fact that herds must move to use pasture available in particular places in different seasons. In **pastoral nomadism,** the entire group—women, men, and children—moves with the animals throughout the year. The Middle East and North Africa provide numerous examples of pastoral nomads (see Salzman 2008). In Iran, for example, the Basseri and the Qashqai ethnic groups traditionally followed a nomadic route more than 300 miles (480 kilometers) long (see Salzman 2004).

With **transhumance,** part of the group moves with the herds, but most people stay in the home village. There are examples from Europe and Africa. In Europe's Alps, it is just the shepherds and goatherds—not the whole hamlet, village, or town—who accompany the flocks to highland meadows in summer. Among the Turkana of Uganda, men and boys take the herds to distant pastures, while much of the village stays put and does some horticultural farming. During their annual trek, pastoral nomads trade for crops and other products with more sedentary people. Transhumants don't have to trade for crops. Because only part of the population accompanies the herds, transhumants can maintain year-round villages and grow their own crops. (Recap 16.1 summarizes the major adaptive strategies.)

MODES OF PRODUCTION

An **economy** is a system of production, distribution, and consumption of resources; *economics* is the study of such systems. Economists focus on modern nations and capitalist systems. Anthropologists have broadened understanding of economic principles by gathering data on nonindustrial economies. *Economic anthropology* brings a comparative perspective to the study of economics (see Carrier 2012; Chibnik 2011; Gudeman 2016; Hann and Hart 2011; Sahlins 2011).

A **mode of production** is a way of organizing production—"a set of social relations through which labor is deployed to wrest energy from nature by means of tools, skills, organization, and knowledge" (Wolf 1982, p. 75). In the *capitalist* mode of production, money buys labor power, and there is a social gap between the people (bosses and workers) involved in the production process. By contrast, in nonindustrial societies, labor is not usually bought but is given as a social obligation. In such a *kin-based* mode of production, mutual aid in production is one among many expressions of a larger web of social relations (see Graca and Zingarelli 2015).

Societies representing each of the adaptive strategies just discussed (e.g., foraging) tend to have roughly similar modes of production. Differences in the mode of production within a given strategy may reflect differences in environments, target resources, or cultural traditions. Thus, a foraging mode of production may be based on individual hunters or teams, depending on whether the game is a solitary or a herd or flocking animal. Gathering is usually more individualistic than hunting, although collecting teams may assemble when abundant resources ripen and must be harvested quickly. Fishing may be done alone (as in ice fishing or spearfishing) or in crews (as with open-sea fishing and hunting of sea mammals).

Production in Nonindustrial Societies

Although some kind of division of economic labor related to age and gender is a cultural universal, the specific tasks assigned to each gender and to people of different ages vary. Many horticultural societies assign a major productive role to women, but some make men's work primary. Similarly, among pastoralists, men generally tend large animals, but in some cultures women do the milking. Tasks that are accomplished through teamwork in some cultivating societies may be carried out by smaller groups or individuals in other societies.

The Betsileo of Madagascar have two stages of teamwork in rice cultivation: transplanting and harvesting. Team size varies with the size of the field. Both transplanting and harvesting feature a traditional division of labor by age and gender that is well known to all Betsileo and is repeated across the generations. The first job in the transplanting process is the trampling of a previously tilled and flooded field by young men driving cattle, in order to mix earth and water. The young men yell at and beat the cattle, striving to drive them into a frenzy, so that they will trample the fields properly. Trampling breaks up clumps of earth and mixes irrigation water with soil to form a smooth mud, into which women will soon transplant seedlings. Once the tramplers leave the field, older men arrive. With their spades, they break up the clumps that the cattle missed. Meanwhile, the owner and other adults uproot rice seedlings and take them to the field, where women will transplant them.

At harvest time, four or five months later, young men cut the rice off the stalks. Young women carry it to the clearing above the field. Older women arrange and stack it. The oldest men and women then stand on the stack, stomping and compacting it. Three days later, young men thresh the rice, beating the stalks against a rock to remove the grain. Older men then attack the stalks with sticks to make sure all the grains have fallen off.

Most of the other tasks in Betsileo rice cultivation are done by individual owners and their immediate families. All household members help weed the rice field. It is a man's job to till the fields with a spade or a plow. Individual men repair the irrigation and drainage systems and the earth walls that separate one plot from the next. Among other agriculturalists, however, repairing the irrigation system is a task involving teamwork and communal labor.

Means of Production

In nonindustrial societies, there is a more intimate relationship between the worker and the means of production than there is in industrial nations. **Means,** or **factors, of production** include land (territory), labor, technology, and capital.

Land

Among foragers, ties between people and land were less permanent than among food producers. Although many bands had territories, the boundaries usually were not marked, and there was no way they could be enforced. The hunter's stake in an animal being stalked or hit with a poisoned arrow was more important than where the animal finally died. A person acquired the rights to use a band's territory by being born in the band or by joining it through a tie of kinship, marriage, or fictive kinship. In Botswana in southern Africa, Ju/'hoansi San women, whose work provided over half the food, habitually used specific tracts of berry-bearing trees. However, when a woman changed bands, she immediately acquired a new gathering area.

Among food producers, rights to the means of production also come through kinship and marriage. Descent groups (groups whose members claim common ancestry) are common among nonindustrial food producers, and those who descend from the founder share the group's territory and resources. If the adaptive strategy is horticulture, the estate includes garden and fallow land for shifting cultivation. With pastoralism, descent group members have access to animals to start their own herds, to grazing land, to garden land, and to other means of production.

Labor, Tools, and Specialization

Like land, labor is a means of production. In nonindustrial societies, access to both land and labor

means (factors) of production
Major productive resources, e.g., land, labor, technology, capital.

Transplanting and harvesting rice in the highlands of Madagascar. On the left, Betsileo women transplant rice seedlings—an arduous task that places considerable strain on the back. On the right, Betsileo women carry sheaves of rice to an open area for threshing.

Left: © RGB Ventures/SuperStock/Alamy Stock Photo; right: © Michele Burgess/Alamy Stock Photo

comes through social links such as kinship, marriage, and descent. Mutual aid in production is merely one aspect of ongoing social relations that are expressed on many other occasions.

Nonindustrial societies contrast with industrial nations in regard to another means of production: technology. Manufacturing often is linked to age and gender. Women may weave and men may make pottery or vice versa. Most people of a particular age and gender share the technical knowledge associated with that age and gender. If married women customarily make baskets, all or most married women know how to make baskets. Neither technology nor technical knowledge is as specialized as it is in states.

However, some tribal societies do promote specialization. Among the Yanomami of Venezuela and Brazil (Figure 16.3), for instance, certain villages manufacture clay pots and others make hammocks. They don't specialize, as one might suppose, because certain raw materials happen to be available near particular villages. Clay suitable for pots is widely available. Everyone knows how to make pots, but not everybody does so. Craft specialization reflects the social and political environment rather than the natural environment. Such specialization promotes trade, which is the first step in creating an alliance with enemy villages (Chagnon 1997, 2013). Specialization contributes to keeping the peace, although it has not prevented intervillage warfare.

Alienation in Industrial Economies

There are some significant contrasts between industrial and nonindustrial economies. When factory workers produce for sale and for their employer's profit, rather than for their own use, they may be alienated from the items they make. Such alienation means they don't feel strong pride in or personal identification with their products. They see their product as belonging to someone else, not to the man or woman whose labor actually produced it. In nonindustrial societies, by contrast, people usually see their work through from start to finish and have a sense of accomplishment in the product. The fruits of their labor are their own, rather than someone else's. (This chapter's "Focus on Globalization" describes the increasingly impersonal nature of today's global economy.)

FIGURE 16.3 Location of the Yanomami.

Our Global Economy

Economic systems are based on production, distribution, and consumption. All these processes now have global, and increasingly impersonal, dimensions. The products, images, and information we consume each day can come from anywhere. How likely is it that the item you last bought from a website, an outlet, or a retail store was made in the United States, rather than Canada, Mexico, Peru, or China?

The national has become international. Consider a few familiar "American" brands: Good Humor, French's mustard, Frigidaire, Adidas, Caribou Coffee, Church's Chicken, Trader Joe's, Holiday Inn, Dial soap, T-Mobile, and Toll House Cookies. All of them have foreign ownership. As well, the following iconic brands have been bought by foreign companies: Budweiser, Alka-Selzer, Hellmann's, IBM ThinkPad, Ben and Jerry's, 7-Eleven, Popsicle, *Woman's Day*, Purina, Gerber, Vaseline, Lucky Strike, Firestone, and *Car and Driver* magazine.

Also foreign owned are such American architectural icons as New York's Plaza Hotel, Flatiron Building, and Chrysler Building, along with the Indiana Toll Road and the Chicago Skyway. A Brazilian billionaire now owns a significant share in Burger King, a whopper of a chain with over 12,000 outlets worldwide.

Much of America, including half our national debt, now belongs to outsiders. According to Bruce Bartlett (2010), the share of the U.S. national debt owned by foreigners has swollen since the 1970s, when it was only 5 percent. Since the 1970s, oil-producing countries have invested their profits in U.S. Treasury securities because of their liquidity and safety. By 1975 the foreign share of U.S. national debt had reached 17 percent, where it remained through the 1990s, when China started buying large amounts of Treasury bills. By 2009, foreigners were financing almost half the total publicly held U.S. national debt.

The Internet is a vital organ in our 21st-century global economy. All kinds of products—music, movies, clothing, appliances, this book, you name it—are produced, distributed, and consumed via the Internet. Economic functions that are spatially dispersed (perhaps continents apart) are coordinated online in real time. Activities that once involved face-to-face contact are now conducted impersonally, often across vast distances. When you order something via the Internet, the only human being you might speak to is the delivery driver. However, even that human contact is in danger of being replaced by a drone. The computers that take and process your order from Amazon can be on different continents. The products you order can come from a warehouse anywhere in the world. Transnational finance has shifted the economic control of local life to outsiders (see Kennedy 2010). Greeks, for example, blame Germans for their austerity.

How different is today's global economy from British poet Henry Wadsworth Longfellow's vision of production—noble, local, and autonomous:

Under a spreading chestnut-tree

The village smithy stands. . . .

Toiling—rejoicing—sorrowing,

Onward through life he goes;

Each morning sees some task begin,

Each evening sees it close.

(Longfellow, "The Village Blacksmith," 1839)

A scene from an Amazon warehouse on Cyber Monday, December 5, 2011, the busiest day of the year for online shoppers. This warehouse could be in a lot of places, but it happens to be in Great Britain.
© Geoffrey Robinson/Rex Features/AP Images

In nonindustrial societies, the economic relation between coworkers is just one aspect of a more general social relation. They aren't just coworkers but kin, in-laws, or celebrants in the same ritual. In industrial nations, people don't usually work with relatives and neighbors. If coworkers are friends, the personal relationship usually develops out of their common employment rather than being based on a previous association.

Thus, industrial workers have impersonal relations with their products, coworkers, and employers. People sell their labor for cash, and the economic domain stands apart from ordinary social life. Work is separate from family. In nonindustrial societies, however, the relations of production, distribution, and consumption are *social relations with economic aspects*. Economy is not a separate entity but is *embedded* in the society.

In a garment factory in Hlaing Tharyar, Myanmar, Burmese women stitch sports clothing for a Taiwanese company. Their average wage is less than one American dollar per day. Throughout Southeast Asia, hundreds of thousands of young women from peasant families now work in factories. Chances are good that you own one of their products.

© Paula Bronstein/Getty Images News/Getty Images

A Case of Industrial Alienation

For decades, the government of Malaysia has promoted export-oriented industry, allowing transnational companies to install labor-intensive manufacturing operations in rural Malaysia. The industrialization of Malaysia is part of a global strategy. In search of cheaper labor, corporations headquartered in Japan, Western Europe, and the United States have been moving labor-intensive factories to developing countries. Malaysia has hundreds of Japanese and American subsidiaries, which produce mainly garments, foodstuffs, and electronics components. In electronics plants in rural Malaysia, thousands of young women from peasant families now assemble microchips and microcomponents for transistors and capacitors. Aihwa Ong (1987, 2010) did a study of electronics assembly workers in an area where 85 percent of the workers were young, unmarried females from nearby villages.

Ong found that, unlike village women, female factory workers had to cope with a rigid work routine and constant supervision by men. The discipline that factories enforce was being taught in local schools, where uniforms helped prepare girls for the factory dress code. Village women wore loose, flowing tunics, sarongs, and sandals, but factory workers had to don tight overalls and heavy rubber gloves, in which they felt constrained. Assembling electronics components requires precise, concentrated labor. Demanding and depleting, labor in these factories illustrates

the separation of intellectual and manual activity—the alienation that Karl Marx considered the defining feature of industrial work. One woman said about her bosses, "They exhaust us very much, as if they do not think that we too are human beings" (Ong 1987, p. 202). Nor does factory work bring women a substantial financial reward, given low wages, job uncertainty, and family claims on wages. Young women typically work just a few years. Production quotas, three daily shifts, overtime, and surveillance take their toll in mental and physical exhaustion.

One response to factory relations of production has been spirit possession (factory women are possessed by spirits). Ong interprets this phenomenon as the women's unconscious protest against labor discipline and male control of the industrial setting. Sometimes possession takes the form of mass hysteria. Spirits have simultaneously invaded as many as 120 factory workers. Weretigers (the Malay equivalent of the werewolf) arrive to avenge the construction of a factory on aboriginal burial grounds. Disturbed earth and grave spirits swarm on the shop floor. First the women see the spirits; then their bodies are invaded. The women become violent and scream abuses. The weretigers send the women into sobbing, laughing, and shrieking fits. To deal with possession, factories employ local medicine men, who sacrifice chickens and goats to fend off the spirits. This solution works only some of the time; possession still goes on. Factory women continue to act as vehicles to express their own frustrations and the anger of avenging ghosts.

Ong argues that spirit possession expresses anguish at, and resistance to, capitalist relations of production. By engaging in this form of rebellion, however, factory women avoid a direct confrontation with the source of their distress. Ong concludes that spirit possession, while expressing repressed resentment, doesn't do much to modify factory conditions. (Other tactics, such as unionization, would do more.) Spirit possession may even help maintain the current system by operating as a safety valve for accumulated tensions.

ECONOMIZING AND MAXIMIZATION

Economic anthropologists have been concerned with two main questions:

1. How are production, distribution, and consumption organized in different societies? This question focuses on *systems* of human behavior and their organization.

2. What *motivates* people in different cultures to produce, distribute or exchange, and consume? Here the focus is not on systems of behavior but on the motives of the *individuals* who participate in those systems.

Anthropologists view both economic systems and motivations in a cross-cultural perspective. Motivation is a concern of psychologists, but it also has been, implicitly or explicitly, a concern of economists and anthropologists. Economists tend to assume that producers and distributors make decisions rationally by using the *profit motive,* as do consumers when they shop around for the best value. Although anthropologists know that the profit motive is not universal, the assumption that individuals try to maximize profits is basic to the capitalist world economy and to much of Western economic theory. In fact, the subject matter of economics often is defined as **economizing,** or the rational allocation of scarce means (resources) to alternative ends (uses) (see Chibnik 2011).

What does that mean? Classical economic theory assumes that our wants are infinite and that our means are limited. Since means are limited, people must make choices about how to use their scarce resources: their time, labor, money, and capital. (This chapter's "Appreciating Diversity" disputes the idea that people always make economic choices based on scarcity.) Economists assume that when confronted with choices and decisions, people tend to make the one that maximizes profit. This is assumed to be the most rational (reasonable) choice.

The idea that individuals choose to maximize profit was a basic assumption of the classical economists of the 19th century and is one that is held by many contemporary economists. However, certain economists now recognize that individuals in Western cultures, as in others, may be motivated by many other goals. Depending on the society and the situation, people may try to maximize profit, wealth, prestige, pleasure, comfort, or social harmony. Individuals may want to realize their personal or family ambitions or those of another group to which they belong (see Chibnik 2011; Sahlins 2011).

Alternative Ends

To what uses do people in various societies put their scarce resources? Throughout the world, people devote some of their time and energy to building up a *subsistence fund* (Wolf 1966). In other words, they have to work to eat, to replace the calories they use in their daily activity. People also must invest in a *replacement fund.* They must maintain their technology and other items essential to production. If a hoe or plow breaks, they must repair or replace it. They also must obtain and replace items that are essential not to production but to everyday life, such as clothing and shelter.

People also have to invest in a *social fund.* They have to help their friends, relatives, in-laws, and neighbors. It is useful to distinguish between a social fund and a *ceremonial fund.* The latter term refers to expenditures on ceremonies or rituals. To prepare a festival honoring one's ancestors, for example, requires time and the outlay of wealth.

Citizens of nation-states also must allocate scarce resources to a *rent fund.* We think of rent as payment for the use of property. However, "rent fund" has a wider meaning. It refers to resources that people must render to an individual or agency that is superior politically or economically. Tenant farmers and sharecroppers, for example, either pay rent or give some of their produce to their landlords, as peasants did under feudalism.

Peasants are small-scale agriculturalists who live in state-organized societies and have rent fund obligations. They produce to feed themselves, to sell their produce, and to pay rent. All peasants have two things in common:

1. They live in state-organized societies.

2. They produce food without the elaborate technology—chemical fertilizers, tractors, airplanes to spray crops, and so on—of modern farming or agribusiness.

In addition to paying rent to landlords, peasants must satisfy government obligations, paying taxes in the form of money, produce, or labor. The rent fund is not simply an *additional* obligation for peasants. Often it becomes their foremost and unavoidable duty. Sometimes, to meet the obligation to pay rent, their own diets suffer. The demands of paying rent may divert resources from subsistence, replacement, social, and ceremonial funds.

Motivations vary from society to society, and people often lack freedom of choice in allocating their resources. Because of obligations to pay rent, peasants may allocate their scarce means toward ends that are not their own but those of government officials. Thus, even in societies where there is a profit motive, people are often prevented from rationally maximizing self-interest by factors beyond their control.

economizing
The allocation of scarce means (resources) among alternative ends.

peasant
A small-scale farmer with rent fund obligations.

DISTRIBUTION, EXCHANGE

The economist Karl Polanyi (1968) stimulated the comparative study of exchange, and several anthropologists followed his lead. To study exchange cross-culturally, Polanyi defined three principles orienting exchanges: the market principle, redistribution, and reciprocity. These principles can all be present in the same society, but in that case they govern different kinds of transactions. In any society, one of them usually dominates. The principle of exchange that dominates in a given society is the one that allocates the means of production (see Chibnik 2011; Hann and Hart 2011).

Scarcity and the Betsileo

In the realm of cultural diversity, perceptions and motivations can change substantially over time. Consider some changes I've observed among the Betsileo of Madagascar during the decades I've been studying them. Initially, compared with modern consumers, the Betsileo had little perception of scarcity. Now, with population increase and the spread of a cash-oriented economy, their perceived wants and needs have increased relative to their means. Their motivations have changed, too, as people increasingly seek profits, even if it means stealing from their neighbors or destroying ancestral farms.

In the late 1960s my wife and I lived among the Betsileo people of Madagascar, studying their economy and social life (Kottak 1980, 2004). Soon after our arrival we met two well-educated schoolteachers (first cousins) who were interested in our research. The woman's father was a congressional representative who became a cabinet minister during our stay. Their family came from a historically important and typical Betsileo village called Ivato, which they invited us to visit with them.

We had traveled to many other Betsileo villages, where often we were displeased with our reception. As we drove up, children would run away screaming. Women would hurry inside. Men would retreat to doorways, where they lurked bashfully. This behavior expressed the Betsileo's great fear of the mpakafo. Believed to cut out and devour his victim's heart and liver, the mpakafo is

the Malagasy vampire. These cannibals are said to have fair skin and to be very tall. Because I have light skin and stand well over 6 feet tall, I was a natural suspect. The fact that such creatures were not known to travel with their wives offered a bit of assurance that I wasn't really a mpakafo.

When we visited Ivato, its people were different—friendly and hospitable. Our very first day there we did a brief census and found out who lived in which households. We learned people's names and their relationships to our schoolteacher friends and to each other. We met an excellent informant who knew all about the local history. In a few afternoons I learned much more than I had in the other villages in several sessions.

Ivatans were so willing to talk because we had powerful sponsors, village natives who had made it in the outside world, people the Ivatans knew would protect them. The schoolteachers vouched for us, but even more significant was the cabinet minister, who was like a grandfather and benefactor to everyone in town. The Ivatans had no reason to fear us because their more influential native son had asked them to answer our questions.

Once we moved to Ivato, the elders established a pattern of visiting us every evening. They came to talk, attracted by the inquisitive foreigners but also by the wine, tobacco, and food we offered. I asked questions about their customs and beliefs. I eventually developed interview schedules about various subjects,

including rice production. I used these forms in Ivato and in two other villages I was studying less intensively. Never have I interviewed as easily as I did in Ivato.

As our stay neared its end, our Ivatan friends lamented, saying, "We'll miss you. When you leave, there won't be any more cigarettes, any more wine, or any more questions." They wondered what it would be like for us back in the United States. They knew we had an automobile and that we could afford to buy products they never would have. They commented, "When you go back to your country, you'll need a lot of money for things like cars, clothes, and food. We don't need to buy those things. We make almost everything we use. We don't need as much money as you, because we produce for ourselves."

The Betsileo weren't unusual for nonindustrial people. Strange as it may seem to an American consumer, those rice farmers actually believed they had all they needed. The lesson from the Betsileo of the 1960s is that scarcity, which economists view as universal, is variable. Although shortages do arise in nonindustrial societies, the concept of scarcity (insufficient means) is much less developed in stable subsistence-oriented societies than in the societies characterized by industrialism, particularly as the reliance on consumer goods increases.

But with globalization over the past few decades, significant changes have affected the Betsileo—and most nonindustrial peoples. On

The Market Principle

market principle
Buying, selling, and valuation based on supply and demand.

In today's world capitalist economy, the **market principle** dominates. It governs the distribution of the means of production: land, labor, natural resources, technology, knowledge, and capital. "Market exchange refers to the organizational process of purchase and sale at money price" (Dalton 1967; see also Hann and Hart 2009). With market exchange, items are bought and sold, using

money, with an eye to maximizing profit, and value is determined by the *law of supply and demand* (things cost more the scarcer they are and the more people want them).

Bargaining is characteristic of market-principle exchanges. The buyer and seller strive to maximize—to get their "money's worth." In bargaining, buyers and sellers don't need to meet personally. But their offers and counteroffers do

my last visit to Ivato, in 2006, the effects of cash and of rapid population increase were evident there—and throughout Madagascar—where the national growth rate has been about 3 percent per year. Madagascar's population doubled between 1966 and 1991—from 6 to 12 million people. Today it exceeds 22 million—almost four times as many people to feed as when I first did fieldwork there. One result of population pressure has been agricultural intensification. In Ivato, farmers who formerly had grown only rice in their rice fields now were using the same land for cash crops, such as carrots, after the annual

rice harvest. Another change affecting Ivato in recent years has been the breakdown of social and political order, fueled by increasing demand for cash.

Cattle rustling is a growing threat. Cattle thieves (sometimes from neighboring villages) have terrorized peasants who previously felt secure in their villages. Some of the rustled cattle are driven to the coasts for commercial export to nearby islands. Prominent among the rustlers are relatively well-educated young men who have studied long enough to be comfortable negotiating with outsiders but who have been

unable to find formal work and are unwilling to work the rice fields as their peasant ancestors did. The formal education system has familiarized them with external institutions and norms, including the need for cash. The concepts of scarcity, commerce, and negative reciprocity now thrive among the Betsileo.

I've witnessed other striking evidence of the new addiction to cash during my most recent visits to Betsileo country. Near Ivato's county seat, people now sell semiprecious stones—tourmalines, which originally were found by chance in local rice fields. We saw an amazing sight: dozens of villagers destroying an ancestral resource, digging up a large rice field, seeking tourmalines—clear evidence of the encroachment of cash on the local subsistence economy. You can't eat gemstones.

Throughout the Betsileo homeland, population growth and density are propelling emigration. Locally, land, jobs, and money are all scarce. One woman with ancestors from Ivato, herself now a resident of the national capital (Antananarivo), remarked that half the children of Ivato now lived in that city. Although she was exaggerating, a census of all the descendants of Ivato reveals a substantial emigrant and urban population.

Ivato's recent history is one of increasing participation in a cash economy. That history, combined with the pressure of a growing population on local resources, has made scarcity not just a concept but a reality for Ivatans and their neighbors.

Women hull rice in a Betsileo village. In the village of Ivato, farmers who traditionally grew only rice in their rice fields now use the same land for commercial crops, such as carrots, after the annual rice harvest.
© Carl D. Walsh/Aurora Photos

need to be open for negotiation over a fairly short time period.

Redistribution

Redistribution operates when products, such as a portion of the annual harvest, move from the local level to a center, from which they eventually flow back out. That center may be a capital, a regional collection point, or a storehouse near a chief's residence. Redistribution typically occurs in societies that have chiefs. To reach the center, where they will be stored, products often move through a hierarchy of officials. Along the way, those officials and their dependents may consume some, but never all, of the products. After reaching the center, the flow of goods eventually will reverse direction—out from the center, down through the

redistribution
The flow of goods from the local level into a center, then back out; characteristic of chiefdoms.

hierarchy, and back to the common people. Redistribution is a way of moving a variety of goods from different areas to a central point, where they are stored and eventually supplied to the public. The custom of tithing encouraged by many religions is a form of redistribution, in that what the church receives can be used (redistributed) to benefit the needy.

One example of redistribution comes from the Cherokee, Native Americans who were the original owners of the Tennessee Valley. The Cherokee were productive cultivators of maize, beans, and squash, which they supplemented by hunting and fishing. They also had chiefs. Each of their main villages had a central plaza, where meetings of the chief's council took place, and where redistributive feasts were held. According to Cherokee custom, each family farm had an area where the family set aside a portion of its annual harvest for the chief. This supply of corn was used to feed the needy, as well as travelers journeying through Cherokee territory. This store of food was available to all who needed it, with the understanding that it "belonged" to the chief and was dispersed through his generosity. The chief also hosted the

redistributive feasts held in the main settlements. On those occasions, ordinary people were able to consume some of the produce they had previously given in the chief's name (Harris 1978).

Reciprocity

Reciprocity is the act of reciprocating—giving back, returning a favor, repaying a debt. More specifically, economic anthropologists use the term **reciprocity** to refer to exchanges between social equals, people who are related by some kind of personal tie, such as kinship or marriage. Because it occurs between social equals, reciprocity is the dominant exchange principle in the more egalitarian societies—among foragers, cultivators, and pastoralists.

There are three forms of reciprocity: generalized, balanced, and negative (Sahlins 1968, 2011; Service 1966). These may be imagined as areas along a continuum defined by these questions:

1. How closely related are the parties to the exchange?

2. How quickly and unselfishly are gifts reciprocated?

The exchanges that occur between the most closely related people illustrate *generalized reciprocity*. There is no expectation of immediate return of a gift or favor. With *balanced reciprocity,* social distance increases, as does the need to reciprocate. In *negative reciprocity,* social distance is greatest and reciprocation is most calculated. This range, from generalized through balanced to negative, is called the **reciprocity continuum.**

With **generalized reciprocity,** someone gives to another person and expects nothing concrete or immediate in return. Such exchanges (including parental gift giving in contemporary North America) are not primarily economic transactions but expressions of personal relationships. Most parents don't keep accounts of all the time, money, and energy they expend on their children. They merely hope that the children will respect their culture's customs involving love, honor, loyalty, and other obligations to parents.

Among foragers, generalized reciprocity—unselfish giving with no immediate expectation of return—tends to govern exchanges. People routinely share with other band members. A study of the Ju/'hoansi San (Figure 16.4) found that 40 percent of the population contributed little to the food supply (Lee 1968/1974). Children, teenagers, and people over 60 depended on other people for their food. Despite the high proportion of dependents, the average worker hunted or gathered less than half as much (12 to 19 hours a week) as the average American works. Nonetheless, there was always food because different people worked on different days.

reciprocity
The principle governing exchanges among social equals.

reciprocity continuum
A continuum running from generalized reciprocity (closely related/deferred return) to negative reciprocity (strangers/immediate return).

generalized reciprocity
Exchanges among closely related individuals.

FIGURE 16.4 Location of the San, Including Ju/'hoansi.

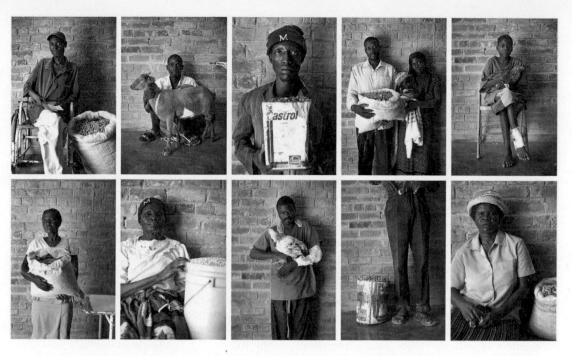

At Zimbabwe's Chidamoyo Hospital, patients often barter farm products for medical treatment. How does barter fit with the exchange principles discussed here?
© Robin Hammond/ Panos Pictures

So strong is the ethic of reciprocal sharing that most foragers have lacked an expression for "thank you." To offer thanks would be impolite because it would imply that a particular act of sharing, which is the keystone of egalitarian society, was unusual. Among the Semai, foragers of central Malaysia (Dentan 1979, 2008), to express gratitude would suggest surprise at a hunter's generosity or success (see also Zhang 2016).

Balanced reciprocity characterizes exchanges between people who are more distantly related than are members of the same band or household. In a horticultural society, for example, a man presents a gift to someone in another village. The recipient may be a cousin, a trading partner, or a brother's fictive kinsman. The giver expects something in return. This may not come immediately, but the social relationship will be strained if there is no reciprocation.

Exchanges in nonindustrial societies also may illustrate **negative reciprocity,** mainly in dealing with people outside or on the fringes of their social systems. To people who live in a world of close personal relations, exchanges with outsiders are full of ambiguity and distrust. Exchange is one way of establishing friendly relations with outsiders, but especially when trade begins, the relationship is still tentative. Often, the initial exchange is close to being purely economic; people want to get something back immediately. Just as in market economies, but without using money, they try to get the best possible immediate return for their investment (see Clark 2010; Hann and Hart 2009).

Generalized and balanced reciprocity are based on trust and a social tie. But negative reciprocity involves the attempt to get something for as little as possible, even if it means being cagey or deceitful or cheating. Among the most extreme and "negative" examples of negative reciprocity was 19th-century horse thievery by North American Plains Indians. Men would sneak into camps and villages of neighboring tribes to steal horses. Such thefts were likely to be reciprocated. A similar pattern of cattle raiding continues today in East Africa, among tribes such as the Kuria (Fleisher 2000). In these cases, the party that starts the raiding can expect reciprocity—a raid on their own village—or worse. The Kuria hunt down cattle thieves and kill them. It's still reciprocity, governed by "Do unto others as they have done unto you."

One way of reducing the tension in situations of potential negative reciprocity is to engage in "silent trade." One example is the silent trade of the Mbuti "pygmy" foragers of the African equatorial forest and their neighboring horticultural villagers. There is no personal contact during their exchanges. A Mbuti hunter leaves game, honey, or another forest product at a customary site. Villagers collect it and leave crops in exchange. The parties can bargain silently. If one feels the return is insufficient, he or she simply leaves it at the trading site. If the other party wants to continue trade, it will be increased.

Coexistence of Exchange Principles

In contemporary North America, the market principle governs most exchanges, from the sale of the means of production to the sale of consumer goods. We also have redistribution. Some of our tax money goes to support the government, but some of it also comes back to us in the form of social services, education, health care, and infrastructure. We also have reciprocity. Generalized

balanced reciprocity
Midpoint on the *reciprocity continuum,* between generalized and negative reciprocity.

negative reciprocity
Potentially hostile exchanges among strangers.

reciprocity characterizes the relationship between parents and children. However, even here the dominant market mentality surfaces in comments about the high cost of raising children and in the stereotypical statement of the disappointed parent: "We gave you everything money could buy."

Exchanges of gifts, cards, and invitations exemplify reciprocity, usually balanced. Everyone has heard remarks like "They invited us to their daughter's wedding, so when ours gets married, we'll have to invite them" and "They've been here for dinner three times and haven't invited us yet. I don't think we should ask them back until they do." Such precise balancing of reciprocity would be out of place in a foraging band, where resources are communal (common to all) and daily sharing based on generalized reciprocity is an essential ingredient of social life and survival.

Generalized reciprocity would appear to be the most widespread form of exchange, because it exists in every kind of society, from foraging bands to industrial nations. Societies with productive economies based on food production have expanded social and economic networks, which allow for wider and more distant exchanges characterized by balanced and even negative reciprocity. Societies with chiefs have redistribution. The market principle tends to dominate exchanges in state-organized societies, to be examined further in Chapter 17, "Political Systems."

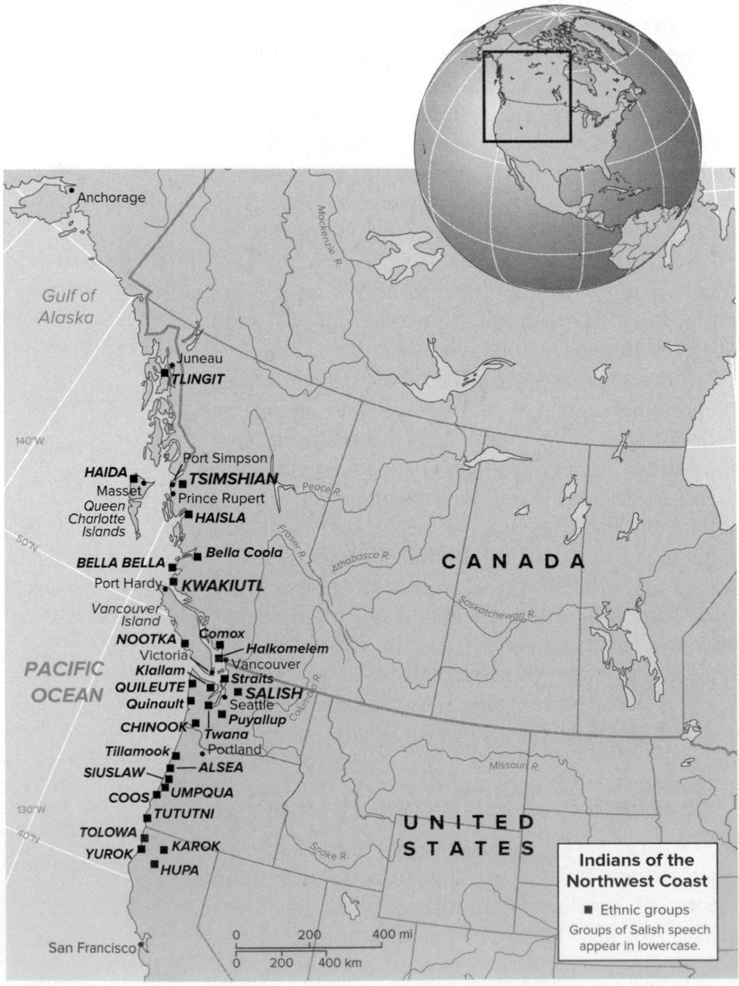

potlatch
A competitive feast on North Pacific Coast of North America.

POTLATCHING

The **potlatch** is a festive event among tribes of the North Pacific Coast of North America, including the Salish and Kwakiutl of Washington and British Columbia and the Tsimshian of Alaska (Figure 16.5). Potlatching is a form of competitive feasting among villages that participate in a regional exchange network. At each potlatch, the sponsoring community gave away food and wealth items, such as blankets and pieces of copper, to visitors from other villages in its network. In return for its giveaway of food and wealth, the sponsoring community received prestige. Prestige increased with the lavishness of the potlatch, the value of the goods distributed. Some North Pacific tribes still practice the potlatch, sometimes as a memorial to the dead (Kan 1986, 1989).

The potlatching tribes were foragers, but not typical ones. Rather than living in nomadic bands, they were sedentary and had chiefs. They enjoyed access to a wide variety of land and sea resources. Among their most important foods were salmon, herring, candlefish, berries, mountain goats, seals, and porpoises (Piddocke 1969).

The economist and social commentator Thorstein Veblen cited potlatching as a prime example of conspicuous consumption in his influential book *The Theory of the Leisure Class* (1934), claiming that potlatching was based on an economically irrational drive for prestige. His analysis emphasized the lavishness and supposed wastefulness, especially of the Kwakiutl displays, to support his contention that in some societies people strive to maximize prestige at the expense of their material well-being. This interpretation has been challenged.

Ecological anthropology, also known as *cultural ecology,* is a theoretical school in anthropology that attempts to interpret cultural practices, such as the potlatch, in terms of their possible long-term role in helping humans adapt to their environments (see Haenn, Wilk, and Harnish 2016). The ecological anthropologists Wayne Suttles (1960) and Andrew Vayda (1961/1968) viewed potlatching not in terms of its apparent wastefulness but in terms of its long-term role as a cultural adaptive mechanism. This view not only helps us understand potlatching; it also helps explain similar patterns of lavish feasting in many other parts of the world. Here is the ecological

FIGURE 16.5 Location of Potlatching Groups.

interpretation: *Customs like the potlatch are cultural adaptations to alternating periods of local abundance and shortage.*

How did this work? The overall natural environment of the North Pacific Coast is favorable, but resources fluctuate from year to year and place to place. Salmon and herring aren't equally abundant every year in a given locality. One village can have a good year while another is experiencing a bad one. Later their fortunes reverse. In this context, the potlatch cycle of the Kwakiutl and Salish had adaptive value; the potlatch was not a competitive display that brought no material benefit.

A village enjoying an especially good year had a surplus of subsistence items, which it could trade for more durable wealth items, such as blankets, canoes, or pieces of copper. Such wealth, in turn, could be given away and thereby converted into prestige. Members of several villages were invited to any potlatch and got to take home the resources that were distributed. In this way, potlatching linked villages together in a regional economy—an exchange system that distributed food and wealth from wealthy to needy communities. In return, the potlatch sponsors and their villages got prestige. The decision to potlatch was determined by the health of the local economy. If there had been subsistence surpluses, and thus a buildup of wealth over several good years, a village could afford a potlatch to convert its food and wealth into prestige.

The long-term adaptive value of potlatching becomes clear when we consider what happened when a formerly prosperous village had a run of bad luck. Its people started accepting invitations to potlatches in villages that were doing better. The tables were turned as the temporarily rich became temporarily poor and vice versa. The newly needy accepted food and wealth items. They were willing to receive rather than bestow gifts and thus to relinquish some of their stored-up prestige. They hoped their luck would eventually improve, so that resources could be recouped and prestige regained.

The potlatch linked local groups along the North Pacific Coast into a regional alliance and exchange network. Potlatching and intervillage exchange had adaptive functions, regardless of the motivations of the individual participants. The anthropologists who stressed rivalry for prestige were not wrong. They were merely emphasizing *motivations* at the expense of an analysis of economic and ecological *systems*.

The use of feasts to enhance individual and community reputations and to redistribute wealth is not unique to populations of the North Pacific Coast. Competitive feasting is widely characteristic of nonindustrial food producers. But among most foragers, who live, remember, in marginal areas, resources are too meager to support feasting on such a level. Among foragers living in

The potlatch then and now. The historic (1904) photo shows guests at a potlatch in Sitka, Alaska. In the photo below, taken in 2004, Tlingit clan members in Sitka celebrate the 100th anniversary of "the Last Potlatch," shown above.

Top: Source: Sitka National Historical Park/National Park Service/U.S. Department of the Interior; bottom: © Daily Sitka Sentinel, James Poulson/AP Images

marginal areas, sharing rather than competition prevails.

The potlatch does not, and did not, exist apart from larger world events. For example, within the spreading world capitalist economy of the 19th century, the potlatching tribes, particularly the Kwakiutl, began to trade with Europeans (fur for blankets, for example). Their wealth increased as a result. Simultaneously, a huge proportion of the Kwakiutl population died from diseases brought by the Europeans. The increased wealth from trade flowed into a drastically reduced population. With many of the traditional potlatch organizers dead (such as chiefs and their families), the Kwakiutl extended the right to give a potlatch to everyone. This resulted in intense competition for prestige, to such an extent that Kwakiutl potlatches began to incorporate the ostentatious destruction of wealth, including blankets, pieces of copper, and even their wooden houses. Blankets and homes were burned, and pieces of copper were buried at sea. Being rich enough to destroy wealth conveyed prestige. European trade and local depopulation caused Kwakiutl potlatching to change its nature. It became much more destructive than it had been previously.

Note, however, that this destructive potlatching also worked to prevent the formation of sharply divided social classes. Wealth relinquished or destroyed was converted into a nonmaterial item: prestige. Under capitalism, we reinvest our profits (rather than burning our cash), with the hope of making an additional profit. The potlatchers, by contrast, were content to relinquish their surpluses rather than use them to widen the social distance between themselves and their fellow tribe members.

for REVIEW

summary

1. Cohen's adaptive strategies include foraging (hunting and gathering), horticulture, agriculture, pastoralism, and industrialism. Foraging was the only human adaptive strategy until the advent of food production (farming and herding) 12,000–10,000 years ago. Food production eventually replaced foraging in most places. Almost all modern foragers have at least some dependence on food production or food producers.

2. Horticulture and agriculture stand at opposite ends of a continuum based on labor intensity and continuity of land use. Horticulture doesn't use land or labor intensively. Horticulturalists cultivate a plot for one or two years and then abandon it. Farther along the continuum, horticulture becomes more intensive, but there is always a fallow period. Agriculturalists farm the same plot of land continuously and use labor intensively. They use one or more of the following: irrigation, terracing, and domesticated animals as means of production and manuring.

3. The pastoral strategy is mixed. Nomadic pastoralists trade with cultivators. Part of a transhumant pastoral population cultivates while another part takes the herds to pasture. Except for some Peruvians and the Navajo, who are recent herders, the New World lacks native pastoralists.

4. Economic anthropology is the cross-cultural study of systems of production, distribution, and consumption. In nonindustrial societies, a kin-based mode of production prevails. One acquires rights to resources and labor through membership in social groups, not impersonally through purchase and sale. Work is just one aspect of social relations expressed in varied contexts.

5. Economics has been defined as the science of allocating scarce means to alternative ends. Western economists assume that the notion of scarcity is universal—which it isn't—and that in making choices, people strive to maximize personal profit. In nonindustrial societies, indeed as in our own, people often maximize values other than individual profit.

6. In nonindustrial societies, people invest in subsistence, replacement, social, and ceremonial funds. States add a rent fund: People must share their output with social superiors. In states, the obligation to pay rent often becomes primary.

7. In addition to studying production, economic anthropologists study and compare exchange systems. The three principles of exchange are the market principle, redistribution, and reciprocity. The market principle, based on supply and demand and the profit motive, dominates in states. With redistribution, goods are collected at a central place, but some of them are eventually given back, or redistributed, to the people. Reciprocity governs exchanges between social equals. It is the characteristic mode of exchange among foragers and horticulturalists. Reciprocity, redistribution, and the market principle may coexist in a society, but the primary exchange mode is the one that allocates the means of production.

8. Patterns of feasting and exchanges of wealth among villages are common among nonindustrial food producers, as well as among the potlatching cultures of North America's North Pacific Coast. Such systems help even out the availability of resources over time.

key terms

critical thinking

1. When considering issues of "human nature," why should we remember that the egalitarian band was a basic form of human social life for most of our history?

2. Intensive agriculture has significant effects on social and environmental relations. What are some of these effects? Are they good or bad?

3. What does it mean when anthropologists describe nonindustrial economic systems as "embedded" in society?

4. What are your scarce means? How do you make decisions about allocating them?

5. Give examples from your own exchanges of different degrees of reciprocity. Why are anthropologists interested in studying exchange across cultures?

Political Systems

▶ **What kinds of political systems have existed worldwide, and what are their social and economic correlates?**

▶ **How does the state differ from other forms of political organization?**

▶ **What is social control, and how is it established and maintained in various societies?**

© imageBROKER/Alamy Stock Photo

The Parliament building in Port Moresby, Papua New Guinea. The inscription at the bottom of the mural states, "Parliament may make laws having effect within and without the country for the peace, order, and good government of Papua New Guinea and the welfare of its people."

understanding OURSELVES

Y ou've probably heard the expression "Big Man on Campus" (BMOC) used to describe a collegian who is very well known and/or popular. BMOC status might be the result of having a large network of friends, a trendy car or way of dressing, good looks, a nice smile, a sports connection, and a sense of humor. "Big man" has a different but related meaning in anthropology. Many indigenous cultures of the South Pacific had a kind of political figure that anthropologists call the "big man." Such a leader achieved his status through hard work, amassing wealth in the form of pigs and other native riches. Characteristics that distinguished the big man from his fellows, enabling him to attract loyal supporters (a large network of friends), included wealth, generosity, eloquence, physical fitness, bravery, and supernatural powers. Those who became big men did so because of their personalities rather than by inheriting their wealth or position.

Do any of the factors that make for a successful big man (or BMOC, for that matter) contribute to political success in a modern nation such as the United States? Although American politicians often use their own wealth, inherited or created, to finance campaigns, they also solicit labor and monetary contributions (rather than pigs) from supporters. And like big men, successful American politicians try to be generous with their supporters. Payback may take the form of a night in the Lincoln bedroom, an invitation to a strategic dinner, an ambassadorship, or largesse to a particular area of the country. Tribal big men amass wealth and then give away pigs. Successful American politicians also dish out "pork."

As with the big man, eloquence and communication skills contribute to political success (e.g., Barack Obama, Bill Clinton, and Ronald Reagan), although lack of such skills isn't necessarily fatal (e.g., either President Bush). What about physical fitness? Hair, height, health (and even a nice smile) are certainly political advantages. Bravery, as demonstrated through distinguished military service, may help political careers, but it certainly isn't required. Nor does it guarantee success. Just ask John McCain or John Kerry. Supernatural powers? Candidates who proclaim themselves atheists are as rare as self-identified witches—or not witches. Almost all political candidates claim to belong to a mainstream religion. Some even present their candidacies or policies as promoting God's will. However, contemporary politics isn't just about personality, as big man systems are. We live in a state-organized, stratified society with inherited wealth, power, and privilege, all of which have political implications. As is typical of states, inheritance and kin connections play a role in political success. Just think of Kennedys, Bushes, and Clintons.

Anthropologists share with political scientists an interest in political systems, power, and politics. Here again, however, the anthropological approach is global and comparative and includes nonstates, while political scientists tend to focus on contemporary and recent nation-states (see Kamrava 2008). Anthropological studies have revealed substantial variation in power, authority, and legal systems in different societies (see Pirie 2013; Walton and Suarez 2016). (**Power** is the ability to exercise one's will over others; *authority* is the formal, socially approved use of power, e.g., by government officials.) (See Schwartz, Turner, and Tuden 2011; Wolf with Silverman 2001.)

WHAT IS "THE POLITICAL"?

Morton Fried offered the following definition of political organization:

> Political organization comprises those portions of social organization that specifically relate to the individuals or groups that manage the affairs of public policy or seek to control the appointment or activities of those individuals or groups. (Fried 1967, pp. 20–21)

This definition certainly fits contemporary North America. Under "individuals or groups that manage the affairs of public policy" come various agencies and levels of government. Those who seek to influence public policy include political parties, unions, corporations, lobbyists, activists, political action committees (including super PACs), religious groups, and nongovernmental organizations (NGOs).

Fried's definition is less applicable to nonstates, where it's often difficult to detect any "public policy." For this reason, I prefer to speak of *sociopolitical* organization in discussing the exercise of power and the regulation of relations among groups and their representatives. Political regulation includes such processes as decision making, dispute management, and conflict resolution. The study of political regulation draws our attention to those who make decisions and resolve conflicts (are there formal leaders?). (See Rhodes and Hart 2014; Schwartz et al. 2011; Stryker and Gonzalez 2014.)

TYPES AND TRENDS

Ethnographic and archaeological studies in hundreds of places have revealed many correlations between the economy and social and political organization. Decades ago, the anthropologist Elman Service (1962) listed four types, or levels, of political organization: band, tribe, chiefdom, and state. Today, none of the first three types can be studied as a self-contained form of political organization, because all now exist within nation-states and are subject to state control. There is archaeological evidence for early bands, tribes, and chiefdoms that existed before the first states appeared. However, because anthropology came into being long after the origin of the state, anthropologists never have been able to observe "in the flesh" a band, tribe, or chiefdom outside the influence of some state. There still may be local political leaders (e.g., village heads) and regional figures (e.g., chiefs) of the sort discussed in this chapter, but all now exist and function within the context of state organization.

A *band* is a small, kin-based group (all its members are related by kinship or marriage) found among foragers. **Tribes** have economies based on horticulture and pastoralism. Living in villages and organized into kin groups based on common descent (clans and lineages), tribes have no formal government and no reliable means of enforcing political decisions. *Chiefdom* refers to a form of sociopolitical organization intermediate between the tribe and the state. In chiefdoms, social relations were based mainly on kinship, marriage, descent, age, generation, and gender—just as in bands and tribes. However, although chiefdoms were kin based, they featured **differential access** to resources (some people had more wealth, prestige, and power than others did) and a permanent political structure. The *state* is a form of sociopolitical organization based on a formal government structure and socioeconomic stratification.

The four labels in Service's typology are much too simple to account for the full range of political diversity and complexity known to archaeology and ethnography. We'll see, for instance, that tribes have varied widely in their political systems and institutions. Nevertheless, Service's typology does highlight some significant contrasts in political organization, especially those between states and nonstates. For example, in bands and tribes—unlike states, which have clearly visible governments—political organization did not stand out as separate and distinct from the total social order. In bands and tribes, it was difficult to characterize an act or event as political rather than merely social.

Service's labels "band," "tribe," "chiefdom," and "state" are categories or types within a *sociopolitical typology*. These types are associated with particular adaptive strategies or economic systems. Thus, foragers (an economic type) tended to have band organization (a sociopolitical

Home healthcare workers rally in support of a minimum wage increase in New York City on April 15, 2015. As anthropologist Margaret Mead once observed about political mobilization, small groups of committed citizens have the capacity to change the world.
© Victor J. Blue/Bloomberg via Getty Images

type). Similarly, many horticulturalists and pastoralists lived in tribes. Although most chiefdoms had farming economies, herding was important in some Middle Eastern chiefdoms. Nonindustrial states usually had an agricultural base.

Food production led to larger, denser populations and more complex economies than was the case among foragers. Many sociopolitical trends reflect the increased regulatory demands associated with cultivation and herding. Archaeologists have studied these trends through time, and cultural anthropologists have observed them among more recent, including contemporary, groups (see Shore, Wright, and Però 2011).

BANDS AND TRIBES

This chapter discusses a series of societies, as case studies with different political systems. A common set of questions will be addressed for each one. What kinds of social groups does the society have? How do those groups represent themselves to each other? How are their internal and external relations regulated?

Foraging Bands

The strong ties that contemporary and recent foragers maintain with sociopolitical groups beyond the band make them markedly different from Stone Age hunter-gatherers. Modern foragers live in nation-states and an interlinked world. All foragers now trade with food producers. The pygmies of Congo, for example, for generations have shared a social world and economic exchanges with their neighbors who are cultivators. Furthermore, most contemporary hunter-gatherers rely on governments and on missionaries for at least part of what they consume.

The San

San speakers ("Bushmen") of southern Africa have been influenced by Bantu speakers (farmers and herders) for 2,000 years and by Europeans for centuries. Edwin Wilmsen (1989) contends that many San descend from herders who were pushed into the desert by poverty or oppression. He sees the San today as a rural underclass in a larger political and economic system dominated by Europeans and Bantu food producers. Within this system, many San now tend cattle for wealthier Bantu rather than foraging independently. San also have their own domesticated animals, further illustrating their movement away from a foraging lifestyle.

Susan Kent (2002) noted a tendency to stereotype foragers, to treat them all as alike. They used to be stereotyped as isolated, primitive survivors of the Stone Age. The developing and more accurate, anthropological view of contemporary and recent foragers sees them as groups forced into

Among tropical foragers, women make an important economic contribution through gathering, as is true among the San shown here in Namibia. What evidence do you see in this photo that contemporary foragers participate in the modern world system?

© Joy Tessman/National Geographic Creative

marginal environments by states, colonialism, and world events.

Kent (2002) focused on variation among foragers, describing considerable diversity in time and space among the San. The nature of San life has changed considerably since the 1950s and 1960s, when a series of anthropologists from Harvard University, including Richard B. Lee, embarked on a systematic study of their lives. Studying the San over time, Lee and others have documented many changes (see Lee 2003, 2012; Silberbauer 1981; Tanaka 1980). Such longitudinal research monitors variation in time, while fieldwork in many San areas has revealed variation in space. One of the most important contrasts is between settled (sedentary) and nomadic groups (Kent and Vierich 1989). Although sedentism has increased substantially in recent years, some San groups (along rivers) have been sedentary for generations. Others, including the Dobe Ju/'hoansi San studied by Lee (1984, 2003, 2012) and the Kutse San whom Kent studied, have retained more of the hunter-gatherer lifestyle.

To the extent that foraging continues to be their subsistence base, groups like the San can illustrate links between a foraging economy and other aspects of life in bands. For example, San groups that still are mobile, or that were so until recently, emphasize social, political, and gender equality, which are traditional band characteristics. A social system based on kinship, reciprocity, and sharing is appropriate for an economy with few people and limited resources. People have to share meat when they get it; otherwise, it rots. The nomadic pursuit of wild plants and animals tends to discourage permanent settlement, wealth accumulation, and status distinctions.

In the past, foraging bands—small nomadic or seminomadic social units—formed seasonally when component nuclear families got together. The particular families might vary from year to year. Marriage and kinship created ties between members of different bands. Trade and visiting also linked them. Band leaders were leaders in name only. In such an *egalitarian* society, they were first among equals (see Solway 2006). Sometimes they gave advice or made decisions, but they had no way to enforce those decisions. Because of the spread of states and globalization, it is increasingly difficult for ethnographers to find and observe such patterns of band organization.

The Inuit

The aboriginal Inuit (Hoebel 1954, 1954/1968), another group of foragers, provide a classic example of methods of settling disputes—**conflict resolution**—in stateless societies. All societies have ways of settling disputes (of variable effectiveness) along with cultural rules or norms about proper and improper behavior. *Norms* are cultural standards or guidelines that enable individuals to distinguish between appropriate and inappropriate behavior in a given society (N. Kottak 2002). While rules and norms are cultural universals, only state societies, those with established governments, have laws that are formulated, proclaimed, and enforced (see Donovan 2007; Pirie 2013).

Foragers lacked formal **law** in the sense of a legal code with trial and enforcement, but they did have methods of social control and dispute settlement. The absence of law did not mean total anarchy. As described by E. A. Hoebel (1954) in a classic ethnographic study of conflict resolution, a sparse population of some 20,000 Inuit spanned 6,000 miles (9,500 kilometers) of the Arctic region (Figure 17.1). The most significant social groups were the nuclear family and the band. Personal relationships linked the families and bands. Some bands had headmen. There also were shamans (part-time religious specialists). However, these positions conferred little power on those who occupied them.

Hunting and fishing by men were the primary Inuit subsistence activities. The diverse and

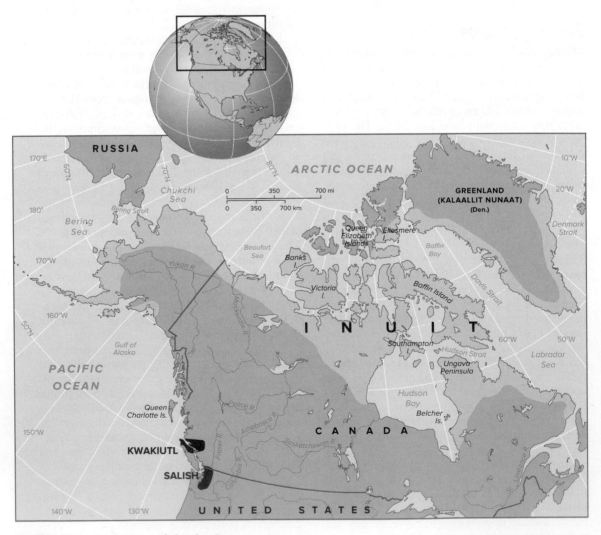

FIGURE 17.1 Location of the Inuit.

abundant plant foods available in warmer areas, where female labor in gathering is important, were absent in the Arctic. Traveling on land and sea in a bitter environment, Inuit men faced more dangers than women did. The traditional male role took its toll in lives, so that adult women outnumbered men. This permitted some men to have two or three wives. The ability to support more than one wife conferred a certain amount of prestige, but it also encouraged envy. (*Prestige* is social esteem, respect, or approval.) If a man seemed to be taking additional wives just to enhance his reputation, a rival was likely to steal one of them. Most Inuit disputes were between men and originated over women, caused by wife stealing or adultery.

A jilted husband had several options. He could try to kill the wife stealer. However, if he succeeded, one of his rival's kinsmen surely would try to kill him in retaliation. One dispute might escalate into several deaths as relatives avenged a succession of murders. No government existed to intervene and stop such a *blood feud* (a murderous feud between families). However, one also could challenge a rival to a song battle. In a public setting, contestants made up insulting songs about each other. At the end of the match, the audience proclaimed the winner. However, if the winner was the man whose wife had been stolen, there was no guarantee she would return. Often she stayed with her abductor.

Thefts are common in societies with marked property differentials, like our own, but thefts are uncommon among foragers. Each Inuit had access to the resources he or she needed to sustain life. Every man could hunt, fish, and make the tools necessary for subsistence. Every woman could obtain the materials needed to make clothing, prepare food, and do domestic work. Inuit men could even hunt and fish in the territories of other local groups. There was no notion of private ownership of territory or animals.

Tribal Cultivators

As is true of foraging bands, there are no totally autonomous tribes in today's world. Still, there are societies, for example, in Papua New Guinea and in South America's tropical forests, in which tribal principles continue to operate. Tribes typically have a horticultural or pastoral economy and are organized into villages and/or *descent groups* (kin groups whose members trace descent from a common ancestor). Tribes lack socioeconomic stratification (i.e., a class structure) and a formal government of their own. A few tribes still conduct small-scale warfare, in the form of intervillage raiding. Tribes have more effective regulatory mechanisms than foragers do, but tribal societies have no sure means of enforcing political decisions. The main regulatory officials are village heads, "big men," descent-group leaders, village councils, and leaders of pantribal associations. All these figures and groups have limited authority.

Like foragers, horticulturalists tend to be egalitarian, although some have marked *gender stratification:* an unequal distribution of resources, power, prestige, and personal freedom between men and women. Horticultural villages usually are small, with low population density and open access to strategic resources. Age, gender, and personal traits determine how much respect people receive and how much support they get from others. Egalitarianism diminishes, however, as village size and population density increase. Horticultural villages usually have headmen—rarely, if ever, headwomen.

The Village Head

The Yanomami (Chagnon 1997, 2013; Ferguson 1995; Ramos 1995) are Native Americans who live in southern Venezuela and the adjacent part of Brazil. When anthropologists first studied them, they numbered about 26,000 people, living in 200 to 250 widely scattered villages, each with a population between 40 and 250. The Yanomami are horticulturalists who also hunt and gather. Their staple crops are bananas and plantains (a banana-like crop). There are more significant social groups among the Yanomami than exist in a foraging society. The Yanomami have families, villages, and descent groups. Their descent groups, which span more than one village, are patrilineal (ancestry is traced back through males only) and exogamous (people must marry outside their own descent group). However, branches of two different descent groups may live in the same village and intermarry.

Traditionally among the Yanomami the only leadership position has been that of **village head** (always a man). His authority, like that of a foraging band's leader, is severely limited. If a headman wants something done, he must lead by example and persuasion. The headman lacks the right to issue orders. He can only persuade, harangue, and try to influence public opinion. For example, if he wants people to clean up the central plaza in preparation for a feast, he must start sweeping it himself, hoping his covillagers will take the hint and relieve him.

When conflict erupts within the village, the headman may be called on as a mediator who listens to both sides. He will give an opinion and advice. If a disputant is unsatisfied, the headman has no power to back his decisions and no way to impose punishments. Like the band leader, he is first among equals.

A Yanomami village headman also must lead in generosity. Expected to be more generous than any other villager, he cultivates more land. His garden provides much of the food consumed when his village hosts a feast for another village. The headman represents the village in its dealings with outsiders, including Venezuelan and Brazilian government agents.

village head
A local tribal leader with limited authority.

The way someone acts as headman depends on his personal traits and the number of supporters he can muster. Napoleon Chagnon (1997) describes how one village headman, Kaobawa, guaranteed safety to a delegation from a village with which a covillager of his wanted to start a war. Kaobawa was a particularly effective headman. He had demonstrated his fierceness in battle, but he also knew how to use diplomacy to avoid offending other villagers. No one in his village had a better personality for the headmanship. Nor (because Kaobawa had many brothers) did anyone have more supporters. Among the Yanomami, when a village is dissatisfied with its headman, its members can leave and found a new village. This happens from time to time and is called *village fissioning*.

With its many villages and descent groups, Yanomami sociopolitical organization is more complicated than that of a band-organized society. The Yanomami face more problems in regulating relations between groups and individuals. Although a headman sometimes can prevent a specific violent act, intervillage raiding has been a feature of some areas of Yanomami territory, particularly those studied by Chagnon (1997, 2013).

big man
Generous tribal entrepreneur with multivillage support.

It's important to recognize as well that the Yanomami are not isolated from outside events. They live in two nation-states, Venezuela and Brazil, and attacks by outsiders, especially Brazilian ranchers and miners, have plagued them (Chagnon 2013; *Cultural Survival Quarterly* 1989; Ferguson 1995). During a Brazilian gold rush between 1987 and 1991, one Yanomami died each day, on average, from such attacks. By 1991, there were some 40,000 miners in the Brazilian Yanomami homeland. Some Yanomami were killed outright. The miners introduced new diseases, and the swollen population ensured that old diseases became epidemic. Brazilian Yanomami were dying at a rate of 10 percent annually, and their fertility rate had dropped to zero. Since then, one Brazilian president has declared a huge Yanomami territory off limits to outsiders. Unfortunately, local politicians, miners, and ranchers have managed to evade the ban. The future of the Yanomami remains uncertain (see Romero 2008).

The "Big Man"

Many societies of the South Pacific, particularly on the Melanesian Islands and in Papua New Guinea, had a kind of political leader that we call the big man. The **big man** (almost always a male) was an elaborate version of the village head, but with one significant difference. Unlike the village head, whose leadership was limited to one village, the big man had supporters in several villages. The big man thus was a regulator of regional political organization.

Consider the Kapauku Papuans, inhabitants of Irian Jaya, Indonesia (located on the island of New Guinea) (see Figure 17.2). Anthropologist Leopold Pospisil (1963) studied the Kapauku (then 45,000 people), who grew crops (with the sweet potato as their staple) and raised pigs. Their cultivation system was too labor intensive to be described as simple horticulture. It required mutual aid in turning the soil before planting. The digging of long drainage ditches, which a big man often helped organize, was even more complex. Kapauku cultivation supported a larger and denser population than does the simpler horticulture of the Yanomami. The Kapauku economy required collective cultivation and political regulation of the more complex tasks.

The key political figure among the Kapauku was the big man. Known as a *tonowi*, he achieved his status through hard work, amassing wealth in the form of pigs and other native riches. The achieved status of big man rested on certain characteristics that distinguished him from his fellows. Key attributes included wealth, generosity, eloquence, physical fitness, bravery, supernatural powers, and the ability to gain the support and loyalty of others. Men became big men because they had certain personalities; they

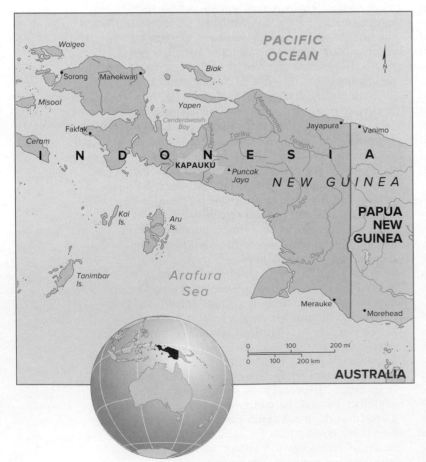

FIGURE 17.2 Location of the Kapauku.

did not inherit their status but created it through hard work and good judgment. Wealth resulted from successful pig breeding and trading. As a man's pig herd and prestige grew, he attracted supporters. He sponsored pig feasts in which pork (provided by the big man and his supporters) was distributed to guests, bringing him more prestige and widening his network of support (see also O'Connor 2015).

The big man's supporters, acknowledging past favors and anticipating future rewards, recognized him as a leader and accepted his decisions as binding. The *tonowi* was an important regulator of regional events in Kapauku life. He helped determine the dates for feasts and markets. He initiated economic projects requiring the cooperation of a regional community.

The Kapauku big man again exemplifies a generalization about leadership in tribal societies: If someone achieves wealth and widespread respect and support, he or she must be generous. The big man worked hard not to hoard wealth but to be able to give away the fruits of his labor, to convert wealth into prestige and gratitude. A stingy big man would lose his support. Selfish and greedy big men sometimes were murdered by their fellows (Zimmer-Tamakoshi 1997).

The "big man," like this one from highland Papua New Guinea, persuades people to organize feasts, which distribute pork and wealth. Big men owe their status to their individual personalities rather than to inherited wealth or position. Does our society have equivalents of big men?

© Edward Reeves/Alamy Stock Photo

Pantribal Sodalities

Big men could forge regional political organization, albeit temporarily, by mobilizing supporters from several villages. Other principles in tribal societies—such as a belief in common ancestry, kinship, or descent—could be used to link local groups within a region. The same descent group, for example, might span several villages, and its dispersed members might recognize the same leader.

Principles other than kinship also can link local groups, especially in modern societies. People who live in different parts of the same nation may belong to the same labor union, sorority or fraternity, political party, or religious denomination. In tribes, nonkin groups called *associations* or *sodalities* may serve a similar linking function. Often, sodalities are based on common age or gender, with all-male sodalities more common than all-female ones.

Pantribal sodalities are groups that extend across the whole tribe, spanning several villages. Such sodalities were especially likely to develop in situations of warfare with a neighboring tribe. Mobilizing their members from multiple villages within the same tribe, pantribal sodalities could assemble a force to attack or retaliate against another tribe.

The best examples of pantribal sodalities come from the Central Plains of North America and from tropical Africa. During the 18th and 19th centuries, Native American populations of the Great Plains of the United States and Canada experienced a rapid growth of pantribal sodalities. This development reflected an economic change that followed the spread of horses, which had

been reintroduced to the Americas by the Spanish, to the area between the Rocky Mountains and the Mississippi River. Many Plains Indian societies changed their adaptive strategies because of the horse. At first they had been foragers who hunted bison (buffalo) on foot. Later they adopted a mixed economy based on hunting, gathering, and horticulture. Finally, they changed to a much more specialized economy based on horseback hunting of bison (eventually with rifles).

As the Plains tribes were undergoing these changes, other tribes also adopted horseback hunting and moved into the Plains. Attempting to occupy the same area, groups came into conflict. A pattern of warfare developed in which the members of one tribe raided another, usually for horses. The economy demanded that people follow the movement of the bison herds. During the winter, when the bison dispersed, a tribe fragmented into small bands and families. In the summer, when huge herds assembled on the Plains, the tribe reunited. They camped together for social, political, and religious activities, but mainly for communal bison hunting.

Two activities demanded strong leadership: organizing and carrying out raids on enemy camps (to capture horses) and managing the summer bison hunt. All the Plains societies developed pantribal sodalities, and leadership roles within them, to police the summer hunt. Leaders coordinated hunting efforts, making sure that people did not cause a stampede with an early shot or an ill-advised action. Leaders imposed severe penalties, including seizure of a culprit's wealth, for disobedience.

pantribal sodalities Non-kin-based groups with regional political significance.

Many tribes that adopted this Plains strategy of adaptation had once been foragers for whom hunting and gathering had been individual or small-group affairs. They never had come together previously as a single social unit. Age and gender were available as social principles that could quickly and efficiently forge unrelated people into pantribal sodalities.

Raiding of one tribe by another, this time for cattle rather than horses, also was common in eastern and southeastern Africa, where pantribal sodalities also developed. Among the pastoral Masai of Kenya, men born during the same four-year period were circumcised together and belonged to the same named group, an *age set,* throughout their lives. The sets moved through *age grades,* the most important of which was the warrior grade. Members of a set felt a strong allegiance to one another. Masai women lacked comparable set organization, but they also passed through culturally recognized age grades: the initiate, the married woman, and the female elder.

In certain parts of western and central Africa, pantribal sodalities are secret societies, made up exclusively of men or women. Like our college fraternities and sororities, these associations have secret initiation ceremonies. Among the Mende of Sierra Leone, men's and women's secret societies were very influential. The men's group, the Poro, trained boys in social conduct, ethics, and religion and it supervised political and economic activities. Leadership roles in the Poro often overshadowed village headship and played an important part in social control, dispute management, and tribal political regulation. Age, gender, and ritual can link members of different local groups into a single social collectivity in a tribe and thus create a sense of ethnic identity, of belonging to the same cultural tradition.

Among the Masai of Kenya and Tanzania, men born during the same four-year period belonged to the same named group, an age set, throughout their lives. The sets moved through grades, of which the most important was the warrior grade. Shown here is the *eunoto* ceremony in which young men become senior warriors and are allowed to choose wives.

© imageBROKER/Alamy Stock Photo

Nomadic Politics

The political systems associated with pastoralism varied considerably, ranging from tribal societies to chiefdoms. The Masai (just discussed) live in a tribal society. The sociopolitical organization of such tribal herders is based on descent groups and pantribal sodalities. Other pastoralists, however, have chiefs and live in nation-states. The scope of political authority among pastoralists expands considerably as regulatory problems increase in densely populated regions (see Salzman 2008). Consider two Iranian pastoral nomadic tribes—the Basseri and the Qashqai (Salzman 1974). Starting each year from a plateau near the coast, these groups took their animals to grazing land 17,000 feet (5,400 meters) above sea level (see Figure 17.3).

Within the nation-state of Iran, the Basseri and the Qashqai shared this route with each other and with several other ethnic groups. Use of the same pastureland at different times of year was carefully scheduled. Ethnic-group movements were tightly coordinated. Expressing this schedule is *il-rah*, a concept common to all Iranian nomads. A group's *il-rah* is its customary path in time and space. It is the schedule, different for each group, of when specific areas can be used in the annual trek.

Each tribe had its own leader, known as the *khan* or *il-khan*. The Basseri *khan*, because he dealt with a smaller population, faced fewer problems in coordinating its movements than did the leaders of the Qashqai. Correspondingly, his rights, privileges, duties, and authority were weaker. Nevertheless, his authority exceeded that of any political figure discussed so far. The *khan's* authority still came from his personal traits rather than from his office. That is, the Basseri followed a particular *khan* not because of a political position he happened to fill but because of their personal allegiance and loyalty to him as a man. The *khan* relied on the support of the heads of the descent groups into which Basseri society was divided.

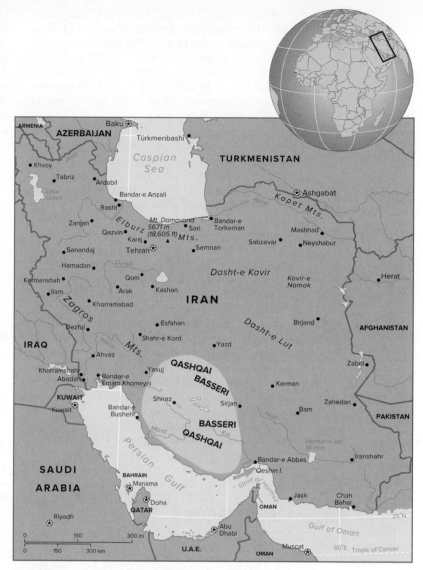

FIGURE 17.3 Location of the Basseri and Qashqai.

The Qashqai are pastoral nomads who traditionally trekked about 300 miles (480 kilometers) from highland summer pastures to lowland winter pastures near the Persian Gulf. The traditional migration is shown on the left; the modern trek, incorporating motor vehicles, on the right.

Left: © Philippe Michel/age fotostock; right: © Kaveh Kazemi/Getty Images News/Getty Images

Among the Qashqai, however, allegiance shifted from the person to the office. The Qashqai had multiple levels of authority and more powerful chiefs or *khans*. Managing 400,000 people required a complex hierarchy. Heading it was the *il-khan,* helped by a deputy, under whom were the heads of constituent tribes, under each of whom were descent-group heads.

A case illustrates just how developed the Qashqai authority structure was. A hailstorm prevented some nomads from joining the annual migration at the appointed time. Although all the nomads recognized that they were not responsible for their delay, the *il-khan* assigned them less favorable grazing land, for that year only, in place of their usual pasture. The tardy herders and other Qashqai considered the judgment fair and didn't question it. Thus, Qashqai authorities regulated the annual migration. They also adjudicated disputes between people, tribes, and descent groups.

These Iranian cases illustrate the fact that pastoralism often is just one among many specialized economic activities within a nation-state. As part of a larger whole, pastoral tribes are constantly pitted against other ethnic groups. Within the context of the modern nation-state, that government becomes a final authority, a higher-level regulator that attempts to limit conflict among ethnic groups. State organization arose not just to manage agricultural economies but also to regulate the activities of ethnic groups within expanding social and economic systems (see Das and Poole 2004).

CHIEFDOMS

The first states emerged in the Old World around 5,500 years ago. The first chiefdoms had developed perhaps a thousand years earlier, but few survive today. In many parts of the world, the chiefdom was a transitional form of organization that emerged during the evolution of tribes into states. State formation began in Mesopotamia (currently Iran and Iraq). It next occurred in Egypt, the Indus Valley of Pakistan and India, and northern China. A few thousand years later states arose in two parts of the Western Hemisphere—Mesoamerica (Mexico, Guatemala, Belize) and the central Andes (Peru and Bolivia). Early states are known as archaic, or nonindustrial, states, in contrast to modern industrial nation-states. Robert Carneiro defines the state as "an autonomous political unit encompassing many communities within its territory, having a centralized government with the power to collect taxes, draft men for work or war, and decree and enforce laws" (1970, p. 733).

The chiefdom and the state, like many categories used by social scientists, are ideal types. That is, they are labels that make social contrasts seem sharper than they really are. In reality there is a continuum from tribe to chiefdom to state. Some societies had many attributes of chiefdoms but retained tribal features. Some advanced chiefdoms had many attributes of archaic states and thus are difficult to assign to either category. Recognizing this "continuous change" (Johnson and Earle 2000), some anthropologists speak of "complex chiefdoms" (Earle 1987, 1997), which are almost states.

Political and Economic Systems

Geographic areas where chiefdoms existed included the circum-Caribbean (e.g., Caribbean islands, Panama, Colombia), lowland Amazonia, what is now the southeastern United States, and Polynesia. Chiefdoms created the megalithic cultures of Europe, including the one that built Stonehenge. Bear in mind that chiefdoms and states can fall (disintegrate) as well as rise. Before Rome's expansion, much of Europe was organized at the chiefdom level, to which it reverted for centuries after the fall of Rome in the fifth century C.E. Much of our ethnographic knowledge about chiefdoms comes from Polynesia (Kirch 2000), where they were common at the time of European exploration. In chiefdoms, social relations are mainly based on kinship, marriage, descent, age, generation, and gender—as they are in bands and tribes. This is a basic difference between chiefdoms and states. States bring nonrelatives together and oblige them to pledge allegiance to a government.

Unlike bands and tribes, however, chiefdoms administer a clear-cut and permanent regional political system. Chiefdoms may include thousands of people living in many villages or hamlets. Regulation is carried out by the chief and his or her assistants, who occupy political offices. An **office** is a permanent position,

Chiefdoms as widespread as Mexico's Olmecs, England's Stonehenge, and Polynesia's Easter Island (Rapanui) are famed for their major works in stone. The statues shown here are Easter Island's major tourist attraction.

© David Madison/The Image Bank/Getty Images

office
A permanent political position.

which must be refilled when it is vacated by death or retirement. Because official vacancies are filled systematically, the political system that is the chiefdom endures across the generations, thus ensuring permanent political regulation.

Polynesian chiefs were full-time specialists whose duties included managing the economy. They regulated production by commanding or prohibiting (using religious taboos) the cultivation of certain lands and crops. Chiefs also regulated distribution and consumption. At certain seasons—often on a ritual occasion, such as a first-fruit ceremony—people would offer part of their harvest to the chief through his or her representatives. Products moved up the hierarchy, eventually reaching the chief. Conversely, illustrating obligatory sharing with kin, chiefs sponsored feasts at which they gave back some of what they had received (see O'Connor 2015). Unlike big men, chiefs were exempt from ordinary work and had rights and privileges unavailable to the masses. Like big men, however, they still returned a portion of the wealth they took in.

Such a flow of resources to and then from a central place is known as *chiefly redistribution,* which offers economic advantages. If different parts of the chiefdom specialized in particular products, chiefly redistribution made those products available to the entire society. Chiefly redistribution also helped stimulate production beyond the basic subsistence level and provided a central storehouse for goods that might become scarce in times of famine (Earle 1987, 1997).

An outdoor portrait of a Maori chief at the Polynesian Cultural Center in Hawaii. Both Hawaii and New Zealand, where the Maori live, were sites of traditional Polynesian chiefdoms. How do chiefs differ from ordinary people?

© Jeff Greenberg/PhotoEdit

Status Systems

Social status in chiefdoms was based on seniority of descent. Polynesian chiefs kept extremely long genealogies. Some chiefs (without writing) managed to trace their ancestry back dozens of generations. All the people in the chiefdom were thought to be related to one another. Presumably, all were descended from a group of founding ancestors.

The status of chief was based on seniority of descent. The chief would be the oldest child (usually son) of the oldest child of the oldest child, and so on. Degrees of seniority were calculated so intricately on some islands that there were as many ranks as people. For example, the third son would rank below the second, who in turn would rank below the first. The children of an eldest brother, however, would all rank above the children of the next brother, whose children in turn would outrank those of younger brothers. However, even the lowest-ranking man or woman in a chiefdom was still the chief's relative. In such a kin-based context, everyone, even a chief, had to share with his or her relatives. Because everyone had a slightly different status, it was difficult to draw a line between elites and common people. Other chiefdoms calculated seniority differently and had shorter genealogies than did those in Polynesia.

Still, the concern for seniority and the lack of sharp gaps between elites and commoners are features of all chiefdoms.

The status systems of chiefdoms, as of states, were associated with differential access to resources. Some men and women had privileged access to power, prestige, and wealth. They controlled strategic resources, such as land and water. Earle characterizes chiefs as "an incipient aristocracy with advantages in wealth and lifestyle" (1987, p. 290).

Compared with chiefdoms, archaic states drew a much firmer line between elites and masses, distinguishing at least between nobles and commoners. Kinship ties did not extend from the nobles to the commoners because of stratum endogamy—marriage within one's own group. Commoners married commoners; elites married elites.

The Emergence of Stratification

The status system of a chiefdom differed from that of a state because of the chiefdom's kinship basis. In the context of differential wealth and power, the chiefly type of status system didn't last very long. Chiefs would start acting too haughty

TABLE 17.1 Max Weber's Three Dimensions of Stratification

wealth	=>	economic status
power	=>	political status
prestige	=>	social status

and try to erode the kinship basis of the chiefdom. In Madagascar they would do this by demoting their more distant relatives to commoner status and banning marriage between nobles and commoners (Kottak 1980). Such moves, if accepted by the society, created separate social strata—unrelated groups that differ in their access to wealth, prestige, and power. (A *stratum* is one of two or more groups that contrast in social status and access to strategic resources. Each stratum includes people of both genders and all ages.) The creation of separate social strata is called *stratification,* and its emergence signified the transition from chiefdom to state. The presence of stratification is one of the key distinguishing features of a state.

The influential sociologist Max Weber (1922/1968) defined three related dimensions of social stratification: (1) Economic status, or **wealth,** encompasses all a person's material assets, including income, land, and other types of property. (2) *Power,* the ability to exercise one's will over others—to get what one wants—is the basis of political status. (3) **Prestige**—the basis of social status—refers to esteem, respect, or approval for acts, deeds, or qualities considered exemplary. Prestige, or "cultural capital" (Bourdieu 1984), gives people a sense of worth and respect, which they may often convert into economic advantage (Table 17.1).

In archaic states—for the first time in human history—there were contrasts in wealth, power, and prestige between entire groups (social strata) of men and women. Each stratum included people of both genders and all ages. The **superordinate** (higher or elite) stratum had privileged access to valued resources. Access to those resources by members of the **subordinate** (lower or underprivileged) stratum was limited by the privileged group.

wealth
All a person's material assets; basis of economic status.

prestige
Esteem, respect, or approval.

superordinate
The upper, privileged group in a stratified society.

subordinate
The lower, underprivileged group in a stratified society.

STATE SYSTEMS

Recap 17.1 summarizes the information presented so far on bands, tribes, chiefdoms, and states. States, remember, are autonomous political units with social strata and a formal government. States tend to be large and populous, and certain statuses, systems, and subsystems with specialized functions are found in all states (see Sharma and Gupta 2006). They include the following:

1. Population control: fixing of boundaries, establishment of citizenship categories, and censusing.

2. Judiciary: laws, legal procedure, and judges.

3. Enforcement: permanent military and police forces.

4. Fiscal support: taxation.

In archaic states, these subsystems were integrated by a ruling system or government composed of civil, military, and religious officials (Fried 1960). Let's look at the four subsystems one by one.

Population Control

To keep track of whom they govern, states conduct censuses. A state demarcates boundaries to separate that state from other societies. Customs agents, immigration officers, navies, and coast guards patrol frontiers. States also regulate population through administrative subdivision: provinces, districts, "states," counties, subcounties, and parishes. Lower-level officials manage the populations and territories of the subdivisions.

States often promote geographic mobility and resettlement, severing longstanding ties among people, land, and kin (Smith 2003). Population displacements have increased with globalization and as war, famine, and job seeking churn up migratory currents. People in states come to identify themselves by new statuses, including residence, ethnicity, occupation, political party, religion, and team or club affiliation—rather than only as members of a descent group or an extended family.

States also manage their populations by granting different rights and obligations to citizens and noncitizens. Status distinctions among citizens also

RECAP 17.1	Economic Basis of and Political Regulation in Bands, Tribes, Chiefdoms, and States		
SOCIOPOLITICAL TYPE	**ECONOMIC TYPE**	**EXAMPLES**	**TYPE OF REGULATION**
Band	Foraging	Inuit, San	Local
Tribe	Horticulture, pastoralism	Yanomami, Kapauku, Masai	Local, temporary regional
Chiefdom	Productive horticulture, pastoral nomadism, agriculture	Qashqai, Polynesia, Cherokee	Permanent regional
State	Agriculture, industrialism	Ancient Mesopotamia, contemporary United States and Canada	Permanent regional

May, 2016: Pearlie Mae Smith, right, reacts after winning a share of a Powerball jackpot valued at $429.6 million—a nice return on a $6 investment. Do lottery winners usually gain prestige, or merely money, as a result of their luck?
© Mel Evans/AP Images

To handle disputes and crimes, all states have courts and judges. Shown here in a 2005 photo, judges in Hong Kong attend the annual ceremonial opening of the Legal Year at Hong Kong city hall. Does this photo say anything about cultural diffusion and/or colonialism?
© Philippe Lopez/AFP/Getty Images

are common. Archaic states granted different rights to nobles, commoners, and slaves. In American history prior to the Emancipation Proclamation, there were different laws for enslaved and free people. In European colonies, separate courts judged cases involving only natives and cases involving Europeans. In contemporary America, a military judiciary coexists alongside the civil system.

Judiciary

All states have laws based on precedent and legislative proclamations. Without writing, laws may be preserved in oral tradition. Crimes are violations of the legal code ("breaking the law"), with specified types of punishment. To handle crimes and disputes, all states have courts and judges (see Donovan 2007; Pirie 2013).

A striking contrast between states and non-states is intervention in internal and domestic disputes, such as violence within and between families. Governments step in to halt blood feuds and regulate previously private disputes. However, states aren't always successful in their attempts to curb internal conflict. About 85 percent of the world's armed conflicts since 1945 have begun within states—in efforts to overthrow a ruling regime or as disputes over ethnic, religious, or human rights issues (see Barnaby 1984; Chatterjee 2004; Nordstrom 2004; Tishkov 2004).

Enforcement

How do states enforce laws and judicial decisions? All states have enforcement agents—some kind of police force. The duties of these enforcement officers may include apprehending and imprisoning criminals (those who have broken the law). Confinement requires prisons and jailers. If there is a death penalty, executioners are needed. Government officials have the power to collect fines and confiscate property. The government

uses its enforcement agents to maintain internal order, suppress disorder, and guard against external threats (with the military and border officials—see Maguire, Frois, and Zurawski 2014). As described in this chapter's "Focus on Globalization," censorship is another tool that governments may employ to secure their authority.

Armies help states subdue and conquer neighboring nonstates, but conquest isn't the only reason state organization has spread. Although states impose hardships, they also offer advantages. States have formal mechanisms (e.g., an army and a police force) designed to protect against external threats and to preserve internal order. When they are successful in promoting internal peace, states enhance production. Their economies can support massive, dense populations, which supply armies and colonists to promote expansion.

Fiscal Support

All states have fiscal systems. States could not maintain the government apparatus and agents just discussed without a secure means of financial support. Governments rely on financial, or **fiscal,** mechanisms (e.g., taxation) to support their officials and numerous other specialists. As in the chiefdom, the state intervenes in production, distribution, and consumption. The state may require a certain area to produce specific things, or ban certain activities in particular places. Like chiefdoms, states have redistribution ("spreading the wealth around"), but less of what comes in from the people actually goes directly back to the people.

In nonstates, people customarily share with their relatives, but people who live in states also have to turn over a significant portion of what

fiscal
Pertaining to finances and taxation.

focus on GLOBALIZATION

The Political Role of New Media

Global forces often face roadblocks to their international spread. Although the Internet makes possible the instantaneous global transmission of information, many countries censor the Internet and other mass media for political or moral reasons. Cuba limits Internet surfing and offers no access to Facebook or Twitter. Many countries limit access to porn sites. China has a sophisticated censorship system—sometimes called the "Great Firewall of China." China's local search engine, Baidu, which observes Chinese censorship rules, dwarfs Google, Bing, and Yahoo in the Chinese market. As of 2015, despite censorship, China had more than twice as many Internet users (almost half its population) as the United States (where over 87 percent have access).

Censorship can be a barrier to international business. The World Trade Organization (WTO) favors freedom of access to the Internet for commercial reasons: to allow free trade. WTO rules allow member nations to restrict trade to protect public morals or ensure public order, but with the understanding that such restrictions will disrupt trade as little as possible.

If the Internet and other media are used to promote free trade, how about free thought? The media have the capacity to enlighten by providing users with unfamiliar information and viewpoints and by offering a forum for dissident voices. On the other hand, the media also spread and reinforce stereotypes and misinformation, and, in doing so, close people's minds to complexity.

The media also promote fear, which often is manipulated for political reasons. Waves of internationally transmitted images and information can reinforce the perception that the world is a dangerous place, with threats to security and order everywhere. Facebook, Twitter, YouTube, cell-phone and digital cameras, and cable/satellite TV link people across the globe. Constant and instantaneous reporting has blurred the distinction between the international, the national, and the local. Geographic distance is obscured, and risk perception is magnified, by the barrage of "bad news" received daily from so many places. Many people have no idea how far away the disasters and threats really are. Was that suspicious package found in Paris or Pasadena? Did that bomb go off in Mumbai or Michigan? Votes in Athens, Greece, or Rome, Italy, can affect the American stock market more than votes in Athens or Rome, Georgia.

The political manipulation of media is not new. (Think of book banning and burning, for example. See http://www.adlerbooks.com/banned-books/ for a list of books that have been banned at some time in the United States.) Would-be guardians of morality and authoritarian regimes always have sought to silence dissident voices. What is new is the potentially instantaneous and global reach of the voices that question authority. New media, including cell phones, Twitter, and YouTube, have been used to muster public opinion and organize protests in places as distant as Istanbul, Turkey; Kiev, Ukraine; and Ferguson, Missouri. Can you think of examples of how new media have been used to question authority?

---

they produce to the state. Markets and trade usually are under at least some state oversight, with officials overseeing distribution and exchange, standardizing weights and measures, and collecting taxes on goods passing into or through the state. Of the revenues the state collects, it reallocates part for the general good and keeps another part (often larger) for itself—its agents and agencies. State organization doesn't bring more freedom or leisure to the common people, who may be conscripted to build monumental public works. Some projects, such as dams and irrigation systems, may be economically necessary, but residents of archaic states also had to build temples, palaces, and tombs for the elites. Those elites reveled in the consumption of sumptuary goods—jewelry, exotic food and drink, and stylish clothing reserved for, or affordable only by, the rich. Peasants' diets suffered as they struggled to meet government demands for produce, currency, or labor. Commoners perished in territorial wars that had little relevance to their own needs. To what extent are these observations true of contemporary states?

Although it offers advantages, we should not think of the state as "better" than other forms of sociopolitical organization. Stratification and the state are antithetical to the egalitarian and free-ranging way of life practiced by our foraging ancestors. We have just considered some of the demands that states place on ordinary people. It should not be surprising, then, that populations in various parts of the world have resisted, and tried to avoid or escape, state organization. We saw in the chapter "Making a Living" that foragers do not necessarily adopt food production just because they know of its existence. Similarly, certain societies have managed to resist or escape state organization by adopting nomadic lifestyles that are difficult for states to supervise. For example, James C. Scott (2009) discusses how a belt of highland societies with economies based on shifting cultivation have in Southeast Asia survived for generations outside the control of states based in the lowlands of the same countries.

SOCIAL CONTROL

In studying political systems, anthropologists pay attention not only to the formal, governmental institutions but to other forms of social control as well. The concept of social control is broader than "the political." **Social control** refers to "those fields of the social system (beliefs, practices, and institutions) that are most actively involved in the maintenance of any norms and the regulation of any conflict" (N. Kottak 2002, p. 290). Norms are cultural standards or guidelines that enable individuals to distinguish between appropriate and inappropriate behavior.

Previous sections of this chapter have focused more on formal political organization than on sociopolitical process. We've seen how the scale and strength of political systems have expanded in relation to economic changes. We've examined means of conflict resolution, or their absence, in various types of society. We've looked at political decision making, including leaders and their limits. We've also recognized that all contemporary humans have been affected by states, colonialism, and the spread of the world system (see Shore et al. 2011).

Sociopolitical was introduced as a key concept at the beginning of this chapter. So far, we've focused mainly on the political part of sociopolitical; now we focus on the social part. In this section we'll see that political systems have their informal, social, and subtle aspects along with their formal, governmental, and public dimensions.

Hegemony and Resistance

In addition to the formal mechanisms discussed in the section "State Systems," what mechanisms do states employ to maintain social order? Antonio Gramsci (1971) developed the concept of **hegemony** for a stratified social order in which subordinates comply with domination by internalizing their rulers' values and accepting the "naturalness" of domination (this is the way things were meant to be). According to Pierre Bourdieu (1977, p. 164), every social order tries to make its own arbitrariness (including its mechanisms of control and domination) seem natural and in everyone's interest—even when that is not the case. Often promises are made (e.g., things will get better if you're patient).

Both Bourdieu (1977) and Michel Foucault (1979) argued that it is easier and more effective to dominate people in their minds than to try to control their bodies. Besides, and often replacing, physical coercion are more insidious forms of social control. These include various techniques of persuading and managing people and of monitoring and recording their beliefs, activities, and contacts.

Hegemony, the internalization of a dominant ideology, is one way in which elites curb resistance to their power and domination. Another way

to discourage resistance is to make subordinates believe they eventually will gain power—as young people usually foresee when they let their elders dominate them. Yet another way to curb resistance is to separate or isolate people while supervising them closely, as is done in prisons (Foucault 1979).

Some contexts enable or encourage public resistance, particularly when people are allowed to assemble. The setting of a crowd offers anonymity, while also reinforcing and encouraging the common sentiments that have brought those people together. The elites, sensing the threat of surging crowds and public rebellion, often discourage such gatherings. They try to limit and control holidays, funerals, dances, festivals, and other occasions that might unite the oppressed. For example, in the American South before the Civil War, gatherings of five or more slaves were prohibited unless a white person was present.

Also working to discourage resistance are factors that interfere with community formation—such as geographic, linguistic, and ethnic separation. Elites want to isolate the oppressed rather than bringing them together in a group. Consequently, southern U.S. plantation owners sought slaves with diverse cultural and linguistic backgrounds, and limited their rights to assemble. Despite the measures used to divide them, the slaves resisted, developing their own popular culture, linguistic codes, and religious vision. The masters stressed portions of the Bible that emphasized compliance (e.g., the book of Job). The slaves, however, preferred the story of Moses and deliverance. The cornerstone of slave religion became the idea of a reversal in the conditions of whites and blacks. Slaves also resisted directly, through sabotage and flight. In many New World areas, slaves managed to establish free communities in the hills and other isolated areas (Price 1973).

Weapons of the Weak

The study of sociopolitical systems also should consider the sentiments and activity that may be hiding beneath the surface of evident, public behavior. In public, the oppressed may seem to accept their own domination, even when they are questioning it in private. Scott (1990) uses the term "public transcript" to describe the open, public interactions between oppressed people and their oppressors. Scott uses "hidden transcript" to describe the critique of the power structure that goes on out of sight of those who hold power. In public, the elites and the oppressed may observe the etiquette of power relations. The dominants act like masters while their subordinates show humility and defer. But resistance often is seething beneath the surface.

Sometimes, the hidden transcript may include active resistance, but it is individual and disguised rather than collective and defiant. Scott (1985)

social control
Maintaining social norms and regulating conflict.

hegemony
A stratified social order in which subordinates accept hierarchy as "natural."

uses Malay peasants, among whom he did field-work, to illustrate small-scale acts of resistance—which he calls "weapons of the weak." The Malay peasants used an indirect strategy to resist an Islamic tithe (religious tax). Peasants were expected to pay the tithe, usually in the form of rice, which was sent to the provincial capital. In theory, the tithe would come back as charity, but it never did. Peasants didn't resist the tithe by rioting, demonstrating, or protesting. Instead, they used a "nibbling" strategy, based on small acts of resistance. For example, they failed to declare their land or lied about the amount they farmed. They underpaid, or they delivered rice contaminated with water, rocks, or mud to add weight. Because of this resistance, only 15 percent of what was due actually was paid (Scott 1990, p. 89).

Hidden transcripts tend to be expressed publicly at certain times (festivals and Carnavals) and in certain places (e.g., markets). Because of its costumed anonymity, Carnaval (Mardi Gras in New Orleans) is an excellent arena for expressing normally suppressed feelings. Carnavals celebrate freedom through immodesty, dancing, gluttony, and sexuality (DaMatta 1991). Carnaval may begin as a playful outlet for frustrations built up during the year. Over time, it may evolve into a powerful annual critique of stratification and domination and thus a threat to the established order (Gilmore 1987). (Recognizing that ceremonial license could turn into political defiance, the Spanish dictator Francisco Franco outlawed Carnaval.)

"Schwellkoepp," or "Swollen Heads," caricature local characters during a Carnaval parade in Mainz, Germany. Because of its costumed anonymity, Carnaval is an excellent arena for expressing typically suppressed speech. Is there anything like Carnaval in your society?

© Daniel Roland/AP Images

Shame and Gossip

Many anthropologists have noted the importance of "informal" processes of social control, such as fear, stigma, shame, and gossip, especially in small-scale societies (see Freilich, Raybeck, and Savishinsky 1991). Gossip and shame, for example, can function as effective processes of social control when a direct or formal sanction is risky or impossible (Herskovits 1937). Gossip can be used to shame someone who has violated a social norm. Margaret Mead (1937) and Ruth Benedict (1946) distinguished between shame as an external sanction (i.e., forces set in motion by others, for example, through gossip) and guilt as an internal sanction, psychologically generated by the individual. They regarded shame as a more prominent form of social control in non-Western societies and guilt as a more dominant emotional sanction in Western societies. Of course, to be effective as a sanction, the prospect of being shamed or of shaming oneself must be internalized by the individual. In small-scale societies, in a social environment where everyone knows everyone else, most people try to avoid behavior that might shame them or otherwise spoil their reputations and alienate them from their social network.

Nicholas Kottak (2002) studied political systems, and social control more generally, among the rural Makua of northern Mozambique (Figure 17.4). Social control mechanisms among the Makua extended well beyond the formal political system, as revealed in conversations about social norms and crimes. The Makua talk easily about norm violations, conflicts, and the sanctions that can follow them. Jail, sorcery, and shame are the main sanctions anticipated by the rural Makua.

Makua ideas about social control emerged most clearly in discussions about what would happen to someone who stole his or her neighbor's chicken. Most Makua villagers have a makeshift chicken coop in a corner of their home. Chickens leave the coop before sunrise each day and wander around, looking for scraps. Villagers may be tempted to steal a chicken when its owner seems oblivious to its whereabouts. The Makua have few material possessions and a meat-poor diet, making free-ranging chickens a real temptation. Their discussions about unsupervised chickens and the occasional chicken theft as community problems clarified their ideas about social control—about why people did *not* steal their neighbor's chickens.

The Makua perceived three main disincentives or sanctions: jail (*cadeia*), sorcery attack (*enretthe*), and shame (*ehaya*). (As used here, a *sanction* refers to a kind of punishment that follows a norm violation.) The main sanctions—sorcery and, above all, shame—came from society rather than from the formal political system. First, sorcery: Once someone discovered his chicken had been stolen, he would, the Makua thought, ask a traditional healer to launch a sorcery attack on his behalf. This would either kill the thief or make him very ill.

According to Nicholas Kottak (2002), the Makua repeatedly mention the existence of sorcerers and sorcery, although they aren't explicit about who the sorcerers are. They see sorcery as based on malice, which everyone feels at some point. Having felt malice themselves, individual Makua probably experience moments of self-doubt about their own potential status as a sorcerer. They recognize that others have similar feelings. Local theories see sickness, social misfortune, and death as caused by malicious sorcery. Life expectancy is short and infant mortality high in a Makua village. Health, life, and existence are far more problematic than they are for most Westerners. Such uncertainty heightens fears relating to sorcery. Any conflict or norm violation is dangerous because it might trigger a sorcery attack. In particular, the Makua see the chicken thief as the inevitable target of a vengeance sorcery attack.

Makua fear sorcery, but they overwhelmingly mentioned shame as the main reason not to steal a neighbor's chicken. The chicken thief, having been discovered, would have to attend a formal, publicly organized village meeting, which would determine the appropriate punishment and compensation. The Makua were concerned not so much with a potential fine as with the intense and enduring shame or embarrassment they would feel as a confirmed chicken thief.

Rural Makua tend to live in one community for their entire lives. Such communities typically have fewer than a thousand people, so that residents can easily keep track of one another's identities and reputations. Tight clustering of homes, markets, and schools facilitates the monitoring process. In this social environment, people

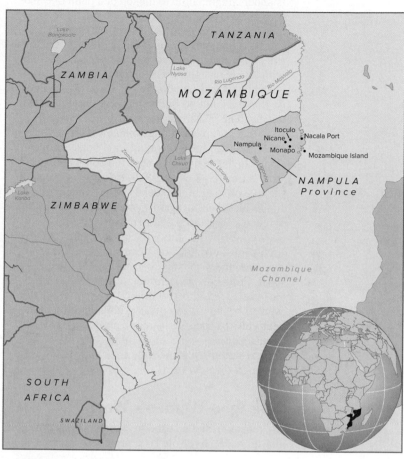

FIGURE 17.4 Location of the Makua and the Village of Nicane in Northern Mozambique.
The Province of Nampula shown here is Makua territory.

Nicholas Kottak (back center) attends a village meeting among the Makua of northern Mozambique. Two chiefs have called the meeting to renegotiate the boundaries of their political jurisdictions.
© Nicholas C. Kottak

try to avoid behavior that might spoil their reputations and alienate them from society.

Shame can be a very powerful sanction. Bronislaw Malinowski (1927) described how Trobriand Islanders might climb to the top of a palm tree and dive to their deaths because they couldn't tolerate the shame associated with public knowledge of some stigmatizing action. Makua villagers tell the story of a man rumored to have fathered a child with his stepdaughter. The political authorities imposed no formal sanctions (e.g., a fine or jail time) on this man, but gossip about the affair circulated widely. The gossip crystallized in the lyrics of a song that groups of young women would perform. After the man heard his name and behavior mentioned in that song, he hanged himself by the neck from a tree (N. Kottak 2002). (Previously we saw the role of song in the social control system of the Inuit. We'll see it again in the case of the Igbo Women's War, discussed in the next section.)

We see from this discussion that people aren't just citizens of governments; they are also members of society, and social sanctions exist alongside governmental ones. Such sanctions also exemplify other "weapons of the weak," because they often are wielded most effectively by people—for example, women or young people—who have limited access to the formal authority structure, as in the Igbo case, to which we now turn.

The Igbo Women's War

Shame and ridicule, used by women against men, played a decisive role in a protest movement in

In Nigeria, contemporary Igbo women collect water from a well standpipe. Political action by organized groups of Igbo women posed the first major challenge to British authority in Nigeria and in West Africa more generally during the colonial period.
© Eye Ubiquitous/SuperStock

southeastern Nigeria in 1929. This is remembered as the "Aba Women's Riots of 1929" in British colonial history and as the "Women's War" in Igbo history (see Dorward 1983; Martin 1988; Mba 1982; Oriji 2000; Van Allen 1971). During this two-month "war," at least 25,000 Igbo women joined protests against British officials, their agents, and their colonial policies. This massive revolt touched off the most serious challenge to British rule in the history of what was then the British colony of Nigeria.

In 1914, the British had implemented a policy of indirect rule by appointing local Nigerian men as their agents—known as "warrant chiefs." These chiefs became increasingly oppressive, seizing property, imposing arbitrary regulations, and imprisoning people who criticized them. Colonial administrators further stoked local outrage when they announced plans to impose taxes on Igbo market women. These women were key suppliers of food for Nigeria's growing urban population; they feared being forced out of business by the new tax. Market women were key organizers of the protests.

After hearing about the tax, thousands of Igbo women assembled in various towns to protest both the warrant chiefs and the taxes on market women. They used a traditional practice of censoring and shaming men through all-night song-and-dance ridicule (called "sitting on a man"). This process entailed constant singing and dancing around the houses and offices of the warrant chiefs. The women also followed the chiefs' every move, forcing the men to pay attention by invading their space (see also Walton and Suarez 2016). Wives of the warrant chiefs also urged their husbands to listen to the protesters' demands.

The protests were remarkably effective. The tax was abandoned, and many of the warrant chiefs resigned, some to be replaced by women. Other women were appointed to the Native courts as judges. The position of women improved in Nigeria, where market women especially remain a powerful political force to this day. Many Nigerian political events in the 1930s, 1940s, and 1950s were inspired by the Women's War, including additional tax protests. This Women's War inspired many other protests in regions all over Africa. The Igbo uprising is seen as the first major challenge to British authority in Nigeria and West Africa during the colonial period. This case shows how women effectively used their social power (through song, dance, noise, and "in-your-face" behavior) to subvert the formal authority structure and, in so doing, gained greater influence within that structure. Can you think of other, perhaps recent, examples? These examples from the Makua and the Igbo show how gossip, ridicule, and shaming can be effective processes of social control, which can even result in governmental change. The Igbo case also shows the importance of community organizing and political mobilization in effective resistance.

Resistance via Social Media: A Case Study

As we saw in this chapter's "Focus on Globalization," new media, including Facebook, Twitter, and smartphones, have been used prominently during uprisings in Turkey, Ukraine, and many other countries. Anthropologists have done research on the role of social media in various places, including Brazil. What some have dubbed Brazil's "Facebook Revolution" took place between June and September 2013. In cities large and small, Brazilians took to the streets (and cyberspace) to protest against the government and its public services policies. The movement began in São Paulo with small-scale demonstrations against bus fare increases. It exploded when images of police brutality—many recorded on cell-phone cameras—flooded first the Internet and then television broadcasts. These raw images recalled memories of the military dictatorship (1964–1985) for the older generation. Younger Brazilians were shocked at scenes of violent repression by agents of the government. The startling image of a young journalist's disfigured eye, caused by a riot police rubber bullet, was a particularly powerful visual shown repeatedly.

Media-borne calls for public action were spurred by citizens' concerns about the direction of Brazil's economic and political policies. The use of Facebook was vital in planning the demonstrations and recruiting protesters. Television news joined in, broadcasting the time and location of protests and then airing the ensuing encounters for nightly viewing. The protesters were overwhelmingly middle-class urbanites. The demonstrations accelerated during the international Confederation's Cup soccer games, which Brazil was hosting, focusing on the government's lavish spending—on stadiums for that competition and for the upcoming World Cup (2014) and Olympic Games (2016)—while ignoring the health, education, and transportation needs of most Brazilians.

While this civil unrest was evolving and expanding, a team of ethnographers from American and Brazilian universities was conducting research on the use and impact of electronic media in five Brazilian communities. (Anthropologist Richard Pace and I are collaborators in this research project conducted in various parts of Brazil, with sponsorship from the U.S. National Science Foundation.) As the protests intensified, our research team was observing how local Brazilians used media to understand the manifestations of these actions and, in some cases, to plan their own parallel protests. How did local Brazilians learn about, interpret, and participate in the discontent being played out at the national level?

Local interest and participation were greatest in Ibirama, a town of almost 15,000 people in Santa Catarina state, southern Brazil. In that community, project researcher Cynthia Pace (University of South Florida) observed extensive use of Facebook and television to both follow and participate in the protests. Ibirama is a tightly knit community founded in the late 19th century by German, Polish, and Russian migrants. Overwhelmingly middle class, it has had quality access to the Internet for more than a decade. Facebook is the preferred form of communication, with people posting daily, and even hourly, to signal people's comings and goings, issue invitations to local events, and advertise local businesses. (Cynthia Pace was chided one week for being invited to only five events instead of the normal 10 or more. She was told she needed more Facebook friends.)

As the protests spread in June 2013, Cynthia Pace's housemate, Pedro, an engineering student, used Facebook to post his plans to protest government corruption and the policies of President Dilma Rousseff. Pedro's Facebook network included thousands of people in Ibirama, and the resulting demonstration attracted hundreds. Cynthia Pace filmed the protest, and Pedro posted the footage on his Facebook page, from which a regional TV station obtained it for the evening news broadcast. The protest focused squarely on political and economic mismanagement by the federal government. Participants felt certain their actions would combine with others across the nation and bring down the Rousseff presidency. (As of this writing, three years after the Ibirama protest, President Rousseff has been suspended from office and replaced by her vice president pending her impeachment trial.)

Far from our other research sites is Gurupá, a community of 9,500 people located on the Amazon River in the state of Pará. Its inhabitants are poor by national standards, but the community has benefited greatly from government programs for poverty alleviation, as well as a recent boom in the export of açaí (a tropical fruit). Gurupá has a history of social activism and protest and strongly supports President Rousseff's Workers' Party. In town, local access to the Internet is unreliable, slow, and regularly interrupted. In Gurupá's rural areas, access is nonexistent. Cell phones (available only since 2011) are used to access Facebook when service allows. Local people watched the distant street protests mainly on television, given the issues with Internet access. According to researcher Monte Talley (Vanderbilt University), the people of Gurupá tended to see the manifestations as political venting by urban residents far removed from

On Rio de Janeiro's Copacabana beach, protesters agitate for political reform and better public services and against PEC37, a proposed law that would have deprived independent public prosecutors of the right to probe crimes and political corruption. (The law was not passed.)

© Yasuyoshi Chiba/AFP/Getty Images

the realities of the Amazon. Eventually, a local protest event was planned and posted on Facebook, although the real organization was accomplished by face-to-face interactions. The event, which drew about 100 people, was photographed and placed on Facebook by its organizers. Framed as a protest against the Rousseff presidency, the real focus of the event became local politics, with participants from the opposition party.

Another community studied by our research team is Turedjam, population 500, which is located in the Kayapó Indigenous Territories near the Brazilian town of Ourilândia do Norte, Pará. The village was established in 2010. Unlike most other Kayapó villages, it has electricity, television, and cell-phone service. Although the community lacks Internet access, some villagers have gone online in nearby Brazilian towns, and a few even have Facebook accounts. According to researcher Glenn Shepard (Goeldi Museum, Belem, Brazil), the villagers watched the demonstrations on television. With limited proficiency in the Portuguese language, however, many Kayapó had trouble following the details of the protest movement. They interpreted the distant street protests as manifestations of general discontent among "whites" with their own government. Opportunistically, the Kayapó seized the national events as an opening to pursue their own longstanding grievances. Local men painted their bodies solid black (a sign of warfooting among these Native Americans) and maintained constant contact with other villages via

short-wave radio and cell phones. Their plan was to block traffic on the Transamazon Highway, in an attempt to force concessions from the Rousseff government. Their main concerns included demarcation of Kayapó lands and a potentially destructive regional dam project. The proposed highway blockage eventually was abandoned in favor of direct talks with government officials.

From these case studies we see that urban events, when broadcast nationally via television, cell phones, and the Internet, also affect people living in small towns and villages far from those urban centers. But the effects are varied, reflecting the particular local context, including its class status and degree of media access. The national "mediascape" gets fragmented locally. For a few months in Brazil in 2013, nationwide knowledge of urban discontent created a momentary imagined solidarity—most strongly among urban, middle-class Brazilians. The protests expressed a general discontent with Brazil's direction, but the goals of political action were unclear and diffuse, and there was no real common enemy (e.g., a brutal dictator). Although the 2013 protests did mobilize large numbers of Brazilians, they resulted in no immediate political change. President Rousseff was reelected president in 2014. By 2016, however, she was embroiled in an impeachment process. Social media certainly plays a role in disseminating political goals and spurring action, but a media campaign cannot in itself guarantee political change.

for REVIEW

1. Although no ethnographer has been able to observe a sociopolitical system uninfluenced by some state, many anthropologists use a typology that classifies societies as bands, tribes, chiefdoms, or states. Foragers tended to live in egalitarian, band-organized societies. Personal networks linked individuals, families, and bands. Band leaders were first among equals, with no sure way to enforce decisions. Disputes rarely arose over strategic resources, which were open to all.

2. Political authority increased with growth in population size and density and in the scale of regulatory problems. More people mean more relations among individuals and groups to regulate. Increasingly complex economies pose further regulatory problems.

3. Heads of horticultural villages are local leaders with limited authority. They lead by example and persuasion. Big men have support and authority beyond a single village. They are regional regulators, but temporary ones. In organizing a feast, they mobilize labor from several villages. Sponsoring such events leaves them with little wealth but with prestige and a reputation for generosity.

4. Age and gender also can be used for regional political integration. Among North America's Plains Indians, men's associations (pantribal sodalities) organized raiding and buffalo hunting. Such sodalities provide offense and defense when there is intertribal raiding for animals. Among pastoralists, the degree of authority and political organization reflects population size and density, interethnic relations, and pressure on resources.

5. The state is an autonomous political unit that encompasses many communities. Its government collects taxes, drafts people for work and war, and decrees and enforces laws. The state is a form of sociopolitical organization based on central government and social stratification. Early states are known as archaic, or nonindustrial, states, in contrast to modern industrial nation-states.

6. Unlike tribes, but like states, chiefdoms had permanent regional regulation and differential access to resources. But chiefdoms lacked stratification. Unlike states, but like bands and tribes, chiefdoms were organized by kinship, descent, and marriage. Chiefdoms emerged in several areas, including the circum-Caribbean, lowland Amazonia, the southeastern United States, and Polynesia.

7. Weber's three dimensions of stratification are wealth, power, and prestige. In early states—for the first time in human history—contrasts in wealth, power, and prestige between entire groups of men and women came into being. A socioeconomic stratum includes people of both genders and all ages. The superordinate—higher or elite—stratum enjoys privileged access to resources.

8. Certain systems are found in all states: population control, judiciary, enforcement, and fiscal. These are integrated by a ruling system or government composed of civil, military, and religious officials. States conduct censuses and demarcate boundaries. Laws are based on precedent and legislative proclamations. Courts and judges handle disputes and crimes. A police force maintains internal order, as a military defends against external threats. A financial, or fiscal, system supports rulers, officials, judges, and other specialists and government agencies.

9. *Hegemony* describes a stratified social order in which subordinates comply with domination by internalizing its values and accepting its "naturalness." Situations that appear hegemonic may have resistance that is individual and disguised rather than collective and defiant. "Public transcript" refers to the open, public interactions between the dominators and the oppressed. "Hidden transcript" describes the critique of power that goes on where the powerholders can't see it. Discontent also may be expressed in public rituals such as Carnaval.

10. Broader than the political is the concept of social control—those fields of the social system most actively involved in the maintenance of norms and the regulation of conflict. Sanctions are social as well as governmental. Shame and gossip can be effective social sanctions. In the Igbo Women's War, women effectively used their social power (through song, dance, noise, and "in-your-face" behavior) to subvert the formal authority structure and, in so doing, gained greater influence within that structure. Urban events, when broadcast nationally via TV, cell phones, and the Internet, also affect people far from those urban centers. Such effects, however, are varied, reflecting the particular local context. Although the media can disseminate political goals and spur action, social media cannot in themselves guarantee political change.

key terms

critical thinking

1. This chapter notes that the labels "band," "tribe," "chiefdom," and "state" are too simple to account for the full range of political diversity and complexity known to archaeologists and ethnographers. Why not get rid of this typology altogether if it does not accurately describe reality? What is the value, if any, of researchers retaining the use of ideal types to study society?

2. Why shouldn't modern hunter-gatherers be seen as representative of Stone Age peoples? What are some of the stereotypes associated with foragers?

3. What are sodalities? Does your society have them? Do you belong to any? Why or why not?

4. What conclusions do you draw from this chapter about the relationship between population density and political hierarchy?

5. This chapter describes population control as one of the specialized functions found in all states. What are examples of population control? Have you had direct experiences with these controls? (Think of the last time you traveled abroad, registered to vote, paid taxes, or applied for a driver's license.) Do you think these controls are good or bad for society?

Gender

- ▶ How are biology and culture expressed in human sex/gender systems?

- ▶ How do gender, gender roles, and gender stratification correlate with other social, economic, and political variables?

- ▶ What is sexual orientation, and how do sexual practices vary cross-culturally?

© Scanpix Sweden, Fredrik Sandberg/AP Images

Gender-neutral "emotion dolls" using in teaching at "Egalia," a preschool in Stockholm, Sweden. The school's staff avoid words like "him" or "her" and address the children as "friends" rather than "girls" and "boys." This public preschool exemplifies Sweden's efforts to engineer lifelong gender equality.

understanding OURSELVES

A table (18.1) in this chapter lists activities that are generally done by the men in a society, generally done by the women in a society, or done by either men or women (swing). In this table, you will see some "male" activities familiar to our own culture, such as building houses, hunting, and butchering, along with activities that we consider typically female, such as doing the laundry and cooking. This list may bring to mind as many exceptions as followers of these "rules." Although it is not typical, it certainly is not unheard of for an American woman to hunt large game or an American man to cook (think of any male celebrity chef). Celebrities aside, women in our culture increasingly work outside the home in a wide variety of jobs—doctor, lawyer, accountant, professor—traditionally considered men's work. It is not true, however, that women have achieved equity in all types of employment. As of this writing, only 20 out of 100 U.S. senators are women. Only four women have ever served on the U.S. Supreme Court.

Ideas about proper gender behavior are changing just as inconsistently as are the employment patterns of men and women. Today's TV shows may feature characters who display nontraditional gender behavior and sexual behavior, while old beliefs, cultural expectations, and gender stereotypes linger.

The American expectation that proper female behavior should be polite, restrained, or meek poses a challenge for women, because American culture also values decisiveness and "standing up for your beliefs." When American men and women display similar behavior—speaking their minds, for example—they are judged differently. A man's assertive behavior may be admired and rewarded, but similar behavior by a woman may be labeled "aggressive"—or worse.

Both men and women are constrained by their cultural training, stereotypes, and expectations. For example, American culture stigmatizes male crying. It's okay for little boys to cry, but becoming a man often means giving up this natural expression of joy and sadness. Why shouldn't men be able to cry when they feel emotions? American men are trained as well to make decisions and stick to them. In our stereotypes, changing one's mind is more associated with women than with men and may be perceived as a sign of weakness. Politicians routinely criticize their opponents for being indecisive, for waffling or "flip-flopping" on issues. What a strange idea—that people shouldn't change their positions if they've discovered there's a better way. Males, females, and humanity may be equally victimized by aspects of cultural training.

Because anthropologists study biology, society, and culture, they are in a unique position to comment on nature (biological predispositions) and nurture (environment) as determinants of human behavior. Human attitudes, values, and behavior are limited not only by our genetic predispositions—which often are difficult to identify—but also by our experiences during enculturation. Our attributes as adults are determined both by our genes and by our environment during growth and development.

SEX AND GENDER

Questions about nature and nurture emerge in the discussion of human sex-gender roles and sexuality. Men and women differ genetically. Women have two X chromosomes, and men have an X and a Y. The father determines a baby's sex because only he has the Y chromosome to transmit. The mother always provides an X chromosome.

The chromosomal difference is expressed in hormonal and physiological contrasts. Humans are sexually dimorphic, more so than some primates, such as gibbons (small, tree-living Asiatic apes), and less so than others, such as gorillas and orangutans. **Sexual dimorphism** refers to differences in male and female biology besides the contrasts in breasts and genitals. Women and men differ not just in primary (genitalia and reproductive organs) and secondary (breasts, voice, hair distribution) sexual characteristics but in average weight, height, strength, and longevity. Women tend to live longer than men and have excellent endurance capabilities. In a given population, men tend to be taller and to weigh more than women do. Of course, there is a considerable overlap between the sexes in terms of height, weight, and physical strength, and there has been a pronounced reduction in sexual dimorphism during human evolution.

Just how far, however, do such genetically and physiologically determined differences go? What effects do they have on the way men and women act and are treated in different societies? Anthropologists have discovered both similarities and differences in the roles of men and women in different cultures. The predominant anthropological position on sex-gender roles and biology may be stated as follows:

> The biological nature of men and women [should be seen] not as a narrow enclosure limiting the human organism, but rather as a broad base upon which a variety of structures can be built. (Friedl 1975, p. 6)

Although in most societies men tend to be somewhat more aggressive than women are, many of the behavioral and attitudinal differences between the sexes emerge from culture rather than biology. Sex differences are biological, but gender encompasses all the traits that a culture assigns to and inculcates in males and females. **Gender**, in other words, refers to the cultural construction of whether one is female, male, or something else.

Given the "rich and various constructions of gender" within the realm of cultural diversity, Susan Bourque and Kay Warren (1987) note that the same images of masculinity and femininity do not always apply. Margaret Mead did an early ethnographic study of variation in gender roles. Her book *Sex and Temperament in Three Primitive Societies* (1935/1950) was based on fieldwork in three societies in Papua New Guinea: the Arapesh, Mundugumor, and Tchambuli. The extent of personality variation in men and women among those three societies on the same island amazed Mead. She found that Arapesh men and women both acted as Americans traditionally have expected women to act: in a mild, parental,

The realm of cultural diversity contains richly different social constructions and expressions of gender roles, as is illustrated by this Wodaabe man at the annual Gerewol male beauty contest in Niger.
© Robert Harding World Imagery/Alamy Stock Photo

responsive way. Mundugumor men and women both, in contrast, acted as she believed we expect men to act: fiercely and aggressively. Finally, Tchambuli men were "catty," wore curls, and went shopping, but Tchambuli women were energetic and managerial and placed less emphasis on personal adornment than did the men. (Drawing on their case study of the Tchambuli, whom they call the Chambri, Errington and Gewertz [1987], while recognizing gender malleability, have disputed the specifics of Mead's account.)

There is a well-established field of feminist scholarship within anthropology (Di Leonardo 1991; Lewin and Silverstein 2016; Rosaldo 1980*b*; Strathern 1988). Anthropologists have gathered systematic ethnographic data about similarities and differences involving gender in many cultural settings (Bonvillain 2007; Brettell and Sargent 2012; Mascia-Lees 2010; Stimpson and Herdt 2014; Ward and Edelstein 2013). Anthropologists can detect recurrent themes and patterns involving gender differences. They also can observe that gender roles vary with environment, economy, adaptive strategy, and type of political system. Before we examine the cross-cultural data, some definitions are in order.

Gender roles are the tasks and activities a culture assigns by gender. Related to gender roles are **gender stereotypes**, which are oversimplified but strongly held ideas about the characteristics of males and females. **Gender stratification** describes an unequal distribution of rewards (socially valued resources, power, prestige, human rights, and personal freedom) between men and women, reflecting their different positions in a social hierarchy. According to Ann Stoler (1977), the "economic determinants of gender status" include freedom or autonomy (in disposing of

sexual dimorphism
Marked differences in male and female biology, beyond breasts and genitals.

gender
The cultural construction of whether one is female, male, or something else.

gender roles
The tasks and activities that a culture assigns to each sex.

gender stereotypes
Oversimplified, strongly held views about the characteristics of males and females.

gender stratification
The unequal distribution of social resources between men and women.

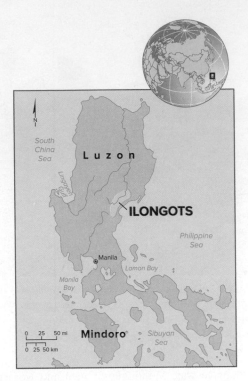

FIGURE 18.1 Location of Ilongots in the Philippines.

one's labor and its fruits) and social power (control over the lives, labor, and produce of others).

In stateless societies, gender stratification often is more obvious in regard to prestige than it is in regard to wealth. In her study of the Ilongots of northern Luzon in the Philippines (Figure 18.1), Michelle Rosaldo (1980a) described gender differences related to the positive cultural value placed on adventure, travel, and knowledge of the external world. More often than women, Ilongot men, as headhunters, visited distant places. They acquired knowledge of the external world, amassed experiences there, and returned to express their knowledge, adventures, and feelings in public oratory. They received acclaim as a result. Ilongot women had inferior prestige because they lacked external experiences on which to base knowledge and dramatic expression. On the basis of Rosaldo's study and findings in other stateless societies, Ong (1989) argues that we must distinguish between prestige systems and actual power in a given society (see also Hodgson 2016). High male prestige does not necessarily entail economic or political power held by men over their families. (For more on Rosaldo's contributions to gender studies, see Lugo and Maurer 2000.)

RECURRENT GENDER PATTERNS

Ethnologists compare ethnographic data from several cultures (i.e., cross-cultural data) to discover and explain differences and similarities.

Data relevant to the cross-cultural study of gender can be drawn from the domains of economics, politics, domestic activity, kinship, and marriage. Review Table 18.1 (on p. 347) for cross-cultural data from 185 randomly selected societies on the division of labor by gender.

The findings in Table 18.1 illustrate cultural generalities rather than absolute cultural universals. That is, among the societies known to ethnography, there is a general, indeed a very strong, tendency for men to build boats, but there are exceptions. One was the Hidatsa, a Native American group in which the women made the boats used to cross the Missouri River. (Traditionally, the Hidatsa were village farmers and bison hunters on the North American Plains; they now live in North Dakota.) Another exception is that Pawnee women worked wood; this is the only Native American group that assigned this activity to women. (The Pawnee, also traditionally Plains farmers and bison hunters, originally lived in what is now central Nebraska and central Kansas; they now live on a reservation in north central Oklahoma.) Among the Mbuti "pygmies" of Africa's Ituri forest, women hunt—by catching small, slow animals, using their hands or a net (Murdock and Provost 1973).

Exceptions to cross-cultural generalizations may involve societies or individuals. That is, a society like the Hidatsa can contradict the cross-cultural generalization that men build boats by assigning that task to women. Or in a society where the cultural expectation is that men build boats, a particular woman or women can contradict that expectation by doing the male activity. Table 18.1 shows that in a sample of 185 societies, certain activities ("swing activities") are assigned to either or both men and women. Among the most important of such activities are planting, tending, and harvesting crops. Some societies customarily assign more farming chores to women, whereas others make men the primary farmers. Among the tasks almost always assigned to men (Table 18.1), some (e.g., hunting large animals on land and sea) seem clearly related to the greater average size and strength of males. Others, such as working wood and making musical instruments, seem more culturally arbitrary. And women, of course, are not exempt from arduous and time-consuming physical labor, such as gathering firewood and fetching water. In Arembepe, Bahia, Brazil, for example, women used to transport water in 5-gallon tins, balanced on their heads, from wells and lagoons located at long distances from their homes.

Notice that Table 18.1 includes no mention of trade and market activity, in which either men or women, or both, are active. Is this table somewhat androcentric (male centered) in detailing more tasks for men than for women? More than men, women do child care, but the study on which Table 18.1 is based does not break down domestic activities to the same extent that it details work

TABLE 18.1 Generalities in the Division of Labor by Gender, Based on Data from 185 Societies

GENERALLY MALE ACTIVITIES	SWING (MALE OR FEMALE) ACTIVITIES	GENERALLY FEMALE ACTIVITIES
Hunting large aquatic animals (e.g., whales, walrus)	Making fire	Gathering fuel (e.g., firewood)
Smelting ores	Body mutilation	Making drinks
Metalworking	Preparing skins	Gathering wild vegetal foods
Lumbering	Gathering small land animals	Dairy production (e.g., churning)
Hunting large land animals	Planting crops	Spinning
Working wood	Making leather products	Doing the laundry
Hunting fowl	Harvesting	Fetching water
Making musical instruments	Tending crops	Cooking
Trapping	Milking	Preparing food (e.g., processing cereal grains)
Building boats	Making baskets	
Working stone	Caring for small animals	
Working bone, horn, and shell	Preserving meat and fish	
Mining and quarrying	Loom weaving	
Setting bones	Gathering small aquatic animals	
Butchering*	Clothing manufacture	
Collecting wild honey	Making pottery	
Clearing land		
Fishing		
Tending large herd animals		
Building houses		
Preparing the soil		
Making nets		
Carrying burdens		
Making mats		
Making rope		

*All the activities above "butchering" are almost always done by men; those from "butchering" through "making rope" usually are done by men.

SOURCE: Adapted from G. P. Murdock and C. Provost, 1973, "Factors in the Division of Labor by Sex: A Cross-Cultural Analysis," *Ethnology* 12(2): 202–225.

done outside the home. Think about this table in terms of today's home and job roles and with respect to the activities done by contemporary women and men. Men still do most of the hunting; either gender can collect the honey from a supermarket, even as most baby-bottom wiping (part of child care and not included in Table 18.1) continues to be in female hands.

Cross-culturally the subsistence contributions of men and women are roughly equal (Table 18.2). But in domestic activities and child care, female labor clearly predominates, as we see in Tables 18.3 and 18.4. Table 18.3 shows that in about half the societies studied, men did virtually no domestic work. Even in societies where men did domestic chores, the bulk of such work was done by women. Adding together their subsistence activities and their domestic work, we see that women tend to

work more hours than men do. Has this changed in the contemporary world?

What about child care? Women tend to be the main caregivers in most societies, but men often play a role. Again there are exceptions, both within and between societies. Table 18.4 uses cross-cultural data to answer the question "Who—men or women—is primarily responsible for the care, handling, and discipline of young children?" Women have primary responsibility for young children in two-thirds of the societies, but there are exceptions. In the United States and Canada today, some men are primary caregivers despite the cultural fact that the female role in child care remains more prominent. Given the critical role of breast-feeding in ensuring infant survival, it makes sense, for infants especially, for the mother to be the primary caregiver.

TABLE 18.2 Time and Effort Expended on Subsistence Activities by Men and Women*

More by men	16
Roughly equal	61
More by women	23

*Percentage of 88 randomly selected societies for which information was available on this variable.

SOURCE: M. F. Whyte, 1978, "Cross-Cultural Codes Dealing with the Relative Status of Women," *Ethnology* 17(2):211–239.

TABLE 18.3 Who Does the Domestic Work?*

Males do virtually none	51
Males do some, but females do most	49

*Percentage of 92 randomly selected societies for which information was available on this variable.

SOURCE: M. F. Whyte, 1978, "Cross-Cultural Codes Dealing with the Relative Status of Women," *Ethnology* 17(2):211–239.

TABLE 18.4 Who Is Primarily Responsible for the Care, Handling, and Discipline of Children?*

Males have more say	18
Roughly equal	16
Females have more say	66

*Percentage of 67 randomly selected societies for which information was available on this variable.

SOURCE: M. F. Whyte, 1978, "Cross-Cultural Codes Dealing with the Relative Status of Women," *Ethnology* 17(2):211–239.

TABLE 18.5 Does the Society Allow Multiple Spouses?*

Only for males	77
For both, but more commonly for males	4
For neither	16
For both, but more commonly for females	2

*Percentage of 92 randomly selected societies for which information was available on this variable.

SOURCE: M. F. Whyte, 1978, "Cross-Cultural Codes Dealing with the Relative Status of Women," *Ethnology* 17(2):211–239.

TABLE 18.6 Is There a Double Standard with Respect to PREMARITAL Sex?*

Yes—females are more restricted	44
No—equal restrictions on males and females	56

*Percentage of 73 randomly selected societies for which information was available on this variable.

SOURCE: M. F. Whyte, 1978, "Cross-Cultural Codes Dealing with the Relative Status of Women," *Ethnology* 17(2):211–239.

TABLE 18.7 Is There a Double Standard with Respect to EXTRAMARITAL Sex?*

Yes—females are more restricted	43
Equal restrictions on males and females	55
Males punished more severely for transgression	3

*Percentage of 73 randomly selected societies for which information was available on this variable.

SOURCE: M. F. Whyte, 1978, "Cross-Cultural Codes Dealing with the Relative Status of Women," *Ethnology* 17(2):211–239.

In many societies women (and children) routinely do hard physical labor, as is illustrated by these stone factory workers in Kathmandu, Nepal.

© Horizons WWP/Alamy Stock Photo

There are differences in male and female reproductive strategies. Women give birth, breast-feed, and assume primary responsibility for infant care. Women ensure that their progeny will survive by establishing a close bond with each baby. It's also advantageous for a woman to have a reliable mate to ease the child-rearing process and help ensure the survival of her children. Women can have only so many babies during the course of their reproductive years, which begin after menarche (the advent of menstruation) and end with menopause (cessation of menstruation). Men have a longer reproductive period, which can last into the elder years. If they choose to do so, men can enhance their reproductive success by impregnating several women over a longer time span. Cross-culturally, men are much more likely to have multiple mates than women are (see Tables 18.5, 18.6, and 18.7). Among the societies known to ethnography, polygyny (multiple wives) is much more common than polyandry (multiple husbands) (see Table 18.5).

Men mate, within and outside marriage, more than women do. Table 18.6 shows cross-cultural data on premarital sex, and Table 18.7 summarizes the data on extramarital sex. In both cases men are less restricted than women are, although the restrictions are equal in about half the societies studied. Double standards that restrict women more than men are one illustration of gender stratification, which we now examine more systematically.

GENDER ROLES AND GENDER STRATIFICATION

Economic roles will affect gender stratification. In one cross-cultural study, Sanday (1974) found that gender stratification decreased when men and women made roughly equal contributions to subsistence.

In foraging societies, gender stratification was most marked when men contributed much more to the diet than women did. This was true among the Inuit and other northern hunters and fishers. Among tropical and semitropical foragers, by contrast, gathering usually provides more food than hunting and fishing do. Gathering generally is women's work. Men usually hunt and fish, and there is no culture in which women are the primary hunters. However, women also do some fishing and may hunt small animals, as is true among the Agta of the Philippines (Griffin and Estioko-Griffin 1985). When gathering is prominent, gender status tends to be more equal than it is when hunting and fishing are the main subsistence activities.

Gender status also is more equal when the domestic and public spheres aren't sharply separated. (*Domestic* means within or pertaining to the home.) Strong differentiation between the home and the outside world is called the **domestic–public dichotomy** or the *private–public contrast.* The outside world can include politics, trade, warfare, or work. Often when domestic and public spheres are clearly separated, public activities have greater prestige than domestic ones do. This can promote gender stratification, because men are more likely to be active in the public domain than women are. Cross-culturally, women's activities tend to be closer to home than men's are. Another reason hunter-gatherers have less gender stratification than farmers and herders do is that the domestic–public dichotomy is less developed among foragers.

We've seen that certain gender roles are more sex-linked than others. Men are the usual hunters and warriors. Given such tools and weapons as spears, knives, and bows, men make better hunters and fighters because they are bigger and stronger on the average than are women in the same population (Divale and Harris 1976). The male hunter-fighter role also reflects a tendency toward greater male mobility.

In foraging societies, women are either pregnant or lactating during most of their childbearing period. Late in pregnancy and after childbirth, carrying a baby limits a woman's movements, even her gathering. However, among the Agta of the Philippines (Griffin and Estioko-Griffin 1985), women not only gather; they also hunt with dogs while carrying their babies with them. Still, given the effects of pregnancy and breast-feeding on mobility, it would be problematic for women to be the primary hunters (Friedl 1975). Warfare, which also requires mobility, is not typical of foraging societies, nor is interregional trade well

Among foragers, gender stratification tends to increase when men contribute much more to the diet than women do—as has been true among the Inuit and other northern hunters and fishers. Shown here, in Foxe Basin, Nunavut (in Canada's Northwest Territories), Inuit hunters load walrus onto their boats.
© Paul Nicklen/National Geographic Creative

Many jobs that men do in some societies are done by women in others, and vice versa. In West Africa, women play a prominent role in trade and marketing. In Togo, shown here, women dominate textile sales. Is there a textile shop near you? Who runs it?
© Pascal Deloche/GODONG/picture-alliance/Newscom

developed. Warfare and trade are two public arenas that can contribute to status inequality of males and females among food producers.

Reduced Gender Stratification—Matrilineal-Matrilocal Societies

Cross-cultural variation in gender status is related to rules of descent and postmarital residence. Many horticultural societies have **matrilineal descent** (descent traced through females only) and *matrilocality* (residence after marriage with the wife's relatives). In such societies, female status tends to be high. Matriliny and matrilocality disperse related males, rather than consolidating them. By contrast, patriliny and patrilocality keep male relatives together, which is advantageous when warfare is present. Matrilineal-matrilocal systems tend to occur in societies where population pressure on strategic resources is minimal and warfare is infrequent.

Women tend to have high status in matrilineal-matrilocal societies for several reasons. Descent-group membership, succession to political positions, allocation of land, and overall social identity all come through female links. In Negeri Sembilan, Malaysia (Peletz 1988), matriliny gave women sole inheritance of ancestral rice fields. Matrilocality created solidary clusters of female kin. Women had considerable influence beyond the household. In such matrilineal contexts, women are the basis of the entire social structure. Although public authority may be (or may appear to be) assigned to the men, much of the power and decision making may actually belong to the senior women.

Matriarchy

Cross-culturally, anthropologists have described tremendous variation in the roles of men and women, and the power differentials between them. If a *patriarchy* is a political system ruled by men, is a matriarchy necessarily a political system ruled by women? Or might we apply the term *matriarchy,* as anthropologist Peggy Reeves Sanday (2002) does, to a political system in which women play a much more prominent role than men do in social and political organization? One example would be the Minangkabau of West Sumatra, Indonesia, whom Sanday has studied for decades.

Sanday considers the Minangkabau a matriarchy because women are the center, origin, and foundation of the social order. Senior women are associated with the central pillar of the traditional house, the oldest one in the village. The oldest village in a cluster is called the "mother village." In ceremonies, women are addressed by the term used for their mythical Queen Mother. Women control land inheritance, and couples reside matrilocally. In the wedding ceremony, the wife collects her husband from his household and, with her female kin, escorts him to hers. If there is a

A Minangkabau bride and groom in West Sumatra, Indonesia, where anthropologist Peggy Reeves Sanday has conducted several years of ethnographic fieldwork.
© Lindsay Hebberd/Corbis

divorce, the husband simply takes his things and leaves. Yet despite the special position of women, the Minangkabau matriarchy is not the equivalent of female rule, given the Minangkabau belief that all decision making should be by consensus.

Increased Gender Stratification—Patrilineal-Patrilocal Societies

Martin and Voorhies (1975) link the decline of matriliny and the spread of the **patrilineal-patrilocal complex** (consisting of patrilineality, patrilocality, warfare, and male supremacy) to pressure on resources. (Societies with **patrilineal descent** trace descent through males only. In *patrilocal* societies a woman moves to her husband's village after marriage.) Faced with scarce resources, patrilineal-patrilocal cultivators such as the Yanomami often wage warfare against other villages. This favors patrilocality and patriliny, customs that keep related men together in the same village, where they make strong allies in battle. Such societies tend to have a sharp domestic–public dichotomy, and men tend to dominate the prestige hierarchy. Men may use their public roles in warfare and trade and their greater prestige to symbolize and reinforce the devaluation or oppression of women.

matrilineal descent
Descent traced through women only.

patrilineal-patrilocal complex
Male supremacy based on patrilineality, patrilocality, and warfare.

patrilineal descent
Descent traced through men only.

In some parts of Papua New Guinea, the patrilineal-patrilocal complex has extreme social repercussions. Regarding females as dangerous and polluting, men may segregate themselves in men's houses (such as this one, located near the Sepik River), where they hide their precious ritual objects from women. Are there places like this in your society?

© George Holton/Science Source

In many societies, especially patriarchal ones, women experience, and fear, intimidation as they increasingly enter the public sphere, especially in impersonal, urban settings. "Ladies Only" lines like this one at the Golden Temple in Amritsar, Punjab, India, are designed to help women move unmolested through public space.

© Conrad P. Kottak

The patrilineal-patrilocal complex characterizes many societies in highland Papua New Guinea. Women work hard growing and processing subsistence crops, raising and tending pigs (the main domesticated animal and a favorite food), and doing domestic cooking, but they are isolated from the public domain, which men control. Men grow and distribute prestige crops, prepare food for feasts, and arrange marriages. The men even get to trade the pigs and control their use in ritual.

In densely populated areas of the Papua New Guinea highlands, male–female avoidance is associated with strong pressure on resources (Lindenbaum 1972). Men fear all female contacts, including sexual acts. They think that sexual contact with women will weaken them. Indeed, men see everything female as dangerous and polluting. They segregate themselves in men's houses and hide their precious ritual objects from women. They delay marriage, and some never marry.

By contrast, the sparsely populated areas of Papua New Guinea, such as recently settled areas, lack taboos on male–female contacts. The image of woman as polluter fades, male–female intercourse is valued, men and women live together, and reproductive rates are high.

Patriarchy and Violence

Patriarchy describes a political system ruled by men in which women have inferior social and political status, including basic human rights. Barbara Miller (1997), in a study of systematic neglect of females, describes women in rural northern India as "the endangered sex." Societies that feature a full-fledged patrilineal-patrilocal complex, replete with warfare and intervillage raiding, also typify patriarchy. Such practices as dowry murders, female infanticide, and clitoridectomy (removal of the clitoris) exemplify patriarchy, which extends from tribal societies such as the Yanomami to state societies such as India and Pakistan.

The gender inequality spawned by patriarchy and violence, which continues into the 21st century, can be deadly. Anyone who follows current events will have heard of recent cases of blatant abuse of women and girls, particularly in the context of warfare and terrorism, for example, in Bosnia, Syria, and Nigeria. In all of these places, rape has been used as a weapon of war or as punishment for transgressions committed by the victim's male relatives. In Afghanistan, Pakistan, and elsewhere, girls have been prevented from, or punished for, attending school. In 2014, Boko Haram, a jihadist rebel group in northern Nigeria, which also opposes female education, kidnapped nearly 300 schoolgirls, whom they subjected to abuse and forced marriages.

Sometimes, thankfully, such abuse fails in its attempt to silence female voices. Consider Malala Yousafzai (born in 1997 in northern Pakistan), who at the early age of 9 years embarked on her ongoing career as a forceful and persuasive advocate for female education. Her courageous early work, including public speaking and a blog for the

patriarchy
Political system ruled by men.

BBC (started when she was 11), criticized the Taliban for its efforts to block girls' education and prompted the Taliban to issue a death threat against her. In October 2012, a gunman shot Malala (then age 14) three times on a school bus as she was traveling home from school. She survived, and has continued to speak out about the importance of education for girls. In 2014 she became the youngest person ever to receive the Nobel Peace Prize.

Although more prevalent in certain social settings than in others, family violence and domestic abuse of women are also worldwide problems. Domestic violence certainly occurs in nuclear family settings, such as Canada and the United States, as well as in more blatantly patriarchal contexts. Cities, with their impersonality and isolation from extended kin networks, are breeding grounds for domestic violence, as also may be rural areas in which women lead isolated lives.

When a woman lives in her own village of birth, she has kin nearby to protect her interests. Even in patrilocal polygynous (multiple wives) settings, women often count on the support of their cowives and sons in disputes with potentially abusive husbands. Settings in which women have a network of support are disappearing from today's world. Isolated families and patrilineal social forms have spread at the expense of matriliny. Many nations have declared polygyny illegal. More and more women, and men, find themselves cut off from their families and extended kin.

With the spread of the women's rights and human rights movements, attention to domestic violence and abuse of women has increased. Laws have been passed, and mediating institutions established. Brazil's female-run police stations for battered women provide an example, as do shelters for victims of domestic abuse in the United States and Canada. A series of "Ladies Only" facilities, including trains and entry lines, can be found throughout India. But patriarchal institutions do persist in what should be a more enlightened world.

GENDER IN INDUSTRIAL SOCIETIES

Attitudes about women's work outside the home have varied historically in response to economic conditions and world events. In the United States, for example, the "traditional" idea that "a woman's place is in the home" actually developed as industrialism spread after 1900. One reason for this change was an influx of European immigrants, providing a male workforce willing to accept low wages for jobs, including factory work, that women previously might have held. Eventually, machine tools and mass production further reduced the need for female labor.

The economic roles of 19th-century American women were varied. Pioneer women worked productively in farming and home industry. As production shifted from home to factory, some women, particularly those who were poor and/or unmarried, turned to factory employment. Young white women might work outside the home for a time, until they married and had children. The experience was different, of course, for African American women, many of whom, after abolition, continued working as field hands and domestics.

Anthropologist Maxine Margolis (2000) describes how gendered work, attitudes, and beliefs have varied in response to American economic needs. For example, when men are off fighting wars, work outside the home has been presented as women's patriotic duty, and the notion that women are biologically unfit for hard physical labor has faded.

The rapid population growth and business expansion that followed World War II created a demand for women to fill jobs in clerical work, public school teaching, and nursing (traditionally defined as female occupations). Inflation and the culture of consumption have also spurred female employment. When demand and/or prices rise, multiple paychecks help maintain family living standards.

Economic changes after World War II set the stage for the contemporary women's movement, marked by the publication of Betty Friedan's influential book *The Feminine Mystique* in 1963 and the founding of NOW, the National Organization for Women, in 1966. Among other things, the movement promoted expanded work opportunities for women, including the goal (as yet unrealized) of equal pay for equal work. Between 1970 and 2014, the female percentage of the American workforce rose from 38 to 47 percent. About 76 million women now have paid employment, compared with about 84 million men. Women fill more than half (52 percent) of all management and professional jobs (Bureau of Labor Statistics 2014). And it's not mainly single women working, as once was the case. Table 18.8 presents figures on the generally increasing cash employment of American wives and mothers, including those with young children.

Note in Table 18.8 that the cash employment of American married men has been falling while that of American married women has been rising. In 1960, 89 percent of all married men worked, compared with just 32 percent of married women—a gap of 57 percent. That gap had narrowed to 13 percent by 2014, as cash employment of husbands declined to 74 percent, while that of wives rose to 61 percent. The median income of American women working full-time, in 2014 was 79 percent of that of a comparably employed male, up from 68 percent in 1989 (Entmacher et al. 2013; DeNavas-Walt and Proctor 2015). The 2014 median annual income of an employed American women was $39,621, versus $50,583 for the comparable man (DeNavas-Walt and Proctor 2015).

As women increasingly work outside the home, ideas about the gender roles of males and females

TABLE 18.8   Cash Employment of American Mothers, Wives, and Husbands, 1960–2014*

YEAR	PERCENTAGE OF MARRIED WOMEN, HUSBAND PRESENT WITH CHILDREN UNDER AGE 6	PERCENTAGE OF ALL MARRIED WOMEN[†]	PERCENTAGE OF ALL MARRIED MEN[‡]
1960	19	32	89
1970	30	40	86
1980	45	50	81
1990	59	58	79
2014	60	61	74

*Civilian population 16 years of age and older.

[†]Husband present.

[‡]Wife present.

SOURCE: DeNavas-Walt, C., and B. D. Proctor, 2015, "Income and Poverty in the United States: 2014." U.S. Census Bureau, Current Population Reports, P60–252. Washington, DC: U.S. Government Printing Office. https://www.census.gov/content/dam/Census/library/publications/2015/demo/p60-252.pdf, p. 11.

have changed. Compare your grandparents and your parents. Chances are you have an employed mother, but your grandmother was more likely to have been a stay-at-home mom. Your grandfather is more likely than your father to have worked in manufacturing and to have belonged to a union. Your father is more likely than your grandfather to have participated in child-care and housework.

Thanks to automation and robotics, jobs have become less demanding in terms of physical labor. With machines to do the heavy work, the smaller average body size and lesser average strength of women are no longer significant impediments to blue-collar employment. But the main reason we don't see more modern-day Rosies working alongside male riveters is that the U.S. workforce itself has been abandoning heavy-goods manufacture. In the 1950s, two-thirds of American jobs were blue-collar, compared with fewer than 15 percent today. The location of those jobs has shifted within the world capitalist economy. Third World countries, with their cheaper labor costs, produce steel, automobiles, and other heavy goods less expensively than the United States can, but the United States excels at services. The American mass education system has many deficiencies, but it does train millions of people for service and information-oriented jobs.

Another important socioeconomic change since the 1960s is the increasing levels of education and professional employment among women. In the United States today, more women than men attend and graduate from college. Women will soon comprise the majority of college-educated workers in the U.S. labor force. Back in 1968, women made up less than 10 percent of the entering classes of MD (medicine), JD (law), and MBA (business) programs. The proportion of female students in those programs has risen to about 50 percent. Nowadays, female college graduates aged 30 to 34 are just as likely to be doctors, dentists, lawyers, professors, managers, and scientists

During the world wars, the notion that women were biologically unfit for hard physical labor faded. World War II's Rosie the Riveter—a strong, competent woman dressed in overalls and a bandana—was introduced as a symbol of patriotic womanhood. Is there a comparable poster woman today? What does her image say about modern gender roles?

SOURCE: National Archives and Records Administration

as they are to be working in traditionally female professions, as teachers, nurses, librarians, secretaries, or social workers. In the 1960s, women were seven times more likely to be in the latter than in the former series of professions.

In 1970, more than 60 percent of occupations were so male-dominated that 80 percent or more of their workers were male. Today that kind of occupational segregation has been reduced substantially. Only about a third of occupations have that degree of overrepresentation by males. On the other hand, the share of occupations in which women make up 80 percent or more of workers has remained relatively constant at 10 percent.

Despite the many gains, female employment continues to lag noticeably in certain highly paid professions, such as computer science and engineering. In those fields, the percentage of female graduates has actually declined, to about 20 percent from 37 percent in 1980. By midcareer, twice the number of women as men leave their jobs in computer science, often because they perceive an uncomfortable and unsupportive workplace environment. Nearly 40 percent of women who left science, engineering, and technology jobs cited a "hostile macho culture" as their primary reason for doing so, versus only 27 percent who cited compensation (Council of Economic Advisers Report, 2014).

Work and Family: Reality and Stereotypes

All humans have work and family obligations, but ideas about how to balance those responsibilities have changed considerably in recent years. Americans, both men and women, increasingly report that work interferes with family—not the other way around. Some 46 percent of working men and women report that job demands sometimes or often interfere with their family lives, up from 41 percent 15 years ago.

Both men and women increasingly are questioning the notion that the man should be the breadwinner while the woman assumes domestic and child-care responsibilities. In the United States today, more than 40 percent of mothers are the primary or sole source of income in their homes. This includes both single mothers and married mothers. Add to the rising percentage of female breadwinners the fact that fathers increasingly are taking on caregiving activities traditionally done by mothers. Seven percent of American families with children now are father-only families. In general, American fathers now spend significantly more time on child care and housework than they did in the past. American fathers now do 4.6 more hours of child care, and 4.4 more hours of housework, per week than they did in 1965.

However, just as there are lingering barriers to women's progress in the workplace, obstacles remain to men's success at home. The reasons for this are both material and cultural. Material factors include the facts that women still do considerably more domestic work than men do, and the average man still works longer hours outside the home and earns more money than the average woman does, even in dual-earner households. There is cultural lag as well. A stereotype that lingers is that of the incompetent male homemaker. Clueless husbands and inept fathers have been a staple of television sitcoms—especially those produced after large numbers of women began to enter the workforce. Women still tend to think they are better homemakers than their husbands. Former Princeton professor Anne-Marie Slaughter (2013, 2015) cites examples of American women who maintain deeply entrenched stereotypes about their own homemaking superiority and men's (lack of) domestic capabilities—from kids to kitchens (Slaughter 2013).

Slaughter discusses how, even when men seek, or are willing to play, a prominent domestic role, women may resist. The same woman who says she wants her husband to do more at home may then criticize him for not "doing things right" when he does pitch in. As Slaughter points out, "Doing things right" means doing things the woman's way. Practice, of course, does make perfect, and women still do a disproportionate share of housework and childcare in 21st-century America. If the woman is the one who usually does the domestic work, and if she assumes she can do it better and faster than her husband, she probably will do so. A stereotype can become a self-fulfilling prophecy, often reinforced by material reality.

When women ask their husbands for "help" around the house or with the kids, they are actually affirming their role as primary homemaker and child-care provider. The husband is viewed as merely a helper, rather than an equal partner. Slaughter (2013, 2015) argues that Americans need to conceive and implement a whole new domestic order. Full gender equality would mean equality both at work and at home. There is still work to be done on both fronts. Men and women need to commit to and value a larger male domestic role, and employers need to make it easier for their employees to balance work and family responsibilities.

Both fathers and mothers increasingly are seeking jobs that offer flexibility, require less travel, and include paid parental leave (including paternity leave). The United States lags behind other developed nations in providing such benefits, which help workers build long-term careers, as they also fulfill family responsibilities. In fact, the United States is the only developed country that has not adopted mandatory paid parental leave policies. Although a few states and local governments do offer such leave to their employees, most workers have to rely on an employer's decision to offer benefits. Only about 11 percent of American private-sector employers offer paid leave specifically for family reasons.

A quarter of American workers report actual or threatened job loss because of an illness- or family-related absence. The work-family balancing act is particularly challenging for low-wage workers. They tend to have the least workplace flexibility, the most uncertain work hours, and the fewest benefits, and they can least afford to take unpaid leave. The toll is especially hard on single mothers.

The Feminization of Poverty

Alongside the economic gains of many American women, especially the college-educated, stands an opposite extreme: the feminization of poverty. This refers to the increasing representation of women (and their children) among America's poorest people. Table 18.9 shows that the average income of married-couple families is more than twice that of families maintained by a single woman. The median female-headed one-earner family had an annual income of $36,151 in 2014, compared with $81,025 for a married-couple household.

The feminization of poverty isn't just a North American phenomenon. The percentage of single-parent (usually female-headed) households has been increasing worldwide. The figure ranges from about 10 percent in Japan, to between 10 and 20 percent in certain South Asian and southeast Asian countries, to almost 50 percent in certain African countries and the Caribbean. Among the developed Western nations, the United States maintains the largest percentage of single-parent households (around 30 percent), followed by the United Kingdom, Canada, Ireland, and Denmark (over 20 percent in each). Globally, households headed by women tend to be poorer than those

New graduates of the School of Medicine at the University of California, Davis, attend their school's commencement ceremony on May 22, 2010. Women are increasingly prominent among graduates of medical, law, and business schools.
© ZUMA Press Inc/Alamy Stock Photo

headed by men. In the United States in 2014, the poverty rate for female-headed households was 43 percent, compared with 6 percent for married-couple families (DeNavas-Walt and Proctor 2015). More than half the poor children in the United States live in families headed by women (Entmacher et al. 2013).

One way to improve the situation of poor women is to encourage them to organize. Membership in a group can help women gain confidence, mobilize resources, and reduce the risks and costs associated with credit (Dunham 2009). This chapter's "Focus on Globalization" describes an index designed to measure, country by country, gender-based disparities and to track progress in reducing them.

TABLE 18.9 Median Annual Income of U.S. Households, by Household Type, 2014

	NUMBER OF HOUSEHOLDS (1,000s)	MEDIAN ANNUAL INCOME (DOLLARS)	PERCENTAGE OF MEDIAN EARNINGS COMPARED WITH MARRIED-COUPLE HOUSEHOLDS
All households	124,587	53,657	66
Family households	81,716	68,426	84
Married-couple households	60,010	81,025	100
Male earner, no wife	6,162	53,684	66
Female earner, no husband	15,544	36,151	45
Nonfamily households	42,871	32,047	40
Single male	20,143	39,181	48
Single female	22,728	26,673	33

SOURCE: DeNavas-Walt, C., and B. D. Proctor, 2015, "Income and Poverty in the United States: 2014." U.S. Census Bureau, Current Population Reports, P60-252. Washington, DC: U.S. Government Printing Office. https://www.census.gov/content/dam/Census/library/publications/2015/demo/p60-252.pdf, p. 6.

Measuring and Reducing Gender Stratification

One clear indication of gender stratification is the existence of a significant gap between males and females in access to economic opportunity, political participation, education, and health. The World Economic Forum, based in Switzerland, attempts to measure this gap, country by country and year by year. The forum began publishing its annual Global Gender Gap Report in 2006 (see Bekhouche, Hausmann, Tyson, and Zahidi 2015). The report includes an index that assesses gender inequality, and progress in reducing it, in 145 countries, from all regions of the world. For each country, the index measures the gap between males and females in four major categories: economic opportunity and participation, educational attainment, health and survival, and political empowerment.

Most of the indexed countries, representing over 90 percent of the world's population, have reduced their gender gaps, but significant gender stratification remains. Worldwide, 96 percent of the gender gap in health has closed, along with 95 percent in education. Only 59 percent of the economic gap, however, and merely 23 percent of the political gap between men and women have closed. In other words, gender stratification remains most marked in the economic and, especially, the political arenas.

Let's focus on politics and power. Worldwide, 22 women were serving as heads of government at the start of 2016. *Forbes* magazine's 2015 list of the world's most powerful people ranked Angela Merkel, Germany's chancellor, in second place (after Russian president Vladimir Putin, and one position ahead of U.S. president Barack Obama). The next woman in the top 10 (placing seventh) was Janet Yellen, chair of the U.S. Federal Reserve. Besides Merkel, no other female head of state ranked in the top 10, or even the top 30! Indeed, Merkel and Yellen were the only women included among the world's 20 most powerful people. Considering a broader measure of political participation, female representation in ministries, parliaments, and houses of Congress has improved gradually, but still stands at only around 20 percent.

North America has been the world's most successful region in terms of correcting gender-based inequality. Next come Europe and Central Asia, followed by Latin America, Africa, and Asia. The Middle East/North Africa has done the least to reduce gender stratification. Four Nordic countries consistently have held the top positions in the index: Iceland, Norway, Finland, and Sweden—joined in 2015 by Ireland. Although no country has yet achieved full gender equality, those five countries have closed over 80 percent of their gender gaps, considering all criteria. Ranking lowest consistently, Yemen has closed less than 50 percent of its gender gap.

The United States ranked 28th overall in the Global Gender Gap Index in 2015. There was virtually no gender gap in educational attainment. U.S. literacy rates are high for both genders. Rates of enrollment for females and males have been comparable, with American women increasingly surpassing men in attained education. The United States fared less well in terms of economics and politics. While ranking sixth overall in economic participation and opportunity, the United States was only 74th in terms of equal pay for equal work, and 72nd in degree of political empowerment.

To summarize: Worldwide (considering all countries), by 2015, 23 percent of the political empowerment gap had been closed, versus just 14 percent in 2006. In terms of economic participation, 59 percent of the gap had been closed, compared with 56 percent in 2006. In 2015, 95 percent of the educational gap had been closed, progressing a bit from 92 percent in 2006. In terms of health, however, there was a small decline between 2006 and 2014, from 97 percent to 96 percent.

These rates of improvement seem slow, and considerable progress remains to be made. A country's overall economic development tends to reflect its degree of gender equality. Because women represent about half of any national talent base, a country's long-run competitiveness depends on the opportunities it offers its women. How might your country act to reduce its gender gap? (For a copy of the 2015 report, see http://www3.weforum.org/docs/GGGR2015/cover.pdf.)

German Chancellor Angela Merkel (center left) takes a "selfie" with a young constituent in Berlin on April 27, 2016. Is Merkel still the world's most powerful woman?
© Krisztian Bocsi/Bloomberg via Getty Images

Work and Happiness

Table 18.10 lists the 13 countries in which female labor-force participation was greatest in 2014. The highest rate, 84 percent, was in Iceland; the lowest rate among the 13 was in the United States, at 67 percent. Turkey is included in Table 18.10 as an example of a low-participation country, with a rate of 34 percent.

There appears to be a relationship between a country's rate of female labor-force participation and its citizens' feelings of well-being. The *World Happiness Report,* which has been published annually since 2012, is an attempt to measure well-being and happiness in 158 countries. Its measurements are based on a set of six key variables, and a series of lesser ones. The six variables that are related most strongly to a country's sense of well-being are its per-capita gross domestic product (GDP, an indicator of its economic strength), social support, healthy life expectancy, freedom to make life choices, generosity in giving, and perceptions of corruption. The first five are positive variables: As they increase, so does the sense of well-being. The last one, perceptions of corruption, is a negative variable. That is, the less people perceive corruption, the happier they are. The 2015 *World Happiness*

A father and son cooking in the kitchen. In married-couple households, American men have assumed a greater share of domestic and childcare responsibilities, and more single fathers are raising their children.

© Hero/Corbis/Glow Images RF

Report, issued by the Sustainable Development Solutions Network (SDSN), can be found at the following website: http://worldhappiness.report/wp-content/uploads/sites/2/2015/04/WHR15.pdf.

Switzerland was the world's happiest country in 2015, followed by Iceland. Canada came in fifth; and the United States, 15th.

TABLE 18.10 Female Labor Force Participation by Country, 2014–2015

COUNTRY	ADULT FEMALE LABOR FORCE PARTICIPATION (2014)	RANK AMONG WORLD'S 15 "HAPPIEST COUNTRIES" (2015)
Iceland	84	2
Switzerland	79	1
Sweden	79	8
Norway	76	4
Denmark	75	3
New Zealand	74	9
Canada	74	5
Finland	74	6
Netherlands	74	7
Germany	73	*
United Kingdom	72	*
Australia	70	10
United States	67	15
Turkey	34	*

*These countries were not among the 15 "happiest countries."
SOURCE: Organization for Economic Cooperation and Development, https://stats.oecd.org/Index.aspx?DataSetCode=LFS_SEXAGE_I_R; Boyer, L., 2015, These Are the 20 Happiest Countries in the World, *U.S. News & World Report,* April 24, http://www.usnews.com/news/articles/2015/04/24/world-happiness-report-ranks-worlds-happiest-countries-of-2015.

A scientist conducting laboratory research in Reykjavík, Iceland. What do you imagine this woman does when she gets home? Is it common for women to work outside the home in Iceland?

© ARCTIC IMAGES/Alamy Stock Photo

All but two of the countries with the highest female employment also were among the world's happiest. One wonders exactly why, as more women work outside the home, citizens might feel greater sense of well-being. The greater financial security associated with dual-earner households may be part of the explanation. The world's happiest countries not only have more employed women, but they also have a higher living standard and a more secure government safety net. Can you think of other factors that might explain a relationship between happiness and work outside the home?

intersex
Pertaining to a group of biological conditions reflecting a discrepancy between external and internal genitals.

BEYOND MALE AND FEMALE

Gender is socially constructed, and societies may recognize more than two genders (see Nanda 2014). The contemporary United States, for example, includes individuals who may self-identify using such labels as "transgender," "intersex," and "transsexual." Such persons contradict dominant male–female gender distinctions by being part male and part female, or neither male nor female. Because people who self-identify as "transgender" are increasingly visible, we must be careful about seeing "masculine " and "feminine" as absolute and binary categories.

Sex, we have seen, is biological, whereas gender is socially constructed. Transgender is a social category that includes individuals who *may or may not* contrast biologically with ordinary males and females. Within the transgender category, intersex people (see below) usually contrast biologically with ordinary males and females, but *transgender also includes people whose gender identity has no apparent biological roots*.

The distinction between the terms *intersex* and *transgender* is like the distinction between sex and gender. *Intersex* refers to biology, while *transgender* refers to an identity that is socially constructed and individually performed (Butler 1988; 1990; 2015). The term **intersex** encompasses a variety of conditions involving a discrepancy between the external genitals (penis, vagina, etc.) and the internal genitals (testes, ovaries, etc.). The older term for this condition, *hermaphroditism,* combined the names of a Greek god and goddess. Hermes was a god of male sexuality (among other things) and Aphrodite a goddess of female sexuality, love, and beauty.

The causes of intersex are varied and complex (Kaneshiro 2009): (1) An XX intersex person has the chromosomes of a woman (XX) and normal ovaries, uterus, and fallopian tubes, but the external genitals appear male. Usually, this results from a female fetus having been exposed to an excess of male hormones before birth. (2) An XY intersex person has the chromosomes of a man (XY), but the external genitals are incompletely formed, ambiguous, or female. The testes may be normal, malformed, or absent. (3) A true gonadal intersex person has both ovarian and testicular tissue. The external genitals may be ambiguous or may appear to be female or male. (4) Intersex also can result from an unusual chromosome combination, such as X0 (only one X chromosome, and no Y chromosome), XXY, XYY, and XXX. In the last three cases there is an extra sex chromosome, either an X or a Y. These chromosomal combinations don't typically produce a discrepancy between internal and external genitalia, but there may be problems with sex hormone levels and overall sexual development.

The XXY configuration, known as *Klinefelter's syndrome,* is the most common of these chromosomal combinations and the second most common condition (after Down syndrome) caused by the presence of extra chromosomes in humans. Effects of Klinefelter's syndrome occur in about 1 of every 1,000 males. One in every 500 males has an extra X chromosome but lacks the main symptoms—small testicles and reduced fertility. With XXX, also known as *triple X syndrome,* there is an extra X chromosome in each cell of a human female. Triple X occurs in about 1 of every 1,000 female births. There usually is no physically distinguishable difference between triple X women and other women. The same is true of XYY compared with other males. *Turner syndrome* encompasses several conditions, of which 0X (absence of one sex chromosome) is most common. In this case, all or

South Africa's Caster Semenya celebrates her gold medal run in the final of the Women's 800 meters during the World Athletics Championships in Berlin in August 2009. Following that victory, questions were raised about her gender, and she was subjected to gender testing. She was sidelined for 11 months while the tests were reviewed before being cleared to run again in 2010.

© David J. Phillip/AP Images

part of one of the sex chromosomes is absent. Girls with Turner syndrome typically are sterile because of nonworking ovaries and amenorrhea (absence of a menstrual cycle).

Biology, remember, isn't destiny; people construct their identities in society. Many individuals affected by one of the biological conditions just described see themselves simply as male or female, rather than transgender. An individual may become **transgender** when their gender identity contradicts their biological sex at birth and the gender identity that society assigned to them in infancy. Feeling that their previous gender assignment was incorrect, they assert or seek to achieve a new one. The transgender category is diverse. Some transgender individuals lean toward male; some, female; and some toward neither of the dominant genders.

The anthropological record attests that gender diversity beyond male and female exists in many societies and has taken many forms across societies and cultures (see Nanda 2014; Peletz 2009). Consider, for example, the eunuch, or "perfect servant" (a castrated man who served as a safe attendant to harems in Byzantium [Tougher 2008]). Hijras, who live mainly in northern India, are culturally defined as "neither men nor women," or as men who become women by undergoing castration and adopting women's dress and behavior. Hijras identify with the Indian mother goddess and are believed to channel her power. They are known for their ritualized performances at births and marriages, where they dance and sing, conferring the mother goddess's blessing on the child or the married couple. Although culturally defined as celibate, some hijras now engage in prostitution, in which their role is as women with men (Nanda 1996, 1998). Hijra social movements have campaigned for recognition as a third gender, and in 2005, Indian passport application forms were updated with three gender options: M, F, and E (for male, female, and eunuch [i.e., hijra], respectively) (*Telegraph* 2005).

Several Native American tribes, including the Zuni of the American Southwest, included gender-variant individuals, described by the term "Two-Spirit." Depending on the society, as many as four genders might be recognized: feminine women, masculine women, feminine men, and masculine men. The Zuni Two-Spirit was a male who adopted social roles traditionally assigned to women and, through performance of a third gender, contributed to the social and spiritual well-being of the community (Roscoe 1991, 1998). Some Balkan societies included "sworn virgins," born females who assumed male gender roles and activities to meet societal needs when there was a shortage of men (Gremaux 1993).

Among the Gheg tribes of North Albania, "virginal transvestites" were biologically female, but locals consider them "honorary men" (Shryock 1988). Some Albanian adolescent girls have

Neither men nor women, hijras constitute India's third gender. Many hijras get their income from performing at ceremonies, begging, or prostitution. The beauty contest shown here was organized by an AIDS prevention and relief organization that works with the local hijra community.

© Maciej Dakowicz/Alamy Stock Photo

Caitlyn Jenner attends a conference in Rancho Palos Verdes, California, on February 2, 2016.

© Jerod Harris/WireImage via Getty Images

transgender
A gender identity that is socially constructed and performed by individuals whose gender identity contradicts their biological sex at birth and the gender identity assigned to them in infancy.

Hidden Women, Public Men—Public Women, Hidden Men

Generations of anthropologists have applied their field's comparative, cross-cultural, and biocultural approaches to the study of sex and gender. To some extent at least, gender, sexual preferences, and even sexual orientation are culturally constructed. Here I describe a case in which popular culture and comments by ordinary Brazilians about beauty and sex led me to an analysis of some striking gender differences between Brazil and the United States.

For several years, one of Brazil's top sex symbols was Roberta Close, whom I first saw in a furniture commercial. Roberta ended her pitch with an admonition to prospective furniture buyers to accept no substitute for the advertised product. "Things," she warned, "are not always what they seem."

Nor was Roberta. Although petite and very feminine, Roberta was actually a man. Furthermore, despite the fact that Roberta was a man posing as a woman, he (or more appropriately, she) won a secure place in Brazilian mass culture. Her photos decorated magazines. She was a panelist on a TV variety show and starred in a

stage play in Rio with an actor known for his supermacho image. Roberta even inspired a well-known, and apparently heterosexual, pop singer to make a video honoring her. In it, she strolled seductively around Rio's Ipanema Beach in a bikini, showing off her ample hips and buttocks.

The video depicted the widespread male appreciation of Roberta's beauty. As confirmation, one heterosexual man told me he had recently been on the same plane as Roberta and had been struck by her looks. Another man said he wanted to have sex with her. These comments, it seemed to me, illustrated striking cultural contrasts about gender and sexuality. In Brazil, a Latin American country noted for its machismo, heterosexual men did not feel that attraction toward a transvestite blemished their masculine identities.

Roberta Close can be understood in relation to a gender-identity scale that jumps from extreme femininity to extreme masculinity, with little in between. In Brazil, masculinity has been stereotyped as active and public, femininity as passive and domestic. The male–female contrast in rights and behavior is much stronger in

Brazil than it is in North America. Brazilians confront a more rigidly defined masculine role than North Americans do.

The active–passive dichotomy also provides a stereotypical model for male–male sexual relations. One man is supposed to be the active, masculine (inserting) partner, whereas the other is the passive, effeminate one. The latter man is derided as a *bicha* (intestinal worm), but little stigma attaches to the inserter. Indeed, many "active" (and heterosexually married) Brazilian men like to have sex with transvestite prostitutes, who are biological males.

If a Brazilian man is unhappy pursuing either active masculinity or passive effeminacy, there is one other choice—active femininity. For Roberta Close and others like her, the cultural demand of ultramasculinity has yielded to a performance of ultrafemininity. These men–women form a third gender in relation to Brazil's polarized male–female identity scale.

Transvestites like Roberta, called *travestis* in Portuguese, are particularly prominent in Rio de Janeiro's annual Carnaval, when an ambience of

chosen to become men, remain celibate, and live among men, with the support of their families and villagers (Young 2000). And consider Polynesia. In Tonga the term *fakaleitis* describes males who behave as women do, thereby contrasting with mainstream Tongan men. Similar to Tonga's *fakaleitis,* Samoan *fa'afafine* and Hawaiian *mahu* are men who adopt feminine attributes, behaviors, and visual markers.

This chapter's "Appreciating Anthropology" describes how Brazilian *travestis* (men dressing and acting as women) form a third gender in relation to Brazil's polarized male–female identity scale (see also Kulick 1998). Transvestites, not uncommon in Brazil, are members of one gender (usually males) who dress as another (female). At the time of the case described in "Appreciating Anthropology," a Brazilian man who wished to have gender reassignment surgery could not

obtain the operation in Brazil. Individuals seeking gender reassignment, such as Roberta Close, as described in "Appreciating Anthropology," traveled to Europe for the procedure. In France, transvestites (men dressing as women) regardless of nationality commonly are referred to as "Brésiliennes" (the feminine form of the French word for *Brazilian*), so common are Brazilians among the transvestites in Europe. In Brazil, many "heterosexual" men do have sexual relations with *travestis,* with little stigma attached, as described in "Appreciating Anthropology."

The category transgender encompasses varied individuals whose gender performance and identity enlarge an otherwise binary gender structure. Transgender individuals are increasingly visible in the media and our everyday lives. The Amazon television series *Transparent,* whose principal character is a transgender

ceremonial inversion rules the city. In the culturally accurate words of the American popular novelist Gregory McDonald, who sets one of his books in Brazil at Carnaval time:

> Everything goes topsy-turvy. . . . Men become women; women become men; grownups become children; rich people pretend they're poor; poor people, rich; sober people become drunkards; thieves become generous. Very topsy-turvy. (McDonald 1984, p. 154)

Most notable in this costumed inversion (DaMatta 1991), men dress as women. Carnaval reveals and expresses normally hidden tensions and conflicts as social life is turned upside down. Reality is illuminated through a dramatic presentation of its opposite.

This is the final key to Roberta Close's cultural meaning. She emerged in a setting in which male–female inversion is part of the year's most popular festival. *Travestis* are featured prominently at Rio's Carnaval balls, where they dress as scantily as the real women do. They wear postage-stamp bikinis, sometimes with no tops. Photos of real women and transformed ones vie for space in the magazines. It is often impossible to tell the born women from the hidden men. Roberta Close is a permanent incarnation of Carnaval—a year-round reminder of the spirit of Carnavals past, present, and yet to come.

Roberta Close, photographed in 1999, at age 35. In 1989, Close underwent sex reassignment surgery in England. Subsequently she was voted the "Most Beautiful Woman in Brazil." She now lives with her husband in Switzerland.
© Ricardo Gomes/Globo via Getty Images

Roberta Close emerged from a Latin culture whose gender roles contrast strongly with those of the United States. From small village to massive city, public areas including streets, bars, soccer fields, and stadiums tend to be dominated by men. Although bikinis adorn Rio's beaches on weekends and holidays, there are many more men than women there on weekdays. The men revel in their ostentatiously sexual displays. As they sun themselves and play soccer and volleyball, they regularly stroke their genitals to keep them firm. They are living publicly, assertively, and sexually in a public world of men.

Brazilian men must work hard at this public image, constantly performing their culture's definition of masculinity and their gender identity as a man. Public life is a play whose strong roles go to men. Roberta Close, of course, has been a public figure. Given that Brazilian culture defines the public world as male, we can perhaps better understand now why a popular Brazilian sex symbol could be a man who excels at performing in public as a woman.

woman, has received several awards. The emergence of Caitlyn Jenner as a transgender woman received considerable media attention in 2015, including her own television show. Facebook now offers more than 50 gender options (Miller 2015). There have been various recent attempts to estimate the transgender population of the United States. The U.S. Census Bureau attempted such an estimate based on census records of people whose name change suggested a gender switch (Miller 2015). Of Americans who participated in the 2010 census, about 90,000 had changed their names to one of the opposite gender. Another estimate examined survey data and estimated that 0.3 percent of the American population, or 700,000 adults, were likely transgender (see Miller 2015).

In recent years, the lesbian and gay rights movement has expanded to include bisexual and transgender individuals. This lesbian, gay, bisexual, and transgender (LGBT) community in the United States works to promote government policies and social practices that protect its members' civil and human rights. In recent years, the LGBT movement and its supporters have achieved many successes, including the repeal of the Defense of Marriage Act (DOMA) and of the "Don't Ask Don't Tell" (DADT) policy of the U.S. armed services. The most notably achievement has been the legalization of same-sex marriage throughout the United States as of 2015. With reference specifically to transgender rights, states that have enacted laws prohibiting discrimination based on sexual identity, such as Washington, Oregon, and Vermont, have larger shares of transgender people than do states without such laws (Miller 2015).

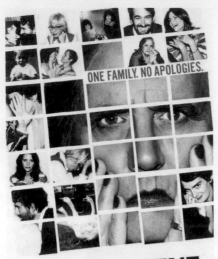

A poster for the TV series Transparent, available through Amazon streaming. Jeffrey Tambor is the cisgender man who plays the lead—a transgender woman—in this series.

© Hand-out/shomi/Newscom

SEXUAL ORIENTATION

gender identity
A person's identification by self and others as male, female, or something else.

sexual orientation
Sexual attraction to persons of the opposite sex, same sex, or both sexes.

Gender identity refers to whether a person feels, acts, and is regarded as, male, female, or something else. One's gender identity does not dictate one's sexual orientation. Men who have no doubt about their masculinity can be sexually attracted to women or to other men. Ditto women with regard to female gender identity and variable sexual attraction. **Sexual orientation** refers to a person's habitual sexual attraction to, and sexual activities with, persons of the opposite sex, *heterosexuality;* the same sex, *homosexuality;* or both sexes, *bisexuality. Asexuality,* indifference toward or lack of attraction to either sex, also is a sexual orientation. All four of these forms are found throughout the world. But each type of desire and experience holds different meanings for individuals and groups. For example, male–male sexual activity may be a private affair in Mexico, rather than public, socially sanctioned, and encouraged as it was among the Etoro of Papua New Guinea.

In any society, individuals will differ in the nature, range, and intensity of their sexual interests and urges (see Blackwood 2010; Herdt and Polen 2013; Hyde and DeLamater 2016; Lyons and Lyons 2011; Nanda 2014). No one knows for sure why such individual sexual differences exist. Part of the answer appears to be biological, reflecting genes or hormones. Another part may have to do with experiences during growth and development. But whatever the reasons for individual variation, culture always plays a role in molding individual sexual urges toward a collective norm. And such sexual norms vary from culture to culture.

What do we know about variation in sexual norms from society to society, and over time? A classic cross-cultural study (Ford and Beach 1951) found wide variation in attitudes about forms of sexual activity. Even in a single society, such as the United States, attitudes about sex vary over time and with socioeconomic status, region, and rural versus urban residence. However, even in the 1950s, prior to the "age of sexual permissiveness" (the pre-HIV period from the mid-1960s through the 1970s), research showed that almost all American men (92 percent) and more than half of American women (54 percent) admitted to masturbation. In the famous Kinsey report (Kinsey, Pomeroy, and Martin 1948), 37 percent of the men surveyed admitted having had at least one sexual experience leading to orgasm with another male. In a later study of 1,200 unmarried women, 26 percent reported same-sex sexual activities. (Because Kinsey's research relied on nonrandom samples, it should be considered merely illustrative, rather than a statistically accurate representation, of sexual behavior at the time.)

In almost two-thirds (63 percent) of the 76 societies in the Ford and Beach study, various forms of same-sex sexual activity were acceptable. Occasionally sexual relations between people of the same sex involved transvestism on the part of one of the partners (see Kulick 1998). Transvestism did not characterize male–male sex among the Sudanese Azande, who valued the warrior role (Evans-Pritchard 1970). Prospective warriors—young men aged 12 to 20—left their families and shared quarters with adult fighting men, who had sex with them. The younger men were considered temporary brides of the older men and did the domestic duties of women. Upon reaching warrior status, these young men took their own younger male brides. Later, retiring from the warrior role, Azande men married women. Flexible in their sexual expression, Azande males had no difficulty shifting from sex with older men (as male brides), to sex with younger men (as warriors), to sex with women (as husbands) (see Murray and Roscoe 1998).

An extreme example of tension involving male–female sexual relations in Papua New Guinea is provided by the Etoro (Kelly 1976), a group of 400 people who subsisted by hunting and horticulture in the Trans-Fly region (Figure 18.2). The Etoro illustrate the power of culture in molding human sexuality. The following account, based on ethnographic fieldwork by Raymond C. Kelly in the late 1960s, applies only to Etoro males and their beliefs. Etoro cultural norms prevented the male anthropologist who studied them from gathering comparable information about female attitudes and behavior. Note, also, that the activities described have been discouraged by

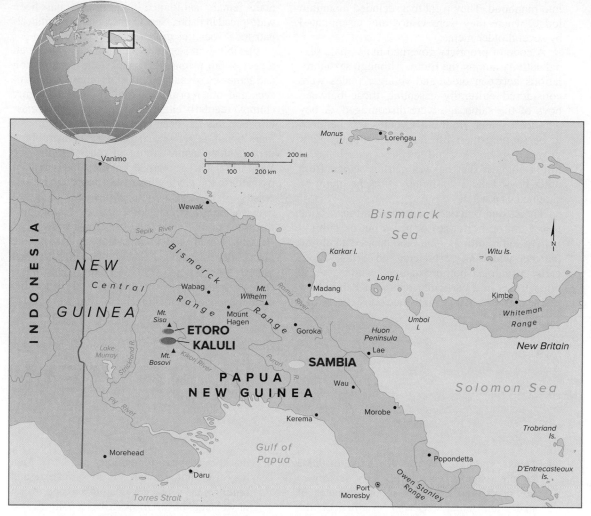

FIGURE 18.2 The Location of the Etoro, Kaluli, and Sambia in Papua New Guinea.
The western part of the island of New Guinea is part of Indonesia. The eastern part of the island is the independent nation of Papua New Guinea, home of the Etoro, Kaluli, and Sambia.

missionaries. Since there has been no restudy of the Etoro specifically focusing on these activities, the extent to which these practices continue today is unknown. For this reason, I'll use the past tense in describing them.

Etoro opinions about sexuality were linked to their beliefs about the cycle of birth, physical growth, maturity, old age, and death. Etoro culture promoted the idea that semen was necessary to give life force to a fetus, which, they believed, was implanted in a woman by an ancestral spirit. A man was required to have sexual intercourse with his wife during her pregnancy in order to nourish the growing fetus. The Etoro believed, however, that men had a limited lifetime supply of semen. Any sex act leading to ejaculation was seen as draining that supply, and as sapping a man's virility and vitality. The birth of children, nurtured by semen, symbolized a necessary sacrifice that would lead to the husband's eventual death. Male–female intercourse, required for reproduction, was otherwise discouraged. Women

who wanted too much sex were viewed as witches, hazardous to their husbands' health. Furthermore, Etoro culture allowed male–female intercourse only about 100 days a year. The rest of the time it was tabooed. Seasonal birth clustering shows the taboo was respected.

So objectionable was male–female sex that it was removed from community life. It could occur neither in sleeping quarters nor in the fields. Coitus could happen only in the woods, where it was risky because poisonous snakes, the Etoro believed, were attracted by the sounds and smells of male–female sex.

Although coitus was discouraged, sex acts between males were viewed as essential. Etoro believed that boys would not produce semen on their own. To grow into men and eventually give life force to their children, boys had to acquire semen orally from older men. No taboos were attached to this. This oral insemination could proceed in the sleeping area or garden. Every three years, young men around the age of 20 were formally initiated into manhood. They went to a secluded mountain lodge, where they were visited and inseminated by several older men.

A code of propriety governed male–male sexual activity among the Etoro. Although sexual relations between older and younger males were considered culturally essential, those between boys of the same age were discouraged. A boy who took semen from other youths was believed to be sapping their life force and stunting their growth. A boy's rapid physical development might suggest that he was getting semen from other boys. Like a sex-hungry wife, he might be shunned as a witch.

The sexual practices described in this section rested not on hormones or genes but on cultural beliefs and traditions. The Etoro shared a cultural pattern, which Gilbert Herdt (ed. 1984, 2006) calls "ritualized homosexuality," with some 50 other tribes in a particular region of Papua New Guinea. These societies illustrate one extreme of a male–female avoidance pattern that has been widespread in Papua New Guinea, and in patrilineal-patrilocal societies more generally.

Flexibility in sexual expression seems to be an aspect of our primate heritage. Both masturbation and same-sex sexual activity exist among chimpanzees and other primates. Male bonobos (pygmy chimps) regularly engage in a form of mutual masturbation that has been called "penis fencing." Female bonobos get sexual pleasure from rubbing their genitals against those of other females (de Waal 1997). Our primate sexual potential is molded by culture, the environment, and reproductive necessity. Male–female coitus is practiced in all human societies—which, after all, must reproduce themselves—but alternatives also are widespread (Rathus, Nevid, and Fichner-Rathus 2014). Like our gender roles, the sexual component of human identity—the ways in which we express our "natural," or biological, sexual urges—is a matter that culture and environment influence and limit.

for REVIEW

summary

1. *Gender roles* are the tasks and activities that a culture assigns to each sex. *Gender stereotypes* are oversimplified ideas about attributes of males and females. *Gender stratification* describes an unequal distribution of rewards by gender, reflecting different positions in a social hierarchy. Cross-cultural comparison reveals some recurrent patterns involving the division of labor by gender and gender-based differences in reproductive strategies. Gender roles and gender stratification also vary with environment, economy, adaptive strategy, level of social complexity, and degree of participation in the world economy.

2. When gathering is prominent, gender status is more equal than it is when hunting or fishing dominates the foraging economy. Gender status is more equal when the domestic and public spheres aren't sharply separated. Foragers lack two public arenas that contribute to higher male status among food producers: warfare and organized interregional trade.

3. Gender stratification also is linked to descent and residence. Women's status in matrilineal societies tends to be high because overall social identity comes through female links. Women in many societies, especially matrilineal ones, wield power and make decisions. Scarcity of resources promotes intervillage warfare, patriliny, and patrilocality. The localization of related males is adaptive for military solidarity. Men may use their warrior role to symbolize and reinforce the social devaluation and oppression of women. *Patriarchy* describes a political system ruled by men in which women have inferior social and political status, including basic human rights.

4. Americans' attitudes toward gender vary with class and region. When the need for female labor declines, the idea that women are unfit for many jobs increases, and vice versa. Factors such as war, falling wages, and inflation help explain female cash employment and Americans' attitudes toward it. The need for flexible employment, permitting a proper balance of work and family responsibilities, is increasingly important to both male and female workers. Despite the increased participation by women in the labor force and higher education, and by men in the domestic realm, including child care, barriers to full equality remain. Countering the economic gains of many American women is the feminization of poverty. This has become a global phenomenon, as impoverished female-headed households have increased worldwide.

5. Societies may recognize more than two genders. The term *intersex* describes a group of conditions, including chromosomal configurations, that may produce a discrepancy between external and internal genitals. Transgender individuals

may or may not contrast biologically with ordinary males and females. Self-identified transgender people tend to be individuals whose gender identity contradicts their biological sex at birth and the gender identity that society assigned to them in infancy.

6. *Gender identity* refers to whether a person feels, and is regarded as, male, female, or something else. One's gender identity does not dictate one's sexual orientation. *Sexual orientation* stands for a person's habitual sexual attraction to, and activities with, persons of the opposite sex (heterosexuality), the same sex (homosexuality), or both sexes (bisexuality). Sexual norms and practices vary widely from culture to culture.

key terms

critical thinking

1. How are sexuality, sex, and gender related to one another? What are the differences between these three concepts? Provide an argument about why anthropologists are uniquely positioned to study the relationships among sexuality, sex, and gender in society.

2. Using your own society, give an example of a gender role, a gender stereotype, and gender stratification.

3. What is the feminization of poverty? Where is this trend occurring, and what are some of its causes?

4. Is intersex the same as transgender? If not, how do they differ? How might biological, cultural, and personal factors influence gender identity?

5. This chapter describes Raymond Kelly's research among the Etoro of Papua New Guinea. What were his findings regarding Etoro male–female sexual relations? How did Kelly's own gender affect some of the content and extent of his study? Can you think of other research projects where the ethnographer's gender would have an impact?

Families, Kinship, and Descent

© Wang Song/Xinhua Press/Corbis

A family reunion celebrating the Chinese Lunar New Year outside a cave dwelling in central China's Henan Province.

▶ Why and how do anthropologists study kinship?

▶ How do families and descent groups differ, and what are their social correlates?

▶ How is kinship calculated, and how are relatives classified, in various societies?

understanding OURSELVES

Although it still is something of an ideal in our culture, the nuclear family (mother, father, and biological children) now accounts for less than one-fifth of all American households. Such phrases as "marriage and the family" and "mom and pop" no longer apply to a majority of American households. What kind of family raised you? Perhaps it was a nuclear family. Or maybe you were raised by a single parent, with or without the help of extended kin. Perhaps your extended kin acted as your parents. Or maybe you had a stepparent and/or step- or half-siblings in a blended family. Your own family may match none of these descriptions, or it may have had different descriptions at different times.

Although contemporary American families may seem amazingly diverse, other cultures offer family alternatives that Americans might have trouble understanding. Imagine a society in which someone doesn't know for sure, and doesn't care much about, who his actual mother was. Consider Joseph Rabe, a Betsileo man who was my field assistant in Madagascar. Illustrating an adoptive pattern common among the Betsileo, Rabe was given as a toddler to his childless aunt, his father's sister. He knew that his birth mother lived far away, but did not know which of two sisters in his birth mother's family was his actual mother. His

mother and her sister both died in his childhood (as did his father), so he didn't really know them. But he was very close to his father's sister, for whom he used the term for mother. Indeed, he had to call her that because the Betsileo have only one kin term, *reny,* for mother, mother's sister, and father's sister. (They also use a single term, *ray,* for father and all uncles.) The difference between "real" (biologically based) and socially constructed kinship didn't matter to Rabe.

Contrast this Betsileo case with Americans' attitudes about kinship and adoption. On family-oriented radio talk shows, I've heard hosts distinguish between "birth mothers" and adoptive mothers, and between "sperm daddies" and "daddies of the heart." The latter may be adoptive fathers or stepfathers who have "been like fathers" to someone. American culture tends to promote the idea that kinship is, and should be, biological. It's increasingly common for adopted children to seek out their birth parents (which used to be discouraged as disruptive), even after a perfectly satisfactory upbringing in an adoptive family. The American emphasis on biology for kinship is seen also in the recent proliferation of DNA testing. Viewing our beliefs through the lens of cross-cultural comparison helps us appreciate that kinship and biology don't always converge, nor do they need to.

FAMILIES

The kinds of societies anthropologists have studied traditionally, including many examples considered in this chapter, have stimulated a strong interest in families, along with larger systems of kinship, descent, and marriage. Cross-culturally, the social construction

of kinship illustrates considerable diversity. Understanding kinship systems has become an essential part of anthropology because of the importance of those systems to the people we study. We are ready to take a closer look at the systems of kinship and descent that have organized human life during much of our history.

family of orientation
The nuclear family in which one is born and grows up.

family of procreation
The nuclear family established when one marries and has children.

descent group
A group based on belief in shared ancestry.

Ethnographers quickly recognize social divisions—groups—within any society they study. During fieldwork, they learn about significant groups by observing their activities and composition. People often live in the same village or neighborhood, or work, pray, or celebrate together because they are related in some way. To understand the social structure, an ethnographer must investigate such kin ties. For example, the most significant local groups may consist of descendants of the same grandfather. These people may live in neighboring houses, farm adjoining fields, and help each other in everyday tasks. Other sorts of groups, based on different or more distant kin links, get together less often.

One kind of kin group that is widespread is the nuclear family, consisting of parents and children, who normally live together in the same household. Other kin groups include extended families and descent groups. Extended families are those that include three or more generations. Members of an extended family get together from time to time, but they don't necessarily live together. **Descent groups** include people who share common ancestry—they *descend* from the same ancestor(s). Descent groups typically are spread out among several villages, so that all their members do not reside together; only some of them do—those who live in a given village. Descent groups tend to be found in societies with economies based on horticulture, pastoralism, or agriculture.

Nuclear and Extended Families

Most people belong to at least two nuclear families at different times in their lives. They are born into a family consisting of their parents and siblings.

Outside their village home (which lacks running water) in Bamyan province, Afghanistan, Noor Ahmad, 15, washes dishes with his sister, Aqila, 8. Siblings play a prominent role in child rearing in many societies. Do your siblings belong to your family of orientation or procreation?

© Majority World/UIG via Getty Images

Reaching adulthood, they may establish a nuclear family that includes their spouse (or domestic partner) and eventually their children. Some people establish more than one family through successive marriages or domestic partnerships.

Anthropologists distinguish between the **family of orientation** (the family in which one is born and grows up) and the **family of procreation** (formed when one has children). From the individual's point of view, the critical relationships are with parents and siblings in the family of orientation and with spouse (or domestic partner) and children in the family of procreation.

In most societies, relations with nuclear family members (parents, siblings, and children) take precedence over relations with other kin. Nuclear family organization is very widespread but not universal, and its significance in society differs greatly from one place to another. In a few societies, such as the classic Nayar case (described on p. 369), nuclear families are rare or nonexistent. In others, the nuclear family plays no special role in social life. Other social units, such as extended families and descent groups, can assume many of the functions otherwise associated with the nuclear family.

The following example from Bosnia illustrates how an extended family—known as the *zadruga*—can be the most important kinship unit, overshadowing the nuclear family. Among the Muslims of western Bosnia (Lockwood 1975), nuclear families did not exist as independent units. People customarily resided in a household called a *zadruga*. Living in this household was an extended family headed by a senior man and his wife, the senior woman. Also living in the *zadruga* were their married sons and their wives and children, as well as unmarried sons and daughters. Each married couple had a sleeping room, decorated and partly furnished from the bride's trousseau. However, possessions—even clothing items—were freely shared by *zadruga* members. Even trousseau items could be used by other *zadruga* members.

Within the *zadruga*, social interaction was more usual among its women, its men, or its children than between spouses, or between parents and children. When the *zadruga* was particularly large, its members ate at three successive settings: for men, women, and children, respectively. Traditionally, all children over 12 slept together in boys' or girls' rooms. When a woman wanted to visit another village, she asked permission not from her husband, but from the male *zadruga* head. Although men may have felt closer to their own children than to those of their brothers, they were obliged to treat all of the *zadruga*'s children equally. Any adult in the household could discipline a child. When a marriage broke up, children under 7 went with the mother. Older children could choose between their parents. Children were considered part of the household where they were born even if their mother left. One widow who remarried had to leave her five children, all over 7, in their father's *zadruga,* headed by his brother.

Another example of an alternative to the nuclear family is provided by the Nayars (or Nair), a large and powerful caste on the Malabar Coast of southern India (Figure 19.1). Their traditional kinship system was matrilineal (descent traced only through females). Nayar lived in matrilineal extended family compounds called *tarawads.* The *tarawad* was a residential complex with several buildings, its own temple, granary, water well, orchards, gardens, and landholdings. Headed by a senior woman, assisted by her brother, the *tarawad* housed children, siblings, her sisters' children, and other matrikin—matrilineal relatives (Gough 1959; Shivaram 1996).

Traditional Nayar marriage was barely more than a formality—a kind of coming-of-age ritual. A young woman would go through a marriage ceremony with a man, after which they might spend a few days together at her *tarawad.* Then the man would return to his own *tarawad,* where he lived with his mother, aunts, uncles, siblings, and other matrikin. Nayar men belonged to a warrior class, who left home regularly for military expeditions, returning permanently to their *tarawad* on retirement. Nayar women could have multiple sexual partners. Children became members of the mother's *tarawad;* they were not considered to be relatives of their biological father. Indeed, many Nayar children didn't even know who their father was. Child care was the responsibility of the *tarawad.* Nayar society therefore reproduced itself biologically without the nuclear family.

Industrialism and Family Organization

The geographic mobility associated with industrialism works to fragment kinship groups larger than the nuclear family. As people move, often for economic reasons, they are separated from their parents and other kin. Eventually, most North Americans will enter a marriage or domestic partnership and establish a family of procreation. With only about 2 percent of the U.S. population now working in farming, relatively few Americans are tied to the land—to a family farm or estate. A nonfarming nation can be a mobile nation. Americans can move to places where jobs are available, even if they have to leave home to do so. Individuals and married couples often live hundreds of miles from their parents. Usually, their jobs have played a major role in determining where they live (see Descartes and Kottak 2009). This pattern of postmarital residence, in which married couples establish a new place of residence away from their parents, is called **neolocality**.

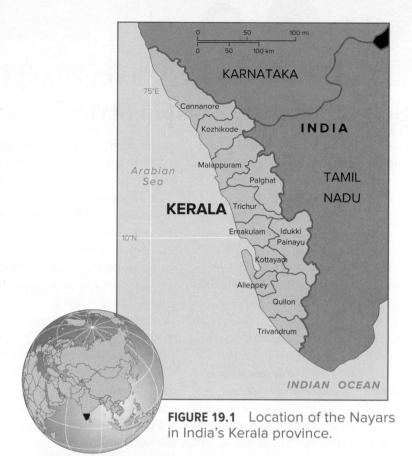

FIGURE 19.1 Location of the Nayars in India's Kerala province.

A matrilineal extended family of the Khasi ethnic group in India's northeastern city of Shillong. The Khasis trace descent through women, taking their maternal ancestors' surnames. Women choose their husbands; family incomes are pooled, and extended family households are managed by older women.
© DINODIA/Dinodia Photo/age fotostock

The prefix *neo* means new; the couple establishes a new residence, a "home of their own." For middle-class North Americans, neolocality is both a cultural preference and a statistical norm. That is, they both want to, and eventually do, establish homes and nuclear families of their own.

neolocality
The living situation in which a couple establishes new residence.

appreciating DIVERSITY

Social Security, Kinship Style

In all societies, people care for others. Sometimes, as in our own state-organized society, social security is a function of government as well as of the individual and the family. In other societies, such as Arembepe, as described here, social security is part of systems of kinship, marriage, and fictive kinship.

My book *Assault on Paradise,* 4th edition (Kottak 2006), describes social relations in Arembepe, the Brazilian fishing community I've studied for many years. When I first studied Arembepe, I was struck by how similar its social relations were to those in the egalitarian, kin-based societies anthropologists have studied traditionally. The twin assertions "We're all equal here" and "We're all relatives here" were offered repeatedly as Arembepeiros' summaries of the nature and basis of local life. Like members of a clan (who claim to share common ancestry but who can't say exactly how they are related), most villagers couldn't trace precise genealogical links to their distant kin. "What difference does it make, as long as we know we're relatives?"

As in most nonindustrial societies, close personal relations were either based or modeled on kinship. A degree of community solidarity was promoted, for example, by the myth that everyone was kin. However, social solidarity was actually less developed in Arembepe than in societies with clans and lineages—which use genealogy to include some people, and exclude others from membership, in a given descent group. Intense social solidarity demands that some people be excluded. By asserting they all were related—that is, by excluding no one— Arembepeiros were actually weakening kinship's potential strength in creating and maintaining group solidarity.

Rights and obligations always are associated with kinship and marriage. In Arembepe, the closer the kin connection and the more formal the marital tie, the greater the rights and obligations. Couples could be married formally or informally. The most common union was a stable common-law marriage. Less common, but with more prestige, was legal (civil) marriage, performed by a justice of the peace and conferring inheritance rights. The union with the most prestige combined legal validity with a church ceremony.

The rights and obligations associated with kinship and marriage constituted the local social security system, but people had to weigh the benefits of the system against its costs. The most obvious cost was this: Villagers had to share in proportion to their success. As people (usually ambitious men) climbed the local ladder of success, they got more dependents. To maintain their standing in public opinion, and to guarantee that they could depend on others in old

An extended family of *cocoteros,* workers on a coconut plantation in the rural town of Barigua in eastern Cuba. Try to guess the relationships among them.
© James Quine/Alamy Stock Photo

It should be noted, however, that there are significant differences involving kinship between middle-class and poorer North Americans. One example is the association between poverty and single-parent households. Another example is the higher incidence of *expanded family households* among Americans who are less well off. An **expanded family household** is one that includes a group of relatives other than, or in addition to, a married couple and their children. Expanded family households take various forms. When the expanded household includes three or more generations, it is an **extended family household**, like the Bosnian *zadruga.* Another type of expanded family household is the *collateral household,* which includes siblings and their spouses and children. Yet another form is a *matrifocal household,* which is headed by a woman and includes other adult relatives and children.

The higher proportion of expanded family households among poorer Americans has been explained as an adaptation to poverty (Stack 1975). Unable to survive economically as independent

age, they had to share. However, sharing was a powerful leveling mechanism. It drained surplus wealth and restricted upward mobility.

How, specifically, did this leveling work? As is often true in stratified nations, Brazilian national cultural norms are set by the upper classes. Middle- and upper-class Brazilians usually marry legally and in church. Even Arembepeiros knew this was the only "proper" way to marry. The most successful and ambitious local men copied the behavior of elite Brazilians. By doing so, they hoped to acquire some of their prestige.

However, legal marriage drained individual wealth, for example, by creating an obligation to offer financial assistance to one's in-laws. Responsibilities involving children also increased with income, because children had better survival chances in wealthier households than in poorer ones. Adequate incomes bought improved diets and provided the means and confidence to seek out better medical attention than was locally available. More living children meant more mouths to feed, and (since the heads of such households usually wanted a better education for their children) increased expenditures on schooling. The correlation between economic success and large families was a siphoner of wealth that restricted individual economic advance. Tomé, a fishing entrepreneur, envisioned a life of constant hard work if he was to feed, clothe, and educate his growing family. Unlike most Arembepeiros, Tomé and his wife had never lost a child. He recognized, however, that his growing family would, in the short run, be a drain on his resources. "But in the end, I'll have successful sons to help their mother and me, if we need it, in our old age."

Arembepeiros knew who could afford to share with others; success can't be concealed in a small community. Villagers based their expectations of others on this knowledge. Successful people had to share with more kin and in-laws, and with more distant kin, than did poorer people. Captains and boat owners were expected to buy beer for ordinary fishermen; store owners had to sell on credit. As in bands and tribes, any well-off person was expected to exhibit a corresponding generosity. With increasing wealth, people also were asked more frequently to enter ritual kin relationships. Through baptism—which took place twice a year when a priest visited, or which could be done outside—a child acquired two godparents. These people became the coparents (compadres) of the baby's parents. The fact that ritual kinship obligations increased with wealth was another factor limiting individual economic advance.

We see that kinship, marriage, and ritual kinship in Arembepe had costs and benefits. The costs were limits on the economic advance of individuals. The primary benefit was social security—guaranteed help from kin, in-laws, and ritual kin in times of need. Benefits, however, came only after costs had been paid—that is, only to those who had lived "proper" lives, not deviating too noticeably from local norms, especially those about sharing.

nuclear family units, relatives band together in an expanded household and pool their resources (see Hansen 2005). (This chapter's "Appreciating Diversity" shows how poor Brazilians use kinship, marriage, and fictive kinship as a form of social security.)

Changes in North American Kinship

The nuclear family may remain a cultural ideal for many Americans, but, as we see in Table 19.1 and Figure 19.2, nuclear families now account for less than one-fifth of American households. Other domestic arrangements now outnumber the "traditional" American household more than five to one (see Golombok 2015). There are several reasons for this changing household composition. Women increasingly have joined men in the cash workforce. Often, this removes them from their family of orientation while making it economically feasible to delay (or even forgo) marriage. Often, job demands compete with romantic attachments.

The median age at first marriage for American women in 2015 was 27 years, compared with 21 years in 1970. For men the comparable ages were 29 and 23. More than a third (35 percent) of American men and 30 percent of American women had never married as of 2015.

What about divorce? The number of divorced Americans increased sixfold, from 1970 to 2015, from 4.3 million to 26 million people. (Note, however, that each divorce creates two divorced people.) Table 19.2 shows the ratio of divorces to marriages in the United States for selected years between 1950 and 2014. The divorce rate jumped between 1960 and 1980 as the ratio of divorces to marriages doubled. Thereafter, between 1980 and 2000, the ratio hovered around 50 percent. That is, each year there were about half as many new divorces as there were new marriages. Since 2000 the rate has stabilized and even declined recently, falling to 46 percent in 2014.

The growth of single-parent families also has outstripped population growth, tripling from fewer than 4 million in 1970 to 12 million in 2015. (The

expanded family household
A household that includes a group of relatives other than, or in addition to, a married couple and their children.

extended family household
A household with three or more generations.

TABLE 19.1 Changes in Family and Household Organization in the United States, 2015 Compared with 1970

	1970	2015
Numbers		
Total number of households	63 million	125 million
Number of people per household	3.1	2.5
Percentages:		
Married couples living with children	40%	19%
Married couples without children	30%	29%
Family households	81%	66%
Households with five or more people	21%	10%
People living alone	17%	28%
Percentage of single-mother families	5%	13%
Percentage of single-father families	0%	5%
Percentage of households with children under 18	45%	29%

SOURCE: Jonathan Vespa, Jamie M. Lewis, and Rose M. Kreider, 2013, "America's Families and Living Arrangements: 2012," Current Population Reports, P20-570, U.S. Census Bureau, Washington, DC. https://www.census.gov/prod/2013pubs/p20-570.pdf; http://www.census.gov/hhes/families/data/cps2015.html

overall American population in 2015 was about 1.6 times its size in 1970.) Most of those single-parent families (83 percent) are single-mother families, leaving 17 percent as single-father families. Fewer than half (47 percent) of American women lived with a husband in 2015, compared with 65 percent in 1950. The proportion of single-person households—people living alone—rose from only 17 percent in 1970 to 28 percent in 2015.

Household size in both the United States and Canada has declined from 2.9 in 1980 to 2.5 today. The typical American family has 3.1 members versus 3.3 in 1980 (see Table 19.3). The trend toward smaller families and living units also is detectable in Western Europe and other industrial nations. To be sure, contemporary Americans maintain social lives through school, work, friendship, sports, clubs, religion, and organized social activities. However, the growing isolation from kin that these figures suggest may well be unprecedented in human history.

The entire range of kin attachments is narrower for North Americans, particularly those in the middle class, than it is for nonindustrial peoples. Although we recognize ties to grandparents, uncles, aunts, and cousins, we have less contact with, and depend less on, those relatives than people in other cultures do. We see this when we answer a few questions: Do we know exactly how we are related to all our cousins? How much do we know about our ancestors, such as their full names and where they lived? How many of the people with whom we associate regularly are our relatives?

Differences in the answers to these questions by people from industrial and

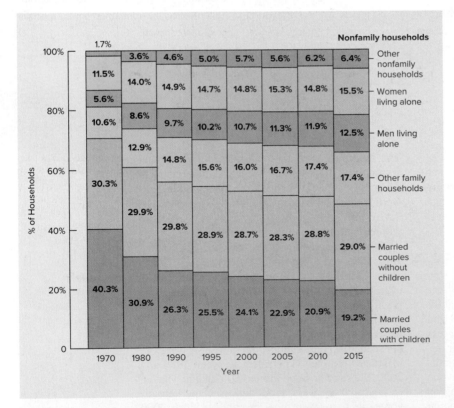

FIGURE 19.2 Households by Type: Selected Years, 1970 to 2015 (Percent Distribution).

SOURCES: Jonathan Vespa, Jamie M. Lewis, and Rose M. Kreider, 2013, "America's Families and Living Arrangements: 2012," Current Population Reports, P20-570, U.S. Census Bureau, Washington, DC. https://www.census.gov/prod/2013pubs/p20-570.pdf; http://www.census.gov/hhes/families/data/cps2015.html

TABLE 19.2 Ratio of Divorces to Marriages per 1,000 U.S. Population, Selected Years, 1950–2014

1950	1960	1970	1980	1990	2000	2014
23%	26%	33%	50%	48%	49%	46%

SOURCE: *Statistical Abstract of the United States 2012,* Table 132, http://www.cdc.gov/nchs/nvss/marriage_divorce_tables.htm

those from nonindustrial societies confirm the declining importance of kinship in contemporary nations. Immigrants are often shocked by what they perceive as weak kinship bonds and lack of proper respect for family in contemporary North America. In fact, most of the people whom middle-class North Americans see every day are either nonrelatives or members of the nuclear family (see also Willie and Reddick 2009).

Interestingly, a recent study (Qian 2013) found that the traditional American nuclear family was best represented among recent immigrants. Sociologist Zhenchao Qian describes several differences involving marriage and the family between recent immigrants and native-born Americans. By 2010, the end point of Qian's 10-year study, immigrants comprised 13 percent of the U.S. population. They brought customs of their cultures of origin with them to the United States. One such pattern was marital stability, although brides tended to be significantly younger than their grooms. Among immigrants in their mid- to late twenties, 62 percent of women were married, compared with just 43 percent of men. At every age, however, the immigrant marriage rate was greater than that of native-born Americans, including those of their own ethnicity. Asian immigrants, for example, were twice as likely to marry as were U.S.-born Asians. Compared with native-born marriages, those of immigrants also tended to be more ethnically homogeneous and less prone to divorce. In 2010, about 30 percent of immigrant children lived in homes with a male breadwinner and a stay-at-home mother. This was nine percentage points higher than the figure for native-born Americans. In general, dual-income families make more than single-income ones.

What does "family" mean in different cultures? Consider a striking contrast between the United States and Brazil, the two most populous nations of the Western Hemisphere, in the meaning of "family." Contemporary North American adults usually define their families as consisting of their spouse (or domestic partner) and their children. However, when Brazilians talk about their families, they mean their parents, siblings, aunts, uncles, grandparents, and cousins. Later they add their children, but rarely the spouse, who has his or her own family. The children are shared by the two families. Because middle-class Americans lack an extended family support system, marriage assumes more importance. The spousal relationship is supposed to take precedence over either spouse's relationship with his or her own parents. This places a significant strain on American marriages (see this chapter's "Appreciating Anthropology" for a study of American family life in the 21st century).

TABLE 19.3 Household and Family Size in the United States and Canada, 1980 versus 2011 (Canada) and 2015 (U.S.)

	1980	MOST RECENT
Average family size		
United States	3.3	3.1
Canada	3.4	3.1
Average household size		
United States	2.9	2.5
Canada	2.9	2.5

SOURCES: J. M. Fields, "America's Families and Living Arrangements: 2003," Current Population Reports, P20-553, November 2004, http://www.census.gov/prod/2004pubs/p20-553.pdf, pp. 3–4; *Statistics Canada, 2011 Census of Canada,* http://www.statcan.gc.ca/tables-tableaux/sum-som/l01/cst01/famil53a-eng.htm; J. Vespa, J. M. Lewis, and R. M. Kreider, 2013, "America's Families and Living Arrangements: 2012," Current Population Reports, P20-570, U.S. Census Bureau, Washington, D.C.; http://www.census.gov/hhes/families/data/cps2015.html

One among many kinds of American family. This single mother, seen here teaching her daughter how to bake, used donor insemination to become pregnant. What do you see as the main differences between nuclear families and single-parent families?

© Steve Russell/Toronto Star via Getty Images

American Family Life in the 21st Century

Anthropologists today increasingly study daily life in the United States, including that of middle-class families. An excellent example is *Life at Home in the Twenty-First Century: 32 Families Open Their Doors* (Arnold et al. 2012), a study of home life in 32 middle-class, dual-income families in Los Angeles, focusing on physical surroundings and material culture, the items owned and used in daily life. The book's authors are three UCLA anthropologists—Jeanne Arnold, Anthony Graesch, and Elinor Ochs—and Italian photographer Enzo Ragazzini. All did research through UCLA's Center on Everyday Lives of Families (CELF), which was founded in 2001 and is directed by Ochs.

The families selected for, and agreeing to participate in, the study on which *Life at Home* was based were all middle-class and owned or were buying their homes. They varied in ethnicity, income level, and neighborhood. Same-sex couples were included. The authors took a systematic approach to their subjects. They videotaped the activities of family members, tracked their movements using positioning devices, measured their stress levels through saliva samples, and took almost 20,000 photographs (approximately 600 per family) of homes, yards, and activities. The researchers also asked family members to narrate tours of their homes and videotaped them as they did so. Over a 4-year period, the project generated 47 hours of family-narrated video home tours and 1,540 hours of videotaped family interactions and interviews (see Arnold et al. 2012; Feuer 2012; Sullivan 2012).

A key finding of the study was the extent of clutter in those homes, a manifestation of a high degree of consumerism among dual-income American families. Never in human history, the researchers conclude, have families accumulated so many personal possessions. Hypothesizing that dealing with so much clutter would have psychological effects, the researchers collected saliva samples from the subjects in order to measure diurnal cortisol, an indicator of stress. Mothers' saliva, it turned out, contained more diurnal cortisol than did fathers'. The researchers also noticed

that, in their video tours, mothers often used words like "mess" and "chaotic" to describe their homes, while fathers rarely mentioned messiness. Author Anthony Graesch reasons that clutter bothers moms so much because it challenges deeply ingrained notions that homes should be tidy and well managed (see Feuer 2012). The role of domestic manager, of course, is traditionally a female one. For dads and kids, more than for moms, possessions appeared to be a source of pleasure, pride, and contentment rather than stress (Arnold et al. 2012; Feuer 2012).

Another finding was that children rarely went outside, despite the overall mild weather in Los Angeles. They used their possessions indoors, resulting in more clutter, including whole walls devoted to displays of dolls and toys. More than half of the 32 households had special rooms designed for work or schoolwork, but even in home offices kids' stuff tended to crowd parental items. The researchers speculate that guilt motivates dual-income parents to overbuy for their children. The parents in the study managed to spend, on an average weekday, no more than

four hours with their kids, perhaps leading them to overcompensate with toys, clothes, and other possessions (Graesch quoted in Feuer 2012).

The study found that the kitchen was the center of home life. In this space, family members met, interacted, exchanged information, and socialized with their children. And in the kitchen, the refrigerator played a key role. Stuck on its doors and sides were pictures, displays of children's achievements, reminders, addresses, and phone lists (including many outdated ones). The typical refrigerator front panel held 52 objects. The most crowded refrigerator had 166 stick-ons. The refrigerator served as a compact representation of that family's history and activities (Feuer 2012; Sullivan 2012).

Researchers found a correlation between the number of objects on the refrigerator and the overall clutter in a home. The refrigerator thus served not only as a chronicler of family life but also as a measure of its degree of consumerism—and perhaps of stress. We might hypothesize that a high number of refrigerator stick-ons indicates that someone in the household needs to take up meditation to lower his or her blood pressure.

As studied by anthropologists in greater Los Angeles, the clutter that typifies many middle-class American homes reflects a high degree of consumerism, especially among dual-income families. Never in human history have non-elite families owned so many possessions.

© The Washington Times/ZUMA Press/Newscom

Living in a less mobile society, Brazilians stay in closer contact with their relatives, including members of the extended family, than North Americans do. Residents of Rio de Janeiro and São Paulo, two of South America's largest cities, are reluctant to leave those urban centers to live away from family and friends. Brazilians find it hard to imagine, and unpleasant to live in, social worlds without relatives. Contrast this with a characteristic American theme: learning to live with strangers.

The Family among Foragers

Foraging societies are far removed from industrial nations in terms of population size and social complexity, but they do feature geographic mobility, which is associated with nomadic or seminomadic hunting and gathering. Here again, a mobile lifestyle favors the nuclear family as the most significant kin group, although in no foraging society is the nuclear family the only group based on kinship. The two basic social units of traditional foraging societies are the nuclear family and the band. Both are based on kinship ties.

Unlike middle-class couples in industrial nations, foragers don't usually reside neolocally. Instead, they join a band in which either the husband or the wife has relatives. However, couples and families may move from one band to another several times (see Hill et al. 2011). Although nuclear families are ultimately as impermanent among foragers as they are in any other society, they are usually more stable than bands are.

Many foraging societies lacked year-round band organization. The Native American Shoshoni of the Great Basin in Utah and Nevada (Figure 19.3) provide an example. The resources available to the Shoshoni were so meager that for most of the year families traveled alone through the countryside, hunting and gathering. In certain seasons families assembled to hunt cooperatively as a band; after just a few months together, they dispersed (see Fowler and Fowler 2008).

In neither industrial nor foraging societies are people tied permanently to the land. The mobility and the emphasis on small, economically self-sufficient family units promote the nuclear family as a basic kin group in both types of societies.

DESCENT

We've seen that the nuclear family is important in industrial nations and among foragers. The descent group, by contrast, is the key kinship group among nonindustrial farmers and herders. Descent groups, remember, are made up of people who share common ancestry—they *descend* from the same ancestor(s). Unlike nuclear families, descent groups are permanent. They last for generations. The group endures even as its membership

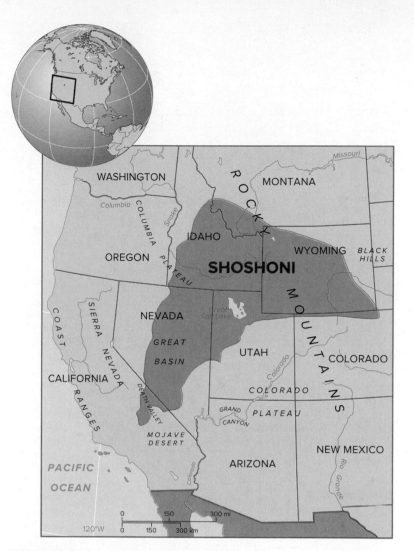

FIGURE 19.3 Location of the Shoshoni.

changes. Individual members are born and die, move in and move out. Descent groups may take their names from an ancestor, or from a familiar animal, plant, or natural feature. If a descent group is known as "Children of Abraham," there will be "Children of Abraham" generation after generation. Ditto for "Wolves," "Willow Trees," or "People of the Bamboo Houses." All of these are actual descent group names.

Attributes of Descent Groups

Descent groups frequently are *exogamous: Exogamy* means to marry outside one's own group. Members of a descent group must marry someone from another descent group. Often, descent group membership is determined at birth and is lifelong. Two common rules admit certain people as descent-group members while excluding others. With a rule of *matrilineal descent,* people join the mother's group automatically at birth and are life members. With *patrilineal descent,* people similarly are born into and have lifetime membership

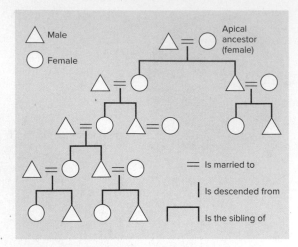

FIGURE 19.4 A Matrilineage Five Generations Deep.

Matrilineages are based on demonstrated descent from a female ancestor. Only the children of the group's women belong to the matrilineage. The children of the group's men are excluded; they belong to their mother's matrilineage.

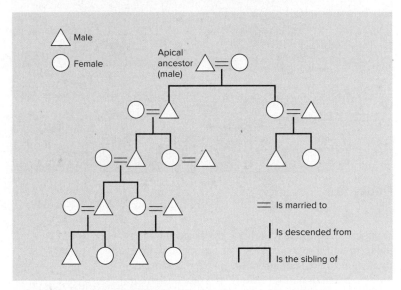

FIGURE 19.5 A Patrilineage Five Generations Deep.

Lineages are based on demonstrated descent from a common ancestor. With patrilineal descent, children of the group's men are included as descent-group members. Children of the group's female members are excluded; they belong to their father's patrilineage.

unilineal descent

Matrilineal or patrilineal descent.

lineage

A unilineal descent group based on demonstrated descent.

clan

A unilineal descent group based on stipulated descent.

Adam stands as the original apical ancestor for the patrilineal genealogies laid out in the Bible.

Lineages and clans are two types of descent group. Clans tend to be larger than lineages and can include lineages. A **lineage** is a descent group based on *demonstrated descent*. Members can demonstrate how they descend from their common ancestor, by naming their forebears in each generation from the apical ancestor through the present. (This doesn't mean the genealogy is accurate, only that lineage members think it is.) In the Bible the litany of men who "begat" other men is a demonstration of descent for a large patrilineage that ultimately includes Jews and Arabs (who share Abraham as their last common apical ancestor).

Unlike lineages, members of a clan do not demonstrate how they descend from their common ancestor; they merely claim, assert, or *stipulate* their common ancestry and descent. They don't try to specify actual genealogical links generation by generation, as members of a lineage do. A **clan,** then, is a descent group based on *stiplulated descent.*

The Betsileo of Madagascar have both lineages and clans. They can demonstrate descent for the most recent 8 to 10 generations. Going further back than that, however, they can only stipulate their descent from particular ancestors. The stipulated founders of Betsileo clans can include vaguely defined foreign royalty or even mythical creatures, such as mermaids (Kottak 1980). Like the Betsileo, many societies have both lineages and clans. When this is true, the clan will have more members and cover a larger geographic area than its component lineages do. Sometimes a clan's apical ancestor is not a human at all but an animal or a plant (called a *totem*). Whether human or not, the ancestor symbolizes the social unity and identity of the members, distinguishing them from other groups.

The economic types that usually have descent-group organization are horticulture, pastoralism, and agriculture. A given society usually has multiple descent groups. Any one of them may be confined to a single village, but they usually span more than one village. Any branch of a descent group that lives in one place is a *local descent group.* Two (or more) local branches of different descent groups may live in the same village.

Lineages, Clans, and Residence Rules

As we've seen, descent groups, unlike nuclear families, are permanent units, with new members gained and lost in each generation. Members have access to the lineage estate, where some of them must live, in order to benefit from and manage that estate across the generations. To endure, descent groups need to keep at least some of their members at home. An easy way to do this is to have a rule about who belongs to the descent group and where they should live after they get married. Patrilineal and matrilineal descent, and the postmarital residence rules that

in the father's group. (In Figures 19.4 and 19.5, which show matrilineal and patrilineal descent groups, respectively, the triangles stand for males and the circles for females.) Matrilineal and patrilineal descent are types of **unilineal descent**. That means they use only *one* line of descent—either the male or the female line.

Members of any descent group believe that they descend from the same *apical ancestor.* That person stands at the apex, or top, of their common genealogy. For example, Adam and Eve, according to the Bible, are the apical ancestors of all humanity. Since Eve is said to have come from Adam's rib,

usually accompany them, ensure that about half the people born in each generation will live out their lives on the ancestral estate.

With patrilineal descent, the typical postmarital residence rule is *patrilocality:* Married couples reside in the husband's father's community, so that the children will grow up in their father's village. It makes sense for patrilineal societies to require patrilocal postmarital residence. If the group's male members are expected to exercise their rights in the ancestral estate, it's a good idea to raise them on that estate and to keep them there after they marry.

A less common postmarital residence rule, associated with matrilineal descent, is *matrilocality:* Married couples live in the wife's mother's community, and their children grow up in their mother's village. Together, patrilocality and matrilocality are known as *unilocal* rules of postmarital residence. Regardless of where one resides after marriage, one remains a member of one's original unilineal descent group for life. This means that a man residing in his wife's village in a matrilineal society keeps his membership in his own matrilineal descent group, and a woman residing in her husband's village is still a member of her own patrilineal descent group.

Ambilineal Descent

With unilineal descent, whether matrilineal or patrilineal, people at birth automatically become lifetime members of one—and only one—descent group. Unilineal descent admits some people while clearly and definitely excluding others. Things aren't always so definite. Unilineal descent isn't the only descent rule known to anthropology. Ambilineal descent is a descent rule that offers more flexibility and choice. With **ambilineal descent**, group membership is neither automatic at birth nor fixed for life. Individuals have a choice about their descent group affiliation, and they can belong to more than one descent group. Ambilineal descent groups do not *automatically* exclude either the children of sons or those of daughters. People can choose the descent group they join (e.g., that of their father's father, father's mother, mother's father, or mother's mother). People also can change their descent-group membership, or belong to two or more groups at the same time.

Family versus Descent

There are rights and obligations associated with kinship and descent. Many societies have both families and descent groups. Obligations to one may conflict with obligations to the other—more so in matrilineal than in patrilineal societies. In the latter, a woman typically leaves home when she marries and raises her children in her husband's community. After leaving home, she has no primary or substantial obligations to her own descent group. She can invest fully in her children, who will become members of her husband's group. In a matrilineal society things are different. A man has strong

obligations both to his family of procreation (his wife and children) and to his closest matrikin (his sisters and their children). The continuity of his own descent group depends on his sisters and their children, since descent is carried by females, and he has descent-based obligations to look out for their welfare. He also has obligations to his wife and children. If a man is sure his wife's children are his own, he has more incentive to invest in them than when he has doubts.

ambilineal descent
A flexible descent rule, neither patrilineal nor matrilineal.

Most societies have a prevailing opinion about where couples should live after they marry; this is called a postmarital residence rule. A common rule is patrilocality: The couple lives with the husband's relatives, so that children grow up in their father's community. The top image shows a young Muslim bride (veiled in pink) in the West African country of Guinea Bissau. On the last day of her three-day wedding ceremony, she will collect laundry from her husband's family, wash it with her friends, and be taken to his village on a bicycle. The bottom image shows the transport of dowry gifts during a wedding ceremony among the Minangkabau people of Sumatra, Indonesia. In this matrilineal society, property and land pass from mother to daughter, and traditional postmarital residence is matrilocal.

Top: © Ami Vitale/Alamy Stock Photo; bottom: © Peter Horree/Alamy Stock Photo

Compared with patrilineal systems, matrilineal societies tend to have higher divorce rates and greater female promiscuity (Schneider and Gough 1961). According to Nicholas Kottak (2002), among the matrilineal Makua of northern Mozambique, a husband is concerned about his wife's potential promiscuity. A man's sister also takes an interest in her brother's wife's fidelity; she doesn't want her brother wasting time on children who may not be his, thus diminishing his investment as an uncle (mother's brother) in her children. A confessional ritual that is part of the Makua birthing process demonstrates the sister's allegiance to her brother. When a wife is deep in labor, the husband's sister, who attends her, must ask, "Who is the real father of this child?" If the wife lies, the Makua believe the birth will be difficult, often ending in the death of the woman and/or the baby. This ritual serves as an important social paternity test. It is in both the husband's and his sister's interest to ensure that his wife's children are indeed his own.

KINSHIP CALCULATION

In addition to studying kin groups, anthropologists also are interested in **kinship calculation:** the relationships based on kinship that people recognize in different societies and how they talk about those relationships (see Sahlins 2013). Who is, and who is not, considered to be a relative—a kinsman or a kinswoman? Like race and gender, kinship is culturally constructed. This means that some genealogical kin are considered to be relatives, whereas others may not be. It also means that even people who aren't genealogical relatives can be constructed socially as kin. We can summarize that kinship calculation, also known as kinship classification, is the system that people in a particular society use to recognize and categorize kinship relationships.

Cultures maintain varied beliefs about biological processes involving kinship, including the role of insemination in creating human life. We know that fertilization of an ovum by a single sperm is responsible for conception. Other cultures have different ideas about procreation. In some societies it is believed that spirits, rather than men, place babies in women's wombs. In others, people think that a fetus must be nourished by continuing insemination during pregnancy. People in many cultures believe that several acts of intercourse are needed to make a baby (see Beckerman and Valentine 2002). The Barí of Venezuela and their neighbors, for example, believe that multiple men can create the same fetus. When a Barí child is born, the mother publicly announces the names of the one or more men she believes to be the father(s). If those men accept paternity, they must provide care for the mother and child. Barí children with more than one official father turn out to be advantaged compared with those who have just one. Anthropologists report that 80 percent of Barí children with multiple dads survived to

adulthood, compared with just 64 percent who had just one (Beckerman and Valentine 2002).

Ethnographers strive to discover, in a given society, the specific genealogical relationships between "relatives" and the person who has named them—the **ego.** *Ego* means *I* (or *me*) in Latin. It's who you, the reader, are in the kin charts that follow. It's your perspective looking out on your kin. By posing the same questions to several local people, the ethnographer learns about the extent and direction of kinship calculation in that society. The ethnographer also begins to understand the relationship between kinship calculation and kin groups: how people use kinship to create and maintain personal ties and to join social groups. In the kinship charts that follow, the gray square labeled "ego" identifies the person whose kinship calculation is being examined.

Kin Terms and Genealogical Kin Types

At this point, we may distinguish between *kin terms* (the words used for different relatives in a particular language) and *genealogical kin types*. **Kin terms** are the specific words used for different relatives in a particular culture and language. Kin terms are cultural, rather than biological, categories. *Genealogical kin types, by contrast,* refer to biology, to an actual genealogical relationship. Father's brother is a genealogical kin type, whereas *uncle* is a kin term (in English) that lumps together, or merges, multiple genealogical kin types, including father's brother, mother's brother, and often the husbands of "blood" aunts. Kin terms reflect the social construction of kinship in a given culture.

We designate genealogical kin types with the letters and symbols shown in Figure 19.6. As with *uncle,* a kin term may (and usually does) lump together multiple genealogical relationships. *Grandfather* includes mother's father and father's father. The term *cousin* lumps together several kin types. Even the more specific *first cousin* includes mother's brother's son (MBS), mother's brother's daughter (MBD), mother's sister's son (MZS), mother's sister's daughter (MZD), father's brother's son (FBS), father's brother's daughter (FBD), father's sister's son (FZS), and father's sister's daughter (FZD). *First cousin* thus lumps together at least eight genealogical kin types.

Even the key kin term father, which is used primarily for one kin type—the genealogical father—can be extended to an adoptive father or stepfather, and even to a priest or a "Heavenly Father."

We use *uncle* to include both mother's brother and father's brother because we perceive them as being the same sort of relative. Calling them *uncles,* we distinguish between them and another kin type, F, whom we call *Father, Dad,* or *Pop.* In many societies, however, it is common to call a father and a father's brother by the same term. Later we'll see why.

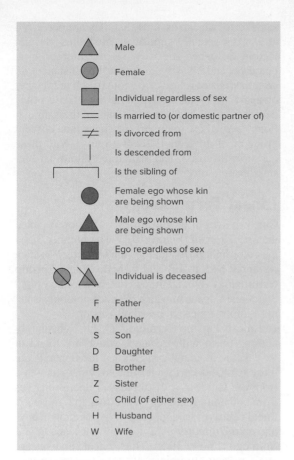

	Male
	Female
	Individual regardless of sex
	Is married to (or domestic partner of)
	Is divorced from
	Is descended from
	Is the sibling of
	Female ego whose kin are being shown
	Male ego whose kin are being shown
	Ego regardless of sex
	Individual is deceased
F	Father
M	Mother
S	Son
D	Daughter
B	Brother
Z	Sister
C	Child (of either sex)
H	Husband
W	Wife

FIGURE 19.6 Kinship Symbols and Genealogical Kin Type Notation.

A neolocal American nuclear family in front of their home. The nuclear family's relative isolation from other kin groups in modern nations reflects geographic mobility within an industrial economy with sale of labor for cash.

© Ariel Skelley/Blend Images LLC RF

Kin Terms in America

It's reasonable for North Americans to distinguish between relatives who belong to their nuclear families and those who don't. We are more likely to grow up with our parents than with our aunts and uncles. We tend to see our parents more often than we see our uncles and aunts, who may live in different towns and cities. We often inherit from our parents, but our cousins have first claim to inherit from our aunts and uncles. If our marriage is stable, we see our children daily as long as they remain at home. They are our heirs. We feel closer to them than to our nieces and nephews.

American kinship calculation and kin terms reflect these social features. Thus, the term *uncle* distinguishes between the kin types MB and FB on the one hand and the kin type F on the other. However, this term also lumps kin types together. We use the same term for MB and FB, two different kin types—one on the mother's side, the other on the father's side. We do this because American kinship calculation is **bilateral**—traced equally on both sides, through males and females, for example, father and mother. Both kinds of uncle are brothers of a parent. We think of both as roughly the same kind of relative.

"No," you may object, "I'm closer to my mother's brother than to my father's brother." That may

be. However, in a representative sample of Americans, we would find a split, with some favoring one side and some favoring the other. We'd actually expect a bit of *matrilateral skewing*—a preference for relatives on the mother's side. This occurs for many reasons. When contemporary children are raised by just one parent, it's much more likely to be the mother than the father. Also, even with intact marriages, the wife tends to play a more active role in managing family affairs, including family visits, reunions, holidays, and extended family relations, than the husband does. This would tend to reinforce her kin network over his and thus favor matrilateral skewing.

Bilateral kinship means that people tend to perceive kin links through males and females as being similar or equivalent. This bilaterality is expressed in interaction with, living with or near, and rights to inherit from relatives. We don't usually inherit from uncles, but if we do, there's about as much chance that we'll inherit from the father's brother as from the mother's brother. We usually don't live with an aunt, but if we do, it might be either the mother's sister or the father's sister.

KINSHIP TERMINOLOGY

People perceive and define kin relations differently in different societies. In any culture, kinship terminology is a classification system, a taxonomy

bilateral kinship calculation
Kin ties calculated equally through both sexes.

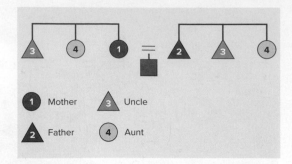

FIGURE 19.7 Lineal Kinship Terminology.

or typology. It is a *native taxonomy,* developed over generations by the people who live in a particular society. A native classification system is based on how people perceive similarities and differences in the things being classified.

However, anthropologists have discovered that there are a limited number of patterns or systems by which people classify their kin (see McConvell, Keen, and Hendery 2013). People who speak very different languages may use exactly the same system of kinship terminology. This section examines the four main ways of classifying kin on the parental generation: lineal, bifurcate merging, generational, and bifurcate collateral. We also consider the social correlates of these classification systems. (Note that each of the systems described here applies to the parental generation. There also are differences in kin terminology used to classify siblings and cousins. There are six such systems, which you can see diagrammed and discussed at the following websites: http://anthro.palomar.edu/kinship/kinship_5.htm and http://anthro.palomar.edu/kinship/kinship_6.htm.)

Kin terms provide useful information about social patterns. If two relatives are designated by the same term, we can assume that they are perceived as sharing socially significant attributes. Several factors influence the way people interact with, perceive, and classify relatives. For instance, do certain kinds of relatives customarily live together or apart? How far apart? What benefits do they derive from each other, and what are their obligations? Are they members of the same descent group or of different descent groups? With these questions in mind, let's examine systems of kinship terminology.

Lineal Terminology

Our own system of kinship classification is called the *lineal system* (Figure 19.7). The number 3 and the color light blue stand for the term *uncle,* which we apply both to FB and to MB. **Lineal kinship terminology** is found in societies such as the United States and Canada in which the nuclear family is the most important group based on kinship.

Lineal kinship terminology has absolutely nothing to do with lineages, which are found in very different social contexts. (What contexts are those?) Lineal kinship terminology gets its name from the fact that it distinguishes lineal relatives from collateral relatives. What does that mean? A **lineal relative** is an ancestor or a descendant, anyone on the direct *line* of descent that leads to and from ego (Figure 19.8). Thus, lineal relatives are one's parents, grandparents, great-grandparents, and other direct forebears. Lineal relatives also include children, grandchildren, and great-grandchildren. **Collateral relatives** are all other kin. They include siblings, nieces and nephews, aunts and uncles, and cousins (Figure 19.8). **Affinals** are relatives by marriage, whether of lineals (e.g., son's wife) or of collaterals (sister's husband).

Bifurcate Merging Terminology

Bifurcate merging kinship terminology (Figure 19.9) *bifurcates,* or splits, the mother's side from the father's side. But it also *merges* same-sex siblings—sisters with sisters and brothers with brothers. Thus, one's mother and mother's sister are lumped together or merged under the

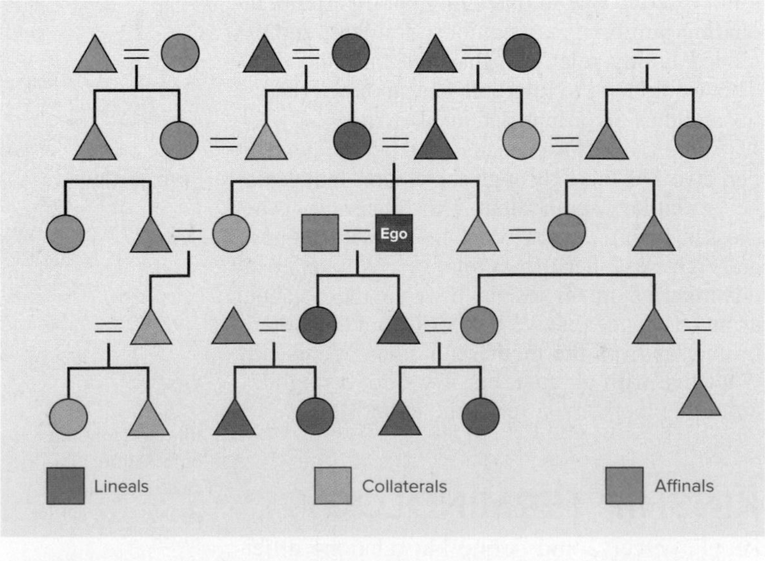

FIGURE 19.8 The Distinctions among Lineals, Collaterals, and Affinals as Perceived by Ego.

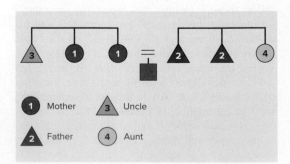

Mother
Father
Uncle
Aunt

FIGURE 19.9 Bifurcate Merging Kinship Terminology.

same term (1), while one's father and father's brother also are merged—into a common term (2). There are different terms for mother's brother (3) and father's sister (4).

Bifurcate merging kinship terminology is found in societies with descent groups. In that context, its logic makes sense: One's mother and father always belong to different descent groups, so the terminology separates them. More specifically, bifurcate merging kinship terminology is found in societies with unilineal (patrilineal and matrilineal) descent groups. It makes sense to use the same term for father and father's brother in a patrilineal society, because they share a common descent group, gender, and generation. Because patrilineal societies usually have patrilocal residence, the father and his brother live in the same local group. Because they share so many attributes that are socially relevant, ego regards them as social equivalents and calls them by the same kinship term—2. However, the mother's brother belongs to a different descent group, lives elsewhere, and has a different kin term—3.

What about mother and mother's sister in a patrilineal society? They belong to the same descent group, the same gender, and the same generation. Often they marry men from the same village and go to live there. These social similarities help explain the use of the same term—1—for both.

Similar observations apply to matrilineal societies. Consider a society with two matrilineal clans, the Ravens and the Wolves. Ego belongs to his or her mother's clan, the Raven clan. Ego's father belongs to the Wolf clan. Ego's mother and her sister are female Ravens of the same generation. If there is matrilocal residence, as there often is in matrilineal societies, they will live in the same village. Because they are so similar socially, ego calls them by the same kin term—1.

The father's sister, however, belongs to a different group, the Wolves; lives elsewhere; and has a different kin term—4. Ego's father and father's brother are male Wolves of the same generation. If they marry women of the same clan and live in the same village, this creates additional social similarities that reinforce this usage.

Generational Terminology

As in bifurcate merging kinship terminology, **generational kinship terminology** uses the same term for parents and their siblings, but the lumping is more complete (Figure 19.10). With generational terminology, there are only two terms for relatives on the parental *generation*. We may translate them as "father" and "mother," but more accurate translations would be "male member of the parental generation" and "female member of the parental generation." The Betsileo of Madagascar use generational terminology. All the men (F, FB, and MB) are called *ray* (pronounced like

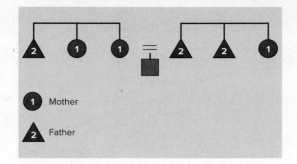

1 ● Mother
2 ▲ Father

FIGURE 19.10 Generational Kinship Terminology.

the English word "rye"), and all the women (M, MZ, and FZ) are called *reny* (sounds like "raynie" in English).

We see that generational kinship terminology does not distinguish between the mother's side and the father's side. It does not bifurcate, but it certainly does merge. It uses just one term for father, father's brother, and mother's brother. In a unilineal society, these three kin types would never belong to the same descent group. Generational kinship terminology also uses a single term for mother, mother's sister, and father's sister. Nor, in a unilineal society, would these three ever be members of the same group.

Nevertheless, generational terminology suggests closeness between ego and his or her aunts and uncles—much more closeness than exists between Americans and these kin types. How likely would you be to call your uncle "Dad" or your aunt "Mom"? We'd expect to find generational terminology in societies in which extended kinship is much more important than it is in our own but in which there is no rigid distinction between the father's side and the mother's side.

It makes sense, then, that generational kin terminology is found in societies with ambilineal descent, where descent-group membership is not automatic. People may choose the group they join, change their descent-group membership, or belong to two or more descent groups simultaneously. Generational terminology fits these conditions. The use of intimate kin terms signals that people have close personal relations with all their relatives on the parental generation. People exhibit similar behavior toward their parents, aunts, and uncles, and may live for variable lengths of time with one or more of those relatives.

Significantly, generational terminology also characterizes certain foraging bands, including Kalahari San groups and several native societies of North America. Use of this terminology reflects certain similarities between foraging bands and ambilineal descent groups. In both societies, people have a choice about their kin-group affiliation. Foragers always live with kin, but they often shift band affiliation and so may be members of several different bands during their lifetimes.

generational kinship terminology
Just two parental kin terms: M=MZ=FZ and F=FB=MB.

KINSHIP TERMINOLOGY	KIN GROUP	RESIDENCE RULE	ECONOMY
Lineal	Nuclear family	Neolocal	Industrialism, foraging
Bifurcate merging	Unilineal descent group—patrilineal or matrilineal	Unilocal—patrilocal or matrilocal	Horticulture, pastoralism, agriculture
Generational	Ambilineal descent group, band	Ambilocal	Agriculture, horticulture, foraging
Bifurcate collateral	Varies	Varies	Varies

Just as in food-producing societies with ambilineal descent, generational terminology among foragers helps maintain close personal relationships with several parental-generation relatives, whom ego may eventually use as a point of entry into different groups.

Bifurcate Collateral Terminology

bifurcate collateral kinship terminology

Six separate parental kin terms: M, F, MB, MZ, FB, and FZ.

Of the four kin classification systems, **bifurcate collateral kinship terminology** is the most specific. It has separate kin terms for each of the six kin types (mother, father, mother's sister, mother's brother, father's brother, and father's sister) on the parental generation (Figure 19.11). Bifurcate collateral terminology isn't as common as the other types. Many of the societies that use it are in North Africa and the Middle East, and many of them are offshoots of the same ancestral group.

Bifurcate collateral terminology also may develop when a child has parents of different ethnic backgrounds and uses terms for aunts and uncles

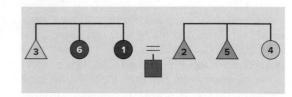

FIGURE 19.11   Bifurcate Collateral Kinship Terminology.

derived from different languages. Thus, if you have a mother who is Latina and a father who is Anglo, you may call your aunts and uncles on your mother's side "tia" and "tio," while calling those on your father's side "aunt" and "uncle." And your mother and father may be "Mom" and "Pop." That's a modern form of bifurcate collateral kinship terminology. Recap 19.1 lists the types of kin group, the postmarital residence rule, and the economic type associated with the four types of kinship terminology.

for REVIEW

summary

1. In nonindustrial societies, kinship, descent, and marriage organize social and political life. In studying kinship, we must distinguish between kin groups, whose composition and activities can be observed, and kinship calculation—how people identify and designate their relatives.

2. One widespread kin group is the nuclear family, consisting of a married couple and their children. There are functional alternatives to the nuclear family. That is, other groups may assume functions usually associated with the nuclear family. Nuclear families tend to be especially important in foraging and industrial societies. Among farmers and herders, other kinds of kin groups, particularly descent groups, often overshadow the nuclear family.

3. In contemporary North America, the nuclear family is a characteristic kin group for the middle class. Expanded households and sharing with extended family kin occur more frequently among the poor, who may pool their resources in dealing with poverty. Today, however, even in the American middle class, nuclear family households are declining as single-person households and other domestic arrangements increase.

4. The descent group is a basic kin group among nonindustrial farmers and herders. Unlike families, descent groups have perpetuity—they last for generations. Descent-group members share and manage a common estate: land, animals, and other resources. There are several kinds of

descent groups. Lineages are based on demonstrated descent; clans, on stipulated descent. Descent rules may be unilineal or ambilineal. Patrilineal and matrilineal descent are associated, respectively, with patrilocal and matrilocal postmarital residence. Obligations to one's descent group and to one's family of procreation may conflict, especially in matrilineal societies.

5. A kinship terminology is a classification of relatives based on perceived differences and similarities. Comparative research has revealed a limited number of ways of classifying kin.

Because there are correlations between kinship terminology and other social practices, we often can predict kinship terminology from other aspects of culture. The four basic kinship terminologies for the parental generation are lineal, bifurcate merging, generational, and bifurcate collateral. Many foraging and industrial societies use lineal terminology, which is associated with nuclear family organization. Cultures with unilocal residence and unilineal descent tend to have bifurcate merging terminology. Generational terminology correlates with ambilineal descent and also occurs in certain foraging societies.

key terms

affinals 380

ambilineal descent 377

bifurcate collateral kinship terminology 382

bifurcate merging kinship terminology 380

bilateral kinship calculation 379

clan 376

collateral relative 380

descent group 368

ego 378

expanded family household 371

extended family household 371

family of orientation 368

family of procreation 368

generational kinship terminology 381

kin terms 378

kinship calculation 378

lineage 376

lineal kinship terminology 380

lineal relatives 380

neolocality 369

unilineal descent 376

critical thinking

1. Why is kinship so important to anthropologists? How might the study of kinship be useful for research in fields of anthropology other than cultural anthropology?

2. What are some examples of alternatives to nuclear family arrangements considered in this chapter? What may be the impact of new (and increasingly accessible) reproductive technologies on domestic arrangements?

3. Although the nuclear family remains the cultural ideal for many Americans, other domestic arrangements now outnumber the "traditional" American household more than five to one. What are some reasons for this? Do you think this trend is good or bad? Why?

4. To what sorts of family or families do you belong? Have you belonged to other kinds of families? How do the kin terms you use compare with the four classification systems discussed in this chapter?

5. Cultures with unilineal descent tend to have bifurcate merging terminology, whereas ambilineal descent is associated with generational terminology. Why does this make sense? How might the terminology used for the parental generation be applied to your own generation?

Marriage

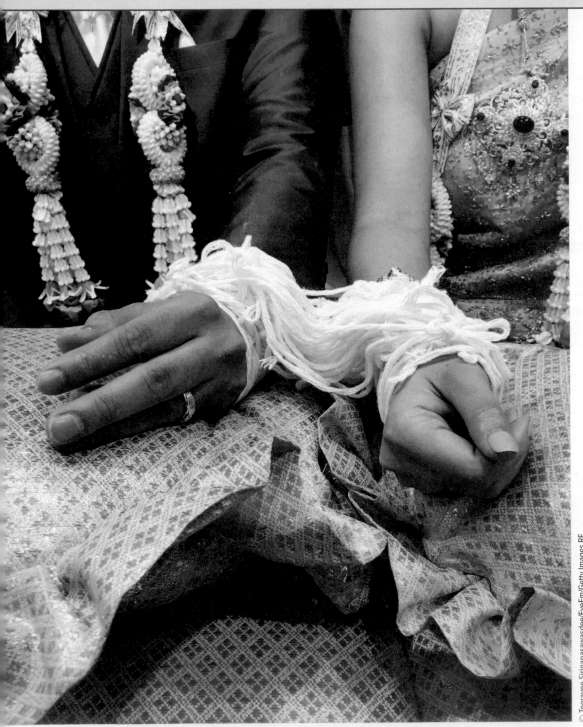

© Teeravee Sirinapasawasdee/EyeEm/Getty Images RF

The White Thread Ceremony, in which white threads soaked in holy water are attached to the wrists of bride and groom, is a feature of this wedding in Thailand.

▶ How is marriage defined and regulated, and what rights does it convey?

▶ What role does marriage play in creating and maintaining group alliances?

▶ What forms of marriage exist cross-culturally, and what are their social correlates?

chapter outline

understanding OURSELVES

According to the radio talk show psychologist (and undergraduate anthropology major) Dr. Joy Browne, parents' job is to give their kids "roots and wings." Roots, she says, are the easier part. In other words, it's easier to raise children than to let them go. Has that been true of your parents with respect to you? I've heard comments about today's "helicopter parents" hovering over even their college-aged kids, using cell phones, texting, e-mail, and even GPS devices to follow their progeny more closely than in prior generations. Do you have any experience with such a pattern?

It can be difficult to make the transition between the family that raised us (our family of orientation) and the family we form if we have children (our family of procreation). In contemporary America, we usually get a head start by "leaving home" long before we establish a family of procreation. We go off to college or find a job that enables us to support ourselves, so that we can live independently or with roommates. In nonindustrial societies people, especially women, may leave home abruptly when they marry. Often, a woman must leave her home village and her own kin and move in with her husband and his relatives. This can be an unpleasant and alienating transition. Many women complain about feeling isolated, or being mistreated, in their husband's village.

In contemporary North America, although neither women nor men typically have to adjust to living with in-laws full-time, conflicts with in-laws aren't at all uncommon. Just read "Dear Abby" or listen to Dr. Joy Browne (cited previously) for a week. Even more of a challenge is learning to live with a spouse. Marriage always raises issues of accommodation and adjustment. Initially, the married couple is just that, unless there are children from a previous marriage. If there are, adjustment issues will involve step-parenthood—and a prior spouse—as well as the new marital relationship. Once a couple has its own child, the family-of-procreation mentality takes over. In the United States, family loyalty shifts, but not completely, from the family of orientation to the family that includes spouse and child(ren). Given our bilateral kinship system, we maintain relations with our sons and daughters after they marry, and grandchildren theoretically are as close to one set of grandparents as to the other set. In practice, grandchildren tend to be a bit closer to their mother's than to their father's families. Can you speculate about why that might be? How is it for you? Are you closer to your paternal or maternal grandparents? How about your uncles and aunts on one side or the other? Why is that?

DEFINING MARRIAGE

"Love and marriage," "marriage and the family": These familiar phrases show how we link the romantic love of two individuals to marriage and how we link marriage to reproduction and family creation. But marriage is an institution with significant roles and functions in addition to reproduction. What is marriage, anyway?

Marriage is difficult to define cross-culturally because of the many forms it can take. It is difficult to find a definition broad enough to subsume marriage in all societies and situations. Consider the following definition from *Notes and Queries on Anthropology:*

> Marriage is a union between a man and a woman such that the children born to the woman are recognized as legitimate offspring of both partners. (Royal Anthropological Institute 1951, p. 111)

This definition isn't universally valid for several reasons. First, in many societies, marriages unite more than two spouses. Here we speak of *plural marriages,* as when a man weds two (or more) women, or a woman weds a group of brothers—an arrangement called *fraternal polyandry* that is characteristic of certain Himalayan cultures.

Second, some societies recognize various kinds of same-sex marriages. In South Sudan, for example, a Nuer woman could take a wife if her father had no sons, who were necessary for the survival of his patrilineage. That father could ask his daughter to stand as a fictive son in order to take a bride. This daughter would become the socially recognized husband of another woman (the wife). This was a symbolic and social relationship rather than a sexual one. The "wife" had sex with a man or men (whom her female "husband" approved) until she became pregnant. The children born to the wife were accepted as the offspring of both the female husband and the wife. Although the female husband was not the actual **genitor,** the biological father of the children, she was their **pater,** or socially recognized father. What's important in this Nuer case is *social* rather than *biological paternity.* We see again how kinship is socially constructed. The bride's children were considered the legitimate offspring of her female "husband," who was biologically a woman but socially a man, and the patrilineal descent line continued.

A third objection to the definition of marriage offered above is that it focuses exclusively on the role of marriage in establishing the legitimacy of children. Does this mean that people who marry after childbearing age, or who do not plan to have children, are not actually married?

In fact, marriage has several roles in society besides legitimating children. The British anthropologist Edmund Leach (1955) observed that, depending on the society, several different kinds of rights are allocated by marriage. According to Leach, marriage can, but doesn't always, accomplish the following:

- Establish legal parentage.

- Give either or both spouses a monopoly on the sexuality of the other.

- Give either or both spouses rights to the labor of the other.

- Give either or both spouses rights over the other's property.

- Establish a joint fund of property—a partnership—for the benefit of the children.

- Establish a socially significant "relationship of affinity" between spouses and their relatives.

EXOGAMY AND INCEST

In nonindustrial societies, a person's social world includes two main categories—friends and strangers. Strangers are potential or actual enemies. Marriage is one of the primary ways of converting strangers into friends, of creating and maintaining personal and political alliances. **Exogamy,** the custom and practice of seeking a mate outside one's own group, has adaptive value, because it links people into a wider social network that nurtures, helps, and protects them in times of need. Incest restrictions (prohibitions on sex with relatives) reinforce exogamy by pushing people to seek their mates outside the local group. Most societies discourage sexual contact involving close relatives, especially members of the same nuclear family.

Incest refers to sexual contact with a relative, but cultures define their kin, and thus incest, differently. In other words, incest, like kinship, is socially constructed. For example, some U.S. states permit marriage, and therefore sex, with first cousins, while others ban those practices as incestuous. Cross culturally, sex, and marriage between first cousins may or may not be considered incestuous, depending on context and the kin type of the first cousin. Many societies distinguish between two types of first cousins: cross cousins and parallel cousins. The children of two brothers or two sisters are **parallel cousins.** The children of a brother and a sister are **cross cousins.** Your mother's sister's children and your father's brother's children are your parallel cousins. Your father's sister's children and your mother's brother's children are your cross cousins.

The American kin term *cousin* doesn't distinguish between cross and parallel cousins, but in many societies, especially those with unilineal descent, the distinction is essential. As an example, consider a community with only two descent groups. This exemplifies what is known as *moiety* organization—from the French *moitié,* which means "half." Descent bifurcates the community so that everyone belongs to one half or the other. Some societies have patrilineal moieties; others have matrilineal moieties.

In Figures 20.1 and 20.2, notice that cross cousins always are members of the opposite moiety and parallel cousins always belong to your (ego's) own moiety. With patrilineal descent (Figure 20.1), people take the father's descent-group affiliation; in a matrilineal society (Figure 20.2), they take the mother's affiliation. You can see from these diagrams that your mother's sister's

exogamy
Marriage outside one's own group.

incest
Sexual relations with a close relative.

genitor
A child's biological father.

pater
One's socially recognized father; not necessarily the genitor.

parallel cousins
Children of two brothers or two sisters.

cross cousins
Children of a brother and a sister.

Among the Yanomami of Venezuela and Brazil (shown here), sex with (and marriage to) cross cousins is proper, but sex with parallel cousins is considered incestuous. With unilineal descent, sex with cross cousins isn't incestuous because cross cousins never belong to ego's descent group.

© Nigel Dickinson/Alamy Stock Photo

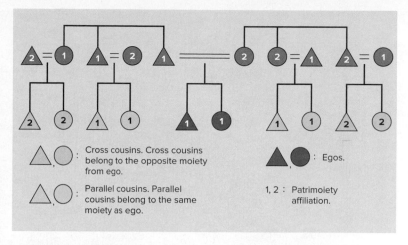

FIGURE 20.1 Parallel and Cross Cousins and Patrilineal Moiety Organization.

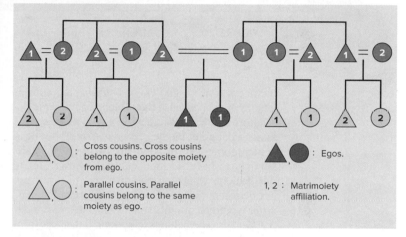

FIGURE 20.2 Matrilineal Moiety Organization.

children (MZC) and your father's brother's children (FBC) always belong to your group. Your cross cousins—that is, FZC and MBC—belong to the other moiety.

Parallel cousins belong to the same generation and the same descent group as ego does, and they are like ego's brothers and sisters. They are called by the same kin terms as brothers and sisters are. Defined as close relatives, parallel cousins, like siblings, are excluded as potential mates; cross cousins are not.

In societies with unilineal moieties, cross cousins always belong to the opposite group. Sex with cross cousins isn't incestuous, because they aren't considered relatives. In fact, in many unilineal societies, people must marry either a cross cousin or someone from the same descent group as a cross cousin. A unilineal descent rule ensures that the cross cousin's descent group is never one's own. With moiety exogamy, spouses must belong to different moieties.

Among the Yanomami of Venezuela and Brazil (Chagnon 2013), boys anticipate eventual marriage to a cross cousin by calling her "wife." They

call their male cross cousins "brother-in-law." Yanomami girls call their male cross cousins "husband" and their female cross cousins "sister-in-law." Here, as in many other societies with unilineal descent, sex with cross cousins is proper but sex with parallel cousins is incestuous.

If cousins can be classified as nonrelatives, how about even closer biological kin types? When unilineal descent is very strongly developed, the parent who belongs to a different descent group than your own isn't considered a relative. Thus, with strict patrilineality, the mother is not a relative but a kind of in-law who has married a member of your own group—your father. With strict matrilineality, the father isn't a relative because he belongs to a different descent group.

The Lakher of Southeast Asia (Figure 20.3) are strictly patrilineal (Leach 1961). Using the male ego (the reference point, the person in question) in Figure 20.4, let's suppose that ego's father and mother get divorced. Each remarries and has a daughter by a second marriage. A Lakher always belongs to his or her father's group, all of whose

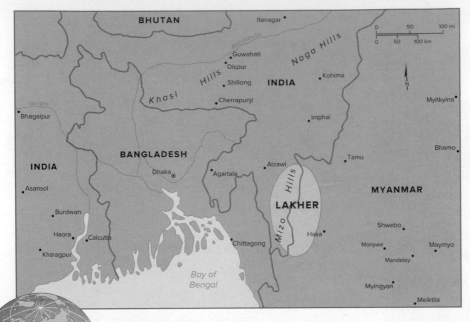

FIGURE 20.3 Location of the Lakher.

members (one's *agnates,* or *patrikin*) are considered relatives, because they belong to the same descent group. Ego can't have sex with or marry his father's daughter by the second marriage, just as in contemporary North America it's illegal for half-siblings to have sex and marry. However, unlike our society, where all half-siblings are restricted, sex between our Lakher ego and his maternal half-sister would be nonincestuous. She isn't ego's relative because she belongs to her own father's descent

group rather than ego's. The Lakher illustrate very well that definitions of relatives, and therefore of incest, vary from culture to culture.

INCEST AND ITS AVOIDANCE

We know from primate research that adolescent males (among monkeys) or females (among apes) often move away from the group in which they were born (see Chapais 2008; Rodseth et al. 1991; and Wade 2011). This emigration reduces the frequency of incestuous unions, but it doesn't stop them. DNA testing of wild chimps has confirmed incestuous unions between adult sons and their mothers, when residing in the same group. Human behavior with respect to mating with close relatives may express a generalized primate tendency, in which we see both urges and avoidance.

The Occurrence of Incest

A cross-cultural study of 87 societies (Meigs and Barlow 2002) suggested that incest occurred in several of them. It's not clear, however, whether the authors of the study controlled for the social construction of incest. They report, for example, that incest occurs among the Yanomami, but they may be considering cross-cousin marriage to be incestuous, when it is not so considered by the Yanomami. Another society in their sample is the Ashanti, for whom the ethnographer Meyer Fortes reports, "In the old days it [incest] was punished by death. Nowadays the culprits are heavily fined" (Fortes 1950, p. 257). This suggests that there really were violations of Ashanti incest restrictions, and that such violations were, and still are, punished. More strikingly, among 24 Ojibwa individuals from whom he obtained information about incest, A. Irving Hallowell found 8 cases of parent–child incest and 10 cases of brother–sister incest (Hallowell 1955, pp. 294–95). Because reported cases of actual parent–child and sibling incest are very rare in the ethnographic literature, questions about the possibility of social construction arise here too. In many cultures, including the Ojibwa, people use the same terms for their mother and their aunt, their father and their uncle, and their cousins and siblings. Could the siblings in the Ojibwa case actually have been cousins, and the parents and children, uncles and nieces?

In ancient Egypt, sibling marriage apparently was allowed for both royalty and commoners, in

Incestuous union   Ego   **Nonincestuous union**

●, ▲ : Ego's patrilineage

●, ▲ : Ego's mother's second husband's patrilineage

○ : Ego's mother's patrilineage

○ : Ego's father's second wife's patrilineage

≠ : Separation or divorce.

FD by second marriage is a comember of ego's descent group and is included within the incest taboo.

MD by second marriage is not a comember of ego's descent group and is not tabooed.

FIGURE 20.4 Patrilineal Descent-Group Identity and Incest among the Lakher.

some districts at least. Based on official census records from Roman Egypt (first to third centuries C.E.), 24 percent of all documented marriages in the Arsinoites district were between "brothers" and "sisters." The rates were 37 percent for the city of Arsinoe and 19 percent for the surrounding villages. These figures are much higher than any other documented levels of inbreeding among humans (Scheidel 1997). Again one wonders if the relatives involved were actually as close biologically as the kin terms would imply.

According to Anna Meigs and Kathleen Barlow (2002), for Western societies with nuclear family organization, "father–daughter incest" is much more common with stepfathers than with biological fathers. But is it really incest if they aren't biological relatives? American culture is unclear on this matter. Incest also happens with biological fathers, especially those who were absent or did little caretaking of their daughters in childhood (Williams and Finkelhor 1995). In a carefully designed study, Linda M. Williams and David Finkelhor (1995) found father–daughter incest to be least likely when there was substantial paternal parenting of daughters. This experience enhanced the father's parenting skills and his feelings of nurturance, protectiveness, and identification with his daughter, thus reducing the chance of incest.

Incest Avoidance

A century ago, early anthropologists speculated that incest restrictions reflect an instinctive horror of mating with close relatives (Hobhouse 1915; Lowie 1920/1961). But why, one wonders, if humans really do have an instinctive aversion to

Discovered in Egypt's Valley of the Kings, a gold and silver inlaid throne from the tomb of Tutankhamun is now on display in Cairo's Egyptian Museum. Sibling marrage was allowed not only for ancient Egyptian royalty but also for commoners in some regions.

© Kenneth Garrett/National Geographic Creative

incest, would formal restrictions be necessary? No one would want to have sexual contact with a relative. Yet as social workers, judges, psychiatrists, and psychologists are well aware, incest is more common than we might suppose.

Why do societies discourage incest? Is it because incestuous unions tend to produce abnormal offspring, as the early anthropologist Lewis Henry Morgan (1877/1963) suggested? Laboratory experiments with animals that reproduce faster than humans do (such as mice and fruit flies) have been used to investigate the effects of inbreeding: A decline in survival and fertility does accompany brother–sister mating across several generations. However, despite the potentially harmful biological results of systematic inbreeding, human marriage patterns are based on specific cultural beliefs rather than universal concerns about a decline in fertility several generations in the future. Biological concerns certainly cannot explain why so many societies promote marriage of cross cousins but not of parallel cousins.

In most societies, people avoid incest by following rules of exogamy, which force them to mate and marry outside their kin group (Lévi-Strauss 1949/1969; Tylor 1889; White 1959). Exogamy is adaptively advantageous because it creates new social ties and alliances. Marrying a close relative, with whom one already is on peaceful terms, would be counterproductive. There is more to gain by extending peaceful relations to a wider network of groups. Marriage within the group would isolate that group from its neighbors and their resources and social networks, and might ultimately lead to the group's extinction. Exogamy helps explain human adaptive success. Besides its sociopolitical function, exogamy also ensures genetic mixture between groups and thus maintains a successful human species.

ENDOGAMY

The practice of exogamy pushes social organization outward, establishing and preserving alliances among groups. In contrast, rules of **endogamy** dictate mating or marriage within a group to which one belongs. Formal endogamic rules are less common but are still familiar to anthropologists. Indeed, most societies *are* endogamous units, although they usually don't need a formal rule requiring people to marry someone from their own society. In our own society, classes and ethnic groups are quasi-endogamous groups. Members of an ethnic or religious group often want their children to marry within that group, although many of them do not do so. The outmarriage rate varies among such groups, with some more committed to endogamy than others are.

Homogamy means to marry someone similar, as when members of the same social class intermarry. In modern societies, there's a correlation

endogamy
Marriage of people from the same social group.

How many fingers do this Indian woman and her child have? Such genetically determined traits as polydactylism (extra fingers) may show up when there is a high incidence of endogamy. Despite the biological effects of inbreeding, marriage preferences and prohibitions are based on specific cultural beliefs rather than universal concerns about future biological degeneration.

© DPA/The Image Works

between socioeconomic status (SES) and education. People with similar SES tend to have similar educational aspirations, to attend similar schools, and to pursue similar careers. For example, people who meet at an elite university are likely to have similar backgrounds and career prospects. Homogamous marriage can work to concentrate wealth in social classes and to reinforce the system of social stratification. In the United States, for example, the rise in female employment, especially in professional careers, when coupled with homogamy, has dramatically increased household incomes in the upper classes. This pattern has been one factor in sharpening the contrast in household income between the richest and poorest quintiles (top and bottom 20 percent) of Americans.

Caste

An extreme example of endogamy is India's caste system, which was formally abolished in 1949, although its structure and effects linger. Castes are stratified groups in which membership is determined at birth and is lifelong. Indian castes are grouped into five major categories, or *varna.* Each is ranked relative to the other four, and these categories extend throughout India. Each *varna* includes a large number of subcastes (*jati*), each of which includes people within a region who may intermarry. All the *jati* in a single *varna* in a given region are ranked, just as the *varnas* themselves are ranked.

Occupational specialization often sets off one caste from another. A community may include castes of agricultural workers, merchants, artisans, priests, and sweepers. The untouchable *varna,* found throughout India, includes subcastes whose ancestry, ritual status, and occupations are considered so impure that higher-caste people consider even casual contact with untouchables to be defiling.

The belief that intercaste sexual unions lead to ritual impurity for the higher-caste partner has been important in maintaining endogamy. A man who has sex with a lower-caste woman can restore his purity with a bath and a prayer. However, a woman who has intercourse with a man of a lower caste has no such recourse. Her act cannot be undone or expiated. Because the women have the babies, these differences protect the purity of the caste line, ensuring the proper ancestry of high-caste children. Although Indian castes are endogamous groups, many of them are internally subdivided into exogamous lineages. Traditionally, this meant that Indians had to marry a member of another descent group from the same caste.

Royal Endogamy

Royal endogamy, based in a few societies on brother–sister marriage, is similar to caste endogamy. Inca Peru, ancient Egypt, and traditional Hawaii all allowed royal brother–sister marriages. In ancient Peru and Hawaii, such marriages were permitted despite the restrictions on sibling incest that applied to commoners in those societies.

Manifest and Latent Functions

To understand royal brother–sister marriage, it is useful to distinguish between the manifest and latent functions of customs and behavior. The *manifest function* of a custom refers to the reasons people in that society give for it. Its *latent function* is an effect the custom has on the society that its members don't mention or may not even recognize.

Royal endogamy illustrates this distinction. Hawaiians and other Polynesians believed in an impersonal force called *mana.* Mana could exist in things or people, in the latter case marking them off from other people and making them sacred. The Hawaiians believed that no one had as much mana as the ruler. Mana depended on genealogy. The person whose own mana was exceeded only by the king's was his sibling. The most appropriate wife for a king was his own full sister. Notice that the brother–sister marriage also meant

estates intact. Power often rests on wealth, and royal endogamy tended to ensure that royal wealth remained concentrated in the same line. Royal sibling marriage had similar results in ancient Egypt and Peru. Other kingdoms, including European royalty, also have practiced endogamy, but based on cousin marriage rather than sibling marriage.

SAME-SEX MARRIAGE

What about same-sex marriage? Such unions, of various sorts, have been recognized in many different historical and cultural settings. We saw earlier that the Nuer of South Sudan allowed a woman whose father lacked sons to take a wife and be socially recognized as her husband and as the father (pater, although not genitor) of her children. Other African cultures, including the Igbo of Nigeria and the Lovedu of South Africa, have permitted women to marry other women. In situations in which women, such as prominent market women in West Africa, are able to amass property and other forms of wealth, they may take a wife. Such marriage allows the prominent woman to strengthen her social status and the economic importance of her household (Amadiume 1987).

Sometimes, when same-sex marriage is allowed, one of the partners is of the same biological sex as the spouse, but is considered to belong to a different, socially constructed gender. Several Native American groups had figures known as "Two-Spirit," representing a gender in addition to male or female (Murray and Roscoe 1998). Sometimes, the Two-Spirit was a biological man who assumed many of the mannerisms, behavior patterns, and tasks of women. Such a Two-Spirit might marry a man and fulfill the traditional wifely role. Also, in some Native American cultures, a marriage of a "manly hearted woman" (a third or fourth gender) to another woman brought the traditional male–female division of labor to their household. The manly woman hunted and

An extreme example of endogamy is India's caste system, which was formally abolished in 1949, although its structure and effects linger. Shown here, a member of the Dalit, or untouchable caste, cleans a sewer drain in a market in Jodhpur, India. The work of sweepers and tanners has been considered so smelly and dirty that they have been segregated residentially.

© Jake Norton/Alamy Stock Photo

that royal heirs would be as *manaful*, or sacred, as possible. The manifest function of royal endogamy in ancient Hawaii was part of that culture's beliefs about mana and sacredness.

Royal endogamy also had latent functions—political repercussions. The ruler and his wife had the same parents. Since mana was believed to be inherited, they were almost equally sacred. When the king and his sister married, their children indisputably had the most mana in the land. No one could question their right to rule. But if the king had taken as a wife someone with less mana than his sister, his sister's children eventually could cause problems. Both sets of children could assert their sacredness and right to rule. Royal sibling marriage therefore limited conflicts about succession by reducing the number of people with claims to rule. Royal endogamy also had a latent economic function: By limiting the number of heirs, it helped keep

Supporters of same-sex marriage celebrate the 2015 Supreme Court decision establishing marriage equality throughout the United States.

© Josh Edelson/Bloomberg via Getty Images

did other male tasks, while the wife played the traditional female role.

As of this writing, same-sex marriage is legal in 23 countries: Argentina, Belgium, Brazil, Canada, Columbia, Denmark, England and Wales, Finland, France, Greenland, Iceland, Ireland, Luxembourg, the Netherlands, New Zealand, Norway, Portugal, Scotland, South Africa, Spain, Sweden, the United States, and Uruguay. (Figure 20.5 is a map showing these countries and the year in which same-sex marriage was legalized.)

Twenty-first-century North America has witnessed a rapid and dramatic shift in public and legal opinions about same-sex marriage. In April 2000, the state of Vermont passed a bill allowing same-sex couples to unite legally in "civil unions," with virtually all the benefits of marriage. In Canada, in June 2003, a court ruling established same-sex marriages as legal in the province of Ontario. Two years later, Canada's House of Commons voted to guarantee full marriage rights to same-sex couples throughout that nation.

Argentina (2010)
Belgium (2003)
Brazil (2013)
Canada (2005)
Colombia (2016)
Denmark (2012)
England and Wales (2013)
Finland (2015)
France (2013)
Greenland (2015)
Iceland (2010)
Ireland (2015)
Luxembourg (2014)
The Netherlands (2000)
New Zealand (2013)
Norway (2009)
Portugal (2010)
Scotland (2014)
South Africa (2006)
Spain (2005)
Sweden (2009)
United States (2015)
Uruguay (2013)

FIGURE 20.5 Countries Allowing Same-Sex Marriage (as of 2016) with Year of Legalization.

In Lagos, Nigeria, women work with green vegetables in a bayside market. In parts of Nigeria, prominent market women may take a wife. Such marriage allows wealthy women to strengthen their social status and the economic importance of their households.
© James Marshall/The Image Works

In May 2004, Massachusetts became the first U.S. state to allow same-sex marriage. Thereafter, legalization spread slowly at first, then rapidly in the wake of a key 2013 Supreme Court decision. The District of Columbia and 19 states—California, Connecticut, Delaware, Hawaii, Illinois, Iowa, Maine, Maryland, Massachusetts, Minnesota, New Hampshire, New Jersey, New Mexico, New York, Oregon, Pennsylvania, Rhode Island, Vermont, and Washington—allowed same-sex marriage as of July 2014. By February 2015, that number had jumped to 37.

The legalization of same-sex marriage throughout the United States in June 2015 was achieved despite considerable opposition. In 1996, the U.S. Congress approved the Defense of Marriage Act (DOMA), which denied federal recognition and benefits to same-sex couples. Voters in at least 29 U.S. states passed measures defining marriage as an exclusively heterosexual union. On June 26, 2013, the U.S. Supreme Court struck down a key part of DOMA and granted to legally married same-sex couples the same federal rights and benefits received by any legally married couple. In June 2015, the Supreme Court upheld the legality of same-sex marriage throughout the United States. Although opposition continues (often on religious grounds), public opinion has followed the judicial shift toward approval of same-sex marriage. (This chapter's "Appreciating Anthropology" discusses the position of the American Anthropological Association on same-sex marriage, based on anthropology's knowledge of marital practices cross-culturally.)

This "I love you" wall is on display in an open area of Monmartre, Paris, France. It shows how to say "I love you" in various languages. Is romantic love a cultural universal?

© Conrad P. Kottak

ROMANTIC LOVE AND MARRIAGE

We think of marriage as an individual matter. Although the bride and groom usually seek their parents' approval, the final choice (to live together, to marry, to divorce) lies with the couple. Contemporary Western societies stress the notion that romantic love is necessary for a good marriage. Increasingly, this idea characterizes other cultures as well. The mass media and human migration spread Western ideas about the importance of love for marriage.

Just how widespread is romantic love, and what role should it play in marriage? A study by anthropologists William Jankowiak and Edward Fischer (1992) found romantic ardor to be very common cross-culturally. Previously, anthropologists had tended to ignore evidence for romantic love in other cultures, probably because arranged marriages were so common. Surveying ethnographic data from 166 cultures, Jankowiak and Fischer (1992) found evidence for romantic love in 147 of them—89 percent (see also Jankowiak 1995, 2008).

Furthermore, recent diffusion of Western ideas about the importance of love for marriage has influenced marital decisions in other cultures. Among villagers in the Kangra valley of northern India, as reported by anthropologist Kirin Narayan (quoted in Goleman 1992), even in the traditional arranged marriages, the partners might eventually fall in love. In that area today, however, the media have spread the idea that young people should choose their own spouse based on romantic love, and elopements now rival arranged marriages.

The same trend away from arranged marriages toward love matches has been noted among Native Australians. Traditionally in the Australian Outback, marriages were arranged when children were very young. Missionaries disrupted that pattern, urging that marriage be postponed to adolescence. Before the missionaries, according to anthropologist Victoria Burbank (1988), all girls married before puberty, some as early as age 9; nowadays the average female age at marriage is 17 years. Parents still prefer the traditional arrangement in which a girl's mother chooses a boy from the appropriate kin group. But more and more girls now choose to elope and get pregnant, thus forcing a marriage to someone they love. In the group Burbank studied, most marriages had become love matches (see Burbank 1988; Goleman 1992).

MARRIAGE AS GROUP ALLIANCE

Whether or not they are cemented by passion, marriages in nonindustrial societies remain the

What Anthropologists Could Teach the Supreme Court about the Definition of Marriage

A majority of Americans today, especially the younger ones, have no trouble accepting the practice and legalization of same-sex marriage. However, opinions on this issue have evolved very rapidly. As recently as 2004, then-president George W. Bush was calling for a constitutional amendment banning gay marriage.

Eleven years later, on June 26, 2015, the U.S. Supreme Court issued one of its most socially significant rulings—legalizing same-sex marriage throughout the United States. In the landmark case *Obergefell v. Hodges,* the Court ruled, in a 5–4 decision, that the right to marry is guaranteed to same-sex couples by both the due process clause and the equal protection clause of the 14th Amendment to the U.S. Constitution.

In his strong dissent to that ruling, Chief Justice John Roberts asked, "Just who do we think we are?"—to so enlarge the definition of marriage. Roberts faulted the court for endorsing "the transformation of a social institution that has formed the basis of human society for millennia, for the Kalahari Bushmen and the Han Chinese, the Carthaginians and the Aztecs."

If Roberts knew more about anthropology, he would realize that these four societies don't really support his claim that marriage has universally been a union between one man and one woman. Although the "Kalahari Bushmen" (San peoples) do have exclusively heterosexual marriages, they also divorce and remarry at will. Nor,

in Han period China, was marriage a lifetime union between one man and one woman. Han men were allowed to divorce, remarry, and consort with concubines. Within the Roman Empire, Carthaginian women who were Roman citizens were allowed to marry and divorce freely. Many members of the final society cited by Roberts—the Aztecs—were polygamists. The Aztecs used matchmakers to arrange marriages and asked widows to marry a brother of their deceased husband (Joyce 2015). I doubt that Chief Justice Roberts intended to endorse frequent divorce, consorting with mistresses and concubines, and polygamy as aspects of "a social institution that has formed the basis of human society for millennia."

Roberts went on to argue that marriage "arose in the nature of things to meet a vital need: ensuring that children are conceived by a mother and father committed to raising them in the stable conditions of a lifetime relationship." Here the focus is on the role of marriage in procreation and raising children. As we have seen, however, marriage confers socially significant rights and obligations other than raising children. Nor is procreation necessary for or within marriage. Is a childless marriage any less legitimate than one with children? Is legal adoption of a child less legitimate than conception of the child by a married heterosexual couple? Every day in contemporary societies, men and women marry without expecting to conceive and raise children.

As John Borneman and Laurie Kain Hart (2015) observe, marriage is an elastic institution whose meaning and value vary from culture to culture and evolve over time. Consider the many examples of families, kinship groups, and marriage types considered in this book. From the Bosnian *zadruga* to the Nayar *tarawad* to matrilineal and patrilineal clans, lineages, local descent groups and extended families, children have been raised in, and have managed to survive and even flourish in, all kinds of kin groups. If we go back millennia, as Chief Justice Roberts would like to trace marriage, we would find "love, marriage, and the baby carriage" to be the exception rather than the rule. That is, the combination of romantic love, marriage, procreation, and raising children mainly, or even exclusively, within a nuclear family is a relatively recent—rather than a universal or ages-old development.

Finally, consider the different forms of marriage that have been considered in this chapter: woman-marriage-to-a-woman among the Nuer, cross-cousin marriage, Lakher marriage to a half-sibling, serial monogamy, and other forms that violate the idea that marriage is a lifetime union of one man and one woman.

I would hope, therefore, that the next time a member of the Supreme Court attempts to justify a practice using terms like "for millennia," "ages-old," "universal," or "basic human," they will first consult an anthropologist.

---

concern of social groups rather than mere individuals. The scope of marriage extends from the social to the political—alliance formation. Strategic marriages are tried-and-true ways of establishing alliances between groups.

Gifts at Marriage

In societies with descent groups, people enter marriage not alone but with the help of the descent group. Often, it is customary for a substantial gift to be given before, at, or after the marriage by the husband and his kin to the wife and her kin. The BaThonga of Mozambique call such a gift *lobola,* and the custom of giving something like **lobola** is very widespread in patrilineal societies (Radcliffe-Brown 1924/1952). This gift compensates the bride's group for the loss of her companionship and labor. More important, it makes the children born to the woman full members of her husband's descent group. In matrilineal societies, children are members of the mother's group anyway, so there is no reason for a lobola-like gift.

Another kind of marital gift, **dowry**, occurs when the bride's family provides substantial wealth when their daughter marries. Traditionally, in rural Greece, the bride received a wealth transfer from her mother, which served as a kind of trust fund during her marriage (Friedl 1962). More typically, however, the dowry goes not to the wife but to the husband's family, and the custom is correlated with low female status. In this latter form of dowry, best known from India, women are perceived as burdens. When a man and his family take a wife, they expect to be compensated with dowry for the added responsibility.

Lobola-like gifts exist in many more cultures than dowry does, but the nature and quantity of transferred items differ. Among the BaThonga of Mozambique, whose name—lobola—I am using for this widespread custom, the gift consists of cattle. Use of livestock (usually cattle in Africa, pigs in Papua New Guinea) for lobola is common, but the number of animals given varies from society to society. We can generalize, however, that the larger the gift, the more stable the marriage. Lobola is insurance against divorce.

Imagine a patrilineal society in which a marriage requires the transfer of about 25 cattle from the groom's descent group to the bride's. Michael, a member of descent group A, marries Sarah from group B. His relatives help him assemble the lobola. He gets the most help from his closest patrilineal relatives: his older brother, father, father's brother, and closest patrilineal cousins.

The distribution of the cattle once they reach Sarah's group mirrors the manner in which they were assembled. Sarah's father, or her oldest brother if the father is dead, receives her lobola. He keeps most of the cattle to use as lobola for his sons' marriages. However, a share also goes to everyone who will be expected to help when Sarah's brothers marry.

When Sarah's brother David gets married, many of the cattle go to a third group: C, which is David's wife's group. Thereafter, they may serve as lobola to still other groups. Men continually use their sisters' lobola cattle to acquire their own wives. In a decade, the cattle given when Michael married Sarah will have been exchanged widely.

In such societies, marriage entails an agreement between descent groups. If Sarah and Michael try to make their marriage succeed but fail to do so, both groups may conclude that the marriage can't last. Here it becomes especially obvious that such marriages are relationships between groups as well as between individuals.

lobola
A substantial marital gift from the husband and his kin to the wife and her kin.

dowry
Substantial gifts to the husband's family from the wife's group.

A bride and groom are escorted back to the bride's home after their wedding ceremony in a village in southwest China's Guizhou province. Having observed traditional wedding customs of their Miao ethnic group, they are congratulated by fellow villagers and tourists.
© Qin Gang/Xinhua Press/Corbis

This photo, taken in South Africa, shows the lobola cattle presented at the 2010 wedding of Mandla Mandela (grandson of former South African president Nelson Mandela) and his French wife, Anais Grimaud.
© Bonile Bam/Gallo Images/Alamy Stock Photo

If Sarah has a younger sister or niece (her older brother's daughter, for example), the concerned parties may agree to Sarah's replacement by a kinswoman.

However, incompatibility isn't the main problem that threatens marriage in societies with lobola customs. Infertility is a more important concern. If Sarah has no children, she and her group have not fulfilled their part of the marriage agreement. If the relationship is to endure, Sarah's group must furnish another woman, perhaps her younger sister, who can have children. If this happens, Sarah may choose to stay with her husband. Perhaps she will someday have a child. If she does stay on, her husband will have established a plural marriage.

Many nonindustrial societies allow **plural marriages,** or *polygamy*. There are two varieties; one is common, and the other is very rare. The more common variant is **polygyny,** in which a man has more than one wife at the same time. The rare variant is **polyandry,** in which a woman has more than one husband at the same time. If the infertile wife remains married to her husband after he has taken a substitute wife provided by her descent group, this is polygyny. Reasons for polygyny other than infertility will be discussed shortly.

Durable Alliances

It is possible to exemplify the group-alliance nature of marriage by examining still another

common practice: continuation of marital alliances when one spouse dies.

Sororate

What happens if Sarah dies young? Michael's group will ask Sarah's group for a substitute, often her sister. This custom is known as the **sororate** (Figure 20.6). If Sarah has no sister or if all her sisters are already married, another woman from her group may be available. Michael marries her,

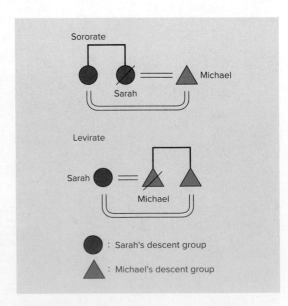

FIGURE 20.6 Sororate and Levirate.

plural marriage
More than two spouses simultaneously; polygamy.

polygyny
Man has more than one wife at the same time.

polyandry
Woman has more than one husband at the same time.

sororate
Widower marries sister of his deceased wife.

there is no need to return the lobola, and the alliance continues. The sororate exists in both matrilineal and patrilineal societies. In a matrilineal society with matrilocal postmarital residence, a widower may remain with his wife's group by marrying her sister or another female member of her matrilineage.

Levirate

What happens if the husband dies? In many societies, the widow may marry his brother. This custom is known as the **levirate.** Like the sororate, it is a continuation marriage that maintains the alliance between descent groups, in this case by replacing the husband with another member of his group. The implications of the levirate vary with age. One study found that in African societies, the levirate, though widely permitted, rarely involves cohabitation of the widow and her new husband. Furthermore, widows don't automatically marry the husband's brother just because they are allowed to. Often, they prefer to make other arrangements (Potash 1986).

DIVORCE

Ease of divorce varies depending on the culture. What factors work for and against divorce? As we've seen, marriages that are political alliances between groups are more difficult to dissolve than are marriages that are more individual affairs, of concern mainly to the married couple and their children. We've seen that a substantial lobola gift may decrease the divorce rate for individuals and that replacement marriages (levirate and sororate) also work to preserve group alliances. Divorce tends to be more common in matrilineal than in patrilineal societies. When residence is matrilocal (in the wife's place), the wife may simply send off a man with whom she's incompatible.

Among the Hopi of the American Southwest, houses were owned by matrilineal clans, with matrilocal postmarital residence. The household head was the senior woman of that household, which also included her daughters and their husbands and children. A son-in-law had no important role there; he returned to his own mother's home for his clan's social and religious activities. In this matrilineal society, women were socially and economically secure, and the divorce rate was high. Consider the Hopi of Oraibi (Orayvi) pueblo, northeastern Arizona (Levy with Pepper 1992; Titiev 1992). In a study of the marital histories of 423 Oraibi women, Mischa Titiev found that 35 percent had been divorced at least once. Jerome Levy found that 31 percent of 147 adult women had been divorced and remarried at least once. For comparison, of all ever-married women in the United States, only

4 percent had been divorced in 1960, 10.7 percent in 1980, and 15 percent in 2013. Much of the instability of Hopi marriages was due to conflicting loyalties to matrikin versus spouse. Most Hopi divorces appear to have been matters of personal choice. Levy generalizes that, cross-culturally, high divorce rates are correlated with a secure female economic position. In Hopi society, women were secure in their homes and land ownership and in the custody of their children. In addition, there were no formal barriers to divorce.

Divorce is more difficult in a patrilineal society, especially when substantial lobola would have to be reassembled and repaid if the marriage failed. A woman residing patrilocally (in her husband's household and community) might be reluctant to leave him. Unlike the Hopi, who let the kids stay with the mother, in patrilineal-patrilocal societies, the children of divorce would be expected to remain with their father, as members of his patrilineage. From the women's perspective this is a strong impediment to divorce.

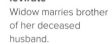

levirate
Widow marries brother of her deceased husband.

Hopi piki bread maker Rebecca Namingha mixes blue corn meal and ashes with water. She'll cook the batter on a hot stone. Traditionally among the matrilineal-matrilocal Hopi, women were socially and economically secure, and the divorce rate was high.

What about divorce in foraging societies? Among foragers, certain factors facilitate divorce, while other factors work to stabilize marriage. Facilitating divorce is the fact that the group alliance functions of marriage are less important, because descent groups are not as characteristic of foragers as of food producers. Also facilitating divorce is the fact that marriages tend to last longer when a couple shares—and would have trouble dissolving—a significant joint fund of property. This usually is not the case among foragers, who have minimal material possessions. Marital stability is favored, however, when the nuclear family is an important year-round unit with a gender-based division of labor, as is true of many foraging societies. Also favoring marital stability is the fact that foragers tend to have sparse populations, so that few alternative spouses are available if a marriage fails.

In contemporary Western societies, when romance fails, so may the marriage. Or it may not fail, if other benefits associated with marriage are compelling. Economic ties and obligations to kids, along with other factors, such as concern about public opinion, or simple inertia, may keep marriages intact after sex, romance, and/or companionship fade. Also, even in modern societies, political leaders and other elites may have strategic marriages similar to the arranged marriages of nonindustrial societies.

The divorce rate tends to rise after wars and to fall when times are bad economically. With more women working outside the home, economic dependence on the husband as breadwinner is weaker, which no doubt facilitates a decision to divorce when a marriage has major problems. Cash employment also places strains on marriage and social life for both partners. Culture and religious factors contribute as well. Culturally, Americans tend to value independence and its modern form, self-actualization. Also, Protestantism (in its various guises) is the most common form of religion in the United States. Of the two major religions in the United States and Canada (where Catholicism predominates), Protestantism has been less stringent in denouncing divorce than has Catholicism.

PLURAL MARRIAGES

In contemporary North America, where divorce is fairly easy and common, polygamy (marriage to more than one spouse at the same time) is against the law. Marriage in industrial nations joins individuals, and relationships between individuals can be severed more easily than can those between groups. As divorce grows more common, North Americans practice *serial monogamy:* Individuals have more than one spouse but never, legally, more than one at the same time. As stated earlier, the two forms of polygamy are polygyny and polyandry. Polyandry is practiced in only a few cultures, notably among certain groups in Tibet, Nepal, and India. Polygyny is much more common.

Polygyny

We must distinguish between the social approval of plural marriage and its actual frequency in a particular society. Many cultures approve of a man's having more than one wife. However, even when polygyny is allowed or encouraged, most men are monogamous, and polygyny characterizes only a fraction of the marriages.

What factors promote, and discourage, polygyny? Polygyny is much more common in patrilineal than in matrilineal societies. The relatively high status that women enjoy in matrilineal societies tends to grant them a degree of independence from men that makes polygyny less likely. Nor is polygyny characteristic of most foraging societies, where a married couple and nuclear family often function as an economically viable team. Most industrial nations have outlawed polygyny.

An equal sex ratio tends to work against polygyny if marriage is an expectation for both men and women. In the United States, about 105 males are born for every 100 females. In adulthood, the ratio of men to women equalizes, and eventually it reverses. The average North American woman outlives the average man. In many nonindustrial societies as well, the male-biased sex ratio among children reverses in adulthood. In some societies, men inherit widows as their plural wives.

The custom of men marrying later than women promotes polygyny. Among the Kanuri people of Bornu, Nigeria, men got married between the ages of 18 and 30; women, between 12 and 14 (Cohen 1967). The age difference between spouses meant that there were more widows than widowers. Most of the widows remarried, some in polygynous unions. Among the Kanuri and in other polygynous societies, widows made up a large number of the women involved in plural marriages (Hart, Pilling, and Goodale 1988). Polygyny is favored in situations in which having plural wives is an indicator of a man's household productivity, prestige, and social position. The more wives, the more workers. Increased productivity means more wealth. This wealth in turn attracts additional wives to the household. Wealth and wives bring greater prestige to the household and its head.

Polygyny also is supported when the existing spouses agree about when another one is to be added, especially if they are to share the same household. In certain societies, the first wife requests a second one to help with household chores. The second wife's status is lower than that of the first; they are senior and junior wives.

Modern-day polygyny is illustrated by this photo (left) of South African President Joseph Zuma and his three wives. In the United States as in South Africa, powerful men often have multiple wives, but not legally at the same time. The three marriages of Donald Trump (shown here with his third wife, Melania) illustrate serial monogamy.

Left: © Mike Hutchings/AP Images; right: © Mary Altaffer/AP Images

The senior wife sometimes chooses the junior one from among her close kinswomen. Polygyny also can work when the cowives live apart. Among the Betsileo of Madagascar, the different wives always lived in different villages. A man's first and senior wife, called "Big Wife," lived in the village where he cultivated his best rice field and spent most of his time. Polygynous men must be able to support multiple wives. High-status Betsileo men with multiple rice fields could have a wife and households near each field. Those men spent most of their time with the senior wife, but they visited the others throughout the year.

Polygyny can also be favored when it is politically advantageous. Plural wives can play important political roles in nonindustrial states. The king of the Merina, a populous society in the highlands of Madagascar, had palaces for each of his 12 wives in different provinces. He stayed with them when he traveled through the kingdom. They were his local agents, overseeing and reporting on provincial matters. The king of Buganda, the major precolonial state of Uganda, took hundreds of wives, representing all the clans in his nation. Everyone in the kingdom became the king's in-law, and all the clans had a chance to provide the next ruler. This was a way of giving the common people a stake in the government.

We see that there is no single explanation for polygyny. Its context and function vary from society to society and even within the same society. Some men are polygynous because they have inherited a widow from a brother (the levirate). Others have plural wives because they seek prestige or want to increase household productivity. Still others use marriage as a political tool or a means of economic advancement. Men and women with political and economic ambitions cultivate marital alliances that serve their aims. In many societies, including the Betsileo

of Madagascar and the Igbo of Nigeria, women arrange the marriages.

Like all institutions studied by anthropologists, customs involving plural marriage are changing in the contemporary world and in the context of nation-states and globalization. In Turkey, for example, polygyny had been allowed for men who could afford multiple wives and many children. Polygyny now is outlawed, but it still is practiced. Because polygynous unions have lost legal status, secondary wives are now at much greater risk if their husband mistreats, neglects, or leaves them (Bilefsky 2006).

Polyandry

Polyandry is rare and is practiced under very specific conditions. Most of the world's polyandrous peoples live in South Asia—Tibet, Nepal, India, and Sri Lanka. In some of these areas, polyandry seems to be a cultural adaptation to mobility associated with customary male travel for trade, commerce, and military operations. Polyandry ensures there will be at least one man at home to accomplish male activities within a gender-based division of labor. Fraternal polyandry is also an effective strategy when resources are scarce. Brothers with limited resources (in land) pool their resources in expanded (polyandrous) households. They take just one wife. Polyandry restricts the number of wives and heirs. Less competition among heirs means that land can be transmitted with minimal fragmentation.

THE ONLINE MARRIAGE MARKET

People today shop for everything online, including romantic relationships, in what has been labeled the online "marriage market." There are huge differences in the marriage markets of industrial versus nonindustrial societies. In some of the latter, potential spouses may be limited to cross cousins or members of the other moiety (see Figures 20.1 and 20.2). Sometimes there are set rules of exogamy, such that, for example, women of descent group A have to marry men from descent group B, while men from A must marry women from C. Often, marriages are arranged by relatives. In almost all cases, however, there is some kind of preexisting social relationship between any two individuals who marry and their kin groups.

Potential mates still meet in person in modern nations. Sometimes friends—rarely relatives—help arrange such meetings. Besides friends of friends, the marriage market includes schools, the workplace, bars, clubs, parties, churches, and hobby groups. Add the Internet, which in contemporary societies has become a new place to seek out and develop "virtual" relationships, including romantic ones that may lead eventually to a face-to-face meeting. As part of the "Me, My Spouse, and the Internet" project at the University of Oxford, Bernie Hogan, Nai Li, and William Dutton (2011) surveyed cohabiting couples in 18 countries (Table 20.1 lists those countries and the sample size for each). This study (conducted online) sampled 12,600 couples (25,200 individuals aged 18 and older), all with home Internet access. Respondents were asked about how they met their partners, their dating strategies, how they maintain their current relationships and social networks, and how they use the Internet.

The Oxford survey found that online dating has become a significant part of the marriage market. The role of the Internet has been complementary, rather than a substitution, for offline partner shopping. That is, people still seek and find partners in the old, familiar places, but they look online as well. One-third of the respondents in the study had some experience with online dating, and about 15 percent were in a relationship that had started online. (Hogan et al. 2011).

Online dating is socially shaped: One's offline social connections influence one's opinions and use of online dating. People who know someone who dates online are themselves more likely to date online and to approve of online dating. Like online banking and online shopping, Internet dating is an "experience technology" (Hogan et al. 2011): One's attitudes about that technology reflect one's experiences with it. The more one is exposed to online dating, the more one approves of it. People don't even need to have been successful at online dating to feel positive about it. Simply trying it enhances their view of the experience.

Who benefits most from the new technology? Is it young, tech-savvy people who go online for

TABLE 20.1 Countries Sampled in the Oxford Internet Institute Project "Me, My Spouse, and the Internet"

COUNTRY	SAMPLE SIZE	PERCENT
Italy	3,515	13.9
France	2,970	11.8
Spain	2,673	10.6
Germany	2,638	10.5
UK	2,552	10.1
Brazil	2,438	9.7
Japan	2,084	8.3
Netherlands	1,491	5.9
Belgium	1,124	4.5
Sweden	794	3.1
Portugal	603	2.4
Finland	508	2.0
Ireland	368	1.5
Norway	317	1.3
Austria	309	1.2
Greece	297	1.2
Switzerland	278	1.1
Denmark	241	1.0
Total	25,200	100.0

SOURCE: Bernie Hogan, Nai Li, and William H. Dutton, *A Global Shift in the Social Relationships of Networked Individuals: Meeting and Dating Online Comes of Age* (February 14, 2011, Table 1.1, p. 5). Oxford Internet Institute, University of Oxford, 2011.

almost everything? Or might it be people who are more socially isolated in the offline world, including divorced, older, and widowed people and others who feel alone in their local community? Interestingly, the Oxford researchers found that older people were more likely than younger ones to use online dating to find their current partner. About 36 percent of people over 40 had done so, versus 23 percent of younger adults.

A country's degree of media exposure influences its citizens' Internet access and use of online resources. In Europe, the media-saturated nations of Northern Europe were most likely to use online dating, which benefits from a critical mass of Internet connectivity (the more people online, the larger the pool of potential contacts). On the other hand, online Brazilians (who tend to be gregarious both on- and offline) were most likely to know someone who either began a relationship online or married someone first met online. Personal knowledge of an online romantic relationship was reported by 81 percent of the

Brazilians in the sample versus less than 40 percent of Germans. Brazilians were most, while Britons and Austrians were least, likely to know someone whose partner had been met online.

The Internet reconfigures access to people in general. More of the respondents in the Oxford study reported making online friends than romantic liaisons. More than half (55 percent) of respondents (considering all 18 countries) had met someone new online (Hogan et al. 2011). The 2,438 Brazilians in the sample were the most likely to move from an online to a face-to-face contact. Fully 83 percent of Internet-enabled Brazilians reported meeting someone face-to-face after first meeting him or her online. Japanese respondents were least likely to meet in person after an online acquaintance. They also were least likely to engage in online dating.

In some countries, Internet penetration is almost total, and social network sites have diffused rapidly. In others, social networking and personal sites are less pervasive. With advanced Internet penetration, the online and offline worlds begin to merge. People grow less suspicious. They include more of their "real-world" contacts in their online network, and they reveal more about themselves.

In countries (and regions) with less Internet access, online contacts remain more impersonal and disguised. They tend to take place on websites where icons, pseudonyms, and handles, rather than personal data and pictures, predominate. In this setting, the online world is more separate and foreign—a place where one goes to meet people who may be (and remain) otherwise inaccessible.

The Internet enhances our opportunities to meet people and to form personal relationships. It lets us connect with old friends, new friends, groups, and individuals. But this accessibility also can be disruptive. It can spur jealousy, for example, when a partner makes new friends or reconnects to old ones—and with good reason. The Oxford researchers found that many people disclosed intimate personal details in online settings with someone other than their spouse or partner (Hogan et al. 2011). The researchers also found that heavy media use did not necessarily enhance—and might even decrease—marital satisfaction (Oxford 2013). At a certain point, the complexity of maintaining many distinct communication threads (e.g., Facebook, e-mails, texts, and instant messages) may start undermining relationship ties (Oxford 2013).

for REVIEW

summary

1. Marriage, which usually is a form of domestic partnership, is difficult to define. Marriage conveys various rights. It establishes legal parentage, and it gives each spouse rights to the sexuality, labor, and property of the other. Marriage also establishes a "relationship of affinity" between each spouse and the other spouse's relatives.

2. Human behavior with respect to mating with close relatives may express generalized primate tendencies, but types, risks, and avoidance of incest also reflect specific kinship structures. The avoidance of incest promotes exogamy, which widens social networks.

3. Endogamic rules are common in stratified societies. One extreme example is India, where castes are the endogamous units. Certain ancient kingdoms encouraged royal incest while prohibiting incest by commoners.

4. In societies with descent groups, marriages are relationships between groups as well as between spouses. In patrilineal societies, the groom and his relatives often transfer wealth to the bride and her relatives. As the value of that transfer increases, the divorce rate declines. Examples of how marital customs create and maintain group alliances include the sororate and the levirate.

5. The ease and frequency of divorce vary across cultures. When marriage is a matter of intergroup alliance, divorce is less common. A large fund of joint property also complicates divorce.

6. Many societies permit plural marriages. The two kinds of polygamy are polygyny and polyandry. The former (and more common) involves multiple wives; the latter, multiple husbands.

7. The Internet, which reconfigures social relations and networks more generally, is an important addition to the marriage market in contemporary nations.

key terms

critical thinking

1. What is homogamy? In countries such as the United States, what are the social and economic implications of homogamy (especially when coupled with other trends such as the rise of female education and employment)?

2. What is dowry? What customs involving gift giving typically occur with marriage in patrilineal societies? Do you have comparable customs in your society? Why or why not?

3. According to Edmund Leach (1955), depending on the society, several different kinds of rights are allocated by marriage. What are these rights? Which among these rights do you consider more fundamental than others in your definition of marriage? Which ones can you do without? Why?

4. Outside industrial societies, marriage is often more a relationship between groups than one between individuals. What does this mean? What are some examples of this?

5. How do you, personally, define marriage? Can you come up with a definition of marriage that would fit all the cases described in this chapter?

Religion

▶ What is religion, and what are its various forms, social correlates, and functions?

▶ What is ritual, and what are its various forms and expressions?

▶ What role does religion play in maintaining and changing societies?

The Hathee Singh Jain temple in Ahmedabad, Gujarat, India.

© Conrad P. Kottak

understanding OURSELVES

Have you ever noticed how much baseball players spit? Outside baseball—even among other male sports figures—spitting is considered impolite. Football players, with their customary headgear, don't spit, nor do basketball players, who might slip on the court. No spitting by tennis players, gymnasts, or swimmers, not even Mark Spitz (a swimmer turned dentist). But watch any baseball game for a few innings and you'll see spitting galore. Since pitchers appear to be the spitting champions, the custom likely originated on the mound. It continues today as a carryover from the days when pitchers routinely chewed tobacco, believing that nicotine enhanced their concentration and effectiveness. The spitting custom spread to other players, who unabashedly spew saliva from the outfield to the dugout steps.

For the student of custom, ritual, and magic, baseball is an especially interesting game, to which lessons from anthropology are easily applied. The pioneering anthropologist Bronislaw Malinowski, writing about Pacific Islanders rather than baseball players, noted they had developed all sorts of magic to use in sailing, a hazardous activity. He proposed that when people face conditions they can't control (e.g., wind and weather), they turn to magic. Magic, in the form of rituals, taboos, and sacred objects, is particularly evident in baseball. Like sailing magic, baseball magic reduces psychological stress, creating an illusion of control when real control is lacking.

In several publications about baseball, the anthropologist George Gmelch makes use of Malinowski's observation that magic is most common in situations dominated by chance and uncertainty. All sorts of magical behaviors surround pitching and batting, which are full of uncertainty. There are fewer rituals for fielding, over which players have more control. (Batting averages of .350 or higher are very rare after a full season, but a fielding percentage below .900 is a disgrace.) Especially obvious are the rituals (like the spitting) of pitchers, who may tug their cap between pitches, spit in a particular direction, magically manipulate the resin bag, talk to the ball, or wash their hands after giving up a run. Batters have their rituals, too. It isn't uncommon to see Houston Astros outfielder Carlos Gomez kiss his bat, which he likes to talk to, smell, threaten—and reward when he gets a hit. Another batter routinely would spit, then ritually touch his gob with his bat, to enhance his success at the plate.

Humans use tools to accomplish a lot, but technology still doesn't let us "have it all." To keep hope alive in situations of uncertainty, and for outcomes we can't control, all societies draw on magic and religion as sources of nonmaterial comfort, explanation, and control. What are your rituals?

WHAT IS RELIGION?

In his book *Religion: An Anthropological View*, Anthony F. C. Wallace defined **religion** as "belief and ritual concerned with supernatural beings, powers, and forces" (1966, p. 5). By "supernatural," Wallace was referring to a nonmaterial realm beyond (but believed to impinge on) the observable world. The supernatural cannot be verified or falsified empirically and is inexplicable in ordinary terms. It must be accepted "on faith." Supernatural *beings* (e.g., deities, ghosts, demons, souls, spirits) dwell outside our material world, which they may visit from time to time. There also are supernatural or sacred *forces,* some of them wielded by deities and spirits, others that simply exist. In many societies, people believe they can benefit from, become imbued with, or manipulate such forces (see Bielo 2015; Bowen 2014; Bowie 2006; Crapo 2003; Hicks 2010; Lambek 2008; Stein and Stein 2011; Warms, Garber, and McGee 2009).

Wallace's definition of religion focuses on beings, powers, and forces within the supernatural realm. Émile Durkheim (1912/2001), one of the founders of the anthropology of religion, focused on the distinction between the sacred (the domain of religion) and the profane (the everyday world). Like the supernatural for Wallace, Durkheim's "sacred" was a domain set off from the ordinary, or the mundane (he used the word *profane*). For Durkheim, although every society recognized a sacred domain, the specifics of that domain varied from society to society. In other words, he saw religion as a cultural universal, while recognizing that specific religious beliefs and practices would vary from society to society. Durkheim believed that Native Australian societies had retained the most elementary, or basic, forms of religion. He noted that their most sacred objects, including plants and animals that served as totems, were not supernatural at all. Rather, they were "real-world" entities (e.g., kangaroos, grubs) that had acquired religious meaning and became sacred objects for the social groups that "worshipped" them. Durkheim saw totemism as the most elemetary or basic form of religion.

Durkheim (1912/2001) focused on groups of people—congregants—who gather together for worship, such as a group of Native Australians worshiping a particular totem. He stressed the collective, social, and shared nature of religion, the meanings it embodies, and the emotions it generates. He highlighted religious *effervescence*, the bubbling up of collective emotional intensity generated by worship. As Michael Lambek (2008, p. 5) remarks, "good anthropology understands that religious worlds are real, vivid, and significant to those who construct and inhabit them."

Congregants who worship together share certain beliefs; they have accepted a particular set of doctrines concerning the sacred and its relationship to human beings. The word *religion* derives from the Latin *religare*—"to tie, to bind"—but it is not necessary for all members of a given religion to meet together as a common body. Subgroups meet regularly at local congregation sites. They may attend occasional meetings with adherents representing a wider region. And they may form an imagined community with people of similar faith throughout the world.

Verbal manifestations of religious beliefs include prayers, chants, myths, texts, and statements about ethics and morality (see Hicks 2010; Moro and Meyers 2012; Stein and Stein 2011; Winzeler

Detroit Tiger first baseman Miguel Cabrera kisses his maple bat before hitting his 42nd home run of 2012 at Comerica Park. Sometimes baseball magic works: Cabrera went on that year to achieve baseball's Triple Crown and win the American League's MVP award. He repeated as AL batting champion and MVP in 2013.
© Stan Grossfeld/The Boston Globe via Getty Images

religion
Belief and ritual concerned with supernatural beings, powers, and forces.

2012). Other aspects of religion include notions about purity and pollution (including taboos involving diet and physical contact), sacrifice, initiation, rites of passage, vision quests, pilgrimages, spirit possession, prophecy, study, devotion, and moral actions (Lambek 2008, p. 9).

Like ethnicity and language, religion both unites and divides. Participation in common rites can affirm, and thus maintain, the solidarity of a group of adherents. Religious differences also can be associated with bitter enmity. Contacts and confrontations have increased between so-called world religions, such as Christianity and Islam, and the more localized forms of religion that missionaries typically lump together under the disparaging term "paganism." Increasingly, ethnic, regional, and class conflicts come to be framed in religious terms. Contemporary examples of religion as a social and political force include the Iranian revolution, the rise of the religious right in the United States, the worldwide spread of Pentecostalism, and various Islamic movements (see Lindquist and Handelman 2013).

Long ago, Edward Sapir (1928/1956) argued for a distinction between "a religion" and "religion." The former term would apply only to a formally organized religion, such as the world religions just mentioned. The latter—religion—is universal; it refers to religious beliefs and behavior, which exist in all societies, even if they don't stand out as a separate and clearly demarcated sphere. Indeed, many anthropologists (e.g., Asad 1983/2008) argue that such categories as "religion," "politics," and "the economy" are arbitrary constructs that apply best, and perhaps only, to Western, Christian, and modern societies. In such contexts religion can be seen as a specific domain,

Illustrating polytheism, this section of the East Frieze of the Parthenon (Athens, Greece) shows Poseidon, Apollo, and Artemis. The frieze dates to ca. 447–432 B.C.E.
© Gianni Dagli Orti/Corbis

animism
The belief in souls, or doubles.

polytheism
The belief in multiple deities, who control aspects of nature.

monotheism
The belief in a single all-powerful deity.

mana
A sacred, impersonal force, so named in Melanesia and Polynesia.

separate from politics and the economy. By contrast, in nonindustrial societies, religion typically is more embedded in society. Religious beliefs can help regulate the economy (e.g., astrologers determine when to plant) or permeate politics (e.g., divine right of kings).

Anthropologists agree that religion exists in all human societies; it is a cultural universal. However, we'll see that it isn't always easy to distinguish the sacred from the profane and that different societies conceptualize divinity, the sacred, the supernatural, and ultimate realities very differently.

EXPRESSIONS OF RELIGION

When did religion begin? No one knows for sure. There are suggestions of religion in Neandertal burials and on European cave walls, where painted stick figures may represent shamans, early religious specialists. Nevertheless, any statement about when, where, why, and how religion arose, or any description of its original nature, can only be speculative. Although such speculations are inconclusive, many have revealed important functions and effects of religious behavior. Several theories will be examined now.

Spiritual Beings

Another founder of the anthropology of religion was the Englishman Sir Edward Burnett Tylor (1871/1958). Religion arose, Tylor thought, as people tried to understand conditions and events they could not explain by reference to daily experience. Tylor believed that ancient humans—and contemporary nonindustrial peoples—were

particularly intrigued with death, dreaming, and trance. People see images they remember when they wake up or come out of a trance state. Tylor concluded that attempts to explain dreams and trances led early humans to believe that two entities inhabit the body. One is active during the day, and the other—a double, or soul—is active during sleep and trance states. Although they never meet, they are vital to each other. When the double permanently leaves the body, the person dies. Death is departure of the soul. From the Latin for soul, *anima*, Tylor named this belief animism. The soul was one sort of spiritual entity; people remembered various other entities from their dreams and trances—other spirits. For Tylor, **animism,** the earliest form of religion, was a belief in spiritual beings.

Tylor proposed that religion evolved through stages, beginning with animism. **Polytheism** (the belief in multiple gods) and then **monotheism** (the belief in a single, all-powerful deity) developed later. Because religion originated to explain things, Tylor thought it would decline as science offered better explanations. To an extent, he was right. We now have scientific explanations for many things that religion once elucidated (see Salazar and Bestard 2015). Nevertheless, because religion persists, it must do something more than explain. It must, and does, have other functions and meanings.

Powers and Forces

In addition to animism—and sometimes coexisting with it in the same society—is a view of the supernatural as a domain of impersonal power, or force, which people can control under certain conditions. (You'd be right to think of *Star Wars*.) Such a conception has been particularly prominent in Melanesia, the area of the South Pacific that includes New Guinea and adjacent islands. Melanesians traditionally believed in **mana,** a sacred, impersonal force existing in the universe. Mana could reside in people, animals, plants, and objects.

Melanesian mana was similar to our notion of good luck. Objects with mana could change someone's luck. For example, a charm or an amulet belonging to a successful hunter could transmit the hunter's mana to the next person who held or wore it. A woman could put a rock in her garden, see her yields improve, and attribute the change to the force contained in the rock.

Beliefs in manalike forces have been widespread, although the specifics of the religious doctrines have varied. Consider the contrast between mana in Melanesia and mana in Polynesia (the islands included in a triangular area marked by Hawaii to the north, Easter Island to the east, and New Zealand to the southwest). In Melanesia, anyone could acquire mana by chance, or by working hard to get it. In Polynesia, however, mana was attached to political offices. Chiefs and nobles had more mana than ordinary people did.

So charged with mana were the highest chiefs that contact with them was dangerous to commoners. The mana of chiefs flowed out of their bodies. It could infect the ground, making it dangerous for others to walk in the chief's footsteps. It could permeate the containers and utensils chiefs used in eating. Because high chiefs had so much mana, their bodies and possessions were **taboo** (set apart as sacred and off-limits to ordinary people). Because ordinary people couldn't bear as much sacred current as royalty could, when commoners were accidentally exposed, purification rites were necessary.

As Horton (1993) and Lambek (2008) point out, there are universals in human thought and experience, common conditions and situations that call out for explanation. One of these universal questions is what happens in sleep and trance, and with death. Another is the question of why do some people prosper, while others fail. A religious explanation blames imbalances in success and prestige on such nonmaterial factors as luck, mana, sorcery, or being one of "God's chosen."

The beliefs in spiritual beings (e.g., animism) and supernatural forces (e.g., mana) fit within Wallace's definition of religion, given at the beginning of this chapter. Most religions include both spirits and impersonal forces. Likewise, the supernatural beliefs of contemporary North Americans can include beings (gods, saints, souls, demons) and forces (charms, talismans, crystals, and sacred objects).

Magic and Religion

Magic refers to supernatural techniques intended to accomplish specific aims. These techniques include magical actions, offerings, spells, formulas, and incantations. Magicians might employ *imitative magic* to produce a desired effect by imitating it. For example, if magicians wish to harm someone, they can imitate that effect on an image of the victim—for instance, by sticking pins in "voodoo dolls." With *contagious magic,* whatever is done to an object is believed to affect a person who once had contact with it. Sometimes practitioners of contagious magic use body products from prospective victims—their nails or hair, for example. The spell performed on the body product is believed eventually to reach the person (see Stein and Stein 2011). Magic exists in societies with diverse religious beliefs, including animism, mana, polytheism, and monotheism.

Uncertainty, Anxiety, Solace

Religion and magic don't just explain things and help people accomplish goals. They are also important to the realm of human feelings. In other words, they serve emotional needs as well as cognitive (e.g., explanatory) ones. For example, supernatural beliefs and practices can help reduce

anxiety. Magical techniques can dispel doubts that arise when outcomes are beyond human control. Similarly, religion helps people face death and endure life crises.

When people face uncertainty and danger, according to Malinowski, they turn to magic.

> [H]owever much knowledge and science help man in allowing him to obtain what he wants, they are unable completely to control chance, to eliminate accidents, to foresee the unexpected turn of natural events, or to make human handiwork reliable and adequate to all practical requirements. (Malinowski 1931/1978, p. 39)

As was discussed in this chapter's "Understanding Ourselves," Malinowski found that the Trobriand Islanders used a variety of magical practices when they went on sailing expeditions, a hazardous activity. He proposed that because people can't control matters such as wind, weather, and the fish supply, they turn to magic. People may call on magic when they come to a gap in their knowledge or ability to control a situation, yet have to continue in a pursuit (Malinowski 1931/1978).

Malinowski noted that it was only when confronted by situations they could not control that Trobrianders, out of psychological stress, turned from technology to magic. Despite our own advanced technical skills, we still can't control every outcome, and magic persists in contemporary societies. As was discussed in "Understanding Ourselves," magic is particularly evident in baseball. George Gmelch (1978, 2001, 2006) describes a

taboo
Sacred and forbidden; prohibition backed by supernatural sanctions.

magic
The use of supernatural techniques to accomplish specific ends.

Trobriand Islanders prepare a traditional trading canoe for use in the Kula, which is a regional exchange system. The women bring trade goods in a basket, while the men prepare the long canoe to set sail. Magic is often associated with uncertainty, such as sailing in unpredictable waters.

© Peter Essick/Aurora Photos

series of rituals, taboos, and sacred objects used in the sport. Like Trobriand sailing magic, these behaviors reduce psychological stress, creating an illusion of magical control when real control is lacking. Baseball magic is especially prevalent in pitching and batting.

According to Malinowski, magic is used to establish control, but religion "is born out of . . . the real tragedies of human life" (1931/1978, p. 45). Religion offers emotional comfort, particularly when people face a crisis. Malinowski saw tribal religions as concerned mainly with organizing, commemorating, and helping people get through such life events as birth, puberty, marriage, and death.

Passage rites are often collective. A group—such as these Maasai initiates in Kenya or these navy trainees in San Diego—passes through the rites as a unit. Such liminal people experience the same treatment and conditions and must act alike. They share communitas, an intense community spirit, a feeling of great social solidarity or togetherness.

© Top: John Warburton-Lee Photography/Alamy Stock Photo; bottom: © Joe McNally/Hulton Archive/Getty Images

Rituals

Several features distinguish **ritual** behavior from other kinds of behavior (Rappaport 1974, 1999). Rituals are formal—stylized, repetitive, and stereotyped. People perform them in special (sacred) places and at set times. Rituals include liturgical orders—sequences of words and actions invented prior to the current performance in which they occur. Rituals convey information about the participants and their traditions. Repeated year after year, generation after generation, rituals translate enduring messages, values, and sentiments into action.

Rituals are social acts. Inevitably, some participants are more committed than others are to the beliefs that lie behind the rites. However, just by taking part in a joint public act, the performers signal that they accept a common social and moral order, one that transcends their status as individuals.

Rites of Passage

Magic and religion, as Malinowski noted, can reduce anxiety and allay fears. Ironically, beliefs and rituals also can create anxiety and a sense of insecurity and danger (Radcliffe-Brown 1962/1965). Anxiety can arise because a rite exists. Indeed, participation in a collective ritual (e.g., circumcision of early teen boys, common among East African pastoralists) can produce stress, whose common reduction, once the ritual is completed, enhances the solidarity of the participants.

Rites of passage can be individual or collective. Traditional Native American vision quests illustrate individual **rites of passage** (customs associated with the transition from one place or stage of life to another). To move from boyhood to manhood, a youth would temporarily separate from his community. After a period of isolation in the wilderness, often featuring fasting and drug consumption, the young man would see a vision, which would become his guardian spirit. He would return then to his community as a socially recognized adult.

Contemporary rites of passage include confirmations, baptisms, bar and bat mitzvahs, initiations, weddings, and application for Social Security and Medicare. Passage rites involve changes in social status, such as from boyhood to manhood and from nonmember to sorority sister. More generally, a rite of passage can mark any change in place, condition, social position, or age.

All rites of passage have three phases: separation, liminality, and incorporation. In the first phase, people withdraw from ordinary society. In the third phase, they reenter society, having completed a rite that changes their status. The second, or liminal, phase is the most interesting. It is the limbo, or "time-out," during which people have left one status but haven't yet entered or joined the next (Turner 1969/1995).

LIMINALITY	NORMAL SOCIAL STRUCTURE
Transition	State
Homogeneity	Heterogeneity
Communitas	Structure
Equality	Inequality
Anonymity	Names
Absence of property	Property
Absence of status	Status
Nakedness or uniform dress	Dress distinctions
Sexual continence or excess	Sexuality
Minimization of sex distinctions	Maximization of sex distinctions
Absence of rank	Rank
Humility	Pride
Disregard of personal appearance	Care for personal appearance
Unselfishness	Selfishness
Total obedience	Obedience only to superior rank
Sacredness	Secularity
Sacred instruction	Technical knowledge
Silence	Speech
Simplicity	Complexity
Acceptance of pain and suffering	Avoidance of pain and suffering

SOURCE: Victor W. Turner, *The Ritual Process: Structure and Anti-Structure* (Chicago: Aldine de Gruyter, 1969), pp. 106–107.

Liminality always has certain characteristics. Liminal people exist apart from ordinary distinctions and expectations; they are living in a time out of time. A series of contrasts demarcate liminality from normal social life. For example, among the Ndembu of Zambia, a chief underwent a rite of passage prior to taking office. During the liminal period, his past and future positions in society were ignored, even reversed. He was subjected to a variety of insults, orders, and humiliations.

Passage rites often are collective. Several individuals—boys being circumcised, fraternity or sorority initiates, men at military boot camps, football players in summer training camps, women becoming nuns—pass through the rites together as a group. Recap 21.1 summarizes the contrasts, or oppositions, between liminality and normal social life. Most notable is the social aspect of collective liminality called **communitas**—an intense community spirit, a feeling of great social solidarity, equality, and togetherness (Turner 1967). Liminal people experience the same treatment and conditions and must act alike. Liminality can be marked ritually and symbolically by reversals of ordinary behavior. For example, sexual taboos may be intensified; conversely, sexual excess may be encouraged. Liminal symbols, such as special clothing or body paint, mark the condition as extraordinary—beyond ordinary society and everyday life.

Liminality is basic to all passage rites. Furthermore, in certain societies, including our own, liminal symbols can be used to set off one (religious) group from another—and from society as a whole. Such "permanent liminal groups" (e.g., sects, brotherhoods, and cults) are found most characteristically in nation-states. Such liminal features as humility, poverty, equality, obedience, sexual abstinence, and silence (see Recap 21.1) may be required for all sect or cult members. Those who join such a group agree to its rules. As if they were undergoing a passage rite—but in this case a never-ending one—they may have to abandon their previous possessions and social ties, including those with family members. Is liminality compatible with Facebook?

Members of a sect or cult often wear uniform clothing. Often they adopt a common hairstyle (shaved head, short hair, or long hair). Liminal groups submerge the individual in the collective. This may be one reason Americans, whose core values include individuality and individualism, are so fearful and suspicious of "cults."

Not all collective rites are rites of passage. Most societies have occasions on which people come together to worship or celebrate and, in doing so, affirm and reinforce their solidarity. Rituals such as

liminality
The in-between phase of a rite of passage.

communitas
An intense feeling of social solidarity.

the totemic ceremonies described in the next section are *rites of intensification:* They intensify social solidarity. The ritual creates communitas and produces emotions (the collective spiritual effervescence described by Durkheim 1912/2001) that enhance social solidarity.

Totemism

totem
An animal, a plant, or a geographic feature associated with a specific social group, to which that totem is sacred or symbolically important.

Totemism was a key ingredient in the religions of the Native Australians. **Totems** could be animals, plants, or geographic features. In each tribe, groups of people had particular totems. Members of each totemic group believed themselves to be descendants of their totem, which they customarily neither killed nor ate. However, this taboo was suspended once a year, when people assembled for ceremonies dedicated to the totem. Only on that occasion were they allowed to kill and eat their totem. These annual rites were believed to be necessary for the totem's survival and reproduction.

Totemism uses nature as a model for society. The totems usually are animals and plants, which are part of nature. People relate to nature through their totemic association with natural species. Because each group has a different totem, social differences mirror natural contrasts. Diversity in the natural order becomes a model for diversity in the social order. However, although totemic plants and animals occupy different niches in nature, on another level they are united because they all are part of nature. The unity of the human social order is enhanced by symbolic association with and imitation of the natural order (Durkheim 1912/2001; Lévi-Strauss 1963; Radcliffe-Brown 1962/1965).

cosmology
A system, often religious, for imagining and understanding the universe.

Totemism is one form of **cosmology**—a system, in this case a religious one, for imagining and understanding the universe. Claude Lévi-Strauss, a prolific French anthropologist and a key figure in the anthropology of religion, is well known for his studies of myth, folklore, totemism, and cosmology. Lévi-Strauss believed that one role of religious rites and beliefs is to affirm, and thus maintain, the solidarity of a religion's adherents. Totems are sacred emblems symbolizing common identity. This is true not just among Native Australians but also among Native American groups of the North Pacific Coast of North America, whose totem poles are well known. Their totemic carvings, which commemorated and told visual stories about ancestors, animals, and spirits, were also associated with ceremonies. In totemic rites, people gather together to honor their totem. In so doing, they use ritual to maintain the social oneness that the totem symbolizes.

Totemic principles continue to demarcate groups, including clubs, teams, and universities, in modern societies. Badgers and Wolverines are animals, and (it is said in Michigan) Buckeyes are some kind of nut (more precisely, buckeye nuts come from the buckeye tree). Differences between natural species (e.g., Lions, and Tigers, and Bears) distinguish sports teams, and even political parties (donkeys and elephants). Although the modern context is more secular, one can still witness, in intense college football rivalries, some of the effervescence Durkheim noted in Australian totemic religion and other rites of intensification.

RELIGION AND CULTURAL ECOLOGY

Another domain in which religion plays a role is cultural ecology. Behavior motivated by beliefs in supernatural beings, powers, and forces can help people survive in their material environment. Beliefs and rituals can function as part of a group's cultural adaptation to its environment.

The people of India revere zebu cattle, which are protected by the Hindu doctrine of *ahimsa*, a principle of nonviolence that forbids the killing of animals generally. Western economic development agents occasionally (and erroneously) cite the Hindu cattle taboo to illustrate the idea that religious beliefs can stand in the way of rational economic decisions. Hindus might seem to be irrationally ignoring a valuable food (beef) because of their cultural or religious traditions. Development agents also have asserted that Indians don't know how to raise proper cattle. They point to the scraggly zebus that wander around town and country. Western techniques of animal husbandry grow bigger cattle that produce more beef and milk. Western planners lament that Hindus are set in their ways. Bound by culture and tradition, they refuse to develop rationally.

However, these assumptions are both ethnocentric and wrong. Sacred cattle actually play an

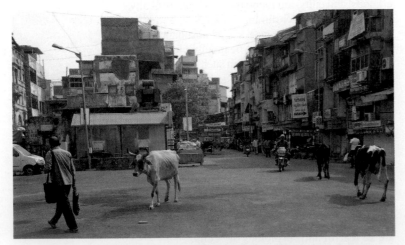

Cows freely walk the streets of any Indian city, including Ahmedabad, Gujarat, shown here. India's zebu cattle are protected by the doctrine of *ahimsa*, a principle of nonviolence that forbids the killing of animals generally.
© Conrad P. Kottak

important adaptive role in an Indian ecosystem that has evolved over thousands of years (Harris 1974, 1978). Peasants' use of cattle to pull plows and carts is part of the technology of Indian agriculture. Indian peasants have no need for large, hungry cattle of the sort that Westerners prefer. Scrawny animals pull plows and carts well enough but don't eat their owners out of house and home. How could peasants with limited land and marginal diets feed super-steers without taking food away from themselves?

Indians use cattle manure to fertilize their fields. Not all the manure is collected, because peasants don't spend much time watching their cattle, which wander and graze at will during certain seasons. In the rainy season, some of the manure that cattle deposit on the hillsides washes down to the fields. In this way, cattle also fertilize the fields indirectly. Furthermore, in a country where fossil fuels are scarce, dry cattle dung, which burns slowly and evenly, is a basic cooking fuel.

Sacred cattle are essential to Indian cultural adaptation. Biologically adapted to poor pasture land and a marginal environment, the scraggly zebu provides fertilizer and fuel, is indispensable in farming, and is affordable for peasants. The Hindu doctrine of *ahimsa* puts the full power of organized religion behind the command not to destroy a valuable resource, even in times of extreme need.

SOCIAL CONTROL

Religion means a lot to people. It helps them cope with uncertainty, adversity, fear, and tragedy. It offers hope that things will get better. Lives can be transformed through spiritual healing. Sinners can repent and be saved—or they can go on sinning and be damned. If the faithful truly internalize a system of religious rewards and punishments, their religion becomes a powerful influence on their attitudes and behavior, as well as what they teach their children.

Many people engage in religious activity because it works for them. Prayers get answered. Native Americans in southwestern Oklahoma use faith healers at high monetary costs, not just because it makes them feel better about the uncertain, but because they believe it works (Lassiter 1998). Each year legions of Brazilians visit a church, Nosso Senhor do Bonfim, in the city of Salvador, Bahia. They vow to repay "Our Lord" (Nosso Senhor) if healing happens. Showing that the vows work, and are repaid, are the thousands of *ex votos,* plastic impressions of every conceivable body part, that adorn the church, along with photos of people who have been cured.

Religion can work by getting inside people and mobilizing their emotions—their joy, their wrath, their righteousness. Adherents can feel a deep sense of shared joy, meaning, experience, communion, belonging, and commitment to their religion. The power of religion affects action. When religions meet, they can coexist peacefully, or their differences can be a basis for enmity and disharmony, even battle. Religious fervor has inspired Christians on crusades against the infidel and has led Muslims to wage holy wars against non-Islamic peoples. Throughout history, political leaders have used religion to promote and justify their views and policies.

How can leaders mobilize communities to support their own policies? One way is by persuasion; another is by hatred or fear. Consider witchcraft accusations. Witch hunts can be powerful means of social control by creating a climate of danger and insecurity that affects everyone. No one wants to seem deviant, to be accused of being a witch. Witch hunts often aim at socially marginal people who can be accused and punished with the least chance of retaliation. During the great European witch craze, during the 15th, 16th, and 17th centuries (Harris 1974), most accusations and convictions were against poor women with little social support.

To ensure proper behavior, religions offer rewards (e.g., the fellowship of the religious community) and punishments (e.g., the threat of being cast out, or excommunicated). Religions, especially the formal, organized ones found in state societies, often prescribe a code of ethics and morality to guide behavior. Moral codes are ways of maintaining

The Right Reverend Kay Goldsworthy during her consecration service and ordination as Australia's first female Anglican bishop at St. George's Cathedral in Perth, Australia.

© Paul Kane/Getty Images News/Getty Images

order and stability that are reinforced continually in sermons, catechisms, and the like. They become internalized psychologically. They guide behavior and produce regret, guilt, shame, and the need for forgiveness, expiation, and absolution when they are not followed.

KINDS OF RELIGION

Although religion is a cultural universal, religions exist in particular societies, and cultural differences show up systematically in religious beliefs and practices. For example, the religions of stratified, state societies differ from those of societies with less marked social contrasts—societies without kings, lords, and subjects. Churches, temples, and other full-time religious establishments, with their monumental structures and hierarchies of officials, must be supported in some consistent way, such as by tithes and taxes. What kinds of societies can support such hierarchies and architecture?

Religious Specialists and Deities

All societies have religious figures—those believed capable of mediating between humans and the supernatural. More generally, all societies have medico-magico-religious specialists. Modern societies can support both priesthoods and health care professionals. Lacking the resources for such specialization, foraging societies typically have only part-time specialists, who often have both religious and healing roles. **Shaman** is the general term encompassing curers ("witch doctors"), mediums, spiritualists, astrologers, palm readers, and other independent diviners. In foraging societies, shamans usually are part-time; that is, they also hunt or gather.

Societies with productive economies (based on agriculture and trade) and large, dense populations—that is, nation-states—can support full-time religious specialists—professional priesthoods. Like the state itself, priesthoods are hierarchically and bureaucratically organized. Anthony Wallace (1966) describes the religions of such stratified societies as "ecclesiastical" (pertaining to an established church and its hierarchy of officials) and Olympian, after Mount Olympus, home of the classical Greek gods. In such religions, powerful anthropomorphic gods have specialized functions, for example, gods of love, war, the sea, and death. Such *pantheons* (collections of deities) were prominent in the religions of many nonindustrial nation-states, including the Aztecs of Mexico, and several African and Asian kingdoms. Greco-Roman religions also were polytheistic, featuring many deities—the Olympian gods.

In monotheism, all supernatural phenomena are believed to be manifestations of, or under the control of, a single eternal, omniscient, omnipotent, and omnipresent being. In the ecclesiastical monotheistic religion known as Christianity, a single supreme being is manifest in a trinity. Robert Bellah (1978, 2011) viewed most forms of Christianity as examples of "world-rejecting religion." According to Bellah, the first world-rejecting religions arose in ancient civilizations, along with literacy and a specialized priesthood. These religions are so named because of their tendency to reject the natural (mundane, ordinary, material, secular) world and to focus instead on a higher (sacred, transcendent) realm of reality. The divine is a domain of exalted morality to which humans can only aspire. Salvation through fusion with the supernatural is the main goal of such religions.

Protestant Values and Capitalism

Notions of salvation and the afterlife dominate Christian ideologies. However, most varieties of Protestantism lack the hierarchical structure of earlier monotheistic religions, including Roman Catholicism. With a diminished role for the priest (minister), salvation is directly available to individuals. Regardless of their social status, Protestants have unmediated access to the supernatural. The individualistic focus of Protestantism offers a close fit with capitalism and with American culture.

In his influential book *The Protestant Ethic and the Spirit of Capitalism* (1904/1958), the social theorist Max Weber linked the spread of capitalism to the values preached by early Protestant leaders. Weber saw European Protestants (and eventually their American descendants) as more successful financially than Catholics. He attributed this difference to the values stressed by their religions. Weber saw Catholics as more concerned with immediate happiness and security. Protestants were more ascetic, entrepreneurial, and future oriented, he thought.

Capitalism, said Weber, required that the traditional attitudes of Catholic peasants be replaced by values befitting an industrial economy based on capital accumulation. Protestantism placed a premium on hard work, an ascetic life, and profit seeking. Early Protestants saw success on Earth as a sign of divine favor and probable salvation. According to some Protestant credos, individuals could gain favor with God through good works. Other sects stressed predestination, the idea that only a few mortals have been selected for eternal life and that people cannot change their fates. However, material success, achieved through hard work, could be a strong clue that someone was predestined to be saved.

Weber also argued that rational business organization required the removal of industrial production from the home, its setting in peasant societies. Protestantism made such a separation possible by emphasizing individualism: Individuals, not families or households, would be saved or not. Interestingly, given the connection that is usually made with morality and religion in contemporary American discourse about family values,

shaman
A part-time medico-magico-religious practitioner.

the family was a secondary matter for Weber's early Protestants. God and the individual reigned supreme.

Today, of course, in North America, as throughout the world, people of many religions and with diverse worldviews are successful capitalists. Furthermore, traditional Protestant values often have little to do with today's economic maneuvering. Still, there is no denying that the individualistic focus of Protestantism was compatible with the severance of ties to land and kin that industrialism demanded. These values remain prominent in the religious background of many of the people of the United States.

WORLD RELIGIONS

Information on the world's major religions in 2010 and projected for 2050 is provided in Figure 21.1, based on recent comprehensive studies by the Pew Research Center (2012, 2015b). Considering data from more than 230 countries, researchers estimated that the world contained about 5.8 billion religiously affiliated people—84 percent of its population of 6.9 billion in 2010.

There were approximately 2.2 billion Christians (31.4 percent of the global population), 1.6 billion Muslims (23.2 percent), 1 billion Hindus (15 percent), nearly 500 million Buddhists (7.1 percent), and 14 million Jews (0.2 percent). In addition, more than 400 million people (5.9 percent) practice folk or traditional religions of various sorts. Some 58 million people, a bit less than 1 percent of the world's population, belong to other religions, including Baha'i, Jainism, Sikhism, Shintoism, Taoism, Tenrikyo, Wicca, and Zoroastrianism.

About 1.1 billion people—16 percent of the world's population—lacked any religious affiliation. The unaffiliated therefore constitute the third-largest group worldwide with respect to religious affiliation, behind Christians and Muslims. There are about as many unaffiliated people as Roman Catholics in the world. Many of the unaffiliated actually hold some religious or spiritual beliefs, even if they don't identify with a particular religion (Pew Research Center 2012, 2015b).

Worldwide, Islam is growing at a rate of about 2.9 percent annually, compared with 2.3 percent for Christianity. Within Christianity, the growth rate is much higher for "born-again" Christians (e.g., Evangelicals/Pentecostals) than for either Catholics or mainline Protestants. Recent demographic projections by the Pew Research Center (2015b, see Figure 21.1) suggest that by 2050 there will be almost as many Muslims (29.7 percent) as Christians (31.4 percent) in the world. In Europe, Muslims will constitute about 10 percent of the population, compared with about 6 percent today. This chapter's "Appreciating Diversity" documents recent religious changes in the United States, including the growth of non-Christian religions and the unaffiliated.

RELIGION AND CHANGE

Like political organization, religion helps maintain social order. And like political mobilization, religious energy can be harnessed not just for change but also for revolution. Reacting to conquest or to actual or perceived foreign domination, for instance, religious leaders may seek to alter or revitalize their society.

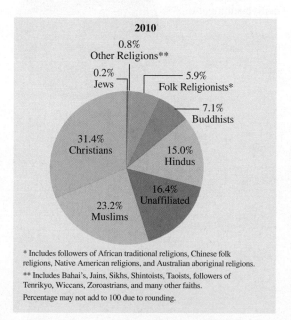

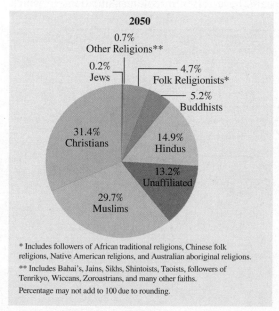

2010

0.8% Other Religions**

0.2% Jews

5.9% Folk Religionists*

7.1% Buddhists

31.4% Christians

15.0% Hindus

16.4% Unaffiliated

23.2% Muslims

* Includes followers of African traditional religions, Chinese folk religions, Native American religions, and Australian aboriginal religions.

** Includes Bahai's, Jains, Sikhs, Shintoists, Taoists, followers of Tenrikyo, Wiccans, Zoroastrians, and many other faiths.

Percentage may not add to 100 due to rounding.

2050

0.7% Other Religions**

0.2% Jews

4.7% Folk Religionists*

5.2% Buddhists

31.4% Christians

14.9% Hindus

13.2% Unaffiliated

29.7% Muslims

* Includes followers of African traditional religions, Chinese folk religions, Native American religions, and Australian aboriginal religions.

** Includes Bahai's, Jains, Sikhs, Shintoists, Taoists, followers of Tenrikyo, Wiccans, Zoroastrians, and many other faiths.

Percentage may not add to 100 due to rounding.

FIGURE 21.1 Major World Religions by Percentage of World Population, 2010, and Projected for 2050.

SOURCE: Pew Research Center. *The Future of World Religions: Population Growth Projections, 2010–2050.* April 2, 2015. http://pewforum.org/files/2015/03/PF_15.04.02_ProjectionsFullReport.pdf.

On the island of Tanna, in Vanuatu, Melanesia, members of the John Frum cargo cult stage a military parade. The young men, who carry fake guns and have "USA" painted on their bodies, see themselves as an elite force within the American army.
© Thierry Falise/LightRocket via Getty Images

Revitalization Movements

revitalization movements
Social movements aimed at altering or revitalizing a society.

Revitalization movements are social movements that occur in times of change, in which religious leaders emerge and undertake to alter or revitalize a society. Christianity originated as a revitalization movement. Jesus was one of several prophets who preached new religious doctrines while the Middle East was under Roman rule. It was a time of social unrest, when a foreign power ruled the land. Jesus inspired a new, enduring, and major religion. His contemporaries were not so successful.

Revitalization movements known as **cargo cults** have arisen in colonial situations in which

cargo cults
Postcolonial, acculturative religious movements in Melanesia.

local people have regular contact with outsiders but lack their wealth, technology, and living standards. Cargo cults attempt to explain European domination and wealth and to achieve similar success magically by mimicking European behavior and manipulating symbols of the desired lifestyle. The cargo cults of Melanesia and Papua New Guinea (see Figure 21.2) are hybrid creations that weave Christian doctrine with aboriginal beliefs. They take their name from their focus on cargo—European goods of the sort natives have seen unloaded from the cargo holds of ships and airplanes.

In one early cult, members believed that the spirits of the dead would arrive in a ship. These ghosts would bring manufactured goods for the natives and would kill all the whites. More recent cults replaced ships with airplanes (Worsley 1959/1985). Many cults have used elements of European culture as sacred objects. The rationale is that Europeans use these objects, have wealth, and therefore must know the "secret of cargo." By mimicking how Europeans use or treat objects, natives hope also to come upon the secret knowledge needed to gain cargo.

For example, having seen Europeans' reverent treatment of flags and flagpoles, the members of one cult began to worship flagpoles. They believed the flagpoles were sacred towers that could transmit messages between the living and the dead. Other natives built airstrips to entice planes bearing canned goods, portable radios, clothing, wristwatches, and motorcycles.

Some cargo cult prophets proclaimed that success would come through a reversal of European domination and native subjugation.

FIGURE 21.2 Location of Melanesia.

The day was near, they preached, when natives, aided by God, Jesus, or native ancestors, would turn the tables. Native skins would turn white, and those of Europeans would turn brown; Europeans would die or be killed.

Syncretisms are cultural, especially religious, mixes that emerge from acculturation. Cargo cults are syncretisms that blend aboriginal and Christian beliefs. Melanesian myths told of ancestors shedding their skins and changing into powerful beings and of dead people returning to life. Christian missionaries also preached resurrection. The cults' preoccupation with cargo is related to traditional Melanesian big man systems. A Melanesian big man was expected to be generous. People worked for the big man, helping him amass wealth, but eventually he had to host a feast and give away all that wealth.

Because of their experience with big man systems, Melanesians believed that all wealthy people eventually had to give their wealth away. For decades, they had attended Christian missions and worked on plantations. All the while they expected Europeans to return the fruits of their labor as their own big men did. When the Europeans refused to distribute the wealth or even to let natives know the secret of its production and distribution, cargo cults developed.

Like arrogant big men, Europeans would be put in their place or leveled, by death if necessary. However, natives lacked the physical means of doing what their traditions said they should do. Thwarted by well-armed colonial forces, natives resorted to magical leveling. They called on supernatural beings to intercede, to kill or otherwise deflate the European big men and redistribute their wealth.

Cargo cults are religious responses to the expansion of the world capitalist economy. However, this religious mobilization had political and economic results. Cult participation gave Melanesians a basis for common interests and activities and thus helped pave the way for political parties and economic interest organizations. Previously separated by geography, language, and customs, Melanesians started forming larger groups as members of the same cults and followers of the same prophets. The cargo cults paved the way for political action through which the indigenous peoples eventually regained their autonomy.

New and Alternative Religious Movements

This chapter's "Appreciating Diversity" describes changing patterns of religious affiliation in the United States, including significant growth in the number of Americans who affiliate with no organized religion. This trend toward nonaffiliation, whether as atheist, agnostic, or "nothing in particular" can also be detected in Canada, Western Europe, China, and Japan. In addition to increasing nonaffiliation, contemporary industrial societies also feature new religious trends and forms of

spiritualism. The New Age movement, which emerged in the 1980s, draws on and blends cultural elements from multiple traditions. It advocates change through individual personal transformation. In the United States and Australia, respectively, some people who are not Native Americans or Native Australians have appropriated the symbols, settings, and purported religious practices of Native Americans and Native Australians for New Age religions. Native American activists decry the appropriation and commercialization of their spiritual beliefs and rituals, as when "sweat lodge" ceremonies are held on cruise ships, with wine and cheese served. They see the appropriation of their ceremonies and traditions as theft. Some Hindus feel similarly about the popularization of yoga.

New religious movements have varied origins. Some have been influenced by Christianity, others by Eastern (Asian) religions, still others by mysticism and spiritualism. Religion also evolves in tandem with science and technology. For example, the Raelian movement, a religious group centered in Switzerland and Montreal, promotes cloning as a way of achieving eternal life (see http://www.rael.org/home).

Many contemporary nations contain unofficial religions. One example is "Yoruba religion," a term applied to perhaps 15 million adherents in Africa as well as to millions of practitioners of syncretic, or blended, religions (with elements of Catholicism and spiritism) in the Western Hemisphere. Forms of Yoruba religion include *santeria* (in the Spanish Caribbean and the United States), *candomblé* (in Brazil), and *vodoun* (in the French Caribbean). Yoruba religion, with roots in precolonial nation-states of West Africa, has spread far beyond its religion of origin, as part of the African diaspora. It remains an influential, identifiable religion today, despite suppression, such as by Cuba's communist government. There are perhaps 3 million practitioners of santeria in Cuba, plus another 800,000 in the United States. At least 1 million Brazilians participate in candomblé, also known as macumba. Voodoo (*vodoun*) has between 2.8 and 3.2 million practitioners (Ontario Consultants 2011), many (perhaps most) of whom would name something else, such as Catholicism, as their religion.

RELIGION AND CULTURAL GLOBALIZATION

Evangelical Protestantism and Pentecostalism

The rapid and ongoing spread of Evangelical Protestantism, which originated in Europe and North America, constitutes a highly successful form of contemporary cultural globalization. A century ago, more than 90 percent of the then approximately 80 million Evangelicals in the world lived in Europe and North America (Pew Research

syncretisms
Cultural, especially religious, mixes, emerging from acculturation.

This New-Time Religion

Because the U.S. Census doesn't gather information about religion, there are no official government statistics on Americans' religious affiliations. To help fill this gap, the Pew Research Center, based in Washington, D.C., carried out "Religious Landscape Studies" in 2007 and 2014. These comprehensive surveys of more than 35,000 adults provide a basis for systematic comparison, enabling us to assess changes in the religious affiliations of Americans between 2007 and 2014 (see Pew Research Center 2015a).

Although the United States continues to have the world's largest Christian population, the number and percentage of Americans affiliated with a Christian church have been declining. Between 2007 and 2014, the Christian share of the U.S. population fell almost 8 points, from 78.4 percent to 70.6 percent. This change was due primarily to declines among Catholics and mainline Protestants, each of which shrank by about three percentage points. (Table 21.1 provides percentages of changes between 2007 and 2014 for all religious categories).

Of the 85 percent of Americans who were raised as Christians, nearly a quarter no longer follow that faith. Former Christians now represent about 19 percent of all U.S. adults. Catholicism has experienced a particularly steep decline. Of the 32 percent of Americans who were raised Catholic, 41 percent no longer practice. Catholics are declining both percentage-wise and in absolute numbers. There were 51 million American Catholics in 2014, 3 million fewer than in 2007.

The absolute number of mainline Protestants—Methodists, Baptists, Lutherans, Presbyterians, and Episcopalians—also fell, from 41 million in 2007 to 36 million in 2014. However, the number of Americans participating in historically black Protestant churches has remained fairly stable in recent years, at around 16 million people. Evangelicals represent the only group of Protestants whose numbers have been increasing, even as their share of the U.S. population has declined by a percentage point. Evangelicals now number around 62 million American adults, an increase of about 2 million since 2007.

As the Christian share of the population has been declining, the percentage of Americans belonging to non-Christian faiths has been rising. Between 2007 and 2014, this percentage rose from 4.7 percent to 5.9, with growth especially strong for Muslims and Hindus.

The most notable increase, however—from 16 percent to 23 percent—has been in the unaffiliated category—Americans with no religious affiliation. These religious "nones" include people who identify as atheists, agnostics, or "nothing in particular." Almost a third (31 percent) of them admit to being atheists or agnostics; they represent 7 percent of the American population overall. Religious nones, at 56 million, now outnumber both Catholics and mainline Protestants. These unaffiliated Americans tend to be young, with a median age of 36 years, compared with 46 years for the U.S. population as a whole, and 52 years for mainline Protestants. The unaffiliated percentage is highest in the West, followed (in order) by the Northeast, Midwest, and South. In the West, the unaffiliated, at 28 percent, outnumber all religious groups. Among ethnic groups, non-Hispanic whites are most likely to be unaffiliated: 24 percent, versus 20 percent for

Latinos and 18 percent for African Americans. Men are much more likely than women to be unaffiliated—27 percent to 19 percent.

How might we explain the growth of the unaffiliated category? One factor may be the decrease in religious in-marriage or endogamy. Of the Americans who have wed since 2010, 39 percent were in a religiously mixed marriage, compared with just 19 percent of Americans who married before 1960. When parents have different religions, or when one is affiliated while the other is not, it may be easier to raise children unaffiliated than to choose between faiths.

It has also becoming increasingly common—and accepted—for people to switch between religions, or to no religion at all. Just over one-third (34 percent) of Americans have a religious identity (or lack thereof) different from the one in which they were raised. If switching from one Protestant church to another, for example, from mainline to Evangelical, is also included, this figure rises to 42 percent. Those raised without any religious affiliations as children are even more likely to switch to a new category in adulthood. About half of the 9 percent of Americans raised in a nonreligious household claim a religious affiliation as adults.

We see that diversity in religious beliefs and practices is on the rise in the United States. Furthermore, the established religions themselves are becoming more racially and ethnically diverse in membership. Minorities now constitute 41 percent of American Catholics, 24 percent of Evangelicals, and 14 percent of mainline Protestants. There is every reason to believe that these trends involving religious affiliation, or lack thereof, will continue in the United States.

Center 2011). Today, estimates of the number of Evangelicals worldwide range from 400 million to well over 1 billion. Most now live outside Europe and North America—in sub-Saharan Africa, the Middle East and North Africa, Latin America, and Asia.

The growth and spread of Evangelical Protestantism has been particularly explosive in Brazil—traditionally (and still) the world's most Catholic country. In 1980, when Pope John Paul II visited the country, 89 percent of Brazil's population claimed to be Roman Catholic. Since then, Evan-

TABLE 21.1 Religious Affiliations of Americans, 2007 and 2014

AFFILIATION	2007	2014	CHANGE (PERCENTAGE POINTS)
Christian	78.4%	70.6%	−7.8
Protestant	51.3%	46.5%	−4.8
Evangelical	26.3%	25.4%	−0.9
Mainline	18.1%	14.7%	−3.4
Historically black	6.9%	6.5%	−0.4
Catholic	23.9%	20.8%	−3.1
Orthodox Christian	0.6%	0.5%	−0.1
Mormon	1.7%	1.6%	−0.1
Jehovah's Witness	0.7%	0.8%	0.1
Other Christian	0.3%	0.4%	0.1
Non-Christian faiths	4.7%	5.9%	1.2
Jewish	1.7%	1.9%	0.2
Muslim	0.4%	0.9%	0.5
Buddhist	0.7%	0.7%	0.0
Hindu	0.4%	0.7%	0.3
Other world religions*	0.3%	0.3%	0.0
Other faiths**	1.2%	1.5%	0.3
Unaffiliated	16.1%	22.8%	6.7
Atheist	1.6%	3.1%	1.5
Agnostic	2.4%	4.0%	1.6
Nothing in particular	12.1%	15.8%	3.7
Don't know/refused	0.8%	0.6%	−0.2

All percentages are of total sample.
*Includes Sikhs, Baha'is, Taoists, Jains, etc.
**Includes Unitarians, New Age religions, Native American religions, etc.

SOURCE: Pew Research Center, Religion and Public Life, "America's Changing Religious Landscape," May 12, 2015, p. 3. http://www.pewforum.org/2015/05/12/americas-changing-religious-landscape/.

gelical Protestantism has spread like wildfire. Having made small inroads during the first half of the 20th century, Evangelical Protestantism grew exponentially in Brazil during the second half. Protestants accounted for less than 5 percent of the population through the 1960s. By 2000, Evangelical Protestants comprised more than 15 percent of Brazilians affiliated with a church. The current estimate of the Evangelical share of Brazil's population is between 20 and 25 percent and growing. Evangelical Protestantism's penetration of Brazil has been mainly at the expense of Catholicism. Among the factors that have worked against Catholicism are these: a declining and mainly foreign priesthood, sharply contrasting political agendas of many of its clerics, and its reputation as mainly a women's religion.

Evangelical Protestantism stresses conservative morality, biblical authority, and a personal ("born-again") conversion experience. Most Brazilian Evangelicals are Pentecostals, who additionally embrace glossolalia (speaking in tongues) and beliefs in faith healing, spirits, exorcism, and miracles.

In its focus on ecstatic and exuberant worship, Pentecostalism has been heavily influenced by— and shares features with—African American Protestantism. In Brazil it shares features with candomblé, which also features chanting and spirit possession (Casanova 2001; Meyer 1999).

Peter Berger (2010) suggests that modern Pentecostalism may be the fastest-growing religion in human history and focuses on its social dimensions to explain why. According to Berger, Pentecostalism promotes strong communities while offering practical and psychological support to people whose circumstances are changing. My own experience in Brazil supports Berger's hypothesis; most new Pentecostals I encountered came from underprivileged, poor, and otherwise marginalized groups in areas undergoing rapid social change.

The British sociologist David Martin (1990) argues that Pentecostalism is spreading so rapidly because its adherents embody Max Weber's Protestant ethic—valuing self-discipline, hard work, and thrift. Others see Pentecostalism as a kind of cargo cult, built on the belief that magic and ritual activity can promote material success (Freston 2008; Meyer 1999). Berger (2010) suggests that today's Pentecostals probably include both types—Weberian Protestants working to produce material wealth as a sign of their salvation along with people who believe that magic and ritual will bring them good fortune.

Converts to Pentecostalism are expected to separate themselves both from their pasts and from the secular social world that surrounds them. In Arembepe, Brazil, for example, the *crentes* ("true believers," as members of the local Pentecostal community are called) set themselves apart by their beliefs, behavior, and lifestyle (Kottak 2006). They worship, chant, and pray. They dress simply and forgo such worldly temptations (seen as vices) as tobacco, alcohol, gambling, and extramarital sexuality, along with dancing, movies, and other forms of popular culture. Pentecostals observe an ascetic moral code and view the surrounding social world as a realm governed by Satan (Robbins 2004).

Pentecostalism strengthens family and household through a moral code that respects marriage and prohibits adultery, gambling, drinking, and fighting. These activities were valued mainly by men in preconversion culture. Pentecostalism has appeal for men, however, because it solidifies their authority within the household. Although Pentecostal ideology is strongly patriarchal, with women expected to subordinate themselves to men, women tend to be more active church members than men are. Pentecostalism promotes services and prayer groups by and for women. In such settings women develop leadership skills, as they also extend their social-support network beyond family and kin (Burdick 1998).

Homogenization, Indigenization, or Hybridization?

Any cultural form that spreads from one society to another—be it a Starbucks, McDonald's, or a

In São Paulo, Brazil, Pastor Rinaldo Pereira conducts a service at Bola de Neve Church. Popular with young people, this church sponsors activities, including surfing, skating, and rock 'n roll and reggae music with religious lyrics. Is evangelical Protestantism. Brazil's major religion?

© Lalo de Almeida/The New York Times/Redux

form of religion—has to fit into the country and culture it enters. We can use the rapid spread of Pentecostalism as a case study of the process of adaptation of foreign cultural forms to local settings.

Joel Robbins (2004) has examined the extent to which what he calls Pentecostal/charismatic Christianity preserves its basic form and core beliefs as it spreads and adapts to various national and local cultures. Pentecostalism is a Western invention: Its beliefs, doctrines, organizational features, and rituals originated in the United States, following the European rise and spread of Protestantism. The core doctrines of acceptance of Jesus as one's savior, baptism with the Holy Spirit, faith healing, and belief in the second coming of Jesus have spread across nations and cultures without losing their basic shape.

Scholars have argued about whether the global spread of Pentecostalism is best understood as (1) a process of Western cultural domination and homogenization (perhaps supported by a right-wing political agenda) or (2) a process in which diffused cultural forms respond to local needs and are differentiated and indigenized. Joel Robbins (2004) takes a middle-ground position, viewing the spread of Pentecostalism as a form of cultural hybridization. Robbins (2004) argues that global and local features appear with equal intensity within these Pentecostal cultures. Churches retain certain core Pentecostal beliefs and behaviors while responding to the local culture and being organized at the local level.

Reviewing the literature, Robbins (2004) finds little evidence that a Western political agenda is propelling the global spread of Pentecostalism. It is true that foreigners (including American pastors and televangelists) have helped introduce Pentecostalism to countries outside North America. There is little evidence, however, that overseas churches are largely funded and ideologically shaped from North America. Pentecostal churches typically are staffed from top to bottom with locals, who run them as organizations that are attentive and responsive to local situations. Conversion is typically a key feature of that agenda. Once converted, a Pentecostal is expected to be an active Evangelist, seeking to bring in new members. This Evangelization is one of the most important activities in Pentecostal culture and certainly aids its expansion.

Pentecostalism spreads as other forces of globalization displace people and disrupt local lives (Martin 1990). To people who feel socially adrift, Pentecostal evangelists offer tightly knit communities and a weblike structure of personal connections within and between Pentecostal communities. Such networks can facilitate access to health care, job placement, educational services, and other resources.

Unlike Catholicism, which is hierarchical, Pentecostalism is egalitarian. Adherents need no special education—only spiritual inspiration—to preach or to run a church. Based on his research in Brazil, John Burdick (1993) notes that many Afro-Brazilians are drawn to the Pentecostal community because others who are socially and racially like them are in the congregation, some serving as preachers. Opportunities for participation and leadership are abundant, for example, as lay preachers, deacons, and leaders of various men's, women's, and youth groups. The churches fund outreach to the needy and other locally relevant social services.

Antimodernism and Fundamentalism

Antimodernism is the rejection of the modern in favor of what is perceived as an earlier, purer, and better way of life. This viewpoint first arose out of disillusionment with the Industrial Revolution and with subsequent developments in science, technology, and consumption patterns. Antimodernists typically consider the use of modern technology to be misguided or think technology should have a lower priority than religious and cultural values. (A related example would be the avoidance of many machines by the Old Order Amish or Pennsylvania Dutch in the United States.)

Religious **fundamentalism** describes antimodernist movements in various religions, including Christianity, Islam, and Judaism. Not only do fundamentalists feel strongly alienated from modern secular culture, but they also have separated from a larger religious group, whose founding principles, they believe, have been corrupted or abandoned. Fundamentalists advocate return and strict fidelity to the "true" (fundamental) religious principles of the larger religion.

Exemplifying their antimodernism, fundamentalists also seek to rescue religion from absorption into modern, Western culture. In Christianity, fundamentalists are "born-again Christians" as opposed to "mainline Protestants." In Islam, they are jama'at (in Arabic, communities based on close fellowship) engaged in jihad (struggle) against a Western culture hostile to Islam and the God-given (shariah) way of life. In Judaism they are Haredi, "Torah-true" Jews. All these fundamentalists see a sharp divide between themselves and other religions, as well as between their own "sacred" view of life and the modern "secular" world (see Antoun 2008).

Both Pentecostalism and Christian fundamentalism preach ascetic morality, the duty to convert others, and respect for the Bible. Fundamentalists, however, tend to cite their success in living a moral life as proof of their salvation, whereas Pentecostals find assurance of their salvation in exuberant, ecstatic experience. Fundamentalists also seek to remake the political sphere along religious lines, whereas Pentecostals tend to have less interest in politics (Robbins 2004).

The Spread of Islam

Islam—whose 1.6 billion followers constitute over a fifth of the world's population—is another rapidly spreading global religion that can be used to illustrate cultural globalization. The globalization of Islam also illustrates cultural hybridization. Islam has adapted successfully to the many nations and cultures it has entered, adopting architectural styles, linguistic practices, and even religious beliefs from host cultures.

For example, while Mosques (Islamic houses of worship) all share certain characteristics (e.g., they face Mecca and have some common architectural features), they also incorporate architectural and decorative elements from their national setting. Although Arabic is Islam's liturgical language, used for prayer, most Muslims' discussion of their faith occurs in their local language. In China, Islamic concepts have been influenced by Confucianism. In India and Bangladesh, the Islamic idea of the prophet has blended with the Hindu notion of the avatar, a deity who takes mortal form and descends to Earth to fight evil and guide the righteous. Islam entered Indonesia by means of Muslim merchants who devised devotional exercises that fit in with preexisting religions—Hinduism and Buddhism in Java and Sumatra and animism in the eastern islands, which eventually became Christian. In Bali, Hinduism survived as the dominant religion. Both Pentecostalism and Islam, we have learned, hybridize and become locally relevant as they spread globally. Although certain core features endure, local people always assign their own meanings to the messages and social forms they receive from outside, including religion. Such meanings reflect their cultural backgrounds, experiences, and prior belief systems. We must consider the processes of hybridization and indigenization in examining and understanding any form of cultural diffusion or globalization.

antimodernism
Rejecting the modern for a presumed earlier, purer, better way of life.

fundamentalism
Advocating strict fidelity to a religion's presumed founding principles.

Indonesian Muslims pray at the Sunda Kelapa port in Jakarta on August 19, 2012. Muslims around the world were celebrating the end of Ramadan, the Muslim calendar's ninth and holiest month.
© Chicarito/AFP/GettyImages

SECULAR RITUALS

In concluding this chapter on religion, we can recognize some problems with the definition of religion given at the beginning of this chapter. The first problem: If we define religion with reference to supernatural beings, powers, and forces, how do we classify ritual-like behavior that occurs in secular contexts? Some anthropologists believe there are both sacred and secular rituals. Secular rituals include formal, invariant, stereotyped, earnest, repetitive behavior and rites of passage that take place in nonreligious settings.

A second problem: If the distinction between the supernatural and the natural is not consistently made in a society, how can we tell what is religion and what isn't? The Betsileo of Madagascar, for example, view witches and dead ancestors as real people who play roles in ordinary life. However, their occult powers are not empirically demonstrable.

On August 27, 2011, this flashmob meditation session was held in London's (England) Trafalgar Square. Does this performance illustrate secular religion?
© Behzad/Demotix/Demotix/Corbis

A third problem: The behavior considered appropriate for religious occasions varies tremendously from culture to culture. One society may consider drunken frenzy the surest sign of faith, whereas another may encourage quiet reverence among the faithful. Who is to say which is "more religious"?

It is possible for apparently secular settings, things, and events to acquire intense meaning for individuals who have grown up in their presence. For example, identities and loyalties based on fandom, football, baseball, and soccer can be powerful, indeed. Rock stars and bands can mobilize many. A World Series win led to celebrations across a "Red Sox nation." Italians and Brazilians are rarely, if ever, as nationally focused and emotionally unified as they are when their teams are competing in the World Cup. The collective effervescence that Durkheim found so characteristic of religion can equally well describe what Brazilians experience when their country wins a World Cup.

In the context of comparative religion, the idea that the secular can become sacred isn't surprising. Long ago, Durkheim (1912/2001) pointed out that almost everything, from the sublime to the ridiculous, has in some societies been treated as sacred. The distinction between sacred and profane doesn't depend on the intrinsic qualities of the sacred symbol. In Australian totemic religion, for example, sacred beings include such humble creatures as ducks, frogs, and grubs, whose inherent qualities could hardly have given rise to the religious sentiment they inspire.

Many Americans believe that recreation and religion are separate domains. From my fieldwork in Brazil and Madagascar and my reading about other societies, I believe that this separation is both ethnocentric and false. Madagascar's tomb-centered ceremonies are times when the living and the dead are joyously reunited, when people get drunk, gorge themselves, and enjoy sexual license. Perhaps the gray, sober, ascetic, and moralistic aspects of many religious events in the United States, in taking the "fun" out of religion, force us to find our religion in fun.

for REVIEW

summary

1. Religion, a cultural universal, consists of belief and behavior concerned with supernatural beings, powers, and forces. Religion also encompasses the feelings, meanings, and congregations associated with such beliefs and behavior. Anthropological studies have revealed many aspects and functions of religion.

2. Tylor considered animism—the belief in spirits or souls—to be religion's earliest and most basic form. He focused on religion's explanatory role, arguing that religion would eventually disappear as science provided better explanations. Besides animism, yet another view of the supernatural also occurs in nonindustrial societies. This sees the supernatural as a domain of raw,

impersonal power or force (called mana in Polynesia and Melanesia). People can manipulate and control mana under certain conditions.

3. When ordinary technical and rational means of doing things fail, people may turn to magic. Often they use magic when they lack control over outcomes. Religion offers comfort and psychological security at times of crisis. However, rites also can create anxiety. Rituals are formal, invariant, stylized, earnest acts in which people subordinate their particular beliefs to a social collectivity. Rites of passage have three phases: separation, liminality, and incorporation. Such rites can mark any change in social status, age, place, or social condition. Collective rites often are cemented by communitas, a feeling of intense solidarity.

4. Besides their psychological and social functions, religious beliefs and practices play a role in the adaptation of human populations to their environments. The Hindu doctrine of *ahimsa,* which prohibits harm to living things, makes cattle sacred and beef a tabooed food. The taboo's force stops peasants from killing their draft cattle, even in times of extreme need.

5. Religion establishes and maintains social control through a series of moral and ethical beliefs, and real and imagined rewards and punishments, internalized in individuals. Religion also achieves social control by mobilizing its members for collective action. Religion helps maintain social order, but it also can promote change. Revitalization movements blend old and new beliefs and have helped people adapt to changing conditions.

6. Protestant values have been important in the United States, as they were in the rise and spread of capitalism in Europe. The world's major religions vary in their growth rates, with Islam expanding more rapidly than Christianity. There is growing religious diversity in the United States and Canada. Religious trends in contemporary North America include religious diversification, declining affiliation with organized religions, rising secularism, and new religions, some inspired by science and technology, some by spiritism. There are secular as well as religious rituals.

7. The spread of Evangelical/Pentecostal Protestantism worldwide illustrates contemporary cultural globalization. Evangelical Protestantism stresses conservative morality, the authority of the Bible, and a personal ("born-again") conversion experience. To people who feel socially adrift, Pentecostalism offers tightly knit communities and a weblike structure of personal connections. Antimodernism is the rejection of the modern, including globalization, in favor of what is perceived as an earlier, purer, and better way of life. Religious fundamentalism describes antimodernist movements in Christianity, Islam, and Judaism. The rapid spread of Islam also illustrates cultural globalization and hybridization. Although certain core features endure, local people always assign their own meanings to the messages and social forms they receive from outside, including religion. The processes of hybridization and indigenization are always associated with cultural diffusion and globalization.

key terms

animism   406

antimodernism   419

cargo cults   414

communitas   409

cosmology   410

fundamentalism   419

liminality   409

magic   407

mana   406

monotheism   406

polytheism   406

religion   405

revitalization movements   414

rites of passage   407

ritual   407

shaman   412

syncretisms   415

taboo   407

totem   410

critical thinking

1. How did anthropologist Anthony Wallace define religion? After reading this chapter, what problems do you think there are with his definition?

2. Describe a rite of passage you (or a friend) have been through. How did it fit the three-phase model given in the text?

3. From the news or your own knowledge, can you provide additional examples of revitalization movements, new religions, or liminal cults?

4. Religion is a cultural universal. But religions are parts of particular cultures, and cultural differences show up systematically in religious beliefs and practices. How so?

5. This chapter notes that many Americans see recreation and religion as separate domains. Based on my fieldwork in Brazil and Madagascar and my reading about other societies, I believe that this separation is both ethnocentric and false. Do you agree with this? What has been your own experience?

Arts, Media, and Sports

▶ What are the arts, and how have they varied historically and cross-culturally?

▶ How does culture influence the media, and vice versa?

▶ How are culture and cultural contrasts expressed in sports?

Whether winter or summer, the Olympics unite arts, media, and sports. Shown here are performers at the opening ceremony for the 2014 Sochi (Russia) Winter Olympics.

© Kyodo via AP Images

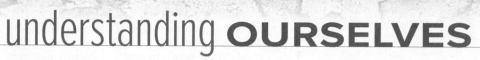

understanding OURSELVES

Imagine a TV broadcast attracting over 70 percent of a nation's viewers. That has happened repeatedly in Brazil as a popular telenovela draws to a close. (Telenovelas are prime-time serial melodramas that run for about 150 episodes.) It happened in the United States in 1953, when 72 percent of all sets were tuned to *I Love Lucy* as Lucy Ricardo went to the hospital to give birth to Little Ricky. It happened even more impressively in 1956, when 83 percent of all sets tuned to *The Ed Sullivan Show* to watch Elvis Presley's TV debut. A single broadcast's largest audience share in more recent years occurred in 1983, when 106 million viewers, representing an audience share of 77 percent, watched the final episode of *M*A*S*H*. In the 21st century, seven successive Super Bowls (2010–2016) topped the viewership, but never the audience share, of the *M*A*S*H* finale. The 2015 Super Bowl (XLIX) between Seattle and New England set a record, with 114.4 million viewers, but the half-time show that year, starring Katy Perry, did even better, attracting 118.5 million viewers. The 2015 Super Bowl also drew a 71 audience share, which means that 71 percent of people who were watching TV that Sunday were watching the Super Bowl. The 2016 Super Bowl between Denver and Carolina declined a bit in viewership—to 111.0 million viewers, but it was still the third most watched program in TV history.

One notable development in the United States over the past few decades has been a shift from mass culture to segmented cultures. An increasingly differentiated nation recognizes, even celebrates, diversity. The mass media join—and intensify—this trend, measuring and catering to various "demographics." Products and messages are aimed less at the masses than at particular segments—target audiences.

As one example, consider the evolution of sports coverage. From 1961 to 1998, ABC offered a weekly sports anthology titled *Wide World of Sports*. On a given Saturday afternoon, Americans might see bowling, track and field, skating, college wrestling, gymnastics, curling, swimming, diving, or another of many sports. It was like having a mini-Olympics running throughout the year. Today, dozens of specialized (often pay-for-view) sports channels cater to every taste, including Major League Baseball, the National Football League, and international soccer. Think of the choices now available through cable and satellite, websites, smartphones, tablets, Netflix, DVRs, and the remote control. Target audiences now have access to a multiplicity of channels, featuring all kinds of music, sports, games, news, comedy, science fiction, soaps, movies, cartoons, old TV sitcoms, programs in Spanish and various other languages, nature shows, travel shows, adventure shows, histories, biographies, and home shopping. News channels (e.g., Fox News or MSNBC) even cater to particular political interests.

It seems likely there is a connection between these media developments and the "special interests" about which politicians perpetually complain. Do you think people might agree more—and Americans be less polarized—if everyone still watched the same TV programs?

WHAT IS ART?

arts
Include visual arts, literature (written and oral), music, and performance arts.

expressive culture
Dance, music, painting, sculpture, pottery, cloth, stories, drama, comedy, etc.

art
An object, event, or other expressive form that evokes an aesthetic reaction.

aesthetics
The appreciation of qualities perceived in art.

The **arts** include music, performance arts, visual arts, and storytelling and literature (oral and written). These manifestations of human creativity sometimes are called **expressive culture.** People express themselves in dance, music, song, painting, sculpture, pottery, cloth, storytelling, verse, prose, drama, and comedy. Many cultures lack terms that can be translated easily as "art" or "the arts." Yet even without a word for art, people everywhere do associate an aesthetic experience—a sense of beauty, appreciation, harmony, pleasure—with sounds, patterns, objects, and events that have certain qualities (see Garcia Canclini 2014). Among the Yoruba of Nigeria, the word for art, *ona,* encompasses the designs made on objects, the art objects themselves, and the profession of the creators of those works. For two Yoruba lineages of leather workers, Otunisona and Osiisona, the suffix *-ona* in their names denotes art (Adepegba 1991).

A dictionary defines **art** as "the quality, production, expression, or realm of what is beautiful or of more than ordinary significance; the class of objects subject to aesthetic criteria" (*Random House College Dictionary* 1982, p. 76). According to the same dictionary, **aesthetics** involves "the qualities perceived in works of art . . . ; the . . . mind and emotions in relation to the sense of beauty" (p. 22). A more recent definition sees art as "something that is created with imagination and skill and that is beautiful or that expresses important ideas or feelings" (Merriam-Webster 2016). We know, however, that a work of art can attract attention, have special significance, and demonstrate imagination and skill without being considered beautiful. Pablo Picasso's *Guernica,* a famous painting of the Spanish Civil War, comes to mind as a scene that, while not beautiful, is indisputably moving and thus a work of art.

In many societies, art isn't viewed as a separate, special activity. But this doesn't stop individuals from being moved by sounds, patterns, objects, and events in a way that we would call aesthetic. Our own society does provide a fairly well-defined role for the connoisseur of the arts. We also have sanctuaries—concert halls, theaters, museums—where people can go to be aesthetically pleased and emotionally moved by objects and performances (see Burt 2013).

Western culture tends to compartmentalize art as something apart from everyday life. This reflects a more general modern separation of institutions like government and the economy from the rest of society. All these fields are considered distinct domains and have their own academic specialists. In non-Western societies, however, the production and appreciation of art are part of everyday life, just as popular culture is in our own society.

This chapter will not attempt to do a systematic survey of all the arts. Rather, the general approach will be to examine topics and issues that apply to expressive culture generally. The term *art* will be used to encompass all the arts, including print and film narratives. In other words, the observations to be made about art are intended to apply to music, theater, film, television, books, stories, and lore, as well as to painting and sculpture. Expressive culture also encompasses such creative forms as jokes, storytelling, dance, children's play, sports, games, and festivals, and anthropologists have written about all of these.

That which is aesthetically pleasing is perceived with the senses. Usually, when we think of art, we have in mind something that can be seen or heard. But others might define art more broadly to include things that can be smelled (scents, fragrances), tasted (recipes), or touched (cloth textures). How enduring must art be? Visual works and written works, including musical compositions, may last for centuries. Can a single noteworthy event, such as a feast, which is not in the least eternal, except in memory, be a work of art? Furthermore, any individual performance, whether in a theater or at a sporting event, can be a "thing of beauty." Nowadays, such performances often are captured on film; otherwise, they would be as ephemeral as a "feast fit for a king."

Many of the high points of Western art had religious inspiration or were done in the service of religion. Consider *The Creation of Adam* (and other frescoes painted from 1508 to 1512) by Michelangelo, on the ceiling of the Sistine Chapel in Vatican City, Rome, Italy.
© Alex Segre/Alamy Stock Photo

Art and Religion

Some of the issues raised in the discussion of religion also apply to art. Definitions of both art and religion mention the "more than ordinary" or the "extraordinary." Religious scholars may distinguish between the sacred (religious) and the profane (secular). Similarly, art scholars may distinguish between the artistic and the ordinary.

If we adopt a special attitude or demeanor when confronting a sacred object, do we display something similar when experiencing a work of art? According to the anthropologist Jacques Maquet (1986), an artwork is something that stimulates and sustains contemplation. It compels attention and reflection. Maquet stresses the importance of the object's form in producing such contemplation. But other scholars stress feeling and meaning in addition to form. The experience of art involves feelings, such as being moved, as well as appreciation of form, such as balance or harmony.

Such an artistic attitude can be combined with and used to bolster a religious attitude. Many of the high points of Western art and music had religious inspiration, or were done in the service of religion, as a visit to a church or a large museum will surely illustrate. Bach and Handel are as well known for their church music as Michelangelo is for his religious painting and sculpture. The buildings (churches and cathedrals) in which religious music is played and in which visual art is displayed may themselves be works of art. Some of the major architectural achievements of Western art are religious structures.

Art may be created, performed, or displayed outdoors in public or in special indoor settings. Just as churches demarcate religion, museums and theaters set art off from the ordinary world, making it special, while inviting spectators in. Buildings dedicated to the arts help create the artistic atmosphere. Architecture may accentuate the setting as a place for works of art to be presented (see Ingold 2013).

The settings of rites and ceremonies, and of art, may be temporary or permanent. State societies have permanent religious structures: churches and temples. So, too, may state societies have buildings and structures dedicated to the arts. Nonstate societies tend to lack such permanently demarcated settings. Both art and religion are more "out there" in society. Still, in bands and tribes, religious settings can be created without churches. Similarly, an artistic atmosphere can be created without museums. At particular times of the year, ordinary space can be set aside for a visual art display or a musical performance. Such special occasions parallel the times set aside for religious ceremonies. In fact, in tribal performances, the arts and religion often mix. For example, masked and costumed performers may imitate spirits. Rites of passage often feature special music, dance, song, bodily adornment, and other manifestations of expressive culture.

Among tribes of the North Pacific Coast of North America, various art forms combined to create a ceremonial atmosphere. Masked and costumed dancers reenacted spirit encounters with human beings, which are part of the origin myths of villages, clans, and lineages. Sometimes, dancers devised intricate patterns of choreography. Their esteem was measured by the number of people who followed them when they danced.

Non-Western art is often, but wrongly, assumed to have an inevitable connection to ritual. In fact, non-Western societies have art for art's sake, just as Western societies do. Even when acting in the service of religion, there is room for individual creative expression (see Osborne and Tanner 2007). In the oral arts, for example, the audience is much more interested in the delivery and performance of the artist than in the particular god for whom the performer may be speaking.

Locating Art

Aesthetic value is one way of distinguishing art. Another way is to consider placement. If something is displayed in a museum, someone must think it's art. Although tribal societies lack museums, they may have special areas where artistic expression takes place. The Tiwi of North Australia, for example, traditionally commissioned the manufacture of commemorative burial poles after a death. The pole artists were sequestered in a work area near the grave. That area was taboo to everyone else. The artists were freed temporarily from the daily food quest. Other community members served as their patrons, supplying the artists with the hard-to-get materials needed for their work (Goodale and Koss 1971).

The French artist known as JR specializes in transforming urban space into art. The image shown here is part of a large-scale 2008–2009 art project, titled "Women Are Heroes," in Rio de Janeiro, Brazil. Here we see a woman's face on steep steps in Rio's Favela Morro da Providência. (See http://www.jr-art.net/projects/women-are-heroes-brazil for more images.)

© JR/Redux

The boundary between what's art and what's not isn't always sharp. The American artist Andy Warhol is famous for transforming Campbell's soup cans, Brillo pads, and images of Marilyn Monroe into art. Many recent artists (see photo previous page) have tried to erase the distinction between art and ordinary life by converting the everyday into a work of art. Objects never intended as art, such as the Valentine Olivetti typewriter, may be transformed into art by being placed in a museum, such as New York's Museum of Modern Art. Jacques Maquet (1986) distinguishes such "art by transformation" from art created and intended to be art, which he calls "art by destination."

In state societies, we have come to rely on critics, judges, and experts to tell us what's art and what isn't. A play titled *Art* is about conflict that arises among three friends when one of them buys an all-white painting. They disagree, as people often do, about the definition and value of a work of art. Such variation in art appreciation is especially common in contemporary society, with its professional artists and critics and great cultural diversity. We'd expect more uniform standards and agreement in less diverse, less stratified societies.

To be culturally relativistic, we need to avoid applying our own standards about what art is to the products of other cultures. Sculpture is art, right? Not necessarily. Previously, we challenged the view that non-Western art always has some kind of connection to religion. The Kalabari case to be discussed now makes the opposite point: that religious sculpture is not always art.

The Kalabari of southern Nigeria (Figure 22.1) carve wooden sculptures for religious, rather than aesthetic, reasons. They produce these sculptures not as works of art, but to serve as "houses" for spirits (Horton 1963). These sculptures will be placed in a cult house, where the spirits can dwell in them. Kalabari sculptures are created not for art's sake, but in order to manipulate and control spirits. The Kalabari do have standards for the carvings, but those standards are not aesthetic; beauty is not a goal. What is required is that a sculpture must be sufficiently complete to represent its spirit, and carvers must base their work on past models. Each spirit has a known image associated with it, and it's risky to deviate too much from that image. Offended spirits may retaliate. As long as they observe these standards of completeness and established images, carvers are free to express themselves. But these images are considered repulsive rather than beautiful.

Art and Individuality

In the creation of art, there is always an interplay between the individual artist and his or her social context. Although it is not unusual for a Western artist to have a reputation as iconoclastic or antisocial, works of art inevitably reflect the artist's cultural background and typically are judged in society. Artists have fans and critics. Discussions of Western art tend to emphasize individual artistic production; a contrary tendency has been to focus on the social context of art in non-Western societies. Those who work with non-Western art have been criticized for ignoring the individual and focusing too much on the social nature and context of art. When art objects from Africa or Papua New Guinea are displayed in museums, often only the name of the tribe and of the Western donor are given, rather than that of the individual artist. This kind of presentation can create the impression that art is produced collectively, rather than by an individual artist. Sometimes it is; sometimes it isn't.

To some extent, there *is* more collective production of art in non-Western societies. In a tribal setting, an artist typically gets more feedback during the creative process than the individual artist typically receives in our own society. In Western societies, the feedback often comes too late, after the product is complete, rather than during production, when it can still be changed. During his fieldwork among Nigeria's Tiv people, Paul Bohannan (1971) found only a few skilled artists, and those individuals preferred to work in private. Mediocre artists, however, typically worked in public, where they routinely got comments from onlookers (critics). Based on suggestions, an artist might change a design, such as a carving, in progress. There was yet another way in which Tiv artists worked socially rather than individually. Sometimes, when artists put their work aside,

Zundert, a small town in the southern Netherlands, is the birthplace of Vincent van Gogh. Corso Zundert, the town's annual flower Parade Festival, is a major event that takes over the streets with gigantic floats, all made with flowers. Commemorating the 125th year of Van Gogh's death, Zundert dedicated its 2015 parade to floats inspired by Vincent's life and art, such as the one shown here in his image.

© CB2/ZOB/Supplied by WENN/Newscom

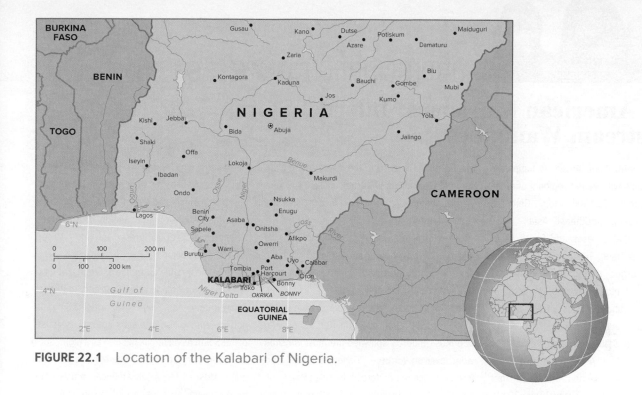

FIGURE 22.1 Location of the Kalabari of Nigeria.

someone else would pick it up and start working on it. The Tiv did not recognize the same kind of connection between individuals and their art that we do.

Even in contemporary societies, artistic creation can be an open and responsive process. Consider the production of Brazilian telenovelas (mentioned in this chapter's "Understanding Ourselves"). As a telenovela progresses, writer(s) typically pay close attention to audience reaction, measured in various ways, from surveys to informal conversations in such locales as beauty salons and other places where people congregate and have the Brazilian equivalent of "water-cooler conversations." Writers then modify, or even change the direction of, a telenovela in view of audience response.

The Tiv example notwithstanding, there *are* well-known individual artists in many non-Western societies. They are recognized as such by other community members, and perhaps by outsiders as well. Their artistic labor may even be conscripted for special displays and performances, including ceremonies, or palace arts and events (see Schneider and Wright 2010).

In Western societies, focus on the individual artist is common, even in collective displays and performances, where, for example, a conductor may be as well, or better, known than their orchestra. Haapala (1998) argues that an artist and his or her works become inseparable: "By creating works of art a person creates an artistic identity for himself. He creates himself quite literally into the pieces he puts into his art. He exists in the works he has created." In this view, Picasso created many Picassos, and he continues to exist

in and through those works, as do William Shakespeare, Jane Austen, and Meryl Streep.

Sometimes, even in Western societies, little is known or recognized about the individual artist responsible for an enduring artwork. We are more likely, for example, to know the name of the recording artist than that of the writer of familiar songs. Sometimes we fail to acknowledge art individually because the artwork was collectively created. To whom should we attribute a pyramid or a cathedral? Should it be the architect, the ruler or leader who commissioned the work, or the master builder who implemented the design?

The Work of Art

The word *opera* is the plural of *opus,* which means a work. For the artist, at least, art is work, albeit creative work. In nonstate societies, artists may have to hunt, gather, herd, fish, or farm in order to eat, but they still manage to find time to work on their art. In state societies, at least, artists have been defined as specialists—professionals who have chosen careers as artists, musicians, writers, or actors. If they manage to support themselves from their art, they may be full-time professionals. If not, they do their art part-time while earning a living from another activity. (This chapter's "Appreciating Diversity" describes talented individuals who pursue musical careers, while holding "day jobs" in other fields.) Sometimes artists associate in professional groups, such as medieval guilds or contemporary unions. Actors Equity in New York, a labor union, is a modern guild, designed to protect the interests of its artist members.

Asian American Musicians: Internet Stars, Mainstream Wannabes

The panethnic term *Asian American* lumps together individuals with varied regional and national backgrounds—East Asian (e.g., Chinese, Japanese, Korean), Southeast Asian (e.g., Filipina/o, Thai, Vietnamese), and South Asian (e.g., Indian, Pakistani). The concept of "Asian American" emerged during the 1960s and 1970s. This panethnic term promotes a sense of common identity and interests among people with diverse national backgrounds.

In the United States, several stereotypes have developed about Asian Americans, from the hard-driving, achievement-oriented "Tiger Mom" and her successful offspring (Chua 2011), to the tech-savvy computer nerd. The fields in which Asian Americans are assumed to (and often do) excel tend to be professional and technical, rather than, say, in sports or entertainment. Our focus here is on a particular group of Asian Americans who have chosen to work outside the stereotype: Asian American performers, especially musicians.

Consider Legaci, a Filipino American R&B "boy band," that appeared on *America's Got Talent* (*AGT*) in July 2014. The show presented them as amateurs despite their having served as backup singers for Justin Bieber, and their visibility as a musical act with several popular videos on YouTube. Spice Girl Mel B, one of the four judges on *AGT*, began by asking the young men about their "day jobs." It turned out that all four members of Legaci worked in tech fields, thus confirming the stereotype of Asian Americans as "computer nerds" and "boring," as judge Howard Stern put it. Only after the group finished performing was their musical talent recognized, and enthusiastically praised, although they did not advance further on *AGT*. While they have enjoyed Internet success, Legaci has been unable to find a place in the mainstream, or to support themselves with their music. The four young men of Legaci still hold jobs outside the music industry.

The mainstream musical insignificance of Asian Americans is particularly striking when we consider the important role that Asia plays in international musical entertainment. India's Bollywood, for example, has a huge presence within global popular culture. South Korea's thriving pop music industry spawned the most watched video ever on YouTube. "Gangnam Style," performed by the South Korean musician Psy, originated as the lead single on his sixth pop album. The song debuted in July 2012 at number one on South Korea's pop chart. By December 21 of that year, "Gangnam Style" had become the first YouTube video to reach one billion views. As of this writing, that video has attracted more than 2.44 billion views.

The availability of YouTube and other social media can be empowering, providing an otherwise unavailable platform for expression and wide recognition. Asian Americans have carved an important niche within the YouTube universe. Among the most successful is the Japanese American comedian Ryan Higa, whose channel is one of YouTube's top 10, with 13.7 million subscribers (Regullano 2015). Two of the top 10 earners on the 2015 *Forbes* list of the World's Highest Paid YouTube Stars are of Asian origin. Ranking seventh was the Vietnamese American Michelle Phan, a make-up demonstrator and entrepreneur whose YouTube channel had over eight million subscribers and 1.1 billion lifetime views. Right after Phan, at number eight, was Lilly Singh, better known by her YouTube name "Superwoman." Singh is Canadian, but her national ethnic origin is Indian, specifically Punjabi.

Her videos, which range from comedy to rap to motivational speaking, have attracted more than one billion views and seven million subscribers since the debut of her channel in 2010. Forbes estimates her 2015 pretax earnings to be around $2.5 million.

With the notable exception of Singh, YouTube tends to favor Americans of East and Southeast Asian, rather than South Asian, origin. Singh is notable among YouTube stars not only because of her South Asian origin, but also as a highly successful female in a domain where males predominate. Most of the Asian American artists who have achieved success on YouTube are male.

Two of the most successful Asian American men on YouTube are Traphik and David Choi. Traphik is a Thai American rapper, also known as Timothy DeLaGhetto. Choi is a Korean American singer-songwriter. With 2.8 million subscribers, Traphik has been able to mount tours based on his Internet renown. He also has appeared on MTV2's hip-hop reality series, *Wild 'N Out*. Choi, whose YouTube presence goes back to the earliest days of that website in 2005, also has toured multiple times, nationally and globally (Regullano 2015).

Researcher Eileen Regullano (2015) concludes that Asian American musicians have used YouTube's democratized platform to create a significant new media presence. What will it take, one wonders, to propel these talents from the Internet into the mainstream? Or perhaps we should ask a different question: whether the Internet itself has become, or is destined to become, the popular culture mainstream. Lilly Singh may not be Beyoncé, Shakira, or Taylor Swift, but, by earning $2.5 million annually as an Internet star, she has little need for any other "day job."

Just how much work is needed to make a work of art? In the early days of French impressionism, many experts viewed the paintings of Claude Monet and his colleagues as too sketchy and spontaneous to be true art. Established artists and critics were accustomed to more formal and classic studio styles. The French impressionists got their name from their sketches—*impressions* in French—of natural and social settings. They took advantage of technological innovations, particularly the availability of oil paints in tubes, to take their palettes, easels, and canvases into the field. There they made the pictures of changing light and color that hang today in so many museums, where they are now fully recognized as art. But before impressionism became an officially recognized "school" of art, its works were perceived by its critics as crude and unfinished. In terms of community standards, the first impressionist paintings were evaluated as harshly as were the crude and incomplete Kalabari wood carvings of spirits.

For familiar genres, such as painting or music, societies tend to have standards by which they judge whether an artwork is complete or fully realized. Most people would doubt, for instance, that an all-white painting could be a work of art. Prevailing standards may pose obstacles to unorthodox or renegade artists, and thus to innovation. But like the impressionists, such artists may eventually succeed. Some societies tend to reward conformity, an artist's skill with traditional models and techniques. Others encourage breaks with the past, or

innovation. Standards may be maintained informally in society, or by specialists, such as art critics.

An interesting feature of contemporary society is that we have all become potential critics. Through the Internet, ordinary individuals are able to express their opinions about a huge variety of topics, including arts, media, and sports. Websites that provide information about movies, for example, now include viewers' comments and reviews, as well as those of "professional critics." Criticism is no longer reserved for the elites, whose opinions may vary significantly from those of "ordinary people" or "viewers like you." A common American expression is "that's just your opinion"—suggesting that anyone's opinion is as valid as anyone else's. The Internet provides an open forum for airing such opinions by anyone savvy enough to post online.

ART, SOCIETY, AND CULTURE

Around 100,000 years ago, some of the world's first artists occupied Blombos Cave, located on a high cliff facing the Indian Ocean at the tip of what is now South Africa. They hunted game and ate fish from the waters below them. In terms of body and brain size, these ancient Africans were anatomically modern humans. They also were turning animal bones into finely worked tools and weapon points. Furthermore, they were engraving

Music is among the most social of the arts, because it so often unites people in groups. Shown here, women in the village of Rhumsiki, Cameroon, Central Africa, offer a folkloristic musical performance.
© imageBROKER/Alamy Stock Photo

artifacts with symbolic marks—manifestations of abstract and creative thought and, presumably, communication through language (Wilford 2002b).

A group led by Christopher Henshilwood of South Africa has analyzed bone tools and other artifacts from Blombos Cave, along with the mineral ocher that may have been used for body painting. The most impressive bone tools are three sharp instruments. The bone appears first to have been shaped with a stone blade, then finished into a symmetrical shape and polished for hours. According to Henshilwood (quoted in Wilford 2002b), "It's actually unnecessary for projectile points to be so carefully made. It suggests to us that this is an expression of symbolic thinking. The people said, 'Let's make a really beautiful object. . . .' Symbolic thinking means that people are using something to mean something else. The tools do not have to have only a practical purpose. And the ocher might be used to decorate their equipment, perhaps themselves."

In Europe, art goes back more than 30,000 years, to the Upper Paleolithic period in western Europe. Cave paintings, the best-known examples of Upper Paleolithic art, were painted in true caves, located deep in the bowels of the Earth. They may have been painted as part of some kind of rite of passage involving retreat from society. Portable art objects carved in stone, bone, and ivory, along with musical whistles and flutes, also confirm artistic expression throughout the Upper Paleolithic (see Lesure 2011). Art is usually more public than the cave paintings. Typically, it is exhibited, evaluated, performed, and appreciated in society. It has spectators or audiences. It isn't just for the artist (see Pink and Abram 2015).

Ethnomusicology

ethnomusicology
The comparative study of music as an aspect of culture and society.

folk
Of the people; e.g., the art, music, and lore of ordinary people.

Ethnomusicology is the comparative study of the musics of the world and of music as an aspect of culture and society. The field of ethnomusicology thus unites music and anthropology. The music side involves the study and analysis of the music itself and the instruments used to create it. The anthropology side views music as a way to explore a culture, to determine the role that music plays in that society, and the specific social and cultural features that influence how music is created and performed.

Ethnomusicology studies non-Western music, traditional and folk music, and even contemporary popular music from a cultural perspective (see Harris and Pease 2015; Rice 2014; Wade 2013). To do this there has to be fieldwork—firsthand study of particular forms of music, their social functions and cultural meanings, within particular societies. Ethnomusicologists talk with local musicians, make recordings in the field, and learn about the place of musical instruments, performances, and performers in a given society (Kirman 1997). Nowadays, given globalization, diverse cultures and musical styles easily meet and mix. Music that draws on a wide range of cultural instruments and styles is called World Fusion, World Beat, or World Music—another topic within contemporary ethnomusicology.

Because music is a cultural universal, and because musical abilities seem to run in families, it has been suggested that a predisposition for music may have a genetic basis (Crenson 2000). Could a "music gene" that arose tens, or hundreds, of thousands of years ago have conferred an evolutionary advantage on those early humans who possessed it? The fact that music has existed in all known cultures suggests that it arose early in human history. Providing direct evidence for music's antiquity is an ancient carved bone flute from a cave in Slovenia. This "Divje babe flute," the world's oldest known musical instrument, dates back more than 43,000 years.

Exploring the possible biological roots of music, Sandra Trehub (2001) notes striking similarities in the way mothers worldwide sing to their children—with a high pitch, a slow tempo, and a distinctive tone. All cultures have lullabies, which sound so much alike they cannot be mistaken for anything else (Crenson 2000). Trehub speculates that music might have been adaptive in human evolution because musically talented mothers had an easier time calming their babies. Calm babies who fell asleep easily and rarely made a fuss might have been more likely to survive to adulthood. Their cries would not attract predators; they and their mothers would get more rest; and they would be less likely to be mistreated. If a gene conferring musical ability appeared early in human evolution, given a selective advantage, musical adults would pass their genes to their children.

Music is among the most social of the arts, because it typically unites people in groups, such as choirs, symphonies, ensembles, and bands. Could it be that early humans with a biological penchant for music were able to live more effectively in social groups—another possible adaptive advantage?

Originally coined for European peasants, **folk** art, music, and lore are the expressive culture of ordinary people, as contrasted with the "high" art, or "classic" art, of the European elites. When folk music is performed (see photo on p. 431), the combination of costumes, music, and often song and dance is supposed to say something about local culture and about tradition. Tourists and other outsiders often perceive rural and folk life mainly in terms of such performances. Community residents themselves often use such performances to display and enact their local culture and traditions for outsiders.

In Planinica, a Muslim village in (prewar) Bosnia, Yvonne Lockwood (1983) studied folksong, which could be heard there day or night. The most active singers were unmarried females aged 16 to 26 (maidens). The social transition from girl to maiden (marriageable female) was signaled by active participation in public song and dance.

In this 2011 photo, musicians play carcaba (iron castanets) and gambri (guitar) in the Kasbah, Tangier, Morocco. For whose pleasure do you suppose this performance is being given? Nowadays, such performances attract tourists as well as local people.

© Nico Tondini/Robert Harding World Imagery/Corbis

Adolescent girls were urged to sing along with women and performing maidens. This was part of a rite of passage by which a little girl (*dite*) became a maiden (*cura*). Marriage, in contrast, moved most women from the public to the private sphere; public singing generally stopped. Married women sang in their own homes or among other women. Only occasionally would they join maidens in public song. After age 50, wives tended to stop singing, even in private. For women, singing thus signaled a series of transitions between age grades: girl to maiden (public singing), maiden to wife (private singing), and wife to elder (no more singing).

Singing and dancing were common at Bosnian *prelos* attended by males and females. In Planinica the Serbo-Croatian word *prelo*, usually defined as "spinning bee," meant any occasion for visiting. *Prelos* were especially common in winter. During the summer, villagers worked long hours, and *prelos* were few. The *prelo* offered a context for play, relaxation, song, and dance. All gatherings of maidens, especially *prelos*, were occasions for song. Married women encouraged them to sing, often suggesting specific songs. If males were also present, a singing duel might occur, in which maidens and young men teased each other. A successful *prelo* was well attended, with much singing and dancing.

Public singing was traditional in many other contexts among prewar Bosnian Muslims. After a day of cutting hay on mountain slopes, parties of village men would congregate at a specific place on the trail above the village. They formed lines according to their singing ability, with the best singers in front and the less talented ones behind. They

proceeded to stroll down to the village together, singing as they went, until they reached the village center, where they dispersed. According to Lockwood, whenever an activity brought together a group of maidens or young men, it usually would end with public singing. The inspiration for parts of *Snow White* and *Shrek* (the movies) can be traced back to such customs of the European countryside.

Representations of Art and Culture

The creative products and images of folk, rural, and non-Western cultures are increasingly spread—and commercialized—by the media and tourism. A result is that many Westerners have come to think of "culture" in terms of colorful customs, music, dancing, and adornments: clothing, jewelry, and hairstyles. A bias toward the arts and religion, rather than the more mundane economic and social aspects of culture, shows up on TV's Discovery Channel, and even in many anthropological films (see Grimshaw and Ravetz 2009; Schneider and Pasqualino 2014). Many ethnographic films start off with music, often drumbeats: "Bonga, bonga, bonga, bonga. Here in [whatever the place or society being depicted], the people are very religious." Such presentations just reinforce the previously critiqued assumption that the arts of nonindustrial societies are always linked to religion. This may create a false impression that non-Western peoples spend much of their time wearing colorful clothes, singing, dancing, and practicing religious rituals. Taken to an extreme, such images portray culture as recreational and ultimately not serious, rather than as something that ordinary people live every day of their lives—not just when they have festivals.

Art and Communication

Art also functions as a form of communication between artist and community or audience. Sometimes, however, there are intermediaries between the artist and the audience. Actors, for example, translate the works and ideas of other artists (writers and directors) into performances. Musicians play and sing compositions of other people along with music they themselves have composed. Using music written by others, choreographers plan and direct patterns of dance, which dancers then execute for audiences.

How does art communicate? We need to know what the artist intends to communicate and how the audience reacts. Often, the audience communicates right back to the artist. Live performers, for instance, get immediate feedback, as may writers and directors by viewing a performance of their own work. In contemporary societies, with increasing diversity in the audience, uniform reactions are rare. Contemporary artists, like businesspeople, are well aware that they have target audiences. Certain segments of the population are more likely to appreciate certain forms of art than other segments are.

Art can transmit several kinds of messages. It can convey a moral lesson or tell a cautionary tale. It can teach lessons the artist, or society, wants told. Like the rites that induce, then dispel, anxiety, the tension and resolution of drama can lead to **catharsis**, intense emotional release, in the audience. Art can move emotions, make us laugh, cry, feel up or down. Art appeals to the intellect as well as to the emotions. We may delight in a well-constructed, nicely balanced, well-realized work of art.

Often, art is meant to commemorate and to last, to carry an enduring message. Like a ceremony, art may serve a mnemonic function, making people remember. Art may be designed to make people remember either individuals or events, such as the AIDS epidemic that has proved so lethal in many world areas or the cataclysmic events of September 11, 2001.

Art and Politics

To what extent should art serve society? Art can be self-consciously prosocial. It can be used to either express or challenge community sentiment and standards. Decisions about what counts as a work of art, or about how to display art, may be political and controversial. Museums have to balance concern over community standards with a wish to be as creative and innovative as the artists and works they display.

Much art that is valued today was received with revulsion in its own time. Children were prohibited from seeing paintings by Matisse, Braque, and Picasso when those works first were displayed in New York in the Armory Show of 1913. Almost a century later, the City of New York and then mayor Rudolph Giuliani took the Brooklyn Museum to court over its 1999–2000 "Sensation" exhibit. After religious groups protested Chris Ofili's *Holy Virgin Mary,* a collage that included elephant dung, Giuliani deemed the work sacrilegious. At the ensuing court trial, art advocates spoke out against the mayor's actions. The museum won the case, but Ofili's work again came under attack when a man smuggled paint inside the Brooklyn exhibition and tried to smear it on the *Virgin* (see Reyburn 2015). According to art professor Michael Davis, Ofili's collage is "shocking," because it deliberately provokes and intends to jolt viewers into an expanded frame of reference. The mayor's reactions may have been based on the narrow definition that art must be beautiful and an equally limited stereotype of a Virgin Mary as depicted in Italian Renaissance paintings.

Today, no museum director can mount an exhibit without worrying that it will offend some politically organized segment of society. In the United States there has been an ongoing battle between liberals and conservatives involving the National Endowment for the Arts. Artists have been criticized as being aloof from society, as creating only for themselves and for elites, as being out of touch with conventional and traditional aesthetic values, and even as mocking the values of ordinary people.

catharsis
Intense emotional release.

Art appreciation must be learned, the earlier the better. How does the placement of art in museums, such as this one, affect art appreciation?

© National Geographic Image Collection/Alamy Stock Photo RF

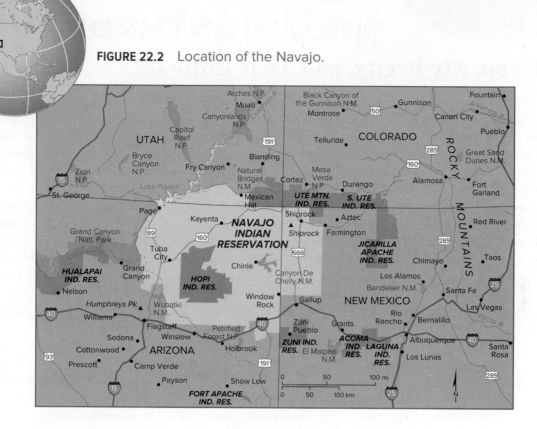

FIGURE 22.2 Location of the Navajo.

The Cultural Transmission of the Arts

Appreciation of the arts reflects one's cultural background. Watch Japanese tourists try to interpret what they are seeing in a Western art museum. Conversely, the form and meaning of a Japanese tea ceremony, or a demonstration of origami (Japanese paper folding), will be alien to a foreign observer. Appreciation of the arts is learned, in particular cultural settings.

For example, music with certain tonalities and rhythm patterns pleases some people but alienates others. In a study of Navajo music, McAllester (1954) found that it reflected the overall culture of that time in three main ways. First, individualism was a key Navajo cultural value: It was up to the individual to decide what to do with his or her songs. Second, the Navajo saw foreign music as dangerous and rejected it. (This second point is no longer true; there are now Navajo rock bands.) Third, a general stress on proper form applied to music. There was, in Navajo belief, a right way to sing every kind of song (see Figure 22.2 for the location of the Navajo).

People learn to appreciate certain kinds of music and other art forms, just as they learn to hear and decipher a foreign language. Unlike Londoners and New Yorkers, Parisians don't flock to musicals. Despite its multiple French origins, even the musical *Les Misérables,* a huge hit in London, New York, and dozens of cities worldwide, bombed in Paris. Humor, too, a form of verbal art, depends on cultural background and setting. What's funny in one culture may not translate as funny in another. When a joke doesn't work, an American may say, "Well, you had to be there at the time." Jokes, like aesthetic judgments, depend on context.

Anthropology's approach to the arts contrasts with the traditional humanities' focus on "fine arts," as in art history, "Great Books," and classical music. Anthropology has extended the definition of "cultured" well beyond the elitist meaning of "high" art and culture (see Sansi-Roca 2015). For anthropologists, everyone acquires culture through enculturation. In academia today, growing acceptance of the anthropological definition of culture has helped broaden the study of the humanities from fine art and elite art to "folk" and non-Western arts, as well as the creative expressions of popular culture.

Using examples from popular culture, this chapter's "Appreciating Anthropology" shows that techniques anthropologists use to analyze myths and folktales can be extended to two fantasy films that most of you have seen: *The Wizard of Oz* and *Star Wars.* "Appreciating Anthropology" also highlights the contributions of the French anthropologist Claude Lévi-Strauss (1967) along with the neo-Freudian psychoanalyst Bruno Bettelheim (1975). Both have made important contributions to the study of myths and fairy tales.

I'll Get You, My Pretty, and Your Little R2

The Wizard of Oz has been telecast regularly for decades. The original *Star Wars* remains one of the most popular films of all time. Both are familiar and significant cultural products with obvious mythic qualities. The contributions of the French structuralist anthropologist Claude Lévi-Strauss (1967) and the neo-Freudian psychoanalyst Bruno Bettelheim (1975) to the study of myths and fairy tales permit the following analysis of visual fairy tales that contemporary Americans know well.

Examining the myths and tales of different cultures, Lévi-Strauss determined that one tale could be converted into another through a series of simple operations—for example, by doing the following:

1. Converting the positive element of a myth into its negative.

2. Reversing the order of the elements.

3. Replacing a male hero with a female hero.

4. Preserving or repeating certain key elements.

Through such operations, two apparently dissimilar myths can be shown to be variations on a common structure—that is, to be transformations of each other.

We'll see that *Star Wars* is a systematic structural transformation of *The Wizard of Oz.* We may speculate about how many of the resemblances were conscious and how many simply reflect a process of enculturation that *Star Wars* writer and director George Lucas shares with other Americans.

The Wizard of Oz and *Star Wars* both begin in arid country, the first in Kansas and the second on the desert planet Tatooine. (Recap 22.1 lists the similarities discussed here.) *Star Wars* converts *The Wizard's* female hero, Dorothy, into a boy, Luke Skywalker. Fairy-tale heroes usually have short, common first names and second names that describe their origin or activity. Thus,

Luke, who travels aboard spaceships, is a Sky-walker, while Dorothy Gale is swept off to Oz by a cyclone (a gale of wind). Dorothy leaves home with her dog, Toto, which is pursued by and has managed to escape from a woman who in Oz becomes the Wicked Witch of the West. Luke follows his "Two-Two" (R2D2), who is fleeing Darth Vader, the witch's structural equivalent.

Dorothy and Luke each start out living with an uncle and an aunt. However, because of the gender change of the hero, the primary relationship is reversed and inverted. Thus, Dorothy's relationship with her aunt is primary, warm, and loving, whereas Luke's relationship with his uncle, though primary, is strained and distant. Aunt and uncle are in the tales for the same reason. They represent home (the nuclear family of orientation), which children (according to American culture norms) must eventually leave to make it on their own. As Bettelheim (1975) points out, fairy tales often disguise parents as uncle and aunt, and this establishes social distance. The child can deal with the hero's separation from aunt and uncle (in *The Wizard of Oz*) or the aunt's and uncle's deaths (in *Star Wars*) more easily than with the separation from or death of real parents. Furthermore, this permits the child's strong feelings toward his or her real parents to be represented in different, more central characters, such as the Wicked Witch of the West and Darth Vader. Both films focus on the child's relationship with the parent of the same sex, dividing that parent into three parts. In *The Wizard,* the mother is split into two parts bad and one part good. They are the Wicked Witch of the East, dead at the beginning of the movie; the Wicked Witch of the West, dead at the end; and Glinda, the good mother, who survives. The original *Star Wars* reversed the proportion of good and bad, giving Luke a good father (his own), the

Jedi knight who is proclaimed dead at the film's beginning. There is another good father, Ben Kenobi, who is ambiguously dead when the movie ends. Third is the evil father figure, Darth Vader. As the good-mother third survives *The Wizard of Oz,* the bad-father third lives on after *Star Wars,* to strike back in the sequel.

The child's relationship with the parent of the opposite sex also is represented in the two films. Dorothy's father figure is the Wizard of Oz, an initially terrifying figure who later is proved to be a fake. Bettelheim notes that the typical fairy-tale father is disguised as a monster or giant. Or else, when preserved as a human, he is weak, distant, or ineffective. Dorothy counts on the wizard to save her but finds that he makes seemingly impossible demands and in the end is just an ordinary man. She succeeds on her own, no longer relying on a father who offers no more than she herself possesses.

In *Star Wars* (although not in the later films), Luke's mother figure is Princess Leia. Bettelheim notes that boys commonly fantasize their mothers to be unwilling captives of their fathers. Fairy tales often disguise mothers as princesses whose freedom the boy-hero must obtain. In graphic Freudian imagery, Darth Vader threatens Princess Leia with a needle the size of the witch's broomstick. By the end of the film, Luke has freed Leia and defeated Vader.

There are other striking parallels in the structure of the two films. Fairy-tale heroes often are accompanied on their adventures by secondary characters who personify the virtues needed in a successful quest. Such characters often come in threes. Dorothy takes along wisdom (the Scarecrow), love (the Tin Woodman), and courage (the Lion). *Star Wars* includes a structurally equivalent trio—Han Solo, C3PO, and Chewbacca—but their association with particular qualities isn't as

RECAP 22.1   *Star Wars* as a Structural Transformation of *The Wizard of Oz*

STAR WARS	THE WIZARD OF OZ
Male hero (Luke Skywalker)	Female hero (Dorothy Gale)
Arid Tatooine	Arid Kansas

Luke follows R2D2:
  R2D2 flees Vader
	Dorothy follows Toto:
	  Toto flees witch

Luke lives with uncle and aunt:
  Primary relationship with uncle
  (same sex as hero)
  Strained, distant relationship with uncle
	Dorothy lives with uncle and aunt:
	  Primary relationship with aunt
	  (same sex as hero)
	  Warm, close relationship with aunt

Tripartite division of same-sex parent:
  2 parts good, 1 part bad father
  Good father dead at beginning
  Good father dead (?) at end
  Bad father survives
	Tripartite division of same-sex parent:
	  2 parts bad, 1 part good mother
	  Bad mother dead at beginning
	  Bad mother dead at end
	  Good mother survives

Relationship with parent of opposite sex
    (Princess Leia Organa):
  Princess is unwilling captive
  Needle
  Princess is freed
	Relationship with parent of opposite sex
	    (Wizard of Oz):
	  Wizard makes impossible demands
	  Broomstick
	  Wizard turns out to be sham

Trio of companions:
  Han Solo, C3PO, Chewbacca
	Trio of companions:
	  Scarecrow, Tin Woodman, Cowardly Lion

Minor characters:
  Jawas
  Sand People
  Stormtroopers
	Minor characters:
	  Munchkins
	  Apple Trees
	  Flying Monkeys

Settings:
  Death Star
  Verdant Tikal (rebel base)
	Settings:
	  Witch's castle
	  Emerald City

Conclusion:
  Luke uses magic to accomplish goal
  (destroy Death Star)
	Conclusion:
	  Dorothy uses magic to accomplish goal
	  (return to Kansas)

precise. The minor characters also are structurally parallel: Munchkins and Jawas, Apple Trees and Sand People, Flying Monkeys and Stormtroopers. And compare settings—the witch's castle and the Death Star, the Emerald City and the rebel base. The endings also are parallel. Luke accomplishes his objective on his own, using the Force (mana, magical power). Dorothy's goal is to return to Kansas. She does that by tapping her shoes together and drawing on the Force in her ruby slippers.

All successful cultural products blend old and new, drawing on familiar themes. They may rearrange them in novel ways and thus win a lasting place in the imaginations of the culture that creates or accepts them. *Star Wars* successfully used old cultural themes in novel ways. It did that by drawing on the American fairy tale, one that had been available in book form since the turn of the 20th century. Have you seen the most recent, and hugely popular, *Star Wars* film, *The Force Awakens*? If so, make an attempt to do your own structural analysis of this new film as a transformation of the original *Star Wars* story. Hints: another arid planet, female rather than male hero closely associated with small droid, evil father replaced by evil son.

Schoolchildren play violins in an orchestra. Does this scene illustrate education, enculturation, or both?
© Richard Mittleman/Alamy Stock Photo RF

A traditional musician and storyteller performs with local children in Panama's Tusipono Embera Community. Are there comparable figures in your society? Does this scene illustrate education, enculturation, or both?
© Kike Calvo/National Geographic Creative

In many societies, myths, legends, tales, and the art of storytelling play important roles in the transmission of culture. Oral traditions may preserve details of history and genealogy, as in many parts of West Africa. Storytelling and music may be combined for drama and emphasis (see lower photo above), much as they are in films and theater.

At what age do children start learning the arts? In some cultures, they start early. Contrast the photo of the violin class (upper photo above) with the photo of the Tusipono Embera Community gathering (lower photo above). The violin scene shows formal instruction. Teachers take the lead in showing students how to play the violin. The lower photo shows a more informal local scene in which children are learning about the arts as part of their overall enculturation. Many of the violin students are learning the arts because their parents

want them to, rather than because they have an artistic temperament they are eager to express. In the United States, performance, often associated with schools, has a strong social, and usually competitive, component. Kids perform with their peers. In the process, they learn to compete, whether for a first-place finish in a sports event or for a first chair in the school orchestra or band.

Continuity and Change

The arts go on changing, although certain art forms have survived for thousands of years. The Upper Paleolithic cave art that has survived for more than 30,000 years was itself a highly developed manifestation of human creativity and symbolism, with a long evolutionary history. Monumental architecture, along with sculpture, ornamental pottery, and written music, literature, and drama, have survived from early civilizations (see Burt 2013; Ingold 2013).

Countries and cultures are known for particular contributions, including the arts. The Balinese are known for dance; the Navajo for sand paintings, jewelry, and weaving; and the French for making cuisine an art form. We still read Greek tragedies and comedies in college, as we also read Shakespeare and Milton and view the works of Michelangelo. Greek theater is among the most enduring of the arts. The words of Aeschylus, Sophocles, Euripides, and Aristophanes have been captured in writing and live on. Who knows how many great preliterate creations and performances have been lost?

Classic Greek theater survives throughout the world. It is read in college courses and performed on stages from Athens to New York. In today's world, the dramatic arts are part of a huge "arts and leisure" industry (encompassing arts, media, and sports), which links Western and non-Western art forms in a global network that has both aesthetic and commercial dimensions (see Marcus and Myers 1995; Root 1996; Schneider and Wright 2013). Non-Western musical traditions and instruments have joined this network. Folk musicians routinely perform for outsiders, including tourists who increasingly visit their villages. And "tribal" instruments such as the Native Australian didgeridoo, a very long, wooden wind instrument, are now exported worldwide. At least one shop in Amsterdam, the Netherlands, sells only didgeridoos. Stores in any world capital hawk "traditional" arts, including musical instruments, from dozens of non-Western countries.

Although American culture values experimentation and innovation, creativity also can be expressed in variations on a traditional form. We see this in "Appreciating Anthropology," in which *Star Wars,* despite its specific story and innovative special effects, is shown to share its structure with a previous narrative. Thanks to globalization, ingredients and flavors from all over the world now combine in modern cuisine. So, too, are elements from many cultures and epochs woven into our contemporary arts and expressive culture, including in modern media.

MEDIA AND CULTURE

Today's mass culture, or popular culture, features cultural forms that have appeared and spread rapidly because of major changes in the material conditions of contemporary life—particularly work organization, transportation, and communication, including the media. Sports, movies, TV shows, video games, digital media, amusement parks, and fast-food restaurants have become powerful elements of national (and international) culture (see Sanjek and Tratner 2016). They offer a framework of common expectations, experiences, and behavior overriding differences in region, class, formal religious affiliation, political sentiment, gender, ethnic group, and place of residence.

Using the Media

Any media-borne image or message can be analyzed in terms of its nature, including its symbolism, and its effects. It also can be analyzed as a **text**—something that can be received, processed, interpreted, and assigned meaning by anyone exposed to it. In this sense, a text doesn't have to be written. The term may refer to a film, an image, or an event. "Readers"—users of the text—make their own interpretations and derive their own feelings from it. "Readers" of media messages constantly produce their own meanings.

According to the media scholar John Fiske (2011), any individual's use of popular culture is a personal creative act (an original "reading" of a "text"). A particular celebrity, movie, game, or TV show means something different to each fan. Fiske argues that the personal meanings one finds in popular culture are most pleasurable when they relate directly and practically to that person's everyday life (Fiske 2011; see also Fiske and Hartley 2003).

Consumers actively select, evaluate, and interpret media in ways that make sense to them. People use media for all sorts of reasons: to validate beliefs, to indulge fantasies, to find messages unavailable in the local setting, to locate information, to make social comparisons, to relieve frustrations, to chart social courses, and to formulate life plans. Popular culture (from hip-hop to comedy) can be used to express discontent and resistance by groups that are or feel powerless or oppressed.

In Ibirama, a town in southern Brazil, anthropologist Alberto Costa found that women and young adults of both sexes were particularly attracted to telenovelas, melodramatic nightly programs often compared to American soap operas, usually featuring sophisticated urban settings (see Kottak 2009; Pace and Hinote 2013). Women and young men in Ibirama used the (socially more liberal) content of telenovelas to challenge conservative

In an ancient amphitheater at Syracuse, Sicily, ancient Greek theater (*Medea*) is being performed for a contemporary audience. Theater is typically a multimedia experience, with visual, aural, and often musical attributes.
© Ingolf Pompe/age fotostock

A synthesis of new and old theater techniques, including puppetry, is used in this production of the stage play *War Horse* at London's Olivier Theatre.
© Elliott Franks/ArenaPal/The Image Works

local norms. In Brazil, elites, intellectuals, educators, the clergy, and older men have tended to be more suspicious and dismissive of mass media than are less powerful people. Often, these groups view media messages as threatening or subverting their traditional authority as guardians of power or cultural capital.

During our fieldwork in a middle-class Michigan town, Lara Descartes and I found that parents selected media messages that supported and reinforced

text
A cultural product that is processed and assigned meaning by anyone exposed to it.

their own opinions and life choices (Descartes and Kottak 2009). Media images of work and family gave parents the chance to identify, or contrast themselves, with media figures. Townfolk compared themselves with people and situations from the media as well as with people in their own lives. We also found, as in Brazil, that some people (traditionalists) were much more dismissive of, distrustful of, or hostile to media than others were.

When people seek certain messages and can't easily find them in their home communities, they are likely to look somewhere else. The media, especially modern social media, allow local people to link in to a rich web of connections that can provide contact, information, entertainment, and potential social validation. In Brazil, we've found that greater use of all media is part of an external orientation, a general wish for information, contacts, models, and support beyond those that are locally and routinely available. For some of the parents (especially mothers) in our Michigan study, media offered a welcome gateway to a wider world. Others, however, were comfortable with, and even sought to enhance, their isolation, limiting both media exposure and the outside social contacts of themselves and their children.

Connection to a wider world, real or imagined, on- or offline, is a way to move beyond local standards and expectations, even if the escape is only temporary and vicarious. David Ignatius (2007) describes the escapist value of 19th-century English novels, whose strong heroines pursued "free thought and personal freedom," rejecting the "easy comforts and arranged marriages of their class" in a quest for something more. Despite (and/or because of) their independent or rebellious temperaments, characters such as Elizabeth Bennett in Jane Austen's *Pride and Prejudice* almost always found a happy ending. Nineteenth-century readers found such a heroine's success "deeply satisfying," because there were so few opportunities in real life (the local community) to see such behavior and choices (all quotes from Ignatius 2007, p. A21).

Another role of the media is to provide social cement—a basis for sharing—as families or friends watch favorite programs or attend events together. The media also can provide common ground for much larger groups, nationally and internationally. Brazilians and Italians can be just as excited, at the same moment but with radically different emotions, by a soccer goal scored in a World Cup match. And they can remember the same winning goal for decades. The common information and knowledge that people acquire through exposure to the same media illustrate *culture* in the anthropological sense (see also Askew and Wilk 2002; Ginsburg, Abu-Lughod, and Larkin 2002).

Assessing the Effects of Television

My co-researchers and I first got the idea that TV might be influencing family planning in Brazil from a brief article in the *New York Times*. Based on interviews with Brazilians, that report suggested that TV (along with other factors) was influencing Brazilians to have smaller families. Fortunately, our research project on media impact in rural Brazil had provided us with the quantitative data we needed to test that hypothesis.

Our findings already had confirmed many other studies showing that the strongest predictor of (smaller) family size is a woman's educational level. However, it turned out that two television variables—current viewing level and especially the number of years of TV presence in the home—were better predictors of (smaller) family size than were many other potential predictors, including income, class, and religiosity.

In the four towns in our study with the longest exposure to television, the average woman had had a TV set in her home for 15 years and had had 2.3 pregnancies. In the three communities where TV had arrived most recently, the average woman had had a home set for 4 years and had had 5 pregnancies. Thus, length of site exposure was a useful predictor of reproductive histories. Of course, television exposure at a site is an aspect of that site's increasing overall access to external systems and resources, which usually include improved methods of contraception. But the impact of longer home TV exposure showed up not only when we compared sites but also within sites, within age cohorts, and among individual women in our total sample.

What social mechanisms were behind these correlations? Family planning opportunities (including contraception) are greater in Brazil now than they used to be. However, experience in Africa, Asia, and Latin America has shown that mere access to contraception does not ensure family planning. Rather, popular demand for contraception must be created. Often, as in India (see photo on p. 439), this is done through "social marketing," including planned multimedia campaigns. In Brazil, however, there has been little direct use of TV to get people to limit their offspring. How, then, has television influenced Brazilians to plan smaller families?

We noticed that Brazilian TV families tend to have fewer children than traditional small-town Brazilians do. Narrative form and production costs limit the number of players in each telenovela (nightly soap opera) to about 50 characters. Telenovelas usually are gender-balanced and include three-generation extended families of different social classes, so that some of the main characters can "rise in life" by marrying up. These narrative conventions limit the number of young children per TV family. We concluded that people's ideas about proper family size are influenced as they see, day after day, nuclear families smaller than the traditional ones in their towns. Furthermore, the aim of commercial television is to sell products and lifestyles. Brazilian TV families routinely are shown enjoying consumer goods and

In some countries, popular demand for birth control has been created through multimedia campaigns, illustrated by this poster in Panaji, Goa, India. In Brazil, there has been little direct use of TV to get people to limit their offspring. How, then, has television influenced Brazilians to plan smaller families?
© Stuart Forster/Alamy Stock Photo

lives of leisure, to which viewers learn to aspire. Telenovelas may convey the idea that viewers can achieve such lifestyles by emulating the apparent family planning of TV characters. The effect of Brazilian television on family planning seems to be a corollary of a more general, TV-influenced shift from traditional toward more liberal social attitudes. Anthropologist Janet Dunn's (2000) further fieldwork in Brazil has demonstrated how TV exposure actually works to influence reproductive choice and family planning.

Networking and Sociability On- and Offline

For generations, anthropologists have stressed the linking social functions (alliance creation) of such ages-old institutions as marriage and trade. Today's world offers some radically new ways to connect socially. Aaron Sorkin chose *The Social Network* as the title for his movie about the founding of Facebook, which is precisely that—a social networking site (SNS), where people go to get linked in cyberspace. Modern media allow local people access to connections that provide contact, information, entertainment, and potential social validation. Among Brazilians, we saw that extensive media use reflects an external orientation, a general wish for connections—a social network—beyond what is locally and routinely available.

Brazil is rapidly increasing its Internet access and its use of social media. As the Brazilian middle class has grown, Internet use has spread across the country, although it remains unreliable in small communities along the Amazon and rural areas in general. About 60 percent of Brazilians have online connectivity, compared with almost 90 percent of Americans (Poushter 2016). Many of those online Brazilians use Facebook, available free of charge on Brazilian smart phones since 2010 (Richard Pace, personal communication). Brazil ranks third in the world in number of Facebook users (after the United States and India). That site's growth rate in Brazil has been phenomenal, with 30 million new users added between 2012 and 2013 alone (Richard Pace, personal communication). Over 70 million Brazilians are now on Facebook. Offline, Brazilians are inherently social people, and they seem to be transferring this sociability to the online world. As in the United States, SNSs (aka social media) reinforce family connections while establishing and maintaining contacts in a wider world of nonrelatives.

Research in the United States provides additional evidence that SNSs enhance social connectivity, rather than (as some have feared) isolating people and truncating their social relationships. Through survey research, the Pew Research Center's ongoing Internet & American Life Project has investigated how the use of social media is related to trust, social support, and political engagement (see Hampton et al. 2011). By 2015, an estimated 89 percent of American adults (aged 18 and over) were online (Poushter 2016). Of them, 74 percent participated in at least one social media

In Jakarta, Indonesia, Ahmad Mustofa Bisri, a prominent moderate Muslim cleric, uses an iPad to check his Twitter feed. Religious leaders increasingly use social media to maintain contact with their followers.

© Bay Ismoyo/AFP/Getty Images

site. Facebook was dominant, attracting 71 percent of online Americans, compared with 28 percent for Pinterest, 26 percent for Instagram, and 23 percent for Twitter (see Pew Research Center 2105c).

A 2010–2011 Pew study found that more than half of Facebook users visited that site at least once a day. The typical visitor was most likely (in this order) to "like" another user's post, comment on a post or status, comment on a posted photo, update his or her own status, or send a private message. In the Pew study, as social media use increased, so did measures of trust, sociability, and political engagement. Internet users overall were twice as likely as nonusers to say people can be trusted, with Facebookers especially trusting and socially oriented. Those who visited Facebook multiple times each day (heavy Facebook users) were 43 percent more likely than other Internet users (and three times as likely as non-Internet users) to say most people can be trusted. The average heavy Facebook user also identified more "close ties" in his or her overall social network than did other Internet users. In terms of support and companionship provided by their social networks, Internet users scored 3 to 6 points higher than nonusers, and heavy Facebookers averaged 5 points higher than Internet users overall. People have to reveal personal and family details on Facebook, so it's not surprising that they would be more trusting and socially oriented.

Furthermore, Internet users, especially those on Facebook, were much more politically engaged than other Americans. The Pew survey was conducted over the November 2010 elections. At that time, 10 percent of respondents had attended a political rally, 23 percent had tried to convince someone to vote for a specific candidate, and 66 percent had voted or intended to vote. Internet users were significantly more likely than offliners to attend political meetings, to vote, and to try to influence someone else's vote. Here again, heavy Facebook users stood out as even more likely than the average Internet user to do those things.

What kind of relationships does Facebook support and reinforce? In this order, one's Facebook "friends" are likely to be a high school friend, an extended family member, a coworker, a college friend, an immediate family member, a member of one's club or group, and, finally, a neighbor. Only 7 percent of Facebook friends are people whom users have never met in person (Hampton et al. 2011).

Internet use, which thrives among the young, educated, and affluent (in the United States and worldwide), is increasing in all countries, age groups, and levels of income and education. Nevertheless, a significant chunk (around 11 percent for the United States) of the populace remains cut off from the connectivity available online (Poushter 2016). In a few (mainly rural) areas of the United States, access remains unavailable or limited. Cost (e.g., of computer and broadband) is another limitation. Among age groups, people over 65 are most likely to lack connectivity. Millions of Americans still remain isolated offline because of their advanced age or limited educations. One-third of the offliners claim to be uninterested in using the Internet, to be unwilling to try, or to not need it. The remainder cite various obstacles to going online, including affordability and availability (Zickuhr 2013). In an increasingly interconnected world, these obstacles and excuses will surely diminish, as an ever greater percentage of the United States and the world goes online.

Indeed, seniors have made significant strides in their use of the Internet, including social media. Usage among Americans 65 and older has mushroomed since 2005, when only 2 percent used social media. Today, that figure exceeds 35 percent (Perrin 2015). In 2005, only 5 percent of rural Americans used social media; that figure approaches 60 percent today.

SPORTS AND CULTURE

We now turn to the cultural context of sports and the cultural values expressed in them. We can recognize links among sports, media, and the arts. Like many artists and media personalities, sports figures are performers, some with celebrity status, who must meet cultural expectations and standards regarding performance and conduct. Because so much of what we know about sports comes from the media, a discussion of sports inevitably provides additional illustration of the pervasive role of the mass media in contemporary life. This section mainly describes how sports and the media *reflect* culture. Sports and the media also *influence* culture, as we saw in the discussion of how Brazilian television modifies social attitudes and family planning. Does it surprise you that the influence of media (and sports) on culture and vice versa are reciprocal?

American Football

On fall Saturdays, millions of Americans travel to and from college football games. Smaller congregations meet in high school stadiums. Millions of Americans watch televised football. Indeed, nearly half the adult population of the United States watches the Super Bowl, which attracts people of diverse ages, ethnic backgrounds, regions, religions, political parties, jobs, social statuses, levels of wealth, and genders.

The popularity of football, particularly professional football, depends directly on the mass media. Is football, with its territorial incursion, hard hitting, and violence, popular because Americans are violent people? Are football spectators vicariously realizing their own hostile and aggressive tendencies? The anthropologist W. Arens (1981) has discounted this interpretation, arguing that if football were a particularly effective channel for expressing aggression, it would have spread (like soccer and baseball) to many other countries, where people have as many aggressive tendencies and hostile feelings as Americans do. He concludes reasonably that the explanation for football's popularity must lie elsewhere.

Arens contends that football is popular because it symbolizes certain key aspects of American life. In particular, it features teamwork based on division of labor, which is a pervasive feature of contemporary life. Susan Montague and Robert Morais (1981) take the analysis a step further. They link football's values, particularly teamwork, to those associated with business. Like corporate workers, the ideal players are diligent and dedicated to the team. Within corporations, however, decision making is complicated, and workers aren't always rewarded for their dedication and good job performance. Decisions are simpler and rewards are more consistent in football, these anthropologists contend, and this helps explain its popularity. Even if we can't figure out how ExxonMobil or Microsoft runs, any fan can become an expert on football's rules, teams, scores, statistics, and patterns of play. Even more important, football suggests that the values stressed by business really do pay off. Teams whose members work the hardest, show the most spirit, and best develop and coordinate their talents can be expected to win more often than other teams do.

What Determines International Sports Success?

Why do countries excel at particular sports? Why do certain nations pile up dozens of Olympic medals, while others win only a handful? It isn't simply a matter of rich and poor, developed and underdeveloped, or even governmental or other institutional support of promising athletes. It isn't even a question of a "national will to win," for although certain nations stress winning even more than Americans do, a cultural focus on winning doesn't necessarily lead to the desired result.

A prominent value in American football is teamwork based on division of labor, which is a pervasive feature of contemporary life. Here the Pittsburgh Steelers huddle during a game against the Baltimore Ravens at Heinz Field in Pittsburgh, Pennsylvania. Is teamwork equally valued in other sports, such as baseball, basketball, or soccer?

© Justin K. Aller/Getty Images Sport/Getty Images

Cultural values, social forces, and the media influence international sports success. We can see this by contrasting the United States and Brazil, two countries with continental proportions and large, physically and ethnically diverse populations. Although each is its continent's major economic power, they offer revealing contrasts in Olympic success: In the 2012 London Summer Olympics, the United States won 104 medals, including 46 gold medals, compared with 17 and 3, respectively, for Brazil.

Americans' interest in sports has been honed over the years by an ever-growing media establishment, which provides a steady stream of games, matches, playoffs, championships, and analyses. Cable and satellite TV offer almost constant sports coverage, including packages for every major sport and season. The Super Bowl is a national event. The Olympic games get extensive coverage and attract significant audiences. Brazilian television, by contrast, traditionally has offered less sports coverage, with no nationally televised annual event comparable to the Super Bowl. The World (soccer) Cup, held every 4 years, is the only sports event that consistently draws huge national audiences.

In international competition, a win by a Brazilian team or the occasional nationally known individual athlete is felt to bring respect to the entire nation, but the Brazilian media are strikingly intolerant of losers. When the now legendary swimmer Ricardo Prado swam for his silver medal in the finals of the 400 Individual Medley (IM), during prime time on national TV in 1984, one newsmagazine observed that "it was as though he was the country with a swimsuit on, jumping in the pool in a collective search for success" (*Isto É* 1984). Prado's own feelings confirmed the magazine,

"When I was on the stands, I thought of just one thing: what they'll think of the result in Brazil." After beating his old world record by 1.33 seconds, in a second-place finish, Prado told a fellow team member, "I think I did everything right. I feel like a winner, but will they think I'm a loser in Brazil?" Prado contrasted the situations of Brazilian and American athletes. The United States has, he said, so many athletes that no single one has to summarize the country's hopes (*Veja* 1984a). Fortunately, Brazil did seem to value Prado's performance, which was responsible for "Brazil's best result ever in Olympic swimming" (*Veja* 1984a). Labeling Prado "the man of silver," the media never tired of characterizing his main event, the 400 IM, in which he once had held the world record, as the most challenging event in swimming. However, the kind words for Ricardo Prado did not extend to the rest of the Brazilian team. The press lamented their "succession of failures" (*Veja* 1984a). (Brazil finally got swimming gold at the 2008 games in Beijing, with César Cielo Filho winning the 50-meter freestyle race.)

Because Brazilian athletes are viewed as stand-ins for their entire country, and because team sports are emphasized, the Brazilian media focus too exclusively on winning. Winning, of course, is also an American cultural value, particularly for team sports, as in Brazil. American football coaches are famous for comments like "Winning isn't everything; it's the only thing" and "Show me a good loser and I'll show you a loser." However, and particularly for sports such as running, swimming, diving, gymnastics, and skating, which focus on the individual, and in which American athletes usually do well, American culture also admires "moral victories," "personal bests," "comeback athletes," and "Special Olympics" and commends those who run good races without finishing first. In amateur and individual sports, American culture tells us that hard work and personal improvement can be as important as winning.

Americans are so accustomed to being told their culture overemphasizes winning that they may find it hard to believe other cultures value it even more. Brazil certainly does. Brazilian sports enthusiasts are preoccupied with world records, probably because only a win (as in soccer) or a best time (as in swimming) can make Brazil indisputably, even if temporarily, the best in the world at something. Prado's former world record in the 400 IM was mentioned constantly in the press prior to his Olympic swim. Such a best-time standard also provides Brazilians with a ready basis to fault a swimmer or runner for not going fast enough, when he or she doesn't make previous times. One might predict, accurately, that sports with more subjective standards would not be very popular in Brazil. Brazilians like to assign blame to athletes who fail them, and negative comments about gymnasts or divers are more difficult, because grace and execution can't be quantified as easily as time can.

Brazilians, I think, value winning so much because it is rare. In the United States, resources are more abundant, chances to achieve more numerous, and poverty less pervasive. American society has room for many winners. Brazilian society is more stratified; together the middle class and the small elite group at the top comprise just about half of the national population. Brazilian sports echo lessons from the larger society: Victories are scarce and usually reserved for the privileged few.

Being versus Doing

The factors believed to contribute to sports success belong to a larger context of cultural values. Particularly relevant is the contrast between ascribed and achieved status. An ascribed status (e.g., age) is based on what one *is* rather than what one *does*. Individuals have more control over their achieved statuses (e.g., student, golfer, tennis player). American culture emphasizes achieved over ascribed status: We are supposed to make of our lives the best we can. Success comes through achievement. An American's identity emerges as a result of what he or she does.

In Brazil, on the other hand, identity rests not so much on doing as on being, on what one is from the start—a strand in a web of personal connections, originating in social class and the extended family. Social position and network membership contribute substantially to individual fortune, and all social life is hierarchical. High-status Brazilians don't stand patiently in line as Americans do. Important people expect their business to be attended to immediately, and social inferiors readily yield. A high-status Brazilian is as likely to say "Do you know who you're talking to?" as an American is to say "Who do you think you are?"—reflecting a more democratic and egalitarian value system (DaMatta 1991).

The following description of a Brazilian judo medalist (as reported by *Veja* magazine) illustrates the importance of ascribed status and privilege.

> Walter Carmona began judo at age six and became a São Paulo champion at twelve. . . . Carmona . . . is fully supported by his father, a factory owner. Walter Carmona's life has been comfortable—he has been able to study and dedicate himself to judo without worries. (*Veja* 1984b, p. 61)

Faced with an athlete from a well-off family, American reporters, by contrast, rarely conclude that privilege is the main reason for success. American media almost always focus on some aspect of doing, some special personal triumph or achievement. Often, this involves the athlete's struggle with adversity (illness, injury, pain, or the death of a parent, sibling, friend, or coach). The featured athlete is presented as not only successful but noble and self-sacrificing as well.

Given the Brazilian focus on ascribed status, the guiding assumption is that one cannot do more than

At the 2012 London Summer Olympics, Brazilian judoist Maria Suelen Altheman celebrates her victory over Gulzhan Issanova of Kazakstan. This win advanced Altheman to the bronze medal judo match in her weight category.

© David Finch/Getty Images Sport/Getty Images

"Special Olympics" commend people who run good races, without necessarily being the best in the world. Shown here, competitors in a heat of the women's 100-meter sprint during the 2015 Special Olympics World Games, in Los Angeles, California. How do national cultural values affect sports performance?

© Mark Ralston/AFP/Getty Images

what one is. One year the Brazilian Olympic Committee sent no female swimmers to the Summer Olympics, because none had made arbitrarily established cutoff times. This excluded a South American record holder, while swimmers with slower times were attending from other countries. No one seemed to imagine that Olympic excitement might spur swimmers to extraordinary efforts.

American culture, supposedly so practical and realistic, has a remarkable faith in the possibility of coming from behind. These values are those of an achievement-oriented society where (ideally) "anything is possible" compared with an ascribed-status society in which it's over before it's begun. In American sports coverage, underdogs and unexpected results, virtually ignored by the Brazilian media, provide some of the "brightest" moments. Brazilian culture has little interest in the unexpected.

Athletes internalize these values. Brazilians assume that if you go into an event with a top seed time, as Ricardo Prado did, you've got a chance to win a medal. Prado's second-place finish made perfect sense back home, because his former world record had been bettered before the race began.

Given the overwhelming value American culture places on work, it might seem surprising that our media devote so much attention to unforeseen results and so little to the years of training, preparation, and competition that underlie Olympic

performance. It probably is assumed that hard work is so obvious and fundamental that it goes without saying. Or perhaps the assumption is that by the time athletes actually enter Olympic competition all are so similar (the American value of equality) that only mysterious and chance factors can explain variable success. The American focus on the unexpected applies to losses as well as wins. Such concepts as chance, fate, mystery, and uncertainty are viewed as legitimate reasons for defeat. Runners and skaters fall; ligaments tear; a gymnast "inexplicably" falls off the pommel horse.

Brazilians place more responsibility on the individual. Less is attributed to factors beyond human control. When individuals who should have performed well don't do so, they are blamed for their failures. It is, however, culturally appropriate in Brazil to use poor health as an excuse for losing. The American media, by contrast, talk much more about the injuries and illnesses of the victors than those of the losers.

The Fall from Grace: The Celebrity Scandal

On the upside of an achievement-oriented society is major success—performing well and consistently, rising to the top, becoming a star; on the downside is failure—a fall from grace. The American expression "the bigger they are, the harder they fall" applies easily to American celebrities, ranging from sports and entertainment figures to politicians. Increasingly familiar to all Americans (because of the growth and ubiquity of the media) is the celebrity scandal and its stages. The media-driven celebrity scandal, whether in politics, entertainment, or sports, can be analyzed as a social drama with four known stages: breech, public reaction, atonement, and reintegration.

First, a transgression of some sort (usually involving sex) becomes publicly known, and a media frenzy follows. After a period of public humiliation and ridicule, the celebrity issues a well-publicized apology, ideally with an aggrieved loved one close at hand. Various other acts of atonement are expected to follow, but they aren't always publicly known. If the apology and atonement are accepted by the public, the scandal begins to fade. If there is no repeat transgression, the celebrity can find eventual redemption through rehabilitation, reform, or a lifestyle change.

Americans have witnessed this process several times in recent years—most often with politicians. Examples include President Bill Clinton, Idaho senator Larry Craig, Louisiana senator David Vitter, New York governor Eliot Spitzer, and vice presidential candidate John Edwards. Former South Carolina governor (and now South Carolina congressman) Mark Sanford famously claimed a fictitious hike on the Appalachian Trail to conceal a visit to Buenos Aires and his Argentinian lover. Serial sexter and former congressman Anthony Weiner has gone through the process (at least) twice. His first fall from grace led to his resignation from the United States Congress. His second round of infractions derailed his 2013 candidacy for mayor of New York City. Initially perceived as appropriately repentant and reformed, Weiner saw his reputation sink again as media reports revealed more recent (and postrepentance) sexting episodes.

Celebrities who fall in this way almost always are men. Female celebrity scandals (e.g., Lindsay Lohan) typically feature media reports of serial erratic and/or unlawful behavior, changes in body image (such as noticeable weight gain or loss), and accusations of being out of control, followed by healing via some form of seclusion and/or rehabilitation. In the luckiest cases, redemption leads to career rejuvenation.

In sports, the most celebrated scandal in recent years features Tiger Woods as its central figure (see Starn 2011). The fall from grace began late in 2009, with media reports of his post-Thanksgiving, post-midnight car crash into a fire hydrant and his wife's use of a golf club to shatter a window of his vehicle. Preceding that crash, a tabloid story had accused the golfer of an extramarital tryst. A media frenzy built up after the crash, as additional extramarital affairs were reported. His fall was particularly steep, because the golfer had been so successful and admired, and because he had managed his image so carefully and effectively.

The golfer's transgression and ensuing public humiliation and trial by media were followed by the inevitable apology and period of atonement (although his marriage did not survive), leading to Wood's gradual reintegration into the world of golf. Signifying his reintegration, he received the 2013 PGA (Professional Golfers' Association) Tour Player of the Year Award. He had won 5 of the 16 tournaments he played in that year and placed in the top 10 in 3 others. Tiger Woods may be back, but he is no longer the untarnished alpha golf champion of yesteryear. This fall from grace, for now at least, seems to have run its course. As of this writing, however, his future is clouded by a series of back surgeries.

for REVIEW

summary

1. Even if they lack a word for "art," people everywhere do associate an aesthetic experience with objects and events having certain qualities. The arts, sometimes called "expressive culture," include the visual arts, literature (written and oral), music, and theater arts. Some issues raised about religion also apply to art. If we adopt a special attitude or demeanor when confronting a sacred object, do we display something similar with art? Much art has been done in association with religion. In tribal performances, the arts and religion often mix. But non-Western art isn't always linked to religion.

2. The special places where we find art include museums, concert halls, opera houses, and theaters. However, the boundary between what's art and what's not may be blurred. Variation in art appreciation is especially common in contemporary society, with its professional artists and critics and great cultural diversity.

3. Those who work with non-Western art have been criticized for ignoring individual artists and for focusing too much on the social context and collective artistic production. Art is work, albeit creative work. In state societies, some people manage to support themselves as full-time artists. In nonstates, artists are usually part-time. Typically, the arts are exhibited, evaluated, performed, and appreciated in society. Music, which often is performed in groups, is among the most social of the arts. Folk art, music, and lore are the expressive culture of ordinary, usually rural, people.

4. Art can stand for tradition, even when traditional art is removed from its original context. Art can express community sentiment, with political goals used to call attention to social issues. Often, art is meant to commemorate and to last. Growing acceptance of the anthropological definition of culture has guided the humanities beyond fine art, elite art, and Western art to the creative expressions of the masses and of many cultures. Myths, legends, tales, and the art of storytelling often play important roles in the transmission of culture.

5. The arts go on changing, although certain art forms have survived for thousands of years. Countries and cultures are known for particular contributions. Today, a huge "arts and leisure" industry links Western and non-Western art forms in an international network with both aesthetic and commercial dimensions.

6. Any media-borne message can be analyzed as a text, something that can be "read"—that is, processed, interpreted, and assigned meaning by anyone exposed to it. People use media to validate beliefs, indulge fantasies, seek out messages, make social comparisons, relieve frustrations, chart social courses, and resist unequal power relations. The media can provide common ground for social groups. Length of home TV exposure is a useful measure of the impact of television on values, attitudes, and beliefs. The effect of Brazilian television on family planning seems to be a corollary of a more general TV-influenced shift from traditional toward more liberal social attitudes. Use of online social media correlates with overall social connectivity and sociability, including measures of trust, companionship, and political involvement.

7. As in the arts and media, performance is a key feature of sports. Much of what we know about sports comes from the media. Like the arts, both sports and the media reflect and influence culture. Football symbolizes and simplifies certain key aspects of American life and values (e.g., hard work and teamwork). Cultural values, social forces, and the media influence international sports success. In amateur and individual sports, American culture tells us that hard work and personal improvement can be as important as winning. Other cultures, such as Brazil, may value winning even more than Americans do. The factors believed to contribute to sports success belong to a larger context of cultural values. Particularly relevant is the contrast between ascribed and achieved status: being versus doing. An American's identity emerges as a result of what he or she does. In Brazil, by contrast, identity rests on being: what one is from the start—a strand in a web of personal connections, originating in social class and the extended family. The media-driven celebrity scandal, whether in politics, entertainment, or sports, can be analyzed as a social drama with four known stages: breech, public reaction, atonement, and reintegration.

key terms

aesthetics 424

art 424

arts 424

catharsis 432

ethnomusicology 430

expressive culture 424

folk 430

text 437

critical thinking

1. Recall the last time you were in an art museum. What did you like, and why? How much of your aesthetic tastes can you attribute to your education, to your culture? How much do you think responds to your own individual tastes? How can you make the distinction?

2. Think of a musical composition or performance you consider to be art, but whose status as such is debatable. How would you convince someone else that it is art? What kinds of arguments against your position would you expect to hear?

3. Can you think of a political dispute involving art or the arts? What were the different positions being debated?

4. Media consumers actively select, evaluate, and interpret media in ways that make sense to them. People use media for all sorts of reasons. What are some examples? Which are most relevant to the way you consume, and maybe even creatively alter and produce, media?

5. This chapter describes how sports and the media *reflect* culture. Can you come up with examples of how sports and media *influence* culture?

The World System, Colonialism, and Inequality

▶ When and why did the world system develop, and what is it like today?

▶ When and how did European colonialism develop, and how is its legacy expressed in postcolonial studies?

▶ How do colonialism, neoliberalism, development, and industrialization exemplify intervention philosophies?

© Jamie Marshall - Tribaleye Images/Photolibrary/Getty Images

The "Flower Hmong," known for their colorful clothing and market activity, are one of many subgroups of the Hmong ethnic group, which inhabits mountainous areas of Southeast Asia and southern China. Show here, a Flower Hmong woman on a mobile telephone call in Bac Ha, Vietnam. The rapid diffusion of the cell phone has transformed communication throughout the world.

understanding OURSELVES

In our 21st-century world system, people are linked as never before by modern means of transportation and communication. Descendants of villages that hosted ethnographers a generation ago now live transnational lives. For me, some of the most vivid illustrations of this new transnationalism come from Madagascar. They begin in Ambalavao, a town in southern Betsileo country, where I rented a small house in 1966–1967.

By 1966, Madagascar had gained independence from France, but its towns still had foreigners to remind them of colonialism. Besides my wife and me, Ambalavao had at least a dozen world-system agents, including an Indian cloth merchant, Chinese grocers, and a few French people. Two young men in the French equivalent of the Peace Corps were there teaching school. One of them, Noel, lived across the street from a prominent local family. Since Noel often spoke disparagingly of the Malagasy, I was surprised to see him courting a young woman from this family. She was Lenore, the sister of Leon, a schoolteacher who became my good friend.

My next trip to Madagascar was a brief visit in February 1981. I had to spend a few days in Antananarivo, the capital. There I was confined each evening to the newly built Hilton hotel by a curfew imposed after a civil insurrection. I shared the hotel with a group of Russian military pilots, there to teach the Malagasy to defend their island, strategically placed in the

Indian Ocean, against imagined enemies. Later, I went down to Betsileo country to visit Leon, my schoolteacher friend from Ambalavao, who had become a prominent politician. Unfortunately for me, he was in Moscow, participating in a 3-month exchange program.

During my next visit to Madagascar, in summer 1990, I met Emily, the 22-year-old daughter of Noel and Lenore, whose courtship I had witnessed in 1967. One of her aunts brought Emily to meet me at my hotel in Antananarivo. Emily was about to visit several cities in the United States, where she planned to study marketing. I met her again just a few months later in Gainesville, Florida. She asked me about her father, whom she had never met. Noel, who had never married Lenore, had left the country before Emily was born. Emily had sent several letters to France, but Noel never responded.

Descendants of Ambalavao are dispersed globally. Emily, a child of colonialism, had aunts in France (Malagasy women married to French men) and another in Switzerland (a retired diplomat). Members of her family, which is not especially wealthy, have traveled to Russia, Canada, the United States, France, Germany, and West Africa. How many of your classmates, including perhaps you, yourself, have recent transnational roots? A descendant of a Kenyan village (although not born there himself) even grew up to become a twice-elected president of the United States.

Although fieldwork in small communities is anthropology's hallmark, isolated groups are impossible to find today. Truly isolated human societies probably never have existed. For thousands of years, human groups have been in contact with one another. Local societies always have participated in a larger system, which today has global dimensions. We call it the *modern world system,* by which we mean a world in which nations are economically and politically interdependent.

THE WORLD SYSTEM

capitalist world economy
A profit-oriented global economy based on production for sale or exchange.

capital
Wealth invested with the intent of producing profit.

The world system and the relations among the countries within it are shaped by the capitalist world economy (see White 2009). A huge increase in international trade during and after the 15th century led to the **capitalist world economy** (Wallerstein 2004; Wallerstein et al. 2013), a single world system committed to production for sale or exchange, with the object of maximizing profits rather than supplying domestic needs. **Capital** refers to wealth or resources invested in business, with the intent of using the means of production to make a profit.

World-System Theory

world-system theory
The idea that a discernible social system, based on wealth and power differentials, transcends individual countries.

World-system theory can be traced to the French social historian Fernand Braudel. In his three-volume work *Civilization and Capitalism, 15th–18th Century* (1981, 1982, 1992), Braudel argued that societies consist of interrelated parts assembled into a system. Societies themselves are subsystems of larger systems, with the world system the largest. The key claim of **world-system theory** is that all the countries of the world belong to a larger, global system, marked by differences in wealth and power. This world system, based on capitalism, has existed at least since the 16th century, when the Old World established regular contact with the Americas.

core
The dominant position in the world system; nations with advanced systems of production.

World-system theory assigns particular countries to one of three different positions, based on their economic and political clout: core, semiperiphery, and periphery (see also Wallerstein 2004). The **core** consists of the strongest and most powerful nations, which have the most productive economies and the greatest concentration of capital. The core monopolizes the most profitable activities, especially the control of world finance

semiperiphery
The position in the world system intermediate between core and periphery.

periphery
The weakest structural and economic position in the world system.

(Arrighi 2010). The **semiperiphery** is intermediate between the core and the periphery. Contemporary nations of the semiperiphery are industrialized. Like core nations, they produce and export both industrial goods and commodities, but they lack the power and economic dominance of core nations. Thus, Brazil, a semiperiphery nation, exports automobiles to Nigeria (a periphery nation) and auto engines, orange juice extract, coffee, and shrimp to the United States (a core nation). The **periphery** includes the world's poorest and least privileged countries. Economic activities there are less mechanized than in the semiperiphery, although some degree of industrialization has reached even periphery nations. The periphery produces mainly raw materials, agricultural commodities, and, increasingly, human labor for export to the core and the semiperiphery (Shannon 1996).

In the United States and Western Europe today, immigration—legal and illegal—from the periphery and semiperiphery supplies cheap labor for agriculture. U.S. states as distant as California, Michigan, and South Carolina make significant use of farm labor from Mexico. The availability of relatively cheap workers from noncore nations such as Mexico (in the United States) and Turkey (in Germany) benefits farmers and business owners in core countries while supplying remittances to families in the semiperiphery and periphery. As a result of 21st-century telecommunications technology, cheap labor doesn't even need to migrate to the United States. Thousands of families in India are being supported as American companies "outsource" jobs—from telephone assistance to software engineering—to nations outside the core (see this chapter's "Focus on Globalization" on p. 452).

The Emergence of the World System

World trade is far older than the modern capitalist world economy. As early as 600 B.C.E., the Phoenicians/Carthaginians sailed around Britain on regular trade routes and circumnavigated Africa. Likewise, Indonesia, the Middle East, and Africa have been linked in Indian Ocean trade for at least 2,000 years. By the 15th century, advances in navigation, mapmaking, and shipbuilding fueled the geographic expansion of trading networks. Europe established regular contact with Asia, Africa, and eventually the New World (the Caribbean and the Americas). Christopher Columbus's first voyage from Spain to the Bahamas and the Caribbean in 1492 was soon followed by additional voyages. These journeys opened the way for a major exchange of people, resources, products, ideas, and diseases, as the Old and New Worlds were forever linked (Crosby 2003; Diamond 2005; Mann 2011; Marks 2015). The *Columbian exchange* is the term for the spread of people, resources, products, ideas, and diseases between Eastern and Western hemispheres after contact.

Today's world capitalist economy features an ongoing migration of manufacturing and jobs across national boundaries. Shown here, an automobile industry worker at a Nissan factory in Resende, Rio de Janeiro state, Brazil. Where did Nissan originate? Where are its vehicles sold?

© Ricardo Funari/Brazil Photos/LightRocket via Getty Images

Previously in Europe as throughout the world, rural people had produced mainly for their own needs, growing their own food and making clothing, furniture, and tools from local products. People produced beyond their immediate needs in order to pay taxes and to purchase trade items, such as salt and iron. As late as 1650 the English diet, like diets in most of the world today, was based on locally grown starches (Mintz 1985). In the 200 years that followed, however, the English became extraordinary consumers of imported goods. One of the earliest and most popular of those goods was sugar (Mintz 1985).

Sugarcane, originally domesticated in Papua New Guinea, was first processed in India. Reaching Europe via the eastern Mediterranean, it was carried to the Americas by Columbus (Mintz 1985, 2007). The climate of Brazil and the Caribbean proved ideal for growing sugarcane, and Europeans built plantations there to supply the growing demand for sugar. This led to the development in the 17th century of a plantation economy based on a single cash crop—a system known as *monocrop* production.

The demand for sugar in a growing international market spurred the development of the trans-Atlantic slave trade and New World plantation economies based on slave labor. By the 18th century, an increased English demand for raw cotton had led to rapid settlement of what is now the southeastern United States and the emergence there of another slave-based monocrop production system. Like sugar, cotton was a key trade item that fueled the growth of the world system.

INDUSTRIALIZATION

By the 18th century the stage had been set for the **Industrial Revolution**—the historical transformation (in Europe, after 1750) of "traditional" into "modern" societies through industrialization. The Industrial Revolution began, in Europe, around 1750. However, the seeds of industrial society had been planted well before the 18th century (Gimpel 1988). For example, a knitting machine invented in England in 1589 was so far ahead of its time that it played a profitable role in factories two and three centuries later.

The Industrial Revolution required capital for investment, and that capital came from the established system of transoceanic commerce, which generated enormous profits. Wealthy people invested in machines and engines to drive machines. Capital investment supported innovation and invention. New industrial machines and techniques increased production in both farming and manufacturing.

European industrialization developed from, and eventually replaced, the *domestic system* of production, also known as the *home-handicraft system*. In the domestic system of production, an organizer-entrepreneur supplied the raw materials

From producer to consumer, in the modern world system. The top photo, taken in the Caribbean nation of Dominica, shows the hard labor required to extract sugar using a manual press. In the bottom photo, an English middle-class family enjoys afternoon tea, sweetened with imported sugar. Which of the ingredients in your breakfast today were imported?

Top: © Bruce Dale/National Geographic Creative; bottom: © Henglein and Steets/Cultura/Getty Images RF

to workers in their homes and collected finished products from them. This entrepreneur, whose sphere of operations might span several homes and even villages, owned the materials, paid for the work, and arranged the marketing.

Causes of the Industrial Revolution

The Industrial Revolution began with machines that manufactured cotton products, iron, and pottery. These were widely used items whose manufacture could be broken down into simple routine motions that machines could perform. When manufacturing

Industrial Revolution
In Europe, after 1750, socioeconomic transformation through industrialization.

moved from homes to factories, where machinery replaced handwork, agrarian societies evolved into industrial ones. As factories produced cheap staple goods, the Industrial Revolution led to a dramatic increase in production. Industrialization fueled urban growth and created a new kind of city, with factories crowded together in places where coal and labor were cheap.

The Industrial Revolution began in England, for several reasons. More than other nations, England needed to innovate in order to meet a demand for staples—at home and from its far-flung colonies. As industrialization proceeded, Britain's population began to increase dramatically. It doubled during the 18th century (especially after 1750) and did so again between 1800 and 1850. This demographic explosion fueled consumption, but British entrepreneurs could not meet the increased demand with the traditional production methods. This spurred experimentation, innovation, further industrialization, and rapid technological change.

Also supporting early English industrialization were Britain's advantages in natural resources. Britain was rich in coal and iron ore and had navigable coasts and waterways. It was a seafaring island-nation located at the crossroads of international trade. These features gave Britain a favored position for importing raw materials and exporting manufactured goods. Another factor in England's industrial growth was the fact that much of its 18th-century colonial empire was occupied by English settler families, who looked to the mother country as they tried to replicate European civilization abroad. These colonies bought large quantities of English staples.

It also has been argued that particular cultural and religious factors contributed to industrialization. Many members of the emerging English middle class were Protestants, whose beliefs and values encouraged industry, thrift, the dissemination of new knowledge, inventiveness, and willingness to accept change (Weber 1904/1958). These cultural values were eminently compatible with the spirit of entrepreneurial innovation that propelled the Industrial Revolution.

Socioeconomic Changes Associated With The Industrial Revolution

The socioeconomic changes associated with industrialization were mixed. English national income tripled between 1700 and 1815 and increased 30 times more by 1939. Standards of comfort rose, but prosperity was uneven. Initially, factory workers got decent wages, until owners started recruiting workers in areas where living standards were low and labor (including that of women and children) was cheap. Smoke and filth from factories polluted 19th-century cities. Housing was crowded and unsanitary. People faced disease outbreaks and rising death rates. This was the world of Ebenezer Scrooge, Bob Cratchit, Tiny Tim—and Karl Marx.

Industrial Stratification

The Industrial Revolution gave rise to a new class system—a new form of socioeconomic stratification. Based on his observations of 19th-century industrial capitalism in England, Karl Marx saw this stratification as a sharp and simple division between two opposed classes: the bourgeoisie (capitalists) and the proletariat (propertyless workers) (Marx and Engels 1848/1976). The bourgeoisie traced its origins to overseas ventures, which had transformed the social structure of northwestern Europe, creating a wealthy commercial class (White 2009).

Industrialization changed society by shifting production from farms and cottages to mills and factories, where mechanical power was available and where workers could be assembled to operate heavy machinery. The **bourgeoisie** owned the factories, mines, estates, and other means of production. Members of the **working class**, or **proletariat**, had to sell their labor to survive.

bourgeoisie
Owners of the means of production.

working class (proletariat)
People who must sell their labor to survive.

The Art of STOCKING-FRAME-WORK-KNITTING.

Engraved for the Universal Magazine 1750 for J. Hinton at the Kings Arms in St. Pauls Church Yard LONDON.

In the home-handicraft, or domestic, system of production, an organizer supplied raw materials to workers in their homes and collected their products. Family life and work were intertwined, as in this English scene. Is there a modern equivalent to the domestic system of production?

© ARPL/Topham/The Image Works

Large paintings of Karl Marx (1818–1883) on display in Tiananmen Square, Beijing, China. © Michael Nichols/ National Geographic Creative

By promoting rural-to-urban migration, industrialization hastened the process of *proletarianization*—the separation of workers from the means of production. The bourgeoisie controlled not only factories, but also schools, the press, and other key institutions. *Class consciousness* (personal identification and solidarity with one's economic group) was a vital part of Marx's view of class. He saw bourgeoisie and proletariat as having radically opposed interests. Marx viewed classes as powerful collective forces that could mobilize human energies to influence the course of history. Based on their common experience, workers, he thought, would develop class consciousness, which could lead to revolutionary change.

Although no proletarian revolution was to occur in England, workers did develop organizations to protect their interests and increase their share of industrial profits. During the 19th century, trade unions and socialist parties emerged, expressing a rising anticapitalist spirit. This early English labor movement worked to remove young children from factories and limit the hours during which women and children could work. The profile of stratification in industrial core nations gradually took shape. Capitalists controlled production, but labor was organizing for better wages and working conditions. By 1900, many governments had factory regulation and social-welfare programs. Mass living standards in core nations rose as population grew.

Today, the existence of publicly traded companies complicates the division between capitalists

and workers. Through pension plans and personal investments, some workers have become part-owners rather than propertyless workers. Today's key capitalist isn't the factory owner, who may have been replaced by stockholders, but the CEO or the chair of the board of directors, neither of whom may actually own the corporation.

The social theorist Max Weber faulted Karl Marx for an overly simple and exclusively economic view of stratification. Weber (1922/1968) looked beyond class and identified three (separate but correlated) dimensions of social stratification: wealth, power, and prestige. Weber also believed that social identities based on nationality, ethnicity, and religion could take priority over class (social identity based on economic status). In fact, the modern world system *is* cross-cut by collective identities based on nationality, ethnicity, and religion. Class conflicts tend to occur within nations, and nationalism has impeded global class solidarity, particularly of proletarians.

Although the capitalist class dominates politically in most countries, growing wealth has made it easier for core nations to benefit their workers. However, the improvement in core workers' living standards wouldn't have occurred without the world system. The wealth that flows from periphery and semiperiphery to core has helped core capitalists maintain their profits while satisfying the demands of core workers. In the periphery and semiperiphery, wages and living standards are lower. The

focus on GLOBALIZATION

Where in the World Are the Jobs?

Throughout the world, young people are abandoning traditional subsistence pursuits and seeking cash. A once popular song asked, "How're you gonna keep 'em down on the farm after they've seen Paree?" Nowadays, most people have seen Paree (Paris, that is), along with other world capitals—maybe not in person but in print or on-screen images. Young people today are better educated and wiser in the ways of the world than ever before. Increasingly, they are exposed to the material and cultural promises of a better life away from the farm. They seek paying jobs, but work is scarce, spurring migration within and across national boundaries. If they can't get cash legally, they seek it illegally.

For the past few years, work also has been scarce in the industrial world, including the United States and Western Europe. As ordinary Americans were struggling to recover from the "Great Recession" of 2007–2009, the U.S. stock market (Dow Jones Industrial Average [DJIA]) was skyrocketing. From a low of 6,457 in March 2009, the DJIA rose to a high of 18,312 in May 2015. During much of that time, however, corporations held on to their rising profits, rather than hiring new workers. The goal of capitalism, after all, is profitability, and paying good wages to fellow citizens isn't necessarily the best way to maximize profits. To reduce labor costs, jobs continue to be outsourced, and machines continue to replace people. Increasingly, corporations offer their customers incentives to bypass humans. Through the Internet, reached via computer or smartphone, we can buy plane tickets (bye bye, travel agents), print boarding passes, reserve hotel rooms, move money, and pay bills. Amazon.com dominates not only "mom and pop" stores but even once powerful chains like Barnes and Noble, Sears, and Radio Shack. Nowadays, when one does manage to speak to an actual human, that person is as likely to be in Mumbai or Manila as Minneapolis or Miami.

What can workers do? Historically, collective bargaining has been the answer, and unions still bring benefits to their workers. Median weekly earnings of American union members—$980 in 2015—remain higher than those of nonunion workers—$776 (U.S. Bureau of Labor Statistics 2015). But effective unions have been national or local—not global like today's job market. How likely is it that a worker in Mumbai would strike in sympathy with one in Detroit?

Companies claim, with some justification, that labor unions limit their flexibility, adaptability, and profitability. In the United States, corporations and the politicians they work to elect have become more open about their opposition to unions and more aggressive in limiting workers' rights to organize and recruit. Union membership in the United States has reached its lowest point in more than 70 years. The unionized percentage of the American workforce fell to 11.1 percent in 2015, compared with 20.1 percent in 1983, and a high of 35 percent during the mid-1950s. The number of unionized private-sector workers stood at 7.6 million in 2015, versus 7.2 million workers in the public sector. However, the union membership rate for public-sector workers (35.2 percent) is significantly higher than that of workers in the private sector (6.7 percent) (U.S. Bureau of Labor Statistics, 2015). One reason for declining union membership overall has been a reduction in public-sector (government) jobs because of austerity measures imposed by politicians. From the United States to Greece to the United Kingdom, such austerity measures have been spreading internationally, reducing employment and workers' benefits.

Max Weber (1864–1920). Did Weber improve on Marx's view of stratification?

General Collections, Prints and Photographs Division, Library of Congress, LC-USZ62-74580

current *world stratification system* features a substantial contrast between both capitalists and workers in the core nations, on the one hand, and workers on the periphery, on the other.

THE PERSISTENCE OF INEQUALITY

Modern stratification systems aren't simple and dichotomous. They include (particularly in core and semiperiphery nations) a middle class of skilled and professional workers. Gerhard Lenski (1966) argued that social equality tends to increase in advanced industrial societies. The masses improve their access to economic benefits and political power. In Lenski's scheme, the shift of political power to the masses reflects the growth of the middle class, which reduces the polarization between owning and working classes. The proliferation of middle-class occupations creates opportunities for social mobility and a more complex stratification system (Giddens 1981).

Wealth Distribution in the United States

Most contemporary Americans claim to belong to the middle class, which they tend to perceive as a vast, undifferentiated group. There are, however, significant, and growing, socioeconomic contrasts within the middle class, and especially between the richest and the poorest Americans. Table 23.1 shows how income varied from the top to the bottom fifth (quintile) of American households in 2014. In that table, we see that the top fifth earned more than half of all income generated in the United States, 17 times the share of the bottom fifth. This 2014 ratio of 17:1 compares with 14:1 in 2000 and 11:1 in 1970. Figure 23.1 examines changes in mean (average) income over time—from 1967 to 2014—for the five quintiles and top 5 percent of American households. Notice the much greater rise for the top quintile, and especially for the top 5 percent, compared with the bottom quintiles.

The top 1 percent have been especially favored. Although incomes for the top 1 percent dropped sharply (about 36 percent) during the Great Recession of 2007–2009, by 2012 those incomes had rebounded by 31 percent. The incomes of the other 99 percent, which dropped 12 percent during the recession, recovered by less than 1 percent during the same period. The top 1 percent have received about 95 percent of the income gains

TABLE 23.1 U.S. National Income by Quintile, 2014

	PERCENT SHARE OF NATIONAL INCOME	MEAN HOUSEHOLD INCOME
Top 5 percent	21.9	$332,347
Top 20 percent	51.2	194,053
Second 20 percent	23.2	87,834
Third 20 percent	14.3	54,041
Fourth 20 percent	8.2	31,087
Bottom 20 percent	3.1	11,676

SOURCE: C. DeNavas-Walt and B. D. Proctor, "Table 2: Income Distribution Measures Using Money Income and Equivalence-Adjusted Income, 2013 and 2014," p. 9, and "Table A-2: Selected Measures of Household Income Dispersion: 1967 to 2014," p. 31. Income and Poverty in the United States: 2014. U.S. Census Bureau, Current Population Reports, P60-252. Washington, DC: U.S. Government Printing Office. https://www.census.gov/content/dam/Census/library/publications/2015/demo/p60-252.pdf.

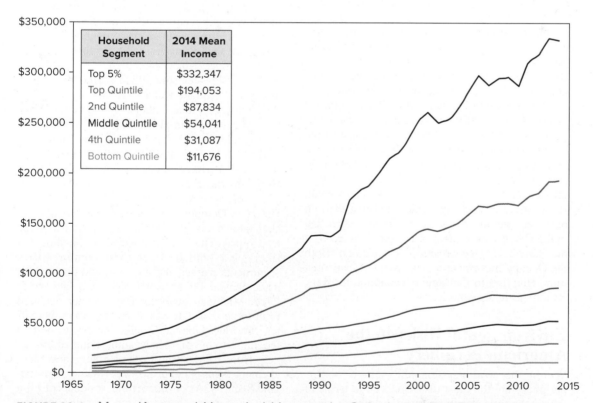

Household Segment	2014 Mean Income
Top 5%	$332,347
Top Quintile	$194,053
2nd Quintile	$87,834
Middle Quintile	$54,041
4th Quintile	$31,087
Bottom Quintile	$11,676

FIGURE 23.1 Mean (Average) Household Income by Quintile and Top 5 Percent, 1967–2014.

SOURCE: C. DeNavas-Walt and B. D. Proctor, "Table H-3: Mean Household Income Received by Each Fifth and Top 5 Percent, All Races: 1967-2014." Income and Poverty in the United States: 2014. U.S. Census Bureau, Current Population Reports, P60-252. Washington, DC: U.S. Government Printing Office. https://www.census.gov/content/dam/Census/library/publications/2015/demo/p60-252.pdf.

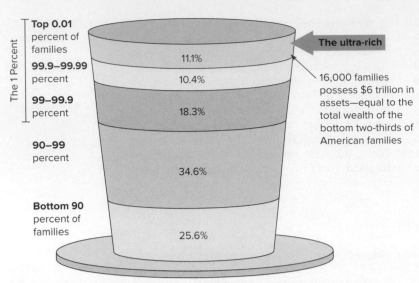

FIGURE 23.2 U.S. Distribution of Wealth, with a Breakdown of the Top 1 Percent into Three Groups—Rich, Very Rich, and Ultra-Rich.

since the recession ended. Higher stock prices, home values, and corporate profits propelled the recovery among affluent Americans, while blue- and white-collar workers continued to feel the effects of high unemployment and stagnant wages (Lowrey 2013).

When we consider wealth (investments, property, possessions, and the like) rather than income, the contrast is even more striking. Figure 23.2 shows that the top 1 percent of American families hold 39.8 percent of the nation's wealth (Coy 2014; Saez and Zucman 2014). The combined assets of the 16,000 ultra-rich families who comprise the top .01 percent hold assets equal to the total wealth of the bottom two-thirds of American families. Figure 23.2 also shows that the bottom 90 percent of American households hold barely a quarter (25.6 percent) of the nation's total wealth. Recognition of such disparities, and that the rich have been getting richer and the poor, poorer, led to the Occupy movement of 2011 and fueled Bernie Sanders's 2016 presidential campaign. Both the Occupy movement and the Sanders campaign drew attention to the lagging economic recovery for a majority of Americans.

Environmental Risks on the American Periphery

Within the world system, the nations on the periphery are the most disadvantaged in terms of their economic development and political clout. Within any nation, including the United States in the 21st century, certain regions and communities are similarly disadvantaged. One expression of this inequality is the degree of exposure to pollution and environmental hazards that a community faces. Communities that are poorer and predominantly minority are more likely to be the victims of toxic waste exposure than are more affluent or even average (middle class) communities.

News reports in 2015 and 2016 highlighted the plight of Flint, Michigan, whose water supply was seriously contaminated following a 2014 cost-cutting switch in its water source. The state of Michigan, which had seized control of Flint's city administration and budget from locally elected officials during a financial emergency, temporarily switched Flint's water source from Lake Huron and the Detroit River to the Flint River. The switch, which took place in April 2014, was to be in effect until completion, in an estimated three years, of a new supply line from Lake Huron. The Flint River had a reputation for nastiness, and, soon after the switch, residents complained their water looked, smelled, and tasted funny (McLaughlin 2016).

Four months after the switch, Flint resident Lee-Anne Walters, concerned about her family's deteriorating health, contacted Marc Edwards, a civil engineering professor and expert on water quality from Virginia Tech University. Ms. Walters previously had sought help from city and state officials, who told her nothing was wrong. However, when Edwards tested the water entering her home, he found lead levels he had never seen in 25 years of testing. Thereafter, Professor Edwards assembled a research team, which confirmed the overall toxicity of Flint's water supply, providing the scientific proof that ultimately led officials to abandon the Flint River (Kozlowski 2016).

The new water source had corroded the lead pipes that brought water into the city's homes. Residents complained about myriad health problems, including skin rashes, hair loss, nausea, dizziness, and pain. A local pediatrician found that lead levels in Flint toddlers had doubled, and in some cases tripled, since the switch from Lake Huron to the Flint River. By the time the city switched back to the Detroit River and Lake Huron in October 2015, irreparable damage had been done not only to public health, but also to the lead pipes. The state responded by handing out filters and bottled water (McLaughlin 2016). Arguments erupted about who should fund the replacement of Flint's water pipes. On January 5, 2016, Michigan governor Rick Snyder declared Flint to be in a state of emergency. Soon thereafter, President Obama declared the city to be in a federal state of emergency, authorizing additional help from FEMA (the Federal Emergency Management Agency) and the Department of Homeland Security. As of this writing, residents of Flint have filed more than a dozen lawsuits, faulting various agencies and individuals, including the city of Flint, the state's Department of Environmental Quality, and Governor Snyder, for violating the U.S. Safe Drinking Water Act.

That this story of toxic endangerment happened in one of Michigan's least affluent cities is no accident. Throughout the United States (as in many other nations), environmental hazards disproportionately endanger poor and minority communities. Flint's population is 57 percent African American. Over 40 percent of its residents live below the poverty line, compared with state and national rates of 17 percent and 15 percent, respectively. One doubts that similar events would have played out in one of Michigan's affluent communities.

Research demonstrates that industries typically target minority and low-income neighborhoods when deciding where to locate polluting facilities (Erickson 2016). Environmental researchers Paul Mohai and Robin Saha (2015) analyzed 30 years of data on the placement of hazardous waste facilities in the United States. Their sample included 319 commercial hazardous waste treatment, storage, and disposal facilities built between 1966 and 1995. Their analysis revealed a clear pattern of racial and socioeconomic bias in the location of environmental hazards. Polluting facilities and other locally unwanted land uses were, and still are, located disproportionately in nonwhite and poor neighborhoods. These communities have fewer resources and political clout to oppose the location of such facilities.

The researchers also examined the demographic composition of neighborhoods at the time polluting facilities were built, as well as the demographic changes that followed the construction of a hazardous waste facility. They found that polluting facilities are often built in neighborhoods in transition. For a decade or two before the project arrived, whites had been moving out, and minorities and poor people moving in. Such demographic and social transition often is accompanied by the loss of community leaders and the weakening of social ties and civic organizations. Potential opposition to placement of hazardous facilities diminishes. Affluent communities, by contrast, are quick to mount organized resistance to environmental threats, and the powers that be take them seriously. Industries choose to follow the path of least resistance and target communities with fewer resources and less political clout. Flint's story garnered headlines, but there are hundreds more stories waiting to be told about environmental threats on the American periphery.

COLONIALISM AND IMPERIALISM

The major forces influencing cultural interactions during the past 500 years have been commercial expansion, industrial capitalism, and the dominance of colonial and core nations (Wallerstein 2004; Wolf 1982). As state formation had done previously, industrialization accelerated local participation in larger networks. According to Bodley (2012),

The presidential candidacy of "Democratic Socialist" Bernie Sanders (shown here at a 2016 rally at Philadelphia's Temple University) critiqued a system advantaging "millionaires and billionaires" and advocated a "political revolution." Did that happen? What demographic groups made up Sanders's constituency?
© Dominick Reuter/AFP/Getty Images

perpetual expansion is a distinguishing feature of industrial economic systems. That expansionist tendency fueled the growth of European colonial empires during and after the 16th century.

Colonialism is the political, social, economic, and cultural domination of a territory and its people by a foreign power for an extended time. The colonial power establishes and maintains a presence in the dominated territory, in the form of colonists and administrative personnel (see Stoler, McGranahan, and Perdue 2007). **Imperialism** refers to a conscious policy of extending the rule of a country or an empire over foreign nations and of taking and holding foreign colonies (see Burbank and Cooper 2010). Imperialism goes back to early states, including Egypt in the Old World and the Incas in the New. A Greek empire was forged by Alexander the Great, and Julius Caesar and his successors spread the Roman empire. More recent examples include the British, French, and Soviet empires (see Burbank and Cooper 2010).

If imperialism is almost as old as the state, colonialism can be traced back to the Phoenicians, who established colonies along the eastern Mediterranean 3,000 years ago. The ancient Greeks and Romans were avid colonizers as well as empire builders (see Pagden 2015; Stearns 2016).

The First Phase of European Colonialism: Spain and Portugal

The first phase of modern colonialism began with the European "Age of Discovery"—of the Americas and of a sea route to the Far East. During the 16th century, Spain, having conquered Mexico (the Aztec empire) and Peru-Bolivia (the Incas), explored and colonized widely in the Caribbean,

colonialism
The long-term foreign control of a territory and its people.

imperialism
A conscious policy aimed at seizing and ruling foreign territory and peoples.

Just before a Republican presidential debate on March 3, 2016 in Detroit, Michigan, demonstrators outside the debate site—the historic Fox theater—advocate for action on the Flint water crisis.
© Chip Somodevilla/Getty Images News/Getty Images

Flint resident LeeAnne Walters shows water samples from her home, taken a week apart, at a forum held at Flint City Hall on January 21, 2015 on health concerns raised by the contaminated water supply.
© William Archie/ZUMA Press/Newscom

the southern portions of what was to become the United States, and Central and South America. In the Pacific, Spain extended its rule to the Philippines and Guam. The Portuguese colonial empire included Brazil, South America's largest colonial territory; Angola and Mozambique in Africa; and Goa in South Asia. Rebellions and wars aimed at independence ended the first phase of European colonialism by the early 19th century. Brazil declared independence from Portugal in 1822. By 1825 most of Spain's colonies had gained their politically independence. Spain held on to Cuba and the Philippines until 1898 but otherwise withdrew from the colonial field. During the first phase of colonialism, Spain and Portugal, along with Britain and France, were the major colonizing nations (see Herzog 2015). The last two (Britain and France) dominated the second phase of colonialism.

Commercial Expansion and European Imperialism

At an accelerating pace during the 19th century, European business interests sought markets overseas. This drive for commercial expansion led to European imperialism in Africa, Asia, and Oceania. During the second half of the 19th century, European imperial expansion was aided by improved transportation, which facilitated the colonization of vast areas of sparsely settled lands in Australia and the interior of North and South America. The new colonies purchased goods from the industrial centers and shipped back wheat, cotton, wool, mutton, beef, and leather. The first phase of European colonialism had been the exploration and exploitation of the Americas and the Caribbean, after Columbus. A second phase began as European nations competed for colonies between 1875 and 1914.

The British Colonial Empire

Like several other European nations, Britain had two stages of colonialism. The first began with the Elizabethan voyages of the 16th century. During the 17th century, Britain acquired most of the eastern coast of North America, Canada's St. Lawrence basin, islands in the Caribbean, slave stations in Africa, and interests in India.

The British shared the exploration and early European settlement of the New World with the Spanish, Portuguese, French, and Dutch. The British by and large left Mexico, along with Central and South America, to the Spanish and the Portuguese. The end of the Seven Years' War in 1763 forced a French retreat from most of Canada and India, where France previously had competed with Britain (Cody 1998). The American Revolution ended the first stage of British colonialism. India, Canada, and various Caribbean islands remained under British control.

The second stage of British colonialism—the British empire, on which the "sun never set," rose from the ashes of the first (see Black 2015). Beginning in 1788, but intensifying after 1815, the British settled Australia. Britain had acquired Dutch South Africa by 1815. By 1819 Singapore anchored a British trade network that extended to much of South Asia and along the coast of China. By this time, the empires of Britain's traditional rivals, particularly Spain, had been severely diminished in scope. Britain's position as imperial power and the world's leading industrial nation was unchallenged.

Britain's colonial expansion continued during the Victorian Era (1837–1901). Queen Victoria's Prime Minister Benjamin Disraeli guided a foreign policy justified by a view of imperialism as shouldering "the white man's burden"—a phrase coined by the poet Rudyard Kipling. People in the empire were seen as incapable of governing

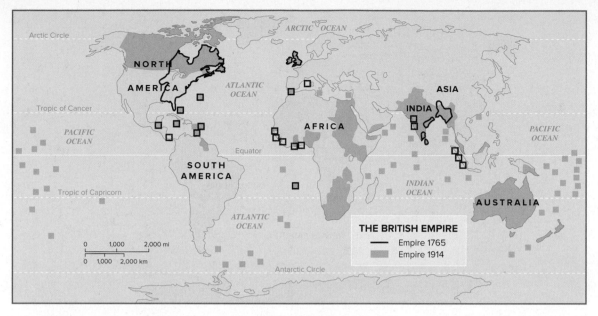

FIGURE 23.3 Map of British Empire in 1765 and 1914.

SOURCE: Academic American Encyclopedia, Vol. 3. 1998 Edition. Grolier, 1998.

themselves, so British guidance was needed to civilize and Christianize them. This paternalistic and racist doctrine was used to legitimize Britain's acquisition and control of parts of central Africa and Asia (Cooper 2014).

The British empire reached its maximum extent around 1914, when it covered a fifth of the world's land surface and ruled a fourth of its population (see Figure 23.3). After World War II, the British empire began to fall apart, with the rise of nationalist movements for independence. India gained its independence in 1947, as did the Republic of Ireland in 1949. The independence movement accelerated in Africa and Asia during the late 1950s (see Buettner 2016). Today, the ties that remain between Britain and its former colonies are mainly linguistic or cultural rather than political (Cody 1998).

French Colonialism

French colonialism also had two phases. The first began with the explorations of the early 1600s. Prior to the French Revolution in 1789, missionaries, explorers, and traders carved out niches for France in Canada, the Louisiana Territory, several Caribbean islands, and parts of India, which were lost along with Canada to Great Britain in 1763 (Harvey 1980).

The foundations of the second French empire were established between 1830 and 1870. In Great Britain the drive for profit led expansion, but French colonialism was spurred more by the state, church, and armed forces than by pure business interests. France acquired Algeria and part of

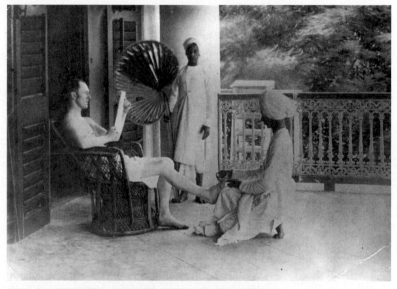

On January 1, 1900, a British officer in India receives a pedicure from a servant. What does this photo say to you about colonialism? Who gives pedicures today?
© Hulton Archive/Getty Images

what eventually became Indochina (Cambodia, Laos, and Vietnam). By 1914, the French empire covered 4 million square miles and included some 60 million people (see Figure 23.4). By 1893, French rule had been fully established in Indochina. Tunisia and Morocco became French protectorates in 1883 and 1912, respectively (Harvey 1980).

To be sure, the French, like the British, had substantial business interests in their colonies, but they also sought, again like the British, international glory and prestige. The French promulgated

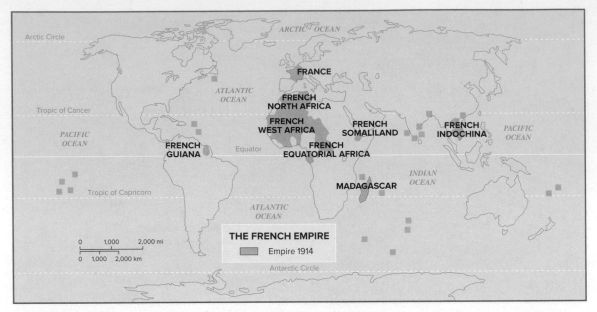

FIGURE 23.4 Map of the French Empire at Its Height around 1914.

SOURCE: Academic American Encyclopedia, Vol. 3. 1998 Edition. Grolier, 1998.

a *mission civilisatrice,* their equivalent of Britain's "white man's burden." The goal was to implant French culture, language, and religion (Roman Catholicism), throughout the colonies (Harvey 1980).

The French used two forms of colonial rule: *indirect rule,* governing through native leaders and established political structures, in areas with long histories of state organization, such as Morocco and Tunisia; and *direct rule* by French officials in many areas of Africa, where the French imposed new government structures to control diverse societies, many of them previously stateless. Like the British empire, the French empire began to disintegrate after World War II. France fought long—and ultimately futile—wars to keep its empire intact in Indochina and Algeria.

Colonialism and Identity

Many geopolitical labels in the news today had no equivalent meaning before colonialism. Whole countries, along with social groups and divisions within them, were colonial inventions. In West Africa, for example, by geographic logic, several adjacent countries could be one (Togo, Ghana, Ivory Coast [Côte d'Ivoire], Guinea, Guinea-Bissau, Sierra Leone, Liberia). Instead, they are separated by linguistic, political, and economic contrasts promoted under colonialism (Figure 23.5).

Hundreds of ethnic groups and "tribes" are colonial constructions (see Ranger 1996). The Sukuma of Tanzania, for instance, were first registered as a single tribe by the colonial administration. Then missionaries standardized a series of dialects into a single Sukuma language, into which they translated the Bible and other religious texts. Thereafter, those texts were taught in missionary schools and to European foreigners and other non-Sukuma speakers. Over time this standardized the Sukuma language and ethnicity (Finnstrom 1997).

As in most of East Africa, in Rwanda and Burundi farmers and herders live in the same areas and speak the same language. Historically, they have shared the same social world, although their social organization is "extremely hierarchical," almost "castelike" (Malkki 1995, p. 24). There has been a tendency to see the pastoral Tutsis as superior to the agricultural Hutus. Tutsis have been presented as nobles, Hutus as commoners. Yet when distributing identity cards in Rwanda, the Belgian colonizers simply identified all people with more than 10 head of cattle as Tutsi. Owners of fewer cattle were registered as Hutus (Bjuremalm 1997). Years later, these arbitrary colonial registers were used systematically for "ethnic" identification during the mass killings (genocide) that took place in Rwanda in 1994 (as portrayed vividly in the film *Hotel Rwanda*).

Postcolonial Studies

In anthropology, history, and literature, the field of postcolonial studies has gained prominence since the 1970s (see Ashcroft, Griffiths, and Tiffin 2013; Nayar 2016). **Postcolonial** studies focus on the past and present interactions between European nations and the societies they colonized (mainly after 1800). In 1914, European empires ruled more than 85 percent of the world (see Streets-Salter 2016). The term *postcolonial* also has been used to describe the second half of the 20th century in general, the period following

postcolonial
Describes relations between European nations and areas they colonized and once ruled.

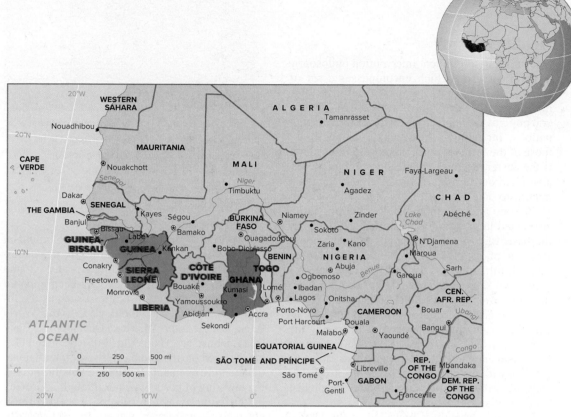

FIGURE 23.5 Small West African Nations Created by Colonialism.

colonialism. Even more generically, *postcolonial* may be used to signify a position against colonialism, imperialism, and Eurocentrism (Buettner 2016; Petraglia-Bahri 1996; Stoler 2013).

The former colonies (*postcolonies*) can be divided into settler, nonsettler, and mixed (Petraglia-Bahri 1996). The settler countries, with large numbers of European colonists and sparser native populations, include Australia and Canada. Examples of nonsettler countries include India, Pakistan, Bangladesh, Sri Lanka, Malaysia, Indonesia, Nigeria, Senegal, and Madagascar. All these had substantial native populations and relatively few European settlers. Mixed countries include South Africa, Zimbabwe, Kenya, and Algeria. Such countries had significant European settlement despite having sizable native populations.

Given the varied experiences of such countries, *postcolonial* has to be a loose term. The United States, for instance, was colonized by Europeans and fought a war for independence from Britain. Is the United States a postcolony? It usually isn't perceived as such, given its current world power position, and its treatment of Native Americans (sometimes called internal colonialism). Research in postcolonial studies has been growing, permitting a wide-ranging investigation of power relations in varied contexts. Broad topics in the field include the formation of empires, the

impact of colonization, and the state of the postcolony today (Petraglia-Bahri 1996; Stoler 2013).

DEVELOPMENT

During the Industrial Revolution, a strong current of thought viewed industrialization as a beneficial process of organic development and progress. Many economists still assume that industrialization increases production and income. They seek to create in "developing" countries a process like the one that first occurred spontaneously in 18th-century Great Britain.

We have seen that Britain used the notion of a white man's burden to justify its imperialist expansion and that France claimed to be engaged in a *mission civilisatrice,* a civilizing mission, in its colonies. Both these ideas illustrate an **intervention philosophy,** an ideological justification for outsiders to guide native peoples in specific directions. Economic development plans also have intervention philosophies. John Bodley (2012) argues that the basic belief behind interventions—whether by colonialists, missionaries, governments, or development planners—has been the same for more than 100 years. This belief is that industrialization, modernization, Westernization, and individualism are desirable evolutionary

intervention philosophy

An ideological justification for outsiders to guide or rule native peoples.

advances and that development schemes that promote them will bring long-term benefits to local people.

Neoliberalism

One currently prominent intervention philosophy is neoliberalism, which encompasses a set of assumptions that have become widespread during the past 30 years (see Carrier 2016). Neoliberal policies are being implemented in developing nations, including postsocialist societies (e.g., those of the former Soviet Union). **Neoliberalism** is the current form of the classic economic liberalism laid out in Adam Smith's famous capitalist manifesto *The Wealth of Nations,* published in 1776, soon after the Industrial Revolution. Smith advocated laissez-faire (hands-off) economics as the basis of capitalism: The government should stay out of its nation's economic affairs. Free trade, Smith argued, is the best way for a nation's economy to develop. There should be no restrictions on manufacturing, no barriers to commerce, and no tariffs. This philosophy is called "liberalism" because it aimed at liberating or freeing the economy from government controls. Economic liberalism encouraged "free" enterprise and competition, with the goal of generating profits. (Ironically, Adam Smith's liberalism is today's capitalist "conservatism.")

Economic liberalism prevailed in the United States until President Franklin Roosevelt's New Deal during the 1930s. The Great Depression produced a turn to Keynesian economics, which challenged liberalism. John Maynard Keynes (1927, 1936) insisted that full employment was necessary for capitalism to grow, that governments and central banks should intervene to increase employment, and that government should promote the common good.

neoliberalism
The principle that governments shouldn't regulate private enterprise; free market forces should rule.

The face of the Scottish economist Adam Smith aptly appears on this English 20-pound banknote. In his famed capitalist manifesto, *The Wealth of Nations,* published in 1776, Smith advocated "free" enterprise and competition, with the goal of generating profits.
© Chris Leslie Smith/PhotoEdit

Especially since the fall of Communism (1989–1991), there has been a revival of neoliberalism, which has been spreading globally. Around the world, neoliberal policies have been imposed by powerful financial institutions such as the International Monetary Fund (IMF), the World Bank, and the Inter-American Development Bank (see Edelman and Haugerud 2005). Neoliberalism entails open (tariff- and barrier-free) international trade and investment. Profits are sought through the lowering of costs, whether through improving productivity, laying off workers, or seeking workers who accept lower wages. In exchange for loans, the governments of postsocialist and developing nations have been required to accept the neoliberal premise that deregulation leads to economic growth, which will eventually benefit everyone through a process sometimes called "trickle down." Accompanying the belief in free markets and the idea of cutting costs is a tendency to impose austerity measures that cut government expenses. This can entail reduced public spending on education, health care, and other social services, as has happened recently with imposed austerity in Greece and elsewhere.

NAFTA's Economic Refugees

In recent decades, many of the migrants seeking work in the United States have come from Mexico. Most Americans are aware of this large-scale Mexican immigration, often of undocumented workers. Most Americans are unaware, however, of the extent to which international forces, including new technologies and the neoliberal North American Free Trade Agreement (NAFTA), are responsible for this migration. Ana Aurelia López (2011) shows how such forces have destroyed traditional Mexican farming systems, degraded agricultural land, and displaced Mexican farmers and small-business people—thereby fueling the migration of millions of undocumented Mexicans to the United States. The following account is a synopsis of her findings.

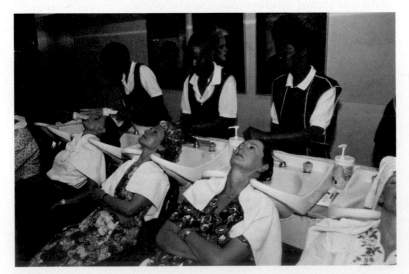

Black workers wash the hair of white customers at a hair salon in Johannesburg's (South Africa) exclusive Hyde Park shopping center. What story does the photo tell you?
© Gideon Mendel/Corbis

To understand what has been happening recently in Mexico, we need to be aware of an agricultural tradition that began at least 7,000 years ago. For thousands of years, Mexican farmers have grown corn (maize) in a sustainable manner. For all those millennia, Mexican farmers planted corn, beans, and squash (known as "the three sisters") together. This polyculture (cultivation of multiple crops) results in corn yields higher than those obtained when corn is cultivated by itself (monoculture). To preserve the fertility of the soil, a "three sisters" plot was allowed to "rest" for five years after being cultivated for two.

Over the generations, Mexican farmers selected diverse strains of corn well adapted to a huge variety of specific microclimates. Mexico became a repository of corn genetic diversity for the world. When corn grown elsewhere developed disease or pest susceptibility or was of poor quality, Mexico provided other countries with genetically superior plants.

Before NAFTA, Mexico supported its farmers by buying a portion of their harvest each year at an elevated cost through price supports. This corn went to a countrywide chain of successful CONASUPO (Compañía Nacional de Subsistencias Populares) stores, which sold corn and other staple foodstuffs below market price to the urban and rural poor. Tariffs protected Mexican farmers from the entrance of foreign corn, such as that grown in the United States.

The first assault on Mexico's sustainable farming culture began in the 1940s when "Green Revolution" technologies were introduced, including seeds that required chemical inputs (e.g., fertilizer). The Mexican government encouraged farmers to replace their traditional, genetically diverse maíz crillo ("creole corn") with the genetically homogenized maíz mejorado ("improved corn"), a hybrid from the United States. Agrochemical companies initially supplied the required chemical inputs free of charge.

Company representatives visited rural villages and offered free samples of seeds and agrochemicals to a few farmers. As news of unusually large first-year crops spread, other farmers abandoned their traditional corn strains for the "improved," chemically dependent corn. As the transition accelerated, the price of both the new seeds and the associated chemical inputs began to rise, and kept on rising. Eventually, farmers no longer could afford either the seeds or the required agrochemicals. When cash-strapped farmers tried to return to planting their former maíz criollo seeds, the plants would grow but corn would not appear. Only the hybrid seeds from the United States would produce corn on the chemically altered soils. Today over 60 percent of Mexico's farmland is degraded due to the spread of agrochemicals—chemical fertilizers and pesticides. (This chapter's "Appreciating Anthropology" on pp. 462–463

On the top, farmers harvest native corn in Oaxaca, Mexico. These are some of the many varieties that were first cultivated in Mesoamerica around 8,000 years ago. On the bottom, demonstrators in Mexico City protest NAFTA's removal of import tariffs on farm goods entering Mexico from the United States and Canada.

Top: © Philippe Psaila/Science Source; bottom: © Eduardo Verdugo/AP Images

describes another case of environmental degradation due to chemical pollution, with mining as the culprit.)

What impact did NAFTA, specifically, have on the Mexican economy? This "free trade" agreement, which went into effect in 1994, produced another major assault on traditional Mexican farming. Loan agreements needed to implement NAFTA forced Mexico to restructure its economy along neoliberal lines. The government had to end its price supports

Is Mining Sustainable?

How can anthropologists help the people they study? The spread of industrialization, illustrated by the mining described here, has contributed to the destruction of indigenous economies, ecologies, and populations. Today multinational conglomerates, along with nations such as Papua New Guinea are repeating—at an accelerated rate—the process of resource depletion that started in Europe and the United States during the Industrial Revolution. Fortunately, however, today's world has some environmental watchdogs, including anthropologists, that did not exist during the first centuries of the Industrial Revolution. Described here is a conundrum confronting a major university. Is a firm whose operations have destroyed the landscapes and livelihoods of indigenous peoples a proper adviser for an institute devoted to ecological sustainability?

In the 1990s, the giant mining company now known as BHP Billiton drew worldwide condemnation for the environmental damage caused by its copper and gold mine in Papua New Guinea. Its mining practices destroyed the way of life of thousands of farming and fishing families who lived along and subsisted on the rivers polluted by the mine, and it was only after being sued in a landmark class-action case that the company agreed to compensate them.

Today several activists and academics who work on behalf of indigenous people around the world say the company continues to dodge responsibility for the problems its mines create.

Yet at the University of Michigan at Ann Arbor, BHP Billiton . . . [became] one of 14 corporate members of an External Advisory Board for the university's new Graham Environmental Sustainability Institute.

Critics at and outside the university contend that Michigan's decision to enlist BHP Billiton as an adviser to an institute devoted to sustainability reflects badly on the institution and allows the company to claim [an undeserved] mantle of environmental and social responsibility.

The arguments echo the discussions about corporate "greenwashing" that have arisen at Stanford University and the University of California at Berkeley over major research grants from ExxonMobil and BP, respectively.

For one BHP Billiton critic at Michigan, the issue is personal. Stuart Kirsch, a professor of anthropology, has spent most of his academic career documenting the damage caused by BHP Billiton's Ok Tedi mine in Papua New Guinea.

Mr. Kirsch, who first visited some of the affected communities as a young ethnographer in 1987, became involved in the class-action lawsuit brought against the company and helped villagers participate in the 1996 legal settlement. "I put my career on hold while being an activist," he says.

He subsequently published several papers related to his work with the Yonggom people as they fought for recognition and compensation from mine operators—scholarship that helped him win tenure. He remains involved with the network of activists and academics who follow mining and its impact on undeveloped communities around the world.

The company's practices polluted the Ok Tedi and Fly Rivers and caused thousands of people to leave their homes because the mining-induced flooding made it impossible for them to grow food to feed themselves, says Mr. Kirsch.

BHP Billiton, based in Australia, later acknowledged that the mine was "not compatible with our environmental values," and spun it off to an independent company that pays all of its mining royalties to the government of Papua New Guinea.

But Mr. Kirsch says that in doing so, the company skirted responsibility for ameliorating the damage it caused. BHP Billiton says it would have preferred to close the mine, but the Papua New Guinea government, in need of the mine revenues, pressed to keep it open. The deal freed BHP Billiton from any future liabilities for environmental damage.

Illtud Harri, a BHP Billiton spokesman, says the company regrets its past with Ok Tedi but considers its pullout from the mine "a responsible exit" that left in place a system that supports educational, agricultural, and social programs for the people of the community.

---

for corn grown by small-scale farmers. Also ended were Mexico's CONASUPO food stores, which had benefited the rural and urban poor.

These terminations caused considerable harm to Mexico's farmers and its urban and rural poor. American agricultural industries, by contrast, have benefited from NAFTA. The U.S.

government continues to subsidize its own corn farmers, who otherwise would go out of business. Prior to NAFTA, Mexico's border tariffs made the sale of U.S. corn in Mexico unprofitable. Under NAFTA, Mexico's corn tariffs were phased out, and corn from the United States began flooding the Mexican markets.

Mr. Talbot, the interim director of the two-year-old sustainability institute, says . . . "We intentionally selected a cross-sector group of organizations" for the advisory board from a list of about 140 nominees, . . . and several companies that "weren't making any serious efforts" toward sustainability were rejected. BHP Billiton, a company formed from the 2001 merger of the Australian mining enterprise Broken Hill Proprietary Company with London-based Billiton, is now the world's largest mining company, with more than 100 operations in 25 countries. The BHP Billiton charter includes a statement that the company has "an overriding commitment to health, safety, environmental responsibility, and sustainable development." But its critics say the company continues to play a key role in mining projects with questionable records on environmental and human rights, even though in many of those cases, it is not directly responsible. BHP Billiton has the resources to present itself as the "golden boy," but, says Mr. Kirsch, "it's much harder to see the people on the Ok Tedi and Fly rivers."

A forum could help to right that imbalance, he says. "Let the students and faculty decide whether this is an appropriate company to advise the University of Michigan," says Mr. Kirsch. "It would be an educational process for everyone involved."

Update: As of this writing (2016), BHP Billiton no longer is listed as a member of the advisory board of Michigan's Graham Institute. And in Papua New Guinea (PNG), after BHP Billiton transferred its ownership of the mine to Ok Tedi Mining Limited, that independent company has spent more than a billion dollars on environmental remediation. The 1996 settlement decreed that BHP would be spared future legal claims in return for giving all its shares to the people of PNG. Those shares are now held in trust (valued at over $1 billion, and growing) in a Singapore-based entity, PNG Sustainable Development Program Limited. The mission of that trust is to promote development in PNG's Western Province, where the mine is located, and across PNG. Today, the provincial and national governments of PNG and the PNG Sustainable Development Program are the only shareholders of Ok Tedi Mining Limited, which pays all its royalties to the PNG government. For hundreds of miles down the Fly River, fishers and farmers still complain about the destruction of their habitat, even as the Ok Tedi mine supplies 16 percent of PNG's national revenue.

Ecological devastation caused by the Ok Tedi copper mine in Papua New Guinea.
© Friedrich Stark/Alamy Stock Photo

SOURCE OF STORY: Goldie Blumenstyk, "Mining Company Involved in Environmental Disaster Now Advises Sustainability Institute at U. of Michigan," *Chronicle of Higher Education,* Vol. 54, Issue 15 (December 7, 2007), p. A22. Copyright 2007, The Chronicle of Higher Education. Reprinted with permission. SOURCES OF UPDATE: http://www.radioaustralia.net.au/pacific/radio/program/pacific-beat/documentary-special-ok-tedi/1069558 and Stuart Kirsch (personal communication).

The NAFTA economy offers Mexico's small-scale corn farmers few options: (1) stay in rural Mexico and suffer, (2) look for work in a Mexican city, or (3) migrate to the United States in search of work. NAFTA did not create a common labor market (i.e., the ability of Mexicans, Americans, and Canadians to move freely across each country's borders and work legally anywhere in North America). Nor did NAFTA make provisions for the predicted 15 million Mexican corn farmers who would be forced off the land as a result of the trade agreement. As could have been expected (and planned for), millions of Mexicans migrated to the United States.

Because of NAFTA, Mexican corn farmers have fled the countryside, and U.S.-subsidized corn has flooded the Mexican market. A declining number of traditional farmers remain to plant and conserve Mexico's unique corn varieties. Between one-third and one-half of Mexico's corn now is imported from the United States, much of it by U.S.-based Archer-Daniels-Midland, the world's largest corporate corn exporter. NAFTA also has facilitated the entrance of other giant U.S. corporations into Mexico: Walmart, Dow Agribusiness, Monsanto, Marlboro cigarettes, and Coca-Cola. These multinationals, in turn, have displaced many small Mexican businesses, creating yet another wave of immigrants—former shopkeepers and their employees—to the United States.

We can summarize the impact of NAFTA on the Mexican economy: destroying traditional small-scale farming, degrading farmland, displacing farmers and small-business people, and fueling massive emigration to the United States. In migrating, these millions of economic refugees continue to face daunting challenges, including separation from their families and homeland, dangerous border crossings, and the ever-present possibility of deportation from the United States.

Within today's world system, comparable effects of neoliberal policies extend well beyond Mexico. As contemporary forces of globalization transform rural landscapes worldwide, rural–urban and transnational migration have become global phenomena. Over and over again, Green Revolution technologies have transformed subsistence into cash economies, fueling a need for money to acquire foreign inputs while hooking the land on chemicals, reducing genetic diversity and sustainability, and forcing the poorest farmers off the land. Few Americans are aware, specifically, of NAFTA's role in ending a 7,000-year-old sustainable farming culture and displacing millions of Mexicans and, more generally, that comparable developments are happening all over the world.

THE SECOND WORLD

The labels "First World," "Second World," and "Third World" represent a common, although ethnocentric, way of categorizing nations. The *First World* refers to the "democratic West"—traditionally conceived in opposition to a "Second World" ruled by "Communism." The *Second World* refers to the former Soviet Union and the socialist and once-socialist countries of Eastern Europe and Asia. Proceeding with this classification, the "less developed countries," or "developing nations," make up the *Third World*.

communism
A social system in which property is owned by the community and people work for the common good.

Communism
The political movement aimed at replacing capitalism with Soviet-style communism.

Communism

The two meanings of communism involve how it is written, whether with a lowercase (small) or an uppercase (large) *c*. Small-*c* **communism** is a social system in which property is owned by the community and in which people work for the common good. Large-*C* **Communism** was a political movement and doctrine seeking to overthrow capitalism and to establish a form of communism such as that which prevailed in the Soviet Union (USSR) from 1917 to 1991. The heyday of Communism was a 40-year period from 1949 to 1989, when more Communist regimes existed than at any time before or after. Today only five Communist states remain—China, Cuba, Laos, North Korea, and Vietnam, compared with 23 in 1985.

Communism, which originated with Russia's Bolshevik Revolution in 1917 and took its inspiration from Karl Marx and Friedrich Engels, was not uniform over time or among countries. All Communist systems were *authoritarian* (promoting obedience to authority rather than individual freedom). Many were *totalitarian* (banning rival parties and demanding total submission of the individual to the state). The Communist Party monopolized power in every Communist state, and relations within the party were highly centralized and strictly disciplined. Communist nations had state ownership, rather than private ownership, of the means of production. Finally, all Communist regimes, with the goal of advancing communism, cultivated a sense of belonging to an international movement (Brown 2001).

Social scientists have tended to refer to such societies as socialist rather than Communist. Today research by anthropologists is thriving in *postsocialist* societies—those that once emphasized bureaucratic redistribution of wealth according to a central plan (Giordano, Ruegg, and Boscoboinik 2014; Verdery 2001). In the postsocialist period, states that once featured planned economies have been following the neoliberal agenda, by divesting themselves of state-owned resources in favor of privatization and marketization. Some of them have moved toward formal liberal democracy, with political parties, elections, and a balance of powers.

Postsocialist Transitions

Neoliberal economists assumed that dismantling the Soviet Union's planned economy would raise gross domestic product (GDP) and living standards. The goal was to enhance production by substituting a free market system and providing incentives through privatization. In October 1991, Boris Yeltsin, who had been elected president of Russia that June, announced a program of radical market-oriented reform, pursuing a

PERIPHERY TO SEMIPERIPHERY	SEMIPERIPHERY TO CORE	CORE TO SEMIPERIPHERY
United States (1800–1860)	United States (1860–1900)	Spain (1620–1700)
Japan (1868–1900)	Japan (1945–1970)	
Taiwan (1949–1980)	Germany (1870–1900)	
S. Korea (1953–1980)		

SOURCE: Thomas R. Shannon, An Introduction to the World-System Perspective, 2nd ed., p. 147. Westview Press, 1989, 1996.

changeover to capitalism. Yeltsin's program of "shock therapy" cut subsidies to farms and industries and ended price controls. During the 1990s, postsocialist Russia endured a series of disruptions, leading to declines in its GDP, average life expectancy, and birthrate, as well as increased poverty. In 2008–2009, Russia shared in the global recession after 10 years of economic growth, but its economy recuperated rapidly and was growing again by 2010, as were its birthrate and average life expectancy. The poverty rate has fallen substantially since the late 1990s but recently has been on the rise—even as Moscow is home to more billionaires than New York City or London (Rapoza 2012). The 2014 Russian poverty rate of 11.2 percent was below the American rate of 14.8 percent the same year.

THE WORLD SYSTEM TODAY

The spread of industrialization continues today, although nations have shifted their positions within the world system. Recap 23.1 summarizes those shifts. By 1900, the United States had become a core nation within the world system and had overtaken Great Britain in iron, coal, and cotton production. In a few decades (1868–1900), Japan had changed from a medieval handicraft economy to an industrial one, joining the semiperiphery by 1900 and moving to the core between 1945 and 1970. India and China have joined Brazil as leaders of the semiperiphery. Figure 23.6 is a map showing the modern world system.

Twentieth-century industrialization added hundreds of new industries and millions of new jobs. Production increased, often beyond immediate demand, spurring strategies, such as advertising, to sell everything industry could churn out. Mass production gave rise to a culture of consumption, which valued acquisitiveness and conspicuous consumption. That culture has become global in scope.

Before and after Communism. Above: on May Day (May 1, 1975), large photos of Politburo members (Communist Party leaders) adorn buildings in Moscow. Below: A Burger King outlet in a Moscow shopping mall. Burger King started opening its outlets in Russia nearly two decades after McDonald's, looking to capitalize on new markets' growing appetite for fast food.

Top: © Bettmann/Corbis; bottom: © Misha Japaridze/AP Images

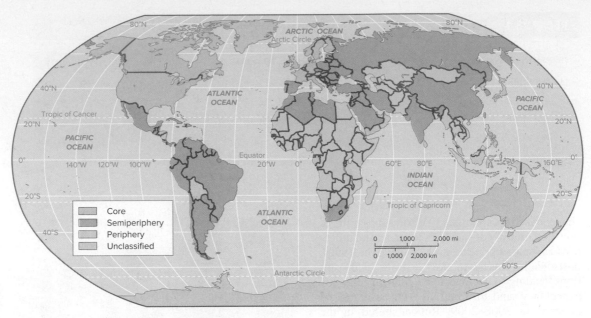

FIGURE 23.6 The World System Today.

for REVIEW

summary

1. Local societies increasingly participate in wider systems—regional, national, and global. The capitalist world economy depends on production for sale, with the goal of maximizing profits. The key claim of world-system theory is that an identifiable social system, based on wealth and power differentials, extends beyond individual countries. That system is formed by a set of economic and political relations that has characterized much of the globe since the 16th century. World capitalism has political and economic specialization at the core, semiperiphery, and periphery.

2. Columbus's voyages opened the way for a major exchange between the Old and New Worlds. Seventeenth-century plantation economies in the Caribbean and Brazil were based on sugar. In the 18th century, plantation economies based on cotton arose in the southeastern United States.

3. The Industrial Revolution began in England around 1750. Transoceanic commerce supplied capital for industrial investment. Industrialization hastened the separation of workers from the means of production. Marx saw a sharp division between the bourgeoisie and the proletariat. Class consciousness was a key feature of Marx's view of this stratification. Weber

believed that social solidarity based on ethnicity, religion, race, or nationality could take priority over class. Today's capitalist world economy maintains the contrast between those who own the means of production and those who don't, but the division is now worldwide. There is a substantial contrast between not only capitalists but also workers in the core nations versus workers on the periphery.

4. Inequality in measures of income and wealth has been increasing in the United States. Another aspect of inequality is in exposure to environmental risks such as pollution and hazardous waste facilities. Communities that are poorer and predominantly minority, such as Flint, Michigan, are most likely to be the victims of toxic waste exposure.

5. Imperialism is the conscious policy of extending the rule of a nation or an empire over other nations and of taking and holding foreign colonies. Colonialism is the domination of a territory and its people by a foreign power for an extended time. European colonialism had two main phases. The first started in 1492 and lasted through 1825. For Britain this phase ended with the American Revolution. For France it ended when Britain won the Seven Years' War, forcing the French to abandon Canada and India.

For Spain it ended with Latin American independence. The second phase of European colonialism extended approximately from 1850 to 1950. The British and French empires were at their height around 1914, when European empires controlled 85 percent of the world. Britain and France had colonies in Africa, Asia, Oceania, and the New World.

6. Many geopolitical labels and identities that were created under colonialism had little or nothing to do with existing social demarcations. The new ethnic or national divisions were colonial inventions, sometimes aggravating conflicts.

7. Like colonialism, economic development has an intervention philosophy that provides a justification for outsiders to guide native peoples toward particular goals. Development usually is justified by the idea that industrialization and modernization are desirable evolutionary advances. Neoliberalism revives and extends classic economic liberalism: the idea that governments should not regulate private enterprise and that free market forces should rule. This intervention philosophy currently dominates aid agreements with postsocialist and developing nations. Neoliberal policies, new

technologies, and the North American Free Trade Agreement (NAFTA) have endangered traditional Mexican farming systems, degraded agricultural land, and displaced Mexican farmers and small-business people—thereby fueling the migration of millions of undocumented Mexicans to the United States.

8. Spelled with a lowercase *c*, communism is a social system in which property is owned by the community and in which people work for the common good. Spelled with an uppercase *C*, Communism indicates a political movement and doctrine seeking to overthrow capitalism and to establish a form of communism such as that which prevailed in the Soviet Union from 1917 to 1991. The heyday of Communism was between 1949 and 1989. The fall of Communism can be traced to 1989–1990 in eastern Europe and 1991 in the Soviet Union. Postsocialist states have followed the neoliberal agenda, through privatization, deregulation, and democratization.

9. By 1900, the United States had become a core nation. Mass production had given rise to a culture, now global in scope, that valued acquisitiveness and conspicuous consumption.

key terms

bourgeoisie 450

capital 448

capitalist world economy 448

colonialism 455

communism 464

Communism 464

core 448

imperialism 455

Industrial Revolution 449

intervention philosophy 459

neoliberalism 460

periphery 448

postcolonial 458

semiperiphery 448

working class (proletariat) 450

world-system theory 448

critical thinking

1. According to world-system theory, societies are subsystems of bigger systems, with the world system as the largest. What are the various systems, at different levels, in which you participate?

2. How does world-system theory help explain why companies hire thousands of workers in India while laying off an equivalent number in Europe and the United States?

3. What were the causes and socioeconomic consequences of the Industrial Revolution? How might knowledge of early industrialization be relevant for an anthropologist interested in investigating the dynamics of industrialization today?

4. Think of a recent case in which a core nation has intervened in the affairs of another nation. What was the intervention philosophy used to justify the action?

5. To what extent is the following statement (p. 451) still true: "The wealth that flows from periphery and semi-periphery to core has helped core capitalists maintain their profits while satisfying the demands of core workers." Are core workers still satisfied? What factors might diminish their level of satisfaction?

CHAPTER 24

Anthropology's Role in a Globalizing World

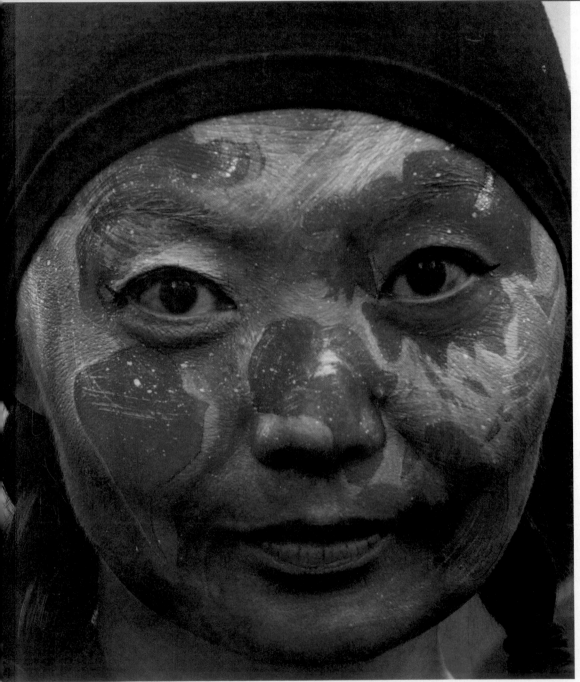

▸ What is global climate change, and how can anthropologists study it, along with other environmental threats?

▸ What is cultural imperialism, and what forces work to favor and oppose it?

▸ What are indigenous peoples, and how and why has their importance increased in recent years?

© Cem Ozdel/Anadolu Agency/Getty Images

One among thousands of people, many wearing colorful costumes, attending the People's Climate March, held in New York City in September 2014 to focus attention on global climate change.

understanding OURSELVES

What's your favorite science fiction movie or TV show? What images of other planets, or of a future Earth, stand out in your memory? Can you visualize *Star Wars*'s Death Star, the two suns of Tatooine, or any other planet in the *Star Wars* galaxy? How about *Avatar*'s Pandora? Such images may be as familiar to you as those of real planets. Think, too, about how extraterrestrials have been portrayed in movies. On the one hand are *ET*'s harmless plant collectors and *Avatar*'s endangered Na'vi. More typical are Earth's would-be conquerors, as shown in two *Independence Day* films, three *Starship Troopers* movies, and a hundred others. Still other films, most notably *The Day the Earth Stood Still* (either the 1951 or the 2008 version), feature omnipotent, omniscient guardians of interplanetary affairs.

If some of our most vivid perceptions of other planets come from fiction, modern technology makes it easier than ever for us to perceive the Earth as both a planet and our world. Anthropologists can use Google Earth to locate communities they have studied in remote corners of the world. My colleagues and I have even used space images to choose communities to study on Earth. Interested in the causes of deforestation in Madagascar, we examined a series of satellite images taken in successive years to determine areas where the forest cover had diminished significantly. Then we traveled to Madagascar to study those areas on the ground. It's interesting to imagine what an alien might "see" in similar images. If these aliens were (as the more benevolent science fiction movies imagine) interested in studying life on Earth, rather than conquering, controlling, or even eating its inhabitants, they would have a lot to interpret. In my work abroad, I've been impressed by two major global trends: population increase and the shift from subsistence to cash economies. These trends have led to agricultural intensification, resource depletion (including deforestation), and emigration and have made it increasingly harder to not think globally when asking ourselves who we are.

I'm struck by the growing number of young people worldwide who have abandoned traditional subsistence pursuits (see Sukarieh and Tannock 2015). They seek jobs for cash, but work is scarce, spurring migration within and across national boundaries. In turn, transnational migration increases cultural diversity, while also generating heated political debates, in the United States and Europe. Every day we encounter people whose ancestral countries and cultures have been studied by anthropologists for generations—making cultural anthropology all the more relevant to our daily lives in an increasingly interconnected world.

This chapter applies an anthropological perspective to contemporary global issues. Let's begin by reviewing two different meanings of the term *globalization*. As used in this book, the primary meaning of globalization is worldwide connectedness. Modern systems of transportation, communication, and finance are global in scope. There are interlinked systems of production, distribution, and consumption that extend across all nations and regions. A second meaning of globalization is political; it has to do with ideology, policy, and neoliberalism (see Kotz 2015). In this more limited sense, globalization refers to efforts by international financial powers to create a global free market for goods and services. This second, political meaning of

Diversity under Siege: Global Forces and Indigenous Peoples

Around the globe, diversity is under siege. In Alaska, which has been warming twice as fast as the rest of the United States, displaced villagers have become climate change refugees—forced to move as rising sea levels have eroded and flooded their settlements. In the South Pacific, Marshall Islanders also face rising seas, which render their villages increasingly uninhabitable and their land too salty for productive agriculture (Davenport and Haner 2015). In the Brazilian Amazon, outside settlers, including farmers, cattle herders, and commercial loggers, are illegally encroaching on areas reserved for indigenous groups. A combination of forces at work globally, including climate change and development, are threatening the lifestyles, livelihoods, and even the lives of indigenous peoples.

We focus now on the Norwegian Arctic, where a Sami (Lapp) population of about 100,000 traditional reindeer herders extends over a vast territory—northern areas of Norway, Sweden, Finland, and Russia's Kola Peninsula.

Sami nomads once moved their herds seasonally across this expanse, paying little attention to national borders. Today, a mere one-tenth of the total Sami population, Western Europe's only indigenous Arctic group, continues to herd reindeer for a living (Wallace 2016).

The Sami way of life is being destroyed incrementally rather than by a major project or event. The cumulative effects of a series of smaller constructions, including roads and pipelines, have reduced Norway's undisturbed reindeer habitat by 70 percent in the past century. Like so many other indigenous peoples, the Sami must compete with powerful external interests for use of their traditional (grazing) lands. For generations, the Sami have lived under state organization. The state allows the Sami to graze their herds, but the land belongs to the national government. The Sami must deal with decisions made at the national level by planners, legislators, and the courts. What is good for the nation and business interests often takes precedence over what may be best for local people.

External inputs have been both positive and negative. The group benefits from the use of GPS collars and smartphone apps to track their animals, and snowmobiles and all-terrain vehicles to round them up. On the negative side, the steady encroachment of industrial infrastructure has reduced their range and freedom of movement. Current threats include dams, roads, live-fire military drills, high-voltage power lines, wind farms, and a copper mine. Many Sami now have to move their herds by truck and boat between summer and winter pastures—a costly operation. When courts approved large-scale projects that negatively affected the Sami, the herders received only a one-time payment as compensation for their losses (Wallace 2016).

Norway is proceeding with plans to extract more resources and build more industry in the Arctic. The Sami fear that their languages and culture, largely sustained by herding, will ultimately be sacrificed to benefit the larger society. The government has ambitious targets for

---

globalization has generated and continues to generate significant opposition. In this book, *globalization* is a neutral term for the fact of global connectedness and linkages, rather than any kind of political position (see also Erikson 2014; Ervin 2014).

The fact that certain practices and risks have global implications warrants a discussion of energy consumption and environmental degradation, including climate change, or global warming. Also considered in this chapter are the threats that deforestation and emerging diseases pose to global biodiversity and human life. The second half of this chapter turns from ecology to the contemporary flows of people, technology, finance, information, messages, images, and ideology that contribute to a global culture of consumption. Part of globalization is intercultural communication, through the media, travel, and migration, which increasingly bring people from different societies into direct contact. Finally, we'll consider how such contacts and external linkages affect indigenous peoples, as well as how those

groups have organized to confront and deal with national and global issues.

It would be impossible in a single chapter (or even book) to do a complete review of all the global issues that are salient today and that anthropologists have studied. Many such issues (e.g., war, displacement, terrorism, NGOs, the media) have been considered in previous chapters, and a series of boxes have "focused on globalization" throughout this book. For timely anthropological analysis of a range of global issues, see recent books by John Bodley (2012, 2015), Shirley Fedorak (2014), and Richard Robbins (2014).

ENERGY CONSUMPTION AND INDUSTRIAL DEGRADATION

Industrialization entailed a shift from reliance on renewable resources to the use of fossil fuels. Earth's supply of oil, gas, and coal is being depleted

renewable energy, including more hydroelectric and wind power projects. These projects, although possibly "good for the globe," negatively affect reindeer herding, as well as Arctic biodiversity, wilderness landscapes, and traditional subsistence activities. A proposed wind farm (now under judicial review) and associated power lines would encroach substantially on the summer grazing lands of a group of herders who still speak South Sami, a language listed by UNESCO as endangered (Wallace 2016).

In addition to the threats from development, the Sami have an ongoing conflict with the military. Since the Cold War, Norwegian soldiers have been a regular presence in Sami country, preparing for a possible Russian incursion across northern Scandinavia. These troops stage regular, often daily, war exercises, including live gunfire. Herders must be vigilant to avoid flying bullets as they go about their activities. (This information about contemporary Sami in this box comes mainly from Wallace 2016.)

Even the most enlightened governments pursue policies that are incompatible with preserving the traditional activities and lifestyles of indigenous peoples. Like certain conservation schemes aimed at preserving biodiversity, efforts that are good for the globe, such as the development of green energy sources, may not be best for local people. Planners must be attentive to the need to seek a delicate balance between what's good for the globe and what's good for the people.

Sami herder Johann Anders Oskal and his brother tend their reindeer herd in Troms County, Norway (January 27th, 2016).
© Scott Wallace/Hulton Archive/Getty Images

to support a previously unknown level of consumption. Americans are the world's foremost consumers of nonrenewable energy. The average American consumes about 35 times more energy than the average forager or tribesperson (Bodley 2015).

Table 24.1 compares energy consumption, total and per capita, in the United States and selected other countries—the top 10 consumers of energy. Overall the United States, which ranks second among the countries, represents about 17 percent of the world's annual energy consumption. China ranks first, accounting for 22 percent of global energy consumption. However, North Americans—Canadians and Americans—rank first and second in per-capita consumption. The average American consumes almost 4 times the energy used by the average Chinese and 16 times the energy used by the average inhabitant of India. Consumption has been rising in China and India, while declining a bit in the United States and Canada, and more dramatically in Europe.

Industrialization has spread to Asia, Latin America, Africa, and the Pacific. One result of industrial expansion is the ongoing destruction of indigenous economies, ecologies, and populations (see this chapter's "Appreciating Diversity"). Two centuries ago, as industrialization was developing, 50 million people still lived in politically independent bands, tribes, and chiefdoms. Around 1800, those nonindustrial societies controlled half the globe and constituted 20 percent of its population (Bodley 2015). Industrialization tipped the balance in favor of state-organized societies (see Hornborg and Crumley 2007).

Many contemporary nations are repeating—at an accelerated rate—the process of resource depletion that began in Europe and the United States during the Industrial Revolution. Fortunately, however, today's world has some environmental watchdogs that did not exist during the Industrial Revolution. Given the appropriate political will, leading to national and international cooperation

TABLE 24.1 Total Energy Consumption, 2012–2013, by Country, Top Ten Countries (in quadrillion BTUs)

	TOTAL	PER CAPITA
World	510.6*	74.4†
China	113.2	82.0
United States	89.9	312.8
Russia	27.7	229.9
India	23.6	19.9
Japan	18.8	163.6
Canada	13.2	396.6
Germany	12.9	160.6
Brazil	11.0	59.0
South Korea	10.8	228.9
France	9.9	165.1

*510.6 quadrillion (510,600,000,000,000,000) BTUs

†74.4 million BTUs

SOURCE: U.S. Energy Information Administration, International Energy Statistics. http://www.eia.gov/cfapps/ipdbproject/IEDIndex3.cfm?tid544&pid544&aid52; Hydrocarbons-technology.com. "Energy Gluttons—The World's Top 10 Energy Consumers." http://www.hydrocarbons-technology.com/features/featureenergy-gluttons-the-worlds-top-10-energy-consumers-4433940/

Methane (CH_4) is a greenhouse gas whose atmospheric concentration has risen due to an increase in various human activities, including livestock raising. Shown here, cattle feeding in Lubbock, Texas. How do cattle produce methane?

© Royalty-Free/Corbis

and sanctions, the modern world may benefit from the lessons of the past (see Hornborg, McNeill, and Martinez-Alier 2007).

There are, however, new dangers in today's world, some of which have become worldwide in scope. Accompanying globalization are significant risks that can spread rapidly beyond individual countries. Thanks to modern transportation systems, diseases that break out in one part of the world can quickly become global threats. Who can forget the Ebola threat of 2014? Furthermore, along with the actual threat that a disease might go global is the heightened risk perception, augmented by the media, that makes people think that anyone anywhere might succumb to a disease that is confined almost entirely to a particular region. Another global threat, which can spread even faster than a disease, is a cyberattack. We should fear cyber viruses as well as real viruses. We have become so reliant on the Internet that anything that might impede or halt the flow of information in cyberspace would have worldwide repercussions. Dangers that can affect people anywhere and everywhere on the planet are part of a *globalization of risk*. Risks are no longer merely local, like the Flint, Michigan, water crisis, or regional, like the California drought. They have become global in scope. People tend to worry more about short-term threats, such as toxic water or Ebola, and middle-term dangers, such as terrorism, than about long-term threats such as global climate change.

greenhouse effect

Warming caused by trapped atmospheric gases.

GLOBAL CLIMATE CHANGE

Each consumer of fossil fuels makes his or her individual contribution (that consumer's "carbon footprint") to global climate change. The fact that there are today about seven billion of those "footprints" has major global significance. The year 2015 surpassed 2014 as the world's hottest year on record. (In the lower 48 United States, 2015 was the second warmest year on record, after 2012). One reason for the heat was an unusually large El Niño weather pattern, which pumped a substantial amount of heat into the atmosphere. Even more significant has been the long-term planetary warming caused by human emissions of greenhouse gases (Gillis 2016b).

The **greenhouse effect** is a natural phenomenon that keeps the Earth's surface warm. The greenhouse gases include water vapor (H_2O), carbon dioxide (CO_2), methane (CH_4), nitrous oxide (N_2O), halocarbons, and ozone (O_3). Without those gases, life as we know it wouldn't exist. Like a greenhouse window, those gases allow sunlight to enter the atmosphere and then trap heat from escaping.

The amount of carbon dioxide in the atmosphere has fluctuated naturally in the past. Every time it increases, the Earth heats up, ice melts, and sea levels rise. Since the Industrial Revolution, humans have been pumping carbon dioxide into the air faster than nature ever did (Gillis 2015). All greenhouse gases have increased since the Industrial Revolution. In fact, the atmospheric concentration of greenhouse gases is now at its highest level in 400,000 years. It will continue to rise, as will global temperatures, without actions to slow it down (National Academy of Sciences 2008; National Research Council 2011).

Global temperatures have risen about 1.8°F since the 19th century (Gillis 2016a). This increase is not due to increased solar radiation. The causes are mainly **anthropogenic**—caused by humans and their activities. Who can reasonably deny that seven billion people, along with their animals, crops, machines, and increasing use of fossil fuels, have a greater environmental impact than the five million or so pre-Neolithic hunter-gatherers estimated to have lived on our planet 12,000 years ago?

Scientists prefer the term **climate change** to *global warming*. The former term points out that, beyond rising temperatures, there have been changes in storm patterns, ecosystem effects, and especially sea levels. The ocean is extremely sensitive to small fluctuations in the Earth's temperature. During the 19th century, as industrialization proceeded, sea levels began to rise; they have climbed about 8 inches since 1880 (Gillis 2016a). The Intergovernmental Panel on Climate Change, a United Nations body that reviews and summarizes climate research, has estimated that continued high emissions are likely to produce a rise in sea level of 1.7 to 3.2 feet during the 21st century (Gillis 2016a). One consequence of rising sea levels has been a worsening of tidal flooding in coastal communities, including the East coast of the United States. In the decade between 1955 and 1964, a tide gauge at Annapolis, Maryland, measured 32 days of flooding. Fifty years later, between 2005 and 2014, that figure jumped to 394 days. In Charleston, South Carolina, flood days increased from 34 in the earlier decade to 219 between 2005 and 2014 (Gillis 2016a).

The precise effects of climate change on regional weather patterns have yet to be fully determined (see DiMento and Doughman 2014). Land areas are predicted to warm more than oceans, with the greatest warming in higher latitudes, such as Canada, the northern United States, northern Europe, and Russia. Climate change may benefit these areas, offering milder winters and extended growing seasons. However, many more people worldwide probably will be harmed (see Cribb 2010). Already we know that in the Arctic, temperatures have risen almost twice as much as the global average. Arctic landscapes and ecosystems are changing rapidly and perceptibly, creating hundreds of "climate refugees" in areas of Alaska where the permafrost is melting and indigenous villages are sinking below sea level (see Yardley 2007). Coastal communities worldwide can anticipate increased flooding and more severe storms and surges. At risk are people, animals, plants, freshwater supplies, and such industries as tour-

ism and farming. (Recap 24.1 summarizes the major factors that work to heat and to cool Earth.)

Global energy demand is the single greatest obstacle to slowing down climate change. Worldwide, energy consumption continues to grow with economic and population expansion. China and India, in particular, are rapidly increasing their use of energy, mainly from fossil fuels, and consequently their emissions. Their cities, most notably Beijing and New Delhi, are now among the most polluted in the world. China currently accounts for about 22 percent of world energy consumption, compared with 9 percent in 2000. The U.S. share fell from 25 percent in 2000 to 17 percent in 2013 (see Table 24.1). Among the alternatives to fossil fuels are nuclear power and such renewable energy technologies as solar, wind, and biomass generators.

In 2015, the American Anthropological Association (AAA) issued a "Statement on Humanity and Climate Change," which can be found at http://www.aaanet.org/cmtes/commissions/ CCTF/upload/AAA-Statement-on-Humanity-and-Climate-Change.pdf. That statement makes several key points, including the following:

- Human cultures and actions are the most important causes of the dramatic environmental changes that have taken place during the last 100 years. Two key factors influencing climate change are (1) reliance on fossil fuels as the primary energy source, and (2) an ever-expanding culture of consumerism.

- Climate change will accelerate migration, destabilize communities, and exacerbate the spread of infectious diseases.

- Most affected will be people living on coasts, in island nations, and in high-latitude (e.g., far north) and high-altitude (e.g., very mountainous) areas.

- The tendency has been to address climate change at the international and national levels. We also need planning at the regional and local levels, because the impacts of climate change vary in specific locales. Affected communities, perhaps working with anthropologists, must be active participants in planning how to adapt to climate change—and in implementing those plans.

ENVIRONMENTAL ANTHROPOLOGY

Anthropology always has been concerned with how environmental forces influence humans and how human activities affect the environment. The 1950s–1970s witnessed the emergence of an area of study known as cultural ecology, or **ecological anthropology** (see Haenn, Wilk, and Harnish

anthropogenic
Caused by humans and their activities.

climate change
Global warming, plus changing sea levels, precipitation, storms, and ecosystem effects.

ecological anthropology
The study of cultural adaptations to environments.

WARMING	
Carbon dioxide (CO_2)	Has natural and human sources; levels increasing due to burning of fossil fuels.
Methane (CH_4)	Has risen due to an increase in human activities, including livestock raising, rice growing, landfill use, and the extraction, handling, and transport of natural gas.
Ozone (O_3)	Has natural sources, especially in the stratosphere, where chemicals have depleted the ozone layer; ozone also produced in the troposphere (lower part of the atmosphere) when hydrocarbons and nitrogen oxide pollutants react.
Nitrous oxide (N_2O)	Has been rising from agricultural and industrial sources.
Halocarbons	Include chlorofluorocarbons (CFCs), which remain from refrigerants in appliances made before CFC ban.
Aerosols	Some airborne particles and droplets warm the planet; black carbon particles (soot) produced when fossil fuels or vegetation are burned; generally have a warming effect by absorbing solar radiation.
COOLING	
Aerosols	Some cool the planet; sulfate (SO_4) aerosols from burning fossil fuels reflect sunlight back to space.
Volcanic eruptions	Emit gaseous SO_2, which, once in the atmosphere, forms sulfate aerosol and ash; both reflect sunlight back to space.
Sea ice	Reflects sunlight back to space.
Tundra	Reflects sunlight back to space.
WARMING/COOLING	
Forests	Deforestation creates land areas that reflect more sunlight back to space (cooling); it also removes trees that absorb CO_2 (warming).

2016). That field initially focused on how cultural beliefs and practices helped human populations adapt to their environments, as well as how people used elements of their culture to maintain their ecosystems. Ecological anthropologists showed that many indigenous groups did a reasonable job of managing their resources and preserving their ecosystems (see Menzies 2006). Such groups had traditional ways of categorizing resources and using them sustainably (see Dagne 2015). The term **ethnoecology** describes a society's set of environmental perceptions and practices (see Vinyeta and Lynn 2013).

Given national and international incentives to exploit and degrade, ethnoecological systems that once preserved local and regional environments increasingly are ineffective or irrelevant (see Dove, Sajise, and Doolittle 2011). Anthropologists routinely witness threats to the people they study and their environments. Among such threats are commercial logging, industrial pollution, and the imposition of external management

ethnoecology
A culture's set of environmental perceptions and practices.

systems on local ecosystems (see Johnston 2009). Today's ecological anthropology, *environmental anthropology,* attempts not only to understand but also to find solutions to environmental problems.

Local people and their landscapes, ideas, values, and traditional management systems face attacks from all sides (see Hornborg, Clark, and Hermele 2011). Outsiders attempt to remake native landscapes and cultures in their own image. The aim of many agricultural development projects, for example, seems to be to make the world as much like a midwestern American agricultural state as possible. Often, there is an attempt to impose mechanized farming and nuclear family ownership, even though these institutions may be inappropriate in areas far removed from the midwestern United States. Anthropologists know that development projects usually fail when they try to replace indigenous institutions with culturally alien concepts (Kottak 1990*b*).

Global Assaults on Local Autonomy

A clash of cultures related to environmental change may occur when development threatens indigenous peoples and their environments (see this chapter's "Appreciating Diversity"). A second clash of cultures related to environmental change may occur when external regulation aimed at conservation confronts indigenous peoples and their ethnoecologies. Like development projects, conservation schemes may ask people to change their ways in order to satisfy planners' goals rather than local goals. In places as different as Madagascar, Brazil, and the Pacific Northwest of the United States, people have been asked, told, or forced to abandon basic economic activities because to do so is good for "nature" or "the globe." "Good for the globe" doesn't play very well in Brazil, whose Amazon has been a focus of international environmentalist attention. Brazilians complain that outsiders (e.g., Europeans and North Americans) promote "global needs" and "saving the Amazon" after having destroyed their own forests for economic growth. Conservation efforts are guaranteed to face local opposition when they promote radical changes without involving local people in planning and carrying out the policies that affect them. When people are asked to give up the basis of their livelihood, they usually resist.

Consider the case of a Tanosy man living on the edge of the Andohahela reserve of southeastern Madagascar. For years he has relied on rice fields and grazing land inside that reserve. Now external agencies are telling him to abandon that land for the sake of conservation. This man is a wealthy *ombiasa* (traditional sorcerer-healer). With four wives, a dozen children, and 20 head of cattle, he is an ambitious, hardworking, and productive peasant. With money, social support, and supernatural authority, he has mounted effective resistance against the park ranger who has been trying to get him to abandon his fields. The *ombiasa* claims he has already relinquished some of his fields, but he is waiting for compensatory land. His most effective resistance has been supernatural. The death of the ranger's young son was attributed to the *ombiasa*'s magic. After that, the ranger became less vigilant in his enforcement efforts.

The spread of environmentalism may reveal radically different notions about the "rights" and value of plants and animals versus humans. In Madagascar, many intellectuals and officials complain that foreigners seem more concerned about lemurs and other endangered species than about the people of Madagascar (the Malagasy). As a geographer there remarked to me, "The next time you come to Madagascar, there'll be no more Malagasy. All the people will have starved to death, and a lemur will have to meet you at the

In early December 2015, people relax on the lawn near government buildings in one of the world's most polluted cities—New Delhi, India.
© Prakash Singh/AFP/Getty Images

A scene from the "great red island" of Madagascar. On that island, the effects of deforestation, water runoff, and soil erosion are visible to the naked eye.
© UNEP-Topham/The Image Works

airport." Most Malagasy perceive human poverty as a more pressing problem than animal and plant survival.

Still, who can doubt that conservation, including the preservation of biodiversity, is a worthy goal? The challenge for applied ecological anthropology is to devise culturally appropriate strategies for achieving biodiversity conservation in the face of unrelenting population growth and commercial expansion. How does one get people to support conservation measures that may—in the short run, at least—diminish their access to resources? Like development plans in general, the most effective conservation strategies pay attention to the needs and wishes of the local people.

Deforestation

Anthropologists know that food producers (farmers and herders) typically do more to degrade the environment than foragers do. Population increase and the need to expand farming caused deforestation in many parts of the ancient Middle East and Mesoamerica (see Cairns 2015; Hornborg and Crumley 2007). Even today, many farmers think of trees as giant weeds to be removed and replaced with productive fields.

Often, deforestation is demographically driven—caused by population pressure. For example, Madagascar's population is growing at a rate of 2.6 percent annually, doubling every generation. The country had 6 million people 50 years ago, compared with 23 million today. Population pressure leads to migration, including rural–urban migration. Madagascar's capital, Antananarivo, had just 100,000 people 50 years ago. Today its population stands at just under two million. Urban growth promotes deforestation if city dwellers rely on fuel wood from the countryside, as is true in Madagascar. As forested watersheds disappear, crop productivity declines. Madagascar is known as the "great red island," after the color of its soil. On that island, the effects of soil erosion and water runoff are visible to the naked eye. From the look of its rivers, Madagascar appears to be bleeding to death. Increasing runoff of water no longer trapped by trees causes erosion of low-lying rice fields near swollen rivers as well as siltation in irrigation canals (Kottak 2007).

Globally, other causes of deforestation include commercial logging, road building, cash cropping, and clearing and burning associated with livestock and grazing. The fact that forest loss has several causes has a policy implication: Different deforestation scenarios require different conservation strategies.

What can be done? On this question applied anthropology weighs in, spurring policy makers to think about new conservation strategies. The traditional approach has been to restrict access to forested areas designated as parks, then employ park guards and punish violators. Modern strategies are more likely to consider the needs, wishes, and abilities of the people (often impoverished) living in and near the forest. Because effective conservation depends on the cooperation of the local people, their concerns must be addressed in devising conservation strategies.

Reasons to change behavior must make sense to local people. In Madagascar, the economic value of the forest for agriculture (as an antierosion mechanism and a reservoir of potential irrigation water) provides a much more powerful incentive against forest degradation than do such global goals as "preserving biodiversity." Most Malagasy have no idea that lemurs and other endemic species exist only in Madagascar. Nor would such knowledge provide much of an incentive

Applied anthropology uses anthropological perspectives to identify and solve contemporary problems that affect humans. Deforestation is one such problem. Here, women take part in a reforestation project in coastal Tanzania near Dar es Salaam.
© Edward Parker/Alamy Stock Photo

for them to conserve the forests if doing so jeopardized their livelihoods.

To curb the global deforestation threat, we need conservation strategies that work. Laws and enforcement may help reduce commercially driven deforestation caused by burning and clear-cutting. But local people also use and abuse forested lands. A challenge for the environmentally oriented applied anthropologist is to find ways to make forest preservation attractive to local people and ensure their cooperation. Applied anthropologists must work to make "good for the globe" good for the people (see Wasson et al. 2012).

Emerging Diseases

A number of potentially lethal infectious diseases have emerged and spread in the past few decades. These *emerging diseases* include HIV/ AIDS, Ebola, West Nile, SARS (severe acute respiratory syndrome), Lyme disease, and Zika. All these diseases have emerged as a result of human activity. Driven by factors including population increase, changing settlement patterns, and commercial expansion, humans have been encroaching on wild lands, particularly forests, and creating conditions that favor the spread of disease pathogens. In the Amazon, for example, one study showed that an increase in deforestation of just 4 percent produced a 50 percent increase in the incidence of malaria. This is because the mosquitoes that transmit malaria thrive in the right mix of sunlight and water in recently deforested areas (Robbins 2012).

Some emerging diseases are *zoonotic*—they spread from animals to humans. The transmission of diseases from wild to domesticated animals and then to humans has been going on since the Neolithic, when animals first were domesticated. Zoonotic diseases pose a huge threat today because of human population increase and forces of globalization. Emerging diseases kill more than two million people annually, and 60 percent of those diseases originate in animals (Robbins 2012).

Among the diseases that have jumped from woods and wildlife to humans through their domesticated animals is the Nipah virus, which began its migration from fruit bats to humans in South Asia. Because fruit bats have co-evolved with the Nipah virus for millions of years, it does little damage to their health. When the virus moves from bats into other species, however, it can be lethal. Fruit bats eat the pulp of fruit and spit out the residue. In rural Malaysia in 1999, an infected bat appears to have dropped a piece of chewed fruit into the food supply of a swine herd (a scenario depicted in the movie *Contagion*). The virus then spread from those pigs to humans. Of 276 people infected in Malaysia, 106 died. Eleven more people died in Signapore, when the virus was exported there via live pigs. South Asia has experienced a dozen smaller Nipah outbreaks in recent years.

Spillovers from wildlife to humans have quadrupled in the last half-century, reflecting increasing

On the left, microbiologists at Atlanta's Centers for Disease Control suit up before entering the CDC's Biosafety Level-4 (BSL-4) laboratory. CDC's Special Pathogens Branch focuses on such emerging disease viruses as Ebola, hantavirus, Nipah, and tickborne encephalitis. On the right, a scientist in Nigeria pursues bats, to test for zoonotic diseases.

Left: James Gathany, CDC/Dr. Scott Smith; right: © Ivan Kuzmin/ Alamy Stock Photo

human encroachment on disease hotspots, especially in the tropics (Robbins 2012). Modern air travel contributes to the potential for a transnational outbreak or even a pandemic. (A *pandemic* is an epidemic with global scope.) The zero patient for the HIV/AIDS pandemic (in North America, at least) was a flight attendant who flew internationally. HIV/AIDS originally jumped from chimpanzees to humans through bush-meat hunters in Africa, who kill and butcher chimps.

Biologists and doctors are acutely aware of the threat posed by zoonotic diseases. One international project, called PREDICT, funds teams of veterinarians, conservation biologists, medical doctors, and epidemiologists to identify disease-causing organisms in wildlife before they spread to humans (see http://www.vetmed.ucdavis.edu/ohi/predict/). PREDICT, which is financed by the United States Agency for International Development (USAID), attempts to "predict," spot, and prevent the spread of zoonotic diseases from world areas with high potential for disease transmission. Some 24 countries in Africa, Latin America, and Asia participate in the program. PREDICT scientists monitor areas where deadly viruses are known to exist and where humans are encroaching. One such locale is a new highway being built to link the Atlantic and Pacific Oceans in South America, traversing Brazil and the Peruvian Andes.

PREDICT scientists also gather blood, saliva, and other samples from wildlife species to create a "library" of viruses, to facilitate identification when a threat is imminent. This library focuses on the animals most likely to carry diseases to people, such as primates, rats, and bats. PREDICT scientists also study ways of preventing disease transmission. Sometimes solutions can be remarkably simple. In Bangladesh, for example, outbreaks of the Nipah virus were contained by placing bamboo screens (which cost 8 cents each) over the containers used to collect date palm sap (Robbins 2012). Because humans, by modifying the environment, create the conditions that allow diseases to emerge and spread, anthropologists can contribute by studying the cultural (including economic) causes of environmental encroachment and in suggesting culturally appropriate and workable solutions.

INTERETHNIC CONTACT

Since at least the 1920s, anthropologists have been interested in changes that take place where there is sustained contact between industrial and nonindustrial societies. The term *acculturation* refers to the cultural changes that occur when different societies come into continuous firsthand contact (Redfield, Linton, and Herskovits 1936). Most acculturation studies have focused on contact between Western and non-Western cultures. Often, this contact reflects Western domination over a non-Western society. In that case, the cultural patterns of the dominant Western society are more likely to be forced upon or accepted by the non-Western society than vice versa. However, the westerners who take up residence in a non-Western setting will also be affected by the cultural practices of that setting. In postcolonial times, people have been migrating from the former colonies to the former colonial nations. Inevitably, these migrants bring along their own cultural practices. It is not uncommon for their foods, music, art, and clothing styles to influence the cultural practices of the former colonial nation. If contact is sustained long enough, acculturation will be reciprocal—influencing both groups, even if one is influenced more than the other.

Acculturation is a form of cultural borrowing, or diffusion, that requires sustained firsthand contact. Diffusion, however, can also occur without direct, firsthand contact between the cultures involved. For example, most North Americans who eat hot dogs ("frankfurters") have never been to Frankfurt, Germany, nor have most North American Toyota owners or sushi eaters ever visited Japan. Although *acculturation* can be applied to any case of cultural contact and change, the term most often has described **Westernization**—the influence of Western expansion on indigenous peoples and their cultures. Thus, local people who wear store-bought clothes, learn Indo-European languages, and otherwise adopt Western customs are called "acculturated." Acculturation may be voluntary or forced, and there may be considerable resistance to the process.

Different degrees of destruction, domination, resistance, survival, adaptation, and modification of native cultures may follow interethnic contact. In the most destructive encounters, native and subordinate cultures face obliteration. When contact with powerful outsiders seriously threatens an indigenous culture, a "shock phase" often follows the initial encounter (Bodley 2012). Outsiders may attack or exploit the native people. Such exploitation may increase mortality, disrupt subsistence, fragment kin groups, damage social support systems, and inspire new religious movements. During the shock phase, there may be civil repression backed by military force. Such factors may lead to the group's cultural collapse (*ethnocide*) or physical extinction (*genocide*).

Cultural Imperialism and Indigenization

Cultural imperialism refers to the spread or advance of one culture at the expense of others, or its imposition on other cultures, which it modifies, replaces, or destroys—usually because of differential economic or political influence. Thus, children in the French colonial empire learned French history, language, and culture from

---

Westernization
The acculturative influence of Western expansion on local cultures worldwide.

cultural imperialism
The spread or advance of one (dominant) culture at the expense of others.

standard textbooks also used in France. Tahitians, Malagasy, Vietnamese, and Senegalese learned the French language by reciting from books about "our ancestors the Gauls."

Some commentators think that modern technology and the mass media are erasing cultural differences, as a common set of products and brands spread globally. Others, however, see a role for modern technology in allowing social groups (local cultures) to express themselves and to survive (see Lule 2015; Mirrlees 2013). For example, radio, TV, film, digital media, and increasingly the Internet (e.g., YouTube) constantly bring local happenings to the attention of a larger public (see Fuchs and Sandoval 2014). For example, Susan Boyle's rendition of "I Dreamed a Dream" on a British TV show soon became an Internet sensation and made her a global star. YouTube similarly fueled the global spread of the hugely popular "Gangnam Style" by the South Korean singer Psy. Without YouTube, appreciation of these performances would be much more limited. Contemporary media play a role in stimulating and organizing local and community activities of many sorts. Think of ways in which this is done by YouTube, Facebook, and Twitter—global networks all.

In Brazil, local practices, celebrations, and performances have changed in the context of outside forces, including the mass media and tourism (see Sharpley and Teller 2015). In the town of Arembepe, Brazil (Kottak 2006), TV coverage stimulated increased participation in a traditional annual performance, the Chegança. This is a danceplay that reenacts the Portuguese discovery of Brazil. Arembepeiros have traveled to the state capital to perform the Chegança before television cameras, for a TV program featuring traditional performances from many rural communities, and cameras have gone to Arembepe to record it.

In several towns along the Amazon River, annual folk ceremonies now are staged lavishly for TV and video cameras. In the Amazon town of Parantíns, for example, boatloads of tourists arriving any time of year are shown a video recording of the town's annual Bumba Meu Boi festival. This is a costumed performance mimicking bullfighting, parts of which have been shown on national TV. This pattern, in which local communities preserve, revive, and intensify the scale of traditional ceremonies to perform for the media and tourists, is expanding. To see whether I could, I just managed to watch snippets of these annual events in Arembepe and Parantíns on YouTube!

Brazilian TV also has aided the national spread of Carnaval beyond its traditional urban centers (Kottak 2009). Still, local reactions to the nationwide broadcasting of Carnaval and its trappings (elaborate parades, costumes, and frenzied dancing) are not simple or uniform responses to external stimuli. Rather than direct adoption of Carnaval, local Brazilians respond in various ways. Often, they don't take up Carnaval itself but modify their local festivities to fit Carnaval images. Others actively spurn Carnaval. One example is Arembepe, where Carnaval has never been important, probably because of its calendrical closeness to the main local festival, which is held

In San Gimignano, Italy, boys and young men don medieval costumes and beat drums in a parade through the streets during one of the town's many pageants. Increasingly, local communities perform "traditional" ceremonies for TV and tourists.
© Paul Seheult/Eye Ubiquitous/Corbis

Illustrating both globalization and indigenization, McDonald's now routinely tries to tailor its offerings to specific cultural appetites. Shown here in downtown Fort de France, Martinique (French West Indies), is a billboard advertising a hamburger topped with Italian cheese (Parmigiano-Reggiano).

© Guiziou Franck/hemis.fr/Getty Images

diaspora
The offspring of an area who have spread to many lands.

indigenization
The process by which borrowed forms are modified to fit the local culture.

in February to honor Saint Francis of Assisi. In the past, villagers couldn't afford to celebrate both occasions. Now, not only do the people of Arembepe reject Carnaval; they also are increasingly hostile to their own main festival. Arembepeiros resent the fact that the Saint Francis festival has become "an outsiders' event," because it draws thousands of tourists to Arembepe each year.

Arembepeiros now prefer the traditional June festivals honoring Saint John, Saint Peter, and Saint Anthony. Formerly, these were observed on a much smaller scale than was the Saint Francis celebration. Arembepeiros observe them now with a new vigor and enthusiasm. The national or the global can become that only if the local populace cooperates.

People constantly make and remake culture as they assign their own meanings to the information, images, and products they get from outside. **Indigenization** refers to the process by which people modify borrowed forms to make them fit into their local culture. Indigenization occurs in cultural domains as different as fast food, music, movies, social media, housing styles, science, terrorism, celebrations, religion, and political ideas and institutions (Ellen, Lycett, and Johns 2013; Fiske 2011; Wilk 2006; Wilk and Barbosa 2012).

A Global System of Images

With globalization, more people in many more places imagine "a wider set of 'possible' lives than they ever did before. One important source of this change is the mass media . . ." (Appadurai 1991, p. 197). The United States as a global media center has been joined by Canada, Japan, Western Europe, Brazil, Mexico, Nigeria, Egypt, India, and Hong Kong.

Like print (see Anderson 2006), modern media can diffuse the cultures of countries within (and often beyond) their borders. Millions of Brazilians, for example, used to be cut off (by geographic isolation or illiteracy) from urban, national, and international events and information; they now participate in a larger "mediascape" (Appadurai 1991) through mass media and the Internet (Kottak 1990*a*, 2009).

Brazil's most popular network (Rede Globo) relies heavily on its own productions, especially telenovelas (nightly serial programs often compared to American soap operas). Globo plays each night to the world's largest and most devoted audience (perhaps 80 million viewers throughout the nation and beyond—via satellite TV). The programs that attract this horde are made by Brazilians, for Brazilians.

The mass media and the Internet also play a prominent role in maintaining ethnic and national identities among people who lead transnational lives. Arabic-speaking Muslims, including migrants in several countries, follow the TV network Al Jazeera, based in Qatar, which helps reinforce ethnic and religious identities. As groups move, they can stay linked to each other and to their homeland through global media. **Diasporas** (people who have spread out from an original, ancestral homeland) have enlarged the markets for media, communication, brands, and travel services targeted at specific ethnic, national, or religious groups who now live in various parts of the world.

A Global Culture of Consumption

In addition to the media, other key global forces are production, commerce, and finance. As Arjun Appadurai (1991, p. 194) puts it, "money, commodities, and persons unendingly chase each other around the world." Residents of many Latin American communities now rely financially on outside cash, which their relatives who have migrated send back home. Also illustrating finance as a global force, the U.S. economy is increasingly influenced by foreign investment, especially from Britain, Canada, Germany, the Netherlands, Japan, and China. The American economy also has increased its dependence on foreign labor—through both the immigration of laborers and the export of jobs.

Business and the media have fueled a global culture of consumption, based on a craving for certain lifestyles and the products that go along with them. People also crave and consume knowledge and information, available through the media and the gadgets that allow media access (see Kennedy 2015). The media also provide connectivity and a forum for expressing shared sentiments. In the Middle East, for example, social media use exploded during the Arab Spring of

2011. In cyberspace Middle Easterners found something missing from their ordinary, offline worlds: platforms permitting social connectivity and the collective airing of grievances. Since then, social media have entered the region commercially, in a big way. Over 40 percent of Middle Easterners have Internet access, and almost 90 percent of them use social media on a daily basis. Facebook is the most popular social network, with 94 percent of Middle Eastern social media users accessing that site. Arabic has become Twitter's fastest-growing language. LinkedIn (a professional social networking and job search site) has almost six million Middle Eastern users (Jazra 2014). (This region has one of the highest youth unemployment rates in the world.) This rapidly rising Middle Eastern Internet presence is occurring in an area where 40 percent of the population (of 380 million) is younger than 30 years. The smartphone is another key element in the Middle Eastern marketing mediascape. Illustrating the spreading culture of consumption, a global survey by Google found that 93 percent of smartphone users notice mobile ads, and 39 percent of those follow up with an online purchase. Saudi Arabia's mobile phone penetration rate is 190 percent, meaning that everyone has almost two cell phones (Hamdan 2013). Media and marketing are the new It couple.

Illustrating the global culture of consumption, few people have never seen a T-shirt advertising a Western product (see Gould 2016). American and English rock stars' recordings blast through the streets of Rio de Janeiro, while taxi drivers from Toronto to Madagascar listen to Brazilian music. The popularity of Korean pop singers spreads internationally via the Internet. Peasants and tribal people participate in the modern world system not only because they have been hooked on cash but also because their products and images are appropriated by world capitalism. They are commercialized by others (like the Quileute nation in the

Twilight series of books and movies). Furthermore, indigenous peoples also market their own images and products, through outlets like Cultural Survival.

PEOPLE IN MOTION

The linkages created through globalization have both enlarged and erased old boundaries and distinctions. Arjun Appadurai (1990, p. 1) characterizes today's world as a "translocal" "interactive system" that is "strikingly new." Whether as refugees, migrants, tourists, pilgrims, proselytizers, laborers, businesspeople, development workers, politicians, terrorists, soldiers, sports figures, or media-borne images, people travel more than ever. The scale of human movement has expanded dramatically. So important is transnational migration that many Mexican villagers are as likely to have friends and relatives living hundreds or thousands of miles away as immediately around them. Migrants maintain their ties with home through social media, by phoning, texting, Skyping, e-mailing, Facebooking, and FaceTiming. Frequently, they send money home; when possible, they also visit. In a sense, they live multilocally—in different places at once. Dominicans in New York City, for example, have been characterized as living "between two islands": Manhattan and the Dominican Republic (Grasmuck and Pessar 1991).

With so many people "in motion," the unit of anthropological study expands from the local community to the diaspora—the offspring of an area who have spread to many lands. Anthropologists increasingly follow descendants of the villages we have studied as they move from rural to urban areas and across national boundaries. For

One mark of globalization is the transnational diffusion of brands—and celebrity. Shown here in Warsaw, Poland, in late October 2015, David Beckham is featured on a billboard advertising for the H&M fashion brand.
© Steven May/Alamy Stock Photo

With so many people on the move, the unit of anthropological study has expanded from the local community to the diaspora, the offspring of an area who have spread to many lands, such as the owners of this falafel shop in Paris, France.
© Lionel Derimais/VISUM/The Image Works

an annual meeting of the American Anthropological Association held in Chicago, the anthropologist Robert Kemper once organized a session of presentations about long-term ethnographic fieldwork. Kemper's own longtime research focus was the Mexican village of Tzintzuntzan, which, with his mentor George Foster, he studied for decades. Eventually, their database expanded to include not only Tzintzuntzan but also its descendants all over the world. Given the Tzintzuntzan diaspora, Kemper was even able to use some of his time in Chicago to visit people from Tzintzuntzan who had established a colony there. In today's world, as people move, they take their traditions and their anthropologists along with them.

Postmodernity describes our time and situation: today's world in flux, these people on the move who have learned to manage multiple identities depending on place and context. In its most general sense, **postmodern** refers to the blurring and breakdown of established canons (rules or standards), categories, distinctions, and boundaries. The word is taken from **postmodernism**—a style and movement in architecture that succeeded modernism, beginning in the 1970s. Postmodern architecture rejected the rules, geometric order, and austerity of modernism. Modernist buildings were expected to have a clear and functional design. Postmodern design is "messier" and more playful. It draws on a diversity of styles from different times and places—including popular, ethnic, and non-Western cultures. Postmodernism extends "value" well beyond classic, elite, and Western cultural forms. *Postmodern* is now used to describe comparable developments in music, literature, and visual art. From this origin, *postmodernity* describes a world in which traditional standards, contrasts, groups, boundaries, and identities are opening up, reaching out, and breaking down.

New kinds of political and ethnic units have emerged along with globalization. In some cases, cultures and ethnic groups have banded together in larger associations. There is a growing pan–Native American identity and an international pantribal movement as well. Thus, in June 1992, the World Conference of Indigenous Peoples met in Rio de Janeiro concurrently with UNCED (the United Nations Conference on the Environment and Development). Along with diplomats, journalists, and environmentalists came 300 representatives of the tribal diversity that survives under globalization—from Lapland to Mali (Brooke 1992; see also Maybury-Lewis 2002; Maybury-Lewis, Macdonald, and Maybury-Lewis 2009).

INDIGENOUS PEOPLES

All too often, conquest, annexation, and development have been associated with **genocide**—the deliberate extermination of a specific ethnic group. Examples of genocide include the Holocaust, Rwanda in 1994, and Bosnia in the early 1990s. Bodley (2015) estimates that an average of 250,000 indigenous people perished annually between 1800 and 1950. The causes included warfare, outright murder, introduced diseases, slavery, land grabbing, and other forms of dispossession and impoverishment.

Remaining in the world today are more than 5,000 distinct groups of indigenous peoples, located in some 90 countries. They comprise more than 5 percent of the world's population, numbering about 370 million people. They remain among the world's most disadvantaged and vulnerable populations. Many of them struggle to hold on to their lands and natural resources (see this chapter's "Appreciating Diversity").

All of the indigenous groups that have survived live today within nation-states. Often, they maintain a distinct ethnic identity, despite having lost their ancestral languages and cultures to varying degrees. Many such groups aspire to autonomy. To describe these original inhabitants of their territories, the term *indigenous people* entered international law in 1982 with the creation of the United Nations Working Group on Indigenous Populations (WGIP). This group meets annually and has members from six continents. The UN General Assembly adopted its Declaration of Indigenous Rights in 2007. Convention 169, a document supporting cultural diversity and indigenous empowerment, had been approved by the International Labor Organization (ILO) in 1989. Such documents, along with the global work of the WGIP, have influenced governments, NGOs, and international agencies to adopt policies favorable to indigenous peoples. In May 2012, the United Nations sponsored a high-level commemoration of the fifth anniversary of the adoption of the UN Declaration on the Rights of Indigenous Peoples (see Doyle 2015; Drahos 2014). In September 2014, the United Nations hosted a World Conference on Indigenous Peoples, to reiterate the U.N.'s ongoing role in promoting and protecting the rights of indigenous peoples (see http://wcip2014.org). Social movements worldwide now use *indigenous people* as a self-identifying label in their quests for social, cultural, and political rights (Brower and Johnston 2007; de la Peña 2005).

In Spanish-speaking Latin America, social scientists and politicians now favor the term *indígena* (indigenous person) over *indio* (Indian), the colonial term that European conquerors used for Native Americans (de la Peña 2005). Until the mid- to late 1980s, Latin American public policy emphasized assimilation. The past 30 years have witnessed a dramatic shift. The emphasis has shifted from biological and cultural assimilation—*mestizaje*—to identities that value difference, especially as indigenous peoples.

In Ecuador, for example, groups seen previously as Quichua-speaking peasants are classified

---

postmodernity
Time of questioning of established canons, identities, and standards.

postmodern
Marked by the breakdown of established canons, categories, distinctions, and boundaries.

postmodernism
Movement after modernism in architecture; now describes comparable developments in music, literature, and visual art.

genocide
The deliberate elimination of a group through mass murder.

now as indigenous communities with assigned territories. Other Andean "peasants" have experienced similar reindigenization as well. Brazil recognized 30 new indigenous communities in the northeast, a region previously seen as having lost its indigenous population. In Guatemala, Nicaragua, Brazil, Colombia, Mexico, Paraguay, Ecuador, Argentina, Bolivia, Peru, and Venezuela, constitutional reforms have recognized those nations as multicultural (Jackson and Warren 2005). Several national constitutions now recognize the rights of indigenous peoples to cultural distinctiveness, sustainable development, political representation, and limited self-government.

The indigenous rights movement exists in the context of globalization, including transnational movements focusing on human rights, women's rights, and environmentalism. Transnational organizations have helped indigenous peoples to influence legislation. Since the 1980s, there has been a general shift in Latin America from authoritarian to democratic rule. Still, inequality and discrimination against indigenous peoples persist.

Ceuppens and Geschiere (2005) comment on an upsurge, in several world areas, of the notion of *autochthony* (being native to, or formed in, the place where found), with an implicit call for excluding strangers. The terms *autochthony* and *indigenous* both go back to classical Greek history, with similar implications. *Autochthony* refers to self and soil. *Indigenous* literally means born inside, with the connotation in classical Greek of being born "inside the house." Both notions stress rights of first-comers to privileged status and protection versus later immigrants—legal or illegal (Ceuppens and Geschiere 2005; Hornborg et al. 2011).

During the 1990s, autochthony became an issue in many parts of Africa, inspiring violent efforts to exclude (European and Asian) "strangers." Simultaneously, autochthony became a key notion in debates about immigration and multiculturalism in Europe. European majority groups have claimed the label *autochthon*. This term highlights the prominence that the exclusion of strangers has assumed in day-to-day politics worldwide (Ceuppens and Geschiere 2005). Familiar contemporary examples include the rise of ethnonationalism in the United States, and the June 2016 Brexit vote (for Britain to leave the European Union).

Essentialism describes the process of viewing an identity (e.g., an ethnic label) as innate, real, and frozen, thus ignoring the historical processes within which that identity developed. Identities, however, are not fixed; they are fluid and multiple. People draw on particular, sometimes competing, self-labels and identities. Some Peruvian groups, for instance, self-identify as *mestizos* but still see themselves as indigenous. Identity is a fluid, dynamic process, and there are multiple ways of being indigenous. Neither speaking an indigenous language nor wearing "native" clothing is required to self-identify as indigenous (Jackson and Warren 2005).

essentialism
Viewing identities that have developed historically as innate and unchanging.

Mary Simat, with the Maasai Women for Education and Economic Development from Kenya, testifies at the Indigenous Peoples' Global Summit on Climate Change in Anchorage, Alaska, in April 2009. The five-day United Nations–affiliated conference attracted about 400 people from 80 nations.
© Al Grillo/AP Images

Seeking official recognition of El Salvador's indigenous peoples, a member of one such group, the Lenca, participates in a 2013 demonstration in the national capital, San Salvador. In 1932, dictator Maximiliano Hernández Martínez, suppressing a peasant uprising, massacred up to 30,000 natives. The survivors, as a result, stopped using their language and hid their traditional customs. Here, as throughout Latin America, things have been changing.
© Jose Cabezas/AFP/Getty Images

ANTHROPOLOGY'S LESSONS

Anthropology teaches us that the adaptive responses of humans are more flexible than those of other species, because our main adaptive means are sociocultural. However, in the face of globalization, the cultural institutions of the past always influence subsequent adaptation, producing continued diversity in the actions and reactions of different groups as they indigenize global inputs. In our globalizing world, anthropology offers a people-centered vision of social change. The existence of anthropology is itself a tribute to the continuing need to understand similarities and differences among human beings throughout the world.

Anthropology offers relevant, indeed powerful, ways of seeing how the world actually works.

Lessons of the past can and should be applied to the present and future, hopefully to benefit humanity. Anthropologists know that civilizations and world powers rise and fall, and that social transformations typically follow major innovations, such as the Neolithic and the Industrial Revolution. There is very little chance that the current world system and the power relations within it will last forever. Whatever it may be, our social future will trace its origins to our social present. That is, future developments will need to build on, modify, and perhaps discard preexisting practices and institutions. What trends observable in the world today are most likely to transform society in the long run? Using your new knowledge of anthropology, try to imagine possible futures for humanity.

for REVIEW

summary

1. Fueling global warming are human population growth and increasing use of fossil fuels. The term *climate change* encompasses global warming along with changing sea levels, precipitation, storms, and ecosystem effects.

2. Anthropologists have studied how environmental forces influence humans and how human activities affect the Earth's atmosphere. An ethnoecology is a society's set of environmental practices and perceptions. Indigenous ethnoecologies increasingly are being challenged by global forces. A challenge for applied ecological anthropology is to devise culturally appropriate strategies for conservation in the face of population growth and commercial expansion.

3. Causes of deforestation include demographic pressure on subsistence economies, commercial logging, road building, cash cropping, urban expansion, and clearing and burning associated with livestock. Infectious diseases such as HIV/AIDS, Ebola, West Nile, SARS, and Zika have emerged and spread because of things that people have done to their environments. Cultural imperialism is the spread of one culture and its imposition on other cultures, which it modifies, replaces, or destroys—usually because of differential economic or political influence. Some critics worry that modern technology, including the mass media, is destroying traditional

cultures. But others see an important role for new technology in allowing local cultures to express themselves.

4. As the forces of globalization spread, they are modified (indigenized) to fit into local cultures. Modern media can help diffuse a national culture within its own boundaries. The media also play a role in preserving ethnic and national identities among people who lead transnational lives.

5. People travel more than ever. But migrants also maintain ties with home, so they live multilocally. *Postmodernity* describes this world in flux, with people on the move who manage multiple social identities depending on place and context. New kinds of political and ethnic units are emerging as others break down or disappear.

6. Governments, NGOs, and international agencies have adopted policies designed to recognize and benefit indigenous peoples. Social movements worldwide have adopted this term as a self-identifying and political label based on past oppression but now signaling a search for social, cultural, and political rights. In Latin America, several national constitutions now recognize the rights of indigenous peoples. Identity is a fluid, dynamic process, and there are multiple ways of being indigenous.

key terms

critical thinking

1. What does it mean to apply an anthropological perspective to contemporary global issues? Can you come up with an anthropological research question that investigates such issues? Imagine you had a year (and the money!) to carry out this project. How would you spend your time and your resources?

2. The topic of global climate change has been hotly debated during the past few years. Why is there so much debate? Are you concerned about global climate change? Do you think everyone on the planet should be equally concerned and share the responsibility of doing something about it? Why or why not?

3. Consider majority and minority rights in the context of contemporary events involving religion, ethnicity, politics, and law. In pluralistic societies, what kind of rights should be granted on the basis of religion? What kinds of groups, if any, within a nation should have special rights? How about indigenous peoples?

4. Do you now live, or have you ever lived, multilocally? If so, how so?

5. What term do anthropologists use to describe the view that identities have developed historically as innate and unchanging? We know, however, that identities are not fixed; they are fluid and multiple. What does this mean? What implications does this have for understanding indigenous political movements?

GLOSSARY

absolute dating Establishing dates in numbers or ranges of numbers.

acculturation An exchange of cultural features between groups in firsthand contact.

Acheulean Lower Paleolithic tool tradition associated with *H. erectus*.

achieved status Social status based on choices or accomplishments.

adaptive Favored by natural selection.

adaptive strategy Means of making a living; productive system.

aesthetics The appreciation of qualities perceived in art.

affinals Relatives by marriage.

African American Vernacular English (AAVE) The rule-governed dialect spoken by some African Americans.

agency The actions of individuals, alone and in groups, that create and transform culture.

agriculture Cultivation using land and labor continuously and intensively.

allele A variant of a particular gene.

Allen's rule Protruding body parts are bigger in warmer areas.

ambilineal descent A flexible descent rule, neither patrilineal nor matrilineal.

AMHs Anatomically modern humans.

analogies Adaptive traits due to convergent evolution.

animism The belief in souls, or doubles.

anthropogenic Caused by humans and their activities.

anthropoids Monkeys, apes, and humans.

anthropological archaeology The study of human behavior through material remains.

anthropology and education The study of students in the context of their family, peers, and enculturation.

anthropology The study of the humans around the world and through time.

anthropometry The measurement of human body parts and dimensions.

antimodernism Rejecting the modern for a presumed earlier, purer, better way of life.

applied anthropology The use of anthropology to solve contemporary problems.

arboreal Living in the trees.

Ardipithecus Earliest recognized hominin genus (5.8–4.4 m.y.a.), Ethiopia.

art An object, event, or other expressive form that evokes an aesthetic reaction.

arts Include visual arts, literature (written and oral), music, and performance arts.

ascribed status Social status based on limited choice.

assimilation Absorption of minorities within a dominant culture.

association An observed relationship between two or more variables.

Au. afarensis Early *Australopithecus* species (3.8–3.0 m.y.a.), Ethiopia ("Lucy"), Tanzania.

Au. africanus Gracile *Australopithecus* species (3.5–2.5 m.y.a.), South Africa.

Au. anamensis Earliest known Australopithecus species (4.2–3.9 m.y.a.), Kenya.

Au. garhi Toolmaking Australopithecus species (2.6–2.5 m.y.a.), Ethiopia.

australopith Common term for all members of the genera *Australopithecus* and *Paranthropus*.

Aztec The last independent Valley of Mexico state (thrived between 1325 and the Spanish Conquest in 1520).

balanced polymorphism Alleles maintain a constant frequency in a population over time.

balanced reciprocity Midpoint on the reciprocity continuum, between generalized and negative reciprocity.

band The basic social unit among foragers; fewer than a hundred people; may split up seasonally.

behavioral ecology The study of the evolutionary basis of social behavior.

behavioral modernity Fully human behavior based on symbolic thought and cultural creativity.

Bergmann's rule Larger bodies are found in colder areas and smaller bodies in warmer ones.

bifurcate collateral kinship terminology Six separate parental kin terms: M, F, MB, MZ, FB, and FZ.

bifurcate merging kinship terminology Four parental kin terms: M5MZ, F5FB, MB, and FZ each stand alone.

big man Generous tribal entrepreneur with multivillage support.

bilateral kinship calculation Kin ties calculated equally through both sexes.

biocultural Combining biological and cultural approaches to a given problem.

biological anthropology The study of human biological variation through time and as it exists today.

bipedal Two-footed; upright locomotion (of hominins).

blade tool Basic Upper Paleolithic tool, hammered off a prepared core.

bone biology The study of bone as a biological tissue.

bourgeoisie Owners of the means of production.

brachiation Under-the-branch swinging.

broad-spectrum revolution Foraging of varied plant and animal foods at end of Ice Age; prelude to Neolithic.

bronze An alloy of copper and arsenic or copper and tin.

call systems Communication systems of nonhuman primates.

capital Wealth invested with the intent of producing profit.

capitalist world economy A profit-oriented global economy based on production for sale or exchange.

cargo cults Postcolonial, acculturative religious movements in Melanesia.

catharsis Intense emotional release.

chiefdom A society with permanent a political structure, hereditary leaders, and social ranking but lacking class divisions.

chromosomes Paired lengths of DNA, composed of multiple genes.

clan A unilineal descent group based on stipulated descent.

climate change Global warming, plus changing sea levels, precipitation, storms, and ecosystem effects.

cline Gradual shift in gene (allele) frequencies between neighboring populations.

Clovis Early American tool tradition; projectile point attached to hunting spear.

collateral relative A relative outside ego's direct line, e.g., B, Z, FB, MZ.

colonialism The long-term foreign control of a territory and its people.

communism A political system in which property is owned by the community and people work for the common good.

Communism A political movement aimed at replacing capitalism with Soviet-style communism.

communitas An intense feeling of social solidarity.

complex societies Large, populous societies (e.g., nations) with social stratification and central governments.

configurationalism The view of culture as integrated and patterned.

conflict resolution Means of settling disputes.

convergent evolution Similar selective forces produce similar adaptive traits.

core The dominant position in the world system; nations with advanced systems of production.

core values Key, basic, or central values that integrate a culture.

correlation An association; when one variable changes, another does, too.

cosmology A system, often religious, for imagining and understanding the universe.

Cro Magnon The first fossil find (1868) of an AMH, from France's Dordogne Valley.

cross cousins Children of a brother and a sister.

crossing over Homologous chromosomes intertwine and exchange DNA.

cultivation continuum Continuum of land and labor use.

cultural anthropology The comparative, cross-cultural study of human society and culture.

cultural colonialism The internal domination by one group and its culture or ideology over others.

cultural consultants People who teach an ethnographer about their culture.

cultural imperialism The spread or advance of one (dominant) culture at the expense of others.

cultural materialism (Harris) The idea that cultural infrastructure determines structure and superstructure.

cultural relativism The idea that behavior should be evaluated not by outside standards but in the context of the culture in which it occurs.

cultural resource management Deciding what needs saving when entire archaeological sites cannot be saved.

cultural rights Rights vested in religious and ethnic minorities and indigenous societies.

cultural transmission Transmission through learning, basic to language.

culture Traditions and customs transmitted through learning.

cuneiform Early Mesopotamian wedge-shaped writing, using stylus on clay.

curer One who diagnoses and treats illness.

daughter languages Languages sharing a common parent language, e.g., Latin.

dendrochronology Tree-ring dating; a form of absolute dating.

descent Social identity based on ancestry.

descent group A group based on belief in shared ancestry.

development anthropology A field that examines the sociocultural dimensions of economic development.

diachronic (Studying societies) across time.

diaspora The offspring of an area who have spread to many lands.

differential access Favored access to resources by super-ordinates over subordinates.

diffusion Borrowing of cultural traits between societies.

diglossia A language with "high" (formal) and "low" (informal, familial) dialects.

discrimination Policies and practices that harm a group and its members.

disease A scientifically identified health threat caused by a known pathogen.

displacement Describing things and events that are not present; basic to language.

domestic–public dichotomy Work at home versus more valued work outside the home.

dominant Term describing an allele that masks another allele in a heterozygote.

dowry Substantial gifts to the husband's family from the wife's group.

ecological anthropology The study of cultural adaptations to environments.

economizing The allocation of scarce means (resources) among alternative ends.

economy A system of resource production, distribution, and consumption.

egalitarian society A society with rudimentary status distinctions.

ego The position from which one views an egocentric genealogy.

emic A research strategy focusing on local explanations and meanings.

empire A mature state that is large, multiethnic, militaristic, and expansive.

enculturation The process by which culture is learned and transmitted across the generations.

endogamy Marriage of people from the same social group.

essentialism Viewing identities that have developed historically as innate and unchanging.

ethnic group One among several culturally distinct groups in a society or region.

ethnicity Identification with an ethnic group.

ethnocentrism Judging other cultures using one's own cultural standards.

ethnocide The deliberate suppression or destruction of an ethnic culture by a dominant group.

ethnoecology A culture's set of environmental perceptions and practices.

ethnography Fieldwork in a particular cultural setting.

ethnology The study of sociocultural differences and similarities.

ethnomusicology The comparative study of music as an aspect of culture and society.

ethnosemantics The study of lexical (vocabulary) categories and contrasts.

etic A research strategy emphasizing the ethnographer's explanations and categories.

evolution Transformation of species; descent with modification.

excavation Digging through layers at a site.

exogamy Marriage outside one's own group.

expanded family household A household that includes a group of relatives other than, or in addition to, a married couple and their children.

expressive culture Dance, music, painting, sculpture, pottery, cloth, stories, drama, comedy, etc.

extended family household A household with three or more generations.

family of orientation The nuclear family in which one is born and grows up.

family of procreation The nuclear family established when one marries and has children.

fiscal Pertaining to finances and taxation.

focal vocabulary A set of words describing particular domains (foci) of experience.

folk Of the people; e.g., the art, music, and lore of ordinary people.

food production An economy based on plant cultivation and/or animal domestication.

foraging An economy and a way of life based on hunting and gathering.

fossils Remains of ancient life.

functionalism An approach that focuses on the role (function) of sociocultural practices in social systems.

fundamentalism Advocating strict fidelity to a religion's presumed founding principles.

gender The cultural construction of whether one is female, male, or something else.

gender identity A person's identification by self and others as male, female, or something else.

gender roles The tasks and activities that a culture assigns to each sex.

gender stereotypes Oversimplified, strongly held views about the characteristics of males and females.

gender stratification The unequal distribution of social resources between men and women.

gene The place (locus) on a chromosome that determines a particular trait.

gene flow Exchange of genetic material through interbreeding.

gene pool All the genetic material in a breeding population.

genealogical method The use of diagrams and symbols to record kin connections.

general anthropology Anthropology as a whole: cultural, archaeological, biological, and linguistic anthropology.

generality Culture pattern or trait that exists in some but not all societies.

generalized reciprocity Exchanges among closely related individuals.

generational kinship terminology Just two parental kin terms: M5MZ5FZ and F5FB5MB.

genetic evolution Change in gene (allele) frequency in a breeding population.

genitor A child's biological father.

genocide The deliberate elimination of a group through mass murder.

genotype An organism's hereditary makeup.

gibbons Small, arboreal, Asiatic apes.

glacials Major advances of continental ice sheets in Europe and North America.

globalization The accelerating interdependence of nations in the world system today.

gracile e.g., *Au. afarensis, Au. africanus*; less robust, i.e., slighter than *Paranthropus*.

greenhouse effect Warming caused by trapped atmospheric gases.

H. erectus Highly successful form of early human; expanded from Africa into Eurasia by 1.77 m.y.a. (1.9-0.4 m.y.a.).

H. habilis Early hominin species (1.9-1.44 m.y.a.), first discovered by L.S.B. and Mary Leakey in 1960; named *habilis,* meaning "able," for their presumed ability to make tools.

H. heidelbergensis Hominin group that lived in Europe, Africa, and Asia from about 850,000 to about 200,000 B.P.

Halafian Early (7500–6500 B.P.), widespread Mesopotamian pottery style.

haplogroup Lineage or branch of a genetic tree marked by one or more specific genetic mutations.

Haplorrhini The primate suborder that includes lemurs, lorises, and their ancestors.

health care systems Beliefs, customs, and specialists concerned with preventing and curing illness.

hegemony A stratified social order in which subordinates accept hierarchy as "natural."

Herto Very early (160,000–154,000 B.P.) AMHs found in Ethiopia.

heterozygous Having dissimilar alleles of a given gene.

hilly flanks Woodland zone just north of Tigris and Euphrates Rivers.

historical linguistics The study of languages over time.

historical particularism (Boas) The idea that histories are not comparable; diverse paths can lead to the same cultural result.

holistic Encompassing past, present, and future; biology, society, language, and culture.

hominid Member of hominid family; any fossil or living human, chimp, or gorilla.

hominins Hominids excluding the African apes; all the human species that ever have existed.

hominoid The zoological superfamily that includes extinct and living apes and hominins.

homologies Traits inherited from a common ancestor.

homozygous Having identical alleles of a given gene.

honorifics Terms of respect; used to honor people.

horticulture Nonindustrial plant cultivation with fallowing.

human rights Rights based on justice and morality beyond and superior to particular countries, cultures, and religions.

hypodescent Children of mixed unions assigned to the same group as their minority parent.

hypothesis A suggested but as yet unverified explanation.

illness A condition of poor health perceived or felt by an individual.

imperialism A conscious policy aimed at seizing and ruling foreign territory and peoples.

incest Sexual relations with a close relative.

increased equity Reduction in absolute poverty, with a more even distribution of wealth.

independent assortment Chromosomes inherited independently of one another.

independent invention The independent development of a cultural feature in different societies.

indigenization The process by which borrowed forms are modified to fit the local culture.

Industrial Revolution In Europe, after 1750, socio-economic transformation through industrialization.

informed consent An agreement to take part in research—after having been informed about its purpose, nature, procedures, and possible impacts.

interglacials Extended warm periods between glacials.

international culture Cultural traditions that extend beyond national boundaries.

interpretive anthropology (Geertz) The study of a culture as a system of meaning.

intersex Pertaining to a group of biological conditions reflecting a discrepancy between external and internal genitals.

intervention philosophy An ideological justification for outsiders to guide or rule native peoples.

interview schedule A form (guide) used to structure a formal, but personal, interview.

IPR Intellectual property rights; an indigenous group's collective knowledge and its applications.

key cultural consultants Experts on a particular aspect of local life.

kin terms The words used for different relatives in a particular language and system of kinship calculation.

kinesics The study of communication through body movements and facial expressions.

kinship calculation How people in a particular society reckon kin relations.

language The primary means of human communication, spoken and written.

law A legal code of a state society, with trial and enforcement.

levirate Widow marries brother of her deceased husband.

lexicon Vocabulary; all the morphemes in a language and their meanings.

life history Of a key consultant; a personal portrait of someone's life in a culture.

liminality The in-between phase of a rite of passage.

lineage A unilineal descent group based on demonstrated descent.

lineal kinship terminology Four parental kin terms: M, F, FB5MB, and MZ5FZ.

lineal relatives Ego's direct ancestors and descendants.

linguistic anthropology The study of language and linguistic diversity in time, space, and society.

lobola A substantial marital gift from the husband and his kin to the wife and her kin.

longitudinal research Long-term study, usually based on repeated visits.

magic The use of supernatural techniques to accomplish specific ends.

maize Corn; first domesticated in tropical southwestern Mexico around 8000 B.P.

mana A sacred, impersonal force, so named in Melanesia and Polynesia.

manioc Cassava; tuber domesticated in the South American lowlands.

market principle Buying, selling, and valuation based on supply and demand.

mater The socially recognized mother of a child.

matrilineal descent Descent traced through women only.

means (factors) of production Major productive resources, e.g., land, labor, technology, capital.

medical anthropology The comparative, biocultural study of disease, health problems, and health care systems.

meiosis The process by which sex cells are produced.

melanin "Natural sunscreen" produced by skin cells responsible for pigmentation.

Mesoamerica Middle America, including Mexico, Guatemala, and Belize.

Mesolithic Stone toolmaking, emphasizing microliths within broad-spectrum economies.

Mesopotamia The area where the earliest states developed, between the Tigris and Euphrates Rivers.

metallurgy The extraction and processing of metals to make tools.

mitosis Ordinary cell division.

mode of production Specific set of social relations that organizes labor.

molecular anthropology DNA comparisons used to determine evolutionary links and distances.

monotheism The belief in a single all-powerful deity.

morphology The (linguistic) study of morphemes and word construction.

Mousterian Middle Paleolithic toolmaking tradition associated with Neandertals.

multiculturalism The view of cultural diversity as valuable and worth maintaining.

mutation Change in DNA molecules.

m.y.a. Million years ago.

nation A society that shares a language, religion, history, territory, ancestry, and kinship.

national culture Cultural features shared by citizens of the same nation.

nationalities Ethnic groups that have, once had, or want their own country.

nation-state An autonomous political entity; a country.

Natufians Widespread Middle Eastern foraging culture (12,800–10,200 B.P.).

natural selection Selection of favored forms through differential reproductive success.

Neandertals Archaic *H. sapiens* group inhabiting Europe and the Middle East from 130,000 to 28,000 B.P.

negative reciprocity Potentially hostile exchanges among strangers.

neoliberalism The principle that governments shouldn't regulate private enterprise; free market forces should rule.

Neolithic Term used to describe economies based on food production (cultivated crops and domesticated animals).

neolocality The living situation in which a couple establishes new residence.

nomadism (pastoral) The annual movement of entire pastoral group with herds.

office A permanent political position.

Oldowan Earliest (2.6–1.2 m.y.a.) stone tools; sharp flakes struck from cores (choppers).

opposable thumb A thumb that can touch all the other fingers.

overinnovation Trying to achieve too much change.

paleoanthropology The study of hominid, hominin, and human life through the fossil record.

Paleolithic Old Stone Age, including Lower (early), Middle, and Upper (late).

paleontology The study of ancient life through the fossil record.

paleopathology The study of disease and injury in skeletons from archaeological sites.

pantribal sodalities Non-kin-based groups with regional political significance.

parallel cousins Children of two brothers or two sisters.

Paranthropus boisei Late, hyperrobust East African australopiths (2.3–1.4 m.y.a.).

Paranthropus robustus Robust South African australopiths (1.9–1.0 m.y.a.).

particularity Distinctive or unique culture trait, pattern, or integration.

pastoralists Herders of domesticated animals.

pater One's socially recognized father; not necessarily the genitor.

patriarchy Political system ruled by men.

patrilineal descent Descent traced through men only.

patrilineal-patrilocal complex Male supremacy based on patrilineality, patrilocality, and warfare.

peasant A small-scale farmer with rent fund obligations.

periphery The weakest structural and economic position in the world system.

phenotype The expressed physical characteristics of an organism.

phenotypical adaptation Adaptive biological changes during an individual's lifetime.

phoneme The smallest sound contrast that distinguishes meaning.

phonemics The study of significant sound contrasts (phonemes) in a language.

phonetics The study of speech sounds—what people actually say.

phonology The study of sounds used in speech in a particular language.

Pleistocene Main epoch (2 m.y.a.–10,000 B.P.) of evolution of *Homo*.

plural marriage More than two spouses simultaneously; polygamy.

plural society A society with economically interdependent ethnic groups.

political economy The web of interrelated economic and power relations in society.

polity A political entity, such as a chiefdom or state.

polyandry Woman has more than one husband at the same time.

polygyny Man has more than one wife at the same time.

polytheism The belief in multiple deities, who control aspects of nature.

population genetics The field that studies genetics of breeding populations.

postcolonial Describes relations between European nations and areas they colonized and once ruled.

postmodern Marked by the breakdown of established canons, categories, distinctions, and boundaries.

postmodernism Movement after modernism in architecture; now describes comparable developments in music, literature, and visual art.

postmodernity Time of questioning of established canons, identities, and standards.

potlatch A competitive feast on North Pacific Coast of North America.

power The ability to exercise one's will over others.

prejudice Devaluing a group because of its assumed attributes.

prestige Esteem, respect, or approval.

primary states States arising through competition among chiefdoms.

primatology The study of apes, monkeys, tarsiers, lemurs, and lorises.

productivity Creating new expressions that are comprehensible to other speakers.

protolanguage A language ancestral to several daughter languages.

public anthropology Efforts to extend anthropology's visibility beyond academia and to demonstrate its public policy relevance.

punctuated equilibrium Long periods of stability, with occasional evolutionary leaps.

questionnaire A form used by sociologists to obtain comparable information from respondents.

race An ethnic group assumed to have a biological basis.

racial classification Assigning humans to categories (purportedly) based on common ancestry.

racism Discrimination against an ethnic group assumed to have a biological basis.

random genetic drift Genetic change due to chance.

random sample A sample in which all population members have an equal statistical chance of inclusion.

ranked society A society with hereditary inequality but lacking social stratification.

recessive Term describing a genetic trait masked by a dominant trait.

reciprocity The principle governing exchanges among social equals.

reciprocity continuum A continuum running from generalized reciprocity (closely related/deferred return) to negative reciprocity (strangers/immediate return).

redistribution The flow of goods from the local level into a center, then back out; characteristic of chiefdoms.

refugees People who flee a country to escape persecution or war.

relative dating Establishing a time frame in relation to other strata or materials.

religion Belief and ritual concerned with supernatural beings, powers, and forces.

remote sensing The use of aerial photos and satellite images to locate sites on the ground.

revitalization movements Social movements aimed at altering or revitalizing a society.

rickets Vitamin D deficiency marked by bone deformation.

rites of passage Rites marking transitions between places or stages of life.

ritual Formal, repetitive, stereotyped behavior; based on a liturgical order.

robust e.g., *Paranthropus robustus* and *Paranthropus boisei*; having large, strong, sturdy bones, muscles, and teeth.

sample A smaller study group chosen to represent a larger population.

Sapir-Whorf hypothesis The theory that different languages produce different patterns of thought.

science A field of study that seeks reliable explanations, with reference to the material and physical world.

scientific medicine A health care system based on scientific knowledge and procedures.

sedentism Settled (sedentary) life.

semantics A language's meaning system.

semiperiphery The position in the world system intermediate between core and periphery.

settlement hierarchy Communities with varying size, function, and building types.

sexual dimorphism Marked differences in male and female anatomy and temperament.

sexual orientation Sexual attraction to persons of the opposite sex, same sex, or both sexes.

sexual selection Selection of traits that enhance mating success.

shaman A part-time medico-magico-religious practitioner.

smelting The high-temperature extraction of metal from ore.

social control Maintaining social norms and regulating conflict.

sociolinguistics The study of language in society.

sororate Widower marries sister of his deceased wife.

speciation Formation of new species.

species A population whose members can interbreed to produce offspring that can live and reproduce.

state A society with a central government, administrative specialization, and social classes.

status Any position that determines where someone fits in society.

stereotypes Fixed ideas—often unfavorable—about what members of a group are like.

stratification The presence of social divisions—strata—with unequal wealth and power.

stratified Class structured, with differences in wealth, prestige, and power.

stratigraphy The study of earth sediments deposited in demarcated layers (strata).

Strepsirrhini The primate suborder that includes tarsiers, monkeys, apes, and humans.

style shifts Varying one's speech in different social contexts.

subcultures Different cultural traditions associated with subgroups in the same complex society.

subgroups (Linguistic) closely related languages.

subordinate The lower, underprivileged group in a stratified society.

superordinate The upper, privileged group in a stratified society.

superorganic (Kroeber) The special domain of culture, beyond the organic and inorganic realms.

survey research The study of society through sampling, statistical analysis, and impersonal data collection.

symbol Something, verbal or nonverbal, that stands for something else.

symbolic anthropology The study of symbols in their social and cultural context.

synchronic (Studying societies) at one time.

syncretisms Cultural, especially religious, mixes, emerging from acculturation.

syntax The arrangement and order of words in phrases and sentences.

systematic survey The study of settlement patterns over a large area.

taboo Sacred and forbidden; prohibition backed by supernatural sanctions.

taphonomy The study of processes affecting remains of dead animals.

taxonomy Classification scheme; assignment to categories (*taxa*; singular, *taxon*).

teosinte Wild ancestor of maize; grows wild in southwestern Mexico.

Teotihuacán The first Valley of Mexico state (100–700 C.E.); earliest Mesoamerican empire.

terrestrial Ground-dwelling.

text A cultural product that is processed and assigned meaning by anyone exposed to it.

theory A set of ideas formulated to explain something.

Thomson's nose rule Average nose length increases in cold areas.

totem An animal, a plant, or a geographic feature associated with a specific social group, to which that totem is sacred or symbolically important.

transgender A gender identity that is socially constructed and individually performed by individuals whose gender identity contradicts their biological sex at birth and the gender identity assigned to them in infancy.

transhumance A system in which only part of a population moves seasonally with herds.

tribe A food-producing society with rudimentary political structure.

tropics Zone between 23 degrees north (Tropic of Cancer) and 23 degrees south (Tropic of Capricorn) of the equator.

underdifferentiation Seeing less-developed countries as all the same; ignoring cultural diversity.

uniformitarianism The belief that natural forces at work today also explain past events.

unilineal descent Matrilineal or patrilineal descent.

unilinear evolutionism The (19th-century) idea of a single line or path of cultural development.

universal Something that exists in every culture.

Upper Paleolithic Blade-toolmaking traditions of early AMHs.

urban anthropology The anthropological study of cities and urban life.

variables Attributes that differ from one person or case to the next.

village head A local tribal leader with limited authority.

wealth All a person's material assets; basis of economic status.

Westernization The acculturative influence of Western expansion on local cultures worldwide.

working class (proletariat) People who must sell their labor to survive.

world-system theory The idea that a discernible social system, based on wealth and power differentials, transcends individual countries.

Zapotec state The first Mesoamerican state, in the Valley of Oaxaca.

BIBLIOGRAPHY

Adams, R. M.
　2008　An Interdisciplinary Overview of a Mesopotamian City and Its Hinterlands. *Cuneiform Digital Library Journal.* http://cdli.ucla.edu/pubs/cdlj/2008/cdlj2008_001.

Adams, S.
　2012　The World's Next Genocide. *New York Times,* November 15.

Adepegba, C. O.
　1991　The Yoruba Concept of Art and Its Significance in the Holistic View of Art as Applied to African Art. *African Notes* 15: 1–6.

Ahmed, A. S.
　2004　*Postmodernism and Islam: Predicament and Promise,* rev. ed. New York: Routledge.

Aiello, L., and M. Collard
　2001　Our Newest Oldest Ancestor? *Nature* 410: 526–527.

Akazawa, T., and C. M. Aikens, eds.
　1986　*Prehistoric Hunter-Gatherers in Japan: New Research Methods.* Tokyo: University of Tokyo Press.

Altmann, J., G. Hausfater, and S. Altmann
　1988　Determinants of Reproductive Success in Savannah Baboons, *Papio cynocephalus.* In *Reproductive Success: Studies of Individual Variation in Contrasting Breeding Systems,* T. H. Clutton-Brock, ed., pp. 403–418. Chicago: University of Chicago Press.

Amadiume, I.
　1987　*Male Daughters, Female Husbands.* Atlantic Highlands, NJ: Zed.

American Anthropological Association
　2004　*Statement on Marriage and the Family.* http://www.americananthro.org/ConnectWithAAA/Content.aspx?ItemNumber=2602.

American Psychiatric Association
　2013　*Diagnostic and Statistical Manual of Mental Disorders: DSM 5,* 5th ed. Washington, DC: American Psychiatric Association.

Amos, T. D.
　2011　*Embodying Difference: The Making of the Burakumin in Modern Japan.* Honolulu: University of Hawaii Press.

Anderson, B.
　2006　(orig. 1991) *Imagined Communities: Reflections on the Origin and Spread of Nationalism,* rev. ed. New York: Verso.

Anderson-Levitt, K. M., ed.
　2012　*Anthropologies of Education: A Global Guide to Ethnographic Studies of Learning and Schooling.* New York: Berghahn Books.

Anemone, R. L.
　2011　*Race and Human Diversity: A Biocultural Approach.* Upper Saddle River, NJ: Prentice Hall/Pearson.

Annenberg/CPB Exhibits
　2000　Collapse, Why Do Civilizations Fall? http://www.learner.org/exhibits/collapse/.

Ansell, A.
　2013　*Race and Ethnicity: The Key Concepts.* New York: Routledge.

Antoun, R. T.
　2008　*Understanding Fundamentalism: Christian, Islamic, and Jewish Movements,* 2nd ed. Lanham, MD: AltaMira.

Appadurai, A.
　1990　Disjuncture and Difference in the Global Cultural Economy. *Public Culture* 2(2): 1–24.
　1991　Global Ethnoscapes: Notes and Queries for a Transnational Anthropology. In *Recapturing Anthropology: Working in the Present,* R. G. Fox, ed. pp. 191–210. Santa Fe: School of American Research Advanced Seminar Series.

Appiah, K. A.
　1990　Racisms. In *Anatomy of Racism,* David Theo Goldberg, ed. pp. 3–17. Minneapolis: University of Minnesota Press.

Arens, W.
　1981　Professional Football: An American Symbol and Ritual. In *The American Dimension: Cultural Myths and Social Realities,* 2nd ed., W. Arens and S. P. Montague, eds. pp. 1–10. Sherman Oaks, CA: Alfred.

Arensberg, C.
　1987　Theoretical Contributions of Industrial and Development Studies. In *Applied Anthropology in America,* E. M. Eddy and W. L. Partridge, eds. New York: Columbia University Press.

Arnold, C.
　2015　New Clues on How and When Wolves Became Dogs. *National Geographic,* December 17. http://news.nationalgeographic.com/2015/12/151217-dogs-domestication-asia-china-genetics-animals-science/.

Arnold, J. E., et al.
　2012　*Life at Home in the Twenty-First Century: 32 Families Open Their Doors.* Los Angeles: Cotsen Institute of Archaeology Press.

Arrighi, G.
　2010　*The Long Twentieth Century: Money, Power, and the Origins of Our Times,* new and updated ed. New York: Verso.

Asad, T.
　2008　(orig. 1983) The Construction of Religion as an Anthropological Category. In *A Reader in the Anthropology of Religion,* M. Lambek, ed., pp. 110–226. Malden, MA: Blackwell.

Asfaw, B., T. White, and O. Lovejoy
　1999　*Australopithecus garhi:* A New Species of Early Hominid from Ethiopia. *Science* 284: 629.

Ashcroft, B., G. Griffiths, and H. Tiffin
　2013　*Postcolonial Studies: The Key Concepts,* 3rd ed. New York: Routledge, Taylor and Francis.

Askew, K. M., and R. R. Wilk, eds.
　2002　*The Anthropology of Media: A Reader.* Malden, MA: Oxford, Blackwell.

Avert.org
　2010　Global HIV and AIDS Epidemic. http://www.avert.org/global-hiv-aids-epidemic.htm.

Baer, H. A., M. Singer, and I. Susser
　2013　*Medical Anthropology and the World System,* 3rd ed. Santa Barbara, CA: Praeger.

Bailey, G., and P. Spikins, eds.
　2008　*Mesolithic Europe.* New York: Cambridge University Press.

Bailey, R. C., et al.
　1989　Hunting and Gathering in Tropical Rain Forests: Is It Possible? *American Anthropologist* 91: 59–82.

Balter, M.
　2010　Romanian Cave Art May Boast Central Europe's Oldest Cave Art. *Science Now,* June 21. http://news.sciencemag.org/sciencenow/2010/06/romanian-cave-may-boast-central.html.

Banton, M.
　2015　*What We Now Know about Race and Ethnicity.* New York: Berghahn Books.

Barfield, T. J.
　2010　*Afghanistan: A Cultural and Political History.* Princeton, NJ: Princeton University Press.

Barnaby, F., ed.
　1984　*Future War: Armed Conflict in the Next Decade.* London: M. Joseph.

Baro, M., and T. F. Deubel
　2006　Persistent Hunger: Perspectives on Vulnerability, Famine, and Food Security in Sub-Saharan Africa. *Annual Review of Anthropology* 35: 521–538.

Baron, D. E.
　2009　*A Better Pencil: Readers, Writers, and the Digital Revolution.* New York: Oxford University Press.
　2015　Singular They Is Word of the Year. The Web of Language, November 19. University of Illinois. https://illinois.edu/blog/view/25/280996.

Barth, F.

1968   (orig. 1958) Ecologic Relations of Ethnic Groups in Swat, North Pakistan. In *Man in Adaptation: The Cultural Present,* Yehudi Cohen, ed., pp. 324–331. Chicago: Aldine.

1969   *Ethnic Groups and Boundaries: The Social Organization of Cultural Difference.* London: Allen and Unwin.

Bartlett, B.

2010   America's Foreign Owned National Debt. *Forbes,* March 12. http://www.forbes.com/2010/03/11/treasury-securities-national-debt-chinatrade-opinions-columnists-bruce-Bartlett_print.html.

Barton, C. M., et al.

2011   Modeling Human Ecodynamics and Biocultural Interactions in the Late Pleistocene of Western Eurasia. *Human Ecology.* doi:10.1007/s10745-011-9433-8.

Bar-Yosef, O.

1987   Pleistocene Connections between Africa and Southwest Asia: An Archaeological Perspective. *African Archaeological Review* 5: 29–38.

Beall, C. M.

2014   Adaptation to High Altitudes: Phenotypes and Genotypes. *Annual Review of Anthropology* 43: 251–272.

Beck, S., and C. A. Maida, eds.

2013   *Toward Engaged Anthropology.* New York: Berghahn Books.

2015   *Public Anthropology in a Borderless World.* New York: Berghahn Books.

Becker, K.

2013   400 Research Chimpanzees to Be Retired. Healthy Pets, March 18. http://healthypets.mercola.com/sites/healthypets/archive/2013/03/18/research-chimpanzees.aspx.

Beckerman, S., and P. Valentine

2002   *Cultures of Multiple Fathers: The Theory and Practice of Partible Paternity in Lowland South America.* Gainesville: University of Florida Press.

Beckhouche, Y., et al.

2015   *The Global Gender Gap Report 2015.* Geneva, Switzerland: World Economic Forum.

Beeman, W.

1986   *Language, Status, and Power in Iran.* Bloomington: Indiana University Press.

Bellah, R. N.

1978   Religious Evolution. In *Reader in Comparative Religion: An Anthropological Approach,* 4th ed., W. A. Lessa and E. Z. Vogt, eds., pp. 36–50. New York: Harper & Row.

2011   *Religion in Human Evolution: From the Paleolithic to the Axial Age.* Cambridge, MA: Belknap Press of Harvard University Press.

Bellwood, P. S.

2005   *The First Farmers: Origins of Agricultural Societies.* Malden, MA: Blackwell.

Benazzi, S., et al.

2011   Early Dispersal of Modern Humans in Europe and Implications for Neanderthal Behaviour. *Nature* 479: 525–528. doi:10.1038/nature10617.

Benedict, R.

1940   *Race, Science and Politics.* New York: Modern Age Books.

1946   *The Chrysanthemum and the Sword.* Boston: Houghton Mifflin.

1959   (orig. 1934) *Patterns of Culture.* New York: New American Library.

Bennett, J. W.

1969   *Northern Plainsmen: Adaptive Strategy and Agrarian Life.* Chicago: Aldine.

Berdan, F. F.

2013   *Aztec Archaeology and Ethnohistory.* New York: Cambridge University Press.

Berger, P.

2010   Pentecostalism—Protestant Ethic or Cargo Cult? Peter Berger's blog, July 29. http://blogs.the-american-interest.com/berger/2010/07/29/pentecostalism-%E2%80%93-protestant-ethic-or-cargo-cult/.

Beriss, D.

2004   *Black Skins, French Voices: Caribbean Ethnicity and Activism in Urban France.* Boulder, CO: Westview Press.

Berlin, B. D., and P. Kay

1991   *Basic Color Terms: Their Universality and Evolution,* 2nd ed. Berkeley: University of California Press.

1999   *Basic Color Terms: Their Universality and Evolution.* Stanford, CA: Center for the Study of Language and Information.

Berna, F., et al.

2012   Microstratigraphic Evidence of in Situ Fire in the Acheulean Strata of Wonderwerk Cave, Northern Cape Province, South Africa. *Proceedings of the National Academy of Sciences.* doi:10.1073/pnas.1117620109.

Bernard, H. R.

2011   *Research Methods in Anthropology: Qualitative and Quantitative Methods,* 5th ed. Lanham, MD: AltaMira.

2013   *Social Science Research Methods: Qualitative and Quantitative Approaches,* 2nd ed. Los Angeles: Sage.

Bernard, H. R., and C. G. Gravlee, eds.

2014   *Handbook of Methods in Cultural Anthropology,* 2nd ed. Lanham, MD: Rowman & Littlefield.

Bettelheim, B.

1975   *The Uses of Enchantment: The Meaning and Importance of Fairy Tales.* New York: Vintage.

Bhanoo, S.

2015   Thigh Bone Suggests Ancient and Modern Humans Overlapped. *New York Times,* December 18. http://www.nytimes.com/2015/12/22/science/thigh-bone-suggests-ancient-and-modern-humans-overlapped.html?_r=0

Bielo, J. S.

2015   *Anthropology of Religion: The Basics.* New York: Routledge.

Bilefsky, D.

2006   Polygamy Fosters Culture Clashes (and Regrets) in Turkey. *New York Times,* July 10.

Binford, L. R.

1968   Post-Pleistocene Adaptations. In *New Perspectives in Archeology,* S. R. Binford and L. R. Binford, eds., pp. 313–341. Chicago: Aldine.

Bjuremalm, H.

1997   Rättvisa kan skipas i Rwanda: Folkmordet 1994 går att förklara och analysera på samma sätt som förintelsen av judarna. *Dagens Nyheter* [06-03-1997, p. B3].

Black, J.

2015   *The British Empire: A History and a Debate.* Burlington, VT: Ashgate.

Blackwood, E.

2010   *Falling into the Lesbi World: Desire and Difference in Indonesia.* Honolulu: University of Hawaii Press.

Blanton, R. E.

1999   *Ancient Oaxaca: The Monte Alban State.* New York: Cambridge University Press.

Boas, F.

1966   (orig. 1940) *Race, Language, and Culture.* New York: Free Press.

Bocquet-Appel, J.-P., and O. Bar-Yosef

2008   *The Neolithic Demographic Transition and Its Consequences.* New York: Springer.

Bodley, J. H.

2012   *Anthropology and Contemporary Human Problems,* 6th ed. Lanham, MD: AltaMira.

2015   *Victims of Progress,* 6th ed. Lanham, MD: Rowman & Littlefield.

Boellstorff, T., et al.

2012   *Ethnography and Virtual Worlds: A Handbook of Method.* Princeton, NJ: Princeton University Press.

Bohannan, P.

1971   Artist and Critic in an African Society. In *Anthropology and Art: Readings in Cross-Cultural Aesthetics,* C. Otten, ed., pp. 172–181. Austin: University of Texas Press.

Bono

2011   A Decade of Progress on AIDS. *New York Times,* November 30, p. 39. http://www.nytimes.com/2011/12/01/opinion/a-decade-of-progress-on-aids.html?scp=1&sq=bono%20world%20aids%20day&st=cse.

Bonvillain, N.

2007   *Women and Men: Cultural Constructs of Gender,* 4th ed. Upper Saddle River, NJ: Prentice Hall.

2012 *Language, Culture, and Communication: The Meaning of Messages,* 7th ed. Boston: Pearson Prentice Hall.

2016 *The Routledge Handbook of Linguistic Anthropology.* New York: Routledge.

Borneman, J., and L.K. Hart

2015 The Institution of Marriage Our Society Needs: Anthropological Investigations over the Last Century Have Shown that Marriage is an Elastic Institution. *Aljazeera America,* July 12. http://america.aljazeera.com/opinions/2015/7/the-institution-of-marriage-our-society-needs.html.

Borofsky, R.

2000 Public Anthropology: Where To? What Next? *Anthropology Newsletter* 41(5): 9–10.

Borofsky, R., and S. Hutson

2016 Maybe "Doing No Harm" Is Not the Best Way to Help Those Who Helped You. *Anthropology News* 57(1-2): 29.

Bouckaert, R., et al.

2012 Mapping the Origins and Expansion of the Indo-European Language Family. *Science* 337: 957–960.

Bourdieu, P.

1977 *Outline of a Theory of Practice.* Translated by Richard Nice. Cambridge, UK: Cambridge University Press.

1982 *Ce Que Parler Veut Dire.* Paris: Fayard.

1984 *Distinction: A Social Critique of the Judgment of Taste.* Translated by R. Nice. Cambridge, MA: Harvard University Press.

Bourque, S. C., and K. B. Warren

1987 Technology, Gender and Development. *Daedalus* 116(4): 173–197.

Bowen, J. R.

2014 *Religion in Practice: An Approach to Anthropology of Religion,* 6th ed. Boston: Pearson/Allyn and Bacon.

Bower, B.

2013 Fossils Point to Ancient Ape-Monkey Split. *Science News* 183(12): 9. http://www.sciencenews.org/view/generic/id/350410/description/Fossils_point_to_ancient_ape-monkey_split.

Bowie, F.

2006 *The Anthropology of Religion: An Introduction.* Malden, MA: Blackwell.

Bowler, J. M., et al.

2003 New Ages for Human Occupation and Climatic Change at Lake Mungo, Australia. *Nature* 421: 837–840.

Brace, C. L.

2005 *"Race" Is a Four-Letter Word: The Genesis of the Concept.* New York: Oxford University Press.

Bradley, B. J., et al.

2004 Dispersed Male Networks in Western Gorillas. *Current Biology* 14: 510–513.

Braidwood, R. J.

1975 *Prehistoric Men,* 8th ed. Glenview, IL: Scott, Foresman.

Braudel, F.

1981 *Civilization and Capitalism, 15th–18th Century.* Volume I: *The Structure of Everyday Life: The Limits.* Translated by S. Reynolds. New York: Harper & Row.

1982 *Civilization and Capitalism, 15th–18th Century.* Volume II: *The Wheels of Commerce.* New York: HarperCollins.

1992 *Civilization and Capitalism, 15th–18th Century.* Volume III: *The Perspective of the World.* Berkeley: University of California Press.

Brenneis, D.

1988 Language and Disputing. *Annual Review of Anthropology* 17: 221–237.

Brettell, C. B., and C. F. Sargent, eds.

2012 *Gender in Cross-Cultural Perspective,* 6th ed. Upper Saddle River, NJ: Pearson/Prentice Hall.

Briggs, C. L.

2005 Communicability, Racial Discourse, and Disease. *Annual Review of Anthropology* 34: 269–291.

Briody, E. K., R. T. Trotter II, and T. L. Meerwarth

2010 *Transforming Culture: Creating and Sustaining a Better Manufacturing Organization.* New York: Palgrave Macmillan.

Brooke, J.

1992 Rio's New Day in Sun Leaves Laplander Limp. *New York Times,* June 1, p. A7.

Brookings Institution

2010 *State of Metropolitan America: On the Front Lines of Demographic Transition.* The Brookings Institution Metropolitan Policy Program. http://www.brookings.edu/~/media/Files/Programs/Metro/state_of_metro_america/metro_america_report1.pdf.

Brower, B., and B. R. Johnston

2007 *Disappearing Peoples? Indigenous Groups and Ethnic Minorities in South and Central Asia.* Walnut Creek, CA: Left Coast Press.

Brown, A.

2001 Communism. *International Encyclopedia of the Social & Behavioral Sciences,* pp. 2323–2326. New York: Elsevier.

Brown, M. F.

2003 *Who Owns Native Culture?* Cambridge, MA: Harvard University Press.

Brown, P. J., and R. L. Barrett

2010 *Understanding and Applying Medical Anthropology,* 2nd ed. New York: McGraw-Hill.

Brownstein, R.

2010 The Gray and the Brown: The Generational Mismatch. *National Journal,* July 24. http://www.nationaljournal.com/njmagazines/cs_20100724_3946php.

Bryant, V. M.

1999 Review of Piperno, D. R., and D. M. Pearsall, *The Origins of Agriculture in the Lowland Neotropics.* Bryant, V. M. (1998), *North American Archaeologist* 26: 245–246.

2003 Invisible Clues to New World Domestication. *Science* February 14, 299(5609): 1029–1030.

2007a Artifact: Maize Pollen. *Archaeology* 60(4). www.archaeology.org/0707/etc/artifact.html.

2007b Little Things Mean a Lot: The Search for Starch Grains at Archaeological Sites. *Mammoth Trumpet* 22(4): 3–4, 16.

2013 Please Don't Wash the Artifacts. *General Anthropology* 20(2): 1–7.

Buettner, E.

2016 *Europe after Empire: Decolonization, Society, and Culture.* Cambridge, UK: Cambridge University Press.

Buikstra, J. E., and L. A. Beck

2006 *Bioarchaeology: The Contextual Analysis of Human Remains.* New York: Academic Press.

Buikstra, J. E., and C. A. Roberts, eds.

2012 *The Global History of Paleopathology; Pioneers and Prospects.* New York: Oxford University Press.

Burawoy, M.

2000 Introduction. *Global Ethnography: Forces, Connections, and Imaginations in a Postmodern World.* Berkeley: University of California Press.

Burbank, J., and F. Cooper

2010 *Empires in World History: Power and the Politics of Difference.* Princeton, NJ: Princeton University Press.

Burbank, V. K.

1988 *Aboriginal Adolescence: Maidenhood in an Australian Community.* New Brunswick, NJ: Rutgers University Press.

Burdick, J.

1993 *Looking for God in Brazil: The Progressive Catholic Church in Urban Brazil's Religious Arena.* Berkeley: University of California Press.

1998 *Blessed Anastácia: Women, Race, and Popular Christianity in Brazil.* New York: Routledge.

Burger, J., et al.

2007 Absence of the Lactase-Persistence Associated Allele in Early Neolithic Europeans. *Proceedings of the National Academy of Sciences* 104(10): 3736–3741.

Burke, H., et al.

2008 *Kennewick Man: Perspectives on the Ancient One.* Walnut Creek, CA: Left Coast Press.

Burley, D. V., and W. R. Dickinson

2001 Origin and Significance of a Founding Settlement in Polynesia. *Proceedings of the National Academy of Sciences* 98: 11829–11831.

Burling, R.

1970 *Man's Many Voices: Language in Its Cultural Context.* New York: Harcourt Brace Jovanovich.

Burt, B.
2013 *World Art: An Introduction to the Art in Artefacts.* New York: Bloomsbury.

Butler, J.
2015 *Notes Toward a Performative Theory of Assembly.* Cambridge: Harvard University Press.
1990 *Gender Trouble: Feminism and the Subversion of Identity.* New York: Routledge.
1988 Performative Acts and Gender Constitution: An Essay in Phenomenology and Feminist Theory. *Theatre Journal* 40(4): 519-531.

Byers, S. N.
2011 *Introduction to Forensic Anthropology,* 4th ed. Boston: Prentice Hall.

Cairns, M. F.
2015 *Shifting Cultivation and Environmental Change: Indigenous People, Agriculture and Forest Conservation.* New York: Routledge.

Callaway, E.
2011 Ancient DNA Reveals Secrets of Human History. *Nature* 476: 136–137.

Cambridge, University of
2015 Millet: The Missing Piece in the Puzzle of Prehistoric Humans' Transition from Hunter-Gatherers to Farmers. *Research News,* December 14. http://www.cam.ac.uk/research/news/millet-the-missing-piece-in-the-puzzle-of-prehistoric-humans-transition-from-hunter-gatherers-to-farmers.

Cameron, N., and B. Bogin, eds.
2012 *Human Growth and Development,* 2nd ed. London: Elsevier/AP.

Campbell, C. J., ed.
2011 *Primates in Perspective,* 2nd ed. New York: Oxford University Press.

Cann, R. L., M. Stoneking, and A. C. Wilson
1987 Mitochondrial DNA and Human Evolution. *Nature* 325: 31–36.

Carballo, D. M.
2016 *Urbanization and Religion in Ancient Central Mexico.* New York: Oxford University Press.

Carey, B.
2007 Washoe, a Chimp of Many Words Dies at 42. *New York Times,* November 1.

Carneiro, R. L.
1956 Slash-and-Burn Agriculture: A Closer Look at Its Implications for Settlement Patterns. In *Men and Cultures,* Selected Papers of the Fifth International Congress of Anthropological and Ethnological Sciences, pp. 229–234. Philadelphia: University of Pennsylvania Press.
1968 (orig. 1961) Slash-and-Burn Cultivation among the Kuikuru and Its Implications for Cultural Development in the Amazon Basin. In *Man in Adaptation: The Cultural Present,* Y. A. Cohen, ed., pp. 131–145. Chicago: Aldine.
1970 A Theory of the Origin of the State. *Science* 69: 733–738.
1990 Chiefdom-Level Warfare as Exemplified in Fiji and the Cauca Valley. In *The Anthropology of War,* J. Haas, ed., pp. 190–211. Cambridge, UK: Cambridge University Press.
1991 The Nature of the Chiefdom as Revealed by Evidence from the Cauca Valley of Colombia. In *Profiles in Cultural Evolution,* A. T. Rambo and K. Gillogly, eds., *Anthropological Papers* 85, pp. 167–190. Ann Arbor: University of Michigan Museum of Anthropology.

Carrier, J. G., ed.
2012 *A Handbook of Economic Anthropology.* Cheltenham, UK: Edward Elgar.
2016 *After the Crisis: Anthropological Thought, Neoliberalism and the Aftermath.* New York: Routledge.

Carter, J.
1988 Freed from Keepers and Cages, Chimps Come of Age on Baboon Island. *Smithsonian,* June, pp. 36–48.

Casanova, J.
2001 Religion, the New Millennium, and Globalization. *Sociology of Religion* 62: 415–441.

Caspari, R., and S.-H. Lee
2004 Older Age Becomes Common Late in Human Evolution. *Proceedings of the National Academy of Sciences* 101(30): 10895–10900.

Caulkins, D., and A. T. Jordan
2013 *A Companion to Organizational Anthropology.* Malden, MA: Wiley-Blackwell.

Cernea, M. M., ed.
1991 *Putting People First: Sociological Variables in Rural Development,* 2nd ed. New York: Oxford University Press (published for the World Bank).

Ceuppens, B., and P. Geschiere
2005 Autochthony: Local or Global? New Modes in the Struggle over Citizenship and Belonging in Africa and Europe. *Annual Review of Anthropology* 34: 385–407.

Chagnon, N. A.
1997 *Yanomamö,* 5th ed. Fort Worth: Harcourt Brace.
2013 *Noble Savages: My Life among Two Dangerous Tribes—the Yanomamo and the Anthropologists.* New York: Simon & Schuster.

Chambers, E.
1987 Applied Anthropology in the Post-Vietnam Era: Anticipations and Ironies. *Annual Review of Anthropology* 16: 309–337.

Chapais, B.
2008 *Primeval Kinship: How Pair Bonding Gave Birth to Human Society.* Cambridge, MA: Harvard University Press.

Chatterjee, P.
2004 *The Politics of the Governed: Reflections on Popular Politics in Most of the World.* New York: Columbia University Press.

Cheney, D. L., and R. M. Seyfarth
1990 In the Minds of Monkeys: What Do They Know and How Do They Know It? *Natural History,* September, pp. 38–46.

Chibnik, M.
2011 *Anthropology, Economics, and Choice.* Austin: University of Texas Press.

Childe, V. G.
1950 The Urban Revolution, *Town Planning Review* 21: 3–17.
1951 *Man Makes Himself.* New York: New American Library.

Choi, C. Q.
2011 Savanna, Not Forest, Was Human Ancestors' Proving Ground. *Live Science,* August 3. http://www.livescience.com/15377-savannas-human-ancestors-evolution.html.

Chomsky, N.
1955 *Syntactic Structures.* The Hague: Mouton.

Chua, A.
2011 *Battle Hymn of the Tiger Mother.* New York: Penguin.

Ciochon, R. L., and J. G. Fleagle, eds.
2012 *Primate Evolution and Human Origin.* New Brunswick, NJ: Transaction.

Ciochon, R. L., J. Olsen, and J. James
1990 *Other Origins: The Search for the Giant Ape in Human Prehistory.* New York: Bantam Books.

Clark, G.
2010 *African Market Women: Seven Life Stories from Ghana.* Indianapolis: Indiana University Press.

Clayton, S. C.
2013 Measuring the Long Arm of the State: Teotihuacan's Relations in the Basin of Mexico. *Ancient Mesoamerica* 24(1): 87–105.

Coburn, N.
2011 *Bazaar Politics: Power and Pottery in an Afghan Market Town.* Stanford, CA: Stanford University Press.

Cody, D.
1998 British Empire. http://www.victorianweb.org/.

Cohen, J. H.
2015 *Eating Soup without a Spoon: Anthropological Theory and Method in the Real World.* Austin: University of Texas Press.

Cohen, M. N., and G. J. Armelagos
2013 *Paleopathology at the Origins of Agriculture,* 2nd ed. Gainesville: University of Florida Press.

Cohen, P.
2008 The Pentagon Enlists Social Scientists to Study Security Issues. *New York Times,* June 18.

Cohen, R.
1967   *The Kanuri of Bornu.* New York: Harcourt Brace Jovanovich.

Cohen, Y. A.
1974   Culture as Adaptation. In *Man in Adaptation: The Cultural Present,* 2nd ed., Y. A. Cohen, ed., pp. 45–68. Chicago: Aldine.

Colson, E., and T. Scudder
1975   New Economic Relationships between the Gwembe Valley and the Line of Rail. In *Town and Country in Central and Eastern Africa,* David Parkin, ed., pp. 190–210. London: Oxford University Press.
1988   *For Prayer and Profit: The Ritual, Economic, and Social Importance of Beer in Gwembe District, Zambia, 1950–1982.* Stanford, CA: Stanford University Press.

Conard, N. J.
2011   *Neanderthal Lifeways, Subsistence, and Technology.* New York: Springer.

Connah, G.
2016   *African Civilizations: An Archaeological Perspective,* 3rd ed. New York: Cambridge University Press.

Cooper, F.
2014   *Africa in the World: Capitalism, Empire, Nation-State.* Cambridge, MA: Harvard University Press.

Coronel-Molina, S. M., and T. L. McCarty
2016   *Indigenous Language Revitalization in the Americas.* New York: Routledge.

Council of Economic Advisers
2014   Nine Facts about American Families and Work. Executive Office of the President of the United States. https://www.whitehouse.gov/sites/default/files/docs/nine_facts_about_family_and_work_real_final.pdf.

Cowgill, G. L.
2008   Teotihuacan as an Urban Place. In *Urbanism in Mesoamerica,* vol. 2, R. H. Cobean, A. G. Mastache, Á. C. Cook, and K. G. Hirth, eds., pp. 85–112. University Park: Pennsylvania State University.
2013   Possible Migrations and Shifting Identities in the Central Mexican Epiclassic. *Ancient Mesoamerica* 24(1): 131–149.

Coy, P.
2014   The Richest Rich Are in a Class by Themselves. Bloomberg News, April 14, 2014. http://www.bloomberg.com/news/articles/2014-04-03/top-tenth-of-1-percenters-reaps-all-the-riches.

Craig, O.
2013   Earliest Evidence for the Use of Pottery. *Nature* 496: 351–354. http://www.nature.com/nature/journal/v496/n7445/full/nature12109.html.

Crapo, R. H.
2003   *Anthropology of Religion: The Unity and Diversity of Religions.* New York: McGraw-Hill.

Crenson, M.
2000   Music—from the Heart or from the Genes. http://www.cis.vt.edu/modernworld/d/musicgenes.html.

Crewe, E., and R. Axelby
2013   *Anthropology and Development: Culture, Morality and Politics in a Globalised World.* Cambridge, UK: Cambridge University Press.

Cribb, J.
2010   *The Coming Famine: The Global Food Crisis and What We Can Do to Avoid It.* Berkeley: University of California Press.

Crick, F. H. C.
1968   (orig. 1962) The Genetic Code. In *The Molecular Basis of Life: An Introduction to Molecular Biology, Readings from Scientific American,* pp. 198–205. San Francisco: W. H. Freeman.

Crosby, A. W., Jr.
2003   *The Columbian Exchange: Biological and Cultural Consequences of 1492.* Westport, CT: Praeger.

Cultural Survival Quarterly
1989   Quarterly journal. Cambridge, MA: Cultural Survival.

Cummings, V., P. Jordan, and M. Zvelebil, eds.
2014   *The Oxford Handbook of the Archaeology and Anthropology of Hunter-Gatherers.* Oxford, UK: Oxford University Press.

Curnoe, D., et al.
2012   Human Remains from the Pleistocene-Holocene Transition of Southwest China Suggest a Complex Evolutionary History for East Asians. *PLOS ONE Online,* March 14. http://www.plosone.org/article/info%3Adoi%2F10.1371%2Fjournal.pone.0031918.

Curry, A.
2009   Climate Change: Sites in Peril. *Archaeology* 62(2). http://archive.archaeology.org/0903/etc/climate_change.html.

Dagne, T. W.
2015   *Intellectual Property and Traditional Knowledge in the Global Economy: Translating Geographical Indications for Development.* New York: Routledge.

Dalton, G., ed.
1967   *Tribal and Peasant Economies.* Garden City, NY: Natural History Press.

Dalton, R.
2006   Ethiopia: Awash with Fossils. *Nature* 439: 14-16. http://www.nature.com/news/2006/060102/full/439014a.html.

DaMatta, R.
1991   *Carnivals, Rogues, and Heroes: An Interpretation of the Brazilian Dilemma.* Translated from the Portuguese by John Drury. Notre Dame, IN: University of Notre Dame Press.

D'Andrade, R.
1984   Cultural Meaning Systems. In *Culture Theory: Essays on Mind, Self, and Emotion,* R. A. Shweder and R. A. Levine, eds., pp. 88–119. Cambridge, UK: Cambridge University Press.

Darnell, R., and F. W. Gleach, eds.
2014   *Anthropologists and Their Traditions across National Borders.* Lincoln: University of Nebraska Press.

Darwin, C.
2009   (orig. 1859) *On the Origin of Species.* Alachua, FL: Bridge-Logos.

Das, V., and D. Poole, eds.
2004   *Anthropology in the Margins of the State.* Santa Fe, NM: School of American Research Press.

Davenport, C., and J. Haner
2015   The Marshall Islands Are Disappearing. *New York Times,* December 1. http://www.nytimes.com/interactive/2015/12/02/world/The-Marshall-Islands-Are-Disappearing.html?_r=0.

Day, E.
2015   #BlackLivesMatter: The Birth of a New Civil Rights Movement. *The Guardian,* July 19. http://www.theguardian.com/world/2015/jul/19/blacklivesmatter-birth-civil-rights-movement.

Degler, C.
1970   *Neither Black nor White: Slavery and Race Relations in Brazil and the United States.* New York: Macmillan.

de la Peña, G.
2005   Social and Cultural Policies toward Indigenous Peoples: Perspectives from Latin America. *Annual Review of Anthropology* 34: 717–739.

De Leon, J.
2015   *The Land of Open Graves: Living and Dying on the Migrant Trail.* Oakland: University of California Press.

deLumley, H.
1976   (orig. 1969) A Paleolithic Camp at Nice. In *Avenues to Antiquity, Readings from Scientific American,* B. M. Fagan, ed., pp. 36–44. San Francisco: W. H. Freeman.

Dembski, W. A.
2004   *The Design Revolution: Answering the Toughest Questions about Intelligent Design.* Downers Grove, IL: InterVarsity Press.

Demeter, F., et al.
2012   Anatomically Modern Humans in Southeast Asia (Laos) by 46 ka. *Proceedings of the National Academy of Sciences,* 109(36): 14375–14380.

DeNavas-Walt, C., and B. D. Proctor
2015   *Income and Poverty in the United States: 2014.* U.S. Census Bureau, Current Population Reports, P60-252. Washington, DC: U.S. Government Printing Office. https://www.census.gov/content/dam/Census/library/publications/2015/demo/p60-252.pdf.

Denny, R. M., and P. L. Sunderland, eds.
 2014 *Handbook of Anthropology in Business.* Walnut Creek, CA: Left Coast Press.

Dentan, R. K.
 1979 *The Semai: A Nonviolent People of Malaya,* fieldwork edition. New York: Harcourt Brace.
 2008 *Overwhelming Terror: Love, Fear, Peace and Violence among the Semai of Malaysia.* Lanham, MD: Rowman & Littlefield.

Descartes, L., and C. P. Kottak
 2009 *Media and Middle-Class Moms.* New York: Routledge.

De Vos, G. A., and H. Wagatsuma
 1966 *Japan's Invisible Race: Caste in Culture and Personality.* Berkeley: University of California Press.

de Waal, F. B. M.
 1995 Bonobo Sex and Society: The Behavior of a Close Relative Challenges Assumptions about Male Supremacy in Human Evolution. *Scientific American,* March, pp. 82–88.
 1997 *Bonobo: The Forgotten Ape.* Berkeley: University of California Press.
 1998 *Chimpanzee Politics: Power and Sex among Apes.* Baltimore: Johns Hopkins University Press.

Diamond, J. M.
 1990 A Pox upon Our Genes. *Natural History,* February, pp. 26–30.
 1997 *Guns, Germs, and Steel: The Fates of Human Societies.* New York: W. W. Norton.
 2005 (orig. 1997) *Guns, Germs, and Steel: The Fates of Human Societies.* New York: W. W. Norton.

Dickau, R. A. J. Ranere, and R. G. Cooke
 2007 Starch Grain Evidence for the Preceramic Dispersals of Maize and Root Crops into Tropical Dry and Humid Forests of Panama. *Proceedings of the National Academy of Sciences of the United States of America* 104(9): 3651–3656. http://www.pnas.org/cgi/content/full/104/9/3651.

Di Leonardo, M., ed.
 1991 *Gender at the Crossroads of Knowledge: Feminist Anthropology in the Postmodern Era.* Berkeley: University of California Press.

DiMento, J. F. C., and P. Doughman
 2014 *Climate Change: What It Means for Us, Our Children, and Our Grandchildren.* Cambridge, MA: MIT Press.

Divale, W. T., and M. Harris
 1976 Population, Warfare, and the Male Supremacist Complex. *American Anthropologist* 78: 521–538.

Donham, D. L.
 2011 *Violence in a Time of Liberation: Murder and Ethnicity at a South African Gold Mine, 1994.* Durham, NC: Duke University Press.

Donovan, J. M.
 2007 *Legal Anthropology: An Introduction.* Lanham, MD: Rowman & Littlefield.

Dorward, D. C., ed.
 1983 *The Igbo "Women's War" of 1929: Documents Relating to the Aba Riots in Eastern Nigeria.* Wakefield, UK: East Ardsley.

Douglas, M.
 1970a *Natural Symbols: Explorations in Cosmology.* London: Barrie and Rockliff, The Crescent Press.
 1970b *Purity and Danger: An Analysis of Concepts of Pollution and Taboo.* Harmondsworth, UK: Penguin.

Dove, M. R., P. E. Sajise, and A. A. Doolittle, eds.
 2011 *Beyond the Sacred Forest: Complicating Conservation in Southeast Asia.* Durham, NC: Duke University Press.

Doyle, C. M.
 2015 *Indigenous Peoples, Title to Territory, Rights, and Resources: The Transformative Role of Free Prior and Informed Consent.* New York: Routledge.

Drahos, P.
 2014 *Intellectual Property, Indigenous People, and Their Knowledge.* Cambridge, UK: Cambridge University Press.

Dressler, W. W., K. S. Oths, and C. C. Gravlee
 2005 Race and Ethnicity in Public Health Research. *Annual Review of Anthropology* 34: 231–252.

Duffield, M., and V. Hewitt, eds.
 2009 *Empire, Development, and Colonialism: The Past in the Present.* Rochester, NY: James Currey.

Dunham, S. A.
 2009 *Surviving Against the Odds: Village Industry in Indonesia.* Durham, NC: Duke University Press.

Dunham, W.
 2016 Diminutive 'Hobbit' People Vanished Earlier than Previously Known. Reuters, March 30. http://www.reuters.com/articles/us-science-hobbit-idUSKCN0WW2EH.

Dunn, J. S.
 2000 *The Impact of Media on Reproductive Behavior in Northeastern Brazil.* Ph.D. dissertation, Department of Anthropology, University of Michigan, Ann Arbor.

Duranti, A., ed.
 2009 *Linguistic Anthropology: A Reader.* Malden, MA: Wiley-Blackwell.

Durkheim, E.
 1951 (orig. 1897) *Suicide: A Study in Sociology.* Glencoe, IL: Free Press.
 2001 (orig. 1912) *The Elementary Forms of the Religious Life.* Translated by Carol Cosman. Abridged with an introduction and notes by Mark S. Cladis. New York: Oxford University Press.

Dürr, E., and R. Jaffe, eds.
 2010 *Urban Pollution: Cultural Meanings, Social Practices.* New York: Berghahn Books.

Earle, T. K.
 1987 Chiefdoms in Archaeological and Ethnohistorical Perspective. *Annual Review of Anthropology* 16: 279–308.
 1997 *How Chiefs Come to Power: The Political Economy in Prehistory.* Stanford, CA: Stanford University Press.

Eckert, P.
 1989 *Jocks and Burnouts: Social Categories and Identity in the High School.* New York: Teachers College Press, Columbia University.
 2000 *Linguistic Variation as Social Practice: The Linguistic Construction of Identity in Belten High.* Malden, MA: Blackwell.

Eckert, P., and S. McConnell-Ginet
 2013 *Language and Gender,* 2nd ed. Cambridge, UK: Cambridge University Press.

Eckert, P., and N. Mendoza-Denton
 2002 Getting Real in the Golden State. *Language,* March 29. http://www.pbs.org/speak/seatosea/americanvarieties/californian/.

Edelman, M., and A. Haugerud
 2005 *The Anthropology of Development and Globalization: From Classical Political Economy to Contemporary Neoliberalism.* Malden, MA: Blackwell.

Edgar, H. J. H., and K. L. Hunley
 2009 Race Reconciled: How Biological Anthropologists View Human Variation. *American Journal of Physical Anthropology* 139(1): 1–4.

Edwards, J.
 2013 *Sociolinguistics: A Very Short Introduction.* New York: Oxford University Press.

Egan, T.
 2005 A Skeleton Moves from the Courts to the Laboratory. *New York Times,* July 19.

Eldred, S. M.
 2013 Chimp Research Curtailed: Will Science Suffer? *Discovery News,* January 23. http://news.discovery.com/animals/zooanimals/chimp-research-curtailed-will-science-suffer-130123.htm.

Eldredge, N.
 2014 *Extinction and Evolution: What Fossils Reveal about the History of Life.* Buffalo, NY: Firefly Books.
 2015 *Eternal Ephemera: Adaptation and the Origin of Species, from the Nineteenth Century through Punctuated Equilibria.* New York: Columbia University Press.

Eldredge, N., and S. Pearson
 2010 *Charles Darwin and the Mystery of Mysteries.* New York: Rb Flash Point/Roaring Brook Press.

Ellen, R., S. J. Lycett, and S. E. Johns, eds.
 2013 *Understanding Cultural Transmission in Anthropology: A Critical Synthesis.* New York: Berghahn.

Ellick, C. J., and J. E. Watkins
 2011 *The Anthropology Graduate's Guide: From Student to a Career.* Walnut Creek, CA: Left Coast Press.

Elson, C.

2007   *Excavations at Cerro Tilcajete: A Monte Alban II Administrative Center in the Valley of Oaxaca.* Memoir 42 of the Museum of Anthropology, University of Michigan, Ann Arbor.

Ember, M., and C. R. Ember

1997   Science in Anthropology. In *The Teaching of Anthropology: Problems, Issues, and Decisions,* C. P. Kottak, J. J. White, R. H. Furlow, and P. C. Rice, eds., pp. 29–33. Mountain View, CA: Mayfield.

Entmacher, J., et al.

2013   *Insecure and Unequal: Poverty and Income among Women and Families 2000–2012.* Washington, DC: National Women's Law Center. http://www.nwlc.org/resource/insecure-unequal-poverty-among-women-and-families-2000-2012.

Erickson, J.

2016   Minority, Low-Income Neighborhoods Targeted for Hazardous Waste. University of Michigan, *The University Record,* January 20.

Erickson, P. A., and L. D. Murphy

2013   *A History of Anthropological Theory,* 4th ed. Toronto: University of Toronto Press.

Eriksen, T. H.

2014   *Globalization: The Key Concepts,* 2nd ed. New York: Bloomsbury Academic.

Errington, F., and D. Gewertz

1987   *Cultural Alternatives and a Feminist Anthropology: An Analysis of Culturally Constructed Gender Interests in Papua New Guinea.* New York: Cambridge University Press.

Ervin, A. M.

2005   *Applied Anthropology: Tools and Perspectives for Contemporary Practice,* 2nd ed. Boston: Pearson/Allyn & Bacon.

2014   *Cultural Transformation and Globalization: Theory, Development and Social Change.* Boulder, CO: Paradigm.

Escobar, A.

2012   *Encountering Development: The Making and Unmaking of the Third World.* Princeton, NJ: Princeton University Press.

Evans-Pritchard, E. E.

1940   *The Nuer: A Description of the Modes of Livelihood and Political Institutions of a Nilotic People.* Oxford: Clarendon Press.

1970   Sexual Inversion among the Azande. *American Anthropologist* 72: 1428–1433.

Ezekiel, E.

2011   Foreign Aid Is Not a Rathole. *New York Times,* November 30. http://opinionator.blogs.nytimes.com/2011/11/30/foreign-aid-is-not-a-rathole/?scp=3&sq=ezekiel%20emanuel%20december%201&st=cse.

Fagan, B. M.

1996   *World Prehistory: A Brief Introduction,* 3rd ed. New York: HarperCollins.

2010   *Cro-Magnon: How the Ice Age Gave Birth to the First Modern Humans.* New York: Bloomsbury.

Fairbanks, D. J.

2015   *Everyone Is African: How Science Explodes the Myth of Race.* New York: Prometheus Books.

Fairclough, N.

2015   *Language and Power.* New York: Routledge.

Fasold, R. W., and J. Connor-Linton.

2014   *An Introduction to Language and Linguistics.* New York: Cambridge University Press.

Fearon, J. D.

2003   Ethnic and Cultural Diversity by Country. *Journal of Economic Growth* 8(2): 195–222.

Feder, K. L.

2014   *Frauds, Myths, and Mysteries: Science and Pseudoscience in Archaeology,* 8th ed. New York: McGraw-Hill.

Fedorak, S.

2014   *Global Issues: A Cross-Cultural Perspective.* Toronto: University of Toronto Press.

Ferguson, D.

2015   First Black Player on PGA Tour Dies. *Associated Press, Post and Courier.* Charleston, SC, February 5.

Ferguson, R. B.

1995   *Yanomami Warfare: A Political History.* Santa Fe, NM: School of American Research Press.

Ferraro, G. P., and E. K. Briody

2013   *The Cultural Dimension of International Business,* 7th ed. Boston: Pearson.

Ferraro, J. V., et al.

2013   Earliest Archaeological Evidence of Persistent Hominin Carnivory. *PLOS ONE Online,* April 5. http://www.plosone.org/article/info%3Adoi%2F10.1371%2Fjournal.pone.0062174.

Feuer, J.

2012   The Clutter Culture, *UCLA Magazine Online,* July 1, 2012. http://magazine.ucla.edu/features/the-clutter-culture/.

Finnstrom, S.

1997   Postcoloniality and the Postcolony: Theories of the Global and the Local. http://www.postcolonialweb.org/.

Fiske, J.

2011   *Reading the Popular,* 2nd ed. New York: Routledge.

Fiske, J., and J. Hartley

2003   *Reading Television,* 2nd ed. New York: Routledge.

Flannery, K. V.

1969   Origins and Ecological Effects of Early Domestication in Iran and the Near East. In *The Domestication and Exploitation of Plants and Animals,* P. J. Ucko and G. W. Dimbleby, eds., pp. 73–100. Chicago: Aldine.

1973   The Origins of Agriculture. *Annual Review of Anthropology* 2: 271–310.

1986   *Guila Naquitz: Archaic Foraging and Early Agriculture in Oaxaca, Mexico.* Orlando, FL: Academic Press.

1999   Chiefdoms in the Early Near East: Why It's So Hard to Identify Them. In *The Iranian World: Essays on Iranian Art and Archaeology,* A. Alizadeh, Y. Majidzadeh, and S. M. Shahmirzadi, eds. Tehran: Iran University Press.

Flannery, K. V., and J. Marcus

2000   Formative Mexican Chiefdoms and the Myth of the "Mother Culture." *Journal of Anthropological Archaeology* 19: 1–37.

2003a   *The Cloud People: Divergent Evolution of the Zapotec and Mixtec Civilizations.* Clinton Corners, NY: Percheron Press.

2003b   The Origin of War: New 14C Dates from Ancient Mexico. *Proceedings of the National Academy of Sciences of the United States of America,* 100(20): 11801–11805.

2012   *The Creation of Inequality: How Our Prehistoric Ancestors Set the Stage for Monarchy, Slavery, and Empire.* Cambridge: Harvard University Press.

Flannery, K. V., J. Marcus, and R. G. Reynolds

1989   *The Flocks of the Wamani: A Study of Llama Herders on the Punas of Ayacucho, Peru.* San Diego: Academic Press.

Fleagle, J. G.

2013   *Primate Adaptation and Evolution,* 3rd ed. San Diego, CA: Elsevier.

Fleisher, M. L.

2000   *Kuria Cattle Raiders: Violence and Vigilantism on the Tanzania/Kenya Frontier.* Ann Arbor: University of Michigan Press.

Fluehr-Lobban, C.

2013   *Ethics and Anthropology: Ideas and Practice.* Lanham, MD: AltaMira.

Ford, C. S., and F. A. Beach

1951   *Patterns of Sexual Behavior.* New York: Harper Torchbooks.

Fortes, M.

1950   Kinship and Marriage among the Ashanti. In *African Systems of Kinship and Marriage,* A. R. Radcliffe-Brown and D. Forde, eds., pp. 252–284. London: Oxford University Press.

Fortier, J.

2009   The Ethnography of South Asian Foragers. *Annual Review of Anthropology* 39: 99–114.

Fossey, D.

1983   *Gorillas in the Mist.* Boston: Houghton Mifflin.

Foster, G. M., and B. G. Anderson

1978   *Medical Anthropology.* New York: McGraw-Hill.

Foucault, M.

1979   *Discipline and Punish: The Birth of the Prison.*
Translated by Alan Sheridan. New York: Vintage Books,
University Press.

1990   *The History of Sexuality,* vol. 2, *The Use of Pleasure.*
Translated by R. Hurley. New York: Vintage.

Foundation for AIDS Research

2015   Statistics: Worldwide. http://www.amfar.org/world-
wide-aids-stats/.

Fouts, R.

1997   *Next of Kin: What Chimpanzees Have Taught Me
about Who We Are.* New York: William Morrow.

Fowler, C.

2015   *The Oxford Handbook of Neolithic Europe.* New
York: Oxford University Press.

Fowler, C. S., and D. D. Fowler, eds.

2008   *The Great Basin: People and Place in Ancient Times.*
Santa Fe, NM: School for Advanced Research Press.

Fowler, S.

2011   Into the Stone Age with a Scalpel: A Dig with Clues
on Early Urban Life. *New York Times,* September 7. http://
www.nytimes.com/2011/09/08/world/europe/08iht-M08C-
TURKEY-DIG.html?pagewanted=all.

Free Dictionary

2004   Honorific (definition of). http://encyclopedia.thefree-
dictionary.com/Honorific.

Freilich, M., D. Raybeck, and J. Savishinsky

1991   *Deviance: Anthropological Perspectives.* Westport,
CT: Bergin and Garvey.

Freston, P., ed.

2008   *Evangelical Christianity and Democracy in Latin
America.* New York: Oxford University Press.

Fricke, T.

1994   *Himalayan Households: Tamang Demography and
Domestic Processes,* 2nd ed. New York: Columbia University
Press.

Fried, M. H.

1960   On the Evolution of Social Stratification and the
State. In *Culture in History,* S. Diamond, ed., pp. 713–731.
New York: Columbia University Press.

1967   *The Evolution of Political Society: An Essay in Political Anthropology.* New York: McGraw-Hill.

Friedan, B.

1963   *The Feminine Mystique.* New York: W. W. Norton.

Friedl, E.

1962   *Vasilika: A Village in Modern Greece:* New York:
Holt, Rinehart, and Winston.

1975   *Women and Men: An Anthropologist's View.* New
York: Harcourt Brace Jovanovich.

Friedman, J., ed.

2003   *Globalization, the State, and Violence.* Walnut Creek,
CA: AltaMira.

Friedman, K. E., and J. Friedman

2008   *The Anthropology of Global Systems.* Lanham, MD:
AltaMira.

Fuchs, C., and M. Sandoval, eds.

2014   *Critique, Social Media, and the Information Society.*
New York: Routledge/Taylor and Francis.

Furuichi, R., and J. Thompson, eds.

2008   *The Bonobos: Behavior, Ecology, and Conservation.*
New York: Springer.

Gal, S.

1989   Language and Political Economy. *Annual Review of
Anthropology* 18: 345–367.

Galdikas, B. M.

2007   The Vanishing Man of the Forest. *International Her-
ald Tribune,* January 7. http://www.nytimes.com/2007/01/07/
opinion/07iht-edgald.4127210.html?_
r=1&scp51&sq=orangutan%20endangered&st=cse.

Garcia Canclini, N.

2014   *Art beyond Itself: Anthropology for a Society
without a Story Line.* Durham, NC: Duke University
Press.

Gardner, R. A., B. T. Gardner, and T. E. Van Cantfort, eds.

1989   *Teaching Sign Language to Chimpanzees.* Albany:
State University of New York Press.

Garraty, C. P.

2013   Market Development and Pottery Exchange under
Aztec and Spanish Rule in Cerro Portezuelo. *Ancient
Mesoamerica* 24(1): 151–176.

Gates, C.

2003   *Ancient Cities: The Archaeology of Urban Life in the
Ancient Near East, Egypt, Greece, and Rome.* New York:
Routledge.

Geertz, C.

1973   *The Interpretation of Cultures.* New York: Basic
Books.

1983   *Local Knowledge.* New York: Basic Books.

Geis, M. L.

1987   *The Language of Politics.* New York: Springer-Verlag.

Gell-Mann, M., and M. Ruhlen

2011   The Origin and Evolution of Word Order. *Proceedings of the National Academy of Sciences* 108(42):
17290–17295. http://www.pnas.org/content/early/2011/
10/04/1113716108.

Gibbons, A.

2001   The Peopling of the Pacific. *Science* 291: 1735. http://
www.familytreedna.com/pdf/Gibbons_Science2001.pdf.

2012   A New Face Reveals Multiple Lineages Alive at the
Dawn of Our Genus *Homo. Science* 337: 635.

Giddens, A.

1981   *The Class Structure of the Advanced Societies,* 2nd
ed. London: Hutchinson.

Gijswijt-Hofstra, M., et al., eds.

2005   *Psychiatric Cultures Compared: Psychiatry and
Mental Health Care in the Twentieth Century.* Amsterdam,
Netherlands: Amsterdam University Press.

Gilmore, D. D.

1987   *Aggression and Community: Paradoxes of Andalusian
Culture.* New Haven, CT: Yale University Press.

Gillis, J.

2015   Short Answers to Hard Questions about Climate
Change. *New York Times,* November 28. http://www.nytimes
.com/interactive/2015/11/28/science/what-is-climate-change
.html.

2016a   2015 Was Hottest Year in Historical Record, Scientists Say. *New York Times,* January 20. http://www.nytimes
.com/2016/01/21/science/earth/2015-hottest-year-global-
warming.html?_r=0.

2016b   Seas Are Rising at Fastest Rate in Last 28 Centuries.
New York Times, February 22. http://www.nytimes
.com/2016/02/23/science/sea-level-rise-global-warming-
climate-change.html.

Gimpel, J.

1988   *The Medieval Machine: The Industrial Revolution of
the Middle Ages,* 2nd ed. Aldershot, Hants, UK: Wildwood
House.

Ginsburg, F. D., L. Abu-Lughod, and B. Larkin, eds.

2002   *Media Worlds: Anthropology on New Terrain.*
Berkeley: University of California Press.

Giordano, C., F. Ruegg, and A. Boscoboinik, eds.

2014   *Does East Go West? Anthropological Pathways
through Postsocialism.* Zurich, Switzerland: Lit Verlag.

Gmelch, G.

1978   Baseball Magic. *Human Nature* 1(8): 32–40.

2001   *Inside Pitch: Life in Professional Baseball.* Washington,
DC: Smithsonian Institution Press.

2006   *Inside Pitch: Life in Professional Baseball.* Lincoln:
University of Nebraska Press.

Gmelch, G., R. V. Kemper, and W. Zenner, eds.

2010   *Urban Life: Readings in the Anthropology of the City,*
5th ed. Long Grove, IL: Waveland.

Goleman, D.

1992   Anthropology Goes Looking for Love in All the Old
Places. *New York Times,* November 24, 1992, p. B1.

1995   Making Room on the Couch for Culture. *New York
Times,* December 5. http://www.nytimes.com/1995/12/05/
science/making-room-on-the-couch-for-culture.
html?pagewanted=all&src=pm.

Golombok, S.

2015   *Modern Families: Parents and Children in New
Family Forms.* New York: Cambridge University Press.

Gonlin, N., and K. D. French, eds.
2015 *Human Adaptation in Ancient Mesoamerica.* Boulder, CO: University Press of Colorado.

Goodale, J., and J. D. Koss
1971 The Cultural Context of Creativity among Tiwi. In *Anthropology and Art: Readings in Cross-Cultural Aesthetics,* C. Otten, ed., pp. 182–203. Austin: University of Texas Press.

Goodall, J.
2009 *Jane Goodall: 50 Years at Gombe, a Tribute to Five Decades of Wildlife Research, Education, and Conservation.* New York: Stewart, Tabori, and Chang.
2010 *In the Shadow of Man,* new ed. Boston: Mariner Books.

Goodman, A. H., et al.
2013 *Race: Are We So Different?* Malden, MA: Wiley-Blackwell.

Gotkowitz, L., ed.
2011 *Histories of Race and Racism: The Andes and Mesoamerica from Colonial Times to the Present.* Durham, NC: Duke University Press.

Gough, E. K.
1959 The Nayars and the Definition of Marriage. *Journal of Royal Anthropological Institute* 89: 23–34.

Gould, S. J.
2007 *Punctuated Equilibrium.* Cambridge, MA: Belknap Press of Harvard University Press.

Gould, T. H. P.
2016 *Global Advertising in a Global Culture.* Lanham, MD: Rowman & Littlefield.

Gowlett, J. A. J.
1993 *Ascent to Civilization: The Archaeology of Early Humans.* New York: McGraw-Hill.

Grabowski, M., et al.
2015 Body Mass Estimates of Hominin Fossils and the Evolution of Human Body Size. *Journal of Human Evolution* 85: 75-93.

Graburn, N. H. H., J. Ertle, and R. K. Tierney, eds.
2008 *Multiculturalism in the New Japan: Crossing the Boundaries Within.* New York: Berghahn Books.

Graca, L. da, and A. Zingarelli, eds.
2015 *Studies on Pre-capitalist Modes of Production.* Boston: Brill.

Gramsci, A.
1971 *Selections from the Prison Notebooks.* Edited and translated by Quenten Hoare and Geoffrey Nowell Smith. London: Wishart.

Grasmuck, S., and P. Pessar
1991 *Between Two Islands: Dominican International Migration.* Berkeley: University of California Press.

Gravlee, C.
2009 How Race Becomes Biology: Embodiment of Social Inequality. *American Journal of Physical Anthropology* 139(1): 47–57.

Green, T.
2006 Archaeologist Makes the Case for Burying Dominant Theory of First Americans. Austin: University of Texas Research. http://www.utexas.edu/research/impact/collins.html.

Gremaux, R.
1993 Woman Becomes Man in the Balkans. In *Third Sex Third Gender: Beyond Sexual Dimorphism in Culture and History,* G. Herdt, ed. Cambridge: MIT Press.

Griffin, P. B., and A. Estioko-Griffin, eds.
1985 *The Agta of Northeastern Luzon: Recent Studies.* Cebu City, Philippines: University of San Carlos.

Grimshaw, A., and A. Ravetz
2009 *Observational Cinema: Anthropology, Film, and the Exploration of Social Life.* Bloomington: Indiana University Press.

Gu, S.
2012 *Language and Culture in the Growth of Imperialism.* Jefferson, NC: McFarland.

Gudeman, S. F.
2016 *Anthropology and Economy.* New York: Cambridge University Press.

Gugliotta, G.
2002 Earliest Human Ancestor? Skull Dates to When Apes, Humans Split. *Washington Post,* July 11, p. A01.

2005 Tools Found in Britain Show Much Earlier Human Existence. *Washington Post,* December 15, p. A-24.

Gupta, A., and J. Ferguson
1997 Beyond "Culture": Space, Identity, and the Politics of Difference. In *Culture, Power, Place: Explorations in Critical Anthropology,* A. Gupta and J. Ferguson, eds., pp. 33–51. Durham, NC: Duke University Press.

Gupta, A., and J. Ferguson, eds.
1997a *Anthropological Locations: Boundaries and Grounds of a Field Science.* Berkeley: University of California Press.
1997b *Culture, Power, Place: Explorations in Critical Anthropology.* Durham, NC: Duke University Press.

Guyot, J., and C. Hughes
2007 Researchers Find Earliest Evidence for Modern Human Behavior. *Arizona State University Research Magazine.* http://researchmag.asu.edu/2008/02researchers_find_earliest_evid.html.

Haapala, A.
1998 Literature: Invention of the Self. *Canadian Aesthetics Journal* 2. http://www.uqtr.ca/AE/vol_2/haapala.html.

Habu, J., et al.
2011 Shell Midden Archaeology in Japan: Aquatic Food Acquisition and Long-term Change in the Jomon Culture. *Quaternary International* 239(1-2): 19–27.

Haenn, N., R. R. Wilk, and A. Harnish, eds.
2016 *The Environment in Anthropology: A Reader in Ecology, Culture, and Sustainable Living.* New York: New York University Press.

Hallowell, A. I.
1955 *Culture and Experience.* Philadelphia: University of Pennsylvania Press.

Hamdan, S.
2013 Social Media Firms Move to Capitalize on Popularity in Middle East. *New York Times,* February 6. http://www.nytimes.com/2013/02/07/world/middleeast/social-media-firms-move-to-capitalize-on-popularity-in-middle-east.html?pagewanted=print.

Hamilton, M. B.
2009 *Population Genetics.* Hoboken, NJ: Wiley-Blackwell.

Hampton, K., et al.
2011 Social Networking Sites and Our Lives. Pew Research Center, Internet and American Life Project, June 16. http://www.pewinternet.org/2011/06/16/social-networking-sites-and-our-lives/.

Hancock, G.
2015 *Magicians of the Gods: The Forgotten Wisdom of Lost Civilization.* New York: Thomas Dunne Books.

Hancock, G., and R. Bauval
1996 *Message of the Sphinx: A Quest for the Hidden Legacy of Mankind.* New York: Three Rivers Press.

Handwerk, B.
2008 Half of Humanity Will Live in Cities by Year's End. *National Geographic News,* March 13. www.nationalgeographic.com/news/pf30472163.html.

Hann, C., and K. Hart
2011 *Economic Anthropology: History, Ethnography, Critique.* Malden, MA: Polity Press.

Hann, C., and K. Hart, eds.
2009 *Market and Society: The Great Transformation Today.* New York: Cambridge University Press.

Hansen, K. V.
2005 *Not-So-Nuclear Families: Class, Gender, and Networks of Care.* New Brunswick, NJ: Rutgers University Press.

Harlan, J. R., and D. Zohary
1966 Distribution of Wild Wheats and Barley. *Science* 153: 1074–1080.

Harlow, H. F.
1971 *Learning to Love.* San Francisco: Albion.

Harmand, S., et al.
2015 3.3-Million-Year-Old Stone Tools from Lomekwi 3, West Turkana, Kenya. *Nature* 521: 310–315.

Harper, K. N., M. K. Zuckerman, and G. J. Armelagos
2014 Syphilis Then and Now. *The Scientist,* February 1. http://www.the-scientist.com/?articles.view/articleNo/38985/title/Syphilis--Then-and-Now/.

Harris, M.
1964   *Patterns of Race in the Americas.* New York: Walker.
1970   Referential Ambiguity in the Calculus of Brazilian Racial Identity. *Southwestern Journal of Anthropology* 26(1): 1–14.
1974   *Cows, Pigs, Wars, and Witches: The Riddles of Culture.* New York: Random House.
1978   *Cannibals and Kings.* New York: Vintage.
2001a   (orig. 1979) *Cultural Materialism: The Struggle for a Science of Culture.* Walnut Creek, CA: AltaMira.
2001b   (orig. 1968) *The Rise of Anthropological Theory.* Walnut Creek, CA: AltaMira.

Harris, M., and C. P. Kottak
1963   The Structural Significance of Brazilian Racial Categories. *Sociologia* 25: 203–209.

Harris, R., and R. Pease
2015   *Pieces of the Musical World: Sounds and Culture.* New York: Routledge.

Harrison, G. G., W. L. Rathje, and W. W. Hughes
1994   Food Waste Behavior in an Urban Population. In *Applying Anthropology: An Introductory Reader,* 3rd ed., A. Podolefsky and P. J. Brown, eds., pp. 107–112. Mountain View, CA: Mayfield.

Harrison, K. D.
2007   *When Languages Die: The Extinction of the World's Languages and the Erosion of Human Knowledge.* New York: Oxford University Press.
2010   *The Last Speakers: The Quest to Save the World's Most Endangered Languages.* Washington, DC: National Geographic.

Hart, C. W. M., A. R. Pilling, and J. C. Goodale
1988   *The Tiwi of North Australia,* 3rd ed. Fort Worth: Harcourt Brace.

Hartigan, J., ed.
2013   *Anthropology of Race: Genes, Biology, and Culture.* Santa Fe, NM: School for Advanced Research Press.
2015   *Race in the 21st Century: Ethnographic Approaches.* New York: Oxford University Press.

Hartl, D. L.
2014   *Essential Genetics: A Genomics Perspective,* 6th ed. Burlington, MA: Jones and Bartlett.

Harvey, D. J.
1980   French Empire. *Academic American Encyclopedia,* vol. 8, pp. 309–310. Princeton, NJ: Arete.

Haugerud, A., M. P. Stone, and P. D. Little, eds.
2011   *Commodities and Globalization: Anthropological Perspectives.* Lanham, MD: Rowman & Littlefield.

Hausfater, G., and S. Hrdy, eds.
2008   *Infanticide: Comparative and Evolutionary Perspectives.* New Brunswick, NJ: Aldine.

Henry, J.
1972   *Jules Henry on Education.* New York: Random House.

Herdt, G.
2006   *The Sambia: Ritual, Sexuality, and Change in Papua New Guinea.* Belmont, CA: Thomson/Wadsworth.

Herdt, G. H., ed.
1984   *Ritualized Homosexuality in Melanesia.* Berkeley: University of California Press.

Herdt, G. H., and N. Polen
2013   *Sexual Literacy: Sexuality in Human Nature, Culture and Society.* New York: McGraw-Hill.

Herskovits, M.
1937   *Life in a Haitian Valley.* New York: Knopf.

Herzog, T.
2015   *Frontiers of Possession: Spain and Portugal in Europe and the Americas.* Cambridge, MA: Harvard University Press.

Hess, E.
2008   *Nim Chimsky: The Chimp Who Would Be Human.* New York: Bantam Books.

Heyerdahl, T.
1971   *The Ra Expeditions.* Translated by P. Crampton. Garden City, NY: Doubleday.

Hicks, D., ed.
2010   *Ritual and Belief: Readings in the Anthropology of Religion,* 3rd ed. Boston: McGraw-Hill.

Higham, T., et al.
2011   The Earliest Evidence for Anatomically Modern Humans in Northwestern Europe. *Nature* 479: 521–524. doi:10.1038/nature10484.

Hill, J. H.
1978   Apes and Language. *Annual Review of Anthropology* 7: 89–112.

Hill, K. R., et al.
2011   Co-residence Patterns in Hunter-Gatherer Societies Show Unique Human Social Structure. *Science* 331: 1286–1289. doi:10.1126/science.1199071.

Hill-Burnett, J.
1978   Developing Anthropological Knowledge through Application. In *Applied Anthropology in America,* E. M. Eddy and W. L. Partridge, eds., pp. 112–128. New York: Columbia University Press.

Hinton, A. L., and K. L. O'Neill, eds.
2009   *Genocide: Truth, Memory, and Representation.* Durham, NC: Duke University Press.

Hirth, K. G.
2016   *The Aztec Economic World: Merchants and Markets in Ancient Mesoamerica.* New York: Cambridge University Press.

Hirth, K. G., and J. Pillsbury, eds.
2013   *Merchants, Markets, and Exchange in the Pre-Columbian World.* Washington, DC: Dumbarton Oaks Research Library and Collection.

Hobhouse, L. T.
1915   *Morals in Evolution,* rev. ed. New York: Holt.

Hodder, I.
2006   *The Leopard's Tale: Revealing the Mysteries of Çatalhöyük.* New York: Thames and Hudson.

Hodder, I., ed.
2013   *Çatalhöyük Excavations: The 2000-2008 Seasons.* London: British Institute of Archaeology at Ankara.

Hodgson, D. L.
2016   *The Gender, Culture, and Power Reader.* New Brunswick, NJ: Rutgers University Press.

Hoebel, E. A.
1954   *The Law of Primitive Man.* Cambridge, MA: Harvard University Press.
1968   (orig. 1954) The Eskimo: Rudimentary Law in a Primitive Anarchy. In *Studies in Social and Cultural Anthropology,* J. Middleton, ed., pp. 93–127. New York: Crowell.

Hogan, B., N. Li, and W. H. Dutton
2011   *A Global Shift in the Social Relationships of Networked Individuals: Meeting and Dating Online Comes of Age* (February 14). Oxford Internet Institute, University of Oxford. http://ssrn.com/abstract=1763884 or http://dx.doi.org/10.2139/ssrn.1763884.

Hole, F., K. V. Flannery, and J. A. Neely
1969   *The Prehistory and Human Ecology of the Deh Luran Plain.* Memoir no. 1. Ann Arbor: University of Michigan Museum of Anthropology.

Holst, I., J. E. Moreno, and D. R. Piperno
2007   The Identification of Teosinte, Maize, and *Tripsacum* in Mesoamerica by Using Pollen, Starch Grains, and Phytoliths. *Proceedings of the National Academy of Sciences USA* 104: 17608–17613.

Hopper, F.
2015   Whale Wars Group vs. Makah: Who Decides If Traditions Are Authentic? Indian Country Network. June 23. http://indiancountrytodaymedianetwork.com/2015/06/23/whale-wars-group-vs-makah-who-decides-if-traditions-are-authentic-160741.

Hornborg, A., B. Clark, and K. Hermele, eds.
2011   *Ecology and Power: Struggles over Land and Material Resources in the Past, Present and Future.* New York: Routledge.

Hornborg, A., and C. L. Crumley, eds.
2007   *The World System and the Earth System: Global Socioenvironmental Change and Sustainability since the Neolithic.* Walnut Creek, CA: Left Coast Press.

Hornborg, A., J. R. McNeill, and J. Martinez-Alier, eds.
2007   *Rethinking Environmental History: World-System History and Global Environmental Change.* Lanham, MD: AltaMira.

Horton, R.
1963   The Kalabari Ekine Society: A Borderland of Religion and Art. *Africa* 33: 94–113.
1993   *Patterns of Thought in Africa and the West: Essays on Magic, Religion, and Science.* New York: Cambridge University Press.

Howell, S., and A Talle, eds.
2012   Returns to the Field: Multitemporal Research and Contemporary Anthropology. Bloomington: Indiana University Press.

Hrdy, S. B.
2009   *Mothers and Others.* Cambridge, MA: Harvard University Press.

Hublin, J.-J.
2012   The Earliest Modern Human Colonization of Europe. *Proceedings of the National Academy of Sciences* 109(34) 13471–13472. http://www.pnas.org/content/109/34/13471.full.

Hudjashov, G., et al.
2007   Revealing the Prehistoric Settlement of Australia by Y Chromosome and mtDNA Analysis. *Proceedings of the National Academy of Sciences* 104(21): 8726–8730.

Hurtado. A. M., et al.
2005   Human Rights, Biomedical Science, and Infectious Diseases among South American Indigenous Groups. *Annual Review of Anthropology* 34: 639–665.

Hyde, J. S., and J. D. DeLamater
2016   *Understanding Human Sexuality*, 13th ed. New York: McGraw-Hill Education.

Iannone, G., ed.
2013   *The Great Maya Droughts in Cultural Context: Case Studies in Resilience and Vulnerability.* Boulder, CO: University Press of Colorado.

Ignatius, D.
2007   Summer's Escape Artists. *Washington Post,* July 26. http://www.washingtonpost.com/wp-dyn/content/article/2007/07/25/AR2007072501879.html.

Ingold, T.
2013   *Making: Anthropology, Archaeology, Art and Architecture.* New York: Routledge.

Inhorn, M. C., and E. A. Wentzell, eds.
2012   *Medical Anthropology at the Intersections: Histories, Activisms, and Futures.* Durham, NC: Duke University Press.

Iqbal, S.
2002   A New Light on Skin Color. *National Geographic Online Extra.* http://magma.nationalgeographic.com/ngm/0211/feature2/online_extra.html.

Isaac, G. L.
1972   Early Phases of Human Behavior: Models in Lower Paleolithic Archaeology. In *Models in Archaeology,* D. L. Clarke, ed., pp. 167–199. London: Methuen.

Isaacson, A.
2012   A Mini-Eden for Endangered Orangutans. *New York Times,* January 6.

Isto É
1984   *Olimpíiadas,* August 8.

Jablonski, N. G.
2006   *Skin: A Natural History.* Berkeley: University of California Press.
2012   *Living Color: The Biological and Social Meaning of Skin Color.* Berkeley: University of California Press.

Jablonski, N. G., and G. Chaplin
2000   The Evolution of Human Skin Coloration. *Journal of Human Evolution* 39: 57–106.

Jackson, J., and K. B. Warren
2005   Indigenous Movements in Latin America, 1992–2004: Controversies, Ironies, New Directions. *Annual Review of Anthropology* 34: 549–573.

Jankowiak, W. R., ed.
1995   *Romantic Passion: A Universal Experience?* New York: Columbia University Press.
2008   *Intimacies: Love and Sex across Cultures.* New York: Columbia University Press.

Jankowiak, W. R., and E. F. Fischer
1992   A Cross-Cultural Perspective on Romantic Love. *Ethnology* 31(2): 149–156.

Jazra, K.
2014   15 Stats about Social Media in the Middle East That You Need to Know. Social4ce/Blog, July 1. http://social4ce.com/blog/2014/07/01/15-stats-you-need-to-know-about-social-media-in-the-middle-east/.

Jenkins, D. L., et al.
2012   Clovis Age Western Stemmed Projectile Points and Human Coprolites at the Paisley Caves. *Science* 13(July): 223–228. doi:10.1126/science.1218443.

Jennings, J.
2016   *Killing Civilization: A Reassessment of Early Urbanism and its Consequences.* Albuquerque: University of New Mexico Press.

Jiao, T.
2007   *The Neolithic of Southeast China: Cultural Transformation and Regional Interaction on the Coast.* Youngstown, NY: Cambria Press.

Jobling, M.
2013   *Human Evolutionary Genetics.* New York: Garland Science.

Johnson, A. W., and T. Earle
2000   *The Evolution of Human Societies: From Foraging Group to Agrarian State,* 2nd ed. Stanford, CA: Stanford University Press.

Johnston, B. R.
2005   Chixoy Dam Legacy Issues Study. http://www.center-forpoliticalecology.org/chixoy.html.
2009   *Life and Death Matters: Human Rights, Environment and Social Justice,* 2nd ed. Walnut Creek, CA: Left Coast Press.

Jolly, C. J., and R. White
1995   *Physical Anthropology and Archaeology,* 5th ed. New York: McGraw-Hill.

Joralemon, D.
2010   *Exploring Medical Anthropology,* 3rd ed. Boston: Pearson.

Jordan, B., ed.
2013   *Advancing Ethnography in Corporate Environments: Challenges and Emerging Opportunities.* Walnut Creek, CA: Left Coast Press.

Joyce, R.
2015   Aztec Marriage: A Lesson for Chief Justicc Roberts. *Psychology Today,* June 26. https://www.psychologytoday.com/blog/what-makes-us-human/201506/aztec-marriage-lesson-chief-justice-roberts.

Jurafsky, D.
2014   *The Language of Food: A Linguist Reads the Menu.* New York: W. W. Norton.

Kahn, J.
2011   *Chimpanzees in Biomedical and Behavioral Research: Assessing the Necessity.* Institute of Medicine (of the National Academies). December 15. http://iom.edu/Reports/2011/Chimpanzees-in-Biomedical-and-Behavioral-Research-Assessing-the-Necessity.aspx.

Kamrava, M.
2008   *Understanding Comparative Politics: A Framework for Analysis,* 2nd ed. New York: Routledge.
2013   *The Modern Middle East: A Political History since the First World War,* 3rd ed. Berkeley: University of California Press.

Kan, S.
1986   The 19th-Century Tlingit Potlatch: A New Perspective. *American Ethnologist* 13: 191–212.
1989   *Symbolic Immortality: The Tlingit Potlatch of the Nineteenth Century.* Washington, DC: Smithsonian Institution Press.

Kaneshiro, N. K.
2009   Intersex. *Medline Plus.* National Institutes of Health, U.S. National Library of Medicine. http://www.nlm.nih.gov/medlineplus/ency/article/001669.htm.

Kaufman, S. R., and L. M. Morgan
2005   The Anthropology of the Beginnings and Ends of Life. *Annual Review of Anthropology* 34: 317–341.

Keim, B.
2014   An Orangutan Has (Some) Basic Human Rights, Argentine Court Rules. *Wired,* December 22. http://www.wired.com/2014/12/orangutan-personhood.

Kelly, R. C.

1976 Witchcraft and Sexual Relations: An Exploration in the Social and Semantic Implications of the Structure of Belief. In *Man and Woman in the New Guinea Highlands*, P. Brown and G. Buchbinder, eds., pp. 36–53. Special Publication, no. 8. Washington, DC: American Anthropological Association.

Kennedy, M. D.

2015 *Globalizing Knowledge: Intellectuals, Universities, and Publics in Transformation*. Stanford, CA: Stanford University Press.

Kennedy, P.

2010 *Local Lives and Global Transformations: Towards a World Society*. New York: Palgrave Macmillan.

Kent, S.

1992 The Current Forager Controversy: Real versus Ideal Views of Hunter-Gatherers. *Man* 27: 45–70.

1996 *Cultural Diversity among Twentieth-Century Foragers: An African Perspective*. New York: Cambridge University Press.

1998 *Gender in African Prehistory*. Walnut Creek, CA: AltaMira.

Kent, S., ed.

2002 *Ethnicity, Hunter-Gatherers, and the "Other": Association or Assimilation in Africa*. Washington, DC: Smithsonian Institution Press.

Kent, S., and H. Vierich

1989 The Myth of Ecological Determinism: Anticipated Mobility and Site Organization of Space. In *Farmers as Hunters: The Implications of Sedentism*, S. Kent, ed., pp. 96–130. New York: Cambridge University Press.

Kershaw, S.

2005 In Petition to Government, Tribe Hopes for Return to Whaling Past. *New York Times,* September 19.

Keynes, J. M.

1927 *The End of Laissez-Faire*. London: L. and Virginia Woolf.

1936 *General Theory of Employment, Interest, and Money*. New York: Harcourt Brace.

Kimmel, M. S., and M. A. Messner, eds.

2013 *Men's Lives*, 9th ed. Boston: Allyn & Bacon.

King, E.

2012 Stanford Linguists Seek to Identify the Elusive California Accent. *Stanford Report,* August 6. http://news.stanford.edu/news/2012/august/california-dialect-linguistics-080612.html.

King, T. F., ed.

2011 *A Companion to Cultural Resource Management*. Malden, MA: Wiley-Blackwell.

Kinsey, A. C., W. B. Pomeroy, and C. E. Martin

1948 *Sexual Behavior in the Human Male*. Philadelphia: W. B. Saunders.

Kirch, P. V.

2000 *On the Road of the Winds: An Archaeological History of the Pacific Islands before European Contact*. Berkeley: University of California Press.

2016 *Unearthing the Polynesian Past: Explorations and Adventures of an Island Archaeologist*. Honolulu: University of Hawaii Press.

Kirman, P.

1997 An Introduction to Ethnomusicology. Inside World Music. http://www.insideworldmusic.com/library/weekly/aa101797.htm.

Kjaerulff, J.

2010 *Internet and Change: An Ethnography of Knowledge and Flexible Work*. Walnut Creek, CA: Left Coast Press.

Klein, R. G.

2013 Modern Human Origins. *General Anthropology* 20(1): 1–4.

Klein, R. G., with B. Edgar

2002 *The Dawn of Human Culture*. New York: Wiley.

Kleinman, A.

1991 *Rethinking Psychiatry: From Cultural Category to Personal Experience*. New York: Free Press.

Kluckhohn, C.

1944 *Mirror for Man: A Survey of Human Behavior and Social Attitudes*. Greenwich, CT: Fawcett.

Kochhar, R., and R. Fry

2014 Wealth Inequality Has Widened Along Racial, Ethnic Lines since End of Great Recession. Pew Research Center. http://www.pewresearch.org/fact-tank/2014/12/12/racial-wealth-gaps-great-recession/.

Konopinski, N., ed.

2014 *Doing Anthropological Research: A Practical Guide*. New York: Routledge.

Kontopodis, M., C. Wulf, and B. Fichtner, eds.

2011 *Children, Development, and Education: Cultural, Historical, and Anthropological Perspectives*. New York: Springer.

Kottak, C. P.

1980 *The Past in the Present: History, Ecology, and Social Organization in Highland Madagascar*. Ann Arbor: University of Michigan Press.

1990a *Prime-Time Society: An Anthropological Analysis of Television and Culture*. Belmont, CA: Wadsworth.

1990b Culture and Economic Development. *American Anthropologist* 92(3): 723–731.

1991 When People Don't Come First: Some Lessons from Completed Projects. In *Putting People First: Sociological Variables in Rural Development*, 2nd ed., ed. M. Cernea, pp. 429–464. New York: Oxford University Press.

1999 The New Ecological Anthropology. *American Anthropologist* 101(1): 23-35.

2004 An Anthropological Take on Sustainable Development: A Comparative Study of Change. *Human Organization* 63(4): 501–510.

2006 *Assault on Paradise: The Globalization of a Little Community in Brazil*, 4th ed. New York: McGraw-Hill.

2007 Return to Madagascar: A Forty Year Retrospective. *General Anthropology: Bulletin of the General Anthropology Division of the American Anthropological Association* 14(2): 1–10.

2009 *Prime-Time Society: An Anthropological Analysis of Television and Culture,* updated ed. Walnut Creek, CA: Left Coast Press.

Kottak, C. P., L. L. Gezon, and G. Green

1994 Deforestation and Biodiversity Preservation in Madagascar: The View from Above and Below. CIESIN Human Dimensions Kiosk. http://www.ciesin.com.

Kottak, C. P., and K. A. Kozaitis

2012 *On Being Different: Diversity and Multiculturalism in the North American Mainstream,* 4th ed. New York: McGraw-Hill.

Kottak, N. C.

2002 *Stealing the Neighbor's Chicken: Social Control in Northern Mozambique*. Ph.D. dissertation. Department of Anthropology, Emory University, Atlanta, GA.

Kotz, D. M.

2015 *The Rise and Fall of Neoliberal Capitalism*. Cambridge, MA: Harvard University Press.

Kozlowski, K.

2016 Virginia Tech Expert Helped Expose Flint Water Crisis. *Detroit News*, January 24. http://www.detroitnews.com/story/news/politics/2016/01/23/virginia-tech-expert-helped-expose-flint-water-crisis/79251004/

Kretchmer, N.

1975 (orig. 1972) Lactose and Lactase. In *Biological Anthropology, Readings from Scientific American*, S. H. Katz, ed., pp. 310–318. San Francisco: W. H. Freeman.

Kroeber, A. L.

1944 *Configurations of Cultural Growth*. Berkeley: University of California Press.

1987 (orig. 1952) *The Nature of Culture*. Chicago: University of Chicago Press.

Krogstad, J. M.

2014 11 Facts for National Hispanic Heritage Month. Pew Research Center, September 16. http://www.pewresearch.org/fact-tank/2014/09/16/11-facts-for-national-hispanic-heritage-month/.

Kronenfeld, D., et al., eds.

2011 *A Companion to Cognitive Anthropology*. Malden, MA: Wiley-Blackwell.

Kuhn, S. L., M. C. Stiner, and D. S. Reese

2001 Ornaments of the Earliest Upper Paleolithic: New Insights from the Levant. *Proceedings of the National Academy of Sciences of the United States of America* 98(13): 7641–7646.

Kulick, D.

1998 *Travesti: Sex, Gender, and Culture among Brazilian Transgendered Prostitutes.* Chicago: University of Chicago Press.

Kuniholm, P. I.

2004 Home page of the Malcolm and Carolyn Wiener Laboratory for Aegean and Near Eastern Dendrochronology at Cornell University. http://www.arts.cornell.edu/dendro/.

Labov, W.

1972a *Language in the Inner City: Studies in the Black English Vernacular.* Philadelphia: University of Pennsylvania Press.

1972b *Sociolinguistic Patterns.* Philadelphia: University of Pennsylvania Press.

2006 *The Social Stratification of English in New York City.* New York: Cambridge University Press.

2012 *Dialect Diversity in America: The Politics of Language Change.* Charlottesville: University of Virginia Press.

Lakoff, R. T.

2004 *Language and Woman's Place.* New York: Harper & Row.

Lambek, M., ed.

2008 *A Reader in the Anthropology of Religion.* Malden, MA: Blackwell.

Landes, D.

1999 *The Wealth and Poverty of Nations. Why Some Are So Rich and Some Are So Poor.* London: Abacus.

Lange, M.

2009 *Lineages of Despotism and Development: British Colonialism and State Power.* Chicago: University of Chicago Press.

Largent, F.

2007a Clovis Dethroned: A New Perspective on the First Americans, Part 1. *Mammoth Trumpet* 22(3): 1–3, 20.

2007b Clovis Dethroned: A New Perspective on the First Americans, Part 2. *Mammoth Trumpet* 22(4): 1–2, 13.

Larsen, C. S.

2015 *Bioarchaeology: Interpreting Behavior from the Human Skeleton,* 2nd ed. New York: Cambridge University Press.

Lassiter, L. E.

1998 *The Power of Kiowa Song: A Collaborative Ethnography.* Tucson: University of Arizona Press.

Laughlin, J. C. H.

2006 *Fifty Major Cities of the Bible.* New York: Routledge.

Leach, E. R.

1955 Polyandry, Inheritance and the Definition of Marriage. *Man* 55: 182–186.

1961 *Rethinking Anthropology.* London: Athlone Press.

1970 (orig. 1954) *Political Systems of Highland Burma: A Study of Kachin Social Structure.* London: Athlone Press.

Leadbeater, C.

1999 Europe's New Economy. London: Centre for European Reform.

Leakey, M. G., Feibel, C.S., et al.

1995 New Four-Million-Year-Old Hominid Species from Kanapoi and Allia Bay, Kenya. *Nature* 376: 565–571.

Leakey, M. G., Spoor, F., et al.

2012 New Fossils from Koobi Fora in Northern Kenya Confirm Taxonomic Diversity in Early *Homo. Nature* 488: 201–204.

Lee, R. B.

1974 (orig. 1968) What Hunters Do for a Living, or, How to Make Out on Scarce Resources. In *Man in Adaptation: The Cultural Present,* 2nd ed., Y. A. Cohen, ed., pp. 87–100. Chicago: Aldine.

1979 *The !Kung San: Men, Women, and Work in a Foraging Society.* New York: Cambridge University Press.

1984 *The Dobe !Kung.* New York: Holt, Rinehart and Winston.

2003 *The Dobe Ju/'hoansi,* 3rd ed. Belmont, CA: Wadsworth.

2012 The !Kung and I: Reflections on My Life and Times with the Ju/'hoansi. *General Anthropology* 19(1): 1–4.

Lee, R. B., and R. H. Daly

1999 *The Cambridge Encyclopedia of Hunters and Gatherers.* New York: Cambridge University Press.

Leman, J.

2001 *The Dynamics of Emerging Ethnicities: Immigrant and Indigenous Ethnogenesis in Confrontation.* New York: Peter Lang.

Lenski, G.

1966 *Power and Privilege: A Theory of Social Stratification.* New York: McGraw-Hill.

Lesure, R. G.

2011 *Interpreting Ancient Figurines: Context, Comparison, and Prehistoric Art.* New York: Cambridge University Press.

LeVine, R. A., ed.

2010 *A Reader on Self in Culture.* Malden, MA: Wiley-Blackwell.

Levinson, B. A. U., and M. Pollock, eds.

2011 *A Companion to the Anthropology of Education.* Malden, MA: Blackwell.

Lévi-Strauss, C.

1963 *Totemism.* Translated by R. Needham. Boston: Beacon Press.

1967 *Structural Anthropology.* New York: Doubleday.

1969 (orig. 1949) *The Elementary Structures of Kinship.* Boston: Beacon Press.

Levy, J. E., with B. Pepper

1992 *Orayvi Revisited: Social Stratification in an "Egalitarian" Society.* Santa Fe, NM: School of American Research Press; Seattle: University of Washington Press.

Lewellen, T. C.

2010 Groping toward Globalization: In Search of Anthropology without Boundaries. *Reviews in Anthropology* 31(1): 73–89.

Lewin, E., and L. M. Silverstein, eds.

2016 *Mapping Feminist Anthropology in the Twenty-First Century.* New Brunswick, NJ: Rutgers University Press.

Lie, J.

2001 *Multiethnic Japan.* Cambridge, MA: Harvard University Press.

Lim, L., and U. Ansaldo.

2016 *Languages in Contact.* New York: Cambridge University Press.

Lindenbaum, S.

1972 Sorcerers, Ghosts, and Polluting Women: An Analysis of Religious Belief and Population Control. *Ethnology* 11: 241–253.

Lindquist, G., and D. Handelman, eds.

2013 *Religion, Politics, and Globalization: Anthropological Approaches.* New York: Berghahn Books.

Livingstone, F. B.

1969 Gene Frequency Clines of the *b* Hemoglobin Locus in Various Human Populations and Their Similarities by Models Involving Differential Selection. *Human Biology* 41: 223–236.

Lockwood, W. G.

1975 *European Moslems: Economy and Ethnicity in Western Bosnia.* New York: Academic Press.

Lockwood, Y. R.

1983 *Text and Context: Folksong in a Bosnian Muslim Village.* Columbus, OH: Slavica.

Loomis, W. F.

1967 Skin-Pigmented Regulation of Vitamin-D Biosynthesis in Man. *Science* 157: 501–506.

López, A. A.

2011 New Questions in the Immigration Debate. *Anthropology Now* 3(1): 47–53.

Loveday, L.

1986 Japanese Sociolinguistics: An Introductory Survey. *Journal of Pragmatics* 10: 287–326.

2001 *Explorations in Japanese Sociolinguistics.* Philadelphia: J. Benjamins.

Lowie, R. H.

1961 (orig. 1920) *Primitive Society.* New York: Harper & Brothers.

Lowrey, A.

2013 The Rich Get Richer through the Recovery. *New York Times,* September 13. http://economix.blogs.nytimes.com/2013/09/10/the-rich-get-richer-through-the-recovery/?_r=0.

Lugo, A.

1997   Reflections on Border Theory, Culture, and the
Nation. In *Border Theory: The Limits of Cultural Politics*,
S. Michaelsen and D. Johnson, eds., pp. 43–67. Minneapolis:
University of Minnesota Press.

2008   *Fragmented Lives, Assembled Parts: Culture, Capitalism, and Conquest at the U.S.-Mexico Border*. Austin:
University of Texas Press.

Lugo, A., and B. Maurer

2000   *Gender Matters: Rereading Michelle Z. Rosaldo*. Ann
Arbor: University of Michigan Press.

Lukas, D., and T. H. Clutton-Brock

2013   The Evolution of Social Monogamy in Mammals.
Science 341: 526–530. http://www.sciencemag.org/
content/341/6145/526.

Lule, J.

2015   *Globalization and Media: Global Village of Babel*.
Lanham, MA: Rowman & Littlefield.

Lupton, D.

2012   *Medicine as Culture: Illness, Disease, and the Body*,
3rd ed. Los Angeles: Sage.

Lyell, C.

1969   (orig. 1830–37) *Principles of Geology*. New York:
Johnson.

Lyons, A. P., and H. D. Lyons, eds.

2011   *Sexualities in Anthropology: A Reader*. Malden, MA:
Blackwell.

Maguire, M., C. Frois, and N. Zurawski, eds.

2014   *The Anthropology of Security: Perspectives from the
Frontline of Policing, Counter-terrorism, and Border Control*.
Sterling, VA: Pluto Press.

Malinowski, B.

1927   *Sex and Repression in Savage Society*. London and
New York: International Library of Psychology, Philosophy
and Scientific Method.

1929   Practical Anthropology. *Africa* 2: 23–38.

1944   *A Scientific Theory of Culture and Other Essays*.
Chapel Hill: University of North Carolina Press.

1961   (orig. 1922) *Argonauts of the Western Pacific*. New
York: Dutton.

1978   (orig. 1931) The Role of Magic and Religion. In
*Reader in Comparative Religion: An Anthropological Ap-
proach*, 4th ed., W. A. Lessa and E. Z. Vogt, eds., pp. 37–46.
New York: Harper & Row.

Malkki, L. H.

1995   *Purity and Exile: Violence, Memory, and National
Cosmology among Hutu Refugees in Tanzania*. Chicago:
University of Chicago Press.

Mann, C. C.

2011   *1493: Uncovering the New World Columbus Created*.
New York: Knopf.

Maquet, J.

1986   *The Aesthetic Experience: An Anthropologist Looks at
the Visual Arts*. New Haven, CT: Yale University Press.

Marcus, G. E., and M. M. J. Fischer

1986   *Anthropology as Cultural Critique: An Experimental
Moment in the Human Sciences*. Chicago: University of
Chicago Press.

Marcus, G. E., and F. R. Myers, eds.

1995   *The Traffic in Culture: Refiguring Art and Anthropology*. Berkeley: University of California Press.

Marcus, J.

1989   From Centralized Systems to City-States: Possible
Models for the Epiclassic. In *Mesoamerica after the Decline
of Teotihuacan: A.D. 700–900*, R. A. Diehl and J. C. Berlo,
eds., pp. 201–208. Washington, DC: Dumbarton Oaks.

Marcus, J., and K. V. Flannery

1996   *Zapotec Civilization: How Urban Society Evolved in
Mexico's Oaxaca Valley*. New York: Thames and Hudson.

Marean, C. W., et al.

2007   Early Human Use of Marine Resources and Pigment
in South Africa during the Middle Pleistocene. *Nature* 449:
905–908. doi:10.1038/nature06204.

Marger, M. N.

2015   *Race and Ethnic Relations: American and Global
Perspectives*, 10th ed. Stamford, CT: Cengage.

Margolis, M.

2000   *True to Her Nature: Changing Advice to American
Women*. Prospect Heights, IL: Waveland.

Marks, R.

2015   *The Origins of the Modern World: A Global and
Environmental Narrative from the Fifteenth to the Twenty-
First Century*, 3rd ed. Lanham, MD: Rowman & Littlefield.

Marshack, A.

1972   *Roots of Civilization*. New York: McGraw-Hill.

Marshall, J. A. R.

2015   *Social Evolution and Inclusive Fitness Theory: An
Introduction*. Princeton, NJ: Princeton University Press

Martin, D.

1990   *Tongues of Fire: The Explosion of Protestantism in
Latin America*. Cambridge, MA: Blackwell.

Martin, D. L., R. P. Harrod, and V. R. Perez

2013   *Bioarchaeology: An Integrated Approach to Working
with Human Remains*. New York: Springer.

Martin, K., and B. Voorhies

1975   *Female of the Species*. New York: Columbia University Press.

Martin, S. M.

1988   *Palm Oil and Protest: An Economic History of the
Ngwa Region, South-Eastern Nigeria, 1800–1980*. New York:
Cambridge University Press.

Marx, K., and F. Engels

1976   (orig. 1848) *Communist Manifesto*. New York: Pantheon.

Mascia-Lees, F.

2010   *Gender & Difference in a Globalizing World: Twenty-
First Century Anthropology*. Long Grove, IL: Waveland.

Masters, J., M. Gamba, and F. Génin

2013   What's in a Name? Higher Level Taxonomy of the
Prosimian Primates. In *Leaping Ahead*, J. Masters et al., eds.,
pp. 3-9. New York: Springer.

Matsuzawa, T., et al., ed.

2011   *The Chimpanzees of Bossou and Nimba*. New York:
Springer.

Maugh, T. H., III

2007   One Language Disappears Every 14 Days; about Half
of the World's Distinct Tongues Could Vanish This Century,
Researchers Say. *Los Angeles Times,* September 19.

Maybury-Lewis, D.

2002   *Indigenous Peoples, Ethnic Groups, and the State,* 2nd
ed. Boston: Allyn & Bacon.

Maybury-Lewis, D., T. Macdonald, and B. Maybury-Lewis, eds.

2009   *Manifest Destinies and Indigenous Peoples*. Cambridge, MA: David Rockefeller Center for Latin American
Studies and Harvard University Press.

Mayell, H.

2004   Is Bead Find Proof Modern Thought Began in Africa?
National Geographic News, March 31. http://news.national-
geographic.com/news/2004/03/0331_040331_ostrichman.
html.

Mazzeo, J., A. Rödlach, and B. P. Brenton

2011   Introduction: Anthropologists Confront HIV/AIDS
and Food Insecurity in Sub-Saharan Africa. American
Anthropological Association, *Annals of Anthropological
Practice* 35(1–7).

Mba, N. E.

1982   *Nigerian Women Mobilized: Women's Political Activity in Southern Nigeria, 1900–1965*. Berkeley: University of
California Press, 1982.

McAllester, D. P.

1954   *Enemy Way Music: A Study of Social and Esthetic
Values as Seen in Navaho Music*. Cambridge, MA: Peabody
Museum of American Archaeology and Ethnology, Papers
41(3).

McBrearty, S., and A. S. Brooks

2000   The Revolution That Wasn't: A New Interpretation of
the Origin of Modern Human Behavior. *Journal of Human
Evolution* 39: 453–563.

McBrearty, S., and C. Stringer

2007   The Coast in Colour. *Nature* 449: 793–794.

McConnell-Ginet, S.

2010   *Gender, Sexuality, and Meaning: Linguistic Practice
and Politics*. New York: Oxford University Press.

McConvell, P., I. Keen, and R. Hendery, eds.
2013 *Kinship Systems: Change and Reconstruction.* Salt Lake City: University of Utah Press.

McDonald, G.
1984 *Carioca Fletch.* New York: Warner Books.

McDougall, I., F. H. Brown, and J. G. Fleagle
2005 Stratigraphic Placement and Age of Modern Humans from Kibish, Ethiopia. *Nature* 433: 733–736.

McElroy, A., and P. K. Townsend
2014 *Medical Anthropology in Ecological Perspective,* 6th ed. Boulder, CO: Westview Press.

McGee, R. J., and R. L. Warms
2012 *Anthropological Theory: An Introductory History,* 5th ed. New York: McGraw-Hill.

McGregor, W.
2015 *Linguistics: An Introduction.* New York: Bloomsbury Academic.

McLaughlin, E. C.
2016 5 Things to Know about Flint's Water Crisis. CNN, January 21. http://www.cnn.com/2016/01/18/us/flint-michigan-water-crisis-five-things/.

Mead, M.
1937 *Cooperation and Competition among Primitive Peoples.* New York: McGraw-Hill.
1950 (orig. 1935) *Sex and Temperament in Three Primitive Societies.* New York: New American Library.
1961 (orig. 1928) *Coming of Age in Samoa.* New York: Morrow Quill.
1977 Applied Anthropology: The State of the Art. In *Perspectives on Anthropology, 1976.* Washington, DC: American Anthropological Association.

Meadow, R. H., and J. M. Kenoyer
2000 The Indus Valley Mystery: One of the World's First Great Civilizations Is Still a Puzzle. *Discovering Archaeology,* April, pp. 38–43.

Meigs, A., and K. Barlow
2002 Beyond the Taboo: Imagining Incest. *American Anthropologist* 104(1): 38–49.

Menzies, C. R., ed.
2006 *Traditional Ecological Knowledge and Natural Resource Management.* Lincoln: University of Nebraska Press.

Mercader, J., M. Panger, and C. Boesch
2002 Excavation of a Chimpanzee Stone Tool Site in the African Rainforest. *Science* 296: 1452–1455.

Merriam-Webster
2013 Art (definition of). From *Merriam-Webster's Collegiate® Dictionary,* 11th Edition ©2016 by Merriam-Webster, Inc. (www.Merriam-Webster.com). Used with permission.

Mesthrie, R., ed.
2011 *The Cambridge Handbook of Sociolinguistics.* New York: Cambridge University Press.

Meyer, B.
1999 *Translating the Devil: Religion and Modernity among the Ewe in Ghana.* Trenton, NJ: Africa World Press.

Meyerhoff, M., E. Schleef, and L. MacKenzie
2015 *Doing Sociolinguistics: A Practical Guide to Data Collection and Analysis.* New York: Routledge.

Michalak, P., ed.
2013 *Speciation: Natural Processes, Genetics and Biodiversity.* New York: Nova Biomedical.

Mielke, J. H., L. W. Konigsberg, and J. H. Relethford
2011 *Human Biological Variation,* 2nd ed. New York: Oxford University Press.

Millaire, J. F.
2010 Primary State Formation in the Viru Valley, North Coast of Peru. *Proceedings of the National Academy of Sciences of the United States of America* 107(14): 6186–6191. http://www.pnas.org/content/107/14/6186.abstract.

Miller, B. D.
1997 *The Endangered Sex: Neglect of Female Children in Rural North India.* New York: Oxford University Press.

Miller, C. C.
2015 The Search for the Best Estimate of the Transgender Population. *New York Times,* June 8. http://www.nytimes.com/2015/06/09/upshot/the-search-for-the-best-estimate-of-the-transgender-population.html?_r=0.

Miller, L.
2004 The Ancient Bristlecone Pine, Dendrochronology. http://www.sonic.net/bristlecone/dendro.html.

Miller, N. F., M. A. Zeder, and S. R. Arter
2009 From Food and Fuel to Farms and Flocks: The Integration of Plant and Animal Remains in the Study of Ancient Agro-Pastoral Economies. *Current Anthropology* 50: 915–924.

Mintz, S. W.
1985 *Sweetness and Power: The Place of Sugar in Modern History.* New York: Viking Penguin.
2007 *Caribbean Transformations.* New Brunswick, NJ: Aldine Transaction.

Mirrlees, T.
2013 *Global Entertainment Media: between Cultural Imperialism and Cultural Globalization.* New York: Routledge.

Mitani, J. C.
2011 Fearing a Planet without Apes. *New York Times,* August 20.

Mitani, J. C., et al., eds.
2012 *The Evolution of Primate Societies.* Chicago: University of Chicago Press.

Moberg, M.
2013 *Engaging Anthropological Theory: A Social and Political History.* New York: Routledge.

Mohai, P., and R. Saha
2015 Which Came First, People or Pollution? Assessing the Disparate Siting and Post-Siting Demographic Change Hypotheses of Environmental Injustice. *Environmental Research Letters* 10: 1-17. http://iopscience.iop.org/article/10.1088/1748-9326/10/11/115008/pdf.

Montague, S., and R. Morais
1981 Football Games and Rock Concerts: The Ritual Enactment. In *The American Dimension: Cultural Myths and Social Realities,* 2nd ed., W. Arens and S. B. Montague, eds., pp. 33–52. Sherman Oaks, CA: Alfred.

Montgomery, H.
2008 *An Introduction to Childhood: Anthropological Perspectives on Children's Lives.* Oxford: Blackwell.

Mooney, A.
2011 *Language, Society, and Power.* New York: Routledge.

Mooney, A., and B. Evans, eds.
2015 *Language Society and Power: An Introduction.* New York: Routledge.

Moore, J. D.
2012 *Visions of Culture: An Introduction to Anthropological Theories and Theorists,* 4th ed. Lanham, MD: AltaMira.

Morgan, L. H.
1963 (orig. 1877) *Ancient Society.* Cleveland: World Publishing.
1966 (orig. 1851) *League of the Ho-dé-no-sau-nee or Iroquois.* New York: B. Franklin.

Morkot, R.
2005 *The Egyptians: An Introduction.* New York: Routledge.

Moro, P. A., and J. E. Myers
2012 *Magic, Witchcraft, and Religion: A Reader in the Anthropology of Religion,* 9th ed. New York: McGraw-Hill.

Mosse, D., ed.
2011 *Adventures in Aidland: The Anthropology of Professionals in International Development.* New York: Berghahn Books.

Motseta, S.
2006 Botswana Gives Bushmen Tough Conditions. *Washington Post,* December 14. http://www.washingtonpost.com/wp-dyn/content/article/2006/12/14/AR2006121401008.html.

Mounier, A., S. Condemi, and G. Manzi
2011 The Stem Species of Our Species: A Place for the Archaic Human Cranium from Ceprano, Italy. *PLOS ONE* 6(4): e18821. doi:10.1371/journal.pone.0018821.

Moyà-Solà , S., et al.
2004 *Pierolapithecus catalaunicus:* A New Middle Miocene Great Ape from Spain. *Science* 306: 1339–1344.

Mukhopadhyay, C. C., R. Henze, and Y. T. Moses
2014 *How Real Is Race? A Sourcebook on Race, Culture, and Biology,* 2nd ed. Lanham, MD: AltaMira.

Mullaney, T.
2011 *Coming to Terms with the Nation: Ethnic Classification in Modern China.* Berkeley: University of California Press.

Murchison, J. M.
2010 *Ethnography Essentials: Designing, Conducting, and Presenting Your Research.* San Francisco: Jossey Bass.

Murdock, G. P., and C. Provost
1973 Factors in the Division of Labor by Sex: A Cross-Cultural Analysis. *Ethnology* 12(2): 203–225.

Murray, S. O., and W. Roscoe, eds.
1998 *Boy-Wives and Female Husbands: Studies in African Homosexualities.* New York: St. Martin's Press.

Mydans, S.
1992 Judge Dismisses Case in Shooting by Officer. *New York Times,* June 4, p. A8.

Nanda, S.
1996 Hijras: An Alternative Sex and Gender Role in India. In *Third Sex Third Gender: Beyond Sexual Dimorphism in Culture and History,* G. Herdt, ed., pp. 373–418. New York: Zone Books.
1998 *Neither Man nor Woman: The Hijras of India.* Belmont, CA: Thomson/Wadsworth.
2014 *Gender Diversity: Crosscultural Variations,* 2nd ed. Long Grove, IL: Waveland.

National Academy of Sciences
2008 Understanding and Responding to Climate Change: Highlights of National Academies Reports. http://dels.nas.edu/dels/rpt_briefs/climate_change_2008_final.pdf.

National Research Council
2011 America's Climate Choices. http://nas-sites.org/americasclimatechoices/sample-page/panel-reports/americas-climate-choices-final-report/.

Nayar, P. K., ed.
2016 *Postcolonial Studies: An Anthology.* Malden, MA: Wiley.

New York Times
2005 Intelligent Design Derailed. Editorial Desk, December 22. http://www.nytimes.com/2005/12/22/opinion/intelligent-design-derailed.html?_r=0.

Ni, X., et al.
2013 The Oldest Known Primate Skeleton and Early Haplorhine Evolution. *Nature* 498: 60–64.

Nielsen, R., and M. Slatkin
2013 *An Introduction to Population Genetics: Theory and Applications.* Sunderland, MA: Sinauer Associates.

Nishida, T.
2012 *Chimpanzees at the Lakeshore: Natural History and Culture at Mahale.* New York: Cambridge University Press.

Nordstrom, C.
2004 *Shadows of War: Violence, Power, and International Profiteering in the Twenty-First Century.* Berkeley: University of California Press.

Northover, A.
2016 Words of 2015 Round-Up. Oxford Dictionaries, January 16. Oxford University Press. http://blog.oup.com/2016/01/words-2015-round-up/.

Nunn, N., and N. Qian
2010 The Columbian Exchange: A History of Disease, Food, and Ideas. *Journal of Economic Perspectives* 24(2): 163–188.

O'Connell, J. F., and J. Allen
2004 Dating the Colonization of Sahul (Pleistocene Australia–New Guinea): A Review of Recent Research. *Journal of Archaeological Science* 31: 835–853.

O'Connor, K.
2015 *The Never-Ending Feast: The Anthropology and Archaeology of Feasting.* New York: Bloomsbury Academic.

Olszewski, D.
2016 *Archaeology and Humanity's Story: A Brief Introduction to World Prehistory.* New York: Oxford University Press.

Omohundro, J. T.
2001 *Careers in Anthropology,* 2nd ed. New York: McGraw-Hill.

Ong, A.
1987 *Spirits of Resistance and Capitalist Discipline: Factory Women in Malaysia.* Albany: State University of New York Press.
1989 Center, Periphery, and Hierarchy: Gender in Southeast Asia. In *Gender and Anthropology: Critical Reviews for Research and Teaching,* S. Morgen, ed., pp. 294–312. Washington, DC: American Anthropological Association.
2010 *Spirits of Resistance and Capitalist Discipline: Factory Women in Malaysia,* 2nd ed. Albany: State University of New York Press.

Ong, A., and S. J. Collier, eds.
2005 *Global Assemblages: Technology, Politics, and Ethics as Anthropological Problems.* Malden, MA: Blackwell.

Ontario Consultants on Religious Tolerance
2011 Religions of the World: Number of Adherents of Major Religions, Their Geographical Distribution, Date Founded, and Sacred Texts. http://www.religioustolerance.org/worldrel.htm.

Opie, C., Q. D. Atkinson, R. I. M. Dunbar, and S. Shultz
2013 Male Infanticide Leads to Social Monogamy in Primates. *Proceedings of the National Academy of Sciences* 110(33): 13328–13332.

Oriji, J. N.
2000 Igbo Women from 1929–1960. *West Africa Review* 2: 1.

Ortner, S. B.
1984 Theory in Anthropology since the Sixties. *Comparative Studies in Society and History* 126(1): 126–166.

Osborne, R., and J. Tanner, eds.
2007 *Art's Agency and Art History.* Malden, MA: Blackwell.

Ottaviani, J., and D. Meconis
2007 *Wire Mothers: Harry Harlow and the Science of Love.* Ann Arbor, MI: G. T. Labs.

Owen, J.
2006 "Lucy's Baby"—World's Oldest Child—Found by Fossil Hunters. *National Geographic News,* September 20. http://news.nationalgeographic.com/news/2006/09/060920-lucys-baby.html.
2012 "Lucy's Baby" a Born Climber, Hinting Human Ancestors Lingered in Trees. *National Geographic News,* October 26. http://news.nationalgeographic.com/news/2012/10/121026-australopithecus-afarensis-human-evolution-lucy-scapula-science/.

Oxford, University of
2013 Social Media: The Perils and Pleasures. http://www.ox.ac.uk/media/news_stories/2013/130411_1.html.

Oxford University Press
2015 Oxford Dictionaries Word of the Year 2015 Is…. http://blog.oxforddictionaries.com/2015/11/word-of-the-year-2015-emoji.

Özdoğan, M., N. Başgelen, and P. Kuniholm
2011 *The Neolithic in Turkey: New Excavations and New Research.* Galatasaray, Istanbul: Archaeology and Art Publications.

Pace, R., and B. P. Hinote
2013 *Amazon Town TV: An Audience Ethnography in Gurupá, Brazil.* Austin: University of Texas Press.

Pagden, A.
2015 *The Burdens of Empire: 1539 to the Present.* New York: Cambridge University Press.

Paine, R.
2009 *Camps of the Tundra: Politics through Reindeer among Saami Pastoralists.* Oslo: Instituttet for sammenlignende kulturforskning.

Pandika, M.
2013 Agriculture Arose in Many Parts of the Fertile Crescent at Once. *Los Angeles Times,* July 5. http://latimes.com/news/science/sciencenow/la-sci-sn-agriculture-fertile-crescent-iran-20130705,0,5657443.story.

Pardo, I., and G. B. Prato, eds.
2012 *Anthropology in the City: Methodology and Theory.* Burlington, VT: Ashgate.

Parrillo, V. N.
2016 *Understanding Race and Ethnic Relations,* 5th ed. Boston: Pearson.

Parsons, J. R.
1974 The Development of a Prehistoric Complex Society: A Regional Perspective from the Valley of Mexico. *Journal of Field Archaeology* 1: 81–108.

Parzinger, H., et al.
2006 Declaration (on the Bosnia Pyramid Hoax). *The European Archaeologist,* December 11. http://www.e-a-a.org/statement.pdf.

Patterson, F.

1978   Conversations with a Gorilla. *National Geographic,* October, pp. 438–465.

1999   *Koko-love! Conversations with a Signing Gorilla.* New York: Dutton.

Paul, R.

1989   Psychoanalytic Anthropology. *Annual Review of Anthropology* 18: 177–202.

Paulson, T. E.

2005   Chimp, Human DNA Comparison Finds Vast Similarities, Key Differences. *Seattle Post-Intelligencer Reporter,* September 1. http://seattlepi.nwsource.com/local/238852_chimp01.html.

Peletz, M.

1988   *A Share of the Harvest: Kinship, Property, and Social History among the Malays of Rembau.* Berkeley: University of California Press.

2009   *Gender Pluralism; Southeast Asia since Early Modern Times.* New York: Routledge.

Pelto, P. J.

2013   *Applied Ethnography: Guidelines for Field Research.* Walnut Creek, CA: Left Coast Press.

Peregrine, P. N., C. R. Ember, and M. Ember

2007   Modeling State Origins Using Cross-Cultural Data. *Cross-Cultural Research* 41: 75–86.

Perrin, A.

2015   Social Media Usage: 2005-2015. Pew Research Center, October 8. http://www.pewinternet.org/2015/10/08/social-networking-usage-2005-2015/.

Petraglia-Bahri, D.

1996   Introduction to Postcolonial Studies. http://www.emory.edu/ENGLISH/Bahri/.

Pew Research Center

2011   The Pew Forum on Religion and Public Life. http://www.pewforum.org/uploadedFiles/Topics/Religious_Affiliation/Christian/Evangelical_Protestant_Churches/Global%20Survey %20of%20Evan.%20Prot.%20Leaders.pdf.

2012   *The Global Religious Landscape: A Report on the Size and Distribution of the World's Major Religious Groups as of 2010, Analysis,* December 18. http://www.pewforum.org/global-religious-landscape-exec.aspx#src=global-footer.

2015a   America's Changing Religious Landscape. Pew Research Center: Religion & Public Life, May 12. http://www.pewforum.org/2015/05/12/americas-changing-religious-landscape/.

2015b   The Future of World Religions: Population Growth Projections, 2010-2050. Pew Research Center: Religion & Public Life, April 2. http://www.pewforum.org/files/2015/03/PF_15.04.02_ProjectionsFullReport.pdf.

2015c   Social Networking Fact Sheet. Pew Research Center. http://www.pewinternet.org/fact-sheets/social-networking-fact-sheet/.

Phillips, D.

2015   Even the Military May Not Be Enough to Protect an Endangered Amazon Tribe. *Washington Post,* November 8. https://www.washingtonpost.com/world/the_americas/even-the-military-may-not-be-enough-to-protect-an-endangered-amazon-tribe/2015/11/07/676c72f2-4789-11e5-9f53-d1e3ddfd0cda_story.html

Piddocke, S.

1969   The Potlatch System of the Southern Kwakiutl: A New Perspective. In *Environment and Cultural Behavior,* A. P. Vayda, ed., pp. 130–156. Garden City, NY: Natural History Press.

Piemmons, D., and A. W. Barker, eds.

2015   *Anthropological Ethics in Context: An Ongoing Dialogue.* Walnut Creek, CA: Left Coast Press.

Pink, S., and S. Abram

2015   *Media, Anthropology and Public Engagement.* New York: Berghahn Books.

Piperno, D. R.

2001   On Maize and the Sunflower. *Science* 292: 2260–2261.

Piperno, D. R., and D. M. Pearsall

1998   *The Origins of Agriculture in the Lowland Neotropics.* San Diego: Academic Press.

Pirie, F.

2013   *Anthropology of Law.* Oxford, UK: Oxford University Press.

Podolefsky, A., and P. J. Brown, eds.

1992   *Applying Anthropology: An Introductory Reader,* 2nd ed. Mountain View, CA: Mayfield.

Pohl, M. E. D., et al.

2007   Microfossil Evidence for Pre-Columbian Maize Dispersals in the Neotropics from San Andrés, Tabasco, Mexico. *Proceedings of the National Academy of Sciences of the United States of America* 104(29): 11874–11881. doi:10.1073/pnas.0701425104.

Polanyi, K.

1968   *Primitive, Archaic and Modern Economies: Essays of Karl Polanyi.* G. Dalton, ed. Garden City, NY: Anchor Books.

Pospisil, L.

1963   *The Kapauku Papuans of West New Guinea.* New York: Harcourt Brace Jovanovich.

Potash, B., ed.

1986   *Widows in African Societies: Choices and Constraints.* Stanford, CA: Stanford University Press.

Potts, D. T.

2015   *The Archaeology of Elam: Formation and Transformation of an Ancient Iranian State.* New York: Cambridge University Press.

Poushter, J.

2016   Smartphone Ownership and Internet Usage Continues to Climb in Emerging Economies. Pew Research Center, February 22. http://www.pewglobal.org/files/2016/02/pew_research_center_global_technology_report_final_february_22__2016.pdf.

Price, D.

2000   Anthropologists as Spies. *Nation,* November 20, 24–27.

Price, R., ed.

1973   *Maroon Societies.* New York: Anchor Press, Doubleday.

Pringle, H.

2008   Did Humans Colonize the World by Boat? Research Suggests Our Ancestors Traveled the Oceans 70,000 Years Ago. *Discover,* May 20. http://discovermagazine.com/2008/jun/20-did-humans-colonize-the-world-by-boat.

Qian, Z.

2013   Divergent Paths of American Families. September 11. Brown University, US2010. http://www.s4.brown.edu/us2010/Data/Report/report09112013.pdf.

Radcliffe-Brown, A. R.

1952   (orig. 1924) The Mother's Brother in South Africa. In A. R. Radcliffe-Brown, *Structure and Function in Primitive Society,* pp. 15–31. London: Routledge & Kegan Paul.

1965   (orig. 1962) *Structure and Function in Primitive Society.* New York: Free Press.

Raffaele, P.

2010   *Among the Great Apes: Adventures on the Trail of Our Closest Relatives.* New York: Smithsonian, Harper.

Ramachandran, S., and N. Rosenberg

2011   A Test of the Influence of Continental Axes of Orientation on Patterns of Human Gene Flow. *Journal of Physical Anthropology* 146(4): 515–529.

Ramos, A. R.

1995   *Sanumá Memories : Yanomami Ethnography in Times of Crisis.* Madison: University of Wisconsin Press.

Random House College Dictionary (1982, revised ed.). New York: Random House.

Ranger, T. O.

1996   Postscript. In *Postcolonial Identities,* R. Werbner and T. O. Ranger, eds. London: Zed.

Rapoza, K.

2012   Disturbing Trend for Putin, Russian Poverty Rising. *Forbes.* April 12. http://www.forbes.com/sites/kenrapoza/2012/04/12/disturbing-trend-for-putin-russian-poverty-rising/.

Rappaport, R. A.

1974   Obvious Aspects of Ritual. *Cambridge Anthropology* 2: 2–60.

1999   *Holiness and Humanity: Ritual in the Making of Religious Life.* New York: Cambridge University Press.

Rathje, W. L., and C. Murphy

2001   *Rubbish!: The Archaeology of Garbage.* Tucson: University of Arizona Press.

Rathus, S. A., J. S. Nevid, and J. Fichner-Rathus
2014 *Human Sexuality in a World of Diversity,* 9th ed. Boston: Allyn & Bacon.

Redfield, R., R. Linton, and M. Herskovits
1936 Memorandum on the Study of Acculturation. *American Anthropologist* 38: 149–152.

Regullano, E.
2015 Asian American Internet Musicking. *Anthropology Now* 7(2): 80-86.

Reiter, R., ed.
1975 *Toward an Anthropology of Women.* New York: Monthly Review Press.

Relethford, J. H.
2009 Race and Global Patterns of Phenotypic Variation. *American Journal of Physical Anthropology* 139(1): 16–22.
2012 *Human Population Genetics.* Hoboken, NJ: Wiley-Blackwell.

Renfrew, C.
1987 *Archaeology and Language: The Puzzle of Indo-European Origin.* London: Pimlico.

Renfrew, C., and P. Bahn
2012 *Archaeology: Theories, Methods, and Practice,* London: Thames and Hudson.

Renfrew, C., and P. Bahn, eds.
2014 *The Cambridge World Prehistory.* New York: Cambridge University Press.

Reyburn, S.
2015 Chris Ofili's 'The Holy Virgin Mary' to Be Sold. *New York Times,* May 28. http://www.nytimes.com/2015/05/29/arts/design/chris-ofilis-the-holy-virgin-mary-to-be-sold.html?_r=0.

Reyhner, J., et al., eds.
2013 *Honoring Our Children: Culturally Appropriate Approaches for Teaching Indigenous Students.* Flagstaff: Northern Arizona University.

Rhodes, R. A. W., and P. 't Hart
2014 *The Oxford Handbook of Political Leadership.* Oxford, UK: Oxford University Press.

Riach, J.
2013 Golf's Failure to Embrace Demographics across Society Is Hard to Stomach. *The Guardian,* May 22. http://www.theguardian.com/sport/blog/2013/may/22/uk-golf-clubs-race-issues.

Rice, P. C.
2002 Paleoanthropology 2001—Part 2. *General Anthropology* 8(2): 11–14.

Rice, T.
2014 *Ethnomusicology: A Very Short Introduction.* New York: Oxford University Press.

Rickford, J. R.
1997 Suite for Ebony and Phonics. http://www.stanford.edu/~rickford/papers/SuiteForEbonyandPhonics.html (also published in *Discover,* December 1997).

Rickford, J. R., and R. J. Rickford
2000 *Spoken Soul: The Story of Black English.* New York: Wiley.

Rilling, J. K.
2013 The Neural and Hormonal Bases of Human Parental Care. *Neuropsychologia* 51: 731–747.

Roach, J.
2007 "Hobbit" Human Was Unique Species, Wrist Bones Suggest. *National Geographic News,* September 20. http://news.nationalgeographic.com/news/pf/65255655.html.

Robbins, J.
2004 The Globalization of Pentecostal and Charismatic Christianity. *Annual Review of Anthropology* 33: 17–143.
2012 The Ecology of Disease. *New York Times,* July 14. http://www.nytimes.com/2012/07/15/sunday-review/the-ecology-of-disease.html?pagewanted5all.

Robbins, R.
2014 *Global Problems and the Culture of Capitalism,* 6th ed. Boston: Pearson.

Roberts, D. F.
1953 Body Weight, Race and Climate. *American Journal of Physical Anthropology* 11: 533–558.

Robertson, J.
1992 Koreans in Japan. Paper presented at the University of Michigan Department of Anthropology, Martin Luther King Jr. Day Panel, January. Ann Arbor: University of Michigan Department of Anthropology (unpublished).

Robson, D.
2013 There Really Are 50 Eskimo Words for Snow. *Washington Post,* January 14. http://articles.washingtonpost.com/2013-01-14/national/36344037_1_eskimo-words-snow-inuit.

Rodseth, L., et al.
1991 The Human Community as a Primate Society. *Current Anthropology* 32: 221–254.

Rojas, J. L., and M. E. Smith
2012 *Tenochtitlan: Capital of the Aztec Empire.* Gainesville: University Press of Florida.

Romero, S.
2008 Rain Forest Tribe's Charge of Neglect Is Shrouded by Religion and Politics. *New York Times,* October 7.

Root, D.
1996 *Cannibal Culture: Art, Appropriation, and the Commodification of Difference.* Boulder, CO: Westview Press.

Roque, R., and K. A. Wagner, eds.
2011 *Engaging Colonial Knowledge: Reading European Archives in World History.* New York: Palgrave Macmillan.

Rosaldo, M. Z.
1980a *Knowledge and Passion: Notions of Self and Social Life.* Stanford, CA: Stanford University Press.
1980b The Use and Abuse of Anthropology: Reflections on Feminism and Cross-Cultural Understanding. *Signs* 5(3): 389–417.

Rosaldo, M. Z., and L. Lamphere, eds.
1974 *Woman, Culture, and Society.* Stanford, CA: Stanford University Press.

Rosenberg, K. R., and W. R. Trevathan
2001 The Evolution of Human Birth. *Scientific American* 285(5): 60–65.

Rothman, J. M., D. Raubenheimer, and C. A. Chapman
2011 Nutritional Geometry: Gorillas Prioritize Non-protein Energy While Consuming Surplus Protein. *Biology Letters* 7: 847–849.

Rothstein, E.
2006 Protection for Indian Patrimony That Leads to a Paradox. *New York Times,* March 29.

Royal Anthropological Institute of Great Britain and Ireland
1951 *Notes and Queries on Anthropology,* 6th ed. London, UK: Routledge and K. Paul.

Ruhlen, M.
1994 *The Origin of Language: Tracing the Evolution of the Mother Tongue.* New York: Wiley.

Ryan, S.
1990 *Ethnic Conflict and International Relations.* Brookfield, MA: Dartmouth.

Ryang, S., and J. Lie
2009 *Diaspora without Homeland: Being Korean in Japan.* Berkeley: University of California Press.

Rylko-Bauer, B., M. Singer, and J. Van Willigen
2006 Reclaiming Applied Anthropology: Its Past, Present, and Future. *American Anthropologist* 108(1): 178–190.

Sabloff, J. A.
2008 *Archaeology Matters: Action Archaeology in the Modern World.* Walnut Creek, CA: Left Coast Press.

Sack, K.
2011 In Tough Times, a Boom in Cremations as a Way to Save Money. *New York Times,* December 8. http://www.nytimes.com/2011/12/09/us/in-economic-downturn-survivors-turning-to-cremations-over-burials.html?_r=0.

Sadig, A. M.
2010 *The Neolithic of the Middle Nile Region: An Archeology of Central Sudan and Nubia.* East Lansing: Michigan State University Press.

Saez, E., and G. Zucman
2014 Wealth Inequality in the United States since 1913: Evidence from Capitalized Income Tax Data. Working Paper 20625, National Bureau of Economic Research, Cambridge, MA. http://gabriel-zucman.eu/files/SaezZucman2014.pdf.

Sahlins, M. D.
1968 *Tribesmen.* Englewood Cliffs, NJ: Prentice Hall.
2011 (orig. 1972) *Stone Age Economics.* New Brunswick, NJ: Transaction.

2013 *What Kinship Is—And Is Not.* Chicago: University of Chicago Press.

Salazar, C., and J. Bestard, eds.
2015 *Religion and Science as Forms of Life: Anthropological Insights into Reason and Unreason.* New York: Berghahn Books.

Salzman, P. C.
1974 Political Organization among Nomadic Peoples. In *Man in Adaptation: The Cultural Present,* 2nd ed., Y. A. Cohen, ed., pp. 267–284. Chicago: Aldine.
2004 *Pastoralists: Equality, Hierarchy, and the State.* Boulder, CO: Westview Press.
2008 *Culture and Conflict in the Middle East.* Amherst, NY: Humanity Books.
2012 *Classic Comparative Anthropology: Studies from the Tradition.* Long Grove, IL: Waveland.

Salzmann, Z.
2012 *Linguistic Anthropology: A Short Introduction.* Prague, Czech Republic: Nezavisle centrum pro studium politiky.

Salzmann, Z., J. M. Stanlaw, and N. Adachi
2015 *Language, Culture, and Society: An Introduction to Linguistic Anthropology,* 6th ed. Boulder, CO: Westview Press. Sample, I. (2012 "Red Deer Cave People" May Be New Species of Human. *The Guardian,* March 14. http://www.guardian.co.uk/science/2012/mar/14/red-deer-cave-people-species-human.

Sanday, P. R.
1974 Female Status in the Public Domain. In *Woman, Culture, and Society,* M. Z. Rosaldo and L. Lamphere, eds., pp. 189–206. Stanford, CA: Stanford University Press.
2002 *Women at the Center: Life in a Modern Matriarchy.* Ithaca, NY: Cornell University Press.
2003 Public Interest Anthropology: A Model for Engaged Social Science. http://www.sas.upenn.edu/anthro/CPIA/PAPERS/SARdiscussion%20paper.65.html.

Sanjek, R.
2004 Going Public: Responsibilities and Strategies in the Aftermath of Ethnography. *Human Organization* 63(4): 444–456.
2014 *Ethnography in Today's World: Color Full before Color Blind.* Philadelphia: University of Pennsylvania Press.

Sanjek, R., and S. W. Tratner, eds.
2016 *eFieldnotes: The Makings of Anthropology in the Digital World.* Philadelphia: University of Pennsylvania Press.

Sansi-Roca, R.
2015 *Art, Anthropology and the Gift.* New York: Bloomsbury Academic.

Sapir, E.
1931 Conceptual Categories in Primitive Languages. *Science* 74: 578–584.
1956 (orig. 1928) The Meaning of Religion. In E. Sapir, *Culture, Language and Personality: Selected Essays.* Berkeley: University of California Press.

Saville, A., ed.
2012 *Flint and Stone in the Neolithic Period.* Oakville, CT: Oxbow Books.

Scarre, C., and B. Fagan
2016 *Ancient Civilizations,* 4th ed. Milton Park, Abingdon, Oxon: Routledge.

Schaefer, R.
2013 *Race and Ethnicity in the United States,* 7th ed. Upper Saddle River, NJ: Prentice Hall.

Schaik, C. V.
2004 *Among Orangutans: Red Apes and the Rise of Human Culture.* Tucson: University of Arizona Press.
2015 *The Primate Roots of Human Nature.* Hoboken, NJ: Wiley.

Scheidel, W.
1997 Brother-Sister Marriage in Roman Egypt. *Journal of Biosocial Science* 29(3): 361–371.

Schneider, A., and C. Pasqualino, eds.
2014 *Experimental Film and Anthropology.* New York: Bloomsbury Academic.

Schneider, A., and C. Wright, eds.
2010 *Between Art and Anthropology: Contemporary Ethnographic Practice.* New York: Berg.
2013 *Anthropology and Art Practice.* New York: Bloomsbury Academic.

Schneider, D. M.
1968 *American Kinship: A Cultural Account.* Englewood Cliffs, NJ: Prentice Hall.

Schneider, D. M., and K. Gough, eds.
1961 *Matrilineal Kinship.* Berkeley: University of California Press.

Schultz, S., C. Opie, and Q. D. Atkinson
2011 Stepwise Evolution of Stable Sociality in Primates. *Nature* 479: 229–222, November 11. http://www.nature.com/nature/journal/v479/n7372/full/nature10601.html.

Schwartz, M. J., V. W. Turner, and A. Tuden, eds.
2011 *Political Anthropology.* New Brunswick, NJ: Aldine Transaction.

Schweingruber, F. H.
2007 *Wood Structure and Environment.* New York: Springer.

Scott, J.
2002 Prehistoric Human Footpaths Lure Archaeologists Back to Costa Rica. University of Colorado Press Release, May 20. http://www.eurekalert.org/pub_releases/2002-05/uoca-phf052002.php.

Scott, J. C.
1985 *Weapons of the Weak.* New Haven, CT: Yale University Press.
1990 *Domination and the Arts of Resistance.* New Haven, CT: Yale University Press.

Scott, S., and C. Duncan
2004 *Return of the Black Death: The World's Greatest Serial Killer.* Hoboken, NJ: Wiley.

Scudder, T., and E. Colson
1980 *Secondary Education and the Formation of an Elite: The Impact of Education on Gwembe District, Zambia.* London: Academic Press.

Scupin, R.
2012 *Race and Ethnicity: The United States and the World,* 2nd ed. Upper Saddle River, NJ: Prentice Hall.

Sebeok, T. A., and J. Umiker-Sebeok, eds.
1980 *Speaking of Apes: A Critical Anthropology of Two-Way Communication with Man.* New York: Plenum Press.

Senut, B., et al.
2001 First Hominid from the Miocene (Lukeino Formation, Kenya *Comptes Rendus de l'Academie des Sciences, Series IIA—Earth and Planetary Science* 332: 137–144.

Service, E. R.
1962 *Primitive Social Organization: An Evolutionary Perspective.* New York: McGraw-Hill.
1966 *The Hunters.* Englewood Cliffs, NJ: Prentice Hall.

Shannon, T. R.
1996 *An Introduction to the World-System Perspective,* 2nd ed. Boulder, CO: Westview Press.

Sharma, A., and A. Gupta, eds.
2006 *The Anthropology of the State: A Reader.* Malden, MA: Blackwell.

Sharpley, R., and D. J. Teller, eds.
2015 *Tourism and Development; Concepts and Issues.* Buffalo, NY: Channel View Publications.

Sheets, P. D.
2006 *The Ceren Site: An Ancient Village Buried by Volcanic Ash.* Belmont, CA: Thomson Higher Education.

Shermer, M.
2011 *In Darwin's Shadow: The Life and Science of Alfred Russel Wallace: A Biographical Study on the Psychology of History.* New York: Oxford University Press.

Shivaram, C.
1996 Where Women Wore the Crown: Kerala's Dissolving Matriarchies Leave a Rich Legacy of Compassionate Family Culture. *Hinduism Today* 96(2). http://www.hinduism-today.com/archives/1996/2/1996-2-03.shtml.

Shore, B.
1996 *Culture in Mind: Meaning, Construction, and Cultural Cognition.* New York: Oxford University Press.

Shore, C., S. Wright, and D. Però eds.
2011   *Policy Worlds: Anthropology and the Analysis of Contemporary Power*. New York: Berghahn Books.

Shreeve, J.
2015   This Face Changes the Human Story. But How? *National Geographic*, September 10. http://news.nationalgeographic.com/2015/09/150910-human-evolution-change/

Shryock, A.
1988   Autonomy, Entanglement, and the Feud: Prestige Structures and Gender Values in Highland Albania. *Anthropological Quarterly* 61(3): 113–118.

Silberbauer, G.
1981   *Hunter and Habitat in the Central Kalahari Desert*. New York: Cambridge University Press.

Simmons, A. H.
2007   *The Neolithic Revolution in the Near East: Transforming the Human Landscape*. Tucson: University of Arizona Press.

Simons, E. L., and P. C. Ettel
1970   *Gigantopithecus. Scientific American*, January, pp. 77–85.

Singer, M.
2015   *The Anthropology of Infectious Disease*. Walnut Creek, CA: Left Coast Press.

Singer, M., and H. Baer
2012   *Introducing Medical Anthropology: A Discipline in Action*, 2nd ed. Lanham, MD: AltaMira.

Singer, M., and P. I. Erickson, eds.
2011   *A Companion to Medical Anthropology*. Malden, MA: Wiley-Blackwell.

Skoglund, P., et al.
2012   Origins and Genetic Legacy of Neolithic Farmers and Hunter-Gatherers in Europe. *Science* 27(April): 336, 6080: 466–469. doi:10.1126/science.1216304.

Slaughter, A-M.
2013   Women Are Sexist, Too: If Women Are Equal at the Office, Why Can't Men Be Equal at Home? http://time.com/women-are-sexist-too/.
2015   *Unfinished Business: Men, Women, Work, Family*. New York: Random House.

Smith, A. T.
2003   *The Political Landscape: Constellations of Authority in Early Complex Polities*. Westport, CT: Praeger.

Smith, C. H., and G. Beccaloni, eds.
2010   *Natural Selection and Beyond: The Intellectual Legacy of Alfred Russel Wallace*. New York: Oxford University Press.

Smith, C. S.
2006   Some See a "Pyramid" to Hone Bosnia's Image. Others See a Big Hill. *New York Times*, May 15.

Smith, M. E.
2009   V. Gordon Childe and the Urban Revolution: A Historical Perspective on a Revolution in Urban Studies. *Town Planning Review* 80(1): 2–29.
2016   *At Home with the Aztecs: An Archaeologist Uncovers Their Daily Life*. New York: Routledge.

Smith, M. K., and M. E. Doyle
2002   "Globalization," *The Encyclopedia of Informal Education*. http://www.infed.org/biblio/globalization.

Smitherman, G.
1986   *Talkin and Testifyin: The Language of Black America*. Detroit: Wayne State University Press.

Snowden, F. M., Jr.
1970   *Blacks in Antiquity: Ethiopians in the Greco-Roman Experience*. Cambridge, MA: Belknap Press of Harvard University Press.
1995   Europe's Oldest Chapter in the History of Black White Relations. *In Racism and Anti-Racism in World Perspective*, B. P. Bowser, ed., pp. 3–26. Thousand Oaks, CA: Sage.

Solway, J., ed.
2006   *The Politics of Egalitarianism*. New York: Berghahn Books.

Solway, J., and R. Lee
1990   Foragers, Genuine and Spurious: Situating the Kalahari San in History (with CA treatment). *Current Anthropology* 31(2): 109–146.

Sotomayor, S.
2009   (orig. 2001) A Latina Judge's Voice. The Judge Mario G. Olmos Memorial Lecture, delivered at the University of California, Berkeley, School of Law in 2001; published in the spring 2002 issue of the *Berkeley La Raza Law Journal*, republished by the *New York Times* on May 14, 2009.

Speer, J. H.
2010   *Fundamentals of Tree-Ring Research*. Tucson: University of Arizona Press.

Spencer, C. S.
2003   War and Early State Formation in Oaxaca, Mexico. *Proceedings of the National Academy of Sciences of the United States of America* 100(20): 11185–11187. http://www.pnas.org/cgi/doi/10.1073/pnas.2034992100.
2010   Territorial Expansion and Primary State Formation. *Proceedings of the National Academy of Sciences* 107:7119-7126.

Spencer, C. S., and E. M. Redmond
2004   Primary State Formation in Mesoamerica. *Annual Review of Anthropology* 33: 173–179.

Spickard, P., ed.
2004   *Race and Nation: Ethnic Systems in the Modern World*. New York: Routledge.
2012   *Race and Immigration in the United States: New Histories*. New York: Routledge.
2013   *Multiple Identities: Migrants, Ethnicity, and Membership*. Bloomington: Indiana University Press.

Spindler, G. D., and L. Hammond, eds.
2006   *Innovations in Educational Ethnography: Theory, Methods, and Results*. Mahwah, NJ: Erlbaum Associates.

Spooner, B., ed.
2015   *Globalization: The Crucial Phase*. Philadelphia: University of Pennsylvania Museum of Archaeology and Anthropology.

Spoor, F., et al.
2007   Implications of New Early Homo Fossils from Ileret, East of Lake Turkana, Kenya. *Nature* 448: 688–691. http://news.nature.com//news/2007/070806/070806-5.html.

Srivastava, J., N. J. H. Smith, and D. A. Forno
1999   *Integrating Biodiversity in Agricultural Intensification: Toward Sound Practices*. Washington, DC: World Bank.

Stack, C. B.
1975   *All Our Kin: Strategies for Survival in a Black Community*. New York: Harper Torchbooks.

Stanish, C., and A. Levine
2011   War and Early State Formation in the Northern Titicaca Basin, Peru. *Proceedings of the National Academy of Sciences* 108(34): 13901–13906.

Starn, O.
2011   *The Passion of Tiger Woods: An Anthropologist Reports on Golf, Race, and Celebrity Scandal*. Durham, NC: Duke University Press.

Statistics Canada
2001   1996 Census. Nation Tables. http://www.statcan.ca/english/census96/nation.htm.
2010   Study: Projections of the Diversity of the Canadian Population. http://www.statcan.gc.ca/daily-quotidien/100309/dq100309a-eng.htm.

Stearns, P. N.
2016   *Globalization in World History*, 2nd ed. New York: Routledge.

Steegmann, A. T., Jr.
1975   Human Adaptation to Cold. In *Physiological Anthropology*, A. Damon, ed., pp. 130–166. New York: Oxford University Press.

Stefoff, R.
2011   *Forensic Anthropology*. New York: Marshall Cavendish Benchmark.

Stein, R. L., and P. L. Stein, eds.
2011   *The Anthropology of Religion, Magic, and Witchcraft*, 3rd ed. Upper Saddle River, NJ: Pearson Prentice Hall.

Stevens, N. J., et al.
2013   Palaeontological Evidence for an Oligocene Divergence between Old World Monkeys and Apes. *Nature* 497: 611–614. http://www.nature.com/nature/journal/v497/n7451/full/nature12161.html.

Steward, J. H.
1955   *Theory of Culture Change*. Urbana: University of Illinois Press.

1956   *The People of Puerto Rico: A Study in Social Anthropology.* Urbana: University of Illinois Press.

Stimpson, C. R., and G. H. Herdt
2014   *Critical Terms for the Study of Gender.* Chicago: University of Chicago Press.

Stodder, A. L. W., and A. M. Palkovich, eds.
2012   *The Bioarchaeology of Individuals.* Gainesville: University of Florida Press.

Stoffel, M., et al., eds.
2010   *Tree Rings and Natural Hazards: A State-of-the-Art.* New York: Springer.

Stoler, A.
1977   Class Structure and Female Autonomy in Rural Java. *Signs* 3: 74–89.
1995   *Race and the Education of Desire: Foucault's History of Sexuality and the Colonial Order of Things.* Durham, NC: Duke University Press.
2002   *Carnal Knowledge and Imperial Power: Race and the Intimate in Colonial Rule.* Berkeley: University of California Press.
2009   *Along the Archival Grain: Epistemic Anxieties and Colonial Common Sense.* Princeton, NJ: Princeton University Press.

Stoler, A. L., ed.
2013   *Imperial Debris: On Ruins and Ruination.* Durham: Duke University Press.

Stoler, A. L., C. McGranahan, and P. C. Perdue, eds.
2007   *Imperial Formations.* Santa Fe, NM: School for Advanced Research Press.

Stoneking, M.
2015   *An Introduction to Molecular Anthropology.* Hoboken, NJ: Wiley.

Strachan, T., and A. P. Read
2011   *Human Molecular Genetics,* 4th ed. New York: Garland Science.

Strassmann, B. I., and W. M. Garrard
2011   Alternatives to the Grandmother Hypothesis: A Meta-Analysis of the Association between Grandparental and Grandchild Survival in Patrilineal Populations. *Human Nature* 22: 201–222.

Strathern, A., and P. J. Stewart
2010   *Kinship in Action: Self and Group.* Boston: Prentice Hall.

Strathern, M.
1988   *Dealing with Inequality: Analysing Gender Relations in Melanesia and Beyond: Essays by Members of the 1983/1984 Anthropological Research Group at the Research School of Pacific Studies, the Australian National University.* New York: Cambridge University Press.

Streets-Salter, H., and T. Getz
2016   *Empires and Colonies in the Modern World: A Global Perspective.* New York: Oxford University Press.

Strier, K. B., ed.
2014   *Primate Ethnographies.* Boston: Pearson.

Stringer, C.
2012a   *Lone Survivors: How We Came to Be the Only Humans on Earth.* New York: Henry Holt.
2012b   Palaeontology: The 100-Year Mystery of Piltdown Man. *Nature* 492: 177–179.

Stryker, R., and R. J. Gonzalez, eds.
2014   *Up, Down, and Sideways: Anthropologists Trace the Pathways of Power.* New York: Berghahn Books.

Subbaraman, N.
2013   Earliest Fish Stews Were Cooked in Japan during Last Ice Age, Experts Say. NBC News, June 22. http://science.nbcnews.com/_news/2013/04/10/17687754-earliest-fish-stews-were-cooked-in-japan-during-last-ice-age-experts-say?lite.

Sukarieh, M., and S. Tannock
2015   *Youth Rising? The Politics of Youth in the Global Economy.* New York: Routledge/Taylor and Francis.

Sullivan, M.
2012   Trouble in Paradise: UCLA Book Enumerates Challenges Faced by Middle-Class L.A. Families. UCLA Newsroom, June 19. http://newsroom.ucla.edu/portal/ucla/trouble-in-paradise-new-ucla-book.aspx.

Sunstein, B. S., and E. Chiseri-Strater
2012   *Fieldworking: Reading and Writing Research,* 4th ed. Boston: Bedford/St. Martin's.

Sussman, R. W., and C. R. Cloninger, eds.
2011   *Origins of Altruism and Cooperation.* New York: Springer.

Sussman, R. W., D. T. Rasmussen, and P. H. Raven
2013   Rethinking Primate Origins Again. *American Journal of Primatology* 75(2): 95-106.

Suttles, W.
1960   Affinal Ties, Subsistence, and Prestige among the Coast Salish. *American Anthropologist* 62: 296–395.

Tanaka, J.
1980   *The San Hunter-Gatherers of the Kalahari.* Tokyo: University of Tokyo Press.

Tannen, D.
1990   *You Just Don't Understand: Women and Men in Conversation.* New York: Ballantine.

Tannen, D., ed.
1993   *Gender and Conversational Interaction.* New York: Oxford University Press.

Tannen, D., and A. M. Trester, eds.
2012   *Discourse 2.0: Language and New Media.* Washington, DC: Georgetown University Press.

Tattersall, I., and R. DeSalle
2011   *Race? Debunking a Scientific Myth.* College Station: Texas A&M University Press.

Tavernise, S.
2012   Whites Account for under Half of Births in U.S. *New York Times,* May 17. http://www.nytimes.com/2012/05/17/us/whites-account-for-under-half-of-births-in-us.html?pagewanted=all&_r=0.

Taylor, C.
1987   Anthropologist-in-Residence. In *Applied Anthropology in America,* 2nd ed., E. M. Eddy and W. L. Partridge, eds. New York: Columbia University Press.

Taylor, P., et al.
2012   When Labels Don't Fit: Hispanics and Their Views of Identity. Pew Research Hispanic Center, April 4. http://www.pewhispanic.org/2012/04/04/when-labels-dont-fit-hispanics-and-their-views-of-identity.

Telegraph
2005   Third Sex Finds a Place on Indian Passport Forms. *The Telegraph,* March 10. http://infochangeindia.org/humanrights/news/third-sex-finds-a-place-on-indianpassport-forms.html.

Terrace, H. S.
1979   *Nim.* New York: Knopf.

Terrell, J. E.
1998   The Prehistoric Pacific. *Archaeology* 51(6). Archaeological Institute of America. http://www.archaeology.org/9811/abstracts/pacific.html.

Tersigni-Tarrant, M. T. A., and N. R. Shirley, eds.
2012   *Forensic Anthropology: An Introduction.* Boca Raton, FL: CRC Press.

Than, K.
2012   Human Ancestors Ate Bark—Food in Teeth Hints at Chimplike Origins. *National Geographic News,* June 12. http://news.nationalgeographic.com/news/2012/06/120627-sediba-teeth-fossils-bark-human-evolution-max-planck-nature/.

Thomson, A., and L. H. D. Buxton
1923   Man's Nasal Index in Relation to Certain Climatic Conditions. *Journal of the Royal Anthropological Institute* 53: 92–112.

Tishkoff, S. A., et al.
2007   Convergent Adaptation of Human Lactase Persistence in Africa and Europe. *Nature Genetics* 39(1): 31–40.

Tishkov, V. A.
2004   *Chechnya: Life in a War-Torn Society.* Berkeley: University of California Press.

Titiev, M.
1992   *Old Oraibi: A Study of the Hopi Indians of Third Mesa.* Albuquerque: University of New Mexico Press.

Tougher, S.
2008   *The Eunuch in Byzantine History and Society.* New York: Routledge.

Trehub, S. E.
2001 Musical Predispositions in Infancy. *Annals of the New York Academy of Sciences* 930(1): 1–16.

Trivedi, B. P.
2001 Scientists Identify a Language Gene. *National Geographic News*, October 4. http://news.nationalgeographic.com/news/2001/10/1004_TVlanguagegene.html.

Trudgill, P.
2010 *Investigations in Sociohistorical Linguistics: Stories of Colonisation and Contact*. New York: Cambridge University Press.

Turnbull, C.
1965 *Wayward Servants: The Two Worlds of the African Pygmies*. Garden City, NY: Natural History Press.

Turner, V. W.
1967 *The Forest of Symbols: Aspects of Ndembu Ritual*. Ithaca, NY: Cornell University Press.
1995 (orig. 1969) *The Ritual Process*. Hawthorne, NY: Aldine.
996 (orig. 1957) *Schism and Continuity in an African Society: A Study of Ndembu Village Life*. Washington, DC: Berg.

Tylor, E. B.
1889 On a Method of Investigating the Development of Institutions: Applied to Laws of Marriage and Descent. *Journal of the Royal Anthropological Institute* 18: 245–269.
1958 (orig. 1871) *Primitive Culture*. New York: Harper Torchbooks.

Ulijaszek, S. J., and H. Lofink
2006 Obesity in Biocultural Perspective. *Annual Review of Anthropology* 35: 337–360.

U.S. Bureau of Labor Statistics
2014 Household Data, Annual Averages, Table 11. http://www.bls.gov/cps/cpsaat11.pdf.
2015 *National Compensation Survey*. Washington, DC: U.S. Department of Labor. http://www.bls.gov/ncs/.

Valentin, F. et al.
2015 Early Lapita Skeletons from Vanuatu Show Polynesian Craniofacial Shape: Implications for Remote Oceanic Settlement and Lapita Origins. *Proceedings of the National Academy of Sciences*, December 28. http://www.pnas.org/content/early/2015/12/22/1516186113.full.pdf.

Vallegia, C. R., and J. J. Snodgrass
2015 Health of Indigenous Peoples. *Annual Review of Anthropology* 44: 117–135.

Van Allen, J.
1971 *"Aba Riots" or "Women's War"?: British Ideology and Eastern Nigerian Women's Political Activism*. Waltham, MA: African Studies Association.

Van Cantfort, T. E., and J. B. Rimpau
1982 Sign Language Studies with Children and Chimpanzees. *Sign Language Studies* 34: 15–72.

Vayda, A. P.
1968 (orig. 1961) Economic Systems in Ecological Perspective: The Case of the Northwest Coast. In *Readings in Anthropology*, 2nd ed., vol. 2, M. H. Fried, ed., pp. 172–178. New York: Crowell.

Veblen, T.
1934 *The Theory of the Leisure Class: An Economic Study of Institutions*. New York: The Modern Library.

Veja
1984a *Olimpíadas*, August 8, pp. 36–50.
1984b *Vitórias no Tatame*. August 15, p. 61.

Vekua, A., D. Lordkipanidze, and G. P. Rightmire
2002 A Skull of Early Homo from Dmanisi, Georgia. *Science*, July 5, pp. 85–89.

Ventkatesan, S., and T. Yarrow, eds.
2014 *Differentiating Development: Beyond an Anthropology of Critique*. New York: Berghahn Books.

Verdery, K.
2001 Socialist Societies: Anthropological Aspects. *International Encyclopedia of the Social & Behavioral Sciences*, pp. 14496–14500. New York: Elsevier.

Viegas, J.
2013 Scientists Say Our Languages Might Preserve Neanderthal Talk. NBC News, July 11. http://www.nbcnews.com/science/scientists-say-our-languages-might-preserve-neanderthal-talk-6C10604072.

Vigil, J. D.
2010 *Gang Redux: A Balanced Anti-gang Strategy*. Long Grove, IL: Waveland.
2012 *From Indians to Chicanos: The Dynamics of Mexican-American Culture*, 3rd ed. Boulder, CO: Westview Press.

Vigne, J.-D., et al.
2012 First Wave of Cultivators Spread to Cyprus at Least 10,600 Years Ago. *Proceedings of the National Academy of Sciences* 109(22): 8445–8449.

Villmoore, B., et al.
2015 Early *Homo* at 2.8 Ma from Ledi-Geraru, Afar, Ethiopia. *Science* 347: 1352-1355. http://www.sciencemag.org/content/347/6228/1352.

Vincent, J.
1990 *Anthropology and Politics: Visions, Traditions, and Trends*. Tucson: University of Arizona Press.

Vinyeta, K., and K. Lynn
2013 *Exploring the Role of Traditional Ecological Knowledge in Climate Change Initiatives*. Portland, OR: U.S. Department of Agriculture, Forest Service, Pacific Northwest Research Station.

von Cramon-Taubadel, N.
2011 Global Human Mandibular Variation Reflects Differences in Agricultural and Hunter-Gatherer Subsistence Strategies. *Proceedings of the National Academy of Sciences* 108(49): 19546–19551.

von Däniken, E.
1971 *Chariots of the Gods: Unsolved Mysteries of the Past*. New York: Bantam.

Wade, B. C.
2013 *Thinking Musically: Experiencing Music, Expressing Culture*, 3rd ed. New York: Oxford University Press.

Wade, N.
2004 New Species Revealed: Tiny Cousins of Humans. *New York Times*, October 28, national edition, pp. A1, A6.
2007 Fossil DNA Expands Neanderthal Range. *New York Times*, October 2.
2011 New View of How Humans Moved Away from Apes. *New York Times*, March 10.
2012 Family Tree of Languages Has Roots in Anatolia, Biologists Say. *New York Times*, August 23.

Wade, P.
2010 *Race and Ethnicity in Latin America*, 2nd ed. New York: Pluto Press.
2015 *Race: An Introduction*. New York: Cambridge University Press.

Walker, S. M., and D. W. Owsley
2012 *Their Skeletons Speak: Kennewick Man and the Paleoamerican World*. Minneapolis, MN: Carolrhoda Books.

Wallace, A. F. C.
1966 *Religion: An Anthropological View*. New York: McGraw-Hill.

Wallace, S.
2016 Dodging Wind Farms and Bullets in the Arctic. *National Geographic*, March 1. http://news.nationalgeographic.com/2016/03/160301-arctic-sami-norway-reindeer/.

Wallerstein, I. M.
2004 *World-Systems Analysis: An Introduction*. Durham, NC: Duke University Press.

Wallerstein, I. M., et al.
2013 *Does Capitalism Have a Future?* New York: Oxford University Press.

Walton, D., and J. A. Suarez, eds.
2016 *Culture, Space, and Power: Blurred Lines*. Lanham, MD: Lexington Books.

Ward, C. V., W. H. Kimbel, and D. C. Johanson
2011 Complete Fourth Metatarsal and Arches in the Foot of *Australopithecus afarensis*. *Science* 331: 750–753.

Ward, M. C., and M. Edelstein
2013 *A World Full of Women*, 6th ed. Upper Saddle River, NJ: Pearson.

Wardhaugh, R., and J. Fuller
2015 *An Introduction to Sociolinguistics*, 7th ed. Malden, MA: Wiley-Blackwell.

Warms, R., J. Garber, and R. J. McGee, eds.
2009 *Sacred Realms: Readings in the Anthropology of Religion*, 2nd ed. New York: Oxford University Press.

Warne, A. D., ed.
2015   *Ethnic and Cultural Identity: Perceptions, Discrimination, and Social Challenges.* Hauppauge, NY: Nova Science.

Wasson, C., M. O. Butler, and J. Copeland-Carson, eds.
2012   *Applying Anthropology in the Global Village.* Walnut Creek, CA: Left Coast Press.

Waters, M. R., and T. W. Stafford, Jr.
2007   Redefining the Age of Clovis: Implications for the Peopling of the Americas. *Science* 315: 1122–1126. doi: 10.1126/science.1137166.

Waters, M. R., et al.
2011   Pre-Clovis Mastodon Hunting 13,800 Years Ago at the Manis Site, Washington. *Science* 334: 351–353. doi:10.1126/science.1207663.

Watson, J. D.
1970   *Molecular Biology of the Gene.* New York: Benjamin.

Watters, E.
2010   The Americanization of Mental Illness. *New York Times,* January 8. http://www.nytimes.com/2010/01/10/magazine/10psyche-t.html?pagewanted=all.

Watzman, H.
2006   The Echoes of Ancient Humans. *Chronicle of Higher Education,* January 27. http://chronicle.com/weekly/v52/i21/(21a01601.htm.

Wayman, E.
2012   Primate Origins Tied to Rise of Flowering Plants. *Smithsonian,* November 28. http://www.smithsonianmag.com/science-nature/primate-origins-tied-to-rise-of-flowering-plants-145971956/?no-ist.

Weber, M.
1958   (orig. 1904) *The Protestant Ethic and the Spirit of Capitalism.* New York: Scribner.
1968   (orig. 1922) *Economy and Society.* Translated by E. Fischoff et al. New York: Bedminster Press.

Webster's New World Encyclopedia
1993   College Edition. Englewood Cliffs, NJ: Prentice Hall.

Week
2013   Should Apes Have Legal Rights? *The Week,* August 3. http://theweek.com/articles/461480/should-apes-have-legal-rights.

Weiner, J. S.
2003   *The Piltdown Forgery.* New York: Oxford University Press.

Weiner, M.
2009   *Japan's Minorities: The Illusion of Homogeneity,* 2nd ed. New York: Routledge.

Weiss, H.
2005   *Collapse.* New York: Routledge.

Wendorf, F., and R. Schild
2000   Late Neolithic Megalithic Structures at Nabta Playa (Sahara), Southwestern Egypt. http://www.comp-archaeology.org/WendorfSAA98.html.

Wenke, R. J., and D. I. Olszewski
2007   *Patterns in Prehistory: Mankind's First Three Million Years,* 5th ed. New York: Oxford University Press.

White, L. A.
1949   *The Science of Culture: A Study of Man and Civilization.* New York: Farrar, Strauss.
1959   *The Evolution of Culture: The Development of Civilization to the Fall of Rome.* New York: McGraw-Hill.
2009   *Modern Capitalist Culture,* abridged ed. Walnut Creek, CA: Left Coast Press.

White, T. D., M. T. Black, and P. A. Folkens
2012   *Human Osteology,* 3rd ed. San Diego: Academic Press.

Whiteford, L. M., and R. T. Trotter II
2008   *Ethics for Anthropological Research and Practice.* Long Grove, IL: Waveland.

Whiting, J. M.
1964   Effects of Climate on Certain Cultural Practices. In *Explorations in Cultural Anthropology: Essays in Honor of George Peter Murdock,* ed. W. H. Goodenough, pp. 511–544. New York: McGraw-Hill.

Whittle, A., and P. Bickle
2014   *Early Farmers*: *The View from Archaeology and Science.* Oxford, UK: Oxford University Press.

Whorf, B. L.x
1956   A Linguistic Consideration of Thinking in Primitive Communities. In *Language, Thought, and Reality: Selected Writings of Benjamin Lee Whorf,* J. B. Carroll, ed., pp. 65–86. Cambridge, MA: MIT Press.

Wiley, A. S., and J. S. Allen
2013   *Medical Anthropology: A Biocultural Approach,* 2nd ed. New York: Oxford University Press.

Wilford, J. N.
2000   Ruins Alter Ideas of How Civilization Spread. *New York Times,* May 23.
2002a   Seeking Polynesia's Beginnings in an Archipelago of Shards. *New York Times,* January 8, Science Desk.
2002b   When Humans Became Human. *New York Times,* February 26, late edition, final, section F, p. 1.
2007a   Fossils in Kenya Challenge Linear Evolution. *New York Times,* August 9, p. A6.
2007b   Fossils Reveal Clues on Human Ancestors. *New York Times,* September 20.
2009a   Fossil Skeleton from Africa Predates Lucy. *New York Times,* October 2, pp. A1, A6.
2009b   Feet Offer Clue about Tiny Hominid. *New York Times,* May 9.
2010   In Syria, a Prologue for Cities. *New York Times,* April 6.
2011a   Fossil Teeth Put Humans in Europe Earlier Than Thought. *New York Times,* November 3, p. A4.
2011b   In African Cave, Signs of an Ancient Paint Factory. *New York Times,* October 13, p. A14.
2011c   Earliest Signs of Advanced Tools Found. *New York Times,* August 31.
2012   Artifacts Revive Debate on Transformation of Human Behavior. *New York Times,* July 30. http://www.nytimes.com/2012/07/31/science/cave-findings-revive-debate-on-human-behavior.html?_r=0.
2013   Palm-Size Fossil Resets Primates' Clock, Scientists Say. *New York Times,* June 5. http://www.nytimes.com/2013/06/06/science/palm-size-fossil-resets-primates-clock-scientists-say.html?pagewanted=all&_r=0.
2015   Stone Tools from Kenya Are Oldest Yet Discovered. *New York Times,* May 20.

Wilk, R. R.
2006   *Fast Food/Slow Food: The Cultural Economy of the Global Food System.* Lanham, MD: AltaMira.

Wilk, R. R., and L. Barbosa
2012   *Rice and Beans: A Unique Dish in a Hundred Places.* New York: Berg.

Williams, L. M., and D. Finkelhor
1995   Paternal Caregiving and Incest: Test of a Biosocial Model. *American Journal of Orthopsychiatry* 65(1): 101–113.

Willie, C. V., and R. J. Reddick
2009   *A New Look at Black Families,* 6th ed. Lanham, MD: Rowman & Littlefield.

Wilmsen, E. N.
1989   *Land Filled with Flies: A Political Economy of the Kalahari.* Chicago: University of Chicago Press.

Wilson, D. S.
2002   *Darwin's Cathedral: Evolution, Religion, and the Nature of Society.* Chicago: University of Chicago Press.

Wilson, M. L., and R. W. Wrangham
2003   Intergroup Relations in Chimpanzees. *Annual Review of Anthropology* 32: 363–392.

Winzeler, R. L.
2012   *Anthropology and Religion,* 2nd ed. Lanham, MD: Rowman & Littlefield.

Wittfogel, K. A.
1957   *Oriental Despotism: A Comparative Study of Total Power.* New Haven, CT: Yale University Press.

Wolcott, H. F.
2010   *Ethnography Lessons: A Primer.* Walnut Creek, CA: Left Coast Press.

Wolf, E. R.
1966   *Peasants.* Englewood Cliffs, NJ: Prentice Hall.
1982   *Europe and the People without History.* Berkeley: University of California Press.

Wolf, E. R., with S. Silverman
  2001 *Pathways of Power: Building an Anthropology of the Modern World.* Berkeley: University of California Press.
Wolpoff, M. H.
  1999 *Paleoanthropology,* 2nd ed. New York: McGraw-Hill.
Wood, B., ed.
  2011 *Wiley-Blackwell Encyclopedia of Human Evolution.* Hoboken, NJ: Wiley-Blackwell.
Worsley, P.
  1985 (orig. 1959) Cargo Cults. In *Readings in Anthropology* 85/86. Guilford, CT: Dushkin.
Wrangham, R., W. McGrew, F. de Waal, and P. Heltne, eds.
  1994 *Chimpanzee Cultures.* Cambridge, MA: Harvard University Press.
Wright, H. T.
  1977 Recent Research on the Origin of the State. *Annual Review of Anthropology* 6: 379–397.
  1994 Prestate Political Formations. In *Chiefdoms and Early States in the Near East: The Organizational Dynamics of Complexity,* ed. G. Stein and M. S. Rothman, *Monographs in World Archaeology* 18: 67–84. Madison, WI: Prehistory Press.
Wu, X., et al.
  2012 Early Pottery at 20,000 Years Ago in Xianrendong Cave, China. *Science* 336: 1696.
Wynn, T., and F. L. Coolidge
  2011 *How to Think Like a Neanderthal.* New York: Oxford University Press.
Yardley, W.
  2007 Victim of Climate Change, a Town Seeks a Lifeline. *New York Times,* May 27. http://www.nytimes.com/2007/05/27/us/27newtok.html?_r=0.
Yellen, J. E., A. S. Brooks, and E. Cornelissen
  1995 A Middle Stone Age Worked Bone Industry from Katanda, Upper Semliki Valley, Zaire. *Science* 268: 553–556.
Yetman, N., ed.
  1991 *Majority and Minority: The Dynamics of Race and Ethnicity in American Life,* 5th ed. Boston: Allyn & Bacon.
Yong, E.
  2015 6 Tiny Cavers, 15 Odd Skeletons, and 1 Amazing New Species of Ancient Human. *The Atlantic,* September 10. http://www.theatlantic.com/science/archive/2015/09/homo-naledi-rising-star-cave-hominin/404362/.

Young, A.
  2000 *Women Who Become Men: Albanian Sworn Virgins.* New York: Berg.
Zeder, M. A.
  1997 The American Archaeologist: Results of the 1994 SAA Census. *SAA Bulletin* 15(2): 12–17.
  2008 Domestication and Early Agriculture in the Mediterranean Basin: Origins, Diffusion, and Impact. *Proceedings of the National Academy of Sciences* 105(33): 11597–11604. http://www.pnas.org/content/early/2008/08/11/0801317105.
Zhang, Y.
  2016 *Trust and Economics: The Co-evolution of Trust and Exchange Systems.* New York: Routledge.
Zickuhr, K.
  2013 Home Broadband 2013. Pew Research Center, Internet and American Life Project, August 26. http://www.pewinternet.org/Press-Releases/2013/Home-Broadband-2013.aspx.
Zimmer, C.
  2010 Siberian Fossils Were Neanderthals' Eastern Cousins, DNA Reveals. *New York Times,* December 22. http://www.nytimes.com/2010/12/23/science/23ancestor.html.
  2013 Monogamy and Human Evolution. *New York Times,* August 2. http://www.nytimes.com/2013/08/02/science/monogamys-boost-to-human-evolution.html.
  2015 Agriculture Linked to DNA Changes in Ancient Europe. *New York Times,* November 23. http://www.nytimes.com/2015/11/24/science/agriculture-linked-to-dna-changes-in-ancient-europe.html?_r=0.
Zimmer-Tamakoshi, L.
  1997 The Last Big Man: Development and Men's Discontents in the Papua New Guinea Highlands. *Oceania* 68(2):107–122.
Zimring, C. A., ed.
  2012 *Encyclopedia of Consumption and Waste: The Social Science of Garbage.* Thousand Oaks, CA: Sage Reference.
Zukin, S., P. Kasinitz, and X. Chen
  2015 *Global Cities, Local Streets: Everyday Diversity from New York to Shanghai.* New York: Routledge.

NAME INDEX

SUBJECT INDEX

Page numbers followed by *f* indicate material in figures and illustrations and their captions; page numbers followed by *t* indicate material in tables and Recap boxes.

totalitarian, 464
totem, 376
totemism, 410
totems, 410
Toumai, 128, 130
trade, 221
 in Valley of Mexico, 225
trampling, 307
transformism, 73
transgender, 358–361
 rights, 361
transhumance, 306
transnational diffusion, 31
Transparent TV series, 360–361
tree-ring chronologies, 62–63
tree-ring dating, 63
tribal cultivators, 325
tribe, 109
triplets, 78
triple X syndrome, 358
Trobriand culture, 237
tropics, 95–96
Turner syndrome, 358

U

Ubaid communities, 216
underdifferentiation, 41–42
underwater archaeology, 60
uneducated speech, 265
uniformitarianism, 73
unilinear evolutionism, 242
universal life-cycle events, 25
universals, 24–25
Upper Paleolithic
 bone tools, 173–174
 cave art, 175–176
Upper Paleolithic traditions, 173
urban anthropology, 43–44
urbanization, 43–44
Uruk period, 217
U.S. Agency for International Development (USAID), 36

V

variables, 238
varna, 390
Venus figurines, 171*f*
vertebrate life, history of, 119
 Cenozoic era, 119
 Mesozoic era, 119
 Paleozoic era, 119
 Quaternary period, 119
 Tertiary period, 119
vertical economy, 190
village fissioning, 326
village head, 325–326
vitamin D, 194
Voices of California, 268
Voodoo *(vodoun)*, 415

W

war, 208–209
wealth distribution in the United States, 452–454
Western culture, 424
Western cultures, 14
Westernization, 478
Western medicine, 46
 physician-patient encounters, 46
 "pros" and "cons," 46
Wizard of Oz, 434, 435*t*
Wonderwerk Cave, 152–153
words of the year, 263
working class, 450
working-class speech, 265
world capitalist economy, 448*f*
world events, 6–7
world religions, 413
World Series (baseball), 7
world stratification system, 452
 inequality, 452–455
 wealth distribution in the United States, 452–454
world system
 emergence of, 448–449
 industrialization and, 449–450
 present times, 465, 466*f*
world-system theory, 448

X

XX intersex person, 358
XY intersex person, 358

Y

Yanomami, 325–326
Yanomami of Venezuela, 308
Yanomami of Venezuela and Brazil, 387, 387*f*
yaws, 84
Y chromosome tree, 94
Yeltsin's program of "shock therapy," 465
Yoruba of Nigeria, 424
Yoruba religion, 415

Z

zadruga, 368–369
Zapotec state, 223
Zhoukoudian cave, 154
zoological taxonomy, 107*f*
 Hominidae (hominoids), 108–109
 homologies and analogies in, 107–109
 place of humans *(Homo sapiens)* in, 108*t*
 Pongidae (pongids), 108–109
Zoonomia, 73
Zuni Two-Spirit, 359

Important Theories

Anthropology: Appreciating Human Diversity provides comprehensive coverage of the major theoretical perspectives at the cor_ anthropological study. The list below indicates specific text chapters in which these concepts are discussed.

GENERAL APPROACHES

Adaptation: *1, 2, 3, 5, 6, 7, 8, 9, 10, 11, 13, 14, 16, 17, 19, 20, 21, 24*

Biocultural approaches: *1, 3, 13, 18*

Comparative approaches: *1, 2, 3, 4, 5, 6, 7, 11, 12, 13, 14, 15, 16, 17, 18, 19, 20, 21, 22, 23, 24*
   Classification and typologies: 2, 6, 7, 8, 9, 10, 11, 12, 13, 16, 17, 18, 19, 20, 21, 22, 23, 24
   Systemic cross-cultural comparison: 1, 2, 13, 18, 21, 22, 23

Ethnography: *1, 2, 3, 11, 13, 16, 17, 18, 19, 20, 21, 23, 24*
   Emic and etic approaches: 13
   Longitudinal and multi-sited approaches:
   Quantitative and qualitative approaches: 13

Ethnological theory: *1, 18, 20*

Evolutionary theory: *5, 6, 7, 8, 9, 10, 13*

Explanation: *1, 2, 3, 5, 6, 7, 8, 10, 11, 12, 13, 15, 16, 18, 19, 20, 21, 22*

Holism: *1*

Scientific theory: *1, 2, 3, 4, 5, 7, 10, 13, 17, 18, 21, 23, 24*

Social theory: *13, 21, 22, 23*

SPECIFIC APPROACHES

Colonialism and postcolonial studies: *2, 3, 13, 15, 17, 21, 23, 24*

Configurationalism/cultural patterning: *2, 13, 16, 17, 22, 23, 24*

Cultural studies and postmodernism: *24*

Ecological anthropology: *16, 17, 18, 21, 22, 23, 24*

Feminist theory: *18, 23*

Functional approaches: *13, 16, 17, 19, 20, 21, 22, 24*

Humanistic approaches: *1, 2, 13, 21, 22, 23, 24*

Integration and patterning: *2, 3, 13, 15, 17, 21, 22, 24*

Interpretive approaches: *2, 13, 17, 22, 24*

Political-economy and world-system approaches: *2, 3, 13, 15, 16, 17, 18, 21, 23, 24*

Political/legal anthropology and power: *2, 3, 12, 13, 15, 17, 18, 20, 21, 22, 23, 24*
   Conflict: 3, 13, 15, 16, 17, 18, 21, 23, 24
   Rise and fall of state, theories for: 12, 16, 23
   Social control: 17, 21, 23, 24

Practice theory: *2, 13, 23, 24*
   Culture as contested: 2, 3, 13, 15, 18, 21, 23, 24
   Public and private culture: 2, 17, 22, 23
   Resistance: 2, 3, 17, 23, 24

Psychological approaches: *13, 16, 17, 21*

Symbolic approaches: *2, 12, 13, 18, 21, 22*

Systemic approaches: *2, 3, 11, 12, 13, 16, 17, 18, 19, 21, 23, 24*

Theories of social construction: *2, 6, 15, 18, 19, 20, 21, 22, 23, 24*
   Identities: 15, 17, 18, 19, 20, 21, 22, 23, 24
   Native theories (folk classification): 2, 3, 13, 15, 17, 18, 19, 20, 21, 22
   Race and ethnicity: 2, 15, 17, 19, 21, 22, 23, 24
   Social status: 2, 15, 16, 17, 18, 19, 20, 21, 22, 23, 24